Shooter's Bible
109TH EDITION

SKYHORSE PUBLISHING

Skyhorse Publishing books may be purchased in bulk at special discounts for sales promotion, corporate gifts, fund-raising, or educational purposes. Special editions can also be created to specifications. For details, contact the Special Sales Department, Skyhorse Publishing, 307 West 36th Street, 11th Floor, New York, NY 10018 or info@skyhorsepublishing.com.

Skyhorse® and Skyhorse Publishing® are registered trademarks of Skyhorse Publishing, Inc.®, a Delaware corporation.

Visit our website at www.skyhorsepublishing.com.

10 9 8 7 6 5 4 3 2 1

Library of Congress Cataloging-in-Publication Data is available on file.

Cover design by Brian Peterson
Cover photos courtesy of Barrett, Browning, and Smith & Wesson

Print ISBN: 978-1-5107-3530-9
Ebook ISBN: 978-1-5107-2691-8
ISSN: 0080 9365

Printed in Canada

CONTENTS

INTRODUCTION

Welcome to the 109th edition of the *Shooter's Bible*, the ultimate reference book for millions of people who want information on new guns, ammunition, and optics, as well as up-to-date prices and specs for thousands of in-production firearms. Since it was first published ninety-two years ago, more than seven million copies of the *Shooter's Bible* have been sold—and we're just warming up!

2016 was a solid year for firearms sales in the United States, and with relaxed laws across much of the country, and with more and more people buying firearms for hunting, self-defense, and just plain shooting, many people are predicting another solid year for the gun industry. According to a spokesperson for the National Shooting Sports Foundation, "Using data from the FBI National Instant Criminal Background Checks System (NICS), which is a popular indicator for estimated firearms sales, background checks increased 94 percent over the past decade, with 2016 being the highest total since recordkeeping began in 1998. Other indicators, such as firearms production and excise tax collection, have shown similar increases."

To meet the growing demand, firearms manufacturers have come out with a slew of new products. As you'll read in Robert A. Sadowski's full new product report, "Guns, Optics and Ammo," beginning on page 3, the news in handguns centers on the renowned 1911, a model that many of us are familiar with. This 106-year-old design continues to be popular and configured into a huge variety of models and calibers. One 1911 of note is the H9, from Hudson Manufacturing, a newcomer on the block. Part 1911, part striker fire, this 9mm handgun has a 1911-style grip and straight pull trigger, which translates to a

Editor Cassell (right) with son James after a morning of clays shooting. Some excellent over-and-unders are in the new product lineup this year.

low bore axis and less felt recoil. It's also modular, using a stainless steel slide and an insert chassis. It has a capacity of fifteen in the clip, plus one in the chamber. In rifles, some of the biggest news comes from Savage, which now has the Modern Savage Rifle (MSR), a new AR platform series of riles that includes the MSR 15 Patrol, MSR 15 Recon, MSR 10 Hunter, and the MSR 10 Long Range. The MSR 15 models are chambered for .223 Rem/5.56x45mm NATO and feature .223 Wylde chambers. The MSR 10 models are chambered in .308 Win and 6.5 Creedmoor. In shotguns, CZ-USA has come out with trap and sporting clays shotguns that feature quality at affordable prices. Meanwhile, Browning has added to its Citori 725 series with high-end, luxurious Grade V and VII trap model shotguns. And there's much more, as you shall see in the new products section.

If you own or want to buy currently produced firearms, then you'll want to check out the existing products section starting on page 109. Here is where you'll find nearly every gun currently in production, with up-to-date prices and specs. If you own a gun that isn't in this section, it is probably out of production, in which case you need to pick up a copy of another Skyhorse publication, the *Gun Trader's Guide*. The thirty-ninth edition just came off the presses, as a matter of fact.

If this is the first time you have picked up a copy of the *Shooter's Bible*, you should know that it has a long, illustrious past. The first numbered edition was published in 1925. It's been published annually, and in some cases biannually, ever since, and continues to be the ultimate reference book for millions of people who want information on new guns, ammunition, and optics.

The Skyhorse staff is proud of this newest edition of the *Shooter's Bible*, a book that has been continually updated and fact-checked for the past twelve months. Now that this edition is off the presses, we're already going back to work on next year's edition. It's an ongoing process, and given all the technological changes going on in the industry, it's one that gets more interesting every year.

Note: For a full listing of *Shooter's Bible* and *Gun Trader's Guide* guidebooks (including the brand-new *Gun Trader's Guide to Handguns*), please visit www.skyhorsepublishing.com.

Jay Cassell
Editorial Director
Skyhorse Publishing

Shooter's Bible researcher Lindsey Breuer-Barnes tried her hand at a new Daniel Defense V7 after a day on the clays course.

GUNS, OPTICS, AND AMMO 2018

By Robert A. Sadowski

The news in rifles is that MSR doesn't stand for Modern Sporting Rifle anymore; it's now Modern Savage Rifle. Legacy Sports International and CZ-USA are producing good quality target shotguns at a price shooters can afford. The biggest news in handguns is the 1911. This one-hundred-six-year-old design continues to be popular and configured into a variety of models and calibers. Perhaps the coolest new handgun is from a new manufacturer named Hudson Mfg. The H9 is Hudson Mfg.'s 9mm pistol that is part 1911 and part striker fire. The new optics are crystal clear with plenty of scopes and red dots for AR-15 platforms. In ammunition, the 6.5 Creedmoor cartridge is see a spike in factory loads. Here are the details.

RIFLES

Barrett (barrett.net)

A lightweight bolt action from Barrett? Yes. The Barrett Fieldcraft (MSRP: $1,799) is a hunting rifle constructed with a carbon fiber stock and 416 stainless steel barreled action. Available in short and long actions. Depending on action length, weight is 5 to 6 pounds without scope.

Bergara (bergarausa.com)

Expect sub 1-MOA groups from the BMP (Bergara Match Precision) (MSRP: $1,699) rifle. The B14 BMP is built with a 7075 T6 aluminum chassis and Bergara B14 action and world-renowned #5 taper barrel. The design incorporates a barrel nut that allows shooters to replace or change barrels. The chassis is compatible with common AR-style parts. The stock is adjustable for LOP and cheek riser. Available in .308 Win. or 6.5 Creedmoor.

Browning (browning.com)

The BAR Mark II Safari 100th Anniversary (MSRP: $2,700) celebrates the BAR from when the full auto military model was first used in World War I. This semiautomatic commemorative features a steel receiver with engraved military and hunting scenes. Only one hundred models will be built

in .30-06. The new BAR MK 3 DBM (MSRP: $1,470) is a multi-purpose rifle chambered in .308 Win. with a detachable box magazine, 18-inch barrel, and matte black synthetic stock and forend. It's well suited for hunting and self-defense applications. The BAR MK 3 is ready to hunt hard, chambered in .243 Win. with a 22-inch barrel in a matte black Stalker (MSRP: $1,270) or Mossy Oak Break-Up Country (MSRP: $1,380) finish. The X-Bolt series has two new models. The X-Bolt Hell's Canyon Long Range (MSRP: $1,230-$2,170) features a 26-inch heavy, fluted barrel mated to a DuraTouch stock with an A-TACS AU camouflage finish available in 6.5 Creedmoor, .270 WSM, .300 WSM, 7mm Rem. Mag., .300 Win. Mag., and 28 Nosler. The X-Bolt Medallion Safari grade (MSRP: $2,000-$2,050) comes equipped with a gloss Grade V/VI walnut Safari/Medallion-style stock with raised cheekpiece, rosewood forend, and pistol grip cap. The metal work is polished,

BROWNING BAR 100 ANNIVERSARY LEFT

BROWNING BAR 100 ANNIVERSARY RIGHT

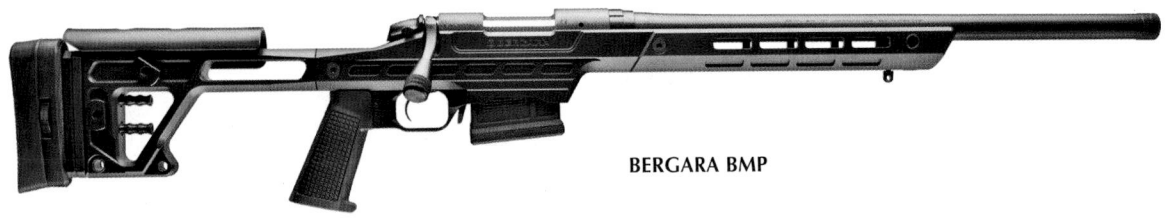

BERGARA BMP

blued steel with gold-accented barrel engraving. Available in numerous calibers from .234 Win. to .375 H&H Mag. The economy AB3 Micro Stalker (MSRP: $600) features a 13-inch LOP on its composite stock and a 20-inch free floated barrel. Calibers include .243 Win., 6.5 Creedmoor, 7mm-08 and .308 Win. A good set up for a young hunter—just be aware, they will be spoiled for life.

Bushmaster (bushmaster.com)

Bushmaster call their new AR-15 the Minimalist-SD (MSRP: $1,170), but it is packed with functional features like the rifle-length AAC SquareDrop handguard, Mission Fist Tactical Minimalist Stock, and 16-inch lightweight contour barrel. The ACR series now has a Designated Marksman Rifle model. The ACR DMR (MSRP: $2,570) is equipped for adventure in harm's way with a heavy 18.5-inch hammer-forged barrel, Magpul PSS2 adjustable stock, Geissele trigger, and a top rail that begs for a sniper scope.

CMMG (cmmging.com)

Drop the hammer with the .458 SOCOM chambered MkW-15 XBE2 Anvil (MSRP: $2150). The Anvil is built on the Mk3 receivers manufactured from 7075-T6 aluminum and features CMMG's proprietary MkW lower receiver plus an SLR adjustable gas block to custom tune your cartridge and equipment.

Colt's Manufacturing (colt.com)

The Colt Combat Unit carbine (MSRP: $1,299) is Colt's first production mid-length gas system. By moving the gas block closer to the muzzle, the felt recoil is more constant with a 14.5-inch barrel M4.

CZ-USA (cz-usa.com)

The 455 American Stainless (MSRP: $434–$451) is CZ-USA's first stainless rimfire and it was designed to be robust. Your great-grandkids will enjoy shooting this rifle. This CZ 455 allows the user to easily change the stock configuration as well as the caliber of the rifle. For entry level, first-time shooters, there is the CZ 455 Scout (MSRP: $339) with a smooth wood stock with an LOP of 12 inches. Available in .22 LR. The CZ 455 Training Rifle Rustic (MSRP: $399) comes with a plainer beech stock. The micro-sized CZ 527 series now has an American model (MSRP: $733) cham-

BROWNING X-BOLT MEDAILLION SAFARI MUZZLE

BROWNING X-BOLT MEDALLION SAFARI RECEIVER

CMMG MKW-15 XBE.2 .458 SOCOM SBN ANVIL

bered in centerfire cartridges ranging from .17 Hornet and .204 Ruger up to 6.5 Grendel and 7.62x39mm. The CZ 527 American Rustic (MSRP: $733) is similar but comes outfitted with an aged beechwood stock and chambered in 6.5 Grendel or 7.62x39mm. The CZ 527 American Synthetic Suppressor-Ready (MSRP: $748) comes with a black synthetic stock and threaded muzzle so this 527 is can ready. Get in the prone position behind the CZ 557 Varmint (MSRP: $865). This short action employs a stout 25.6-inch heavy profile barrel mated to a newly designed walnut stock with palm swell, laser-cut stippling, and a flat forend for shooting off bags. The CZ 805 Bren S1 Carbine (MSRP: $1,999–$2,099) comes with a 16.2-inch barrel, folding adjustable stock, flip-up adjustable iron sights and uses standard AR15-style magazines. Available in .223 Rem./5.56x45mm NATO or .300 Blackout.

FN (fnamerica.com)

The legendary SAW is now available as FN M249S (MSRP: $8,800-$9,200) which is the semiauto version of the M249 SAW light. It features an 18-inch barrel and collapsible buttstock. This civilian friendly SAW accepts magazines or a linked belt. The new FN 15 series has a streamlined approach featuring the new FN handguard with M-LOK technology. Models include the FN 15 DMR II (MSRP: $1,999) and FN 15 Tactical Carbine .300 BLK II (MSRP: $1,599).

Legacy Sports International (legacysports.com)

The Howa KUIU Rifle (MSRP: $782–$811) are available with 20- or 22-inch barrels in a variety of popular hunting calibers and feature a Hogue pillar-bedded overmold stock in Verde and Vias camo finishes. New to the United States is the Australian-made Lithgow Arms Crossover LA101 (MSRP: $1,079–$1,215) rimfire with a polymer or wood laminate stock with butt hook and chambered in either .17 HMR, .22 LR, or .22 WMR.

Mossberg (mossberg.com)

The new MMRs include the MMR Tactical (MSRP: $1,399) with a six-position buttstock and Magpul MOE grip and trigger guard. The model comes with a factory-installed Vortex red/green dot sight (MSRP: $1,400). The MMR Pro (MSRP: $1,393) features an 18-inch barrel with a Silencerco ASR muzzle brake. The MVP FLEX (MSRP: $765) system permits tool-less takedown and has an optional scope package.

CZ USA CZ 455 TRAINING RIFLE

CZ USA CZ 805 BREN S1 CARBINE

FN AMERICA M249S

Remington (remington.com)

The Model 700 AWR (MSRP: $1,150) features a tough Cerakote finish on the barreled action that is mated to lightweight yet rigid fiber/epoxy stock. Calibers available include .270 Win., .30-06, and .300 Win. Mag. The Model 700 Magpul (MSRP: $1,750) features an aluminum reinforced polymer Magpul stock with an adjustable length of pull and cheek comb in either .308 Win. or .260 Rem.

Ruger (ruger.com)

The American Rimfire line (MSRP: $499) is now available with laminated wood stocks. The Predator is the latest addition to the American Centerfire line of bolt action rifles. It features a moss green synthetic stock, heavy taper threaded barrel, and factory installed Vortex Crossfire II 4-12x44mm rifle scope. Available in .2o4 Ruger, .223 Rem., 6.5 Creedmoor or .308 Win.

Savage (savagearms.com)

The MSR series from Savage is the new AR platform series of rifles that includes the MSR 15 Patrol (MSRP: $868), MSR 15 Recon (MSRP: $999), MSR 10 Hunter (MSRP: $1,481), and MSR 10 Long Range (MSRP: $2,284). MSR 15 models are chambered for .223 Rem./5.56x45mm NATO and have a .223 Wylde chamber. The MSR 10 models are chambered in .308 Win. or 6.5 Creedmoor. These new rifles feature BlackHawk! furniture. The new B series (MSRP: $281–$329) of rimfire bolt-action rifles features ergonomic synthetic stocks. Calibers range from .17 HMR, .22 LR and .22 WMR, and all include Savage's AccuTrigger.

Uberti (uberti-usa.com)

The 1886 Sporting Big-Bore (MSRP: $1,995) in .45/70 features a 26-inch octagon barrel and case color receiver. The 1886 Hunter Lite Big-Bore (MSRP: $1,899) has a 22-inch tapered round barrel and half magazine.

Weatherby (weatherby.com)

The Vanguard Adaptive Composite or VAC (MSRP: $1,269) is built on a Vanguard barrel action and features a composite stock with adjustable LOP and cheek comb. A 20-in. barrel has a #3 taper and is threaded at the muzzle. Available in .223 Rem., 6.5 Creedmoor, or .308 Win. The Vanguard Camilla (MSRP: $849) is equipped with a stock specifically designed for women.

LITHGOW ARMS CROSSOVER LA01 RIMFIRE LAMINATE THREADED

HOWA KUIU VERDE

REMNGTON 700 AWR STOCK

SAVAGE ARMS MSR PATROL

UBERTI 1886 HUNTER LITE BIG-BORE

WEATEHRBY VANGUARD CAMILLA

Winchester Repeating Arms (winchesterguns.com)

The new XPR centerfire bolt-action series now includes a Compact model (MSRP: $549–$599) in matte black and Break-Up Country with a 20-inch barrel. The XPR Hunter Mountain Country Range (MSRP: $599) rifle features Winchester's MOA trigger system, detachable box magazine, dipped Mossy Oak Mountain Country Range camo stock, and Perma-Cote Matte Black Barrel. The legendary Model 1873 Sporter model (MSRP: $1,739) is now available in .38 Special/.357 Magnum. The Yellow Boy Model 1866 Short Rifle (MSRP: $1,299) has a 20-inch round barrel, brass receiver, station walnut stock, and is chambered in .44-40 Win.

SHOTGUNS

Benelli (benelliusa.com)

The Super Black Eagle 3 (MSRP: $1,899–$1,999) has been enhanced with better ergonomics, a beveled loading port, redesigned carrier, and a new two-piece carrier latch to make loading the magazine easier. Available in 26- or 28-inch barrels and chambered for 2 ¾-, 3-, and 3 ½-inch shells. Yes, this shotgun devours 12-gauge shells when the ducks come in fast.

Browning (browning.com)

The Citori 725 series has expanded with luxurious Grade V and Grade VII trap model shotguns. The Trap Golden Clays ($5,739) features Grade V/VI walnut stock, ventilated top and side ribs, blued barrel finish, and a 32-inch barrel. The Cynergy CX Composite (MSRP: $1,669) features crossover barrel design with a 60/40 point of impact, ventilated top and side ribs, and charcoal gray composite stock with black rubber overmolding in grip areas. The Cynergy CX (MSRP: $1,739) is also a crossover barrel design with a 60/40 POI and with Grade I walnut stock. The new BT-99 with Adjustable Buttplate and Comb (MSRP: $1,799) takes Browning's single-shot, break-action, trap shotgun and makes it fit-customizable with a Graco Pro Fit adjustable comb and butt pad plate. What better for duck hunting that an A5 or Maxus semiauto? Here's an A5 and Maxus with finishes that resist the water and mud a duck blind can dole out. The A5 and Maxus Wicked Wing (MSRP: $1,869–$1,979) finishes include a Mossy Oak Shadow Grass, Mossy Oak Bottom Lands, A-TACS, and Real Tree on the stock and forend and a Cerakote burnt bronze on the metal. The new gas-operated auto-

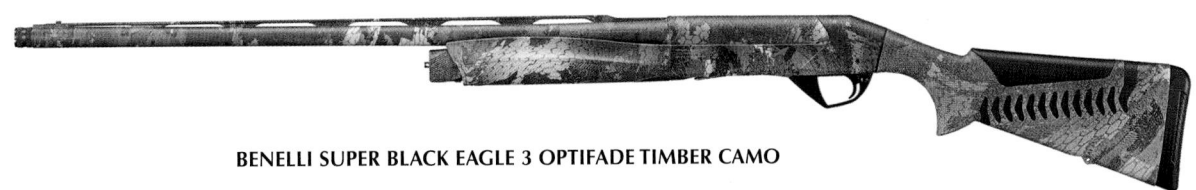

BENELLI SUPER BLACK EAGLE 3 OPTIFADE TIMBER CAMO

BROWNING A5 WICKED WING

CZ USA CZ SWAMP MAGNUM BLACK

MOSSBERG 590A1 COMPACT CRUISER AOW

loading Silver series has introduced new models. The Silver Black Lightning (MSRP: $1,260) features a gloss black and deep blued metal. The Silver Hunter Matte (MSRP: $1,150) has a silver and matte black bi-tone finish. The Silver Rifled Deer Matte (MSRP: $1,340) was designed for deer hunting with a rifled barrel for sabot type slugs, cantilever scope mount, and walnut stock.

CZ-USA (cz-usa.com)

CZ has trap shooters covered. The affordable CZ 612 Target (MSRP: $549) gets select grade wood with Monte Carlo stock and a glossy oil finish while the metal gets a deep polished blue. The CZ All-American (MSRP: $2,499) is pups built for clay sports featuring drop-in locking blocks for shooting tens of thousands of rounds a year, plus a four-way comb combined with adjustable buttplate hardware that is adjustable for cast, toe, as well as LOP. Available in either 28- or 20-gauge, the CZ 628 (MSRP: $429) and CZ620 (MSRP: $429), respectively, are classic pump guns built with elect-grade Turkish walnut and gloss blued metal. The CZ Swamp Magnum (MSRP: $929–$1,029) is a hard-hunting and hard-hitting over/under. Chambered for 3-½-

inch shells, the CZ Swamp Magnum comes in a matte black or cam finish.

Mossberg (mossberg.com)

The Model 590 Shockwave (MSR: $455) was designed for defense and ease of use with a 14-inch barrel and Shockwave Raptor bird's-head-style pistol grip. The cool thing about the Shockwave is it is completely BATF compliant—no tax stamp needed. It features a heavy wall barrel and six-round capacity magazine for 2-¾ inch shells. The Model 500 Persuader (MSRP: $467) is now available in .410 bore with a black synthetic stock and fixed cylinder bore choke. The Flex line now includes the 500 Flex Combo Field/Security (MSRP: $597) that features a synthetic stock and pistol grip along with a 26-inch Accu choke barrel and an 18-inch barrel with a fixed cylinder bore choke. Go from hunting birds to protecting the homestead in seconds due to the unique Flex system. Get eight shots of firepower with the 930 Tactical 8 Shot (MSRP: $612). The factory-installed extended magazine tube adds bite to this 930. Mini bore hunters will appreciate the 28-gauge SA-28 All Purpose Field (MSRP: $654) with blue steel and checkered wood stock.

Stevens (savagearms.com)

The affordable 555 series of over-and-unders now includes the new 555 Enhanced (MSRP: $863) with a laser-engraved receiver and Imperial walnut stock. Available in .410 bore, 28-, 20-, or 12-gauge. The 320 pump gun series now includes new Mossy Oak Shadow Grass camo model (MSRP: $238–$273). The new S1200 series of semiautomatic shotguns features an inertia-driven system at an affordable price. The S1200 (MSRP: $571) is outfitted with a black synthetic stock, the S1200 Walnut (MSRP: $681) features a checkered walnut stock, and the MO Bottomland and MO Shadow Grass Blades (MSRP: $626) have a full camo finish.

Stoeger (stoegerindustries.com)

The intertia-driven M3000 Sporting (MSRP: $699) comes tricked out for busting clays with a 30-inch ported barrel with extended choke tubes and a red-bar front sight plus over-sized, anodized aluminum bolt release and bolt handle. Need a home defender? The M3000 Defense (MSRP: $599–$649) features an 18.5-inch barrel and either a standard or pistol grip black synthetic stock. The P3500 (MSRP: $399-449) is a 3-½-inch pump gun made to handle 12-gauge magnum loads. Available in matte black or Realtree Max-5 camo and either a 26- or 28-inch barrel. Get affordable home protection with the P3000 Defense pump guns (MSRP: $299-$349) featuring an 18-½-inch barrel and either a standard or pistol grip stock.

TriStar (tristararms.com)

The ViperMax series (MSRP: $640–$730) of semiautomatics is chambered for 3-½-inch shells, offer a variety of barrel length, and are available in either a matte black or camo finish. Plus, they come with five Beretta Mobil chokes. The TT-15 DT (MSRP: $1,450) offers a raised target rib with three adjustment points, adjustable comb, palm swell, fiber optic sight, and color-coded extended Beretta/Benelli Mobil chokes.

Winchester Repeating Arms (winchesterguns.com)

The SX3 line has evolved into the SX4 with improved ergonomics like the pistol grip, which is slimmer and lighter. The controls are oversize, so they are glove-friendly. The new models include the SX4 Waterfowl Hunter (MSRP: $939–$1070), with the option of Mossy Oak Shadow Grass Blades, Mossy Oak Bottomlands, and Realtree MAX-5 camo. Models are available with a 26- or 28-inch barrel. The pump-action SXP series now includes the SXP Shadow Marine Defender (MSRP: $480–$510) with an 18-inch barrel, composite pistol grip stock, chrome-plated barrel, and magazine tube. The 20-gauge SXP Black Shadow Deer (MSRP: $550) features a 22-inch rifled barrel, 3-inch chamber, and a black synthetic stock and forearm. The receiver is drilled and tapped for optics. The SXP Turkey (MSRP: $440) comes in either 20- or 12-gauge with a synthetic stock, 24-inch barrel, and Truglo fiber optic adjustable sights.

HANDGUNS

Arex (fimegroup.com)

Serbian firearms manufacturer Arex has added the Rex Zero 1CP (MSRP: $670), a compact version of the Rex Zero 1. This is a 3.85-inch barrel all-metal 9mm pistol with a traditional DA/SA trigger, decocker, and thumb safety. Finishes include matte black and FDE. If the compact version is anything like the larger Rex Zero 1, then expect it to be well made, accurate, and reliable.

AREX REX ZERO 1CP

Browning (browning.com)

Browning's scaled down 1911 platforms—the 1911-380 and 1911-22 chambered in .380 Auto and .22 LR, respectively—are now part of the Black Label series with matte black receiver and a blackened stainless steel slide. The Black Label 1911-380 (MSRP: $800–$880) features a 4.25-inch barrel and checkered rosewood grips. Nights sights are available on some models. The Buck Mark Lite Flute UFX (MSRP: $560) is super lightweight with a 5.5-inch steel barrel encased in an aluminum sleeve that's fluted. It also includes target sights and Ultragrip Fx ambidextrous style grips. A similar Buck Mark Lite UFX (MSRP: $590) model has a matte black finish with the Buckmark symbol in silver on top side of barrel.

Colt's Manufacturing Company (colt.com)

Colt is back in the double-action revolver business with a well-known snake. The new Cobra (MSRP: $699) is a stainless six-shot revolver chambered in .38 Special and +P capable. Colt has tweaked their line of 1911 pistols with features shooters expect in a 1911. The Stainless Steel Colt Competition Pistol (MSRP: $999–$1099) features a dual-spring recoil system that reduces felt recoil. Sights consist of Novak adjustable rear sight and fiber optic front sight. It is available in .45 Auto, 9mm, and .38 Super. The 10mm auto Delta Elite (MSRP: $1099) now has low-profile Novak sights, upswept beavertail grip safety, extended thumb safety, composite grips with Delta medallions, and a receiver with or without an accessory rail. The compact Defender (MSRP: $899–$949) now has a slide tapered at the muzzle to reduce weight and comes in a black Cerakote finish.

CZ-USA (cz-usa.com)

The new CZ P-10 (MSRP: $499–$541) is a striker-fire pistol with a trigger designed for a crisp break. The P-10 has interchangeable backstraps and is chambered in either 9mm or .40 S&W with a seventeen- or fifteen-round magazine, respectively. A suppressor-ready variant is available. You can choose from black and FDE finish choices. The Phantom (MSRP: $636) is based on the SP-01 pistol series and features a polymer receiver with interchangeable backstraps. The Phantom also accepts standard CZ 75 magazines. The Shadow 2 (MSRP: $1,299) is factory tuned and competition ready. The new Shadow has a higher beavertail and undercut trigger guard for closer bore axis. The slide is contoured, it has a full dust cover and accessory rail, and the trigger is turned for better DA and SA pull. The 9mm Scorpion EVO 3 S1 (MSRP: $949) is compatible with many suppressors due to the extended forend. It features a 7.7-inch barrel and 5-inch flash can. The 805 Bren S1 (MSRP: $1,799-$1,899) has an 11-inch barrel with a two-port muzzle brake. Aftermarket arms braces are compatible with this pistol. It is chambered in 5.56 NATO and uses any AR15-style magazine.

Dan Wesson (danwessonfirearms.com)

The 1911 platform Valor (MSRP: $1,766) now comes in a blued finish with black double-diamond checkered G10 grips. Available in 9mm or .45 AUTO. The Specialist Commander (MSRP: $1,701–$2012) has a matte stainless or Duty Black finish, ambidextrous safety, extended magazine release, and flared magwell plus an accessory rail. The Pointman Carry (MSRP: $1,597) is designed for concealed carry. Chambered in 9mm only, it features a reduced barrel length and grip. From Dan Wesson's Elite Series pistols comes The Fury (MSRP: $4,899) a 1911 equipped with a Trijicon RMR optic, threaded muzzle, tall sights, and a double-stack magazine in either 9mm or 10mm Auto.

FN America (fnamerica.com)

Now the concealed carry FNS-9 Compact (MSRP: $599) comes in an FDE finish.

FN AMERICA FNS 9 COMPACT FDE

Hudson Mfg. (hudsonmfg.com)

This new manufacturer builds a pistol that combines features of a 1911 with a striker fire pistol. The H9 (MSRP: $1147) has a 1911-style grip and straight pull trigger in a striker fire. This translates to a low bore axis so there is less felt recoil. The H9 is modular using a stainless steel slide and an insert chassis. Chambered in 9mm with a 15+1 capacity.

DAN WESSON VALOR BLUE

HUDSON H9

Kimber (kimberamerica.com)

The new Custom TLE/RL II (EM) (MSRP: $1164) has an all-business matte blue finish, extended magwell, 3-dot tritium night sights, and is chambered in .45 Auto. The updated Eclipse Custom Target (MSRP: $1393) features tritium night sights, G10 Cyclone grips, and the trademark brush-polished finish slide, matte black small parts, and a gray frame. Available in .45 Auto. The Ultra+ CDP (MSRP: $1173) features a Carry Melt treatment to make it snag free, plus low-profile tritium sights, rounded main spring housing for less palm bite, and rosewood double diamond grips. The Covert series (MSRP: $1427) has a new gray finish Pro Covert model outfitted with Crimson Trace digital camo grips and 3-dot tritium iron sights. The Super Jägare (MSRP: $2688) comes out of Kimber's Custom Shop enhanced for hunting in 10mm Auto with a 6-inch ported barrel and a Leupold Delta Point reflex sight mounted to the slide. The new Micro Desert Night (MSRP: $626) has a matte black slide and desert tan receiver and Brown and black G10 grips.

KIMBER SUPER JÄGARE

Remington (remington.com)

Remington's RP9 (MSRP: $489) is a full size, striker firer, polymer-frame pistol chambered in 9mm. The R1 10mm Hunter Long Slide (MSRP: $1,310) comes with a 6-inch stainless match-grade barrel, adjustable sights, ambidextrous thumb safety, and PVD DLC finish.

Ruger (ruger.com)

Ruger has enhanced two of their popular revolver models. The GP100 (MSRP: $829) has been configured as a five-shooter and chambered in .44 Special. The Redhawk (MSRP: $1,079) has been chambered in .357 Magnum and configured to an eight-shooter. The new Mark IV rimfire pistol has been redesigned so it is easier to field strip and clean with one-button disassembly and re-assembly. The upper barre assembly pivots up at the press of a button. The new Mark IV is available in several models, including Target (MSRP: $529–$689), Hunter (MSRP: $769–$799), and 22/45 Lite (MSRP: $559). The new America Compact (MSRP: $579) has a 3.5-inch barrel chambered in either 9mm or .45 Auto. The next generation LCP II (MSRP: $349) features a short, crisp single-action trigger, better sights, and a larger grip. The SR1911 Target (MSRP: $1019) is constructed of stainless steel and equipped with Bomar-style adjustable sights.

RUGER LCP II

SIG Sauer (sigsauer.com)

The P220 Legion (MSRP: $1413) is chambered in .45 Auto and comes with three magazines, a very cool Legion Gray PVD finish, G10 grips, and a P-SAIT trigger from Grayguns, Inc. It is available in SAO and DA/SA configurations. The P226 RX (MSRP: $1440–$1549) comes optic-equipped with a ROME01 reflex sight installed and iron sights that co-witness with the optic. The polymer frame P320 RX (MSRP: $1040) in Full Size and Compact configurations also feature a factory-installed ROME01 reflex sight and taller iron sights that co-witness with the optic. The P320 Tacops Carry (MSRP: $830) is outfitted with a threaded muzzle, tall sights to clear a suppressor, and comes with four twenty-one-round magazines. The 5-inch bull barrel P320 X-Five (MSRP: $1,005) has an enhanced flat trigger, lightening cut in the slide, adjustable sights, and an extended removable magwell. The 3.9-inch barrel P320 X-Carry (MSRP: $862) has an enhanced flat trigger and a slide mount that accepts a reflex sight.

Smith & Wesson (smith-wesson.com)

The M&P M2.0 series (MSRP: $599) is the next generation of M&P pistols featuring an extended stainless-steel chassis molded into the polymer frame for reduced muzzle flip and faster recovery. Other changes are a crisp trigger with lighter pull and a tactile, audible reset, plus an aggressively-textured grip and four inter-changeable palmswell inserts. The M&P M2.0 series is available in 9mm, .40 S&W, and .45 Auto with 4.25-, 4.5-, and 5-inch barrel variants with black and FDE finishes available. The subcompact M&P Bodyguard is now available in an FDE frame equipped with or without a Crimson Trace Integral Laser (MSRP: $449). The M&P Shield (MSRP: $479–$579) has been released in .45 Auto with and without a thumb safety and tritium 3-dot night sights. The rimfire M&P line now has a M&P 22 Compact (MSRP: $429) with a threaded barrel and features a Cerakote FDE finish frame. The 686 series of .357 Magnum revolvers now has 686 Plus Deluxe models (MSRP: $899) with bright stainless finishes and textured wood grips. The .44 Magnum 629 Deluxe line (MSRP: $1,029) features a bright stainless finish, wood grips, and either a 3- or 6-inch barrel. The Model 66 Combat Magnum (MSRP: $849) is 6-shot .357 Magnum revolver with matte stainless finish, 2.75 inch barrel, and rubber grip. The .44 Mag. Model 69 Combat Magnum (MSRP: $849) is now available with a 2.75-inch barrel and rubber grip.

Springfield Armory (springfield-armory.com)

The new EMP Lightweight Champion with Concealed Carry Contour (MSRP: $1,220) features a bevel cut on the mainspring housing that prevents "palm bite" in the shooter's hand while reducing printing under clothing. The original sub-compact 3-inch barrel 1911, the EMP (MSRP: $1,104), is now available in a black hard coat finish. The TRP Operator (MSRP: $1,730) now has a Tactical Gray finish on the receiver with matte black slide. The XD(M) OSP, or Optical Sight Pistol, (MSRP: $979) is equipped with a slide milled to accept three different adapter plates for various reflex optics. The XD MOD.2 GripZone texture is now available on the .45 Auto 4-Inch Service Model (MSRP: $593) and the 5-Inch Tactical Model (MSRP: $637).

**SPRINGFIELD ARMORY XD(M) OSP
FULL SIZE 9MM**

Taurus (taurususa.com)

The Spectrum (MSRP: $289-$305) is a sub compact pistol chambered in .380 Auto and designed for conceal carry. The grip incorporates soft-touch polymer and has rounded edges for a more comfortable grip. The Spectrum is available in a wide range of finish options including eight standard colors and multiple color combinations. The unique bended Curve (MSRP: $419) now comes with a more powerful Viridian laser/light that punches holes int he darkness.

Walther (waltherarms.com)

The new and affordable Creed (MSRP: $399) offers shooters conceal carry firepower in a compact polymer frame 9mm pistol. Using a pre-cocked double-action trigger system, the Creed offers a smooth consistent trigger pull and a bobbed hammer. No snags when drawing the Creed from conceal cover.

WALTHER CREED

OPTICS

Bushnell (bushnell.com)

The compact Elite Tactical DMR II-i 3.5-21x50mm (MSRP: $1,932–$1,999) is built for long-range, precision shooting and features the new G3 illuminated reticle which provides

**BUSHNELL ELITE TACTICAL
LRTSI FLAT DARK EARTH**

precision holdovers at any range. The Elite Tactical LRTSi (MSRP: $1616–$1867) in 3-12x44mm and 4.5-18x44mm are built for precision shooting on AR-15 platforms. For 3-gun competitors is the Elite Tactical SMRS (MSRP: $1822) designed for short- and mid-range shooting with an illuminated BTR-2 reticle. The AR Optics series has introduced new models. The Enrage Red Dot (MSRP: $240) features a 2-MOA dot with 8-brightness settings and a hi-rise mount. The Incinerate Red Dot (SRP: $240) is a tube design with a circle-dot reticle.

Crosman/Centerpoint (crosman.com)

The new affordable Spectrum series rifle scopes have a first-focal plane reticle and include a 1-4x24mm model (MSRP: $180) and a side parallax adjustment models a 4-12x44mm (MSRP: $225).

Leupold (leupold.com)

The flagship VX-6 line has been improved and renamed the VX-6HD series with six new models: 1-6x24mm (MSRP: $1,689), 1-6x24mm MultiGun (MSRP: $1,819), 2-12x42mm (MSRP: $1,819), 3-18x44mm (MSRP: $2,079), 3-18x50mm (MSRP: $2,209), and 4-24x52mm (MSRP: $2,599). All feature the Twilight Max Light Management System, new automatic reticle-leveling feature and new custom dial system elevation adjustment.

LEUPOLD VX-6HD

Meopta (meoptasportsoptics.com)

The MeoTac 3-12x50mm (MSRP: $2530) rifle scope is built for tactical use and features a 34mm tube and windage and elevation ranges of 100 MOA and 55 MOA respectively with click adjustments of 1/3 MOA. Plus, the illuminated Mil-Dot 3 RD reticle is located in the first focal plane.

SIG Sauer (sigsauer.com)

Now the TANGO6 riflescope line is built with LevelPlex (an anti-cant system), new T120 turrets, and a Dev-L a

hold-over style reticle is now being offered. Most models have a shortened 34mm tube so they are more compact. Models include 1-6x24mm (MSRP: $1,680), 2-12x40mm (MSRP: $1,920), 3-18x44mm (MSRP: $2,040), 4-24x50mm (MSRP: $2,760), and a 5-30x56mm (MSRP: $3,000). The WHISKEY5 Gen2 line of hunting scopes have a 30mm tube and locking turrets. Models include 1-5x20mm (MSRP: $840), 2-10x42mm (MSRP: $960), 2.4-12x56mm (MSRP: $1,500), and 3-15x44mm (MSRP: $1,200).

Swarovski (swarovskioptik.com)

The new Z8i riflescope series offers 8x zoom magnification with a large field of view. Available models include a 1-8x24mm (MSRP: $2,688–$2,899), Z8i 1.7-13.3x42mm P (MSRP: $3,354), Z8i 2-16x50mm P (MSRP: $3,188–$3,266), and Z8i 2.3-18x56mm P (MSRP: $3,443–$3,521). An option on the Z8i line is the ballistic turret flex (BTF), which can be configured separately using several different types of ballistic compensation correction and be attached and removed at any time without tools.

SWAROVSKI Z8I

Trijicon (trijicon.com)

The MGRS or Machine Gun Reflex Sight (MSRP: $4,999) was created to withstand the constant, violent battering of machine guns and features a large objective lens with a 3-inch-by-2-inch viewing area and a 35 MOA segmented circle reticle. Centered within the reticle is a 3 MOA dot for precise aiming at close combat to extended ranges. The unit is powered by a single CR123A battery that lasts about one thousand hours of continuous operation.

Vortex (vortexoptics.com)

The Razor AMG UH-1 (MSRP: $700) is the first holographic sight to combine the durability, reliability, and energy efficiency of a red dot with the sight picture and zero-distortion of a holographic sight.

VORTEX RAZOR AMG UH-1

Browning Ammunition (browningammo.com)

Browning has increased their shotshell line with loads for turkey hunters, slug hunters, and clay target shooters. The BXD Turkey Extra Distance comes in 3- and 3-½-inch 12-gauge shells in #4, 5, or 6 shot, and 20-gauge 3-inch shells. For deer hunters who use slugs, the BXS Deer shells in either 20- or 12-gauge offers a solid copper slug with polymer tip. The cartridge line includes four new BXV Predator and Varmint loads, all of which come with nickel-plated cases and polymer-tipped bullets for rapid expansion.

Federal Premium (federalpremium.com)

Gold Medal Grand target shotshells produce less felt recoil and have more reliable ignition, improved shot hardness, and excellent reloadability—all you expect from Gold Medal shotshells. Hi-Bird shotshells are loaded with a two-piece wad that features SoftCell technology to decrease perceived recoil and produce more consistent long-range patterns. In rifle cartridges, the new Edge TLR was designed for hunting at long range using Slipstream polymer tip bullets that initiate expansion at long range, and at close range, the bullet's copper shank and bonded lead core retain weight for consistent, lethal penetration. New Gold Medal Berger cartridges feature an advanced boat-tail bullet with a high ballistic coefficient to provide the flattest trajectories, less wind drift and surgical long-range accuracy. In rimfire ammunition the new Hunter Match .22 Long Rifle provides long-range accuracy and terminal performance. The 40-gr. hollow-point lead bullet has been tuned for optimum penetration and expansion out to 100 yards.

FEDERAL PREMIUM GOLD MEDAL GRAND

Hornady (hornady.com)

The new Black ammunition line is designed to fit, feed, and function in a variety of AR platforms—direct impingement, gas piston, suppressed, unsuppressed, inertia, bolt, pump, supersonic, subsonic, rifle, mid-length, carbine, or pistol. Custom Rifle ammo now loads the classic .218 Bee (45-gr. HP InterLok) as well as the .250 Savage (100-gr. InterLok) and .264 Win. Mag. (140-gr. InterLok).

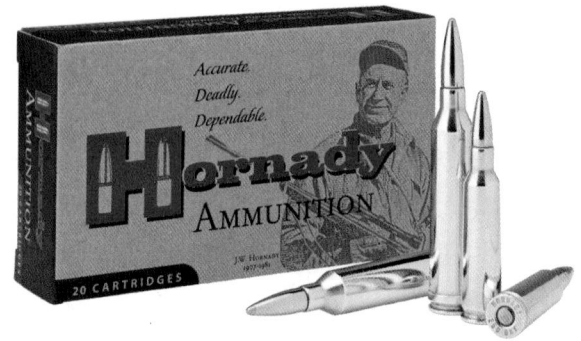

HORNADY CUSTOM RIFLE

Nosler (nosler.com)

Nosler has developed two new calibers: the .22 Nosler and .33 Nosler. The .22 Nosler amps up your AR platform with 55- to 77-gr. bullets. It offers 30 percent more energy and 300 fps more speed than the .223 Re./5.56 NATO. The .33 Nosler is designed for hunting in standard length actions and is capable of propelling a 225-gr. AccuBond bullet at 3025 fps. That's 275 fps faster than the .338 Win. Mag. using the same length action and 25 fps faster than the .338 Lapua at the muzzle while burning 18 percent less powder.

SIG Sauer (sigsauer.com)

SIG's Varmint & Predator line of rifle cartridges includes three loads: a .223 Rem. (40 gr.), .22-250 (40 gr.), and .243 Win. (55 gr.).

Winchester (winchester.com)

The new Varmint X Lead Free is a lead-free option of predator-dedicated ammunition. Available in .223 Rem. (38 gr.), .22-250 Rem. (38 gr.), and .243 Win. (55 gr.). The Super X Subsonic Power Point line of ammunition delivers the ideal balance between high performance and superior value in .308 Win. (185-gr.) and 300 BLK (200-gr.) for improved terminal performance at subsonic velocities.

NEW Products: **Rifles**

ANSCHÜTZ 1416 AMERICAN VARMINTER

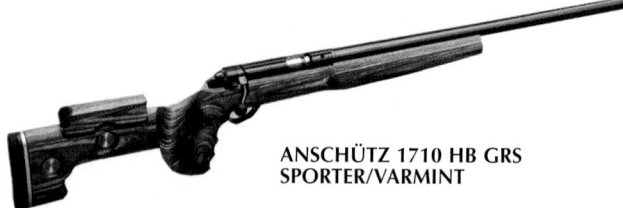

ANSCHÜTZ 1710 HB GRS SPORTER/VARMINT

ANSCHÜTZ 1771 D

AMERICAN SPIRIT ARMS 9MM SIDE CHARGER RIFLE GLOCK MAGAZINE COMPATIBLE

ARMSCOR/ROCK ISLAND ARMORY M22 TCM TACTICAL

AUTO-ORDNANCE THOMPSON 1927 A-1 T1B-14

ANSCHÜTZ 1416 AMERICAN VARMINTER

Action: Bolt
Stock: Thumbhole walnut
Barrel: 18 in.
Sights: None
Weight: 5 lb. 10 oz.
Caliber: .22 LR
Magazine: 5 rounds
Features: 64 bolt-action repeater; 5098 two-stage trigger; blued finish; hex-key bolts; medium-weight barrel threaded ½ in. x 28 tpi; no iron sight provision; counter-bored crown
MSRP **$1650.00**

ANSCHÜTZ 1710 HB GRS SPORTER/VARMINT

Action: Bolt
Stock: GRS Sporter/Varmint
Barrel: 23 in.
Sights: None
Weight: 9 lb.
Caliber: .22 LR
Magazine: 5 rounds
Features: Standard 1710 HB barreled action; two-stage 5109/2 trigger; GRS Sporter/Varmint stock; bottom metal included, as well as hex-keyed action screws
MSRP **$2395.00**

ANSCHÜTZ 1771 D

Action: Bolt
Stock: Germany-styled walnut
Barrel: 21.5 in.
Sights: None
Weight: 7 lb. 7 oz.
Caliber: .222 Rem., .223 Rem., .204 Ruger
Magazine: 4 rounds
Features: 1771 bolt action repeater; six front locking lugs; blued finish; heavy barrel; no iron sight provision
MSRP **$2195.00**

AMERICAN SPIRIT ARMS 9MM SIDE CHARGER RIFLE GLOCK MAGAZINE COMPATIBLE

Action: Semiautomatic
Stock: Synthetic
Barrel: 16 in.
Sights: None
Weight: N/A
Caliber: 9mm
Magazine: 17 rounds
Features: ASA side charging upper receiver; Mil-Std 1913 rail; M-LOK rail; dedicated 9mm Glock magazine lower; six-position collapsible Magpul MOE stock; Glock 17 magazine and hard carrying case
MSRP **$1349.99**

ARMSCOR/ROCK ISLAND ARMORY M22 TCM TACTICAL

Action: Bolt
Stock: Polymer
Barrel: 22.76 in.
Sights: None
Weight: N/A
Caliber: .22 TCM
Magazine: 5 rounds
Features: Good companion to TCM series pistol; bipod installed, top rail, threaded muzzle; interchange the Rock Island 22 TCM 1911 seventeen-round magazine
MSRP **$531.00**

AUTO-ORDNANCE THOMPSON 1927 A-1 T1B-14

Action: Semiautomatic
Stock: Walnut
Barrel: 14.5 in. finned (16.5 in. with compensator)
Sights: Pinned front blade, open adjustable rear
Weight: 12 lb. 8 oz.
Caliber: .45 ACP
Magazine: 20 rounds
Features: Detachable buttstock and vertical foregrip; blowback action, fires from closed bolt; will accept drum magazines
MSRP **$1910.00**

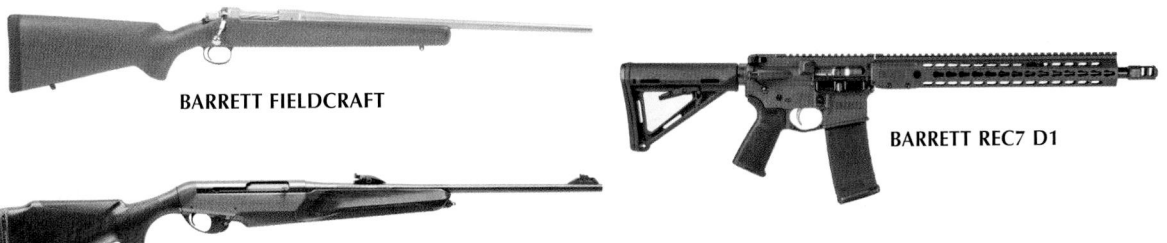

BARRETT FIELDCRAFT

BARRETT REC7 D1

BENELLI R1 PRO

BERGARA BMP (BERGARA MATCH PRECISION)

BERGARA HMR (HUNTING AND MATCH RIFLE)

BERGARA LONG RANGE

BARRETT FIELDCRAFT

Action: Bolt
Stock: Carbon fiber
Barrel: 21 in. or 24 in. by caliber
Sights: None
Weight: 5 lb.–6 lb.
Caliber: .243 Win., .22-250 Rem., 6.5 Creedmoor, 7mm-08 Rem., .308 Win., .25-06 Rem., .270 Win., .30-06 Spfd., 6.5x55 Swede
Magazine: 4 rounds
Features: Carbon fiber stock bedded to action; short or long action scaled to specific caliber; bolts made of 410 heat-treated steel and NP3 coated; 416 stainless steel barrels and receivers
MSRP $1799.00

BARRETT REC7 D1

Action: Semiautomatic
Stock: Synthetic
Barrel: 16 in. and 18 in. (6.8 SPC and 5.56 NATO), 10.25 in. and 16 in. (.300 BLK)
Sights: None
Weight: 5 lb. 8 oz.–6 lb. 8 oz.
Caliber: 16 in. and 18 in. (6.8 SPC and 5.56 NATO), 10.25 in. and 16 in. (.300 BLK)
Magazine: 10, 20, 30 rounds
Features: Hand-built, lightweight, direct impingement; Magpul MOE six-position stock, Barrett designed 15-in. KeyMod handguard, Bravo Company Gunfighter charging handle, and ALG Defense ACT trigger; bolt

carrier group plated in nickel boron finish; six receiver colors: black, tungsten grey, OD green, flat dark earth, multi-role brown, and burnt bronze
MSRP $1899.00

BENELLI R1 PRO

Action: Semiautomatic
Stock: Walnut
Barrel: 22 in.
Sights: Fiber optic front, adjustable rear
Weight: 7 lb. 3.2 oz.
Caliber: .30-06 Spfd.
Magazine: 4 rounds
Features: Includes Benelli's Progressive Comfort technology; AA walnut satin finish stock; receiver drilled and tapped for scope mount, Picatinny rail and shim kit included; CRIO treated barrel
MSRP $1499.00

BERGARA BMP (BERGARA MATCH PRECISION)

Action: Bolt
Stock: Bergara BMP chassis (machined aluminum)
Barrel: 24 in. (6.5 Creedmoor); 20 in. (.308 Win.)
Sights: None
Weight: 10 lb. 2 oz.–11 lb.
Caliber: 6.5 Creedmoor, .308 Win.
Magazine: 5 rounds
Features: Drilled and tapped for Remington 700 scope mounts;

removable buttstock adjustable for cheekpiece and LOP, allowing for a standard AR-style stock and buffer tube to be installed; detachable magazine, threaded muzzle
MSRP $1699.00

BERGARA HMR (HUNTING AND MATCH RIFLE)

Action: Bolt
Stock: Bergara BMP HMR molded with mini-chassis
Barrel: 20 in. (.308 Win.), 22 in. (6.5 Creedmoor)
Sights: None
Weight: 9 lb. 2.4 oz.–9 lb. 4 oz.
Caliber: 6.5 Creedmoor, .308 Win.
Magazine: 5 rounds
Features: Field or competition use; buttstock has adjustable cheekpiece and LOP spacers, integrated mini-chassis; one-piece Bergara B-14 action, Bergara Performance trigger, AICS detachable magazine, threaded muzzle and thread protector
MSRP $1150.00

BERGARA LONG RANGE

Action: Bolt
Stock: Carbon fiber
Barrel: 20 in., 24 in., 26 in. by caliber
Sights: None
Weight: 9 lb. 10 oz.–10 lb. 2 oz.
Caliber: .308 Win., 6.5 Creedmoor, .300 Win. Mag., .280 Ackley Improved, .30-06 Sprg., .270 Win.
Magazine: 5 rounds
Features: Proprietary Bergara Premier action; 416 stainless steel barrel with Cerakote finish; pre-threaded muzzle; four integrated QD flush cup sling mounts, integrated mini-chassis for repeatable bedding, free-floating barrel, buttstock with fully adjustable cheekpiece and adjustable LOP spacers; 20 MOA Picatinny scope mount rail
MSRP $2775.00

BERGARA MOUNTAIN

BLASER R8 INTUITION

BROWNING AB3 MICRO STALKER

BROWNING BAR MARK II SAFARI
100TH ANNIVERSARY

BROWNING BAR MK 3 DBM

BROWNING BAR MK 3 STALKER

BERGARA MOUNTAIN

Action: Bolt
Stock: Carbon fiber
Barrel: 22 in.; .24 in. .300 Win. Mag.
Sights: None
Weight: 6 lb. 3 oz.–6 lb. 6 oz.
Caliber: .308 Win., 6.5 Creedmoor, .300 Win. Mag., .280 Ackley Improved, .30-06 Sprg., .270 Win.
Magazine: 3 (magnum), 4 rounds
Features: Proprietary Bergara Premier action with nonrotating gas shield, coned bolt nose, and sliding plate extractor; 416 stainless steel barrel with Cerakote finish; Timney trigger, two-position safety; sub 1.0 MOA accuracy guaranteed
MSRP **$2190.00**

BLASER R8 INTUITION

Action: Bolt
Stock: Wood (various grades)
Barrel: Varies
Sights: Varies
Weight: N/A
Caliber: All common short-action, long-action, and magnum centerfire calibers from .204 Ruger to .338 Lapua.
Magazine: 1, 2, 3, 4, 5 rounds by caliber
Features: Designed specifically for women with a shorter length of pull and a buttstock designed to fit a woman's unique anatomy, including a higher comb, slimmer pistol grip, and a reduction of distance between the

trigger and the grip; available in all R8 wood stock configurations
MSRP . . . . **$4385.00 and up**

BROWNING AB3 MICRO STALKER

Action: Bolt
Stock: Composite
Barrel: 20 in.
Sights: None
Weight: 6 lb. 6 oz.–6 lb. 8 oz.
Caliber: .243 Win., 6.5 Creedmoor, 7mm-08 Rem., .308 Win.
Magazine: 5 rounds
Features: Intended for smaller-statured hunters; 13 in. length of pull; Pachmayr Decelerator recoil pad; drilled and tapped for scope mounts
MSRP **$599.99**

BROWNING BAR MARK II SAFARI 100TH ANNIVERSARY

Action: Semiautomatic
Stock: Walnut
Barrel: 22 in.
Sights: None
Weight: 7 lb. 14 oz.
Caliber: .30-06 Spfd.
Magazine: 4 rounds
Features: Commemorating the 100th anniversary of the BAR; every rifle produced in 2017 will receive a limited edition serial number; Safari Grade with oil finish Grade V Turkish walnut stock, polished blued finish,

and scroll engraving commemorating the military and sporting history of the BAR; hammer-forged barrel; drilled and tapped for scope mounts; detachable box magazine on hinged floor plate
MSRP **$2699.99**

BROWNING BAR MK 3 DBM (DETACHABLE BOX MAGAZINE)

Action: Semiautomatic
Stock: Composite
Barrel: 18 in.
Sights: None
Weight: 6 lb. 10 oz.
Caliber: .308 Win.
Magazine: 10 rounds
Features: Detachable box magazine with a magwell instead of the standard hinged floor plate design; QD swivel cups (QD sling swivels included); 1913 Picatinny rail scope bases; hammer-forged barrel
MSRP **$1469.99**

BROWNING BAR MK 3 STALKER

Action: Semiautomatic
Stock: Composite
Barrel: 22 in., 23 in., 24 in.
Sights: None
Weight: 6 lb. 10 oz.–7 lb. 8 oz.
Caliber: .243 Win., 7mm-08 Rem., .308 Win., .270 Win., .30-06 Spfd., 7mm Rem. Mag., .300 Win. Mag., .300 WSM, .270 WSM
Magazine: 3, 4 rounds
Features: Composite stock with contemporary design; shim-adjustable for cast and drop at comb; gas-piston operation; lightweight aluminum alloy receiver drilled and tapped for scope mounts; hinged floor plate with detachable box magazine
MSRP . . . . **$1269.99–$1359.99**
Mossy Oak Break-Up
Country: . . . . . **$1399.99–$1499.99**

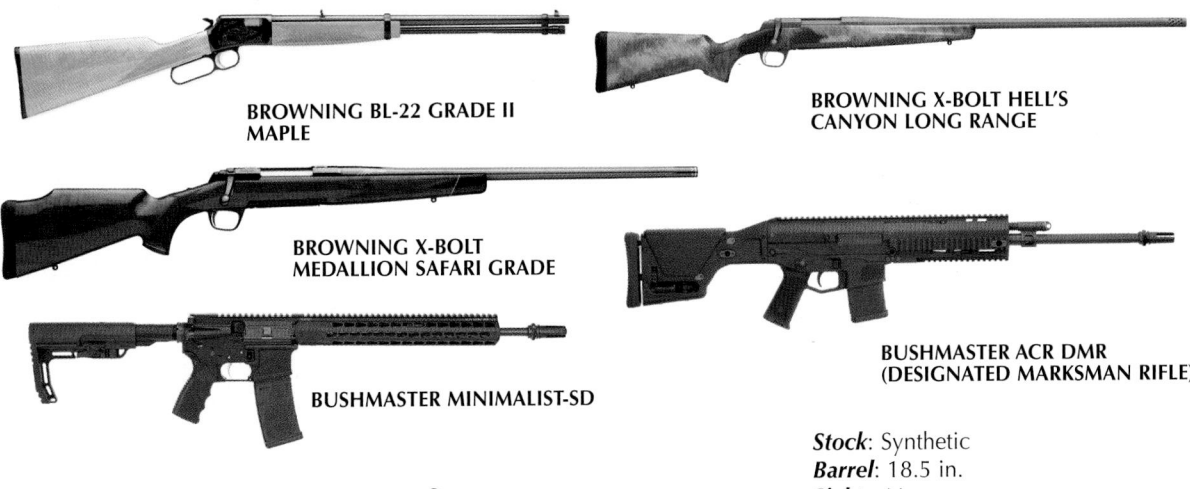

BROWNING BL-22 GRADE II MAPLE

BROWNING X-BOLT HELL'S CANYON LONG RANGE

BROWNING X-BOLT MEDALLION SAFARI GRADE

BUSHMASTER ACR DMR (DESIGNATED MARKSMAN RIFLE)

BUSHMASTER MINIMALIST-SD

CARACAL CAR814 A2

BROWNING BL-22 GRADE II MAPLE

Action: Lever
Stock: Maple
Barrel: 20 in.
Sights: Front bead, adjustable rear
Weight: 5 lb.
Caliber: .22 LR
Magazine: 15 rounds
Features: Classic .22 lever-action offered in a Grade II Maple stock; blued finish and scroll engraving; grooved for scope mounts
MSRP................ **$799.99**

BROWNING X-BOLT HELL'S CANYON LONG RANGE

Action: Bolt
Stock: Composite
Barrel: 26 in.
Sights: None
Weight: 7 lb. 3 oz.–7 lb. 8 oz.
Caliber: 6.5 Creedmoor, .270 Win., .300 WSM, .26 Nosler, 7mm Rem. Mag., .300 Win. Mag., .28 Nosler, 6mm Creedmoor
Magazine: 4 rounds
Features: Heavy sporter contour barrel for increased long-range accuracy; exclusive A-TACS AU camouflage with DuraTouch Armor Coating; free-floated, fluted barrel and receiver metal are in burnt bronze Cerakote; barrel is threaded for

suppressor use; bolt unlock button, Inflex recoil pad 60-degree short bolt lift, and detachable rotary magazine
MSRP........ **$1299.00–$2169.00**

BROWNING X-BOLT MEDALLION SAFARI GRADE

Action: Bolt
Stock: Walnut
Barrel: 24 in.
Sights: None (open sights on .300 and .375 H&H Mag.)
Weight: 7 lb. 8 oz.–7 lb. 12 oz.
Caliber: .300 WSM, .243 Win., .308 Win., 6.5 Creedmoor, .270 Win., .30-06 Sprg., 7mm Rem. Mag., .300 Win. Mag., .338 Win. Mag., .300 H&H Mag., .375 H&H Mag.
Magazine: 3 rounds
Features: Gloss grade V/VI walnut, Safari/Medallion style stock with raised cheekpiece, and rosewood forend and pistol grip cap; polished blued steel with gold-accented barrel engraving; detachable rotary magazine, short throw bolt, adjustable trigger
MSRP........ **$1999.00–$2049.00**

BUSHMASTER ACR DMR (DESIGNATED MARKSMAN RIFLE)

Action: Semiautomatic

Stock: Synthetic
Barrel: 18.5 in.
Sights: None
Weight: 10 lb. 6.4 oz.
Caliber: 5.56 NATO
Magazine: 20 rounds
Features: Modular rifle designed for instant changeout of barrels and calibers; AAC 51T flash hider; heavy barrel treated with Melonite; two-position gas piston operating system; Magpul PR52 stock; Geissele trigger
MSRP............... **$2569.00**

BUSHMASTER MINIMALIST-SD

Action: Semiautomatic
Stock: Synthetic
Barrel: 16 in.
Sights: None
Weight: 6 lb.
Caliber: .300 BLK, 5.56 NATO
Magazine: 30 rounds
Features: Ultralightweight MSR; AAC SquareDrop rail and handguard; Mission First Tactical minimalist stock, grip and magazine; ALG Advanced Combat Trigger (ACT) with 5.5-lb. pull; and AAC 51T flash hider
MSRP............... **$1169.00**

CARACAL CAR814 A2

Action: Semiautomatic
Stock: Synthetic
Barrel: 16 in.
Sights: A2 front sight, flip-up rear
Weight: 7 lb.
Caliber: 6.8 SPC, 5.56 NATO, .300 BLK
Magazine: 30 rounds
Features: Direct impingement gas-operated system; Magpul MOE handguard; two-point QD sling; cleaning kit
MSRP............... **$1300.00**

CARACAL CAR816 A2

CHIAPPA FIREARMS 1886 LEVER ACTION DELUXE

CHIAPPA FIREARMS 1886 LEVER ACTION
RIDGE RUNNER TAKEDOWN

CHIAPPA FIREARMS 1892
LEVER ACTION ALASKAN TD

CHIAPPA FIREARMS M1-9

CHIAPPA FIREARMS M6

CARACAL CAR816 A2

Action: Semiautomatic
Stock: Synthetic
Barrel: 10.5 in., 14.6 in., 16 in.
Sights: Flip-up front and rear
Weight: 7 lb. 6.4 oz.
Caliber: .300 BLK, 5.56 NATO
Magazine: 30 rounds
Features: Short-stroke push rod gas
piston system; three-position
adjustable gas valve; Caracal
handguard; full-length 1913 Picatinny
rail; Modified M4 barrel contour;
Magpul STR Carbine stock; A2-style
flash hider; select-fire option available
MSRP **$1850.00**

CHIAPPA FIREARMS 1886 LEVER ACTION DELUXE

Action: Lever
Stock: Walnut
Barrel: 26 in.
Sights: Dovetail front, buckhorn rear
Weight: 9 lb.
Caliber: .45-70 Govt.
Magazine: 8 rounds
Features: High-grade current
production of Browning's classic 1886
rifle; color case finished receiver;
select walnut; checkering at wrist and
forend; octagonal barrel
MSRP **$1939.00**

CHIAPPA FIREARMS 1886 LEVER ACTION RIDGE RUNNER TAKEDOWN

Action: Lever
Stock: Black-rubber-coated walnut
Barrel: 18.5 in.
Sights: Fiber optic front, Skinner peep
rear
Weight: 7 lb. 12.8 oz.
Caliber: .45-70 Govt.
Magazine: 4 rounds
Features: Takedown lever rifle with D
lever; semi-octagonal barrel; matte
blue finish; and forward-mounted
Picatinny rail; muzzle brake included
MSRP **$1413.00**

CHIAPPA FIREARMS 1892 LEVER ACTION ALASKAN TD

Action: Lever
Stock: Black-rubber-coated walnut
Barrel: 20 in.
Sights: Blade front, Skinner peep rear
Weight: 6 lb. 9.6 oz.
Caliber: .44 Mag.
Magazine: 10 rounds
Features: Takedown rifle with hard-
chromed finish and octagonal barrel
MSRP **$1250.00**

CHIAPPA FIREARMS M1-9

Action: Semiautomatic
Stock: Polymer, wood
Barrel: 18 in.
Sights: Winged front, sliding rear
Weight: 5 lb. 14.4 oz.–6 lb. 4.8 oz.
Caliber: 9mm
Magazine: 10 rounds
Features: Classic M1 carbine taking
Beretta 9mm magazines; metals matte
blue; two magazines included
Polymer: **$599.00**
Wood: **$679.00**

CHIAPPA FIREARMS M6

Action: Lever
Stock: Polypropylene closed cell foam
Barrel: 18.5 in.
Sights: Fiber optic front, military
adjustable rear
Weight: 5 lb. 12.8 oz.–6 lb.
Caliber: 12 ga./.22 LR, 20 ga./.22 LR,
12 ga./.22 WMR, 20 ga./.22 WMR
Magazine: 2 rounds
Features: Combo gun, shotgun barrel
top, .22 rimfire barrel bottom; folding
stock, interchangeable choke tubes,
and dedicated triggers for each barrel;
cleaning kit and 4–8 additional
rounds stored in the stock
MSRP **$729.00**

CHIAPPA FIREARMS MFOUR -22 GEN II PRO 11.8"

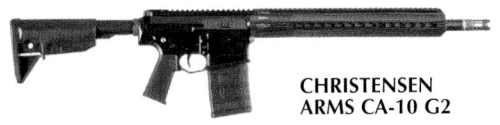

CHRISTENSEN ARMS CA-10 G2

CHRISTENSEN ARMS CA-15 G2

CHRISTENSEN ARMS MESA

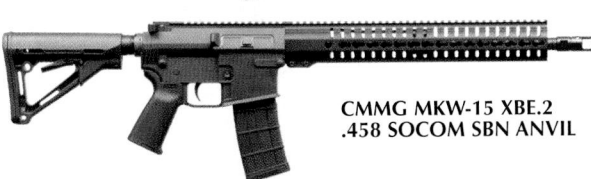

CMMG MKW-15 XBE.2 .458 SOCOM SBN ANVIL

COLT COMBAT UNIT CARBINE

Weight: 6 lb. 8 oz.–6 lb. 11.2 oz.
Caliber: 6.5 Creedmoor, 7mm-08 Rem., 7mm Rem. Mag., .308 Win., .300 Win. Mag.
Magazine: 3 (magnum), 4 rounds
Features: Featherweight contour barrel with removable stainless radial muzzle brake and tungsten Cerakote finish; skeletonized bolt handle; Limbsaver recoil pad; Invar pillars and spot bedding; match chamber and trigger; and button rifled, free-floating barrel
MSRP **$1295.00**

CHIAPPA FIREARMS MFOUR -22 GEN II PRO 11.8"

Action: Semiautomatic
Stock: Synthetic
Barrel: 18 in.
Sights: None
Weight: 5 lb. 11.2 oz.
Caliber: .22 LR
Magazine: 28 rounds
Features: Fully equipped MSR in .22 LR; eight-position Picatinny rail; six-position adjustable buttstock; heavy barrel profile; two magazines
MSRP **$609.00**

CHRISTENSEN ARMS CA-10 G2

Action: Semiautomatic
Stock: Synthetic
Barrel: 18 in., 20 in., 22 in., or 24 in. by caliber
Sights: None
Weight: 7 lb. 12.8 oz.–8 lb. 3.2 oz.
Caliber: .243 Win., 6.5 Creedmoor, .260 Rem., .308 Win.
Magazine: N/A
Features: Upper and lower of billet 7075 aluminum; integrated undercut trigger guard on lower, aerograde carbon fiber handguard on an upper with KeyMod or M-Lok configurations; match chamber and trigger; direct impingement system;

Magpul adjustable STR stock; 416R stainless barrel wrapped in steel aerograde carbon fiber; Titanium side baffle brake
MSRP **$3245.00**

CHRISTENSEN ARMS CA-15 G2

Action: Semiautomatic
Stock: Synthetic
Barrel: 16 in.
Sights: None
Weight: 5 lb. 12.8 oz.
Caliber: .223 Wylde
Magazine: N/A
Features: Custom-built AR optimized for weight and accuracy; newly designed matched receiver with a contour-matching carbon fiber handguard; single-stage match trigger; match chamber; flared magwell; button rifled, threaded, and carbon fiber-wrapped barrel; BCM Gunfighter adjustable stock; stainless steel flash hider; in stainless steel or carbon fiber
Stainless steel: **$1749.00**
Carbon fiber: **$2295.00**

CHRISTENSEN ARMS MESA

Action: Bolt
Stock: Carbon fiber composite
Barrel: 22 in., 24 in.
Sights: None

CMMG MKW-15 XBE.2 .458 SOCOM SBN ANVIL

Action: Semiautomatic
Stock: Synthetic
Barrel: 16.1 in.
Sights: None
Weight: 7 lb. 8 oz.
Caliber: .458 SOCOM
Magazine: N/A
Features: CMMG's mid-size MUTANT platform receiver in billet 7075-T6 aluminum; SLR adjustable gas block; Magpul MOE grip; CTR carbine stock with six-position Mil-Spec extension; Geissele SSA trigger
MSRP **$2149.95**

COLT COMBAT UNIT CARBINE

Action: Semiautomatic
Stock: Synthetic
Barrel: 16.1 in.
Sights: None
Weight: 6 lb. 7 oz.
Caliber: 5.56 NATO
Magazine: 30 rounds
Features: M-LOK capable handguard and flat top upper receiver ready for the addition of optical sights and accessories; mid-length gas system; lightweight profile barrel; extended handguard; black Magpul MOE SL buttstock; black pistol grip
MSRP **$1299.00**

CONNECTICUT VALLEY ARMS (CVA) SCOUT V2

COOPER FIREARMS MODEL 52 XLR LONG RANGE

COOPER FIREARMS MODEL 58 DANGEROUS GAME

COOPER FIREARMS MODEL 92 BACKCOUNTRY

CZ-USA CZ 455 TRAINING RIFLE

CZ-USA CZ 455 SCOUT

CONNECTICUT VALLEY ARMS (CVA) SCOUT V2

Action: Break-open single-shot
Stock: Synthetic
Barrel: 25 in.
Sights: None
Weight: 5 lb. 13 oz.
Caliber: .444 Mag.
Magazine: N/A
Features: New in caliber, this addition to the Scout lineup of takedown single shot rifles wears a stock of Realtree Xtra Green with stainless hardware; muzzle brake and DEAD-ON Mount included
Black:...............**$460.00**
Realtree Xtra Green: **$525.00**

COOPER FIREARMS MODEL 52 XLR LONG RANGE

Action: Bolt
Stock: Composite
Barrel: N/A
Sights: None
Weight: N/A
Caliber: Most long-range magnum calibers
Magazine: 3 rounds
Features: Detachable magazine; muzzle brake; 10 MOA Picatinny rail; tactical bolt handle
MSRP...............**$2755.00**

COOPER FIREARMS MODEL 58 DANGEROUS GAME

Action: Bolt
Stock: Various
Barrel: 24 in.
Sights: Express
Weight: N/A
Caliber: .375 H&H Mag., .416 Rigby, .416 Rem., .404 Jeffery, .458 Win. Mag., .505 Gibbs
Magazine: Hinged single-stack
Features: Front-locking lug bolt repeater with controlled round feed and mechanical ejection; Timney trigger; Wilson Arms premium match grade barrel; available in Classic, Custom Classic, Western Classic, Schnabel, and Mannlicher stock styles
MSRP..................**POR**

COOPER FIREARMS MODEL 92 BACKCOUNTRY

Action: Bolt
Stock: Composite
Barrel: 24 in.
Sights: None
Weight: 5 lb. 12 oz.
Caliber: All standard long-action calibers and magnums up to .338 caliber
Magazine: 3 rounds
Features: Lightweight Cooper Model 92 all-stainless steel action (Chromoly available on request); detachable magazine; Jewell trigger; Wilson Arms

fluted barrel with muzzle brake; guaranteed ½-MOA accuracy
MSRP...............**$2795.00**

CZ-USA CZ 455 SCOUT

Action: Bolt
Stock: Beechwood
Barrel: 16.5 in.
Sights: Blade front elevation adjustable, leaf rear windage adjustable
Weight: 5 lb.
Caliber: .22 LR
Magazine: 5–25 rounds
Features: 12-inch length of pull for youth/small-statured shooters; dovetailed receiver grooves for scope mounting; threaded barrel; single-shot adaptor shipped with firearm
MSRP..................**$339.00**

CZ-USA CZ 455 TRAINING RIFLE

Action: Bolt
Stock: Beechwood
Barrel: 24.8 in.
Sights: Blade front, tangent rear
Weight: 6 lb. 13 oz.
Caliber: .22 LR
Magazine: 5 rounds
Features: Schnabel forend and dovetail cuts for scope mounting; ability to swap barrels and stocks as with other 455s; single-shot adaptor and 10-round magazines available; Rustic version has laser cut stars and stripes checkering at the grip
MSRP...............**$399.00**

CZ-USA CZ 527 AMERICAN/
AMERICAN RUSTIC

CZ-USA CZ 577 VARMINT

CZ-USA CZ 527 AMERICAN SYNTHETIC
SUPPRESSOR-READY

CZ-USA CZ 805 BREN
S1 CARBINE

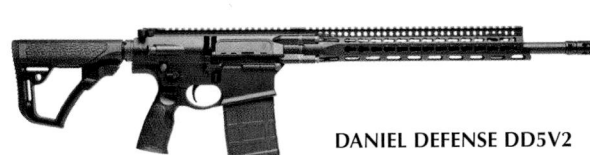

DANIEL DEFENSE DD5 AMBUSH

DANIEL DEFENSE DD5V2

CZ-USA CZ 527 AMERICAN/AMERICAN RUSTIC

Action: Bolt
Stock: Turkish walnut (American); beechwood (American Rustic)
Barrel: 24 in.
Sights: None
Weight: 6 lb. 6.6 oz.
Caliber: .223 Rem., .204 Ruger, 7.62x39, 6.5 Grendel, .222 Rem., .22 Hornet, .17 Hornet (American); 6.5 Grendel and 7.62x39 (American Rustic)
Magazine: 5 rounds
Features: This "micro-Mauser" features a classic American pattern stock, a sporter-weight hammer-forged barrel, a single set trigger, and a recessed target crown; made to be used with optics, it ships with 1-in. steel scope rings
MSRP **$733.00**

CZ-USA CZ 527 AMERICAN SYNTHETIC SUPPRESSOR-READY

Action: Bolt
Stock: Synthetic
Barrel: 16.5 in.
Sights: None
Weight: 5 lb. 14 oz.
Caliber: .300 BLK, 7.62x39
Magazine: 5 rounds

Features: Threaded 5/8×24 for a suppressor; 13.5 in. length of pull; cold hammer-forged barrel; two-position safety; single set trigger; detachable magazine; integral 16mm scope bases
MSRP **$748.00**

CZ-USA CZ 577 VARMINT

Action: Bolt
Stock: Turkish walnut, target-style
Barrel: 25.625 in.
Sights: None
Weight: 10 lb. 14.25 oz.
Caliber: .308 Win., .243 Win.
Magazine: 10 rounds
Features: Built on the 557 short action; heavy profile that tapers to a 0.863-in. at the muzzle; palm swell, laser-cut stippling, flat forend; integral 19mm dovetail scope mount cuts
MSRP **$865.00**

CZ-USA CZ 805 BREN S1 CARBINE

Action: Semiautomatic
Stock: Synthetic
Barrel: 16.2 in.
Sights: Post front, flip-up rear
Weight: 8 lb. 7 oz.
Caliber: .300 BLK, 5.56 NATO/.223 Rem.
Magazine: 10, 30 rounds
Features: Now available in carbine form with a 16.2-in. barrel; CZ

factory's folding adjustable stock; flip-up adjustable iron sights; top and bottom Picatinny rails; two-port muzzle brake
MSRP . . . . **$1999.00–$2099.00**

DANIEL DEFENSE DD5 AMBUSH

Action: Semiautomatic
Stock: Synthetic
Barrel: 18 in.
Sights: None
Weight: 8 lb. 9.6 oz.
Caliber: .308 Win.
Magazine: DD magazine
Features: Robust four-bolt connection system with patent-pending barrel extension that securely attaches the free-floating cold-hammer-forged barrel; KeyMod handguard to upper without a barrel nut; lower receiver features integral oversized trigger guard and flared magwell for SR-25 type magazines; Geissele SSA two-stage trigger; enhanced extractor geometry; dual ejectors; Kryptek Highlander or Realtree Xtra finishes
MSRP . . . . **$3044.00–$3096.00**

DANIEL DEFENSE DD5V2

Action: Semiautomatic
Stock: Synthetic
Barrel: 18 in.
Sights: None
Weight: 8 lb. 9.6 oz.
Caliber: .308 Win.
Magazine: 20 rounds Magpul PMAG
Features: Four-bolt connection system utilizing a unique barrel extension; ambidextrous controls; configurable modular charging handle; cold-hammer-forged barrel; Geissele SSA two-stage trigger; DD Superior Suppression Device; 15-in. Picatinny top rail
MSRP **$3044.00**

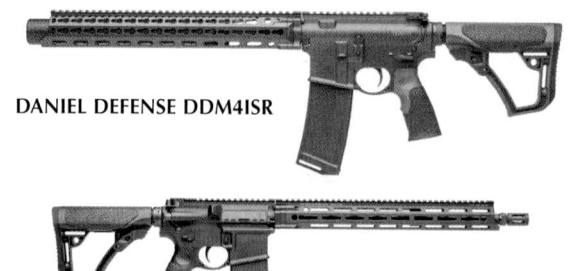

DANIEL DEFENSE DDM4ISR

DANIEL DEFENSE DDM4V7

DANIEL DEFENSE DDM4V7 LW

DANIEL DEFENSE DDM4V7 PRO

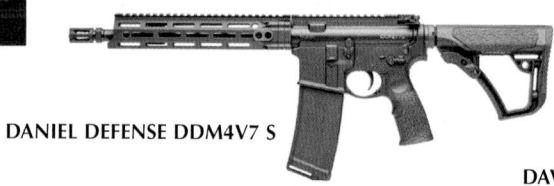

DANIEL DEFENSE DDM4V7 S

DAVIDE PEDERSOLI 1886 HUNTER LIGHT

DANIEL DEFENSE DDM4ISR

Action: Semiautomatic
Stock: Synthetic
Barrel: 9 in.
Sights: None
Weight: 7 lb. 9 oz.
Caliber: .300 BLK
Magazine: DD magazine
Features: Integrally suppressed weapon system optimized for the .300 BLK cartridge; cold-hammer-forged barrel is fluted, has a target crown; standard pistol length gas system; direct impingement; MFR XL 15.0 rail with KeyMod attachments on sides and bottom; Mil-Spec with enhanced flared magwell; rear receiver QD swivel attachment point; available in black and Mil-Spec+
MSRP **$3198.00**

DANIEL DEFENSE DDM4V7

Action: Semiautomatic
Stock: Synthetic
Barrel: 16 in.
Sights: None
Weight: 6 lb. 3.2 oz.
Caliber: 5.56 NATO
Magazine: DD magazine
Features: First rifles in the DDM4 lineup to feature the M-LOK attachment technology with the Daniel Defense MFR XS 15.0 rail;

improved flash suppressor; mid-length gas system; free-floating MFR XS 15.0 handguard; M-LOK attachment points run along seven positions; uninterrupted 1913 Picatinny rail on top; black, Daniel Defense Tornado, or Mil-Spec+ finishes
MSRP . . . . **$1679.00–$1847.00**

DANIEL DEFENSE DDM4V7 LW

Action: Semiautomatic
Stock: Synthetic
Barrel: 16 in.
Sights: None
Weight: 6 lb. 1 oz.
Caliber: 5.56 NATO
Magazine: DD magazine
Features: First rifles in the DDM4 lineup to feature the M-LOK attachment technology with the Daniel Defense MFR XS 15.0 rail; improved flash suppressor; mid-length gas system; free-floating MFR XS 15.0 handguard; M-LOK attachment points run along seven positions; uninterrupted 1913 Picatinny rail on top
MSRP **$1679.00**

DANIEL DEFENSE DDM4V7 PRO

Action: Semiautomatic
Stock: Synthetic
Barrel: 18 in.
Sights: None
Weight: 7 lb. 6.4 oz.
Caliber: 5.56 NATO

Magazine: DD magazine
Features: Designed for multi-gun competitors; 18-in. Strength-to-Weight (S2W), cold-hammer-forged barrel; rifle-length gas system; Muzzle Climb Mitigator; Geissele Automatics Super Dynamic 3 Gun trigger; MFR XS 15.0 rail with M-LOK attachment system; larger Vltor BCM Gunfighter Mod 4 Charging Handle latch; DD buttstock and pistol grip
MSRP **$1941.00**

DANIEL DEFENSE DDM4V7 S

Action: Semiautomatic
Stock: Synthetic
Barrel: 11.5 in.
Sights: None
Weight: 5 lb. 9.6 oz.
Caliber: 5.56 NATO
Magazine: DD magazine
Features: Short-barreled rifle featuring M-LOK attachment technology; free-floating, cold-hammer-forged barrel; carbine-length gas system; free-floating MFR XS 10.0 rail; M-LOK attachment points that run along seven positions; uninterrupted 1913 Picatinny rail on top
MSRP **$1679.00**

DAVIDE PEDERSOLI 1886 HUNTER LIGHT

Action: Lever
Stock: Walnut
Barrel: 22 in.
Sights: Ramped front, buckhorn rear
Weight: 7 lb. 2 oz.
Caliber: .45-70 Govt., .444 Marlin
Magazine: 3 rounds
Features: Lighter, shorter version of standard 1886 lever-action; designed to accommodate a left side-mounted Creedmoor sight; barrel is broach rifled; sling swivels included
MSRP **$1815.00**

DAVIDE PEDERSOLI SHARPS 1877
OVERBAUGH LONG RANGE

DAVIDE PEDERSOLI SHARPS SMALL GAME

ESCORT ARMS RIMFIRE

FN AMERICA FN 15 DMR II

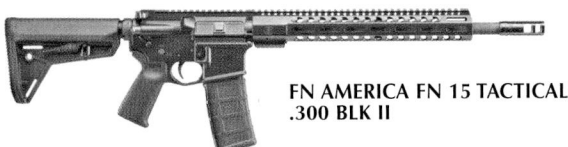

FN AMERICA FN 15 TACTICAL
.300 BLK II

FN AMERICA FN M249S PARA

DAVIDE PEDERSOLI SHARPS 1877 OVERBAUGH LONG RANGE

Action: Sharps
Stock: Walnut
Barrel: 30 in.
Sights: Blade front, military-style rear
Weight: 8 lb. 4.8 oz.
Caliber: .45-70 Govt.
Magazine: N/A
Features: Designed to meet the 10-lb. weight limitations in NRA competition; forged frame and parts; oil-finished American walnut stock with checkering; double set triggers are standard; rifle is drilled and tapped for Creedmoor sights
MSRP $2185.00

DAVIDE PEDERSOLI SHARPS SMALL GAME

Action: Sharps
Stock: Walnut
Barrel: 24 in.
Sights: Brass bead front, buckhorn rear
Weight: 7 lb. 9.6 oz.
Caliber: .22 LR, .22 Hornet
Magazine: N/A
Features: Lighter, slimmer version of standard 1874 Sharps; half-octagon,
half-round barrel styling; overall length is under 42 in.; match barrel and double-set triggers
.22 LR: $1550.00
.22 Hornet: $1580.00

ESCORT ARMS RIMFIRE

Action: Bolt
Stock: Walnut
Barrel: 25 in.
Sights: Fiber optic front, windage/elevation adjustable fiber optic rear
Weight: 6 lb. 8 oz.
Caliber: .22 LR
Magazine: 10 rounds
Features: Rimfire; chrome-plated all-steel receiver and barrel with blued finish; manual safety, cocking indicator, and ventilated rubber recoil pad
MSRP $229.00

FN AMERICA FN 15 DMR II

Action: Semiautomatic
Stock: Synthetic
Barrel: 18 in.
Sights: None
Weight: 7 lb.
Caliber: 5.56 NATO
Magazine: 30 rounds
Features: Direct impingement; FN Rail System with M-LOK that allows accessories to be mounted without any shift to zero; cold-hammer-forged, chrome lined, and free floating barrel; hard anodized aluminum flat-top receiver; match-grade Timney trigger; Magpul MOE grip; STR buttstock; Surefire ProComp 556 muzzle brake
MSRP $1999.00

FN AMERICA FN 15 TACTICAL .300 BLK II

Action: Semiautomatic
Stock: Synthetic
Barrel: 16 in.
Sights: None
Weight: 6 lb. 14.5 oz.
Caliber: .300 BLK
Magazine: 30 rounds
Features: Direct impingement; FN Rail System with M-LOK that allows accessories to be mounted without any shift to zero; cold-hammer-forged, chrome lined, and free floating barrel; FN Combat trigger; hard anodized aluminum flat-top receiver; Magpul MOE grip; MOE SL buttstock; Surefire ProComp 762 muzzle brake
MSRP $1599.00

FN AMERICA FN M249S PARA

Action: Semiautomatic
Stock: Metal
Barrel: 16.1 in.
Sights: Graduated 1000-meter front and rear combo
Weight: 17 lb.
Caliber: 5.56 NATO
Magazine: 30, 200 rounds
Features: Semiauto version of the full-auto M249 Para light machine gun; originally developed by FN Herstal as the FN MINIMI and adopted by the U.S. military in 1988; features signature 16-in. FN cold-hammer-forged, chrome-lined barrel in a quick-change configuration; formed steel frame receiver with claw extractor and fixed, pivoting ejector that ejects to the side; rotating, telescoping stock assembly with a hydraulic recoil buffer system; operates from a closed bolt and will accept both magazine and linked ammunition belts; Picatinny top rail and integral Mil-Std bipod; black or Flat Dark Earth finishes
Black: $8799.00
Flat Dark Earth: $9199.00

HENRY REPEATING ARMS BIG BOY CARBINE .327 FED. MAG. & .41 MAG.

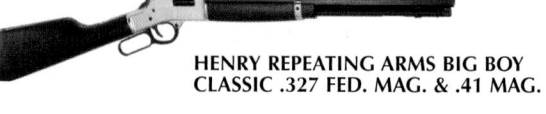

HENRY REPEATING ARMS BIG BOY CLASSIC .327 FED. MAG. & .41 MAG.

HENRY REPEATING ARMS FRONTIER MODEL LONG BARREL 24″

HENRY REPEATING ARMS FRONTIER MODEL THREADED BARREL 24″

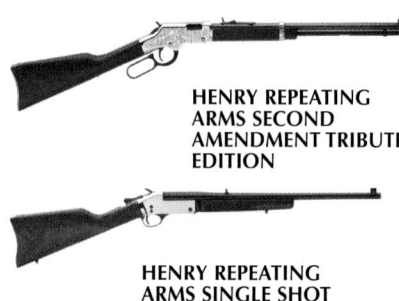

HENRY REPEATING ARMS SECOND AMENDMENT TRIBUTE EDITION

HENRY REPEATING ARMS SINGLE SHOT RIFLE IN STEEL & BRASS

HENRY REPEATING ARMS BIG BOY CARBINE .327 FED. MAG. & .41 MAG.

Action: Lever
Stock: Walnut
Barrel: 16.5 in., 20 in.
Sights: Brass bead front, fully adjustable semi-buckhorn rear with adjustable white diamond insert
Weight: 7 lb. 12 oz.
Caliber: .44 Mag., .45 Colt, .357 Mag., .41 Mag., .327 Fed. Mag.
Magazine: 7 rounds
Features: Classic brass receiver; octagonal carbine-length barrel; now available in .327 Fed. Mag. and .41 Mag. chamberings
MSRP $899.95

HENRY REPEATING ARMS BIG BOY CLASSIC .327 FED. MAG. & .41 MAG.

Action: Lever
Stock: Walnut
Barrel: 20 in.
Sights: Brass bead front, fully adjustable semi-buckhorn rear with adjustable white diamond insert
Weight: 8 lb. 11 oz.
Caliber: .44 Mag., .45 Colt, .357 Mag., .41 Mag., .327 Fed. Mag.
Magazine: 10 rounds
Features: Classic brass receiver; octagonal barrel; now available in

.327 Fed. Mag. and .41 Mag. chamberings
MSRP $899.95

HENRY REPEATING ARMS FRONTIER MODEL LONG BARREL 24″

Action: Lever
Stock: Walnut
Barrel: 24 in.
Sights: Brass bead front, fully adjustable semi-buckhorn rear with adjustable white diamond insert
Weight: 7 lb.
Caliber: .22 LR, .22 Mag.
Magazine: 12, 16, 21 rounds by caliber
Features: Merge of Henry's Lever Octagon and Frontier models; octagonal barrel adds weight, rigidity, and stability; grooved receiver for scope mounting
MSRP . . . . $470.00–$570.00

HENRY REPEATING ARMS FRONTIER MODEL THREADED BARREL 24″

Action: Lever
Stock: Walnut
Barrel: 24 in.
Sights: Brass bead front, fully adjustable semi-buckhorn rear with adjustable white diamond insert
Weight: 7 lb.
Caliber: .22 LR, .22 Mag.
Magazine: 12, 16, 21 rounds by caliber
Features: Similar to the standard Frontier Long Barrel 24-in. model but with a ½x28 threads for suppressor use
MSRP . . . . $502.00–$596.00

HENRY REPEATING ARMS SECOND AMENDMENT TRIBUTE EDITION

Action: Lever

Stock: Walnut
Barrel: 20 in.
Sights: Brass bead front, fully adjustable semi-buckhorn rear with adjustable white diamond insert
Weight: 6 lb. 12 oz.
Caliber: .22 LR
Magazine: 12, 16, 21 rounds by caliber
Features: Hi-gloss silver-toned finish on receiver cover, barrel band, and carbine-style buttplate; cover is embellished on both side flats with 19th century floral engraving set off by 24K gold-plated and raised-relief symbology that includes on its right side a flintlock rifle above the now-famous FROM MY COLD DEAD HANDS statement made by Charlton Heston (NRA president from 1998–2003) at the 2000 NRA convention, and on the smaller panel the NRA seal; the left side shows a gold American eagle in flight, the Second Amendment in a gold shield, and the Bill of Rights in a gold scroll
MSRP $1099.00

HENRY REPEATING ARMS SINGLE SHOT RIFLE IN STEEL & BRASS

Action: Break-open single-shot
Stock: Walnut
Barrel: 22 in.
Sights: Brass bead front, fully adjustable folding leaf rear
Weight: 6 lb. 15 oz.
Caliber: .223 Rem., .243 Win., .308 Win., .44 Mag., .45-70 Govt. (brass version .44 Mag./.45-70 Govt. only).
Magazine: N/A
Features: Centerfire top-lever rifle; matte finish on steel frame or a high-polished finish on hardened brass frame; steel models get curved pistol grip and rubber recoil pad; brass version have straight English grip and and brass buttplate; top lever is ambidextrous
MSRP . . . . $427.00–$549.00

HENRY REPEATING ARMS THE LONG RANGER WITH SIGHTS

HOWA CHASSIS RIFLE

HOWA KUIU RIFLE

KIMBER HUNTER

HOWA LONG RANGE RIFLE

KIMBER MONTANA

HENRY REPEATING ARMS THE LONG RANGER WITH SIGHTS

Action: Lever
Stock: Walnut
Barrel: 20 in.
Sights: Ramp ivory bead front, fully adjustable folding rear
Weight: 7 lb.
Caliber: .22 Rem., .243 Win., .308 Win.
Magazine: 4 rounds
Features: Henry's first long-range hunting rifle; exposed hammer and forged steel lever; geared action that drives a machined and chromed steel bolt with a six-lug rotary head into a rear extension of the barrel; side-ejection from alloy receiver; drilled and tapped for scope mounts; laser-cut checkering
MSRP **$1014.95**

HOWA CHASSIS RIFLE

Action: Bolt
Stock: Synthetic
Barrel: 20 in., 24 in., 26 in.
Sights: None
Weight: 9 lb. 14.4 oz.–10 lb. 3.2 oz.
Caliber: .223 Rem., .243 Win., 6.5 Creedmoor, .308 Win.
Magazine: 10 rounds
Features: CNC-machined Accurate mag 6061-T6 aluminum billet chassis accepts AR-style furniture for customization; LUTH-AR MBA-3 buttstock mounted on a six-position buffer tube; standard, heavy, and threaded barrel options; scope package includes Nikko Stirling Diamond Long Range 4-16x50 scope, with bases and rings; in black or MultiCam
MSRP . . . . **$1239.00–$1725.00**

HOWA KUIU RIFLE

Action: Bolt
Stock: Synthetic
Barrel: 20 in., 22 in., 24 in.
Sights: None
Weight: 7 lb.–8 lb.
Caliber: .204 Ruger, .223 Rem., .22-250 Rem., .243 Win., 6.5 Creedmoor, 7mm-08, .308 Win.
Magazine: 5 rounds
Features: KUIU camo on Hogue pillar-bedded stock and recoil pad; Cerakote Tactical Gray finish on barrel and action; KUIU Vias or Verde camo finishes
MSRP . . . . **$782.00–$811.00**

HOWA LONG RANGE RIFLE

Action: Bolt
Stock: Synthetic
Barrel: 26 in.
Sights: None
Weight: 9 lb. 8 oz.
Caliber: 6.5 Creedmoor, .308 Win.
Magazine: 5 rounds
Features: Bell and Carlson varmint/tactical style; vented forend; raised cheekpiece; full aluminum bedding block; 1-in. Pachmayr Decelerator buttpad; dual front sling studs; scope package includes Nikko Stirling Diamond First Focal Plane 4-16x44 scope, with rings and bases
MSRP . . . . **$1015.00–$1299.00**

KIMBER HUNTER

Action: Bolt
Stock: FDE composite
Barrel: 22 in., 24 in.
Sights: None
Weight: 5 lb. 10 oz.
Caliber: .243 Win., .257 Roberts, 6.5 Creedmoor, .270 Win., .280 Ackley Imp., 7mm-08 Rem., .308 Win., .30-06 Spfd.
Magazine: 3 rounds
Features: Lightweight stock; match-grade adjustable trigger; match-grade chamber; sporter contour stainless barrel; removable box magazine
MSRP **$891.00**

KIMBER MONTANA

Action: Bolt
Stock: Reinforced carbon fiber
Barrel: 22 in., 24 in., 26 in.
Sights: None
Weight: 5 lb. 2 oz.–6 lb. 13 oz.
Caliber: .223 Rem., .22-250 Rem., .243 Win., 6.5 Creedmoor, .25-06 Rem., .257 Roberts, .270 Win., .270 WSM, .280 Ackley Imp., .308 Win., 7mm-08 Rem., .30-06 Spfd., .300 Win., Mag., .300 WSM, .338 Win. Mag.
Magazine: 4, 5 rounds
Features: A Montana rifle with Kimber enhancements; match-grade chamber; threaded barrel; sling swivel studs; pillar bedding; sporter contour stainless barrel with satin finish; adjustable trigger
MSRP **$1359.00**

KIMBER MOUNTAIN ASCENT

KIMBER OPEN COUNTRY

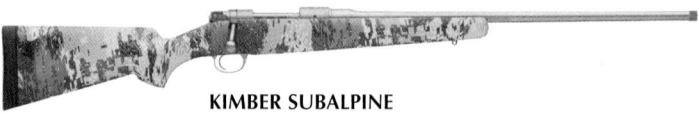

KIMBER SUBALPINE

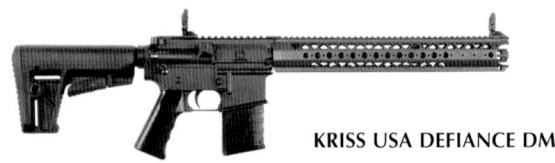

KRISS USA DEFIANCE DMK

LITHGOW ARMS LA101 CROSSOVER RIMFIRE

LWRCI REPR MK II

KIMBER MOUNTAIN ASCENT

Action: Bolt
Stock: Reinforced carbon fiber
Barrel: 22 in., 24 in., 26 in.
Sights: None
Weight: 4 lb. 13 oz.–6 lb. 7 oz.
Caliber: .280 Ackley Imp., .308 Win., .30-06 Spfd., .300 Win. Mag.
Magazine: 4 rounds
Features: Stainless fluted barrel with muzzle brake and thread protector; adjustable trigger; 1-inch Pachmayr Decelerator pad; three-position M70-type safety; Mauser claw extractor; match-grade chamber; 84M action; Moss Green stock
MSRP. **$2040.00**

KIMBER OPEN COUNTRY

Action: Bolt
Stock: Reinforced carbon fiber
Barrel: 24 in.
Sights: None
Weight: 6 lb. 15 oz.
Caliber: 6.5 Creedmoor
Magazine: 5 rounds
Features: Fluted barrel; match-grade chamber; pillar bedding; stock has Gore Optifade Open Country soft touch treatment
MSRP. **$2269.00**

KIMBER SUBALPINE

Action: Bolt
Stock: Reinforced carbon fiber
Barrel: 22 in., 24 in., 26 in.
Sights: None
Weight: 4 lb. 13 oz.–5 lb. 7 oz.
Caliber: .280 Ackley Imp., .308 Win., .30-06 Spfd., .300 WSM, .300 Win. Mag.
Magazine: 3, 4 rounds
Features: Designed specifically for elk hunters; fluted barrel; match-grade chamber; satin stainless metal finish; Gore Subalpine Optifade soft touch stock
MSRP. **$1701.00**

KRISS USA DEFIANCE DMK22

Action: Semiautomatic
Stock: Polymer
Barrel: 16.5 in.
Sights: Flip-up adjustable front and rear
Weight: 6 lb. 9.6 oz.
Caliber: .22 LR
Magazine: 10, 15 rounds
Features: All-new line of AR-platform .22 LR firearms, in partnership with War Sport Manufacturing; 4140 chrome moly barrels with 1:16 twist; threaded barrel; 13-inch free-floating handguard; 1913 Picatinny top rail with modular rail section attachments at 3, 6, and 9 o'clock positions; full metal construction; DEFIANCE DS150 Mil-Spec six-position buttstock; patented barrel adapter allows for the installation of aftermarket Ruger

10/22 barrels; black, Flat Dark Earth, OD Green, and Alpine finishes; LVOA-C option provides longer rail
MSRP. . . . . **$699.00–$799.00**

LITHGOW ARMS LA101 CROSSOVER RIMFIRE

Action: Bolt
Stock: Synthetic, laminate
Barrel: 20.9 in.
Sights: None
Weight: 6 lb. 9.6 oz.–7 lb. 3.2 oz.
Caliber: .22 LR, .22 WMR, .17 HMR
Magazine: N/A
Features: Free-floating barrel; integral molded trigger guard; length of pull adjustment spacers; Cerakote-finished barrel; receiver, bolt handle, and integral scope bases; black synthetic and laminate stock options
MSRP. . . . . **$1079.00–$1215.00**

LWRCI REPR MK II

Action: Semiautomatic
Stock: Synthetic
Barrel: 16 in., 20 in.
Sights: None
Weight: 9 lb. 4.8 oz.
Caliber: 7.62x39
Magazine: N/A
Features: Rapid Engagement Precision Rifle utilizes patented Short Stroke Gas Piston System; billet 7075 aluminum upper and lower; 12.5-in. modular rail system; gas system normal and suppressed settings; side-mounted non-reciprocating charging handle; NiCorr-treated cold-hammer-forged heavy barrel; Patriot Brown, OD Green, Flat Dark Earth, and black anodized finishes available, plus many custom options
MSRP. . . . . **$4150.00–$4253.00**

LWRCI SIX8 A5

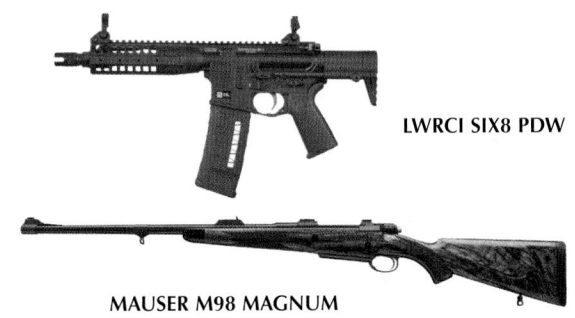

LWRCI SIX8 PDW

MAUSER M12 SOLID

MAUSER M98 MAGNUM

MERKEL MHR 16

**MONTANA RIFLE COMPANY
AMERICAN LEGENDS RIFLE**

LWRCI SIX8 A5

Action: Semiautomatic
Stock: Synthetic
Barrel: 10.5 in., 12.7 in., 14.7 in., 16 in.
Sights: LWRCI Skirmish Backup Iron Sights
Weight: 6 lb. 8 oz.–7 lb. 4 oz.
Caliber: 6.8 SP II
Magazine: N/A
Features: Short-stroke gas-piston operation with low-profile, two-position adjustable gas block; upper and lower have enlarged ejection port, upper rail with cutback scallop design, and full 12-in. modular rails; enhanced fire control group; ambidextrous sling mount; ambidextrous charging handle; Magpul MOE+ grip; LWRCI adjustable compact stock; LWRCI A2 birdcage flash hider; spiral-fluted Nicorr-treated barrel; LWRCI Mark II Advanced Combat Bolt with nickel-boron coating; Magpul PMAG magazine with high-visibility follower
MSRP . . . . approx. $2490.00

LWRCI SIX8 PDW

Action: Semiautomatic
Stock: Synthetic
Barrel: 8.5 in.
Sights: LWRCI Skirmish Backup Iron Sights
Weight: 5 lb. 14.4 oz.
Caliber: 6.8 SP II
Magazine: N/A
Features: Short-stroke gas-piston operation with low-profile, two-position adjustable gas block; upper and lower have enlarged ejection port, upper rail with cutback scallop design, and full 12-in. modular rails; enhanced fire control group; ambidextrous sling mount;

ambidextrous charging handle; Magpul MOE+ grip; LWRCI adjustable compact stock; LWRCI A2 birdcage flash hider; spiral-fluted Nicorr-treated barrel; LWRCI Mark II Advanced Combat Bolt with nickel-boron coating; Magpul PMAG magazine with high-visibility follower
MSRP . . . . approx. $2649.00

MAUSER M12 SOLID

Action: Bolt
Stock: Wood, synthetic
Barrel: 20 in.
Sights: None
Weight: 7 lb.
Caliber: .243 Win., .308 Win., .30-06 Spfd., 8x57 IS, 9.3x62
Magazine: 5
Features: Solid steel construction; Mauser's wide loading breech; thick, short barrel; three-position safety; staggered-round detachable magazine; wood or synthetic stock; open sights available at no charge
MSRP . . . . N/A

MAUSER M98 MAGNUM

Action: Bolt
Stock: Wood
Barrel: 24.4 in.
Sights: Windage and elevation adjustable two-leaf express sights.
Weight: 9 lb. 7 oz.–10 lb. 1.6 oz.
Caliber: .375 H&H Mag., .416 Rigby
Magazine: 4, 5 rounds
Features: Premium steel construction with plasma nitriding; long extractor; controlled round feed; double recoil lugs; pillar bedding; newly designed horizontal safety; double square bridge system designed for swing-off scope mounts; wood upgrades available; .416 Rigby can option heavy barrel profile
MSRP . . . . N/A

MERKEL MHR 16

Action: Bolt
Stock: Walnut, synthetic
Barrel: 22 in (standard), 24 in. (magnum)
Sights: None
Weight: 6 lb. 9.8 oz.–7 lb. 4.4 oz.
Caliber: .243 Win., 6.5x55, .270 Win., .308 Win., .30-06 Spfd., 9.3x62, .300 Win. Mag., 7mm Rem. Mag.
Magazine: 2 (magnum), 3 rounds
Features: Standard contour cold-forged barrel; precision-machined receiver; full-bodied bolt with three lugs; 60-degree bolt throw; direct trigger; chamber lock; accommodates Savage scope mount bases
Synthetic: $799.00
Walnut: $899.00

MONTANA RIFLE COMPANY AMERICAN LEGENDS RIFLE

Action: Bolt
Stock: Black walnut
Barrel: 24 in.
Sights: None
Weight: N/A
Caliber: .270 Win., .30-06 Spfd., 7mm Rem. Mag., .300 Win. Mag., .338 Win. Mag.
Magazine: N/A
Features: Released in limited quantities in 2016, this rifle is more generally available for 2017; raised cheekpiece; AA black walnut stock; black forend tip and grip cap; wrap-around checkering; barrel is free-floated, button rifled, and hand-lapped; glass bedded and sports control round feed action; Mauser-style ejector; three-position safety; right or left hand; blue or stainless steel finish
Blued: $1502.00
Stainless: $1623.00

NEW Products: **Rifles**

MONTANA RIFLE COMPANY MSR (MOUNTAIN SNOW RIFLE)

MOSSBERG MMR PRO

MOSSBERG MMR TACTICAL (VORTEX RED/GREEN DOT COMBO)

MOSSBERG MVP FLEX

NOSLER M48 LONG-RANGE

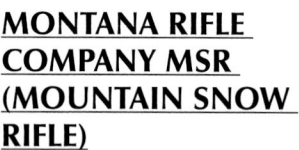

MOSSBERG MVP VARMINT

MONTANA RIFLE COMPANY MSR (MOUNTAIN SNOW RIFLE)

Action: Bolt
Stock: MRC premium synthetic
Barrel: 18 in., 20 in., 22 in., 24 in. by caliber
Sights: None
Weight: N/A
Caliber: .223 Wylde, .204 Ruger, .300 BLK, .243 Win., 6mm Creedmoor, 6.5 Creedmoor, .308 Win.
Magazine: N/A
Features: Built on MRC's X2 platform; detachable magazine box; quick-release flush cup swivel studs; Hydro-Dipped in Kryptek Pontus camo pattern
MSRP **$1731.00**

MOSSBERG MMR PRO

Action: Semiautomatic
Stock: Synthetic
Barrel: 18 in.
Sights: None
Weight: 7 lb.
Caliber: 5.56 NATO/.223
Magazine: 30 rounds
Features: Designed for 3-Gun competition; full-length direct impingement gas system; 18-in. free floating stainless barrel with M-LOK

15-in. forend; forward assist; ejection port dust cover; six-position stock; interchangeable FLEX pad
MSRP **$1393.00**

MOSSBERG MMR TACTICAL (VORTEX RED/GREEN DOT COMBO)

Action: Semiautomatic
Stock: Synthetic
Barrel: 16 in.
Sights: Red/green dot 30mm Vortex optic
Weight: 7 lb.
Caliber: 5.56 NATO/.223
Magazine: 30 rounds
Features: Direct impingement system; phosphate and hard-coat anodized metalwork; barrel gets 13-in. slim forend with M-LOK functionality; JM Pro Drop-In Match Trigger; Magpul MOE grip and trigger guard; an optics-ready version leaves out Vortex scope
MSRP **$1399.00**

MOSSBERG MVP FLEX

Action: Bolt
Stock: Synthetic
Barrel: 18.5 in.
Sights: None
Weight: 7 lb.–7 lb. 8 oz.
Caliber: 5.56 NATO/.223 Rem., .308 Win.
Magazine: 10 rounds
Features: FLEX system permits tool-less takedown; compatibility with

other FLEX stocks, including new four-position stock with dual comb; pillar-bedded stock; user-adjustable LBA trigger; Picatinny top rail; Vortex scoped package available
MSRP **$765.00**

MOSSBERG MVP VARMINT

Action: Bolt
Stock: Laminate
Barrel: 24 in.
Sights: None
Weight: 7 lb. 4.8 oz.–8 lb. 4.8 oz.
Caliber: .204 Ruger, .308 Win., 5.56 NATO/.223 Rem.
Magazine: 6, 11 rounds
Features: Laminate benchrest stock; medium blue fluted barrel, threaded and capped; matte blue finish; optional Vortex Scope package
MSRP **$754.00**

NOSLER M48 LONG-RANGE

Action: Bolt
Stock: Manners MCS-T
Barrel: 26 in.
Sights: None
Weight: N/A
Caliber: 6.5 Creedmoor, .26 Nosler, .28 Nosler, .300 Win. Mag., .30 Nosler, .33 Nosler
Magazine: 3, 4 rounds
Features: Custom Nosler 48 bedded action; aluminum pillars; free-floating Shilen stainless steel barrel; machined action rails; single stage Timney trigger
MSRP **$2495.00**

NOSLER M48 WESTERN

PATRIOT ORDNANCE FACTORY P308 EDGE

PATRIOT ORDNANCE FACTORY P415 EDGE

REMINGTON 700 AWR (AMERICAN WILDERNESS RIFLE)

REMINGTON 700 MAGPUL

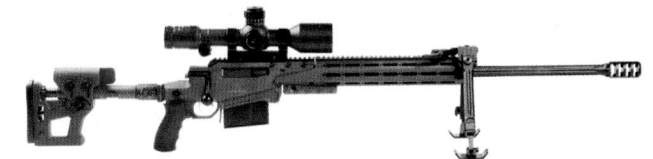

RITTER & STARK SX-1 MTR (MODULAR TACTICAL RIFLE)

steel action; X-Mark Pro trigger is externally adjustable
MSRP **$1150.00**

NOSLER M48 WESTERN

Action: Bolt
Stock: Aramid fiber reinforced composite stock
Barrel: 24.5 in.
Sights: None
Weight: 7 lb. 10.4 oz.
Caliber: 6.5 Creedmoor, .26 Nosler, .280 Ackley Imp., 7mm Rem. Mag., .28 Nosler, .300 Win. Mag., .30 Nosler, .33 Nosler
Magazine: 3, 4 rounds
Features: Designed in conjunction with Cabela's rifle department for western big-game hunting; helical barrel fluting; light contour barrel; removable muzzle brake; glass and aluminum pillar bedding; Cerakote All-Weather finish; Timney trigger; available only through Cabela's
MSRP . . . . **POR**

PATRIOT ORDNANCE FACTORY P308 EDGE

Action: Semiautomatic
Stock: Synthetic
Barrel: 16.5 in.
Sights: None
Weight: 8.1 lb.
Caliber: .308 Win.
Magazine: N/A
Features: Short-stroke gas piston action; five-position adjustable gas block; nitride heat-treated barrel; 14 ½-in. M-LOK rail; triple port muzzle break; seven-position anti-tilt buffer tube; chrome-plated bolt; Mission First Tactical furniture; E2 Dual Extraction Technology chamber; POF

drop-in trigger group; black, NP3, Burnt Bronze, and Tungsten finishes
MSRP . . . . **$2399.00–$2549.00**

PATRIOT ORDNANCE FACTORY P415 EDGE

Action: Semiautomatic
Stock: Synthetic
Barrel: 16.5 in.
Sights: None
Weight: 7 lb.
Caliber: 5.56 NATO/.223 Rem.
Magazine: N/A
Features: Short-stroke gas piston action; nitride heat-treated barrel; 14 ½-in. M-LOK rail; triple port muzzle break; six-position anti-tilt buffer tube; chrome-plated bolt; Mission First Tactical furniture; E2 Dual Extraction Technology chamber; POF drop-in trigger group; black, NP3, Burnt Bronze, and Tungsten finishes
MSRP . . . . **$1999.00–$2149.00**

REMINGTON 700 AWR (AMERICAN WILDERNESS RIFLE)

Action: Bolt
Stock: Grayboe fiberglass composite
Barrel: 24 in.
Sights: None
Weight: 7 lb. 6 oz.
Caliber: .270 Win., .30-06 Spfd., 7mm Rem., Mag., .300 Win. Mag.
Magazine: 3, 4 rounds
Features: Black Cerakote finish on a free-floated 5R rifled barrel; stainless

REMINGTON 700 MAGPUL

Action: Bolt
Stock: Magpul
Barrel: 22 in.
Sights: None
Weight: 8 lb. 12 oz.
Caliber: .260 Rem., .308 Win.
Magazine: 5 rounds
Features: Reinforced polymer Magpul Hunter stock with anodized aluminum bedding block; adjustable length of pull kit; comb height adjustment inserts; detachable magazine; carbon fiber threaded steel barrel with Cerakote finish
MSRP **$1750.00**

RITTER & STARK SX-1 MTR (MODULAR TACTICAL RIFLE)

Action: Bolt
Stock: Synthetic
Barrel: 24.5 in.
Sights: None
Weight: 13 lb.
Caliber: .308 Win., .300 Win. Mag., .338 Lapua
Magazine: 10 rounds
Features: Patented caliber conversion system; bolt locks directly into the barrel breech; aluminum receiver; fully adjustable right/left folding stock with 1913 Picatinny rail for monopod use; top-side MIL-STD 1913 Picatinny rail with 12, 20, or 40 MOA forward inclination and installed directly on the barrel; three-position safety; R&S muzzle brake; free-floating barrels available in fluted or bull barrel configurations; choice of adjustable triggers; adaptor allows use of single- and double-stack magazines
MSRP . . . . **$5555.00–$6555.00**

NEW Products: **Rifles**

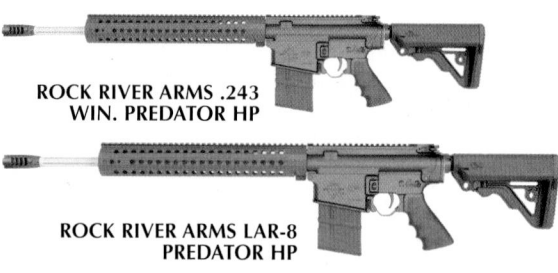

ROCK RIVER ARMS .243 WIN. PREDATOR HP

ROCK RIVER ARMS 6.5 CREEDMOOR PREDATOR HP

ROCK RIVER ARMS LAR-8 PREDATOR HP

ROCK RIVER ARMS LAR-8 PREDATOR HP MID-LENGTH

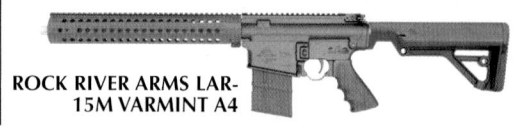

ROCK RIVER ARMS LAR-15M VARMINT A4

ROCK RIVER ARMS LAR-15 QMC RIFLE (QUICK MAGAZINE CHANGE)

ROCK RIVER ARMS .243 WIN. PREDATOR HP

Action: Semiautomatic
Stock: Synthetic
Barrel: 20 in.
Sights: None
Weight: 9 lb. 3.2 oz.–9 lb. 8 oz.
Caliber: .243 Win.
Magazine: N/A
Features: Rifle features a forged, multi-caliber marked LAR-8M lower and a forged A4 upper; stainless steel barrel has 1:10 twist, is fluted, and cryogenically treated; Rock River's Operator muzzle brake available; low-profile gas block; two-stage match trigger with a winter trigger guard; RRA Operator A2 or CAR stock; RRA LAR-8 DLX free-floating rifle-length handrail with three short accessory rails; Hogue pistol grip
MSRP . . . . **$1950.00–$2000.00**

ROCK RIVER ARMS 6.5 CREEDMOOR PREDATOR HP

Action: Semiautomatic
Stock: Synthetic
Barrel: 20 in.
Sights: None
Weight: 9 lb. 3.2 oz.–9 lb. 6.4 oz.
Caliber: 6.5 Creedmoor
Magazine: N/A
Features: Rifle features a forged, multi-caliber marked LAR-8M lower and a forged A4 upper; barrel has 1:8 twist, is bead blasted, and cryogenically treated; Rock River's

Operator muzzle break available; low-profile gas block; two-stage match trigger with a winter trigger guard; RRA Operator A2 stock; RRA LAR-8 DLX free-float handrail with three short accessory rails; Hogue pistol grip
MSRP . . . . **$1950.00–$2000.00**

ROCK RIVER ARMS LAR-8 PREDATOR HP

Action: Semiautomatic
Stock: Synthetic
Barrel: 20 in.
Sights: None
Weight: 9 lb. 3.2 oz.–9 lb. 8 oz.
Caliber: .308 Win.
Magazine: N/A
Features: Rifle features a forged LAR-8 lower with integral Magwell and a forged A4 upper; stainless steel barrel has 1:10 twist, is fluted, bead-blasted, and cryogenically treated; available with or without muzzle brake; two-stage match trigger with winter trigger guard, RRA Operator CAR or A2 buttstock; RRA LAR-8 DLX rifle-length free-floating handguard with three short accessory rails; Hogue pistol grip
MSRP . . . . **$1950.00–$2000.00**

ROCK RIVER ARMS LAR-8 PREDATOR HP MID-LENGTH

Action: Semiautomatic
Stock: Synthetic
Barrel: 16 in.
Sights: None
Weight: 8 lb. 14.4 oz.–9 lb. 3.2 oz.
Caliber: .308 Win.
Magazine: N/A
Features: Forged LAR-8 lower and A4 upper; stainless steel barrel has 1:10 twist, is fluted, bead-blasted, and cryogenically treated; available with

or without muzzle brake; two-stage match trigger with winter trigger guard; RRA Operator CAR or A2 buttstock; RRA LAR-8 DLX rifle-length free-floating handguard with three short accessory rails; Hogue pistol grip
MSRP . . . . **$1900.00–$1950.00**

ROCK RIVER ARMS LAR-15M VARMINT A4

Action: Semiautomatic
Stock: Synthetic
Barrel: 20 in.
Sights: None
Weight: 9 lb. 1.6 oz.
Caliber: .204 Ruger
Magazine: N/A
Features: Forged, multi-caliber marked LAR-15M lower and A4 upper; stainless steel bull barrel has 1:12 twist, is fluted, air gauged, and cryogenically treated; low-profile gas block; two-stage match trigger with a winter trigger guard; A2 buttstock; RRA TRO-STD free-floating handrail with octagonal top rail providing one STD and two short accessory rails; Hogue pistol grip
MSRP **$1400.00**

ROCK RIVER ARMS LAR-15 QMC RIFLE (QUICK MAGAZINE CHANGE)

Action: Semiautomatic
Stock: Synthetic
Barrel: 16 in.
Sights: None
Weight: 7 lb. 14.4 oz.
Caliber: 5.56 NATO
Magazine: 10, 30 rounds
Features: Forged LAR-15 lower and forged A4 upper with a BCM Gunfighter charging handle; chrome moly HBAR carbine barrel with a 1:9 twist; Rock River Beast muzzle brake; two-stage match trigger; winter trigger guard; RRA MAG CAR buttstock; RRA TRO-STD free-floating handguard rail featuring an octagonal top rail with one STD and two short accessory rails
MSRP . . . . **$1400.00–$1450.00**

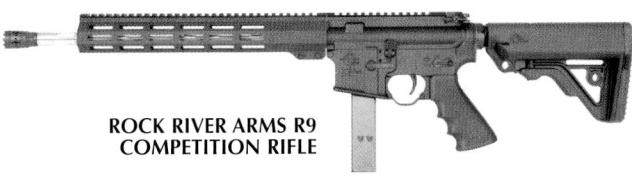

ROCK RIVER ARMS R9 COMPETITION RIFLE

RUGER AMERICAN RIFLE PREDATOR WITH VORTEX CROSSFIRE II SCOPE

RUGER AMERICAN RIMFIRE TARGET

SAKO A7 BIG GAME

SAKO A7 LONG RANGE

SAVAGE ARMS 11/111 DOA HUNTER XP

ROCK RIVER ARMS R9 COMPETITION RIFLE

Action: Semiautomatic
Stock: Synthetic
Barrel: 16 in.
Sights: None
Weight: 7 lb. 6.4 oz.
Caliber: 9mm
Magazine: N/A
Features: Forged LAR-9 lower with integral Magwell and a forged A4 upper; barrel has 1:10 twist, is chain-link fluted, and cryogenically treated; wears a 9mm Mini-Break; two-stage match trigger; RRA Operator CAR stock; RRA Lightweight Extended Mid-Length handguard; Hogue pistol grip
MSRP. **$1565.00**

RUGER AMERICAN RIFLE PREDATOR WITH VORTEX CROSSFIRE II SCOPE

Action: Bolt
Stock: Synthetic
Barrel: 18 in., 22 in.
Sights: None
Weight: 7 lb. 3 oz.–7 lb. 10 oz.
Caliber: .223 Rem., .204 Ruger, 6.5 Creedmoor, .308 Win.
Magazine: 3, 4 rounds
Features: Moss green lightweight stock; forend with grip serrations; Ruger Marksman Adjustable trigger; patented Power Bedding integra

bedding block; topped with Picatinny rail; Vortex 4-12x44mm scope with Dead Hold BDC reticle
MSRP. **$699.00**

RUGER AMERICAN RIMFIRE TARGET

Action: Bolt
Stock: Laminate
Barrel: 18 in.
Sights: None
Weight: 6 lb. 8 oz.–6 lb. 11 oz.
Caliber: .17 HMR, .22 LR, .22 WMR
Magazine: 9, 10 rounds
Features: Black laminate stock has Alexander Henry forend; Ruger Marksman Adjustable trigger; aluminum Picatinny rail; cold-hammer-forged bull barrel with installed knurled thread protector
MSRP. **$499.00**

SAKO A7 BIG GAME

Action: Bolt
Stock: Roughtech
Barrel: 24.25 in. (6.5 Creedmoor), 26 in. (all other calibers)
Sights: None
Weight: 7 lb. 8 oz.
Caliber: 6.5 Creedmoor, .270 Win., .30-06 Spfd., 7mm Rem. Mag., .300 Win. Mag.
Magazine: 3 rounds
Features: Roughtech stock features roughened external surfaces for improved grip; high-energy dissipation HiViz recoil pad; two 5mm spacers; three-lug, push feed bolt action; single-stage adjustable trigger; stainless finish barrel is fluted and has a hand-cut target crown; full

aluminum skeleton machined from extrusion; aluminum Weaver-style rails; synthetic single-stack magazine metal insert for top loading
MSRP. **$1275.00**

SAKO A7 LONG RANGE

Action: Bolt
Stock: Roughtech
Barrel: 24.25 in. (6.5 Creedmoor), 26 in. (all other calibers)
Sights: None
Weight: 9 lb. 3.2 oz.
Caliber: 6.5 Creedmoor, .308 Win., 7mm Rem. Mag., .300 Win. Mag.
Magazine: 3 rounds
Features: Roughtech stock features wider forend for prone shooting support without a bipod; fully integrated aluminum bedding; roughened external surfaces for improved grip; three-lug, push feed bolt action; single-stage adjustable trigger; aluminum Weaver-style rails; HiViz recoil pad
MSRP. **$1425.00**

SAVAGE ARMS 11/111 DOA HUNTER XP

Action: Bolt
Stock: Synthetic
Barrel: 22 in., 24 in. by caliber
Sights: 3-9x40 Bushnell Trophy scope
Weight: 7 lb. 4 oz.–8 lb. 4 oz.
Caliber: .243 Win., .25-06 Rem., .260 Rem., .270 Win., .270 WSM, .30-06 Spfd., .300 Win. Mag., .300 WSM, .308 Win., .338 Fed., .338 Win. Mag., 6.5 Creedmoor, 6.5x284 Norma, 7mm Rem. Mag., 7mm-08 Rem.
Magazine: 2, 3, 4 rounds
Features: Bushnell Trophy scope that comes mounted on Weaver Grand Slam rings and boresighted; detachable box magazine
MSRP. . . . . **$684.00–$712.00**

NEW Products: **Rifles**

SAVAGE ARMS A22

SAVAGE ARMS B SERIES (B17, B22, B22 MAGNUM)

SAVAGE ARMS MODEL 10 APO (ASHBURY PRECISION)

SAVAGE ARMS MSR 10 HUNTER

SAVAGE ARMS MSR 10 LONG RANGE

SAVAGE ARMS MSR 15 PATROL

SAVAGE ARMS A22

Action: Semiautomatic
Stock: Synthetic
Barrel: 21 in.
Sights: Adjustable
Weight: 5 lb. 10 oz.
Caliber: .22 LR
Magazine: 10 rounds
Features: Modeled after the A17, but chambered for .22 LR; straight blowback action; steel billet receiver; user-adjustable AccuTrigger
MSRP **$281.00**

SAVAGE ARMS B SERIES (B17, B22, B22 MAGNUM)

Action: Bolt
Stock: Synthetic
Barrel: 16.25 in., 21 in.
Sights: None
Weight: 5 lb. 8 oz.–6 lb.
Caliber: .17 HMR, .22 LR, .22 WMR
Magazine: 10 rounds
Features: Ergonomically designed stock with a higher comb and vertical pistol grip; top tang safety; 10-round rotary magazine; adjustable AccuTrigger; twelve new models in the series include sporter, heavy, heavy threaded (suppressor ready), and heavy stainless barrel options
MSRP . . . . **$281.00–$459.00**

SAVAGE ARMS MODEL 10 APO (ASHBURY PRECISION)

Action: Semiautomatic
Stock: Synthetic
Barrel: 24 in.
Sights: None
Weight: 10 lb. 5 oz.
Caliber: 6.5 Creedmoor, .308 Win.
Magazine: 5 rounds
Features: A partnership with Ashbury Precision Ordnance, this is a long-range chassis rifle with a factory blueprinted Model 10 barreled action mated to Ashbury's SABER MRCS-AR folding chassis
MSRP **$1799.00**

SAVAGE ARMS MSR 10 HUNTER

Action: Semiautomatic
Stock: Synthetic
Barrel: 16.125 in.
Sights: None
Weight: 7 lb. 13 oz.–8 lb.
Caliber: 6.5 Creedmoor, .308 Win.
Magazine: 20 rounds
Features: Light, compact sporting platform with 5R rifled upgraded barrel; target chamber; BLACKHAWK! AR Blaze trigger; Melonite QPQ finish
MSRP **$1481.00**

SAVAGE ARMS MSR 10 LONG RANGE

Action: Semiautomatic
Stock: Synthetic
Barrel: 20 in.
Sights: None
Weight: 9 lb. 12 oz.
Caliber: 6.5 Creedmoor, .308 Win.
Magazine: 10 rounds
Features: Long distance capabilities built on a compact frame; non-reciprocating side-charging handle; fluted heavy barrel; BLACKHAWK! two-stage target trigger; Magpul PRS adjustable stock; target chamber
MSRP **$2284.00**

SAVAGE ARMS MSR 15 PATROL

Action: Semiautomatic
Stock: Synthetic
Barrel: 16.125 in.
Sights: Custom gas block front, BLACKHAWK! flip-up rear
Weight: 6 lb. 8 oz.
Caliber: .223 Rem.
Magazine: 30 rounds
Features: BLACKHAWK! pistol grip, forend, and buttstock; .223 Wylde target chamber; 5R rifling
MSRP **$868.00**

SAVAGE ARMS MSR 15 RECON

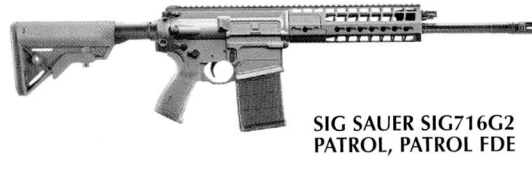

SIG SAUER SIG716G2
PATROL, PATROL FDE

SIG SAUER SIGM400
ELITE PSB

SIG SAUER SIGM400 V-TAC

SIG SAUER SIG MCX PATROL
R, PATROL FDE

SIG SAUER SIG MPX
CARBINE FDE

SAVAGE ARMS MSR 15 RECON

Action: Semiautomatic
Stock: Synthetic
Barrel: 16.125 in.
Sights: BLACKHAWK! flip-up
Weight: 7 lb.
Caliber: .223 Rem.
Magazine: 30 rounds
Features: BLACKHAWK! AR Blaze trigger; free-floating forend; upgraded Savage barrel with a 223 Wylde target chamber; 5R rifling; Melonite QPQ finish
MSRP **$999.00**

SIG SAUER SIG716G2 PATROL, PATROL FDE

Action: Semiautomatic
Stock: Synthetic
Barrel: 16 in.
Sights: None
Weight: 6 lb. 8 oz.
Caliber: 7.62 NATO
Magazine: 20 roumds
Features: Short-stroke gas piston with two-position adjustable gas valve; hammer-forged barrel; KeyMod lightweight handguard; six-position telescoping stock;black or Flat Dark Earth finishes
Black: **$2385.00**
Flat Dark Earth: **$2521.00**

SIG SAUER SIGM400 ELITE PSB

Action: Semiautomatic
Stock: Synthetic
Barrel: 11.5 in. (5.56 NATO), 9 in. (.300 BLK)
Sights: None
Weight: N/A
Caliber: 5.56 NATO, .300 BLK
Magazine: 30 rounds
Features: Direct impingement gas system; designed for single-handed firing with Pistol Stabilizing Brace (PSB); 30-round polymer magazine provided
MSRP **$1650.00**

SIG SAUER SIGM400 V-TAC

Action: Semiautomatic
Stock: Synthetic
Barrel: 16 in.
Sights: None
Weight: N/A
Caliber: 5.56 NATO
Magazine: 30 rounds
Features: Designed by Kyle Lamb; Taper-Lok flash hider; laser-engraved V-TAC logo on lower receiver; aluminum free-float V-TAC handguard; V-TAC adjustable sling; rifle bag
MSRP **$1699.00**

SIG SAUER SIG MCX PATROL R, PATROL FDE

Action: Semiautomatic
Stock: Synthetic
Barrel: 16 in.
Sights: None
Weight: 6 lb. 14.4 oz.
Caliber: 5.56 NATO, .300 BLK, 7.62x39
Magazine: 30 rounds
Features: Optimized for use with the .300 BLK cartridge and silencer; aluminum KeyMod handguard; Picatinny rail; aluminum forend; completely ambidextrous controls; telescoping three-position folding stock; three-prong flash hider; Flat Dark Earth finish available
Black: **$2131.00**
Flat Dark Earth: **$2267.00**

SIG SAUER SIG MPX CARBINE FDE

Action: Semiautomatic
Stock: Synthetic
Barrel: 16 in.
Sights: None
Weight: 7 lb. 9.6 oz.
Caliber: 9mm
Magazine: 30 rounds
Features: Gas piston-operated action; fixed gas valve; two-position collapsible stock; alloy KeyMod forend; ambidextrous charging handle; Flat Dark Earth or black finish
MSRP **$2152.00**

NEW Products: **Rifles**

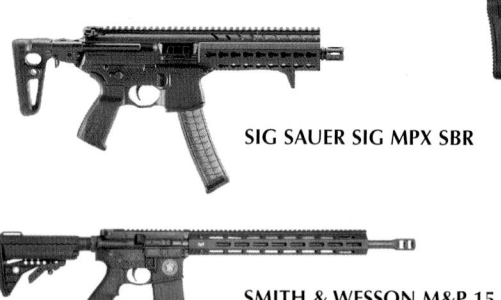

SIG SAUER SIG MPX SBR

SMITH & WESSON M&P 10 6.5 CREEDMOOR

SMITH & WESSON M&P 15 COMPETITION

SMITH & WESSON M&P 15 MOE SL MID

SMITH & WESSON M&P 15T WITH M-LOK, M&P 15T WITH M-LOK AND CRIMSON TRACE LINQ SYSTEM

SPRINGFIELD ARMORY SAINT 5.56 NATO

SIG SAUER SIG MPX SBR

Action: Semiautomatic
Stock: Synthetic
Barrel: 4.5 in., 8 in.
Sights: None
Weight: 6 lb.
Caliber: 9mm
Magazine: 30 rounds
Features: Gas piston-operated action; fixed gas valve; two-position collapsible stock; alloy KeyMod forend; user interchangeable barrels in two lengths have A2 compensator; black finish; 30-round polymer magazine
4.5-in. barrel: $1957.00
8-in. barrel: $2123.00

SMITH & WESSON M&P 10 6.5 CREEDMOOR

Action: Semiautomatic
Stock: Synthetic
Barrel: 20 in.
Sights: None
Weight: 9 lb.
Caliber: 6.5 Creedmoor
Magazine: 10 rounds
Features: MSR flattop platform; threaded muzzle with thread protector; two-stage match trigger; 15-in. free-floating Troy Alpha M-LOK handguard; 2-in. aluminum M-LOK accessory rail; Magpul MOE stock; gas-operated
MSRP $2035.00

SMITH & WESSON M&P 15 COMPETITION

Action: Semiautomatic
Stock: Synthetic
Barrel: 18 in.
Sights: None
Weight: 7 lb. 6 oz.
Caliber: 5.56 NATO
Magazine: 30 rounds
Features: Performance Center muzzle brake; two-stage match trigger; 15-in. free-floating Troy Alpha M-LOK handguard; 2-in. aluminum M-Lok rail; VLTOR I-Mod stock; Hogue pistol grip; aluminum frame; gas-operated
MSRP $1579.00

SMITH & WESSON M&P 15 MOE SL MID

Action: Semiautomatic
Stock: Synthetic
Barrel: 16 in.
Sights: Magpul MBUS rear only, standard AR-type front
Weight: 6 lb. 11.2 oz.
Caliber: 5.56 NATO
Magazine: 30 rounds
Features: Mid-length gas system; co-branded S&W/Magpul lower receiver; chromed firing pin; barrel finished inside and out with Armonite; black, Flat Dark Earth, or Stealth Gray finish
MSRP $1239.00

SMITH & WESSON M&P 15T WITH M-LOK, M&P 15T WITH M-LOK AND CRIMSON TRACE LINQ SYSTEM

Action: Semiautomatic
Stock: Synthetic
Barrel: 16 in.
Sights: Magpul MBUS flip-up front and rear
Weight: 6 lb. 11.2 oz.
Caliber: 5.56 NATO
Magazine: 30 rounds
Features: Gas-operated semiautomatic; 13-in. M&P modular free-float rail system; M-LOK capability; 2-in. M-LOK Picatinny rail; lightweight barrel with 5R rifling; Crimson Trace LiNQ System combo green laser and light available
MSRP . . . . $1189.00–$1799.00

SPRINGFIELD ARMORY SAINT 5.56 NATO

Action: Semiautomatic
Stock: Synthetic
Barrel: 16 in.
Sights: Standard post front, Springfield Armory low profile flip-up dual aperture rear
Weight: 6 lb. 11 oz.
Caliber: 5.56 NATO
Magazine: 30 rounds
Features: Type III aircraft-grade 7075 T6 aluminum upper and lower receivers are joined using the Accu-Tite system; 16-inch chrome moly vanadium barrel treated with Melonite; 1:8-inch twist; mid-length gas system paired with a heavier carbine "H" heavy tungsten buffer; Bravo Company Mod 0 pistol grip and Bravo Company buttstock; QD and fixed sling swivels; Bravo PKMT two-piece handguard; aluminum heat shields
MSRP $899.00

STEYR ARMS PRO TACTICAL
HEAVY BARREL .308

TIKKA T3X ARCTIC

TIKKA T3X COMPACT TACTICAL

TIKKA T3X FOREST

TIKKA T3X HUNTER,
HUNTER STAINLESS

TIKKA T3X LAMINATED
STAINLESS

STEYR ARMS PRO TACTICAL HEAVY BARREL .308

Action: Bolt
Stock: Synthetic
Barrel: 20 in.
Sights: None
Weight: N/A
Caliber: .308 Win.
Magazine: N/A
Features: Heavy contour threaded barrel with Mannox finish; tactical bolt knob; 20 MOA Picatinny rail; and stock spacers; two-stage magazine securing mechanism
MSRP **$1265.00**

TIKKA T3X ARCTIC

Action: Bolt
Stock: Laminate
Barrel: 20 in.
Sights: Open with range dial
Weight: 8 lb. 2 oz.
Caliber: .308 Win.
Magazine: N/A
Features: Chosen by the Canadian Rangers special forces unit; oiled laminated stock with aluminum spacers; threaded mid-contour, cold-hammer-forged barrel; open sights with range dial; mounted Picatinny rail; three-position safety; adjustable two-stage trigger; double locking lugs; plunger ejection; oversized bolt knob; detachable staggered two-row steel magazine
MSRP . . . . **N/A**

TIKKA T3X COMPACT TACTICAL

Action: Bolt
Stock: Synthetic
Barrel: 20 in.
Sights: None
Weight: 5 lb. 14.4 oz.
Caliber: .204 Ruger, .223 Rem., .22-250 Rem., .243 Win., .308 Win.
Magazine: 3, 4 rounds
Features: Designed specifically for low-recoiling centerfire rifle rounds; 30mm spacer and larger recoil pad to further improve fit and reduce felt recoil; black synthetic stock; stainless steel barrel; single-stage adjustable trigger; integral 17mm rail; drilled and tapped for scope mounts
MSRP **$725.00**

TIKKA T3X FOREST

Action: Bolt
Stock: Synthetic
Barrel: 20 in., 22.4 in., 24.4 in.
Sights: Optional open
Weight: 6 lb. 9.8 oz.–7 lb.
Caliber: .22-250 Rem., .222 Rem., .223 Rem., .243 Win., 6.5x55mm, .260 Rem., .270 Win., .270 WSM, .308 Win., 7mm Rem. Mag., 7x64mm, 7mm-08, .30-06 Spfd., 8x57 IS, 9.3x62mm,
Magazine: 3, 4 rounds
Features: Designed for hunter using scopes with large variable optics that require higher mounting; modular synthetic stock has interchangeable pistol grip and optional attachment point that allows the user to change the width of the forend; asymmetrical grip pattern provides solid grip in adverse conditions; stocks without cheekpieces have foam insert that

lowers stock-generated noise; widened ejection port improves cycling; extra top-side receiver screw permits Picatinny rail mounting; set and standard triggers available
MSRP . . . . **N/A**

TIKKA T3X HUNTER, HUNTER STAINLESS

Action: Bolt
Stock: Walnut
Barrel: 22.4 in.
Sights: None
Weight: 6 lb. 12.8 oz.
Caliber: .243 Win., 6.5x55mm, .260 Rem., .270 Win., .308 Win., .30-06 Spfd., 7mm Rem. Mag., .300 WSM
Magazine: 3 rounds
Features: Classic walnut stock has improved checkering and enhanced recoil pad; stainless finish barrel is fluted and has hand-cut target crown; receiver has widened ejection port; integral 17mm rail drilled and tapped to accept standard scope mounts or Picatinny rail
MSRP **$1100.00**

TIKKA T3X LAMINATED STAINLESS

Action: Bolt
Stock: Laminate
Barrel: 22.4 in., 24.3 in.
Sights: None
Weight: 6 lb. 9.6 oz.–7 lb.
Caliber: .243 Win., .260 Rem., .270 Rem., .270 WSM, .308 Win., .30-06 Spfd., 7mm Rem. Mag, .300 WSM
Magazine: N/A
Features: Weather-resistant gray laminate stock; cold-hammer-forged stainless steel free-floating barrel with hand-cut target crown; receiver has widened ejection port; integral 17mm rail drilled and tapped to accept standard scope mounts or Picatinny rail
MSRP . . . . **$1050.00–$1100.00**

NEW Products: **Rifles**

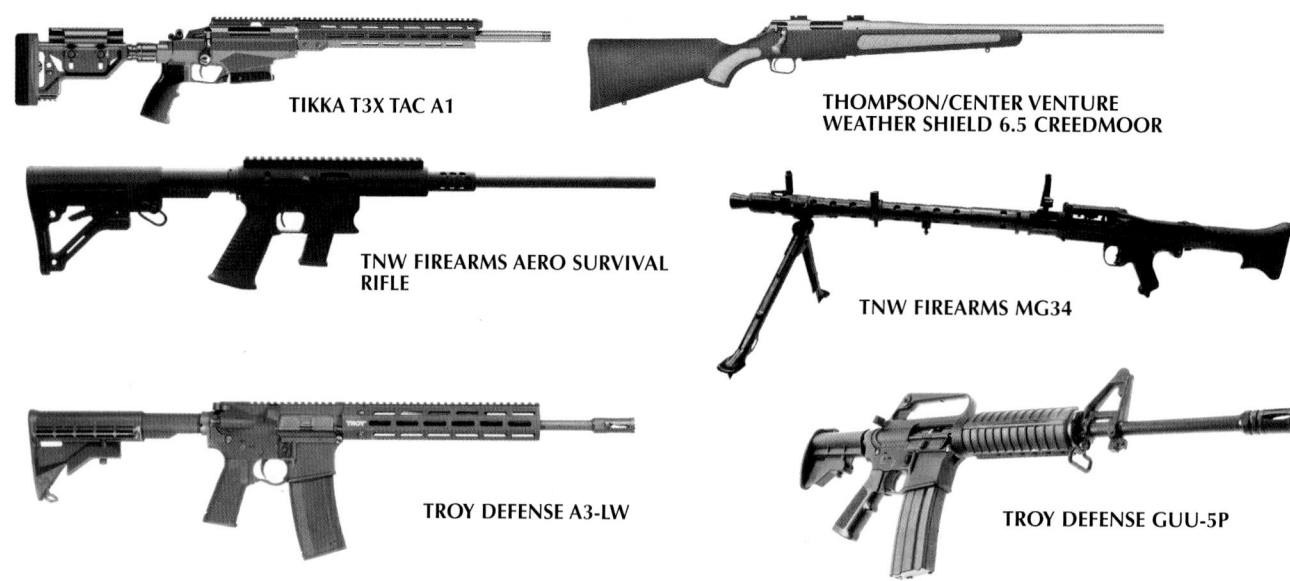

TIKKA T3X TAC A1

THOMPSON/CENTER VENTURE WEATHER SHIELD 6.5 CREEDMOOR

TNW FIREARMS AERO SURVIVAL RIFLE

TNW FIREARMS MG34

TROY DEFENSE A3-LW

TROY DEFENSE GUU-5P

TIKKA T3X TAC A1

Action: Bolt
Stock: Aluminum rear stock and middle chassis
Barrel: 16 in., 20 in., 24 in.
Sights: None
Weight: 10 lb. 5.7 oz.–11 lb. 4 oz.
Caliber: .260 Rem., 6.5 Creedmoor, .308 Win.
Magazine: 10 rounds
Features: Long-range chassis rifle; aluminum rear stock with height- and angle-adjustable cheekpiece; adjustable-height recoil pad; Picatinny rail for monopod attachment; aluminum middle chassis with modular, removable forend connector; AR-15 buffer tube-compatible interface; AR-15 pistol grip compatible slot; barrel is threaded and mid-contour; trigger is two-stage and adjustable; detachable magazine; two-way safety with bolt release lever; topside Picatinny rail
MSRP **$1900.00**

THOMPSON/CENTER VENTURE WEATHER SHIELD 6.5 CREEDMOOR

Action: Bolt
Stock: Composite with Hogue panels
Barrel: 22 in.
Sights: None
Weight: 7 lb.
Caliber: 6.5 Creedmoor
Magazine: 3 rounds
Features: Weaver-style bases factory installed; adjustable trigger;

detachable magazine; Hogue Overmolded panels; nitride-coated bolt; Weather Shield finish
MSRP **$578.00**

TNW FIREARMS AERO SURVIVAL RIFLE

Action: Semiautomatic
Stock: Synthetic
Barrel: 16.25 in.
Sights: None
Weight: 5 lb.
Caliber: .22 LR, 9mm, 10mm, .40 S&W, .357 SIG, .45 ACP
Magazine: 10, 15, 24, 29, 31 rounds by caliber
Features: Specialty survival/home-defense rifle; removable barrel and collapsible AR stock; calibers can easily be converted; TNW offers barrel threading services for suppressor use; black, Tiger Green, Pink Attitude, Dark Earth, and OD Green finishes
MSRP **$799.00**

TNW FIREARMS MG34

Action: Semiautomatic
Stock: Synthetic
Barrel: 24.5 in.
Sights: None
Weight: 10 lb.
Caliber: 8mm
Magazine: 50 rounds
Features: Semiauto version of the German lightweight machine gun that saw service in the Spanish Civil War;

belt-fed rifle fires from a closed bolt position; available with a modified grip that meets California restrictions and 10-round belt for states with magazine/belt capacity restrictions
MSRP **$4699.00**

TROY DEFENSE A3-LW

Action: Semiautomatic
Stock: Synthetic
Barrel: 16 in.
Sights: None
Weight: 5 lb. 9.6 oz.
Caliber: 5.56 NATO
Magazine: N/A
Features: Chrome-lined lightweight barrel; 13-in. Troy M-LOK BattleRail; Troy Medieval Flash suppressor; Mil-Spec trigger
MSRP **$849.00**

TROY DEFENSE GUU-5P

Action: Semiautomatic
Stock: Synthetic
Barrel: 16 in.
Sights: Front peep, A1 drum rear
Weight: 5 lb. 8 oz.
Caliber: 5.56 NATO
Magazine: N/A
Features: MSR platform with traditional looks; forged upper with carry handle; no forward assist; chrome-lined lightweight steel barrel; carbine handguard with single heat shield; A2 flash suppressor; A-frame gas block
MSRP **$999.00**

TROY DEFENSE MK-12 MOD 1

TROY DEFENSE SFOD-D M16A2 CARBINE

TROY DEFENSE SOCC CARBINE, CQB, PDW

UBERTI USA 1886 SPORTING BIG-BORE

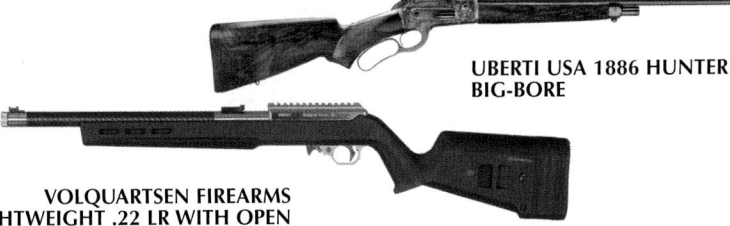

UBERTI USA 1886 HUNTER LITE BIG-BORE

VOLQUARTSEN FIREARMS LIGHTWEIGHT .22 LR WITH OPEN SIGHTS

TROY DEFENSE MK-12 MOD 1

Action: Semiautomatic
Stock: Synthetic
Barrel: 18 in.
Sights: None
Weight: 9 lb. 6.4 oz.
Caliber: 5.56 NATO
Magazine: N/A
Features: Part of Troy Defense's My Service Rifle Commemorative Series; model honors the units of Operation Enduring Freedom, Operation Iraqi Freedom, and the global War on Terror; twice-lapped 18-in. stainless steel barrel; aircraft aluminum quad rail handguard; A2 buttstock; Harris bipod with mount; Troy sling swivel mount; Troy two-piece scope mount; Ergo grip; two-point sling; 12th Model muzzle brake with suppressor mount and thread protector; polymer rail covers and forward grip; crane-style gas block; U.S. Government marking appear on the lower receiver; a portion of the proceeds from the sale of this rifle will be donated to the Lone Survivor Foundation
MSRP **$2599.00**

TROY DEFENSE SFOD-D M16A2 CARBINE

Action: Semiautomatic
Stock: Synthetic
Barrel: 14.9 in.

Sights: A2 square front post, A1 windage wheel w/ A2 peep
Weight: N/A
Caliber: 5.56 NATO
Magazine: N/A
Features: Part of Troy Defense's My Service Rifle Commemorative Series; model commemorates the 1993 Battle of Mogadishu in Somalia; forged A1 upper, large forward assist; shell deflector; chrome-lined barrel; A2 flash hider (bringing barrel length to 16 in.); fires in Safe and Semi modes but marked for authenticity with an Auto marking; carbine handguard with single heat shield; two-point adjustable sling; scope mounting bracket; 2.5-in. rail section; a portion of the proceeds of this rifle will be donated to various Special Forces family charities
MSRP **$1299.00**

TROY DEFENSE SOCC CARBINE, CQB, PDW

Action: Semiautomatic
Stock: SOCC Airborne
Barrel: 14.5 in. (Carbine), 10.5 in. (CQB), 7.5 in. (PDW)
Sights: SOCC front and rear folding
Weight: 6 lb. 12 oz.
Caliber: 5.56 NATO
Magazine: N/A
Features: Special Operations Compatible Carbines are available in three configurations; all feature G2S Geissele triggers, SOCC charging handles and rails, and Troy's own mulitposition SOCC Airborne Stock
MSRP **$1599.00**

UBERTI USA 1886 SPORTING BIG-BORE

Action: Lever
Stock: Walnut
Barrel: 26 in.
Sights: Front post, adjustable rear
Weight: 9 lb. 1.6 oz.
Caliber: .45-70 Govt.
Magazine: 8 rounds
Features: Blued full-length octagonal barrel; A-grade walnut stock; color case receiver; drilled and tapped for Lyman receiver-mounted peep sights
MSRP **$1959.00**

UBERTI USA 1886 HUNTER LITE BIG-BORE

Action: Lever
Stock: Walnut
Barrel: 20 in.
Sights: Front post, adjustable rear
Weight: 7 lb. 1.6 oz.
Caliber: .45-70 Govt.
Magazine: 3 rounds
Features: Blued round barrel; A-grade walnut stock; match-grade accuracy; receiver is color case finished
MSRP **$1899.00**

VOLQUARTSEN FIREARMS LIGHTWEIGHT .22 LR WITH OPEN SIGHTS

Action: Semiautomatic
Stock: Synthetic
Barrel: 16.5 in.
Sights: HiViz fiber optic front, TL tritium rear
Weight: 6 lb.
Caliber: .22 LR
Magazine: 10 rounds
Features: CNC-machined stainless steel receiver; carbon fiber THM tension barrel; TG2000 trigger guard; Magpul X-22 Hunter stock; black, OD Green, or Flat Dark Earth stock colors
MSRP **$1450.00**

NEW Products: **Rifles**

WEATHERBY MARK V
ACCUMARK, ACCUMARK RC

WEATHERBY MARK V ARROYO,
ARROYO RC

WEATHERBY
MARK V DELUXE

WEATHERBY MARK V LAZERMARK

WEATHERBY MARK V OUTFITTER,
OUTFITTER RC

WEATHERBY
MARK V SAFARI

WEATHERBY MARK V ACCUMARK, ACCUMARK RC

Action: Bolt
Stock: Composite
Barrel: 24 in., 26 in., 28 in. by caliber
Sights: None
Weight: 7 lb. 4 oz.–8 lb. 8 oz.
Caliber: .240 Wby. Mag., .257 Wby. Mag., 6.5 Creedmoor, 6.5-3000 Wby. Mag., .270 Win., .270 Wby. Mag., 7mm Rem. Mag., 7mm Wby. Mag., .308 Win., .30-06 Spfd., .300 Win. Mag., .300 Wby. Mag., .30-378 Wby. Mag., .338 Lapua, .338-378 Wby. Mag., .340 Wby Mag.
Magazine: 2, 3, 4, 5 rounds by caliber
Features: Overhauled Mark V line; enhanced ergonomic stock; reduced grip diameter with added palm swell; overall weight reduction; LXX Trigger; fluted #3 contour barrel; Accubrake available
MSRP . . . . $2300.00–$2600.00
RC: . . . . $2700.00–$3000.00

WEATHERBY MARK V ARROYO, ARROYO RC

Action: Bolt
Stock: Composite
Barrel: 24 in., 26 in., 28 in. by caliber
Sights: None
Weight: 7 lb. 4 oz.–8 lb. 8 oz.
Caliber: .240 Wby. Mag., .257 Wby. Mag., 6.5 Creedmoor, 6.5-3000 Wby. Mag., .270 Wby. Mag., 7mm Wby. Mag., .300 Win. Mag., .300 Wby. Mag., .30-378 Wby. Mag., .338 Lapua, .338-378 Wby. Mag.
Magazine: 2, 3, 4, 5 rounds by caliber
Features: Overhauled Mark V line; enhanced ergonomic stock; reduced grip diameter with added palm swell; overall weight reduction; LXX Trigger;

fluted #3 contour free-floating barrel; KUIU camo stock and two-tone Brown Sand/Flat Dark Earth Cerakote; Accubrake available
MSRP . . . . $2800.00–$3000.00
RC: . . . . $3200.00–$3400.00

WEATHERBY MARK V DELUXE

Action: Bolt
Stock: Walnut
Barrel: 24 in., 26 in., 28 in. by caliber
Sights: None
Weight: 6 lb. 12 oz.–10 lb.
Caliber: .240 Wby. Mag., .257 Wby. Mag., 6.5-3000 Wby. Mag., .270 Win., .270 Wby. Mag., 7mm Wby. Mag., .308 Win., .30-06 Spfd., .300 Wby. Mag., .340 Wby. Mag., .378 Wby. Mag., .416 Wby. Mag., .460 Wby. Mag.
Magazine: 2, 3, 4, 5 rounds by caliber
Features: Overhauled Mark V line; enhanced ergonomic stock; reduced grip diameter with added palm swell; overall weight reduction; LXX Trigger; AA fancy Claro walnut stock with fine line diamond checkering; rosewood forend; pistol grip caps with maple spacers; French walnut standard on .460 Wby. Mag.; Accubrake standard on .378, .416, and .460 Wby. Mags., optional on other calibers
MSRP . . . . $2600.00–$3500.00

WEATHERBY MARK V LAZERMARK

Action: Bolt
Stock: Walnut
Barrel: 26 in.
Sights: None
Weight: 8 lb.
Caliber: .257 Wby. Mag., .270 Wby. Mag., .300 Wby. Mag.
Magazine: 3 rounds

Features: Overhauled Mark V line; enhanced ergonomic stock; reduced grip diameter with added palm swell; overall weight reduction; LXX Trigger; #2 contour barrel; Claro walnut stock with five-panel laser-carved oak motif; high-luster blue metalwork
MSRP $2800.00

WEATHERBY MARK V OUTFITTER, OUTFITTER RC

Action: Bolt
Stock: Composite
Barrel: 22 in., 24 in., 26 in., 28 in. by caliber
Sights: None
Weight: 5 lb. 8 oz.–6 lb. 12 oz.
Caliber: .240 Wby. Mag., .257 Wby. Mag., 6.5 Creedmoor, 6.5-3000 Wby. Mag., .270 Win., .270 Wby. Mag., 7mm Wby. Mag., .308 Win., .30-06 Spfd., .300 Wby. Mag.
Magazine: 3, 4, 5 rounds by caliber
Features: Overhauled Mark V line; enhanced ergonomic stock; reduced grip diameter with added palm swell; LXX Trigger; fluted barrel; High Desert camo stock and Armor Black Cerakote; Accubrake available
MSRP . . . . $2800.00–$3000.00
RC: . . . . $3200.00–$3400.00

WEATHERBY MARK V SAFARI

Action: Bolt
Stock: Walnut
Barrel: 24 in., 26 in., 28 in. by caliber
Sights: Post and hood front, classic adjustable rear
Weight: 8 lb. 12 oz.–10 lb.
Caliber: .257 Wby. Mag., .270 Wby. Mag., 7mm Wby. Mag., .300 Wby. Mag., .340 Wby. Mag., .375 H&H Mag., .375 Wby. Mag., .378 Wby.

WEATHERBY MARK V TACMARK

WEATHERBY MARK V TERRAMARK, TERRAMARK RC

WEATHERBY MARK V WEATHERMARK

WEATHERBY MARK V TACMARK ELITE

WEATHERBY MARK V ULTRA LIGHTWEIGHT

Mag., .416 Wby. Mag., .460 Wby. Mag.
Magazine: 2, 3 rounds by caliber
Features: Overhauled Mark V line; enhanced ergonomic stock; reduced grip diameter with added palm swell; overall weight reduction; LXX Trigger; #2, #3, or #4 contour barrel depending on caliber; AAA fancy French walnut stock with ebony forend and hand-cut fleur-de-lis pattern checkering; Damascened bolt and follower; floorplate is engraved with "Safari Custom"; left-hand versions, Accubrake available
MSRP . . . . **$6900.00–$7300.00**

WEATHERBY MARK V TACMARK

Action: Bolt
Stock: Composite
Barrel: 28 in.
Sights: None
Weight: 11 lb. 4 oz.
Caliber: .30-378 Wby. Mag., .338 Lapua, .338-378 Wby. Mag.
Magazine: 5 rounds
Features: Overhauled Mark V line; enhanced ergonomic stock; reduced grip diameter with added palm swell; overall weight reduction; LXX Trigger; fluted free-floating barrel; fully adjustable composite stock with CNC-machined aluminum bedding plate; Accubrake
MSRP **$3600.00**

WEATHERBY MARK V TACMARK ELITE

Action: Bolt
Stock: Composite
Barrel: 28 in.
Sights: None
Weight: 11 lb. 12 oz.
Caliber: .30-378 Wby. Mag., .338 Lapua, .338-378 Wby. Mag.
Magazine: 5 rounds

Features: Overhauled Mark V line; enhanced ergonomic stock; reduced grip diameter with added palm swell; overall weight reduction; LXX Trigger; hand-lapped Krieger Custom match-grade, cut-rifled, free-floating #3 contour barrel; hand-lapped action; fully adjustable composite stock with CNC-machined aluminum bedding plate; DD Ross tactical bolt knob; muzzle brake has 90-degree lateral dispersion ports; Range Certified model comes with Oehler Ballistic Imaging System printout signed and certified by Ed or Adam Weatherby
MSRP **$5000.00**

WEATHERBY MARK V TERRAMARK, TERRAMARK RC

Action: Bolt
Stock: Composite
Barrel: 24 in., 26 in., 28 in. by caliber
Sights: None
Weight: 7 lb. 4 oz.–8 lb. 8 oz.
Caliber: .240 Wby. Mag., .257 Wby. Mag., 6.5 Creedmoor, 6.5-3000 Wby. Mag., .270 Wby. Mag., 7mm Wby. Mag., .300 Win. Mag., .300 Wby. Mag., .30-378 Wby. Mag., .338 Lapua, .338-378 Wby. Mag.
Magazine: 2, 3, 4, 5 rounds by caliber
Features: Overhauled Mark V line; enhanced ergonomic stock; reduced grip diameter with added palm swell; overall weight reduction; LXX Trigger; fluted #3 contour free-floating barrel; Range Certified version comes with Oehler Ballistic Imaging System printout signed and certified by Ed or Adam Weatherby; Flat Dark Earth Cerakote finish; Accubrake available
MSRP . . . . **$2800.00–$3000.00**
RC: . . . . **$3200.00–$3400.00**

WEATHERBY MARK V ULTRA LIGHTWEIGHT

Action: Bolt
Stock: Composite
Barrel: 22 in., 24 in., 26 in., 28 in. by caliber
Sights: None
Weight: 5 lb. 12 oz.–6 lb. 12 oz.
Caliber: .240 Wby. Mag., .257 Wby. Mag., 6.5 Creedmoor, 6.5-3000 Wby. Mag., .270 Win., .270 Wby. Mag., 7mm Rem. Mag., 7mm Wby. Mag., .308 Win., .30-06 Spfd., .300 Win. Mag., .300 Wby. Mag.
Magazine: 3, 4, 5 rounds by caliber
Features: Overhauled Mark V line; enhanced ergonomic stock; reduced grip diameter with added palm swell; overall weight reduction; LXX Trigger; six lugs in standard calibers, nine in magnum; fluted barrel; Accubrake available
MSRP . . . . **$2300.00–$2400.00**

WEATHERBY MARK V WEATHERMARK

Action: Bolt
Stock: Composite
Barrel: 24 in., 26 in., 28 in. by caliber
Sights: None
Weight: 6 lb. 4 oz.–8 lb. 4 oz.
Caliber: .240 Wby. Mag., .257 Wby. Mag., 6.5-3000 Wby. Mag., .270 Win., .270 Wby. Mag., 7mm Rem. Mag., 7mm Wby. Mag., .308 Win., .30-06 Spfd., .300 Win. Mag., .300 Wby. Mag., .30-378 Wby. Mag., .338-378 Wby. Mag., .340 Wby. Mag., .375 H&H Mag.
Magazine: 2, 3, 5 rounds by caliber
Features: Overhauled Mark V line; enhanced ergonomic stock; reduced grip diameter with added palm swell; overall weight reduction; LXX Trigger; non-fluted barrel in #1, #2, or #3 contour depending on caliber; Tactical Gray Cerakote finish; Accubrake available
MSRP . . . . **$1700.00–$2000.00**

WEATHERBY VANGUARD ADAPTIVE
COMPOSITE (VAC)

WEATHERBY VANGUARD CAMILLA

WINCHESTER REPEATING ARMS
MODEL 1866 SHORT RIFLE

WINCHESTER REPEATING ARMS MODEL
1873 SPORTER

WINCHESTER REPEATING ARMS MODEL
1892 125TH ANNIVERSARY SPORTER

WEATHERBY VANGUARD ADAPTIVE COMPOSITE (VAC)

Action: Bolt
Stock: Composite
Barrel: 20 in.
Sights: None
Weight: 8 lb. 12 oz.
Caliber: .223 Rem., 6.5 Creedmoor, .308 Win.
Magazine: 4, 5 rounds
Features: Stock features quick and easy push button system for adjusting both length of pull and height of the comb; full and lowered forend offers an improved grip for shooting while standing as well as a stud to which a bipod and/or sling can be attached
MSRP **$1269.00**

WEATHERBY VANGUARD CAMILLA

Action: Bolt
Stock: Walnut
Barrel: 20 in.
Sights: None
Weight: 6 lb. 8 oz.
Caliber: .243 Win., 6.5 Creedmoor, 7mm-08 Rem., .308 Rem.
Magazine: 4, 5 rounds
Features: Designed specifically for women by a select team of women hunters and shooters; stock made to fit women; length-of-pull shortened to 13 in.; higher comb to align shooter's eye with optics; shorter, slimmer forearm and grip
MSRP **$849.00**

WINCHESTER REPEATING ARMS MODEL 1866 SHORT RIFLE

Action: Lever
Stock: Walnut
Barrel: 20 in.
Sights: Marble Arms gold bead front, folding leaf rear
Weight: 7 lb.
Caliber: .38 Spl., .44-40 Win.
Magazine: 10, 11 rounds by caliber
Features: Crescent brass buttplate; full-length tube magazine; open top ejection; bright polished blue finish; American walnut straight grip stock
MSRP **$1299.99**

WINCHESTER REPEATING ARMS MODEL 1873 SPORTER

Action: Lever
Stock: Walnut
Barrel: 24 in.
Sights: Marble Arms gold bead front, semi-buckhorn rear
Weight: 8 lb.
Caliber: .357 Mag., .44-40 Win., .45 Colt
Magazine: 14 rounds
Features: Classic lever has octagon barrel; pistol grip Grade II/III walnut stock; top tang drilled and tapped for tang-mounted rear sight; crescent buttplate; deep-polished blue finish
MSRP **$1739.99**

WINCHESTER REPEATING ARMS MODEL 1892 125TH ANNIVERSARY SPORTER

Action: Lever
Stock: Walnut
Barrel: 24 in.
Sights: Front post, folding leaf rear
Weight: 6 lb.
Caliber: .357 Mag., .44 Rem. Mag., .44-40 Win., .45 Colt
Magazine: 13 rounds
Features: Half-octagon/half-round button rifled barrel in gloss blue finish; grade IV/V walnut with top tang safety; scroll engraving on receiver; top tang is drilled and tapped for optional peep sight
MSRP **$1799.99**

WINCHESTER REPEATING ARMS MODEL 70 FEATHERWEIGHT HIGH GRADE MAPLE

WINCHESTER REPEATING ARMS MODEL 94 DELUXE CARBIN

WINCHESTER REPEATING ARMS MODEL 70 SUPER GRADE MAPLE

WINCHESTER REPEATING ARMS XPR COMPACT

WINCHESTER REPEATING ARMS XPC CHASSIS RIFLE

WINCHESTER REPEATING ARMS XPR HUNTER COMPACT BREAK-UP COUNTRY

WINCHESTER REPEATING ARMS MODEL 70 FEATHERWEIGHT HIGH GRADE MAPLE

Action: Bolt
Stock: Maple
Barrel: 22 in.
Sights: None
Weight: 6 lb. 12 oz.–7 lb.
Caliber: .243 Win., .308 Win., .25-06 Rem., .270 Win., .30-06 Spfd.
Magazine: 5 rounds
Features: Gloss-finished AAAA maple stock with cut checkering and a schnabel forearm; MOA Trigger System; pre-64 action; controlled round feed; controlled ejection
MSRP. **$1329.99**

WINCHESTER REPEATING ARMS MODEL 70 SUPER GRADE MAPLE

Action: Bolt
Stock: Maple
Barrel: 24 in., 26 in.
Sights: None
Weight: 7 lb. 12 oz.–8 lb. 6 oz.
Caliber: .243 Win., .308 Win., .270 Win., .30-06 Spfd., .264 Win. Mag., 7mm Rem. Mag., .300 Win. Mag.
Magazine: 3, 5 rounds
Features: Gloss-finished AAA maple stock with ebony forend tip; Shadowline cheekpiece; Super Grade engraved hinged floorplate; jeweled

bolt body; knurled bolt handle; pre-64 action with MOA Trigger System; hammer-forged, free-floating steel barrel with target crown
MSRP. **$1699.99**

WINCHESTER REPEATING ARMS MODEL 94 DELUXE CARBINE

Action: Lever
Stock: Walnut
Barrel: 20 in.
Sights: Marble Arms iron sights
Weight: 6 lb. 8 oz.–6 lb. 12 oz.
Caliber: .30-30 Win., .38-55 Win.
Magazine: 7 rounds
Features: Limited edition; grade IV/V checkered walnut stock and forend; gloss blued steel; left-side saddle ring; hammer spur; receiver is drilled and tapped for scope mounting
MSRP. **$1329.99**

WINCHESTER REPEATING ARMS XPC CHASSIS RIFLE

Action: Bolt
Stock: Composite
Barrel: 20 in., 24 in.
Sights: None
Weight: 10 lb.
Caliber: .308 Win., .243 Win., 6.5 Creedmoor
Magazine: 5, 10 rounds
Features: Designed for long-range work; machined alloy chassis frame; Magpul PRS Gen 3 stock; threaded muzzle; target crown; M-LOK rail; 20 MOA scope base; full-length

Picatinny rail; 10-round Magpul P-MAG AICS magazine and five-round MDT metal magazine
MSRP. **$1599.99**

WINCHESTER REPEATING ARMS XPR COMPACT

Action: Bolt
Stock: Composite
Barrel: 20 in., 22 in., 24 in.
Sights: None
Weight: 6 lb. 12 oz.–7 lb.
Caliber: .243 Win., 7mm-08 Rem., .308 Win., .270 WSM, .300 WSM, .325 WSM
Magazine: 3 rounds
Features: Shorter 13-in. length of pull; advanced polymer stock in black, matte blue metal finish; detachable box magazine
MSRP. **$549.99**

WINCHESTER REPEATING ARMS XPR HUNTER COMPACT BREAK-UP COUNTRY

Action: Bolt
Stock: Composite
Barrel: 20 in., 22 in.
Sights: None
Weight: 6 lb. 12 oz.–7 lb.
Caliber: .243 Win., 7mm-08 Rem., .308 Win., .270 WSM, .300 WSM, .325 WSM
Magazine: 3 rounds
Features: New XPR has shorter 13-in. length of pull; Mossy Oak Break-Up Country camo; Permakote mattel black button-rifled, free-floating barrel and receiver; bolt unlock button; MOA Trigger System; drilled and tapped for scope mount
MSRP. **$599.99**

WINCHESTER REPEATING ARMS XPR HUNTER
MOUNTAIN COUNTRY RANGE

WINCHESTER REPEATING ARMS XPR HUNTER VIAS, HUNTER
VERDE, HUNTER HIGHLANDER

WINCHESTER REPEATING ARMS XPR MUDDY GIRL COMPACT

WINCHESTER REPEATING ARMS XPR THUMBHOLE VARMINT
SUPPRESSOR READY

WINCHESTER REPEATING ARMS XPR HUNTER MOUNTAIN COUNTRY RANGE

Action: Bolt
Stock: Composite
Barrel: 22 in., 24 in., 26 in.
Sights: None
Weight: 6 lb. 5.44 oz.–7 lb. 4 oz.
Caliber: .243 Win., 7mm-08 Rem., .308 Win., .270 WSM, .300 WSM, .325 WSM, .270 Win., .30-06 Spfd., 7mm Rem. Mag., .300 Win. Mag., .338 Win. Mag.
Magazine: 3 rounds
Features: Matte black finish on metal; Mossy Oak Mountain Country Range camo stock; detachable magazine; MOA Trigger System
MSRP $599.99

WINCHESTER REPEATING ARMS XPR HUNTER VIAS, HUNTER VERDE, HUNTER HIGHLANDER

Action: Bolt
Stock: Composite
Barrel: 22 in., 24 in., 26 in.

Sights: None
Weight: 6 lb. 12 oz.–7 lb. 4 oz.
Caliber: .243 Win., 7mm-08 Rem., .308 Win., .270 WSM, .300 WSM, .325 WSM, .270 Win., .30-06 Spfd., 7mm Rem. Mag., .300 Win. Mag., .338 Win. Mag., 6.5 Creedmoor
Magazine: 3 rounds
Features: XPR rifle featuring steel receiver and free-floating, button rifled barrel in Permacote gray finish; Kuiu's Vias macro or Verde composite patterns on stock; Highlander version has metal in Flat Dark Earth Permacote and wears Kryptek's Highlander camo
MSRP $599.99

WINCHESTER REPEATING ARMS XPR MUDDY GIRL COMPACT

Action: Bolt
Stock: Composite
Barrel: 20 in., 22 in.
Sights: None
Weight: 6 lb. 12 oz.–7 lb. 4 oz.
Caliber: .243 Win., 7mm-08 Rem., .308 Win., .270 WSM, .300 WSM, .270 Win., .30-06 Spfd., 6.5 Creedmoor

Magazine: 3 rounds
Features: Shorter 13-in. length of pull; composite stock in Muddy Girl camo with textured grip panels; button-rifled, free-floating barrel in Permacote gray finish; detachable magazine; MOA Trigger
MSRP $599.99

WINCHESTER REPEATING ARMS XPR THUMBHOLE VARMINT SUPPRESSOR READY

Action: Bolt
Stock: Laminate
Barrel: 24 in.
Sights: None
Weight: 6 lb. 12 oz.
Caliber: .243 Win., 6.5 Creedmoor, .308 Win., .270 Win., .30-06 Spfd.
Magazine: 3 rounds
Features: Laminate thumbhole stock; raised cheekpiece; vented forearm aids cooling; two front sling swivels accommodate sling and bipod simultaneously; metal is matte blue finished; barrel is threaded
MSRP $799.99

BERETTA APX

CROSMAN AIRMASTER

CROSMAN BENJAMIN TRAIL NP2 WOOD

CROSMAN BUSHMASTER ACR DUAL AMMO
AIR RIFLE

BERETTA APX

Power: CO2
Stock: N/A
Overall length: 7.25 in.
Sights: Fixed front and rear
Weight: 1 lb. 12 oz.
Caliber: BB
Features: Semiautomatic; 20-shot;
double-action repeater has realistic
recoil action; CO2 cartridge housed
in grip; drop-free steel BB magazine;
integrated Picatinny rail
MSRP **$69.99**

CROSMAN AIRMASTER

Power: Variable pump
Stock: Synthetic
Overall length: 39.75 in.
Sights: Fiber optic front, adjustable
rear
Weight: 4 lb. 12 oz.
Caliber: BB, .177
Features: Variable pump; rifled steel
barrel; single-stage trigger; crossbolt

safety; 4x15mm scope; optional kit
includes metal swinging target, 500
pellets, 1,500 BBs, and safety glasses
AirMaster: **$99.99**
AirMaster Kit: **$114.99**

CROSMAN BENJAMIN TRAIL NP2 WOOD

Power: Nitro Piston 2
Stock: Wood
Overall length: 45.6 in.
Sights: None
Weight: 8 lb. 4.8 oz.
Caliber: .177
Features: Break-barrel action with
Nitro Piston 2 powerplant; all
hardwood stock with thumbhole
configuration; two-stage adjustable
trigger; Picatinny rail; shoots 15
percent faster and delivers double the
effective range of original Trail series;
includes CenterPoint 3-9x32mm
scope
MSRP **$339.99**

CROSMAN BUSHMASTER ACR DUAL AMMO AIR RIFLE

Power: Variable pump
Stock: Synthetic
Overall length: 33 in.
Sights: Elevation adjustable pin front,
windage adjustable dual aperture rear
Weight: 3 lb. 8 oz.
Caliber: BB, .177
Features: Bolt-action air rifle with
pump-action powerplant modeled
after Bushmaster's ACR (Adaptive
Combat Rifle); Picatinny rail; pistol
grip stock; five-shot Firepow'r pellet
clip; 18-shot internal magazine; 200-
shot reservoir
MSRP **$124.99**

CROSMAN DPMS CLASSIC A4 NITRO PISTON

CROSMAN MARLIN CLASSIC (BB)

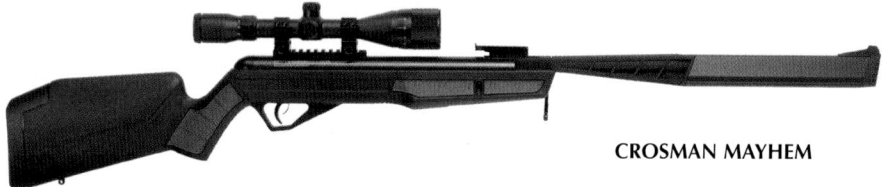

CROSMAN MAYHEM

CROSMAN REMINGTON 1875

CROSMAN DPMS CLASSIC A4 NITRO PISTON

Power: Nitro Piston 2
Stock: Synthetic
Overall length: 40 in.
Sights: None
Weight: 5 lb. 12.8 oz.
Caliber: .177
Features: Break-barrel action modeled after DPMS A4 platform; two-stage adjustable trigger; Picatinny rail; CenterPoint 4x32mm scope included
MSRP **$219.99**

CROSMAN MARLIN CLASSIC (BB)

Power: Spring
Stock: Resin
Overall length: N/A

Sights: Fixed blade front, adjustable notch rear
Weight: 2 lb. 10 oz.
Caliber: BB
Features: Lever-action modeled after traditional Marlin rifle; ratcheting lever; 700-BB reservoir
MSRP **$49.99**

CROSMAN MAYHEM

Power: Nitro Piston 2
Stock: Synthetic
Overall length: 46.5 in.
Sights: Fixed front, windage/elevation adjustable rear
Weight: 7 lb. 6 oz.
Caliber: .177, .22
Features: Break-barrel action with Nitro Piston 2 powerplant; ambidextrous stock with soft-touch inserts; rifled and shrouded barrel;

two-stage trigger; rubber buttpad; sling mounts; Picatinny rail; includes 3-9x40mm AO scope and Crosman's SBD (Silencing Barrel Device)
MSRP **$339.99**

CROSMAN REMINGTON 1875

Power: CO2
Stock: Faux ivory
Overall length: 13.125 in.
Sights: Fixed blade front, fixed notch rear
Weight: 2 lb. 4.8 oz.
Caliber: BB, .177
Features: Replica of Remington 1875 revolver; single-action; functional hammer, load gate, and extractor; nickel finish
MSRP **$139.99**

CROSMAN REMINGTON RP45

CROSMAN ROGUE

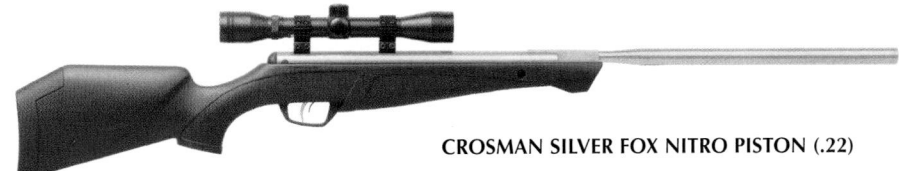

CROSMAN SILVER FOX NITRO PISTON (.22)

CROSMAN STEALTH SHOT NITRO PISTON (.177)

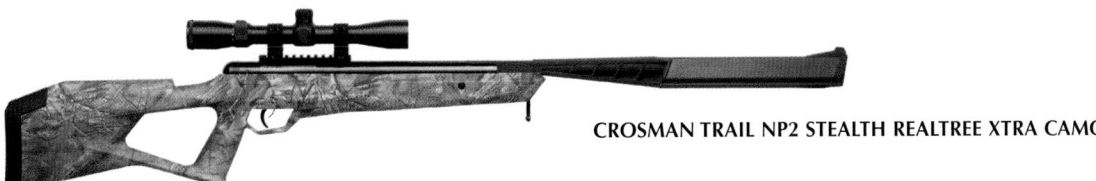

CROSMAN TRAIL NP2 STEALTH REALTREE XTRA CAMO

CROSMAN REMINGTON RP45

Power: CO2
Stock: Synthetic
Overall length: 7.7 in.
Sights: Fixed blade front, fixed notch rear
Weight: 1 lb. 11 oz.
Caliber: BB
Features: Modeled after Remington's RP45 handgun; semiauto repeater; Picatinny rail; slide safety
MSRP **$69.99**

CROSMAN ROGUE

Power: Nitro Piston 2
Stock: Synthetic
Overall length: 48 in.
Sights: Fixed front, adjustable rear
Weight: 7 lb. 6 oz.
Caliber: .177, .22
Features: Break-barrel action with Nitro Piston 2 powerplant; rifled steel barrel; 3-9x32mm scope; Crosman's SBD (Silencing Barrel Device)
MSRP **$299.99**

CROSMAN SILVER FOX NITRO PISTON (.22)

Power: Nitro Piston
Stock: Synthetic
Overall length: 43.5 in.
Sights: None
Weight: 6 lb.
Caliber: .22
Features: Break-barrel action; dovetail mounting rail; two-stage trigger; CenterPoint 4x32mm scope
MSRP **$199.99**

CROSMAN STEALTH SHOT NITRO PISTON (.177)

Power: Nitro Piston
Stock: Synthetic
Overall length: 43.5 in.
Sights: Fiber optic front, adjustable notch rear

Weight: 6 lb.
Caliber: .177
Features: Break-barrel action; two-stage trigger; 4x32mm scope
MSRP **$189.99**

CROSMAN TRAIL NP2 STEALTH REALTREE XTRA CAMO

Power: Nitro Piston 2
Stock: Synthetic
Overall length: 45.6 in.
Sights: Front post
Weight: 8 lb. 4.8 oz.
Caliber: .22
Features: Break-barrel action; rifled steel barrel; adjustable two-stage trigger; ambidextrous stock in Realtree Xtra Camo; 3-9x32mm scope; Crosman SBD (Silencing Barrel Device); available in wood or black synthetic stocks in choice of .177- or .22-caliber
MSRP . . . . **$294.99–$339.99**

NEW Products: Airguns

CROSMAN TRAIL NP MARK II PISTOL

GAMO SWARM MAXXIM IGT

GAMO WHISPER FUSION MACH 1

GLETCHER M712

GLETCHER M1891

GLETCHER M1944

GLETCHER PM 1951

GLETCHER NGT F, NGT R

MSRP $199.99

GLETCHER M1944
Power: CO2
Stock: Imitation wood
Overall length: 52.75 in.
Sights: Post front, tangent rear
Weight: 8 lb. 3 oz.
Caliber: .177
Features: Reproduction of M44
Russian Mosin-Nagant carbine; barrel,
bolt mechanism, and magazine are
metal; action operates like the
original firearm; integral folding
bayonet; built-in hex wrench for CO2
cartridge installation
MSRP $299.99

GLETCHER NGT F, NGT R
Power: CO2
Stock: Plastic
Overall length: 9 in.
Sights: Front post, cutout rear
Weight: 1 lb. 8 oz.
Caliber: .177
Features: Reproduction of the Belgian
Nagant revolver; steel BBs fired
through decorative snap cap
"cartridges"; seven-shot true revolving
action; blue or silver finishes; rifled
barrel options available in both
finishes
MSRP . . . . $134.99–$179.99

GLETCHER PM 1951
Power: CO2
Stock: Plastic
Overall length: 6.3 in.
Sights: Low-profile integral front and
rear
Weight: 1 lb. 10 oz.
Caliber: .177
Features: Reproduction of Russian
Makarov sidearm; metal body and
slide; safety lever; magazine pinky
finger extension
MSRP $99.99

CROSMAN TRAIL NP MARK II PISTOL
Power: Nitro Piston
Stock: Synthetic
Overall length: N/A
Sights: Fiber optic front, adjustable
notch rear
Weight: 3 lb. 7 oz.
Caliber: .177
Features: Break-barrel action; rifled
steel barrel; tactical frame; removable
cocking aid
MSRP $109.99

GAMO SWARM MAXXIM IGT
Power: IGT Mach 1
Stock: Synthetic
Overall length: 45.3 in.
Sights: Fixed fiber optic front, fully
adjustable fiber optic rear
Weight: 5 lb. 10.24 oz.
Caliber: .177, .22
Features: Break-barrel; 10-round
rotary magazine; rifled steel barrel;
11mm scope rail with scope stop;
adjustable first- and second-stage CAT
trigger; ambidextrous stock with
height-adjustable cheekpiece;
equipped with 3-9x40mm scope
MSRP $249.99

GAMO WHISPER FUSION MACH 1
Power: IGT Mach 1

Stock: Synthetic
Overall length: 46.5 in.
Sights: Fiber optic front, adjustable
rear
Weight: 8 lb.
Caliber: .177
Features: Break-barrel, single-cocking
action; single-shot; fluted polymer
jacketed steel barrel; Custom Action
Trigger; Recoil Reducing Rail; 3-9x40
air rifle scope
MSRP $249.99

GLETCHER M712
Power: CO2
Stock: Wood
Overall length: 23 in.
Sights: Post front, tangent rear
Weight: 3 lb.
Caliber: .177
Features: Reproduction of WWII 1932
broomhandle Mauser; breech
mechanism moves when firing; full-
auto functionality and blowback
system
MSRP $179.99

GLETCHER M1891
Power: CO2
Stock: Imitation wood
Overall length: 22.43 in.
Sights: Hooded front post, tangent
rear
Weight: 5 lb. 9.6 oz.
Caliber: .177
Features: Reproduction of Russian
Civil War "Obrez" model, a sawed-off
Mosin-Nagant; mechanism works as
in the original; built-in hex key for
CO2 cartridge installation

GLETCHER STECHKIN

HATSANUSA BARRAGE

HATSANUSA BULLMASTER

LEGENDS MP

GLETCHER STECHKIN

Power: CO2
Stock: Plastic
Overall length: 8.8 in.
Sights: Low-profile integral front, adjustable rear
Weight: 2 lb. 4.8 oz.
Caliber: .177
Features: Limited edition (100 units) reproduction of Soviet Stretchkin pistol; weight is identical to the firearm version; double-action, with gold finish, engraving on slide and frame; comes in a presentation box
MSRP **$259.99**

HATSANUSA BARRAGE

Power: PCP
Stock: Synthetic
Overall length: 19.7 in.
Sights: Fiber optic front and rear
Weight: 10 lb. 1.6 oz.
Caliber: .177, .22
Features: Semiautomatic; fitted with a 500cc air bottle mounted to the forearm; barrel is precision rifled, choked, and fully shrouded; ambidextrous thumbhole stock; Picatinny rail on the forearm; includes magazines for both calibers (.177 mag holds 14 shots, .22 holds 12 shots); TruGlo sights; HatSan's patented anti-knock system that prevents gas discharge and waste if the rifle is knocked or bounced
MSRP **$1299.99**

HATSANUSA BULLMASTER

Power: PCP
Stock: Synthetic
Overall length: 19.7 in.
Sights: None
Weight: 10 lb. 4.8 oz.
Caliber: .177, .22
Features: Semiautomatic bullpup design; 500cc air bottle mounted to the forearm; barrel is precision rifled, choked, and fully shrouded; includes magazines for both calibers (.177 mag holds 14 shots, .22 holds 12 shots);

topside and and under forearm Picatinny rails; elevation adjustable cheekpiece; HatSan's patented anti-knock system that prevents gas discharge and waste if the rifle is knocked or bounced
MSRP **$1399.99**

LEGENDS MP

Power: CO2
Stock: Metal
Overall length: 33 in.
Sights: Fixed front, elevation adjustable rear
Weight: N/A
Caliber: .177
Features: Distinctive German replication; 10-in. barrel; folding stock; full-auto blowback action; 60-shot drop-free steel BB magazine; two CO2 cartridges housed in the magazine
MSRP **$199.99**

SIG SAUER 1911 MAX CO2 BB GUN

SIG SAUER 1911 SPARTAN CO2 BB GUN

SIG SAUER P320 ASP, ASP COYOTE TAN

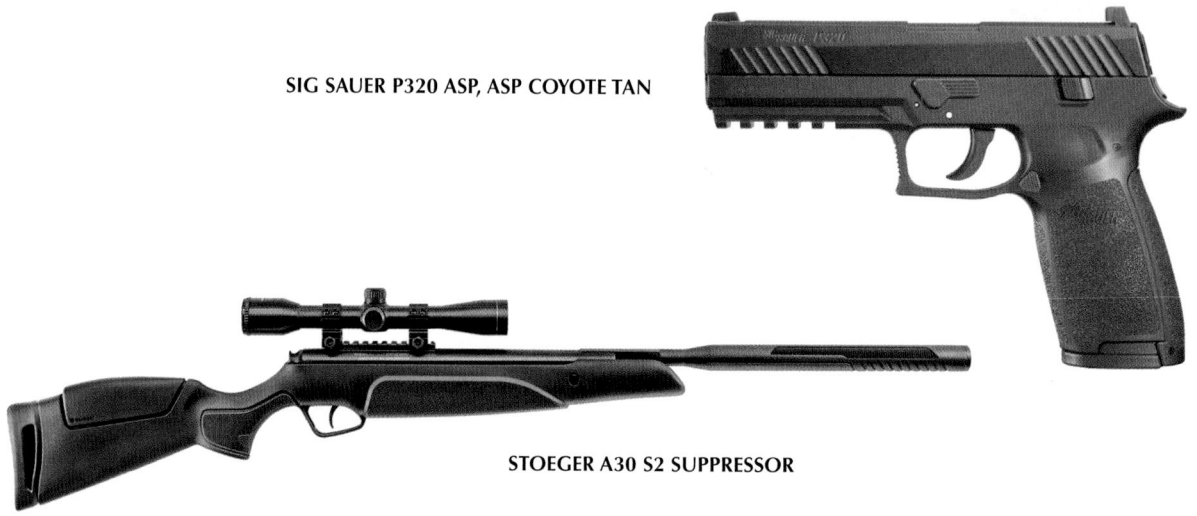

STOEGER A30 S2 SUPPRESSOR

SIG SAUER 1911 MAX CO2 BB GUN

Power: CO2
Stock: Cust Max Michael
Overall length: 8.7 in
Sights: White dot front and rear
Weight: 2 lb. 9.6 oz.
Caliber: BB (4.5mm)
Features: CO2-operated BB gun replication of SIG Max Michael 1911 pistol; accessory rail; skeletonized trigger; cam-lever CO2 loading port; functional grip safety; full blowback metal slide; 16-round magazine; natural alloy finish
MSRP **$109.99**

SIG SAUER 1911 SPARTAN CO2 BB GUN

Power: CO2
Stock: Custom Spartan
Overall length: 8.7 in.
Sights: White dot front and rear

Weight: 2 lb. 9.6 oz.
Caliber: BB (4.5mm)
Features: CO2-operated BB gun replication of SIG Spartan 1911 pistol; MOLON LABE engraved slide; custom Spartan grips; skeletonized trigger; cam-lever CO2 loading port; functional grip safety; full blowback metal slide; 16-round magazine; oil-rubbed bronze finish
MSRP **$110.99**

SIG SAUER P320 ASP, ASP COYOTE TAN

Power: CO2
Stock: Polymer
Overall length: 7.9 in.
Sights: White dot front and rear
Weight: 1 lb. 11 oz.
Caliber: .177
Features: CO2-operated airgun model of SIG's P320 carry gun; rotary magazine holds 30 rounds; rifled steel

barrel; manual safety; all-metal slide; black or Coyote Tan finishes
MSRP **$119.99**

STOEGER A30 S2 SUPPRESSOR

Power: Gas Ram piston
Stock: Synthetic
Overall length: 42.5 in.
Sights: 4x32mm scope
Weight: 7 lb.
Caliber: .177, .22
Features: Stoeger's A30 now with Dual-Stage Noise Reduction System suppressor; suppressor shroud works as cocking grip; .177-caliber has velocities up to 1,200 fps, .22-caliber up to 1,000 fps; two-stage adjustable trigger; automatic ambidextrous safety; break-action Gas Ram piston
MSRP **$219.00**

UMAREX FORGE

UMAREX DX17

UMAREX GAUNTLET

UMAREX OCTANE ELITE

UMAREX SA10

UMAREX STRIKE POINT

UMAREX TREVOX

UMAREX DX17

Power: Spring-powered
Stock: Synthetic
Overall length: 9.5 in.
Sights: Fixed fiber optic front, fixed rear
Weight: 1 lb.
Caliber: BB
Features: Single-action air pistol shoots steel BBs; built-in BB reservoir; integrated accessory rail; 15-shot capacity; includes 200 steel BBs
MSRP **$19.99**

UMAREX FORGE

Power: T.N.T. Turbo Nitrogen Technology gas piston
Stock: Wood
Overall length: 44.8 in.
Sights: 4x32mm scope
Weight: 7 lb. 13 oz.
Caliber: .177
Features: T.N.T. fast piston system; spring piston break barrel with a single-shot cocking mechanism and automatic safety; adjustable trigger; integrated rail platform; 4x32 airgun

scope; rifled barrel; enhanced SilencAir noise dampener
MSRP **$159.99**

UMAREX GAUNTLET

Power: Pre-charged pneumatic
Stock: Synthetic
Overall length: 46.75 in.
Sights: N/A
Weight: 8 lb. 8 oz.
Caliber: .177, .22
Features: Bolt-action repeater; removable 3000 psi 13 cubic in. tank; 1100 psi regulator; adjustable stock comb; pressure key release; rotary magazine; single-shot tray
MSRP **$299.99**

UMAREX OCTANE ELITE

Power: ReAxis gas-powered piston
Stock: Synthetic
Overall length: 48.6 in.
Sights: 3-9x40mm scope
Weight: 9 lb. 8 oz.
Caliber: .177, .22
Features: Lockdown rail mounting system; 3-9x40mm airgun scope with adjustable objective; Stopshox anti-recoil system; SilencAir 5 chamber noise dampener; all-weather stock; rifled barrel; single-shot cocking mechanism
MSRP **$249.99**

UMAREX SA10

Power: CO2
Stock: Synthetic
Overall length: 9.25 in.

Sights: None
Weight: 2 lb. 1 oz.
Caliber: BB, .177
Features: Dual-ammo air pistol accommodating both BBs and .177-caliber pellets; uses one CO2 cartridge; blowback action; DA/SA trigger; eight-round rotary magazine; integrated accessory rail; gold-colored barrel; includes 1 polymer and three metal bonus magazines
MSRP **$89.99**

UMAREX STRIKE POINT

Power: Multi-pump pneumatic
Stock: Synthetic
Overall length: 14 in.
Sights: Fiber optic
Weight: 2 lb. 10 oz.
Caliber: .177, .22
Features: Variable pump power; easy grip pump-action; easy load bolt-action; SilencAir 3 chamber noise dampener
MSRP **$49.99**

UMAREX TREVOX

Power: T.N.T. Turbo Nitrogen Technology gas piston
Stock: Synthetic
Overall length: 18.11 in.
Sights: Fiber optic
Weight: 3 lb. 2 oz.
Caliber: .177
Features: Rifled barrel accuracy with an easy-grip; single-stroke cocking mechanism; SilencAir 3 chamber noise dampener; 11mm dovetail cuts for optics mounting; blued finish
MSRP **$79.99**

ARMSCOR/ROCK ISLAND ARMORY PA 3-IN-1 CHROME SHOTGUN

ARMSCOR/ROCK ISLAND ARMORY SA SHOTGUN LONG STANDARD

ARMSCOR/ROCK ISLAND ARMORY SA SHOTGUN TACT

ARMSCOR/ROCK ISLAND ARMORY VR60 PLUS 1

ARMSCOR/ROCK ISLAND ARMORY PA 3-IN-1 CHROME SHOTGUN

Action: Pump
Stock: Polymer
Barrel: 18.5 in., 28 in.
Chokes: S, F, M, IC
Weight: 6 lb. 2.7 oz.
Bore/Gauge: 12
Magazine: 4 shells
Features: 28-in. vent rib barrel with removable chokes; 18.5-in. cylinder bored barrel with front post sight; full polymer stock; add-on pistol grip; aluminum receiver; metalwork finished in Marine Chrome
MSRP. **$375.00**

ARMSCOR/ROCK ISLAND ARMORY SA SHOTGUN LONG STANDARD

Action: Semiautomatic
Stock: Polymer
Barrel: 28 in.

Chokes: F, M, IC
Weight: 7 lb. 2.5 oz.
Bore/Gauge: 12
Magazine: 4 shells
Features: Inertia-driven semiautomatic; aluminum receiver; front bead; vent rib; black chrome finish
MSRP. **$399.00**

ARMSCOR/ROCK ISLAND ARMORY SA SHOTGUN TACT

Action: Semiautomatic
Stock: Polymer
Barrel: 18.5 in.
Chokes: F, M, IC
Weight: 7 lb.
Bore/Gauge: 12
Magazine: 4 shells
Features: Economical shotgun for home-defense or 3-Gun competition; flash hider at the muzzle; fiber optic front sight, rear sight; Picatinny rail;

aluminum receiver in black chrome finish; polymer stock with pistol grip
MSRP. **$399.00**

ARMSCOR/ROCK ISLAND ARMORY VR60 PLUS 1

Action: Semiautomatic
Stock: Polymer
Barrel: 20 in.
Chokes: F, M, IC
Weight: 8 lb.
Bore/Gauge: 12
Magazine: 5 shells
Features: AR-type platform; conventional gas operation; aluminum receiver; polymer pistol grip stock with molded cheekpiece; A2-type front sight; removable A2-type carry handle; ventilated handguard; Picatinny rail; left-side manual safety; chambered for 2 ¾- or 3-in. shells; brown, red, or black finishes
Black:. **$529.00**
Brown and red: **$549.00**

ARMSCOR/ROCK ISLAND ARMORY
VR60 SHOTGUN STANDARD

BARRETT SOVEREIGN BELTRAMI

BARRETT SOVEREIGN B-XPRO

BARRETT SOVEREIGN RUTHERFORD

ARMSCOR/ROCK ISLAND ARMORY VR60 SHOTGUN STANDARD
Action: Semiautomatic
Stock: Polymer
Barrel: 20 in.
Chokes: F, M, IC
Weight: 7 lb. 6.2 oz.
Bore/Gauge: 12
Magazine: 5 shells
Features: AR-platform semiautomatic; conventional gas-operated action; removable carry handle; full-length Picatinny rail
MSRP **$489.00**

BARRETT SOVEREIGN BELTRAMI
Action: Side-by-side
Stock: Walnut
Barrel: 26 in., 28 in., 30 in.
Chokes: F, IM, M, IC, C
Weight: N/A
Bore/Gauge: 12, 20, 28

Magazine: 2 shells
Features: Grade 3A Turkish walnut stock in straight English configuration; steel box lock receiver with coin-finished, engraved sideplates; tapered solid ribs; steel-shot rated barrels; 12- and 20-ga. models have splinter forends and 3-in. chambers, 28-ga. has semi-beavertail forend and 2 ¾-in. chamber; single non-selective trigger
MSRP **$6150.00**

BARRETT SOVEREIGN B-XPRO
Action: Over/under
Stock: Walnut
Barrel: 30 in., 32 in.
Chokes: Extended (F, IM, M, IC, C)
Weight: N/A
Bore/Gauge: 12
Magazine: 2 shells
Features: A+ walnut stock with pistol grip; 10mm-7mm tapered vent rib; fiber optic front bead; 3-in. chambers;

rounded forend; box lock action; receiver has coin-finished engraving; single selective trigger; automatic ejectors
MSRP **$3075.00**

BARRETT SOVEREIGN RUTHERFORD
Action: Over/under
Stock: Walnut
Barrel: 26 in., 28 in.
Chokes: F, IM, M, IC, C
Weight: N/A
Bore/Gauge: 12, 16, 20, 28
Magazine: 2 shells
Features: Round body box lock; stock is A+ walnut; receiver is coin finished and engraved; single selective trigger; automatic ejectors; Prince of Wales grip; 30mm forcing cones; 6mm vent rib; 12-, 16-, and 20-ga. have 3-in. chambers, 28-ga. is 2 ¾-in.
MSRP . . . . **$2200.00–$2520.00**

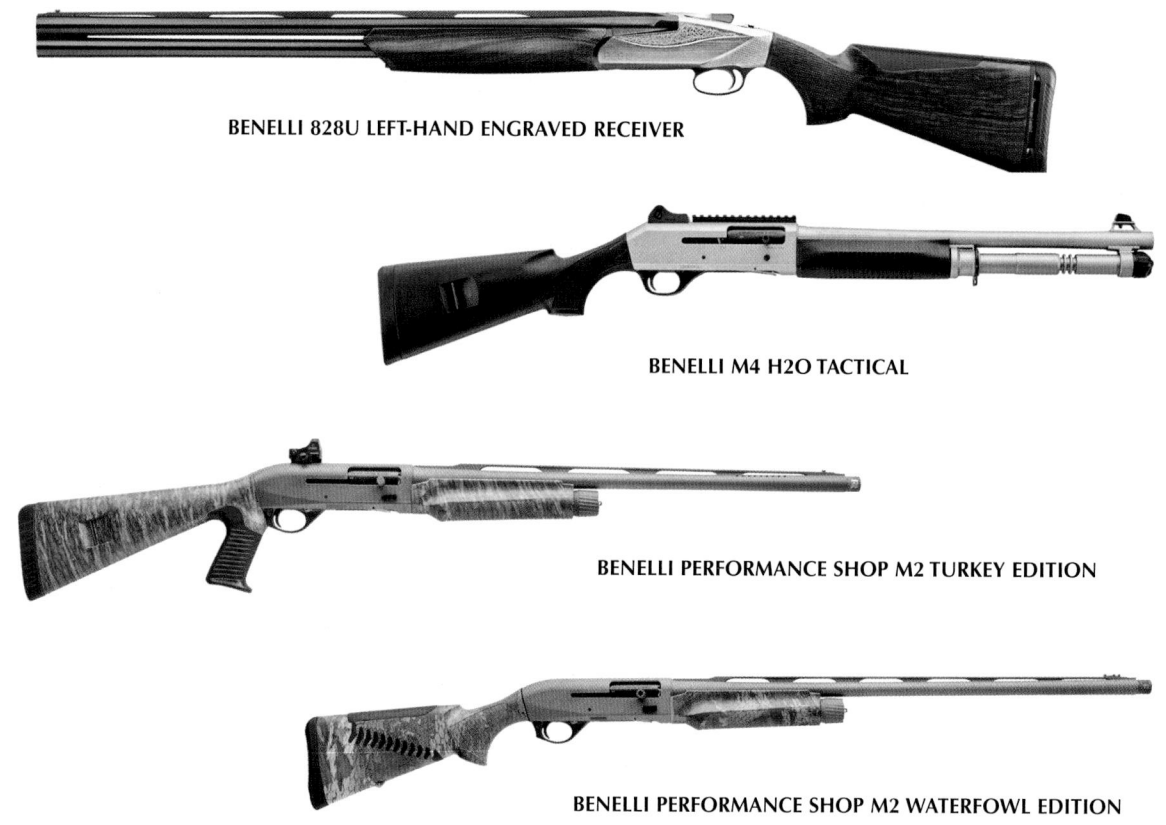

BENELLI 828U LEFT-HAND ENGRAVED RECEIVER

BENELLI M4 H2O TACTICAL

BENELLI PERFORMANCE SHOP M2 TURKEY EDITION

BENELLI PERFORMANCE SHOP M2 WATERFOWL EDITION

BENELLI 828U LEFT-HAND ENGRAVED RECEIVER

Action: Over/under
Stock: Walnut
Barrel: 26 in., 28 in.
Chokes: Crio (C, IC, M, IM, F)
Weight: 6 lb. 8 oz.–6 lb. 9.6 oz.
Bore/Gauge: 12
Magazine: 2 shells
Features: Left-hand stock orientation with engraved nickel-plated receiver
MSRP **$2999.00**

BENELLI M4 H2O TACTICAL

Action: Pump
Stock: Synthetic
Barrel: 18.5 in.
Chokes: M
Weight: 7 lb. 12.8 oz.
Bore/Gauge: 12
Magazine: 5 shells
Features: Titanium Cerakote finish on barrel, receiver, and magazine tube; black Cerakote on bolt; internal components receive corrosion-resistant coatings; ghost ring sights; Picatinny rail; standard or pistol grip stocks
MSRP **$2299.00**

BENELLI PERFORMANCE SHOP M2 TURKEY EDITION

Action: Semiautomatic
Stock: Synthetic
Barrel: 24 in.
Chokes: Benelli (C, IC, M, IM, F), Custom XFT Extended
Weight: 6 lb. 3.2 oz. (20-ga.), 7 lb. (12-ga.)
Bore/Gauge: 12, 20
Magazine: 3 shells
Features: 3-in. chambers and lengthened forcing cones on both gauges; Burris FastFire II sight and ported Crio barrels; 12-ga. supplied with ComforTech field and Steady Grip stocks in Mossy Oak Bottomlands, metal finished in Patriot Brown Cerakote; 20-ga. has only ComforTech field stock and Realtree APG all-over coverage
MSRP . . . . **$2599.00–$3399.00**

BENELLI PERFORMANCE SHOP M2 WATERFOWL EDITION

Action: Semiautomatic
Stock: Synthetic
Barrel: 28 in.
Chokes: 3 Rob Roberts Custom Triple Threat
Weight: 5 lb. 14.4 oz. (20-ga.), 7 lb. 3.2 oz. (12-ga.)
Bore/Gauge: 12, 20
Magazine: 3 shells
Features: Custom-tuned trigger group; lengthened and polished forcing cones; HIVIZ Comp front sight; oversized bolt handle and release button; 3-in. chambers; 12-ga. has ComforTech stock in GORE OPTIFADE Waterfowl Timber and metal in Texas Tan Cerakote finish; 20-ga. has ComforTech stock and all-over Realtree MAX-5 finish
MSRP . . . . **$2399.00–$2699.00**

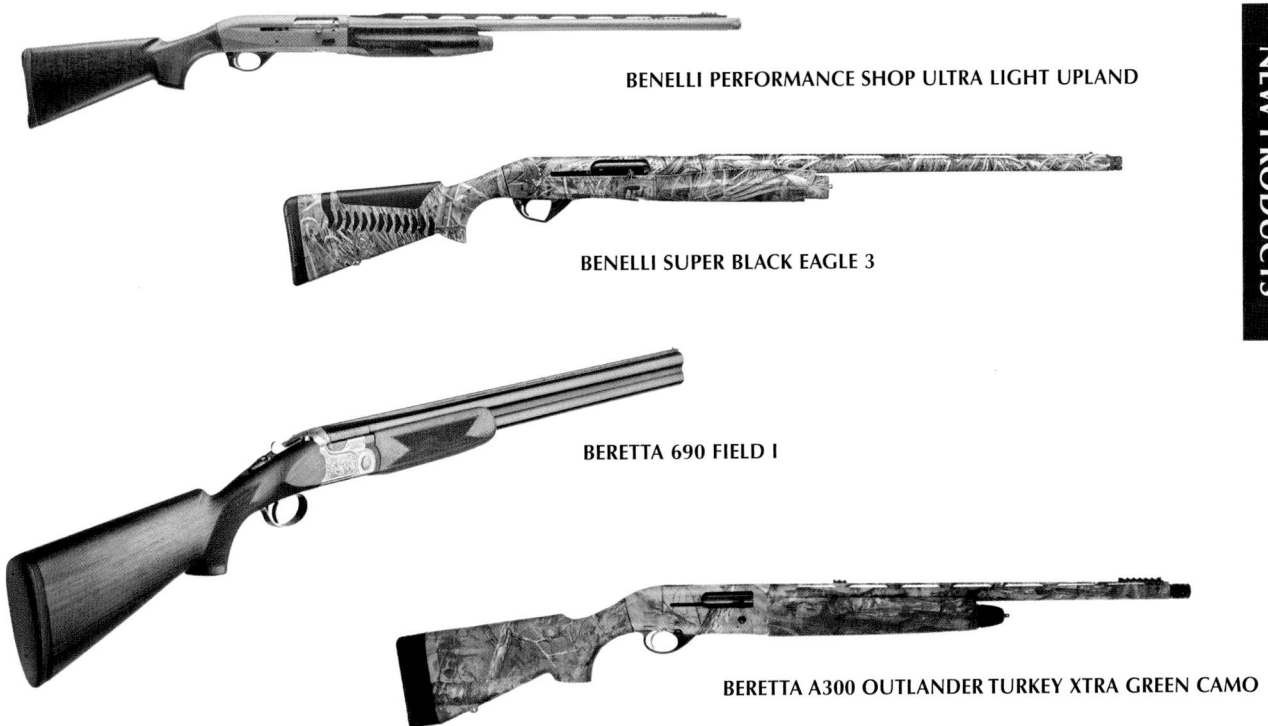

BENELLI PERFORMANCE SHOP ULTRA LIGHT UPLAND

BENELLI SUPER BLACK EAGLE 3

BERETTA 690 FIELD I

BERETTA A300 OUTLANDER TURKEY XTRA GREEN CAMO

BENELLI PERFORMANCE SHOP ULTRA LIGHT UPLAND

Action: Semiautomatic
Stock: Walnut
Barrel: 24 in. (20-ga.), 26 in. (12-ga.)
Chokes: Crio (C, IC, M), 3 Rob Roberts Custom Triple Threat
Weight: 5 lb. 3.2 oz. (20-ga.), 6 lb. 1.6 oz. (12-ga.)
Bore/Gauge: 12, 20
Magazine: 2 shells
Features: Alloy receivers; shortened magazine tubes; carbon fiber ribs; enlarged bolt handles and bolt release buttons; lengthened forcing cones; EDM porting; Burnt Bronze Cerakote finish
MSRP **$2799.00**

BENELLI SUPER BLACK EAGLE 3

Action: Semiautomatic
Stock: Synthetic
Barrel: 26 in., 28 in.
Chokes: Crio (C, IM, F), Extended Crio (IC, M)
Weight: 7 lb.–7 lb. 3 oz.

Bore/Gauge: 12
Magazine: 2 shells
Features: Inertia-driven action with 3 ½-in. chamber; Easy Locking System; oversized safety, bolt handle, and bolt release button; new magazine cap, trigger, stock, and forend designs; enlarged loading port; Easy Fitting System shim kit allows for eight different drop and cast configurations; ComforTech stock; Combtech cheek pad; Crio-treated barrel; black synthetic, Realtree Max-5, GORE OPTIFADE Timber, or Mossy Oak Bottomlands; red bar front sight, mid-bead; receiver drilled and tapped for 93A Weaver scope mounts
Black: **$1899.00**
Camo: **$1999.00**

BERETTA 690 FIELD I

Action: Over/under
Stock: Walnut
Barrel: 28 in.
Chokes: Optima-Choke HP
Weight: 7 lb. 6 oz.
Bore/Gauge: 12, 20
Magazine: 2 shells

Features: Steelium cold-hammer-forged and chrome-lined barrels; oiled Grade 2.5 walnut stock with pistol grip and semi-beavertail forend; receiver has rolled floral pattern engraving
MSRP **$2950.00**

BERETTA A300 OUTLANDER TURKEY XTRA GREEN CAMO

Action: Semiautomatic
Stock: Synthetic
Barrel: 24 in.
Chokes: Extended TruGlo Turkey Choice choke
Weight: 7 lb. 9.6 oz.
Bore/Gauge: 12
Magazine: 3 shells
Features: Chambered for 3 in.; Truglo fiber optic sights mid-rib and muzzle; adjustable drop and cast; reversible safety; aluminum alloy receiver milled for Beretta Optics Mount; sling swivel studs front and back; Realtree Xtra Green camo
MSRP **$900.00**

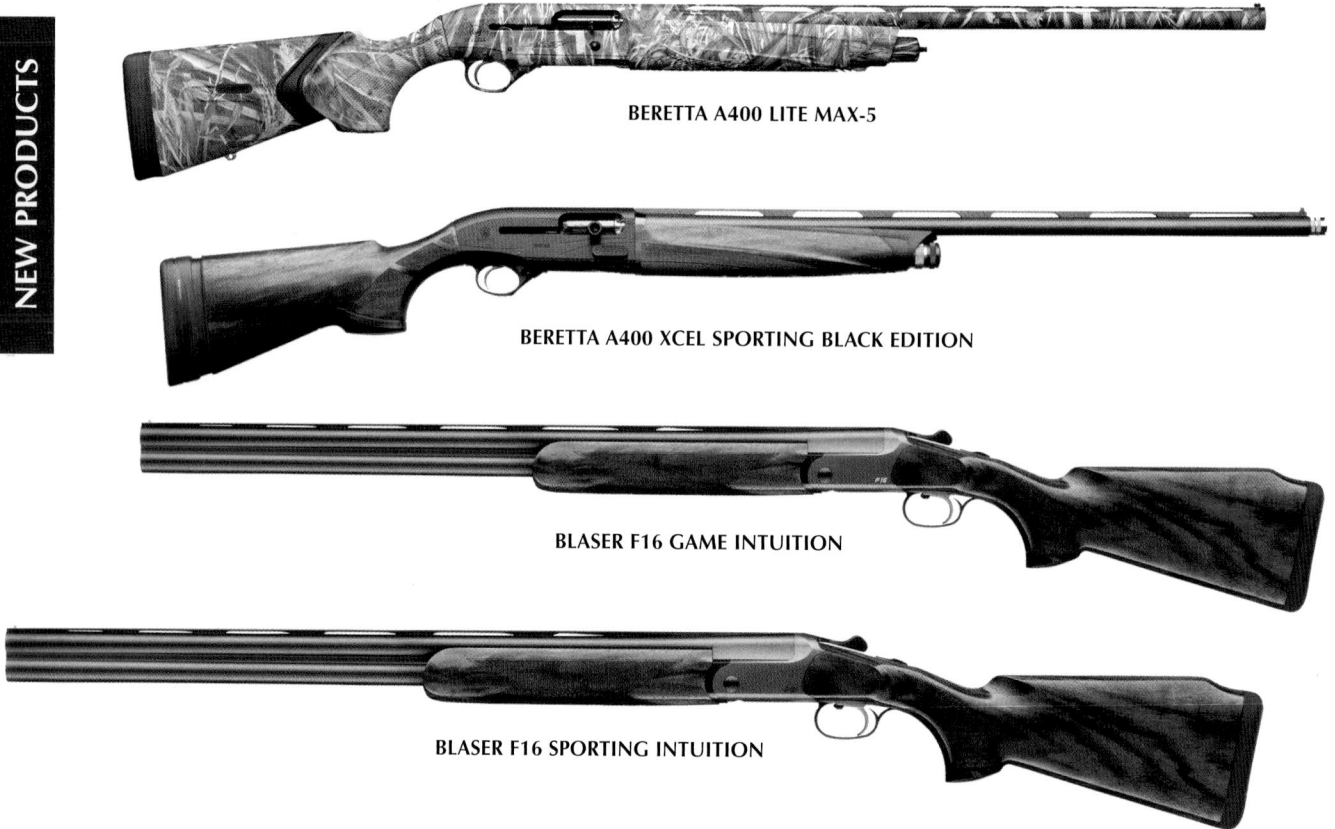

BERETTA A400 LITE MAX-5

BERETTA A400 XCEL SPORTING BLACK EDITION

BLASER F16 GAME INTUITION

BLASER F16 SPORTING INTUITION

BERETTA A400 LITE MAX-5

Action: Semiautomatic
Stock: Synthetic
Barrel: 26 in., 28 in.; 30 in. (12-ga. only)
Chokes: Optima-Choke HP
Weight: 6 lb. 9.6 oz.
Bore/Gauge: 12, 20
Magazine: 2 shells
Features: 3-in. chambers; Beretta Blink gas system; stock features Kick-Off Plus system, adjustable shims, and S-Grip checkering pattern for improved grip; safety is crossbolt type and reversible; black or Realtree Max-5 camo; fiber optic front sight
Black: **$1600.00**
Realtree Max-5: **$1700.00**

BERETTA A400 XCEL SPORTING BLACK EDITION

Action: Semiautomatic
Stock: Walnut
Barrel: 30 in.
Chokes: Optima HP Extended Black
Weight: 7 lb. 6.4 oz.

Bore/Gauge: 12
Magazine: 3 shells
Features: 3-in. chambers; MicroCore recoil pad; reversible safety; oversized bolt handle and release; medium weight forend balancing cap; 10mm carbon fiber rib; matte black receiver finish; black weighted forend cap; carbon fiber 10x10 rib
MSRP **$2200.00**

BLASER F16 GAME INTUITION

Action: Over/under
Stock: Wood grade II
Barrel: 28 in., 30 in.
Chokes: Three flush chokes ($\frac{1}{4}$, $\frac{1}{2}$, $\frac{3}{4}$)
Weight: 6 lb. 10 oz.
Bore/Gauge: 12
Magazine: 2 shells
Features: Designed specifically for women, with a specially designed buttstock tailored to the female anatomy, including a more slender pistol grip, higher comb, and reduced pitch; non-adjustable trigger; 13.8-in. length of pull; sling swivel (not mounted); silver F16 logo and silver

front bead; many options available, including upgraded wood and weight balancer
MSRP . . . . **$4195.00 and up**

BLASER F16 SPORTING INTUITION

Action: Over/under
Stock: Wood grade II
Barrel: 30 in., 32 in.
Chokes: Three flush chokes ($\frac{1}{4}$, $\frac{1}{2}$, $\frac{3}{4}$)
Weight: 7 lb. 5 oz.–8 lb. 3 oz.
Bore/Gauge: 12
Magazine: 2 shells
Features: Designed specifically for women, with a specially designed buttstock tailored to the female anatomy, including a more slender pistol grip, higher comb, and reduced pitch; non-adjustable trigger; 13.8-in. length of pull; Blaser Comfort recoil pad; adjustable trigger length; prep for barrel balancer and stock balancer; red F16 logo and red fiber optic front bead; many options available, including upgraded wood and barrel balancer weights
MSRP . . . . **$4195.00 and up**

BROWNING A5 HUNTER HIGH GRADE

BROWNING A5 WICKED WING

BROWNING BT-99 MICRO WITH ADJUSTABLE BUTTPLATE AND COMB

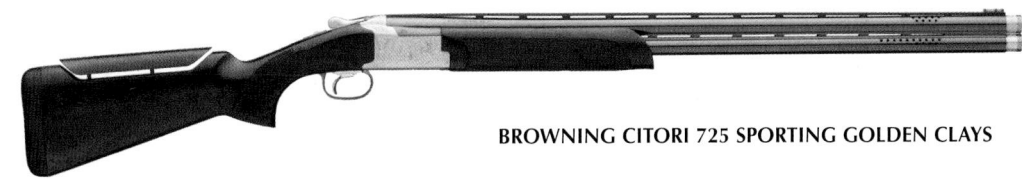

BROWNING CITORI 725 SPORTING GOLDEN CLAYS

BROWNING A5 HUNTER HIGH GRADE

Action: Semiautomatic
Stock: Walnut
Barrel: 26 in., 28 in.
Chokes: Invector-DS (F, M, IC)
Weight: 6 lb. 11 oz.–6 lb. 13 oz.
Bore/Gauge: 12
Magazine: 4 shells
Features: 3-in. chambered gun; gloss finished barrel; receiver with intricate scrollwork, pheasant and mallard engraving; grade 2.5 gloss varnish finish walnut stock with 22 lines-per-inch checkering; lightweight profile barrel; aluminum alloy receiver; recoil-operated Kinematic drive; Vector Pro lengthened forcing cones
MSRP **$1859.99**

BROWNING A5 WICKED WING

Action: Semiautomatic
Stock: Composite
Barrel: 26 in., 28 in.
Chokes: Extended Invector-DS Banded (F,M,IC)
Weight: 7 lb. 3 oz.–7 lb. 5 oz.

Bore/Gauge: 12
Magazine: 4 shells
Features: Chambered for 3.5-in. shells; Cerakote Burnt Bronze camo finish on the receiver and Burnt Bronze on the barrel; Briley extended bolt handle and oversize bolt release; fully chromed bore; recoil operated Kinematic Drive; Vector Pro lengthened forcing cone; fiber-optic front sight and ivory mid-bead; A-TACS AU, Mossy Oak Bottomlands, Realtree Max-5, and Mossy Oak Shadow Grass Blades finishes
MSRP **$1979.99**

BROWNING BT-99 MICRO WITH ADJUSTABLE BUTTPLATE AND COMB

Action: Break-open single-shot
Stock: Black walnut
Barrel: 30 in., 32 in.
Chokes: Invector-Plus flush (M)
Weight: 7 lb. 12 oz.–7 lb. 13 oz.
Bore/Gauge: 12
Magazine: 1 shell
Features: For youth/smaller-framed shooters; fit-customizable single shot,

break action, trap shotgun; Graco Pro Fit adjustable comb and butt pad plate; high-post ventilated floating rib; beavertail forearm; 13.75-in. length of pull; 2¾ in. chamber
MSRP **$1799.99**

BROWNING CITORI 725 SPORTING GOLDEN CLAYS

Action: Over/under
Stock: Walnut
Barrel: 30 in., 32 in.
Chokes: Extended Invector-DS (F, IM, M, IC, Skeet)
Weight: 7 lb. 13 oz.
Bore/Gauge: 12
Magazine: 2 shells
Features: Unique "Golden Clays" accented gold engraving; Pro Fit adjustable comb; ported barrels with vented top and side ribs; HiViz Pro-Comp fiber optic front side and ivory mid-bead; grade V/VI walnut stock; low-profile silver nitride finish steel receiver; FireLite mechanical trigger
MSRP **$5349.99**

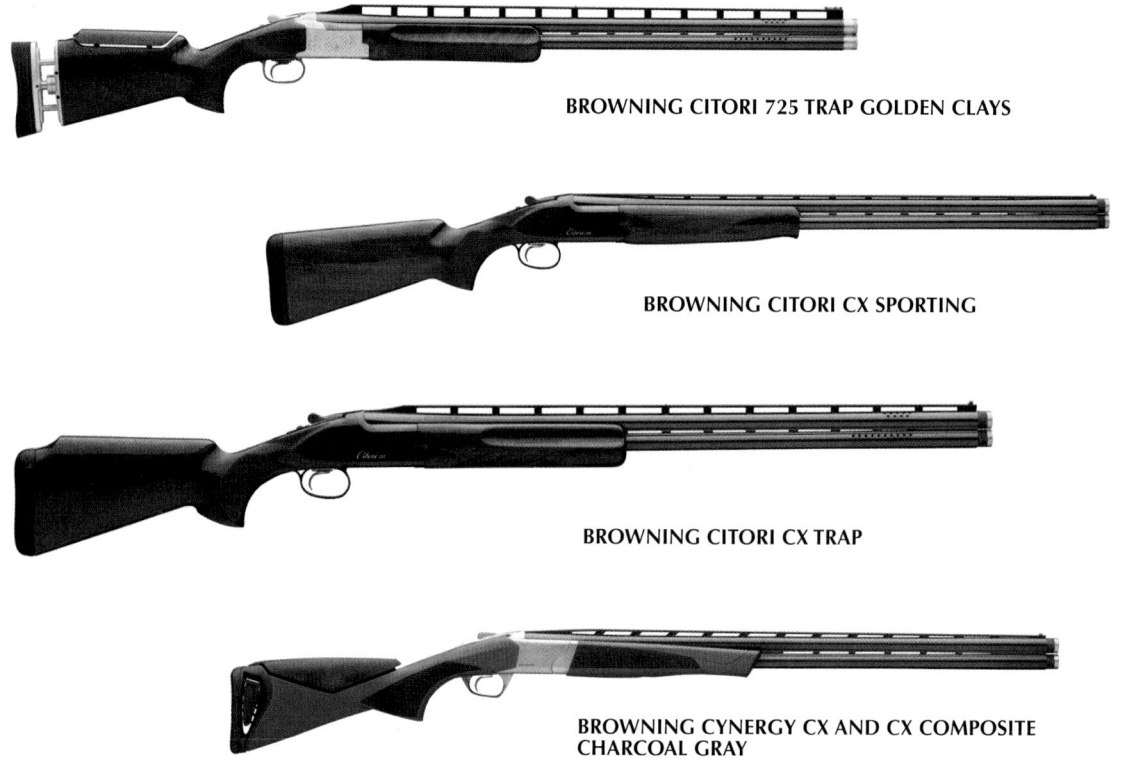

BROWNING CITORI 725 TRAP GOLDEN CLAYS

BROWNING CITORI CX SPORTING

BROWNING CITORI CX TRAP

BROWNING CYNERGY CX AND CX COMPOSITE
CHARCOAL GRAY

BROWNING CITORI 725 TRAP GOLDEN CLAYS

Action: Over/under
Stock: Walnut
Barrel: 30 in., 32 in.
Chokes: Extended Invector-DS (F, LF, IM, IM, M)
Weight: 8 lb. 8 oz.–8 lb. 11 oz.
Bore/Gauge: 12
Magazine: 2 shells
Features: 2¾ in. chamber; Fire Lite Mechanical trigger system; hammer ejectors and top-tang barrel selector/safety; gloss grade V/VI walnut stock with close radius pistol grip and right-hand palm swell; receiver has a silver nitride finish and gold-accented engraving; adjustable Monte Carlo comb; Pachmayr Decelerator XLT Trap recoil pad; ventilated top and side ribs; Vector Pro lengthened forcing cones; GraCoil recoil reduction system; Triple Trigger System; HiViz Pro-Comp front sight and ivory mid-bead
MSRP **$5739.99**

BROWNING CITORI CX SPORTING

Action: Over/under

Stock: Walnut
Barrel: 28 in., 30 in., 32 in.
Chokes: Midas grade extended Invector Plus (F, IM, C)
Weight: 6 lb. 10 oz.–6 lb. 14 oz. (20-ga.); 8 lb. 2 oz.–8 lb. 6 oz. (12-ga.)
Bore/Gauge: 12, 20
Magazine: 2 shells
Features: Crossover design with lightweight profile barrels; flat point of impact; vented rib and side ribs; grade II American walnut stock in gloss finish; Inflex recoil pad; ivory front and mid-beads; 3-inch chambers; flat floating rib
MSRP **$2139.99**

BROWNING CITORI CX TRAP

Action: Over/under
Stock: Walnut
Barrel: 30 in., 32 in.
Chokes: Midas grade extended Invector-Plus (F,M, IC)
Weight: 8 lb. 3 oz.–8 lb. 5 oz.
Bore/Gauge: 12
Magazine: 2 shells
Features: Crossover design with lightweight ported barrels; vented high post rib and side ribs; Vector Pro lengthened forcing cones; high rib

trap model with 3-in. chamber; three optional trigger shoes available
MSRP **$2069.99**

BROWNING CYNERGY CX AND CX COMPOSITE CHARCOAL GRAY

Action: Over/under
Stock: Black walnut, composite
Barrel: 30 in., 32 in.
Chokes: Invector-Plus Midas Grade (F, M, IC)
Weight: 7 lb. 14 oz.–8.0 lb. (CX); 7 lb. 11 oz.–7 lb. 13 oz. (CX Composite)
Bore/Gauge: 12
Magazine: 2 shells
Features: Crossover barrel design with a 60/40 POI; ventilated top and side ribs; ivory front and mid-bead sights; steel ultra-low profile receiver with MonoLock Hinge engraved with a silver nitride finish; reverse striker ignition system; mechanical trigger design; Impact Ejectors; top-tang barrel selector/safety; 3-in. chamber; composite version features black rubber overmolding at grip points and adjustable comb
CX: **$1739.99**
CX Composite: **$1669.99**

BROWNING MAXUS WICKED WING

BROWNING SILVER BLACK LIGHTNING AND SILVER HUNTER MATTE

BROWNING SILVER RIFLED DEER MATTE

CHARLES DALY TRIPLE THREAT

BROWNING MAXUS WICKED WING

Action: Semiautomatic
Stock: Composite
Barrel: 26 in., 28 in.
Chokes: Banded Invector-Plus Extended
Weight: 7.0 lb.–7 lb. 2 oz.
Bore/Gauge: 12
Magazine: 4 shells
Features: 3.5-in. autoloader; A-TACS US, Mossy Oak Bottomlands, or Shadow Grass Blades stocks; Browning's Dura-Touch Armor Coating and burnt bronze Cerakote finish on receiver and barrel; Briley extended bolt handles; oversized bolt release come
MSRP **$1869.99**

BROWNING SILVER BLACK LIGHTNING AND SILVER HUNTER MATTE

Action: Semiautomatic
Stock: Turkish walnut
Barrel: 26 in., 28 in.
Chokes: Invector-Plus (F, M, IC)

Weight: 7 lb. 4 oz.–7 lb. 6 oz.
Bore/Gauge: 12
Magazine: 4 shells
Features: Gloss black and deep blued metal with gloss finish walnut Lightweight aluminum alloy receiver; Active Valve System regulates light and heavy loads; semi-humpback receiver styling; brass front bead; back-bored barrel; matte version features satin finish stock and bi-tone matte black and silver finish on the receiver
Silver Hunter: **$1259.99**
Silver Hunter Matte: **$1149.99**

BROWNING SILVER RIFLED DEER MATTE

Action: Semiautomatic
Stock: Turkish walnut
Barrel: 22 in.
Chokes: N/A
Weight: 6 lb. 12 oz.
Bore/Gauge: 12
Magazine: 4 shells
Features: Fully rifled barrel for sabot slugs; top cantilever scope mount; gas operation; 3-in. chamber; satin finish stock
MSRP **$1339.99**

CHARLES DALY TRIPLE THREAT

Action: Over/under
Stock: Walnut, synthetic
Barrel: 18.5 in.
Chokes: Rem Choke (SK, IC, M, IM, F)
Weight: 8 lb. 3.2 oz. (walnut), 7 lb. 1.6 oz. (synthetic)
Bore/Gauge: 12, 20, .410 (walnut), 12-ga. only (synthetic)
Magazine: 3 shells
Features: Over/under 12-gauge with one barrel over two for three shots total; wood stock version has removable buttstock that can be used for storage or removed so that the shotgun may be used pistol grip style; synthetic stock is not removable; firing sequence is right barrel, left barrel, top barrel; red fiber optic front bead; synthetic stock model has Picatinny rail
MSRP . . . . **$1909.00–$2079.00**

CZ-USA CZ 612 TARGET

CZ-USA CZ 620/628 FIELD SELECT

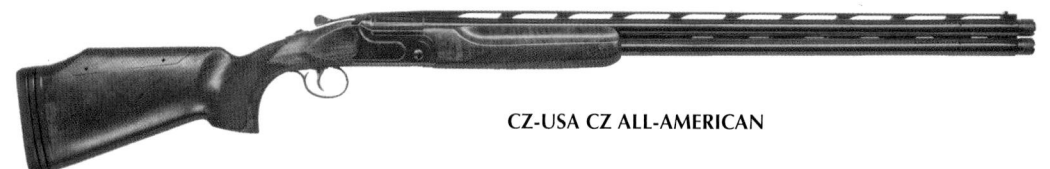

CZ-USA CZ ALL-AMERICAN

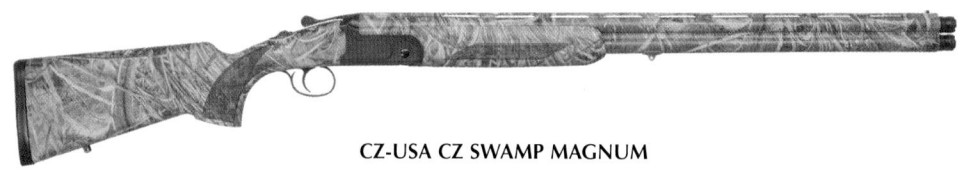

CZ-USA CZ SWAMP MAGNUM

CZ-USA CZ 612 TARGET

Action: Pump
Stock: Turkish walnut
Barrel: 32 in.
Chokes: Extended knurled
Weight: 7 lb. 5 oz.
Bore/Gauge: 12
Magazine: 4 shells
Features: Select grade wood with a glossy oil finish; metal is a deep polished blue; tuned trigger system; raised rib; comfortable Monte Carlo stock; pair of Bradley-style white beads
MSRP **$549.00**

CZ-USA CZ 620/628 FIELD SELECT

Action: Pump
Stock: Turkish walnut
Barrel: 28 in.
Chokes: F, M, C
Weight: 5 lb. 6 oz.
Bore/Gauge: 28 (628); 20 (620)
Magazine: 4 shells
Features: Gauge-specific 7075 aluminum action; deep glossy blue finish; select grade Turkish Walnut; full forend
MSRP **$429.00**

CZ-USA CZ ALL-AMERICAN

Action: Over/under
Stock: Turkish walnut
Barrel: 30 in., 32 in.
Chokes: Extended black
Weight: 8 lb. 8 oz.
Bore/Gauge: 12
Magazine: 2 shells
Features: CNCed throughout; drop-in replacement parts (including locking blocks for those who shoot tens of thousands of rounds a year); four-way comb; adjustable buttplate hardware; barrels have lengthened forcing cones and are ported; 3-in. chambers
MSRP **$2499.00**

CZ-USA CZ SWAMP MAGNUM

Action: Over/under
Stock: Polymer
Barrel: 30 in.
Chokes: Extended black
Weight: 7 lb. 2 oz.
Bore/Gauge: 12
Magazine: 2 shells
Features: Only over/under in CZ's line with an automatic safety, which engages every time the action is opened; polymer stocks in either black or Realtree Max-5 camo; all metal work blacked out; chambered for 3 ½ in.
Black: **$929.00**
Realtree Max-5: **$1029.00**

HENRY REPEATING ARMS LEVER ACTION .410 SHOTGUN

HENRY REPEATING ARMS SINGLE SHOT SHOTGUN IN STEEL & BRASS

IVER JOHNSON IJ700

KEL-TEC KSG-25

LEGACY SPORTS POINTER SEMI-AUTO

HENRY REPEATING ARMS LEVER ACTION .410 SHOTGUN

Action: Lever
Stock: Walnut
Barrel: 20 in., 24 in.
Chokes: None
Weight: 7 lb. 5 oz.–7 lb. 8 oz.
Bore/Gauge: .410
Magazine: 5 shells
Features: Available in standard and carbine barrel lengths; brass bead front sight; pistol grip stock; long version has a smooth Full constriction; carbine length has a smooth Cylinder constriction
MSRP . . . . $850.00-$902.00

HENRY REPEATING ARMS SINGLE SHOT SHOTGUN IN STEEL & BRASS

Action: Break-open single-shot
Stock: Walnut
Barrel: 26 in., 28 in.
Chokes: 1 (varies with gauge)

Weight: 6 lb. 10 oz.–6 lb. 12 oz.
Bore/Gauge: 12, 20, .410
Magazine: 1 shell
Features: Sharing the same action as the single-shot rifle but chambered for 12-ga. 20-ga., and .410-bore shotshells; front brass bead; steel models have pistol grip, brass models sport a straight grip; Rem-Choke style threaded chokes
MSRP . . . . $427.00-$549.00

IVER JOHNSON IJ700

Action: Break-open single-shot
Stock: Walnut
Barrel: 18 in., 26 in.
Chokes: None
Weight: 4 lb. 8 oz.–4 lb. 14 oz.
Bore/Gauge: .410
Magazine: 1 shell
Features: Silver receiver; blued barrel; single extractor; sling swivels
MSRP $175.00

KEL-TEC KSG-25

Action: Pump
Stock: Synthetic

Barrel: 30 in.
Chokes: None
Weight: 9 lb. 4 oz.
Bore/Gauge: 12
Magazine: 21, 25 shells
Features: Magpul MBUS and an RVG vertical grip on the pump; 3-in. chambers; holds a full box of 2 3/4-in. or 3-in. shells
MSRP $1400.00

LEGACY SPORTS POINTER SEMI-AUTO

Action: Semiautomatic
Stock: Walnut, laminate
Barrel: 28 in.
Chokes: F, M, IM, IC, C
Weight: 5 lb. 12.8 oz.–7 lb.
Bore/Gauge: 12, 20, 28
Magazine: 5 shells
Features: Gas-actuated; Turkish walnut in all gauges plus a gray laminate stock option for the 12-ga.; barrels are chrome-moly lined; chambers are 3-in.; fiber optic front sight
MSRP . . . . $674.00–$796.00

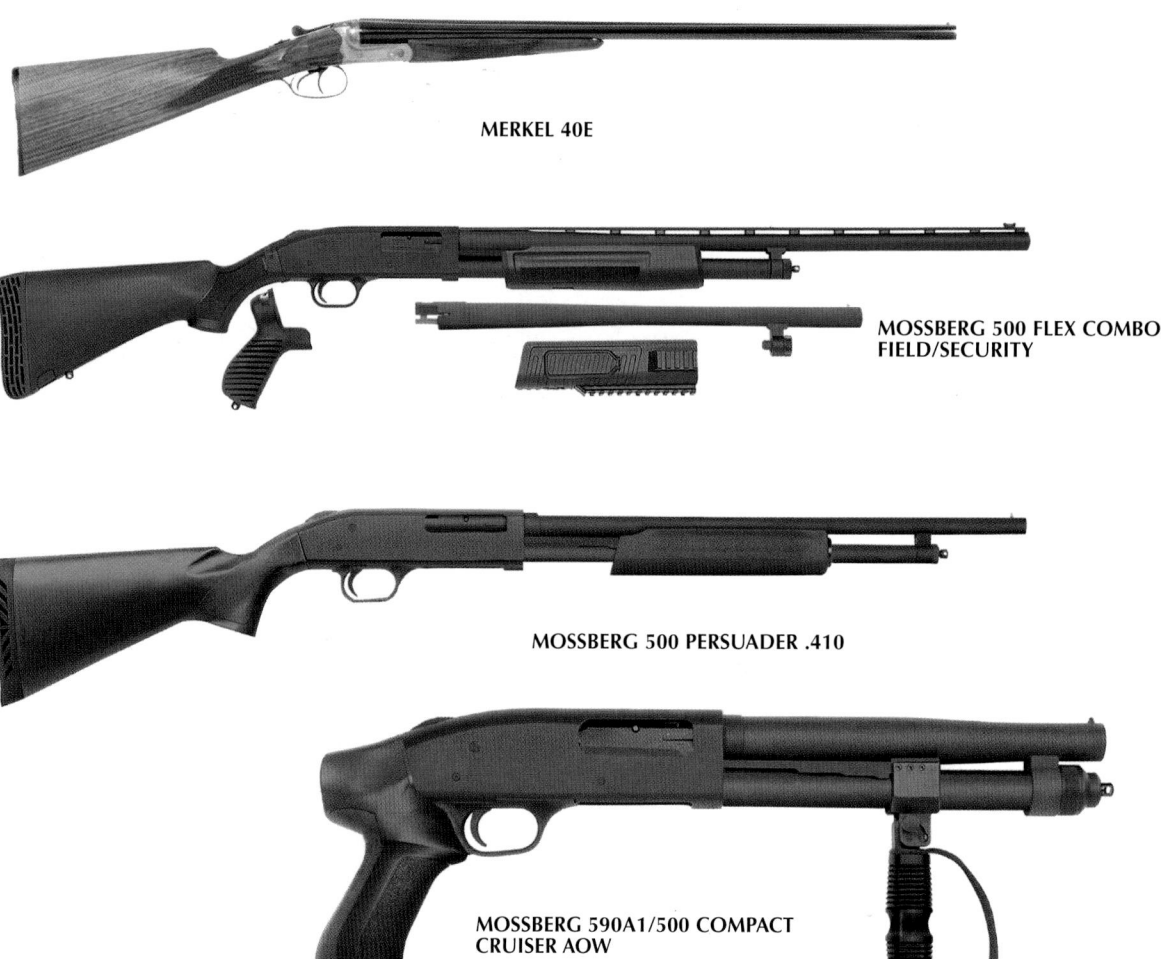

MERKEL 40E

MOSSBERG 500 FLEX COMBO FIELD/SECURITY

MOSSBERG 500 PERSUADER .410

MOSSBERG 590A1/500 COMPACT CRUISER AOW

MERKEL 40E

Action: Side-by-side
Stock: Wood
Barrel: 28 in.
Chokes: None
Weight: 6 lb. 3 oz.
Bore/Gauge: 12, 20, 28
Magazine: 2 shells
Features: Merkel's first new shotgun in nearly a decade; Anson & Deeley boxlock action; Greener crossbolt; Holland & Holland ejectors and monoblock barrel construction; steel receiver is silver nitrite finished with laser engraving; double or single triggers; 3-in. chambers; straight or pistol grip stocks on 12- and 20-ga.; 28-ga. is on the 20-ga. frame with single trigger and 2 ¾-in. chamber
MSRP **$4595.00**

MOSSBERG 500 FLEX COMBO FIELD/SECURITY

Action: Pump
Stock: Synthetic
Barrel: 18.5 in., 26 in.
Chokes: Accu-Set
Weight: 5 lb. 12 oz.–7 lb.
Bore/Gauge: 20
Magazine: 6 shells
Features: Interchangeable FLEX system full stock; pistol grip stock; 26-in. vent rib field barrel; non-ribbed 18.5-in. barrel; two handguards; case
MSRP **$597.00**

MOSSBERG 500 PERSUADER .410

Action: Pump
Stock: Synthetic
Barrel: 18.5 in.

Chokes: None
Weight: 5 lb. 8 oz.
Bore/Gauge: .410
Magazine: 6 shells
Features: Fixed cylinder bore; matte blue finish; bead front sight
MSRP **$467.00**

MOSSBERG 590A1/500 COMPACT CRUISER AOW

Action: Pump
Stock: Synthetic
Barrel: 7.5 in., 10.25 in.
Chokes: None
Weight: 4 lb. 14.4 oz.–5 lb. 4.8 oz.
Bore/Gauge: 12
Magazine: 4, 3 shells
Features: Mossberg's classic pumps in Compact Cruiser versions; dual extractors; twin action bars; anti-jam elevators
500: **$910.00**
590A1: **$980.00**

MOSSBERG 590 SHOCKWAVE

MOSSBERG 930 TACTICAL 8 SHOT

MOSSBERG INTERNATIONAL SA-28 ALL PURPOSE

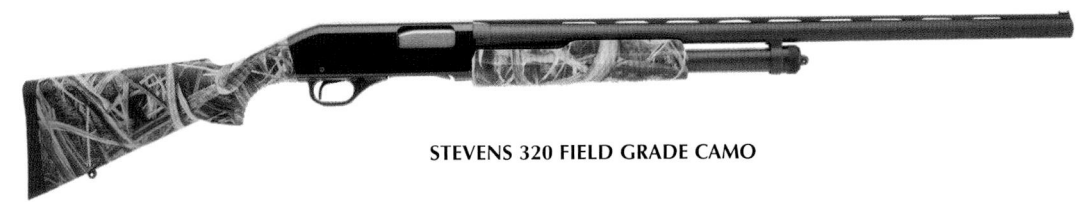

STEVENS 320 FIELD GRADE CAMO

MOSSBERG 590 SHOCKWAVE

Action: Pump
Stock: Synthetic
Barrel: 14 in.
Chokes: None
Weight: 5 lb. 4.8 oz.
Bore/Gauge: 12
Magazine: 6 shells
Features: Features unique Raptor pistol grip
MSRP **$455.00**

MOSSBERG 930 TACTICAL 8 SHOT

Action: Semiautomatic
Stock: Synthetic
Barrel: 18.5 in.
Chokes: None

Weight: 6 lb. 12 oz.
Bore/Gauge: 12
Magazine: 8 shells
Features: The popular 930 tactical autoloader gets an extended eight-shot magazine
MSRP **$612.00**

MOSSBERG INTERNATIONAL SA-28 ALL PURPOSE

Action: Semiautomatic
Stock: Walnut
Barrel: 26 in.
Chokes: Sport Set
Weight: 6 lb. 8 oz.
Bore/Gauge: 28
Magazine: 5 shells

Features: Lightweight field gun in 2 3/4-in.; front bead; high-polish blue metal; high-gloss walnut stock
MSRP **$654.00**

STEVENS 320 FIELD GRADE CAMO

Action: Pump
Stock: Synthetic
Barrel: 26 in., 28 in.
Chokes: M
Weight: 6 lb. 15.2 oz.–7 lb. 7.2 oz.
Bore/Gauge: 12, 20
Magazine: 5 shells
Features: Stocked in Mossy Oak Shadow Grass Blades; compact model available with 13.25-in. length of pull
MSRP . . . . **$238.00–$273.00**

STEVENS 320 FIELD GRADE MUDDY GIRL

STEVENS 320 SECURITY

STEVENS 555 ENHANCED

STEVENS S1200 SYNTHETIC

STEVENS 320 FIELD GRADE MUDDY GIRL

Action: Pump
Stock: Synthetic
Barrel: 22 in., 26 in.
Chokes: M
Weight: 6 lb. 15.2 oz.–7 lb. 4 oz.
Bore/Gauge: 20
Magazine: 5 shells
Features: Designed for youth and women with shorter length of pull (13.25 in.); bottom load; right-eject pump; dual rails; rotary bolt; Muddy Girl camo
MSRP **$273.00**

STEVENS 320 SECURITY

Action: Pump
Stock: Synthetic
Barrel: 18.5 in.

Chokes: M
Weight: 6 lb. 13.6 oz.–7lb.
Bore/Gauge: 12, 20
Magazine: 5 shells
Features: Security version of reliable 320 pump; pistol grip; ghost sight option
MSRP . . . . **$236.00–$264.00**

STEVENS 555 ENHANCED

Action: Over/under
Stock: Walnut
Barrel: 28 in. (12-ga.); 26 in. (20- and 28-ga, .410)
Chokes: SK, IC, M, IM, F
Weight: 5 lb. 8 oz.–6 lb.
Bore/Gauge: 12, 20, 28, .410
Magazine: 2 shells
Features: Lightweight aluminum receiver is scaled to gauge; imperial walnut stock; automatic shell ejectors;

laser-engraved filigree decoration on the receiver
MSRP **$863.00**

STEVENS S1200

Action: Semiautomatic
Stock: Synthetic
Barrel: 26 in., 28 in.
Chokes: C, IC, M, I, F
Weight: 6 lb. 12.8 oz.–7 lb.
Bore/Gauge: 12
Magazine: 5 shells
Features: Steven's first semiautomatic shotgun; inertia-driven system; accepts Beretta Mobilchokes; black synthetic stock (26- or 28-in.), Mossy Oak Bottomlands (26-in.), Mossy Oak Shadow Grass Blades (28-in.), or walnut (28 in.)
Black: **$571.00**
Camo: **$626.00**
Walnut: **$685.00**

STOEGER CONDOR COMBO

STOEGER M3000 DEFENSE

STOEGER M3000 SPORTING

STOEGER P3000 DEFENSE

STOEGER CONDOR COMBO

Action: Over/under
Stock: Walnut
Barrel: 26 in., 28 in.
Chokes: IC, M
Weight: 6 lb. 9.6 oz.–7 lb. 3.2 oz.
Bore/Gauge: 12, 20
Magazine: 2 shells
Features: Two-gauge combo has barrels for 12- and 20-ga.; satin finished walnut stock; 3-in. chambers; brass front bead
MSRP **$679.00**

STOEGER M3000 DEFENSE

Action: Semiautomatic
Stock: Synthetic
Barrel: 18.5 in.

Chokes: Cylinder fixed
Weight: 7 lb.
Bore/Gauge: 12
Magazine: 4 shells
Features: 3-in. chamber; blade front sight; field or pistol grip stock
Pistol grip: $649.00
Standard: $599.00

STOEGER M3000 SPORTING

Action: Semiautomatic
Stock: Synthetic
Barrel: 30 in.
Chokes: SK1, SK2, IC
Weight: 7 lb. 8 oz.
Bore/Gauge: 12
Magazine: 4 shells

Features: Built for clay game competition; 3-in. chamber; fiber optic front sight; extended choke tubes
MSRP **$699.00**

STOEGER P3000 DEFENSE

Action: Pump
Stock: Synthetic
Barrel: 18.5 in.
Chokes: Cylinder fixed
Weight: 6 lb. 8 oz.
Bore/Gauge: 12
Magazine: 4 shells
Features: Blade front sight; 3-in. chamber; field or pistol grip stock
Pistol grip: $349.00
Standard: $299.00

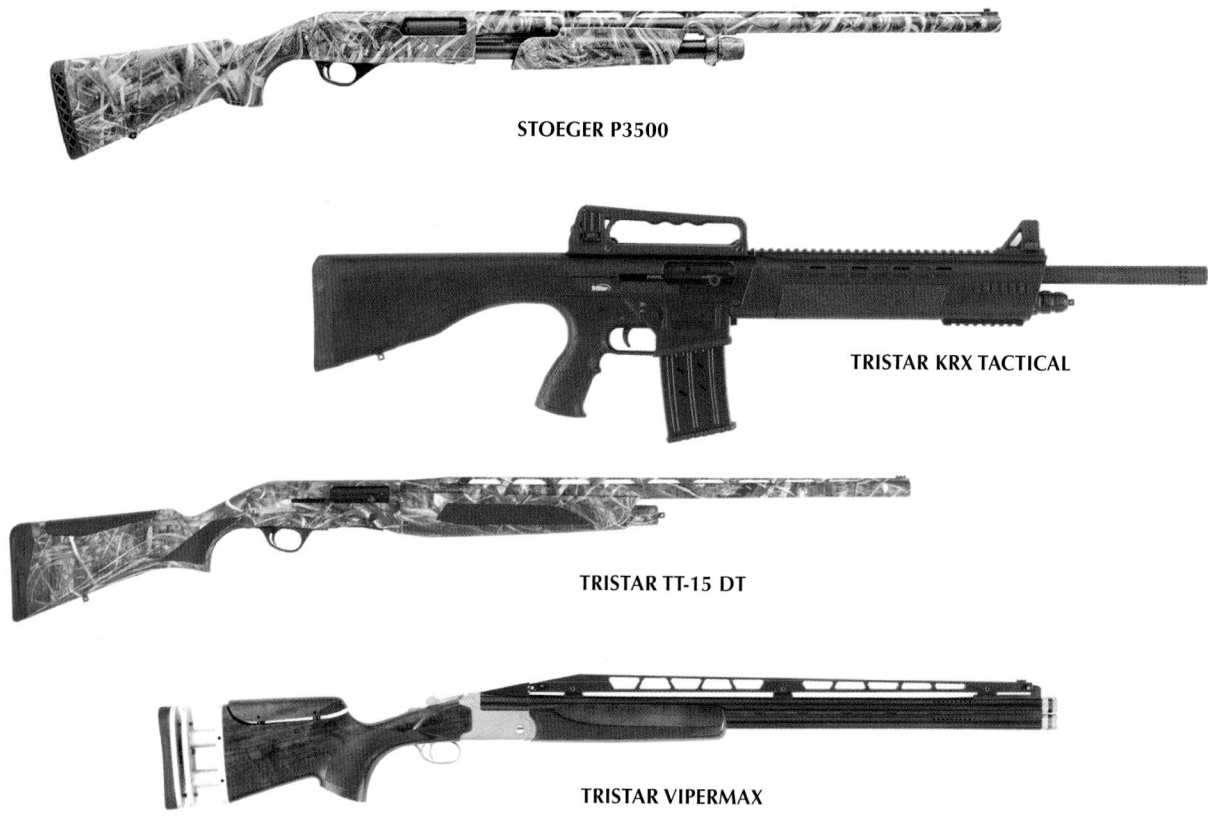

STOEGER P3500

TRISTAR KRX TACTICAL

TRISTAR TT-15 DT

TRISTAR VIPERMAX

STOEGER P3500

Action: Pump
Stock: Synthetic
Barrel: 26 in., 28 in.
Chokes: M
Weight: 6 lb. 14 oz.–7 lb.
Bore/Gauge: 12
Magazine: 4 shells
Features: Chambered for 2 ¾-, 3-, and 3 ½-in.; mechanical rotating bolt; dual action rails; red fiber optic front sight; chrome-lined steel barrel; black or Realtree Max-5
Black:...................**$399.00**
Camo: **$449.00**

TRISTAR KRX TACTICAL

Action: Semiautomatic
Stock: Synthetic
Barrel: 20 in.
Chokes: Extended tactical choke
Weight: 7 lb. 6.4 oz.
Bore/Gauge: 12
Magazine: 5 shells
Features: AR-platform with a 3-in. chamber; controls similar to those of an actual AR; gas-operated; full-length Picatinny rail; removable carry handle; bridge front sight; injection-molded stock and forearm; two detachable magazines
MSRP................. **$595.00**

TRISTAR TT-15 DT

Action: Over/under
Stock: Walnut
Barrel: 30 in.
Chokes: 5 Beretta Mobil (F, IM, M, IC, SK)
Weight: 8 lb. 11.2 oz.
Bore/Gauge: 12
Magazine: 2 shells
Features: The newest addition to TriStar's TT-15 line of dedicated trap guns; back-bored barrels; 2 ¾-in. chambers; adjustable high trap rib; four-way fully adjustable buttstock; red fiber optic front sight. Supplied with color-coded, extended Beretta Mobil Chokes
MSRP............... **$1450.00**

TRISTAR VIPERMAX

Action: Semiautomatic
Stock: Synthetic
Barrel: 26 in., 28 in., 30 in.
Chokes: Beretta Mobil (SK, IC, M, F)
Weight: 7 lb. 6.4 oz.
Bore/Gauge: 12
Magazine: 4 shells
Features: Gas-operated; 3 ½-in. chamber; heavy and light load pistons; extra piston can be stored in the forearm for instant in-the-field change-out; fiber optic front sight; sling swivel studs; magazine cut-off; Quick Shot plug removal; chrome-lined barrel and chamber; black or Realtree Max-5 HD camo; camo version available in all three barrel lengths, black version with 28-in. barrel only
Black:...................**$640.00**
Realtree MAX-5 HD: **$730.00**

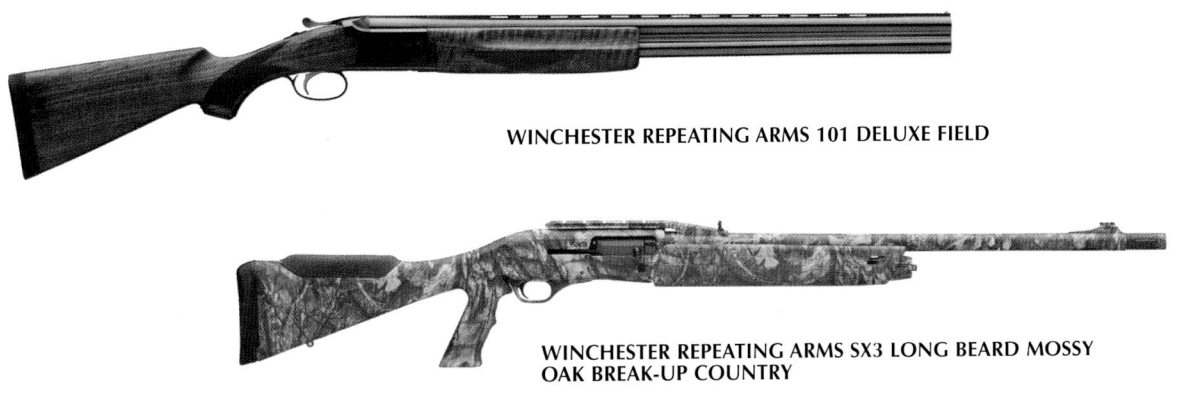

WINCHESTER REPEATING ARMS 101 DELUXE FIELD

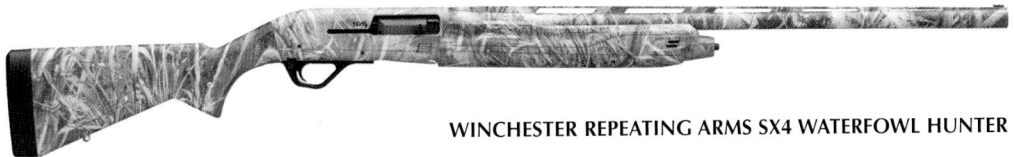

WINCHESTER REPEATING ARMS SX3 LONG BEARD MOSSY
OAK BREAK-UP COUNTRY

WINCHESTER REPEATING ARMS SX4 WATERFOWL HUNTER

WINCHESTER REPEATING ARMS SXP BLACK SHADOW DEER
20-GAUGE

WINCHESTER REPEATING ARMS 101 DELUXE FIELD

Action: Over/under
Stock: Walnut
Barrel: 26 in., 28 in.
Chokes: Invector-Plus (F, M, IC)
Weight: 6 lb. 12 oz.
Bore/Gauge: 12
Magazine: 2 shells
Features: Grade III European walnut stock; detailed engraving on steel receiver; back-bored, hard-chromed barrels; front bead; 3-in. chambers
MSRP **$1999.99**

WINCHESTER REPEATING ARMS SX3 LONG BEARD MOSSY OAK BREAK-UP COUNTRY

Action: Semiautomatic
Stock: Synthetic
Barrel: 24 in.
Chokes: Invector-Plus Briley Extra-Full Long Beard
Weight: 7 lb. 8 oz.
Bore/Gauge: 12

Magazine: 4 shells
Features: Synthetic pistol grip stock with textured gripping surfaces; TruGlo front sight; adjustable rear sight; back-bored barrel with hard chrome plated bore and chamber; cantilever scope mount; Quadra-Vent ports; drop-out trigger assembly
MSRP **$1269.99**

WINCHESTER REPEATING ARMS SX4 WATERFOWL HUNTER

Action: Semiautomatic
Stock: Synthetic
Barrel: 26 in., 28 in.
Chokes: Invector-Plus (F, M, IC)
Weight: 6 lb. 12 oz.–7 lb.
Bore/Gauge: 12
Magazine: 4 shells
Features: Improved stock ergonomics with smaller pistol grip and textured gripping surfaces; back-bored barrels; vent rib; Active Valve gas system; Quadra-Vent ports; drop-out trigger group; oversized bolt handle; stock spacers; ambidextrous crossbolt

safety; Mossy Oak Bottomlands, Mossy Oak Shadow Grass Blades, or Realtree Max-5 camo finishes; 3- and 3 ½-in. chambers
MSRP . . . . **$939.99–$1069.99**

WINCHESTER REPEATING ARMS SXP BLACK SHADOW DEER 20-GAUGE

Action: Pump
Stock: Synthetic
Barrel: 22 in.
Chokes: None
Weight: 6 lb. 10 oz.
Bore/Gauge: 20
Magazine: 4 shells
Features: Rotary-bolt pump; fully rifled barrel; alloy receiver; TruGlo fiber optic front sight; adjustable rear sight; three-shot Speed Plug adaptor; drop-out trigger; ambidextrous crossbolt safety; drilled and tapped for scope mounts; 12-gauge also available
MSRP **$549.99**

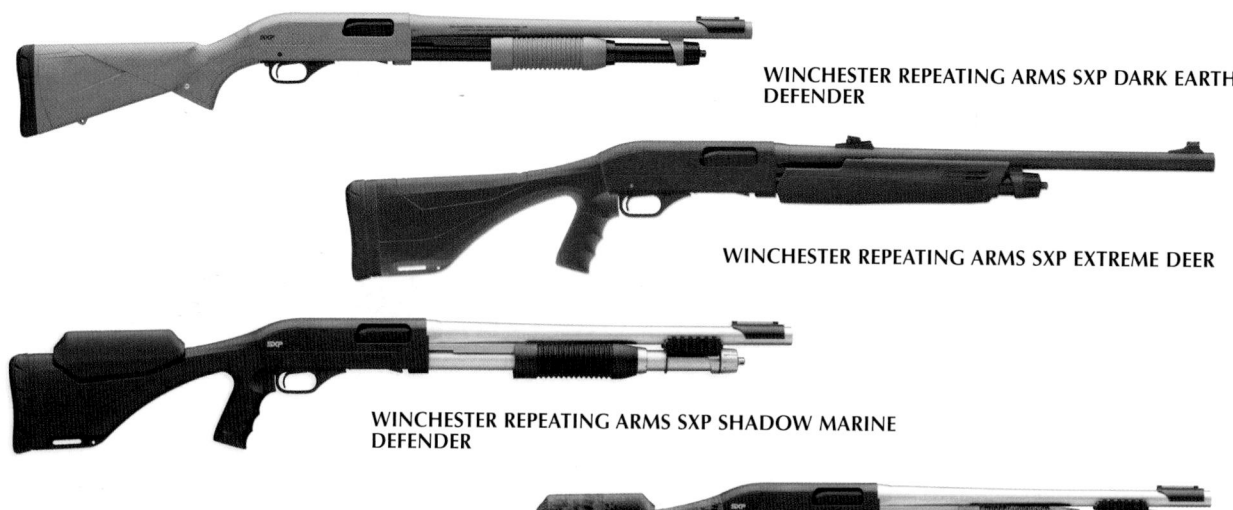

WINCHESTER REPEATING ARMS SXP DARK EARTH DEFENDER

WINCHESTER REPEATING ARMS SXP EXTREME DEER

WINCHESTER REPEATING ARMS SXP SHADOW MARINE DEFENDER

WINCHESTER REPEATING ARMS SXP SHADOW TYPHON MARINE DEFENDER

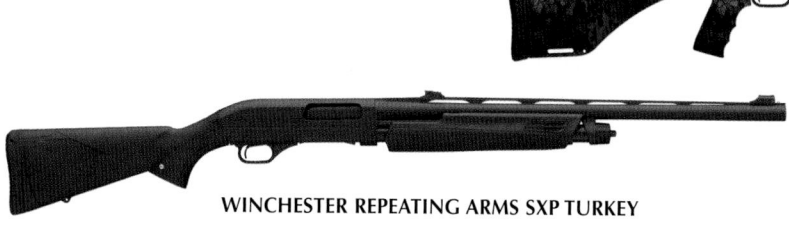

WINCHESTER REPEATING ARMS SXP TURKEY

WINCHESTER REPEATING ARMS SXP DARK EARTH DEFENDER

Action: Pump
Stock: Synthetic
Barrel: 18 in.
Chokes: Fixed cylinder
Weight: 6 lb. 4 oz.
Bore/Gauge: 12, 20
Magazine: 5 shells
Features: Aluminum alloy receiver; 3-in. chamber; front brass bead with removable TruGlo fiber optic sight; finished in Dark Earth
MSRP . . . . $379.99–$399.99

WINCHESTER REPEATING ARMS SXP EXTREME DEER

Action: Pump
Stock: Synthetic
Barrel: 22 in.
Chokes: None
Weight: 7 lb.
Bore/Gauge: 12
Magazine: 4 shells
Features: Rotary-bolt pump with fully rifled barrel; alloy receiver; TruGlo fiber optic front sight; adjustable rear sight; three-shot Speed Plug adaptor; drop-out trigger; ambidextrous crossbolt safety; drilled and tapped for scope mounts; 3-in. chamber; synthetic pistol grip stock has textured grip surfaces, two interchangeable cheek pieces, and two length-of-pull spacers
MSRP $559.99

WINCHESTER REPEATING ARMS SXP SHADOW MARINE DEFENDER

Action: Pump
Stock: Synthetic
Barrel: 18 in.
Chokes: Invector-Plus (C)
Weight: 7 lb. 8 oz.
Bore/Gauge: 12, 20
Magazine: 5 shells
Features: Hard chrome plating on most exterior metal surfaces and bore; alloy receiver is drilled and tapped for scope mounts; 3-in. chamber; synthetic pistol grip stock has textured grip surfaces; two interchangeable cheek pieces; two length-of-pull spacers
MSRP . . . . $479.99–$509.99

WINCHESTER REPEATING ARMS SXP SHADOW TYPHON MARINE DEFENDER

Action: Pump
Stock: Synthetic
Barrel: 18 in.
Chokes: Invector-Plus (C)
Weight: 7 lb. 8 oz.
Bore/Gauge: 12, 20
Magazine: 5 shells
Features: Hard chrome plating on most exterior metal surfaces and bore; alloy receiver is drilled and tapped for scope mounts; 3-in. chamber; synthetic pistol grip stock has textured grip surfaces; two interchangeable cheekpieces; two length-of-pull spacers; stock in dipped Kryptek Typhon camo
MSRP $499.99

WINCHESTER REPEATING ARMS SXP TURKEY

Action: Pump
Stock: Synthetic
Barrel: 24 in.
Chokes: Invector-Plus Extra Full Turkey
Weight: 6 lb. 4 oz. (20-ga.), 6 lb. 10 oz. (12-ga.)
Bore/Gauge: 12, 20
Magazine: 4 shells
Features: Hard chrome plated chamber and bore; back-bore technology; TruGlo fiber optic adjustable sights; 12-ga. has 3 ½-in. chamber; 20-ga. has 3-in. chamber
MSRP $439.99

AREX (FIME GROUP)
REX ZERO 1CP

ARMSCOR/ROCK ISLAND
ARMORY MAPP MS TCM9R
HC, MAPP FS TCM9R HC

ARMSCOR/ROCK
ISLAND ARMORY
ROCK ULTRA CCO

AREX (FIME
GROUP) REX ZERO
1S

ARMSCOR/ROCK
ISLAND ARMORY
BBR ULTRA CS
WARRIOR

AREX (FIME GROUP) REX ZERO 1CP

Action: Semiautomatic
Grips: Polymer
Barrel: 3.85 in.
Sights: White dot
Weight: 25.2 oz.
Caliber: 9mm, .40 S&W, .32 Auto
Capacity: 17 rounds
Features: Produced in Slovenia, this is the company's first entry into the U.S. market; DA/SA semiauto with a short-recoil, modified Browning linkless locking design; combo slide stop/decocker; hard anodized T7075 aluminum frame; nitrocarburized steel slide and cold-hammer-forged barrel; ambidextrous safety and magazine release; loaded chamber indicator; Picatinny rail; oversized trigger guard for use with gloves
MSRP $670.00

AREX (FIME GROUP) REX ZERO 1S

Action: Semiautomatic
Grips: Polymer
Barrel: 4.3 in.
Sights: White dot
Weight: 29 oz.
Caliber: 9mm, .40 S&W, .32 Auto
Capacity: 17 rounds
Features: Produced in Slovenia, this is the company's first entry into the U.S. market; DA/SA semiauto with short-recoil, modified Browning linkless locking design; combo slide stop/decocker; hard anodized T7075 aluminum frame; nitrocarburized steel slide and cold-hammer-forged barrel; ambidextrous safety and magazine release; loaded chamber indicator; Picatinny rail; oversized trigger guard for use with gloves
MSRP $670.00

ARMSCOR/ROCK ISLAND ARMORY BBR ULTRA CS WARRIOR

Action: Semiautomatic
Grips: G10
Barrel: 3.15 in.
Sights: Dovetail standard front, fixed snag-free rear
Weight: N/A
Caliber: .45 ACP
Capacity: 10 rounds
Features: Compact 1911 design; parkerized frame and slide; comfort dovetail grip safety; stable low profile angled sight design for consistent accuracy and reliability
MSRP $814.00

ARMSCOR/ROCK ISLAND ARMORY MAPP MS TCM9R HC, MAPP FS TCM9R HC

Action: Semiautomatic
Grips: Polymer
Barrel: 3.8 in.
Sights: Integrated front post, LPA MPS2 adjustable rear
Weight: 35.5 oz.–37.1 oz.
Caliber: TCM9R
Capacity: 16 rounds
Features: Brings Armscor centerfire, bottlenecked .22-caliber, 9mm length cartridge to the company's MAPP platform in both mid-sized (MS) and full-sized (FS) frames; DA/SA; parkerized finish on frame and slide
MS: $429.00
FS: $449.00

ARMSCOR/ROCK ISLAND ARMORY ROCK ULTRA CCO

Action: Semiautomatic
Grips: G10
Barrel: 4.25 in.
Sights: Dovetail fiber optic front, LPA MPS1-type adjustable rear
Weight: N/A
Caliber: .45 ACP
Capacity: 8 rounds
Features: Officer's grip; aluminum frame; Commander-length slide; full-length guide rod; button-rifled barrel; skeletonized hammer; trigger with overtravel; frame has black oxide finish; slide is parkerized
MSRP $760.00

NEW Products: **Handguns**

ARMSCOR/ROCK ISLAND ARMORY ROCK ULTRA CS

ARMSCOR/ROCK ISLAND ARMORY TCM ROCK ULTRA CCO

ARMSCOR/ROCK ISLAND ARMORY TCM ROCK ULTRA CS-L

ARMSCOR/ROCK ISLAND ARMORY XT 22 MAGNUM

AVIDITY ARMS PD10

BERETTA 92FSR_22 SNIPER GRAY

Weight: 46.4 oz.
Caliber: .22 TCM9R/9mm
Capacity: 8 rounds
Features: Aluminum frame with a short barrel; drop-in 9mm accessory barrel
MSRP **$837.00**

ARMSCOR/ROCK ISLAND ARMORY XT 22 MAGNUM

Action: Semiautomatic
Grips: Rubber
Barrel: 5 in.
Sights: Fixed dovetail front and rear
Weight: 49 oz.
Caliber: .22 WMR
Capacity: 15 rounds
Features: Full-size 1911 platform; pinned barrel; delayed blowback action; low-profile anti-snag sights; all-over parkerized finish
MSRP **$598.00**

AVIDITY ARMS PD10

Action: Semiautomatic
Grips: Polymer
Barrel: 4 in.
Sights: Ameriglo Luma Glow front, I.C.E. Claw Emergency Manipulation rear
Weight: 18.8 oz.
Caliber: 9mm
Capacity: 10 rounds
Features: Personal Defense (PD) carry gun; ergonomic polymer frame; aggressive slide serrations; loaded chamber indicator
MSRP **$499.00**

BERETTA 92FSR 22 SNIPER GRAY

Action: Semiautomatic
Grips: Plastic
Barrel: 4.9 in.
Sights: Dovetailed front and rear
Weight: 26.08 oz.
Caliber: .22 LR
Capacity: 10, 15 rounds
Features: DA/SA .22 LR version of maker's famed 9mm; open slide design; reversible magazine release; ambidextrous decocker/safety; combat trigger guard; 1913 Picatinny rail; Sniper Gray frame finish
MSRP **$450.00**

ARMSCOR/ROCK ISLAND ARMORY ROCK ULTRA CS

Action: Semiautomatic
Grips: Rubber
Barrel: 3.62 in.
Sights: Dovetail standard front, low-profile, snag-free rear
Weight: 46.4 oz.
Caliber: .45 ACP
Capacity: 7 rounds
Features: Traditional 70-series 1911 design in a compact concealed carry package; snag-free features; checkered rubber grips; all-over parkerized matte finish
MSRP **$618.00**

ARMSCOR/ROCK ISLAND ARMORY TCM ROCK ULTRA CCO

Action: Semiautomatic

Grips: G10
Barrel: 4.25 in.
Sights: Dovetail fiber optic front, LPA MPS1-type adjustable rear
Weight: N/A
Caliber: .22 TCM9R/9mm
Capacity: 8 rounds
Features: Officer's grip; aluminum frame; Commander-length slide; full-length guide rod; button-rifled barrel; skeletonized hammer; beveled magazine well; drop-in 9mm accessory barrel
MSRP **$845.00**

ARMSCOR/ROCK ISLAND ARMORY TCM ROCK ULTRA CS-L

Action: Semiautomatic
Grips: G10
Barrel: 3.62 in.
Sights: Dovetail fiber optic front, LPA MPS1-type adjustable rear

BERETTA 92FSR_22
SUPPRESSOR
READY KIT

BERETTA PX4
COMPACT CARRY

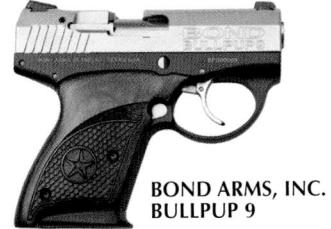

BOND ARMS, INC.
BULLPUP 9

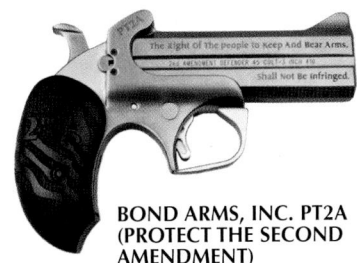

BOND ARMS, INC. PT2A
(PROTECT THE SECOND
AMENDMENT)

BOND ARMS, INC.
TEXAN

BROWNING 1911-
380 BLACK LABEL
MEDALLION STAINLESS
COMPACT, FULL-SIZE

BERETTA 92FSR_22 SUPPRESSOR READY KIT

Action: Semiautomatic
Grips: Plastic
Barrel: 4.9 in.
Sights: Suppressor-height front and rear
Weight: 26.08 oz.
Caliber: .22 LR
Capacity: 10, 15 rounds
Features: DA/SA .22 LR version of maker's famed 9mm; open slide design; reversible magazine release; ambidextrous decocker/safety; combat trigger guard; 1913 Picatinny rail; suppressor-height sights; extended threaded barrel with thread protector and mock suppressor
MSRP **$495.00**

BERETTA PX4 COMPACT CARRY

Action: Semiautomatic
Grips: Polymer
Barrel: 3.2 in.
Sights: Three-dot night sights
Weight: 27.3 oz.
Caliber: 9mm
Capacity: 15 rounds

Features: Designed with handgun and shooting expert Ernest Langdon; compact concealed carry; accessory rail; low-profile slide stop; integral and retractable lanyard loop; PX4's rotating barrel system
MSRP **$899.00**

BOND ARMS, INC. BULLPUP 9

Action: Semiautomatic
Grips: Rosewood
Barrel: 3.35 in.
Sights: Dovetail drift-adjustable non-illuminated three-dot
Weight: 17.5 oz.
Caliber: 9mm Luger
Capacity: 7 rounds
Features: Based on the XR-9 by Boberg Arms; Bond Arms purchased the patents and rights to that gun in 2016, basing its new Bullpup on it
MSRP **$977.00**

BOND ARMS, INC. PT2A (PROTECT THE SECOND AMENDMENT)

Action: Break-top

Grips: Rosewood
Barrel: 4.25 in.
Sights: Front blade, fixed rear
Weight: 23.5 oz.
Caliber: .45 LC/.410-bore, .357 Mag.
Capacity: 2 rounds
Features: Custom extended rosewood grips; "The Right of the People to Keep and Bear Arms" is emblazoned on right side of top barrel; "shall not be infringed" on right side of bottom barrel; cross-bolt safety; stainless steel barrels; compatibility with all Bond barrels; automatic spent casing extractors; BAD premium leather driving holster
MSRP **$887.00**

BOND ARMS, INC. TEXAN

Action: Break-top
Grips: Rosewood
Barrel: 6 in.
Sights: Front ramp
Weight: 23.5 oz.
Caliber: .45 LC/.410-bore
Capacity: 2 rounds
Features: Bond's first six-inch production model; patented rebounding hammer; cross-bolt safety; automatic spent casing extractor; spring-loaded cammed locking lever; compatible with all Bond Arms barrels; rosewood grips are extended and engraved
MSRP **$700.00**

BROWNING 1911-380 BLACK LABEL MEDALLION STAINLESS COMPACT, FULL-SIZE

Action: Semiautomatic
Grips: Laminate
Barrel: 3.625 in. (compact), 4.25 in. (full-size)
Sights: Steel three-dot combat or steel bar-dot combat night sights
Weight: 16 oz. (compact), 18 oz. (full-size)
Caliber: .380 ACP
Capacity: 8 rounds
Features: 85 percent-scale 1911 pistol; compact and full-size versions; stainless steel slide and rosewood laminate grips; ambidextrous manual thumb safety; extended slide release beavertail grip safety; two magazines; Commander hammer; target crown; grips are grooved and checkered
MSRP **$799.99**
Night sights: **$879.99**

BROWNING 1911-380 BLACK LABEL PRO STAINLESS FULL SIZE WITH RAIL

BROWNING BUCK MARK LITE UFX

BROWNING BUCK MARK PLUS UDX, STAINLESS UDX, ROSEWOOD UDX

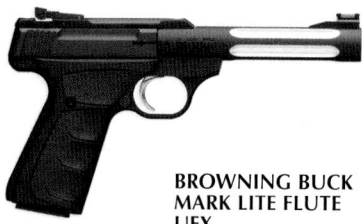

BROWNING BUCK MARK LITE FLUTE UFX

BROWNING BUCK MARK PLUS PRACTICAL URX

CABOT GUNS THE AMERICAN JOE COMMANDER

BROWNING 1911-380 BLACK LABEL PRO STAINLESS FULL SIZE WITH RAIL

Action: Semiautomatic
Grips: Textured G10
Barrel: 4.25 in.
Sights: Steel three-dot combat or steel bar-dot combat night sights
Weight: 18 oz.
Caliber: .380 ACP
Capacity: 8 rounds
Features: 85 percent-scale 1911 pistol; 1913 Picatinny rail; composite frame; ergonomic and skeletonized controls; two magazines; fully machined 7075 aluminum sub-frame and slide rails; target crown; satin silver finish
MSRP..................**$829.99**
Night sights:..........**$909.99**

BROWNING BUCK MARK LITE FLUTE UFX

Action: Semiautomatic
Grips: Ultragrip FX
Barrel: 5.5 in.
Sights: Pro-Target adjustable rear, Marble Arms violet fiber-optic front

Weight: 35 oz.
Caliber: .22 LR
Capacity: 10 rounds
Features: Thin steel barrel wrapped in a high-strength, lightweight, aluminum alloy sleeve; machined flutes in the barrel sleeve further; grips are overmolded polymer; ambidextrous finger grooves
MSRP..................**$559.99**

BROWNING BUCK MARK LITE UFX

Action: Semiautomatic
Grips: Ultragrip FX
Barrel: 5.5 in.
Sights: Pro-Target adjustable rear, Marble Arms violet fiber-optic front
Weight: 35 oz.
Caliber: .22 LR
Capacity: 10 rounds
Features: Blowback action; steel barrel with aluminum alloy outer sleeve; alloy frame; matte black finish with Buckmark symbol in silver on top side of barrel; ambidextrous grip; black rubber overmolding
MSRP..................**$589.99**

BROWNING BUCK MARK PLUS PRACTICAL URX

Action: Semiautomatic
Grips: Nitrite rubber
Barrel: 5.5 in.
Sights: Pro-Target white outline adjustable rear, TRUGLO/Marble Arms fiber-optic front
Weight: 34 oz.
Caliber: .22 LR
Capacity: 10 rounds
Features: Soft nitrile rubber Ultragrip RX (URX) grips with finger grooves; top 1913 Picatinny rail optic base; round tapered bull barrel; matte gray finish
MSRP..................**$479.99**

BROWNING BUCK MARK PLUS UDX, STAINLESS UDX, ROSEWOOD UDX

Action: Semiautomatic
Grips: Laminate
Barrel: 5.5 in.
Sights: TruGlo fiber optic front; white outline Pro-Target rear
Weight: 34 oz.
Caliber: .22 LR
Capacity: 10 rounds
Features: Wood laminate UDX grips (Utragrip Deluxe); stainless steel frame and slabside barrel with polished flats; SA trigger; Picatinny top rail for optics; grip frame machined with finger grooves that match up to textured wood grips; slab-side barrel has high-polished flats
Stainless:..............**$599.99**
Buckmark UDX, Rosewood:...**$549.99**

CABOT GUNS THE AMERICAN JOE COMMANDER

Action: Semiautomatic
Grips: Aluminum
Barrel: 4.25 in.
Sights: Cabot reverse dovetail white-dot front, low-mount fixed rear
Weight: 33.5 oz.
Caliber: .45 ACP
Capacity: 8 rounds
Features: The original American Joe now in Commander-length slide; "Tire Tread" USA engraving at front of slide; wing and spiderweb engraving designed by Joe Faris covering the rest of the slide; special flag grips
MSRP..........**$4500.00 and up**

CABOT GUNS THE DRAKO GARRA

CABOT GUNS VINTAGE CLASSIC

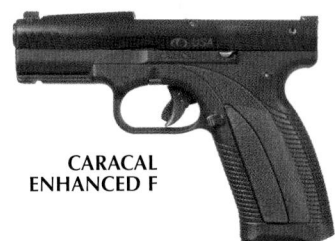

CARACAL ENHANCED F

CHARLES DALY AK-9

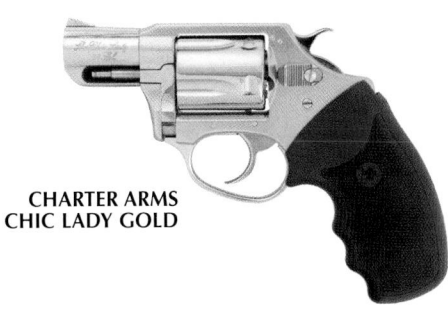

CHARTER ARMS CHIC LADY GOLD

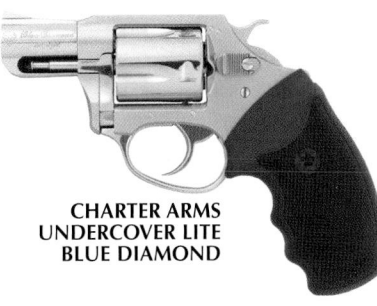

CHARTER ARMS UNDERCOVER LITE BLUE DIAMOND

Features: Striker-fired polymer frame; integrated trigger safety; firing pin safety; drop safety; rail interface for light and laser mounting; full-length steel slide guide; fully supported chamber; cold-hammer-forged barrel; available Quick Sight option
MSRP $599.00

CHARLES DALY AK-9

Action: Semiautomatic
Grips: Synthetic
Barrel: 6.3 in.
Sights: A2-style front sight
Weight: 96 oz.
Caliber: 9mm
Capacity: 10 rounds
Features: AK-style platform reduced to a pistol configuration; steel frame; interchangeable magazine adaptor sold separately allows user to convert between Beretta and Glock magazines without tools
MSRP $529.00

CHARTER ARMS CHIC LADY GOLD

Action: Revolver
Grips: Rubber, compact
Barrel: 2 in.
Sights: Fixed
Weight: 12 oz.
Caliber: .38 Spl.
Capacity: 5 rounds
Features: Smooth, anodized gold frame; hi-polish stainless steel barrel and cylinder; faux gold colored alligator case
MSRP $483.00

CHARTER ARMS UNDERCOVER LITE BLUE DIAMOND

Action: Revolver
Grips: Rubber, compact
Barrel: 2 in.
Sights: Fixed
Weight: 12 oz.
Caliber: .38 Spl.
Capacity: 5 rounds
Features: Smooth, anodized blue frame; hi-polish stainless steel barrel and cylinder
MSRP $446.00

CABOT GUNS THE DRAKO GARRA

Action: Semiautomatic
Grips: Ebony
Barrel: 5 in.
Sights: Gold bead Cabot reverse dovetail front, low-mount fixed rear
Weight: N/A
Caliber: 9mm, .45 ACP
Capacity: 8 rounds
Features: 1911 with "claw mark" front and rear slide cocking serrations in negative/positive relief that extends to the frame; Cabot's radiused, precision-fit trigger with an all-new electric-discharge wire cut design of twin claws; hand-polished ebony grips; mammoth grips optional; night sights available
MSRP . . . . $4950.00 and up

CABOT GUNS VINTAGE CLASSIC

Action: Semiautomatic
Grips: Walnut
Barrel: 5 in.

Sights: Gold bead Cabot reverse dovetail front, low-mount fixed rear
Weight: N/A
Caliber: .45 ACP
Capacity: 8 rounds
Features: Cabot frame and slide from 416 stainless steel billet; proprietary hardening and vintage "classic" finish; Cabot Trinity Stripes rear slide serrations; beveled magazine well; lowered and flared ejection port; Cabot aluminum Tristar trigger; match-grade hand-fit barrel; rhombus-cut front strap and mainspring housing checkering; sight and grip options
MSRP . . . . $3995.00 and up

CARACAL ENHANCED F

Action: Semiautomatic
Grips: Polymer
Barrel: 4 in.
Sights: Three-dot
Weight: 28 oz.
Caliber: 9mm
Capacity: 10, 18 rounds

NEW Products: **Handguns**

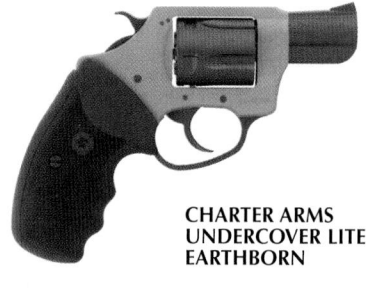

CHARTER ARMS UNDERCOVER LITE EARTHBORN

CHARTER ARMS UNDERCOVER LITE ROSEBUD

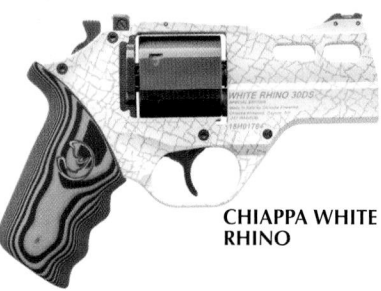

CHIAPPA WHITE RHINO

CHRISTENSEN ARMS 1911 A5, A5-TR, A4

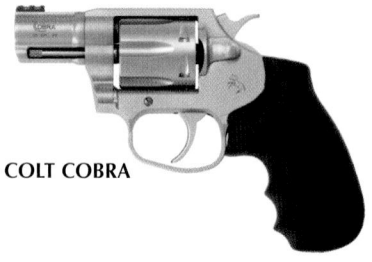

COLT COBRA

COLT COMBAT UNIT RAIL GUN

CHARTER ARMS UNDERCOVER LITE EARTHBORN

Action: Revolver
Grips: Rubber, compact
Barrel: 2 in.
Sights: Fixed
Weight: 12 oz.
Caliber: .38 Spl.
Capacity: 5 rounds
Features: Matte black barrel; Cerakote earth-tone frame and cylinder
MSRP **$422.00**

CHARTER ARMS UNDERCOVER LITE ROSEBUD

Action: Revolver
Grips: Rubber, compact

Barrel: 2 in.
Sights: Fixed
Weight: 12 oz.
Caliber: .38 Spl.
Capacity: 5 rounds
Features: Smooth, anodized rose gold frame; hi-polish stainless steel barrel and cylinder; tough aircraft-grade aluminum and steel; standard hammer for SA/DA
MSRP **$446.00**

CHIAPPA WHITE RHINO

Action: Revolver
Grips: Laminate
Barrel: 3 in.
Sights: Red fiber optic front, green fiber optic rear
Weight: 21 oz.
Caliber: 9mm, .5357 Mag.
Capacity: 6 rounds

Features: Newest addition to Rhino line; Cerakoted and laser-etched frame designed to look like rhinoceros hide; black matte cylinder; gray and black laminate grips
MSRP **$1465.00**

CHRISTENSEN ARMS 1911 A5, A5-TR, A4

Action: Semiautomatic
Grips: G10
Barrel: 4 in., 5 in.
Sights: Raised night sights, suppressor sights
Weight: 32 oz. (A4), 35.2 oz. (A5), 38.4 oz. (A5-TR)
Caliber: 9mm
Capacity: 9 rounds
Features: Aluminum frame machined from 7075 billet aluminum; A5s have raised night sights, A4 has 4-in. threaded barrel and suppressor height sights as well as tactical rail and flared magwell
MSRP **$1995.00**

COLT COBRA

Action: Revolver
Grips: Rubber
Barrel: 2 in.
Sights: Fiber optic front
Weight: 25 oz.
Caliber: .38 Spl.
Capacity: 6 rounds
Features: DA revolver with all-steel contruction; small frame and barrel ideal for concealed carry; Hogue Overmolded grip has been moved rearward to manage recoil
MSRP **$699.00**

COLT COMBAT UNIT RAIL GUN

Action: Semiautomatic
Grips: G10
Barrel: 5 in.
Sights: Novak night sight front, Novak Low Mount Carry rear
Weight: 40 oz.
Caliber: 9mm, .45 ACP
Capacity: 8 rounds (.45 ACP), 9 rounds (9mm)
Features: Upgraded duty-ready 1911 with 1913 Picatinny rail; checkered and scalloped gray G10 grips; designed with Special Forces trainers Daryl Holland and Ken Hackathorn
MSRP **$1499.00**

COLT DEFENDER SERIES

COLT DELTA ELITE RAIL GUN

COLT M45 A1

COLT STAINLESS STEEL COLT COMPETITION PISTOL

COONAN ARMS MOT-10

CZ-USA CZ 75 SP-01 PHANTOM

COONAN ARMS MOT-45

Sights: Novak red fiber optic front, Novak adjustable rear
Weight: 36 oz.
Caliber: 9mm, .38 Super, .45 ACP
Capacity: 8 rounds (.45 ACP), 9 rounds (9mm, .38 Super)
Features: National Match barrel; all stainless construction and finish; undercut trigger guard; blue and scalloped G10 grips
MSRP . . . . **$999.00–$1099.00**

COONAN ARMS MOT-10
Action: Semiautomatic
Grips: Black walnut, black aluminum
Barrel: 5 in.
Sights: Fixed, adjustable; white-dot or tritium night sight
Weight: 40 oz.
Caliber: 10mm
Capacity: 8 rounds
Features: Full-length dust cover; linkless chromed barrel; stainless slide and frame; pivoting trigger; external extractor; extended slide catch and thumb lock
MSRP . . . . **$1399.00–$1683.00**

COONAN ARMS MOT-45
Action: Semiautomatic
Grips: Walnut
Barrel: 5 in.
Sights: Novak-style
Weight: N/A
Caliber: .45 ACP
Capacity: 7 rounds
Features: Linkless barrel; external extractor; pivoting trigger; stainless steel finish
MSRP . . . . **$1399.00–$1633.00**

CZ-USA CZ 75 SP-01 PHANTOM
Action: Semiautomatic
Grips: Polymer, interchangeable
Barrel: 4.6 in.
Sights: Three-dot
Weight: 29.4 oz.
Caliber: 9mm
Capacity: 18 rounds
Features: Essentially a polymer-framed SP-01 Tactical; same fiber-reinforced polymer formula used in P-09 and P-07 frames; interchangeable backstraps and mag compatibility with the standard 75 platform; ambidextrous decocking lever; firing pin block safety
MSRP $636.00

COLT DEFENDER SERIES
Action: Semiautomatic
Grips: G10
Barrel: 3 in.
Sights: Novak white-dot front, Novak Low Mount Carry rear
Weight: 24 oz.
Caliber: 9mm, .45 ACP
Capacity: 7 rounds (.45 ACP), 8 rounds (9mm)
Features: Aluminum alloy frame; forged steel slide; partially checkered black cherry G10 grips; matte blue finish; .45 ACP also available in brushed stainless finish
Matte blue: **$949.00**
Brushed stainless .45 ACP: . . . **$899.00**

COLT DELTA ELITE RAIL GUN
Action: Semiautomatic
Grips: Composite
Barrel: 5 in.
Sights: Novak white-dot front, Novak Low Mount Carry rear
Weight: 38 oz.
Caliber: 10mm
Capacity: 8 rounds

Features: Integrated accessory rail; stainless steel construction with brushed stainless finish; Series 80 firing pin safety
MSRP $1299.00

COLT M45 A1
Action: Semiautomatic
Grips: G10
Barrel: 5 in.
Sights: Novak night sights
Weight: 40 oz.
Caliber: .45 ACP
Capacity: 7 rounds
Features: Selected by the US Marine Corps as their Close Quarters Battle Pistol; available in Decobond Brown finish; checkered Desert Tan G10 grip panels; underside Picatinny rail
MSRP $1699.00

COLT STAINLESS STEEL COLT COMPETITION PISTOL
Action: Semiautomatic
Grips: G10
Barrel: 5 in.

NEW Products: **Handguns**

CZ-USA CZ 805 BREN S1 PISTOL

CZ-USA CZ P-07 SUPPRESSOR-READY

CZ-USA CZ P-10 C

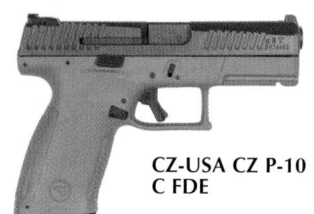

CZ-USA CZ P-10 C FDE

CZ-USA CZ P-10 C SUPPRESSOR-READY

CZ-USA CZ SCORPION EVO 3 S1 PISTOL W/FLASH CAN

CZ-USA CZ 805 BREN S1 PISTOL

Action: Semiautomatic
Grips: Polymer
Barrel: 11 in.
Sights: Post front, flip-up rear
Weight: 107.2 oz.
Caliber: .223/5.56 NATO, .300 BLK
Capacity: 10, 30 rounds
Features: Imported from the Czech Republic as a pistol; popular SBR candidate for conversion to an NFA firearm; adapter kit allows easy installation of aftermarket arm braces or other devices meant to help stabilize large format pistols; STANAG magazine from the AR15/M16; top and bottom Picatinny rails; two-port muzzle brake
MSRP . . . . **$1799.00–$1899.00**

CZ-USA CZ P-07 SUPPRESSOR-READY

Action: Semiautomatic
Grips: Polymer
Barrel: 4.36 in.
Sights: High tritium thee-dot
Weight: 28.7 oz.
Caliber: 9mm
Capacity: 17 rounds
Features: Updated version of the CZ 75 P-07 Duty; interchangeable backstraps; nitrided finish on the slide; frame has been dehorned; interchangeable safety and decocker; muzzle is threaded ½×28 to accept suppressors
MSRP **$537.00**

CZ-USA CZ P-10 C

Action: Semiautomatic
Grips: Polymer
Barrel: 4.02 in.

Sights: Metal three-dot
Weight: 26 oz.
Caliber: 9mm, .40 S&W
Capacity: 10, 12 rounds
Features: Striker-fired pistol; ergonomically designed with a mild palm swell, deep beavertail, and three interchangeable backstraps; trigger engineered to break at 4–4.5 lb.with a short reset; fiber-reinforced polymer frame with nitride finish; barrel is cold-hammer-forged
9mm: **$499.00**
.40 S&W: **$516.00**

CZ-USA CZ P-10 C FDE

Action: Semiautomatic
Grips: Polymer
Barrel: 4.02 in.
Sights: Metal night sights
Weight: 26 oz.
Caliber: .40 S&W
Capacity: 12 rounds
Features: Striker-fired pistol; all-over flat dark earth finish
MSRP **$541.00**

CZ-USA CZ P-10 C SUPPRESSOR-READY

Action: Semiautomatic
Grips: Polymer
Barrel: 4.61 in.
Sights: High metal night sights
Weight: 26 oz.
Caliber: 9mm
Capacity: 17 rounds
Features: Striker-fired pistol; similar to other P-10s but with extended/threaded barrel with ½×28 threads; high night sights; extended magazine capacity
MSRP **$519.00**

CZ-USA CZ SCORPION EVO 3 S1 PISTOL W/FLASH CAN

Action: Semiautomatic
Grips: Polymer
Barrel: 7.72 in.
Sights: Post front, low-profile fully adjustable aperture rear
Weight: 91.2 oz.
Caliber: 9mm
Capacity: 10, 20 rounds
Features: Extended forend; M-LOK attachment points; boosted the sight radius; dual threads of 18×1 and ½×28 provide options
MSRP **$949.00**

CZ-USA CZ
SHADOW 2

DAN WESSON
FURY SUPPRESSOR
READY

DAN WESSON
SPECIALIST
COMMANDER

DAN WESSON A2,
A2 COMMANDER

DAN WESSON
POINTMAN CARRY
(PM-C)

DAN WESSON
VALOR BLUE

CZ-USA CZ SHADOW 2

Action: Semiautomatic
Grips: Aluminum
Barrel: 4.89 in.
Sights: Fiber optic front, HAJO rear
Weight: 46.5 oz.
Caliber: 9mm
Capacity: 17 rounds
Features: The original Shadow improved upon; higher beavertail; undercut trigger guard; contoured slide; increased weight at the dust cover/rail helps keep muzzle down; steel frame with nitride finish; blue aluminum grips are checkered to match front and backstraps; reversible mag release is both extended and three-position adjustable
MSRP **$1299.00**

DAN WESSON A2, A2 COMMANDER

Action: Semiautomatic
Grips: Wood
Barrel: 5 in., 4.25 in.
Sights: Fixed front and rear
Weight: 40 oz.
Caliber: .45 ACP
Capacity: 8 rounds

Features: Dan Wesson's vision of a 3rd Generation military 1911; lowered and flared ejection port; modern combat sights; match barrel; tactical beavertail; extended thumb safety; frame and slide are forged steel finished in a bead-blasted matte blue; Commander-length option available
MSRP **$1363.00**

DAN WESSON FURY SUPPRESSOR READY

Action: Semiautomatic
Grips: G10
Barrel: 5.5 in.
Sights: High front night sight, RMR red dot rear
Weight: 48.5 oz.
Caliber: 9mm, 10mm
Capacity: 18 rounds (9mm), 14 rounds (10mm)
Features: Double-stack, suppressor-ready; single-action equipped; super-short reset Elite Series trigger; skeletonized hammer; underside accessory rail; ambidextrous thumb safety
MSRP **$4899.00**

DAN WESSON POINTMAN CARRY (PM-C)

Action: Semiautomatic
Grips: Wood
Barrel: 4.25 in.
Sights: Fiber optic front, ledge rear
Weight: 36.7 oz.
Caliber: 9mm
Capacity: 8 rounds
Features: Single-stack; carry configuration; Commander-length slide; Officer frame; full stainless; front and back straps are stippled
MSRP **$1597.00**

DAN WESSON SPECIALIST COMMANDER

Action: Semiautomatic
Grips: G10
Barrel: 4.25 in.
Sights: Fixed night sight front, tactical night sight rear
Weight: 40 oz.
Caliber: 9mm, .45 ACP
Capacity: 10 rounds (9mm), 8 rounds (.45 ACP)
Features: Designed with features specified by law enforcement agencies; forged stainless slide; Clark-style serrated rib; green lamp/target white ring front sight and single amber tritium rear dot; integral 1913 Picatinny; 25 lines-per-inch front strap checkering; undercut trigger guard; recessed slide stop to enable the installation of laser grips; ambidextrous thumb safety; extended magazine release; detachable two-piece magwell; available in matte stainless or Duty Black finish
Stainless: **$1701.00**
Duty black: **$2012.00**

DAN WESSON VALOR BLUE

Action: Semiautomatic
Grips: G10
Barrel: 5 in.
Sights: Fixed night sight front, tactical night sight rear
Weight: 40.1 oz.
Caliber: 9mm, .45 ACP
Capacity: 10 rounds (9mm), 8 rounds (.45 ACP)
Features: Blued steel version of previously offered Valor model; flats are polished; rounds are bead-blasted; G10 grips are red and black
MSRP **$1766.00**

NEW Products: **Handguns**

DAVIDE PEDERSOLI HOWDAH

FN AMERICA FNS 9 COMPACT FDE

HECKLER & KOCH SP5K

HUDSON MFG. H9

IVER JOHNSON 1911 CHROME, CHROME AND PEARL

IVER JOHNSON THRASHER

NEW PRODUCTS

DAVIDE PEDERSOLI HOWDAH

Action: Break-open
Grips: Wood
Barrel: 10 in.
Sights: Dovetail front dot, flip-up leaf rear
Weight: 63 oz.
Caliber: .45 LC/.410-bore
Capacity: 2 rounds/shells
Features: Reproduction of famous Auto & Burglar pistol produced by Ithaca Company in the 1920s; rifled barrels; special cartridge chamber enabling interchangeable use of either the .45 LC or .410 shotshells; manual extractors; automatic safety; case-hardened action; oil-finished walnut stock
MSRP **$1395.00**

FN AMERICA FNS 9 COMPACT FDE

Action: Semiautomatic
Grips: Polymer
Barrel: 3.6 in.

Sights: Fixed three-dot
Weight: 23.4 oz.
Caliber: 9mm
Capacity: 10, 12, 17 rounds
Features: Striker-fired compact autoloader; Flat Dark Earth allover finish; polymer frame with replaceable steel slide rails; stainless steel slide with front and rear cocking serrations; 1913 accessory rail; serrated trigger guard; two interchangeable backstraps with lanyard eyelets
MSRP **$599.00**

HECKLER & KOCH SP5K

Action: Semiautomatic
Grips: N/A
Barrel: 4.53 in.
Sights: None
Weight: 67 oz.
Caliber: 9mm
Capacity: 10, 30 rounds
Features: Civilian "sporting pistol" (SP) version of HK's MP5 full-auto; rolling delayed blowback system; overall length 14 in.; elasticized

"bungee" sling; Picatinny rail scope mount
MSRP **$2699.00**

HUDSON MFG. H9

Action: Semiautomatic
Grips: G10 VZ
Barrel: 4.28 in.
Sights: Trijicon HD front, drift-adjustable notch rear
Weight: 34 oz.
Caliber: 9mm
Capacity: 15 rounds
Features: Striker-fired pistol; all-steel construction; configurable safeties; interchangeable grips; ambidextrous operation; accessory rail; front and rear slide serrations; G10 Hogue lower backstrap
MSRP **$1147.00**

IVER JOHNSON 1911 CHROME, CHROME AND PEARL

Action: Semiautomatic
Grips: Black Dymondwood, black synthetic pearl
Barrel: 5 in.
Sights: GI fixed dovetail front and rear
Weight: 38 oz.
Caliber: .45 ACP
Capacity: 8 round
Features: Polished chrome finish; black Dymondwood grips or synthetic black pearl grips; slightly beveled magazine well; slide sports rear gripping serrations
Dymondwood: **$630.00**
Pearl: **$645.00**

IVER JOHNSON THRASHER

Action: Semiautomatic
Grips: Wood
Barrel: 3.125 in.
Sights: Dovetail front, low-profile Novak-style rear
Weight: 30.4 oz.
Caliber: 9mm, .45 ACP
Capacity: 7, 8 rounds
Features: Officer-length slide, longer grip; tops and sides of slide are polished chrome; frame is satin finished; thin-line serrations at front and rear of slide; beveled magazine well; lowered and flared ejection port; available with Trijicon night sights
Standard sights: **$730.00**
Trijicon sights: **$835.00**

78 • Shooter's Bible 109th Edition

www.skyhorsepublishing.com

KAHR ARMS CT380, CW380 GOLD CERAKOTE LIMITED EDITION

KAHR ARMS GEN 2 PREMIUM TP45, TP9

KIMBER CAMP GUARD 10

KIMBER CUSTOM TLE/RL II (EM)

KIMBER K6S FIRST EDITION

KIMBER ECLIPSE TARGET

KIMBER MICRO 9 BEL AIR

KIMBER CUSTOM TLE/RL II (EM)

Action: Semiautomatic
Grips: G10
Barrel: 5 in.
Sights: Fixed low-profile
Weight: 39 oz.
Caliber: .45 ACP
Capacity: 7 rounds
Features: Tactical Law Enforcement family; matte black-finished steel frame and slide; match-grade stainless bushing; 1913 Picatinny rail
MSRP $1164.00

KIMBER ECLIPSE TARGET

Action: Semiautomatic
Grips: G10
Barrel: 5 in.
Sights: Kimber adjustable bar/dot tritium night sights
Weight: 38 oz.
Caliber: .45 ACP
Capacity: 8 rounds
Features: Front strap checkering at 30 lines per inch; aluminum trigger; match-grade bushing; brush-polished flats on a charcoal gray finish
MSRP $1393.00

KIMBER K6S FIRST EDITION

Action: Revolver
Grips: Pau Ferro wood
Barrel: 2 in.
Sights: Black serrated
Weight: 23 oz.
Caliber: .357 Mag.
Capacity: 6 rounds
Features: Hi-polished stainless frame; snub-nosed DAO revolver; concealed hammer; limited range serial numbers
MSRP $2039.00

KIMBER MICRO 9 BEL AIR

Action: Semiautomatic
Grips: Ivory micarta
Barrel: 3.15 in.
Sights: Three-dot white
Weight: 15.6 oz.
Caliber: 9mm
Capacity: 6 rounds
Features: Kimber's unique Bel Air Blue finish on the aluminum frame; mirror-polished stainless slide; stainless steel barrel; bull-length guide rod; single-action
MSRP $864.00

KAHR ARMS CT380, CW380 GOLD CERAKOTE LIMITED EDITION

Action: Semiautomatic
Grips: Textured polymer
Barrel: 3 in. (CT380), 2.58 in. (CW380)
Sights: Pinned polymer front, drift-adjustable white bar rear
Weight: 12.8 oz. (CT380), 11.5 oz (CW380)
Caliber: .380 ACP
Capacity: 7 rounds (CT380), 6 rounds (CW380)
Features: Concealed carry .380 ACP models in a limited edition featuring gold Cerakote coated stainless steel slide
MSRP $419.00

KAHR ARMS GEN 2 PREMIUM TP45, TP9

Action: Semiautomatic
Grips: Textured polymer
Barrel: 4 in., 5 in., 6 in.
Sights: TruGlo green TFX sights
Weight: 20.1 oz.–26.4 oz.
Caliber: 9mm, .45 ACP
Capacity: 8 rounds (9mm), 7 rounds (.45 ACP)
Features: Tightened tolerances; serrations machined in front of slide (5- and 6-in. barrels); shortened trigger stroke; accessory rail; 5- and 6-in. barrels have integral compensators and are optics ready
MSRP $697.00

KIMBER CAMP GUARD 10

Action: Semiautomatic
Grips: Rosewood
Barrel: 5 in.
Sights: Tactical wedge
Weight: 38 oz.
Caliber: 10mm
Capacity: 8 rounds
Features: Designed in partnership with Rocky Mountain Elk Foundation for use in the backcountry; stainless steel frame, slide, and barrel; front strap checkering at 30 lines per inch
MSRP $1228.00

NEW Products: **Handguns**

KIMBER MICRO 9
CDP (LG)

KIMBER MICRO 9
DESERT TAN (LG)

KIMBER MICRO 9 SAPPHIRE

KIMBER MICRO AMETHYST

KIMBER MICRO DESERT NIGHT

KIMBER ROSE GOLD ULTRA II

KIMBER PRO COVERT

Grips: G10
Barrel: 2.75 in.
Sights: Three-dot tritium night sights
Weight: 13.4 oz.
Caliber: .380 ACP
Capacity: 6 rounds
Features: Concealed carry gun in vibrant purple PVD finish; engraved scroll accents; aluminum frame; stainless steel barrel; bull-length guide rod; single-action
MSRP **$1014.00**

KIMBER MICRO DESERT NIGHT

Action: Semiautomatic
Grips: G10
Barrel: 2.75 in.
Sights: Three-dot white
Weight: 13.4 oz.
Caliber: .380 ACP
Capacity: 6 rounds
Features: Concealed carry gun; Desert Tan KimPro finish; black-finished slide; stainless steel slide and barrel; bull-length guide rod
MSRP **$626.00**

KIMBER PRO COVERT

Action: Semiautomatic
Grips: Urban Camouflage Crimson Trace laser grips
Barrel: 4 in.
Sights: Tactical wedge tritium night sights
Weight: 28 oz.
Caliber: .45 ACP
Capacity: 7 rounds
Features: Carry Melt treatment; 30 lines per inch checkering on front strap; Charcoal Gray and KimPro II finish; aluminum frame
MSRP **$1427.00**

KIMBER ROSE GOLD ULTRA II

Action: Semiautomatic
Grips: G10
Barrel: 3 in.
Sights: Tactical wedge
Weight: 25 oz.
Caliber: .45 ACP
Capacity: 7 rounds
Features: Personal defense gun; finished in Rose Gold PVD coating; solid aluminum trigger; aluminum round-heel frame; ambidextrous thumb safety; ball-milled front strap
MSRP **$1652.00**

KIMBER MICRO 9 CDP (LG)

Action: Semiautomatic
Grips: Rosewood Crimson Trace laser grips
Barrel: 3.15 in.
Sights: Three-dot tritium night sights
Weight: 15.6 oz.
Caliber: 9mm
Capacity: 6 rounds
Features: Custom Defense Package of features, including: ambidextrous thumb safety; front strap checkering at 30 lines per inch; Carry Melt treatment rounds; smooth edges for snag-free carry
MSRP **$1142.00**

KIMBER MICRO 9 DESERT TAN (LG)

Action: Semiautomatic
Grips: Crimson Trace laser grips
Barrel: 3.15 in.
Sights: White-dot
Weight: 15.6 oz.
Caliber: 9mm
Capacity: 6 rounds

Features: Super slim, super lightweight concealed carry pistol; stainless barrel; bull-length guide rod; aluminum frame; single-action
MSRP **$790.00**

KIMBER MICRO 9 SAPPHIRE

Action: Semiautomatic
Grips: G10
Barrel: 3.15 in.
Sights: Three-dot tritium night sights
Weight: 15.6 oz.
Caliber: 9mm
Capacity: 6 rounds
Features: Brilliant blue PVD finish on slide; coordinated blue and black G10 grips; slide has scroll engraving enhancements; aluminum frame; stainless steel barrel; bull-length guide rod; single-action
MSRP **$1061.00**

KIMBER MICRO AMETHYST

Action: Semiautomatic

NEW Products: Handguns

KIMBER SUPER JÄGARE

KIMBER WARRIOR SOC (TFS)

KIMBER ULTRA+ CDP

LLAMA MAX-1

MAGNUM RESEARCH DESERT EAGLE BLACK TIGER STRIPE

MAGNUM RESEARCH DESERT EAGLE WHITE MATTE DISTRESSED

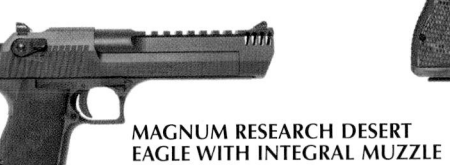

MAGNUM RESEARCH DESERT EAGLE WITH INTEGRAL MUZZLE BRAKE

LLAMA MAX-1

Action: Semiautomatic
Grips: G10
Barrel: 5.5 in.
Sights: Mil-Spec
Weight: 36.96 oz.
Caliber: .38 Super
Capacity: 9 rounds
Features: 1911-type pistol; steel frame; blue or hard-chrome finishes
Blued: **$565.00**
Hard chrome: **$660.00**

MAGNUM RESEARCH DESERT EAGLE BLACK TIGER STRIPE

Action: Semiautomatic
Grips: Hard rubber
Barrel: 6 in.
Sights: Fixed combat style
Weight: 70 oz.–71 oz.
Caliber: .50 AE, .44 Mag.
Capacity: 8 rounds
Features: Desert Eagle in unique black tiger stripe finish
MSRP **$1922.00**

MAGNUM RESEARCH DESERT EAGLE WHITE MATTE DISTRESSED

Action: Semiautomatic
Grips: Hard rubber
Barrel: 6 in.
Sights: Fixed combat style
Weight: 70 oz.–71 oz.
Caliber: .50 AE, .44 Mag.
Capacity: 8 rounds
Features: Desert Eagle in unique White Matte Distressed finish
MSRP **$1922.00**

MAGNUM RESEARCH DESERT EAGLE WITH INTEGRAL MUZZLE BRAKE

Action: Semiautomatic
Grips: Hard rubber
Barrel: 6 in.
Sights: Fixed combat style
Weight: 71 oz.–74 oz.
Caliber: .50 AE, .44 Mag., .357 Mag.
Capacity: 8 rounds
Features: Three-port integral muzzle brakel; Weaver-style accessory rail; black or stainless finish
MSRP . . . . **Black: $1742.00**
Stainless: **$2060.00**

KIMBER SUPER JÄGARE

Action: Semiautomatic
Grips: Micarta
Barrel: 6 in.
Sights: DeltaPoint Pro optic
Weight: 42 oz.
Caliber: 10mm
Capacity: 8 rounds
Features: Designed for close-range big-game and varmint hunting; stainless steel frame and slide; frame has round heel and high cut trigger guard; finished in KimPro and Charcoal Gray; slide has carbon coating and Super Carry pattern on its flat top; Carry Melt treatment; match-grade bushing; solid aluminum trigger
MSRP **$2688.00**

KIMBER ULTRA+ CDP

Action: Semiautomatic
Grips: Rosewood
Barrel: 3 in.
Sights: Fixed low-profile tritium night sights
Weight: 27 oz.
Caliber: .45 ACP
Capacity: 7 rounds

Features: Custom Defense Package; 30 lines-per-inch checkering on front strap and under trigger guard; match-grade bushingless bull barrel; Carry Melt treatment
MSRP **$1173.00**

KIMBER WARRIOR SOC (TFS)

Action: Semiautomatic
Grips: Kimber G10 tactical
Barrel: 5.5 in.
Sights: Suppressor-height tritium night sights, Desert Tan Crimson Trace Rail Master laser
Weight: 40 oz.
Caliber: .45 ACP
Capacity: 7 rounds
Features: Service Melt treatment; ambidextrous thumb safety; standard military length guide rod; 1913 Picatinny rail; stainless match-grade bushing; match-grade aluminum trigger; barrel threaded for suppressor use; frame and slide finished in KimPro II & trade Dark Earth/Dark Green
MSRP **$1605.00**

MAGNUM RESEARCH MAGNUM LITE ULTRA BARREL WITH THREADED MUZZLE

NIGHTHAWK CUSTOM COMPLETE CUSTOM STIPPLE

NIGHTHAWK CUSTOM BORDER SPECIAL

NIGHTHAWK CUSTOM NHC CLASSIC

NIGHTHAWK CUSTOM CARRY +

NIGHTHAWK CUSTOM THE BULL

MAGNUM RESEARCH MAGNUM LITE ULTRA BARREL WITH THREADED MUZZLE

Action: Semiautomatic
Grips: None
Barrel: 10 in.
Sights: None
Weight: 43.2 oz.
Caliber: .22 LR
Capacity: 10 rounds
Features: Rimfire pistol based on Magnum Lite rifles; optic rail; threaded muzzle; thread protector; Barracuda Nutmeg stock
MSRP . . . . **N/A**

NIGHTHAWK CUSTOM BORDER SPECIAL

Action: Semiautomatic
Grips: Cocobolo
Barrel: 4.25 in.
Sights: Gold bead post front, Heinie Black Slant-Pro rear
Weight: 34.1 oz.
Caliber: .45 ACP
Capacity: 8 rounds

Features: Built on concealed carry cut; Commander-sized frame and slide; frame and mainspring housing dehorned for carry; match-grade barrel; ultra high-cut front strap; fluted barrel hood; Elite Midnight Cerakote finish; optional black, two-tone, or all-stainless upgrades available
MSRP . . . . **$3650.00 and up**

NIGHTHAWK CUSTOM COMPLETE CUSTOM STIPPLE

Action: Semiautomatic
Grips: Cocobolo
Barrel: 5 in.
Sights: Nighthawk tritium front, Heinie 2-Dot Slant-Pro tritium rear
Weight: 38.8 oz.
Caliber: .45 ACP
Capacity: 8 rounds
Features: Aggressively stippled on top and rear of slide, front strap, mainspring housing, hammer top, slide stop, mag release, recoil spring plug, thumb safety, and grip safety pad; heavy French border; round butt mainspring housing; beveled frame;

front and rear cocking serrations; bead-blasted stainless finish with polished flats
MSRP . . . . **$4295.00 and up**

NIGHTHAWK CUSTOM NHC CLASSIC

Action: Semiautomatic
Grips: Cocobolo
Barrel: 5 in.
Sights: Gold bead front post, Heinie Black Ledge rear
Weight: 36.9 oz.
Caliber: .45 ACP
Capacity: 8 rounds
Features: Custom offering; slide top has been flattened and accented with arrow pattern and French border; curved slide stop; round butt mainspring housing; frame dehorning; ultra high-cut front strap; stainless finish with script engraving at slide rear; threaded barrel upgrade available
MSRP . . . . **$3895.00 and up**

NIGHTHAWK CUSTOM CARRY +

Action: Semiautomatic
Grips: G10
Barrel: 3.8 in.
Sights: Nighthawk tritium front, Heinie Slant-Pro Straight Eight tritium rear
Weight: 28.5 oz.
Caliber: 9mm
Capacity: 8 rounds
Features: Ultra lightweight Officer frame of forged aluminum; fluted barrel hood; thinned front strap and mainspring housing with Gregory treatment; Everlast Recoil System; bow tie plug; thin G10 ETC Frag grips with thumb scoop; dehorned frame
MSRP . . . . **$3795.00 and up**

NIGHTHAWK CUSTOM THE BULL

Action: Semiautomatic
Grips: Carbon fiber
Barrel: 5 in.
Sights: Nighthawk tritium front, Heinie Ledge Straight Eight tritium rear
Weight: 38.8 oz.
Caliber: .45 ACP
Capacity: 8 rounds
Features: Government frame with French border; bow tie plug; match-grade bull barrel; frame dehorning; Elite Smoke Cerakote finish
MSRP . . . . **$3795.00 and up**

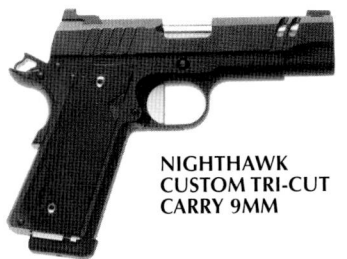

NIGHTHAWK CUSTOM TRI-CUT CARRY 9MM

NIGHTHAWK CUSTOM TURNBULL VIP 1

NIGHTHAWK CUSTOM/KORTH MONGOOSE .357

NIGHTHAWK CUSTOM/ KORTH SKY HAWK 9MM

NIGHTHAWK CUSTOM/ KORTH SUPER SPORT .357

REMINGTON 1911 R1 10MM HUNTER LONG SLIDE

NIGHTHAWK CUSTOM TRI-CUT CARRY 9MM

Action: Semiautomatic
Grips: Aluminum
Barrel: 4.25 in.
Sights: Nighthawk tritium front, Heinie Ledge Straight Eight tritium rear
Weight: 34.7 oz.
Caliber: 9mm
Capacity: 10 rounds
Features: Commander-sized frame with custom tri-cut angled design; pneumatic stippling; slide ports; flat-faced Nighthawk Custom trigger; angled mag release
MSRP . . . . **$4495.00 and up**

NIGHTHAWK CUSTOM TURNBULL VIP 1, TURNBULL VIP 2

Action: Semiautomatic
Grips: Mastodon ivory
Barrel: 5 in.

Sights: Gold bead front, Heinie solid black Slant-Pro rear
Weight: 37.4 oz.
Caliber: .45 ACP
Capacity: 8 rounds
Features: Very Impressive Pistol is a collaboration between Nighthawk Custom and Doug Turnbull; mastodon ivory grips; custom display case; all-over charcoal blue finish; VIP II has case-hardened frame
Turnbull VIP I: **$7495.00**
Turnbull VIP II: **$7195.00**

NIGHTHAWK CUSTOM/ KORTH MONGOOSE .357

Action: Revolver
Grips: Hogue
Barrel: 3 in., 4 in., 5.25 in., 6 in.
Sights: Gold bead front post, adjustable rear
Weight: 37.6 oz.
Caliber: .357 Mag.
Capacity: 6 rounds

Features: Partnership with German manufacturer Korth; revolver has an AISI 4140 aluminum frame; skeletonized high-speed hammer; easy access cylinder release; optional 9mm cylinder designed for use without moon clips
MSRP **$3499.00**

NIGHTHAWK CUSTOM/ KORTH SKY HAWK 9MM

Action: Revolver
Grips: Hogue
Barrel: 2 in., 3 in.
Sights: Ramp front, adjustable rear
Weight: 19.7 oz.
Caliber: 9mm
Capacity: 6 rounds
Features: Partnership with German manufacturer Korth; 7075 aluminum frame; designed for use without moon clips
MSRP **$1699.00**

NIGHTHAWK CUSTOM/ KORTH SUPER SPORT .357

Action: Revolver
Grips: Hogue
Barrel: 6 in.
Sights: Fully adjustable front and rear
Weight: 58.24 oz.
Caliber: .357 Mag.
Capacity: 6 rounds
Features: Partnership with German manufacturer Korth; Lothar Walther cold-forged polygonal barrel; five-way adjustable DA mechanism; Roller Trigger; Picatinny rails; optional 9mm/.38 Spl. conversion cylinder available
MSRP **$4799.00**

REMINGTON 1911 R1 10MM HUNTER LONG SLIDE

Action: Semiautomatic
Grips: VZ Operator II G10
Barrel: 6 in.
Sights: Fully adjustable match sights
Weight: 41 oz.
Caliber: 10mm
Capacity: 8 rounds
Features: Long-slide SA 1911-type handgun; extended beavertail safety; wide rear and front slide cocking serrations
MSRP **$1310.00**

REMINGTON 1911 R1 LIMITED

REMINGTON 1911 R1 TACTICAL

REMINGTON RP9

RUGER AMERICAN COMPACT

RUGER GP100

RUGER LCP II

RUGER MARK IV 22/45 LITE

REMINGTON 1911 R1 LIMITED

Action: Semiautomatic
Grips: VZ Operator G10
Barrel: 5 in.
Sights: Fiber optic front, fully adjustable rear
Weight: 38 oz.–48 oz.
Caliber: 9mm, .40 S&W, .45 ACP
Capacity: 8, 9, 16, 18, 19 rounds
Features: Competition-ready SA 1911-style pistol; ambidextrous extended thumb safety; match-grade barrel; oversized magwell standard; single and double stack versions available; semi-custom Tomasie model
MSRP . . . . **$1250.00–$1650.00**

REMINGTON 1911 R1 TACTICAL

Action: Semiautomatic
Grips: VZ Operator G10
Barrel: 5 in.
Sights: Trijicon night sights
Weight: 38 oz.–41 oz.
Caliber: .45 ACP
Capacity: 8, 15 rounds
Features: Single-stack 1911-type pistol; ambidextrous extended thumb

safety; match-grade trigger and barrel; checkered mainspring housing; railed frame; double-stack frame in threaded and unthreaded options available
MSRP . . . . **$1250.00–$1299.00**

REMINGTON RP9

Action: Semiautomatic
Grips: Polymer
Barrel: 4.5 in.
Sights: Drift-adjustable front and rear
Weight: 26.4 oz.
Caliber: 9mm
Capacity: 18 rounds
Features: Service Melt treatment; ambidextrous thumb safety; standard military-length guide rod; 1913 Picatinny rail; stainless match-grade bushing; match-grade aluminum trigger; barrel threaded for suppressor use; frame and slide finished in KimPro II & trade Dark Earth/Dark Green
MSRP **$489.00**

RUGER AMERICAN COMPACT

Action: Semiautomatic
Grips: Glass-filled nylon

Barrel: 3.55 in.–3.75 in.
Sights: Novak LoMount Carry three-dot
Weight: 28.7 oz.–29.2 oz.
Caliber: 9mm, .45 ACP
Capacity: 17, 10 rounds
Features: Compact version of Ruger's polymer-framed American striker-fired pistol; recoil-reducing barrel cam; low-mass slide; ambidextrous slide and mag releases; grip modules; 1913 Picatinny rail; two Teflon-coated magazines
MSRP **$579.00**

RUGER GP100

Action: Revolver
Grips: Hogue monogrip
Barrel: 3 in.
Sights: Fiber optic front, adjustable rear
Weight: 36 oz.
Caliber: .44 Spl.
Capacity: 5 rounds
Features: Ruger's long-standing GP100 mid-size DA/SA revolver now available as a five-shot .44 Special
MSRP **$829.00**

RUGER LCP II

Action: Semiautomatic
Grips: Glass-filled nylon
Barrel: 2.75 in.
Sights: Fixed front and rear
Weight: 10.6 oz.
Caliber: .380 ACP
Capacity: 6 rounds
Features: Updated from the original; improved sights and trigger; last round hold open; larger grip surface
MSRP **$349.00**

RUGER MARK IV 22/45 LITE

Action: Semiautomatic
Grips: Polymer
Barrel: 4.4 in.
Sights: Fixed front, adjustable rear
Weight: 25 oz.
Caliber: .22 LR
Capacity: 10 rounds
Features: .22 LR pistol based on the 1911 .45 frame; newest version has ventilated aluminum receiver; threaded barrel; polymer frame; one-button takedown; available in black or bronze anodized finishes
MSRP **$559.00**

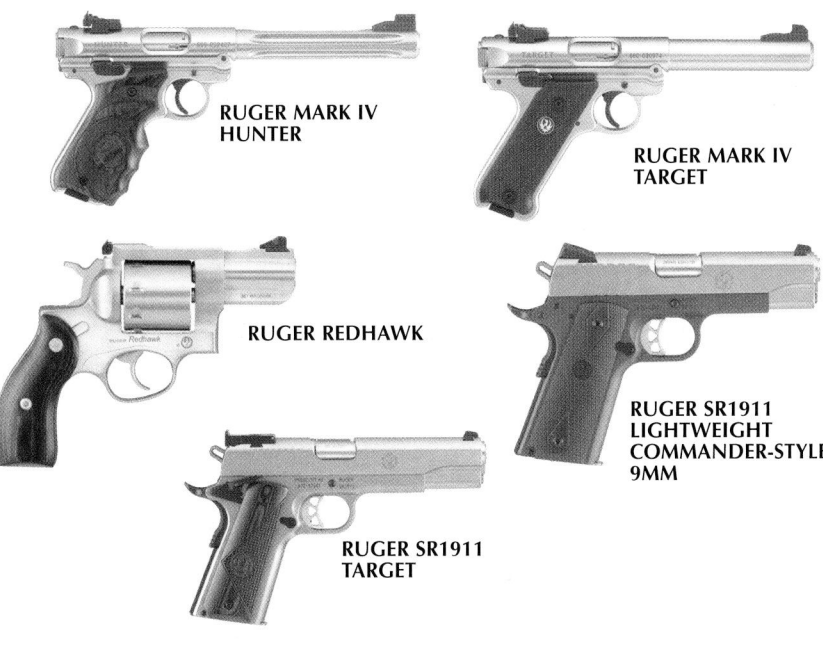

RUGER MARK IV HUNTER

RUGER MARK IV TARGET

RUGER REDHAWK

RUGER SR1911 LIGHTWEIGHT COMMANDER-STYLE 9MM

RUGER SR1911 TARGET

SIG SAUER P220 LEGION

SIG SAUER P226 RX FULL-SIZE

Grips: G10
Barrel: 4.25 in.
Sights: Novak drift-adjustable three-dot
Weight: 29.3 oz.
Caliber: .45 ACP, 9mm
Capacity: 9 rounds
Features: Classic 1911 70-series style in Commander-length slide
MSRP **$979.00**

RUGER SR1911 TARGET

Action: Semiautomatic
Grips: G10
Barrel: 5 in.
Sights: Bomar-style adjustable
Weight: 39 oz.–40.4 oz.
Caliber: .45 ACP, 10mm
Capacity: 8 rounds
Features: Classic 1911 70-series style; oversized ejection port; skeletonized aluminum trigger
MSRP **$1019.00**

SIG SAUER P220 LEGION

Action: Semiautomatic
Grips: G10
Barrel: 3.5 in., 4.4 in., 5 in.
Sights: XRAY3 day/night sights
Weight: 30.4 oz.
Caliber: .45 ACP, 10mm
Capacity: 8 rounds
Features: P220 frame joins the Legion lineup in .45 and 10mm; match, full-size, and carry frames available; SAO 5-lb. trigger available; Legion Gray PVD slide and frame; three magazines
MSRP **$1413.00**

SIG SAUER P226 RX FULL-SIZE

Action: Semiautomatic
Grips: Polymer, E2
Barrel: 4.4 in.
Sights: ROMEO1 reflex sight, co-witness backup suppressor sights
Weight: 34 oz.
Caliber: 9mm
Capacity: 15 rounds
Features: Nitron stainless steel slide; alloy frame; one-piece ergonomic grips; accessory rail; polymer grips in SAO or E2 grips in DA/SA
DA/SA: **$1440.00**
SAO: **$1549.00**

RUGER MARK IV HUNTER

Action: Semiautomatic
Grips: Laminate, synthetic
Barrel: 6.88 in.
Sights: Fiber optic front, adjustable rear
Weight: 44 oz.–44.2 oz.
Caliber: .22 LR
Capacity: 10 rounds
Features: Latest version of Ruger's esteemed .22-caliber SA handguns; one-piece CNC-machined frame; ambidextrous manual safety; drop-free mag design; magazine disconnect; one-button takedown; two magazines; hunter model has fluted bull barrel, option of checkered or target laminated grips
MSRP . . . . **$769.00–$799.00**

RUGER MARK IV TARGET

Action: Semiautomatic
Grips: Laminate, synthetic
Barrel: 5.5 in.
Sights: Fixed front, adjustable rear
Weight: 35.6 oz.–42.8 oz.
Caliber: .22 LR
Capacity: 10 rounds
Features: Latest version of Ruger's esteemed .22-caliber SA handguns; one-piece CNC-machined frame; ambidextrous manual safety; drop-free mag design; magazine disconnect; one-button takedown; two magazines; blued or stainless steel options
Blued: . . . . **$529.00–$569.00**
Stainless steel: **$689.00**

RUGER REDHAWK

Action: Revolver
Grips: Hardwood
Barrel: 2.75 in.
Sights: Ramp front, adjustable rear
Weight: 44 oz.
Caliber: .357 Mag.
Capacity: 8 rounds
Features: Ruger's large-frame DA/SA Redhawk offered as an eight-shot, short-barreled .357 Magnum
MSRP **$1079.00**

RUGER SR1911 LIGHTWEIGHT COMMANDER-STYLE 9MM

Action: Semiautomatic

SIG SAUER P320 RX COMPACT

SIG SAUER P320 RX FULL-SIZE

SIG SAUER P320 TACOPS CARRY

SIG SAUER P320 TACOPS FULL

SIG SAUER P320 X-CARRY

SIG SAUER P320 X-FIVE

SIG SAUER P320 X V-TAC

SIG SAUER P320 RX COMPACT

Action: Semiautomatic
Grips: Polymer
Barrel: 3.8 in.
Sights: ROME01 reflex sight and choice of contrast or SIGLITE night sights
Weight: 26.1 oz.
Caliber: 9mm
Capacity: 15 rounds
Features: Modular striker-fired pistol; interchangeable grip modules and trigger group; nitron stainless steel slide; serialized stainless steel frame
MSRP $1040.00

SIG SAUER P320 RX FULL-SIZE

Action: Semiautomatic
Grips: Polymer
Barrel: 4.7 in.
Sights: ROME01 reflex sight and choice of contrast or SIGLITE night sights
Weight: 30.3 oz.

Caliber: 9mm
Capacity: 17 rounds
Features: Modular striker-fired pistol; interchangeable grip modules and trigger group; nitron stainless steel slide; serialized stainless steel frame
MSRP $1040.00

SIG SAUER P320 TACOPS CARRY

Action: Semiautomatic
Grips: Polymer
Barrel: 3.9 in.
Sights: SIGLITE suppressor sights
Weight: 25.8 oz.
Caliber: 9mm
Capacity: 21 rounds
Features: Striker-fired pistol; compact-length slide; threaded barrel; full-length grip; accessory rail; four extended 21-round magazines
MSRP $830.00

SIG SAUER P320 TACOPS FULL

Action: Semiautomatic

Grips: Polymer
Barrel: 4.7 in.
Sights: Truglo front, SIGLITE rear
Weight: 29.5 oz.
Caliber: 9mm
Capacity: 21 rounds
Features: Modular striker-fired pistol; interchangeable trigger group; nitron stainless steel slide; serialized stainless steel frame; full-length grip; four 21-round magazines
MSRP $762.00

SIG SAUER P320 X-CARRY

Action: Semiautomatic
Grips: Polymer
Barrel: 3.9 in.
Sights: XRAY3 day/night sights
Weight: 26.5 oz.
Caliber: 9mm
Capacity: 17 rounds
Features: Striker-fired pistol; X-Carry Grip Module; X-RAY3 Day/Night Sights; accessory rail; reduced slide catch lever; lightning slide cuts; four-sided beveled magwell; three magazines; ROMEO1 optic compatible
MSRP $862.00

SIG SAUER P320 X-FIVE

Action: Semiautomatic
Grips: Polymer
Barrel: 4.7 in.
Sights: Dawson fiber optic front, Dawson adjustable rear
Weight: 35 oz.
Caliber: 9mm, .40 S&W
Capacity: 21 rounds (9mm), 18 rounds (.40 S&W)
Features: Striker-fired pistol; X Grip Module; bull barrel; extended slide catch lever; four-sided beveled magwell; ROMEO1 optic compatible; four magazines
MSRP $1005.00

SIG SAUER P320 X V-TAC

Action: Semiautomatic
Grips: Polymer
Barrel: 5 in.
Sights: VTAC day/night sights
Weight: 29.5 oz.
Caliber: 9mm
Capacity: 17 rounds
Features: Striker-fired pistol designed by Kyle Lamb; X-Carry Grip Module; stainless slide in Flat Dark Earth finish; lightning slide cuts; ROMEO1 optic compatible; three magazines
MSRP $918.00

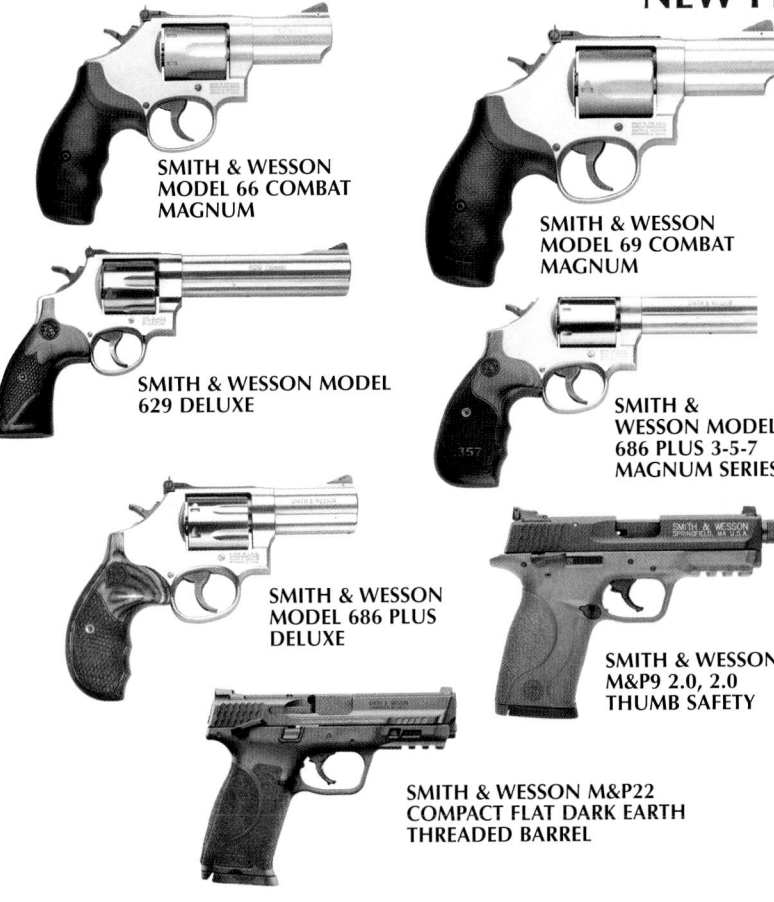

SMITH & WESSON
MODEL 66 COMBAT
MAGNUM

SMITH & WESSON
MODEL 69 COMBAT
MAGNUM

SMITH & WESSON MODEL
629 DELUXE

SMITH &
WESSON MODEL
686 PLUS 3-5-7
MAGNUM SERIES

SMITH & WESSON
MODEL 686 PLUS
DELUXE

SMITH & WESSON
M&P9 2.0, 2.0
THUMB SAFETY

SMITH & WESSON M&P22
COMPACT FLAT DARK EARTH
THREADED BARREL

Caliber: .357 Mag.
Capacity: 7 rounds
Features: Collector's Model 686
L-frame; custom black/silver wood grips
bearing "357"; cylinder is unfluted
MSRP **$899.00**

SMITH & WESSON
MODEL 686 PLUS DELUXE

Action: Revolver
Grips: Wood
Barrel: 3 in., 6 in.
Sights: Red ramp front, white outline
adjustable rear
Weight: 36.8 oz. (3-in. barrel), 44.9
oz. (6-in. barrel)
Caliber: .357 Mag.
Capacity: 7 rounds
Features: S&W's classic 686 L-frame
revolver; all stainless steel
construction; textured wood grips
MSRP **$899.00**

SMITH & WESSON M&P9
2.0, 2.0 THUMB SAFETY

Action: Semiautomatic
Grips: Polymer
Barrel: 4.25 in.
Sights: White three-dot
Weight: 24.7 oz.
Caliber: 9mm
Capacity: 17 rounds
Features: Updated M&P striker-fire
pistol; extended stainless steel chassis;
high grip-to-bore axis; crisper trigger;
lighter pull; tactile and audible reset;
four interchangeable palm swell; two
magazines included; matte black or
Flat Dark Earth finish; with or without
manual thumb safety
MSRP **$599.00**

SMITH & WESSON M&P22
COMPACT FLAT DARK
EARTH THREADED
BARREL

Action: Semiautomatic
Grips: Polymer
Barrel: 3.5 in.
Sights: White three-dot
Weight: 15.3 oz.
Caliber: .22 LR
Capacity: 10 rounds
Features: Reduced scale version of full-
size M&P pistols; ambidextrous manual
safety; reversible magazine release;
Picatinny accessory rail; magazine
safety; threaded barrel; two magazines
MSRP **$429.00**

SMITH & WESSON
MODEL 66 COMBAT
MAGNUM

Action: Revolver
Grips: Synthetic
Barrel: 2.75 in.
Sights: Red ramp front, white outline
adjustable rear
Weight: 33.5 oz.
Caliber: .357 Mag., .38 Spl. +P
Capacity: 6 rounds
Features: K-frame revolver; full top
strap and barrel serration; ball detent
lockup; two-piece barrel; full-length
extractor rod
MSRP **$849.00**

SMITH & WESSON
MODEL 69 COMBAT
MAGNUM

Action: Revolver
Grips: Synthetic
Barrel: 2.75 in.
Sights: Red ramp front, white outline
adjustable rear
Weight: 34.4 oz.
Caliber: .44 Mag.
Capacity: 5 rounds
Features: S&W's first L-frame in .44
Mag.; full top strap and barrel

serration; ball detent lockup; two-
piece barrel; full-length extractor rod
MSRP **$849.00**

SMITH & WESSON
MODEL 629 DELUXE

Action: Revolver
Grips: Wood
Barrel: 3 in., 6.5 in.
Sights: Red ramp front, white outline
adjustable rear
Weight: 39.6 oz. (3-in. barrel), 51.2
oz. (6.5-in. barrel)
Caliber: .44 Mag., .44 S&W Spl.
Capacity: 6 rounds
Features: N-frame revolver; all-stainless
construction; textured wood grips
3-in. barrel: **$999.00**
6.5-in. barrel: **$1029.00**

SMITH & WESSON
MODEL 686 PLUS 3-5-7
MAGNUM SERIES

Action: Revolver
Grips: Wood
Barrel: 3 in., 5 in., 7 in.
Sights: Red ramp front, white outline
adjustable rear
Weight: 37.4 oz. (3-in. barrel), 37.4
oz. (5-in. barrel)

SMITH & WESSON M&P40 2.0, 2.0 THUMB SAFETY

SMITH & WESSON M&P45 2.0, 2.0 THUMB SAFETY

SMITH & WESSON M&P45 SHIELD WITH NIGHT SIGHTS, NO THUMB SAFETY

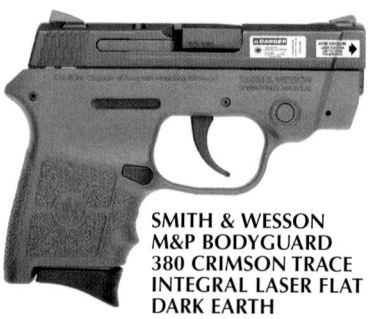

SMITH & WESSON M&P BODYGUARD 380 CRIMSON TRACE INTEGRAL LASER FLAT DARK EARTH

SMITH & WESSON M&P BODYGUARD 380 ENGRAVED

SMITH & WESSON PERFORMANCE CENTER MODEL 586 L-COMP

SMITH & WESSON M&P40 2.0, 2.0 THUMB SAFETY

Action: Semiautomatic
Grips: Polymer
Barrel: 5 in.
Sights: White three-dot
Weight: 27.4 oz.
Caliber: .40 S&W
Capacity: 15 rounds
Features: Updated M&P striker-fire pistol; extended stainless steel chassis; high grip-to-bore axis; crisper trigger; lighter pull; tactile and audible reset; four interchangeable palm swell; two magazines; matte black or Flat Dark Earth finish; with or without manual thumb safety
MSRP **$599.00**

SMITH & WESSON M&P45 2.0, 2.0 THUMB SAFETY

Action: Semiautomatic
Grips: Polymer
Barrel: 4.6 in.

Sights: White three-dot
Weight: 27 oz.
Caliber: .45 ACP
Capacity: 10 rounds
Features: Updated M&P striker-fire pistol; extended stainless steel chassis; high grip-to-bore axis; crisper trigger; lighter pull; tactile and audible reset; four interchangeable palm swell; two magazines; matte black or Flat Dark Earth finish; with or without manual thumb safety
MSRP **$599.00**

SMITH & WESSON M&P45 SHIELD WITH NIGHT SIGHTS, NO THUMB SAFETY

Action: Semiautomatic
Grips: Polymer
Barrel: 3.3 in.
Sights: Tritium night sights
Weight: 20.5 oz.
Caliber: .45 ACP

Capacity: 6, 7 rounds
Features: Thinner, lighter weight version of the standard M&P; striker-fired; without a thumb safety; three magazines, two with extended capacity for a full grip
MSRP **$579.00**

SMITH & WESSON M&P BODYGUARD 380 CRIMSON TRACE INTEGRAL LASER FLAT DARK EARTH

Action: Semiautomatic
Grips: Polymer
Barrel: 2.75 in.
Sights: Drift adjustable front and rear, Crimson Trace laser
Weight: 12.5 oz.
Caliber: .380 ACP
Capacity: 6 rounds
Features: Ultra-compact carry gun; black matte slide; polymer frame in Flat Dark Earth
MSRP **$449.00**

SMITH & WESSON M&P BODYGUARD 380 ENGRAVED

Action: Semiautomatic
Grips: Polymer
Barrel: 2.75 in.
Sights: Drift adjustable front and rear
Weight: 12 oz.
Caliber: .380 ACP
Capacity: 6 rounds
Features: Ultra-compact carry gun; DAO; custom machine-engraved matte silver slide
MSRP **$385.00**

SMITH & WESSON PERFORMANCE CENTER MODEL 586 L-COMP

Action: Revolver
Grips: Rosewood
Barrel: 3 in.
Sights: Tritium night front, adjustable black board rear
Weight: 37.5 oz.
Caliber: .357 Mag.
Capacity: 7 rounds
Features: L-frame with ported full-lug barrel; Performance Center-tuned action; first mid-size seven-shot revolver offered in blue by S&W; carbon steel construction
MSRP **$1208.00**

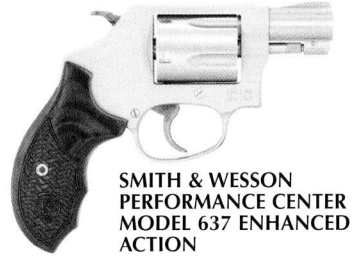

SMITH & WESSON PERFORMANCE CENTER MODEL 637 ENHANCED ACTION

SMITH & WESSON PERFORMANCE CENTER MODEL 642 ENHANCED ACTION

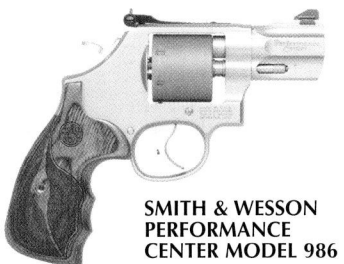

SMITH & WESSON PERFORMANCE CENTER MODEL 986

SPRINGFIELD ARMORY 1911 EMP 4-INCH LIGHTWEIGHT CHAMPION CONCEALED CARRY CONTOUR

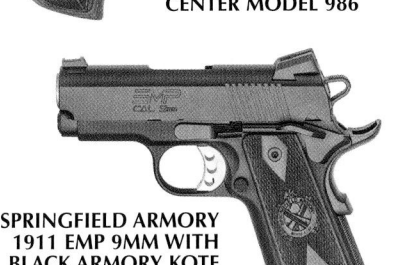

SPRINGFIELD ARMORY 1911 EMP 9MM WITH BLACK ARMORY KOTE

SPRINGFIELD ARMORY 1911 TRP OPERATOR TACTICAL GRAY

SMITH & WESSON PERFORMANCE CENTER MODEL 637 ENHANCED ACTION

Action: Revolver
Grips: Wood
Barrel: 1.875 in.
Sights: Integral ramp front
Weight: 15 oz.
Caliber: .38 Spl. +P
Capacity: 5 rounds
Features: J-frame with Performance Center-tuned action; stainless steel barrel; aluminum alloy frame; matte silver finish; custom wood grips
MSRP **$525.00**

SMITH & WESSON PERFORMANCE CENTER MODEL 642 ENHANCED ACTION

Action: Revolver
Grips: Wood
Barrel: 1.875 in.
Sights: Integral ramp front
Weight: 15 oz.
Caliber: .38 Spl. +P
Capacity: 5 rounds
Features: J-frame with Performance Center-tuned action; stainless steel barrel; aluminum alloy frame; matte

silver finish; custom wood grips; DAO has concealed hammer
MSRP **$525.00**

SMITH & WESSON PERFORMANCE CENTER MODEL 986

Action: Revolver
Grips: Wood
Barrel: 2.5 in.
Sights: Red ramp front, adjustable rear
Weight: 31.7 oz.
Caliber: 9mm
Capacity: 7 rounds
Features: L-frame 9mm with unfluted cylinder; custom barrel with recessed crown; trigger overstop travel; bossed mainspring; Performance Center-tuned action; stainless steel barrel and frame; titanium cylinder; moon clips
MSRP **$1129.00**

SPRINGFIELD ARMORY 1911 EMP 4-INCH LIGHTWEIGHT CHAMPION CONCEALED CARRY CONTOUR

Action: Semiautomatic
Grips: G10

Barrel: 4 in.
Sights: Fiber optic front, low-profile combat rear
Weight: 30.5 oz.
Caliber: 9mm
Capacity: 9 rounds
Features: Combines a longer barrel with a frame trimmed for concealment; bevel-cut mainspring housing; contouring to prevent snagging and printing; stainless steel match-grade bull barrel; fully supported feed ramp; satin finished slide; black hard coat anodized aluminum alloy frame; Posi-Lok texturing on rear and front straps; premium carry case; three magazines
MSRP **$1220.00**

SPRINGFIELD ARMORY 1911 EMP 9MM WITH BLACK ARMORY KOTE

Action: Semiautomatic
Grips: Cocobolo
Barrel: 3 in.
Sights: Fiber optic front, low-profile combat rear
Weight: 27 oz.
Caliber: 9mm
Capacity: 9 rounds
Features: 1911 EMP with new black Armory Kote allover finish; grips are 1.12-in. Thinline Cross Cannon Double Diamond Cocobolo; three slam pad magazines
MSRP **$1104.00**

SPRINGFIELD ARMORY 1911 TRP OPERATOR TACTICAL GRAY

Action: Semiautomatic
Grips: G10
Barrel: 5 in.
Sights: Fully adjustable three-dot tritium
Weight: 45 oz.
Caliber: .45 ACP
Capacity: 7 rounds
Features: Precision fit slide and frame; match-grade stainless steel barrel and bushing; checkered mainspring housing; 20 lines per inch front strap checkering; Gray Armory Kote finish; two slam pad magazines
MSRP **$1730.00**

NEW Products: **Handguns**

SPRINGFIELD ARMORY XD MOD.2 4-INCH SERVICE MODEL .45 ACP, 5-INCH TACTICAL MODEL .45 ACP

SPRINGFIELD ARMORY XD(M) 4.5-INCH OSP FULL SIZE 9MM

STI INTERNATIONAL DVC CARRY

STI INTERNATIONAL DVC TACTICAL

STI INTERNATIONAL HEXTAC 3.0 DS

STI INTERNATIONAL H.O.S.T.

SPRINGFIELD ARMORY XD MOD.2 4-INCH SERVICE MODEL .45 ACP, 5-INCH TACTICAL MODEL .45 ACP

Action: Semiautomatic
Grips: GripZone
Barrel: 4 in., 5 in.
Sights: Fiber optic front, low-profile combat rear
Weight: 30 oz.–31 oz.
Caliber: .45 ACP
Capacity: 13 rounds
Features: New shorter 4-in. Service Model and longer 5-in. barreled Tactical Model; double-stack polymer frame; striker-fired with striker status and loaded chamber indicator; grip safety; Ultra Safety Assurance (USA) Action Safety Trigger standard; two magazines
Service: **$593.00**
Tactical: **$637.00**

SPRINGFIELD ARMORY XD(M) 4.5-INCH OSP FULL SIZE 9MM

Action: Semiautomatic
Grips: None

Barrel: 4.5 in.
Sights: Vortex Venom red-dot, fiber optic front, low-profile combat rear
Weight: 29 oz.
Caliber: 9mm
Capacity: 19 rounds
Features: Milled slide; three adapter plates support popular optics such as, but not limited to: #1 Plate – Vortex Venom, Burris FastFire 2, Burris FastFire 3; #2 Plate – Leupold DeltaPoint, Leupold DeltaPoint Pro, JPoint Sights; #3 Plate – Trijicon RMR; pistol ships with Vortex Venom red installed; full-size pistol with three replaceable backstrap panels; match-grade barrel
MSRP **$979.00**

STI INTERNATIONAL DVC CARRY

Action: Semiautomatic
Grips: 2011 DVC
Barrel: 3.9 in.
Sights: Low-profile tritium front, fixed ledge rear
Weight: N/A
Caliber: 9mm
Capacity: 15 rounds
Features: Light and narrow aluminum 2011 frame for concealability; grip

stippled by Extreme Shooters; slide lightening cuts; second magazine has two-round extension; black DLC-coated frame and slide; copper-colored barrel
MSRP **$2999.00**

STI INTERNATIONAL DVC TACTICAL

Action: Semiautomatic
Grips: 2011 DVC
Barrel: 5 in.
Sights: Tritium fixed ledge
Weight: N/A
Caliber: 9mm, .45 ACP
Capacity: 20 rounds (9mm), 14 rounds (.45 ACP)
Features: Threaded bull barrel; STI Tactical Magwell; tool-less guide rod; full-length tactical dust cover; Picatinny rail
MSRP **$2999.00**

STI INTERNATIONAL HEXTAC 3.0 DS

Action: Semiautomatic
Grips: 1911 VZ, 2011 molded
Barrel: 3.7 in.
Sights: Fiber optic front, fixed ledge rear
Weight: N/A
Caliber: 9mm
Capacity: 7 rounds (1911), 15 rounds (2011)
Features: Trimmed down, aluminum-framed version of Hex Tactical 3.0. 2011 version has VIP grip length; 1911 is Officer's length frame; black Cerakote finish
1911: **$2199.00**
2011: **$2599.00**

STI INTERNATIONAL H.O.S.T.

Action: Semiautomatic
Grips: 1911 VZ, 2011 stippled TreeBark
Barrel: 4.15 in., 5 in.
Sights: Suppressor-height tritium
Weight: N/A
Caliber: 9mm, .45 ACP, 10mm
Capacity: Varies by caliber
Features: Suppressor- and optics-ready pistol; choice of 1911 or 2011 frames; cover plate and adaptor plates for Leupold Delta Point, Vortex Viper, and Trijicon RMR sights; 9mm and .45 ACP have choice of 4.15- or 5-in. barrel, 10mm available only with 5-in.
1911: **$2599.00**
2011: **$3199.00**

TAURUS 180 CURVE

TAURUS SPECTRUM

TNW FIREARMS AERO SURVIVAL PISTOL

TROY DEFENSE XM177P

UBERTI USA SHORT STROKE SASS PRO NICKEL

WALTHER CREED

TAURUS 180 CURVE

Action: Semiautomatic
Grips: None
Barrel: 2.7 in.
Sights: None, built-in Veridian LED light/laser combo
Weight: 13 oz.
Caliber: .380 ACP
Capacity: 6 rounds
Features: World's first curved firearm; designed to fit bod contours and prevent printing through clothes; first handgun to have the Veridian instant-on light and laser built into frame; ultralightweight; Taurus Security System; magazine disconnect; loaded chamber indicator
MSRP. **$404.20**

TAURUS SPECTRUM

Action: Semiautomatic
Grips: Soft-touch overmold
Barrel: 2.8 in.
Sights: Integral low-profile front and rear

Weight: 10 oz.
Caliber: .380 ACP
Capacity: 6 rounds
Features: Ultralight striker-fired micro-pistol; soft-touch overmold grip; rear slide inserts; slide serrations; soft-edged frame; reversible magazine release; highly customizable color options
Standard:. **$289.00**
House color combinations:. **$305.00**

TNW FIREARMS AERO SURVIVAL PISTOL

Action: Semiautomatic
Grips: Synthetic
Barrel: 8 in.
Sights: Flip-up front and rear
Weight: 88 oz.
Caliber: 9mm, 10mm, .40 S&W, .45 ACP, .357 SIG
Capacity: Varies with magazine
Features: Reduced SBR version of TNW's Aero Survival Rifle; compact,

lightweight, and easily disassembled; takes Glock-style magazines; hard black anodized or variegated finishes in pink/black or green/black; some restricted state versions available
MSRP. **$799.00**

TROY DEFENSE XM177P

Action: Semiautomatic
Grips: Synthetic
Barrel: 10 in.
Sights: A1 front, A1 drum rear
Weight: 77 oz.
Caliber: 5.56 NATO
Capacity: N/A
Features: Ultra-short PDW barrel length in traditional MSR platform; carbine handguard with single heat shield; Troy pistol buffer tube; forged upper with tear-drop forward assist; overall length is 25 in.
MSRP. **$999.00**

UBERTI USA SHORT STROKE SASS PRO NICKEL

Action: Revolver
Grips: Simulated ivory
Barrel: 4.75 in., 5.5 in.
Sights: Blade front
Weight: 36.8 oz.
Caliber: .357 Mag., .44 Mag.
Capacity: 6 rounds
Features: Single-action short-stroke SASS competition revolver; low, wide, and checkered hammer; custom-grade mainspring; wider rear channel Easy View sights; shortened hammer travel; mirror nickel finish
MSRP. **$869.00**

WALTHER CREED

Action: Semiautomatic
Grips: None
Barrel: 4 in.
Sights: Three-dot, low profile
Weight: 26.6 oz.
Caliber: 9mm
Capacity: 16, 10 rounds
Features: Economically priced, polymer frame; DAO pre-set trigger pistol; firing pin and drop safeties; ambidextrous magazine release button; 1913 Picatinny rail
MSRP. **$399.00**

NEW Products: **Black Powder**

CONNECTICUT VALLEY ARMS (CVA) ACCURA MR BLACKOUT

CONNECTICUT VALLEY ARMS (CVA) ACCURA PR (PLAINS RIFLE)

COOPER FIREARMS MODEL 22-ML EXCALIBUR

DAVIDE PEDERSOLI 1854 LORENZ INFANTRY RIFLE TYPE II

DAVIDE PEDERSOLI 1860 VOLUNTEER

CONNECTICUT VALLEY ARMS (CVA) ACCURA MR BLACKOUT

Action: Break-action
Stock: Synthetic
Barrel: 25 in.
Sights: None
Weight: 6 lb. 5.6 oz.
Caliber: .50
Features: Previous limited-run model available only through Muzzle-Loaders.com; 416 stainless steel, fluted, nitride-treated Bergara barrel; break-action is easy opening; disassembly can be performed by removing a single screw; Quick Release breech plug; reversible hammer spur; adjustable trigger; Palm Saver ramrod; Quake Claw sling; CrushZone recoil pad; ambidextrous soft-touch stock; drilled and tapped for scope mounts; DuraSight DEAD-ON one-piece mount
MSRP $450.00

CONNECTICUT VALLEY ARMS (CVA) ACCURA PR (PLAINS RIFLE)

Action: Break-action
Stock: Synthetic
Barrel: 28.in.
Sights: None
Weight: 6 lb. 14.4 oz.
Caliber: .50

Features: 416 stainless steel, fluted, nitride-treated Bergara barrel; break-action is easy opening; disassembly can be performed by removing a single screw; Quick Release breech plug; reversible hammer spur; adjustable trigger; Palm Saver ramrod; Quake Claw sling; CrushZone recoil pad; ambidextrous soft-touch stock; drilled and tapped for scope mounts; DuraSight DEAD-ON one-piece mount; black or Realtree Max-1 camo; several available combo packages include a choice of Nikon or Leupold scopes and soft case
MSRP . . . . $508.00–$818.00

COOPER FIREARMS MODEL 22-ML EXCALIBUR

Action: Inline
Stock: Composite
Barrel: 26 in.
Sights: None
Weight: N/A
Caliber: .50
Features: Modern inline with sealed breech design; Timney trigger; match-grade fluted barrel; removable plug; 200-grain charge capable; wood model supplied with Easton Aluminum Ram Rod and stock styles include Classic, Custom Classic, Western Classic and Schnabel
Composite: $1775.00
Wood: . . . . .POR

DAVIDE PEDERSOLI 1854 LORENZ INFANTRY RIFLE TYPE II

Action: Percussion
Stock: Walnut
Barrel: 37 in.
Sights: N/A
Weight: 9 lb.
Caliber: .54
Features: Conceived by the Austrian Lieutenant Joseph Lorenz; rifle's official production started in 1854, replacing the Augustin rifle among the Austrian troops; used in Italy during the second Independence War, as well as in the Balkans; then largely exported to America, equipping both the Union and the Confederate armies, becoming one of the most used rifles during the years of the American Civil War
MSRP $1875.00

DAVIDE PEDERSOLI 1860 VOLUNTEER

Action: Percussion
Stock: Walnut
Barrel: 33 in.
Sights: Tunnel front, Creedmoor rear
Weight: 8 lb. 13 oz.
Caliber: .451
Features: The British N.R.A., for the first time, organized a national event held at Wimbledon in 1860; taking inspiration from this historical sporting event is Pedersoli's Volunteer Rifle featuring a .451-caliber barrel, broach rifled with an optimal twist for target shooting at 100-150 meters; tunnel front sight and high precision Creedmoor sight, oil-finished, hand-checkered stock
MSRP $1815.00

DAVIDE PEDERSOLI CONTINENTAL TARGET PISTOL

DAVIDE PEDERSOLI GIBBS SHORT RIFLE

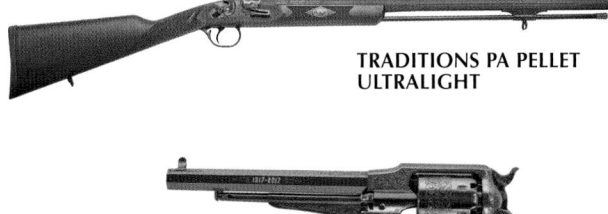

DAVIDE PEDERSOLI MUZZLELOADING ROLLING BLOCK WITH KONUS SCOPE

DAVIDE PEDERSOLI TRADITIONAL HAWKEN

TRADITIONS PA PELLET ULTRALIGHT

UBERTI USA 1858 BUFFALO BILL LIMITED EDITION

lightweight alloy; microcell buttpad; optional Konus scope has illuminated reticle

MSRP . . . . **N/A**

DAVIDE PEDERSOLI TRADITIONAL HAWKEN

Action: Percussion, flintlock
Stock: Walnut
Barrel: 28.375 in.
Sights: Front post, adjustable buckhorn rear
Weight: 8 lb. 9.6 oz.–9 lb. .64-oz.
Caliber: .50, .54
Features: Lighter version of Pedersoli's Rocky Mountain and Missouri River Hawken rifles; double-set triggers; brass patch box; brass furniture; percussion or flintlock configurations; left-hand versions available

MSRP . . . . **$685.00–$765.00**

TRADITIONS PA PELLET ULTRALIGHT

Action: Flintlock
Stock: Wood, synthetic
Barrel: 26 in.
Sights: Alloy fiber optic
Weight: N/A
Caliber: .50
Features: Differs from standard PA Pellet flintlock by changing to a lightweight premium grade chrome-moly steel; 1:28 twist and nitride-treated barrel; hardwood, black, or Mossy Oak Breakup stocks; left-hand version available in hardwood only

MSRP . . . . **$426.00–$506.00**

UBERTI USA 1858 BUFFALO BILL LIMITED EDITION

Action: Revolver
Stock: Simulated ivory
Barrel: 8 in.
Sights: Front post
Weight: 2 lb.11 oz.
Caliber: .44
Features: Six-round cap-and-ball .44 caliber 1858 revolver commemorating the 100th year anniversary of the passing of William Frederick "Buffalo Bill" Cody; hand-chased engraving over the entire metal surface; brass trigger; blue barrel; color case hammer; gold inscriptions on barrel; 500 produced

MSRP **$1049.00**

DAVIDE PEDERSOLI CONTINENTAL TARGET PISTOL

Action: Percussion, flintlock
Stock: Walnut
Barrel: 11 in.
Sights: Front, windage adjustable rear
Weight: 2 lb. 3 oz.
Caliber: .45, .44
Features: Reproduction of target pistol of Central European style; flintlock and percussion versions; limited weight and set trigger; octagonal barrel; chromed finished; front and rear sight adjustable for windage; .44-caliber is a smoothbore

MSRP . . . . **$530.00–$610.00**

DAVIDE PEDERSOLI GIBBS SHORT RIFLE

Action: Percussion
Stock: Walnut
Barrel: 32 in.
Sights: Tunnel front, Creedmoor rear
Weight: 10 lb. 9.6 oz.
Caliber: .451
Features: Modeled on the original Gibbs; equipped with a barrel made for target shooting at 100-150 meters

MSRP **$2090.00**

DAVIDE PEDERSOLI MUZZLELOADING ROLLING BLOCK WITH KONUS SCOPE

Action: Rolling block
Stock: Walnut
Barrel: 28 in.
Sights: Fiber optic front, integrated rear on Picatinny rail; Konus Pro M30 1.5-6x44mm scope
Weight: 8 lb. 9.6 oz.
Caliber: .50
Features: Fast-twist rifling designed for conical and sabot bullets; frame is

NEW Products: Optics
SCOPES

BURRIS MTAC PRYM1 CAMO

BUSHNELL ELITE TACTICAL DMR III

BURRIS RT-6

BUSHNELL ELITE TACTICAL LRTSI

BUSHNELL ELITE TACTICAL SMRS

CROSMAN/CENTERPOINT 4–12X42MM WITH INTEGRATED LASER

CROSMAN/CENTERPOINT 1–4X24MM

BURRIS MTAC PRYM1 CAMO
Weight: 14.5 oz.
Length: 11.3 in.
Power: 1–4x24mm
Obj. Diameter: 24mm
Exit Pupil: 24–32mm
Eye Relief: 3.5–4 in.
Field of View: 32–100 ft @ 100 yds
Features: Compact scope for 3-gun, CQB, or big-game stalking use; Blackout or Sandstorm camo finishes; ballistic QC or AR reticle; 30mm tube; available as part of tactical kit
MSRP . . . . $479.00–$719.00

BURRIS RT-6
Weight: 17.4 oz.
Length: 10.3 in.
Power: 1–6x24mm
Obj. Diameter: 24mm
Exit Pupil: 11.5 mm–5.2mm
Eye Relief: 3.3–4 in.
Field of View: 18.5–106 in.
Features: Intended for 3-gun competition; illuminated reticle; integrated adjustable throw lever; eleven brightness levels; tube is 30mm; ballistic AR mil reticle with trajectory compensation to 600 yards
MSRP . . . . $419.00–$659.00

BUSHNELL ELITE TACTICAL DMR III
Weight: 34 oz.
Length: 13.2 in.
Power: 3.5–21x50mm
Obj. Diameter: 50mm
Exit Pupil: 10.4–2.4mm
Eye Relief: 3.74 in.
Field of View: 25.3–5.1 ft @ 100 yds
Features: G3 illuminated reticle; illumination brightness control integrated on side parallax focus; ThrowHammer Lever allows instant magnification changes; elevation turret provides 10 mils of adjustment per revolution and is equipped with the RevLimiter Zero Stop; available with non-illuminated G3 or Horus H-59 reticles
MSRP . . . . $1932.00–$1998.67

BUSHNELL ELITE TACTICAL LRTSI
Weight: 27.3 oz.–28 oz.
Length: 13.1 in.–14.3 in.
Power: 3–12x44mm, 4.5–18x44mm
Obj. Diameter: 44mm
Exit Pupil: 12.1–2.5mm
Eye Relief: 3.74–3.94 in.
Field of View: 34.8–6 ft @ 100 yds
Features: Illuminated reticle; illumination brightness control integrated on the side parallax focus;

ThrowHammer Lever allows instant magnification changes; elevation turret provides 10 mils of adjustment per revolution and is equipped with the RevLimiter Zero Stop; black or Flat Dark Earth; non-illuminated G3 reticle available
MSRP . . . . $1616.00–$1866.77

BUSHNELL ELITE TACTICAL SMRS
Weight: 23 oz.
Length: 10.5 in.
Power: 1–6.5x24mm
Obj. Diameter: 24mm
Exit Pupil: 11.4–3.7mm
Eye Relief: 3.74 in.
Field of View: 107.1–16.8 ft @ 100 yds
Features: Designed with input form 3-gun competitors, military, and law enforcement experts; short midrange riflescope; folding ThrowDown PCL (power change lever) allows lightning-fast magnification changes; mil-based illuminated BTR-2 reticle provides precise holdovers, regardless of caliber; T-Lok locking target turrets
MSRP $1822.45

CROSMAN/CENTERPOINT 1–4X24MM
Weight: N/A
Length: N/A
Power: 1–4x24mm
Obj. Diameter: 24mm
Exit Pupil: N/A
Eye Relief: N/A
Field of View: N/A
Features: Fully multi-coated lenses; nitrogen purged; turret caps
MSRP $179.99

CROSMAN/CENTERPOINT 4–12X42MM WITH INTEGRATED LASER
Weight: N/A
Length: N/A
Power: 4–12x44mm
Obj. Diameter: 44mm
Exit Pupil: N/A
Eye Relief: N/A
Field of View: N/A
Features: TAG reticle; integral Class 3R laser fully windage and elevation adjustable; fogproof, shockproof, waterproof
MSRP $134.99

CROSMAN/CENTERPOINT 4–12X44MM

CROSMAN/CENTERPOINT 4–16X56MM

GPO GPOTAC

GPO PASSION 3X

GPO PASSION 8X

GPO PASSION 6X

GPO PASSION 4X

Weight: 22.6 oz.–23.3 oz.
Length: 13.4 in. (3–12x56mm), 15.5 in. (6–24x50mm)
Power: 3–12x56mm, 6–24x50mm
Obj. Diameter: 50mm, 56mm
Exit Pupil: 19–4.7mm
Eye Relief: 3.54 in.
Field of View: 37–14 ft @ 100 yds
Features: Entry-level scopes; 30mm tubes; generous eye relief; fast focus ocular lenses; proprietary lens coatings; metal turret caps; clicks are .36-in. in the 3-12x model, ¼-MOA in the 6-24x model; 3-12x models come with standard or illuminated G4 reticle; 6-24X has Plex reticle; parallax free at 100m for 3-12x; 6-24mm has side-adjustment parallax correction
MSRP . . . . **$666.66–$999.99**

CROSMAN/CENTERPOINT 4–12X44MM

Weight: N/A
Length: N/A
Power: 4–12x44mm
Obj. Diameter: 44mm
Exit Pupil: 11–3.7mm
Eye Relief: 4.4–3.6 in.
Field of View: N/A
Features: First focal plane; side parallax adjustment; nitrogen purged; turret caps; 25.4mm tube
MSRP **$224.99**

CROSMAN/CENTERPOINT 4–16X56MM

Weight: N/A
Length: N/A
Power: 4–16x56mm
Obj. Diameter: 56mm
Exit Pupil: 8.0–2.4mm
Eye Relief: 3.1–2.8 in.
Field of View: 12.8–3.6 yds
Features: Mil-dot reticle; side parallax adjustment; fully multi-coated lenses; second focal plane; 30mm tube
MSRP **$199.99**

GPO GPOTAC

Weight: N/A
Length: 10.6 in.–15.5 in.
Power: 1–6x24mm, 1–8x24mm, 5–30x56mm, 6–24x50mm
Obj. Diameter: 24mm, 50mm, 56mm

Exit Pupil: Varies with model/magnification
Eye Relief: 3.54–4.33 in.
Field of View: Varies with model/magnification
Features: GPOTAC line features four scopes; 1-6x and 6-24x feature 30mm tubes, while the 1-8x and 5-30x have 34mm tubes; 1-8x is a first focal plane optic, while the other three are are second focal planes; 1-6x and 1-8x have illuminated HS horseshoe reticle and are parallax free at 100m, while the two larger scopes feature Mil-Spec mil-dot reticles and side-adjustment parallax correction
MSRP . . . . **$1111.10–$2222.21**

GPO PASSION 3X

Weight: 13.8 oz.–18.2 oz.
Length: 11.7 in.–13.2in.
Power: 3–9x40mm, 3–9x42mm, 4–12x40mm, 4–12x42mm
Obj. Diameter: 40mm, 42 mm
Exit Pupil: Varies with model/magnification
Eye Relief: 3.54–3.74 in.
Field of View: Varies with model/magnification
Features: Entry-level scopes; 1-in. tubes; generous eye relief; fast focus ocular lenses; proprietary lens coatings; metal turret caps; clicks are ¼-MOA; with or without illuminated reticles
MSRP . . . . **$333.32–$722.21**

GPO PASSION 6X

Weight: 18.7 oz.–27.5 oz.
Length: 10.6 in. (1–6x24mm), 15 in. (both 2.5–15x models)
Power: 1–6x24mm, 2.5–15x50mm, 2.5–15x56mm
Obj. Diameter: 24mm, 50mm, 56mm
Exit Pupil: Varies with model/magnification
Eye Relief: 3.94 in. (1–6x24mm), 3.74 in. (both 2.5–15x models)
Field of View: Varies with model/magnification
Features: Entry-level scopes; 30mm tubes; generous eye relief; fast focus ocular lenses; proprietary lens coatings; metal turret caps; clicks are .36-in.; illuminated G4 reticles; 1-6x model is parallax free at 100 meters, while both 2.5-15x models features side-adjustment parallax correction
MSRP . . . . **$1277.77–$1444.44**

GPO PASSION 8X

Weight: 18 oz.
Length: 10.7 in.
Power: 1–8x24mm
Obj. Diameter: 24mm
Exit Pupil: 24–3mm
Eye Relief: 3.54 in.
Field of View: 108–14 ft @ 100 yds
Features: Premium optic; 30mm tube; generous eye relief; Super Zoom technology; proprietary lens coatings; PassionTrac quick-zero target turrets; G4 illuminated reticle; clicks are .36-in.; illuminated G4 reticles; optic is parallax free at 100 meters
MSRP **$1666.66**

NEW Products: Optics

LEICA ER 5

LEICA MAGNUS I

LEICA VISUS I LW

LEUPOLD MARK 8
3.5–25X56MM

LEUPOLD MARK 8 1.1–
8X24MM CQBSS M5B1
FRONT FOCAL PLANE

LEUPOLD VX-6HD

LEICA ER 5

Weight: 12 oz.–25.5 oz.
Length: 10.7 in.–17 in.
Power: 1–5x24mm, 1.5–8x32mm, 2–10x50mm, 3–15x56mm, 4–20x50mm, 5–25x56mm,
Obj. Diameter: 24mm, 32mm, 50mm, 56mm
Exit Pupil: Varies with model
Eye Relief: 3.8 in.
Field of View: Varies with model
Features: Compact, lightweight 1-5x24mm for close-quarters work and designed to allow both-eyes-open viewing; all-around 1.5-8x32mm ideal for lightweight rifles; 2-10x50mm has large objective and side parallax adjustment; 3-15x56mm is designed for low-light work, especially with small targets or at distance; extended range use is perfect for the 4-20x50mm with specialized ballistic reticles; 5-25x56mm is perfect for distance work at low light; all ER 5 reticles are second focal plane, all have 30mm tubes
MSRP . . . . **N/A**

LEICA MAGNUS I

Weight: 19.2 oz.–27.7 oz.
Length: 10.7 in.–14.1 in.
Power: 1–6.3x24mm, 1.5–10x42mm, 1.8–12x50mm, 2.4–16x56mm,
Obj. Diameter: 24mm, 42mm, 50mm, 56 mm
Exit Pupil: Varies with model
Eye Relief: 3.5 in.
Field of View: Varies with model
Features: Zoom factor up to 6.7; bright day/night reticle illumination with brightness control; high contrast images and superior light transmission; new tooless scale zeroing; reduced dot subtensions; improved battery lifetime and exchange; slimmed eyepiece; redesigned illumination activation to prevent accidental on/off
MSRP . . . . **N/A**

LEICA VISUS I LW

Weight: 18.3 oz. (2.5–10x42mm), 21.9 oz. (3–12x50mm)
Length: 12.76 in. (2.5–10x42mm), 13.4 in. (3–12x50mm)
Power: 2.5–10x42mm, 3–12x50mm
Obj. Diameter: 42mm, 50mm
Exit Pupil: Varies with model
Eye Relief: 3.9 in.
Field of View: Varies with model
Features: Generous eye relief; 4x zoom; long center tubes; adjustable day/night reticle illumination; choice of L-4 a or L-Ballistic reticles; glossy or matte finishes
MSRP . . . . **N/A**

LEUPOLD MARK 8 1.1– 8X24MM CQBSS M5B1 FRONT FOCAL PLANE

Weight: 23.2 oz.
Length: 11.75 in.
Power: 1.1–8x24mm
Obj. Diameter: 24mm
Exit Pupil: N/A
Eye Relief: 3.3–3.7 in.
Field of View: 14.7–92 ft @ 100 yds
Features: CQBSS = Close Quarters Battle Sniper Scope. Front focal plane illuminated reticle, 34mm main tube, 8:1 zoom ratio, blackened lens edges, extreme fast focus eyepiece, and Auto-Locking Pinch/Turn adjustments; four reticle choices
MSRP . . . . **$3899.99–$4939.99**

LEUPOLD MARK 8 3.5– 25X56MM

Weight: 37 oz.
Length: 16 in.
Power: 3.5–25x56mm
Obj. Diameter: 56mm
Exit Pupil: N/A
Eye Relief: 3.3–3.7 in.
Field of View: 4.4–32.5 ft @ 100 yds
Features: Front focal plane illuminated reticle for long-range use; second generation Argon/Krypton waterproofing; lockable fast-focus eyepiece; side focus; Xtended Twilight (XT) and Index Matched lens systems; 8:1 zoom ratio; multiple reticle options; non-illuminated option available
Illuminated: . . . . **$5374.99–$6109.99**
Non-illuminated: . . . **$3899.00–$4289.00**

LEUPOLD VX-6HD

Weight: 13.4 oz.–23.4 oz.
Length: 11.2 in.–14.6 in.
Power: 1–6x24mm, 2–12x42mm, 3–18x44mm, 3–18x50mm, 4–24x52mm
Obj. Diameter: 24mm, 42mm, 44mm, 50mm, 52mm
Exit Pupil: N/A
Eye Relief: Varies with model
Field of View: Varies with model
Features: High-definition lenses; Twilight Max Light Management System; CDS-ZL2 dial locks; in-scope cant indicator; fast-change magnification throw lever; flip-up rear lens cover; 30mm tubes; Custom Ballistic Dial
MSRP . . . . **$1689.00–$2599.00**

LUCID OPTICS MLX RIFLE
SCOPE

LUCID OPTICS
P7 4X COMBAT
OPTIC

MEOPTA MEOTAC
3–12X50MM RD

NIKKO STIRLING DIAMOND
FPP

NIKON BUCKMASTERS II
3–9X50MM

NIKON BLACK
FORCE1000

NIKON BLACK
X1000

Obj. Diameter: 44mm, 50mm
Exit Pupil: N/A
Eye Relief: 3.9 in., 3.5 in.
Field of View: Varies with model
Features: First focal plane (FFP) optics allow for shot corrections via reticle at any magnification with corresponding 1/10 MIL click value; 30mm main body tube; glass-etched illuminated skeleton HMD reticle; Waterproof, shockproof, nitrogen-filled; Microlux ETE Gen III glass coatings, fully multi-coated
MSRP **$459.00–490.00**

NIKON BLACK FORCE1000

Weight: 16.4 oz.
Length: 10.5 in.
Power: 1–4x24mm
Obj. Diameter: 24mm
Exit Pupil: 6–24mm
Eye Relief: 3.8–4.1 in.
Field of View: 27.2–110.1 ft @ 100 yds
Features: Designed for use with AR platforms; true 1x magnification with 4x zoom designed for both eyes open engagement; tube is 30mm; illuminated Speedforce reticle in the second focal plane
MSRP **$399.95**

NIKON BLACK X1000

Weight: 23.8 oz.
Length: 14.8 in.
Power: 4–16x50mm
Obj. Diameter: 50mm
Exit Pupil: 3.1–12.5mm
Eye Relief: 3.6–4 in.
Field of View: 6.8–27.2 ft @ 100 yds
Features: Dedicated precision long-range AR-platform scope; available with illuminated X-MOA or X-MRAD reticles or non-illuminated X-MOA reticle in the second focal plane
MSRP **$499.95**

NIKON BUCKMASTERS II 3–9X50MM

Weight: 13.1 oz.
Length: 12.4 in.
Power: 3–9x50mm
Obj. Diameter: 50mm
Exit Pupil: 5.6mm (@9x)
Eye Relief: 3.6 in.
Field of View: 11.3–33.8 ft @ 100 yds
Features: Economy scope has new 50mm objective; 1-in. tube; BDC reticle; ¼-in. click adjustments
MSRP **$159.95**

LUCID OPTICS MLX RIFLE SCOPE

Weight: 26 oz.
Length: 13.89 in.
Power: 4.5–18x44mm
Obj. Diameter: 44mm
Exit Pupil: 2.4–11mm
Eye Relief: 3.1–3.6 in.
Field of View: 8.5–25 ft @ 100 yds
Features: First focal plane scope; one-piece 6063 aluminum 30mm tube; Mil-based reticle; side parallax adjustment; 1/10 Mil tactile and audible click adjustments
MSRP **$649.00**

LUCID OPTICS P7 4X COMBAT OPTIC

Weight: 19 oz.
Length: 6.5 in.
Power: 4x30mm
Obj. Diameter: 30mm
Exit Pupil: 9mm
Eye Relief: 3.25 in.
Field of View: 25 ft @ 100 yds
Features: Fixed 4x illuminated reticle scope for close-quarters work; one-piece aluminum construction; manual and auto modes of operation; 50

MOA windage and elevation adjustments; re-zeroable turrets; P7 reticle
MSRP **$439.00**

MEOPTA MEOTAC 3–12X50MM RD

Weight: 34.2 oz.
Length: 12.6 in.
Power: 3–12x50mm
Obj. Diameter: 50mm
Exit Pupil: 16–4.2mm
Eye Relief: 4.5–3.5 in.
Field of View: 37–9 ft @ 100 yds
Features: Features RD illuminated, etched glass, Mil-Dot 3 reticle system with 16 illumination levels; MeoShield abrasion resistance coating; MeoQuick fast-focus eyepiece; side-focus parallax adjustment; oversized zero-stop tactical turrets; 34mm tube
MSRP **$2529.99**

NIKKO STIRLING DIAMOND FPP

Weight: 24.2 oz.–24 oz.
Length: 13 in.–14.2 in.
Power: 4–16x44mm, 6–24x50mm

SIG SAUER TANGO6

SWAROVSKI X5(I) 5-25X56 P L 1/4 MOA

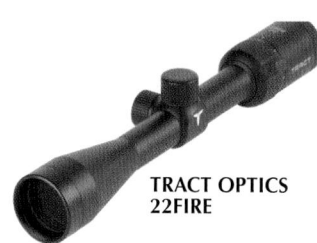

TRACT OPTICS 22FIRE

SIG SAUER WHISKEY5

SWAROVSKI Z8I

TRACT OPTICS RESPONSE

SIG SAUER TANGO6

Weight: 20.9 oz.–42 oz.
Length: 10.25 in.–14.38 in.
Power: 1–6x24mm, 2–12x40mm, 3–18x44mm, 4–24x50mm, 5–30x56mm
Obj. Diameter: 24mm, 44mm, 50mm, 56mm
Exit Pupil: Varies with model
Eye Relief: Varies with model
Field of View: Varies with model
Features: Super-zoom 6x; LevelPlex digital anti-cant; Motion Activated Reticle Illumination; user-configured elevation zero stop; fiber optic power indicator; 34mm tube; HellFire Reticle fiber optics intensity is variable at center point; designed for AR/MSR and bolt-action platforms, long-range applications
MSRP . . . . **$1679.99–$2999.99**

SIG SAUER WHISKEY5

Weight: 19 oz.–29.6 oz.
Length: 10.1 in.–14.1 in.
Power: 1–5x24mm, 2–10x42mm, 2.4–12x56mm, 3–15x52mm
Obj. Diameter: 24mm, 42mm, 56mm, 44mm, 52mm, 52mm (in order of power listing)
Exit Pupil: Varies with model

Eye Relief: 3.8–4.1 in. depending on model
Field of View: Varies with model
Features: Super-zoom 5x; Stealth ID deflection armor coating; SpectraCoat reflection reduction; HellFire fiber optic reticles; fast-focus eyepiece; hunting applications
MSRP . . . . **$839.99–$1499.99**

SWAROVSKI X5(I) 5–25X56 P L 1/4 MOA

Weight: 32.1 oz.
Length: 14.8 in.
Power: 5–25x56mm
Obj. Diameter: 56mm
Exit Pupil: 2.3–9.5mm
Eye Relief: N/A
Field of View: 4.5–21 ft @ 100 yds
Features: High-luminosity rifle scope with 25x magnification; three reticle options; 30mm tube; 10 illumination brightness settings
MSRP **$3666.00**

SWAROVSKI Z8I

Weight: 18.2 oz.–25.6 oz.
Length: 14 in.–14.3 in.
Power: 1–8x24mm, 1.7–13.3x42mm, 2–16x50mm, 2.3–18x56mm
Obj. Diameter: 24, 42, 50, 56mm

Exit Pupil: Varies with model
Eye Relief: N/A
Field of View: Varies with model
Features: Illuminated 8x zoom in a 30mm tube; Flexchange, a switchable reticle; multiple reticles to choose from
MSRP . . . . **$2688.00–$3521.00**

TRACT OPTICS 22FIRE

Weight: 15.2 oz. (3–9x40mm), 16 oz. (4–12x40mm)
Length: 12.2 in. (3–9x40mm), 13.9 in. (4–12x40mm)
Power: 3–9x40mm, 4–12x40mm
Obj. Diameter: 40mm
Exit Pupil: Varies with model
Eye Relief: 3.5 in.
Field of View: Varies with model
Features: Tract Optics delivers premium optics shipped straight to the customer's door; 22Rifle line, designed specifically to maximize accuracy with .22-caliber rifles; Impact BDC or T-Plex reticle; BDC is designed for longer-distance work, while T-Plex is suitable for target practice and small-game hunting
3–9x40mm: **$174.00**
4–12x40mm: **$194.00**

TRACT OPTICS RESPONSE

Weight: 18 oz. (2.5–10x42mm), 19.6 oz. (4–16x42mm)
Length: 11.7 in. (2.5–10x42mm), 13.1 in. (4–16x42mm)
Power: 2.5–10x42mm, 4–16x42mm,
Obj. Diameter: 42mm
Exit Pupil: Varies with model
Eye Relief: 3.5 in.
Field of View: Varies with model
Features: Tract Optics delivers premium optics shipped straight to the customer's door; Response line consists of three scopes, a 2.5-10x42mm with an Impact BDC .223/5.56 reticle, and a 4-16x42mm available with either an Impact BDC .308/7.62 or .223/5.56 reticle; intended for use with ARs/MSRs in the .223 reticles and the AR10 platform with the .308 reticle; fully coated optics; exposed tactical type turrets; glass-etched reticles with windage correction; 1-in. one-piece tubes purged with argon
2.5–10x42mm: **$354.00**
4–16x42mm: **$394.00**

TRACT OPTICS TEKOA

TRACT OPTICS TORIC

TRACT OPTICS TURION

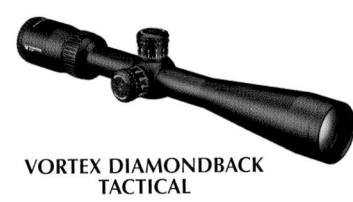

VORTEX DIAMONDBACK TACTICAL

VORTEX VIPER PST GEN II

WEAVER CLASSIC T SERIES XR RIFLESCOPES

TRACT OPTICS TEKOA

Weight: Varies with model
Length: Varies with model
Power: 2.5–10x42mm, 3–12x42mm, 3–12x50mm, 4–16x44mm
Obj. Diameter: 42mm, 44mm, 50mm
Exit Pupil: Varies with model
Eye Relief: 3.5 in.
Field of View: Varies with model
Features: Tract Optics delivers premium optics straight to the customer's door; Impact BDC or T-Plex reticles; 1-in., one-piece, Argon-purged tubes; SCHOTT HT (high transmission glass) for superior low light transmission; 4-16x44mm available with Impact BDC or T-Plex reticles and is designed for long-range applications with Tract's HD Optical Technology; Tekoa scopes are Japanese-made with precision components and built to extremely high tolerances
MSRP . . . . **$494.00–$594.00**

TRACT OPTICS TORIC

Weight: Varies with model
Length: Varies with model
Power: 2–10x42mm, 3–15x42mm, 3–15x50mm
Obj. Diameter: 42mm, 50mm
Exit Pupil: Varies with model
Eye Relief: 3.5 in.

Field of View: Varies with model
Features: Tract Optics delivers premium optics straight to the customer's door; Tract's Ultra High Definition (UHD) optical system; SCHOTT HT (high transmission) glass; fully multi-coated lens system; Impact BDC and T-Plex reticles; all but the 2-10x42mm models feature locking side-focus parallax adjustment; Toric scopes are Japanese-made with precision components and built to extremely high tolerances
2–10x42mm and
3–15x42mm: **$654.00**
3–15x50mm: **$724.00**

TRACT OPTICS TURION

Weight: 15.2 oz.
Length: 12.45 in.
Power: 3–9x40mm
Obj. Diameter: 40mm
Exit Pupil: 13.3–4.4mm
Eye Relief: 3.9 in.
Field of View: 33.2–11 ft @ 100 yds
Features: Tract Optics delivers premium optics straight to the customer's door; Impact BDC or T-Plex reticle; Tract's High Definition optical system; SCHOTT HT (high transmission) glass; suitable for use on centerfire rifles, slug shotguns, and muzzleloaders
MSRP **$394.00**

VORTEX DIAMONDBACK TACTICAL

Weight: 15.9 oz. (3–9x), 16.2 oz. (4–12x)
Length: 12.5 in. (3–9x), 14.2 (4–12x)
Power: 3–9x40mm, 4–12x40mm
Obj. Diameter: 40mm
Exit Pupil: N/A
Eye Relief: 3.8 in.
Field of View: 11.3–3.7 ft @ 100 yds (3–9x), 7.9–23.6 ft @ 100 yds (4–12x)
Features: Second focal plane VMR-1 reticle; 1-in. tube; fast-focus eyepiece; fiber optic radius bar
3–9x: **$379.99**
4–12x: **$399.99**

VORTEX VIPER PST GEN II

Weight: 22.7 oz.–31.2 oz.
Length: 10.9 in.–16 in.
Power: 1–6x24mm, 2–10x32mm, 3–15x44mm, 5–25x50mm
Obj. Diameter: 24mm, 32mm, 44mm, 50mm
Exit Pupil: N/A
Eye Relief: 3.4–3.8 in.
Field of View: Varies with model
Features: Extra-low dispersion (XD) glass; multiple anti-reflection coatings on all air-to-glass surfaces; second focal plane; glass-etched, illuminated reticles; reticle selection varies with magnification
MSRP . . . . **$999.99–$1399.99**

WEAVER CLASSIC T SERIES XR RIFLESCOPES

Weight: 13.2 oz.–24.5 oz.
Length: 16.1 in.
Power: 24x40mm, 36x40mm, 46x48mm
Obj. Diameter: 40mm, 48mm
Exit Pupil: 1.7mm (24x), 1.1mm (35x), 1mm (46x)
Eye Relief: 3.25 in. (24x), 3.2 in. (36x, 46x)
Field of View: 4.32 ft @ 100 yds (24x), 2.87 ft @ 100 yds (36x), 22.4 ft @ 100 yds (46x)
Features: Large magnification fixed-power scopes; side-focus parallax adjustment system; Micro-Trac adjustment system provides independent windage and elevation control in 1/8-in. click values; matte black or silver finishes; three reticle choices
MSRP . . . . **$981.45–$1444.95**

WEAVER TACTICAL RIFLE SCOPE WITH DUAL FOCAL PLANES

WEAVER GRAND SLAM RIFLESCOPE WITH MULTISTOP TURRET

ZEISS VICTORY V8 RAIL MOUNTS

WEAVER GRAND SLAM RIFLESCOPE WITH MULTISTOP TURRET

Weight: N/A
Length: 11 in. (4–16x44mm), 13.4 in. (5–20x50mm)
Power: 4–16x44mm, 5–20x50mm
Obj. Diameter: 44mm, 50mm
Exit Pupil: 10–2.8mm (4–16x44mm), 8.4–2.5mm (5–20x50mm)
Eye Relief: 3.46 in. (4–16x44mm), 3.4 (5–20x50mm)
Field of View: 23.4–6.3 ft @ 100 yds (4–16x44mm), 19.9–4.97ft @ 100 yds (5–20x50mm)
Features: Multistop Turret system allows the user to build their own custom ballistic turret; turret has color-coded bands to match any load/distance; one-piece 1-in. tube; scope

is Argon-purged and has multi-coated lenses
4–16x44mm: $1214.95
5–20x50mm: $1424.95

WEAVER TACTICAL RIFLE SCOPE WITH DUAL FOCAL PLANES

Weight: 21.9 oz.
Length: N/A
Power: 1–7x24mm
Obj. Diameter: 24mm
Exit Pupil: 11.7–3.4mm
Eye Relief: 3.9 in.
Field of View: 95–3.6 ft @ 100 yds
Features: Part of the Super Slam series; illuminated reticle; dual focal plane with 4 MOA red dot and mil-dot ranging; 34mm tube
MSRP $1798.95

ZEISS VICTORY V8 RAIL MOUNTS

Weight: 21.9 oz.–30.2 oz.
Length: 11.9 in.–13.8 in.
Power: 1–8x30mm, 1.8–14x50mm, 2.8–2–x56mm
Obj. Diameter: 36mm, 56mm, 62mm
Exit Pupil: 10.3–2.8mm
Eye Relief: 3.74 in.
Field of View: 39.6–5.4 m @ 100m, 23–3.1m @ 100m, 15.5–2.1m @ 100m
Features: LotuTec protective coating; come with a rail; BDC LongRange standard on the 2.8–20x56 and available for the 1.8–14x50; laterally adjustable BDC is also available; 1.8–14x50 and 2.8–20x56 equipped with parallax compensation
MSRP . . . . $2699.00–$3599.00

SIGHTS

BUSHNELL AR OPTICS ENGULF

BUSHNELL AR OPTICS ENRAGE

BUSHNELL AR OPTICS ENGULF

Weight: N/A
Power: 1x
Features: Micro reflex red dot sight small enough to fit on a pistol; projects a 5-MOA dot; compact design compatible with a large selection of semiautomatic pistols
MSRP $254.95

BUSHNELL AR OPTICS ENRAGE

Weight: 9.8 oz.
Power: 1x
Obj. Diameter:
Features: Battery life that lasts twice as long as previous Bushnell red-dots; eight brightness settings lock in with a single click and there's an off setting between each; 2-MOA red-dot is housed in multi-coated optics; optional hi-rise mount
MSRP $239.99

BUSHNELL AR OPTICS INCINERATE

MEOPTA MEORED

SIG SAUER ROMEO4H

SIG SAUER ROMEO4T

SIG SAUER ROMEO4S

SIG SAUER ROMEO6H, 6T

TRIJICON MACHINE GUN REFLEX SIGHT (MGRS)

VORTEX RAZOR AMG UH-1

BUSHNELL AR OPTICS INCINERATE

Weight: 10.2 oz.
Power: 1x
Features: Circle dot reticle, 25-MOA circle, and 2-MOA center dot work with both tactical rifles and shotguns; rear sight is compatible with Glock dovetail sights; eight brightness settings with off setting between each
MSRP $239.99

MEOPTA MEORED

Weight: 1 oz.
Length: 1.85 in.
Power: 1x
Features: Ultra compact reflex red-dot sight; parallax free and designed for use on handguns with cut-out slides, AR platforms, or shotguns; dot size is 3 MOA; integrated MIL-STD 1913 mount; interface plate accepts a Docter mount; windage adjustment up to 180 MOA; elevation adjustment to 120 MOA; simple on/off button on left side of optic allows the user to adjust brightness level; one CR 2302 battery with a life of up to 300 hours; optic will auto-off after three hours of continuous operation if the on/off

button hasn't been activated; MeoBright, MeoDrop, and MeoShield coatings are all featured
MSRP $517.49

SIG SAUER ROMEO4H

Weight: 3.4 oz.
Power: 1x
Obj. Diameter: 20mm
Features: Designed for a AR-platform pistols, MSRs, and shotguns; four reticle options; side-loading battery has 50,000+ hours of life
MSRP . . . . N/A

SIG SAUER ROMEO4S

Weight: 3.4 oz.
Power: 1x
Obj. Diameter: 20mm
Features: Solar powered red-dot runs in excess of 100,000+ with solar and battery usage; designed for AR-platform pistols, MSRs, and shotguns; lens caps and quick-release mount; four reticle choices
MSRP . . . . N/A

SIG SAUER ROMEO4T

Weight: 3.2 oz.
Power: 1x
Obj. Diameter: 20mm
Features: Solar powered red dot runs in excess of 100,000+ with solar and battery usage; designed for AR-platform pistols, MSRs, and shotguns; lens caps and quick-release mount; four reticle choices; tactical version designed for harsh environments
MSRP . . . . N/A

SIG SAUER ROMEO6H, 6T

Weight: 9.6 oz.
Power: 1x
Obj. Diameter: 30mm
Eye Relief: Unlimited
Features: 6H is battery only, 6T is solar powered; full-size 1x30mm red-dots runs in excess of 100,000+ with solar and battery usage; side-loading battery; 2 MOA red dot; four reticle choices
MSRP . . . . N/A

TRIJICON MACHINE GUN REFLEX SIGHT (MGRS)

Weight: 66.9 oz.
Length: 8.78 in.
Power: 1x
Features: Created to withstand the constant, violent battering of machine guns; large objective lens with a 3-inch-by-2-inch viewing area; 35 MOA segmented circle reticle; centered 3 MOA dot for precise aiming at close combat to extended ranges; powered by a single CR123A battery that lasts 1000 hours of continuous operation
MSRP $4499.00

VORTEX RAZOR AMG UH-1

Weight: 11.8 oz.
Length: 3.5 in.
Power: 1x
Eye Relief: Unlimited
Features: Fusion Hologram with Quantum Well Light Control (FHQ); red-dot size is 1 MOA; fifteen brightness levels; rear-facing controls; integrated mount; micro USB port for use with rechargeable battery
MSRP $699.99

NEW Products: **Optics**

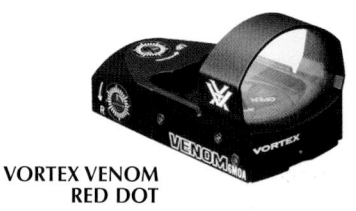

**VORTEX VENOM
RED DOT**

**WEAVER
TACTICAL
RAPID FIRE
RED DOT
1X25MM**

VORTEX VENOM RED DOT

Weight: 1.1 oz.
Length: 1.9 in.
Power: 1x
Eye Relief: Unlimited
Features: Parallax-free red-dot optic; 6 MOA dot size; 130 MOA elevation adjustment; 100 MOA windage adjustment; waterproof; 14-hour automatic shutdown feature; ten brightness level settings
MSRP $329.99

WEAVER TACTICAL RAPID FIRE RED DOT 1X25MM

Weight: 3.4 oz.
Power: 1x
Obj. Diameter: 25mm
Exit Pupil: 22mm
Eye Relief: Unlimited
Field of View: Unlimited
Features: Lightweight rugged body; removable Tactical Mount with TorqueKnob tool-less thumbscrew; 2 MOA red dot; .5-MOA click adjustments; dot has six illumination settings, two of which are night-compatible; tethered windage and elevation caps; low battery indicator
MSRP $239.95

RANGEFINDERS

**NIKON MONARCH
7I VR**

1250

KILO850

SIG SAUER
KILO2200MR

NIKON MONARCH 7I VR

Weight: 7.1 oz.
Length:
Power: 6x
Obj. Diameter: 21mm
Exit Pupil: 3.5mm
Eye Relief: 18mm
Field of View:
Features: First rangefinder with optical vibration reduction; two ranging modes; incline/decline functionality; readings from eight to 1,000 yards in .1-yard increments; yard/meter readings; waterproof
MSRP $399.95

SIG SAUER KILO850

Weight: 5 oz.
Length: 3.9 in.
Power: 4x
Obj. Diameter: 20mm
Exit Pupil: 5mm
Eye Relief: 24mm
Field of View: 43.77 ft @ 100 yds
Features: LightWave DSP Technology ranges up to 1,200 yards; fine line of sight or angle modified range selection; high-transmittance LCD display; user-selectable target modes featuring last or best reading; simple user interface features range or mode buttons only; black or Viper Western Camouflage finishes
MSRP $239.99

SIG SAUER KILO1250

Weight: 5 oz.
Length: 3.9 in.
Power: 6x
Obj. Diameter: 20mm
Exit Pupil: 3.33mm
Eye Relief: 15mm
Field of View: 34.18 ft @ 100 yds
Features: LightWave DSP Technology ranges up to 1,600 yards; fine line of sight or angle modified range selection; high-transmittance LCD display; user-selectable target modes featuring last or best reading; simple user interface features range or mode buttons only; black or Viper Western Camouflage finishes
MSRP $359.99

SIG SAUER KILO2200MR

Weight: 7.5 oz.
Length: 4.2 in.
Power: 7x
Obj. Diameter: 25mm
Exit Pupil: 3.6mm
Eye Relief: 15mm
Field of View: 35.67 ft @ 100 yds
Features: LightWave DSP Technology ranges up to two miles; SpectraCoat anti-reflection coatings; HyperScan technology with four range updates per second in scan mode; RangeLock reports last range result when ranging distant targets; smaller aiming circle has milling features
MSRP $599.99

SIG SAUER KILO2400ABS

SIG SAUER KILO2400ABS

Weight: 7.5 oz.
Length: 4.2 in.
Power: 7x
Obj. Diameter: 25mm

Exit Pupil: 3.6mm
Eye Relief: 15mm
Field of View: 35.67 ft @ 100 yds
Features: LightWave DSP Technology ranges up to two miles; embedded applied ballistics calculator; integrated temperature, humidity, pressure, and compass; Milling reticle with 2.4 MRAD inner diameter and 3 MRAD outer diameter; user-selectable target modes feature last and best readings; Lumatic OLED display constantly monitors light conditions and adjusts display brightness accordingly; multi-position twist-up eyecup provides custom fit; tripod adaptor; smartphone jack WindMETER; stylus pen; lanyard; three spare batteries; ballistic nylon molle kit; nylon carry pouch; configurable reticle with three viewing options: center aiming circle only, center aiming circle and horizontal milling grid, or center aiming circle with horizontal and vertical milling grids; ranges up to two miles
MSRP. **$1799.99**

BROWNING BXD TURKEY EXTRA DISTANCE

BROWNING BXV PREDATOR & VARMINT

CCI A22 MAGNUM GAMEPOINT

BROWNING BXS DEER

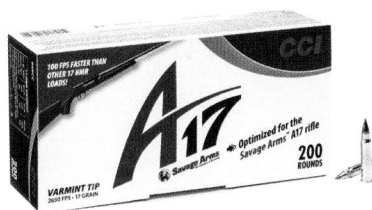

CCI A17 VARMINT TIP

CCI BIG 4

BROWNING BXD TURKEY EXTRA DISTANCE

Features: Improved downrange patterns with high velocity retention; buffered nickel-plated shot; aerodynamically stable wad
Available in: 12 (3 in., 3.5 in.), 20 (3 in.); Shot sizes: 4, 5 (12 ga. only), 6
Box 10:. . . . .**$14.99–$17.99**

BROWNING BXS DEER

Features: Solid copper expansion sabot slug designed to increase accuracy, penetration, and energy transfer
Available in: 12 (2.75 in., 1 oz. slug), 20 (2.75 in., 0.75 oz. slug)
Box 5:. . . . .**$12.99–$14.99**

BROWNING BXV PREDATOR & VARMINT

Features: Polymer tip improves BC and results in flatter trajectory and higher downrange velocity
Available in: .223 Win., .243 Win., .22 Hornet, .22-250
Box 20:. . . . .**$19.99–$25.99**

CCI A17 VARMINT TIP

Features: Designed for Savage's semiautomatic A17 rifle; Varmint Tip bullet
Available in: .17 HMR
Box 50, 200: . . . .**$14.99–$64.99**

CCI A22 MAGNUM GAMEPOINT

Features: GamePoint bullet; designed around Savage's semiautomatic A22 Magnum rifle
Available in: .22 WMR (35 gr.)
Box 200:. **$59.99**

CCI BIG 4

Features: Centerfire handgun shotshells with larger No. 4 pellets for extended range and penetration
Available in: 9mm, .38 Spl., .44 Spl., .45 Colt
Box 10:. . . . .**$14.95–$19.95**

NEW PRODUCTS

NEW Products: Ammunition

DANIEL DEFENSE FIRST CHOICE AMMUNITION

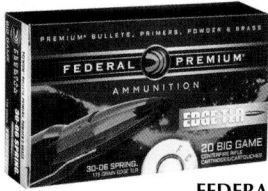

FEDERAL PREMIUM EDGE TLR

FEDERAL PREMIUM GOLD MEDAL BERGER

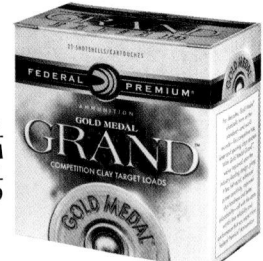

FEDERAL PREMIUM GOLD MEDAL GRAND

FEDERAL PREMIUM HI-BIRD

FEDERAL PREMIUM HUNTER MATCH .22 LONG RIFLE

FEDERAL PREMIUM TACTICAL TIP MATCHKING

HORNADY AMERICAN GUNNER SHOTGUN

DANIEL DEFENSE FIRST CHOICE AMMUNITION

Features: Subsonic round; for target shooting or home defense; manufactured using durable brass cases and precision 220-grain Lapua-Scenar-L OTM bullets; every round stamped with "DD" must undergo and pass a thorough inspection to ensure critical dimensions that affect accuracy are met before it leaves the factory
Available in: .300 BLK
Box 30: **$50.00**

FEDERAL PREMIUM EDGE TLR

Features: Uses the exclusive Slipstream polymer tip to initiate expansion at long range; at close range, the bullet's copper shank and bonded lead core retain weight for consistent, lethal penetration; long, sleek profile offers an extremely high BC; AccuChannel groove technology improves accuracy and reduces drag
Available in: .308 Win., .30-06 Spfd., .300 Win. Mag., .300 WSM
Box 20: . . . .**$47.95–$59.95**

FEDERAL PREMIUM GOLD MEDAL BERGER

Features: Rounds feature a Berger bullet with a high BC to provide flat trajectories, less wind drift, and surgical long-range accuracy; Gold Medal match primers; Federal brass; specially formulated propellants
Available in: .223 Rem., 6.5 Grendel, 6.5 Creedmoor, .308 Win.
Box 20: . . . .**$32.95–$34.95**

FEDERAL PREMIUM GOLD MEDAL GRAND

Features: Gold Medal Grand competition clay target loads feature two-piece wad; SoftCell technology decreases felt recoil and produces more uniform patterns; rigid PrimerLock head improves primer sensitivity
Available in: 12 ga. (2.75 in.); Shot sizes: 7.5, 8
Box 25: **$10.95**

FEDERAL PREMIUM HI-BIRD

Features: Two-piece wad features SoftCell technology to decrease perceived recoil and produce more consistent long-range patterns; dense long-range patterns and increased down-range energy
Available in: 12 ga. (2.75 in.); Shot sizes: 6, 7.5, 8
Box 25: . . . .**$10.95–$12.95**

FEDERAL PREMIUM HUNTER MATCH .22 LONG RIFLE

Features: High-velocity long-range round; hollowpoint designed for optimum expansion at 100 yards; nickel-plated case
Available in: .22 LR
Box 50: **$7.95**

FEDERAL PREMIUM TACTICAL TIP MATCHKING

Features: Polymer tip; tapered jacket allows rapid, controlled expansion on impact to maximize terminal effect; designed for use in semiautomatic rifle; low- ash propellants
Available in: .308 Win.
Box 20: **$27.95**

HORNADY AMERICAN GUNNER SHOTGUN

Features: Reduced recoil rifled slugs or 00 buckshot; rifled slug is 1 oz., 00 buck holds eight high-antimony swaged pellets
Available in: 12 ga.
Box 5, slug: **$8.27**
Box 5, 00 buckshot: **$11.01**

HORNADY BLACK

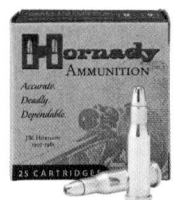

HORNADY CUSTOM RIFLE

HORNADY PRECISION HUNTER

HORNADY SUPERFORMANCE MATCH

LAPUA NATURALIS (3RD GENERATION)

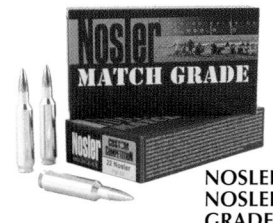

NOSLER .22 NOSLER TROPHY GRADE/MATCH GRADE

NOSLER .33 NOSLER TROPHY GRADE

POLYCASE INCEPTOR SPORT UTILITY

HORNADY BLACK

Features: Designed to function across a wide variety of platforms including direct impingement, gas piston, suppressed, unsuppressed, inertia, bolt, pump, supersonic, subsonic, rifle, mid-length, carbine, or pistol; seven bullet types; 00 buckshot comes in a box of 10
Available in: 5.45x39, .223 Rem., 5.56 NATO, 6.5 Grendel, 6.8mm SPC, .300 BLK, .300 Win., 7.62x39, .450 Bushmaster, 12-ga. 00 Buckshot
Box 20: . . . . **$15.00–$38.33**

HORNADY CUSTOM RIFLE

Features: Depending on caliber, Custom ammo is loaded with Hornady SST, InterBond, InterLock, or V-MAX bullets

Available in: .218 Bee, .250 Savage, .264 Win. Mag.
Box 20: . . . . **$42.55–$54.24**

HORNADY PRECISION HUNTER

Features: Best-in-class BCs, match-accurate hunting loads, topped with ELD-X Heat Shield Tip bullets
Available in: .270 Win., 7mm-08 Rem., .280 Rem., .300 WSM, .300 Wby. Mag.
Box 20: . . . . **$43.28 –$63.92**

HORNADY SUPERFORMANCE MATCH

Features: Achieves muzzle velocity 100 to 200 fps faster than conventional .308 Win. loads; AMAX

or Hornady Boattail Hollowpoint Match bullets featuring AMP (Advanced Manufacturing Process) jackets
Available in: .308 Win.
Box 20: **$43.59**

LAPUA NATURALIS (3RD GENERATION)

Features: Updated bullet design has monolithic pure copper body that can produce weight retention up to 100 percent; new boattail design eases reloading and improves ballistics; controlled expansion is procured via a polymer valve tip
Available in: .222 Rem. (55 gr.), 7x65R (156 gr.), .308 Win. (170 gr.)
MSRP . . . . **N/A**

NOSLER .22 NOSLER TROPHY GRADE/MATCH GRADE

Features: Centerfire cartridge with 25 percent more capacity, more than 30 percent more energy, and more than 300 fps than .223 Rem.; Trophy Grade: 55-grain BTV bullet; Match Grade: 77-grain CC bullet
Available in: .22 Nosler
Box 20: **$29.95**

NOSLER .33 NOSLER TROPHY GRADE

Features: Propels a 225-grain Accubond at 3025 fps, 265-grain AccuBond Long Range at 2775 fps; uses 18 percent less powder than comparable .338 Win. Mag. and .339 Lapua cartridges
Available in: .33 Nosler (225 gr., 265 gr.)
Box 20: **$77.50**

POLYCASE INCEPTOR SPORT UTILITY

Features: Lead-free injection-molded copper-polymer projectiles loaded to tight specifications in high-quality brass cases; RNP (Round Nose Precision) profile in handgun cartridges or with the SRR (Short-Range Rifle) in rifle cartridges
Available in: .380 ACP, 9mm, .38 Spl., .40 S&W, .45 ACP, .300 BLK
Box 50: . . . . **$17.99–$39.99**

NEW Products: **Ammunition**

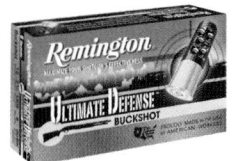

REMINGTON ULTIMATE DEFENSE BUCKSHOT

WINCHESTER POWER-POINT SUBSONIC

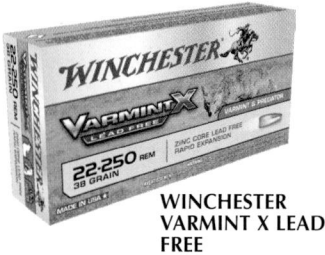

WINCHESTER VARMINT X LEAD FREE

SIG SAUER VARMINT & PREDATOR

WINCHESTER SUPER X SUBSONIC RIMFIRE

REMINGTON ULTIMATE DEFENSE BUCKSHOT

Features: Dense patterns and big knock-down power; short-range patterns through smoothbores are tight; .410-bore loads house four lead 000 buckshot pellets
Available in: 12, .410
Box 5, 15: **$5.99**

SIG SAUER VARMINT & PREDATOR

Features: Single-based extruded powders; smoke gray-tipped projectiles designed for expansion; match-grade accuracy; flat trajectories
Available in: .223 Rem. (40 gr.), .22-250 Rem. (40 gr.), .243 Win. (55 gr.)
Box 20: . . . . **N/A**

WINCHESTER POWER-POINT SUBSONIC

Features: Designed for improved terminal performance at subsonic velocities; radical profile delivers expansion; alloyed lead core helps retain weight
Available in: .300 BLK, .308 Win.
Box 20: . . . . **N/A**

WINCHESTER SUPER X SUBSONIC RIMFIRE

Features: New to the SuperX lineup; subsonic .22 WMR for varmint hunters; reduced noise with and without suppressor use; lead hollowpoint
Available in: .22 WMR (45 gr.)
Box 50: . . . . **N/A**

WINCHESTER VARMINT X LEAD FREE

Features: Features zinc core technology used in Winchester's Super Clean pistol ammo
Available in: .22-250 Rem., .223 Rem., .243 Rem.
Box 20: . . . . **N/A**

NEW Products: **Bullets**

BERGER CLASSIC HUNTER

Features: Three new bullets have been added to this line, which are designed specifically for factory rifle applications where SAAMI-length loaded rounds are mandatory
Available in: 6mm (135 gr.), .270 (140 gr.), 7mm (150 gr.)
Box 100: . . . . **$53.80–$57.80**

BERGER ELITE HUNTER

Features: Three new bullets have been added to this line, which has the same hybrid profile as Berger's Hybrid Target bullets

Available in: 6.5mm (140 gr.), 7mm (175 gr.) .30 (180 gr.)
Box 100: . . . . **$54.20–$60.80**

HORNADY ELD-X

Features: The ELD-X (Extremely Low Drag - eXpanding) bullet is a technologically advanced, match-accurate, all-range hunting bullet featuring highest-in-class ballistic coefficients and consistent, controlled expansion at all practical hunting distances; Heat Shield tip
Available in: .277, .284
Box 100: **$48.33**

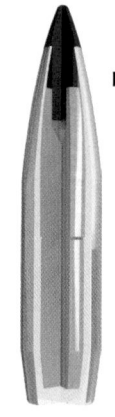

HORNADY ELD-X

HORNADY FTX HANDGUN

HORNADY FTX RIFLE

LAPUA NATURALIS (3RD GENERATION)

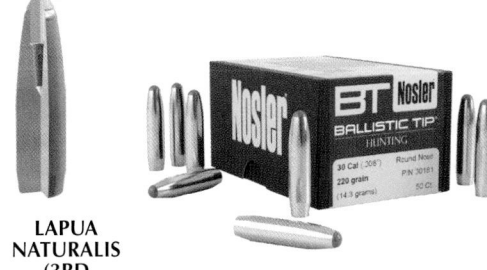

NOSLER BALLISTIC TIP HUNTING .30-CALIBER SUBSONIC

NOSLER ACCUBOND LONG RANGE

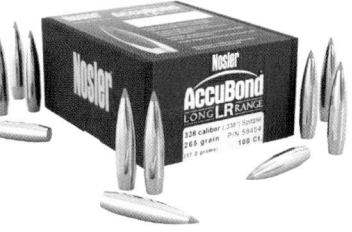

NOSLER VARMAGEDDON

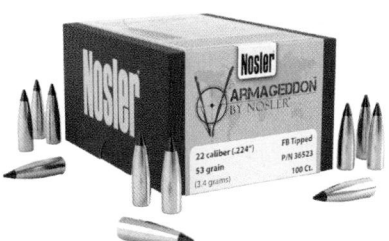

BERGER ELITE HUNTER

PEREGRINE PLAINSMASTER

NOSLER BALLISTIC TIP HUNTING BULLET

Features: Streamlined polymer tip color-coded by caliber resists deformation in the magazine and begins expansion upon impact; heavy jacketed brass acts as a platform for large-diameter mushrooming; solid brass boattail
Available in: .30 (220 gr.)
Box 50: **$25.10**

NOSLER BALLISTIC TIP HUNTING .30-CALIBER SUBSONIC

Features: Only available previously in loaded ammunition, the new bullet was created to maximize effective terminal performance for the .300 BLK cartridge at subsonic velocities; at 1000 fps, the ballistic tip bullet reliably exhibits controlled, double-diameter expansion, 90 percent weight retention, and 18 in. of penetration in ballistic gelatin; round nose
Available in: .30 (220 gr.)
Box 50: **$25.10**

NOSLER RDF (REDUCED DRAG FACTOR)

Features: Very high BCs via a compound ogive; long drag-reducing boattail; very small hollowpoint meplat
Available in: .22 (70 gr.), 6mm (105 gr.), 6.5mm (140 gr.), .30 (175 gr.)
Box 100, 500: . . . . . . **$29.15–$168.50**

NOSLER VARMAGEDDON

Features: Created for high-volume varmint shooting
Available in: .22 (53 gr.), 7.62x39 (123 gr.)
Box 100, 250: . . . . **N/A**

PEREGRINE PLAINSMASTER

Features: Hand manufactured, lead-free, spitzer-type monolithic hunting bullets; high BCs result in flat trajectories; unique driving band increases velocities; PlainsMaster's patented brass plunger works on the principle of pneumatic expansion; meat damage is very limited since

HORNADY FTX HANDGUN

Features: Features Flext Tip technology
Available in: .410
Box 100: **$43.13**

HORNADY FTX RIFLE

Features: Flex Tip, InterLock features; designed for use in lever-action/tubular magazine firearms
Available in: .257, .308
Box 100: . . . .**$34.97–$42.57**

LAPUA NATURALIS (3RD GENERATION)

Features: Joining other updated third-generation Naturalis bullets; monolithic pure copper body that can produce weight retention up to 100 percent; new boattail design eases reloading and improves ballistics; consistent, controlled expansion is procured via a polymer valve tip
Available in: .224 (55 gr.)
MSRP . . . . **N/A**

NOSLER ACCUBOND LONG RANGE

Features: Features unique gray polymer tip and tangent ogive designed to be reliable and accurate in a variety of firearms without having to be close in or in contact with the lands; high-performance boattail
Available in: .30 (168 gr.), .338 (265 gr.)
Box 100: . . . .**$62.70–$74.10**

NEW Products: **Bullets**

SIERRA MATCHKING 6MM 110-GRAIN

SIERRA MATCHKING 7MM 197-GRAIN

SIERRA TIPPED MATCHKING

bullets don't disintegrate upon impact, instead delivering most of their energy in the targeted animal whether impacting bone or flesh
Available in: Dozens of calibers and weights from .224 (50 gr.) to .458 (380 gr.)
Box 25, 50: . . . . **$30.25–$60.05**

RAINIER LEADSAFE

Features: Hollowpoints and roundnose flatpoint bullets; swaged lead cores totally encapsulated by Rainier LeadSafe full copper plating with pure virgin copper
Available in: .300 BLK (180 gr.)
MSRP . . . . **N/A**

SIERRA MATCHKING 6MM 110-GRAIN

Features: Hollowpoint boattail with a sleek, .27-caliber ogive and a final meplat improves BC, wind resistance, and velocity retention; bearing surface-to-ogive junction uses the same 1.5-degree angle commonly found in many match rifle chamber throats; requires a twist rate of 1:7 or faster
Available in: 6mm (110 gr.)
Box 100: **$42.36**
Box 500: **$208.75**

SIERRA MATCHKING 7MM 197-GRAIN

Features: Hollowpoint boatttail with a sleek, .27-caliber ogive and a final meplat improves BC, wind resistance, and velocity retention; bearing surface-to-ogive junction uses the same 1.5-degree angle commonly found in many match rifle chamber throats; requires a twist rate of 1:7.5 or faster
Available in: 7mm (197 gr.)
Box 100: **$54.20**
Box 500: **$264.21**

SIERRA TIPPED MATCHKING

Features: Enhanced MatchKing with acetal resin tip that reduces drag and improves BC; designed for F-class competition; requires a barrel twist rate of 1:10 or faster
Available in: .308 (195 gr.)
Box 100: **$51.19**

NEW Products: **Muzzleloading Components**

FEDERAL PREMIUM 209 MUZZLELOADING PRIMERS

FEDERAL PREMIUM LEAD MUZZLELOADER BULLET

UMAREX ARX

FEDERAL PREMIUM 209 MUZZLELOADING PRIMERS

Features: Complements Federal's B.O.R. Lock MZ bullets; superior resistance to moisture and hot, reliable ignition
Available in: N/A
Box 100: **$8.95**

FEDERAL PREMIUM LEAD MUZZLELOADER BULLET

Features: Polymer tip; expanding polymer base cup that engages rifling and seals the bore; fouling cutting ring reduces cleaning between shots
Available in: .50 (350 gr.)

Box 15: **$24.95**

UMAREX ARX

Features: Designed in conjunction with PolyCase Ammunition Development Lab; SpeedBand sabot available calibers include .357, .40, and .45, while a .45-caliber option has Umarex's base-style SpeedBelt; acceptable for use in large-bore airguns, including Umarex's Hammer .50-caliber; (Hammer information not available prior to publication; introduction expected mid-to late-2017)
Available in: .357, .40, .45
Box 20: **$21.99**

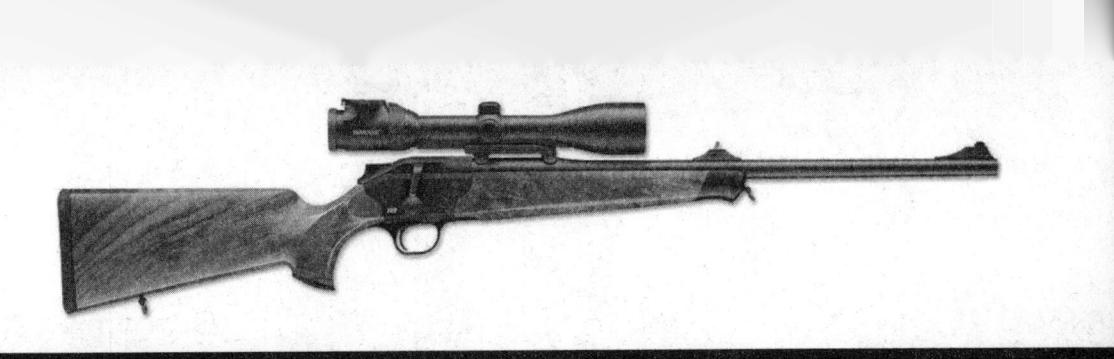

Adcor Defense

ADCOR DEFENSE A-556 ELITE

ADCOR DEFENSE ADCOR ELITE

A-556 ELITE
Action: Semiautomatic
Stock: Synthetic
Barrel: 10.5 in.–20 in.
Sights: None
Weight: 6 lb. 7 oz.–7 lb. 13 oz.
Caliber: 5.56 NATO
Magazine: Detachable box, 30 rounds
F*eatures*: Custom rifle stock; custom ergonomic rifle grip with aggressive texturing; forward placed, reversible/ambidextrous charging handle; gas piston system with multi-position regulator; free-floating barrel; ejection port dust wiper; two-piece keyed quad-rail system; tool-free field strip design
MSRP.................$2295.00

ADCOR ELITE
Action: Semiautomatic
Stock: Synthetic
Barrel: 16 in.
Sights: None
Weight: 10 lb.
Caliber: 7.62x39, .300 BLK

Magazine: 30 rounds
Features: Gas piston action, billet upper and lower, free-floating chrome-lined barrel and forward charging handle are standard. Choice of Quad or Key Mod rails; black, Flat Dark Earth, Olive Drab Green, or Patriot Brown
MSRP.................$2395.00

Advanced Armament Corp.

ADVANCED ARMAMENT CORP. MULTI PURPOSE WEAPON (MPW)

MULTI PURPOSE WEAPON (MPW)
Action: Semiautomatic
Stock: Magpul CTR
Barrel: 9 in., 12.5 in., 16 in.
Sights: None
Weight: N/A
Caliber: 7.62x35mm (.300 BLK)
Magazine: Detachable box, 30 rounds
Features: Bolt carrier features a proprietary design with a modified cam path and nickel-boron finish to enhance reliability and ease of cleaning; bolt machined from Carpenter 158 steel; freefloating forearm; lower receiver features a Geissele two-stage trigger; six-position Mil-Spec collapsing stock
MSRP................................$1599.95

American Spirit Arms

18" SIDE CHARGING RIFLE

18" SIDE CHARGING RIFLE
Action: Semiautomatic
Stock: Synthetic
Barrel: 18 in.
Sights: None
Weight: 8 lb. 13 oz.
Caliber: .556 NATO
Magazine: Detachable box
Features: Mil-Std 1913 rail; barrel threaded for flash suppressor; nitrided carrier; 12 in. Samson evolution rail; ergo grip; Choice of ASA 4 or 3 lb. single-stage trigger; A2 flash hider; VLTOR collapsible buttstock with Ergo grip. Optional flip-up sights, Samson bipod stud, and 15-in. Samson Evolution rail available.
MSRP................................$1499.99

American Tactical Imports

AMERICAN TACTICAL GSG MP-40 CARBINE

GSG MP-40
Action: Semiautomatic
Stock: Metal
Barrel: 17.2 in.
Sights: Fixed

Weight: 9 lb.
Caliber: .22 LR
Magazine: Detachable box, 10 or 23 rounds
Features: Bakelite support under the barrel; adjustable iron sights; simple safety features; all metal construction; blued finish
MSRP **$539.95**

**AMERICAN TACTICAL
OMNI HYBRID 5.56**

OMNI HYBRID 5.56
Action: Semiautomatic
Stock: Synthetic
Barrel: 16 in.
Sights: None
Weight: 7 lb.
Caliber: 5.56 NATO
Magazine: Detachable box, 10 or 30 rounds
Features: Picatinny rail; retractable stock
MSRP **$684.95**

OMNI HYBRID MAXX
Action: Semiautomatic
Stock: Synthetic
Barrel: 16 in.
Sights: None
Weight: 6 lb. 4 oz., 6 lb. 8 oz.
Caliber: .223 Rem./5.56 NATO, .22 LR, .300 BLK
Magazine: Detachable box, 30 round
Features: Retractable stock; metal-reinforced polymer lower and upper receiver; Picatinny rail
.22 LR **$494.95**
.223/5.56 NATO . . . . **$609.95–$729.95**
.300 BLK **$699.95**

AMERICAN TACTICAL OMNI HYBRID MAXX

Anschütz (J.G. Anschütz)

ANSCHÜTZ 1416 D HB CLASSIC

1416 D HB CLASSIC
Action: Bolt
Stock: Walnut
Barrel: 23 in.
Sights: None
Weight: 6 lb. 7 oz.
Caliber: .22 LR
Magazine: Detachable box, 5 rounds
Features: Heavy barrel; lacquered walnut wood stock (optional beavertail); pistol grip; black buttplate; studs for sling swivel; lateral sliding safety
MSRP **$1099.00**

Anschütz (J.G. Anschütz)

ANSCHÜTZ 1416 D HB THUMBHOLE

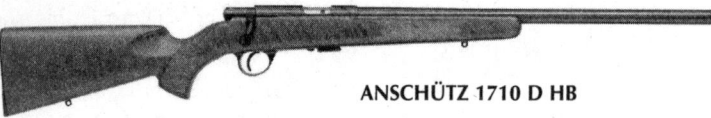

ANSCHÜTZ 1517 D HB

ANSCHÜTZ 1710 D HB

ANSCHÜTZ 1727F

ANSCHÜTZ 1771D GRS

1416 D HB THUMBHOLE
Action: Bolt
Stock: Walnut
Barrel: 23 in.
Sights: None
Weight: 6 lb. 7 oz.
Caliber: .22 LR
Magazine: Detachable box, 5 rounds
Features: Luxus repeating rifle; single-stage trigger; black buttplate; carved German checkering on the pistol grip; sling swivel studs; wave-style V-block dovetail rail for telescopic sight
MSRP $1599.99

1517 D HB, 1517 D HB BEAVERTAIL
Action: Bolt
Stock: Walnut, hardwood
Barrel: 22 in.
Sights: None
Weight: 6 lb.–6 lb. 6 oz.
Caliber: .17 HMR
Magazine: Detachable box, 4 rounds
Features: Single- or two-stage adjustable trigger; optional beavertail stock
Classic stock $1249.00
Beavertail $1199.00

1710 D HB
Action: Bolt
Stock: Walnut
Barrel: 23 in.
Sights: Open
Weight: 7 lb. 11 oz.
Caliber: .22 LR
Magazine: Detachable box, 5 rounds
Features: Drilled and tapped for scope mounts; sliding safety catch; two-stage or single-stage trigger; adjustable folding leaf sights and pear front adjustable ramp; Meistergrade has engraved forestock and trigger guard; black plastic buttplate
MSRP: $2089.00

1727F
Action: Bolt
Stock: Walnut German stock
Barrel: 18 in., 22 in.

Sights: None
Weight: 7 lb. 11 oz.
Caliber: .17 HMR, .22 LR
Magazine: Internal, 4 rounds
Features: Unique straight-pull bolt combines with traditional German-shaped stock in walnut; .22 LR is available in both barrel lengths, .17 HMR in 22-in only; 18-in. .22 LR features a threaded, tapered heavy weight barrel, 22-in. .22LR available left-hand.
.22 LR 18 in.: $3595.00
.22 LR 23 in.: $3495.00
.17 HMR: $3495.00

1770D
Action: Bolt
Stock: Walnut
Barrel: 22 in.
Sights: Drilled and tapped for scopes
Weight: 7 lb. 7 oz.
Caliber: .223 Rem.

Magazine: Detachable, 3-shot, in-line
Features: Six locking lug action for strength and reliability; adjustable, single-stage match trigger; hand checkered stock with oval cheekpiece and rubber buttpad; detachable sling swivel studs
MSRP $2595.00

1771D GRS
Action: Bolt
Stock: Laminated birch
Barrel: 22 in.
Sights: None
Weight: 8 lb. 6 oz.
Caliber: .204 Ruger, .222 Rem., .223 Rem., .300 BLK
Magazine: Detachable box, 4 rounds
Features: Butt plate speed lock adjustment; GRS-rubber butt plate; cheek piece speed lock adjustment; ergonomical and gripping forend; precision barrel
MSRP $2899.00

Anschütz (J.G. Anschütz)

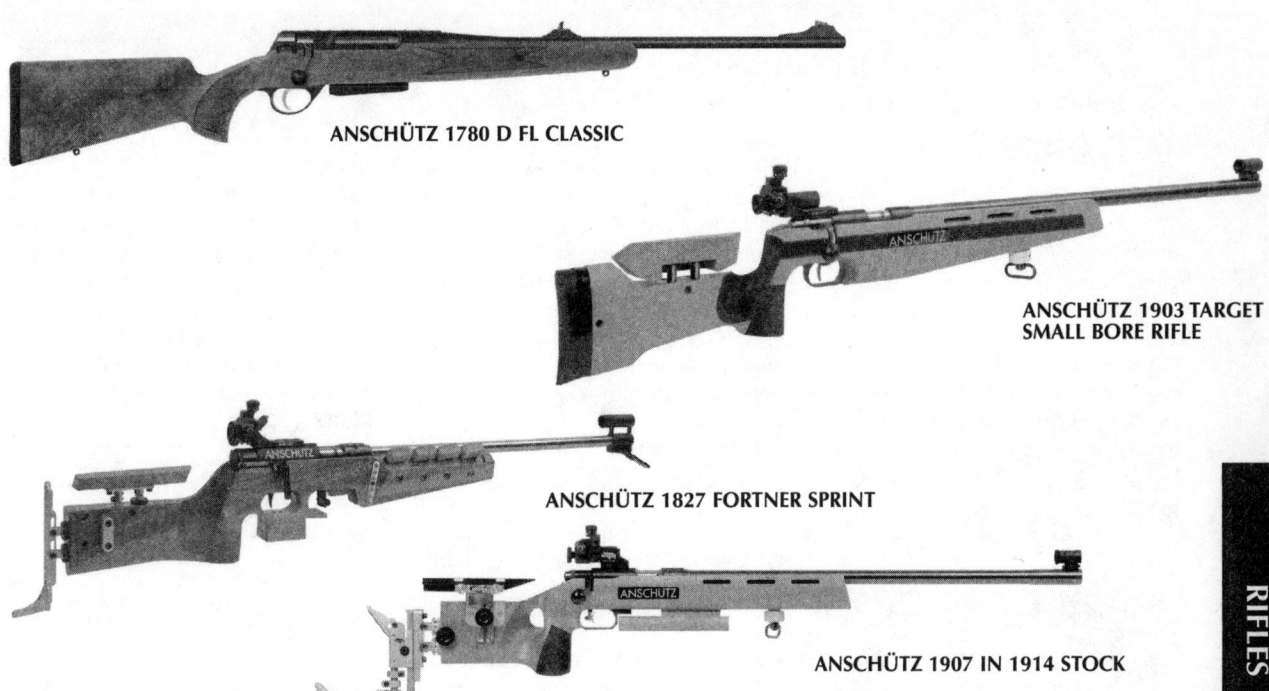

ANSCHÜTZ 1780 D FL CLASSIC

ANSCHÜTZ 1903 TARGET SMALL BORE RIFLE

ANSCHÜTZ 1827 FORTNER SPRINT

ANSCHÜTZ 1907 IN 1914 STOCK

ANSCHÜTZ 2013/690 WITH 2018 PRECISE STOCK

1780 D FL CLASSIC

Action: Bolt
Stock: Walnut
Barrel: 23 in.
Sights: Drilled and tapped for scopes
Weight: 7 lb. 2 oz.
Caliber: .308 Win., .30-06 Spfd., 8x57 IS, 9.3x62 Mauser
Magazine: Detachable box, 5 rounds
Features: Single-stage trigger; fast acquisition sight; sliding safety catch; available in a variety of stock options, including wood Monte Carlo, German, thumbhole and classic stocks, and classic stocks in soft grip wood orange camo, wood green camo, and black
MSRP: $3495.00

1827 FORTNER SPRINT

Action: Bolt
Stock: Biathlon, walnut
Barrel: 22 in.

Sights: None
Weight: 8 lb. 2 oz.
Caliber: .22 LR
Magazine: Detachable box, 5 rounds
Features: Combination of an extra light 1827 Fortner barreled action with the stock of the 1827 model; lacquered walnut stock with stippled checkering; heavy, cylindrical match barrel; match stage two or single trigger
MSRP. $3495.00

1903 TARGET SMALL BORE RIFLE

Action: Bolt
Stock: Hardwood
Barrel: 26 in., heavy
Sights: None
Weight: 9 lb. 11 oz.
Caliber: .22 LR
Magazine: None
Features: A match rifle for small bore shooters; anatomically perfect walnut

stock with vertically adjustable cheek piece; optional aluminum, hook, or rubber buttplate; aluminum accessories rail
Right-hand $1275.00
Left-hand $1335.00

1907 IN 1914 STOCK

Action: Bolt
Stock: Walnut
Barrel: 32.28 in.
Sights: None
Weight: 10 lb. 12 oz.
Caliber: .22 LR
Magazine: None
Features: Match 54 action; heavy, cylindrical barrel; match two-stage or single-stage trigger; safety signal pin
MSRP. $3149.00

2013/690 WITH 2018 PRECISE STOCK

Action: Bolt
Stock: Aluminum
Barrel: 32 in., 33 in.
Sights: None
Weight: 13 lb., 13 lb. 10 oz.
Caliber: .22 LR
Magazine: None
Features: Single loader; two-stage trigger; optional buttplate; new backend offers large range of adjustment for small shooters
MSRP. $4295.00

Anschütz (J.G. Anschütz)

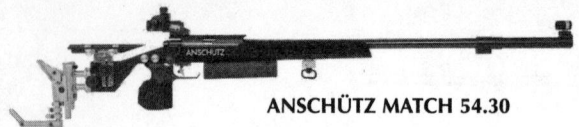

ANSCHÜTZ MATCH 54.30

ANSCHÜTZ MSR RX 22 BLACKHAWK

MATCH 54.30

Action: Barreled
Stock: Aluminum or walnut
Barrel: 26 in.
Sights: None
Weight: 11 lb. 3 oz.
Caliber: .22 LR
Magazine: 8 rounds
Features: Improved ergonomics; reduced weight of firing pin for increase in velocity and shorter lock time; newly designed target chamber for better accuracy; threaded receiver and barrel connection; available in aluminum or walnut stock
MSRP . . . . $3490.00–$4160.00

MSR RX 22 BLACKHAWK

Action: Semiautomatic
Stock: Laminated wood, plastic
Barrel: 16.5 in.
Sights: None
Weight: 7 lb.
Caliber: .22 LR
Magazine: Detachable box, 10 rounds
Features: Folding stock; aluminum grooved Picatinny rail for accessories; six possible positions for cocking lever; optional buttplate and sight set; black, desert, aluminum colors available
MSRP $699.99

ArmaLite

ARMALITE AR-10 COMPETITION RIFLE

ARMALITE AR-10 A-SERIES DEFENSIVE SPORTING RIFLE

ARMALITE AR-10 SUPER SASS

AR-10 A-SERIES DEFENSIVE SPORTING RIFLE

Action: Semiautomatic
Stock: Synthetic
Barrel: 13 in., 16 in.
Sights: Front
Weight: 7 lb. 14 oz.
Caliber: 7.62 NATO, .308 Win.
Magazine: 10, 20 rounds
Features: No-frills rifle built for sporting or defensive use; mid-length gas system, six-position collapsible stock, forged flat top with Mil-Std 1913 rail, 7075 forged aluminum lower and receiver, standard charging handle, single-stage trigger are standard; supplied with one 20-round Magpul Pmag; Colorado-compliant version comes with 10-round Magpul Pmag
MSRP $1099.00

AR-10A SUPER SASS

Action: Semiautomatic
Stock: Synthetic
Barrel: 20 in.
Sights: Adjustable front
Weight: 11 lb. 13 oz.
Caliber: 7.62 NATO, .308 Win.
Magazine: Detachable box, 20 rounds
Features: Functionally identical to the AR-10B family, the AR-10A family is designed to accept early ArmaLite AR-10 "Waffle" magazines and good quality magazines copied from them, including Magpul PMAG 20LR, Knight's Armament, and DPMS; adjustable gas block front sight; black synthetic stock; sling, hard case, and sling swivel mounts included
MSRP $3099.00

AR-10 COMPETITION RIFLE

Action: Semiautomatic
Stock: Synthetic
Barrel: 18 in.
Sights: None
Weight: 8 lb. 3 oz.–8 lb. 14 oz.
Caliber: .308 Win./7.62 NATO
Magazine: Detachable box, 25 rounds
Features: Picatinny rail; Armalite tunable brake pinned and welded; 12-in. free-floating handguard; stock adjustable for length-of-pull and comb height; ambidextrous safety and charging handle
MSRP $2199.00

RIFLES

ArmaLite

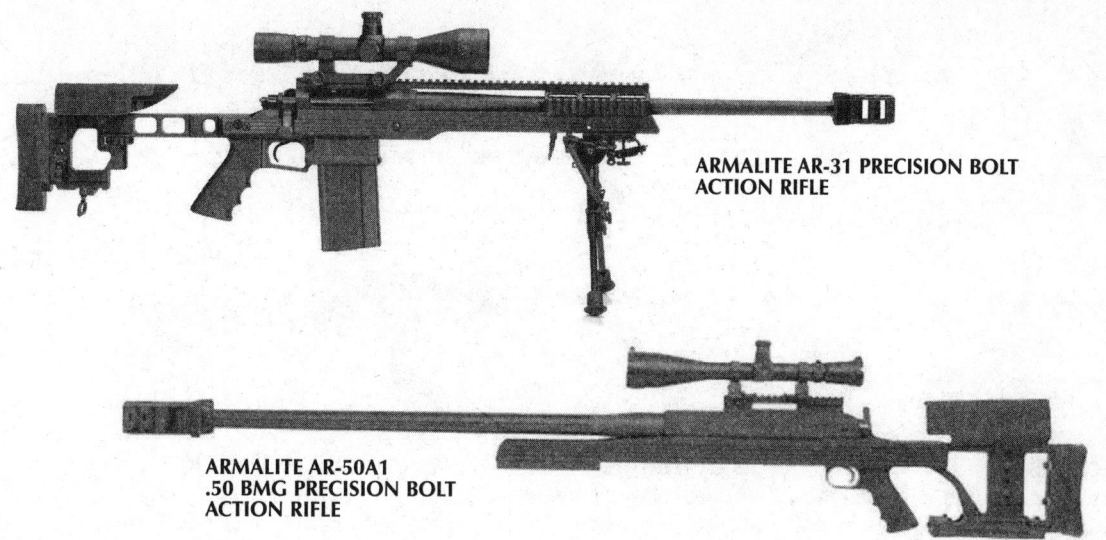

ARMALITE AR-31 PRECISION BOLT ACTION RIFLE

ARMALITE AR-50A1 .50 BMG PRECISION BOLT ACTION RIFLE

AR-31 PRECISION BOLT ACTION RIFLE

Action: Bolt
Stock: Synthetic
Barrel: 24 in.
Sights: None
Weight: 14 lb.
Caliber: .308 Win.
Magazine: Detachable box, 10 rounds

Features: Can use 5, 10, 15, 20, and 25 round magazines
MSRP . Call manufacturer for pricing

AR-50A1 .50 BMG PRECISION BOLT ACTION RIFLE

Action: Bolt
Stock: Synthetic
Barrel: 33 in.
Sights: None
Weight: 33 lb. 3 oz.
Caliber: .50 BMG
Magazine: None
Features: Chromoly barrel; muzzle-brake; 15 minute rail; single-stage trigger
MSRP . Call manufacturer for pricing

Arsenal, Inc.

ARSENAL, INC. SAM7R

SAM7UF

Action: Semiautomatic
Stock: Metal underfolding
Barrel: 16.25 in.
Sights: Adjustable
Weight: 7 lb. 8 oz.
Caliber: 7.62x39 Warsaw
Magazine: Detachable box, 10 rounds
Features: Milled and forged receiver; chrome lined hammer forged barrel; muzzle nut, bayonet/accessory lug; reinforced underfolding buttstock; black polymer pistol grip and hand-guards; stainless steel heat shield
MSRP $1299.00

SAM7R

Action: Semiautomatic
Stock: Polymer
Barrel: 16.25 in.
Sights: Scope rail
Weight: 8 lb.
Caliber: 7.62x39 Warsaw
Magazine: Detachable box, 10 rounds
Features: Milled receiver; chrome-lined, hammer-forged barrel; muzzle brake; cleaning rod; intermediate length US-made 10 in. trapdoor butt-stock
MSRP $1299.00

ARSENAL, INC. SAM7UF

Arsenal, Inc.

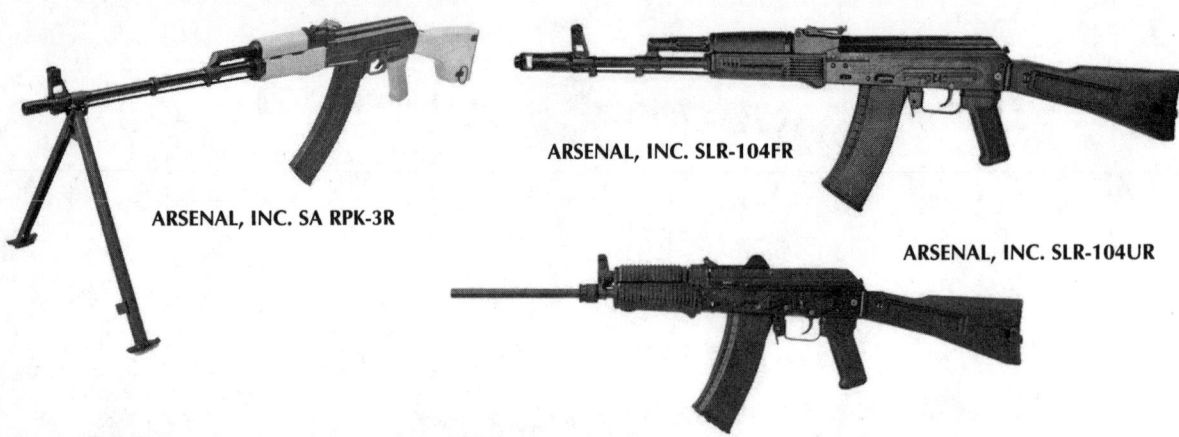

ARSENAL, INC. SA RPK-3R

ARSENAL, INC. SLR-104FR

ARSENAL, INC. SLR-104UR

SA RPK-3R
Action: Gas-operated semiautomatic
Stock: Black polymer or blond wood
Barrel: 23.2 in.
Sights: Open
Weight: 10 lb. 8 oz.
Caliber: 5.45x39 Warsaw
Magazine: Detachable box, 45 rounds
Features: RPK heavy barrel; milled receiver; U.S.-made; paddle style buttstock and scope rail; includes sling, oil bottle, and cleaning kit
MSRP. **$2500.00**

SLR-104FR
Action: Semiautomatic
Stock: Synthetic
Barrel: 16.25 in.
Sights: Adjustable
Weight: 6 lb. 2 oz.
Caliber: 5.45x39 Warsaw
Magazine: Detachable box, 30 rounds
Features: Left-sided folding stock; muzzle brake; bayonet and accessory lugs; scrope rail; sling; two-stage trigger; available in 5.56 NATO and 7.62x39 Warsaw
MSRP. **$1099.00**

SLR-104UR
Action: Semiautomatic
Stock: Synthetic
Barrel: 16.25 in.
Sights: Fixed
Weight: 6 lb.
Caliber: 5.45x39 Warsaw
Magazine: Detachable box, 30 rounds
Features: Stamped receiver; short gas system; front sight block/gas block combination; black polymer furniture; stainless steel heat shield; left-side folding polymer stock; two stage trigger; scope rail
MSRP. **$1299.00**

Auto-Ordnance

AUTO-ORDNANCE AOM150

AUTO-ORDNANCE
M1SB THOMPSON
M1 SBR

AOM150
Action: Semiautomatic
Stock: Walnut; handguard
Barrel: 18 in.
Sights: Blade front; flip style rear
Weight: 5 lb. 6 oz.
Caliber: .30
Magazine: Detachable stick, 15 rounds

Features: Folding stock; Parkerized finish
MSRP. **$941.00**

M1SB THOMPSON M1 SBR
Action: Semiautomatic
Stock: Walnut, vertical foregrip
Barrel: 10.5 in.

Sights: Blade front, fixed battle rear
Weight: 10 lb. 8 oz.
Caliber: .45 ACP
Magazine: Detachable stick, 30 rounds
Features: Will not accept drum magazines; frame and receiver made from solid steel
MSRP. **$2027.00**

Auto-Ordnance

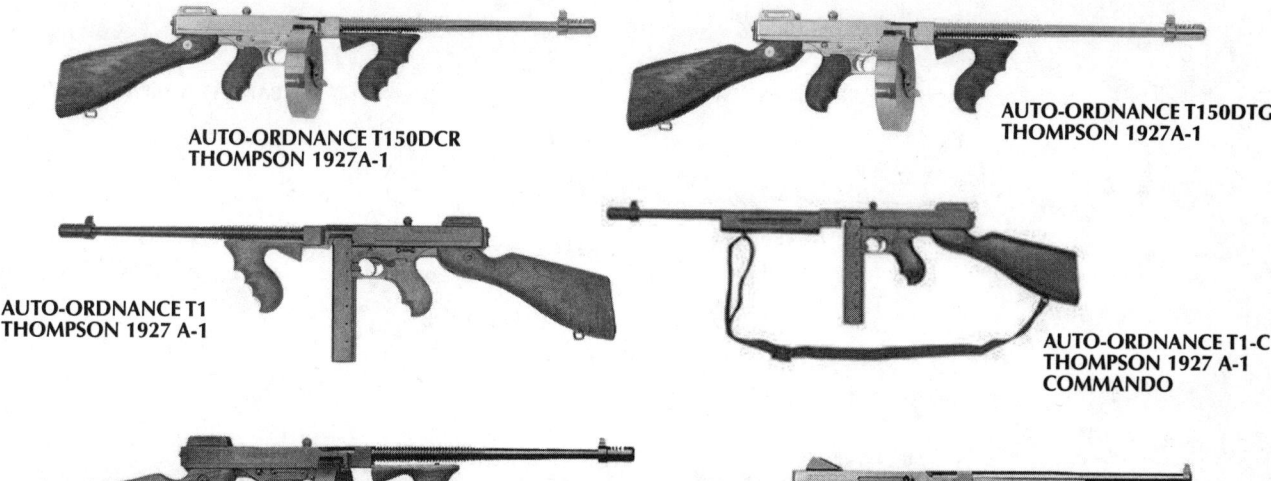

AUTO-ORDNANCE T150DCR
THOMPSON 1927A-1

AUTO-ORDNANCE T150DTG
THOMPSON 1927A-1

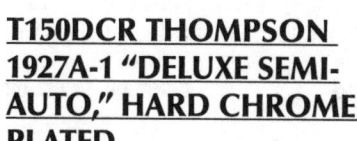

AUTO-ORDNANCE T1
THOMPSON 1927 A-1

AUTO-ORDNANCE T1-C
THOMPSON 1927 A-1
COMMANDO

AUTO-ORDNANCE T1SB THOMPSON
1927 A-1 SBR SHORT BARREL RIFLE

AUTO-ORDNANCE TM1
THOMPSON M1 CARBINE

T150DCR THOMPSON 1927A-1 "DELUXE SEMI-AUTO," HARD CHROME PLATED

Action: Semiautomatic
Stock: Walnut
Barrel: 16.5 in.
Sights: Blade front, open rear adjustable
Weight: 13 lb.
Caliber: .45 ACP
Magazine: One each round 50 drum and 20 stick magazines
Features: Finned barrel; fixed stock with vertical foregrip
MSRP **$2963.00**

T150DTG THOMPSON 1927A-1 "DELUXE SEMI-AUTO," TITANIUM GOLD PLATED

Action: Semiautomatic
Stock: Walnut
Barrel: 16.5 in.
Sights: Blade front, open rear adjustable
Weight: 13 lb.
Caliber: .45 ACP
Magazine: One each round 50 drum and 20 stick magazines
Features: Finned barrel; fixed stock with vertical foregrip
MSRP **$2963.00**

T1 THOMPSON 1927 A-1

Action: Semiautomatic
Stock: Walnut, vertical foregrip
Barrel: 16.5 in.
Sights: Blade front, open rear adjustable
Weight: 13 lb.
Caliber: .45 ACP
Magazine: Detachable stick, 30 rounds
Features: Frame and receiver made from solid steel; compensator; optional 50-round drum magazine
MSRP **$1461.00**

T1-C THOMPSON 1927 A-1 COMMANDO

Action: Semiautomatic
Stock: Black finish stock and forend
Barrel: 16.5 in.
Sights: Blade front, open rear adjustable
Weight: 13 lb.
Caliber: .45 ACP
Magazine: Detachable stick, 30 rounds
Features: Frame and receiver made from solid steel; compensator; black nylon sling
MSRP **$1393.00**

T1SB THOMPSON 1927 A-1 SBR SHORT BARREL RIFLE

Action: Semiautomatic
Stock: Walnut, vertical foregrip

Barrel: 10.5 in.
Sights: Blade front, open rear adjustable
Weight: 12 lb.
Caliber: .45 ACP
Magazine: Detachable stick, 30 rounds
Features: Frame and receiver made from solid steel; blued steel finish
MSRP **$2114.00**
Detachable butt stock: . . . **$2630.00**

TM1 THOMPSON M1

Action: Semiautomatic
Stock: Walnut, vertical foregrip
Barrel: 16.5 in.
Sights: Blade front, fixed battle rear
Weight: 8 lb., 11 lb. 8 oz.
Caliber: .45 ACP
Magazine: Detachable stick, 30 rounds
Features: Side bolt action; frame and receiver made from solid steel; lightweight model features a frame and receiver made from solid aluminum
MSRP **$1329.00**

Barrett

BARRETT 82A1

BARRETT M107A1

BARRETT 95

BARRETT 98B

BARRETT 99

BARRETT MRAD

BARRETT REC7 GEN II

MODEL 82A1

Action: Semiautomatic
Stock: Synthetic
Barrel: 20 in., 29 in.
Sights: Flip-up iron sights or Leupold scope
Weight: 30 lb. 14 oz.
Caliber: .416, .50 BMG
Magazine: Detachable box, 10 rounds
Features: Pelican case; detachable adjustable bipod legs; cleaning kit; carry handle; muzzlebrake; Picatinny rail; chrome-lined barrel
MSRP . . . . $9119.00–$9323.00

M107A1

Action: Semiautomatic
Stock: Synthetic
Barrel: 20 in., 29 in.
Sights: Flip-up iron sights
Weight: 30 lb. 14 oz.
Caliber: .50 BMG
Magazine: Detachable box, 10 rounds
Features: Chrome-lined barrel, Flat Dark Earth stock finish; suppressor-ready muzzlebrake; pelican case; M1913 optics rail; detachable adjustable lightweight bipod legs; lightweight monopod
MSRP $12281.00

MODEL 95

Action: Semiautomatic
Stock: Synthetic
Barrel: 29 in.

Sights: Flip-up iron sights
Weight: 25 lb.
Caliber: .50 BMG
Magazine: Detachable box, 5 rounds
Features: Pelican case; detachable adjustable bipod legs; cleaning kit; Picatinny rail
MSRP $6671.00

MODEL 98B TACTICAL, 98B LIGHTWEIGHT

Action: Bolt
Stock: Synthetic
Barrel: 16 in., 18 in., 22 in., 24 in.
Sights: None
Weight: 9 lb. 4 oz.–13 lb. 8 oz.
Caliber: .308 Win., .300 Win. Mag. .338 Lapua (Tactical); 6.5 Creedmoor, .260 Rem., .308 Win., 7mm Rem. Mag., .300 Win. Mag., .338 Lapua (Lightweight)
Magazine: Detachable box, 10 rounds
Features: Ergonomic pistol grip; muzzlebrake; heavy or fluted barrel; Harris bipod; monopod; cleaning kit; side accessory rail; air/watertight hard case; black stock
Tactical: . . . . $4419.00–$4699.00
Lightweight: . . . . $4113.00–$4499.00

MODEL 99

Action: Bolt
Stock: Synthetic
Barrel: 29 in., 32 in.
Sights: None
Weight: 25 lb.
Caliber: .416 Barrett, .50 BMG

Magazine: None
Features: Picatinny rail; pelican case; detachable adjustable bipod; cleaning kit
MSRP . . . . $3967.00–$4222.00

MRAD

Action: Bolt action repeater
Stock: Synthetic
Barrel: 17 in.–22 in.
Sights: None
Weight: 14 lb. 13 oz.
Caliber: .300 Win. Mag., .308 Win. Mag., .338 Lapua Mag.
Magazine: Detachable box, 10 rounds
Features: Fluted or heavy barrel; multi-role brown finish stock; folding stock; adjustable cheekpiece and butt-plate; includes two 10-round magazines, two sling loops, and three adjustable accessory rails
MSRP . . . . $6000.00–$6975.00

REC7 GEN II

Action: Semiautomatic
Stock: Synthetic
Barrel: 9.25 in.–18 in.
Sights: Adjustable
Weight: 6 lb.–7 lb. 3 oz.
Caliber: 5.56 NATO, 6.8 SPC
Magazine: Detachable box, 30 rounds
Features: Forged 7075 aluminum upper and lower receivers are Type 3 hard-coat anodized; free-floated, hammer-forged, chrome-lined barrel with M4 feed ramps machined into the receiver and the barrel extension; mil-spec A2 flash hider protects the muzzle
MSRP . . . . $2199.00–$2799.00

Benelli USA

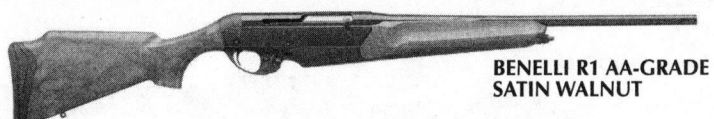

BENELLI R1 AA-GRADE SATIN WALNUT

R1
Action: Semiautomatic
Stock: AA-grade satin walnut, synthetic or Realtree APG

Barrel: 22 in., 24 in.
Sights: None
Weight: 7 lb. 2 oz.–7 lb. 5 oz.
Caliber: .30-06 Spfd., .300 Win. Mag., .338 Win. Mag.

Magazine: Detachable box, 3+1 or 4+1 rounds
Features: Picatinny rail; synthetic and APG finish come with GripTight coating; raised comb; auto-regulating gas-operated system
Walnut: **$1019.00**
ComforTech: ... **$1139.00–$1249.00**

Beretta USA

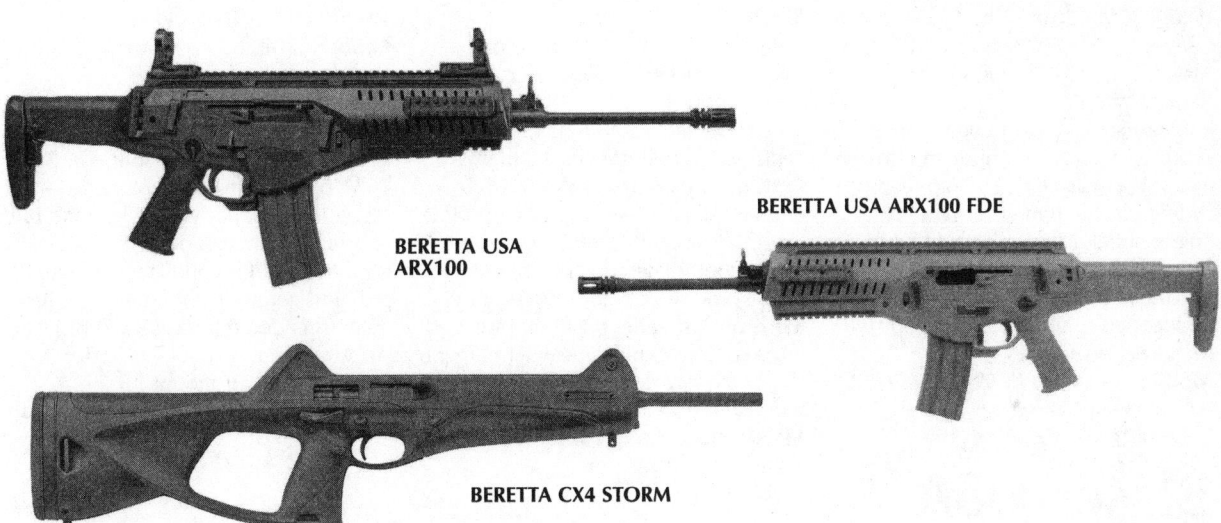

BERETTA USA ARX100

BERETTA USA ARX100 FDE

BERETTA CX4 STORM

ARX100
Action: Semiautomatic
Stock: Telescopic folding
Barrel: 12 in., 16 in.
Sights: Removable back-up sights
Weight: 6 lb. 13 oz.
Caliber: 5.56 NATO (other barrels available)
Magazine: Detachable box, 30 rounds
Features: Cold hammer forged barrel can be replaced with barrels in different lengths and calibers; case ejection switches from right to left at a button push; completely ambidextrous; technopolymer receiver; contains no pins and can be disassembled without the use of tools; optional .300 Black Out kit available
MSRP **$1950.00**

ARX100 FDE
Action: Semiautomatic
Stock: Synthetic
Barrel: 16 in.
Sights: Folding backup sights
Weight: 6 lb. 13 oz.
Caliber: 5.56x45
Magazine: 30 rounds
Features: Telescopic folding stock; ambidextrous charging handle, AR15-style two-position safety, and magazine releases; full-length Picatinny rail; quick-change barrel
MSRP **$1950.00**

CX4 STORM
Action: Single-action
Stock: Synthetic
Barrel: 16.6 in.
Sights: Front sight post
Weight: 5 lb. 12 oz.
Caliber: 9mm, .40 S&W, .45 ACP
Magazine: Detachable box, 10, 15, 17, 20 (9mm); 10, 11, 12, 14, 17 (40 S&W); 8 (.45 ACP) rounds
Features: Picatinny rail; allows for reverse ejection and extraction; ideal for left-handed shooters; adjustable length-of-pull; easy to accessorize
MSRP ....**$800.00–$915.00**

Bergara

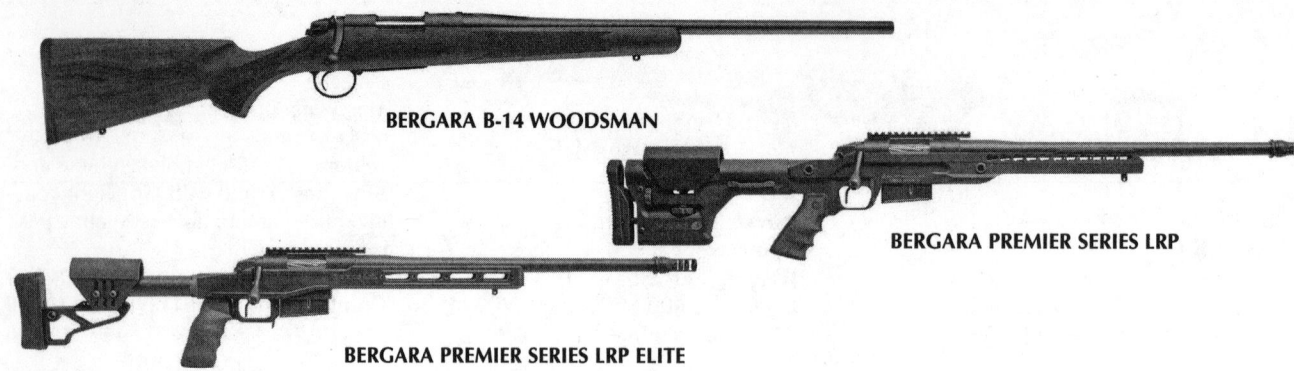

BERGARA B-14 WOODSMAN

BERGARA PREMIER SERIES LRP

BERGARA PREMIER SERIES LRP ELITE

B-14 WOODSMAN
Action: Bolt
Stock: Walnut
Barrel: 22 in., 24 in.
Sights: None
Weight: 7 lb. 2 oz.–7 lb. 6 oz.
Caliber: .270, .30-06 Spfd., .300 Win. Mag., .308, 6.5 Creedmoor, 7mm Rem., Mag.
Magazine: Detachable box
Features: Coned bolt nose and breech ensuring consistently smooth feeding; sliding plate extractor for proper alignment; stocks are bedded with integral pillars for stability and enhanced accuracy; factory drilled and tapped to fit Remington 700 style rings and bases.
MSRP . . . . $945.00–$975.00

PREMIER SERIES LRP
Action: Bolt
Stock: Aluminum chassis
Barrel: 20 in., 22 in., 24 in.
Sights: None
Weight: 9 lb. 13 oz.–10 lb. 6 oz.
Caliber: .308, 6.5 Creedmoor, 6mm Creedmoor
Magazine: Detachable box, 5 rounds
Features: Aluminum chassis that is CNC machined from solid 6061 T6 aluminum; AR15-style grip; adjustable length of pull; adjustable comb height; butt plate can be canted to give a precise fit to the shooter in virtually any shooting position; threaded muzzle (5/8X24); Dead Air Armament Key Lock muzzle brake/suppressor mount
MSRP . . . . $2000.00 and up

PREMIER SERIES LRP ELITE
Action: Bolt
Stock: Aluminum chassis
Barrel: 20 in., 22 in., 24 in.
Sights: None
Weight: 10 lb. 8 oz.–11 lb. 2 oz.
Caliber: .308, 6.5 Creedmoor, 6mm Creedmoor
Magazine: Detachable box, 5 rounds
Features: Aluminum chassis stock that is CNC machined from solid 7075-T651 billet aluminum; self-adjusting recoil lug locking system; keymod rail sections for accessories; AR15-style grip; Magpul PRS butt stock; length of pull and comb height are fully adjustable; threaded muzzle (5/8X24); Dead Air Armament Key Lock muzzle brake/suppressor mount
MSRP . . . . $2850.00 and up

Blaser USA

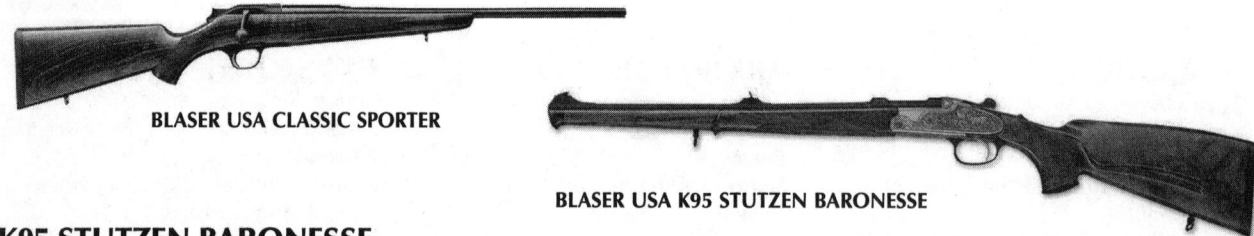

BLASER USA CLASSIC SPORTER

BLASER USA K95 STUTZEN BARONESSE

K95 STUTZEN BARONESSE
Action: Single shot
Stock: Walnut
Barrel: 19.75 in.
Sights: None
Weight: 5 lb. 11 oz.
Caliber: .222 Rem., 5.6R Mag., .243 Win., 6.5x57R, 7x57 R, .308 Win., .30-06 Spfd., 8x57 IRS
Magazine: None
Features: Octagonal barrel standard, barrels are interchangeable; available from grade Lexus; split forearm for continuous precision even in extreme weather; black forearm tip; range of ornamentation and game engravings
MSRP $2066.00

R8 CLASSIC SPORTER
Action: Bolt
Stock: Turkish walnut
Barrel: Variable
Sights: None
Weight: Variable
Caliber: Variable
Magazine: Variable
Features: Manual cocking bolt; interchangeable caliber system; trigger magazine housing combination; Prince of Wales grip
MSRP $4699.00

BLASER R8 JAEGER

BLASER R8 PROFESSIONAL

BLASER R8 PROFESSIONAL SUCCESS

R8 JAEGER

Action: Straight-pull bolt-action
Stock: Walnut, pistol grip
Barrel: 20.5 in., 23 in., 25.75 in.
Sights: None
Weight: 6 lb. 6 oz.
Caliber: .222 Rem. to .338 Win. Mag.
Magazine: Detachable box, 3 rounds with lock
Features: Cold-hammer-forged barrels and chambers; black forearm tip; synthetic stock in dark green or walnut, straight comb; manual cocking system; integrated trigger/magazine unit; original Blaser saddle mount
MSRP. $4386.00

R8 PROFESSIONAL

Action: Straight-pull bolt-action
Stock: Matte dark green synthetic stock, pistol grip
Barrel: 20.5 in., 23 in., 25.75 in.
Sights: None
Weight: 6 lb. 6 oz.
Caliber: .222 Rem. to .338 Win. Mag.
Magazine: Detachable box, 3 rounds with lock
Features: Shatter-proof, synthetic dark green stock; detachable magazine/trigger unit; single-stage trigger; quick-release scope mount; ergonomically optimized pistol grip; kickstop optional; precision trigger; black forearm tip; integrated receiver
MSRP. $3787.00

R8 PROFESSIONAL SUCCESS

Action: Bolt
Stock: Synthetic
Barrel: 22.8 in., 25.6 in.
Sights: Open
Weight: 7 lb.
Caliber: .222 Rem., .204 Ruger, .223 Rem., .22–250 Rem., .243 Win., 6XC, 6.5x55 Swedish, 6.5x57, 6.5x65 RWS, .270 Win., 7x64 Brenneke, .308 Win., .30-06 Spfd., 8x57 IS, 8.5x63, 9.3x57, 9.3x62 Mauser, 6.5x68, 7.5x55 Suisse, 8x68 S, .257 Wby. Mag., .270 Wby. Mag., .270 WSM, 7mm Blaser Mag., 7mm Rem. Mag., .300 Blaser Mag., .300 Win. Mag., .300 Wby. Mag., .300 WSM, .338 Blaser Mag., .338 Win. Mag., .375 Blaser Mag., .375 H&H
Magazine: 3+1, 4+1, 5+1 rounds
Features: Blaser precision trigger; radial locking system; ergonomically optimized stock in dark green or dark brown and elastomer grips; double loading option; leather model available
MSRP. $4337.00

Browning

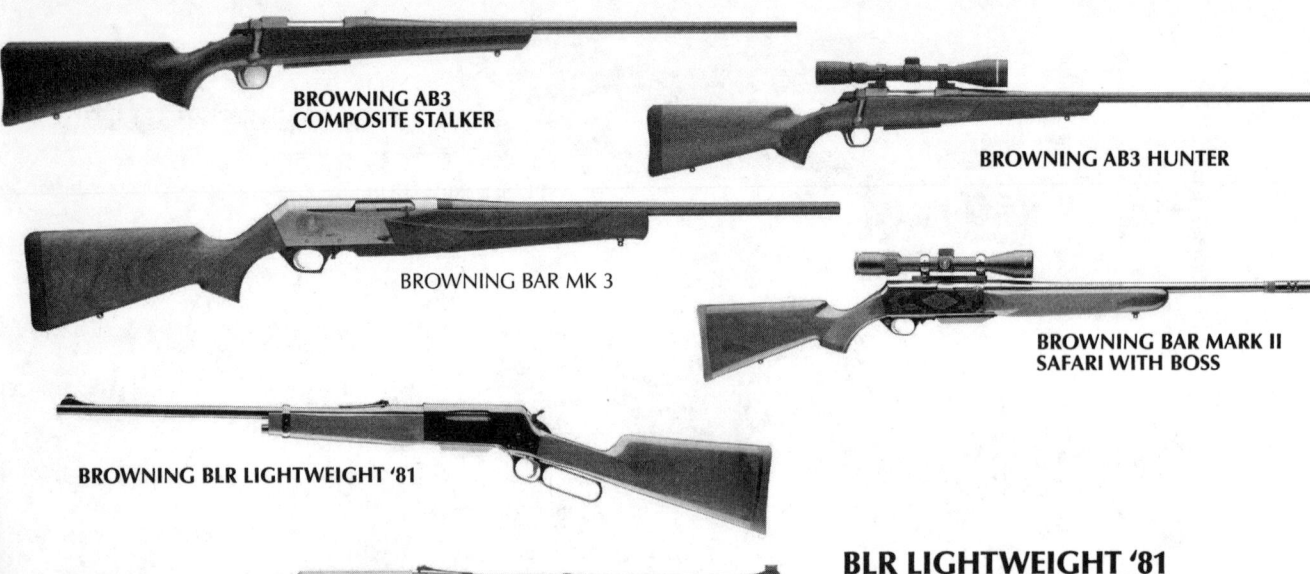

BROWNING AB3 COMPOSITE STALKER

BROWNING AB3 HUNTER

BROWNING BAR MK 3

BROWNING BAR MARK II SAFARI WITH BOSS

BROWNING BLR LIGHTWEIGHT '81

BROWNING BLR LIGHTWEIGHT '81 STAINLESS TAKEDOWN

AB3 COMPOSITE STALKER

Action: Bolt
Stock: Synthetic
Barrel: 22 in., 26 in.
Sights: None
Weight: 6 lb. 9 oz.–7 lb. 3 oz.
Caliber: .243 Win., .270 Win., .270 WSM, .30-06 Spfd., .300 Win. Mag., .300 WSM, .308 Win., 6.5 Creedmoor, 7mm Rem. Mag., 7mm-08 Rem.
Magazine: Detachable box, 4 rounds
Features: Inflex Technology recoil pad; top tang safety; blued barrel and action
MSRP **$599.99**

AB3 HUNTER

Action: Bolt
Stock: Satin
Barrel: 22 in.
Sights: Drilled and tapped for sights
Weight: 6 lb. 11 oz.–7 lb. 6 oz.
Caliber: .243 Win., .270 Win., .270 WSM, .30-06 Spfd., .300 Win. Mag., .300 WSM, .308 Win., 6.5 Creedmoor, 7mm Rem. Mag., 7mm-08 Rem.
Magazine: Detachable box
Features: 5-round mag capacity; steel barrel; polished finish
MSRP **$669.99**

BAR MARK II SAFARI WITH BOSS

Action: Gas-operated semiautomatic
Stock: Walnut
Barrel: 22 in., 24 in.
Sights: None
Weight: 8 lb. 1.6 oz.–8 lb. 3 oz.
Caliber: .270 Win., .30-06 Spfd., .300 Win. Mag., .338 Win. Mag.
Magazine: Detachable box
Features: Checkered, select gloss finish walnut stock; steel receiver with blued finish and scroll engraving; drilled and tapped for scope mounts; multi-lug rotary bolt; recoil pad sling swivel studs installed
MSRP . . . . **$1389.00–$1499.99**

BAR MK 3

Action: Semiautomatic
Stock: Walnut
Barrel: 22 in., 23 in., 24 in.
Sights: None
Weight: 7 lb. 2 oz.–7 lb. 11 oz.
Caliber: .243 Win., .270 Win., .270 WSM, .30-06 Spfd., .300 Win. Mag., .300 WSM, .308 Win., 7mm Rem. Mag., 7mm-08 Rem.
Magazine: Detachable rotary, 3 or 4 rounds
Features: Completely new styling; fine oil-finished walnut; precision alloy receiver; hammer-forged barrel; drilled and tapped for scope; gold trigger guard engraving
MSRP . . . . **$1239.99–$1339.99**

BLR LIGHTWEIGHT '81

Action: Lever
Stock: Walnut, straight grip
Barrel: 20 in., 22 in., 24 in.
Sights: None
Weight: 6 lb. 8 oz.–7 lb. 12 oz.
Caliber: .22-250 Rem., .223 Rem., .243 Win., .270 Win., .270 WSM, .30-06 Spfd., .300 Win. Mag., .300 WSM, .308 Win., .325 WSM, .358 Win., .450 Mar, 7mm Rem. Mag., 7mm WSM, 7mm-08 Rem.
Magazine: Detachable box
Features: Aircraft-grade alloy receiver; drilled and tapped for scope mounts; crowned muzzle; adjustable sights; gloss finish walnut stock; recoil pad
MSRP . . . . **$959.99–$1039.99**

BLR LIGHTWEIGHT '81 STAINLESS TAKEDOWN

Action: Lever-action
Stock: Laminate, straight grip
Barrel: 20 in., 22 in., 24 in.
Sights: Open
Weight: 6 lb. 8 oz.–7 lb. 12 oz.
Caliber: .223 Rem., .22-250 Rem., .243 Win., 7mm-08 Rem., .308 Win., .358 Win., .270 Win., .30-06 Spfd., 7mm Rem. Mag., .300 WSM, .270 WSM, .450 Marlin
Magazine: Detachable box
Features: Aircraft-grade alloy receiver; drilled and tapped for scope mounts; stainless steel barrel with matte finish; gray laminate wood stock in satin finish; recoil pad; separates for storage or transportation; optional Scout-style scope mount; TRUGLO/Marble's fiber optic front sight
MSRP . . . . **$1229.99–$1279.99**

RIFLES

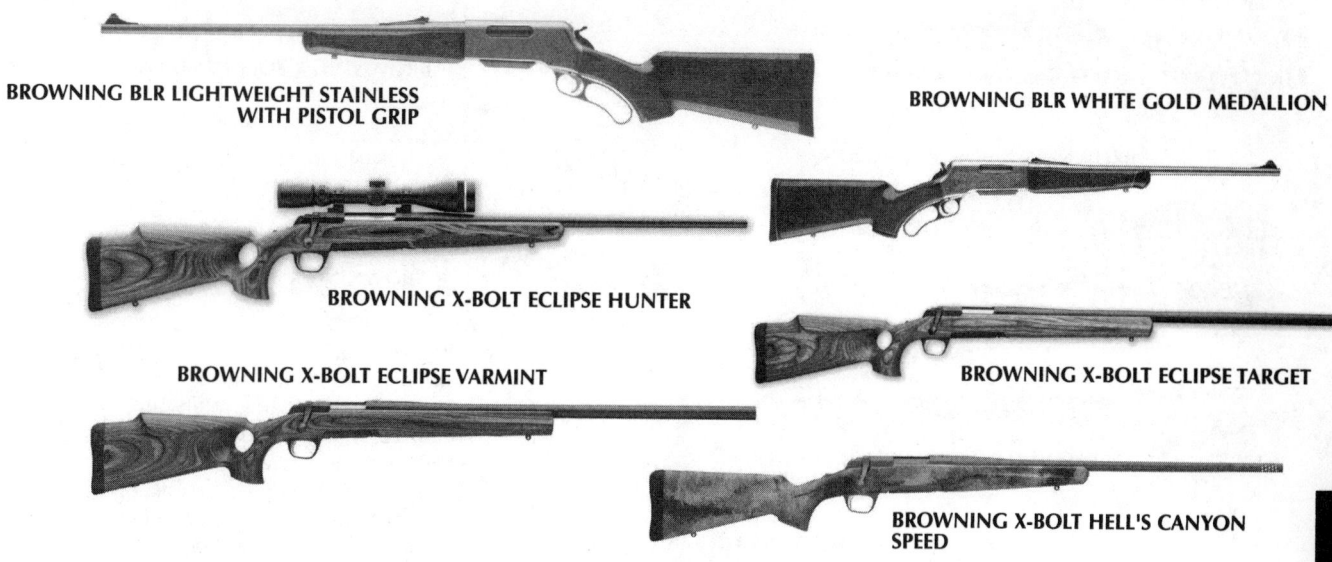

BROWNING BLR LIGHTWEIGHT STAINLESS WITH PISTOL GRIP

BROWNING BLR WHITE GOLD MEDALLION

BROWNING X-BOLT ECLIPSE HUNTER

BROWNING X-BOLT ECLIPSE VARMINT

BROWNING X-BOLT ECLIPSE TARGET

BROWNING X-BOLT HELL'S CANYON SPEED

BLR LIGHTWEIGHT STAINLESS WITH PISTOL GRIP

Action: Lever-action
Stock: Walnut, pistol grip
Barrel: 20 in., 22 in., 24 in.
Sights: None
Weight: 6 lb. 8 oz.–7 lb. 12 oz.
Caliber: .223 Rem., .22-250 Rem., .243 Win., 7mm–08 Rem., .308 Win., .358 Win., .270 Win., .30-06 Spfd., .300 Win. Mag., .300 WSM, .270 WSM, 7mm WSM, .450 Marlin, .325 WSM

Magazine: Detachable box
Features: Aircraft-grade alloy receiver; drilled and tapped for scope mounts; steel barrel with matte finish; crowned muzzle; adjustable sights; gloss finish walnut stock with pistol grip; sling swivel studs installed; recoil pad
MSRP . . . . **$1099.99–$1179.99**

BLR WHITE GOLD MEDALLION

Action: Lever-action
Stock: Walnut, pistol grip
Barrel: 20 in., 22 in.
Sights: Open
Weight: 6 lb. 8 oz.–6 lb. 12 oz.
Caliber: .243 Win., 7mm-08 Rem., .308 Win., .300 WSM, .270 WSM
Magazine: Detachable box
Features: Aircraft-grade aluminum receiver with nickel finish; high-relief engraving on receiver; drilled and tapped for scope mounts; crowned muzzle; stainless steel barrel; stock comes in grade IV/V walnut with a

checkered pistol grip and forearm; rosewood forend cap; silver pistol grip cap; adjustable sights; recoil pad; sling swivel studs installed; limited availability
MSRP . . . . **$1469.99–$1549.99**

X-BOLT ECLIPSE HUNTER

Action: Bolt
Stock: Wood laminate
Barrel: 22 in., 23 in., 24 in., 26 in.
Sights: None
Weight: 6 lb. 7 oz.–7 lb. 8 oz.
Caliber: .25-06 Rem., .243 Win., .270 Win., .270 WSM, .30-06 Spfd., .300 Win. Mag., .300 WSM, .308 Win., 7mm Rem. Mag., 7mm-08 Rem.
Magazine: Detachable box, 4 rounds
Features: Inflex Technology recoil pad
MSRP . . . . **$1019.99–$1059.99**

X-BOLT ECLIPSE TARGET

Action: Bolt
Stock: Satin
Barrel: 28 in.
Sights: None
Weight: 10 lb.–10 lb. 3 oz.
Caliber: .308 Win., 6mm Creedmoor, 6.5 Creedmoor
Magazine: Detachable box
Features: Steel barrel; short action; drilled and tapped for scope
MSRP . . . . **$1069.99–$1399.99**

X-BOLT ECLIPSE VARMINT

Action: Bolt
Stock: Satin
Barrel: 26 in.
Sights: None

Weight: 9 lb. 5 oz.– 9 lb. 6 oz.
Caliber: .204 Ruger., .223 Rem., .22-250 Rem.
Magazine: Detachable box
Features: Steel barrel; super short action; steel barrel
MSRP **$1069.99**

X-BOLT HELL'S CANYON SPEED

Action: Bolt
Stock: Composite
Barrel: 22 in., 23, in. 26 in.
Sights: None
Weight: 6 lb. 5 oz.–6 lb. 13 oz.
Caliber: .26 Nosler, .243 Win., .270 Win., .270 WSM, .30-06 Spfd., 300 Win. Mag., .300 WSM, .308 Win., 6.5 Creedmoor, 7mm Rem. Mag., 7mm-08 Rem.

Magazine: Detachable rotary, 3 or 4 rounds
Features: A-TACS AU (Arid/Urban) camouflage; Dura-Touch finish; composite stock; Cerakote finish; fluted; sporter barrel with threaded muzzle brake; detachable rotary magazine; short throw bolt; adjustable trigger; Inflex Technology recoil pad
MSRP . . . . **$1199.99–$1269.99**

Browning

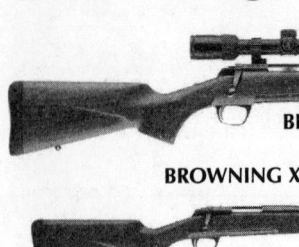

BROWNING X-BOLT HUNTER

BROWNING X-BOLT MEDALLION

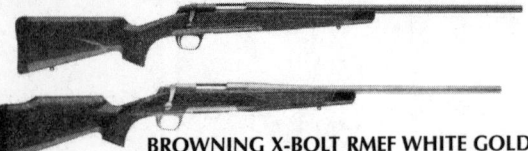

BROWNING X-BOLT RMEF WHITE GOLD

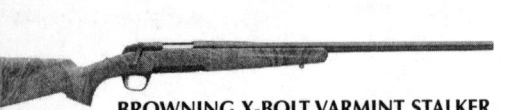

BROWNING X-BOLT VARMINT STALKER, MOSSY OAK BRUSH

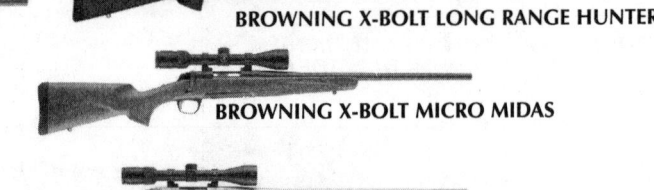

BROWNING X-BOLT LONG RANGE HUNTER

BROWNING X-BOLT MICRO MIDAS

BROWNING X-BOLT STAINLESS STALKER

X-BOLT HUNTER
Action: Bolt
Stock: Satin finish walnut stock
Barrel: 22 in., 23 in., 24 in., 26 in.
Sights: None
Weight: 6 lb. 13 oz.–7 lb.
Caliber: .243 Win., 7mm-08 Rem., .308 Win., .25-06 Rem., .270 Win., .280 Rem., .30-06 Spfd., 7mm Rem. Mag., .375 HH Mag., .388 Win. Mag., .300 Win. Mag., .300 WSM, .270 WSM, 7mm WSM, .325 WSM, .223 Rem., .22-250 Rem.
Magazine: Detachable rotary box
Features: Adjustable feather trigger; top-tang safety with bolt unlock button; sling swivel studs installed; Inflex technology recoil pad
MSRP. . . . .**$899.99–$949.99**

X-BOLT LONG RANGE HUNTER STAINLESS
Action: Bolt
Stock: Composite
Barrel: 26 in.
Sights: None
Weight: 7 lb. 3 oz.–7 lb. 8 oz.
Caliber: .26 Nosler, .270 Win., .300 Win. Mag., .300 WSM, 6.5 Creedmoor, 7mm Rem. Mag.
Magazine: Detachable rotary
Features: Stainless steel receiver; drilled and tapped for scope mounts; threaded barrel includes muzzle brake and accepts suppressor (5/8 in. x 24 threads); fluted free-floated barrel; palm swell and carbon fiber finish; sling swivel studs
MSRP. **$1469.99**

X-BOLT MEDALLION
Action: Bolt
Stock: Walnut
Barrel: 22 in., 23 in., 24 in., 26 in.
Sights: Open
Weight: 6 lb. 6 oz.–7 lb.
Caliber: .223 Rem., .22-250 Rem., .243 Win., .308 Win., .25-06 Rem., .270 Win., .280 Rem., .30-06 Spfd., 7mm Rem. Mag., .300 Win. Mag., .338 Win. Mag., .300 WSM, .270 WSM, 7mm WSM, .325 WSM, .375 H&H Mag.
Magazine: Detachable rotary box
Features: Gloss finish walnut stock, rosewood forend grip and pistol cap; Inflex technology recoil pad; adjustable feather trigger; drilled and tapped for scope mounts; left-hand option
MSRP. . . . . **$1039.99–$1079.99**
Left-hand: . . . . . **$1069.99–$1099.99**

X-BOLT MICRO MIDAS
Action: Bolt
Stock: Walnut
Barrel: 20 in.
Sights: None
Weight: 6 lb. 1 oz–6 lb. 6 oz.
Caliber: .243 Win., 7mm-08 Rem., .270 WSM, .300 WSM, .308 Win., .22-250 Rem.
Magazine: Detachable rotary magazine
Features: Drilled and tapped for scope mounts, low-luster blued finish, free-floating barrel; adjustable feather trigger; top-tang safety; left-hand option
MSRP. . . . .**$859.99–$899.99**

X-BOLT RMEF WHITE GOLD
Action: Bolt
Stock: Walnut
Barrel: 26 in.
Sights: None

Weight: 7 lb.
Caliber: .300 Win. Mag.
Magazine: Detachable rotary box
Features: Monte Carlo stock; stainless steel barrel and receiver, receiver etched in gold; raised cheekpiece; Inflex technology recoil pad; adjustable feather trigger; top-tang safety
MSRP. **$1539.99**

X-BOLT STAINLESS STALKER
Action: Bolt
Stock: Composite
Barrel: 22 in., 23 in., 24 in., 26 in.
Sights: None
Weight: 6 lb. 3 oz.–6 lb. 13 oz.
Caliber: .243 Win., 7mm-08 Rem., .308 Win., .25-06 Rem., .270 Win., .280 Rem., .30-06 Spfd., 6.5 Creedmoor, .300 H&H Mag., 7mm Rem. Mag., .300 Win. Mag., .388 Win. Mag., .300 WSM, .270 WSM, 7mm WSM, .325 WSM, .223 Rem., .22-250 Rem.
Magazine: Detachable rotary box
Features: Composite stock in matte black with textured gripping surfaces; Dura-Touch armor coating; adjustable feather trigger; top-tang safety; bolt unlock button; palm swell
MSRP. . . . . **$1139.99–$1179.99**

X-BOLT VARMINT STALKER, MOSSY OAK BRUSH
Action: Bolt
Stock: Synthetic
Barrel: 24 in., 26 in.
Sights: None
Weight: 6 lb. 13 oz.–7 lb. 2 oz.
Caliber: .204 Ruger, .22-250 Rem., .223 Rem., .243 Win., .308 Win.
Magazine: Detachable box, 4 rounds
Features: Intended to take advantage of lighter bullets and faster velocities; sporter contour barrel; standard style X-Bolt stock
MSRP. **$939.99**

Bushmaster Firearms

BUSHMASTER .450 RIFLE & CARBINE

BUSHMASTER TARGET MODEL RIFLE A2

BUSHMASTER XM-15 MOE 16" MID-LENGTH

BUSHMASTER XM-15 QUICK RESPONSE CARBINE (QRC)

BUSHMASTER XM-15 STANDARD 16-IN. A3 PATROLMAN'S CARBINE WITH QUAD-RAIL

.450 RIFLE & CARBINE

Action: Semiautomatic
Stock: Synthetic, A2 pistol grip
Barrel: 16 in. (carbine), 20 in. (rifle)
Sights: None
Weight: 8 lb. 2 oz. (carbine), 8 lb. 8 oz. (rifle)
Caliber: .450 Bushmaster
Magazine: Detachable box, 5 rounds
Features: Chromoly steel barrels; free-floating aluminum forends; forged aluminum receivers; solid A2 buttstock with trapdoor storage compartment; Pictatinny rail; black web sling included; shipped in lockable hard plastic case with orange safety block
Rifle: $1299.00
Carbine: $1299.00

PREDATOR RIFLE COMPLIANT

Action: Semiautomatic
Stock: Synthetic, ambidextrous pistol grip
Barrel: 20 in.
Sights: None
Weight: 8 lb.
Caliber: 5.56 NATO, .223 Rem.
Magazine: Detachable box, 5 rounds (accepts all M16/AR 15 type)
Features: Non-chrome lined fluted barrel with 1:8 twist; two-stage trigger; Magpul MOE stock; one five-round magazine supplied
MSRP. $1159.00

TARGET MODEL RIFLES

Action: Semiautomatic
Stock: Synthetic

Barrel: 20 in
Sights: None
Weight: 8 lb. 7 oz.
Caliber: 5.56 NATO, .223 Rem.
Magazine: Detachable box, 30 rounds (accepts all M16 / AR15 type)
Features: A2 upper receiver 300–800 meter rear sight system; chromoly steel or polished stainless steel barrels; shipped in a lockable hard case with orange safety block
A2: $969.00
A3: $999.00

XM-15 MOE 16-IN. MID-LENGTH

Action: Semiautomatic
Stock: Synthetic
Barrel: 16 in.
Sights: Magpul MSBUS rear flip sight
Weight: 6 lb. 2 oz.
Caliber: .308 Win., 7.62 NATO
Magazine: Detachable box, 20 rounds
Features: Receiver length Picatinny rail; Magpul MOE polymer mid-length handguard; Magpul MOE adjustable buttstock with strong A-frame design; rubber buttplate; Magpul MOE vertical grip; MOE enhanced trigger guards; shipped in lockable hard case with yellow safety block; stock comes in black, Flat Dark Earth, or OD green
MSRP. $1099.00

XM-15 QUICK RESPONSE CARBINE (QRC)

Action: Semiautomatic
Stock: Synthetic
Barrel: 16 in.

Sights: Mini red-dot
Weight: 6 lb.
Caliber: 5.56 NATO
Magazine: 30 rounds
Features: AR-15-style rifle has super-light contour, chrome-moly, Melonite-coated barrel, six-position collapsible stock, and A2 birdcage flash hider; supplied with quick-detach mini red-dot optic and one 30-round Magpul PMag
MSRP $769.00

XM-15 STANDARD 16-IN. A3 PATROLMAN'S CARBINE WITH QUAD-RAIL

Action: Semiautomatic
Stock: Synthetic
Barrel: 16 in.
Sights: None
Weight: 8 lb. 5 oz.
Caliber: 5.56 NATO, .223 Rem.
Magazine: Detachable box, 30 rounds
Features: Chrome-lined barrel; A2 birdcage-type suppressor; free-float quad rail forend; six-position telestock for light weight and quick handling; ships with lockable hard case and yellow safety block
A3: $1099.00

Bushmaster Firearms

BUSHMASTER XM-15 STANDARD 16" HEAVY BARREL CARBINE A2

XM-15 STANDARD 16-IN. HEAVY BARREL CARBINE A2

Action: Semiautomatic
Stock: Synthetic
Barrel: 16 in.
Sights: Open
Weight: 6 lb. 3 oz.
Caliber: 5.56 NATO, .223 Rem.

Magazine: Detachable box, 30 rounds (accepts all M16/AR15 type)
Features: 16-in. chrome-lined HBAR-profile heavy barrel with A2 flash hider; M16 bolt carrier, M4 feed ramp, six-position stock
A2: **$895.00**

C&H Precision Firearms

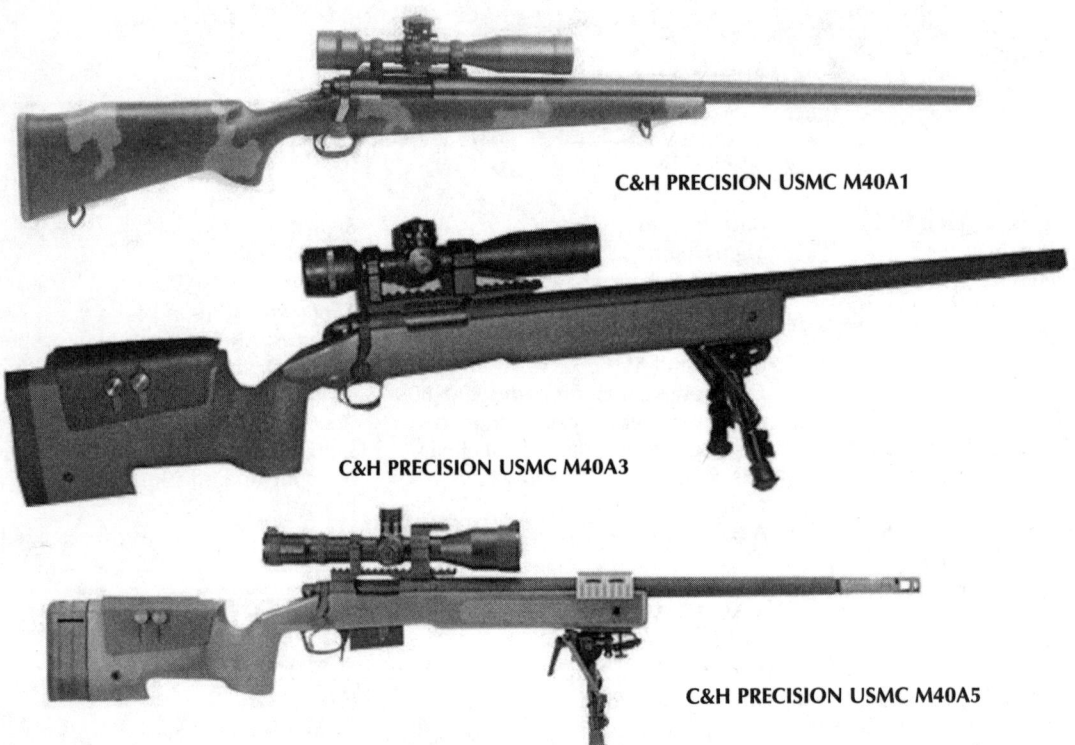

C&H PRECISION USMC M40A1

C&H PRECISION USMC M40A3

C&H PRECISION USMC M40A5

M40A1
Action: Bolt
Stock: Synthetic
Barrel: 25 in.
Sights: None
Weight: N/A
Caliber: .308 Win., 7.62 NATO
Magazine: N/A
Features: USMC stainless steel contour barrel; McMillan M40A1-HTG stock in forest camo; USMC spec. trigger guard custom made from Winchester model 70 steel trigger guard and floor plate; matte black finish
MSRP **$3825.00**

M40A3
Action: Bolt
Stock: Synthetic
Barrel: 25 in.
Sights: None
Weight: N/A
Caliber: .308 Win., 7.62 NATO
Magazine: N/A
Features: USMC stainless steel contour barrel; McMillan A4 stock with adjustable saddle cheek and spacer system in olive drab green; DD Ross trigger guard; matte black finish
MSRP **$4205.00**

M40A5
Action: Bolt
Stock: Synthetic
Barrel: 25 in.
Sights: None
Weight: N/A
Caliber: .308 Win., 7.62 NATO
Magazine: Detachable box, 5 rounds
Features: USMC stainless steel contour barrel with Surefire muzzle brake/suppressor adapter; McMillan A4 stock with adjustable saddle cheek, spacer system, and PGW PVS-22 night vision mount, in olive drab green; Badger Ordnance M5 DBM with five round magazine; matte black finish
MSRP **$4625.00**

RIFLES

Century Arms

CENTURY NTERNATIONAL
ARMS C39V2

CENTURY NTERNATIONAL
ARMS RAS47 SBR

C39V2
Action: Semiautomatic
Stock: Synthetic or wood
Barrel: 10.6 in., 12.4 in.
Sights: Standard AKM sights
Weight: 7 lb. 15 oz.–8 lb. 3 oz.
Caliber: 7.62 x 39mm
Magazine: 30 rounds
Features: 100 percent American made; barrel 1:10 twist; larger T-shaped magazine catch; bolt hold-open notch on the safety selector; front sight gas block and birdcage-style flash hider; bolt carrier tail heat treated to ensure maximum performance and life; accepts all standard AK mags
MSRP.................$749.99

RAS47 SBR
Action: Semiautomatic
Stock: Synthetic or wood
Barrel: 10.6 in., 12.4 in.
Sights: Standard AKM sights
Weight: 7 lb. 9.6 oz.–7 lb. 13 oz.
Caliber: 7.62 x 39mm
Magazine: 30 rounds
Features: 100 percent American made; barrel 1:10 twist; larger T-shaped magazine catch; bolt hold-open notch on the safety selector ; front sight gas block and birdcage-style flash hider; bolt carrier tail heat treated to ensure maximum performance and life; accepts all standard AK mags
MSRP.................$1073.73

Chiappa Firearms

CHIAPPA FIREARMS RAK-22

RAK-22
Action: Semiautomatic
Stock: Wood
Barrel: 17.25 in.
Sights: Adjustable
Weight: 6 lb.
Caliber: .22 LR
Magazine: Detachable box, 10 rounds
Features: Steel blued receiver and barrel
MSRP.................$529.00

Chiappa Firearms

CHIAPPA FIREARMS 1892 MARE'S LEG THIRD VERSION

CHIAPPA FIREARMS DOUBLE BADGER

CHIAPPA FIREARMS LA 322 DELUXE TAKE DOWN BLACK CHROME

CHIAPPA FIREARMS LA 322 KODIAK CUB TAKE DOWN

CHIAPPA FIREARMS LA 322 STANDARD TAKE DOWN MATTE BLUE

1892 MARE'S LEG THIRD VERSION

Action: Lever action
Stock: Walnut
Barrel: 9 in.
Sights: Adjustable
Weight: 4 lb. 13 oz.
Caliber: .357 Mag., .45 Colt, .44/.40
Magazine: 4 rounds
Features: Walnut pistol grip stock and forend; octagonal barrel, steel receiver, barrel band, large lever loop, and saddle ring give authentic antique look and feel
MSRP $1479.00

DOUBLE BADGER

Action: Over-under with rifled rimfire barrel
Stock: Beechwood
Barrel: 36 in.
Sights: Williams fiber optic ghost ring and front sight
Weight: 6 lb. 13 oz.
Caliber: 20 ga/.22 LR, .410 ga/.22 LR, .410 ga/.22 WMR
Magazine: 2 rounds
Features: Rimfire rifle-shotgun combo; 3/8 in. dovetail rail for mounting optics; pushing the trigger guard down allows the Double Badger to fold in half for easy travel; each barrel is selectively fired by its own trigger and controlled by a top tang safety that is easy to use quickly and reliably
MSRP . . . . $429.00–$499.00

LA 322 DELUXE TAKE DOWN BLACK CHROME

Action: Lever action
Stock: Walnut
Barrel: 18.5 in.
Sights: Hooded front, adjustable rear
Weight: 5 lb. 8 oz.
Caliber: .22 LR
Magazine: 15 rounds
Features: 3/8 in. dovetail into top of receiver; take down design; deluxe stock with pistol grip and checkering
MSRP $619.00

LA 322 KODIAK CUB TAKE DOWN

Action: Lever action
Stock: English-style black soft touch

Barrel: 18.5 in.
Sights: Hooded front, adjustable rear
Weight: 5 lb. 8 oz.
Caliber: .22 LR
Magazine: 15 rounds
Features: Matte hard chrome finish that is durable and corrosion-resistant; black soft touch coating makes the stock easier to grip and protects from the elements; easy take down
MSRP $809.00

LA 322 STANDARD TAKE DOWN MATTE BLUE

Action: Lever action
Stock: English-style wood
Barrel: 18.5 in.
Sights: Hooded front, adjustable rear
Weight: 5 lb. 8 oz.
Caliber: .22 LR
Magazine: 15 rounds
Features: 3/8 in. dovetail into top of receiver; take down design
MSRP $469.00

Chiappa Firearms

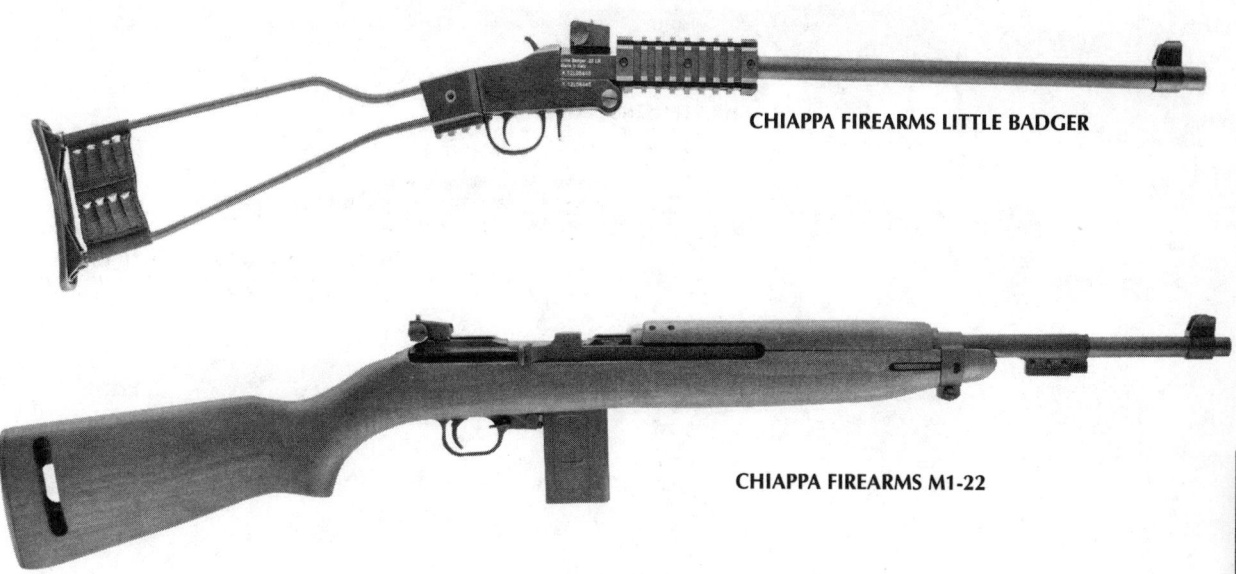

CHIAPPA FIREARMS LITTLE BADGER

CHIAPPA FIREARMS M1-22

LITTLE BADGER
Action: Single shot
Stock: Metal foldable
Barrel: 16.5 in.
Sights: Adjustable rear
Weight: 3 lb. 8 oz.
Caliber: .22 LR, .22WMR, .17 HMR
Magazine: None
Features: Single barrel; foldable rifle; extremely light for comfortable carry; folds to 16.5 in. total length; nylon carry bag and special cartridge holder available
MSRP . . . . **$229.00–$249.00**

M1-22
Action: Semiautomatic
Stock: Polymer
Barrel: 18 in.
Sights: Adjustable rear
Weight: 5 lb. 8 oz.
Caliber: .22 LR
Magazine: Detachable box, 10 rounds
Features: The M1 carbine is a light-weight, easy-to-use semiautomatic carbine that became a standard firearm for the U.S. military during World War II, the Korean War, and the Vietnam War, and was produced in several variants
Synthetic: **$309.00**
Wood: **$409.00**

Chipmunk Rifles

CHIPMUNK
Action: Bolt
Stock: Walnut, laminated
Barrel: 16.125 in.
Sights: Target
Weight: 2 lb. 8 oz.
Caliber: .22 LR
Magazine: None
Features: Designed with younger shooters in mind; single-shot; manual-cocking action; receiver-mounted rear sights; metal with blued finish or stainless steel; post sight on ramp front, fully adjustable peep rear; adjustable trigger; extendable buttplate and front rail; available in black, walnut, deluxe walnut, camo laminate, and brown laminate
Standard Chipmunk: . . . . **$209.00–$245.00**
Barracuda: . . . . **$258.00–$294.00**

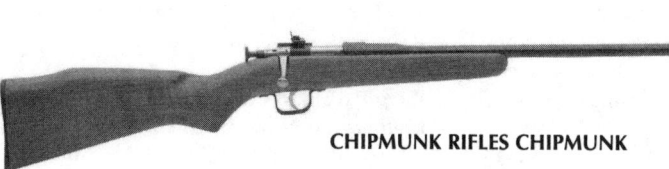

CHIPMUNK RIFLES CHIPMUNK

Christensen Arms

CHRISTENSEN ARMS BA TACTICAL

CHRISTENSEN FIREARMS CA-10 DMR

CHRISTENSEN CA-15 VTAC

CHRISTENSEN ARMS CA-15 G2 3G

CHRISTENSEN ARMS ELR

BA TACTICAL

Action: Bolt
Stock: Hand-laid fiberglass
Barrel: 20 in.–27 in.
Sights: None
Weight: 7 lb. 11 oz.–8 lb. 2 oz.
Caliber: .223 Rem., .300 Win. Mag., .308 Win., 6.5 Creedmoor, .338 Lapua, .300 Norma, .338 Norma
Magazine: Detachable box, 5 rounds
Features: Integral full-length rail incorporates a 20 MOA taper; front stud with five flush cups; adjustable cheek piece via inserts; stainless steel side-port muzzle brake
MSRP **$2795.00**

CA-10 DESIGNATED MARKSMAN RIFLE (DMR)

Action: Semiautomatic
Stock: Synthetic
Barrel: 24 in.
Sights: None
Weight: 8.2 lb.
Caliber: .243 Win., .308 Win., 6.5 Creedmoor
Magazine: Detachable box

Features: Picatinny rail; OSS suppressor; ambidextrous magazine release; Magpul stock; various finishes available
MSRP **$3245.00**

CA-15 VTAC

Action: Semiautomatic
Stock: Synthetic
Barrel: 16 in.
Sights: None
Weight: 5 lb. 5 oz.–5 lb. 8 oz.
Caliber: 5.56 NATO
Magazine: Detachable box
Features: Flared magwell; Picatinny rails; steel fluted barrel or carbon wrapped barrel; flash hider; 1:8-inch barrel twist
MSRP **$2845.00**

CA-15 G2 3G

Action: Semiautomatic
Stock: Carbon fiber
Barrel: 16 in., 18 in.
Sights: None
Weight: 5 lb. 11 oz.
Caliber: .223 Wylde
Magazine: 30 rounds

Features: Christensen Arms 416R stainless steel, carbon fiber-wrapped, button rifled barrel, match chamber, threaded muzzle, adjustable titanium side baffle brake; receiver is 7075 aluminum, stock is BCM gunfighter adjustable; direct impingement gas system and Hiperfire trigger are standard
MSRP **$2845.00**

ELR

Action: Bolt
Stock: Hand-laid carbon fiber
Barrel: 26 in.–27 in.
Sights: None
Weight: 7 lb. 8 oz.
Caliber: .26 Nosler, .28 Nosler, .30 Nosler, 30-06 Spfd., .300 RUM, .300 Win. Mag., .300 WSM, .308 Win., 6.5 Creedmoor, 6.5-284, .338 Lapua, 7mm Rem. Mag.
Magazine: 4 rounds
Features: Machined aluminum hinged floorplate; dual front studs with flush cups; adjustable cheek piece via inserts; titanium side-port muzzle brake
MSRP **$2795.00**

Christensen Arms

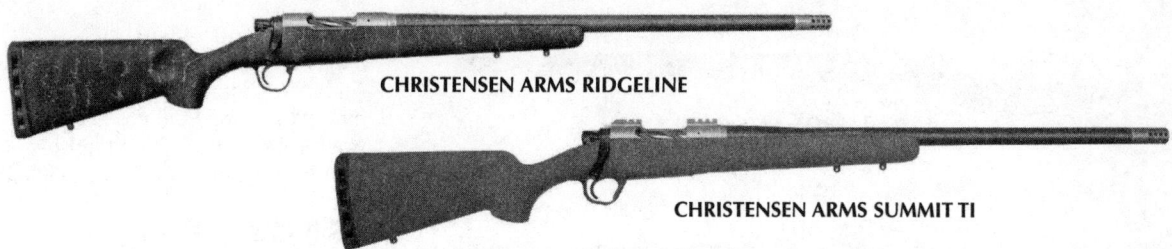

CHRISTENSEN ARMS RIDGELINE

CHRISTENSEN ARMS SUMMIT TI

RIDGELINE

Action: Bolt
Stock: Hand-laid fiberglass with carbon fiber reinforced stock
Barrel: 22 in.–26 in.
Sights: None
Weight: 6 lb. 5 oz.–6 lb. 11 oz.
Caliber: .22-250 Rem., .243 Win., 26 Nosler, .270 Win., .270 WSM, .28 Nosler, .280 Ackley, .30 Nosler, 30-06 Spfd., .300 RUM, .300 Win. Mag., .300 WSM, .308 Win., 6.5 Creedmoor, 6.5-284, 7mm Rem. Mag., 7mm-08 Rem.
Magazine: 4 rounds
Features: Carbon fiber–wrapped barrel; a spiral fluted bolt; scalloped bolt knob; dual front studs; SUB MOA accuracy; bedded recoil lug and invar pillar inserts; machined aluminum hinged floorplate
MSRP $1995.00

SUMMIT TI AND SUMMIT TI-TH

Action: Bolt
Stock: Aerograde carbon fiber
Barrel: 24 in.–27 in.
Sights: None
Weight: 5 lb. 8 oz.–6 lb.
Caliber: 25-06 Rem., 26 Nosler, .270 Win., .270 WSM, .28 Nosler, .280 Ackley, .30 Nosler, 30-06 Spfd., .300 RUM, .300 Win. Mag., .300 WSM, 6.5 Creedmoor, 6.5-284, .308 Win., .300 RUM, .338 Lapua, .375 H&H, 7mm Rem. Mag.
Magazine: 3 rounds
Features: 416R stainless steel, aerograde carbon fiber-wrapped barrel is hand lapped and button rifled and sports a removable radial titanium muzzle brake; trued receiver has integrated Picatinny rail; fully adjustable match trigger, Nitride-treated bolt with fluted knob, enlarged ejection port, full-length bedding with carbon fiber pillars are standard; sporter or thumbhole stock
MSRP $5495.00

Cimarron Firearms Co.

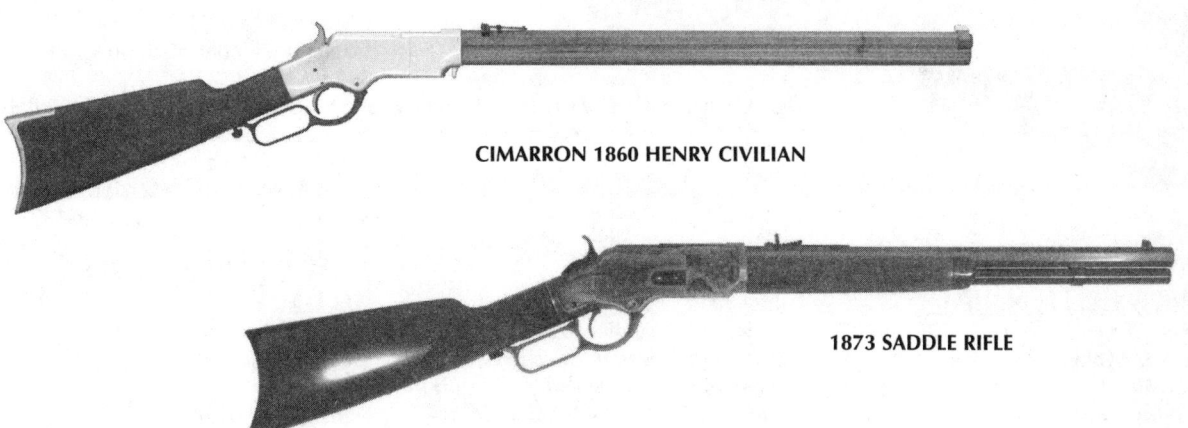

CIMARRON 1860 HENRY CIVILIAN

1873 SADDLE RIFLE

1860 HENRY CIVILIAN

Action: Lever
Stock: Walnut
Barrel: 24 in.
Sights: Open
Weight: 9 lb. 2 oz.
Caliber: .44 WCF
Magazine: Under-barrel tube, 12 rounds

Features: Reproduction of 1860 Civil War Henry rifle; includes military sling swivels; frame comes in charcoal blue or original finish
MSRP 1459.90

1873 SADDLE RIFLE

Action: Lever
Stock: Wood
Barrel: 18 in.
Sights: Open
Weight: 8 lb.
Caliber: .357 Mag., .38 Spl., .45 Colt, .44 WCF
Magazine: Fixed tube
Features: Full octagon barrel; straight stock with checkered forearm and stock
MSRP $1363.70

Cimarron Firearms Co.

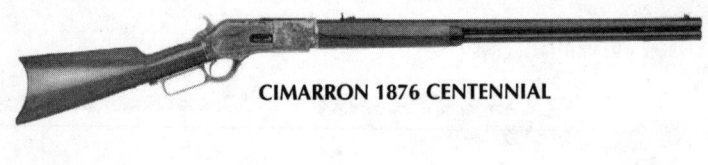

CIMARRON 1876 CENTENNIAL

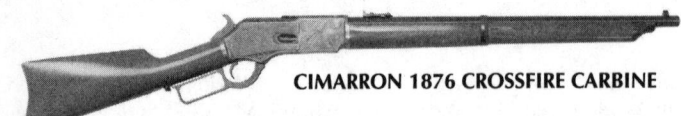

CIMARRON 1876 CROSSFIRE CARBINE

CIMARRON 1885 HIGH WALL SPORTING RIFLE

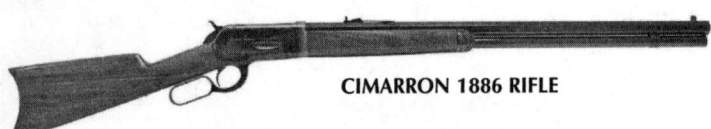

CIMARRON 1886 RIFLE

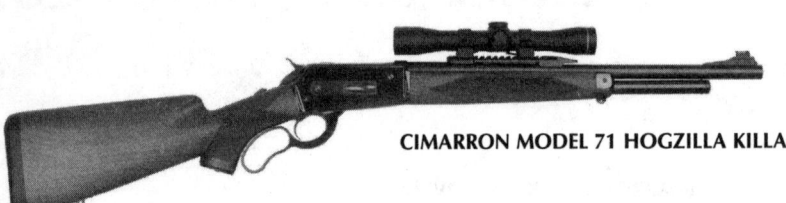

CIMARRON MODEL 71 HOGZILLA KILLA

1876 CENTENNIAL

Action: Lever
Stock: Walnut
Barrel: 28 in.
Sights: Open
Weight: 9 lb. 15 oz.–10 lb. 2 oz.
Caliber: .45-60, .45-75, .40-60, .50-95
Magazine: Under-barrel tube, 12 rounds
Features: Originally dubbed the "Centennial Model" because of its introduction during America's 100th anniversary of the Declaration of Independence from British rule, and featured at Philadelphia's Centennial Exposition, this enlarged version of the famed 1873 Winchester was designed to handle stronger loads than its predecessor; finished in a standard blue octagonal barrel, tubular magazine, barrel band and fore-end, with a color case hardened receiver, lever, trigger, hammer and butt plate
MSRP . . . . $1605.46–$1688.70

1876 CROSSFIRE CARBINE

Action: Lever
Stock: Walnut
Barrel: 22 in.
Sights: None
Weight: 8 lb. 15 oz.
Caliber: .45-60, .45-75
Magazine: Under-barrel tube, 8 rounds
Features: Gun was glorified in the movie *Crossfire Trail;* case-hardened stock with standard blued finish
MSRP $1852.50

1885 HIGH WALL SPORTING RIFLE

Action: Dropping block
Stock: Walnut, pistol grip
Barrel: 30 in.
Sights: Open
Weight: 9 lb. 4 oz.–10 lb. 6 oz.
Caliber: .45-70 Govt., .40-65, .38-55, .45-90, .30-40 KRAG, .348 Win., .405 Win.
Magazine: None
Features: Reproduction of the Winchester single-shot hunting rifle popular in 1880s; standard blued finish on octagonal barrel; single- or double- set triggers
MSRP $1129.70

1886 RIFLE

Action: Lever
Stock: Walnut
Barrel: 22 in., 26 in.
Sights: None
Weight: 8 lb.–9 lb.
Caliber: .45-70 Govt.
Magazine: Under-barrel tube, 7+1, 8+1 rounds
Features: Made by Armi Sport in Italy; color case-hardened receiver and buttplate; octagonal barrel; standard blued finish; carbine version available
MSRP $1597.70

MODEL 71 HOGZILLA KILLA

Action: Lever
Stock: Walnut
Barrel: 19 in.
Sights: Fiber optic
Weight: 7 lb. 9.6 oz.
Caliber: .45-70 Govt.
Magazine: Fixed tube
Features: Carbine model; scout rail; pistol grip stock
MSRP $1846.48

Cimarron Firearms Co.

CIMARRON MODEL 71 CLASSIC

CIMARRON PEDERSOLI SHARPS BUSINESS RIFLE

MODEL 71 CLASSIC
Action: Lever
Stock: Walnut
Barrel: 24 in.
Sights: Open
Weight: 8 lb. 11 oz.
Caliber: .45-70 Govt.
Magazine: Fixed tube
Features: Blued receiver; pistol grip stock

MSRP $2047.50

PEDERSOLI SHARPS BUSINESS RIFLE
Action: Sharps
Stock: Wood
Barrel: 32 in.
Sights: Adjustable
Weight: 11 lb. 14 oz.
Caliber: .45-70 Govt.
Magazine: N/A
Features: Octagonal barrel; color case hardened framel; walnut stock and forearm; standard blue finish; double set triggers

MSRP $1506.70

CMMG, Inc.

CMMG MK47 AKS8, SBN, NFA, MUTANT

CMMG MK47 AKS13 SBN, MUTANT

MK47 AKS8 SBN, NFA, MUTANT
Action: Semiautomatic
Stock: Synthetic
Barrel: 8 in.
Sights: None
Weight: 6 lb. 13 oz.
Caliber: 7.62X39
Magazine: 30 rounds
Features: KRINK muzzle device; pinned on gas block; mid-sized receiver based on CMMG's MK3 platform; improved 9 in. handguard; lower receiver readily accepts all standard AK magazines

MSRP $1649.95

MK47 AKS13 SBN, MUTANT
Action: Semiautomatic
Stock: Synthetic
Barrel: 13 in.
Sights: None
Weight: 7 lb. 6 oz.
Caliber: 7.62x39
Magazine: 30 rounds
Features: KRINK muzzle device pinned and welded to a 13 in. barrel to meet the 16 in. legal requirement; improved 15 in. handguard; pinned on gas block; mid-sized receiver based on CMMG's MK3 platform; lower receiver readily accepts all standard AK magazines

MSRP $1749.95

CMMG, Inc.

CMMG MK47 MUTANT AKM

CMMG MK47 MUTANT T

MK47 MUTANT AKM

Action: Semiautomatic
Stock: Synthetic
Barrel: 16.1 in.
Sights: None
Weight: 7 lb. 3 oz.
Caliber: 7.62x39mm
Magazine: Detachable box
Features: Combining the accuracy and modularity of the AR-15 with the reliability of the AK47, the Mk47 features all new mid-sized receivers based on a Mk3 platform carved from billet 7075-T6 aluminum; designed to harness the power and reliability of the 7.62x39mm cartridge utilizing a robust bolt; unique Mk47 lower receiver readily accepts all standard AK magazines; equipped with a MOE pistol grip, SV muzzle brake, 30rd AK PMAG, and lifetime quality guarantee
MSRP **$1649.95**

MK47 MUTANT T

Action: Semiautomatic
Stock: Synthetic
Barrel: 16.1 in.
Sights: None
Weight: 7 lb.
Caliber: 7.62 Warsaw
Magazine: Detachable box, 30 rounds
Features: Features all new mid-sized receivers based on a Mk3 platform carved from billet 7075-T6 aluminum; designed to harness the power and reliability of the 7.62 Warsaw cartridge utilizing a robust bolt; unique Mk47 lower receiver readily accepts all standard AK magazines; equipped with a MOE pistol grip, and SV muzzle brake
MSRP **$1499.95**

Colt's Manufacturing Company

COLT EXPANSE M4 CARBINE

EXPANSE M4 CARBINE

Action: Semiautomatic
Stock: Synthetic
Barrel: 16.1 in.
Sights: Adjustable front sight
Weight: 6 lb. 7 oz.
Caliber: 5.56x45 NATO
Magazine: 3 rounds
Features: Aluminum magazine; 1/7 RH rifling; non-chrome-lined bore
MSRP **$749.00**

RIFLES

Colt's Manufacturing Company

COLT LE6940

COLT LE901-16SE

LE901-16SE

Action: Semiautomatic
Stock: Combat-style, synthetic
Barrel: 16.1 in.
Sights: Flip-up front, adjustable post, flip-up rear
Weight: 9 lb. 6 oz.
Caliber: .308 Win.
Magazine: Detachable box, 20 rounds
Features: Matte black, monolithic upper receiver; .308 Winchester upper

receiver group can be swapped out for Mil-Spec Colt upper in 5.56 NATO; ambidextrous controls on magazine release, bolt catch and safety selector; back up iron sights; full floated barrel; bayonet lug and flash hider
MSRP $1999.00

LE6940

Action: Semiautomatic
Stock: Combat-style, synthetic
Barrel: 16.1 in.
Sights: Flip-up front flip-up rear

Weight: 6 lb. 11 oz.
Caliber: 5.56 NATO
Magazine: Detachable box, 20, 30 rounds
Features: Incorporates a continuous Picatinny rail from the rear of the upper receiver to the front sight, free-floating chrome-line barrel, folding locking front sight, Magpul MBUS rear sight, integrated quad-rail; single-stage trigger, direct gas impingement system are standard
MSRP $1339.00

Connecticut Valley Arms (CVA)

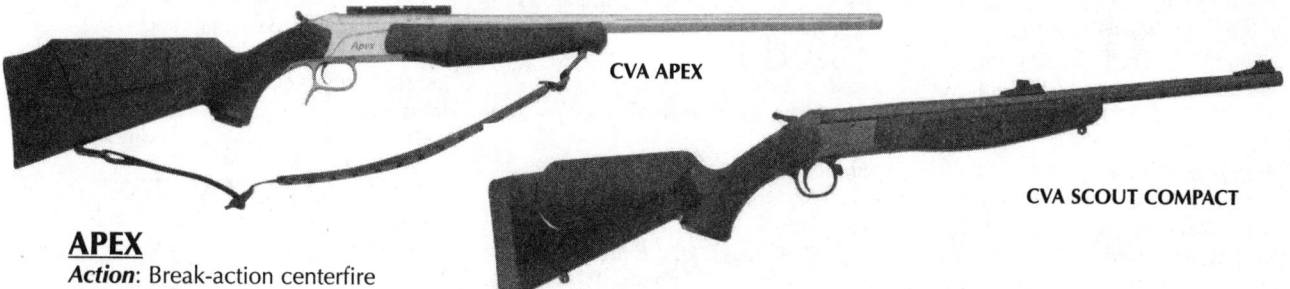

CVA APEX

CVA SCOUT COMPACT

APEX

Action: Break-action centerfire
Stock: Synthetic
Barrel: 25 in.
Sights: None
Weight: 7 lb. 8 oz.
Caliber: .45-70 Govt., 7mm-08 Rem., .308 Win., .30-06 Spfd., .300 Win. Mag., .35 Whelen, .270 Win., .243 Win., .223 Rem., .222 Rem., .22-250 Rem.
Magazine: None
Features: Ambidextrous synthetic stock with rubber grip panels; comes in black or Realtree APG camo; stainless steel, fluted Bergara barrel; adjustable trigger; interchangeable

barrels; CrushZone recoil pad; DuraSight rail mount; QRBP (Quick Release Breech Plug); reversible hammer spur; Quake Claw Sling; also available in muzzleloading models
MSRP . . . . $651.20–$731.95

SCOUT

Action: Centerfire, single shot
Stock: Synthetic
Barrel: 20 in. (compact), 22 in. (standard fluted barrels)
Sights: None

Weight: 5 lb. 13 oz.
Caliber: .223 Rem., .243 Win., .300 BLK, .35 Rem., .35 Whelen, .44 Mag., .444 Marlin, .45-70 Govt.
Magazine: None
Features: Stainless steel or blued barrel; ambidextrous black synthetic stock; DuraSight Dead-On integral scope rail; CrushZone recoil pad; reversible hammer spur; compact and alternate length stocks available
MSRP . . . . $413.60–$525.00

Cooper Firearms

COOPER FIREARMS MODEL 21
VARMINT EXTREME

COOPER FIREARMS MODEL 21
VARMINTER (LAMINATE STOCK]

COOPER FIREARMS MODEL 51

COOPER FIREARMS MODEL 52 WESTERN CLASSIC

COOPER FIREARMS
MODEL 57M CLASSIC

COOPER FIREARMS MODEL 57 LIGHT VARMINT
TARGET - LVT

MODEL 21 CLASSIC

Action: Bolt
Stock: AA Claro Walnut
Barrel: N/A
Sights: None
Weight: 6 lb. 8 oz.–7 lb. 8 oz.
Caliber: .17 Rem., .19-233, .20
VarTarg, .20 Tactical, .204 Ruger, .221
Fireball, .222 Rem., .222 Rem. Mag.,
.223 Rem., .223 Rem. AI, 6x45, 6x47,
.300 BLK
Magazine: None
Features: Hand-rubbed oil-finished
stock with four-panel hand checker-
ing, Pachmayer recoil pad, chrome-
moly premium match grade Wilson
Arms barrel, steel grip cap are
standard
Right-hand: **$2225.00**
Left-hand: **$2425.00**

MODEL 22 CLASSIC

Action: Bolt
Stock: AA Claro Walnut
Barrel: N/A
Sights: None
Weight: N/A
Caliber: .More than 30 calibers avail-
able, from .22 BR to .338 Federal
Magazine: None
Features: Hand-rubbed oil-finished

stock with four-panel hand checkering, Pachmayer recoil pad, chrome-
moly premium match grade Wilson
Arms barrel, steel grip cap are
standard
MSRP **$2229.00**

MODEL 51

Action: Bolt
Stock: AA Claro Walnut
Barrel: N/A
Sights: None
Weight: N/A
Caliber: .17 Rem., .19-223, Tactical
.20, .204 Ruger, .222 Rem., .222
Rem. Mag., .223 Rem., .223 Rem. AI,
6x45, 6x47, .300 BLK
Magazine: None
Features: Longer barrel standard on
all varmint models; fully adjustable
single-stage trigger; Sako style extrac-
tion machined from solid bar stock
MSRP **$2275.00**

MODEL 52 WESTERN CLASSIC

Action: Bolt
Stock: AAA+ Claro Walnut
Barrel: N/A
Sights: None
Weight: N/A

Caliber: More than 30 available calibers from .257 Wby. to .416 Rem.
Mag.
Magazine: 3 rounds
Features: Stock has shadowline beaded cheekpiece, African ebony tip, and
western fleur wraparound checkering.
Steel grip cap, sling swivels, and case
coloring on selected metal work are
standard
MSRP **$3895.00**

MODEL 57-M CLASSIC

Action: Bolt
Stock: N/A
Barrel: N/A
Sights: None
Weight: N/A
Caliber: .17 Mach 2, .22 LR, .22
WMR, .17 HMR
Magazine: 4, 5 rounds
Features: Hand-rubbed oil-finished
stock with four-panel hand checkering,
Pachmayer recoil pad, chrome-moly
premium match grade Wilson Arms
barrel, steel grip cap are standard
Right-hand: **$2295.00**
Left-hand: **$2495.00**

RIFLES

COOPER FIREARMS MODEL 57 LIGHT VARMINT TARGET - LVT

COOPER FIREARMS EXCALIBUR

MODEL 54 CLASSIC
Action: Bolt
Stock: AA Claro Walnut
Barrel: N/A
Sights: None
Weight: N/A
Caliber: .22-250 Rem., .22-250 AI, .243 Win., .243 Win. AI, .250 Savage, .250 Savage AI, .260 Rem., 6.5 Creedmoor, 6.5-57 Lapua, 7mm-08, .300 Savage, .308 Win., .338 Federal, .358 Win.
Magazine: 3 rounds
Features: Three-rear locking lug bolt action magazine fed repeater; center-fire action, also available in stainless steel; Sako style extraction machined from solid bar stock; plunger style ejector machined form solid bar; fully adjustable single-stage trigger
Right-hand: $2275.00
Left-hand: $2525.00

MODEL TRP-3
Action: Bolt
Stock: Synthetic
Barrel: N/A
Sights: None
Weight: N/A
Caliber: .22 LR
Magazine: N/A
Features: Dual recoil plane synthetic stock with wide beavertail forearm; stainless steel straight taper premium match grade Wilson Arms barrel; all metal work is matte finish; single-shot.
MSRP $2175.00

"VARIATIONS"

1. Classic
AA Claro walnut; steel grip; four-panel hand checkering; oil finish; matte metal finish; no options; available in all Cooper models

2. Custom Classic
AAA Claro walnut stock, shadowline beaded cheekpiece, African ebony tip, and western fleur wraparound checkering; sling swivel studs and chorome-moly premium match-grade Wilson Arms barrel are standard; all metal work has high gloss finish; available in all models

3. Excalibur
Hand-laid synthetics with Kevlar reinforcing material surrounding an aircraft-grade aluminum bedding block. Spiral fluted bolt, chrome-moly premium match grade Wilson Arms fluted barrel are standard; all metal work is matte finish; available for models 51, 52, and 54

4. Jackson Game
AA+ Claro walnut stock, rollover cheekpiece, semi-beavertail forearm. VE hand checkered grip in crossover multi-point pattern; stainless steel premium match grade Wilson Arms barrel; laminate version available; available for Models 51, 52, and 54

5. Jackson Hunter
Hand-laid synthetics with Kevlar reinforcing material surrounding an aircraft-grade aluminum bedding block; stainless steel premium match grade Wilson Arms barrel is standard; all metal work is matte finish; available for models 51, 52, 54, and 57-M

6. Jackson Squirrel
AA+ Claro walnut stock with rollover cheekpiece and semi-beavertail forearm. Grip has VE hand checkering in a crossover multi-point pattern; stainless steel premium match Wilson Arms barrel; also available in laminate; all metal work is matte finish; available in Model 57-M only

7. Mannlicher
AAA+ Claro walnut, shadowline beaded cheekpiece, African ebony tip, western fleur wraparound hand checking, chrome-moly premium match grade Wilson Arms octagonal barrel; all metal work is high gloss finish; available in all models

8. Montana Varminter
AA+ Claro walnut stock, hand-checkered grip, stainless steel straight taper premium match grade Wilson Arms barrel; all metal work is matte finish; available in models 21, 22, 38, 51, 52, 54, and 57-M

9. Phoenix
Hand-laid synthetics with Kevlar reinforcing material surrounding an aircraft-grade aluminum bedding block; spiral fluted bolt, chrome-moly premium match grade Wilson Arms fluted barrel are standard; all metal work is matte finish; available for models 21, 22, 38, 51, 54; left-hand options only in models 21 and 38

10. Schnabel
Available in models 52, 54, 56, and 57; AA+ Claro walnut; raised comb; slim taper forearm; multi-point two panel hand checkering; oil finish; standard grade sling swivel studs; Pachmayr pad; steel grip cap; chromoly premium match grade barrel; metal work is matte finished; available in Models 51, 52, 54, 57-M, 58, and muzzleloader

11. Varminter
AA Claro walnut stock, hand checkered grip, stainless steel straight taper premium match grade Wilson Arms barrel; all metal work is matte finish; available in Models 21, 22, 38, 51, 52, 54, and 57-M

12. Varmint Extreme
AAA Claro walnut stock, hand checkered grip in a crossover western fleur pattern; stainless steel straight taper matte finish premium match grade Wilson Arms barrel; all blued steel is high gloss finish; available in models 21, 22, 38, 51, 52, 54, and 57-M

13. Western Classic
AAA+ Claro walnut, shadowline beaded cheekpiece, African ebony tip, western fleur wraparound hand checking, chrome-moly premium match grade Wilson Arms octagonal barrel; all metal work is high gloss finish, selected metal work is highlighted with case coloring

CZ-USA (Ceska Zbrojovka)

CZ-USA 455 AMERICAN

CZ-USA 455 AMERICAN SYNTHETIC SUPPRESSOR READY

CZ-USA 455 FS

CZ-USA 455 LUX

CZ-USA 455 TRAINING RIFLE

CZ-USA 455 ULTRA LUX

455 FS

Action: Bolt
Stock: Walnut
Barrel: 20.6 in.
Sights: Adjustable iron sights
Weight: 6 lb. 6 oz.
Caliber: .22 LR, .17 HMR
Magazine: Detachable box, 5 rounds
Features: Action machined from bar stock; adjustable trigger; detachable feed magazine; cold-hammer-forged barrels; standard 11mm optic-mounting dovetail; full length Mannlicher walnut stock; adjustable iron sights
MSRP . . . . **$514.00–$540.00**

455 LUX

Action: Bolt
Stock: Walnut
Barrel: 20.6 in.
Sights: Open
Weight: 6 lb. 2 oz.
Caliber: .22 LR, .22 WMR
Magazine: Detachable box, 5 rounds
Features: Interchangeable barrel system; adjustable trigger; hammer-forged barrel and billet machined receiver; adjustable iron sights; lux pattern walnut stock
MSRP . . . . **$440.00–$469.00**

455 TRAINING RIFLE

Action: Bolt
Stock: Beechwood
Barrel: 24.8 in.
Sights: Adjustable
Weight: 6 lb. 5 oz.
Caliber: .17 HMR, .22 LR
Magazine: Detachable box, 5 or 10 rounds
Features: Ability to swap the barrel and/or stock; single-shot adapter and 10 round magazine are available
.22 LR: **$374.00**
.17 HMR: **$399.00**

455 ULTRA LUX

Action: Bolt
Stock: Beechwood, European with cheekpiece
Barrel: 26.6 in.
Sights: Tangent adjustable
Weight: 6 lb. 13 oz.
Caliber: .22 LR
Magazine: Detachable box
Features: Long barreled rimfire; tangent rear sight; 10-round magazine
MSRP **$449.00**

455 AMERICAN

Action: Bolt
Stock: Walnut, black polymer
Barrel: 20.5 in.
Sights: None
Weight: 5 lb. 13 oz.–6 lb. 2 oz.
Caliber: .17 HMR, .22 LR, .22 WMR, Combo .22 LR with .17 HMR replacement barrel
Magazine: Detachable box, 5 rounds
Features: Cold hammer-forged barrel; blued receiver and barrel finish; integrated dovetail scope base; interchangeable barrel system; adjustable trigger
Single caliber: . . . . **$421.00–$438.00**
Combo: **$557.00**

455 AMERICAN SYNTHETIC SUPPRESSOR READY

Action: Bolt
Stock: Synthetic
Barrel: 16.5 in.
Sights: None
Weight: 5 lb. 8 oz.
Caliber: .22 LR
Magazine: Detachable box, 5 rounds
Features: High, flat comb for scope; suppressor not included
MSRP **$421.00**

RIFLES

CZ-USA (Ceska Zbrojovka)

CZ-USA 455 VARMINT

CZ-USA 455 VARMINT EVOLUTION

CZ-USA 455 VARMINT PRECISION TRAINER SUPPRESSOR READY

CZ-USA 455 VARMINT TACTICOOL SUPRESSOR READY

CZ–USA 512 AMERICAN

455 VARMINT

Action: Bolt
Stock: Walnut
Barrel: 20.5 in.
Sights: Optic mounting dovetail
Weight: 7 lb. 1 oz.
Caliber: .22 LR, .22 WMR, .17 HMR
Magazine: Detachable box, 5 rounds
Features: Action machined from bar stock; adjustable trigger; detachable feed magazine; cold-hammer-forged barrels; standard 11mm optic-mounting dovetail; heavier and stiffer barrel for enhanced accuracy; accepts all accessory barrels for the 455 models
MSRP . . . . **$469.00–$497.00**

455 VARMINT EVOLUTION

Action: Bolt
Stock: Laminate
Barrel: 20.5 in.
Sights: Optic mounting dovetail
Weight: 7 lb. 2 oz.
Caliber: .17 HMR, .22 LR
Magazine: Detachable box, 5 rounds
Features: Action machined from bar stock; adjustable trigger; detachable feed magazine; cold-hammer-forged barrels; standard 11mm optic-mounting dovetail; sky blue/gray laminated stock; ambidextrous; free floated barrel; accepts all accessory barrels for the 455 models
MSRP . . . . **$538.00–$565.00**

455 VARMINT PRECISION TRAINER SUPPRESSOR READY

Action: Bolt
Stock: Carbon fiber
Barrel: 20.5 in.
Sights: None
Weight: 7 lb. 13 oz.
Caliber: .22 LR
Magazine: Detachable box, 5 rounds
Features: Camo stock; blued finish; two supressor-ready versions available, a 24-in. and a 16-in., both in .22 LR
20.5 in, 16 in.: **$940.00**
24 in.: **$967.00**

455 VARMINT TACTICOOL SUPRESSOR READY

Action: Bolt
Stock: Laminate
Barrel: 16.5 in.
Sights: None
Weight: 6 lb. 10 oz.
Caliber: .22 LR
Magazine: Detachable box, 5 rounds
Features: Suppressor not included
MSRP **$549.00**

512 AMERICAN

Action: Semiautomatic
Stock: Turkish walnut
Barrel: 20.5 in.
Sights: None
Weight: 5 lb. 0.6 oz.
Caliber: .22 LR, .22 WMR
Magazine: Detachable box, 5 rounds
Features: Aluminum alloy upper receiver; fiberglass-reinforced polymer lower receiver; easy fieldstripping; Turkish walnut stock with laser-cut checkering
MSRP . . . . **$510.00–$541.00**

CZ-USA (Ceska Zbrojovka)

CZ–USA 512 CARBINE

CZ-USA 512 SEMI-AUTOMATIC

CZ-USA 527 VARMINT

CZ-USA 550 MAGNUM H.E.T. II
(HIGH ENERGY TACTICAL)

CZ-USA 550 SAFARI MAGNUM

CZ-USA 550 "WESTERN SERIES" BADLANDS

RIFLES

512 CARBINE

Action: Semiautomatic
Stock: Black beechwood
Barrel: 16.5 in.
Sights: Adjustable tangent
Weight: 5 lb. 2 oz.
Caliber: .22 LR
Magazine: Detachable box, 5 rounds
Features: Aluminum alloy upper receiver; fiberglass-reinforced polymer lower receiver; easy fieldstripping
MSRP **$493.00**

512 SEMI-AUTOMATIC

Action: Semiautomatic
Stock: Lacquered beech wood
Barrel: 20.7 in.
Sights: Adjustable
Weight: 5 lb. 14 oz.
Caliber: .22 LR, .22 WMR
Magazine: Detachable box, 5 rounds
Features: Aluminum alloy upper receiver and fiberglass reinforced polymer lower half; dual guide rods; hammer-forged CZ barrel; integral 11mm dovetail for mounting optics
MSRP . . . .**$480.00–$510.00**

527

Action: Bolt
Stock: Walnut
Barrel: 18.5 in.–24 in.
Sights: Open

Weight: 5 lb. 14 oz.–7 lb. 13 oz.
Caliber: American .223 Rem., .204 Ruger, 7.62x39, 6.5 Grendel, .222 Rem., .22 Hornet, .17 Hornet; Carbine .223 Rem., 7.62x39; FS .223 Rem.; Lux .223 Rem., .22 Hornet, .222 Rem.; Lux left-hand .223 Rem.; Varmint .223 Rem., .204 Ruger, .17 Hornet
Magazine: Detachable box, 5 rounds
Features: Hammer-forged barrel; controlled round feed; single-set trigger; each model comes in a variety of calibers and a different stock
American: . . . . **$733.00–$787.00**
Carbine: **$733.00**
FS: **$784.00**
Lux: . . . . **$733.00–$778.00**
Varmint: . . . . **$725.00–$775.00**

550 MAGNUM H.E.T. II (HIGH ENERGY TACTICAL)

Action: Bolt
Stock: Carbon fiber
Barrel: 25 in.
Sights: None
Weight: 14 lb.
Caliber: .338 Lapua
Magazine: Detachable box, 5 rounds
Features: Adjustable cheekpiece; molded-in midnight camo; low-mount Picatinny rail; Badger Ordinance FTE muzzle brake
MSRP **$3929.00**

550 SAFARI MAGNUM

Action: Bolt
Stock: Walnut
Barrel: 25 in.
Sights: Express sights
Weight: 9 lb. 6 oz.
Caliber: 416 Rigby, .458 Lott, .458 Win. Mag., .505 Gibbs
Magazine: 5 rounds
Features: Known worldwide as the 602 BRNO; hammer-forged barrel; single-set trigger; controlled round feed and fixed ejector make the rifle reliable enough for heavy and dangerous game; express sights (1 standing, 2 folding); select Trukish walnut stock with classic safari shape
MSRP **$1318.00**

550 "WESTERN SERIES" BADLANDS

Action: Bolt
Stock: Kevlar
Barrel: 25 in.
Sights: None
Weight: 9 lb. 3 oz.
Caliber: .338 Lapua
Magazine: Internal, 4 rounds
Features: Blued finish; muzzle break
MSRP **$2599.00**

CZ-USA (Ceska Zbrojovka)

CZ-USA 550 "WESTERN SERIES" SONORAN

CZ-USA 557 SPORTER

CZ-USA 557 SPORT MANNERS

CZ-USA 557 SPORTER SHORT ACTION

CZ-USA 557 URBAN COUNTER SNIPER

550 "WESTERN SERIES" SONORAN
Action: Bolt
Stock: Carbon fiber
Barrel: 24 in., 26 in. (Mag.)
Sights: None
Weight: 7 lb. 10 oz., 7 lb. 13 oz. (Mag.)
Caliber: .26 Nosler, .30-06 Spfd., .270 Win., .300 Win. Mag., 7mm Rem. Mag.
Magazine: Internal, 5 or 3 (Mag.) rounds
Features: Fluted barrel; high corrosion and wear resistence
MSRP $3199.00

557 CARBINE
Action: Bolt
Stock: Walnut
Barrel: 20.5 in.
Sights: Fixed
Weight: 7 lb. 4 oz.
Caliber: .30-06 Spfd., .243 Win., .308 Win., .270 Win., 6.5x55 Swedish
Magazine: Internal, 4 rounds

Features: Integral 19mm dovetails
MSRP $812.00

557 SPORTER
Action: Bolt
Stock: Walnut
Barrel: 20.5 in.
Sights: None
Weight: 7 lb. 4 oz.
Caliber: .30-06 Spfd., .270 Win., 6.5x55 Swedish
Magazine: Internal, 4 rounds
Features: Integral 19mm dovetails
MSRP $792.00

557 SPORTER MANNERS
Action: Bolt
Stock: Carbon fiber
Barrel: 20.5 in.
Sights: None
Weight: 6 lb. 11 oz.
Caliber: .30-06 Spfd., .270 Win., 6.5x55 Swedish
Magazine: Internal, 4 rounds
Features: Features a Manners composite stock with a 100-percent carbon fiber shell and aluminum

bedding pillars; 19mm dovetails, fully adjustable match trigger, hinged floorplate, and two-position safety are standard
MSRP $1268.00

557 SPORTER SHORT ACTION
Action: Short action
Stock: Turkish walnut
Barrel: 20.5 in.
Sights: None
Weight: 7 lb.
Caliber: .243 Win., .308 Win.
Magazine: Detachable box, 4 rounds
Features: CNCed billet action; cold hammer-forged barrel
MSRP $792.00

557 URBAN COUNTER SNIPER
Action: Bolt
Stock: Carbon fiber composite
Barrel: 16 in.
Sights: None
Weight: 10 lb. 8 oz.
Caliber: .308 Win.
Magazine: Detachable box, 10 rounds
Features: Built for compactness; designed to excel at engaging targets within 400 yards; three-prong flash hider serves as a QD for a suppressor
MSRP $1899.00

CZ-USA (Ceska Zbrojovka)

CZ–USA 557 VARMINT

CZ-USA 750 SNIPER

CZ–USA 805 BREN S1 CARBINE

CZ–USA SCORPION EVO 3 S1 CARBINE

CZ-USA ULTIMATE HUNTING RIFLE

557 VARMINT

Action: Bolt
Stock: Walnut
Barrel: 25.6 in.
Sights: None
Weight: 10 lb. 14 oz.
Caliber: .243 Win., .308 Win.
Magazine: Detachable box
Features: Heavy, straight profile barrel tapering to a 0.863 in. muzzle; healthy palm swell; laser-cut stippling; flat forend
MSRP $865.00

750 SNIPER

Action: Bolt
Stock: Synthetic thumbhole
Barrel: 26 in.
Sights: Open
Weight: 11 lb. 14 oz.
Caliber: .308 Win.
Magazine: Detachable box, 10 rounds
Features: Adjustable comb; underside of forend is fitted with a 220mm-long rail for bipod attachment; muzzle-brake; thread protector; mirage shield; blued barrel; single-stage trigger
MSRP $1999.00

805 BREN S1 CARBINE

Action: Semiautomatic
Stock: Synthetic
Barrel: 16.2 in.
Sights: Flip up, 2 rear aperture sizes
Weight: 8 lb. 0.3 oz.
Caliber: .223; 5.56
Magazine: 10 or 30 rounds
Features: Factory folding adjustable stock; flip-up adjustable iron sights; STANAG magazine; two-port muzzle keeping the Bren solidly on target and reducing recoil and muzzle flip
MSRP . . . .$1999.00–$2099.00

SCORPION EVO 3 S1 CARBINE

Action: Semiautomatic
Stock: Synthetic
Barrel: 16.2 in.
Sights: Low-profile fully adjustable aperture and post, 4 rear aperture sizes
Weight: 7 lb.
Caliber: 9mm
Magazine: 10 or 30 rounds
Features: 16.2 in. barrel fitted with either a compensating muzzle brake or a faux suppressor built specifically for CZ-USA by SilencerCo; newly designed forend covered in M-LOK attachment points to keep the profile slim while still being big enough to swallow most pistol-caliber suppressors; top Picatinny rail; low-profile aluminum adjustable sights; ambidextrous controls; swappable non-reciprocating charging handle; adjustable trigger
MSRP . . . . $999.00–$1049.00

ULTIMATE HUNTING RIFLE

Action: Bolt
Stock: Walnut
Barrel: 23.6 in.
Sights: Open
Weight: 7 lb. 11 oz.
Caliber: .300 Win. Mag.
Magazine: Fixed, 3 rounds
Features: Hammer-forged, blued barrel; single-stage trigger
MSRP $1361.00

Dakota Arms

DAKOTA MODEL 10

DAKOTA MODEL 76 CLASSIC

DAKOTA MODEL 97

DAKOTA SHARPS

DAKOTA VARMINTER

MODEL 10

Action: Falling block
Stock: Walnut
Barrel: 23 in.
Sights: None
Weight: 6 lb.–7 lb.
Caliber: .22 LR to .300 Win., .338 to .375 H&H Mag.
Magazine: None
Features: Point wrap checkering; scope ring bases installed; custom length of pull; barrel break in
MSRP . . . . **from $5260.00**
Deluxe: . . . . **from $6690.00**

MODEL 76 CLASSIC

Action: Bolt
Stock: Walnut
Barrel: 23 in.
Sights: None
Weight: 6 lb. 8 oz.–9 lb. 8 oz.
Caliber: Classic: .257 Roberts, .260 Rem., .270 Win., .280 Rem., .30-06 Spfd., .300 Dakota, .300 Win. Mag., .300 WSM, .308 Win., .330 Dakota, .416 Rem., 7mm Rem. Mag., 7mm-08 Rem.; Safari: .300 H&H, .375 Dakota, .416 Rem., 7mm Dakota; African: .338 Win. Mag., .375 H&H, .416 Rem., .404 Jeffery, .416 Rigby, .450 Dakota, .458 Lott
Magazine: Box, 4 rounds
Features: Barrel break in; custom length of pull; optional engraving; point panel checkering; Dakota swivel studs; 1-inch recoil pad; straddle floor plate; right- or left-hand configurations; Safari model has front island sight with flip-up night sight; African model has quarter rib sights with banded front sights and flip-up night sights
Classic: . . . . **from $6030.00**
Safari: . . . . **from $8010.00**
African: . . . . **from $8890.00**

MODEL 97

Action: Bolt
Stock: Fiberglass, composite, walnut
Barrel: 22 in. (short action), 25 in. (long action)
Sights: None
Weight: 7 lb.
Caliber: All-Weather: .30-06 Spfd., .338 Win. Mag., .375 H&H, 7mm Rem. Mag., 7mm-08 Rem.; Long Range: .280 Rem., .338 Win. Mag., 7mm Rem. Mag., 7mm-08 Rem.
Magazine: Blind box
Features: Stainless Douglas barrel; black composite stock with two inletted Ken Howell swivel studs; stainless trigger bow
All-weather: . . . . **from $4050.00**
Deluxe: . . . . **from $4820.00**
Long Range: . . . . . . **from $3720.00**

SHARPS

Action: Falling block
Stock: Walnut
Barrel: 26 in.
Sights: Open
Weight: 8 lb. 4 oz.
Caliber: .17 HMR, .22 Hornet, .30-30 Win., .30-40 Krag., .375 H&H
Magazine: None
Features: Octagon barrel; steel buttplate; single blade rear sight with front bead; matte blued metal finish
Sharps: . . . . **from $4490.00**
Miller: . . . . **from $5590.00**

VARMINTER

Action: Bolt
Stock: Walnut
Barrel: 22 in.
Sights: None
Weight: 8 lb. 4 oz.
Caliber: .17 VarTag, .17 Rem., .17 Tactical, .20 PPC, .204 Ruger, .221 Rem. Fireball, .22 PPC, .223 Rem., 6mm PPC, 6.5 Grendel
Magazine: None
Features: Available in walnut sporter-style stock or XXX walnut varmint style stock with semi-beavertail forend; checkered grip; recessed target crown; vapor hone matte bead blast finish on stainless; stainless steel barrel
MSRP . . . . **from $2840.00**
All-weather: . . . . **from $3390.00**
Deluxe: . . . . **from $3390.00**
Heavy: . . . . **from $2840.00**

Daniel Defense

DANIEL DEFENSE DDM4V4S

DANIEL DEFENSE DDM4V7

DANIEL DEFENSE DDM4V9

DANIEL DEFENSE DDM4V7LW

DANIEL DEFENSE DDM4V11 PRO

DANIEL DEFENSE DD5V1

DDM4V4S

Action: Semiautomatic
Stock: Synthetic
Barrel: 11.5 in.
Sights: None
Weight: 5 lb. 14 oz.
Caliber: 5.56 NATO
Magazine: Detachable box, 30 rounds
Features: Lightweight, ergonomic rail system affords ample room for securely mounting multiple accessories and offers the longest possible sight radius with iron sights; three removable high-temperature-resistant Daniel Defense Rail Panels for a secure, comfortable grip while also protecting the support hand from heat; compatibility with a wide variety of muzzle devices and sound suppressors; freefloating, cold hammer-forged barrel
MSRP **$1733.00**

DDM4V7

Action: Semiautomatic
Stock: Synthetic
Barrel: 16 in.
Sights: None
Weight: 6 lb. 3 oz.
Caliber: 5.56 NATO
Magazine: Detachable box, 30 rounds
Features: M-LOK attachment technology with Daniel Defense MFR XS

15.0 rail; DD improved flash suppressor; mid-length gas system; uninterrupted 1913 Picatinny rail; black, Mil Spec+, or Daniel Defense Tornado finishes
MSRP . . . . **$1679.00–$1847.00**

DDM4V7 LW

Action: Semiautomatic
Stock: Synthetic
Barrel: 16 in.
Sights: None
Weight: 6 lb. 1 oz.
Caliber: 5.56 NATO
Magazine: Detachable box, 30 rounds
Features: M-LOK attachment technology with Daniel Defense MFR XS 15.0 rail; DD improved flash suppressor; mid-length gas system; uninterrupted 1913 Picatinny rail
MSRP **$1679.00**

DDM4V9

Action: Semiautomatic
Stock: Synthetic
Barrel: 16 in.
Sights: None
Weight: 6 lb. 10 oz.
Caliber: 5.56 NATO
Magazine: Detachable box, 30 rounds
Features: Daniel Defense stock, pistol and vertical grips, flash suppressor, and M4 rail
MSRP **$1773.00**

DDM4V11 PRO

Action: Semiautomatic
Stock: Synthetic
Barrel: 18 in.
Sights: None
Weight: 7 lb. 8 oz.
Caliber: 5.56 NATO
Magazine: Detachable box, 30 rounds
Features: Picatinny rails; muzzle climb mitigator; freefloat rail; Geissele automatics super dynamic 3-gun trigger; flared magazine well
MSRP **$2099.00**

DD5V1

Action: Semiautomatic
Stock: Synthetic
Barrel: 16 in.
Sights: None
Weight: 8 lb. 5 oz.
Caliber: .308 Win./7.62x51 mm
Magazine: 20 rounds
Features: Four-bolt connection system utilizing a unique barrel extension; optimized upper receiver; improved bolt carrier group; ambidextrous controls; configurable modular charging handle; cold hammer-forged barrel; Geissele SSA two-stage trigger for precise fire control; DD Superior Suppression Device; 15 in. Picatinny top rail; black, Mil-Spec+, or Daniel Defense Tornado finishes
MSRP . . . .**$3044.00–$3198.00**

Davide Pedersoli & C.

PEDERSOLI 1874 SHARPS OLD WEST

PEDERSOLI 1886 SPORTING RIFLE

PEDERSOLI MODEL 86/71 LEVER ACTION BOARBUSTER CAMO

PEDERSOLI MODEL 86/71 LEVER ACTION CLASSIC

PEDERSOLI MODEL 86/71 LEVER ACTION STAINLESS STEEL

1874 SHARPS OLD WEST MAPLE

Action: Dropping block
Stock: Maple
Barrel: 30 in.
Sights: None
Weight: 11 lb. 7 oz.
Caliber: .45-70 Govt.
Magazine: None
Features: Optional Creedmoor and tunnel sights; brass plate on right side of butt stock can be personalized; forend has wedge plates; pistol grip cap is made of hardened steel
MSRP **$2340.00**

1886 SPORTING RIFLE

Action: Lever
Stock: Wood
Barrel: 26 in.
Sights: Adjustable rear, fixed front
Weight: 9 lb. 13 oz.
Caliber: .45-70 Govt.
Magazine: N/A
Features: PMG quality barrel; forged

and CNC machined frame; American selected walnut stock; blade front sight and adjustable rear sight; drilled and tapped to assemble the aperture bolt sight
MSRP **$2015.00**

MODEL 86/71 LEVER ACTION BOARBUSTER

Action: Lever
Stock: Walnut
Barrel: 19 in.
Sights: Drilled and tapped for scopes
Weight: 7 lb. 4 oz.
Caliber: .444 Marlin, .45-70 Govt.
Magazine: 5 rounds
Features: Barrel equipped with European Picatinny style base with integral rear sight; half cock safety on hammer; safety slide catch at the rear of the frame; checkered pistol grip stock and forend are made from walnut; also available in soft touch orange camo color; metal parts are blued; drilled and tapped for sights
MSRP . . . . **$1940.00–$1975.00**

MODEL 86/71 LEVER ACTION CLASSIC

Action: Lever
Stock: Walnut
Barrel: 24 in.
Sights: Drilled and tapped for scopes
Weight: 8 lb. 3 oz.
Caliber: .45-70 Govt.
Magazine: 5 rounds
Features: Last "big frame" rifle for Winchester; drilled and tapped for scopes; broach rifled barrel and magazine are blued finished; checkered walnut pistol grip; frame is forged and CNC-machined, with a blued finish on the standard version and case-hardened frame and buttcap on the Premium model with select walnut stock and forend
Standard Classic: **$1905.00**
Premium: **$1950.00**

MODEL 86/71 LEVER ACTION STAINLESS STEEL

Action: Lever
Stock: Synthetic
Barrel: 19 in.
Sights: Adjustable rear, fixed front
Weight: 7 lb. 15 oz.
Caliber: .45-70 Govt.
Magazine: N/A
Features: PMG barrel, broach rifled; fiber optic front sight and Weaver/Picatinny base with integrated rear sight; stock is made of American walnut covered with a camouflage film; microcell thick butt plate and swivel stud
MSRP **$2590.00**

Davide Pedersoli & C.

PEDERSOLI MODEL 86/71 LEVER ACTION WILDBUSTER

PEDERSOLI KODIAK MARK IV

PEDERSOLI ROLLING BLOCK MISSISSIPPI CLASSIC

PEDERSOLI ROLLING BLOCK TARGET

PEDERSOLI SHARPS LITTLE BESTY

MODEL 86/71 LEVER ACTION WILDBUSTER

Action: Lever
Stock: Walnut
Barrel: 24 in.
Sights: Drilled and tapped for scopes
Weight: 8 lb. 3 oz.
Caliber: .45-70 Govt.
Magazine: 5 rounds
Features: Ramp rear sight; walnut forend and pistol grip stock with checkered buttplate; blued finish on metal parts; drilled and tapped for scopes
MSRP **$1765.00**

KODIAK MARK IV

Action: Breech loading
Stock: Walnut
Barrel: 22 in., 24 in.
Sights: Open
Weight: 9 lb. 11 oz.–10 lb. 5 oz.
Caliber: .450 NE, .45-70 Govt. 8x57JRS, 9.3x74R
Magazine: None
Features: Double-leave rear sight in a dovetail; tapered round barrels made of blued steel; select walnut stock with checkering and oil finish; available with an interchangeable 20-gauge barrel in all calibers except

the .450 NE
Rifle calibers only: . . . **$6145.00–$8260.00**
With 20-gauge barrel: . **$8370.00–$8425.00**

ROLLING BLOCK MISSISSIPPI CLASSIC

Action: N/A
Stock: Wood
Barrel: 26 in.
Sights: Adjustable rear, fixed front
Weight: 7 lb. 8 oz.
Caliber: .357 Mag, .38-55, .45 Colt
Magazine: N/A
Features: High carbon steel barrel is broach rifled; alloy frame is embellished with a engraving; old silver colour finishing; equipped with a blade front sight and an adjustable rear sight, drilled to assemble the Creedmoor sight; stock and forend are made of American walnut with brass fittings
MSRP **$1005.00**

ROLLING BLOCK TARGET

Action: Dropping block
Stock: Walnut
Barrel: 30 in.
Sights: Open
Weight: 10 lb. 9 oz.
Caliber: .357 Mag., .45–70 Govt.

Magazine: None
Features: Octagonal, conical blued barrel; case-hardened color frame is equipped with ramp rear sight adjustable in elevation; steel buttplate and trigger guard; straight stock and forend made of walnut with oil finish; Deluxe grade also available
Standard Target: **$1230.00**
Deluxe Target: **$2590.00**

SHARPS LITTLE BETSY

Action: N/A
Stock: Wood
Barrel: 24 in.
Sights: Creedmoor
Weight: 7 lb. 10 oz.
Caliber: .17 HRM, .22LR, .22 Hornet, .357 Mag, .30-30 Win.
Magazine: N/A
Features: Forged and CNC machined frame features a floral engraving; stock is made of American walnut; barrel PMG quality features a matt blue finish; sights includes a tunnel front sight and the folding Creedmoor sight; with double set trigger
MSRP . . . . **$1795.00–$1955.00**

Del-Ton

DEL-TON DT SPORT OR

DEL-TON DTI ECHO 7.62X39

DEL-TON DTI EVOLUTION

DEL–TON DTI EXTREME DUTY 316

DEL-TON ECHO 316H OR

RIFLES

DT SPORT OR

Action: Semiautomatic
Stock: M4 six-position
Barrel: 16 in.
Sights: None
Weight: 5 lb. 13 oz.
Caliber: 5.56 NATO
Magazine: Detachable box, 30 rounds
Features: Low profile gas block; six-position M4 stock; CAR handguards with single heat shields; A2 flash hider; anodized receiver; gun lock included
MSRP **$717.95**

DTI ECHO 7.62X39

Action: Semiautomatic
Stock: Synthetic
Barrel: 16 in.
Sights: Adjustable front sight
Weight: 6 lb. 10 oz.
Caliber: 7.62x39
Magazine: Detachable box, 30 rounds
Features: Carbine gas system; phosphated under F-marked front sight

base; chrome-lined carrier interior; carbine-length hand guards; aluminum delta ring; single heat shield
MSRP **$753.42**

DTI EVOLUTION

Action: Semiautomatic
Stock: Magpul CTR Mil-Spec
Barrel: 16 in.
Sights: Folding front, flip rear
Weight: 7 lb. 3 oz.
Caliber: 5.56 NATO
Magazine: Detachable box, 30 rounds
Features: Chrome-lined barrel; Samson Evolution free-float rail; Quick Flip Dual Aperture rear sight; Magpul MOE+ grip
MSRP **$1319.05**

DTI EXTREME DUTY 316

Action: Semiautomatic
Stock: M4 reinforced fiber
Barrel: 16 in.
Sights: Samson quick flip dual aperture rear sight

Weight: 6 lb. 6.4 oz.
Caliber: 5.56 NATO
Magazine: Detachable box
Features: Hammer forged CMV chrome-lined barrel; H-buffer
Standard: **$1119.05**
California-compliant: **$1333.33**

ECHO 316H OR

Action: Semiautomatic
Stock: M4 five-position
Barrel: 16 in.
Sights: None
Weight: 6 lb. 10 oz.
Caliber: 5.56 NATO
Magazine: Detachable box, 30 rounds
Features: Single rail gas block; CAR handguards with single heat shields; A2 flash hider; forged 7075 T6 aluminum upper and lower receivers
MSRP **$816.44**

Dixie Gun Works

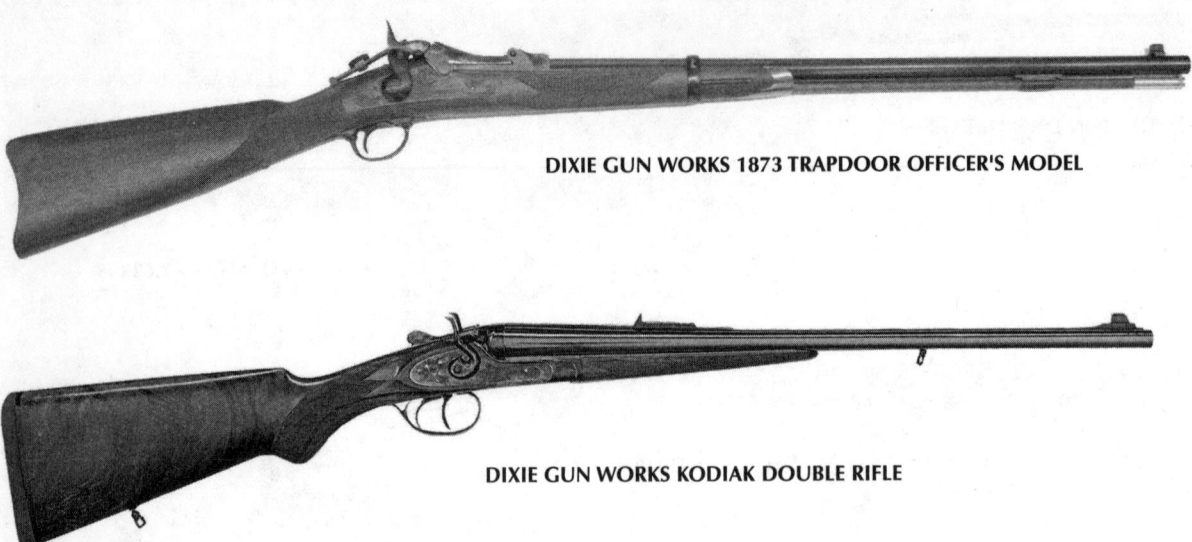

DIXIE GUN WORKS 1873 TRAPDOOR OFFICER'S MODEL

DIXIE GUN WORKS KODIAK DOUBLE RIFLE

1873 TRAPDOOR OFFICER'S MODEL BY PEDERSOLI

Action: Breechloading
Stock: Walnut
Barrel: 26 in.
Sights: Adjustable
Weight: 8 lb.
Caliber: .45-70 Govt.
Magazine: None
Features: Single-shot rifle; front sight is blued steel with brass bead; rear sight is adjustable tang sight; color case-hardened steel furniture, pewter nose cap; single set trigger; chambered for black powder cartridges or factory-loaded smokeless ammo
MSRP **$1950.00**

KODIAK DOUBLE RIFLE BY PEDERSOLI

Action: Lever
Stock: Walnut, pistol grip
Barrel: 24 in.
Sights: Flip up sights
Weight: 10 lb.–10 lb. 12 oz.
Caliber: .50, .54, .58 Kodiak, .45-70 Mark IV, .72 Express
Magazine: None
Features: Express has dovetail, steel ramp with brass bead as front sight; blued barrels; external hammers are rebounding style; double triggers; sling is included; English walnut buttstock and forearm are checkered; rubber recoil pad; chambered for black powder cartridges or factory-loaded smokeless ammo
MSRP . . . . **$1495.00–$5250.00**

Doublestar Corp.

DOUBLESTAR CORP STAR 10-B

STAR 10-B

Action: Semiautomatic
Stock: Synthetic
Barrel: 18 in.
Sights: None
Weight: 9 lb. 13 oz.
Caliber: .308 cal
Magazine: 20 rounds
Features: Hogue pistol grip; Wilson air gauged stainless steel barrel (fluted); Samson Evolution handguard; brass deflector and dust cover; integrated trigger guard
MSRP **$2566.69**

.22 BULL BARREL

Action: Semiautomatic
Stock: Fixed A2 synthetic
Barrel: 16 in.
Sights: None
Weight: 7 lb. 5 oz.
Caliber: .22 LR
Magazine: Detachable box, 10 rounds
Features: Capable of accepting after-market stocks, grips, fire control components; integral feed ramp; fixed ejector
MSRP...............**$1029.00**

DPMS .22 BULL BARREL

DPMS 24 SPECIAL

DPMS 3G2

DPMS A2 CLASSIC

24 SPECIAL

Action: Semiautomatic
Stock: Synthetic; pistol grip
Barrel: 24 in.
Sights: None
Weight: 10 lb. 4 oz.
Caliber: .233 Rem
Magazine: Detachable box, 30 rounds
Features: Aircraft aluminum alloy, A3 style flattop receiver coated in black Teflon; aluminum trigger guard; black standard A2 Zytel Mil-Spec stock with Panther Tactical grip; aluminum ribbed free-float tube; nylon web sling included; adjustable buttplate
MSRP...............**$1229.00**

3G2

Action: Semiautomatic
Stock: Synthetic
Barrel: 16 in.
Sights: Magpu Gen 2 BUS
Weight: 7 lb. 1.6 oz.
Caliber: 5.56 NATO
Magazine: Detachable box, 30 rounds
Features: Stainless lightweight barrel with Miculek compensator; full length M111 handguard allows for the placement of back-up sights either on the top rail or on a 45-degree angle for rapid close-range target acquisition; Ergo grip and Magpul STR stock round out this range-ready carbine; pistol grip stock
MSRP...............**$1239.00**

A2 CLASSIC

Action: Semiautomatic
Stock: Synthetic
Barrel: 20 in.
Sights: Open
Weight: 9 lb.
Caliber: 5.56 NATO
Magazine: Detachable box, 30 rounds
Features: Chromoly steel barrel with A2 flash hider; forged aircraft aluminum alloy receiver with A2 fixed carry handle; black standardized A2 black style Mil-Spec stock; standard A2 round handguards; dual aperture adjustable rear sights, Mil-Spec front sight post
MSRP...............**$869.00**

RIFLES

DPMS Panther Arms

DPMS AP4 CARBINE

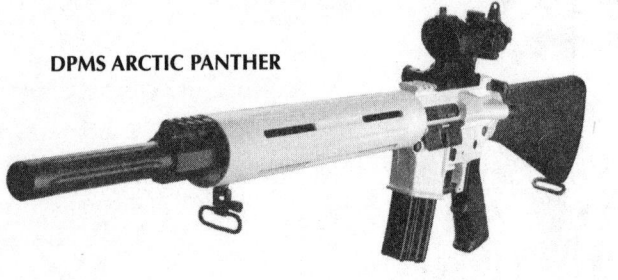

DPMS ARCTIC PANTHER

DPMS CARBINE 16

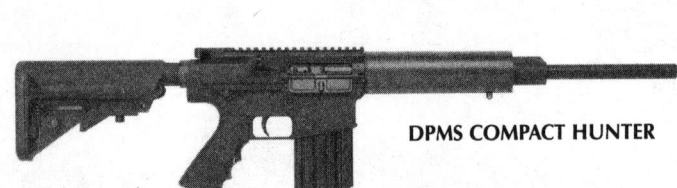

DPMS COMPACT HUNTER

DPMS DCM

AP4 CARBINE

Action: Semiautomatic
Stock: Synthetic
Barrel: 16 in.
Sights: Open
Weight: 7 lb. 2 oz.
Caliber: 5.56 NATO
Magazine: Detachable box, 30 rounds
Features: Chromoly steel barrel with A2 Flash hider; A3 aircraft aluminum alloy receiver with detachable carrying handle; adjustable rear sight and A2 front sight assembly; black AP4–6 position, telescoping fiber reinforced polymer stock; oval, carbine length GlacierGuards
MSRP **$959.00**

ARCTIC PANTHER

Action: Semiautomatic
Stock: Synthetic
Barrel: 20 in.
Sights: None
Weight: 9 lb.
Caliber: .223 Rem.
Magazine: Detachable box, 30 rounds
Features: Fluted and black Teflon coated barrel; aircraft aluminum alloy, A3 style flattop receiver coated

in white; standard A2 black Zytel Mil-Spec stock; aluminum ribbed free-float handguard tube (coated white)
MSRP **$1129.00**

CARBINE 16

Action: Semiautomatic
Stock: Synthetic
Barrel: 16 in.
Sights: Open
Weight: 6 lb. 14 oz.
Caliber: 5.56 NATO
Magazine: Detachable box, 30 rounds
Features: Chromoly steel barrel with flash hider; A3 aircraft aluminum alloy receiver with detachable carrying handle; adjustable rear sight and A2 front sight assembly; DPMS Pardus black stock; oval, carbine length GlacierGuards
MSRP **$829.00**

COMPACT HUNTER

Action: Semiautomatic
Stock: Synthetic
Barrel: 16 in.
Sights: None
Weight: 7 lb. 12 oz.
Caliber: .308 Win.

Magazine: Detachable box, 4, 10, 20 rounds
Features: Designed for smaller statures and suitable for youth, female, and hunters who prefer a compact firearm; Teflon-coated stainless steel barrel; carbon fiber free-float tube; Hogue pistol grip; B5 Systems-Special Operations Peculiar Modification (SOPMOD) stock
MSRP **$1499.00**

DCM

Action: Semiautomatic
Stock: Synthetic
Barrel: 20 in.
Sights: Adjustable NM
Weight: 9 lb. 6 oz.
Caliber: .233 Rem.
Magazine: Detachable box, 30 rounds
Features: National Match dual aperture rear sight, NM front sight post; A2 fixed carry handle; forged aircraft aluminum alloy receiver; receiver coated in Teflon; aluminum trigger guard; standard black A2 style Mil-Spec stock with trap door assembly; DCM free-float handguard system
MSRP **$1129.00**

DPMS Panther Arms

DPMS PANTHER ARMS GII AP4

DPMS PANTHER ARMS GII BULL

DPMS PANTHER ARMS GII RECON

DPMS PANTHER ARMS GII SASS

DPMS LR-204

DPMS LITE LR-308

GII AP4

Action: Semiautomatic
Stock: Synthetic
Barrel: 16 in.
Sights: F marked front sight base
Weight: 7 lb. 4 oz.
Caliber: 7.62 NATO
Magazine: Detachable box
Features: A2 pistol grip; cancellation brake; 34.25 in. collapsed; six position collabsible stock; muzzle brake; receiver mounted Picatinny rail
MSRP.................$1499.00

GII BULL 24

Action: Semiautomatic
Stock: Synthetic
Barrel: 24 in.
Sights: None
Weight: 10 lb.
Caliber: 7.62 NATO
Magazine: Detachable box
Features: 416 stainless steel bull barrel; A2 MII Spec buttstock; receiver mounted Picatinny rail
MSRP.................$1399.00

GII RECON

Action: Semiautomatic
Stock: Synthetic
Barrel: 16 in.
Sights: Front and rear BUIS
Weight: 8 lb. 8 oz.
Caliber: 7.62 NATO
Magazine: Detachable box
Features: 416 stainless steel barrel; bead blasted mid-length glass; six position collapsible stock; Advanced Armament 51T Blackout flash hider; handguard and receiver mounted Picatinny rails
MSRP.................$1759.00

GII SASS

Action: Semiautomatic
Stock: Synthetic
Barrel: 18 in.
Sights: Front and rear BUIS
Weight: 10 lb. 8 oz.
Caliber: 7.62 NATO
Magazine: Detachable box
Features: 416 stainless steel barrel; teflon coated; fluted bull barrel; mid-length glass; Magpul PRS stock; Panther flash hider; Harris bipod; handguard and receiver mounted Picatinny rails
MSRP.................$2379.00

LONG RANGE LITE

Action: Semiautomatic
Stock: Synthetic
Barrel: 24 in.
Sights: None
Weight: 10 lb. 4 oz.
Caliber: .308 Win.
Magazine: Detachable box, 4, 10, 20 rounds
Features: 416 stainless steel lightweight fluted barrel; improved 2012 carbon fiber free-float tube; A3 receiver
MSRP.................$1499.00

LR-204

Action: Semiautomatic
Stock: Synthetic
Barrel: 24 in.
Sights: None
Weight: 10 lb. 4 oz.
Caliber: .204 Ruger
Magazine: Detachable box, 30 rounds
Features: Fluted barrel; standard A2 black stock; aluminum ribbed freefloat tube; aircraft aluminum alloy, Teflon coated, forged A3 style receiver; nylon web sling included
MSRP.................$1059.00

DPMS Panther Arms

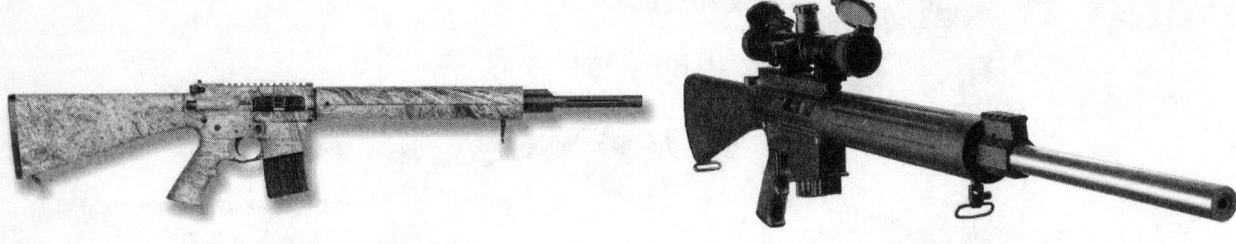

DPMS PRAIRIE PANTHER CAMO

DPMS LR-308

DPMS LR-260

DPMS RECON

DPMS NATO REPR

LR-260/LR-65

Action: Semiautomatic
Stock: Synthetic
Barrel: 24 in.
Sights: None
Weight: 11 lb. 4 oz.
Caliber: .260 Rem.
Magazine: Detachable box, 19 rounds
Features: 416 Stainless steel bull barrel; A3 style flattop receiver made of thick walled aluminum; standard AR-15 trigger group; standard A2 black style Mil-Spec stock with trap door assembly; standard length ribbed free-float handguard tube
MSRP. $1239.00

LR-308

Action: Semiautomatic
Stock: Synthetic
Barrel: 24 in.
Sights: None
Weight: 11 lb. 3 oz.
Caliber: .308 Win.
Magazine: Detachable box, 19 rounds
Features: 416 Stainless steel bull barrel; thick walled aluminum receiver coated with Teflon; internal trigger guard; raised Picatinny rail for easy scope mounting; standard A2 Black Zytel Mil-Spec stock
MSRP. $1199.00

NATO REPR

Action: Semiautomatic
Stock: Synthetic
Barrel: 20 in.
Sights: None
Weight: 9 lb. 12 oz.
Caliber: 7.62 NATO
Magazine: Detachable box, 19 rounds
Features: Two-stage match grade trigger; dark earth Magpul PRS stock; Hogue rubber grip with finger grooves; A3 style flattop; ambi-selector installed; milled from solid billet of aluminum; AAC flash hider/suppressor adapter
MSRP. $2589.00

PRAIRIE PANTHER CAMO

Action: Semiautomatic
Stock: Synthetic
Barrel: 20 in.
Sights: None
Weight: 7 lb. 2 oz.
Caliber: .223 Rem.
Magazine: Detachable box, 20 rounds
Features: Target crowned, stainless steel heavy barrel; A3 flattop aircraft aluminum alloy receiver; Magpul winter trigger guard; King's Desert Shadow camo, King's Snow Shadow camo, or Mossy Oak Brush camo stock; receiver features durable ceramic over coat in either type of camo; nylon web sling included
MSRP. $1289.00

RECON

Action: Semiautomatic
Stock: Synthetic
Barrel: 16 in.
Sights: Magpul BUIS
Weight: 9 lb.
Caliber: 5.56 NATO
Magazine: Detachable box, 30 rounds
Features: Bead-blasted stainless, mid length gas system; semi-auto trigger group; Magpul MOE stock in Teflon black
MSRP. $1129.00

DPMS Panther Arms

DPMS SWEET 16

DPMS TACTICAL 16

SWEET 16, BULL 20, BULL 24

Action: Semiautomatic
Stock: Synthetic
Barrel: 16 in., 20 in., 24 in.
Sights: None
Weight: 7 lb. 14 oz.–9 lb. 13 oz.
Caliber: .223 Rem.
Magazine: Detachable box, 30 rounds
Features: Aircraft aluminum alloy, A3 style flattop receiver coated in black Teflon; aluminum trigger guard; black standard A2 Zytel Mil-Spec stock; aluminum ribbed free-float tube; Nylon web sling included

Bull Sweet 16:	**$939.00**
Bull 20:	**$969.00**
Bull 24:	**$999.00**

TACTICAL 16

Action: Semiautomatic
Stock: Synthetic
Barrel: 16 in.
Sights: Open
Weight: 8 lb. 3 oz.
Caliber: 5.56 NATO
Magazine: Detachable box, 30 rounds
Features: Chromoly steel barrel with A3 Flash hider; A2 front and rear sight assembly; forged aircraft aluminum alloy receiver coated in Teflon; black standard A2 style mil stock; nylon web sling included

MSRP **$859.00**

E.R. Shaw

MK. VII CUSTOM

Action: Bolt
Stock: Walnut, laminate wood, or synthetic
Barrel: 16.25 in.–26 in.
Sights: None
Weight: Depending on specifications
Caliber: 92 calibers to choose from, from .17 Rem. to .450 Marlin
Magazine: Fixed magazine
Features: In addition to nearly 100 caliber choices, customers may select the twist rate (choices vary between caliber families), choose between nutmeg laminate, pepper laminate, walnut, or black synthetic stocks, and a host of other features

Starting price: **$775.00**

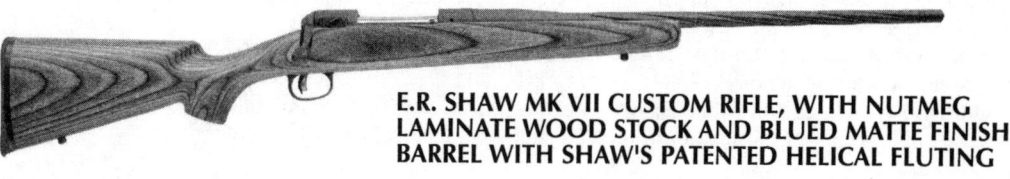

E.R. SHAW MK VII CUSTOM RIFLE, WITH NUTMEG LAMINATE WOOD STOCK AND BLUED MATTE FINISH BARREL WITH SHAW'S PATENTED HELICAL FLUTING

Excel Arms

EXCEL ARMS ACCELERATOR RIFLE

EXCEL ARMS X-5.7R

EXCEL ARMS X-22R

ACCELERATOR RIFLE
MR-22, MR-5.7

Action: Semiautomatic
Stock: Polymer composite, pistol grip
Barrel: 18 in.
Sights: Standard includes Red/Green dot optic
Weight: 8 lb.
Caliber: .22 WMR, .17 HMR
Magazine: Detachable box, 9 rounds
Features: Corrosion-resistant 17-4 stainless steel, including its fluted barrel; features manual and firing pin safeties, a last-round fired hold open bolt, flat-top accessory rail. A number of options are available:

Basic: supplied with one 9-round magazine; Standard: supplied with two 9-round magazines and red-dot optic; Limited Edition Zanders: supplied with two 9-round magazines, grey shroud, and two side-mounted Picatinny rails; P1 Package: supplied with two 9-round magazines, nylong sling, detachable sling swivels, detachable iron sights; P2 Package: same as P1 Package, but with 3-9x40 scope and scope rings instead of iron sights; P3 Package: same as Package 1, but with the addition of a 6 in.–9-in. bipod; P4 Package: same as P2 Package, but with the addition of a 6-in.–9-in. bipod

Basic MR-22:	**$538.00**
Basic MR 5.7:	**$672.00**
Standard MR-22:	**$577.00**
Limited Edition (Zanders Sporting Goods):	**$538.00**
Pacagke P-1 MR-22:	**$700.00**
Package P-2 MR-22:	**$700.00**
Package P-2 MR 5.7:	**$835.00**
Package P-3 MR-22:	**$793.00**
Package P-4 MR-22:	**$793.00**
Package P-5 MR-22:	**$984.00**

X-5.7R

Action: Semiautomatic
Stock: Synthetic
Barrel: 18 in.
Sights: None
Weight: 6 lb. 4 oz.
Caliber: 5.7x28mm
Magazine: Detachable box, 25, 10 rounds
Features: CNC-machined aluminum; Picatinny rail; tactical AR styling; collapsible stock; tapped holes in the hand guard for mounting accessory rails

MSRP	**$795.00**
Iron sights:	**$916.00**

X-22R RIFLE

Action: Semiautomatic
Stock: Synthetic
Barrel: 18 in.
Sights: None
Weight: 4 lb. 12 oz.
Caliber: .22 LR HV
Magazine: Detachable box, 25 rounds, (10 rounds optional)
Features: CNC-machined aluminum frame; optional 3–9x40 scope; tapped holes in hand guard for mounting accessory rails; integral weaver base to mount scopes, sights, and optics

Basic:	**$504.00**
Scoped:	**$594.00**
10 RD:	**$504.00**

FN America

FN AMERICA BALLISTA

FN AMERICA FN 15 COMPETITION

FN AMERICA FN SPR A5M XP

FN AMERICA FNAR STANDARD HEAVY BARREL

BALLISTA
Action: Bolt
Stock: Collapsible
Barrel: 26 in.
Sights: N/A, scope compatible
Weight: 15 lb.
Caliber: .308 Win., .300 Win. Mag.,
.338 Lapua Mag.
Magazine: Detachable box, 8 or 15
rounds (.308 Win.), 6 or 10 rounds
(.300 Win. Mag.), 5 or 8 rounds (.338
Lapua)
Features: Modular, multi-caliber
designed for long-range precision
work; aluminum alloy receiver;
adjustable trigger; ambidextrous stock;
vibration-isolated aluminum alloy
receiver; Picatinny rail
MSRP **$7499.00**

FN 15 COMPETITION
Action: Semiautomatic
Stock: Synthetic
Barrel: 18 in.
Sights: None

Weight: 8 lb. 2 oz.
Caliber: 5.56x45mm
Magazine: 30 rounds
Features: Alloy-steel, cold-hammer
forged, and chrome-lined match-grade
barrel with muzzle break; Mega Arms
16 in. rail system with M-LOK;
Magpul MOE furniture; Timney
Competition single stage trigger; ergo-
nomic safety lever and magazine
release
MSRP **$2249.00**

FN SPR A5M XP
Action: Bolt
Stock: McMillan fiberglass
Barrel: 20 in., 24 in.
Sights: None
Weight: 11 lb. 5 oz.–11 lb. 13 oz.
Caliber: .300 WSM, .308 Win.
Magazine: Detachable box, 4 or 5
rounds
Features: Threaded tactical bolt knob;
barrel threaded muzzle; Picatinny rail;
external claw extractor with con-

trolled round feeding; integral recoil
lug; three-position safety; knurled bolt
handle
MSRP **$2899.00**

FNAR STANDARD
Action: Gas-operated semiautomatic
Stock: Synthetic
Barrel: 16 in., 20 in. standard fluted,
20 in. heavy fluted
Sights: Receiver mounted rail
Weight: 8 lb. 13 oz.–10 lb.
Caliber: .308 Win., 7.62 NATO
Magazine: Detachable box, 10, 20
rounds
Features: Extended bolt handle, hammer-forged barrel with crown; comes
with one magazine, three interchangeable recoil pads, three comb
inserts and shims for adjusting for
cast-on, cast-off, and drop at comb;
stock is matte black synthetic with
pistol grip and adjustable comb
MSRP . . . . **$1199.00–$1767.00**

FN America

FN AMERICA SCAR 17S
CARBINE

SCAR 16S AND 17S CARBINE

Action: Gas-operated semiautomatic
Stock: Polymer
Barrel: 16.25 in.
Sights: Adjustable, folding, removable
Weight: 8 lb.
Caliber: .308 Win., 7.62 NATO
Magazine: Detachable box, 10, 20 rounds
Features: Fully adjustable stock; Picatinny rail plus three accessory rails for attaching a variety of sights and lasers; free-floating, cold-hammer-forged barrel; available in black or Flat Dark Earth tactical, telescoping, side-folding polymer stock
MSRP. . . . . **$2995.00–$3349.00**

Heckler & Koch

RIFLES

HECKLER & KOCH MR556A1

HECKLER & KOCH MR762A1

HECKLER & KOCH MR762A1
LONG RIFLE PACKAGE II

MR556A1

Action: Semiautomatic
Stock: Synthetic
Barrel: 14 in., 16.5 in.
Sights: Troy microsights
Weight: 8 lb. 10 oz.
Caliber: 5.56 NATO, .223 Rem.
Magazine: Detachable box, 30 rounds
Features: Free-floating Picatinny rail; gas operated piston system
Standard, Standard
 w/Raddlock:. **$3399.00**
Competition, Competition
 w/ Raddlock: **$3199.00**

MR762A1

Action: Semiautomatic
Stock: Synthetic
Barrel: 16.5 in.
Sights: None
Weight: 9 lb. 15 oz.
Caliber: 7.62 NATO
Magazine: Detachable box, 10, 20 rounds
Features: Match rifle features; direct descendant of HK416/417 series, but made for civilians; uses a piston and a solid operating "pusher" rod in place of the common gas tube normally used in AR-style rifles; cold-hammer-forged barrel; adjustable stock
MSRP. **$3999.00**

MR762A1 LONG RIFLE PACKAGE II

Action: Semiautomatic
Stock: Synthetic
Barrel: 16.5 in.
Sights: 3–9x40mm scope
Weight: 10 lb. 7 oz.
Caliber: 7.62 NATO
Magazine: Detachable box, 10, 20 rounds
Features: Rifle; Leupold 3–9 VX-R Patrol scope and mount; HK G28 buttstock; LaRue Tactical BRM-S bipod; ERGO Pistol Grip; Blue Force Gear sling; Manta rail covers; OTIS cleaning kit; a 10- and 20-round magazine; Model 1720 Pelican case
Without scope
 and mount: **$6399.00**
With scope and mount: . . . **$6899.00**

Henry Repeating Arms

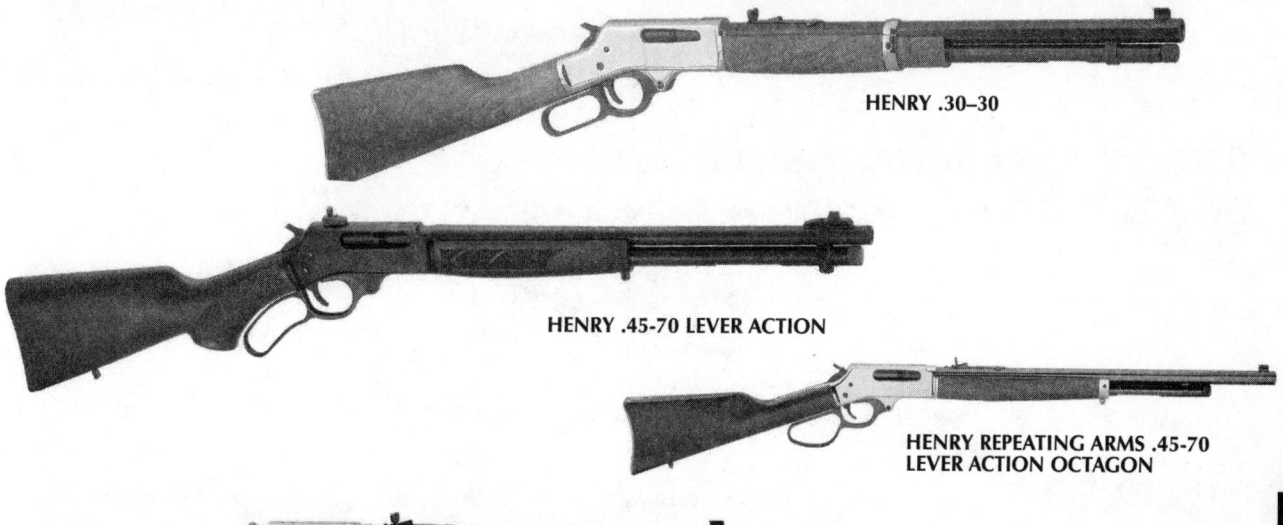

HENRY .30–30

HENRY .45-70 LEVER ACTION

HENRY REPEATING ARMS .45-70
LEVER ACTION OCTAGON

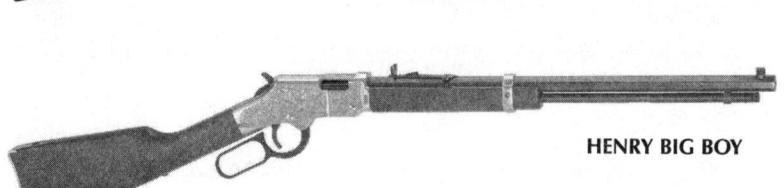

HENRY REPEATING ARMS ALL-WEATHER
LEVER ACTION

HENRY BIG BOY

.30-30

Action: Lever
Stock: Walnut
Barrel: 20 in.
Sights: Open
Weight: 7 lb.
Caliber: .30-30 Win.
Magazine: Under-barrel tube, 5 rounds
Features: Steel round barrel: deluxe checkered American walnut with rubber buttpad; XS Ghost Rings sights; blued steel receiver, drilled and tapped for easy scope mounting. Brass octagon barrel: straight-grip American walnut with buttplate; marble fully adjustable semi-buckhorn rear sight, with diamond insert, beaded front sight; brass receiver, drilled and tapped for easy scope mounting
Steel: **$850.00**
Brass: **$950.00**

.45-70 LEVER ACTION

Action: Lever
Stock: Walnut
Barrel: 18.43 in.

Sights: Closed rear, blade front
Weight: 7 lb. 1 oz.
Caliber: .45-70 Govt.
Magazine: Under-barrel tube, 4 rounds
Features: Pistol-grip American walnut with buttplate; blued steel drilled and tapped for easy scope mounting; XS Ghost Rings rear sight with blade front
MSRP **$850.00**

.45-70 LEVER ACTION OCTAGON

Action: Lever
Stock: Wood
Barrel: 22 in.
Sights: Adjustable
Weight: 8 lb. 2 oz.
Caliber: .45-70 Govt.
Magazine: 4 rounds
Features: Straight-grip American Walnut stock with brass buttplate; fully adjustable semi-buckhorn rear, and brass beaded front sight; brass drilled and tapped for a Weaver 63B mount
MSRP **$950.00**

ALL-WEATHER LEVER ACTION

Action: Lever
Stock: Stained hardwood
Barrel: 18.43 in., 20 in.
Sights: Adjustable semi-buckhorn rear, brass bead front
Weight: 7 lb.–7 lb. 1 oz.
Caliber: .30-30, .45-70
Magazine: Under-barrel tube, 4 or 5 rounds
Features: Adjustable buckhorn/bead sights; straight-grip in the .30-30 and pistolgrip in the .45-70; hard chrome plating on all metal surfaces (except springs and sights); durable industrial-grade coating on hardwood furniture; low-gloss look that won't spook game
MSRP **$999.95**

BIG BOY

Action: Lever
Stock: Walnut
Barrel: 20 in.
Sights: Open
Weight: 8.68 lb.
Caliber: .41 Mag., .327 Fed. Mag., .44 Mag., .45 Colt, .357 Mag.
Magazine: Under-barrel tube, 10 rounds
Features: Adjustable marble semi-buckhorn rear with white diamond insert and brass beaded front sight; solid top brass receiver, brass buttplate and brass barrel band; straight-grip American walnut stock; octagonal barrel
MSRP **$899.95**

Henry Repeating Arms

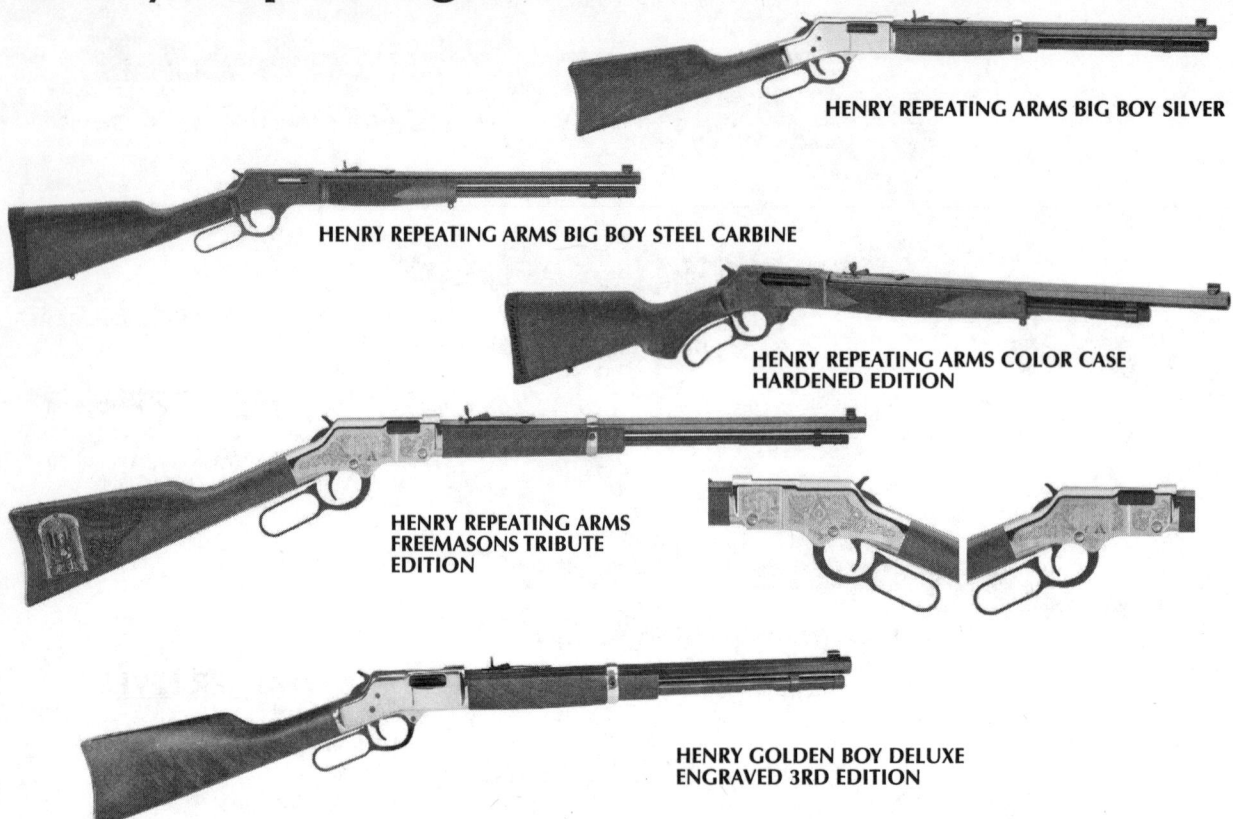

HENRY REPEATING ARMS BIG BOY SILVER

HENRY REPEATING ARMS BIG BOY STEEL CARBINE

HENRY REPEATING ARMS COLOR CASE HARDENED EDITION

HENRY REPEATING ARMS FREEMASONS TRIBUTE EDITION

HENRY GOLDEN BOY DELUXE ENGRAVED 3RD EDITION

BIG BOY SILVER
Action: Lever
Stock: Walnut
Barrel: 20 in.
Sights: Semi-buckhorn rear, brass bead front
Weight: 8 lb. 11 oz.
Caliber: .44 Magnum, .45 Colt, .357 Mag/.38 Spl.
Magazine: Under-barrel tube, 10 rounds
Features: Nickel plating; octagon barrel; buckhorn/bead sights; drilled and tapped scope option; straight stock wrist; carbine-style buttplate; okay for left-handed shooters
MSRP. **$990.00**

BIG BOY STEEL CARBINE
Action: Lever
Stock: Checkered walnut
Barrel: 16.5 in.
Sights: Adjustable semi-buckhorn rear with adjustable white diamond insert, brass bead front
Weight: 6 lb. 9 oz.
Caliber: .44 Magnum, .45 Colt, .357 Mag/.38 Spl., .327 Fed., .41 Mag.
Magazine: Under-barrel tube, 7 rounds
Features: Sliding transfer bar safety

system in its hammer; lighter steel frame; ventilated rubber recoil pad; sling swivel studs; rifle-style fore-end cap; glove-friendly oversized lever
MSRP. **$850.00**

COLOR CASE HARDENED EDITION
Action: Lever
Stock: Walnut
Barrel: 20 in., 22 in.
Sights: Semi-buckhorn rear, brass bead front
Weight: 8 lb. 2 oz.–8 lb. 8 oz.
Caliber: .30-30, .45-70
Magazine: Under-barrel tube, 4 or 5 rounds
Features: Deep bluing, dark walnut, and mottled case colors achieved through a genuine case-hardening process; octagonal barrels; transfer bar safety; sling swivel studs; drilled and tapped frame; ventilated rubber recoil pad; okay for left-handed shooters
MSRP. **$995.00**

FREEMASONS TRIBUTE EDITION
Action: Lever
Stock: Walnut
Barrel: 20 in.

Sights: Adjustable semi-buckhorn rear with adjustable white diamond insert, brass bead front
Weight: 6 lb. 12 oz.
Caliber: .22 S/L/LR
Magazine: 16 rounds (long range), 21 rounds (short)
Features: Receiver engraving with 24K gold plating; engraved/painted stock; depicts our first president in full Masonic regalia
MSRP. **$1020.00**

GOLDEN BOY DELUXE ENGRAVED 3RD EDITION
Action: Lever
Stock: Walnut
Barrel: 20 in.
Sights: Fully adjustable rear, brass-beaded front
Weight: 6 lb. 12 oz.
Caliber: .22 LR, .22 WMR, .17 HMR
Magazine: Under-barrel tube, 16 rounds (LR), 12 rounds (Short)
Features: American walnut stock; adjustable buckhorn rear sight, beaded front sight; brasslite receiver, brass buttplate, and blued barrel
.22 LR: **$1499.95**
.22 WMR: **$1549.95**
.17 HMR: **$1575.00**

Henry Repeating Arms

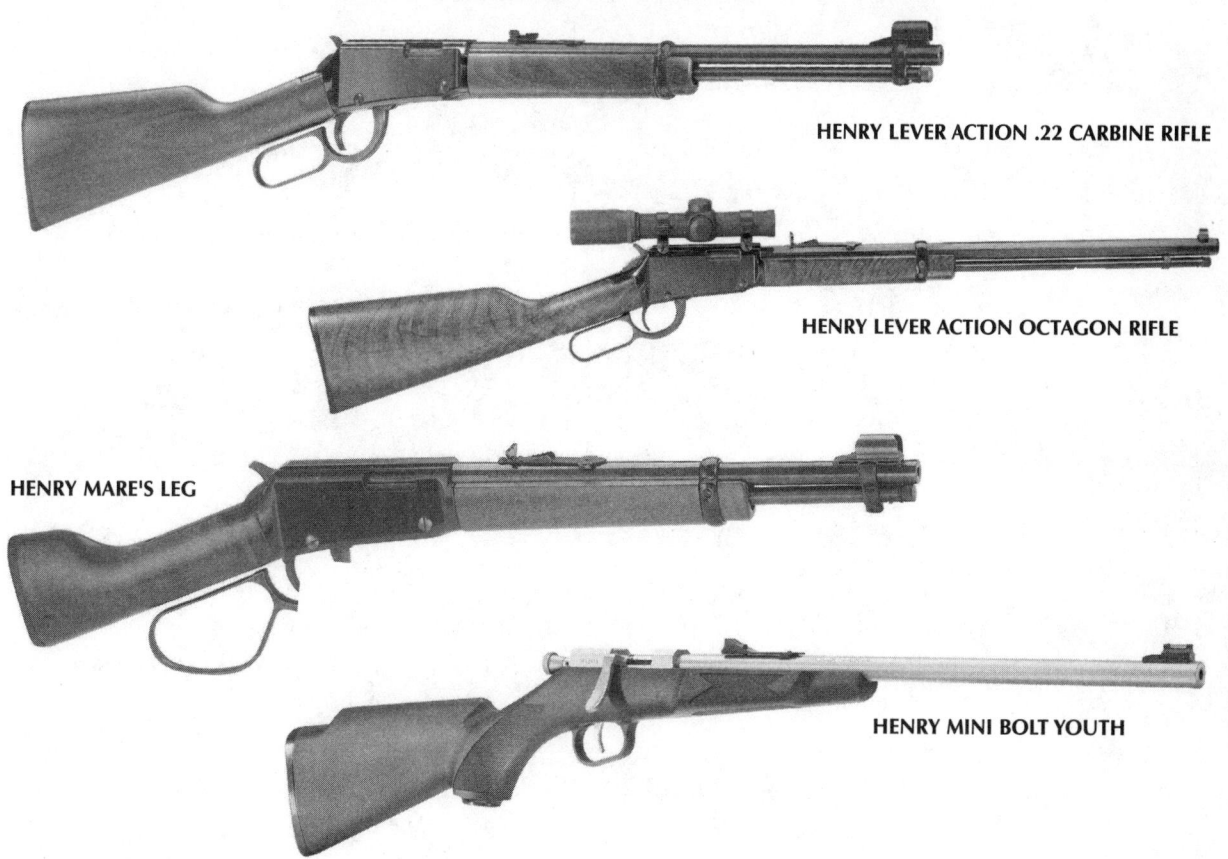

HENRY LEVER ACTION .22 CARBINE RIFLE

HENRY LEVER ACTION OCTAGON RIFLE

HENRY MARE'S LEG

HENRY MINI BOLT YOUTH

LEVER ACTION .22 CARBINE RIFLE

Action: Lever
Stock: Walnut
Barrel: 16.13 in.
Sights: Open
Weight: 4 lb. 8 oz.
Caliber: .22 LR
Magazine: 15 rounds (.22 LR), 17 rounds (.22 L), 18 rounds (.22 S), 21 rounds (.22)
Features: Straight-grip American walnut stock; adjustable rear, hooded front sight; blued round barrel and lever
MSRP $375.00

LEVER ACTION OCTAGON RIFLE

Action: Lever
Stock: Walnut
Barrel: 20 in.
Sights: Open
Weight: 6 lb. 4 oz.
Caliber: .22 LR, .22 WMR, .17 HMR
Magazine: Under-barrel tube, 21 rounds (.22 S), 16 rounds (.22 LR); 12 rounds (.22 Mag.); 11 rounds (.17 HMR)
Features: American walnut; marble fully adjustable semi-buckhorn rear with reversible white diamond insert and brass beaded front sight; blued barrel and lever
.22 LR, ...$450.00
.22 WMR: $550.00
.17 HMR: $550.00

MARE'S LEG

Action: Lever
Stock: Walnut
Barrel: 12.5 in.–12.9 in.
Sights: Open
Weight: 4 lb. 7 oz.–5 lb. 13 oz.
Caliber: .22 LR, .22 WMR, .357 Mag., .44 Mag., .45 Colt
Magazine: 5–10 rounds depending on caliber
Features: .45 Colt: American walnut; marble fully adjustable semi-buckhorn rear with reversible white diamond insert and brass beaded front sights; brasslite receiver, brass buttplate, and blued barrel; .22 S/L/

LR: American . . . . ole rear, with hooded front sight; blued metal barrel and lever
.22 Magnum $450.00
.22 LR: $440.00
.45 Colt, .44 Mag.,
   .357 Mag.: $975.00

MINI BOLT YOUTH

Action: Bolt
Stock: Synthetic
Barrel: 16.25 in.
Sights: Open
Weight: 3 lb. 4 oz.
Caliber: .22 LR, .22 S
Magazine: None
Features: Single-shot; one-piece fiberglass synthetic stock in orange or black; Williams fire sights; stainless steel receiver and barrel; black or Muddy Girl Camo stock finishes
MSRP $275.00

Henry Repeating Arms

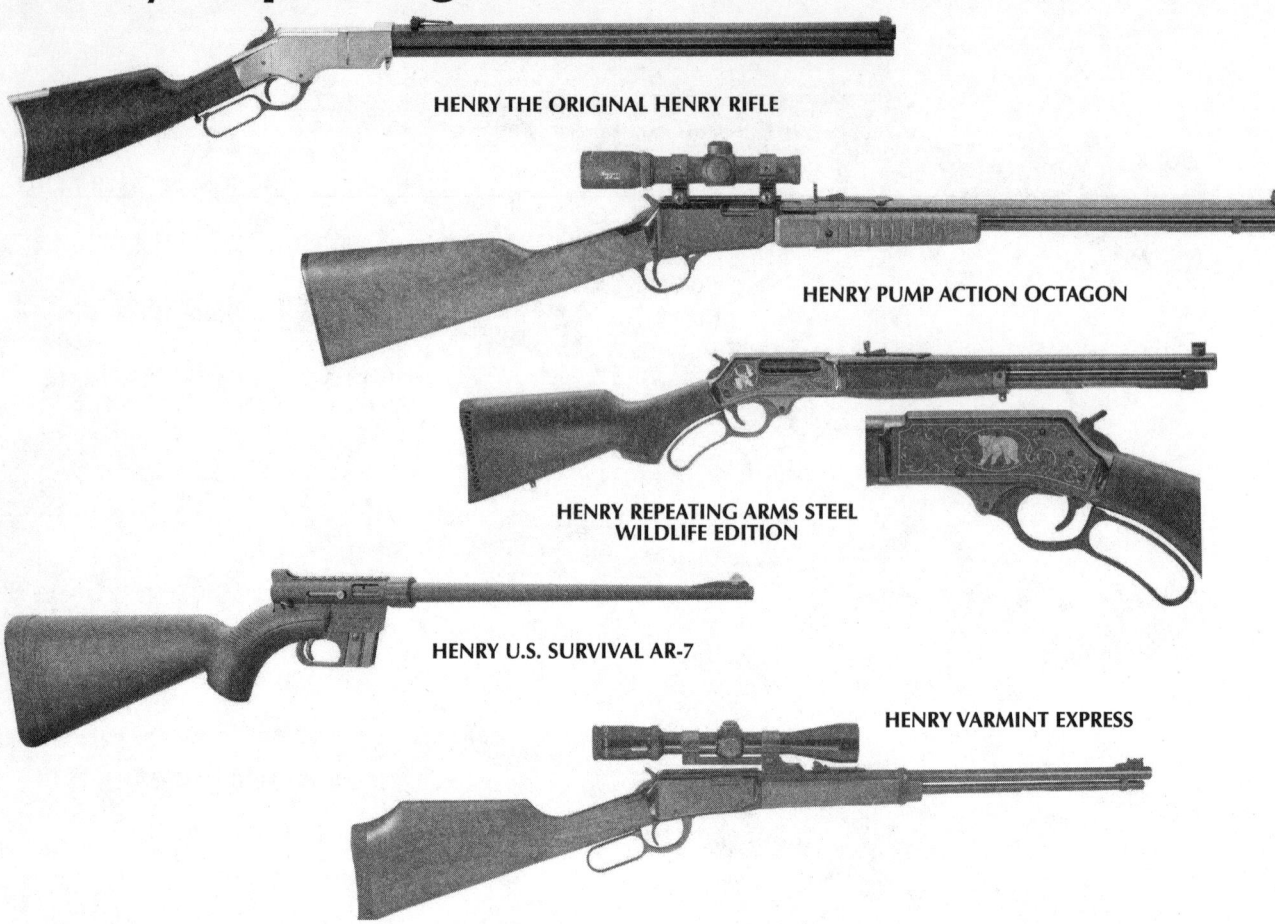

HENRY THE ORIGINAL HENRY RIFLE

HENRY PUMP ACTION OCTAGON

HENRY REPEATING ARMS STEEL WILDLIFE EDITION

HENRY U.S. SURVIVAL AR-7

HENRY VARMINT EXPRESS

ORIGINAL HENRY RIFLE

Action: Lever
Stock: Walnut
Barrel: 24.5
Sights: Folding ladder rear
Weight: 9 lb.
Caliber: .44-40, .45 Colt
Magazine: Under-barrel tube, 13+1 rounds
Features: True to original specifications; first time the Original Henry has been offered in the U.S. by an American manufacturer in 150 years
MSRP **$2300.00**

PUMP ACTION OCTAGON

Action: Pump
Stock: Walnut
Barrel: 19.75 in.
Sights: Open
Weight: 6 lb.
Caliber: .22 LR, .22 WMR
Magazine: Under-barrel tube, 15 rounds (.22 LR), 12 rounds (.22 WMR)
Features: American walnut stock; adjustable rear, beaded front sight; blued octagonal barrel

.22 LR: **$550.00**
.22 WMR: **$590.00**

STEEL WILDLIFE EDITION

Action: Lever
Stock: Walnut
Barrel: 18.43 in., 20 in.
Sights: Semi-buckhorn rear, brass bead front
Weight: 7 lb.–7 lb. 1 oz.
Caliber: .30-30, .45-70
Magazine: Under-barrel tube, 4 or 5 rounds
Features: Swivel studs; engraved receiver with 24K gold plating; lighter steel frame; straight-wristed walnut stock with checkering fore and aft; black rubber recoil pad; frame drilled and tapped for scope mounts; center-fire in-hammer transfer bar; American vine, scroll, and braided borders surrounding a circular buck's head portrait in 24K gold relief on the right side behind the ejection port and an oval-framed leaping buck on the left
MSRP **$1450.00**

US SURVIVAL AR-7

Action: Semiautomatic
Stock: ABS Plastic
Barrel: 16 in.
Sights: Adjustable rear, blade front
Weight: 3 lb. 8 oz.
Caliber: .22 LR
Magazine: Detachable box, 8 rounds
Features: ABS plastic in black; Teflon coated receiver and coated steel barrel; black or Mossy Oak Break-Up camo
Black: **$290.00**
Camo: **$350.00**

VARMINT EXPRESS

Action: Lever
Stock: Walnut
Barrel: 20 in.
Sights: Open
Weight: 5 lb. 12 oz.
Caliber: .17 HMR
Magazine: Under-barrel tube, 11 rounds
Features: Checkered American walnut stock; Williams fire sights; blued round barrel and lever
MSRP **$550.00**

High Standard

HIGH STANDARD ENFORCER

ENFORCER

Action: Semiautomatic
Stock: Synthetic
Barrel: 16 in.
Sights: A2 front sight, Magpul MBUS rear

Weight: 7 lb. 6 oz.
Caliber: 5.56 NATO
Magazine: Detachable box, 30 rounds
Features: A2 flash hider; YHM quad rail with smooth side; YHM same plane flip-up sights; ergonomic grip;

two-stage match trigger upgrades include hard-chrome barrel lining, nitride dipped barrel, Diamond T-Break flash hider and various laser etchings
MSRP. **$999.99**

Hi-Point Firearms

HI-POINT FIREARMS MODEL 995TS

HI-POINT FIREARMS 4095TS

995TS

Action: Blow-back semiautomatic
Stock: Black, skeleton-style, all-weather molded polymer
Barrel: 16.5 in.
Sights: Adjustable
Weight: 7 lb.
Caliber: 9mm, .40 S&W, .45 ACP
Magazine: Detachable box, 10 rounds
Features: Sling, swivels, and base mount included; last round lock-open latch; multiple Picatinny rails; internal

recoil buffer; also available in digital tan, pink, and woodland camos
MSRP. . . . . **$315.00–$480.00**

4095TS

Action: Semiautomatic
Stock: Polymer
Barrel: 17.5 in.
Sights: Adjustable
Weight: 7 lb.
Caliber: .45 ACP
Magazine: 9 rounds

Features: All-weather; black polymer skeletonized stock sling; swivels and scope base internal recoil buffer in stock weaver style rails; fully adjustable sights ("ghost ring" rear peep and post front); quick on/off thumb safety; grip-mounted clip release; also available in digital tan, pink, and woodland camos
MSRP. . . . . **$325.00–$479.00**

Howa by Legacy Sports

HOWA HOGUE KRYPTEK

HOWA/HOGUE RANCHLAND COMPACT PACKAGE

HOWA HOGUE RIFLE

HOWA MINI ACTION

HOWA BY LEGACY SPORTS SCOUT

HOGUE KRYPTEK
Action: Bolt
Stock: Synthetic
Barrel: 20 in., 22 in., 24 in.
Sights: None
Weight: 7 lb. 12 oz.–8 lb.
Caliber: .22-250 Rem., .25-06 Rem., .204 Ruger, .223 Rem., .243 Win., .270 Win., .30-06 Spfd., .300 Win. Mag., .308 Win., .338 Win. Mag., .375 Ruger, 6.5 Creedmoor, 6.5x55 Swedish, 7mm Rem. Mag.
Magazine: Internal
Features: Available in three different stock patterns: Highlander, Typhon
MSRP . . . . $782.00–$816.00

HOGUE RANCHLAND COMPACT PACKAGE
Action: Bolt
Stock: Synthetic
Barrel: 20 in.
Sights: None
Weight: 8 lb. 12 oz.
Caliber: .223 Rem., .204 Ruger, .22-250 Rem., .243 Win., .308 Win., 6.5 Creedmoor, 7mm-08 Rem.
Magazine: Internal box
Features: Hogue pillar-bedded stock and recoil pad, two-stage HACT trigger, three-position safety, one-piece scope base, rings, and Nikko Stirling 2.5-10x42mm scope; hollow bolt handle and shaved receiver; full-dip firearm including scope, rings, base, stock, barrel and receiver; available in black, OD Green, Yote camo, and Kings Desert Shadow camo
MSRP . . . . $762.00–$840.00

HOGUE RIFLES
Action: Bolt
Stock: Synthetic
Barrel: 20 in., 22 in., 24 in.
Sights: None
Weight: 7 lb. 12 oz.
Caliber: Standard Blue, Stainless: .223 Rem., .204 Ruger, .22-250 Rem., .243 Win., .308 Win., 7mm–08, 6.5x 55 Swedish, .25-06 Rem., .270 Win., .30-06 Spfd.; Magnum Blue, Stainless: .300 Win. Mag., .375 Ruger, .338 Win. Mag, 7mm Rem. Mag.
Magazine: Internal box
Features: Stainless or blued barrel; synthetic stock comes in black, sand, or green with matching Hogue Soft Grip; recoil pad; hinged floor plate; sling; swivel studs; optional lightweight #1 barrel in blue, as well as #2 barrel in Cerakote Gun Metal Gray; all models available in black or green stock finishes; Cerakote options also available in Typhon finish

Standard #2 barrel, blue: . . . . $608.00–$637.00
Lightweight #1 barrel, blue: $637.00
Cerakote Gun Metal Gray: . . . . $724.00–$811.00

MINI ACTION
Action: Bolt
Stock: Synthetic
Barrel: 20 in., 22 in.
Sights: None
Weight: 5 lb. 11 oz.–6 lb. 10 oz.
Caliber: .222 Rem., .223 Rem., .204 Ruger, 6.5 Grendel, 7.62x39
Magazine: Detachable box, 10 rounds
Features: HOWA's Mini Action is only 6 in. long and weighs just 10.2 oz., 3 oz. and almost a full inch less than a standard short action and two ounces nearly 1.5 in. less than a long-action; barrels in lightweight (#1), standard (#2), and heavy (#6) options, as well as stocks in black, OD Green, Kryptek Highlander, Multicam and Yote camo finishes; package includes Nikko Stirling 3-9x40mm scope and one-piece base and rings
Rifle only #1: . . . . . $652.00–$724.00
Rifle only #2: . . . . . $608.00–$681.00
Rifle only #6: . . . . . $681.00–$753.00
Scope package #1: . . .$753.00–$840.00
Scope package #2: . . .$724.00–$829.00
Scope package #3: . . .$782.00–$885.00

SCOUT
Action: Bolt
Stock: Synthetic
Barrel: 18.5 in.
Sights: Optional scope
Weight: 7 lb.–8 lb.
Caliber: .308 Win.
Magazine: Detachable box, 10 rounds
Features: Williams one-piece rail and peep sight; Williams hooded, fiber optic front blade sight; Hogue pillar-bedded stock and recoil pad; Cerakote tactical gray finish on barrel, action, and origional steel floorplate; A2 flash hider; forged one-piece bolt with two locking lugs; three-position safety; sling swivel studs; available in Feral Thunder Mountain camouflage, black, and green finishes; optional package comes with Nikko Stirling Panamax 3–9x40mm scope and one-piece base and rings
MSRP . . . . $797.00–$1029.00

H-S Precision

H-S PRECISION HTR

H-S PRECISION PHR

HTR (HEAVY TACTICAL RIFLE)

Action: Bolt
Stock: Synthetic
Barrel: 20 in., 22 in., 24 in., 26 in., 28 in.
Sights: None
Weight: 10 lb. 12 oz.–11 lb. 4 oz.
Caliber: Any standard SAAMI, LR calibers
Magazine: Detachable box, 3, 10 rounds
Features: Pro-Series 2000; fully adjustable synthetic stock comes in a wide range of colors combinations including sand, black, olive, gray, and spruce green; heavy fluted barrel
MSRP................$3895.00

PHR (PROFESSIONAL HUNTER RIFLE)

Action: Bolt
Stock: Synthetic
Barrel: 20 in., 22 in., 24 in., 26 in., 28 in.
Sights: None
Weight: 7 lb. 12 oz.–8 lb. 4 oz.
Caliber: All popular magnum calibers up to .375 H&H and .338 Lapua
Magazine: Detachable box, 3, 4 rounds
Features: Pro-Series 2000; cheekpiece and built-in recoil reduction system; steel barrel; optional muzzlebrake; synthetic stock comes in a wide range of color combinations including sand, black, olive, gray, and spruce green; left-hand available for additional cost
MSRP................$3795.00

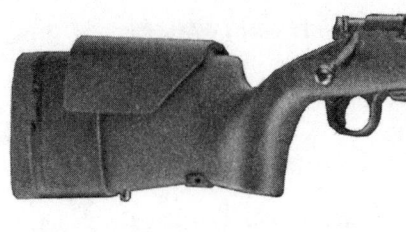

H-S PRECISION TTD

TTD (TACTICAL TAKE-DOWN RIFLE)

Action: Bolt
Stock: Composite
Barrel: 22 in., 24 in.
Sights: None
Weight: 11 lb. 4 oz.–11 lb. 12 oz.
Caliber: Available in all standard SA SAAMI and LR calibers
Magazine: Detachable box, 3, rounds
Features: Stainless steel barrel and floor plate; synthetic stock with full length bedding block chassis system; metal parts are finished in matte black Teflon; wide variety of stock colors including sand, black, olive, gray, and spruce green
MSRP................$6095.00

I.O. Inc.

I.O. INC. M214

M214

Action: Semiautomatic
Stock: Synthetic
Barrel: 16 in.
Sights: Adjustable
Weight: N/A
Caliber: 7.62x39 Warsaw
Magazine: Detachable box, 30 rounds
Features: Americanized version of the AK-47; Phantom flash hider; gas block/front sight combo; recoil buffer; nitrided barrel; optional folding stick
MSRP................ $739.95

Jarrett Rifles

JARRETT BEANFIELD

JARRETT PROFESSIONAL HUNTER

JARRETT SHIKAR SERIES

JARRETT WIND WALKER

BEANFIELD

Action: Bolt
Stock: Synthetic
Barrel: Various lengths available
Sights: None
Weight: Varies depending on options
Caliber: Any popular standard or magnum chambering
Magazine: Comes with 20 rounds
Features: Can build rifle on any receiver provided; optional caliber, stock style, color, muzzlebrake, barrel size, and taper; includes load data and 20 rounds of custom ammo
MSRP . . . . starting at $6050.00

PROFESSIONAL HUNTER

Action: Bolt
Stock: Synthetic or walnut
Barrel: Various lengths available
Sights: None

Weight: Varies depending on options
Caliber: .375 H&H, .416 Rem., .416 Rigby, .450 Rigby
Magazine: Comes with 40 rounds
Features: Includes 40 rounds of soft pointed bullets and solids created custom for each gun; ballistics print-out and last three targets the gun shot also provided; optional scopes; .416 Rem. comes with Jarrett Tri-Lock receiver
MSRP . . . . starting at $11700.00

SHIKAR SERIES

Action: Bolt
Stock: Wood
Barrel: N/A
Sights: None
Weight: 8 lb.
Caliber: Any long action, standard or magnum caliber
Magazine: N/A

Features: Muzzle brake; decelerator pad; hand checkering; trap door plate; Shilen or Jewell trigger; aged American black walnut stock; Jarrett Tri-Lock left or right hand receiver
MSRP . . . . starting at $10,320.00

WIND WALKER

Action: Bolt
Stock: Synthetic
Barrel: Up to 24 in.
Sights: None
Weight: 7 lb. 8 oz.
Caliber: Any popular short-action
Magazine: Comes with 20 rounds
Features: Jarrett Tri-Lock action; muzzlebrake; Tally scope mounting system; phenolic resin metal finish with choice of stock colors; ballistic print out included
MSRP . . . . starting at $8320.00

J. P. SAUER & SOHN S 101

J. P. SAUER & SOHN S 101 ARTEMIS

J.P. SAUER S 303 ELEGANCE

S 101
Action: Bolt
Stock: Walnut
Barrel: 22 in., 24 in.
Sights: Adjustable open sights optional
Weight: 6 lb. 12 oz.
Caliber: .22-250 Rem., .243 Win., .270 Win., .308 Win., .30-06 Spfd., 6.5x55 Swedish, 7x64 Brenneke, 8x57IS, 9.3x62 Mauser, 7mm Rem. Mag., .300 Win. Mag., .338 Win. Mag.
Magazine: 5+1 rounds (standard), 4+1 rounds (magnum)
Features: 60-degree bolt lift; six locking lugs; available in standard and magnum calibers; matte black finish; DURA SAFE firing pin safety; EVER REST action bedding; ambidextrous stock
MSRP . . . . $1499.00–$1699.00

S 101 ARTEMIS
Action: Bolt
Stock: Wood
Barrel: 20 in.
Sights: Adjustable
Weight: 6 lb. 6 oz.
Caliber: .243 Win., .270 Win., .308 Win., 7x64 Brenneke, .30-06 Spfd., 8x57IS, 9.3x62 Mauser
Magazine: 5+1 rounds
Features: Designed for individuals with small hands and frames; walnut ERGO MAX stock; laserline stock grain; exclusive jeweled bolt; DURA SAFE direct firing pin safety; walnut bolt knob; super crisp 2-lb. trigger pull; fully adjustable iron sights
MSRP $1969.00

S 303 ELEGANCE
Action: Semiautomatic
Stock: Walnut
Barrel: 20 in., 22 in.
Sights: High contrast
Weight: 7 lb. 3 oz.–7 lb. 6 oz.
Caliber: .30-06 Spfd., .300 Win. Mag.
Magazine: Detachable box, 2, 5 rounds
Features: Manual cocking at the upper wrist; crisp single-stage trigger; four bolt lugs engage directly into the barrel; free-floating barrel
MSRP $4752.00

J.P. Sauer & Sohn

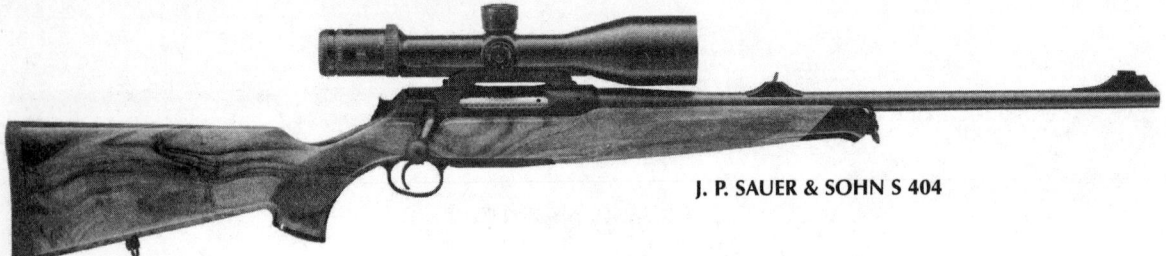

J. P. SAUER & SOHN S 404

S 404

Action: Bolt
Stock: Wood
Barrel: 20–24.4 in.
Sights: Adjustable
Weight: 7 lb.–7 lb. 3 oz.
Caliber: .243 Win., 6.5x55 Swedish, .270 Win., 7x64 Brenneke, .308 Win., .30-06 Spfd., 8x57IS, 9.3x62 Mauser, 7mm Rem. Mag., .300 Win. Mag., 8x68 S, .338 Win. Mag., .375 H&H Mag.
Magazine: 2–3 rounds
Features: ERGO LUX stock in grade-5 figured walnut; aviation-grade high-alloy aluminum receiver; perfectly placed ergonomic manual cocking slide on the bolt shroud; easily replaceable bolt head makes switching from standard to magnum calibers a snap; twin ejectors for a precisely perpendicular ejection pattern; 6-lug bolt locks directly into the barrel; jeweled bolt body; SAUER Quattro trigger with choice of four trigger pull weights: 550 g (1.2 lbs), 750 g (1.7 lbs), 1000 g (2.2 lbs) and 1250 g (2.7 lbs); infinitely adjustable trigger blade with 8 mm (0.3 in) adjustment range for length of pull and a left-to-right swivel range of 5 degrees; SAUER Universal Mount (SUM) integral to with receiver for an extremely low build height; SAUER universal key (SUS) integrated into the front sling swivel for forend and buttstock removal, barrel removal or replacement, and selection of trigger pull weight; MagLock magazine safety
MSRP . . . . **$3200.00–$3900.00**

Kel-Tec

KEL-TEC RFB

KEL-TEC SUB-2000

RFB

Action: Semiautomatic
Stock: Synthetic
Barrel: 18 in., 24 in.
Sights: None
Weight: 8 lb.–8 lb. 11 oz.
Caliber: 7.62 NATO
Magazine: Detachable box, 10 or 20 rounds
Features: Picatinny rail; short-stroke gas piston operation; A2-style flash hider
MSRP **$1929.99**

SUB-2000

Action: Semiautomatic
Stock: Polymer
Barrel: 16.1 in.
Sights: Target
Weight: 4 lb.
Caliber: 9mm, .40 S&W
Magazine: 10+1 rounds
Features: Accepts Smith & Wesson M&P an SIG P226 magazines in 9mm or .40 S&W, Beretta 92 and 96 magazines, and Glock 17, 19, 22, and 23 magazines; folds away for storage and transportation
MSRP **$500.00**

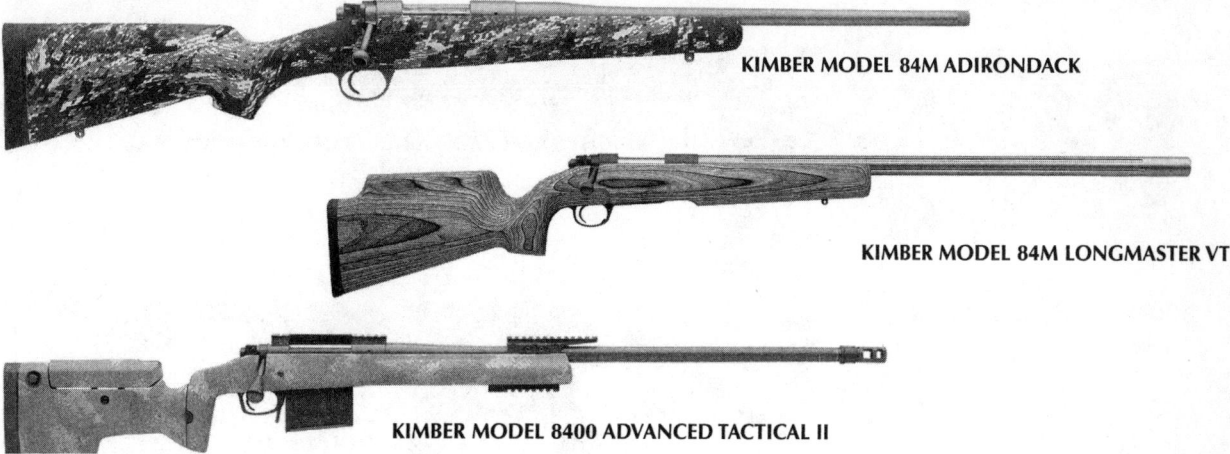

KIMBER MODEL 84M ADIRONDACK

KIMBER MODEL 84M LONGMASTER VT

KIMBER MODEL 8400 ADVANCED TACTICAL II

KIMBER MODEL 8400 ADVANCED TACTICAL SOC

KIMBER MODEL 8400 PATROL TACTICAL

MODEL 84M ADIRONDACK

Action: Bolt
Stock: Synthetic
Barrel: 18 in.
Sights: None
Weight: 4 lb. 13 oz.
Caliber: .308 Win., 7mm-08 Rem., 6.5 Creedmoor, .300 BLK
Magazine: Internal, 4 rounds
Features: Kevlar/carbon fiber stock with Optifade Forrest finish; recoil pad; fluted barrel threaded for muzzle break/suppressor
MSRP $1768.00

MODEL 84M LONGMASTER CLASSIC, LONGMASTER VT

Action: Bolt
Stock: Laminate
Barrel: 26 in.
Sights: None
Weight: 7 lb. 5 oz.–10 lb.
Caliber: Classic: .223 Rem., .308 Win.; VT: .22-250 Rem.
Magazine: Internal box, 5 rounds
Features: Satin-finished stainless metalwork, heavy sporter barrel contour,

adjustable trigger, 20 lines-per-inch checkering on A-grade walnut, match grade chamber, pillar and glass bedding, Mauser claw extractor, three-position Model 70-type safety are standard
Classic: $1291.00
VT: $1427.00

MODEL 8400 ADVANCED TACTICAL II

Action: Bolt
Stock: Synthetic
Barrel: 22 in.
Sights: None
Weight: 10 lb. 10 oz.
Caliber: .300 Win. Mag.
Magazine: Detachable box, 5 rounds
Features: Manners MCS-TF4 folding stock with adjustable comb; fluted barrel with muzzle brake/suppressor thread; adjsutable trigger
MSRP $4351.00

MODEL 8400 ADVANCED TACTICAL SOC

Action: Bolt
Stock: Synthetic

Barrel: 22 in.
Sights: None
Weight: 11 lb. 6 oz.
Caliber: 6.5 Creedmoor, .308 Win.
Magazine: Detachable box, 5 rounds
Features: Fluted barrel threaded and fitted with SureFire muzzle break/suppressor adapter; Picatinny rails; side folding stock; Harris bipod adapter included
MSRP $4419.00

MODEL 8400 PATROL TACTICAL

Action: Bolt
Stock: Synthetic
Barrel: 24 in., 26 in.
Sights: None
Weight: 8 lb. 12 oz.
Caliber: .300 Win. Mag., .308 Win.
Magazine: Internal, 5 rounds
Features: Manners MCS-T6 reinforced carbon fiber stock; sling swivel studs; front swivel stud for bipod; recoil pad
MSRP $2447.00

Knight's Armament Company

KNIGHT'S ARMAMENT SR-15 E3 CARBINE MOD 2 M-LOK

KNIGHT'S ARMAMENT SR-15 E3 CQB MOD 2 M-LOK

KNIGHT'S ARMAMENT SR-15 E3 LPR MOD 2 M-LOK

KNIGHT'S ARMAMENT SR-15 E3 MOD 2 M-LOK

SR-15 E3 CARBINE MOD 2 M-LOK

Action: Semiautomatic
Stock: Synthetic
Barrel: 14.5 in.
Sights: Adjustable
Weight: 6 lb. 6.4 oz.
Caliber: 5.56mm NATO
Magazine: 30 rounds
Features: Free-floated barrel inside a URX4 M-LOK handguard; improved E3 round-lug bolt design; ambidextrous bolt release, selector lever, and magazine release; drop-in two-stage trigger; 3-prong flash eliminator
MSRP **$2575.56**

SR-15 E3 CQB MOD 2 M-LOK

Action: Semiautomatic
Stock: Synthetic
Barrel: 11.5 in.
Sights: Adjustable
Weight: 6 lb. 8 oz.
Caliber: 5.56mm NATO
Magazine: 30 rounds
Features: Free-floated barrel inside a URX4 M-LOK handguard; improved E3 round-lug bolt design; ambidextrous bolt release, selector lever, and magazine release; drop-in two-stage trigger; 3-prong flash eliminator
MSRP **$2575.56**

SR-15 E3 LPR MOD 2 M-LOK

Action: Semiautomatic
Stock: Synthetic
Barrel: 18 in.
Sights: Adjustable
Weight: 7 lb. 6.4 oz.
Caliber: 5.56mm NATO
Magazine: 30 rounds
Features: Free-floated barrel inside a URX4 M-LOK handguard; improved E3 round-lug bolt design; ambidextrous bolt release, selector lever, and magazine release; drop-in two-stage trigger; 3-prong flash eliminator
MSRP **$2700.56**

SR-15 E3 MOD 2 M-LOK

Action: Semiautomatic
Stock: Synthetic
Barrel: 16 in.
Sights: Adjustable
Weight: 6 lb. 9 oz.
Caliber: 5.56mm NATO
Magazine: 30 rounds
Features: Free-floated barrel inside a URX4 M-LOK handguard; improved E3 round-lug bolt design; ambidextrous bolt release, selector lever, and magazine release; drop-in two-stage trigger; 3-prong flash eliminator
MSRP **$2450.56**

RIFLES

Knight's Armament Company

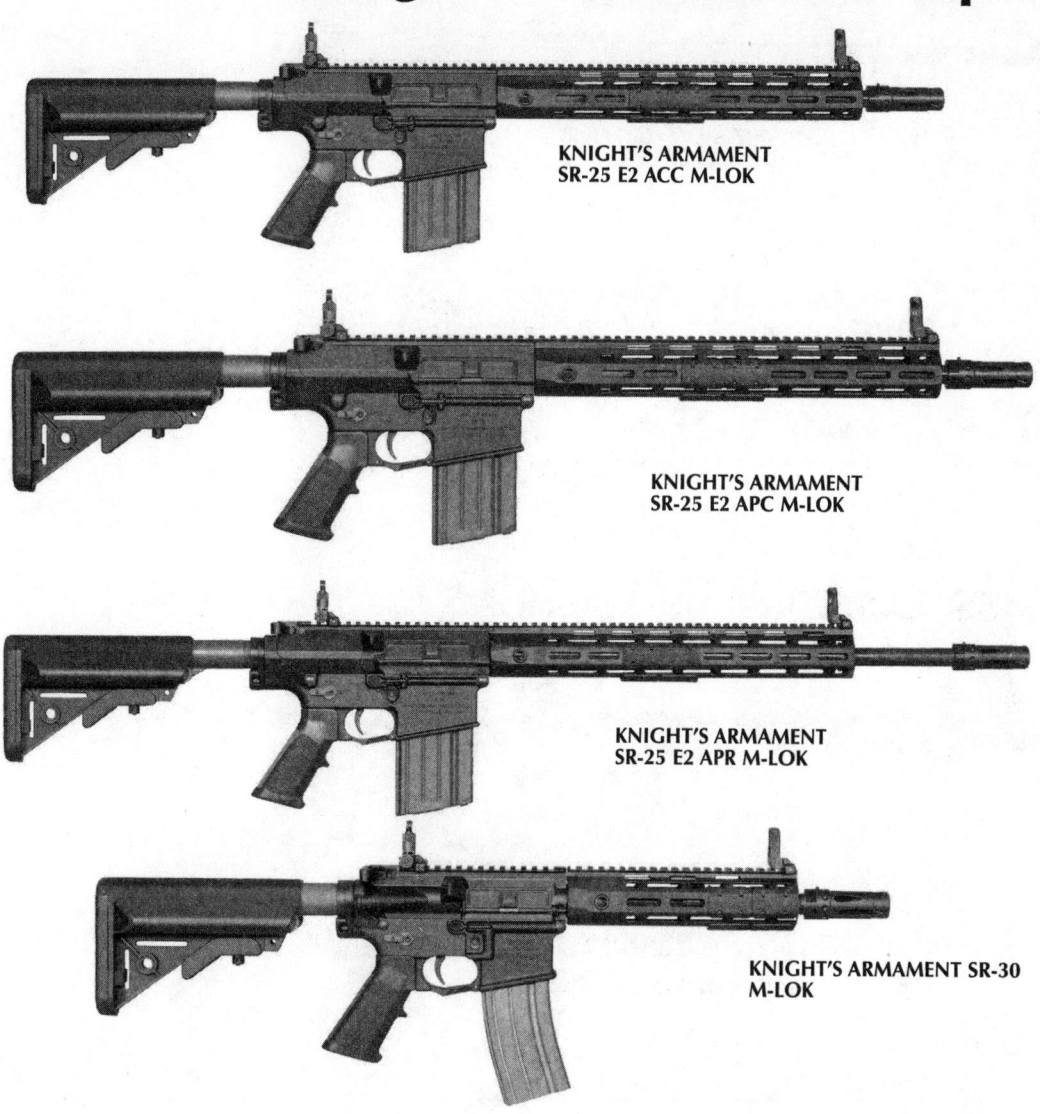

KNIGHT'S ARMAMENT
SR-25 E2 ACC M-LOK

KNIGHT'S ARMAMENT
SR-25 E2 APC M-LOK

KNIGHT'S ARMAMENT
SR-25 E2 APR M-LOK

KNIGHT'S ARMAMENT SR-30
M-LOK

SR-25 E2 ACC M-LOK

Action: Semiautomatic
Stock: Synthetic
Barrel: 16 in.
Sights: Adjustable
Weight: 8 lb. 6.4 oz.
Caliber: 7.62mm NATO/.308 Win.
Magazine: 20 rounds
Features: Ambidextrous bolt release, selector, and magazine release; drop-in 2-stage trigger; 7.62 QDC flash suppressor
MSRP................$4861.11

SR-25 E2 APC M-LOK

Action: Semiautomatic
Stock: Synthetic
Barrel: 16 in.
Sights: Adjustable
Weight: 9 lb.
Caliber: 7.62mm NATO/.308 Win.

Magazine: 20 rounds
Features: Ambidextrous bolt release, selector, and magazine release; drop-in 2-stage trigger; 7.62 QDC flash suppressor
MSRP................$4861.11

SR-25 E2 APR M-LOK

Action: Semiautomatic
Stock: Synthetic
Barrel: 20 in.
Sights: Adjustable
Weight: 10 lb. 8 oz.
Caliber: 7.62mm NATO/.308 Win.
Magazine: 20 rounds
Features: Ambidextrous bolt release, selector, and magazine release; drop-in 2-stage trigger; 7.62 QDC flash suppressor
MSRP................$4861.11

SR-30 M-LOK

Action: Semiautomatic
Stock: Synthetic
Barrel: 9.5 in.
Sights: Adjustable
Weight: 6 lb. 3 oz.
Caliber: .300 BLK (7.62x35mm)
Magazine: 30 rounds
Features: QDC-compatible flash hider will mount any of the KAC 7.62mm QDC suppressors; ambidextrous controls; two-stage match trigger; M-Lok accessory mounting system
MSRP................$2631.94

Krieghoff

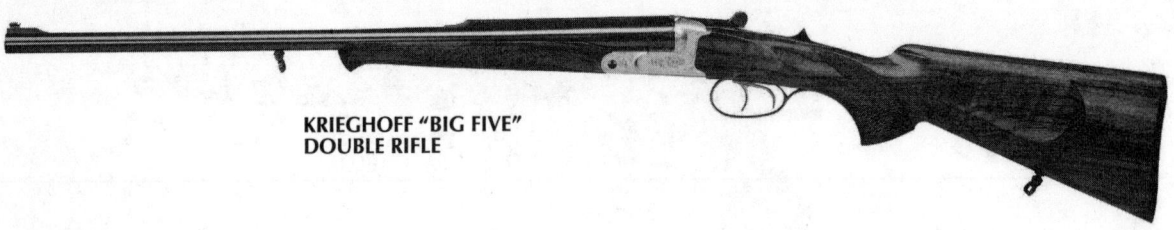

KRIEGHOFF "BIG FIVE" DOUBLE RIFLE

"BIG FIVE" DOUBLE RIFLE

Action: Hinged breech
Stock: Walnut
Barrel: 23.5 in.
Sights: Open
Weight: 9 lb. 8 oz.–10 lb. 8 oz.
Caliber: .375 H&H Mag., .375

Flanged Magnum N.E., .450/.400 NE, .500/.416 N.E., .470 N.E., .500 N.E.
Magazine: None
Features: Double triggers; V-shaped rear sight with a white, vertical middle line and a pearl front sight; optional Super-Express sight; Monte

Carlo style cheekpiece; European walnut stock with small game scene engraving; steel trigger and floor plate; straight comb and large recoil pad
MSRP $13995.00

Kriss USA

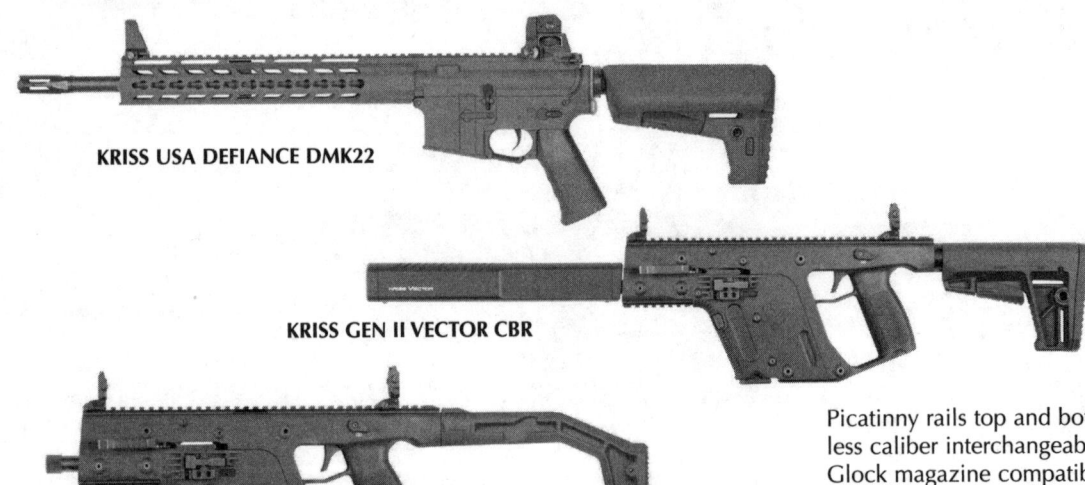

KRISS USA DEFIANCE DMK22

KRISS GEN II VECTOR CBR

KRISS VECTOR GEN II SBR

KRISS USA DEFIANCE DMK22

Action: Semiautomatic
Stock: Synthetic
Barrel: 16 in.
Sights: Adjustable
Weight: N/A
Caliber: .22 LR
Magazine: 10 or 15 rounds
Features: Full-metal construction; compatible with aftermarket barrels, magazines, stocks, pistol grips, handguards, and some AR-15 trigger upgrades; available in black, Flat Dark Earth, OD Green, Alpine, and

LVOA Black (LVOA version has extended LVOA-C rail from War Sport Manufacturing, LLC)
MSRP . . . . $699.00–$799.00

VECTOR GEN II CBR

Action: Semiautomatic
Barrel:16 in., 18.6 in.
Sights: Low-profile folding front and rear
Weight: 8 lb.
Caliber: 9mm, 9x21, .45 ACP, 10mm, .40 S&W, .357 SIG
Magazine: Glock magazines
Features: Patented Kriss Super V recoil mitigation system, ambidextrous short-throw safety lever, Mil-Std 1913

Picatinny rails top and bottom, toolless caliber interchangeability and Glock magazine compatibility are standard
MSRP . . . .$1499.00–$1519.00

VECTOR GEN II SBR

Action: Semiautomatic
Stock: Polymer
Barrel: 5.5 in.
Sights: Custom flip-up iron
Weight: 5 lb. 10 oz.
Caliber: .45 ACP, 9mm, 9x21, 10mm, .40 S&W, .357 SIG
Magazine: Glock magazines
Features: Gen II iteration has sidefolding stock, Kriss's Super V recoil management system, tool-less caliber interchangeability, Glock magazine compatibility, and a barrel threaded for attachments. Available in black, Flat Dark Earth, OD Green, Combat Grey, and Alpine finishes
MSRP . . . .$1549.00–$1569.00

Lazzeroni Arms, Inc.

LAZZERONI L2012LT-XTLR MOUNTAIN-LITE LONG RANGE

LAZZERONI L2012SP-XTLR SPORTER EXTRA LONG RANGE

LAZZERONI L2012TH-XTLR THUMBHOLE EXTRA LONG RANGE

RIFLES

L2012LT-XTLR MOUNTAIN-LITE LONG RANGE

Action: Bolt
Stock: Graphite/composite
Barrel: 26 in.
Sights: None
Weight: 7 lb. 5 oz.
Caliber: 7.82 (.308) Warbird, 7.21 (.284) Firebird
Magazine: 4 rounds
Features: All new precision CNC-machined chromoly receiver; one-piece diamond-fluted bolt shaft; stainless steel match-grade button-barrel; custom molded hand-bedded graphite/composite stock designs; precision-machined aluminum alloy floor plate/trigger guard assembly; jewel competition trigger; Vais muzzlebrake; Limbsaver recoil pad
MSRP **$5499.99**

L2012SP-XTLR SPORTER EXTRA LONG RANGE

Action: Bolt
Stock: Graphite/composite
Barrel: 28 in.
Sights: None
Weight: 8 lb. 13 oz.
Caliber: 7.82 (.308) Warbird, 7.21 (.284) Firebird, 8.59 (.338) Titan
Magazine: Detachable box, 4 rounds
Features: Heavy barrel contour; recoil reducing roll-over cheekpiece incorporated into stock design; 20 MOA Picatinny rail; 34mm or 30mm rings
MSRP **$6999.99**

L2012TH-XTLR THUMBHOLE EXTRA LONG RANGE

Action: Bolt
Stock: Graphite/composite
Barrel: 25 in.
Sights: None
Weight: 7 lb. 11 oz.
Caliber: 7.82 (.284) Warbird, 7.21 (.284) Firebird, 8.59 (.338) Titan
Magazine: 4 rounds
Features: 20 MOA Picatinny style rail; 34mm or 30mm ring sets; right hand only
MSRP **$6699.99**

Les Baer Custom

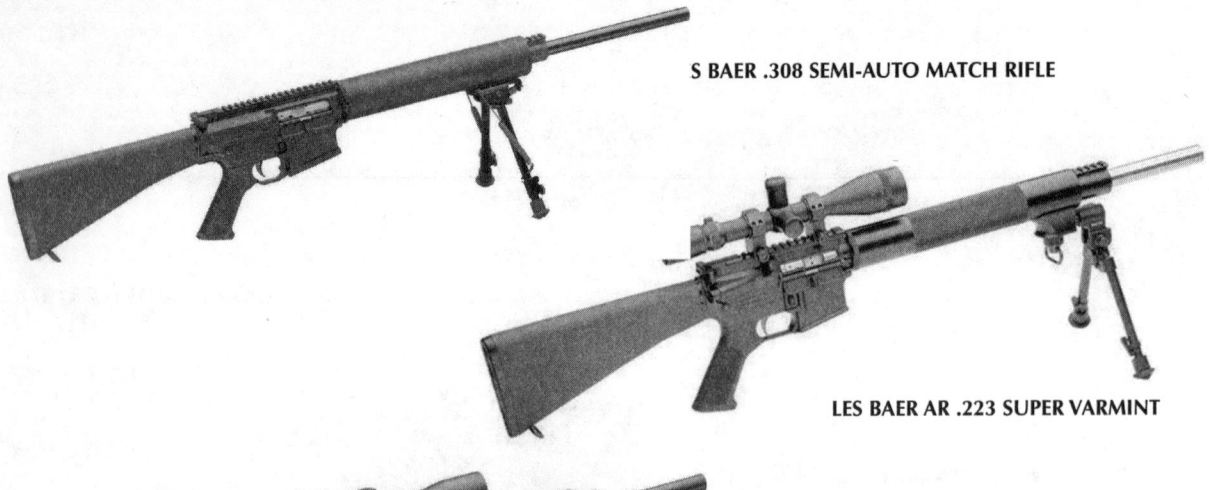

S BAER .308 SEMI-AUTO MATCH RIFLE

LES BAER AR .223 SUPER VARMINT

LES BAER MID-LENGTH MONOLITH .308 SEMI-AUTO SWAT MODEL

LES BAER MONOLITH .308 SEMI-AUTO SWAT

.308 SEMI-AUTO MATCH RIFLE

Action: Semiautomatic
Stock: Synthetic
Barrel: 18 in. or 20 in.
Sights: None
Weight: 11 lb. 3 oz.
Caliber: .308 Win., 6.5 Creedmoor
Magazine: Detachable box, 20 round
Features: No forward assist; Picatinny style flat top rail; LBC carrier, chromed; chromed precision bolt; Geissele two-stage trigger group; steel gas block; LBC Custom grip; Harris bipod; DuPont S coating on barrel; enforcer muzzlebrake; Magpul stock
MSRP **$3640.00**

AR .223 SUPER VARMINT

Action: Semiautomatic
Stock: Synthetic
Barrel: 20 in. (optional 18 in., 22 in., 24 in.)
Sights: None
Weight: 9 lb.
Caliber: .223 Rem.
Magazine: Detachable box, 20 rounds

Features: Includes targets; LBC forged and precision machined upper and lower receivers; Picatinny style flat top rail; LBC National Match chromed carrier; LBC chromed bolt; LBC extractor; Geissele two-stage trigger group; adjustable free-float handguard with locking ring; aluminum gas block; stainless steel barrel; Versa Pod installed
MSRP **$2640.00**

MID-LENGTH MONOLITH .308 SEMI-AUTO SWAT MODEL

Action: Semiautomatic
Stock: Synthetic
Barrel: 16 in.
Sights: Optional scope and rings
Weight: 11 lb. 5 oz.
Caliber: .308 Win.
Magazine: Detachable box, 20 rounds

Features: LBC carrier, chromed; LBC precision chromed bolt; Geissele two-stage trigger group; LBC steel gas block with Picatinny rail; LBC bench rest 416R stainless steel barrel with rifling; Magpul PRS stock; two twenty-round Magpul magazines
MSRP **$4390.00**

MONOLITH .308 SEMI-AUTO SWAT

Action: Semiautomatic
Stock: Synthetic
Barrel: 20 in. (optional 18 in., 24 in.)
Sights: None
Weight: 9.04 lb.
Caliber: .308 Win.
Magazine: Detachable box, 20 round
Features: Geissele two-stage trigger group; LBC Steel gas block with Picatinny rail on top; LBC bench rest, stainless steel barrel; Magpul PRS stock in black; special Versa Pod and adapter; DuPont S coating in barrel
MSRP **$4390.00**

Lewis Machine & Tool Company

LEWIS MACHINE & TOOL LM8PDW556

LM8PDW556
Action: Semiautomatic
Stock: Synthetic
Barrel: 16 in.
Sights: Adjustable flip up front and rear
Weight: 7 lb. 3.2 oz.
Caliber: 5.56x45 NATO
Magazine: 30 rounds
Features: Completely ambidextrous features; flared magazine well; winter trigger guard; ¼ MOA windage adjustable rear sight; SOPMOD buttstock; easily field strips with no special tools
MSRP **$2849.00**

LWRC International

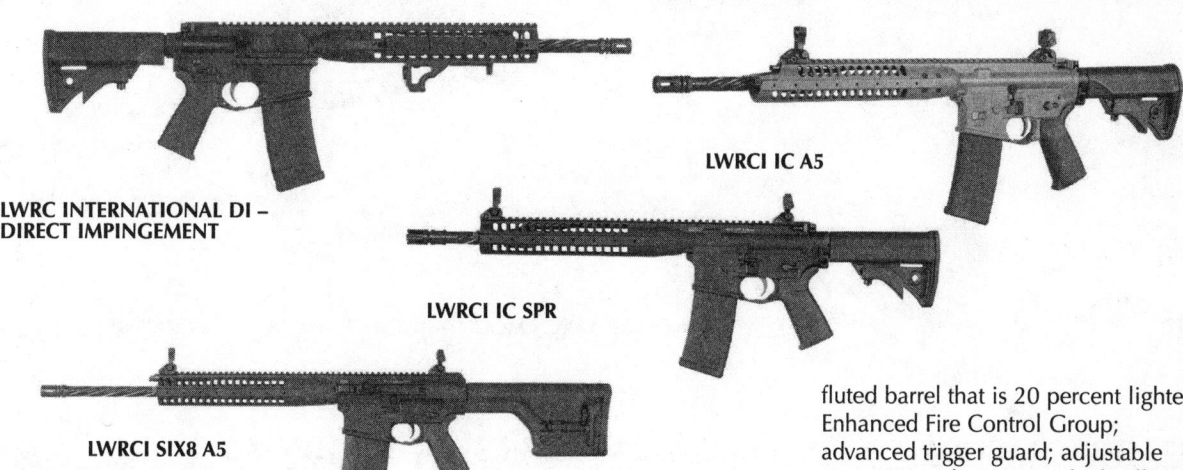

LWRC INTERNATIONAL DI – DIRECT IMPINGEMENT

LWRCI IC A5

LWRCI IC SPR

LWRCI SIX8 A5

DI – DIRECT IMPINGEMENT
Action: Semiautomatic
Stock: Synthetic
Barrel: 16.1 in.
Sights: None
Weight: 6 lb. 10 oz.
Caliber: 5.56 NATO
Magazine: Detachable box
Features: Direct impingement system; modular, one-piece free-float rail; angled ergonomic fore grip with QD sling point; fully ambidextrous lower controls; A2 birdcade flash hider
MSRP **$1599.00**

IC A5
Action: Semiautomatic
Stock: Composite
Barrel: 10.5 in., 14.7 in., 16.1 in.
Sights: Skirmish back up iron sights
Weight: 6 lb. 8 oz.–7 lb. 5 oz.
Caliber: .5.56 NATO

Magazine: 10 or 30 rounds
Features: Enhanced Fire Control Group; dual-control fully ambidextrous lower receiver; Magpul MOE grip; NiCorr treated cold hammer-forged barrel; ambidextrous charging handle; Monoforge upper receiver with modular rail system; adjustable two-position gas block; A2 birdcage flash hider
MSRP . . . . **$2651.00–$2804.00**

IC SPR
Action: Semiautomatic
Stock: Composite
Barrel: 14.7 in., 16.1 in.
Sights: Skirmish back up iron sights
Weight: 7 lb.–7 lb. 5 oz.
Caliber: 5.56 NATO
Magazine: 10 or 30 rounds
Features: Monoforge upper receiver with user-configurable 12-inch rail system; cold hammer-forged spiral

fluted barrel that is 20 percent lighter; Enhanced Fire Control Group; advanced trigger guard; adjustable compact stock; compact high-efficiency flash hider; patented short-stroke gas piston system; Magpul MOE grip
MSRP . . . .**$2396.00–$2549.00**

IC SIX8 A5
Action: Semiautomatic
Stock: Composite
Barrel: 10.5 in., 12.7 in., 14.7 in., 16.1 in.
Sights: Skirmish back up iron sights
Weight: 6 lb. 8 oz.–7 lb. 5 oz.
Caliber: 6.8 SPC II
Magazine: 10 or 30 rounds
Features: Cold hammer-forged barrel; 12-inch user-configurable rail with scallop cut design; compact stock with integral sling attachment point; short-stroke piston operation; Enhanced Fire Control Group; adjustable two-position gas block; ambidextrous charging handle; Magpul MOE grip; enlarged ejection point
MSRP . . . .**$2396.00–$2549.00**

Magnum Research

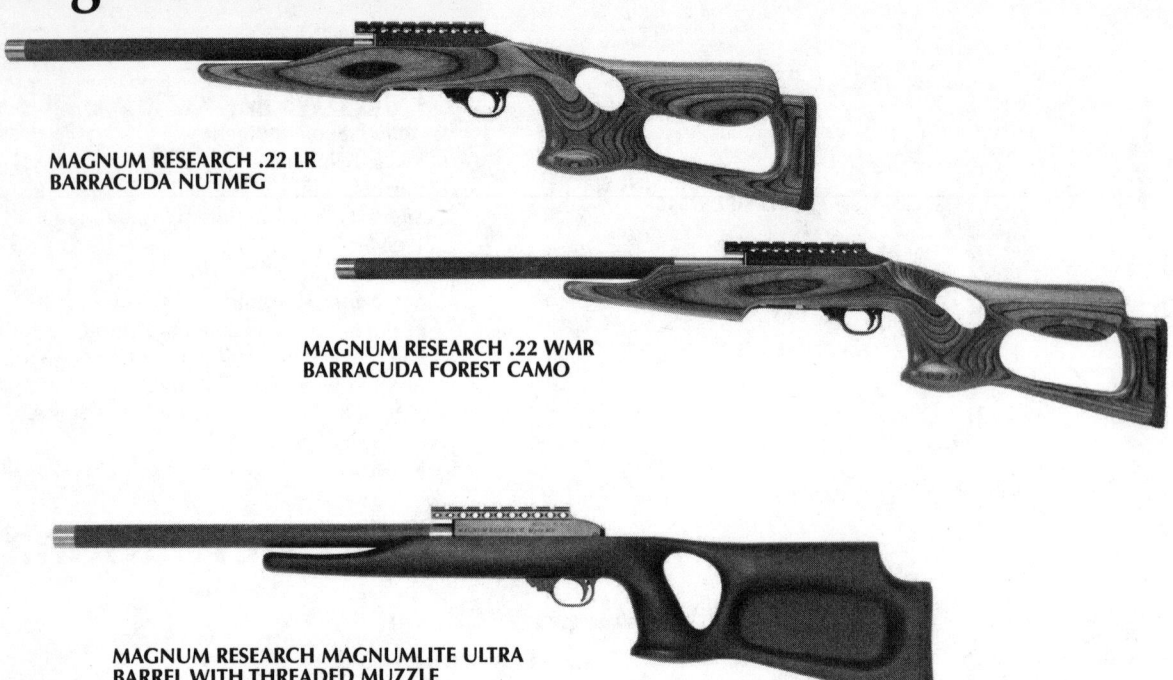

MAGNUM RESEARCH .22 LR BARRACUDA NUTMEG

MAGNUM RESEARCH .22 WMR BARRACUDA FOREST CAMO

MAGNUM RESEARCH MAGNUMLITE ULTRA BARREL WITH THREADED MUZZLE

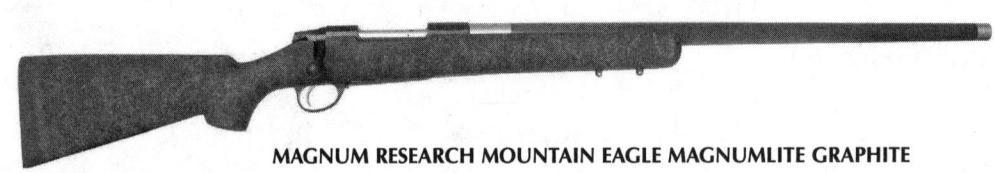

MAGNUM RESEARCH MOUNTAIN EAGLE MAGNUMLITE GRAPHITE

.22 LR BARRACUDA NUTMEG, BARRACUDA PEPPER

Action: Bolt
Stock: Barracuda American black walnut
Barrel: 17 in.
Sights: Rail for weaver style rings on receiver
Weight: 4 lb. 5 oz.
Caliber: .22 LR
Magazine: One 10 round magazine
Features: Patented graphite barrel; light weight; great accuracy
MSRP $819.00

.22 WMR BARRACUDA FOREST CAMO

Action: Bolt
Stock: Barracuda forest camo
Barrel: 19 in.
Sights: Rail for weaver style rings on receiver
Weight: 6 lb. 10 oz.
Caliber: .22 Win. Mag.
Magazine: One 9 round

Features: Gas-assisted blowback; graphite or stainless steel barrel
MSRP $935.00

MAGNUMLITE ULTRA BARREL WITH THREADED MUZZLE

Action: Semiatuomatic
Stock: Synthetic
Barrel: 17 in.
Sights: None
Weight: 4 lb. 4 oz.
Caliber: .22 LR
Magazine: 10+1
Features: Ambidextrous lightweight thumbhole stock made of polypropylene with fiber additives; semi palm swell on both sides of the pistol grip; molded-to-fit hard rubber buttplate attached with screws; graphite bull barrel with uni-directional graphite fibers parallel to the bore axis; full floating barrel; French gray anodized finish
MSRP $569.00

MOUNTAIN EAGLE MAGNUMLITE GRAPHITE

Action: Bolt
Stock: Composite
Barrel: 24 in., 26 in.
Sights: None
Weight: 7 lb. 4 oz.–9 lb. 2 oz.
Caliber: .30-06 Spfd., .223 Rem., .308 Win., .280 Rem., 7mm Rem. Mag., .300 Win. Mag., .22-250 Rem., .300 WSM, 7mm WSM
Magazine: Box, 4, 5 rounds
Features: Adjustable trigger; Kevlar-graphite stock in H-S Precision or Hogue Overmolded; open grip; free-floating match-grade barrel; hinged floor plate of solid steel; recoil pad; sling swivel studs; left-hand available for most calibers; action has been drilled and tapped for scope
MSRP . . . .$2173.00–$2475.00

Marlin Firearms

MARLIN 60

MARLIN 70PSS

MARLIN 336C

MARLIN 336XLR

MARLIN 336SS

60
Action: Semiautomatic
Stock: Laminated hardwood
Barrel: 19 in.
Sights: Open
Weight: 5 lb. 8 oz.
Caliber: .22 LR
Magazine: Under-barrel tube, 14 rounds
Features: Manual and automatic "last-shot" bolt hold-opens; receiver top has serrated, non-glare finish; cross-bolt safety; steel charging handle; Monte Carlo walnut-finished laminated hardwood; Model 60C is blue with walnut-finished hardwood stock; Model 60C is blue with a Realtree HardwoodsTM synthetic stock; Model 60SB is stainless with walnut-finished hardwood stock; Model 60SN is blue with black synthetic stock and also comes as a scope package option; and 60SS is stainless with a laminated black/gray hardwood stock
60: **$209.00**
60C: **$246.00**
60SB: **$265.00**
60SN: **$201.00**
60SN with scope: **$217.00**
60SS: **$316.00**

70PSS
Action: Semiautomatic
Stock: Synthetic
Barrel: 16.25 in.

Sights: Open
Weight: 3 lb. 4 oz.
Caliber: .22 LR
Magazine: Detachable clip, 7 rounds
Features: Automatic "last-shot" bolt hold-open; manual bolt hold-open; Monte Carlo black fiberglass-filled synthetic stock with abbreviated forend; nickel plated swivel studs; molded-in checkering; adjustable open rear sight; front ramp sight with high visibility orange post and cut-away wide-scan hood
MSRP **$345.00**

336C
Action: Lever
Stock: Walnut
Barrel: 20 in.
Sights: Open
Weight: 7 lb.
Caliber: .30-30 Win., .35 Rem.
Magazine: Under-barrel tube, 6 rounds
Features: Deeply blued surfaces; hammer block safety; American black walnut stock with pistol grip and checkering
MSRP **$635.00**

336SS
Action: Lever
Stock: Walnut
Barrel: 20 in.
Sights: Open

Weight: 7 lb.
Caliber: .30-30 Win., .35 Rem.
Magazine: Under-barrel tube, 6 rounds
Features: Stainless steel receiver, barrel, lever, and trigger guard; hammer block safety; American black walnut pistol grip stock with fluted comb and cut checkering; rubber rifle buttpad; adjustable semi-buckhorn folding rear, ramp front sight with brass bead and wide-scan hood; solid top receiver tapped for scope mount; offset hammer spur for scope use
MSRP **$779.00**

336XLR
Action: Lever
Stock: Laminated hardwood
Barrel: 24 in.
Sights: Open
Weight: 7 lb.
Caliber: .30-30 Win.
Magazine: Under-barrel tube, 5 rounds
Features: Stainless steel receiver, barrel, lever, and trigger guard plate; black/gray laminated hardwood stock with pistol grip and checkering; deluxe recoil pad; nickel plates swivel studs; adjustable semi-buckhorn folding rear sight and brass bead front sight with wide-scan hood; receiver tapped for scope mount
MSRP **$969.00**

Marlin Firearms

RIFLES

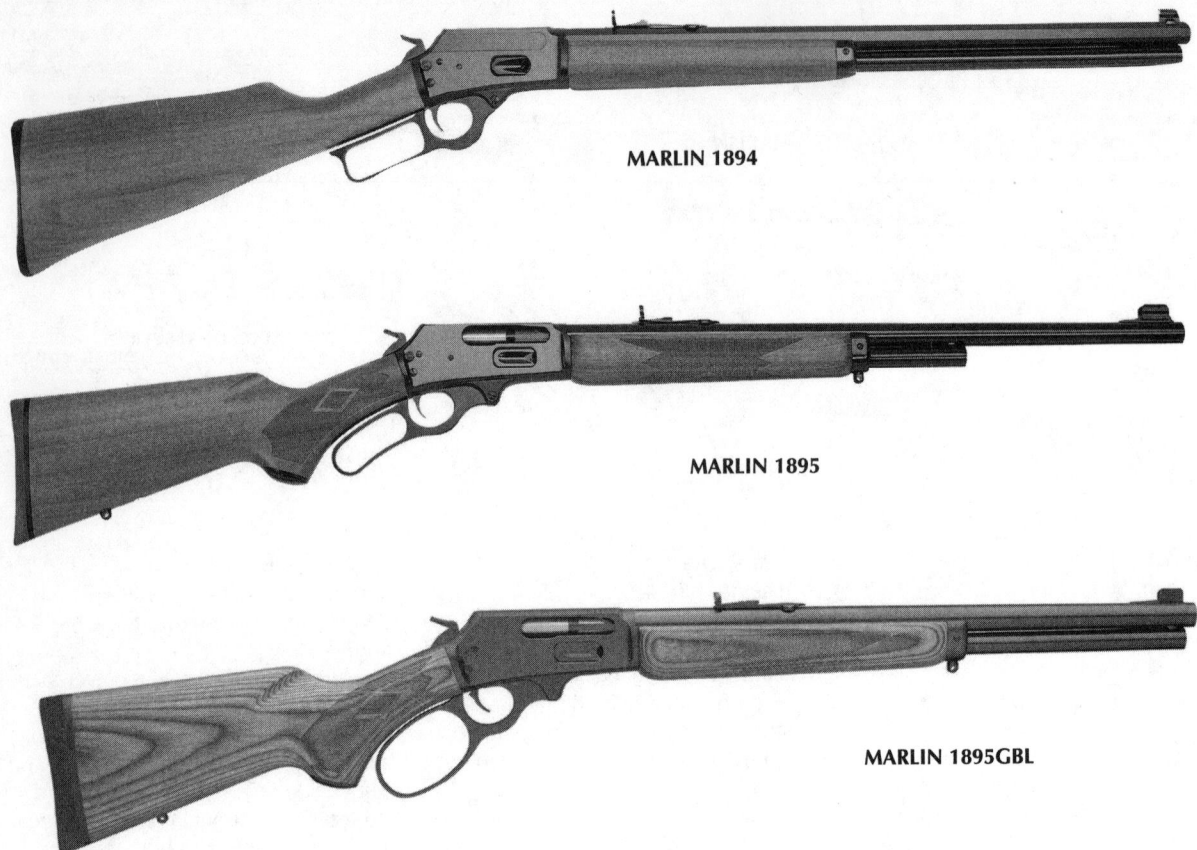

MARLIN 1894

MARLIN 1895

MARLIN 1895GBL

1894

Action: Lever
Stock: Walnut
Barrel: 20 in.
Sights: Open
Weight: 6 lb. 8 oz.
Caliber: .45 Colt, .44 Mag./.44 Spl.
Magazine: Under-barrel tube, 10 rounds
Features: Lever action with squared finger lever; deeply blued metal surfaces; straight-grip American black walnut stock; hard rubber buttplate; tough Mar-Shield finish; blued steel forend cap; tapered octagon barrel; adjustable marble semi-buckhorn rear sight and marble carbine front sight; solid top receiver tapped for scope mount
MSRP **$789.00**

1895

Action: Lever
Stock: Walnut
Barrel: 22 in.

Sights: Open
Weight: 7 lb. 8 oz.
Caliber: .45-70 Govt.
Magazine: Under-barrel tube, 4 rounds
Features: Standard 1895 has American black walnut pistol grip stock, 22-in. barrel, and blued metal; 1895CB has American walnut straight grip stock and 26-in. octagonal barrel, and blued metal; 1895CBA has 18.5 tapered octagonal barrel, blued metal and black walnut straight grip stock; 1895G has a black walnut straight grip stock, 18.5-in. barrel, and blued metal; 1895GS has 18.5-in barrel, walnut straight grip stock, and stainless steel metal;1895GSBL has blued metal, 18.5-in. barrel, and green laminate pistol grip stock with black webbing
1895: **$745.00**
1895CB: **$786.00**
1895 CBA: **$899.00**
1895G: **$750.00**

1895GS: **$896.00**
1895GSBL: **$1232.00**

1895GBL

Action: Lever
Stock: Laminate
Barrel: 18.5 in.
Sights: Open
Weight: 7 lb.
Caliber: .45-70 Govt.
Magazine: Full length tubular magazine, 6 rounds
Features: Lever action with big loop finger lever; deeply blued metal surfaces; hammer block safety; American pistol grip two-tone brown laminate stock with cut checkering; ventilated recoil pad; tough Mar-Shield finish; swivel studs; adjustable semi-buckhorn folding rear sight and ramp front sight with brass bead; receiver tapped for scope mount; offset hammer spur for scope use
MSRP **$786.00**

Marlin Firearms

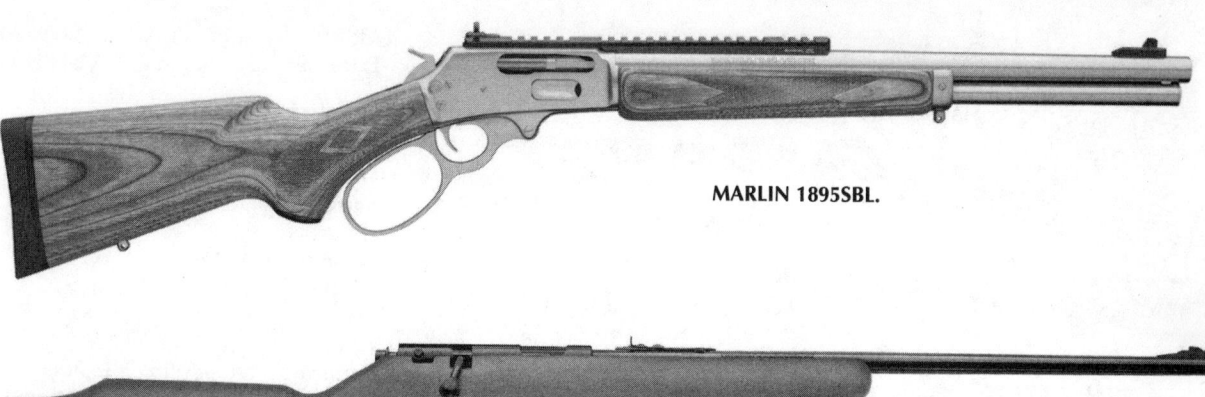

MARLIN 1895SBL.

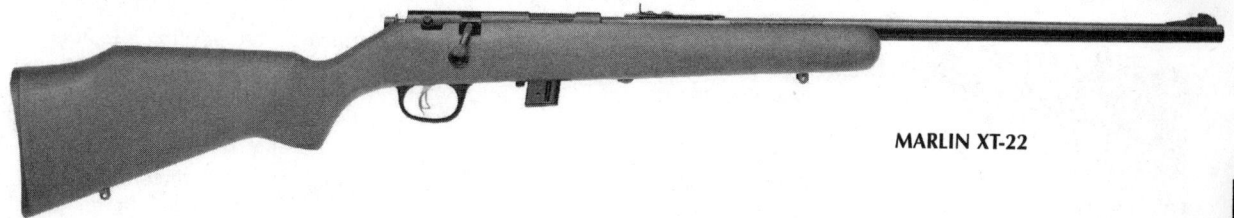

MARLIN XT-22

1895SBL

Action: Lever
Stock: Laminated hardwood
Barrel: 18.5 in.
Sights: Open
Weight: 8 lb.
Caliber: .45-70 Govt.
Magazine: Under-barrel tube, 6 rounds
Features: Lever action with big loop finger lever; deeply blued metal surfaces; stainless steel barrel and receiver; black/gray laminated hardwood with pistol-grip stock and cut checkering; fluted comb; deluxe recoil pad; compact version available
MSRP **$1146.00**

XT-22

Action: Bolt
Stock: Hardwood
Barrel: 22 in.
Sights: Open
Weight: 6 lb.
Caliber: .22 LR
Magazine: Detachable clip, 7 rounds
Features: Pro-Fire adjustable trigger; Micro-Groove rifling; blued bolt action; thumb safety; red cocking indicator; Monte Carlo walnut-finished hardwood with swivel studs; full pistol grip; tough Mar-Shield finish; adjustable rear sight and front ramp sights; receiver grooved for scope mount, drilled and tapped for scope bases
MSRP **$239.00**

MasterPiece Arms

MASTERPIECE ARMS
MPAR 556 RIFLE

MPAR 556 RIFLE

Action: Semiautomatic
Stock: Synthetic
Barrel: 16 in.
Sights: None
Weight: 7 lb. 13 oz.
Caliber: 5.56 NATO, .223 Rem.
Magazine: Detachable box, 30 rounds
Features: Short stroke piston design; lightweight, free-floating, two-piece aluminum handguard; user located Picatinny rails; side-folding collapsible stock; full length top rail
MSRP **$950.99**

Mauser

MAUSER M03 EXPERT

MAUSER M12

MAUSER M12 IMPACT

MAUSER M12 TRAIL

M03 EXPERT

Action: Bolt
Stock: Wood or synthetic
Barrel: 20.5 in., 23.5 in. (Mag.)
Sights: Fixed
Weight: 8 lb.
Caliber: .30-06 Spfd., .300 Win. Mag., 8x57IS, 9.3x62 Mauser, .308 Win., .338 Blaser Mag., 8x68S
Magazine: Internal, 5+1 or 4+1 (Mag.) rounds
Features: Muzzle-Safe and Mag-Safe; three-dot sight
MSRP $6822.00

M12

Action: Bolt
Stock: Wood, Synthetic
Barrel: 22 in., 24.5 in.
Sights: None
Weight: 7 lb.
Caliber: .22-250 Rem., .243 Win., 6.5x55 Swedish, .270 Win., 7x64 Brenneke, .308 Win., .30-06 Spfd., 8x57 IS, 9.3x62 Mauser, 7mm Rem., .300 Win. Mag., .338 Win. Mag.
Magazine: 5+1 rounds
Features: 60-degree bolt lift; detachable magazine; open sights available; drilled and tapped for scopes; stock extension available

MSRP $1799.00
Extreme: $1499.00

M12 IMPACT

Action: Bolt
Stock: Synthetic
Barrel: 20 in.
Sights: None
Weight: 6 lb. 12 oz.
Caliber: .243 Win., .308 Win.
Magazine: Detachable box, 5+1 rounds
Features: Three-position SRS firing pin safety; solid-steel 20 MOA Picatinny rail; uncompromising, crisp single-stage trigger; ergonomic extended bolt handle with 60-degree bolt lift; high accuracy thanks to direct locking in the cold hammer-forged barrel; Ilaflon coating for maximum rust protection
MSRP . . . . $1503.00–$1674.00

M12 TRAIL

Action: Bolt
Stock: Synthetic
Barrel: 18.5 in.
Sights: Three dot hunt drive sights
Weight: 6 lb. 12 oz.
Caliber: .308 Win., 8x57 IS, 9.3x62
Magazine: 5+1 rounds
Features: Removable sling swivel at muzzle; moveable snap-ball sling loop on hear stock; barrel and action surfaces are finished in matte black Ilaflon; signal orange-grey synthetic camo stock
MSRP $1900.00

McMillan

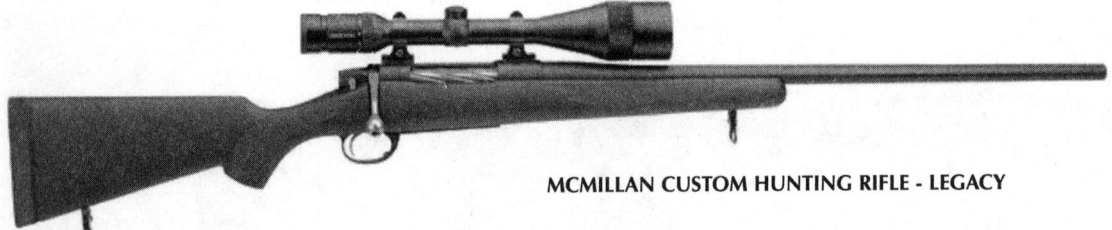

MCMILLAN CUSTOM HUNTING RIFLE - LEGACY

CUSTOM HUNTING RIFLES - LEGACY

Action: Bolt
Stock: Nutmeg laminate
Barrel: 22 in., 24 in.
Sights: None
Weight: 6 lb. 8 oz.–7 lb.
Caliber: .223 Rem., .243 Win., .260 Rem., .308 Win., .300 WSM
Magazine: Fixed
Features: Today's Legacy model features McMillan's G31 short-action and a match grade stainless steel barrel with a target crown; five stock options available: McMillan Dynasty, McMillan Hunter, McMillan A3, stan- dard walnut, XX walnut, and Nutmeg laminate; barreled action and bolt are dressed in black Cerakote; muzzle brake can be optioned; supplied with a rollered travel case
MSRP . . Call manufacturer for pricing

McMillan

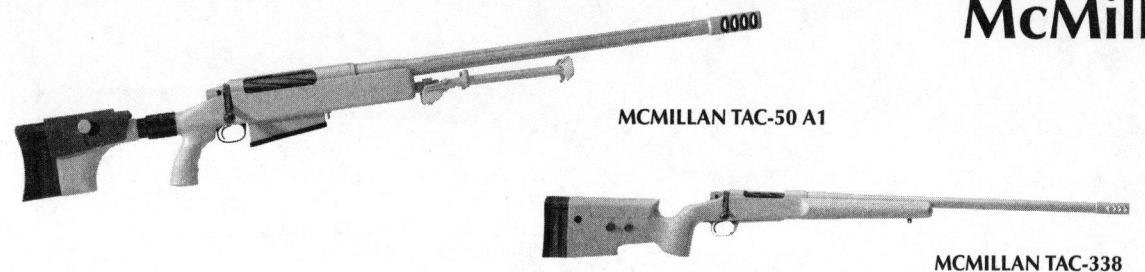

MCMILLAN TAC-50 A1

MCMILLAN TAC-338

TAC-50 A1

Action: Semiautomatic
Stock: Synthetic
Barrel: 29 in.
Sights: Drilled and tapped for scopes
Weight: 26 lb.
Caliber: .50 BMG
Magazine: Detachable box, 5 rounds
Features: McMillan's TAC-50A1 features the company's TAC-50A1 removable stock with an adjustable cheekpiece, Decelerator recoil pad, bipod, and four flush-mount cups with 1.25-in. sling loops; barrel is a 29-in. Navy contour 1:15 twist, free-floating, match grade, hand-lapped, and fluted with a threaded muzzle and threaded McMillan muzzle brake; metal finish made to match stock color, available in black, olive, gray, tan, and Dark Earth
MSRP $9990.00

TAC-338

Action: Bolt
Stock: Composite
Barrel: 27 in.
Sights: None
Weight: 11 lb.
Caliber: .338 Alpha Mag.
Magazine: Detachable box, 1 to 5 rounds

Features: Featuring McMillan's own TAC-338 action designed for the .338 Lapua; the 27-in. barrel has a medium-heavy contour, is match grade and stainless steel, and has a muzzle brake with ¾-24 threads; McMIllan's Tactical stock with adjustable cheekpiece, length-of-pull spacers, one stud, and six flush-mount cups with ¼-in. sling loops; 20 MOA 1913 Mil-Std rail is standard; metalwork finished to match the stock, available in black, OD Green, and Flat Dark Earth
MSRP $5699.00

Merkel

AFRICAN SAFARI SERIES MODEL 140AE

Action: Boxlock
Stock: Walnut
Barrel: 23.6 in.
Sights: Bead front, four-leaf express rear
Weight: 10 lb. 8 oz.
Caliber: .375 H&H, .416 Rigby, .470 NE, .500 NE
Magazine: None
Features: Classic styling with cheekpiece, half luxus Turkish walnut; hand-engraved, English-style arabesque, gold relief Cape buffalo; tapered, octagonal barrel with rust blued finish
MSRP $18995.00

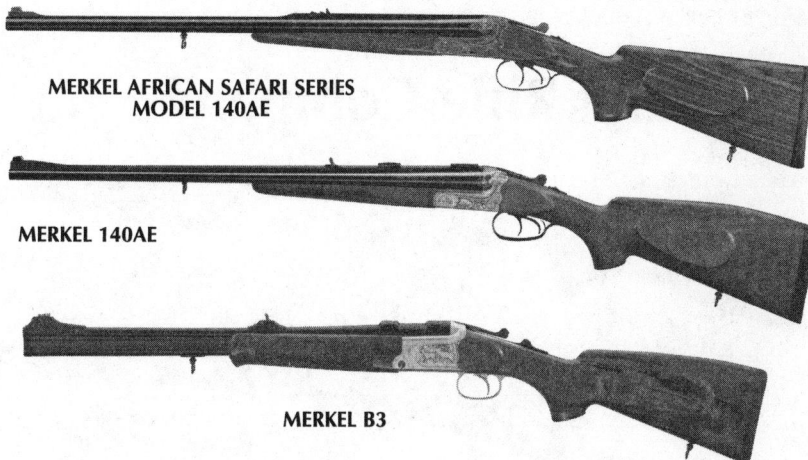

MERKEL AFRICAN SAFARI SERIES MODEL 140AE

MERKEL 140AE

MERKEL B3

140

Action: Side-by-side
Stock: Wood
Barrel: 23.6 in.
Sights: None
Weight: 7 lb. 8 oz.
Caliber: 7x65R, .30-06 Spfd., .30R Blaser, 8x57IRS, 9.3x74R
Magazine: None
Features: Anson & Deeley locks; steel action; Greener-style cross-bolt and double bottom bite; double trigger with front set trigger, optional single trigger; automatic trigger safety; optional with ejectors; hard soldered barrels with muzzle adjustment; engraving English arabesque or game scene "JAGD"; rubber buttplate; pistol grip; cheekpiece and hogback comb
MSRP $13995.00

B3

Action: Over/under
Stock: Checkered walnut
Barrel: 21.6 in.

Sights: Driven-hunt sight with integrated light elements
Weight: 6 lb. 6 oz.
Caliber: .30-06 Spfd., 9.3x74R, .30R Blaser, 8x57IRS
Magazine: None
Features: Short, light, and responsive; manual cocking mechanism; tilting breech block can be removed without tools; adjustable single trigger; pistol grip; cheekpiece and hogback comb; rubber buttpad
Hunting: . . . . . . $5495.00–$6495.00

Merkel

MHR 16

Action: Bolt
Stock: Synthetic or wood
Barrel: 22 in., 24 in.
Sights: None
Weight: 6 lb. 9.8 oz.–7 lb. 6 oz.
Caliber: .243 Win., .270 Win., .30-06 Spfd., .300 Win. Mag., .308 Win., 6.5x55, 7mm Rem. Mag., 9.3x62
Magazine: Detachable box, 3+1 rounds
Features: Two-position trigger safety with separate chamber lock; newly designed receiver that is cold-forged and precision machined; 60-degree bolt throw; direct trigger with a weight of just less than three pounds
Synthetic stock: **$799.00**
Wood stock: **$899.00**

RX HELIX

Action: Straight-pull bolt
Stock: Walnut
Barrel: 20 in., 22 in., 24 in.
Sights: Fixed fiber optic
Weight: 6 lb. 6 oz.
Caliber: .222 Rem., .223 Rem., .243 Win., .270 Win., .300 Win. Mag., .308 Win., 6.5x55 Swedish, 7mm Rem. Mag., 7x64 Brenneke, .30-06 Spfd., 8x57 IS, 9.3x62 Mauser

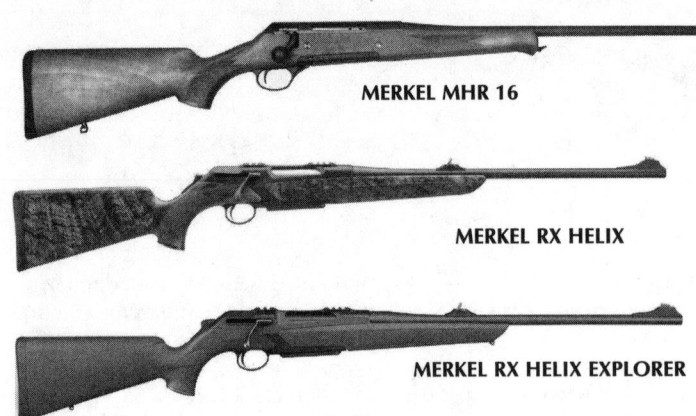

MERKEL MHR 16

MERKEL RX HELIX

MERKEL RX HELIX EXPLORER

Magazine: Detachable box, 3, 5 rounds
Features: Fully enclosed action with integral rail; interchangeable barrels and mags for tool-free caliber change in 60 seconds; tang-mounted safety; aluminum action; Weaver mounting rail; European walnut stock; manual cocking system; Elastomer recoil pad; checkering on forend and pistol grip
Standard: . . . . . . $3995.00–$4995.00

RX HELIX EXPLORER

Action: Straight-pull bolt
Stock: Synthetic
Barrel: 20 in., 22 in., 24 in.

Sights: Fixed fiber optic
Weight: 6 lb.–6 lb. 3 oz.
Caliber: .222 Rem., .223 Rem., 6.5x55 Swedish, .270 Win., 7x64 Brenneke, .308 Win, .30-06 Spfd., 8x57 IS, 9.3x62 Mauser, 7mm Rem. Mag., .300 Win. Mag.
Magazine: Detachable box, 3, 5 rounds
Features: Fully enclosed action with integral rail; interchangeable barrels and mags for tool-free caliber change in 60 seconds; tang-mounted safety; aluminum action; Weaver rail; manual cocking system; Elastomer recoil pad
MSRP **$3295.00**

Montana Rifle Company

MONTANA RIFLE COMPANY
AMERICAN VANTAGE RIFLE (AVR)

MONTANA RIFLES COLORADO BUCK SPECIAL EDITION (CBSE) WITH SCOPE

AMERICAN VANTAGE RIFLE (AVR)

Action: Bolt
Stock: Walnut, Synthetic
Barrel: 24 in.
Sights: Marble replaceable front and rear
Weight: 9 lb.
Caliber: .35 Whelen, .375 H&H, .375 Ruger, .416 Rem. Mag., .416 Ruger, .458 Lott, .458 Win. Mag.

Magazine: N/A
Features: Matte blued chrome moly steel or stainless steel barreled actions; available in right or left hand configurations
Blue: $1636.00
Stainless: $1756.00

COLORADO BUCK SPECIAL EDITION (CBSE) WITH SCOPE

Action: Bolt

Stock: Carbon fiber
Barrel: 24 in.
Sights: Leupold VX-6 1–6x24mm CDS turret with Warne ringmounts
Weight: 8 lb. 9 oz.
Caliber: .22-250 Rem., 7mm Rem. Mag., .300 Win. Mag., .375 H&H
Magazine: 3 rounds
Features: Carbon fiber kevlar reenforced stock; match-grade, hand lapped, 100 percent stainless steel

Montana Rifle Company

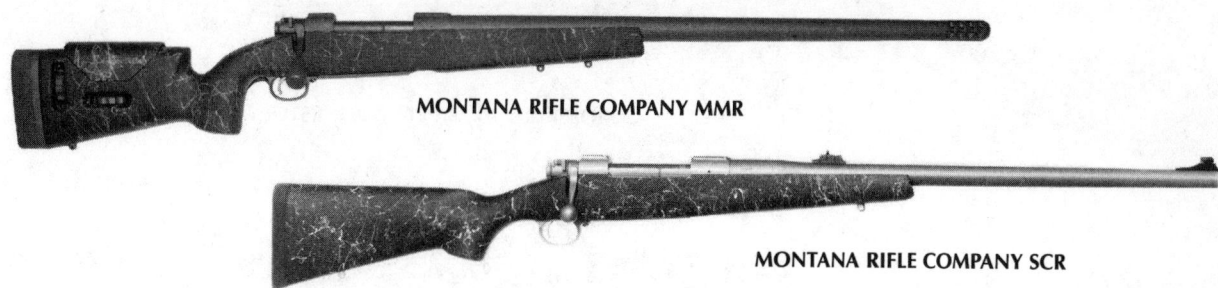

MONTANA RIFLE COMPANY MMR

MONTANA RIFLE COMPANY SCR

barrel, Cerakoted Tungsten grey barrel for imperviousness; muzzle brake for decreased felt recoil; included scope is a Nikon Monarch 3 4-16x42mm Custom XR Turret; available without scope

With scope:...........$2799.00
Without scope:........$2299.00

MONTANA MARKSMAN RIFLE (MMR)

Action: Bolt
Stock: Synthetic
Barrel: 22 in.–26 in.
Sights: None
Weight: 13 lb.
Caliber: .300 Win. Mag., .300 WSM, .308 Win., 6.5-284 Norma, 6.5

Creedmoor, 6.5x55
Magazine: N/A
Features: Long-range tactical rifle; fluted and nitrided barrel; detachable muzzle brake; adjustable stock
MSRP.................$3510.00

SEVEN CONTINENT RIFLE (SCR)

Action: Bolt
Stock: Synthetic
Barrel: 24 in.–26 in.
Sights: None
Weight: 9 lb.–10 lb.
Caliber: .338 Lapua, .338 Norma, .416 Rigby, .378 Wby. Mag., .460 Wby. Mag., .505 Gibbs
Magazine: N/A

Features: Built around Montana Rifle's Professional Hunter action, this rifle features a match-grade, hand-lapped barrel that is free-floated and button rifled, custom carbon fiber Kevlar-reinforced synthetic stock, and steel Marble replaceable front and rear open sights with a dual screw-in system; the trigger is an adjustable old-style M70, and the action features a double square bridge, control round feed, three-position safety, Mauser-style claw extractor, and is glass bedded
MSRP.................$2839.00

Mossberg (O. F. Mossberg & Sons)

MOSSBERG 464 LEVER-ACTION RIFLE

MOSSBERG 464 SPX LEVER-ACTION RIMFIRE RIFLE

464 LEVER-ACTION RIFLE

Action: Lever
Stock: Walnut
Barrel: 20 in.
Sights: Adjustable rifle sights or three-dot adjustable fiber optic
Weight: 6 lb. 12 oz.
Caliber: .30-30 Win.
Magazine: Under-barrel tube, 7–14 rounds
Features: Ejection port designed for cases to clear optics, top tang safety are standard; three-dot adjustable fiber optic sights or adjustable rifle

sights; receiver is drilled and tapped for Weaver #403 bases; pistol grip or straight stock; pistol grip has diamond pattern fine-line checkering on the grip and wrapped around edge-to-edge on the forearm
Straight grip:...........$518.00
Pistol grip:.............$558.00

464 SPX LEVER-ACTION RIMFIRE RIFLE

Action: Lever
Stock: Synthetic
Barrel: 18 in.

Sights: Rifle sights
Weight: 6 lb.
Caliber: .22 LR
Magazine: Under-barrel tube, 14 rounds
Features: 6-position adjustable stocks; tri-rail forends with rail covers; adjustable fiber optic sights; flash suppressor and muzzlebrake; top-tang safety; dovetail receiver, Picatinny tri-rail fore-end
MSRP.................$525.00

Mossberg (O. F. Mossberg & Sons)

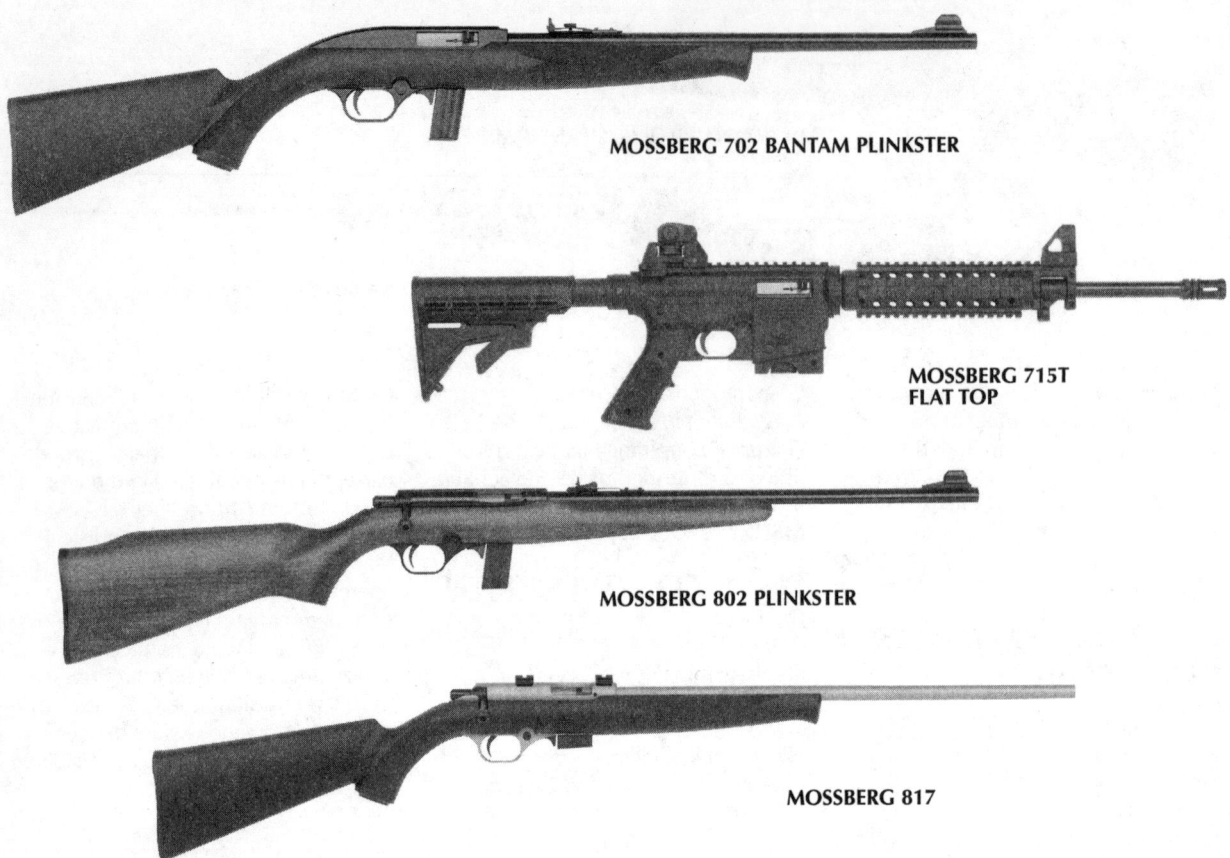

MOSSBERG 702 BANTAM PLINKSTER

MOSSBERG 715T FLAT TOP

MOSSBERG 802 PLINKSTER

MOSSBERG 817

702 BANTAM PLINKSTER

Action: Semiautomatic
Stock: Synthetic
Barrel: 18 in.
Sights: Adjustable rifle sights
Weight: 4 lb.
Caliber: .22 LR
Magazine: Detachable box, 11 rounds
Features: Youth rifle has 13-in. length of pull, black synthetic stock, and blued metal work; available with adjustable rifle sights only, or as a scoped package with a 4X rifle scope
Rifle sights only: $192.00
Scoped package: $202.00

715T FLAT TOP

Action: Semiautomatic
Stock: Synthetic
Barrel: 16.25 in.
Sights: Mounted front, adjustable rear; rail mount and adjustable front and rear; 30mm red-dot
Weight: 5 lb. 8 oz.
Caliber: .22 LR
Magazine: Detachable box, 11 or 26 rounds
Features: Four versions available with a mounted front sight and adjustable rear: fixed 13-in. length of pull black synthetic, 11-round mag; A2 adjustable black synthetic stock with 11-round mag; A2 adjustable black synthetic stock with 26-round mag; and A2 adjustable stock in Moonshine Muddy Girl camo with 26-round mag, rail mount, and adjustable front and rear sights; three versions equipped with a 30mm red dot sight, one fixed stock with an 11-round mag, and two A2 adjustable stocks, with either an 11- or 26-round mag, all in black
Sights only: . . . . . $383.00–$439.00
Red-dot sight package: . . . $373.00

802 PLINKSTER

Action: Bolt
Stock: Synthetic or wood
Barrel: 18 in.
Sights: Adjustable rifle sights
Weight: 4 lb.–4 lb. 8 oz.
Caliber: .22 LR
Magazine: Detachable box, 11 rounds
Features: Three configurations, Sport Grip synthetic stock model in black or Pink Marble, or a traditionally styled wood stock; all three have 14.25-in. length of pull, adjustable sights, 11-round magazines, and blued metal work
MSRP . . . . $191.00–$234.00

817

Action: Bolt
Stock: Synthetic or wood
Barrel: 21 in.
Sights: None
Weight: 4 lb. 8 oz.–5 lb.
Caliber: .17 HMR
Magazine: Detachable box, 6 rounds
Features: Factory-mounted Weaver-style scope bases; cross-bolt safety and magazine release buttons; free gun lock included; stock available in black synthetic or wood; varmint option has heavier bull barrel and comes only in the Sport Grip configuration
Standard barrel: . . . $223.00–$266.00
Varmint barrel: . . . $275.00–$285.00

Mossberg (O. F. Mossberg & Sons)

MOSSBERG BLAZE-47

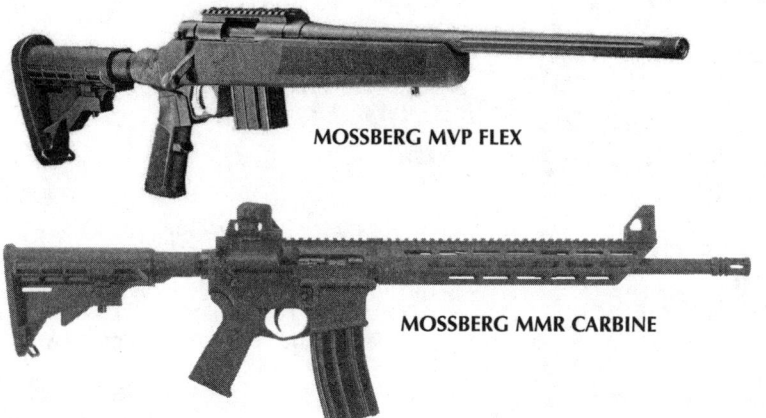

MOSSBERG BLAZE
AUTOLOADING RIMFIRE RIFLE

MOSSBERG MVP FLEX

MOSSBERG MMR CARBINE

BLAZE-47

Action: Semiautomatic
Stock: Wood or synthetic
Barrel: 16.5 in.
Sights: Adjustable
Weight: 4 lb. 8 oz.–4 lb. 12 oz.
Caliber: .22 LR
Magazine: Detachable box, 11–26 rounds
Features: Adjustable fiber optic rear sight and raised front rifle sights; choice of fixed wood stocks with 13 ½-inch length-of-pull (LOP) or lever-activated, 6-position adjustable LOP synthetic stock (11 ¼–14 inch); optional 10 or 25- round capacity magazines
Synthetic stock: **$357.00**
Wood stock: **$408.00**

BLAZE AUTOLOADING RIMFIRE RIFLE

Action: Semiautomatic
Stock: Synthetic
Barrel: 16.5 in.
Sights: Fixed
Weight: 3 lb. 8 oz.
Caliber: .22 LR
Magazine: Detachable box, 11–26 rounds

Features: All Blaze rifles feature free-floating 16.5-inch barrels with fixed front sight; 1:16 twist rate; 3/8-inch dovetail for ease of scope mounting; and blue metal finishes; optional sight systems include adjustable rifle rear sight for windage and elevation; barrel-mounted, top Picatinny rail to easily add the optic of your choice; or as a field-ready option, scoped combos come with a rail-mounted, Dead Ringer Green Dot adjustable sight featuring four optional reticle configurations; synthetic stocks feature vented forends and choice of black or camo-dipped finishes (Kryptek Highlander, Muddy Girl or Wildfire Camouflage patterns); the Blaze Bantam, available in black synthetic, features a shortened, 12-inch length-of-pull (LOP) to comfortably fit a younger shooter or any adult requiring a reduced LOP; Blaze 10- and 25-round magazines and top Picatinny rails are available
Standard rifle: **$203.00**
Green dot combo: **$273.00**
Kryptec Highlander: **$293.00**
Muddy Girl and Wildfire: . . .**$261.00**
Youth Bantam: **$203.00**

MVP FLEX

Action: Bolt
Stock: Synthetic
Barrel: 18.5 in., 20 in.
Sights: None
Weight: 6 lb. 8 oz.–8 lb. 4 oz.
Caliber: 5.56 NATO, 7.62 NATO
Magazine: Detachable box, 10+1 rounds
Features: Lightning Bolt trigger system; compatible with all FLEX buttstocks featuring the tool-less locking system; fluted medium bull barrel or sporter barrel; threaded, removable A2-style flash suppressor and thread protector included on bull barrel model; Picatinny rail; optional scope package available
MSRP . . . . **$725.00–$858.00**

MMR CARBINE

Action: Semiautomatic
Stock: Synthetic
Barrel: 16.25 in.
Sights: Rail-mounted adjustable
Weight: 6 lb. 12 oz.
Caliber: 5.56mm NATO/.223 Rem.
Magazine: 10 or 30 rounds
Features: Direct-impingement gas system; 13 in. handguard that combines a comfortable, slim profile with the versatile Magpul M-LOK system and a full-length top rail; Magpul MOE polymer trigger guard; 6-position adjustable or optional fixed length-of-pull stock; free-floating, button-rifled, carbon steel barrel; black phosphate/anodized metal finishes for enhanced durability; CA-compliant versions available
MSRP **$938.00**

Mossberg (O. F. Mossberg & Sons)

MOSSBERG MVP LC (LIGHT CHASSIS) SERIES

MOSSBERG MVP LR (LONG RANGE) SERIES

MOSSBERG MVP PATROL

MOSSBERG MVP PREDATOR

RIFLES

MVP LC (LIGHT CHASSIS) SERIES

Action: Bolt
Stock: Synthetic
Barrel: 16.25 in., 18.5 in., 22 in.
Sights: None
Weight: 8 lb.–10 lb.
Caliber: 5.56 NATO, 6.5 Creedmoor, 7.62 NATO
Magazine: Detachable box, 11 rounds
Features: Housed in an aluminum, tan-finished, light chassis stock designed by MDT that provides a modular, ergonomic base; free-floating, medium bull barrel is threaded and comes with a SilencerCo Saker muzzle brake, utilizing the Trifecta quick-detach mounting system (thread cap included); the barrels, constructed of carbon steel, are button-rifled with 16.25-inch length and 1:7 twist rate in the 5.56 NATO (.223 Rem.) chambering and the 7.62 NATO (.308 Win.) sports an 18.5-inch barrel with a 1:10 twist rate; both barrels feature a matte blue finish on all metalwork; Mossberg's Lightning Bolt Action (LBA) Trigger System is user-adjustable from 3 to 7 pounds and is machined from aircraft-grade aluminum and hard-coat anodized to military spec; spiral fluted bolt; oversized tactical-style bolt handle; Picatinny top rail; adjustable bipod; Magpul P-Mag 10-round magazines standard; 6.5 Creedmoor with a 22-in. barrel added to the unscoped LC line in 2017
MVP LC rifle: **$1407.00**
Vortex HS-T scoped combo: . . **$1995.00**

MVP LR (LONG RANGE) SERIES

Action: Bolt
Stock: Synthetic
Barrel: 16.25 in., 20 in., 22 in.
Sights: None or fixed
Weight: 7 lb.–8 lb.
Caliber: 5.56 NATO, 6.5 Creedmoor, 7.62 NATO
Magazine: Detachable box, 11 rounds
Features: MVP-LR feature a benchrest-style Mosscote stock with ergonomically-designed pistol grip with palm swell and deeply-relieved area behind the pistol grip; 20-inch fluted, medium bull barrels with 1:7 (5.56 NATO/.223 Rem.) and 1:10 (7.62 NATO/.308 Win.) twist rates; and dual front and single rear sling swivel studs; MVP-LR Tactical feature a classically-styled, Mosscote stock; 16.25-inch medium bull barrel with respective twist rates as above; adjustable fiber optic sights; and single front and rear sling swivel studs; 6.5 Creedmoor with a 22-in. barrel added 2017
MSRP **$975.00**

MVP PATROL

Action: Bolt
Stock: Synthetic
Barrel: 16.25 in.
Sights: Adjustable
Weight: 7 lb.–7 lb. 8 oz.
Caliber: 5.56 NATO, 7.62 NATO
Magazine: Detachable box, 10+1 rounds

Features: Picatinny rail; threaded barrel for flash suppressor; Lightning Bolt action adjustable trigger system; Standard Patrol rifles have 16.25-in. barrels and come in black or tan textured stocks; Thunder Ranch options feature 18.5-in. barrel. and come with OD Green stocks; 7.62x39 option with threaded 16.25-in. barrel and A2 flash hider, black synthetic stock with cheekpiece and longer 13.75-in. length of pull, and Vortex Crossfire II 2-7x32mm scope added to lineup in 2017
Standard Patrol: **$733.00**
Thunder Ranch Patrol: **$755.00**
7.62x39 with Vortex scope: . . . **$866.00**

MVP PREDATOR

Action: Bolt
Stock: Laminate
Barrel: 18.5 in., 20 in.
Sights: None
Weight: 7 lb.–7 lb. 8 oz.
Caliber: 5.56 NATO, 6.5 Creedmoor, 7.62 NATO
Magazine: Detachable box, 11 rounds
Features: Predator models feature a sporter-style laminate stock, optional scope package, choice of barrel lengths, contour and threading; rifles can use AR-15/AR-10 style and M1A-M14 magazines, action is pillar bedded, and the LBA trigger is adjustable; 6.5 Creedmoor added in 2017
Standard rifle: **$733.00**
Vortex scope package (7.62 and 5.56 NATO only): **$873.00**

Mossberg (O. F. Mossberg & Sons)

MOSSBERG MVP SCOUT

MOSSBERG PATRIOT SERIES

MOSSBERG MVP SCOUT
WITH VORTEX SCOPE

MOSSBERG PATRIOT KRYPTEK HIGHLANDER

MVP SCOUT

Action: Bolt
Stock: Synthetic
Barrel: 16.25 in.
Sights: Fiber optic front ghost ring
Weight: 6 lb. 12 oz.
Caliber: 7.62 NATO
Magazine: Detachable box, 11 rounds
Features: Has an 11-inch receiver/barrel-mounted Picatinny rail; an integrated, rail-mounted, Ghost Ring rear sight is paired with a barrel-mounted, fiber optic front sight; two Picatinny side rails, located near the front of the forend; a compact 16 ¼-inch medium bull, carbon steel button-rifled, threaded barrel with an A2-style suppressor, with a 1:10 twist rate; a protective thread cap is provided; an adjustable rifle sling; scoped package includes Vortex 2-7x32 rifle scope
Standard rifle: **$761.00**
Vortex scope package:. **$931.00**

MVP SCOUT WITH VORTEX SCOPE

Action: Bolt
Stock: Synthetic
Barrel: 16.25 in.
Sights: Ghost ring rear, fiber optic front, mounted scope 2–7x32mm
Weight: 9 lb.
Caliber: 7.62mm NATO/.308 Win.
Magazine: 10 rounds
Features: M1A- and AR10-style magazines; bull barrel threaded with removable A2-style flash suppressor; adjustable trigger; Picatinny rail; scoped version includes Vortex 2-7x32mm optic; available without scope

With scope:. **$931.00**
Without scope: **$761.00**

PATRIOT KRYPTEK HIGHLANDER

Action: Bolt
Stock: Synthetic
Barrel: 22 in.
Sights: None
Weight: 7 lb.
Caliber: .243 Win., .270 Win., .300 Win. Mag., .308 Win., .30-06 Spfd.
Magazine: 4 or 5 rounds
Features: Kryptek Highlander stocks feature a camouflage pattern specially designed for hunting in varied terrain and elevation; textured stippling on the grip and the three surface areas of the forend; straight comb with rounded edges, raised cheekpiece, and traditional rubber butt pad for greater comfort and reduced recoil; streamlined bolt handle provides additional clearance for gloved or larger hands; aggressively checkered bolt knob
MSRP. **$436.00**

PATRIOT SERIES

Action: Bolt
Stock: Wood, synthetic, or laminate
Barrel: 20 in., 22 in., 24 in.
Sights: None or rifle sights
Weight: 6 lb. 8 oz.–9 lb.
Caliber: .243 Win., .22-250 Rem., 7mm-08 Rem., .308 Win., .25-06 Rem., .270 Win., .30-06 Spfd., 7mm Rem. Mag., .300 Win. Mag., .338 Win. Mag., .375 Ruger, 6.5 Creedmoor
Magazine: Detachable box, 4–5 rounds
Features: Twin-lug, push-feed

machined-steel action which is fed from a lightweight polymer, flush box magazine with 4 or 5-round total capacity (magnum and standard calibers respectively); button-rifled, standard contour, free-floating 22-inch barrels (20-inch barrels on Bantam/Super Bantam) are constructed of carbon steel, feature straight-edge fluting (375 Ruger versions have non-fluted barrels) and recessed crowns; metal finishes include a choice of Matte Blue or Mossberg's Marinecote protective finish; every Patriot rifle also features Mossberg's LBA (Lightning Bolt Action) Adjustable Trigger System for consistent shot placement and is user-adjustable from 2 to 7 pounds; standard features include distinctive, spiral-fluted bolts; receiver-mounted, weaver-style scope bases; adjustable, fiber optic sights (select calibers); and sling swivel studs

Kryptek Highlander: **$436.00**
Laminate
  Marinecote: . . . . **$591.00–$609.00**
Night Train: . . . . . . **$621.00–$794.00**
Patriot Predator: **$441.00**
Patriot Revere:. **$823.00**
Scoped Combo Synthetic:. .**$436.00**
Scoped Combo Walnut: . . .**$566.00**
Synthetic: **$397.00**
Synthetic Marinecote,
  rifle sights:. **$462.00**
Synthetic Vortex Scoped
  Combo: **$537.00**
Walnut: **$525.00**
Walnut Vortex Scoped
  Combo: **$665.00**
Walnut Adjustable Sights: . .**$545.00**
Youth Bantam:. **$525.00**
Youth Super
  Bantam: . . . . **$397.00–$436.00**
Youth Super Bantam Scoped
  Combo: . . . . **$436.00–$474.00**

Nesika

NESIKA LONG RANGE

NESIKA SPORTER

NESIKA TACTICAL

LONG RANGE

Action: Bolt
Stock: Synthetic
Barrel: 26 in.
Sights: None
Weight: 9 lb. 12 oz.
Caliber: .300 Win. Mag., 6.5x284, 7mm Rem. Mag.
Magazine: Internal
Features: Nesika stainless Hunter action; receiver made from 15-5 stainless steel; one-piece bolt from 4340 CM steel; Douglas air-gauged stainless steel barrel; fluted Varmint contour; Timney trigger set at a 3 lbs.; Leupold QRW bases
MSRP $3999.00

SPORTER

Action: Bolt
Stock: Synthetic
Barrel: 24 in., 26 in.
Sights: None
Weight: 8 lb.
Caliber: .260 Rem., 7mm-08 Rem., .308 Win., .30-06 Spfd., .280 Rem., 7mm Rem. Mag., .300 Win. Mag., 6.5x284
Magazine: Internal
Features: Nesika stainless Hunter action; receiver made from 15-5 stainless steel; one-piece bolt from 4340 CM steel; Douglas air-gauged stainless steel barrel; fluted Varmint contour; Timney trigger set at a 3 lbs.; Leupold QRW bases
MSRP $3499.00

TACTICAL

Action: Bolt
Stock: Synthetic
Barrel: 26 in., 28 in.
Sights: None
Weight: 13 lb. 12 oz.
Caliber: .300 Win. Mag., .338 Lapua
Magazine: Detachable box, 5 rounds
Features: Picatinny rail; all metal coated with Cerakoted matte black finish; tactical hand laid-up composite stock with aluminum bedding block, spacer adjuster system, and adjustable cheekpiece; Timney trigger set at 3 lbs.
MSRP $4499.00

New Ultra Light Arms

NEW ULTRA LIGHT ARMS MODEL 20 RIMFIRE

NEW ULTRA LIGHT ARMS MODEL 20 ULTIMATE MOUNTAIN RIFLE

MODEL 20 RIMFIRE

Action: Bolt
Stock: Kevlar/graphite composite
Barrel: 22 in.
Sights: None
Weight: 5 lb. 4 oz.
Caliber: .22 LR
Magazine: None or detachable box, 5 rounds
Features: Single-shot or repeater; drilled and tapped for scope; recoil pad; sling swivels; color stock options; left-hand models available for no extra charge
Single shot: **$1800.00**
Repeater: **$1850.00**

MODEL 20 ULTIMATE MOUNTAIN RIFLE

Action: Bolt
Stock: Kevlar/graphite composite
Barrel: 22 in.
Sights: None
Weight: 5 lb.
Caliber: .308 Win., .243 Win., 6mm Rem., .257 Roberts, 7mm-08, .284 Win.
Magazine: Detachable box
Features: Available in left-hand; choice of stock colors; 20-oz. action; two-position safety
MSRP $3500.00
Left-handed: **$3600.00**

RIFLES

Nosler

NOSLER M48 CUSTOM RIFLE

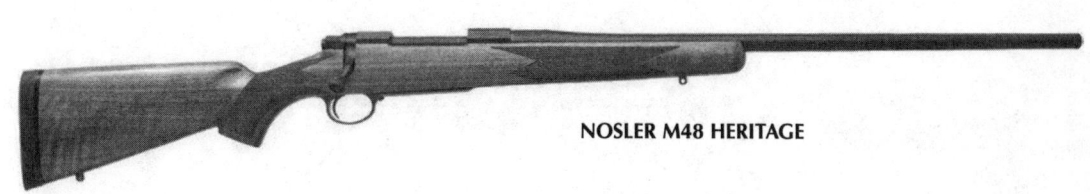

NOSLER M48 HERITAGE

M48 CUSTOM RIFLE
Action: Bolt
Stock: Walnut
Barrel: 24 in., 24.75 in.
Sights: Open
Weight: 8 lb. 4 oz.–8 lb. 12 oz.
Caliber: .30 Nosler, .300 WSM, .280 Ack. Imp., .338 Win. Mag.
Magazine: Internal, 3, 4 rounds
Features: Leupold Custom Shop; match-grade stainless, fully free-floated hand lapped barrel; three-stage safety; glass pillar-bedded fancy wal-

nut stock; custom case cruzer by Pelican; custom leather sling
MSRP . . . . $2495.00–$3145.00

M48 HERITAGE
Action: Bolt
Stock: Wood
Barrel: 24 in.–26 in.
Sights: None
Weight: 7 lb. 4 oz.–7 lb. 13 oz.
Caliber: .22 Nosler, .243 Win., 6.5 Creedmoor, 6.5-284 Norma, .26 Nosler, .270 Win., .280 AI, 7mm

Rem. Mag., .28 Nosler, .308 Win., .30-06 Spfd., .300 WSM, .300 Win. Mag., .30 Nosler, .338 Win. Mag., .33 Nosler
Magazine: N/A
Features: Nosler Model 48 Custom action; stainless match-grade barrel; fancy walnut stock with heckering; hinged floor-plate; two-position Rocker safety; Cerakote all-weather finish
MSRP $1895.00

Noveske

NOVESKE GEN 3 SERIES

GEN 3 SERIES
Action: Semiautomatic
Stock: Synthetic
Barrel: 7.5 in.–18 in.
Sights: Adjustable

Weight: N/A
Caliber: .300 BLK, 5.56 NATO, 7.62 NATO
Magazine: Detachable box, 30 rounds

Features: Numerous barrel lengths, rail, stock and finish options available across three calibers; current Gen III models include OMW (One More Wave), Leonidas and Leonidas Switchblock N6 and N6 Switchblock, 5.56 Diplomat and .300 BLK Pistols, 10.5-in barreled Rifle, 13.7-in barreled Infidel, 14.5-in. barreled Afghan, 16- and 18-in. Rifles, 10.5-in. Switchblock, 16-in. Switchblock, Noveske Bazooka Green Wide Open Armory Exclusive, and 13.7-in. Infidel FDE (Flat Dark Earth; RSR exclusive)
MSRP . . . . $2095.00–$3800.00

Patriot Ordnance Factory

PATRIOT ORDNANCE FACTORY P300

PATRIOT ORDNANCE FACTORY RENEGADE

PATRIOT ORDNANCE FACTORY RENEGADE PLUS

RIFLES

P300
Action: Semiautomatic
Stock: Synthetic
Barrel: 18 in., 24 in.
Sights: None
Weight: 9 lb. 3 oz.–9 lb. 13 oz.
Caliber: .300 Win. Mag.
Magazine: Detachable box
Features: Adjustable gas piston system; extended handguard; completely ambidextrous lower receiver; 14.5 in. M-LOK compatible rail handguard; M rail allows for additional rails to be mounted or removed based on shooter's preference; adjustable Magpul CTR stock on the 18 in. variant and a Magpul MOE rifle length installed on the 24 in. variant; EFP drop in trigger; completely ambidextrous safety selector, bolt catch, bolt release, and magazine release; E² extraction technology
MSRP $3499.00

RENEGADE
Action: Semiautomatic
Stock: Synthetic
Barrel: 16.5 in.
Sights: None
Weight: 6 lb. 5 oz.
Caliber: 5.56 NATO, 7.62x39
Magazine: Detachable box
Features: M-LOK compatible Renegade rail; heat sink barrel nut; Dictator 9-position adjustable gas block with straight gas tube; nitride heat-treated barrel
MSRP $1499.00

RENEGADE PLUS
Action: Semiautomatic
Stock: Synthetic
Barrel: 16.5 in. (5.56 NATO), 18.5 in. (.223 Wylde)
Sights: None
Weight: 6 lb. 6 oz. (5.56 NATO), 7 lb. 11 oz. (.223 Wylde)
Caliber: 5.56 NATO, .223 Wylde
Magazine: Detachable box
Features: M-LOK compatible Renegade rail; heat sink barrel nut; Dictator 9-position adjustable gas block with straight gas tube; nitride heat-treated barrel; Gen 4 POF-USA ambidextrous billet lower receiver and POF-USA Ultimate Bolt Carrier Group; flat 3.5 lb match-grade trigger with KNS Precision anti-walk pins; NP3 coated for maximum protection and reliability; integrated gas key (no screws required)
MSRP . . . . $1899.00–$2029.00

Primary Weapons Systems

PRIMARY WEAPONS SYSTEMS
(PWS) MK1 MOD 2

PRIMARY WEAPONS SYSTEMS MK216

PRIMARY WEAPONS SYSTEMS MK220

MK1 MOD 2
Action: Semiautomatic
Stock: Synthetic
Barrel: 7.75 in.–18 in.
Sights: None
Weight: 5 lb. 8.8 oz.–6 lb. 10.2 oz.
Caliber: .223 Rem.
Magazine: Detachable box
Features: Forged upper and lower
receivers; includes PicMod
technology, which allows for the
mounting of any KeyMod attachment
anywhere on the rail while being able
to mount most Picatinny accessories
directly to the rail in the areas where
the PicMod feature is present;
adjustable gas block; new handguard

mounting system features a trunnion
machined into the upper receiver;
enhanced trigger; anodized in mil
spec type 3; ambidextrous controls for
the safety selector
MSRP **$2049.95**

MK216
Action: Semiautomatic
Stock: Synthetic
Barrel: 16 in.
Sights: Adjustable
Weight: 8 lb. 10 oz.
Caliber: .308 Win., 7.62 NATO
Magazine: Detachable box, 10 or 20
rounds
Features: FSC muzzle brake and

suppressor; Picatinny rail; adjustable
stock
MSRP **$2199.95**

MK220
Action: Semiautomatic
Stock: Synthetic
Barrel: 20 in.
Sights: Adjustable
Weight: 9 lb. 7 oz.
Caliber: .308 Win., 7.62 NATO
Magazine: Detachable box, 10 or 20
rounds
Features: PRC muzzle brake;
Picatinny rail; adjustable stock
MSRP **$2199.95**

PTR Industries

PTR INDUSTRIES PTR 32 KFR GEN 2

PTR 32 KFR GEN 2
Action: Semiautomatic
Stock: Synthetic
Barrel: 16 in.
Sights: Fixed
Weight: 9 lb. 8 oz.

Caliber: 7.62 Warsaw
Magazine: Detachable, 30 rounds
Features: H&K Navy-type polymer
trigger group housing, HK 91-length
handguards, cocking tube, welded
scope mount, paddle magazine

release, delayed blowback roller lock
system are standard; now with 5/8-24
barrel threading.
MSRP **$1265.00**

PTR Industries

PTR INDUSTRIES PTR 91 FR

PTR 91 FR

Action: Semiautomatic
Stock: Synthetic
Barrel: 18 in.
Sights: Fixed
Weight: 9 lb. 12 oz.

Caliber: .308, 7.62 NATO
Magazine: 20 rounds
Features: Flash hider; H&K navy-type polymer trigger group housing; black tactical handguard with one 6 in. rail at 6 o'clock; welded scope mount;

black powder-coat finish; New Jersey- and California-compliant versions available
MSRP **$1299.00**

Purdey

PURDEY BOLT ACTION RIFLE

PURDEY DOUBLE RIFLE

BOLT ACTION RIFLES

Action: Bolt
Stock: Walnut
Barrel: 25 in.
Sights: Open
Weight: 10 lb. 8 oz.
Caliber: Available in all calibers up to .505 Gibbs
Magazine: None
Features: Original Mauser '98 or modern Mauser type magnum square bridge; model 70 type safety catch for use with telescopic sights; quick detachable claw or Purdey rail

mounts depending on the type of action and telescopic sight chosen; Purdey's rail mount system with integral recoil bar; Turkish walnut stock with pistol grip; cheekpiece and rubber recoil pad; single trigger
MSRP . . . .**Custom built, call manufacturer for pricing**

DOUBLE RIFLES

Action: Self-Opening
Stock: Walnut
Barrel: 23 in.–26 in.
Sights: Open

Weight: 12 lb. 4 oz.
Caliber: .375, .470, .500, .600
Magazine: None
Features: Hinged front trigger; bolted non-automatic safety catch; sling swivels optional; full pistol grip; cheekpiece and leather covered recoil pad; chopper lump barrel construction; express rear sights with bead foresight with flip-up moon sight; optional beavertail forend and telescopic sights
MSRP . . . . **Custom built, call manufacturer for pricing**

Remington Arms Company

REMINGTON MODEL 552 BDL SPEEDMASTER

REMINGTON MODEL 572 BDL FIELDMASTER

REMINGTON MODEL 597 WITH SCOPE

REMINGTON MODEL 597 HB

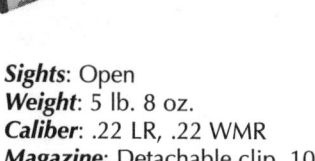

REMINGTON MODEL 597 MOSSY OAK PINK

MODEL 552 BDL SPEEDMASTER

Action: Semiautomatic
Stock: Walnut
Barrel: 22 in.
Sights: Open
Weight: 5 lb. 12 oz.
Caliber: .22 S, L, LR
Magazine: Under-barrel tube
Features: Adjustable iron sights for open sight plinking; grooved receiver for scope mounts; high-gloss American walnut stock and forend checkering; richly blued carbon-steel barrel; positive cross-bolt safety
MSRP **$707.00**

MODEL 572 BDL FIELDMASTER

Action: Pump
Stock: Walnut
Barrel: 21 in.
Sights: Open
Weight: 5 lb. 12 oz.
Caliber: .22 S, L, LR
Magazine: Under-barrel tube
Features: Smooth classic side action; high-gloss American walnut stock and forend with cut checkering; richly blued carbon-steel barrel; adjustable iron sights for open slight plinking; receiver grooved for scope mounts; positive cross-bolt safety
MSRP **$723.00**

MODEL 597

Action: Semiautomatic
Stock: Synthetic
Barrel: 22 in.

Sights: Open
Weight: 5 lb. 8 oz.
Caliber: .22 LR, .22 WMR
Magazine: Detachable clip, 10 rounds
Features: Bolt-guidance system features twin, tool-steel guide rails; sear and hammer are Teflon/nickel-plated; non-glare matte finish; adjustable big game iron sights; last-shot "hold open" bolt for added safety
MSRP . . . . **$213.00–$257.00**

MODEL 597 HEAVY BARREL

Action: Semiautomatic
Stock: Synthetic
Barrel: 22 in.
Sights: None
Weight: 5 lb. 12 oz.
Caliber: .22 LR
Magazine: Detachable clip, 10 rounds
Features: Heavy barrel with rugged green synthetic stock; bolt-guidance system features twin tool-steel guide

rails; Teflon nickel plated sear and hammer; patented drop-out staggered stack, detachable metal magazine; last-shot "hold open" bolt; scope rail
MSRP **$254.00**

MODEL 597 MOSSY OAK PINK

Action: Semiautomatic
Stock: Synthetic
Barrel: 20 in.
Sights: Fiber optic front
Weight: 5 lb. 8 oz.
Caliber: .22 LR
Magazine: Detachable box, 10 rounds
Features: Matte blue barrel with Mossy Oak Pink synthetic stock; bolt-guidance system features twin tool-steel guide rails; Teflon nickel plated sear and hammer; patented drop-out staggered stack, detachable metal magazine; last-shot "hold open" bolt; scope rail
MSRP **$306.00**

Remington Arms Company

REMINGTON MODEL 700 BDL

REMINGTON MODEL 700 CDL

REMINGTON MODEL 700 LONG RANGE

REMINGTON MODEL 700 MOUNTAIN SS

REMINGTON MODEL 700 200TH ANNIVERSARY LIMITED EDITION

REMINGTON MODEL 700 ADL 200TH ANNIVERSARY OMMEMORATIVE

MODEL 700 BDL

Action: Bolt
Stock: Walnut
Barrel: 22 in., 24 in.
Sights: Open
Weight: 7 lb. 4 oz.–7 lb. 8 oz.
Caliber: .243 Win., .270 Win., .30-06 Spfd., 7mm Rem. Mag.
Magazine: Internal
Features: Adjustable X-Mark Pro Trigger system; walnut stock with black forend cap; Monte Carlo comb with raised cheekpiece and skipline cut checkering; hinged magazine floor plate; sling swivel studs; hooded ramp front sight and adjustable rear sight; cylindrical receiver machined from solid-steel bar
MSRP . . . . $994.00–$1024.00

MODEL 700 CDL

Action: Bolt
Stock: Walnut
Barrel: 24 in., 26 in.
Sights: None
Weight: 7 lb. 5 oz.–7 lb. 10 oz.
Caliber: .243 Win., .25-06 Rem., .270 Win., 7mm-08 Rem., 7mm Rem. Mag., .300 Win. Mag., .30-06 Spfd.
Magazine: Internal
Features: Adjustable X-Mark Pro Trigger system; cylindrical receiver machined from solid-steel bar stock; walnut stock with oil finish
MSRP . . . . $1029.00–$1059.00

MODEL 700 LONG RANGE

Action: Bolt
Stock: Synthetic
Barrel: 26 in.
Sights: None
Weight: 9 lb.
Caliber: .25-06 Rem., .30-06 Spfd., .300 Rem. Ultra Mag., .300 Win. Mag., 7mm Rem. Mag.
Magazine: Internal, 4 or 3 (Mag.) rounds
Features: Bell and Carlson M40 tactical stock; heavy varmint barrel with matte finish; X-Mark Pro externally adjustable trigger system
MSRP $879.76

MODEL 700 MOUNTAIN SS

Action: Bolt
Stock: Synthetic
Barrel: 22 in.
Sights: Drilled and tapped for scopes
Weight: 6 lb. 8 oz.
Caliber: .25-06 Rem., .270 Win., .280 Rem., .30-06 Spfd., 7mm-08 Rem., .308 Win.
Magazine: Internal
Features: Bell & Carson aramid fiber reinforced stock; X-Mark Pro trigger system; cylindrical receiver design; sling swivel studs; stainless steel barrel and action; hinged magazine floor plate
MSRP $1152.00

MODEL 700 200TH ANNIVERSARY LIMITED EDITION

Action: Bolt
Stock: Walnut
Barrel: 24 in.
Sights: Fixed
Weight: 7 lb. 8 oz.
Caliber: 7mm Rem. Mag.
Magazine: 3 rounds
Features: C-grade walnut stock with fleur de lis checkering; classic American-style engraving and 24k gold inlay portraying founder Eliphalet Remington; steel floorplate; medallion in grip; limited to quantity of 2016; special serial number; New England custom sights ; custom box
MSRP $2399.00

MODEL 700 ADL 200TH ANNIVERSARY COMMEMORATIVE

Action: Bolt
Stock: Walnut
Barrel: 24 in., 26 in.
Sights: Fixed
Weight: 7 lb. 6 oz.–7 lb. 10 oz.
Caliber: .243 Win., .270 Win., .30-06 Spfd., .300 Win. Mag.
Magazine: 3 or 4 rounds
Features: A-grade walnut stock with fleur de lis checkering; medallion in grip; X-Mark Pro externally adjustable trigger
MSRP $695.00

Remington Arms Company

MODEL 700 SENDERO SF II
Action: Bolt
Stock: Composite
Barrel: 26 in.
Sights: None
Weight: 8 lb. 8 oz.
Caliber: .25-06 Rem., .264 Win. Mag., 7mm Rem. Mag., .300 Win. Mag., .300 Rem. Ultra Mag.
Magazine: Internal
Features: Composite stock in black with gray webbing, reinforced with aramid fibers; features contoured beavertail forend with ambidextrous finger grooves and palm swells; heavy contour barrels are fluted for rapid cooling; full-length aluminum bedding stocks; twin front swivel studs for sling and bipod; concave target-style barrel crown
MSRP. $1502.00

MODEL 700 SPS
Action: Bolt
Stock: Synthetic
Barrel: 24 in., 26 in.
Sights: None
Weight: 7 lb.–7 lb. 10 oz.
Caliber: .270 WSM, .260 Rem., .300 WSM, .223 Rem., .243 Win., 7mm-08 Rem., .308 Win., .270 Win., .30-06 Spfd., .300 Win. Mag., .300 Rem. Ultra Mag., 7mm Rem. Mag., .338 Win. Mag.
Magazine: Internal box
Features: Black ergonomic synthetic stock; carbon steel sight drilled and tapped for scope mounts; exterior metal-work features matte blued finish; hinged floor plate; swivel studs
MSRP. $731.00

MODEL 700 SPS CAMO
Action: Bolt
Stock: Synthetic
Barrel: 20 in., 22 in., 24 in.
Sights: None
Weight: 7 lb.–7 lb. 6 oz.
Caliber: .270 Win., .30-06 Spfd., 7mm Rem. Mag., .300 Win. Mag.
Magazine: None
Features: Hammer-forged barrel; X-Mark Pro externally adjustable trigger system; SuperCell recoil pad; synthetic stock in Mossy Oak Break-Up Infinity pattern; Hogue over-molded grips; receivers tapped and drilled
MSRP. $809.00

REMINGTON MODEL 700 SENDERO SF II

REMINGTON MODEL 700 SPS LEFT-HAND

REMINGTON MODEL 700 SPS CAMO

REMINGTON MODEL 700 SPS TACTICAL

REMINGTON MODEL 700 SPS TACTICAL AAC-SD

REMINGTON MODEL 700 SPS VARMINT

MODEL 700 SPS TACTICAL
Action: Bolt
Stock: Synthetic
Barrel: 20 in.
Sights: None
Weight: 7 lb. 4 oz.–7 lb. 11 oz.
Caliber: .223 Rem., .300 BLK, .308 Win.
Magazine: Detachable box
Features: Ergonomic tactical stock in black; sling swivel studs; carbon steel barrel is drilled and tapped for sights; metal features blued finish; X-Mark Pro adjustable trigger; SuperCell recoil pad; semi-beavertail forend; hinged floor plate
MSRP. . . . . $788.00–$842.00

MODEL 700 SPS TACTICAL AAC-SD
Action: Bolt
Stock: Synthetic
Barrel: 20 in.
Sights: None
Weight: 7 lb. 5 oz.
Caliber: .308 Win.

Magazine: Internal box
Features: Heavy barrel with threaded muzzle; accepts AAC and other threaded flash hiders, muzzlebrakes and suppressors; Hogue overmolded hillier green pillar bedded stock; X-Mark Pro adjustable trigger; optional Leupold Mark IV scope
MSRP. $842.00

MODEL 700 SPS VARMINT
Action: Bolt
Stock: Synthetic
Barrel: 26 in.
Sights: None
Weight: 8 lb. 8 oz.
Caliber: .204 Ruger, .223 Rem., .22-250 Rem., .243 Win., .308 Win.
Magazine: Internal
Features: Ergonomic black synthetic stock has a vented beavertail forend; non-reflective matte blued finish on barrel and receiver; hinged floor plate; sling swivel studs; drilled and tapped for scope mounts
MSRP. $761.00

Remington Arms Company

REMINGTON MODEL 700 TACTICAL CHASSIS

REMINGTON MODEL 700 VLS

REMINGTON MODEL 700 VTR

REMINGTON MODEL 783 SCOPED

REMINGTON MODEL 7600

MODEL 700 TACTICAL CHASSIS
Action: Bolt
Stock: Synthetic
Barrel: 24 in., 26 in.
Sights: None
Weight: 11 lb. 12 oz.–12 lb. 4 oz.
Caliber: .300 Win. Mag., .308 Win., .338 Lapua Mag.
Magazine: Detachable box
Features: MDT TAC21 tactical chassis constructed out of aluminum anodized to Mil-Spec Type III; top full-length Picatinny rail; stainless steel barreled action with black cerakote finish; Magpul MAG307 PRS adjustable stock and pistol grip; target tactical bolt handle; AAC 51-T ratchet mount muzzle brake; X-Mark Pro externally adjustable trigger
MSRP . . . . $2900.00–$3500.00

MODEL 700 VLS
Action: Bolt
Stock: Laminate
Barrel: 26 in.
Sights: Target
Weight: 9 lb. 6 oz.
Caliber: .204 Ruger, .22-250 Rem., .223 Rem., .243 Win., .308 Win.

Magazine: Internal
Features: Varmint laminated stock; Monte Carlo cheekpiece; beavertail shape forend; blued, satin finish metal; concave target-style barrel crown
MSRP $1056.00

MODEL 700 VTR
Action: Bolt
Stock: Synthetic
Barrel: 22 in.
Sights: None
Weight: 7 lb. 10 oz.
Caliber: .22-250 Rem., .223 Rem., .260 Rem., .308 Win.
Magazine: Internal
Features: Integral muzzle brake; Picatinny rail; detachable bipod; stainless steel barrel available
MSRP $930.00

MODEL 783 SCOPED
Action: Bolt
Stock: Black synthetic
Barrel: 20 in., 22 in., 24 in.
Sights: None
Weight: 8 lb. 4 oz.–8 lb. 10 oz.
Caliber: .22-250 Rem., .223 Rem., .243 Win., .270 Win., .30-06 Spfd., .300 Win. Mag., .308 Win., 7mm Rem. Mag.

Magazine: 3–5 rounds
Features: CrossFire trigger system; carbon steel magnum contour button rifled barrel; pillar-bedded stock and free-floated barrel; SuperCell recoil pad; available in Mossy Oak Break-Up Country in .223, .243, .308, and .30-06 only; both stock options come with a pre-mounted and bore-sighted 3-9x40mm scope
Black: $399.00
Camo: $451.00

MODEL 7600
Action: Pump
Stock: Wood
Barrel: 18.5 in., 22 in.
Sights: Open
Weight: 7 lb. 8 oz.
Caliber: .270 Win., .30-06 Spfd., .308 Win.
Magazine: Detachable box, 4 rounds
Features: Free-floated barrel; Monte Carlo walnut stock with satin finish as standard; metal work has black non-reflective finish; iron sights and drilled and tapped receiver for scope mounts; rotary-bolt lock-up
MSRP $918.00

RIFLES

Remington Arms Company

REMINGTON MODEL 7600 200TH ANNIVERSARY LIMITED EDITION

REMINGTON R-25 GII

REMINGTON MODEL SEVEN CDL

REMINGTON MODEL SEVEN SYNTHETIC

MODEL 7600 200TH ANNIVERSARY LIMITED EDITION

Action: Pump
Stock: Walnut
Barrel: 22 in.
Sights: Fixed
Weight: 7 lb. 8 oz.
Caliber: .30-06 Spfd.
Magazine: 4 rounds
Features: C-grade walnut stock with fleur de lis checkering; classic American-style engraving and 24k gold inlay portraying founder Eliphalet Remington; steel floorplate; medallion in grip; limited to quantity of 2016; special serial number; New England custom sights ; custom box
MSRP **$1999.00**

MODEL R-25 GII

Action: Semiautomatic
Stock: Synthetic
Barrel: 18 in.
Sights: None
Weight: 7 lb. 10 oz.
Caliber: 7.62x51mm
Magazine: 4 rounds
Features: Stainless steel, Teflon-coated barrel, target crown muzzle; fixed, lightweight stock with SuperCell Recoil pad, available in Mossy Oak Breakup Infinity; Hogue pistol grip; carbon fiber vented free float handguard; two stage match trigger
MSRP **$1697.00**

MODEL SEVEN CDL

Action: Bolt
Stock: Walnut
Barrel: 20 in.
Sights: Open
Weight: 6 lb. 8 oz.
Caliber: .243 Win., .260 Rem., 7mm-08 Rem., .308 Win.
Magazine: Internal box

Features: SuperCell recoil pad; American walnut CDL stock with sat-in-finished barrel; compact design for fast handling; cylindrical receiver; available in Rem. short-action magnum and Winchester short magnum
MSRP **$1039.00**

MODEL SEVEN SYNTHETIC

Action: Bolt
Stock: Synthetic
Barrel: 18 in., 20 in.
Sights: None
Weight: 6 lb. 2 oz.–6 lb. 8 oz.
Caliber: .243 Win., .260 Rem., 7mm-08 Rem., .308 Win.
Magazine: Internal
Features: Synthetic black stock; compact design for fast handling; cylindrical receiver design
MSRP **$731.00**

Rifles Inc.

RIFLES INC. CANYON

RIFLES INC. CLASSIC

RIFLES INC. LIGHTWEIGHT STRATA

RIFLES INC. MASTER'S SERIES

RIFLES INC. SAFARI

CANYON

Action: Bolt
Stock: McMillan HTG
Barrel: 24 in.
Sights: None
Weight: 10 lb.
Caliber: Most popular calibers
Magazine: Internal
Features: Blind or hinged floor plate; customer-supplied Rem. 700 action; match grade stainless steel Lilja number 6 barrel; optional muzzlebrake; matte stainless metal finish, optional black Teflon; adjustable cheekpiece; custom buttpad
MSRP $3500.00

CLASSIC

Action: Bolt
Stock: Laminated fiberglass
Barrel: 24 in.–26 in.
Sights: None
Weight: 6 lb. 8 oz.
Caliber: All popular chamberings up to .375 H&H
Magazine: Internal
Features: Customer-supplied Rem. 700 action; match grade stainless steel Lilja barrel; blind or hinged floor plate; matte stainless metal finish, optional Black Teflon finish; black laminated fiberglass, pillar glass bedded stock
MSRP $2900.00

LIGHTWEIGHT STRATA

Action: Bolt
Stock: Laminate
Barrel: 22 in.–26 in.
Sights: None
Weight: 4 lb. 8 oz.–5 lb. 12 oz.
Caliber: All popular chamberings up to .375 H&H
Magazine: Internal
Features: Customer-supplied Rem. 700 action; match grade stainless steel Lilja barrel; fluted bolt and hollowed-handle; blind or hinged floor plate; matte stainless metal finish, optional black Teflon finish; hand-laminated blend of Kevlar/graphite and boron, pillar glass bedded stock; Titanium Strata has hand-laminated

graphite stock with pillar glass bedded; custom buttpad; Quiet Slimbrake II muzzlebrake
Lightweight Strata: $3200.00
Lightweight 70: $3100.00

MASTER'S SERIES

Action: Bolt
Stock: Laminated fiberglass
Barrel: 24 in.–27 in.
Sights: None
Weight: 7 lb. 12 oz.
Caliber: All popular chamberings up to .375 H&H
Magazine: Internal
Features: Customer-supplied Rem. 700 action; match grade stainless steel Lilja number 5 barrel; hinged floor plate; matte stainless metal finish, optional black Teflon finish; black laminated fiberglass, pillar glass bedded stock; optional muzzlebrake
MSRP $3200.00

SAFARI

Action: Bolt
Stock: Laminated fiberglass
Barrel: 23 in.–25 in.
Sights: Optional Express Sights
Weight: 8 lb. 8 oz.
Caliber: .375 H&H, .416 Rem. Mag., and other large game cartridges
Magazine: 4 rounds
Features: Customer-supplied Winchester Model 70 Classic action; lapped and face trued bolt; match grade stainless steel Lilja barrel; Quiet Slimbrake II muzzlebrake; hinged floor plate or optional drop box; matte stainless finish, optional black Teflon; double laminated fiberglass, pillar glass bedded stock; Pachmayr decelerator; optional barrel band
MSRP $3500.00

Rock River Arms

ROCK RIVER ARMS LAR-6.8 COYOTE CARBINE

ROCK RIVER ARMS LAR-6.8 X-1

ROCK RIVER ARMS LAR-8 PREDATOR HP

ROCK RIVER ARMS LAR-8 X-1

LAR-6.8 COYOTE CARBINE
Action: Semiautomatic
Stock: Synthetic
Barrel: 16 in.
Sights: None
Weight: 7 lb.
Caliber: 6.8 SPC II
Magazine: 1 round
Features: Smith Vortex flash hider; chromoly barrel; RRA two-stage match trigger
MSRP $1310.00

LAR-6.8 X-1
Action: Semiautomatic
Stock: Synthetic
Barrel: 18 in.
Sights: None
Weight: 7 lb. 13 oz.
Caliber: 6.8 SPC II
Magazine: Detachable box, 25 rounds
Features: RRA Beast of Hunter muzzle brake; available in black or tan; available with A2 or CAR stocks
MSRP . . . . $1595.00–$1655.00

LAR-8 PREDATOR HP
Action: Semiautomatic
Stock: Synthetic
Barrel: 20 in.
Sights: None
Weight: 8 lb. 10 oz.
Caliber: .308 Win., 7mm-08 Rem., .243 Win.
Magazine: Detachable box
Features: Forged A4 receiver with forward assist and port door; stainless steel barrel; gas block sight Base; two-stage trigger; Hogue rubber grip; RRA aluminum free-float tube; A2 buttstock or operator stock
MSRP . . . . $1950.00–$2000.00

LAR-8 X-1
Action: Semiautomatic
Stock: Synthetic
Barrel: 18 in.
Sights: None
Weight: 9 lb. 8 oz.
Caliber: .308 Win., 7.62 NATO
Magazine: Detachable box, 20 rounds
Features: RRA Beast of Hunter muzzle brake; available in black or tan; available with A2 or CAR stocks
MSRP . . . . $1845.00–$1895.00

Rock River Arms

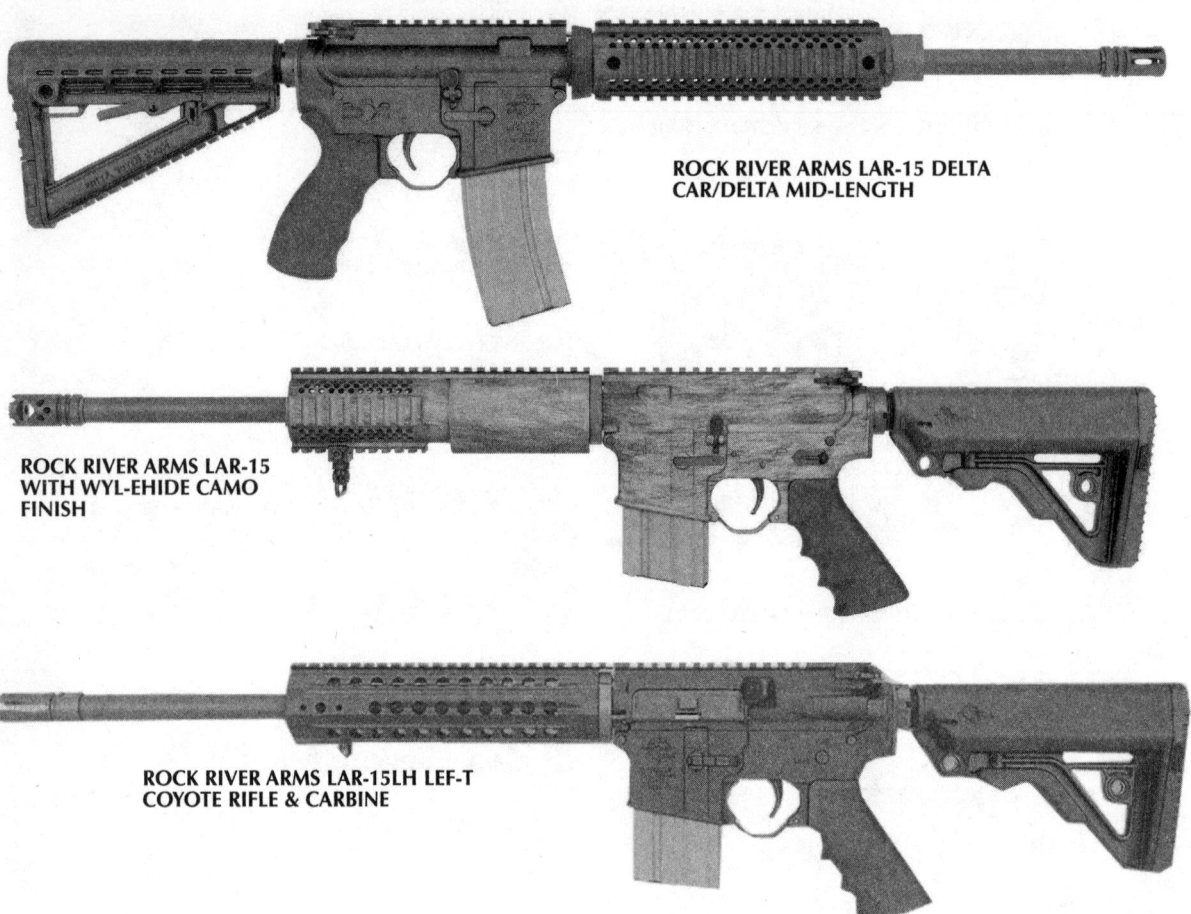

ROCK RIVER ARMS LAR-15 DELTA CAR/DELTA MID-LENGTH

ROCK RIVER ARMS LAR-15 WITH WYL-EHIDE CAMO FINISH

ROCK RIVER ARMS LAR-15LH LEF-T COYOTE RIFLE & CARBINE

LAR-15 DELTA CAR/DELTA MID-LENGTH

Action: Semiautomatic
Stock: Synthetic
Barrel: 16 in.
Sights: None
Weight: 7 lb.–7 lb. 4.8 oz.
Caliber: 5.56 NATO, .223 Rem.
Magazine: Detachable box, 30 rounds
Features: Delta Quad Rail two piece drop-in and gas system, available in CAR or Mid-length; low profile gas block; Ergo SureGrip; two stage trigger
MSRP . . . . $1085.00–$1100.00

LAR-15 WITH WYL-EHIDE CAMO FINISH

Action: Semiautomatic
Stock: Synthetic
Barrel: 16 in.
Sights: None
Weight: 7 lb. 10 oz.
Caliber: 5.56 NATO, .223 Rem.
Magazine: Detachable box, 20 rounds
Features: Camo anodized to the lower receiver, upper receiver, charging handle, trigger guard, and RRA half quad rail handguard; Hogue rubber pistol grip; low profile gas block; RRA operator CAR stock
MSRP $1550.00

LAR-15LH LEF-T COYOTE RIFLE & CARBINE

Action: Semiautomatic
Stock: Synthetic A2
Barrel: 16 in., 20 in.
Sights: None
Weight: 7 lb.-8 lb. 6.4 oz.
Caliber: 5.56 NATO, .223 Rem.
Magazine: Detachable box, 20 rounds
Features: Smith Vortex Flash Hider; Hogue free float tube; Hogue grip; two stage trigger
Carbine: $1445.00
Rifle: $1500.00

Rock River Arms

ROCK RIVER ARMS LAR-15 R3 COMPETITION RIFLE

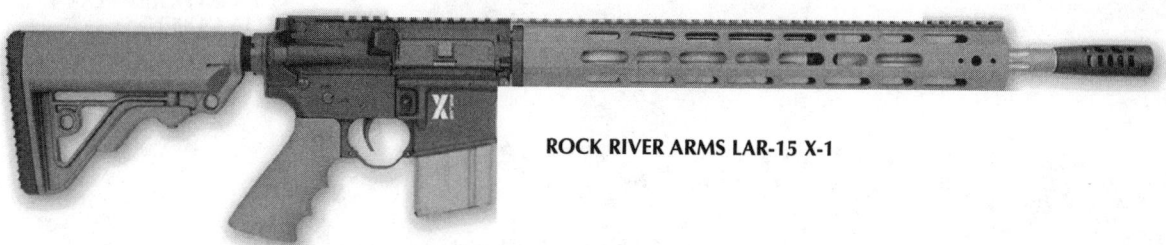

ROCK RIVER ARMS LAR-15 X-1

ROCK RIVER ARMS LAR-40 MID-LENGTH A4

LAR-15 R3 COMPETITION RIFLE
Action: Semiautomatic
Stock: Synthetic A2 or CAR
Barrel: 18 in.
Sights: None
Weight: 7 lb. 9.6 oz.
Caliber: 5.56 NATO, .223 Rem.
Magazine: Detachable box, 30 rounds
Features: RRA tuned and ported muzzle brake; low profile gas block; two stage trigger; Hogue Rubber grip
MSRP . . . . $1355.00–$1365.00

LAR-15 X-1
Action: Semiautomatic
Stock: Synthetic
Barrel: 18 in.
Sights: None
Weight: 7 lb. 13 oz.
Caliber: 5.56 NATO, .223 Rem.
Magazine: Detachable box, 30 rounds
Features: RRA Beast of Hunter muzzle brake; available in black or tan; available with A2 or CAR stocks
MSRP . . . . $1495.00–$1555.00

LAR-40 MID-LENGTH A4
Action: Semiautomatic
Stock: Synthetic
Barrel: 16 in.
Sights: None
Weight: 7 lb. 2 oz.
Caliber: .40 S&W
Magazine: Detachable clip
Features: Flash hider; single-stage trigger; RRA tactical CAR stock with Hogue grip
A4: $1260.00

Rock River Arms

**ROCK RIVER ARMS
LAR-47 CAR A4**

**ROCK RIVER ARMS LAR-47
DELTA CARBINE**

ROCK RIVER ARMS LAR-47 X-1

ROCK RIVER ARMS LAR-300 AAC X-1

LAR-47 CAR A4
Action: Semiautomatic
Stock: Synthetic
Barrel: 16 in.
Sights: None
Weight: 6 lb. 6 oz.
Caliber: 7.62x39 Warsaw
Magazine: Detachable box, 30 rounds, standard AK-47 mag
Features: RRA 6-postion tactical CAR stock; A2 pistol grip; CAR handguards; RRA two-stage trigger; A2 flash hider; ambidextrous mag release
MSRP $1270.00

LAR-47 DELTA CARBINE
Action: Semiautomatic
Stock: Synthetic
Barrel: 16 in.

Sights: None
Weight: 7 lb. 12 oz.
Caliber: 7.62x39 Warsaw
Magazine: Detachable box, 30 rounds, standard AK-47 mag
Features: RRA 6-position delta CAR stock; RRA delta pistol grip; RRA 2-piece quad rail; RRA delta muzzlebrake; RRA two-stage trigger; ambidextrous mag release
MSRP $1545.00

LAR-47 X-1
Action: Semiautomatic
Stock: Synthetic
Barrel: 18 in.
Sights: None
Weight: 8 lb. 3 oz.
Caliber: 7.62 Warsaw
Magazine: Detachable box

Features: Available in black or tan; RRA Operator A2 Stock; RRA Beast muzzle brake
MSRP . . . . $1600.00–$1660.00

LAR-300 AAC X-1
Action: Semiautomatic
Stock: Synthetic
Barrel: 18 in.
Sights: None
Weight: 7 lb. 14 oz.
Caliber: .300 BLK
Magazine: Detachable box
Features: Stainless steal cryo treated barrel; RRA two stage trigger; RRA beast muzzle break; A2 or CAR stock
MSRP . . . . $1585.00–$1645.00

ROCK RIVER ARMS LAR-458 CAR A4

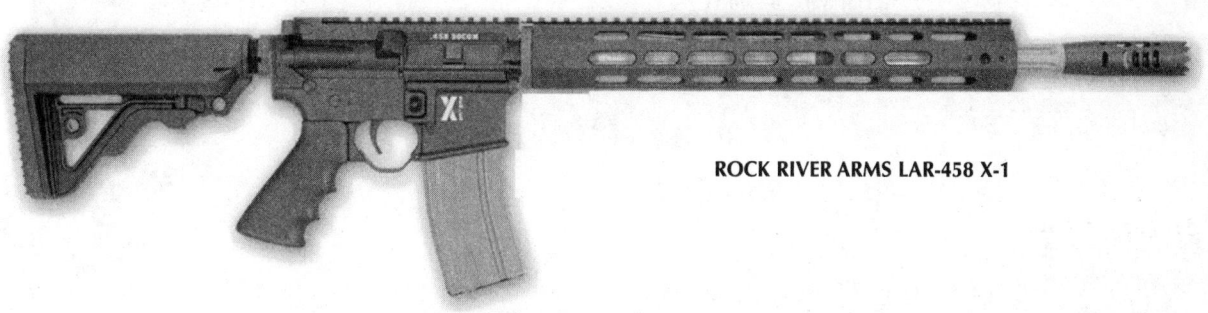

ROCK RIVER ARMS LAR-458 X-1

ROCK RIVER ARMS LAR-PDS CARBINE

LAR-458 CAR A4

Action: Semiautomatic
Stock: Synthetic
Barrel: 16 in.
Sights: None
Weight: 7 lb. 10 oz.
Caliber: .458 SOCOM
Magazine: Detachable box
Features: Forged A4 receiver; A2 flash hider; chromoly bull barrel; varmint gas block with sight rail; RRA two-stage trigger; RRA aluminum free-float tube; A2 pistol grip; A2 buttstock
MSRP $1230.00

LAR-458 X-1

Action: Semiautomatic
Stock: Synthetic
Barrel: 18 in.
Sights: None
Weight: 8 lb. 12 oz.
Caliber: .458 SOCOM
Magazine: Detachable box, 30 rounds
Features: RRA Beast of Hunter muzzle brake; available in black or tan; available with A2 or CAR stocks
MSRP . . . . $1595.00–$1655.00

LAR-PDS CARBINE

Action: Semiautomatic
Stock: Synthetic
Barrel: 16 in.
Sights: None
Weight: 7 lb. 6 oz.
Caliber: .223 Rem.
Magazine: Detachable box
Features: Ambidextrous non-reciprocating charging handle; A2 flash hider; RRA two-stage trigger; Hogue rubber grip; tri-rail handguard available
MSRP . . . . $1595.00–$1750.00

Rossi

ROSSI FULL SIZE CENTERFIRE MATCHED PAIR

ROSSI M92 .44-40 WIN.

ROSSI RIO GRANDE

ROSSI SINGLE SHOT RIFLE

FULL SIZE CENTERFIRE MATCHED PAIR

Action: Break Open, single-shot
Stock: Synthetic
Barrel: 23 in., 28 in.
Sights: Adjustable sights
Weight: 5 lb. 4 oz.–6 lb. 4 oz.
Caliber: 20-gauge paired with choice of .223 Rem., .243 Win., .44 Mag.
Magazine: None
Features: Quick-interchangeable rifle and shotgun barrels; single shot; recoil pad; sling swivels; black synthetic stock; steel barrel with matte blued finish; button rifled barrel
MSRP . . . . **$344.98–$352.00**

M92

Action: Lever
Stock: Wood
Barrel: 20 in., 24 in.
Sights: None
Weight: 5 lb.–7 lb.

Caliber: .38/.357 Mag., .44 Mag., .45 Colt,
.44-40 Win.
Magazine: Under-barrel tube, 10+1 or 12+1 rounds
Features: Octagonal barrel with a variety of metal finishes: blued, blued/case-hardened, blued/brass, and stainless; authentic curved buttplate with finish matched to receiver
MSRP . . . . **$627.38–$726.89**

RIO GRANDE

Action: Lever
Stock: Hardwood
Barrel: 20 in.
Sights: Open
Weight: 5 lb. 13 oz.–7 lb.
Caliber: .30-30 Win.
Magazine: Under-barrel tube, 6+1 rounds
Features: Blued or stainless steel barrel; authentic buckhorn sights; Taurus Safety System
MSRP **$673.33**

SINGLE SHOT RIFLE

Action: Break-open, single-shot
Stock: Synthetic
Barrel: 23 in.
Sights: Adjustable fiber optic front
Weight: 6 lb. 4 oz.–7 lb.
Caliber: .223 Rem., .243 Win.
Magazine: None
Features: Steel barrel in matte blued finish; equipped with scope rail and hammer extension that accommodates all popular optics; black synthetic stock with removable cheekpiece; soft recoil pad; white line spacer; button rifled barrels; sling swivels
MSRP **$306.82**

Ruger (Sturm, Ruger & Co.)

RUGER 10/22 CARBINE

RUGER 10/22 TAKEDOWN

RUGER 10/22 TARGET

10/22 CARBINE

Action: Semiautomatic
Stock: Synthetic or hardwood
Barrel: 18.5 in.
Sights: Gold bead front sight, adjustable rear
Weight: 5 lb.
Caliber: .22 LR
Magazine: Detachable rotary, 10 rounds
Features: Stock comes in black synthetic and hardwood; extended magazine release; push-button manual safety; combination scope base adapter; hammer-forged barrel; polymer trigger housing; aluminum receiver; contoured buttpad; barrel band; available LaserMax laser
MSRP . . . . **$309.00–$339.00**

10/22 TAKEDOWN

Action: Semiautomatic
Stock: Black synthetic
Barrel: 16.12 in.–18.5 in.
Sights: Gold bead front, adjustable rear
Weight: 4 lb. 9.6 oz.–5 lb. 5 oz.
Caliber: .22 LR
Magazine: Detachable rotary, 10 rounds
Features: Built of alloy steel with satin black finish; easy takedown and reassembly; detachable rotary magazine; extended magazine release; combination scope base adapter; push-button manual safety; available in three configurations: black synthetic stock with 18-in. stainless barrel; black synthetic stock with 16.6-in. barrel in blue; black synthetic Ruger modular stock with 16.12-in. satin black threaded, fluted target barrel
MSRP . . . . **$439.00–$629.00**

10/22 TARGET

Action: Semiautomatic
Stock: Laminate
Barrel: 20 in.
Sights: None
Weight: 7 lb. 8 oz.
Caliber: .22 LR
Magazine: Detachable rotary, 10 rounds
Features: Stock comes in black or brown laminate; extended magazine release; push-button manual safety; combination scope base adapter; hammer-forged barrel; polymer trigger housing; aluminum receiver; target trigger; flat buttplate
MSRP . . . . **$579.00–$629.00**

Ruger (Sturm, Ruger & Co.)

RUGER AMERICAN RIFLE

RUGER AMERICAN RIFLE RANCH

RUGER AR-556

RUGER AMERICAN RIMFIRE WITH WOOD STOCK

RUGER GUIDE GUN

AMERICAN RIFLE

Action: Bolt
Stock: Synthetic
Barrel: 22 in.
Sights: Drilled and tapped for scopes
Weight: 6 lb. 2 oz.–6 lb. 4 oz.
Caliber: .22-250 Rem., .223 Rem., 6.5 Creedmoor, 7mm-08 Rem., .243 Win., .270 Win., .30-06 Spfd., .308 Win.
Magazine: Detachable rotary, 4 rounds
Features: Ruger Marksman adjustable trigger; ergonomic, lightweight stock; soft rubber recoil pad; three-lug 70 degree bolt; Power Bedding positively locates the receiver and free-floats the barrel; hammer-forged barrel; tang safety; round rotary magazine
MSRP $489.00

AMERICAN RIFLE RANCH

Action: Bolt
Stock: Synthetic
Barrel: 16.1 in.
Sights: None
Weight: 6 lb.–6 lb. 8 oz.
Caliber: .223/5.56 NATO, .300 BLK, .450 Bushmaster

Magazine: Detachable rotary, 3–5 rounds
Features: Ruger Marksman Adjustable trigger offers a pull weight that is adjustable between 3 and 5 pounds; ergonomic, lightweight flat dark earth composite stock with modern forend contouring and grip serrations and swivel studs; soft rubber recoil pad; Power Bedding positively locates the receiver and free-floats the barrel for outstanding accuracy; threaded barrel is cold hammer-forged; tang safety; rotary magazine; factory installed one-piece aluminum scope rail
MSRP . . . . $529.00–$599.00

AMERICAN RIMFIRE WITH WOOD STOCK

Action: Bolt
Stock: Wood
Barrel: 22 in.
Sights: Fiber optic front, adjustable rear
Weight: 6 lb. 2 oz.
Caliber: .22 LR
Magazine: 10 rounds

Features: Extended magazine release; patent-pending Power Bedding integral bedding block system; Ruger Marksman Adjustable trigger offers a crisp release with a pull weight that is user adjustable between 3 and 5 lb.; wood stock with checkering on the grip and forend and a rubber buttpad for a comfortable length of pull; cold hammer-forged barrel
MSRP $459.00

AR-556

Action: Semiautomatic
Stock: Synthetic
Barrel: 16.1 in.
Sights: Adjustable
Weight: 6 lb. 8 oz.
Caliber: .223 Rem./5.56 NATO
Magazine: Detachable box, 30 rounds
Features: The milled gas block is located at a carbine length (M4) position; multiple attachment points include a QD socket and bayonet lug; front sight post is elevation adjustable, and a front sight tool is included; A-2 Style F-Height allows co-witness with many optics; Ruger Rapid Deploy folding rear sight provides windage adjustability; six-position telescoping M4-style buttstock and Mil-Spec buffer tube; barrel is cold hammer-forged; Ruger flash suppressor; matte black oxide finish on the exterior of the bolt carrier
MSRP $799.00

GUIDE GUN WITH MUZZLE BRAKE SYSTEM

Action: Bolt
Stock: Green Mountain laminate
Barrel: 20 in.
Sights: Bead front, adjustable rear
Weight: 8 lb.-8 lb. 2 oz.
Caliber: .300 RCM, .300 Win. Mag., .30-06 Spfd., .338 RCM, .338 Win. Mag., .375 Ruger, .416 Ruger
Magazine: 3 rounds (4 rounds in .30-06 Spfd.)
Features: LC6 Trigger; Mauser-type extractor; muzzle brake system; three-position safety; manner-forged barrel; integral scope mounts; stainless steel bolt; swivel studs;
MSRP $1269.00

Ruger (Sturm, Ruger & Co.)

RUGER GUNSITE SCOUT RIFLE

RUGER HAWKEYE PREDATOR

RUGER M77 HAWKEYE

RUGER MINI-14 RANCH RIFLE

RUGER MINI-14 TACTICAL

RIFLES

GUNSITE SCOUT RIFLE

Action: Bolt
Stock: Laminate
Barrel: 16.50 in.
Sights: Post front sight, adjustable rear
Weight: 7 lb.
Caliber: .308 Win., 5.56 NATO, .450 Bushmaster
Magazine: Detachable box, 10 rounds
Features: Flash suppressor, Picatinny rail; recoil pad; accurate sighting system; integral scope mounts; Mauser-type extractor; developed with Gunsite and features their logo
MSRP . . . . $1139.00–$1199.00

HAWKEYE PREDATOR

Action: Bolt
Stock: Laminate
Barrel: 22 in., 24 in.
Sights: None
Weight: 7 lb. 11 oz.–8 lb. 2 oz.
Caliber: .22-250 Rem., .223 Rem., .204 Ruger, .308 Win., 6.5 Creedmor
Magazine: 4 rounds
Features: Non-rotating, Mauser-type controlled round feed extractor; hinged solid-steel floorplate; cold hammer-forged barrel; patented integral scope mounts
MSRP . . . . $1139.00–$1159.00

HAWKEYE STANDARD

Action: Bolt
Stock: Walnut
Barrel: 22 in., 24 in.
Sights: None
Weight: 7 lb.–8 lb. 3 oz.
Caliber: .204 Ruger, .223 Rem., .243 Win., .270 Win., 7mm Rem. Mag., 7mm-08 Rem., .30-06 Spfd., .300 Win. Mag., .308 Win.
Magazine: 3–5 rounds
Features: American walnut stock; alloy steel, satin blued barrel; LC6 trigger; positive floor plate latch; integral scope mounts; three-position safety
MSRP $979.00

MINI-14 RANCH RIFLE

Action: Semiautomatic
Stock: Hardwood, synthetic
Barrel: 18.5 in.
Sights: Blade front sight, adjustable rear
Weight: 6 lb. 12 oz.–7 lb.
Caliber: 5.56 NATO, .223 Rem.
Magazine: 5 rounds, or detachable box, 20 rounds
Features: Stock comes in hardwood

or black synthetic; Garand style action; hammer-forged barrel; sighting system; integral scope mounts; flat buttpad; integral sling swivels on hardwood or black synthetic stocks
MSRP . . . . $999.00–$1139.00

MINI-14 TACTICAL

Action: Semiautomatic
Stock: Synthetic
Barrel: 16.1 in.
Sights: Adjustable
Weight: 6 lb. 12 oz.–7 lb. 4 oz.
Caliber: 5.56 NATO, .223 Rem., .300 BLK
Magazine: Detachable box, 5, 20 rounds
Features: Black synthetic stock; blued barrel with a flash suppressor; adjustable ghost ring rear sight, non-glare protected-post front sight
MSRP . . . . $1089.00–$1169.00

Ruger (Sturm, Ruger & Co.)

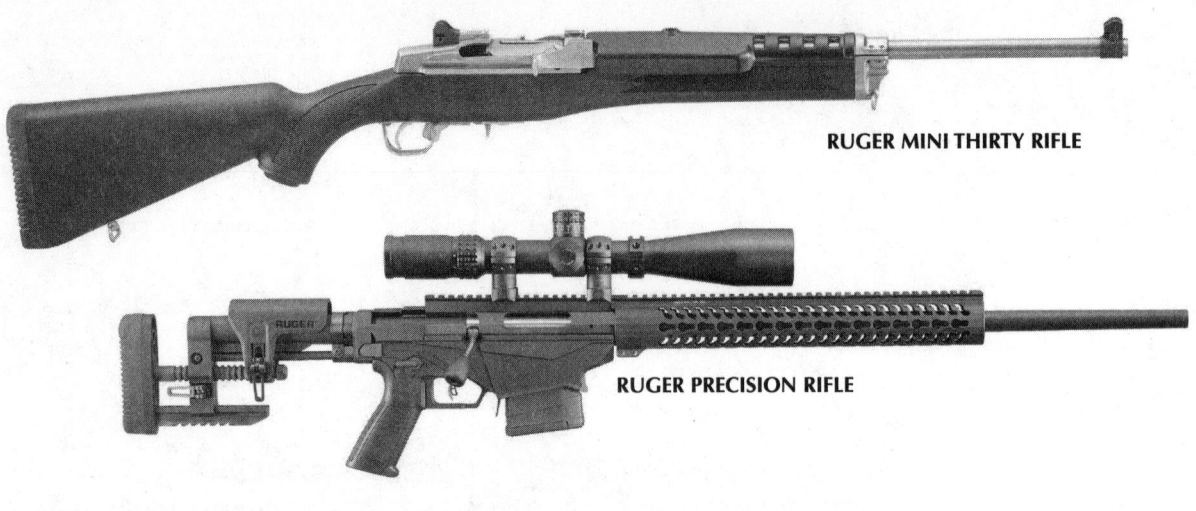

RUGER MINI THIRTY RIFLE

RUGER PRECISION RIFLE

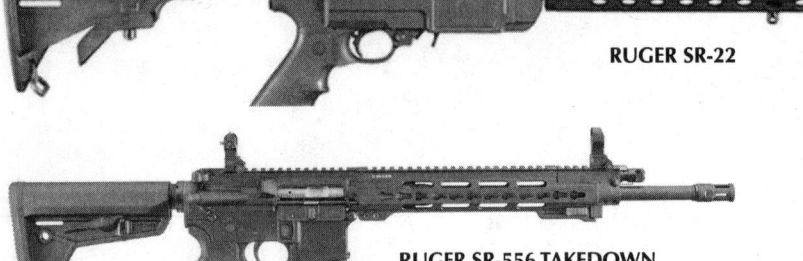

RUGER SR-22

RUGER SR-556 TAKEDOWN

MINI THIRTY RIFLE

Action: Semiautomatic
Stock: Synthetic
Barrel: 16.12 in., 18.5 in.
Sights: Blade front sight, adjustable rear
Weight: 6 lb. 11 oz.
Caliber: 7.62x39 Warsaw
Magazine: 5 rounds, or detachable box, 20 rounds
Features: Garand style action, hammer-forged barrel; sighting system; integral scope mounts; black synthetic stock; sling swivels; stainless steel or alloy steel barrel in matte or blued finish as well as a newer version in stainless steel with a 16.12-in. barrel
MSRP . . . . **$1069.00–$1169.00**

PRECISION RIFLE

Action: Bolt
Stock: Synthetic
Barrel: 20 in., 24 in.
Sights: None
Weight: 9 lb. 12 oz.–10 lb. 12 oz.

Caliber: .308 Win., 6.5 Creedmoor, 6mm Creedmoor
Magazine: 10 rounds
Features: Cold hammer-forged chrome-moly steel barrel with 5R rifling at minimum bore and groove dimensions, minimum, headspace and centralized chamber; Samson Evolution KeyMod™ handguard; 20 MOA Picatinny rail; in-line recoil path manages recoil directly from the rear of the receiver to the buttstock; patent-pending multi-magazine interface functions interchangeably with M110, SR25, DPMS, and Magpul-style magazines and AICS magazines (works with some M14 magazines); Ruger Marksman Adjustable trigger
MSRP **$1599.00**

SR-22

Action: Semiautomatic
Stock: Synthetic
Barrel: 16.12 in.
Sights: None

Weight: 6 lb. 8 oz.–6 lb. 14 oz.
Caliber: .22 LR
Magazine: Detachable rotary, 10 rounds
Features: Black laminate stock in standard or collapsible; AR-style ergonomic Hogue Monogrip and six-position telescoping buttstock; hammer-forged barrel; round handguard; barrel support block
MSRP **$709.00**

SR-556 TAKEDOWN

Action: Semiautomatic
Stock: Synthetic
Barrel: 16.12 in.
Sights: Folding iron
Weight: 7 lb. 2 oz.
Caliber: .223 Rem., 5.56 NATO
Magazine: 30 rounds
Features: Patented chrome-plated, two-stage piston with multi-stage regulator; two-stage trigger that offers a smooth, crisp, 4.5 lb. trigger pull; full-strength hammer spring for consistent primer ignition and a lightweight hammer; front sight is both elevation- and windage-adjustable; lower receiver fitted with the Magpul MOE grip and MOE SL collapsible buttstock on the mil-spec buffer tube; flash suppressor; slim, lightweight KeyMod handguard for reduced overall weight
MSRP **$2199.00**

Sako

SAKO 85 BAVARIAN

SAKO 85 BAVARIAN LEFT-HANDED

SAKO 85 BLACK BEAR

SAKO 85 BROWN BEAR

85 BAVARIAN

Action: Bolt
Stock: Walnut
Barrel: 22 in., 24 in.
Sights: None
Weight: 7 lb.–7 lb. 8 oz.
Caliber: .308 Win., .270 Win., .30-06 Spfd., .300 Win. Mag., .270 WSM, .300 WSM, 6.5x55 Swedish, 7mm-08 Rem., 7mm Rem. Mag.
Magazine: 4, 5 rounds
Features: High grade walnut stock in traditional European style; single-set trigger
MSRP $2225.00

85 BAVARIAN LEFT-HANDED

Action: Bolt
Stock: Wood
Barrel: 20–22.4 in.
Sights: Fixed
Weight: 7 lb.–7 lb. 4 oz.
Caliber: .25-06 Rem., .30-06 Spfd., .270 Win., 6.5x55 Swedish, 7x64 Brenneke, 8x57IS, 9.3x62 Mauser
Magazine: Detachable box, 5+1 rounds

Features: Oil finished walnut stock with Schnabel-type forend and pistol grip endplate in rosewood
MSRP $2275.00

85 BLACK BEAR

Action: Bolt
Stock: Black composite
Barrel: 21.25 in.
Sights: Adjustable Express "V" rear, white bead front and integral dovetail for scope mounts
Weight: 6 lb. 13 oz.–7 lb.
Caliber: .308 Win., .338 Fed., .30-06 Spfd., 8x57IS, 9.3x62 Mauser, 9.3x66 Sako
Magazine: Detachable box, 5 rounds
Features: Purpose built weapon for bear and wild boar hunters; adjustable single-stage trigger; adjustable shallow "V" Express style rear sight with white bead front sight for fast target acquisition and a barrel band for front swivel; patented Total Control Magazine Latch (TCL) prevents accidental release of the stain-

less steel magazine under the heaviest recoil or harshest hunting conditions
MSRP $1850.00

85 BROWN BEAR

Action: Bolt
Stock: Brown laminate
Barrel: 21.25 in.
Sights: Adjustable open rear, blade style front and integral dovetail for scope mounts
Weight: 7 lb. 15 oz.
Caliber: .338 Win. Mag., .375 H&H Mag.
Magazine: Detachable box, 4 rounds
Features: Open adjustable rear sight and blade style front sight; short free-floated bull barrel has a band type front swivel; forged one-piece bolt with three locking lugs offers fast, smooth cycling with controlled round feed and mechanical case ejection; patented Total Control Magazine Latch (TCL) prevents accidental release of the stainless steel magazine
MSRP $2500.00

Sako

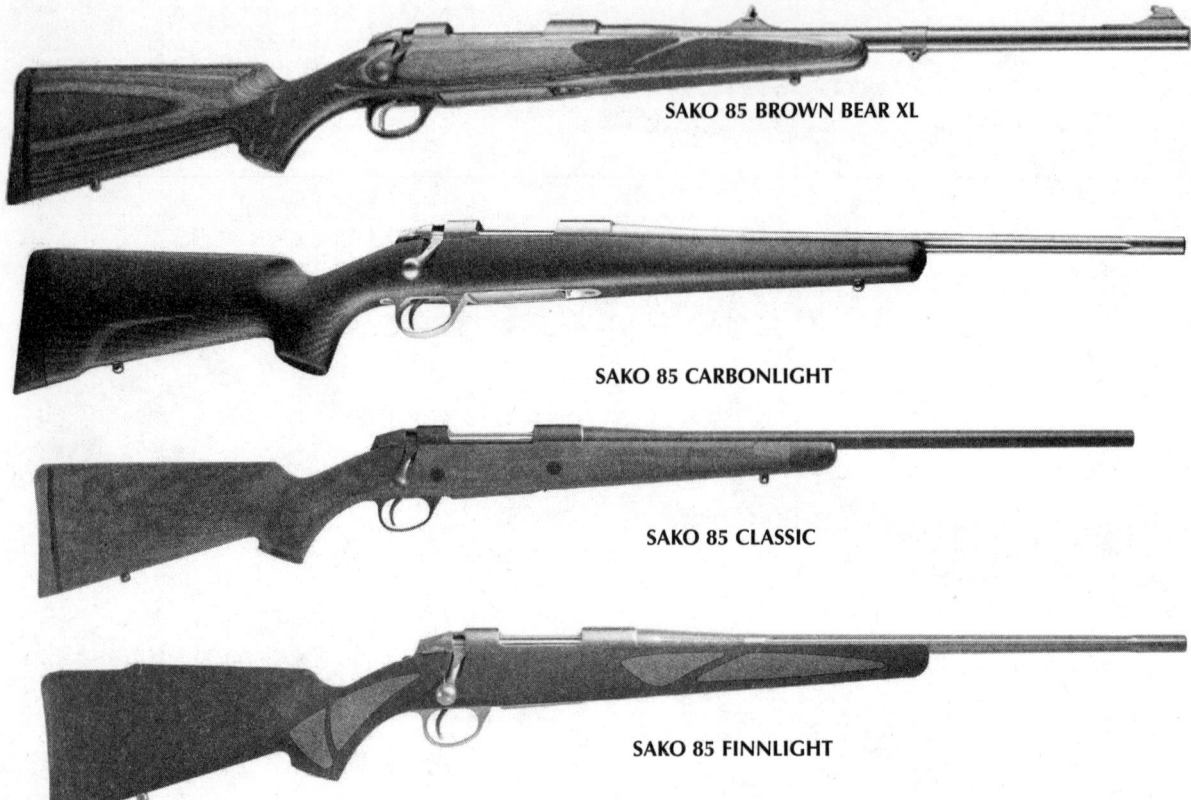

SAKO 85 BROWN BEAR XL

SAKO 85 CARBONLIGHT

SAKO 85 CLASSIC

SAKO 85 FINNLIGHT

85 BROWN BEAR XL

Action: Bolt
Stock: Wood
Barrel: 22 in.
Sights: Adjustable
Weight: 9 lb. 8 oz.
Caliber: .416 Ridgby, .450 Ridgby, .500 Jeffery
Magazine: Detachable box, 4+1 rounds
Features: Brown laminated hardwood, straight classic stock, black action and 540mm semi heavy barrel; purpose built weapons for bear and bruise hunters; adjustable special fast target acquisition iron sights; detachable staggered two-row steel magazine; can be top-loaded; integral Dovetail rails for secure scope mounting
MSRP $2295.00

85 CARBONLIGHT

Action:Bolt
Stock: Carbon fiber
Barrel: 20 in.
Sights: None
Weight: 5 lb. 5 oz.
Caliber: .22-250 Rem., .243 Win., .260 Rem., 7mm-08 Rem., .308 Win.
Magazine: Detachable box, 5 rounds
Features: Fluted barrel; stainless steel action; stainless steel barrel; single stage trigger; single set trigger available
MSRP $3175.00

85 CLASSIC

Action: Bolt
Stock: Walnut
Barrel: 22.4 in., 24.4 in.
Sights: Open
Weight: 7 lb.–7 lb. 12 oz.
Caliber: (Short): .243 Win., .260 Rem., 7mm-08 Rem., .308 Win., .338 Federal; (SM) .270 Win. S Mag., .300 Win. S Mag.; (Medium) .25-06 Rem., 6.5x55 Swedish, .270 Win., .30-06 Spfd., 9.3x66 Sako; (Long): 7mm Rem. Mag., .300 Win. Mag., .338 Win. Mag., .375 H&H Mag.
Magazine: Detachable box, S/M 6 rounds, SM/L 5 rounds
Features: Comes in short actions Extra Short (XS), Short (S) and Short Magnum (SM), medium action (M), and long action (L); straight, classic walnut stock with rosewood forend tip and pistol grip cap; integral rails for scope mounts; free-floating barrel is cold-hammer-forged; adjustable single-stage trigger
MSRP $2325.00

85 FINNLIGHT

Action: Bolt
Stock: Synthetic
Barrel: 20.25 in., 22.4 in.
Sights: None
Weight: 6 lb. 3 oz.–6 lb. 13 oz.
Caliber: (Short): .22-250 Rem., .243 Win., .260 Rem., .7mm-08 Rem., .308 Win.; (SM) .270 Win. Short Mag., .300 Win. Short Mag.; (Medium): .25-06 Rem., 6.5x55 Swedish, .270 Win., .30-06 Spfd.; (Long) 7mm Rem. Mag., .300 Win. Mag.
Magazine: Detachable box, S/M 6 rounds, SM/L 5 rounds
Features: Comes in short actions Short (S) and Short magnum (SM), Medium action (M), and Long action (L); single-stage trigger; two-way Sako safety locks both trigger and bolt handle; black synthetic stock with soft gray grip areas; pistol grip stock; integral rails for scope mounts; free-floating barrel is cold-hammer-forged of stainless steel
MSRP $1800.00

SAKO 85 HUNTER LEFT-HANDED

SAKO 85 KODIAK

SAKO 85 LONG RANGE

SAKO 85 SAFARI

SAKO 85 SYNTHETIC BLACK

85 HUNTER LEFT-HANDED

Action: Bolt
Stock: Wood
Barrel: 24.4 in.
Sights: None
Weight: 7 lb. 12 oz.
Caliber: .300 Win. Mag., .338 Win. Mag., .375 H&H Mag., 7mm Rem. Mag.
Magazine: Detachable box, 4+1 rounds
Features: High-grade walnut stock and satin-like blued finish on the barrel and receiver
MSRP **$2125.00**

85 KODIAK

Action: Bolt
Stock: Laminated hardwood
Barrel: 12.25 in.
Sights: Open
Weight: 7 lb. 15 oz.
Caliber: .338 Win. Mag., .375 H&H Mag.

Magazine: Detachable box, 5 rounds
Features: Adjustable single-stage trigger; barrel band for front swivel; integral dovetail rails for secure scope mounting; straight stock made of gray matte-lacquered laminated hardwood and reinforced with two cross-bolts; free-floating "bull" barrel
MSRP **$1950.00**

85 LONG RANGE

Action: Bolt
Stock: Wood
Barrel: 26 in.
Sights: None
Weight: 9 lb. 12 oz.
Caliber: .300 Win. Mag., .338 Lapua Mag.
Magazine: Detachable box, 4+1 rounds
Features: Flush design muzzle brake; designed for long range hunting
MSRP **$2865.00**

85 SAFARI

Action: Bolt
Stock: Walnut
Barrel: 24.2 in.

Sights: Front bead, adjustable iron sights rear
Weight: 9 lb.
Caliber: .375 H&H Mag.
Magazine: Detachable box, 6 rounds
Features: Free-floating barrel; ergonomic walnut stock with checkering; staggered, two-row magazine with total control latch; single-set adjustable trigger; steel trigger guard; two-way Sako safety locks both trigger and bolt handle; Pachmayr recoil pad; limited models imported to U.S.
MSRP . . . . **$10000.00–$10500.00**

85 SYNTHETIC BLACK

Action: Bolt
Stock: Synthetic
Barrel: 22.4 in.
Sights: None
Weight: 6 lb.–6 lb. 6 oz.
Caliber: .270 Win., .308 Win., 6.5x55 Swedish, 7x64 Brenneke
Magazine: Detachable box, 5+1 rounds
Features: Matte black, fluted barrel
MSRP **$1750.00**

Sako

SAKO 85 VARMINT LAMINATED ST

SAKO A7 ROUGHTECH PRO

SAKO A7 ROUGHTECH RANGE

SAKO FINNFIRE II

SAKO TRG 22

SAKO TRG M10

85 VARMINT LAMINATED STAINLESS

Action: Bolt
Stock: Laminated hardwood
Barrel: 20 in., 23.6 in.
Sights: None
Weight: 8 lb. 10 oz.–9 lb.
Caliber: (XS) .204 Ruger, .222 Rem., .223 Rem.; (Short) .22-250 Rem., .243 Win., .260 Rem., 7mm-08 Rem., .308 Win., .338 Federal
Magazine: Detachable box, XS 7 rounds, S 6 rounds
Features: Comes in short actions Extra Short (XS) and Short (S); single-set trigger; two-way Sako safety locks both trigger and bolt handle; straight stock with wide forend is made of brown matte laquered laminated hardwood; integral rail for scope mounts
MSRP **$2025.00**

A7 ROUGHTECH PRO

Action: Bolt
Stock: Synthetic
Barrel: 24.4 in.
Sights: None
Weight: 6 lb. 13 oz.
Caliber: .30-06 Spfd., .243 Win., .270 Win., .300 Win. Mag., .300 WSM, .308 Win., 7mm Rem. Mag.
Magazine: Detachable box
Features: Stocks are coated with rough surface texture to offer a solid grip in all weather conditions, have a full integrated aluminum bedding; stocks are equipped with advanced high energy dissipation recoil pad and come with two 5mm spacers for length of pull adjustment; mounting rail
MSRP **$1200.00**

A7 ROUGHTECH RANGE

Action: Bolt
Stock: Synthetic
Barrel: 26 in.
Sights: None
Weight: 8 lb.
Caliber: .25-06 Rem., .300 Win. Mag., .300 WSM, .308 Win., 7mm Rem. Mag.
Magazine: Detachable box
Features: Stocks are coated with rough surface texture to offer a solid grip in all weather conditions, have a full integrated aluminum bedding; stocks are equipped with advanced high energy dissipation recoil pad and come with two 5mm spacers for length of pull adjustment; mounting rail
MSRP **$1425.00**

FINNFIRE II

Action: Bolt
Stock: Wood
Barrel: 22 in.
Sights: None
Weight: 6 lb. 3 oz.
Caliber: .17 HMR, .22 LR
Magazine: Detachable box, 5+1 rounds
Features: Oiled stock; single stage trigger; muzzle thread
MSRP **$1095.00**

TRG 22

Action: Bolt
Stock: Synthetic
Barrel: 20 in., 26 in., 27.1 in.
Sights: None
Weight: 10 lb. 4 oz.–10 lb. 12 oz.
Caliber: .308 Win, .300 Win. Mag., .338 Lapua Mag.
Magazine: Detachable box, 5, 7, 10 rounds
Features: Double-stage trigger; two-way Sako safety locks both trigger and bolt handle; base of stock is made of polyurethane with aluminum skeleton; adjustable cheekpiece and buttplate; Ambidextrous stock in green or desert tan color; includes integral dovetail on receiver and is drilled and tapped for Picatinny rail mounting
MSRP . . . . **$3500.00–$7100.00**

TRG M10

Action: Bolt
Stock: Synthetic
Barrel: 20–27 in.
Sights: None
Weight: 13 lb. 4 oz.–14 lb. 5 oz.
Caliber: .308 Win., .338 Lapua Mag.
Magazine: Detachable box, 8 or 11 rounds
Features: Threaded muzzle; muzzle break available; phosphatized steel parts; stainless steel barrel; double stage trigger; Picatinny or Weaver rail; fully adjustable rear stock; ambidextrous controls
MSRP **$10500.00**

Savage Arms

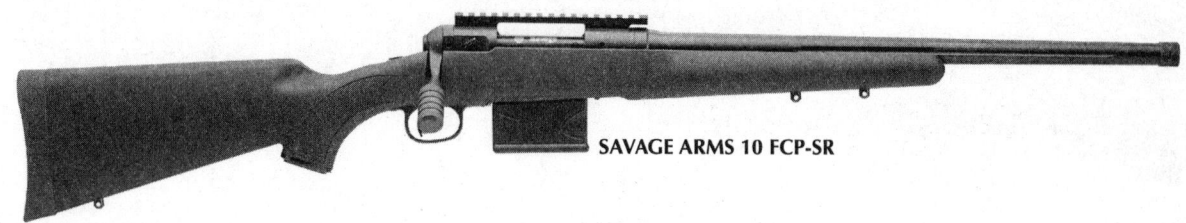

SAVAGE ARMS 10 FCP-SR

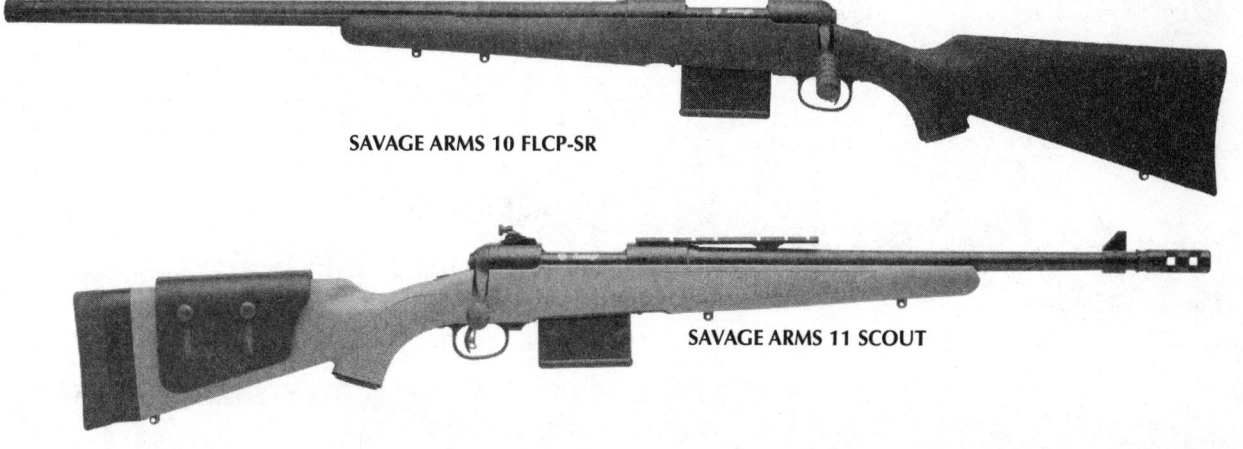

SAVAGE ARMS 10 FLCP-SR

SAVAGE ARMS 11 SCOUT

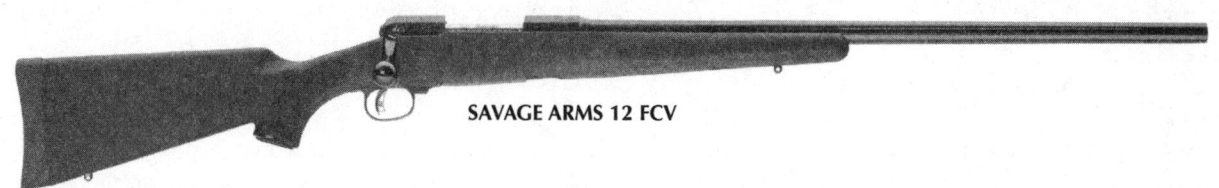

SAVAGE ARMS 12 FCV

10 FCP-SR
Action: Bolt
Stock: Synthetic
Barrel: 20 in.
Sights: None
Weight: 8 lb. 12 oz.
Caliber: .308 Win.
Magazine: Detachable box
Features: Carbon steel barrel; matte barrel finish
MSRP $785.00

10 FLCP-SR
Action: Bolt
Stock: Synthetic
Barrel: 24 in.
Sights: None
Weight: 9 lb.
Caliber: .308 Win.

Magazine: Detachable box
Features: Carbon steel barrel; matte barrel finish
MSRP $785.00

11 SCOUT
Action: Bolt
Stock: Synthetic
Barrel: 18 in.
Sights: Front fixed
Weight: 7 lb. 13 oz.
Caliber: .308 Win.
Magazine: Detachable box
Features: Carbon steel barrel; matte barrel finish
MSRP $818.00

12 FCV
Action: Bolt
Stock: Synthetic
Barrel: 26 in.
Sights: None
Weight: 9 lb.
Caliber: .204 Ruger, .22-250, .223 Rem.
Magazine: Detachable box
Features: Carbon steel barrel; matte barrel finish
MSRP $781.00

Savage Arms

SAVAGE ARMS 12 VARMINT SERIES BTCSS

SAVAGE ARMS 14/114 AMERICAN CLASSIC

SAVAGE ARMS 16/116 LIGHTWEIGHT HUNTER

SAVAGE ARMS 25 LIGHTWEIGHT VARMINTER

12 VARMINT SERIES BTCSS

Action: Bolt
Stock: Laminate
Barrel: 26 in.
Sights: None
Weight: 10 lb.
Caliber: .204 Ruger, .223 Rem., .22-250 Rem.
Magazine: Detachable box, 4 rounds
Features: Drilled and tapped for scope mounts; stainless steel barrel with high luster finish; AccuTrigger; wood laminate with thumbhole and satin finish
MSRP $1293.00

14/114 AMERICAN CLASSIC

Action: Bolt
Stock: Wood
Barrel: 22 in., 24 in.
Sights: None
Weight: 7 lb. 4 oz.–7 lb. 12 oz.
Caliber: .243 Win., .270 Win., .30-06 Spfd., .300 Win. Mag., .308 Win., 7mm Rem. Mag., 7mm-08 Rem.
Magazine: Hinged floor plate, 2, 4 rounds
Features: Drilled and tapped for scope mounts; carbon steel barrel with matte blued finish; short action; AccuTrigger; satin finish wood stock
MSRP $979.00

16/116 LIGHTWEIGHT HUNTER

Action: Bolt
Stock: Synthetic
Barrel: 20 in.
Sights: None
Weight: 5 lb. 10 oz.
Caliber: .223 Rem., .243 Win., .270 Win., .308 Win., 6.5 Creedmoor, 7mm-08 Rem.
Magazine: Detachable box, 4 rounds
Features: Compact, flyweight design; matte black finish; stainless steel barrel
MSRP $752.00

25 LIGHTWEIGHT VARMINTER

Action: Bolt
Stock: Wood laminate
Barrel: 24 in.
Sights: None
Weight: 8 lb. 4 oz.
Caliber: .17 Hornet, .204 Ruger, .22 Hornet, .223 Rem.
Magazine: Detachable box, 4 rounds
Features: Drilled and tapped for scope mounts; carbon steel barrel with blued satin finish; wood laminate stock with satin finish
MSRP $772.00

Savage Arms

SAVAGE ARMS 25 WALKING VARMINTER

SAVAGE ARMS 93 FV-SR LANDRY

SAVAGE ARMS 112 MAGNUM TARGET

SAVAGE ARMS A17

SAVAGE ARMS A17 TARGET SPORTER LAMINATE

25 WALKING VARMINTER
Action: Bolt
Stock: Synthetic
Barrel: 22 in.
Sights: None
Weight: 6 lb. 14 oz.
Caliber: .17 Hornet, .204 Ruger, .22 Hornet, .222 Rem., .223 Rem.
Magazine: Detachable box, 4 rounds
Features: Matte black synthetic stock; matte black carbon steel barrel; AccuTrigger
MSRP $620.00

93 FV-SR LANDRY
Action: Bolt
Stock: Synthetic
Barrel: 16.5 in.
Sights: None
Weight: 5 lb. 8 oz.
Caliber: .22 WMR
Magazine: Detachable box
Features: Carbon steel barrel; matte barrel finish
MSRP $432.00

112 MAGNUM TARGET
Action: Bolt
Stock: Wood laminate
Barrel: 26 in.
Sights: None
Weight: 12 lb.
Caliber: .338 Lapua Mag.
Magazine: Single shot
Features: Carbon steel barrel; matte barrel finish
MSRP $1177.00

A17
Action: Semiautomatic
Stock: Synthetic
Barrel: 22 in.
Sights: Drilled and tapped for scope mounts
Weight: 5 lb. 7 oz.
Caliber: .17 HMR
Magazine: Detachable rotary
Features: Carbon steel barrel; high luster barrel finish; Delayed Blowback Action, Hard Chromed Bolt with Dual Controlled Round Feed, Case Hardened Receiver, Button-Rifled Barrel
MSRP $473.00

A17 TARGET SPORTER LAMINATE
Action: Semiautomatic
Stock: Wood laminate
Barrel: 22 in.
Sights: None
Weight: N/A
Caliber: .17 HMR
Magazine: Detachable rotary, 10 rounds
Features: Delayed blowback action; hard chromed bolt with dual controlled round feed; case hardened receiver; button-rifled barrel
MSRP $571.00

Savage Arms

SAVAGE ARMS A17 TARGET THUMBHOLE

SAVAGE ARMS A17 XP

SAVAGE ARMS A22 MAGNUM

SAVAGE ARMS AXIS

SAVAGE ARMS AXIS XP CAMO COMPACT

A17 TARGET THUMBHOLE

Action: Semiautomatic
Stock: Wood laminate
Barrel: 22 in.
Sights: None
Weight: N/A
Caliber: .17 HMR
Magazine: Detachable rotary, 10 rounds
Features: Grey laminate thumbhole stock; delayed blowback action; hard chromed bolt with dual controlled round feed; case hardened receiver; button-rifled barrel
MSRP $631.00

A17 XP

Action: Semiautomatic
Stock: Synthetic
Barrel: 22 in.
Sights: 3.5–10x36mm Bushnell Rimfire Optics A17 scope
Weight: N/A
Caliber: .17 HMR
Magazine: Detachable rotary, 10 rounds
Features: Delayed blowback action;

hard chromed bolt with dual controlled round feed; case hardened receiver; button-rifled barrel
MSRP $578.00

A22 MAGNUM

Action: Semiautomatic
Stock: Synthetic
Barrel: 21 in.
Sights: None
Weight: 5 lb. 9 oz.
Caliber: .22 WMR
Magazine: Detachable rotary, 10 rounds
Features: Delayed blowback action; hard chromed bolt with dual controlled round feed; case hardened receiver; button-rifled barrel
MSRP $473.00

AXIS

Action: Bolt
Stock: Synthetic
Barrel: 22 in.
Sights: None
Weight: 6 lb. 8 oz.
Caliber: .22-250 Rem., .223 Rem.,

.243 Win., .25-06 Rem., .270 Win., .30–06 Spfd., .308 Win., 6.5 Creedmoor, 7mm-08 Rem.
Magazine: Detachable box, 4 rounds
Features: New modern design, smooth bolt operation; drilled and tapped for scope mounts; carbon steel barrel with black matte finish; synthetic stock with matte black finish
MSRP $368.00

AXIS XP CAMO COMPACT

Action: Bolt
Stock: Synthetic
Barrel: 20 in.
Sights: Scope included
Weight: 6 lb. 13 oz.
Caliber: .223 Rem., .243 Win., 7mm-08 Rem.
Magazine: Detachable box, 4 rounds
Features: Made with cooperation from the Youth Shooting Sports Alliance; carbon steel barrel with matte black finish; availble in black, Mossy Oak Break-Up camo, and Muddy Girl camo
MSRP $485.00

Savage Arms

SAVAGE ARMS B.MAG

SAVAGE ARMS B.MAG TARGET

SAVAGE ARMS HUNTER SERIES 11/111 BTH

SAVAGE ARMS LANDRY RASCAL

SAVAGE ARMS MAGNUM SERIES 93 BRJ

RIFLES

B.MAG

Action: Bolt
Stock: Synthetic
Barrel: 22 in.
Sights: None
Weight: 5 lb.
Caliber: .17 WSM
Magazine: Detachable box, 8 rounds
Features: Drilled and tapped for scope mounts; AccuTrigger; stainless steel barrel with matte finish
MSRP **$379.00**

B.MAG TARGET

Action: Bolt
Stock: Synthetic
Barrel: 22 in.
Sights: None
Weight: N/A
Caliber: .17 WSM
Magazine: Detachable rotary, 8 rounds
Features: Stainless steel barrel; matte barrel finish
MSRP **$578.00**

HUNTER SERIES 11/111 BTH

Action: Bolt
Stock: Wood laminate
Barrel: 22 in.
Sights: None
Weight: 6 lb. 12 oz.–7 lb.
Caliber: .22-250 Rem., .243 Win., .223 Rem., .25-06 Rem., .270 Win., .30-06 Spfd., .308 Win.
Magazine: Hinged floor plate, 4 rounds
Features: Drilled and tapped for scope mounts; carbon steel barrel with blued satin finish; AccuTrigger; wood laminate stock with thumbhole in satin finish
MSRP **$982.00**

LANDRY RASCAL

Action: Bolt
Stock: Synthetic
Barrel: 16 in.
Sights: Adjustable peep
Weight: 2 lb. 11 oz.
Caliber: .22 LR
Magazine: Single shot
Features: Carbon steel barrel; satin barrel finish
MSRP **$233.00**

MAGNUM SERIES 93 BRJ

Action: Bolt
Stock: Wood laminate
Barrel: 21 in.
Sights: None
Weight: 7 lb.
Caliber: .22 WMR
Magazine: Detachable box, 5 rounds
Features: Carbon steel barrel in blued satin finish; wood laminate stock; AccuTrigger
MSRP **$542.00**

Savage Arms

SAVAGE ARMS MARK II SERIES BTV

SAVAGE ARMS MARK II SERIES FV-SR LANDRY

SAVAGE ARMS MODEL 42 TAKEDOWN, COMPACT

SAVAGE ARMS RASCAL SINGLE SHOT

MARK II SERIES BTV

Action: Bolt
Stock: Wood laminate
Barrel: 21 in.
Sights: None
Weight: 6 lb. 8 oz.
Caliber: .22 LR
Magazine: Detachable box, 5 rounds
Features: Carbon steel barrel with blued satin finish; wood laminate stock with thumbhole; AccuTrigger
MSRP $461.00

MARK II SERIES FV-SR LANDRY

Action: Bolt
Stock: Synthetic
Barrel: 16.5 in.
Sights: None
Weight: 5 lb. 8 oz.
Caliber: .22 LR
Magazine: Detachable box
Features: Carbon steel barrel; matte barrel finish
MSRP $345.00

MODEL 42 TAKEDOWN, COMPACT

Action: Over/under
Stock: Synthetic
Barrel: 20 in.
Sights: Adjustable
Weight: 6 lb.
Caliber: .22 LR, .410
Magazine: 2 rounds
Features: Carbon steel barrel; matte barrel finish; break-open combination gun, .22 LR over .410
MSRP $500.00

RASCAL SINGLE SHOT

Action: Bolt
Stock: Synthetic, hardwood
Barrel: 16.125 in.
Sights: Adjustable
Weight: 2 lb. 10 oz.–2 lb. 15 oz.
Caliber: .22 LR
Magazine: None
Features: Matte synthetic stock available in seven colors; adjustable peep sights; drilled and tapped for scope mounts; AccuTrigger; carbon steel barrel with satin blued finish
MSRP . . . . $191.00–$238.00

SEMI-AUTOMATIC SERIES 64 F

Action: Semiautomatic
Stock: Synthetic
Barrel: 20.5 in.
Sights: Open
Weight: 5 lb.
Caliber: .22 LR
Magazine: Detachable box, 10 rounds
Features: Drilled and tapped for scope mounts; carbon steel barrel with satin blued finish; synthetic matte black stock
MSRP $140.00

SPECIALTY SERIES 11/111 HOG HUNTER

Action: Bolt
Stock: Synthetic
Barrel: 20 in.
Sights: Adjustable
Weight: 7 lb. 4 oz.–8 lb.
Caliber: .223 Rem., .308 Win., .338 Fed.
Magazine: Internal box, 4 rounds
Features: Green composite synthetic stock; matte black carbon steel barrel; LPA adjustable sights; threaded barrel; AccuTrigger
MSRP $595.00

SPECIALTY SERIES 11/111 LADY HUNTER

Action: Bolt
Stock: Wood
Barrel: 20 in.
Sights: None
Weight: 6 lb.–6 lb. 8 oz.
Caliber: .223 Rem., .243 Win., .270 Win., .30-06 Spfd., .308 Win., 6.5 Creedmoor, 7mm-08 Rem.
Magazine: Detachable box, 4 rounds
Features: Oil-finish American walnut stock with ladies-specific geometry; carbon steel barrel in matter black
MSRP $899.00

SPECIALTY SERIES 11/111 LONG RANGE HUNTER

Action: Bolt
Stock: Synthetic
Barrel: 26 in.
Sights: None
Weight: 8 lb. 6 oz.
Caliber: .260 Rem., .300 Win. Mag., .300 WSM, .308 Win., .338 Lapua Mag., .338 Fed., 6.5 Creedmoor, 6.5-284 Norma, 7mm Rem. Mag.
Magazine: Hinged floor plate, 2, 4 rounds
Features: Drilled and tapped for scope mounts; carbon steel barrel with black matte finish; synthetic stock with black matte finish; AccuTrigger
MSRP . . . . $1171.00–$1421.00

SAVAGE ARMS SEMI-AUTOMATIC SERIES 64 F

SAVAGE ARMS SPECIALTY SERIES 11/111 HOG HUNTER

SAVAGE ARMS SPECIALTY SERIES 11/111 LADY HUNTER

SAVAGE ARMS SPECIALTY SERIES 11/111 LONG RANGE HUNTER

Savage Arms

**SAVAGE ARMS SPECIALTY SERIES
16/116 BEAR HUNTER**

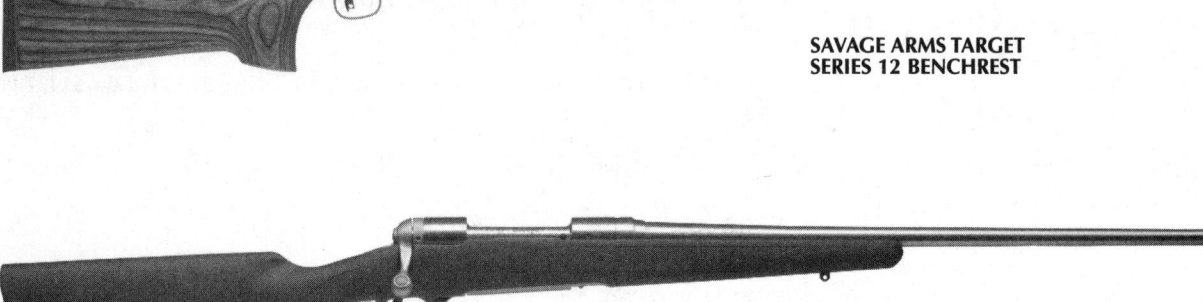

**SAVAGE ARMS TARGET
SERIES 12 BENCHREST**

**SAVAGE ARMS WEATHER WARRIOR
SERIES 16/116 FCSS**

SPECIALTY SERIES 16/116 BEAR HUNTER

Action: Bolt
Stock: Synthetic
Barrel: 23 in.
Sights: None
Weight: 7 lb. 8 oz.
Caliber: .300 Win. Mag., .300 WSM, .338 Fed., .338 Win. Mag., .375 Ruger
Magazine: Hinged floor plate, 2 rounds
Features: Drilled and tapped for scope mounts; adjustable muzzle-brake; stainless steel barrel; synthetic stock with matte camo finish; AccuTrigger; AccuStock
MSRP . . . . $1098.00–$1135.00

TARGET SERIES 12 BENCHREST

Action: Bolt, single shot
Stock: Wood laminate
Barrel: 29 in.
Sights: None
Weight: 12 lb. 12 oz.
Caliber: .308 Win., 6.5-284 Norma, 6 Norma BR
Magazine: None
Features: Drilled and tapped for scope mounts; stainless steel barrel with high luster finish; wood laminate stock with satin finish; AccuTrigger
MSRP $1678.00

WEATHER WARRIOR SERIES 16/116 FCSS

Action: Bolt
Stock: Synthetic
Barrel: 22 in., 24 in.
Sights: None
Weight: 6 lb. 14 oz.–7.15 lb.
Caliber: .22-250 Rem., .223 Rem., .243 Win., .270 Win., .30-06 Spfd., .300 Win. Mag., .308 Win., 7mm Rem. Mag., .7mm-08 Rem.
Magazine: Detachable box, 2, 4 rounds
Features: Drilled and tapped for scope mounts; stainless steel barrel with high luster finish; synthetic stock with black matte finish; AccuTrigger
MSRP $939.00

SIG SAUER M400 PREDATOR

SIG SAUER MPX CARBINE

SIG SAUER SIG516 PATROL

SIG SAUER SIGM400 PREDATOR

SIG SAUER SIG716GR DMR

SIG SAUER SIG716G2 PATROL

M400 PREDATOR

Action: Semiautomatic
Stock: Synthetic
Barrel: 16 in., 18 in.
Sights: None
Weight: 7 lb. 4 oz.
Caliber: 5.56mm, 300 BLK
Magazine: 5 rounds
Features: Two-stage match trigger; hammer-forged stainless steel barrel; barrels come threaded for the addition of muzzle devices or silencers; top Picatinny rail; ALG aluminum free-floating handguard features M-Lok attachment points, allowing for lights, lasers, and bipods to be mounted; tough, durable hard coat anodized upper and lower receivers
MSRP . . . . **$1446.00–$1582.00**

MPX CARBINE

Action: Semiautomatic
Stock: Synthetic
Barrel: 16 in.
Sights: Adjustable
Weight: 7 lb. 8 oz.
Caliber: 9mm
Magazine: 30 rounds
Features: Closed, fully locked short stroke pushrod gas system; skeletonized low-profile side-folding stock;

AR-style trigger; ambidextrous selector, mag release, and bolt release; aluminum Add-A-Rail or KeyMod handguard
MSRP **$2016.00**

SIG516 PATROL

Action: Semiautomatic
Stock: Tactical synthetic
Barrel: 16 in.
Sights: None
Weight: 7 lb. 5 oz.
Caliber: 5.56 NATO
Magazine: Detachable box, 30 rounds
Features: Gas piston operating system; three-position gas regulator; free-floating military grade chrome-lined barrel; Picatinny flat top upper; aircraft grade aluminum upper and lower receiver with hard coat anodize finish.
MSRP: . . . Black $1888.00; Flat Dark Earth $2024.00

SIG716GR DMR

Action: Semiautomatic
Stock: Synthetic
Barrel: 16 in.
Sights: None
Weight: 8 lb. 3 oz.
Caliber: 7.62 NATO
Magazine: 20 rounds
Features: Taper-Lok muzzle brake; aluminum KeyMod handguard with

continuous M1913 top rail; two-position adjustable gas valve; two-stage match trigger; sub-MOA performance; available in black or flat dark earth
MSRP **$3108.00**

SIG716G2 PATROL

Action: Semiautomatic
Stock: Tactical synthetic
Barrel: 16 in.
Sights: None
Weight: 9 lb. 5 oz.
Caliber: 7.62 NATO
Magazine: Detachable box, 20 rounds
Features: Second generation is a short-stroke gas piston operating system with a free-floating barrel, aluminum fore-end, telescoping stock, and M1913 Mil-Std rail; one 20-round polymer AR-10 mag included; available in black and Flat Dark Earth
Black: **$2385.00**
Flat Dark Earth: **$2521.00**

SIGM400 PREDATOR

Stock: Synthetic
Barrel: 18 in. (5.56 NATO), 16 in. (.300 BLK)
Sights: None
Weight: 4 lb. 8 oz.
Caliber: 5.56 NATO, .300 BLK
Magazine: 5 round
Features: Based on direct-impingement AR-15 platform, the rifle features a top Picatinny rail, hard coat anodized upper and lower, six-position Mil-Std telescoping stock, and aluminum magazine
California-compliant: **$1446.00**
Standard: **$1582.00**

Smith & Wesson

SMITH & WESSON M&P10

SMITH & WESSON M&P15

SMITH & WESSON M&P15-22 SPORT

M&P10
Action: Gas-operated semiautomatic
Stock: Synthetic
Barrel: 22 in.
Sights: None
Weight: 7 lb. 11 oz.
Caliber: .308 Win., 7.62 NATO
Magazine: Detachable box, 20 rounds
Features: Ambidextrous magazine catch; bolt catch; reversible, ambidextrous safety selector; S&W enhanced flash hider; gas block with integral Picatinny rail; QD sling swivel attachment point (bottom of gas block); 5R rifling
MSRP. $1619.00

M&P15
Action: Semiautomatic
Stock: Synthetic
Barrel: 16 in.
Sights: Troy adjustable front post, folding rear battle sight
Weight: 6 lb. 12 oz.
Caliber: 5.56 NATO, .223 Rem.
Magazine: Detachable box, 30 rounds
Features: Six-position telescopic black stock; chrome-lined gas key and bolt carrier; flash suppressor compensator; two-position safety lever
MSRP. $1249.00

M&P 15-22 SPORT, SPORT M-LOK
Stock: Synthetic
Barrel: 16.5 in.
Sights: Folding Magpul MBUS front and rear
Weight: 4 lb. 12 oz.
Caliber .22 LR
Capacity: 10, 25 rounds
Features: Updated version of the original M&P 15-22, with a slightly shorter barrel; six-position collapsible stock, 10-in. slim handguard, M-LOK compatible, functioning charging handle, shell deflector, two-position receiver-mounted safety, and Armonite barrel finish are standard; available in black, matte black, Kryptek, Flat Dark Earth, and Muddy Girl finishes; California Compliant and Magpul MOE variants also available
MSRP. . . . . $449.00–$709.00

SMITH & WESSON M&P15 300 WHISPER

SMITH & WESSON M&P15 MOE SL MID MAGPUL SPEC SERIES

SMITH & WESSON M&P15 PC

SMITH & WESSON M&P15 VTAC II

SMITH & WESSON M&P15 SPORT II

M&P15 300 WHISPER

Action: Semiautomatic
Stock: Synthetic
Barrel: 16 in.
Sights: None
Weight: 6 lb. 6 oz.
Caliber: .300 Whisper, .300 BLK
Magazine: Detachable box, 10 rounds
Features: Sub-sonic and super-sonic capabilities; 4140 chromoly steel barrel; forged 7075 aluminum receivers coated with Realtree APG finish; gas-operated rifle; single-stage trigger; integral one-piece trigger guard; six-position collapsible CAR stock; optics ready
MSRP **$1119.00**

M&P15 MOE SL MID MAGPUL SPEC SERIES

Action: Semiautomatic
Stock: Synthetic
Barrel: 16 in.
Sights: M4-A2 post front, folding Magpul rear
Weight: 6 lb. 8 oz.
Caliber: 5.56 NATO
Magazine: Detachable box, 30 rounds

Features: Mid-length operating system, patent-pending flash hider; available in black and dark earth finish; Magpul designed forged lower receiver with flared magazine; one-piece integrated trigger guard; Melonite finish on barrel; MOE six-position collapsible buttstock
MSRP **$1239.00**

M&P15 SPORT II

Action: Semiautomatic
Stock: Synthetic
Barrel: 16 in.
Sights: Adjustable front, Magpul MBUS rear
Weight: 6 lb. 7 oz.
Caliber: 5.56 NATO
Magazine: 30+1 rounds
Features: Forged, integral trigger guard; Armornite finish (durable corrosion-resistant finish); chromed firing pin; forward assist; dust cover
MSRP **$739.00**

M&P15 PC

Action: Semiautomatic
Stock: Synthetic
Barrel: 20 in.
Sights: None
Weight: 8 lb. 2 oz.
Caliber: 5.56 NATO, .223 Rem.

Magazine: Detachable box, 10 rounds
Features: Hogue Green pistol grip; A2 buttstock; two-stage trigger; Realtree Advantage Max-1 Camo finish stock; chromed gas key and bolt carrier
Black: **$1549.00**
Camo: **$1589.00**

M&P15 VTAC II

Action: Semiautomatic
Stock: Synthetic
Barrel: 16 in.
Sights: None
Weight: 6 lb. 4 oz.
Caliber: 5.56 NATO
Magazine: Detachable box, 30 rounds
Features: Mid-length operating system, patent-pending flash hider; 4150 CMV steel barrel with Melonite finish; VTAC/Troy Extreme TRX handguard that reduces heat transfer; packaged with 2-inch adjustable Picatinny rails; Geissele Super V trigger
MSRP **$1949.00**

Springfield Armory

SPRINGFIELD ARMORY LOADED M1A

SPRINGFIELD ARMORY M1A SOCOM 16

SPRINGFIELD ARMORY M1A SOCOM 16 CQB

SPRINGFIELD ARMORY NATIONAL MATCH M1A

SPRINGFIELD ARMORY SCOUT SQUAD

LOADED M1A

Action: Semiautomatic
Stock: Synthetic
Barrel: 22 in.
Sights: Adjustable
Weight: 11 lb. 4 oz.
Caliber: 7.62 NATO
Magazine: 10 rounds
Features: 1:11 inch barrel twist; match grade aperture with ½ MOA adjustment for windage and 1 MOA for elevation; FDE precision adjustable stock
MSRP . . . . **$1846.00–$2061.00**

M1A SOCOM 16

Action: Semiautomatic
Stock: Composite
Barrel: 16.25 in.
Sights: Tritium front sight
Weight: 8 lb. 13 oz.
Caliber: 7.62 NATO, .308 Win
Magazine: Detachable box, 10 rounds
Features: Muzzlebrake; forward mounted scope base; two-stage military trigger; composite black or green stock
MSRP . . . . **$1985.00–$2420.00**

M1A SOCOM 16 CQB

Action: Semiautomatic
Stock: Synthetic

Barrel: 16.25 in.
Sights: XS Post with tritium insert front, adjustable rear
Weight: 9 lb. 3 oz.
Caliber: .308 Win., 7.62x51mm NATO
Magazine: 10 or 20 rounds
Features: Adjustable buttstock; five-position length and two-position adjustable cheek piece; standard AR-type commercial buffer tube; AK-style pistol grip; accepts any standard AK-style replacement; M-Lok compatible system; fixed top rail
MSRP . . . . **$2121.00–$2420.00**

NATIONAL MATCH M1A

Action: Semiautomatic
Stock: Walnut
Barrel: 22 in.
Sights: National Match front military post sight; rear National Match hooded aperture
Weight: 9 lb. 13 oz.
Caliber: 7.62 NATO, .308 Win.
Magazine: Detachable box, 10 rounds

Features: Glass bedded; NM gas cylinder; NM recoil spring guide; NM flash suppressor; walnut stock; stainless steel or carbon barrel; two-stage military trigger
Carbon barrel: **$2359.00**
Stainless steel barrel: **$2414.00**

SCOUT SQUAD

Action: Semiautomatic
Stock: Walnut, composite
Barrel: 18 in.
Sights: National Match front military post sight; rear military aperture
Weight: 9 lb. 5 oz.
Caliber: 7.62 NATO, .308 Win.
Magazine: Detachable box, 10 rounds
Features: Mounted optical sight base; muzzle stabilizers; black or green fiberglass composite, American walnut stock or Mossy Oak camo stock; two-stage military trigger
MSRP . . . . **$1849.00–$1985.00**

Springfield Armory

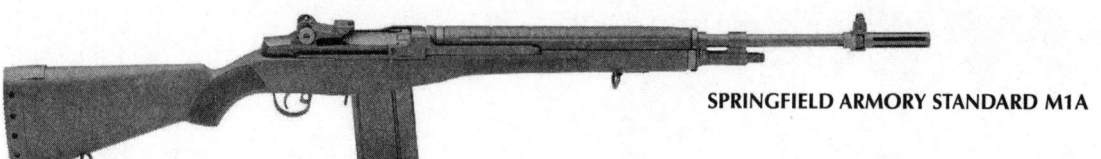

SPRINGFIELD ARMORY STANDARD M1A

STANDARD M1A

Action: Semiautomatic
Stock: Composite or walnut
Barrel: 22 in.
Sights: National Match military front post, adjustable rear aperture sight
Weight: 9 lb. 5 oz.
Caliber: 7.62 NATO, .308 Win.
Magazine: Detachable box, 10 rounds
Features: Black fiberglass with rubber buttplate, Mossy Oak stock with metal buttplate or American walnut with original military buttplate; two-stage military trigger
MSRP . . . . **$1685.00–$1786.00**

Stag Arms

STAG ARMS MODEL 3G

STAG ARMS MODEL 8 (PISTON)

MODEL 3G

Action: Semiautomatic
Stock: Synthetic
Barrel: 18 in.
Sights: None
Weight: N/A
Caliber: 5.56 NATO, .223 Rem.
Magazine: Detachable box, 30 rounds
Features: A2 flash hider; Picatinny rail; Magpul ACS buttstock; enhanced semiauto with a manganese phosphate coating
MSRP **$1459.00**

MODEL 8 (PISTON)

Action: Gas-operated piston semiautomatic
Stock: Synthetic
Barrel: 20 in.
Sights: Midwest Industries front and rear flip-up
Weight: 6 lb. 14 oz.
Caliber: 5.56 NATO
Magazine: Detachable box, 30 rounds
Features: Right and left-hand available; six-position collapsible stock; chrome-lined barrel
MSRP **$1145.00**

Steyr Arms

STEYR ARMS AUG A3 M1

STEYR ARMS MANNLICHER DUETT

STEYR ARMS MANNLICHER PRO HUNTER

STEYR ARMS SCOUT

STEYR ARMS SSG 08

AUG A3 M1

Action: Semiautomatic
Stock: Synthetic
Barrel: 16 in.
Sights: None
Weight: 7 lb. 11 oz.–8 lb. 13. oz.
Caliber: 5.56 NATO, .223 Rem.
Magazine: Detachable box, 30 rounds
Features: Bullpup rifle has adjustable short-stroke gas piston, hard Eloxal-coated aircraft aluminum receiver, chrome-lined CHF barrel with muzzle brake, two-position trigger-blocking safety; short rail, high rail, and optics configurations; available in white/black, OD Green, or MUD
MSRP................$2099.00

MANNLICHER DUETT

Action: Break-action
Stock: Walnut
Barrel: 23.6 in.
Sights: Open sights, 11mm prismatic scope mount rail
Weight: 6 lb. 6 oz.
Caliber: Rifle: .222 Rem., .243 Win., .308 Win., 7x65R, .30-06 Spfd., .30R Blaser, 8x57 IRS, 9.3x74R; Shotgun: 12 Ga./3-in.
Magazine: None

Features: Break-action over-under combination rifle/shotgun; dual gold-plated single-stage triggers; free-floated cold-hammer-forged barrels, Mannox finish; tang-mounted manual cocking lever; 5 models available; manual cocking system; European walnut stock; checkered forend and pistol grip
Standard:...... **$3995.00–$7495.00**

PRO HUNTER

Action: Bolt
Stock: Synthetic
Barrel: 20 in., 23.6 in., 25.6 in.
Sights: None
Weight: 7 lb. 5 oz.–8 lb. 3 oz.
Caliber: .308 Win., 7mm-08 Rem., .270 Win., .30-06 Spfd., .300 Win. Mag.
Magazine: Detachable box
Features: Direct trigger, optionally set trigger; durable synthetic stock adjusted by spacers; Mannotm metal surface finish protects against corrosion; three-position safety
MSRP................. **$850.00**
Stainless:............. **$950.00**

SCOUT

Action: Bolt
Stock: Synthetic

Barrel: 19 in.
Sights: None
Weight: 6 lb. 10 oz.
Caliber: .308 Win.
Magazine: Detachable box, 5 rounds (optional 10 round magazine)
Features: Weaver scope mounting rail; set trigger or direct trigger; synthetic stock in black or gray wood imitation; optional bipod integrated into forearm; matte black or stainless steel finish on barrel
MSRP................$1699.00

SSG 08

Action: Bolt
Stock: Synthetic
Barrel: 20 in., 23.6 in.
Sights: None
Weight: 5 lb. 8 oz.–5 lb. 11 oz.
Caliber: .300 Win. Mag., .308 Win.
Magazine: Detacable box, 10 rounds
Features: Direct trigger; Mannox TM system; high grade aluminum folding stock; adjustable cheekpiece and buttplate with height marking; ergonomic exchangeable pistol grip; UIT rail and Picatinny rail; muzzlebrake; Versa-Pod
MSRP........ **$5899.00–$6495.00**

Szecsei & Fuchs Fine Guns

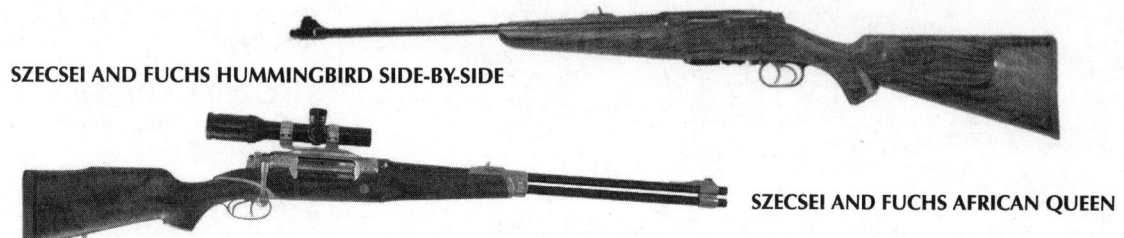

SZECSEI AND FUCHS HUMMINGBIRD SIDE-BY-SIDE

SZECSEI AND FUCHS AFRICAN QUEEN

DOUBLE-BARREL BOLT ACTION REPEATING RIFLE

Action: Double-barrel bolt
Stock: Hand selected, exclusive grade, Turkish walnut
Barrel: 20 in.–24 in.
Sights: Options of scopes or open sights
Weight: Small caliber rifles: approx. 7 lb. 8 oz.; Large caliber rifles: 9 lb. 12 oz.–12 lb.
Caliber: Available in many popular calibers, starting with .17 HMR all the way up to large game calibers, like Szecsei & Fuchs' custom .700 SSS
Magazine: Detachable box, 4+2

rounds
Features: The DBR, only custom built to personal taste, is crafted with great care and handiwork from the finest materials. Incorporating a design remarkable for its cleverness, the six-shot magazine feeds two rounds simultaneously, both of which can be fired by two quick pulls of the trigger. The triggers have integrated, noiseless double firing safety catches, the barrels may be requested in either octagon or round profile, and a one-piece bolt reloads two rounds with each cycle of the action. Starting with the selection of either side-by-side or over-and-under, the rifle can be

personalized with exquisite custom engravings, optics, mounts and rings, extra magazines, and custom leather-bound cases. *As these rifles are custom order only, and with the fluctuation of the U.S. dollar, it is best to contact the sales representative listed in back to obtain a firm quotation. Average product delivery currently 16 months.
MSRP . . . . . . Small caliber rifles are $25000.00 and up. Large caliber rifles are approximately $100000.00 and up. Both small and large calibers are available in side-by-side and over/under rifle configurations (African Queen $190k as shown).

Tactical Rifles

TACTICAL RIFLES CLASSIC SPORTER

TACTICAL RIFLES TACTICAL L.R.

CLASSIC SPORTER

Action: Chimera bolt
Stock: Walnut
Barrel: 22 in.
Sights: None
Weight: 8 lb. 14 oz.
Caliber: .308 Win., .260 Rem., 6.5 Creedmoor and Lapua, .243 Win., 7mm-08 Rem. (short action), .25-06,.30-06 Spfd., .270 Win., .300 Win. Mag., 7mm Rem. Mag. (long action)
Magazine: 4+1 rounds
Features: Chimera action is constructed from stainless steel with a hand-fitted spiral-groove bolt and "Magnum"

extractor; Picatinny rail; XXX grade English walnut stock with 22 lpi checkering at grip and forearm; extreme environment matte black finish
MSRP $5895.00

TACTICAL L.R.

Action: Bolt, 700 Rem.
Stock: Synthetic
Barrel: 18 in.-26 in.
Sights: None
Weight: 12 lb.–13 lb. 6 oz.
Caliber: 7.62 NATO, .308 Win., .260 Rem., 6.5 Creedmoor, 6.5 Lapua, .243 Win., 7mm-08, .30-06 Spfd.,

.270 Win., .25-06; other calibers can be custom ordered
Magazine: Detachable box, 5 or 10 rounds
Features: Ergonomic thumbhole stock comes in black or green; raised cheekpiece; free-floating chromoly match grade barrel; ambidextrous sling swivel studs; soft rubber recoil pad; Picatinny rail; aluminum block chassis stock system; optional bipod
MSRP $3450.00

Taurus

TAURUS CTG29 CARBINE

TAURUS CTG240 CARBINE

CTG29 CARBINE

Action: Semiautomatic
Stock: Synthetic
Barrel: 16 in.
Sights: Adjustable
Weight: 6 lb. 10 oz.

Caliber: 9mm
Magazine: Detachable box, 10 rounds
Features: Close quarter carbine platform with a blowback-operated system that fires from the closed-bolt position; fixed front, adjustable rear sights; Picatinny rail; ambidextrous charging handle
MSRP $879.00

CTG240 CARBINE

Action: Semiautomatic
Stock: Synthetic
Barrel: 16 in.
Sights: Adjustable
Weight: 6 lb. 10 oz.
Caliber: .40 S&W
Magazine: Detachable box, 10 rounds
Features: Close quarter carbine platform with a blowback-operated system that fires from the closed-bolt position; fixed front, adjustable rear sights; Picatinny rail; ambidextrous charging handle
MSRP $879.00

Taylor's & Co. Firearms

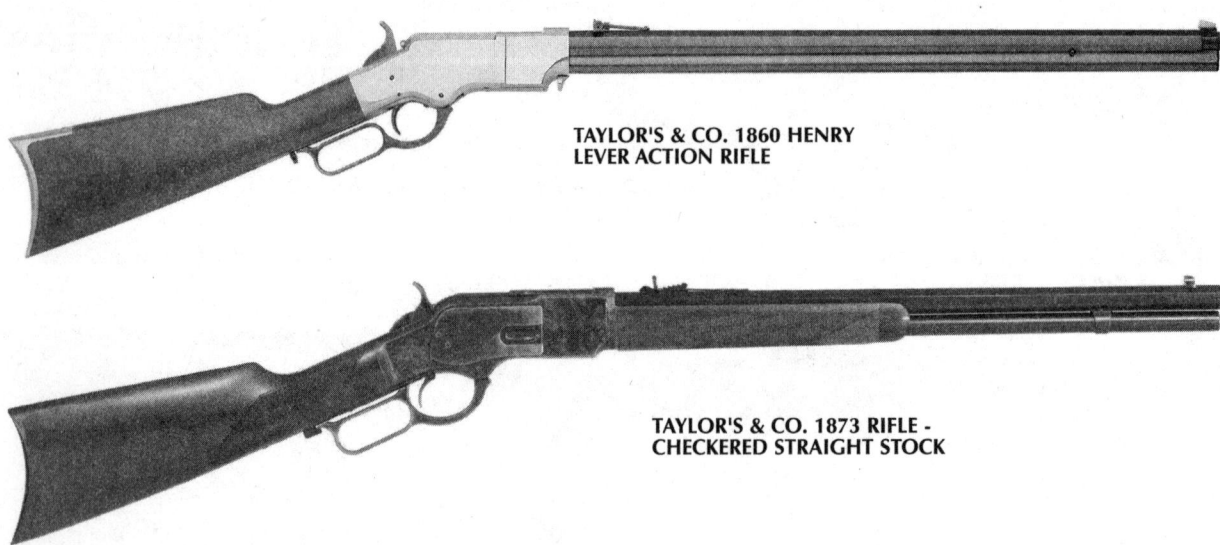

TAYLOR'S & CO. 1860 HENRY LEVER ACTION RIFLE

TAYLOR'S & CO. 1873 RIFLE - CHECKERED STRAIGHT STOCK

1860 HENRY LEVER ACTION RIFLE

Action: Lever
Stock: Walnut
Barrel: 24.25 in.
Sights: Open
Weight: 9 lb. 3 oz.
Caliber: .44-40 Win.
Magazine: Under-barrel tube, 9–13 rounds
Features: Brass frame; octagonal barrel with blued finish; includes sling swivels
MSRP $1508.00

1873 RIFLE - CHECKERED STRAIGHT STOCK

Action: Lever
Stock: Walnut
Barrel: 20 in.
Sights: Open
Weight: 8 lb. 8 oz.
Caliber: .357 Mag., .45 LC
Magazine: Under-barrel tube, 10+1 rounds
Features: Case-hardened frame; straight stock with checkering; available with full octagon barrel
MSRP $1375.00

Taylor's & Co. Firearms

TAYLOR'S & CO. 1886 RIDGE RUNNER

TAYLOR'S & CO. ALASKAN TAKE-DOWN MODEL

TAYLOR'S & CO. LIGHTNING SLIDE ACTION RIFLE

RIFLES

1886 RIDGE RUNNER

Action: Lever
Stock: Wood or synthetic
Barrel: 18.5 in.
Sights: Skinner rear peep sight, fiber optic front
Weight: 7 lb. 13 oz.
Caliber: .45-70 Govt.
Magazine: 4, 8 rounds
Features: Available in two versions, either matte blue or matte chrome metal work. Stock is wood with soft-touch rubber overmold; Integrated Skinner rear peep sight, Weaver rail, front fiber optic sight, D-shaped lever, muzzle brake, and half-octagonal barrel are standard
Blue: $1728.00
Chrome: $1830.00

1892 ALASKAN TAKE-DOWN MODEL

Action: Lever
Stock: Synthetic
Barrel: 16 in., 20 in.
Sights: Skinner rear
Weight: 6 lb. 10 oz.
Caliber: .357 Mag., .44RM, .45 LC
Magazine: Under-barrel tube, 10 rounds
Features: Matte chrome finish; soft touch stock
.357, .45 LC (16-in. barrel): . . . $1412.00
.44 Mag. (20-in. barrel): . . . $1483.00

LIGHTNING SLIDE ACTION RIFLE

Action: Slide
Stock: Walnut
Barrel: 20 in., 24.25 in., 26 in.
Sights: Open
Weight: 6 lb. 6 oz.–6 lb. 14 oz.
Caliber: .45 LC, .44-40, .357 Mag.
Magazine: Under-barrel tube
Features: Lightning Baby Carbine has 20-in. round barrel and blued receiver; Lightning Standard has 26-in round barrel with blued receiver; Lightning Rifle Premium has 24-in. octagonal barrel and case-hardened receiver
Lightning Baby Carbine: . . . $1655.00
Lightning Rifle Standard: . . . $1688.00
Lightning Rifle Premium: . . . $1968.00

Thompson/Center Arms

THOMPSON/CENTER COMPASS

THOMPSON/CENTER DIMENSION

THOMPSON/CENTER PROHUNTER PREDATOR

THOMPSON/CENTER VENTURE COMPACT

THOMPSON/CENTER VENTURE PREDATOR SNOW

COMPASS

Action: Bolt
Stock: Composite
Barrel: 22 in., 24 in.
Sights: None
Weight: 7 lb. 4 oz.–7 lb. 8 oz.
Caliber: .22-50 Rem., .204 Ruger, .223/5.56, .243 Win., .270 Win., .30-06 Spfd., .300 Win. Mag., .308 Win., 6.5 Creedmoor, 7mm Rem. Mag., 7mm-08 Rem.
Magazine: Detachable box, 5+1 rounds
Features: Adjustable trigger; ergonomic, lightweight stock; textured grip panels; soft rubber recoil pad; aluminum pillar bedding system that positively locates the receiver and free-floats the barrel for outstanding accuracy; easy-to-use three-position safety; rotary magazine fits flush with the stock and provides smooth feeding; drilled and tapped receiver for scope mounting with bases included
MSRP $399.00

DIMENSION

Action: Bolt
Stock: Composite
Barrel: 22 in., 24 in.
Sights: None

Weight: 7 lb.
Caliber: .204 Ruger, .223 Rem., .22-250 Rem., .243 Win., 7mm-08 Rem., .308 Win., .270 Win., .30-06 Spfd., 7mm Rem. Mag., .300 Win. Mag.
Magazine: Detachable box, 3 rounds
Features: A bolt action platform you can build on season after season; switch out barrels, bolts, magazines, and and other components such as scopes and mounts; stocks are black compositi, metal work is blued; left-hand versions available
MSRP $689.00

PROHUNTER PREDATOR

Action: Single-shot, break-open
Stock: Composite
Barrel: 28 in.
Sights: None
Weight: 7 lb. 12 oz.
Caliber: .204 Ruger, .223 Rem., .22-250 Rem., .308 Win.
Magazine: None
Features: Realtree MAX-1 camo composite stock and barrel; FlexTech; mounted and drilled for scopes
MSRP $882.00

VENTURE COMPACT

Action: Bolt
Stock: Composite

Barrel: 20 in.
Sights: None
Weight: 6 lb. 12 oz.
Caliber: .22-250 Rem., .223 Rem., .243 Win., .308 Win., 7mm-08 Rem.
Magazine: Detachable box, 3+1 rounds
Features: Adjustable trigger; included spacer and buttpad; Hogue traction inlays; Melanite coated bolt; two position safety
MSRP $537.00

VENTURE PREDATOR SNOW

Action: Bolt
Stock: Composite
Barrel: 22 in., 24 in.
Sights: Bases for mounting scopes
Weight: 6 lb. 12 oz.
Caliber: 7mm-08 Rem., .243 Rem., .22-250 Rem., .308 Win.
Magazine: Detachable box, 3+1 rounds
Features: Adjustable trigger; Hogue rubber inlays; sling swivel studs; Weather Shield bolt handle
MSRP $638.00

TIKKA T3 LITE ADJUSTABLE

TIKKA T3 SPORTER LEFT-HANDED

T3 LITE ADJUSTABLE
Action: Bolt
Stock: Synthetic
Barrel: 20.1 in.–24.4 in.
Sights: None
Weight: 6 lb.–6 lb. 6 oz.
Caliber: .22-250 Rem., .25-06 Rem., .30-06 Spfd., .204 Rem., .222 Rem., .223 Rem., .243 Win., .260 Rem., .270 Win., .270 WSM, .300 Win. Mag., .300 WSM, .308 Win., .338 Fed., .338 Win. Mag., 6.5x55 Swedish, 7mm Rem. Mag., 7mm-08 Rem., 7x64 Brenneke, 8x57IS, 9.3x62 Mauser

Magazine: 3–6 rounds
Features: Adjustable cheek piece; left-handed available; optional magazine; muzzle threaded for silencer on some calibers
MSRP $775.00

T3 SPORTER
Action: Bolt
Stock: Laminated wood, oiled
Barrel: 20 in., 24 in.
Sights: Scope rail and threads for Weaver-type scope rail
Weight: 9 lb.–9 lb. 11 oz.

Caliber: .222 Rem., .223 Rem., 6.5x55 Swedish, .260 Rem., .308 Win.
Magazine: 5 or 6 rounds
Features: Adjustable cheekpiece; adjustable recoil pad in length and height; various rail placements that allow rifle to be carried in biathlon style; metal parts are matte blued; limited number of left-handed models imported to U.S.
MSRP $1595.00
Left-handed: $1755.00

Troy Defense

TROY DEFENSE M5 9MM RIFLE
Action: Semiautomatic
Stock: Polymer
Barrel: 16 in.
Sights: Standard rear and M4 front folding battlesights
Weight: 6 lb. 7 oz.
Caliber: 9mm
Magazine: 17 rounds
Features: Upper receiver designed to prevent over insertion of Glock magazines; Troy Medieval muzzle brake; lightweight Troy BattleAx CQB stock
MSRP $1299.00

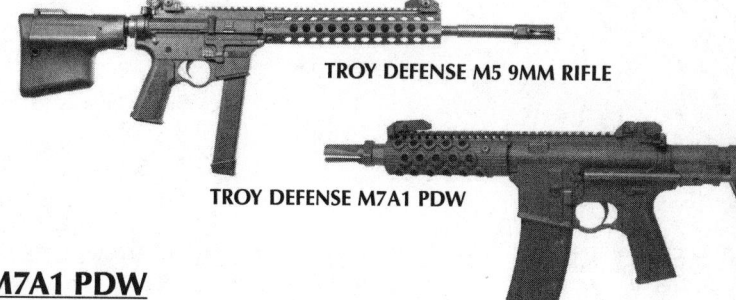

TROY DEFENSE M5 9MM RIFLE

TROY DEFENSE M7A1 PDW

M7A1 PDW
Action: Semiautomatic
Stock: Synthetic
Barrel: 7.5 in.
Sights: Adjustable
Weight: 5 lb. 13 oz.
Caliber: 5.56 NATO
Magazine: Detachable box, 30 rounds

Features: Ambidextrous safety selector; nickel boron PDW bolt carrier group; Picatinny rail
MSRP . . . .$1649.00–$1749.00

Turnbull Manufacturing Co.

TURNBULL MFG. CO. TAR-15

TAR-15
Action: Semiautomatic
Stock: Black Walnut
Barrel: 16 in.
Sights: None

Weight: 8 lb. 8 oz.
Caliber: .223 Rem.
Magazine: Detachable box, 5 or 10 rounds
Features: AR-15 gas impingement system; 8620 carbon steel receivers;

color case hardened steel; oversized integral trigger guard; picatinny rail; screw on muzzle brake
MSRP . . . Call manufacturer for pricing

Uberti

UBERTI 1860 HENRY RIFLE

UBERTI 1866 YELLOWBOY

UBERTI 1873 COMPETITION

UBERTI 1873 CARBINE

UBERTI 1874 CAVALRY CARBINE SHARPS

RIFLES

1860 HENRY RIFLE

Action: Lever
Stock: Walnut
Barrel: 18.5 in., 24.5 in.
Sights: Adjustable
Weight: 9 lb.
Caliber: .45 Colt, .44-40 Win.
Magazine: Under-barrel tube, 8+1 or 13+1 rounds
Features: Several versions: Trapper has 18.5-in barrel, brass frame/buttplate, and case-hardened lever, .45 LC only; Rifle is available in both calibers, has 24.5-in. barrel, brass frame/buttplate, and case-hardened receiver; Steel Rifle is available in both calibers, has 24.5-in. barrel, case-hardened frame/lever, blue buttplate
MSRP . . . . **$1429.00–$1459.00**

1866 YELLOWBOY

Action: Lever
Stock: Walnut
Barrel: 19 in., 20 in., 24.25 in.
Sights: Adjustable
Weight: 8 lb. 3 oz.

Caliber: .45 Colt, .44-40 Win., .38 Spl.
Magazine: Under barrel tube, 10+1 or 13+1 rounds
Features: Three versions, all calibers available in all three: Carbine, 19-in. barrel; Short Rifle, 20-in. barrel; Sporting Rifle, 24.25-in. barrel. All have brass frames and buttplates, case-hardened levers
MSRP . . . . **$1189.00–$1209.00**

1873 COMPETITION

Action: Lever
Stock: Wood
Barrel: 20 in.
Sights: Adjustable
Weight: 8 lb.
Caliber: .357 Mag., .45 Colt
Magazine: Under-barrel tube, 10+1 rounds
Features: Octagonal barrel; A-grade walnut; lever lock; side loading gate for ease of loading
MSRP **$1499.00**

1873 RIFLE & CARBINE

Action: Lever
Stock: Walnut
Barrel: 16.1 in., 18 in., 19 in., 20 in., 24.5 in.
Sights: Adjustable
Weight: 7 lb. 3 oz.–8 lb. 3 oz.
Caliber: .45 Colt, .357 Mag., .44-44
Magazine: Under-barrel tube, 9+1, 10+1 or 13+1 rounds
Features: Octagonal barrel on rifle; round barrel on carbine and trapper; A-grade walnut with checkered pistol grip and forend
Trapper: **$1259.00**
Rifle: **$1259.00**
Carbine: . . . . . . **$1219.00–$1309.00**
Sporting: **$1259.00**

1874 CAVALRY CARBINE SHARPS

Action: Falling block
Stock: Walnut
Barrel: 22 in.
Sights: Creedmoor Sight
Weight: 8 lb.
Caliber: .45-70 Govt.
Magazine: None
Features: Round blued barrel; case-hardened levers and blued buttplate
MSRP **$1809.00**

UBERTI 1874 SHARPS RIFLE

UBERTI 1876 CENTENNIAL

UBERTI 1885 HIGH-WALL SINGLE-SHOT
SPECIAL SPORTING MODEL

UBERTI SPRINGFIELD TRAPDOOR CARBINE

UBERTI SPRINGFIELD TRAPDOOR RIFLE

1874 SHARPS RIFLE

Action: Falling block
Stock: Walnut
Barrel: 32 in., 34 in.
Sights: Creedmoor Sight
Weight: 10 lb. 4 oz.–11 lb.
Caliber: .45-70 Govt.
Magazine: None
Features: Blued octagonal barrel;
checkered walnut stock; case-hard-
ened, except Extra Deluxe model;
double-set trigger; pewter forend cap
Special: $2019.00
Deluxe: $3129.00
Down Under: $2579.00
Buffalo Hunter: $2539.00
Extra Deluxe: $4999.00

1876 CENTENNIAL

Action: Lever
Stock: Walnut
Barrel: 28 in.
Sights: Adjustable
Weight: 10 lb.
Caliber: .45-60, .45-75, .50-95

Magazine: Under-barrel tube, 11+1
rounds
Features: Case-hardened frame and
lever; blued buttplate; octagonal
barrel; straight stock
MSRP $1609.00

1885 HIGH-WALL SINGLE-SHOT

Action: Falling block
Stock: Walnut
Barrel: 28 in., 30 in., 32 in.
Sights: Adjustable
Weight: 9 lb. 5 oz. (carbine), 10 lb.
Caliber: .45-70 Govt., .45-90,
.45-120
Magazine: None
Features: Case-hardened frame and
lever; blued buttplate; octagonal bar-
rel; carbine model has round barrel;
carbine and sporting rifle have straight
stock
Big Game: $1119.00
Carbine: $1009.00
Sporting Rifle: . . $1079.00–$1139.00
Special Sporting: . . . $1209.00–$1279.00

SPRINGFIELD TRAPDOOR CARBINE

Action: Hinged breech
Stock: Walnut
Barrel: 22 in.
Sights: Adjustable
Weight: 7 lb. 5 oz.
Caliber: .45-70 Govt.
Magazine: None
Features: Blued steel, case-hardened
breechblock and buttplate; fitted with
sliding ring and bar for cavalryman to
carry it clipped to carbine sling
MSRP $1669.00

SPRINGFIELD TRAPDOOR RIFLE

Action: Hinged breech
Stock: Walnut
Barrel: 32.5 in.
Sights: Adjustable
Weight: 8 lb. 13 oz.
Caliber: .45-70 Govt.
Magazine: None
Features: Blued steel, case-hardened
breechblock and buttplate
MSRP $1949.00

Volquartsen Firearms

TF-17 & TF-22

Action: Semiautomatic
Stock: Ambidextrous birch
Barrel: 18.5 in.
Sights: Picatinny rail
Weight: 8 lb. 8 oz.
Caliber: .17 HMR, .22 WMR
Magazine: Rotary mag, 9 rounds
Features: Blowback design, TG2000 trigger unit with 2.25-lb. pull; black stainless barrel
MSRP **$1265.00**

VOLQUARTSEN FIREARMS TF-17

Walther Arms

WALTHER HK G36 RIMFIRE

HK G36 RIMFIRE

Action: Semiautomatic
Stock: Synthetic, telescoping
Barrel: 18 in.
Sights: Fixed front, adjustable back
Weight: 6 lb. 12 oz.
Caliber: .22 LR
Magazine: Detachable box, 20 rounds
Features: Ambidextrous safety; Picatinny rail; 10- and 30-round magazines available
MSRP **$599.00**

Weatherby

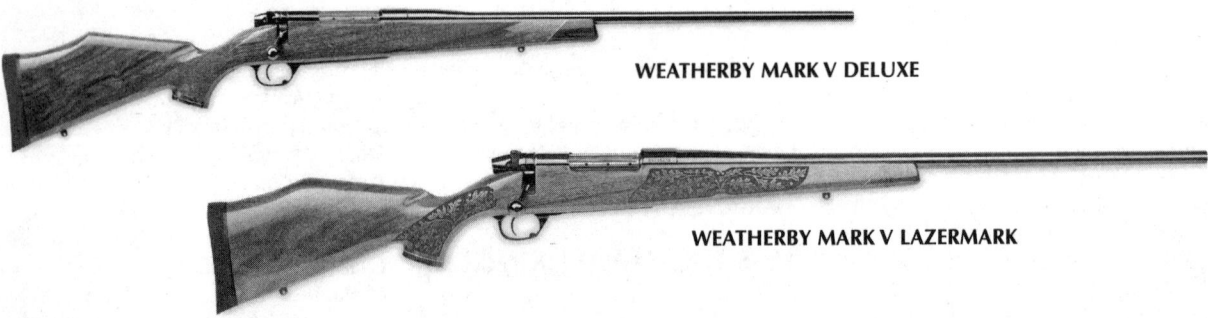

WEATHERBY MARK V DELUXE

WEATHERBY MARK V LAZERMARK

MARK V DELUXE

Action: Bolt
Stock: Walnut
Barrel: 24 in., 26 in., 28 in.
Sights: None
Weight: 6 lb. 12 oz.–10 lb.
Caliber: .270 Win., .308 Win., .30–06 Spfd., .257 Wby. Mag., .270 Wby. Mag., 7mm Wby. Mag., .300 Wby. Mag., .340 Wby. Mag., .378 Wby. Mag., .416 Wby. Mag., .460 Wby. Mag.
Magazine: 2+1, 3+1, 5+1 rounds
Features: Adjustable trigger; walnut Monte Carlo stock with rosewood forend and pistol grip cap and maple-wood spacers; blued metalwork in high luster finish; Pachmayr decelerator pad
MSRP . . . . **$2600.00–$3500.00**

MARK V LAZERMARK

Action: Bolt
Stock: Walnut
Barrel: 26 in.
Sights: None
Weight: 8 lb. 8 oz.
Caliber: .257 Wby. Mag., .270 Wby. Mag., 7mm Wby. Mag., .300 Win. Mag., .300 Wby. Mag.
Magazine: 3+1 rounds
Features: Adjustable trigger; hand-selected, raised comb Monte Carlo stock with laser-carved oak leaf pattern; blued metalwork in high luster finish; Pachmayr decelerator pad
MSRP **$2800.00**

RIFLES

Weatherby

WEATHERBY MARK V SPORTER

WEATHERBY VANGUARD BACK COUNTRY

WEATHERBY VANGUARD CAMILLA

WEATHERBY VANGUARD DANGEROUS GAME RIFLE

WEATHERBY VANGUARD SPORTER

WEATHERBY VANGUARD SPORTER DBM

MARK V SPORTER
Action: Bolt
Stock: Walnut
Barrel: 24 in., 26 in.
Sights: None
Weight: 8 lb.
Caliber: .257 Wby. Mag., .270 Wby. Mag., 7mm Rem. Mag., 7mm Wby. Mag., .300 Win. Mag., .300 Wby. Mag., .340 Wby. Mag.
Magazine: 3+1 rounds
Features: Adjustable trigger; raised comb Monte Carlo walnut stock with satin finish; features fine line diamond point checkering and rosewood forend and grip cap; bead blasted, blued metalwork with low luster finish; Pachmayr decelerator pad
MSRP $1800.00

VANGUARD BACK COUNTRY
Action: Bolt
Stock: Monte Carlo composite
Barrel: 24 in.
Sights: None
Weight: 6 lb. 12 oz.
Caliber: .240 Wby. Mag., .270 Win., .257 Wby. Mag., .30-06 Spfd., .300 Win. Mag., .300 Wby. Mag.
Magazine: 5+1 or 3+1 rounds
Features: SUB-MOA guarantee; chrome moly metalwork with Cerakote Tactical Grey finish; pillar-bedded stock; two-stage trigger; 3-position safety; auxiliary trigger sear; Pachmayr Decelerator pad
MSRP $1429.00

VANGUARD CAMILLA
Action: Bolt
Stock: Turkish walnut
Barrel: 20 in.
Sights: None
Weight: 6 lb. 4 oz.
Caliber: .223 Rem., .243 Win., .308 Win., 7mm-08 Rem.
Magazine: N/A
Features: SUB-MOA accuracy guarantee; "creep-free," match-quality, two-stage trigger; three-position safety; slimmer grip angle; shorter, slimmer forearm and grip with right side palm swell for better balance and fit; fleur de lis checkering pattern; recoil pad has been given a negative angle, reduced in size, and the toe canted away from the body to better fit a woman's shoulder
MSRP $849.00

VANGUARD DANGEROUS GAME RIFLE
Action: Bolt
Stock: Composite
Barrel: 24 in.
Sights: Adjustable rear, hooded front
Weight: 7 lb. 12 oz.
Caliber: .375 H&H
Magazine: 3+1 rounds
Features: Guaranteed SUB-MOA accuracy; hand-laminated, raised comb, Monte Carlo composite stock with full-length aluminum bedding plate, matte gel coat finish, and spiderweb accents; matte, bead blasted, blued finish; NECG adjustable rear sight and Williams Gun Sight Company hooded front sight
MSRP $1299.00

VANGUARD SPORTER
Action: Bolt
Stock: Walnut
Barrel: 24 in.
Sights: None
Weight: 7 lb. 4 oz.–7 lb. 8 oz.
Caliber: .223 Rem., .22-250 Rem., .240 Wby., .243 Win., .25-06 Rem., .270 Win., 7mm-08 Rem., .308 Win., .30-06 Spfd., .257 Wby. Mag., 7mm Rem. Mag., .300 Win. Mag., .300 Wby. Mag.
Magazine: 3+1, 5+1 rounds
Features: Two-stage trigger; raised comb, Monte Carlo stock with satin urethane finish; hand-selected A fancy grade Turkish walnut; rosewood forend; low luster, matte blued metalwork; fine line diamond point checkering; low density recoil pad
MSRP $849.00

VANGUARD SPORTER DBM
Action: Bolt
Stock: Walnut Monte Carlo
Barrel: 24 in.
Sights: None
Weight: 7 lb. 4 oz.
Caliber: .240 Wby.,.25-06 Rem., .270 Win., .30-06 Spfd.
Magazine: Detachable box, 3 rounds
Features: Rosewood forend; raised comb; satin urethane finish; matte blued metalwork; adjustable trigger
MSRP $849.00

Weatherby

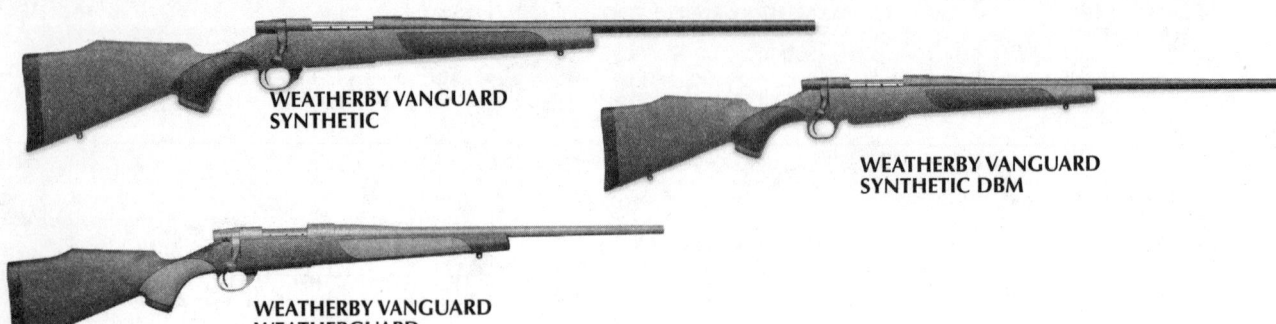

WEATHERBY VANGUARD SYNTHETIC

WEATHERBY VANGUARD SYNTHETIC DBM

WEATHERBY VANGUARD WEATHERGUARD

VANGUARD SYNTHETIC

Action: Bolt
Stock: Synthetic
Barrel: 24 in.
Sights: None
Weight: 7 lb. 4 oz.
Caliber: .25-06 Rem., .30-06 Spfd., .223 Rem.,.240 Wby. Mag., .243 Win., .257 Wby. Mag., .300 Wby. Mag., .300 Win. Mag., .308 Win., .338 Win. Mag., 7mm Rem. Mag., and 7mm-08 Rem., 6.5 Creedmoor, .22-250 Rem., .270 Win., .375 H&H
Magazine: Internal, 6+1 rounds
Features: Lightweight, composite Monte Carlo Griptonite stock; matte bead blasted blued finish; three-position safety.
MSRP . . . . **$649.00–$799.00**

VANGUARD SYNTHETIC DBM

Action: Bolt
Stock: Injection-molded Monte Carlo
Barrel: 24 in.
Sights: None
Weight: 7 lb. 4 oz.
Caliber: .240 Wby., .25-06 Rem., .270 Win., .30-06 Spfd.
Magazine: Detachable box, 3 rounds
Features: Matte bead blasted blued metalwork; low density recoil pad; two-stage trigger
MSRP **$649.00**

VANGUARD WEATHERGUARD

Action: Bolt
Stock: Monte Carlo Griptonite
Barrel: 24 in.

Sights: None
Weight: 7 lb. 12 oz.
Caliber: .25-06 Rem., .22-250 Rem., .30-06 Spfd., .223 Rem., .240 Wby Mag., .243 Win., .257 Wby Mag., .270 Win., .300 Win. Mag., .300 Wby Mag., .308 Win., 7mm Rem. Mag., 7mm-08 Rem.
Magazine: 3+1 or 5+1 rounds
Features: Guaranteed SUB-MOA accuracy; Monte Carlo Griptonite stock features pistol grip, forend inserts, and right-side palm swell (aids shooter's comfort and control); tactical grey Cerakote finish for exceptional weather and corrosion resistance; fluted bolt body; three-position safety; hinged floorplate; cold hammer-forged barrel; match quality two-stage trigger
MSRP **$749.00**

Webley & Scott

WEBLEY & SCOTT EMPIRE

WEBLEY & SCOTT RIMFIRE

WEBLEY & SCOTT EMPIRE

Action: Bolt
Stock: Walnut
Barrel: 22 in.
Sights: Optional scope
Weight: 7 lb. 13 oz.–9 lb.

Caliber: .243 Win., .270 Win., .308 Win., .30-06 Spfd., 7mm-08
Magazine: Detachable box, 5 rounds
Features: Cold hammer-forged barrel provides top accuracy; two-stage trigger; fully jeweled bolt and knurled handle; pillar-bedded, Italian walnut

wood stock with cheek weld; optional package includes Nikko Stirling Panamax 3–9x40mm scope and one-piece base and rings
MSRP . . . . $956.00–$1043.00

XOCET RIMFIRE RIFLE

Action: Bolt
Stock: Synthetic
Barrel: 19 in.
Sights: None
Weight: 7 lb. 9 oz.
Caliber: .17 HMR, .22 WMR, .22 LR
Magazine: Detachable box, 10 rounds
Features: Carbon/kevlar composite bull barrel or carbon-steel standard barrel; threaded barrel with knurled cap; skeletonized trigger; Picatinny rail; sling swivel studs
MSRP . . . . $365.00–$465.00

Wilson Combat

WILSON COMBAT .308 SUPER SNIPER

WILSON COMBAT RECON TACTICAL

WILSON COMBAT URBAN SUPER SNIPER

.308 SUPER SNIPER
Action: Semiautomatic
Stock: Synthetic, telescoping
Barrel: 20 in.
Sights: None
Weight: 10 lb. 11 oz.
Caliber: .308 Win.
Magazine: 10 rounds, 20 rounds
Features: Barrel is precision button rifled from 416-R stainless steel; 1:10 twist; Picatinny rail; BILLet-AR machined aluminum upper and lower receivers; 12 inch or 14 inch free-floating TRIM rail; available with a fluted or non-fluted barrel
MSRP . . . .$3095.00–$3145.00

RECON TACTICAL
Action: Semiautomatic
Stock: Synthetic tactical
Barrel: 16 in.
Sights: Optional rail
Weight: 7 lb.
Caliber: .308 Win., .338 Fed., 6.5 Creedmoor,.204 Ruger, 5.56 NATO, 6.8 SPC, .300 BLK, 7.62x40 WT, .458 SOCOM
Magazine: Detachable box, 30 rounds
Features: Match grade medium weight stainnless steel barrel; forged 7075 upper (flat top) and lower receiver; mid-length gas system with low-profile gas block; Wilson Combat T.R.I.M. rail; ergo pistol grip
MSRP . . . Starting at $2250.00–$3234.95

URBAN SUPER SNIPER
Action: Semiautomatic, mid-length gas system with low-profile gas block
Stock: Synthetic, telescoping
Barrel: 18 in.
Sights: None
Weight: 7 lb. 5 oz.
Caliber: 6.8 SPC
Magazine: 10, 20, or 30 rounds
Features: Medium heavy-weight, fluted, stainless steel premium match-grade barrel; 1:8 twist; Picatinny rail; 10.4 inch free-floating TRIM rail
MSRP $2225.00

Winchester Repeating Arms

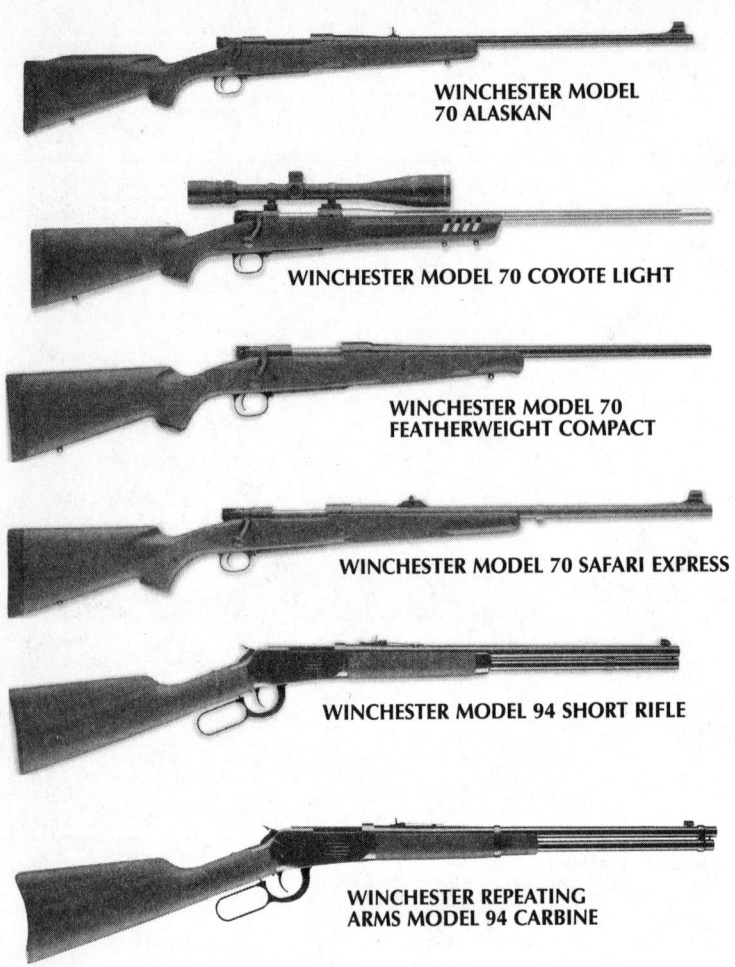

WINCHESTER MODEL
70 ALASKAN

WINCHESTER MODEL 70 COYOTE LIGHT

WINCHESTER MODEL 70
FEATHERWEIGHT COMPACT

WINCHESTER MODEL 70 SAFARI EXPRESS

WINCHESTER MODEL 94 SHORT RIFLE

WINCHESTER REPEATING
ARMS MODEL 94 CARBINE

MODEL 70 ALASKAN

Action: Bolt
Stock: Walnut
Barrel: 25 in.
Sights: Open
Weight: 8 lb. 8 oz.
Caliber: .30-06 Spfd., .300 Win. Mag. .338 Win. Mag., .375 HH Mag.
Magazine: None
Features: Satin finish Monte Carlo walnut stock with cut checkering; folding adjustable rear sight with hooded gold bead front sight; recessed target crown
MSRP . . . . **$1339.99–$1379.99**

MODEL 70 COYOTE LIGHT

Action: Bolt
Stock: Composite
Barrel: 24 in.
Sights: None
Weight: 7 lb. 8 oz.
Caliber: .22-250 Rem., .243 Win., .308 Win., .300 WSM, .270 WSM,

325 WSM
Magazine: 3 rounds
Features: Bipod mounting studs; matte-blued receiver and medium-heavy fluted stainless barrel mount; Pachmayr Decelerator
MSRP . . . . **$1999.99–$1239.99**

MODEL 70 FEATHERWEIGHT COMPACT

Action: Bolt
Stock: Walnut
Barrel: 20 in.
Sights: None
Weight: 6 lb. 8 oz.
Caliber: .22-250 Rem., .243 Win., 7mm-08 Rem., .308 Win.
Magazine: 5 rounds
Features: Pachmayr decelerator recoil pad; action is drilled and tapped for optics
MSRP **$939.99**

MODEL 70 SAFARI EXPRESS

Action: Bolt
Stock: Satin-finished checkered walnut with deluxe cheekpiece
Barrel: 24 in.
Sights: Hooded-blade front and express-style rear
Weight: 9 lb.
Caliber: .375 H&H Mag., .416 Rem. Mag., .458 Win. Mag.
Magazine: 3 rounds
Features: Pre-'64 type claw extractor; Pachmayr decelerator recoil pad; barrel band front swivel base; dual recoil lugs and three-position safety; MOA trigger system; matte blued finish; two steel cross-bolts and one-piece steel trigger guard and hinged floor plate
MSRP **$1499.99**

MODEL 94 CARBINE

Action: Lever
Stock: Walnut
Barrel: 20 in.
Sights: Adjustable semi-buckhorn rear, Marble Arms front
Weight: 6 lb. 8 oz.
Caliber: .25-35, .30-30 Win., .38-55 Win.
Magazine: Under-barrel tube
Features: Triple-checked button rifled barrel; round locking bolt trunnions; top-tang safety; rebounding hammer; bolt relief cut; steel loading gate; articulated cartridge stop; available knurled hammer spur extension
MSRP **$1199.99**

MODEL 94 SHORT RIFLE

Action: Lever
Stock: Walnut
Barrel: 20 in.
Sights: Front, adjustable rear
Weight: 6 lb. 12 oz.
Caliber: .30-30 Win., .450 Marlin, .25-35 Win., .38-55 Win.
Magazine: Under-barrel tube, 7 rounds
Features: Straight grip; rifle-style forearm and black grip cap; semi-buckhorn rear sights, Marble Arms gold-bead front sight; drilled and tapped for optics
MSRP **$1229.99**

Winchester Repeating Arms

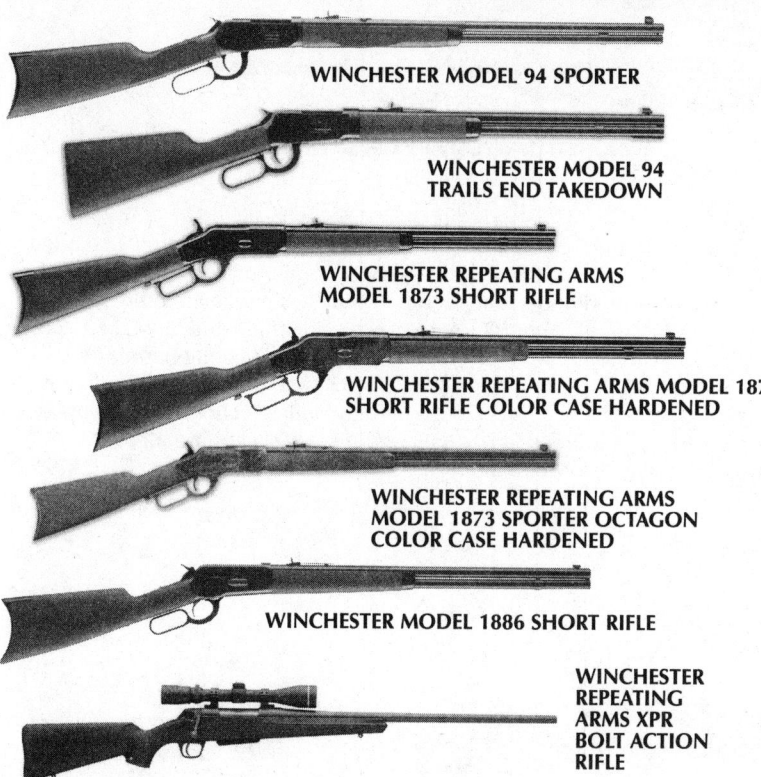

WINCHESTER MODEL 94 SPORTER

WINCHESTER MODEL 94 TRAILS END TAKEDOWN

WINCHESTER REPEATING ARMS MODEL 1873 SHORT RIFLE

WINCHESTER REPEATING ARMS MODEL 1873 SHORT RIFLE COLOR CASE HARDENED

WINCHESTER REPEATING ARMS MODEL 1873 SPORTER OCTAGON COLOR CASE HARDENED

WINCHESTER MODEL 1886 SHORT RIFLE

WINCHESTER REPEATING ARMS XPR BOLT ACTION RIFLE

MODEL 94 SPORTER

Action: Lever
Stock: Walnut
Barrel: 24 in.
Sights: Marble Arms front, adjustable rear
Weight: 7 lb. 8 oz.
Caliber: .25-35 Win., .30-30 Win., .38-55 Win.
Magazine: Under-barrel tube, 8 rounds
Features: Half-round, half-octagon blued barrel; straight grip stock with a crescent butt and finely checkered blued-steel buttplate with double-line bordering; drilled and tapped for optics
MSRP. $1399.99

MODEL 94 TRAILS END TAKEDOWN

Action: Lever
Stock: Walnut
Barrel: 20 in.
Sights: Adjustable
Weight: 6 lb. 12 oz.
Caliber: .30-30 Win., .38-55 Win., .450 Marlin
Magazine: Under-barrel tube, 6 rounds
Features: Walnut stock and forearm with satin finish and straight-grip styling; blued steel receiver and barrel; Marble Arms front sight with semi-buckhorn rear sight; Pachmayr Decelerator recoil pad (450 model)
MSRP. $1459.99

MODEL 1873 SHORT RIFLE

Action: Lever
Stock: Wood
Barrel: 20 in.
Sights: Adjustable
Weight: 7 lb. 4 oz.
Caliber: .357 Mag., .45 Colt, .44-40 Win.
Magazine: Under-barrel tube, 10 rounds
Features: Walnut straight grip stock with satin oil finish; classic rifle style forearm with blued steel cap; semi-buckhorn rear sight with Marble Arms gold bead front sights; steel loading gate; receiver rear tang drilled and tapped for optional tang-mounted rear sight
MSRP. $1299.99

MODEL 1873 SHORT RIFLE CASE HARDENED

Action: Lever
Stock: Wood
Barrel: 20 in.
Sights: Adjustable
Weight: 7 lb. 4 oz.
Caliber: .357 Mag., .38 Spl., .44-40 Win., .45 Colt
Magazine: 10–11 rounds
Features: Steel receiver, color case hardened; steel loading gate; rear tang is drilled and tapped for scope mount; steel barrel, polished blued finish; full-length magazine tube; grade II/III walnut stock; straight grip; classic rifle-style forearm; steel forend cap;

semi-buckhorn rear sight; Marble's gold bead front sight; color case hardened crescent buttplate, lever, forend cap, and loading gate
MSRP. $159.99

MODEL 1873 SPORTER OCTAGON COLOR CASE HARDENED

Action: Lever
Stock: Wood
Barrel: 24 in.
Sights: Adjustable
Weight: 7 lb. 8 oz.
Caliber: .357 Mag., .38 Spl., .44-40 Win.
Magazine: 13–14 rounds
Features: Steel reciver, color case hardened; steel loading gate; rear tang is drilled and tapped for scope mount; full octagon barrel, polished blued finish; full-length magazine tube; grade II/III walnut stock; straight grip; classic rifle-style forearm; steel fore-end cap; semi-buckhorn rear sight; Marble's gold bead front sight; color case hardened crescent buttplate, lever, fore-end cap, and loading gate; production limited to 250 units
MSRP. $1739.99

MODEL 1886 SHORT RIFLE

Action: Lever
Stock: Walnut
Barrel: 20 in., 24 in.
Sights: Front with brass bead, adjustable rear
Weight: 8 lb. 6 oz.
Caliber: .45-70 Govt.
Magazine: Under-barrel tube, 8 rounds
Features: Deeply blued receiver and lever; end cap and steel crescent buttplate; straight grip
MSRP. $1339.99

XPR

Action: Bolt
Stock: Composite polymer
Barrel: 24 in., 26 in.
Sights: None
Weight: 7 lb.
Caliber: .243 Win., 7mm-08, .308 Win., .270 WSM, .300 WSM, .325 WSM, .270 Win., .30-06 Spfd., 7mm Rem. Mag., .300 Win. Mag., .338 Win. Mag., 6.5 Creedmoor
Magazine: Detachable box, 3 rounds
Features: Chromoly steel barrel; matte blue finish; hardened steel components; recessed target-style crown; Inflex recoil pad
MSRP. . . . . $549.00–$549.99

Winchester Repeating Arms

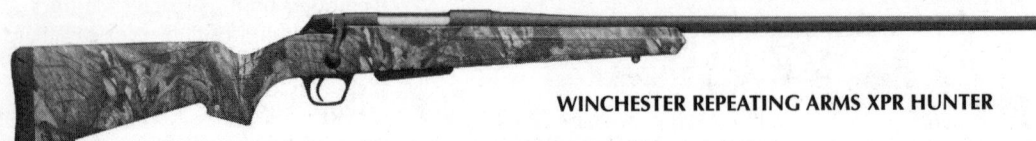

WINCHESTER REPEATING ARMS XPR HUNTER

XPR HUNTER, XPR HUNTER COMPACT

Action: Bolt
Stock: Composite
Barrel: 24 in.
Sights: None
Weight: 6 lb. 5.44 oz.
Caliber: .270 Win., 30-06 Spfd., .300 Win. Mag., .338 Win. Mag., .243

Win. 7mm-08 Rem., .308 Win., .270 WSM, .300 WSM, .325 WSM, 7mm Rem. Mag., 6.5 Creedmoor; Compact available in .243 Win., 7mm-08 Rem., .308 Win., .270 WSM, .300 WSM, .325 WSM
Magazine: 3 rounds
Features: Mossy Oak Break-Up Country or Mossy Oak Mountain

Range camo finish on full-size rifles, Mossy Oak Break-up only on Hunter Compact; steel, matte blued finish receiver; drilled and tapped for scope mounts; free-floating barrel; MOA trigger system; two- position thumb safety; Inflex technology recoil pad; swing swivel stud installed
MSRP **$599.99**

Windham Weaponry

WINDHAM WEAPONRY 300 BLACKOUT

WINDHAM WEAPONRY R20FFTM-308

300 BLACKOUT

Action: Semiautomatic gas impingment system
Stock: Synthetic, telescoping
Barrel: 16 in.
Sights: None
Weight: 7 lb.
Caliber: .300 BLK, 7.62x35
Magazine: Detachable box, 30+1 rounds
Features: Hogue six-position telescoping buttstock; 1:7 inch twist; Diamondhead VRS-T 13.5 inch free-float forend; two quick detachable

sling swivels included; Hogue beavertail pistol grip; hardcoat black anodize receiver finish; Picatinny rail; chrome-lined barrel with Diamondhead T brake
MSRP **$1680.00**

R20FFTM-308

Action: Semiautomatic
Stock: Synthetic
Barrel: 20 in.
Sights: None
Weight: 9 lb. 0.8 oz.
Caliber: .308 Win.

Magazine: 5+1 rounds
Features: Magpul fixed length buttstock with multiple sling attachments; comfortable rubber recoil pad under which is a handy storage compartment; multiple attachment options for M-Lok accessory rails; internal heat shielding; Hogue overmolded rubber pistol grip; Mil Std 1913 Picatinny rails on both receiver and gas block
MSRP **$1667.50**

Windham Weaponry

**WINDHAM WEAPONRY
RMCS-2 (MULTI-CALIBER
SYSTEM) RIFLE KIT**

**WINDHAM WEAPONRY
RMCS-3 (MULTI-CALIBER
SYSTEM) RIFLE KIT**

RMCS-2 (MULTI-CALIBER SYSTEM) RIFLE KIT

Action: Semiautomatic
Stock: Synthetic
Barrel: 16 in.
Sights: None
Weight: N/A
Caliber: .223 Rem./5.56 NATO–300 BLK
Magazine: 30 rounds
Features: Two calibers in the same AR platform by simply switching out the barrel; chrome-lined barrels; Mil Std

1913 railed gas block; receivers are CNC machined from forged 7075 T6 aircraft aluminum and finished in hardcoat black anodize; twist rates differ depending on barrel
MSRP **$1738.00**

RMCS-3 (MULTI-CALIBER SYSTEM) RIFLE KIT

Action: Semiautomatic
Stock: Synthetic
Barrel: 16 in.
Sights: None

Weight: N/A
Caliber: .223 Rem./5.56 NATO–300 BLK–7.62x36mm
Magazine: Standard 30 rd. for .223 Rem./5.56 NATO; standard Magpul for 7.62x39mm; standard Colt type Mag for 9mm
Features: Two calibers in the same AR platform by simply switching out the barrels and magazine wells; chrome-lined barrels; Mil Std 1913 railed gas block; receivers are CNC machined from forged 7075 T6 aircraft aluminum and finished in hardcoat black anodize; twist rates differ depending on barrel
MSRP **$2391.00**

Windham Weaponry

**WINDHAM WEAPONRY
RMCS-4 (MULTI-CALIBER
SYSTEM) RIFLE KIT**

RMCS-4 (MULTI-CALIBER SYSTEM) RIFLE KIT

Action: Semiautomatic
Stock: Synthetic
Barrel: 16 in.
Sights: None
Weight: N/A

Caliber: .223 Rem./5.56 NATO–300 BLK–7.62x36mm–9mm
Magazine: Standard 30 rd. for .223 Rem./5.56 NATO; standard Magpul for 7.62x39mm; standard Colt type Mag for 9mm
Features: Two calibers in the same AR platform by simply switching out the barrels and magazine wells; chrome-lined barrels; Mil Std 1913 railed gas block; receivers are CNC machined from forged 7075 T6 aircraft aluminum and finished in hardcoat black anodize; twist rates differ depending on barrel
MSRP **$2971.00**

AirForce Airguns

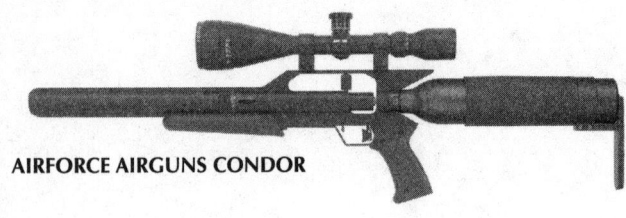

AIRFORCE AIRGUNS CONDOR

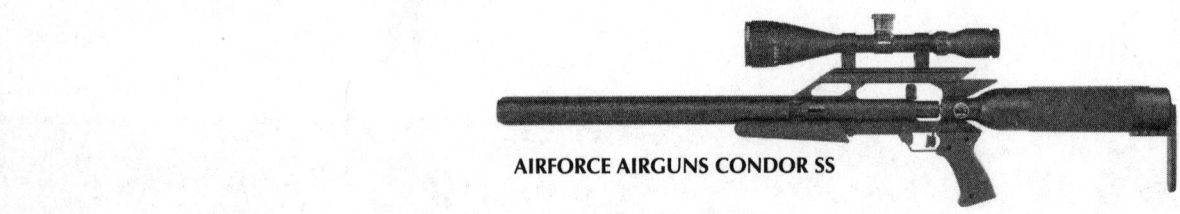

AIRFORCE AIRGUNS CONDOR SS

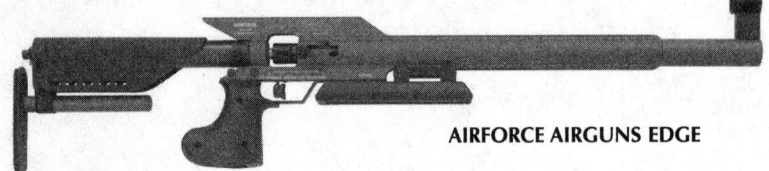

AIRFORCE AIRGUNS EDGE

AIRFORCE AIRGUNS ESCAPE

CONDOR

Power: Pre-charged pneumatic, user adjustable
Stock: Composite
Overall Length: 38.7 in.
Sights: None
Weight: 6 lb. 8 oz.
Caliber: .25, .22, .20, .177
Features: Black, red, or blue composite stock; integral extended scope rail; detachable air tank; Lothar Walther barrel; pressure relief device; adjustable power; scopes optional
Spin-Loc: **$744.95**

CONDOR SS

Power: Compressed air
Stock: Composite
Overall Length: 38.125 in.
Sights: Open or optical may be installed
Weight: 6 lb. 2 oz.
Caliber: .177, .20, .22, .25
Features: CondorSS combines the major attributes of the TalonSS's quiet operation and the Condor's high power levels; new sound reduction technology; 18-inch barrel blue, red, or original black; 600–1300 fps; two-stage trigger; single shot
MSRP **$774.95**

EDGE

Power: Pre-charged pneumatic
Stock: Composite
Overall Length: 35–40 in.
Sights: TS1 peep sight system
Weight: 6 lb. 2 oz.
Caliber: .177
Features: Ambidextrous cocking knob; regulated air system; adjustable length of pull; adjustable forend; hooded front sight only or front and rear sight available; two-stage adjustable trigger; composite stock in red or blue finish; scopes optional
Front sight: **$556.95**
Rear & front sights: **$694.95**

ESCAPE

Power: Compressed air
Stock: Synthetic
Overall Length: 34.5 in.–39 in.
Sights: Open or optical
Weight: 5 lb. 4.8 oz
Caliber: .22, .25
Features: Lothar Walther Barrels; Quick-Detach or Spin-Loc air tanks; lightweight and compact; geared for survival situations; user adjustable length
MSRP **$694.95**

AIRGUNS

AirForce Airguns

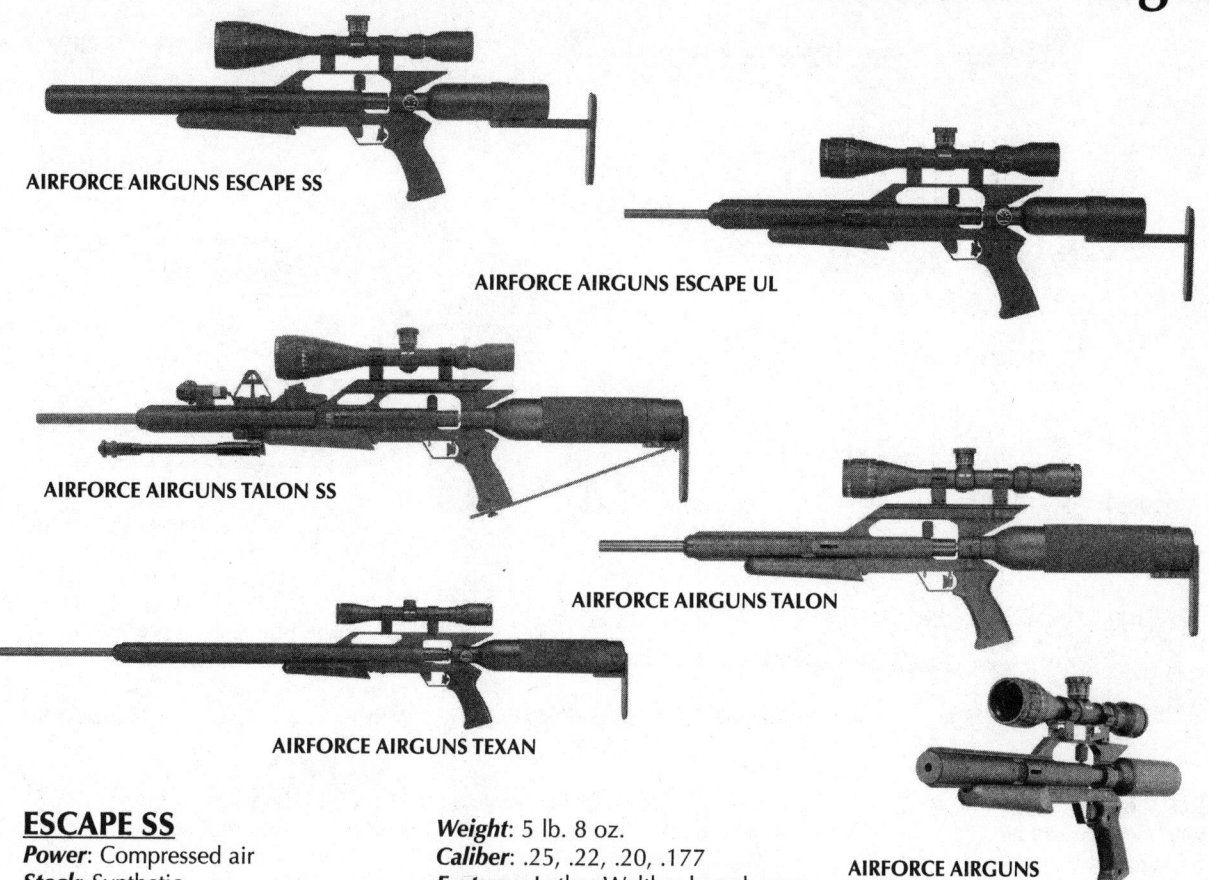

AIRFORCE AIRGUNS ESCAPE SS

AIRFORCE AIRGUNS ESCAPE UL

AIRFORCE AIRGUNS TALON SS

AIRFORCE AIRGUNS TALON

AIRFORCE AIRGUNS TEXAN

AIRFORCE AIRGUNS TALON P

ESCAPE SS
Power: Compressed air
Stock: Synthetic
Overall Length: 27.75 in.–32.25 in.
Sights: Open or optical
Weight: 4 lb. 4.8 oz
Caliber: .22, .25
Features: Lothar Walther Barrels;
Quick-Detach or Spin-Loc air tanks;
lightweight and compact; geared for
survival situations; user adjustable
length; Sound-Loc sound reduction
technology installed
MSRP **$684.95**

ESCAPE UL
Power: Compressed air
Stock: Synthetic
Overall Length: 28.5 in.–33 in.
Sights: Open or optical
Weight: 4 lb. 4 oz
Caliber: .22, .25
Features: Lothar Walther Barrels;
Quick-Detach or Spin-Loc air tanks;
lightweight and compact; geared for
survival situations; user adjustable
length
MSRP **$642.95**

TALON
Power: Compressed air
Stock: Composite
Overall Length: 32.6 in.
Sights: None

Weight: 5 lb. 8 oz.
Caliber: .25, .22, .20, .177
Features: Lothar Walther barrel; pressure relief device; adjustable power;
detachable air tank; black composite
stock; scopes optional
MSRP **$609.95**

TALON P
Power: Compressed air
Stock: Composite
Overall Length: 24 in.
Sights: None
Weight: 3 lb. 8 oz.
Caliber: .25
Features: Designed to deliver over 50
ft.-lbs. of energy with a .25-caliber
hunting pellet; integral extended
scope rail; Lothar Walther barrels;
scopes optional
MSRP **$479.95**

TALON SS
Power: Compressed air
Stock: Composite
Overall Length: 32.7 in.
Sights: None
Weight: 5 lb. 4 oz.
Caliber: .25, .22, .20, .177
Features: Improved sound reduction;
Lothar Walther barrel; pressure relief
device; adjustable power; detachable
air tank; black, red, or blue composite
stock; multiple mounting rails; two-

stage trigger; innovative muzzle cap
that strips away air turbulence and
reduces discharge sound levels;
scopes optional
MSRP **$652.95**

TEXAN
Power: Compressed air
Stock: Synthetic
Overall Length: 48 in.
Sights: Open or optical
Weight: 8 lb.
Caliber: .308, .357, .45
Features: With the ability to launch
.45 caliber projectiles at over 1000
feet per second and generating energy
levels of over 500 foot pounds, the
Texan takes its place as the world's
most powerful production air rifle.
Easy to load and simple to use, this
Big Bore air rifle will let you focus on
hunting with the knowledge you have
enough power to get the job done.
MSRP **$1054.95**

Anschütz (J.G. Anschütz)

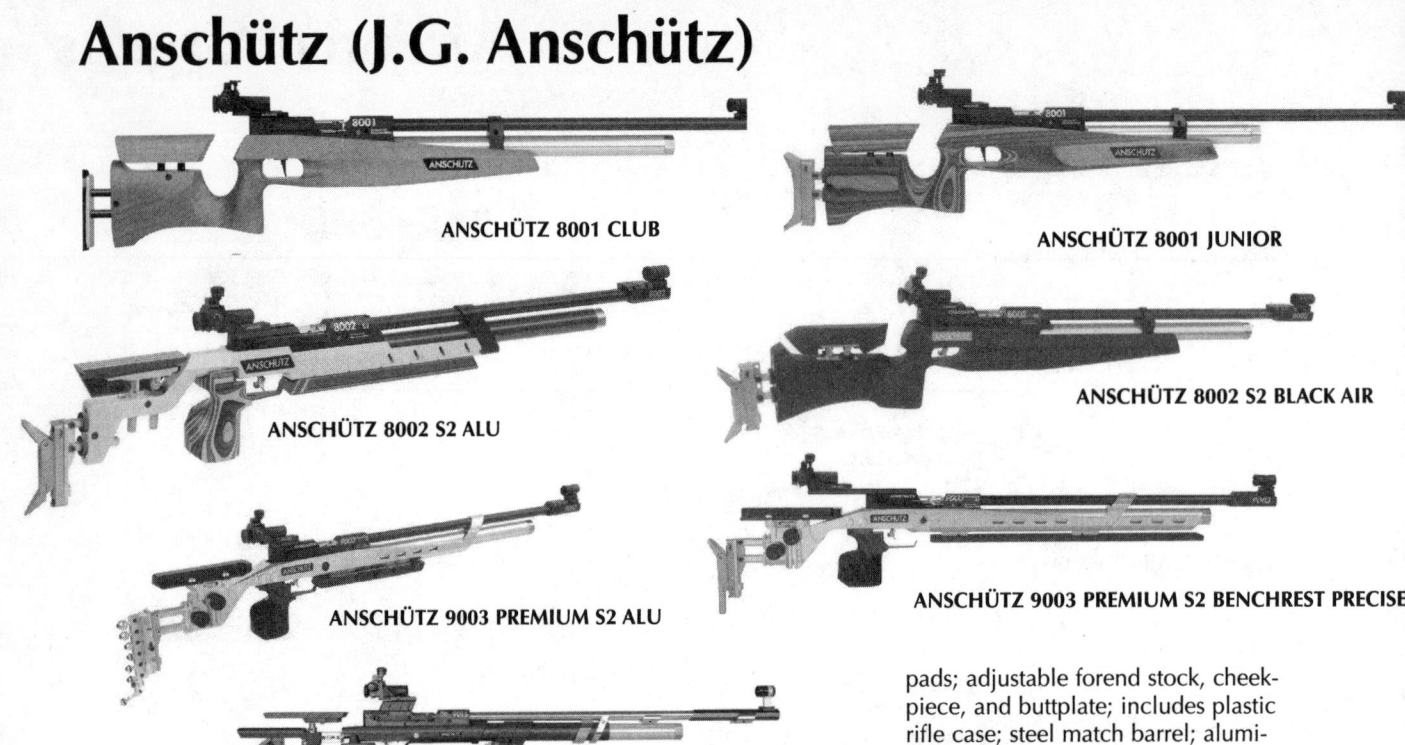

ANSCHÜTZ 8001 CLUB

ANSCHÜTZ 8001 JUNIOR

ANSCHÜTZ 8002 S2 ALU

ANSCHÜTZ 8002 S2 BLACK AIR

ANSCHÜTZ 9003 PREMIUM S2 ALU

ANSCHÜTZ 9003 PREMIUM S2 BENCHREST PRECISE

J. G. ANSCHÜTZ 9015 ONE

8001 CLUB
Power: Compressed air
Stock: Walnut
Overall Length: 42.1 in.
Sights: Open, includes sight set 6834
Weight: 8 lb. 6 oz.
Caliber: .177
Features: Walnut stock with stippled checkering and non-stained aluminum or rubber buttplate; adjustable trigger; match grade barrel
MSRP **$2000.00**

8001 JUNIOR
Power: Compressed air
Stock: Laminate
Overall Length: 37.4 in.
Sights: Open, includes sight set 6834
Weight: 8 lb. 2 oz.
Caliber: .177
Features: Laminated wood in blue and orange with aluminum buttplate stock; cylindrical match grade barrel; comes with accessory box
MSRP **$1859.00**

8002 S2 ALU
Power: Compressed air
Stock: Aluminum and synthetic pistol grip or laminated wood pistol grip
Overall Length: 42.1 in.
Sights: Open, includes sight set 6834
Weight: 10 lb. 2 oz.
Caliber: .177

Features: Aluminum stock in silver and blue with laminated wood or synthetic pistol grip; blue air cylinder; ProGrip cheekpiece and forend; includes accessory box; aluminum accessory rail
Aluminum: **$2564.00**
Wood: **$2244.00**

8002 S2 BLACK AIR
Power: Compressed air
Stock: Plastic
Length: 43.3 in.
Sights: Rear, turnable front
Weight: 9 lb. 8 oz.
Caliber: .177
Features: IWA special edition equipped with new Anschütz SOFT-Grip stock, combining the vibration damping and recoil absorbing characteristics of a naturally grown wooden stock with the characteristics of an easy-care and weather-proof plastic stock; match barrel; aluminum buttplate; cheekpiece; two-stage trigger
MSRP **$2350.00**

9003 PREMIUM S2 PRECISE
Power: Compressed air
Stock: Aluminum
Overall Length: 43.7 in.
Sights: Open, includes sight set 6834
Weight: 9 lb. 15 oz.
Caliber: .177
Features: Silver/black aluminum stock pistol grip; Soft Link shock absorber

pads; adjustable forend stock, cheekpiece, and buttplate; includes plastic rifle case; steel match barrel; aluminum accessory rail on stock
MSRP **$3895.95**

9003 PREMIUM S2 BENCHREST PRECISE
Power: Compressed air
Stock: Aluminum
Length: 39.96 in.
Sights: Open, includes sight set 6834
Weight: 11 lb. 11 oz.
Caliber: .177
Features: Aluminum stock with wedgeshaped design; pistol grip; Soft Link shock absorber pads; adjustable forend stock, cheekpiece and buttplate; includes plastic rifle case; valve and valve body coated with gold; steel match barrel; aluminum accessory rail on stock
MSRP **$4040.00**

9015 ONE
Power: Barreled action
Stock: Aluminum; stainless steel; carbon
Overall Length: 39 in.–47.2 in.
Sights: Adjustable
Weight: 10.1 lb.
Caliber: .177
Features: New patented 5065 4K trigger with ball bearings and versatile adjustable trigger blade; a stainless steel barrel unit; thin, special coated barrel extension; maintenance free stabilizer; air filter against pollutions; cocking lever mountable left and right; adjustable cheekpiece; scalloped grip
MSRP **$3449.95**

AIRGUNS

Beeman Precision Airguns

BEEMAN PRECISION AIRGUNS BEAR CLAW

BEEMAN PRECISION AIRGUNS ELKHORN

BEEMAN PRECISION AIRGUNS GRIZZLY X2 DUAL CALIBER

BEEMAN PRECISION AIRGUNS MACH 12.5

BEEMAN PRECISION AIRGUNS PREDATOR

AIRGUNS

BEAR CLAW
Power: Spring piston
Stock: Wood
Overall Length: 45.5 in.
Sights: Scope
Weight: 8 lb. 8 oz.
Caliber: .177, .22
Features: 3–9x32 scope included; break barrel action; available as dual caliber version
MSRP . . . . **$199.99–$259.99**

ELKHORN
Power: Spring piston
Stock: Wood
Overall Length: 46.5 in.
Sights: Scope
Weight: 9 lb.–10 lb
Caliber: .177, .22

Features: 3–9x32 scope included; break barrel action; fluted barrel
MSRP **$249.99**

GRIZZLY X2 DUAL CALIBER
Power: Spring piston
Stock: Wood
Overall Length: 45.5 in.
Sights: Fixed and scope
Weight: 8 lb. 8 oz.
Caliber: .177, .22
Features: 4x32 scope and fiber optics sights; break barrel action; inter-changeable barrels; available with case
MSRP . . . . **$179.99–$199.99**

MACH 12.5
Power: Spring piston
Stock: Wood
Overall Length: 46.5 in.
Sights: Scope
Weight: 10 lb.
Caliber: .177, .22
Features: 3–9x40 scope included; break barrel action; muzzle break
MSRP **$299.99**

PREDATOR
Power: Spring piston
Stock: Synthetic
Overall Length: 45.5 in.
Sights: Fixed and scope
Weight: 8 lb. 8 oz.
Caliber: .177, .22
Features: 3–9x32 scope and fiber optic sights; break barrel action
MSRP . . . . **$199.99–$219.99**

Beeman Precision Airguns

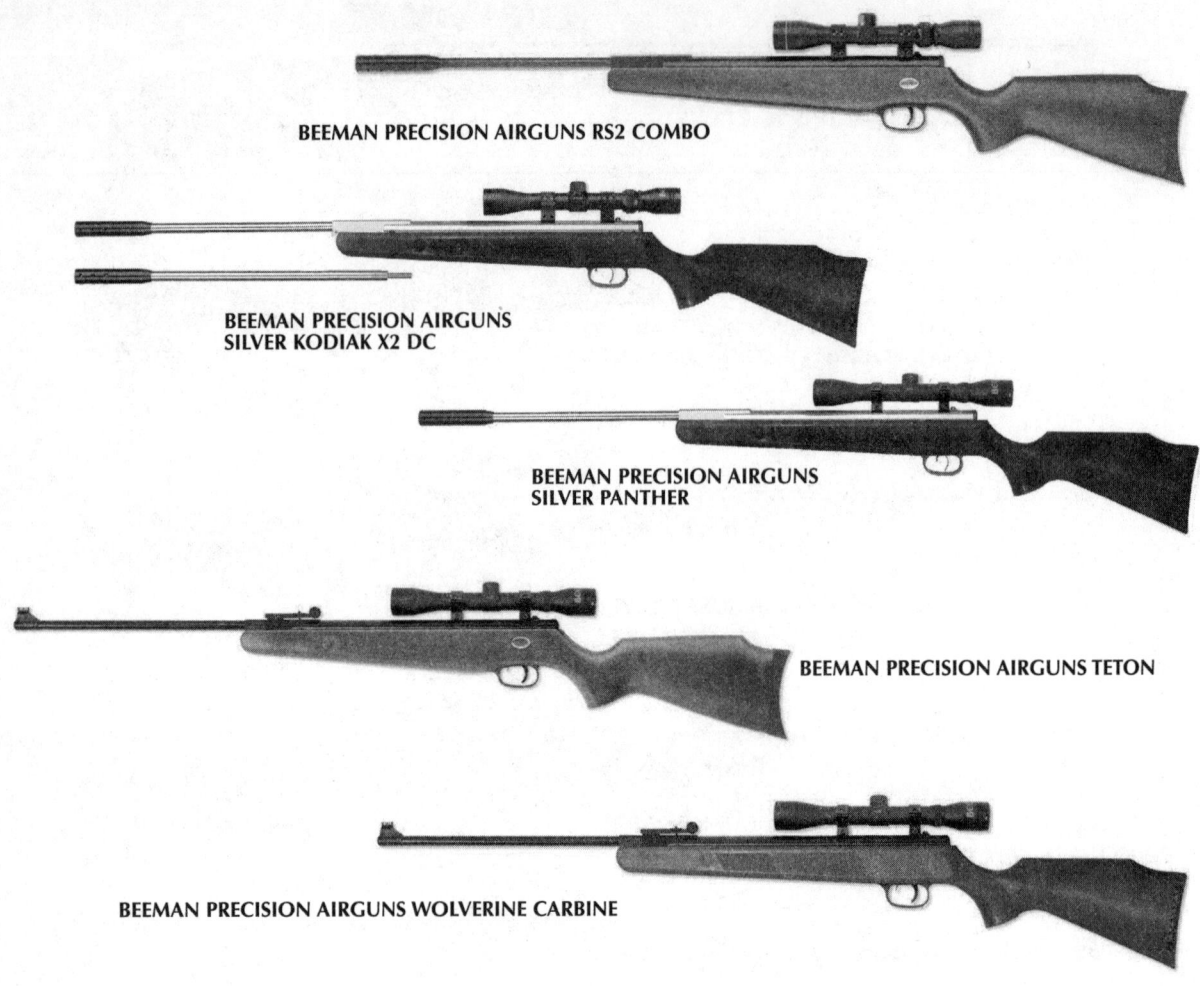

BEEMAN PRECISION AIRGUNS RS2 COMBO

BEEMAN PRECISION AIRGUNS
SILVER KODIAK X2 DC

BEEMAN PRECISION AIRGUNS
SILVER PANTHER

BEEMAN PRECISION AIRGUNS TETON

BEEMAN PRECISION AIRGUNS WOLVERINE CARBINE

RS2 COMBO
Power: Spring piston
Stock: Wood
Overall Length: 46.5 in.
Sights: Scope
Weight: 10 lb.
Caliber: .177, .22
Features: 3–9x32 scope inlcuded;
break barrel action; rifled barrel
MSRP $199.99

SILVER KODIAK X2 DC
Power: Break action, spring piston
Stock: All-weather synthetic
Overall Length: 47.5 in.
Sights: 3–9x32 or 4x32 scope
Weight: 8 lb. 12 oz.
Caliber: .177, .22
Features: Two airguns in one; satin
nickel plated barrel and receiver;
ported muzzle brake; 1000 fps max
velocity
MSRP . . . . $168.00–$219.99

SILVER PANTHER
Power: Break action, spring piston
Stock: All-weather synthetic
Overall Length: 47.5 in.
Sights: 4x32 scope
Weight: 8 lb. 12 oz.
Caliber: .177, .22
Features: Satin nickel plated barrel
and receiver; ported muzzle brake;
1000 fps max velocity
MSRP . . . . $149.99–$188.92

TETON
Power: Spring piston
Stock: Wood
Overall Length: 44.5 in.
Sights: Fixed and scope
Weight: 9 lb.
Caliber: .177, .22

Features: 4x32 scope and fiber optic
sights; break barrel action; rifled barrel
MSRP $149.99

WOLVERINE CARBINE
Power: Spring piston
Stock: Synthetic
Overall Length: 45.5 in.
Sights: Fixed and scope
Weight: 8 lb. 8 oz.
Caliber: .177, .22
Features: 4x32 scope and fiber optic
sights; break barrel action; rifled
barrel; rubber recoil pad
MSRP $149.99

CROSMAN BENJAMIN ARMADA

CROSMAN BENJAMIN ARMADA MAGPUL EDITION

CROSMAN BENJAMIN BULLDOG .357 TROPHY GAME HUNTING AIR RIFLE

CROSMAN BENJAMIN DISCOVERY

CROSMAN BENJAMIN TITAN NP

BENJAMIN ARMADA

Power:Multi-shot pneumatic, bolt
Stock: Synthetic
Overall Length: 42 in.
Sights: None
Weight: 7 lb. 5 oz.
Caliber: .177, .22, .25
Features: Modular, versatile design; backwards compatible with Mil-Spec AR-15 grips and stocks; machined receiver featuring 5 inches of Picatinny rail space; delivers over 30 consistent shots per fill (up to 16 in .25 cal); bolt action is reversible; integrated resonance dampener; 10-round magazine delivers fast follow up shots (8-rd magazine in .25 cal); rifled barrel, choked and shrouded; optics and bipod not included
MSRP $649.99

BENJAMIN ARMADA MAGPUL EDITION

Power: Multi-shot pneumatic, bolt
Stock: Synthetic
Overall Length: 42 in.
Sights: 4–16x56mm scope included
Weight: 8 lb. 3 oz.
Caliber: 0.22
Features: The Magpul Edition includes an M-LOK licensed aluminum hand-rail with picatinny rails and Magpul MOE grip; Magpul MOE 6-position stock with cheek riser; CenterPoint 4-16x56mm scope with co-witness rings and sunshade; bipod adjustable from 6 in. to 9 in.
MSRP $999.99

BENJAMIN BULLDOG .357

Power:Multi-shot pneumatic, bolt
Stock: Synthetic
Overall Length: 36 in.
Sights: None
Weight: 7 lb. 11 oz.
Caliber: .357
Features: Bullpup configuration; 26 inches of picatinny rail; Baffle-less SoundTrap shroud for big bore sound suppression; sidelever bolt reversible for left hand shooters; intuitive, easy to load 5-shot magazine; reversible bolt; 10 shots per fill; now available in Realtree Xtra camo, Sportsman's Pack, and Big Game Hunter's Pack

Black:	$849.99
Realtree Xtra:	$899.99
Sportsman's Pack:	$1099.99
Big Game Hunter's Pack:	$1199.99

BENJAMIN DISCOVERY

Power: Dual fuel compressed air
Stock: Walnut
Overall Length: 39 in.
Sights: Fiber optic front, adjustable rear
Weight: 5 lb. 2 oz.–5 lb. 3 oz.
Caliber: .22, .177
Features: Rifled steel barrel; velocity up to 900 fps; cross-bolt safety; built-in pressure gauge; high pressure pump included
MSRP . . . . $269.95–$279.95

BENJAMIN TITAN NP

Power: Nitro piston
Stock: Hardwood
Length: 43 in., 44.5 in.
Sights: 4x32mm scope included
Weight: 6 lb. 10 oz.–6 lb. 14 oz.
Caliber: .177, .22
Features: Powered by Nitro Piston technology; delivers velocities up to 1200 fps (.177) with alloy pellets; included 4x32mm scope; ambidextrous hardwood stock with thumbhole; two-stage adjustable trigger; ventilated rubber recoil pad
MSRP . . . . $139.99–$159.99

AIRGUNS

Crosman

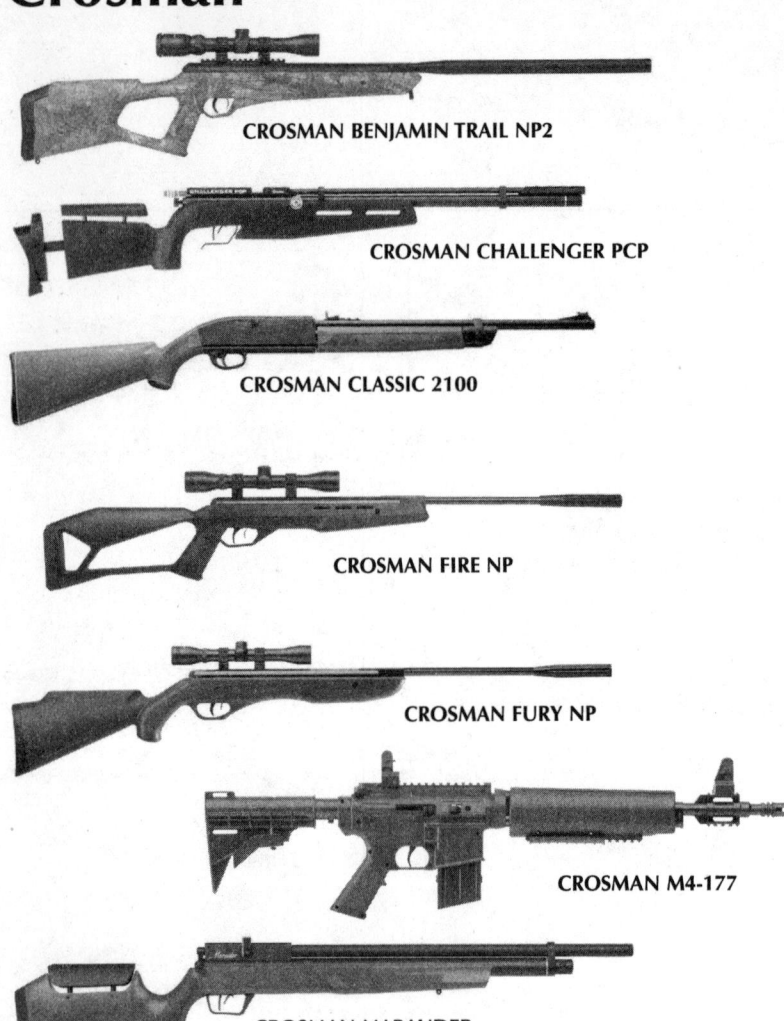

CROSMAN BENJAMIN TRAIL NP2

CROSMAN CHALLENGER PCP

CROSMAN CLASSIC 2100

CROSMAN FIRE NP

CROSMAN FURY NP

CROSMAN M4-177

CROSMAN MARAUDER

BENJAMIN TRAIL NP2

Power: NP2 nitro piston
Stock: Synthetic or wood
Overall Length: 46.25 in.
Sights: CenterPoint 3–9x32mm scope
Weight: 8 lb. 5 oz.
Caliber: .177, .22
Features: Break barrel; first to feature new NP2 power system; enhanced Clean Break Trigger; integrated sound suppression system; shoots up to 1200 fps alloy, 900 fps pellet; .22 available in hardwood, synthetic, and Realtree Xtra; now available with SBD, Crosman's Silencing Barrel Device
Hardwood: . . . . . . $289.99–$339.99
Realtree: . . . . $279.99–$339.99
Synthetic: . . . . $249.99–$299.99

CHALLENGER PCP

Power: Pneumatic pump and CO2
Stock: Synthetic
Overall Length: 41.5 in.

Sights: Open
Weight: 7 lb. 2 oz.
Caliber: .177
Features: Two-stage match grade adjustable trigger; Lothar Walther barrel; adjustable cheekpiece and buttpiece; black synthetic stock; 11mm scope mount rails; ambidextrous
Without sights: $529.99
Sights: $629.99

CLASSIC 2100

Power: Pneumatic pump
Stock: Synthetic
Overall Length: 39.75 in.
Sights: Visible impact front, adjustable rear
Weight: 4 lb. 13 oz.
Caliber: .177
Features: Cross-bolt safety; BB up to 755 fps, pellet up to 725 fps
MSRP $69.99

FIRE NP

Power: Nitro piston
Stock: Synthetic
Overall Length: 43.5 in.
Sights: None
Weight: 6 lb.
Caliber: .177
Features: Rifled steel barrel; two-stage, adjustable trigger; CenterPoint 4x32mm scope
MSRP $149.99

FURY NP

Power: Break action Nitro Piston
Stock: Synthetic all-weather
Overall Length: 45 in.
Sights: 4x32mm scope
Weight: 6 lb. 6 oz.
Caliber: .177
Features: Velocities up to 1200 fps; rifled steel barrel; adjustable two-stage trigger; Nitro Piston technology delivers smooth cocking, reduced vibration and shoots with 70 percent less noise
MSRP $139.99

M4-177 RIFLE

Power: Multi-pump pneumatic
Stock: Synthetic
Length: 34 in.
Sights: Adjustable front and rear
Weight: 3 lb. 9 oz.
Caliber: .177
Features: Rifled steel barrel; shoots both pellets and BBs; variable pump action easy to use for right- or left-handed shooters; Picatinny rails; front and rear sights and stock are removable for upgrades; adjustable stock; velocities up to 660 fps with BBs and 625 fps with 7.9gr, .177 caliber pellets
MSRP $79.99

MARAUDER

Power: Compressed air
Stock: Wood
Overall Length: 42.8 in.
Sights: None
Weight: 8 lb. 3 oz.
Caliber: .177, .22, .25
Features: Bolt action; ten round magazine; reversable bolt; dovetail mounting rail; available in wood, black synthetic, and Realtree Max1, Realtree Xtra, and Muddy Girl camo stocks
MSRP . . . . $539.99–$579.99

Crosman

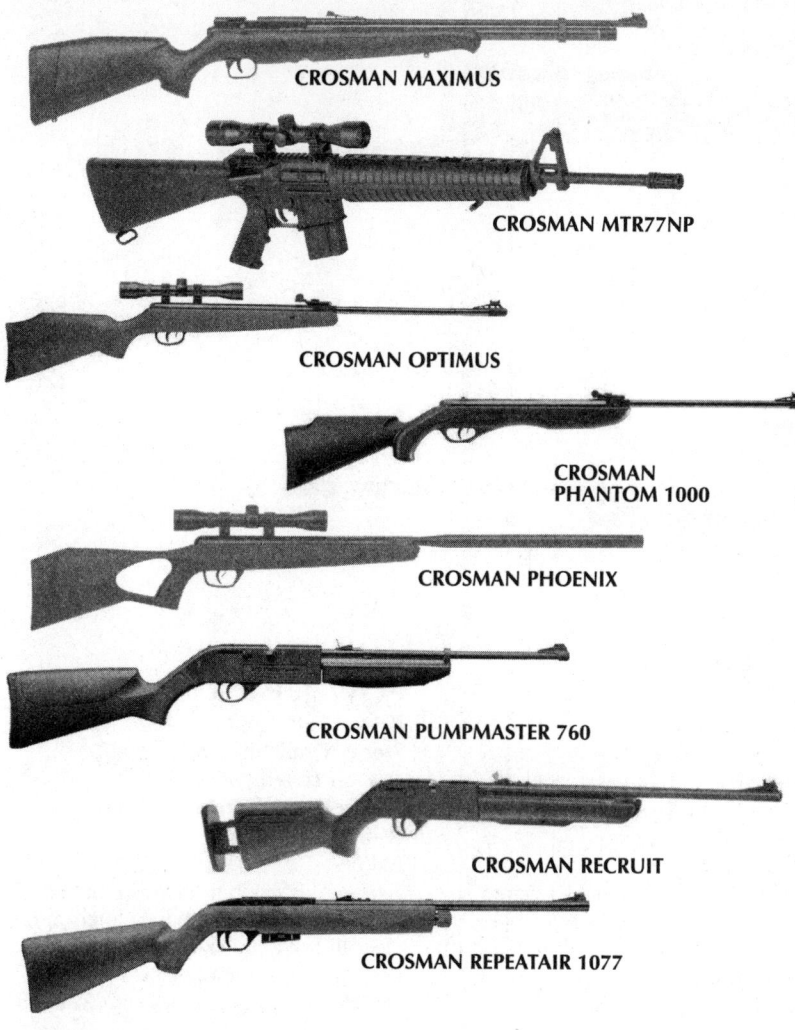

CROSMAN MAXIMUS

CROSMAN MTR77NP

CROSMAN OPTIMUS

CROSMAN PHANTOM 1000

CROSMAN PHOENIX

CROSMAN PUMPMASTER 760

CROSMAN RECRUIT

CROSMAN REPEATAIR 1077

MAXIMUS
Power: Bolt
Stock: Synthetic
Overall Length: N/A
Sights: Fiber optic front and rear
Weight: N/A
Caliber: .22, .177
Features: Easy filling 2000 PSI reservoir; rifled barrel; up to 30 effective shots per fill
MSRP $219.99

MTR77NP
Power: Break action Nitro Piston
Stock: Synthetic all-weather
Overall Length: 40 in.
Sights: 4x32mm scope
Weight: 6 lb. 2 oz.
Caliber: .177
Features: Nitro Piston technology delivers smooth cocking, reduced vibration and shoots with 70 percent less noise; sling mounts; storage in false magazine; up to 1200 fps; carry handle and carry handle/scope combo also available
MSRP . . . . $199.95–$245.99

OPTIMUS
Power: Break action
Stock: Hardwood
Overall Length: 43 in.
Sights: 4x32mm CenterPoint scope
Weight: 6 lb. 8 oz.
Caliber: .177, .22
Features: Ambidextrous hardwood stock; relatively light cocking force and a two-stage adjustable trigger; velocities of up to 1200 fps with alloy pellets; barrel incorporates a micro-adjustable rear sight and fiber optic front sight; .177 also available without scope
MSRP . . . . $109.99–$139.99

PHANTOM 1000
Power: Spring piston
Stock: Synthetic
Overall Length: 44.5 in.
Sights: Fiber optic front, adjustable rear
Weight: 6 lb.
Caliber: .177, .22
Features: All-weather, synthetic black stock and forearm; checkered grip and forearm; velocity up to 1000 fps; rifled steel barrel; two-stage adjustable trigger; scoped package available on .177-caliber
MSRP . . . . $89.99–$149.99

PHOENIX
Power: NP2 nitro piston
Stock: Synthetic
Overall Length: 45.8 in.
Sights: CenterPoint 4x32mm scope
Weight: 8 lb.
Caliber: .22, .177
Features: Velocities up to 1400 fps; enhanced two-stage Clean Break Trigger; precision rifled steel barrel; integrated sound suppression system; dovetail rail
MSRP $199.99

PUMPMASTER
Power: Pneumatic pump
Stock: Synthetic
Overall Length: 33.5 in.
Sights: Fiber optic front, adjustable rear
Weight: 2 lb. 12 oz.
Caliber: .177/BB
Features: Cross-bolt safety; BB up to 625 fps; pellet up to 600 fps
MSRP $44.99

RECRUIT
Power: Pneumatic pump
Stock: Synthetic
Overall Length: 38.25 in.
Sights: Scope
Weight: 2 lb. 15 oz.
Caliber: .177
Features: Adjustable buttstock; adjustable synthetic stock; 11mm dovetail scope rail; cross-bolt safety
MSRP $79.99

REPEATAIR 1077
Power: CO2
Stock: All-weather, synthetic, wood
Overall Length: 36.88 in.
Sight: Fiber optic front, adjustable rear
Weight: 3 lb. 11 oz.
Caliber: .177
Features: Exclusive 12-shot rotary pellet clip lets you shoot longer; maximum velocity 625 fps; cross-bolt safety
Synthetic: $69.96
Wood: $114.95

Crosman

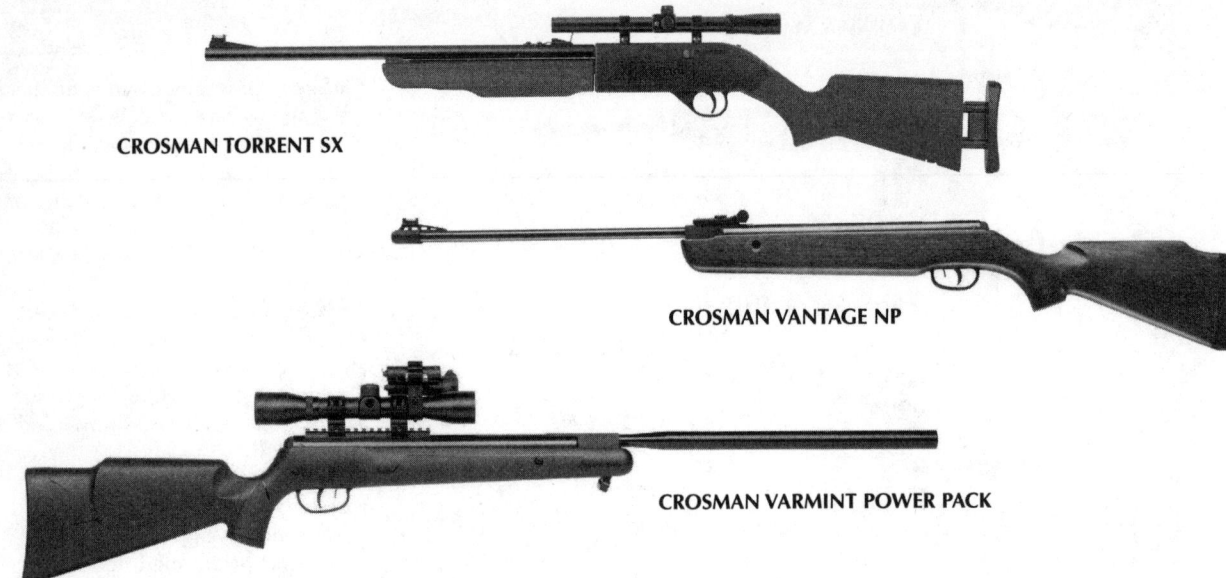

CROSMAN TORRENT SX

CROSMAN VANTAGE NP

CROSMAN VARMINT POWER PACK

TORRENT SX
Power: Variable pump
Stock: Synthetic
Overall Length: 36.75 in.
Sights: Fiber optic front, adjustable rear
Weight: 2 lb. 15 oz.
Caliber: .177
Features: Lightweight, variable pump BB/pellet rifle; adjustable stock; customized length of pull; up to 695 fps; five-shot clip; olive-drab stock and forearm
MSRP **$49.95**

VANTAGE NP
Power: Break action
Stock: Hardwood
Length: 45 in.
Sights: Fiber optic front, adjustable rear 4x32mm scope included
Weight: 7 lb. 2 oz.
Caliber: .177
Features: Crosman's own version of the Bantage NP; hardwood stock; fiber optic front sight and fully adjustable rear sight
MSRP **$160.00**

VARMINT POWER PACK
Power: Nitro piston
Stock: Synthetic
Overall Length: 44.5 in.
Sights: CenterPoint 4x32mm scope
Weight: 7 lb. 6 oz.
Caliber: .22
Features: Break barrel; 90 lumen LED flashlight with a red flip-up filter; red, class III fast acquisition laser with push on/off or remote tape switch
MSRP **$249.99**

Daisy

DAISY AVANTI MODEL 887 GOLD MEDALIST

AVANTI MODEL 887 GOLD MEDALIST
Power: CO2 single shot bolt
Stock: Laminated hardwood
Overall Length: 39.5 in.

Sights: Front globe with changeable aperture inserts, rear diopter with micrometer
Weight: 7 lb. 5 oz.
Caliber: .177

Features: Laminated hardwood stock; Lothar Walther rifled high-grade steel barrel; manual, cross-bolt trigger block; includes scope rail adapter
MSRP **$499.99**

Daisy

DAISY POWERLINE MODEL 880

DAISY POWERLINE MODEL 901

DAISY WINCHESTER M-14

DAISY WINCHESTER MODEL 77XS

DAISY WINCHESTER MODEL 1100SS

DAISY WINCHESTER MODEL 1250WS

WINCHESTER M-14
Power: CO2 semiautomatic
Stock: Composite
Length: 44.5 in.
Sights: Blade front, adjustable rear
Weight: 4 lb. 6 oz.
Caliber: .177
Features: Dual ammo BB or pellet rifle; rifled steel barrel; adjustable rear sight, fixed front sight; brown composite stock; 700 fps maximum velocity
MSRP **$99.99**

WINCHESTER MODEL 77XS
Power: Multi-pump pneumatic
Stock: Composite
Length: 37.6 in.
Sights: TruGlo fiber optic front, adjustable rear
Weight: 3 lb. 2 oz.
Caliber: .177
Features: Rifled steel barrel; TruGlo fiber optic front, adjustable rear sight; 4x32mm air rifle scope included; black composite stock; 800 fps maximum velocity
MSRP **$129.99**

WINCHESTER MODEL 1100SS
Power: Break action/spring piston
Stock: Composite
Overall Length: 46.25 in.
Sights: Blade front, micro-adjustable rear
Weight: 6 lb. 10 oz.
Caliber: .177
Features: Rifled steel barrel; 1100 fps with alloy pellets; single shot; thumb safety engages when rifle is cocked
MSRP **$129.99**

WINCHESTER MODEL 1250WS
Power: Break action/spring piston
Stock: Hardwood
Overall Length: 46.25 in.
Sights: Fiber optic front, 3–9x32mm scope
Weight: 6 lb. 10 oz.
Caliber: .177
Features: Rifled steel barrel; 1250 fps; thumb safety engages when cocked
MSRP **$179.99**

POWERLINE MODEL 880
Power: Multi-pump pneumatic
Stock: Molded wood grain
Overall Length: 37.6 in.
Sights: TruGlo fiber optic front, adjustable rear
Weight: 3 lb. 11 oz.
Caliber: .177
Features: Wood-grained, Monte Carlo stock and forearm; rifled steel barrel; cross-bolt trigger block; velocity up to 750 fps; engineering resin with dovetail mount for scope
MSRP **$49.99**

POWERLINE MODEL 901
Power: Multi-pump pneumatic
Stock: Composite
Overall Length: 37.5 in.
Sights: Fiber optic front, adjustable rear
Weight: 3 lb. 11 oz.
Caliber: .177
Features: Rifled steel barrel; black advanced composite stock; dovetail mounts for optics
MSRP **$69.99**

Gamo USA

GAMO BIG CAT 1250

GAMO USA BIG CAT 1400

BONE COLLECTOR MAXXIM

COYOTE WHISPER FUSION

GAMO MAGNUM

HORNET MAXXIM

BIG CAT 1250
Power: Break action/spring piston
Stock: Synthetic
Overall Length: 43.3 in.
Sights: 4x32mm scope
Weight: 6 lb. 2 oz.
Caliber: .177
Features: Tough all-weather molded synthetic stock; ventilated rubber pad for recoil; twin cheekpads; non-slip texture design on grip and forearm; manual trigger system; fluted barrel; two-stage adjustable trigger
MSRP $199.95

BIG CAT 1400
Power: Break action/spring piston
Stock: Synthetic
Overall Length: 43.3 in.
Sights: 4x32 scope
Weight: 6 lb. 2 oz.
Caliber: .177
Features: 33mm power plant enabling it to shoot at up to 1,400 fps with PBA Platinum Ammo; Smooth Action Trigger to maximize pinpoint accuracy; all-weather synthetic stock with rubberized grips; Shock Wave Absorber recoil pad
MSRP $229.95

BONE COLLECTOR MAXXIM
Power: Inert Gas Technology
Stock: Synthetic
Overall length: 45.3 in.
Sights: 3-9X air rifle scope

Weight: 5 lb. 11.5 oz.
Caliber: .177, .22
Features: Designed in collaboration with Michael Waddell, Nick Mundt, and Travis "T Bone" Turner of the "Bone Collector" TV series; single-shot; features a single-cocking system, fluted polymer jacketed steel barrel with Whisper Maxxim technology, two-stage adjustable Custom Action Trigger, all-weather stock, double-sided cheekpiece, and Shock Wave Absorber recoil pad
MSRP $199.99

COYOTE WHISPER FUSION
Power: PCP
Stock: Beechwood
Overall length: 42.9 in.
Sights: None
Weight: 7 lb. 13.6 oz.
Caliber: .177, .22
Features: An entry-level PCP-power plant bolt-action air rifle that boasts a 10-pellet rotary clip, hammer forged rifled barrel, selve-regulating valve, Custom Action Trigger, Shock Wave Absorber, double-sided molded cheekpiece, and Whisper Fusion technology
MSRP $559.99

GAMO MAGNUM
Power: Inert Gas Technology Mach 1
Stock: Synthetic
Overall length: 49.2 in.

Sights: 3-9X air rifle scope
Weight: 6 lb. 14 oz.
Caliber: .177, .22
Features: The power plant system substitutes the traditional spring for a gas cylinder that delivers more power; single-shot, single-cocking air rifle is designed for pest control and features a fluted polymer jacketed steel barrel with Whisper Maxxim technology, two-stage adjustable Custom Action Trigger, all-weather stock, double-sided cheekpiece, and Shock Wave Absorber recoil pad
MSRP $299.99

HORNET MAXXIM
Power: Inert Gas Technology
Stock: Synthetic
Overall length: 45.3 in.
Sights: 3-9X air rifle scope
Weight: 5 lb. 11.5 oz.
Caliber: .177, .22
Features: Break-barrel air rifle is single-cocking, allows 10 shots before reloading, has cocking safety system, fluted polymer jacketed steel barrel with Whisper Maxxim technology, two-stage adjustable Custom Action Trigger, all-weather stock, and Shock Wave Absorber recoil pad. Includes Whisper Maxxim silencing technology and Recoil Reducing Rail
MSRP $159.99

Gamo USA

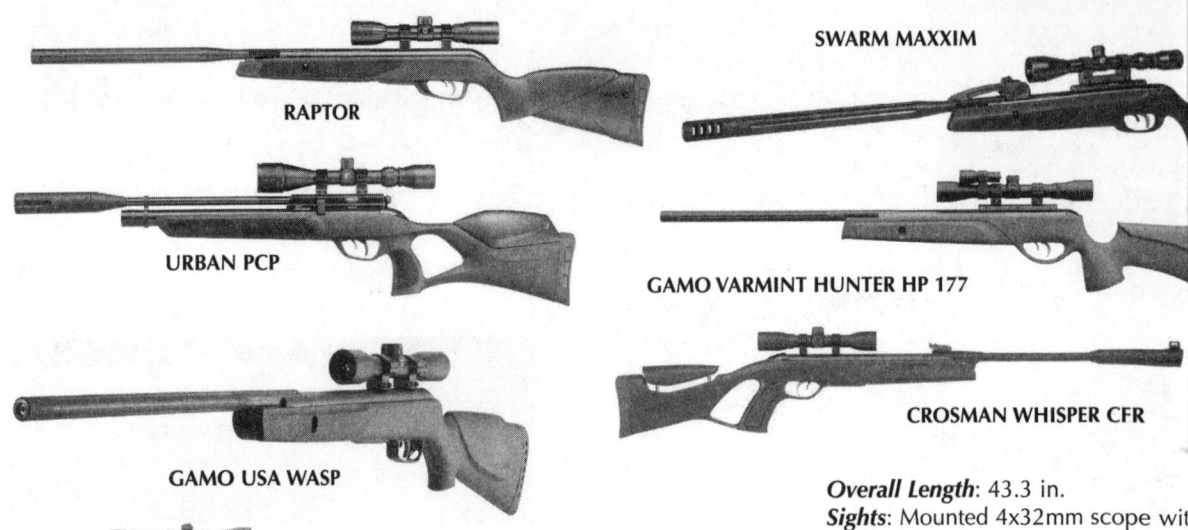

RAPTOR

SWARM MAXXIM

URBAN PCP

GAMO VARMINT HUNTER HP 177

GAMO USA WASP

CROSMAN WHISPER CFR

GAMO WHISPER
SILENT CAT

RAPTOR

Power: Single-cocking
Stock: Synthetic
Overall length: 46 in.
Sights: Fiber optic front and rear sights, 3-9X air rifle scope
Weight: 7 lb. 8 oz.
Caliber: .177
Features: This single-shot air rifle features Gamo's Turbo Stabilizing System technology and an adjustable ambidextrous cheekpiece, in addition to a two-stage adjustable Smooth Action Trigger
MSRP **$259.95**

RECON WHISPER

Power: Break action/spring piston
Stock: Synthetic
Overall Length: 37.2 in.
Sights: 4x20mm scope
Weight: 4 lb. 10 oz.
Caliber: .177
Features: All-weather black molded synthetic stock; ventilated rubber buttpad; twin cheekpads; automatic cocking safety system; 525 fps maximum velocity
MSRP **$120.00**

SWARM MAXXIM

Power: Inert Gas Technology
Stock: Synthetic
Overall length: 45.3 in.
Sights: 3-9X air rifle scope
Weight: 5 lb. 10 oz.
Caliber: .177
Features: Break-barrel air rifle is sin-

gle-cocking, allows 10 shots before reloading, has cocking safety system, fluted polymer jacketed steel barrel with Whisper Maxxim technology, two-stage adjustable Custom Action Trigger, all-weather stock, and Shock Wave Absorber recoil pad
MSRP **$199.99**

URBAN PCP

Power: PCP
Stock: Synthetic
Overall length: 42.9 in.
Sights: None
Weight: 6 lb. 11.2 oz.
Caliber: .22
Features: Bolt-action air rifle features Whisper Fusion technology multi-shot mechanism, Custom Action Trigger, hammer forged barrel, and thumbhole stock with double-sided molded cheekpiece
MSRP **$399.99**

VARMINT HUNTER HP 177

Power: Break action/spring piston
Stock: Synthetic
Length: 43.78 in.
Sights: 4x32mm scope
Weight: 6 lb. 10 oz.
Caliber: .177
Features: Lightweight synthetic stock; match grade fluted barrel; 1400 fps maximum velocity; 4x32mm air rifle scope with laser sight and flashlight; break barrel single cocking system
MSRP **$289.95**

USA WASP

Power: Single shot
Stock: Synthetic

Overall Length: 43.3 in.
Sights: Mounted 4x32mm scope wit rings
Weight: 6 lb. 1 oz.
Caliber: .177
Features: Fluted polymer jacketed steel barrel; all-weather black color stock; automatic cocking safety system; manual trigger safety; twin raise cheek pads
MSRP . . . .**$189.**

WHISPER CFR

Power: Single shot/spring piston
Stock: Synthetic
Length: 46.85 in.
Sights: Fiber optic sights, mounted 4x32 standard reticle scope
Weight: 8 lb.
Caliber: .177
Features: First Whisper Air Rifle with a fixed barrel; integrated ND52 noise dampener system; fixed rifled steel barrel; capable of 1100 fps; newly designed recoil pad with 74 percent more recoil absorbing pressure; all-weather synthetic molded stock with thumbhole
MSRP **$299.95**

WHISPER SILENT CAT

Power: Break action/spring piston
Stock: Synthetic
Overall Length: 37.2 in.
Sights: Mounted scope with rings
Weight: 4 lb. 10 oz.
Caliber: .177
Features: Raised rail scope mount with 39x40mm scope; two-stage adjustable trigger; manual safety; non-removable noise dampener; black synthetic all-weather stock; ventilated rubber buttplate; non-slip checkering on grip and forearm
MSRP **$269.95**

RWS

RWS MODEL 34

RWS MODEL 48 WITH SCOPE

RWS MODEL 54

RWS MODEL 350 MAGNUM

MODEL 34
Power: Break action/spring piston
Stock: Hardwood, synthetic
Overall Length: 45 in.
Sights: 4x32mm scope
Weight: 7 lb. 8 oz.–8 lb.
Caliber: .177, .22
Features: Polished with blued metalwork; full-sized hardwood stock; two-stage adjustable trigger; automatic safety; finely rifled barrel; 34 Pro large muzzlebrake
MSRP $332.01
With scope: $452.81

MODEL 48
Power: Side lever/spring piston
Stock: Hardwood
Overall Length: 42.5 in.

Sights: Adjustable rear
Weight: 8 lb. 8 oz.
Caliber: .177
Features: Extended breech stock to reduce recoil; fixed barrel system; adjustable trigger; automatic safety; optional RWS 4x32mm scope and mounts
MSRP $526.60
With scope: $680.70

MODEL 54
Power: Side lever/spring piston
Stock: Hardwood
Overall Length: 43.75 in.
Sights: Adjustable rear
Weight: 9 lb.
Caliber: .177, .22, .25
Features: Adjustable trigger; scope

rail; Monte Carlo hardwood stock with cheekpiece and checkering; automatic safety; 1100 fps maximum velocity
MSRP $739.04
With scope: $850.65

MODEL 350 MAGNUM
Power: Break action/spring piston
Stock: Hardwood
Overall Length: 48.3 in.
Sights: 4x32mm scope
Weight: 8 lb. 3 oz.
Caliber: .177, .22
Features: Two-stage trigger; mounted scope rail
MSRP $492.25
With scope: $593.85

AIRGUNS

Stoeger Airguns

STOEGER AIRGUNS A30

STOEGER AIRGUNS ATAC SUPPRESSOR S2

STOEGER AIRGUNS X3-TAC

STOEGER X-5

STOEGER X-20 SUPPRESSOR S2

STOEGER X-50 AIR RIFLE COMBO

A30
Power: Gas operated
Stock: Synthetic
Overall Length: 42.5 in.
Sights: Fiber optic sights and 4x32 scope
Weight: 8 lb. 5 oz.
Caliber: .177, .22
Features: Gas-Ram Technology system, or GRT; fully CNC machined precision breech; velocities are up to 1,200 fps for .117 cal and up to 1,000 fps for .22 cal
MSRP $199.00

ATAC SUPPRESSOR S2
Power: Break action/gas-operated
Stock: Synthetic
Overall Length: 42.5 in.
Sights: 4–16x40mm scope
Weight: 8 lb. 14 oz.
Caliber: .177, .22
Features: Airflow control technology and dual-stage noise reduction system; automatic ambidextrous safety; black tactical stock; up to 1200 fps with alloy pellets (.177); adjustable length of pull; integral Picatinny rails
MSRP $259.00

X3-TAC
Power:Air-operated break action
Stock: Synthetic
Overall Length: 36 in.
Sights: Fiber optic sights
Weight: 5 lb. 5 oz.
Caliber: .177
Features: Features a single-shot air rifle chambered for .177-caliber pellets; powered by a fast break-action, spring-and-piston mechanism that requires only 16 pounds of force to cock; incorporates an ambidextrous automatic safety located at the rear of the receiver; features a skeletonized tactical-style black synthetic stock; has an 11¾″ length of pull
MSRP $89.00

X-5
Power: Break action/spring piston
Stock: Hardwood, black synthetic
Overall Length: 41 in.
Sights: Hooded front with red, fiber optic insert; rear fiber optic
Weight: 5 lb. 11 oz.
Caliber: .177
Features: Automatic, ambidextrous safety mounted on back of receiver; Monte Carlo-style stock; integral dovetail scope rail on receiver
MSRP . . . . $109.00–$149.00

X-20 SUPPRESSOR S2
Power: Break action/spring piston
Stock: Black synthetic
Overall Length: 43 in.
Sights: 4x32mm illuminated red green scope
Weight: 7 lb.
Caliber: .177
Features: Air Flow Control system; adjustable two-stage trigger; integral dovetail scope rail on receiver; non-slip, deluxe rubber recoil pad; Monte Carlo-style, black synthetic stock with checkering; rifled, blued steel barrel
MSRP $179.00

X-50
Power: Break action/spring piston
Stock: Black synthetic
Overall Length: 50 in.
Sights: 3–9x40mm parallax adjustable scope with rings
Weight: 9 lb. 14 oz.
Caliber: .177
Features: Ergonomic cocking grip; rifled blued steel barrel; synthetic Monte Carlo-style stock; ambidextrous automatic safety
MSRP . . . . $319.00–$359.00

AIRGUNS

SHOTGUNS

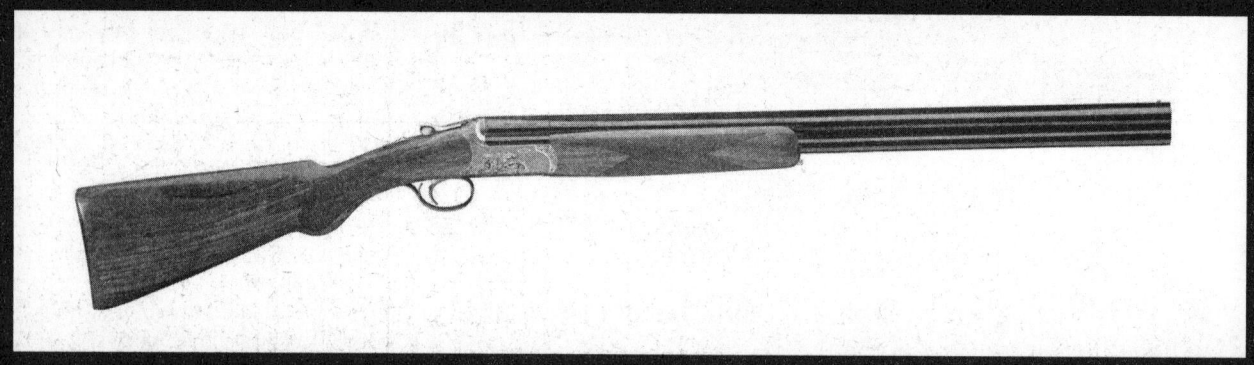

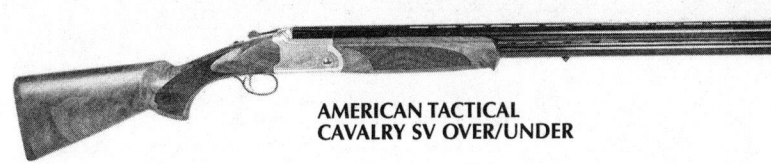

**AMERICAN TACTICAL
CAVALRY SV OVER/UNDER**

CAVALRY SV OVER/UNDER

Action: Over/under
Stock: Turkish walnut
Barrel: 26 in., 28 in.
Chokes: C, IC, M, IM, F
Weight: N/A
Bore/Gauge: 12, 20, 28, .410
Magazine: 2 shells
Features: Brass front bead sights, available with auto ejector, chambered for 3-in. Mag. shells, single selective trigger
MSRP **$659.95**

AYA (Aguirre y Aranzabal)

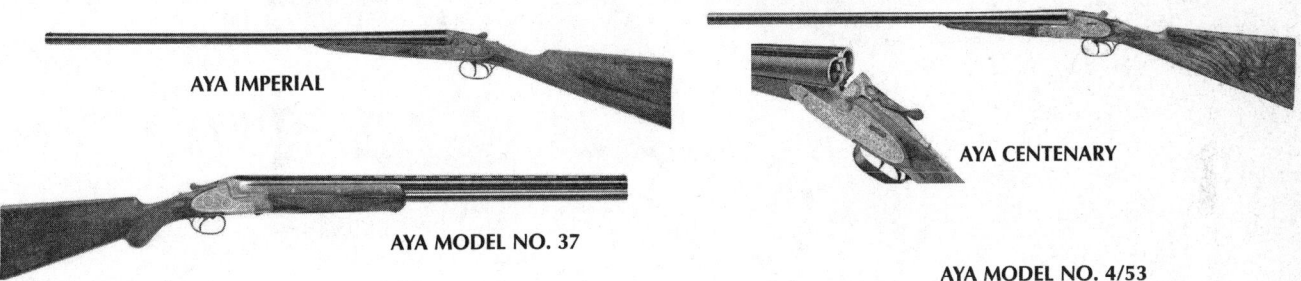

AYA IMPERIAL

AYA CENTENARY

AYA MODEL NO. 37

AYA MODEL NO. 4/53

CENTENARY

Action: Side-by-side
Stock: Wood
Barrel: 28 in.
Chokes: N/A
Weight: 6 lb. 12 oz.
Bore/Gauge: 12, 16, 20, 28, .410
Magazine: 2 shells
Features: Forged steel action with double locking mechanism and gas vents; hardened steel intercepting safety sears; gold lined cocking indicators; double trigger with hinged front trigger; optional selective or non-selective single trigger; chopper lump steel barrels; concave rib; straight hand, finely chequered oil finished walnut stock; exhibition wood; custom Centenary engraving, gold inlays; initial oval; automatic safety
MSRP . . . . . . **Contact manufacturer for pricing**

IMPERIAL

Action: Side-by-side hammerless sidelock
Stock: Walnut
Barrel: 28 in., with other lengths to order

Chokes: Screw-in tubes
Weight: 6 lb. 12 oz.
Bore/Gauge: 12, 16, 20, 28, .410
Magazine: None
Features: Forged steel action with double locking mechanism and gas vents; gold washed internal lock parts; gold lined cocking indicators; optional selective or non-selective single trigger; concave rib; straight hand, finely checkered walnut stock; gold initial oval
From . . . . . . **Contact manufacturer for pricing**

MODEL NO. 4/53

Action: Side-by-side hammerless boxlock ejector
Stock: Walnut
Barrel: 28 in., with other lengths to order
Chokes: Screw-in tubes
Weight: 6 lb. 10 oz.
Bore/Gauge: 12, 16, 20, 28, .410
Magazine: None
Features: Double locking mechanism with replaceable hinge pin; disk set firing pins; double trigger; chopper

lump barrels with concave rib; light scroll engraving; metal finish available in hardened, old silver, or white finish; automatic safety
From . . . . . . **Contact manufacturer for pricing**

MODEL NO. 37

Action: Over/under sidelock
Stock: Walnut
Barrel: 28 in.
Chokes: Screw-in tubes
Weight: 7 lb. 8 oz.
Bore/Gauge: 12
Magazine: None
Features: Double underlocking lugs and double crossbolt; chopper lump chrome nickel steel barrels; hardened steel intercepting safety sears; gold line cocking indicators; gold washed internal lock parts; double trigger with hinged front trigger; fine rose and scroll, game scene, or bold relief engraving on action plates; full pistol grip walnut stock
From . . . . . . **Contact manufacturer for pricing**

SHOTGUNS

Benelli USA

BENELLI 828U

BENELLI CORDOBA

BENELLI ETHOS

BENELLI LEGACY SPORT

BENELLI M2 FIELD 12 GA.

828U

Action: Over/under
Stock: Wood
Barrel: 26 in., 28 in.
Chokes: C, IC, M, IM, F, wrench
Weight: 6 lb. 8 oz.
Bore/Gauge: 12
Magazine: 2 shells
Features: Patented steel locking system and plate; easily removable trigger group receiver; adjustable drop and cast; ergonomic opening lever; impulse activated ejectors
MSRP . . . . $2499.00–$2999.00

CORDOBA

Action: Inertia operated semiautomatic
Stock: Synthetic
Barrel: 28 in., 30 in.
Chokes: Extended Crio Chokes
Weight: 7 lb.
Bore/Gauge: 12, 20
Magazine: 4+1 shells
Features: Black synthetic stock with GripTight; Crio ported barrels; ComforTech gel recoil pad and comb insert; heavy duty magazine cap
MSRP $2099.00

ETHOS

Action: Inertia-operated semiautomatic
Stock: Walnut
Barrel: 26 in., 28 in.
Chokes: C, IC, M, IM, F
Weight: 5 lb.–6 lb. 5 oz.
Bore/Gauge: 12, 20, 28
Magazine: 4+1 shells
Features: Progressive Comfort recoil reduction system; two-part carrier latch for easy reloading; interchangerable fiber optic sights; available with engraved nickel-plated receiver
MSRP . . . . $1999.00–$2199.00

LEGACY SPORT, SPORT II

Action: Inertia operated semiautomatic
Stock: Walnut
Barrel: 28 in., 30 in.
Chokes: Extended Crio Chokes (C, CI, M, IM, F)
Weight: 7 lb. 6 oz.–7 lb. 8 oz.
Bore/Gauge: 12
Magazine: 4+1 shells
Features: Aesthetically enhanced clay competition shotguns. All versions have Inertia Drive system, gel recoil pad, and ported Crio chokes; Legacy Sport has AA-walnut satin-finished stock and engraved receiver; it is

available in 12-gauge 2 ¾-, 3-in.; Sport II has an A-walnut satin-finished stock; it is available in 12- and 20-gauge 2 ¾-, 3-in.; both 12-gauge models are available with 28- or 30-in. barrels; 20-gauge comes only with a 28-in. barrel
Sport: $2439.00
Sport II: $1899.00

M2 FIELD 12 GA.

Action: Inertia operated semiautomatic
Stock: Synthetic, Realtree APG
Barrel: 21 in., 24 in., 26 in., 28 in.
Chokes: Crio Chokes (IC, M, F)
Weight: 6 lb. 14 oz.–7 lb. 3 oz.
Bore/Gauge: 12
Magazine: 3+1 shells
Features: ComforTech gel recoil pad and comb insert; ComforTech shim kit; red bar front sight; stock comes in black synthetic, Realtree APG, and Realtree MAX-5 Camo; Straight Field model available in left-hand; also availabe in Compact and Rifled Slug versions; all 12-gauge models chamber 3-in. shells
Camo: . . . . $1549.00–$1649.00
Synthetic: . . . . . $1449.00–$1549.00

Benelli USA

BENELLI M2 FIELD 20 GA.

BENELLI MONTEFELTRO BLACK SYNTHETIC

BENELLI NOVA TACTICAL

SUPER BLACK EAGLE II 25TH ANNIVERSARY
FLYWAY, 25TH ANNIVERSARY LIMITED EDITION,
LEFT-HAND

M2 FIELD 20 GA.
Action: Inertia operated semiautomatic
Stock: Synthetic
Barrel: 24 in., 26 in.
Chokes: Crio Chokes (IC, M, F)
Weight: 5 lb. 13 oz.–6 lb. 8 oz.
Bore/Gauge: 20
Magazine: 3+1 shells
Features: ComforTech gel recoil pad
and comb insert; ComforTech shim
kit; red bar front sight; synthetic stock
in Realtree Max-5 camo, Realtree
APG camo or black finish. Now available
in Compact, Rifled Slug, and left-
hand versions (left-hand in black syn-
thetic only); chambered for 3-in.
shells
MSRP . . . . $1499.00–$1599.00
Camo: . . . . $1599.00–$1649.00

MONTEFELTRO BLACK SYNTHETIC
Action: Semiautomatic
Stock: Black synthetic
Barrel: 26 in.
Chokes: IC, M, F
Weight: 6 lb. 14 oz.
Bore/ Gauge: 12
Magazine: 4 +1 shells
Features: Traditional Monetefeltro
styling in a more economical version,

with a black synthetic stock, three
choke tubes, and minus the
ComforTech technology; chambered
for 3-in. shells
MSRP $1139.00

NOVA TACTICAL
Action: Pump
Stock: Synthetic
Barrel: 18.5 in.
Chokes: Fixed cylinder choke
Weight: 7 lb. 3 oz.
Bore/Gauge: 12
Magazine: 4+1 shells
Features: Available with ghost-ring or
open rifle sights; push-button shell
stop; grooved grip surface stocks in
black synthetic stock; available with
H2O technology, including a matte
nickel-plated metal work
MSRP . . . . $419.00–$669.00

SUPER BLACK EAGLE II 25TH ANNIVERSARY FLYWAY, 25TH ANNIVERSARY LIMITED EDITION, LEFT-HAND
Action: Semiautomatic
Stock: walnut, synthetic
Barrel: 28 in.
Weight: ;7 lb. 3 oz.–7 lb. 5 oz.

Chokes: 5
Bore/Gauge: 12
Magazine: 3 shells
Features: As the Super Black Eagle II
is phased out and replaced by the
Super Black Eagle III in 2017, three
models remain in the II lineup; the
25th Anniversary Flyway chambers 3
½-in. shells and is released in four
versions, one for each of the flyways
(Mississippi, Atlantic, Central, and
Pacific); all have AAA satin-finished
walnut stocks and flyway-specific
engravings on their nickel-plated
receivers, red bar front sight and mid-
rib bead, and C, IC, M, IM, and F
Crio chokes; the 25th Anniversary
Limited Edition chambers 3 ½-in.
shells and comes in choice of black
Cerakote or Realtree MAX5 camo,
with IC, M, and F extended chokes
and IC and M flush chokes; the Left-
Hand model also chambers 3 ½-in.
shells, is available with a black,
Realtree MAX5, or Realtree APG
synthetic stock, and comes with C, IC,
M, IM, and F Crio chokes
25th Anniversary Flyway: . . $3199.00
25th Anniversary
   Limited Edition: $1999.00
Left-Hand. $1899.00

Benelli USA

SUPERNOVA PUMP SHOTGUN

Action: Pump
Stock: Synthetic
Barrel: 24 in., 26 in., 28 in.
Chokes: Standard choke (IC, M, F)
Weight: 7 lb. 13 oz.–8 lb.
Bore/Gauge: 12
Magazine: 4+1 shells
Features: Stock comes in black synthetic, Realtree APG camo, or Realtree Max-5 camo; receiver drilled and tapped for scope mounting; standard chokes; vented recoil pad; standard model chambers up to 3 ½- in. shells; rifled slug version chambers only up to 3-in. shells, comes only with a 24-in. barrel, and is available only in black or Realtree APG
Standard: . . . . $549.00–$669.00
Rifled slug: . . . . $829.00–$929.00

SUPERSPORT

Action: Inertia operated semiautomatic
Stock: Synthetic
Barrel: 28 in., 30 in.
Chokes: Extended Crio Chokes(C, IC, M, IM, F)
Weight: 6 lb. 5 oz.–7 lb. 5 oz.
Bore/Gauge: 12, 20
Magazine: 4+1 shells
Features: Stock comes in black SuperSport carbon fiber finish; red bar front sight and metal bead mid sight; Crio ported barrels; ComforTech gel recoil pad and comb insert
MSRP $2199.00

SUPER VINCI

Action: Inertia operated semiautomatic
Stock: Synthetic, Realtree APG
Barrel: 26 in., 28 in.
Chokes: Crio Chokes (C, IC, M, IM, F)
Weight: 6 lb. 14 oz.–7 lb.
Bore/Gauge: 12
Magazine: 3+1 shells
Features: In-line inertia driven system; enlarged trigger and trigger guard for use with gloves; ComforTech Plus recoil pad; QuadraFit shim kit; drilled and tapped for scopes; available in black, Realtree Max-5 or Realtree APG synthetic stocks in both barrel lengths, as well as Gore Optifade Concealment-Marsh in a 28-in. barrel only; all models chamber up to 3 ½- in. shells
MSRP . . . . $1599.00–$1699.00

ULTRA LIGHT

Action: Inertia operated semiautomatic
Stock: Walnut
Barrel: 24 in., 26 in.
Chokes: Crio Chokes (IC, M, F)
Weight: 5 lb. 3 oz.–6 lb. 2 oz.
Bore/Gauge: 12, 20, 28
Magazine: 2+1 shells
Features: Weather-coated walnut stock; red bar front sight and metal bead mid sight; gel recoil pad; option of checkered Montefeltro forend or ultra light forend
MSRP . . . . $1669.00–$1799.00

VINCI

Action: Inertia operated semiautomatic
Stock: Synthetic
Barrel: 26 in., 28 in.
Chokes: Crio Chokes (C, IC, M, IM, F)
Weight: 6 lb. 13 oz.–6 lb. 14 oz.
Bore/Gauge: 12
Magazine: 3+1 shells
Features: Stock in black, Realtree APG, or Realtree MAX-5 camo; red bar front sight and metal bead mid sight; drilled and tapped for scope mounting; ComforTech Plus recoil pads
MSRP . . . . $1449.00–$1549.00

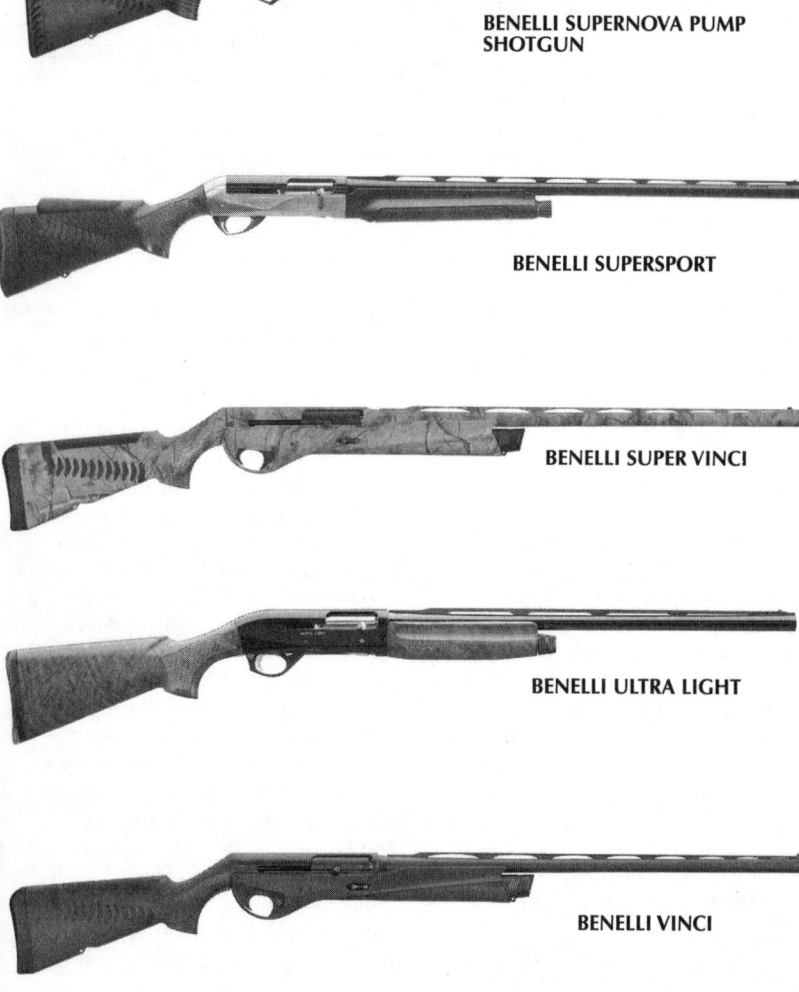

BENELLI SUPERNOVA PUMP SHOTGUN

BENELLI SUPERSPORT

BENELLI SUPER VINCI

BENELLI ULTRA LIGHT

BENELLI VINCI

Beretta USA

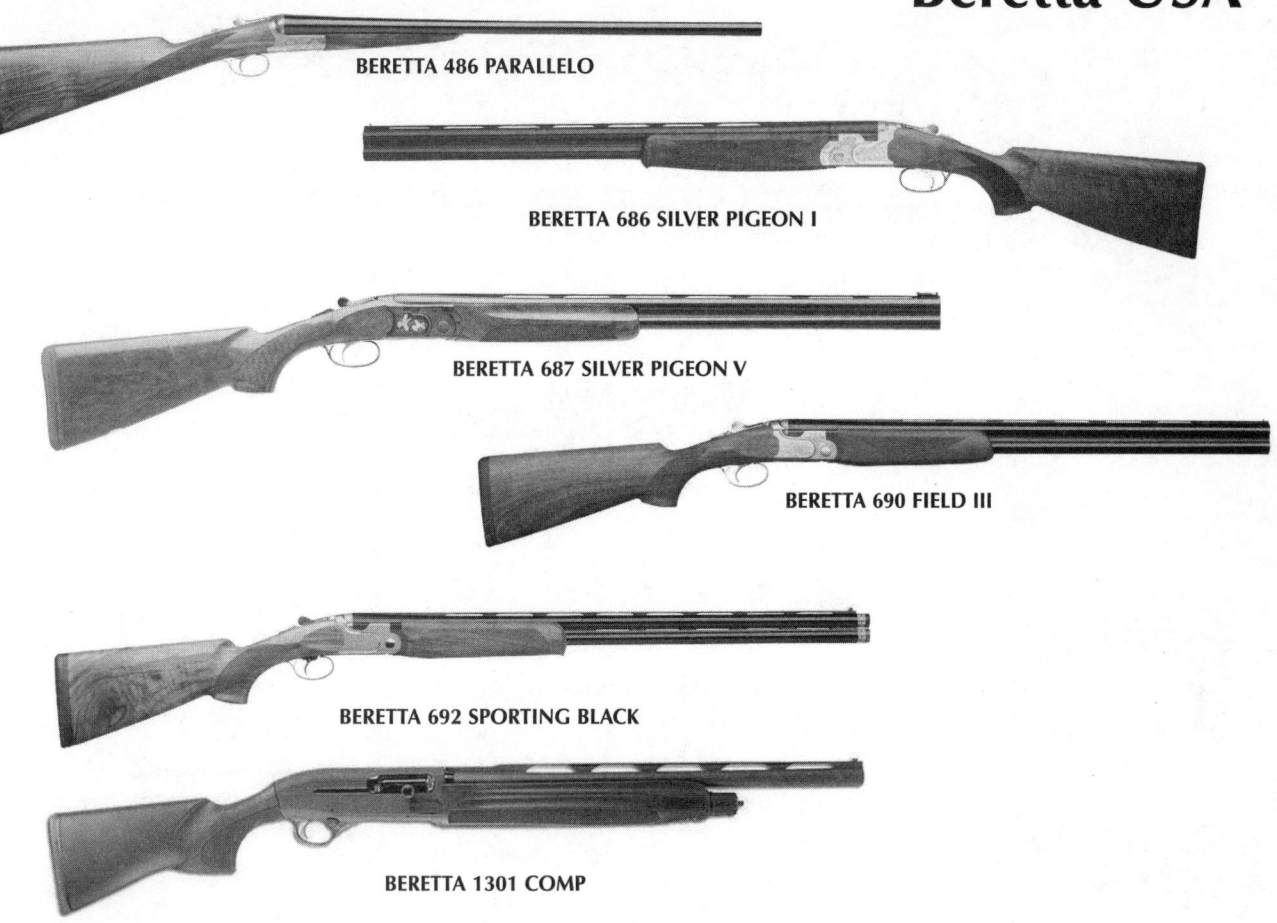

BERETTA 486 PARALLELO

BERETTA 686 SILVER PIGEON I

BERETTA 687 SILVER PIGEON V

BERETTA 690 FIELD III

BERETTA 692 SPORTING BLACK

BERETTA 1301 COMP

486 PARALLELO
Action: Side-by-side
Stock: Wood
Barrel: 28 in., 30 in.
Chokes: Fixed, Optima-Choke
Weight: 7 lb.
Bore/Gauge: 12
Magazine: 2 shells
Features: Round action with lavish scroll engraving; new leaf springs, trigger group, barrel technology
MSRP **$5350.00**

686 SILVER PIGEON I
Action: Over/under
Stock: Walnut
Barrel: 26 in., 28 in., 30 in.
Chokes: MC
Weight: 6 lb. 13 oz.
Bore/Gauge: 12, 20, 28, .410
Magazine: 2 shells
Features: Extensive but refined floral and scroll decoration on the frame; dual-conical locking mechanism; automatic safety; oil finish on checkered walnut stock and forend; metal bead sight
MSRP **$2350.00**

687 SILVER PIGEON V
Action: Over/under
Stock: Walnut
Barrel: 28 in.
Chokes: Screw-in tubes
Weight: 6 lb. 13 oz.
Bore/Gauge: 12, 20, 28, .410
Magazine: 2 shells
Features: Oil-finished walnut stock detailed with gold game bird inlays and a gold Beretta medallion underneath; color-case finish; single selective trigger; 3-inch chambers; available with English stock or standard stock with pistol grip
MSRP **$4075.00**

690 FIELD III
Action: Over/under
Stock: Wood
Barrel: 28 in.
Chokes: Optima-Choke
Weight: 7 lb. 6 oz.
Bore/Gauge: 12
Magazine: 2 shells
Features: Micro Core recoil pad; adjustable Extraction-ejection; double top receiver and shoulder design
MSRP **$3475.00**

692 SPORTING BLACK
Action: Over/under
Stock: Walnut
Barrel: 30 in., 32 in.
Chokes: 5 OCHP
Weight: 7 lb. 11 oz.
Bore/ Gauge: 12
Magazine: 2 shells
Features: Steelium Plus barrels; longer forcing cone; Beretta Fast Adjustment System Technology; Adjustable Balance System; adjustable trigger
MSRP . . . . **$5250.00–$5750.00**

1301 COMP
Action: Gas-operated semiautomatic
Stock: Synthetic
Barrel: 21 in., 24 in.
Chokes: IC
Weight: 7 lb. 2 oz.
Bore/Gauge: 12
Magazine: 5+1 shells
Features: Fiber optic sights; oversized bolt release and handle; Optima Bore HP interchangable choke system
MSRP **$1275.00**

Beretta USA

BERETTA 1301 TACTICAL

BERETTA A300 OUTLANDER

BERETTA A300 OUTLANDER TURKEY

BERETTA A350 EXTREMA

BERETTA A400 XPLOR ACTION

1301 TACTICAL
Action: Gas-operated semiautomatic
Stock: Synthetic
Barrel: 18.5 in.
Chokes: F
Weight: 7 lb. 2 oz.
Bore/Gauge: 12
Magazine: 5+1 shells
Features: Ghost ring sight; front blade sight; Picatinny rail; oversized bolt release and handle; fixed cylinder choke
MSRP. $1075.00

A300 OUTLANDER
Action: Gas-operated semiautomatic
Stock: Synthetic, camo, walnut
Barrel: 28 in.
Chokes: MC3
Weight: 7 lb. 10 oz.
Bore/Gauge: 12
Magazine: 3+1 shells
Features: Gas operation with compensating exhaust valve and self-cleaning piston; adjustable shim system on stock; aluminum alloy receiver; crossbolt safety with ergonomics; front metal bead sight; black synthetic, camo, or oiled wood stock finish

Camo: $900.00
Synthetic: $800.00
Wood: $900.00

A300 OUTLANDER TURKEY
Action: Semiautomatic
Stock: Synthetic
Barrel: 24 in.
Chokes: 3 chokes (F, M, IC)
Weight: 7 lb. 9 oz.
Bore/Gauge: 12
Magazine: 3+1 shells
Features: TRUGLO fiber optic sights; Realtree XTRA camo finish; adjustable drop cast; reliable/clean gas operating system; sling attachment
MSRP. $900.00

A350 EXTREMA
Action: Semiautomatic
Stock: Synthetic
Barrel: 28 in.
Chokes: Optima HP
Weight: 7 lb. 2 oz.
Bore/Gauge: 12
Magazine: N/A
Features: Adjustable shim system for drop and right-hand or left-hand configuration; 3.5 in. chamber; steelium barrel; fiber optic bead front sight; sling points; Micro Core recoil pad; Max-5 camo finish
MSRP. $1150.00

A400 XPLOR ACTION
Action: Gas-operated semiautomatic
Stock: Walnut
Barrel: 26 in., 28 in.
Chokes: F
Weight: 5 lb. 8 oz.
Bore/Gauge: 12, 20, 28
Magazine: 3+1 shells
Features: Fiber optic sights; Gun Pod shell counter, cartridge tester, and temperature display; Kick-Off recoil reduction system; Optima Bore interchangable bore system
MSRP. . . . .$1600.00–$1700.00

SHOTGUNS

Beretta USA

BERETTA A400 LITE (SYNTHETIC)

BERETTA A400 XPLOR UNICO

BERETTA A400 XTREME UNICO

BERETTA DT11 SPORTING BLACK

A400 LITE (SYNTHETIC)
Action: Semiautomatic
Stock: Walnut and polymer
Barrel: 26 in., 28 in., 30 in.
Chokes: OptimaChoke screw-in tube
Weight: 6 lb. 3 oz.–6 lb. 10 oz.
Bore/Gauge: 12
Magazine: 3+1 or 2+1 shells
Features: Steelium barrel design, walnut stock with polymer forend insert, trigger guard and kick-off interface; 3-in. chamber; blink operating system; Micro-Core recoil pad; available with kick-off damper system
MSRP $1600.00

A400 XPLOR UNICO
Action: Semiautomatic
Stock: Walnut or polymer
Barrel: 26 in., 28 in., 30 in.
Chokes: OptimaChoke screw-in tube
Weight: 6 lb. 10 oz.–7 lb.
Bore/Gauge: 12
Magazine: 3+1 or 2+1 shells
Features: Single-selective trigger; green receiver; walnut stock with

polymer forend insert, trigger guard and kick-off interface; 3.5-in. chamber; metal bead front sight; camo or green anodized available
MSRP . . . . $1750.00–$1850.00

A400 XTREME UNICO, UNICO CAMO
Action: Semiautomatic
Stock: Synthetic or camo
Barrel: 26 in., 28 in., 30 in.
Chokes: Optima Bore HP (C, Mod, Full)
Weight: 7 lb. 10 oz.
Bore/Gauge: 12
Magazine: 4+1 or 3+1 shells
Features: Adjustable buttstock shim kits, anti-corrosion coatings on the barrel, Beretta's fast-cycling Blink technology, fast-assembly B-Lock fore-end cap, Kick-Off 3/Kick-Off Mega recoil reduction system, and Steelium Optma Bore HP barrels; chamber 3 ½-in. shells; camo version available in Realtree Max-5; left-hand available in either finish but only with 28-in. barrel

Synthetic: . . . . . $1750.00–$1800.00
MAX-5: $1900.00

DT11 SPORTING BLACK
Action: Over/under
Stock: Walnut
Barrel: 30 in., 32 in.
Chokes: OCHPe
Weight: 9 lb.
Bore/ Gauge: 12
Magazine: 2 shells
Features: Steelium Pro barrel; top rib with hollowed bridges; ergonomic top lever; safety selector switch; increased receiver side wall thickness; select high-quality walnut wood finished in oil; stock and forend can be fitted to customer's measurement; pistol grip and forend are hand-checkered; B-Fast adjustable stock available; left-hand model available in both barrel lengths, but without B-Fast stock option
MSRP . . . . $10999.00–$11300.00

SHOTGUNS

Blaser USA

BLASER F3 SPORTING

BLASER F16 GAME

BLASER F16 SPORTING

F3 SPORTING

Action: Over/under
Stock: Walnut
Barrel: 28 in., 30 in., 32 in., 34 in.
Chokes: Briley Spectrum chokes (SK, IC, M., IM, F)
Weight: 7 lb. 5 oz.
Bore/Gauge: 12, 20, 28, .410
Magazine: 2 shells
Features: Sporting stock, forearm with Schnabel; internal block system; ergonomically optimized, adjustable trigger blade; Triplex Bore design; ejection-ball-system; balancer

Standard:. $7613.00
Luxus: $9340.00
Grand Luxus:. $12233.00
Super Luxus: $13913.00
Baronesse:. $15010.00
Exclusive:. . . . . . . **Price on request**
Super Exclusive:. . **Price on request**
Imperial: . . . . **Price on request**

F16 GAME

Action: Over/under
Stock: Walnut
Barrel: 28 in., 30 in.
Chokes: Blaser chokes flush to muzzle
Weight: 6 lb. 13 oz.
Bore/Gauge: 12

Magazine: 2 shells
Features: Sleak English-style forearm design; crisp trigger pull; Triplex bore design; tapered rib; proven Blaser ejection system; Inertial Block System (IBS) prevents an involuntary second shot or the unintentional triggering of a second shot while maintaining a superb trigger pull
MSRP. $3795.00

F16 SPORTING

Action: Over/under
Stock: Walnut
Barrel: 30 in., 32 in.
Chokes: Blaser chokes flush to muzzle
Weight: 7 lb. 8 oz.–8 lb. 6 oz.

Bore/Gauge: 12
Magazine: 2 shells
Features: Balancer system allows the adjustment of the weight distribution to shooter's personal needs; sleak English-style forearm design; crisp trigger pull; Triplex bore design; tapered rib; proven Blaser ejection system; Inertial Block System (IBS) prevents an involuntary second shot or the unintentional triggering of a second shot while maintaining a superb trigger pull
MSRP. $4195.00

Browning

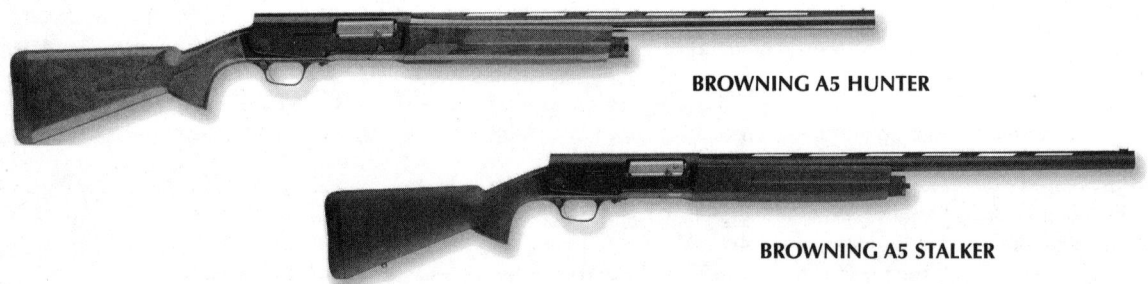

BROWNING A5 HUNTER

BROWNING A5 STALKER

A5 HUNTER

Action: Semiautomatic
Stock: Walnut
Barrel: 26 in., 28 in., 30 in.
Chokes: Invector-DS
Weight: 6 lb. 15 oz.
Bore/Gauge: 12
Magazine: None
Features: Strong, lightweight aluminum alloy; black anodized bi-tone finish; flat, ventilated rib; recoil operated Kinematic Drive is ultra-reliable and cycles a wide range of loads; gloss finish walnut with close radius pistol grip; 22 lines-per-inch checkering; shim adjustable for length of pull, cast and drop; Vector Pro lengthened forcing cone; three invector-DS™ choke tubes; Inflex II technology recoil pad; brass front bead sight; ivory mid-bead sight; included ABS case
MSRP. . . . .$1629.99–$1759.99

A5 STALKER

Action: Semiautomatic
Stock: Composite
Barrel: 26 in., 28 in., 30 in.
Chokes: Invector-DS
Weight: 7 lb. 3 oz.–7 lb. 7 oz.
Bore/Gauge: 12

Magazine: None
Features: Strong, lightweight aluminum alloy; flat, ventilated rib; recoil operated Kinematic Drive is ultra-reliable and cycles a wide range of loads; composite with close radius pistol grip; textured gripping surfaces; shim adjustable for cast and drop; matte black finish; Dura-Touch armor coating; Vector Pro lengthened forcing cone; Inflex II technology recoil pad; fiber-optic front sight; included ABS case
MSRP. . . . .$1499.99–$1629.99

SHOTGUNS

Browning

BROWNING A5 SWEET SIXTEEN

BROWNING A-BOLT SHOTGUN STALKER

BROWNING BPS HUNTER

BROWNING BPS MICRO MIDAS

A5 SWEET SIXTEEN
Action: Semiautomatic
Stock: Turkish walnut
Barrel: 28 in.
Chokes: Invector-DS flush
Weight: 5 lb. 13 oz.
Bore/Gauge: 16
Magazine: 4 shells
Features: Gloss walnut stock; brass bead front sight; humbpack receiver; ergo balanced; short recoil-operated Kinematic Drive System; auto-loader shotgun; Invector-DS choke tubes; built on a smaller, lighter receiver for reduced weight
MSRP $1699.99

A-BOLT SHOTGUN STALKER
Action: Bolt
Stock: Composite
Barrel: 22 in.

Chokes: None
Weight: 7 lb.
Bore/Gauge: 12
Magazine: Detachable, 2+1 shells
Features: Black composite; textured gripping surfaces; Dura-touch armor coating; sling swivel studs installed; recoil pad; Truglo/Marble's fiber optic front sight, adjustable rear sight
MSRP $1149.99

BPS HUNTER
Action: Pump
Stock: Walnut
Barrel: 26 in., 28 in.
Chokes: Three Invector-Plus choke tubes with 12 and 20 gauges; Standard Invectors with 16, 28, and .410
Weight: 6 lb. 15 oz.–7 lb. 11 oz.
Bore/Gauge: 12, 16, 20, 28, .410
Magazine: None

Features: Satin finish walnut stock; forged and machined steel receiver; ventilated rib barrel; top-tang safety
MSRP . . . . $699.99–$729.99

BPS MICRO MIDAS
Action: Pump
Stock: Walnut
Barrel: 24 in., 26 in.
Chokes: 3 Invector-Plus (12, 20 Ga.), 3 Standard Invector (28, .410 Ga.)
Weight: 6 lb. 15 oz.–7 lb. 10 oz.
Bore/ Gauge: 12, 20, 28, .410
Magazine: None
Features: Ventilated rib barrel; dual steel action bars; top-tang safety; scaled down for smaller shooters; Inflex Technology recoil; silver colored front bead sight; stock spacers
MSRP . . . . $699.99–$729.99

Browning

BPS RIFLED DEER HUNTER
Action: Pump
Stock: Walnut
Barrel: 22 in.
Chokes: Screw-in tubes
Weight: 7 lb. 4 oz.–7 lb. 10 oz.
Bore/Gauge: 12, 20
Magazine: None
Features: Satin finish walnut stock; forged and machined steel receiver; thick-walled barrel for slug ammunition only; dual steel action bars
MSRP . . . . $829.99–$839.99

BPS TRAP
Action: Pump
Stock: Walnut
Barrel: 30 in.
Chokes: Three Invector-Plus choke tubes
Weight: 8 lb. 2 oz.
Bore/Gauge: 12
Magazine: None
Features: Satin finish walnut stock with raised comb; forged and machined steel receiver with engraving; dual steel action bars; top-tang safety; magazine cut-off; HiViz ProComp fiber optic sight with mid-bead
MSRP $839.99

BT-99
Action: Pump
Stock: Walnut
Barrel: 32 in., 34 in.
Chokes: Screw-in tubes
Weight: 8 lb. 3 oz.–8 lb. 5 oz.
Bore/Gauge: 12
Magazine: None
Features: Satin finish walnut stock with beavertail forearm; steel receiver with blued finish; high-post ventilated rib
MSRP $1429.99

BT-99 MICRO MIDAS
Action: Pump
Stock: Walnut
Barrel: 28 in., 30 in.
Chokes: 1 Invector-Plus
Weight: 7 lb. 11 oz
Bore/ Gauge: 12
Magazine: None
Features: Blued finish; high-post ventilated rib barrel; beavertail forearm; scaled down for smaller shooters; Vector-Pro lengthed forcing cone; recoil pad; ivory front and mid-bead sights
MSRP $1429.99

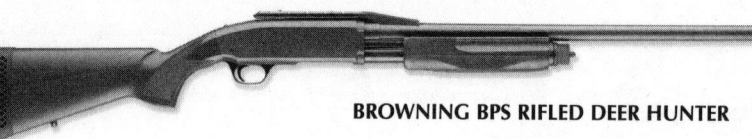

BROWNING BPS RIFLED DEER HUNTER

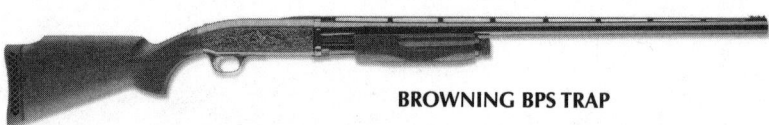

BROWNING BPS TRAP

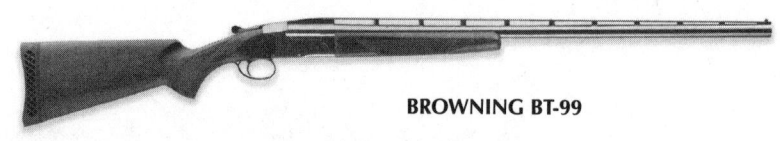

BROWNING BT-99

BROWNING BT-99 MICRO MIDAS

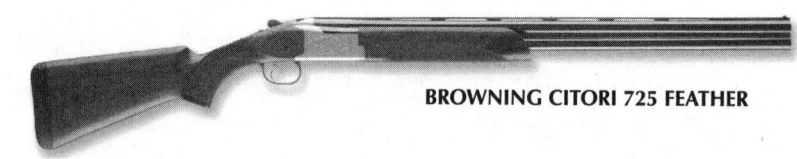

BROWNING CITORI 725 FEATHER

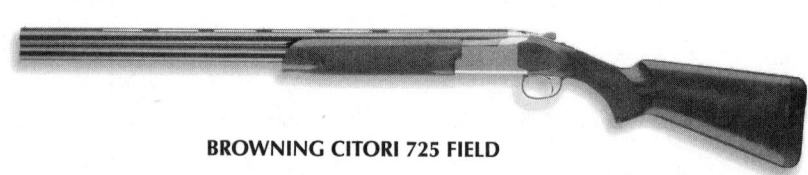

BROWNING CITORI 725 FIELD

CITORI 725 FEATHER
Action: Over/under
Stock: Walnut
Barrel: 26 in., 28 in.
Chokes: 3 Invector-DS
Weight: 5 lb. 14 oz.–6 lb. 9 oz.
Bore/ Gauge: 12, 20
Magazine: 2 shells
Features: Lightweight alloy receiver; low-profile; silver nitride finish; ventilated top rib barrel; Fire Lite Mechanical Trigger system; hammer ejectors; ivory front and mid-bead sights
MSRP $2549.99

CITORI 725 FIELD
Action: Over/under
Stock: Walnut
Barrel: 26 in., 28 in., 30 in.
Chokes: Invector-DS
Weight: 6 lb. 7 oz.–7 lb. 8 oz.
Bore/Gauge: 12, 20, 28, .410
Magazine: 2 shells
Features: Steel receiver with silver nitride finish; accented, high-relief engraving; ventilated top rib action; mechanical trigger system; hammer ejectors; top-tang barrel selector/safety; gloss oil finish Grade II/III walnut with close radius pistol grip; Vector Pro lengthened forcing cones; ivory front and mid-bead sights
MSRP . . . . $2469.99–$2539.99

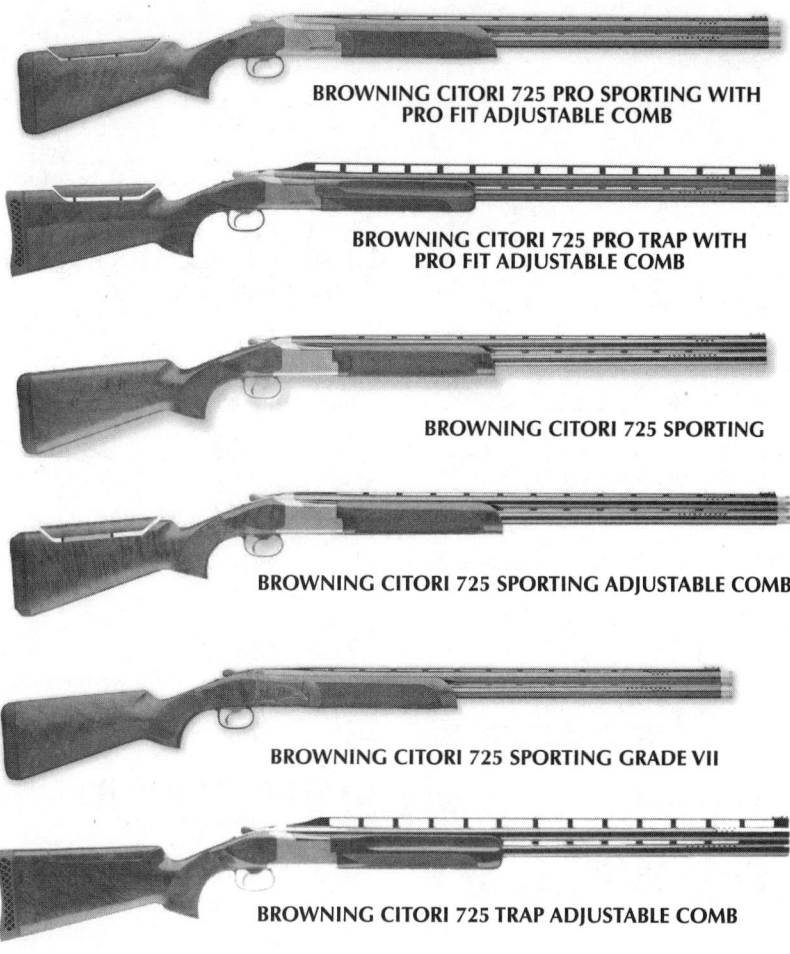

BROWNING CITORI 725 PRO SPORTING WITH PRO FIT ADJUSTABLE COMB

BROWNING CITORI 725 PRO TRAP WITH PRO FIT ADJUSTABLE COMB

BROWNING CITORI 725 SPORTING

BROWNING CITORI 725 SPORTING ADJUSTABLE COMB

BROWNING CITORI 725 SPORTING GRADE VII

BROWNING CITORI 725 TRAP ADJUSTABLE COMB

CITORI 725 PRO SPORTING WITH PRO FIT ADJUSTABLE COMB

Action: Over/under
Stock: Wood
Barrel: 30 in., 32 in.
Chokes: F, IM, M, IC, S
Weight: 7 lb. 5 oz.–7 lb. 13 oz.
Bore/Gauge: 12, 20
Magazine: 2 shells
Features: Polished blue barrel finish; grade III/IV black walnut stock with gloss oil finish; HiViz ProComp sights; vented ribs; drilled and tapped for scopes
MSRP $3999.99

CITORI 725 PRO TRAP WITH PRO FIT ADJUSTABLE COMB

Action: Over/under
Stock: Wood
Barrel: 30 in., 32 in.
Chokes: F, LF, M, 2IM
Weight: 8 lb. 8 oz., 8 lb. 11 oz.
Bore/Gauge: 12

Magazine: 2 shells
Features: Polished blue barrel finish; grade III/IV black walnut stock with gloss oil finish; HiViz ProComp sights; vented ribs; drilled and tapped for scopes
MSRP $3999.99

CITORI 725 SPORTING

Action: Over/under
Stock: Walnut
Barrel: 28 in., 30 in., 32 in.
Chokes: Invector-DS
Weight: 6 lb. 4 oz.–7 lb. 10 oz.
Bore/Gauge: 12, 20, 28, .410
Magazine: 2 shells
Features: Steel receiver with silver nitride finish; gold accented engraving; ventilated top and side rib action; mechanical trigger system; hammer ejectors; top-tang barrel selector/safety; gloss oil finish Grade III/IV walnut with close radius pistol grip; Vector Pro lengthened forcing cones; five Invector-DS choke tubes; HiViz Pro-Comp sight and ivory mid-bead
MSRP . . . . $3069.99–$3199.99

CITORI 725 SPORTING ADJUSTABLE COMB

Action: Over/under
Stock: Wood
Barrel: 30 in., 32 in.
Chokes: F, IM, M, IC, S
Weight: 7 lb. 13 oz.
Bore/Gauge: 12
Magazine: 2 shells
Features: Steel low-profile receiver with silver nitride finish and gold accented engraving; ventilated barrel with top and side ribs; Fire Lite mechanical trigger system; top-tang barrel selector/safety; gloss oil finish Grade III/IV walnut stock with close radius pistol grip and adjustable comb; HiViz Pro-Comp sight and ivory mid-bead
MSRP $3529.99

CITORI 725 SPORTING GRADE VII

Action: Over/under
Stock: Wood
Barrel: 28 in., 30 in., 32 in.
Chokes: F, IM, M, IC, S
Weight: 7 lb.–7 lb. 10 oz.
Bore/Gauge: 12, 20, 28, .410
Magazine: 2 shells
Features: Polished blue barrel finish; grade VI/VII black walnut stock with gloss oil finish; HiViz ProComp sights; large Inflex 2 recoil pad; limited availability
MSRP $6269.99

CITORI 725 TRAP ADJUSTABLE COMB

Action: Over/under
Stock: Wood
Barrel: 30 in., 32 in.
Chokes: F, IM, M
Weight: 8 lb. 8 oz.–8 lb. 11 oz.
Bore/Gauge: 12
Magazine: 2 shells
Features: Steel low-profile receiver with silver nitride finish and gold accented engraving; ventilated barrel with top and side ribs; Fire Lite mechanical trigger system; top-tang barrel selector/safety; gloss oil finish Grade III/IV walnut stock with close radius pistol grip and Monte Carlo or adjustable straight comb; HiViz Pro-Comp sight and ivory mid-bead
MSRP $3739.99

SHOTGUNS

Browning

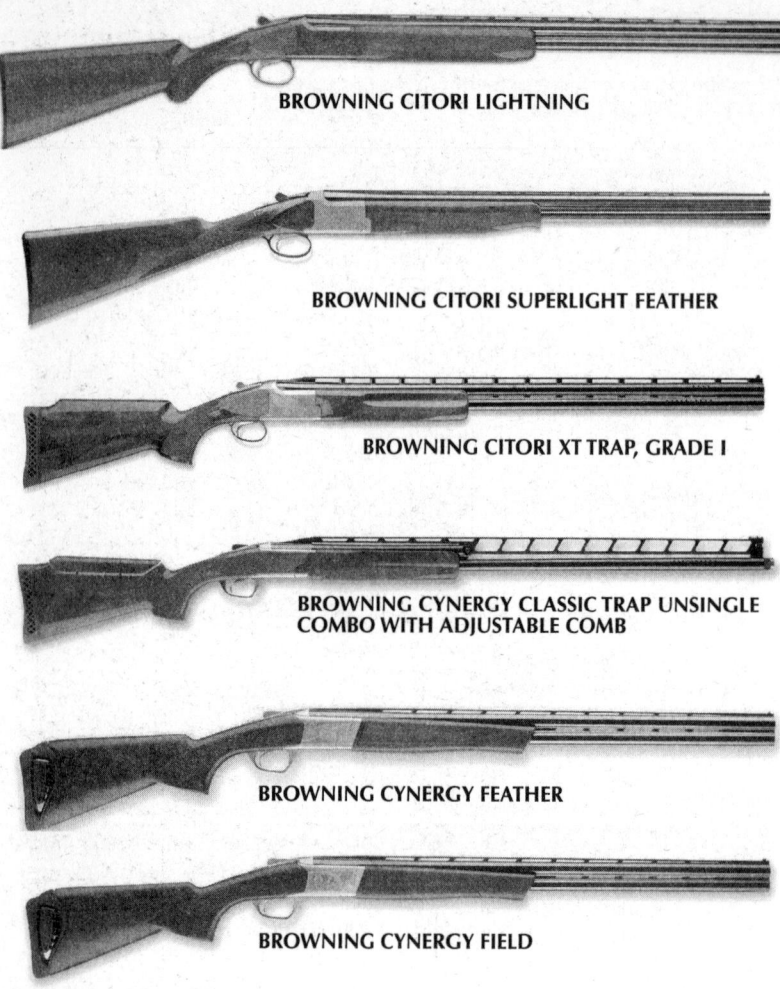

BROWNING CITORI LIGHTNING

BROWNING CITORI SUPERLIGHT FEATHER

BROWNING CITORI XT TRAP, GRADE I

BROWNING CYNERGY CLASSIC TRAP UNSINGLE COMBO WITH ADJUSTABLE COMB

BROWNING CYNERGY FEATHER

BROWNING CYNERGY FIELD

CITORI LIGHTNING

Action: Over/under
Stock: Walnut
Barrel: 26 in., 28 in., 30 in., 32 in.
Chokes: Three Invector-Plus choke tubes on 12 and 20, three standard Invector tubes on 28 and .410
Weight: 6 lb. 7 oz.–8 lb. 9.6 oz.
Bore/Gauge: 12, 20, 28, .410
Magazine: 2 shells
Features: Walnut stock with pistol grip; ventilated rib; single selective trigger; hammer ejectors; top-tang barrel selector/safety; ivory front bead sight
MSRP . . . . **$1989.99–$2069.99**

CITORI SUPERLIGHT FEATHER

Action: Over/under
Stock: Walnut
Barrel: 26 in.
Chokes: Invector-Plus
Weight: 5 lb. 11 oz.–6 lb. 12 oz.

Bore/Gauge: 12, 20
Magazine: 2 shells
Features: Lightweight alloy receiver with steel breech face and hinge pin; high-relief engraving; single selective trigger; hammer ejectors; top-tang barrel selector/safety; gloss finish walnut, English-style straight grip stock, Schnabel forearm; three Invector-Plus choke tubes
MSRP **$2389.99**

CITORI XT TRAP, GRADE I

Action: Over/under
Stock: Walnut
Barrel: 30 in., 32 in.
Chokes: Three Invector-plus choke tubes
Weight: 8 lb. 6 oz.–8 lb. 8 oz.
Bore/Gauge: 12
Magazine: 2 shells
Features: Triple-trigger system; HiViz Pro-Comp sight; steel receiver with gold accented engravings; ventilated

barrel; walnut stock with close radius pistol grip and right-hand palm swell; semi-beavertail forearm with finger grooves
MSRP **$2649.99**

CYNERGY CLASSIC TRAP UNSINGLE COMBO WITH ADJUSTABLE COMB

Action: Single shot and over/under
Stock: Walnut
Barrel: 32/32 in., 30/34 in., 32/34 in.
Chokes: Four Invector-Plus Midas Grade choke tubes
Weight: 8 lb. 13 oz.–8 lb. 15 oz.
Bore/Gauge: 12
Magazine: 1 or 2 shells
Features: Steel receiver with MonoLock hinge; double- and single-barrel sets included; reverse striker ignition system; impact ejectors; top-tang barrel selector/safety; gloss finish Monte Carlo grade III/IV walnut stock with right-hand palm swell
MSRP **$4269.99**

CYNERGY FEATHER

Action: Over/under
Stock: Walnut
Barrel: 26 in., 28 in.
Chokes: Three Invector-Plus choke tubes on 12 and 20, Standard Invector on 28 and .410
Weight: 5 lb. 12 oz.–6 lb. 12 oz.
Bore/Gauge: 12, 20
Magazine: 2 shells
Features: Lightweight alloy receiver; gold enhanced grayed finish; MonoLock hinge; reverse striker ignition system; top-tang barrel selector/safety; Inflex technology recoil pad system; ivory front and mid-bead sights
MSRP . . . . **$2139.99–$2199.99**

CYNERGY FIELD

Action: Over/under
Stock: Walnut
Barrel: 26 in., 28 in.
Chokes: Three Invector-Plus choke tubes on 12 and 20; Standard Invector on 28 and .410
Weight: 6 lb. 1 oz.–7 lb. 11 oz.
Bore/Gauge: 12, 20, 28, .410
Magazine: 2 shells
Features: Steel receiver with MonoLock hinge; reverse striker ignition system; impact ejectors; oil finish walnut stock; ivory front and mid-bead sights
MSRP . . . . **$1869.99–$1939.99**

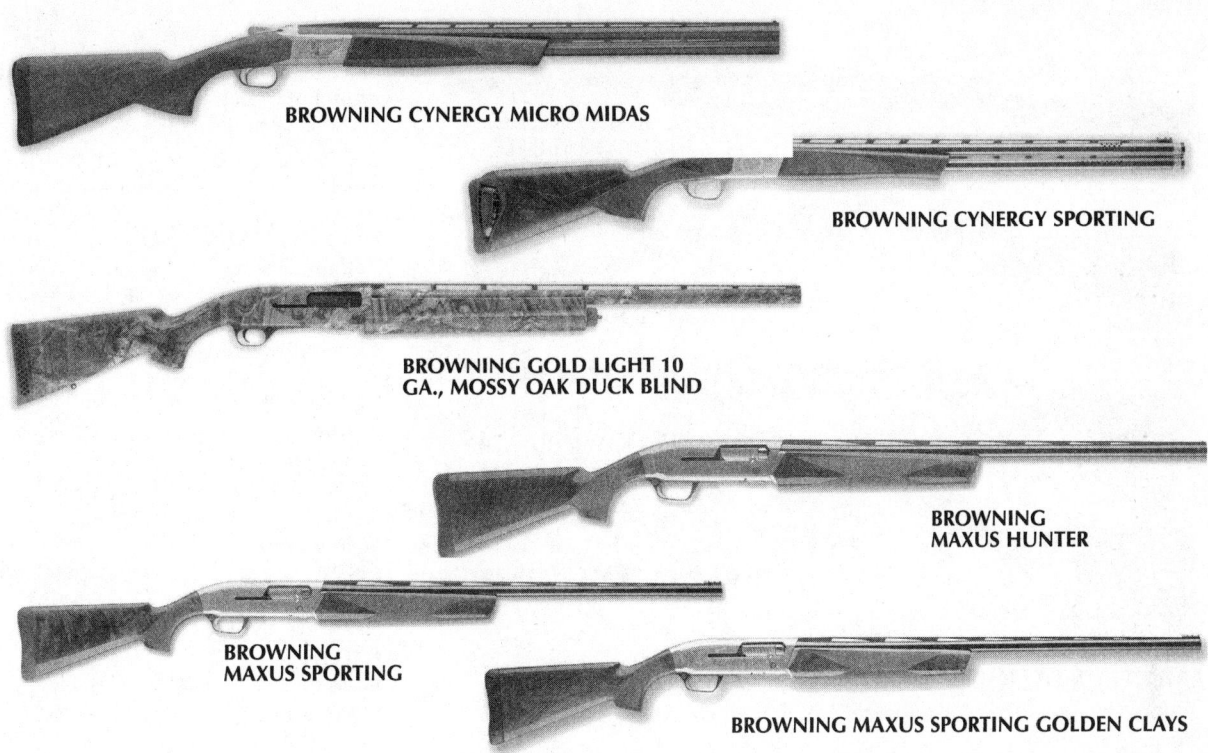

BROWNING CYNERGY MICRO MIDAS

BROWNING CYNERGY SPORTING

BROWNING GOLD LIGHT 10 GA., MOSSY OAK DUCK BLIND

BROWNING MAXUS HUNTER

BROWNING MAXUS SPORTING

BROWNING MAXUS SPORTING GOLDEN CLAYS

CYNERGY MICRO MIDAS
Action: Over/under
Stock: Wood
Barrel: 24 in., 26 in.
Chokes: F, M, IC
Weight: 6 lb.–6 lb. 2 oz.
Bore/Gauge: 20
Magazine: 2 shells
Features: Matte blued barrel finish; grade I/II black walnut stock with satin finish; ivory bead front sight; Cynergy Inflex recoil pad
MSRP $1869.99

CYNERGY SPORTING
Action: Over/under
Stock: Walnut
Barrel: 30 in., 32 in.
Chokes: Three Invector-Plus choke tubes
Weight: 7 lb. 14 oz.–8 lb.
Bore/Gauge: 12
Magazine: 2 shells
Features: Reverse striker ignition system; impact ejectors; top-tang barrel selector/safety; gloss oil finish on grade III/IV walnut; steel receiver; Inflex technology recoil pad system; HiViz Pro-Comp fiber optic sight
MSRP $2399.99

GOLD LIGHT 10 GA.
Action: Gas-operated semiautomatic
Stock: Composite
Barrel: 26 in., 28 in.
Chokes: Three Standard Invector choke tubes
Weight: 9 lb. 9 oz.–9 lb. 10 oz.
Bore/Gauge: 10
Magazine: 4+1 shells
Features: Aluminum alloy receiver; ventilated rib barrel; composite stock and forearm in MO Break-Up Country or MO Shadow Grass Blades; DuraTouch armor coating
MSRP $1739.99

MAXUS HUNTER
Action: Gas-operated semiautomatic
Stock: Composite
Barrel: 26 in., 28 in., 30 in.
Chokes: Three Invector-Plus
Weight: 6 lb. 15 oz.–7 lb. 1 oz.
Bore/Gauge: 12
Magazine: None
Features: Aluminum alloy receiver with durable satin nickel finish; laser engraving of pheasant and mallard on receiver; Inflex technology recoil pad; ivory front bead sight
MSRP . . . . $1549.99–$1699.99

MAXUS SPORTING
Action: Gas-operated semiautomatic
Stock: Walnut
Barrel: 28 in., 30 in.
Chokes: Five Invector-Plus choke tubes
Weight: 7 lb.–7 lb. 1 oz.
Bore/Gauge: 12
Magazine: None
Features: Aluminum alloy receiver with durable satin nickel finish; laser engraving of game birds transforming into clay birds; speed lock forearm; ivory mid bead sight, HiVix Tri-Comp fiber optic front sight
MSRP $1759.99

MAXUS SPORTING GOLDEN CLAYS
Action: Gas-operated semiautomatic
Stock: Walnut
Barrel: 28 in., 30 in.
Chokes: 5 Invector-Plus
Weight: 7 lb. 3 oz.–7 lb. 4 oz.
Bore/ Gauge: 12
Magazine: None
Features: Gold-enhanced engraving; lightweight aluminum alloy; flat, ventilated rib; 3 in. chamber; Power Drive Gas System; Speed Lock Forearm; Vector Pro lengthened forcing cone; HiViz Pro-Comp fiber optic front sight
MSRP $2069.99

Browning

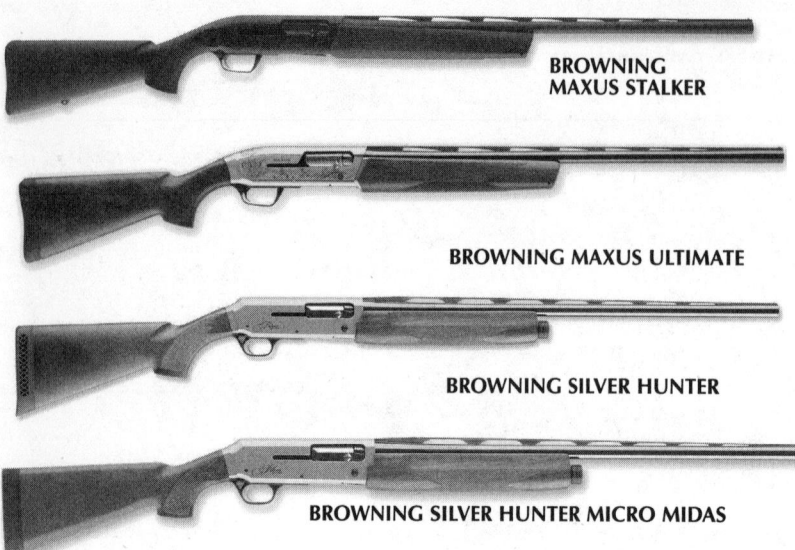

BROWNING MAXUS STALKER

BROWNING MAXUS ULTIMATE

BROWNING SILVER HUNTER

BROWNING SILVER HUNTER MICRO MIDAS

MAXUS STALKER

Action: Gas-operated semiautomatic
Stock: Composite
Barrel: 26 in., 28 in.
Chokes: Three Invector Plus choke tubes
Weight: 6 lb. 14 oz.–7 lb. 2.08 oz.
Bore/Gauge: 12
Magazine: None
Features: Magazine cut-off, matte black composite stock with pistol grip; speed lock forearm; textured gripping surfaces; Dura Touch armor coating; Inflex technology recoil pads; lightning trigger system; ventilated rib
MSRP . . . . $1379.99–$1549.99

MAXUS ULTIMATE

Action: Gas-operated semiautomatic
Stock: Walnut
Barrel: 26 in., 28 in., 30 in.
Chokes: Invector Plus (F, M, IC)
Weight: 7 lb. 1 oz.–7 lb. 4 oz.
Bore/Gauge: 12
Magazine: None
Features: Strong, lightweight aluminum alloy receiver; durable satin nickel finish; laser engraved (pintails on the left-hand side and pheasants on the right); gloss blued finish; ventilated rib; gloss oil finished grade III walnut with close radius pistol grip; speed lock forearm; shim

adjustable for length of pull, cast, and drop; Inflex technology recoil pad; brass bead front sight; ABS case included
MSRP $1939.99

SILVER HUNTER

Action: Gas-operated semiautomatic
Stock: Walnut
Barrel: 26 in., 28 in., 30 in.
Chokes: Three Invector-Plus choke tubes
Weight: 6 lb. 5 oz.–7 lb. 9 oz.
Bore/Gauge: 12, 20
Magazine: None
Features: Aluminum alloy receiver; ventilated rib barrel; satin finish walnut stock
MSRP . . . . $1199.99–$1359.99

SILVER HUNTER MICRO MIDAS

Action: Gas-operated semiautomatic
Stock: Walnut
Barrel: 24 in., 26 in.
Chokes: Three Invector-Plus choke tubes
Weight: 6 lb.–7 lb. 5 oz.
Bore/Gauge: 12, 20
Magazine: None
Features: Semi-humpback receiver design with silver finish; ivory front bead sight
MSRP $1199.99

Caesar Guerini

CHALLENGER ASCENT

Action: Over/under
Stock: Hand-rubbed oil
Barrel: 30 in., 32 in.
Chokes: 6 MAXIS competition chokes
Weight: 8 lb. 6 oz.–8 lb. 8 oz.
Bore/ Gauge: 12
Magazine: 2 shells
Features: 10mm high tapered top rib is designed to shoot at 50/50 percent point-of-impact; White Bradley style front sight, with brass center bead; DTS trigger system; manual safety
Right-hand: $6295.00
Left-hand: $6530.00

ELLIPSE

Action: Round body
Stock: Hand-rubbed oil on walnut
Barrel: 28 in.
Chokes: 5 nickel plated, flush fitting
Weight: 6 lb. 1 oz.–7 lb. 4 oz.
Bore/ Gauge: 12, 20, 28

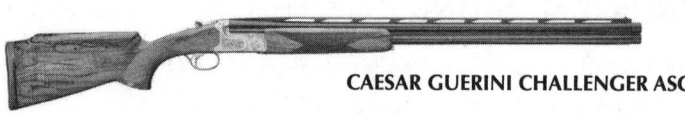

CAESAR GUERINI CHALLENGER ASCENT

Magazine: 2 shells
Features: Engraving pattern coated with Invisalloy; brass front bead sight; single (selective optional) trigger; manual safety; tapered, solid top rib
Standard right-hand: $4650.00
Left-hand or English
   stocks: . . . . add $235.00

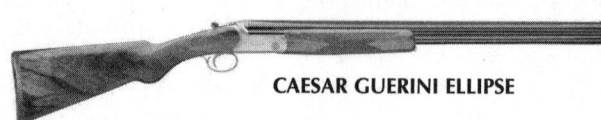

CAESAR GUERINI ELLIPSE

Caesar Guerini

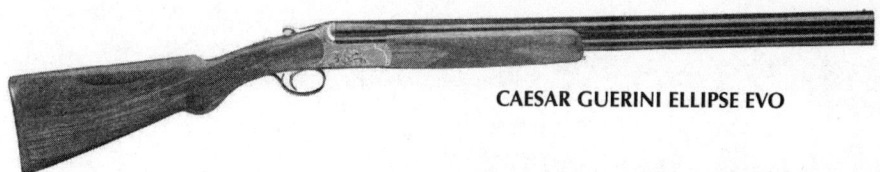

CAESAR GUERINI ELLIPSE EVO

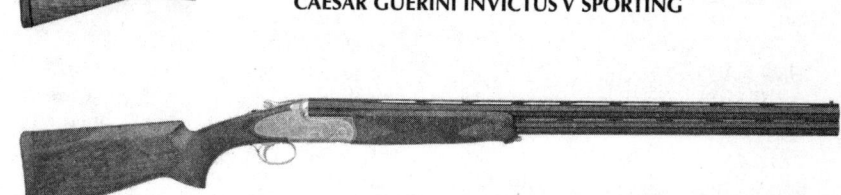

CAESAR GUERINI INVICTUS I SPORTING

CAESAR GUERINI INVICTUS V SPORTING

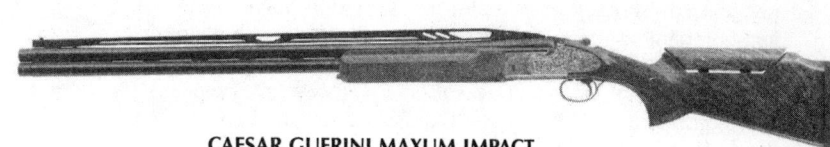

CAESAR GUERINI MAGNUS SPORTING

CAESAR GUERINI MAXUM IMPACT

ELLIPSE EVO

Action: Over/under
Stock: Walnut
Barrel: 28 in.
Chokes: 5 choke tube options
Weight: 6 lb.–7 lb.
Bore/Gauge: 12, 20, 28
Magazine: None
Features: Single trigger; rounded forend; chrome-lined barrel; non-ventilated center rib; hand-polished coin finish receiver with Invisalloy protective finish
Standard right-hand 12- or 20-ga.: . $6450.00
20/28-ga. combo: $8605.00
Left-hand or English
   stocks: . . . . add $235.00

INVICTUS I SPORTING

Action: Over/under
Stock: Wood
Barrel: 30 in., 32 in.
Chokes: 6 MAXIS competition chokes
Weight: 8 lb. 1 oz.–8 lb. 3 oz.
Bore/Gauge: 12
Magazine: 2 shells
Features: White Bradley style front silver center bead; manual safety (automatic optional); DTS-2 trigger system with two trigger pull weight options, take up, over travel and length of pull adjustments
Standard right-hand: $6995.00
Left-hand or English
   stock: . . . . add $235.00

INVICTUS V SPORTING

Action: Over/under
Stock: Wood
Barrel: 30 in., 32 in.
Chokes: 6 MAXIS competition chokes
Weight: 8 lb. 1 oz.–8 lb. 3 oz.
Bore/Gauge: 12
Magazine: 2 shells
Features: DPS2 trigger system; factory selective release triggers available in single and double release; contemporary Italian Ornato-style engraving

with deep relief game scenes; white Bradley-style front silver center bead
MSRP $8795.00

MAGNUS SPORTING

Action: Over/under
Stock: Hand-rubbed oil on walnut
Barrel: 30 in., 32 in., 34 in.
Chokes: 6 CCP competition chokes (6 MAXIS for 12 Ga. models)
Weight: 7 lb. 6 oz.–8 lb. 2 oz.
Bore/ Gauge: 12, 20, 28, .410
Magazine: 2 shells
Features: Single selective trigger; manual safety; ventilated center rib; available 20/28 gauge combo and 20/28/.410 gauge combo
Standard right-hand: $5450.00
20/28-ga. combo: $7975.00
20/28/.410 combo: $10,635.00
Left-hand stock: . . . . . . add $235.00
Adjustable comb: . . . . add $355.00
Case-hardened
   receiver: . . . . add $295.00

MAXUM IMPACT

Action: Over/under
Stock: Checkered walnut with adjustable cheekpiece
Barrel: 30 in., 32 in.
Chokes: Maxis choke system
Weight: 7 lb. 11 oz.–8 lb. 7 oz.
Bore/Gauge: 12, 20
Magazine: 2 shells
Features: Engraved receiver; 17mm-tall D.T.S. rib for more upright shooting; 5 in. dual conical forcing cones; selective and non-selective triggers available; left-hand available
Standard: $8795.00
Left-hand: $9030.00

SHOTGUNS

Caesar Guerini

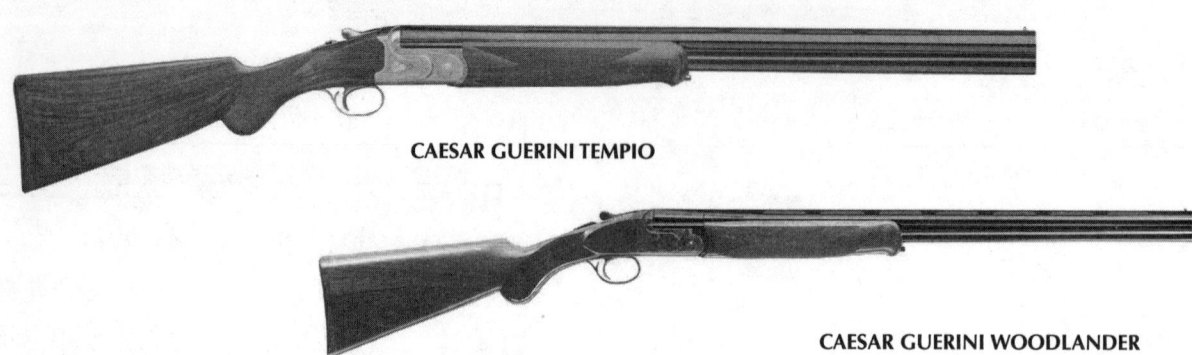

CAESAR GUERINI TEMPIO

CAESAR GUERINI WOODLANDER

TEMPIO

Action: Over/under
Stock: Turkish walnut
Barrel: 26 in., 28 in., 30 in.
Chokes: 5 nickel plated, flush fitting chokes
Weight: 6 lb.–7 lb.
Bore/Gauge: 12, 20, 28, .410
Magazine: 2 shells
Features: Designed to be a sleek and fast pointing shotgun in the field; perfect companion for upland game hunters; low-profile receiver matched with a trim stock, classic Prince-of-Wales grip and schnabel forend make the gun a perfect match for fast game birds; contemporary style of "ornato" style scroll with tasteful gold accents; Invisalloy protective coating

Standard:..............	$4075.00
20/28-ga. combo:........	$6145.00
20/28/.410 combo:	$8395.00
Left-hand or English stock:...........	add $235.00

WOODLANDER

Action: Over/under
Stock: English walnut
Barrel: 26 in., 28 in., 30 in.
Chokes: Five precision patterned flush chokes (CYL, IC, M, IM, F)
Weight: 6 lb.–7 lb.
Bore/Gauge: 12, 20, 28, .410
Magazine: 2 shells
Features: Gun reflects passion for fall coverts, autumn foliage, wet gun dogs, and the smell of wood; understated elegance of color case hardening and nicely figured, oil-finished English walnut that speaks of quality from a bygone era; a superior-handling upland game gun that's perfect for tight cover and fast-flushing birds

Standard:..............	$3595.00
20/28 combo:...........	$5665.00
20/28/.410 combo:	$7915.00
Left-hand or English stock:...........	add $235.00

Chiappa Firearms

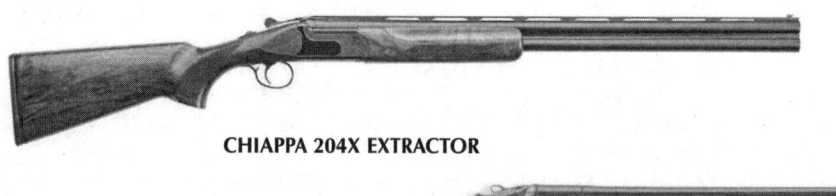

CHIAPPA 204X EXTRACTOR

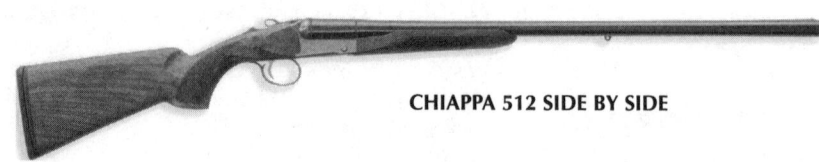

CHIAPPA 512 SIDE BY SIDE

204X

Action: Over/under
Stock: Walnut
Barrel: 26 in., 28 in.
Chokes: Skeet, IC, MOD, IM, F
Weight: 6 lb. 6 oz.–6 lb. 13 oz.
Bore/Gauge: 20, 12
Magazine: 2 shells
Features: Fiber optic sights; matte black receiver; 12-ga. with walnut stock offered in 26- or 28-in. barrels and 3-in. chambers, Realtree Xtra Green camo version has 24-in. barrels and chambers 3 ½-in. shells

Camo:	$1089.00
Walnut:	$999.00

512 SIDE BY SIDE

Action: Break-action side-by-side
Stock: Walnut
Barrel: 28 in.
Chokes: Rem-choke in all barrels
Weight: 6 lb. 2 oz.
Bore/Gauge: 12, 20, 28
Magazine: 2 shells
Features: Interchangeable choke tubes in each barrel; white receiver

MSRP................	$1169.00

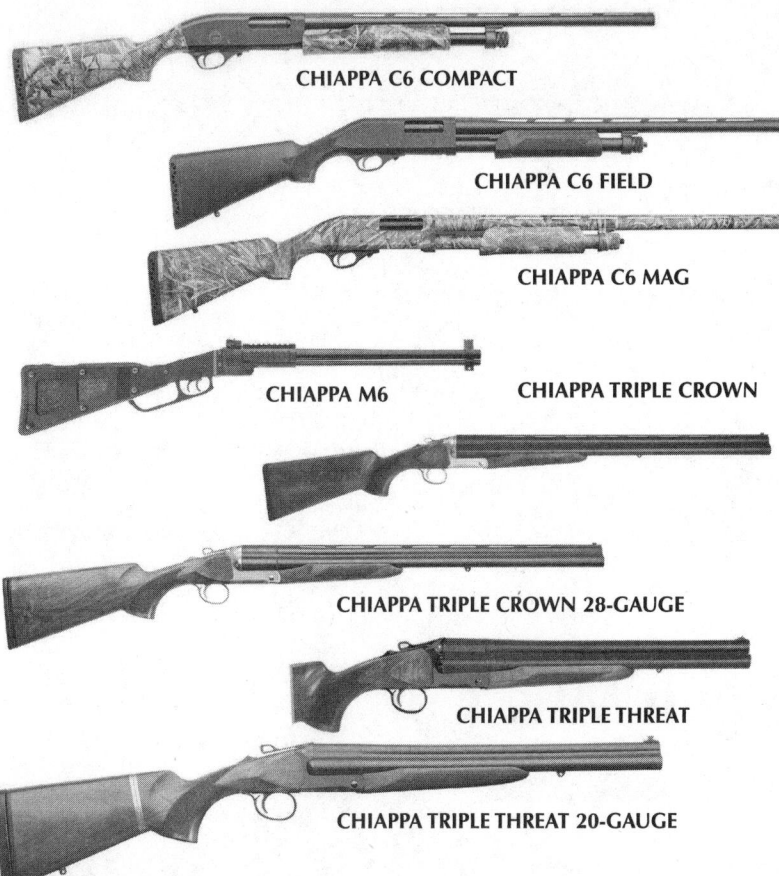

CHIAPPA C6 COMPACT

CHIAPPA C6 FIELD

CHIAPPA C6 MAG

CHIAPPA M6

CHIAPPA TRIPLE CROWN

CHIAPPA TRIPLE CROWN 28-GAUGE

CHIAPPA TRIPLE THREAT

CHIAPPA TRIPLE THREAT 20-GAUGE

C6 COMPACT

Action: Pump
Stock: Synthetic
Barrel: 22 in.
Chokes: RemChoke MOD
Weight: 5 lb.
Bore/Gauge: 20
Magazine: 5+1 shells
Features: Black receiver, camo stock and forend
MSRP **$439.00**

C6 FIELD

Action: Pump
Stock: Synthetic
Barrel: 26 in.
Chokes: MC-3
Weight: 5 lb. 6 oz.–6 lb. 6 oz.
Bore/Gauge: 12, 20
Magazine: 5+1 shells
Features: Dual pump action bars; drilled and tapped for rails; interchangeable choke tubes; has full RealTree XTRA GREEN camo in 20-gauge model; fiber optic front sight
MSRP **$409.00**

C6 MAG

Action: Pump
Stock: Synthetic

Barrel: 24 in., 28 in.
Chokes: MC-3
Weight: 6 lb. 11 oz.
Bore/Gauge: 12
Magazine: 5+1 shells
Features: Dual pump action bars; drilled and tapped for rails; interchangeable choke tubes; fiber optic front sight; comes in RealTree camo or RealTree XTRA GREEN camo
MSRP **$519.00**

M6

Action: Over/under
Stock: Foam and steel
Barrel: 18.5 in.
Chokes: N/A
Weight: 6 lb.
Bore/Gauge: 20-ga./.22LR, 12-ga./.22LR, 12-ga./.22WMR, 20-ga./.22WMR
Magazine: 2 shells
Features: Three Picatinny rails; cleaning kit included in stock; folds for transportation; top tang manual safety; adjustable iron type with fiber optics
MSRP . . . .**$729.00–$949.00**

TRIPLE CROWN

Action: Break-action
Stock: Wood

Barrel: 26 in., 28 in.
Chokes: Rem-choke in all barrels
Weight: 8 lb. 11 oz.
Bore/Gauge: 12, 20
Magazine: 3 shells
Features: Side-by-side and middle arrangement sporting model with three shotgun barrels; chokes in all three barrels; sling swivel studs
MSRP **$2039.00**

TRIPLE CROWN 28-GAUGE

Action: Break-action
Stock: Walnut
Barrel: 26 in.
Chokes: Rem-choke in all barrels
Weight: 7 lb.
Bore/Gauge: 28
Magazine: 3 shells
Features: Compact barrels; a removal buttstock for easy storage or use as a pistol grip; interchangeable choke tubes; side-by-side and middle arrangement defense model with three shotgun barrels; sling swivel studs
MSRP **$2039.00**

TRIPLE THREAT

Action: Break-action
Stock: Wood
Barrel: 18.5 in.
Chokes: Rem-choke in all barrels
Weight: 8 lb.
Bore/ Gauge: 12
Magazine: 3 shells
Features: Side-by-side and middle arrangement defense model with three shotgun barrels; chokes in all three barrels; sling swivel studs; wooden stock can be partly disassembled
MSRP **$2079.00**

TRIPLE THREAT 20-GAUGE

Action: Break-action
Stock: Walnut
Barrel: 18.5 in.
Chokes: Rem-choke in all barrels
Weight: 7 lb. 3 oz.
Bore/Gauge: 20
Magazine: 3 shells
Features: Compact barrels; a removal buttstock for easy storage or use as a pistol grip; interchangeable choke tubes; side-by-side and middle arrangement defense model with three shotgun barrels; sling swivel studs
MSRP **$2079.00**

Cimarron Firearms Co.

CIMARRON 1878 COACH GUN

1878 COACH GUN
Action: Side-by-Side
Stock: Wood
Barrel: 20 in., 26 in.

Chokes: Open
Weight: 8 lb.–8 lb. 15 oz.
Bore/ Gauge: 12
Magazine: 2 shells

Features: 3 in. blue steel real working hammers; available in standard blue, original finish, or USA finish
MSRP . . . . **$596.70–$879.90**

Connecticut Shotgun Mfg. Co.

CONNECTICUT SHOTGUN MFG. CO.
A-10 AMERICAN

CONNECTICUT SHOTGUN MFG.
CO. CSMC MODEL 21

A-10 AMERICAN
Action: Sidelock over/under
Stock: Checkered American black walnut
Barrel: 26 in.–32 in.
Chokes: 5 TruLock tubes
Weight: 6 lb. 8 oz.–7 lb. 8 oz.
Bore/Gauge: 12, 20, 28
Magazine: 2 shells
Features: Finely engraved, cut checkering; ventilated rib; pistol grip or straight grip; auto ejectors, single selective trigger; Galazan pad
MSRP . . . . . . **Contact manufacturer for pricing**

CSMC MODEL 21
Action: Sidelock over/under
Stock: American black walnut
Barrel: 28 in., 30 in.
Chokes: 5 included

Weight: 7 lb. 9 oz.
Bore/Gauge: 20
Magazine: 2 shells
Features: Available in Standard grade with a blued receiver, a #6 Pigeon grade, and a Grand American grade.
MSRP . . . . . . **Contact manufacturer for pricing**

CZ-USA (Ceska Zbrojovka)

CZ-USA 612 FIELD

612 FIELD
Action: Pump
Stock: Walnut
Barrel: 28 in.
Chokes: 3 chokes

Weight: 6 lb. 3 oz.
Bore/Gauge: 12
Magazine: 4+1 shells
Features: Satin chrome finish; capable of shooting 2 ¾-in. and 3-in. shells; supplied with three chokes
MSRP **$389.00**

CZ-USA (Ceska Zbrojovka)

CZ-USA 620 BIG GAME

CZ-USA 620 YOUTH

CZ-USA 712 ALS G2

CZ–USA 712 GREEN G2

CZ–USA 712 SYNTHETIC CAMO G2

CZ-USA 712 G2

CZ-USA 712 TARGET G2

620 BIG GAME

Action: Pump
Stock: Synthetic
Barrel: 22 in.
Chokes: 1 chokes
Weight: 5 lb. 3 oz.
Bore/Gauge: 20
Magazine: 4 shells
Features: Weaver rail
MSRP **$399.00**

620 YOUTH

Action: Pump
Stock: Synthetic
Barrel: 24 in.
Chokes: 3 chokes
Weight: 5 lb. 3 oz.
Bore/Gauge: 20
Magazine: 4 shells
Features: Brass bead sight; capable of shooting 2 ¾-in. and 3-in. shells; supplied with three chokes
MSRP **$349.00**

712 ADJUSTABLE LENGTH STOCK (ALS) G2

Action: Gas-operated semiautomatic
Stock: Polymer
Barrel: 26 in., 28 in.
Chokes: Interchangeable chokes (F, M, IC)
Weight: 7 lb. 13 oz.
Bore/Gauge: 12
Magazine: 4+1 shells
Features: Polymer ATI adjsutable stock; fiber optic front sight; adjustable length of pull from 12 to 14 inches
MSRP **$579.00**

712 G2

Action: Semiautomatic
Stock: Turkish walnut
Barrel: 26 in., 28 in.
Chokes: 5 included
Weight: 7 lb. 5 oz.–7 lb. 6 oz.
Bore/Gauge: 12
Magazine: 4+1 shells
Features: Accepting 2¾ and 3-inch shells, it is an all-arounder, a great choice for upland game, waterfowl, or clays; barrel is chrome-lined and

has a matte black hard chrome exterior that will resist corrosion for many seasons in the field; G2 stock adds new laser-engraved checkering, right-hand palm swell as well as a barrel lock-ring to make assembly easier
MSRP **$499.00**

712 GREEN G2

Action: Semiautomatic
Stock: Turkish walnut
Barrel: 28 in.
Chokes: 5 chokes
Weight: 7 lb. 6 oz.
Bore/Gauge: 12
Magazine: 4+1 shells
Features: Green anodized receiver; laser-cut checkering; healthy palm swell; smooth gas-operating system
MSRP **$499.00**

712 SYNTHETIC CAMO G2

Action: Semiautomatic
Stock: Synthetic
Barrel: 28 in.
Chokes: 3 extended black
Weight: 6 lb. 11 oz.
Bore/Gauge: 12
Magazine: 4+1 shells
Features: Weatherproof; durable polymer stocks
MSRP **$679.00**

712 TARGET G2

Action: Gas-operated semiautomatic
Stock: Walnut
Barrel: 30 in.
Chokes: Interchangeable chokes (F, M, IC)
Weight: 7 lb. 10 oz.
Bore/Gauge: 12
Magazine: 4+1 shells
Features: Gas operated aluminum alloy action with target-grade enhancements; chrome-lined barrel; fiber optic front sight on a 10mm stepped rib; Schnabel forend; smooth rounded heel; Monte Carlo buttstock
MSRP **$680.00**

SHOTGUNS

CZ-USA (Ceska Zbrojovka)

CZ-USA 712 UTILITY G2

CZ-USA 720 ALS G2

CZ-USA 912

CZ–USA ALL AMERICAN TRAP COMBO

CZ–USA DRAKE

CZ-USA LADY STERLING

CZ–USA REDHEAD PREMIER

712 UTILITY G2
Action: Semiautomatic
Stock: Synthetic
Barrel: 20 in.
Chokes: Screw-in chokes (F, IM, M, IC, C)
Weight: 6 lb. 10 oz.
Bore/Gauge: 12
Magazine: 4+1 shells
Features: 3-in. chamber cross-bolt safety; black synthetic stock; matte chrome black barrel
MSRP $499.00

720 ALS G2
Action: Semiautomatic
Stock: Synthetic
Barrel: 24 in.
Chokes: 3 chokes
Weight: 6 lb. 10 oz.
Bore/Gauge: 20

Magazine: 4 shells
Features: Fully-adjustable ATI Akita stock; capable of shooting 2 ¾-in. and 3-in. shells; ejector
MSRP $599.00

912
Action: Recoil-operated semiautomatic
Stock: Walnut
Barrel: 28 in.
Chokes: 5 interchangeable choke tubes
Weight: 7 lb. 5 oz.
Bore/Gauge: 12
Magazine: 4+1 shells
Features: Fiber optic front bead; features a gloss black finish on metalwork; cross-bolt safety; chrome-lined barrel; aluminum frame
MSRP $544.00

ALL AMERICAN TRAP COMBO
Action: Over/under
Stock: Turkish walnut
Barrel: 32 in.
Chokes: 1 Skeet, 1 IC, 2 M, 1 IM, 2 F
Weight: 8 lb. 8 oz.
Bore/Gauge: 12
Magazine: 2 shells
Features: Comes with a single-shot un-single with a dial-adjustable aluminum rib (adjustable from 50/50 up to 90/10 point of impact) and a standard set of barrels with stepped rib (50/50 point of impact); surface hardened CNC-milled action; firing pins that ride in bushings; replaceable locking blocks; adjustable parallel comb; competition trigger; auto ejectors
MSRP $3,399.00

DRAKE
Action: Over/under
Stock: Turkish walnut
Barrel: 28 in.
Chokes: 5 chokes
Weight: 6 lb. 8 oz.–7 lb. 6 oz.
Bore/Gauge: 12, 20
Magazine: 2 shells
Features: CNCed action; extractor operation; single selectable trigger; mid-rib delete; laser-cut checkering
MSRP $629.00

LADY STERLING
Action: Over/under
Stock: Turkish walnut
Barrel: 28 in.
Chokes: 5 chokes
Weight: 7 lb. 8 oz.
Bore/Gauge: 12
Magazine: 2 shells
Features: Capable of shooting both 2¾-in. and 3-in. shells
MSRP $1321.00

REDHEAD PREMIER
Action: Over/under
Stock: Turkish walnut
Barrel: 26 in., 28 in.
Chokes: 5 flush-mount
Weight: 6 lb. 14 oz.
Bore/Gauge: 12, 20, 28, .410
Magazine: 2 shells
Features: The tried-and-true Redhead also gets CZ's new 1-piece CNCed receiver; laser-cut checkering, solid mid-ribs, pistol grip, and a classy white bead; silver receiver and ejectors that kick out the spent shells automatically, hard plastic case included
MSRP . . . . $959.00–$1057.00

SHOTGUNS

CZ-USA (Ceska Zbrojovka)

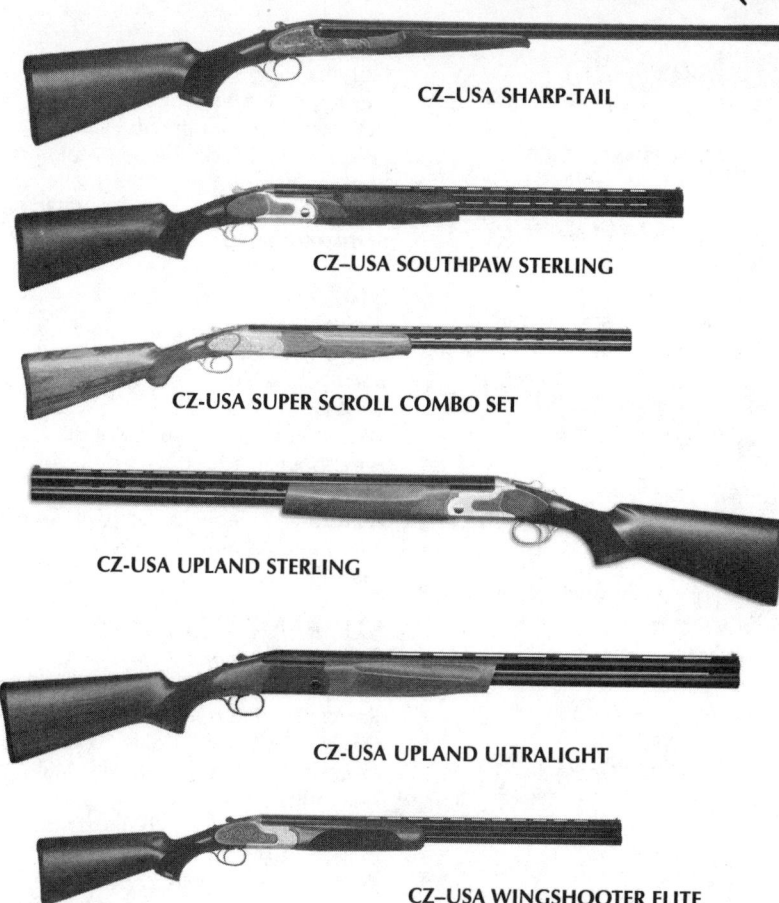

CZ–USA SHARP-TAIL

CZ–USA SOUTHPAW STERLING

CZ-USA SUPER SCROLL COMBO SET

CZ-USA UPLAND STERLING

CZ-USA UPLAND ULTRALIGHT

CZ–USA WINGSHOOTER ELITE

SHARP-TAIL
Action: Side-by-side
Stock: Wood
Barrel: 28 in.
Chokes: 5 flush interchangeable
Weight: 6 lb.– 7 lb. 5 oz.
Bore/Gauge: 12, 20, 28, .410
Magazine: 2 shells
Features: Black hard chrome barrel finish; color case hardened receiver finish; semi-beavertail forend; extractor; manual safety
MSRP . . . . $1022.00–$1229.00

SOUTHPAW STERLING
Action: Over/under
Stock: Turkish walnut with laser stippling
Barrel: 30 in.
Chokes: 5 flush-mount
Weight: 7 lb. 8 oz.
Bore/Gauge: 12
Magazine: 2 shells
Features: Cast on for left-handed shooters; shares most of the other features of the Upland Sterling, but with a more universal 29-inch barrel; a mechanical trigger and safety with

selectable barrels; a regular right-handed top lever latch; plastic case
MSRP $999.00

SUPER SCROLL COMBO SET
Action: Over/under
Stock: Grade 5 Turkish walnut
Barrel: 30 in.
Chokes: 5 per gauge
Weight: 6 lb. 11 oz.
Bore/ Gauge: 20, 28
Magazine: 2 shells
Features: Intended for the hunter or sporting clays shooter who wants to carry an absolutely gorgeous shotgun; ornate hand-engraved scrollwork on receiver, faux sideplates, trigger guard and mono-block; both barrel sets are equipped with ejectors; five chokes per gauge and a full grip, making it an excellent crossover gun between clay and feather
MSRP $3899.00

UPLAND STERLING
Action: Over/under
Stock: Turkish walnut

Barrel: 28 in.
Chokes: 5 screw-in
Weight: 7 lb. 8 oz.
Bore/ Gauge: 12
Magazine: 2 shells
Features: Built on a new platform featuring a CNC-milled steel receiver, resulting in mechanical components that operate with clockwork precision and consistency; Turkish walnut stock features a stippled grip area on the wrist and forend rather than the traditional checkering
MSRP $999.00

UPLAND ULTRALIGHT, ULTRALIGHT GREEN
Action: Over/under
Stock: Turkish walnut
Barrel: 26 in., 28 in.
Chokes: F, IM, M, IC, C
Weight: 6 lb.
Bore/Gauge: 12, 20
Magazine: 2 shells
Features: Lightweight, black alloy receiver; vent rib; matte-blued model available in 12-gauge only; green model features a unique green anodized receiver and is available in 12- or 20-gauge, both with 28-in. barrels
MSRP $762.00

WINGSHOOTER ELITE
Action: Over/under
Stock: Turkish walnut
Barrel: 28 in.
Chokes: 5 flush-mount
Weight: 7 lb. 6 oz.
Bore/Gauge: 12, 20
Magazine: 2 shells
Features: Replaces the Wingshooter; new CNCed 1-piece receiver; fully hand-engraved side-plates, reminiscent of custom-grade Super Scroll; single selectable trigger, solid mid-ribs, ejectors, and two-tone chromed finish; laser-cut checkering, solid mid-ribs, pistol grip stock, white bead; hard plastic case
MSRP $1059.00

Escort by Legacy Sports

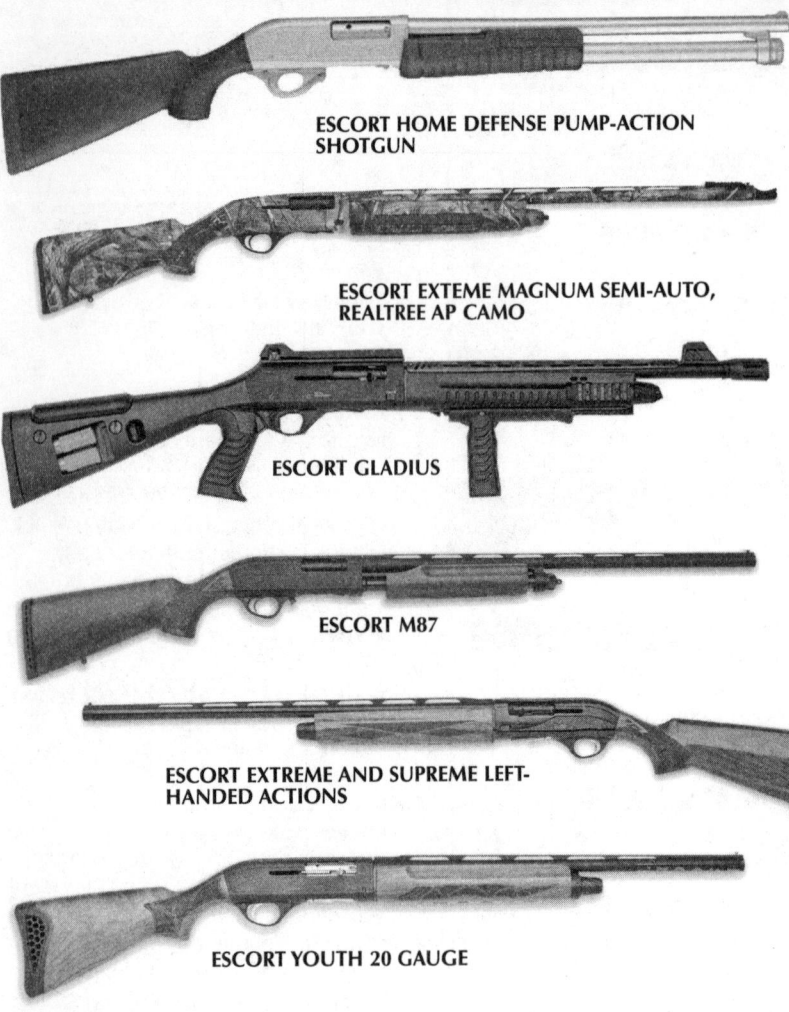

ESCORT HOME DEFENSE PUMP-ACTION SHOTGUN

ESCORT EXTEME MAGNUM SEMI-AUTO, REALTREE AP CAMO

ESCORT GLADIUS

ESCORT M87

ESCORT EXTREME AND SUPREME LEFT-HANDED ACTIONS

ESCORT YOUTH 20 GAUGE

HOME DEFENSE PUMP-ACTION SHOTGUN

Action: Pump
Stock: Synthetic
Barrel: 18 in.
Chokes: Cylinder bore
Weight: 6 lb. 4 oz.
Bore/Gauge: 12
Magazine: 5 shells
Features: Rifle-style front sight; black synthetic stock; AimGuard has black metal finish, MarineGuard has water resistant nickel finish; sling swivel studs; dovetail receiver for mounting accessory sights
AimGuard: $319.00
MarineGuard: $385.00

EXTREME MAGNUM

Action: Semiautomatic
Stock: Synthetic
Barrel: 22 in., 24 in., 26 in., 28 in.
Chokes: 3, 5, 6 chokes depending on model

Weight: 7 lb.–7 lb. 10.4 oz.
Bore/Gauge: 12, 20
Magazine: 5+1 shells
Features: Non-slip grip pads on the forend and pistol grip; SMART Valve gas pistons; HiVis MagniSight fiber optic, magnetic sight; available in black synthetic and the following camo patterns: Realtree Max-5HD, Realtree APHD camo, Realtree APHD Turkey, Foxy Woods, and Yote. Left-hand models available in the Realtree camos and black synthetic in both 3- and 3 ½-in. models
3-in.: . . . . $565.00–$753.00
3 1/2-in.: . . . . $655.00–$825.00

GLADIUS

Action: Pump or semiautomatic
Stock: Synthetic
Barrel: 18 in.
Chokes: C
Weight: 6 lb. 13 oz.
Bore/Gauge: 20

Magazine: 5+1 shells
Features: Fiber optic front sight with elevation adjustment; ghost ring rear sight with full adjustment; Picatinny rails; muzzle break; forend pistol grip; built-in holder for two extra shells
Pump: $485.00
Semiautomatic: $590.00

M87

Action: Pump
Stock: Wood
Barrel: 22–28 in.
Chokes: Multi-3
Weight: 5 lb. 13 oz.–6 lb. 13 oz.
Bore/Gauge: .12, 20
Magazine: 4 +1 shells
Features: Available in youth; all come with 3-inch chambers
MSRP $359.00

SUPREME (LEFT-HAND)

Action: Semiautomatic
Stock: Wood
Barrel: 26 in., 28 in.
Chokes: F, M, IM, IC, Skeet (Extreme Camo models also come with MR Waterfowl)
Weight: 6 lb. 8 oz.–7 lb. 6 oz.
Bore/ Gauge: 12, 20
Magazine: 5+1 shells
Features: Turkish walnut stock, chome moly-lined barrels, fiber optic sight, receiver dovetailed accessory rail, stock shim adjustments, single-round magazine cut-off, SMART valve self-regulating gas piston, and FAST loading system; left-hand available in both gauges
MSRP $629.00

YOUTH SEMI-AUTO SHOTGUN

Action: Semiautomatic
Stock: Wood, synthetic
Barrel: 22 in.
Chokes: Multi-3
Weight: 6 lb. 6 oz.
Bore/ Gauge: 20
Magazine: Cut-off for single round loading
Features: Youth model based on Standard Magnum semiauto series; chambers 3-in. shells, features TRIO recoil pad, 12.5-in. length of pull; wood stock, plus synthetic stocks available in black or camos Realtree Max-5HD, Realtree APHD, Yote, and Foxy Woods; left-hand models available in all but the two Realtree patterns
MSRP . . . . $535.00–$569.00

Fabarm

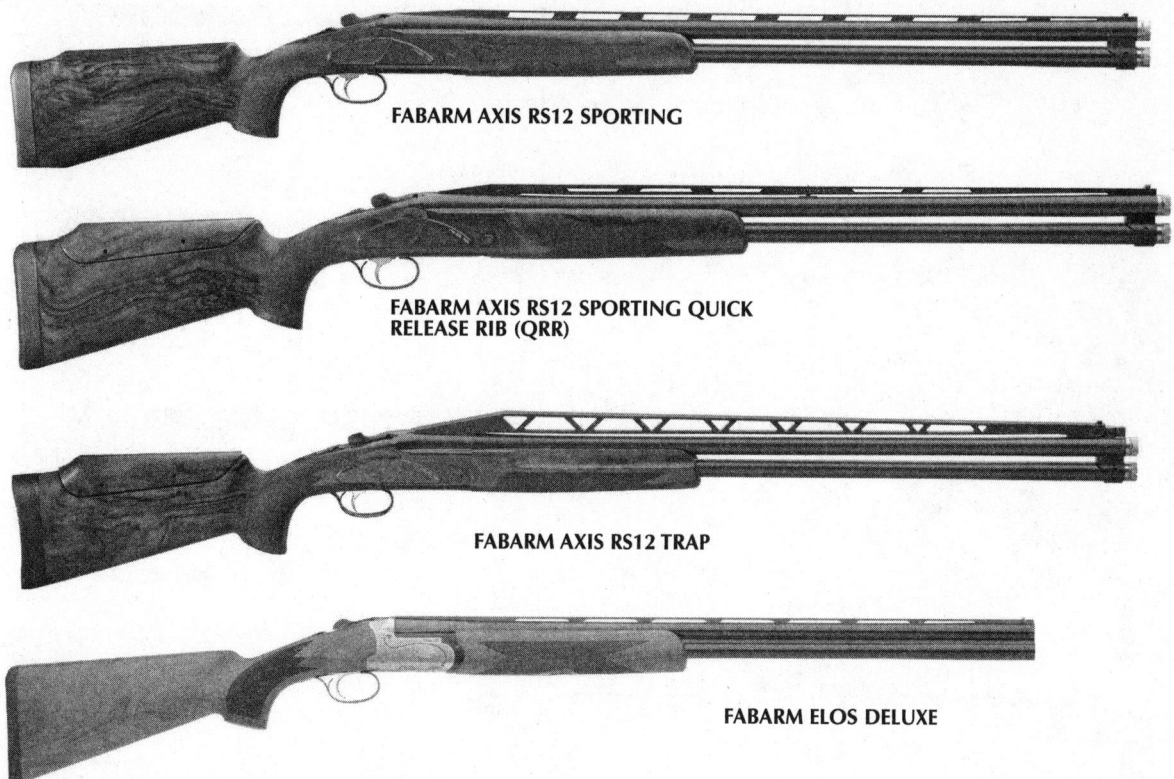

FABARM AXIS RS12 SPORTING

FABARM AXIS RS12 SPORTING QUICK RELEASE RIB (QRR)

FABARM AXIS RS12 TRAP

FABARM ELOS DELUXE

AXIS RS12 SPORTING
Action: Over/under
Stock: Wood
Barrel: 30 in., 32 in.
Chokes: 5 Exis HP
Weight: 8 lb. 4 oz.
Bore/Gauge: 12
Magazine: 2 shells
Features: Axis free-floating barrels feature Tribore HP tapered bores that lower recoil and reduce the need for excessively long forcing cones; blued action; Fabarm Micro Metric adjustable comb and left hand stocks available
Standard: **$3215.00**
Left-hand: . . . . **add $125.00**
Adjustable stock: . . . . . **add $355.00**

AXIS RS12 SPORTING QUICK RELEASE RIB (QRR)
Action: Over/under
Stock: Wood
Barrel: 30–32 in.
Chokes: 5 Exis HP
Weight: 8 lb. 6 oz.
Bore/Gauge: 12

Magazine: 2 shells
Features: Quick Release Rib design allows configuration for varying shooting styles and disciplines; standard offering includes two 10mm high ramp style ribs—one with a 50/50 percent point-of-impact and a second for a higher 65/35 percent; includes Tribore free floating barrels for improved balance and performance; 97mm Exis HP hyperbolic choke tubes; integrated recoil reducer; adjustable trigger; Triwood enhanced stock finish; Micro Metric adjustable stock comb
Standard: **$4280.00**
Left-hand stock: . . . . . . **add $125.00**
Adjustable stock: . . . . . **add $355.00**

AXIS RS12 TRAP
Action: Over/under
Stock: Wood
Barrel: 32 in., 34 in. (unsingle)
Chokes: 5 Exis HP
Weight: 8 lb. 14 oz.
Bore/Gauge: 12
Magazine: 1 or 2 shells
Features: Free-floating over-and-under

barrels; adjustable ribs on all barrels; tapered bores; integrated recoil reducer; adjustable comb; optional release triggers; 97mm Exis HP hyperbolic choke tubes; adjustable trigger; Triwood enhanced stock finish
Over/under or Unsingle: . . . **$4280.00**
Combo: **$5995.00**
Left-hand stock: . . . . . . **add $125.00**

ELOS DELUXE, DELUXE AL
Action: Over/under
Stock: European walnut
Barrel: 28 in.
Chokes: 5 Inner HP
Weight: 5 lb. 14 oz.–7 lb. 1 oz.
Bore/ Gauge: 12, 20, 28
Magazine: 2 shells
Features: Round action with pistol grip and semi-schnabel fore-end; AL version is nearly a pound lighter than the standard Deluxe
12, 20-gauge: **$3055.00**
28-gauge: **$3185.00**
Left-hand stock: . . . . . . **add $125.00**

Fabarm

FABARM L4S INITIAL HUNTER

FABARM L4S SERIES

FABARM XLR5 VELOCITY FR COMPACT

FABARM XLR5 WATERFOWLER

L4S INITIAL HUNTER

Action: Semiautomatic
Stock: Turkish walnut
Barrel: 26 in., 28 in.
Chokes: 3 inner HP
Weight: 6 lb. 5 oz.–6 lb. 13 oz
Bore/Gauge: 12
Magazine: 4 shells
Features: Pulse Piston system; TRIBORE HP tapered barrels; innovative new design that allows the fore-end to be removed without disassembling the shotgun; gas-operating system that significantly reduces recoil; stock shim system for adjusting fit; left-hand versions available in both barrel lengths; model chambers 3-in. shells
Right-hand: $1275.00
Left-hand: $1455.00

L4S SERIES

Action: Semiautomatic
Stock: Wood
Barrel: 26 in., 28 in.
Chokes: 3 Inner HP
Weight: 6 lb. 5 oz.–6 lb. 13 oz.

Bore/Gauge: 12
Magazine: 4 shells
Features: Stock shim system for adjusting fit; Tribore HP tapered barrels; available in three grades: Initial Hunter (black action), Grey Hunter (silver action with game scene), and Deluxe Hunter (silver action with detailed game scene with gold inlays and upgraded wood); Initial Hunter available in left-hand
Deluxe Hunter: $2145.00
Grey Hunter: $1730.00
Initial Hunter: . . $1275.00–$1455.00

XLR5 VELOCITY FR COMPACT

Action: Semiautomatic
Stock: Wood
Barrel: 28 in., 30 in.
Chokes: 5 Exis HP
Weight: 7 lb. 6 oz.
Bore/Gauge: 12
Magazine: 5 shells
Features: Tapered Tribore HP barrel; oversized bolt handle; oversized bolt release; three optional magazine cap weights to adjust the balance point;

barrel features a tapered top rib; stock features Triwood enhanced finish
Right-hand: $2050.00
Left-hand: $2230.00

XLR5 WATERFOWLER

Action: Semiautomatic
Stock: Synthetic
Barrel: 28 in., 30 in.
Chokes: 3 inner HP, 1 EXIS DK
Weight: 7 lb.
Bore/Gauge: 12
Magazine: 5 shells
Features: Pulse Piston system; TRIBORE HP barrel design for reduced recoil and improved pattern performance; special competition choke tube, the EXIS DK, tuned for non-toxic ammo in the most popular pellet sizes; a top rib increases the sighting plain by 4 in. and allows the shooter to see down the rib with a more comfortable head-up posture; chrome plated barrel extension and bores; left-hand versions available in both barrel lengths; model chambers 3-in. shells
Right-hand: $1695.00
Left-hand: $1875.00

FAUSTI USA CALEDON L4

FAUSTI CLASS

FAUSTI ITALYCO

FAUSTI MAGNIFICENT

FAUSTI MAGNIFICENT

CALEDON L4

Action: Over/under
Stock: Walnut
Barrel: 26 in., 28 in., 30 in.
Chokes: Fixed or interchangeable choke tubes
Weight: 5 lb. 12 oz.–7 lb. 4 oz.
Bore/Gauge: 12, 16, 20, 28, .410
Magazine: 2 shells
Features: Single selectable trigger; A+ Turkish walnut stock with oil finish; laser-engraved lower receiver; automatic ejectors; metallic bead sight
MSRP . . . . $2999.00–$3569.00

CLASS

Action: Over/under
Stock: Walnut
Barrel: 26 in., 28 in., 30 in.
Chokes: Fixed or interchangeable choke tubes
Weight: 5 lb. 12 oz.–7 lb. 5 oz.
Bore/Gauge: 12, 16, 20, 28, .410
Magazine: 2 shells

Features: Features automatic ejectors; metallic bead; single-selectable trigger; 14–3/8-in. length of pull; timeless AA walnut oil-polished stock; Prince of Wales style stock; receiver laser-engraved with flushing quail
MSRP . . . . $2449.00–$2999.00

ITALYCO

Action: Over/under
Stock: Wood
Barrel: 23–32 in.
Chokes: Fixed
Weight: N/A
Bore/Gauge: 12 (2 ¾ in., 3 in.), 16 (2 ¾ in.), 20 (2 ¾ in., 3 in.), 28 (2 ¾ in.), .410 (3 in.)
Magazine: 2 shells
Features: Single selective trigger (double trigger available); automatic ejector (manual ejector available); box lock round body; pistol grip with steel grip cap or Prince of Wales or English
MSRP . . . . $8960.00–$12600.00

MAGNIFICENT

Action: Over/under
Stock: Walnut
Barrel: 26 in., 28 in., 30 in.
Chokes: Fixed or interchangeable choke tubes
Weight: 5 lb. 12 oz.–7 lb. 6 oz.
Bore/Gauge: 12, 16, 20, 28, .410
Magazine: 2 shells
Features: AAA+ walnut stock with oil finish; precision scroll engraving accompanies Aphrodite, the Greek goddess of love and beauty, on the receiver; the Crest of the city of Brescia, Italy, where all Fausti shotguns are produced, is on the underside of the receiver; single selectable trigger; automatic ejectors; metallic bead sight
Field: . . . .$4999.00–$5559.00
Sporting: . . . .$5999.00–$6559.00

Franchi

FRANCHI AFFINITY 20 GA. - REALTREE APG

FRANCHI INSTINCT L 12 GA.

FRANCHI INSTINCT SL 20 GA.

FRANCHI INTENSITY

FRANCHI AFFINITY CATALYST

FRANCHI INSTINCT CATALYST

FRANCHI INSTINCT L 28 GAUGE
AND .410 GAUGE

AFFINITY

Action: Inertia driven semiautomatic
Stock: Black synthetic, Realtree Max-4, Realtree APG
Barrel: 26 in., 28 in.
Chokes: Interchangeable (IC, M, F)
Weight: 5 lb. 8 oz.–6 lb. 12 oz.
Bore/Gauge: 12, 20
Magazine: 4+1 shells
Features: Red fiber optic bar; durable synthetic stock impervious to all-weather elements as well as gun solvents and lubricants; newly designed recoil pad; aluminum alloy receiver strengthened with steel inserts
MSRP . . . . **$849.00–$949.00**

AFFINITY CATALYST

Action: Semiautomatic
Stock: Walnut
Barrel: 28 in.
Chokes: IC, M, F
Weight: 6 lb. 10 oz.
Bore/Gauge: 12
Magazine: 4+1 shells
Features: Drop, cast, pitch, and length-of-pull are all tailored to a woman's build; fiber optic red-bar front sight
MSRP **$999.00**

INSTINCT CATALYST

Action: Over/under
Stock: Walnut
Barrel: 28 in.
Chokes: IC, M, F
Weight: 7 lb. 3 oz.
Bore/Gauge: 12
Magazine: 2 shells
Features: Redesigned stock with a drop, cast, pitch, length-of-pull, and grip length that better align with a woman's body; red, fiber optic front sights; auto ejectors; automatic safety
MSRP **$1599.00**

INSTINCT L

Action: Over/under
Stock: Walnut
Barrel: 26 in., 28 in.
Chokes: Interchangeable (IC, M, F)
Weight: 6 lb. 2 oz.–6 lb. 6 oz.
Bore/Gauge: 12, 20, 28, .410
Magazine: 2 shells
Features: Ventilated raised rib; red fiber optic front sight; blued and color-case-hardened finish on the receiver, with gold inlay; A-grade walnut stock in Prince-of-Wales style with cut checkering on the forend and pistol grip; satin oil finish; single gold-plated trigger; chrome-lined barrels proofed for steel shot; hard-shell custom-fitted gun case included
MSRP . . . . **$1399.00–$1699.00**

INSTINCT L 28-GAUGE, .410-BORE

Action: Over/under
Stock: Walnut
Barrel: 28 in.
Chokes: Extended (C, F, IC, IM, M), F, IC, M, Skeet 1 & 2
Weight: 6 lb.
Bore/Gauge: 28, .410
Magazine: 2 shells
Features: Auto ejectors, barrel selector, auto safety; color case hardened receiver; red fiber optic front bead
MSRP **$1699.00**

INSTINCT SL

Action: Over/under
Stock: Walnut
Barrel: 26 in., 28 in.
Chokes: Interchangeable (IC, M, F)
Weight: 5 lb. 6 oz.–5 lb. 11 oz.
Bore/Gauge: 12, 20
Magazine: 2 shells
Features: Vent rib; red fiber optic front bead; aluminum alloy receiver; blued barrels; AA-grade satin walnut stock in Prince-of-Wales style with cut checkering and oil finish; tang-mounted automatic safety; custom-fitted, hard-shell gun case included
MSRP **$1699.00**

INTENSITY

Action: Inertia driver semiautomatic
Stock: Black synthetic, Realtree Max-5, Mossy Oak Bottomlands
Barrel: 26 in., 28 in., 30 in.
Chokes: IC, M, F
Weight: 6 lb. 11 oz.
Bore/ Gauge: 12
Magazine: 4+1 shells
Features: Inertia Driven system; recoil spring encircles the magazine tube forward the receiver; stepped, venti-lated-rib, red fiber optic front sight; three extended choke tubes
MSRP . . . . **$1099.00–$1199.00**

SHOTGUNS

Ithaca Gun Company

ITHACA DEERSLAYER II

ITHACA DEERSLAYER III

ITHACA MODEL 37 DEFENSE SYNTHETIC

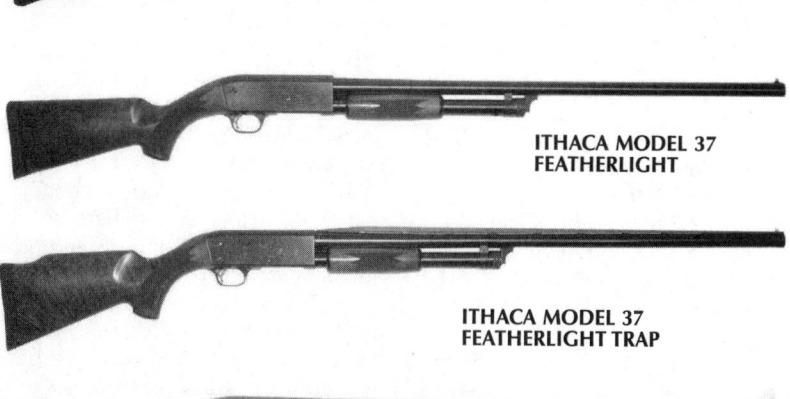

ITHACA MODEL 37 FEATHERLIGHT

ITHACA MODEL 37 FEATHERLIGHT TRAP

ITHACA MODEL 37 WATERFOWL

DEERSLAYER II

Action: Pump
Stock: Walnut
Barrel: 24 in.
Chokes: None
Weight: 6.8 lb.–8 lb. 6 oz.
Bore/Gauge: 12, 20
Magazine: 4+1 shells
Features: Solderless barrel system; thumbhole or standard black walnut Monte Carlo stock; fat deluxe checkered forend; sling swivel studs; Pachmayr 750 Decelerator recoil pad; matte blued finish on barrel; gold-plated trigger; Marble Arms rifle sights; drilled and tapped for Weaver #62 scope rail
MSRP **$1150.00**

DEERSLAYER III

Action: Pump
Stock: Walnut

Barrel: 20 in., 26 in., 28 in.
Chokes: None
Weight: 8.1 lb.–9 lb. 8 oz.
Bore/Gauge: 12, 20
Magazine: 4+1 shells
Features: Heavy-walled, fluted, fixed barrel in blue matted finish; walnut Monte Carlo stock with optional thumbhole; Pachmayr 750 Decelerator recoil pad; sling swivel studs; gold-plated trigger; Weaver #62 rail pre-installed on receiver
MSRP **$1350.00**

MODEL 37 DEFENSE

Action: Pump
Stock: Walnut
Barrel: 18.5 in., 20 in.
Chokes: None
Weight: 6.5 lb.–7 lb. 2 oz.
Bore/Gauge: 12, 20

Magazine: 4+1 or 7+1 shells
Features: Choice of walnut or black synthetic stock; 3 in. chamber; matte blued finish barrel; Pachmayr decelerator recoil pad
MSRP . . . . **$784.00–$855.00**

MODEL 37 FEATHERLIGHT

Action: Pump
Stock: Walnut
Barrel: 26 in., 28 in., 20 in.
Chokes: 3 Briley Choke tubes (F, M, IC, and wrench)
Weight: 6.1 lb.–7 lb. 10 oz.
Bore/Gauge: 12, 16, 20, 28
Magazine: 4+1 rounds
Features: Solderless shells system; classic game scene engraving; black walnut stock with semi-pistol butt stock; TruGlo red front sight; Pachmayr 752 Decelerator recoil pad
MSRP **$895.00**

MODEL 37 FEATHERLIGHT TRAP

Action: Pump
Stock: Walnut
Barrel: 30 in.
Chokes: Briley Choke tubes
Weight: 7 lb. 13 oz.
Bore/Gauge: 12
Magazine: 4+1 shells
Features: Bottom ejection; 3 in. chamber; gold plated tubes; walnut Monte Carlo stock; vent rib barrel; classic game scene engraving
MSRP **$1020.00**

MODEL 37 WATERFOWL

Action: Pump
Stock: Camo, synthetic black
Barrel: 28 in., 30 in.
Chokes: Briley choke tubes
Weight: 7 lb. 3 oz.–7 lb. 6 oz.
Bore/ Gauge: 12, 20
Magazine: 4+1 shells
Features: 3 in. chamber; gold plated trigger; gamescene engraving; permaguard protection
MSRP **$865.00**

SHOTGUNS

Iver Johnson Arms, Inc.

IVER JOHNSON HP 18

IVER JOHNSON IJ500

IVER JOHNSON IJ600

HP 18

Action: Semiautomatic
Stock: Synthetic
Barrel: 18.5 in.
Chokes: N/A
Weight: 6 lb. 6 oz.
Bore/Gauge: 12, 20
Magazine: 5+1 shells
Features: High grade alloy receiver for reduced weight; two-piece detachable pistol grip stock; rubber buttpad on the stock to help reduce felt recoil; Picatinny rail on top of the receiver, with a fully adjustable white dot rear sight; fiber optic front sight; finger grooves on the forend to ensure a solid grip while firing; muzzle break externally threaded onto the barrel; 12-ga. available in black or Digital Tan, 20-ga. in black only
Black:................**\$420.00**
Digital Tan 12-ga.: **\$499.00**

IJ500

Action: Semiautomatic
Stock: Walnut
Barrel: 28 in.
Chokes: 3 internally threaded choke tubes (F, IM, M)
Weight: 7 lb. 2 oz.
Bore/Gauge: 12, 20
Magazine: 5+1 shells
Features: Front brass bead sight; checkered stock and forend; chambered for 2 ¾" and 3" shotshells. —12-ga. now available in synthetic stock in Max-4 camo.
Wood stock: **\$420.00**
12-ga. Max-4 camo: **\$499.00**

IJ600

Action: Over/under
Stock: Walnut
Barrel: 28 in.
Chokes: 5 internal (F, IM, M, IC, C)
Weight: 6 lb. 1 oz.–7 lb. 5 oz.
Bore/Gauge: 12, 20, .410
Magazine: N/A
Features: Vent rib on top and bottom barrel; extractors on both barrels; engraved receiver with birds accented in gold colored coating; selector switch located on the safety for choosing which barrel fires first; checkered stock and forend; sling swivel on barrel and stock; 20 gauge has a scaled down receiver, stock, and forend
MSRP.................**\$540.00**

Kel-Tec

KEL-TEC KSG

KEL-TEC KSG-NR

KSG

Action: Pump
Stock: Glass reinforced nylon
Barrel: 18.5 in.
Chokes: Cylinder bore
Weight: 6 lb. 14.4 oz.-8 lb. 8 oz.
Bore/Gauge: 12 gauge (3 in.)
Magazine: 6+6+1
Features: KSG receiver is made from hardened steel and includes the magazine tubes which have been welded in place; pump action feeds from either the left or right tube
MSRP...................**\$990.00**

KSG-NR

Action: Pump
Stock: Polymer
Barrel: 18.5 in.
Chokes: Choke adapter
Weight: 6 lb. 13 oz.
Bore/Gauge: 12
Magazine: 4+4+1
Features: Shortened forend and magazine tubes; integral vertical foregrip; built-in flashlight
MSRP................**\$1299.00**

Krieghoff

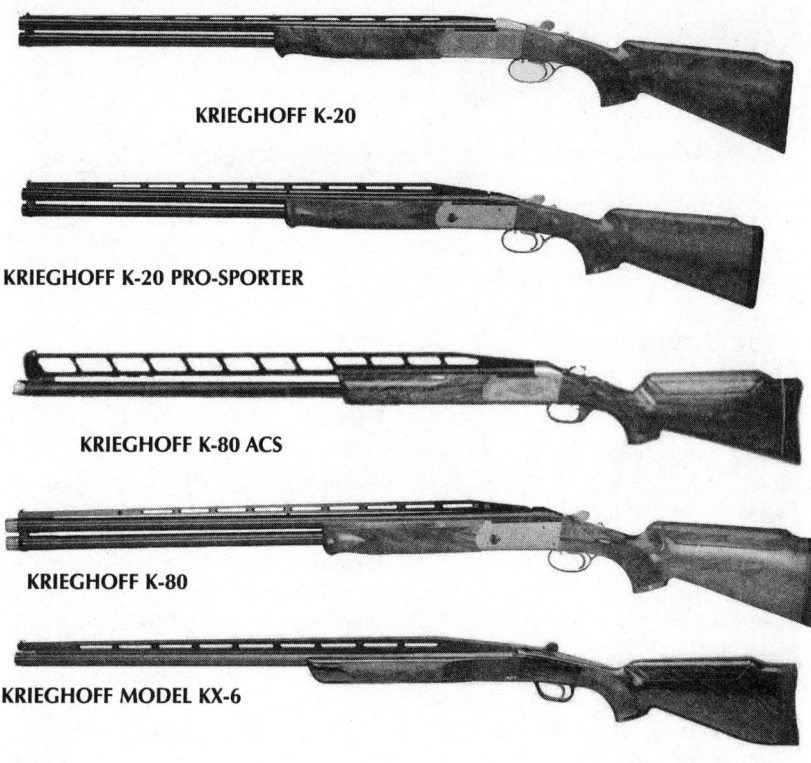

KRIEGHOFF K-20

KRIEGHOFF K-20 PRO-SPORTER

KRIEGHOFF K-80 ACS

KRIEGHOFF K-80

KRIEGHOFF MODEL KX-6

K-20

Action: Over/under
Stock: Walnut
Barrel: 30 in., 32 in.
Chokes: 5 choke tubes (C, S, IC, LM, M, LIM, IM, F)
Weight: 7 lb. 8 oz.
Bore/Gauge: 20, 28, .410
Magazine: 2 shells
Features: Top-tang push safety button; classic scroll engraving; white pearl front bead and metal center bead; single-selective mechanical trigger; hand-checkered select European walnut stock with satin epoxy finish
20 Ga.: $11395.00
28 Ga.: $11495.00
.410: $11495.00
20/28 Ga. Set: $15890.00
Set of 3: $20405.00

K-20 PRO-SPORTER

Action: Over/under
Stock: Walnut
Barrel: 30 in., 32 in.
Chokes: Titanium choke tubes
Weight: 8 lb.
Bore/Gauge: 20, 28, .410
Magazine: 2 shells
Features: Higher rib and stock allows shooter to keep their head more erect, increasing sight range, allowing for quicker target acquisition, reduced neck fatigue, and perceived recoil; high rib easily adjustable
MSRP . . . . . . $11695.00–$11795.00
20/28 Ga. Set: $16390.00
3 Ga. Set: $21105.00

K-80

Action: Over/under
Stock: Walnut
Barrel: 30 in., 32 in., 34 in.
Chokes: Steel or Titanium choke tubes (C, S, IC, LM, M, LIM, IM, F, SF)
Weight: 8 lb. 4 oz.
Bore/Gauge: 12
Magazine: 2 shells
Features: White pearl front sight and metal center bead; nickel-plated steel receiver with satin grey finish; single select trigger; top-tang push button safety; fine-checkered Turkish walnut
From: . . . . $10595.00–$13000.00

K-80 ACS

Action: Single barrel
Stock: Walnut
Barrel: 30 in., 32 in., 34 in.
Chokes: 8 factory steel choke tubes
Weight: 8 lb. 12 oz.
Bore/Gauge: 12
Magazine: 2 shells
Features: White pearl front bead and metal center bead sight; case-hardened action, nickel-plated steel receiver with nitride silver finish; single selective trigger; over/under available
From: $17370.00

KX-6

Action: Single-shot trap
Stock: Walnut
Barrel: 34 in.
Chokes: IM, LIM, F
Weight: 8 lb. 12 oz.
Bore/ Gauge: 12
Magazine: 1 shell
Features: White pearl front sight and metal center bead; case hardened, long lasting black nitro carbonized finish; semiautomatic ejector; adjustable tapered rib; available choke tubes: CY, SK, IC, M, SF
MSRP $5490.00

K-Var

K-VAR VEPR 12

VEPR 12

Action: Semiautomatic
Stock: Synthetic
Barrel: 19 in.
Chokes: Cylinder
Weight: 6 lb. 14 oz.
Bore/Gauge: 12
Magazine: 5+1 shells
Features: AK safety selector with levers on both sides for easy operation; ability to insert magazines straight into the magazine well without canting; RPK-style windage adjustable rear sights; windage and elevation adjustable front sights integrated to the gas block; Picatinny rail incorporated into the hinged dust cover; left-side folding tubular buttstock with cheek rest and sling loop
MSRP $1199.00

Ljutic

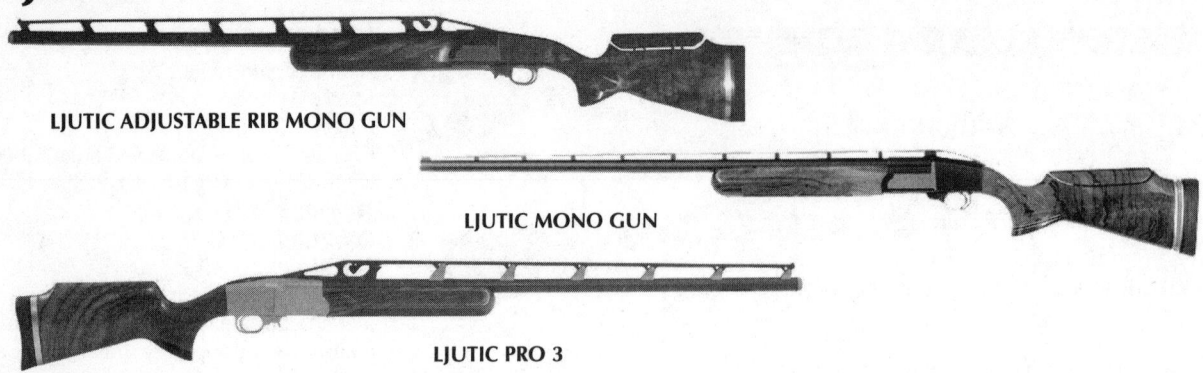

LJUTIC ADJUSTABLE RIB MONO GUN

LJUTIC MONO GUN

LJUTIC PRO 3

ADJUSTABLE RIB MONO GUN
Action: Single barrel
Stock: Walnut
Barrel: 34 in.
Chokes: Fixed or Ljutic SIC
Weight: 10 lb.
Bore/Gauge: .740, 12
Magazine: 1 shell
Features: "One Touch" adjustable rib allows you to change your point-of-impact; adjustable comb stock
Adjustable Rib: **$7495.00**
Stainless Adjustable: **$8495.00**

MONO GUN
Action: Single barrel
Stock: Walnut
Barrel: 32 in.–34 in.
Chokes: Optional screw in chokes (Fixed, Ljutic SIC, Briley SIC)
Weight: 10 lb.
Bore/Gauge: .740, 12
Magazine: 1 shell
Features: Comes with American walnut wood; optional roll over combs and cheek pieces; various upgrades available
Mono: **$7495.00**
Stainless: **$8495.00**

PRO 3
Action: Single barrel
Stock: Walnut
Barrel: 34 in.
Chokes: 4 Briley Series 12 chokes
Weight: 9 lb.
Bore/Gauge: .740, 12
Magazine: 1 shell
Features: Aluminum baseplate; interchangeable two-pad system; adjustable comb; English or American walnut stock; screw in hinge pin; stainless or blued barrel
Blued barrel: **$8495.00**
Stainless: **$8995.00**

Marocchi

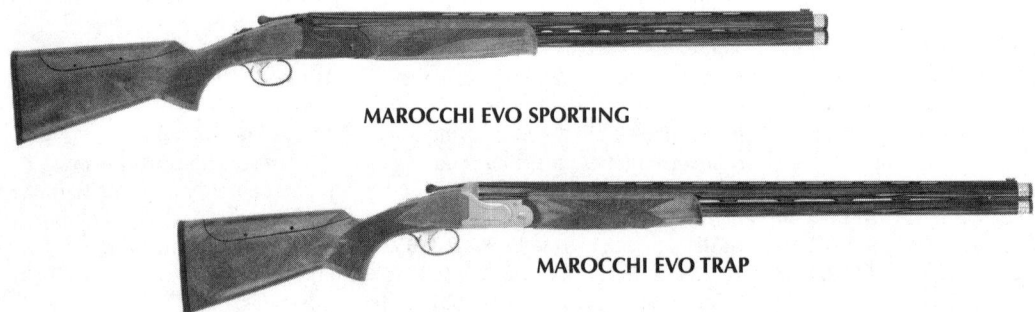

MAROCCHI EVO SPORTING

MAROCCHI EVO TRAP

EVO SPORTING

Action: Over/under
Stock: Wood
Barrel: 18.5 in.
Chokes: 5, interchangeable
Weight: 7 lb. 5 oz.
Bore/Gauge: 12
Magazine: 2 shells
Features: Schnabel designed forearm; rubber recoil pad; adjustable blade trigger in three positions; adjustable comb; hand polished and blued barrel finishing; available in black or nickel receiver; optional upgraded Alien2025 stock, which is made by an Italian crafter and improves recoil by reducing vibrations
MSRP **$1950.00**
With Alien2025 Stock: **$4450.00**

EVO TRAP
Action: Over/under
Stock: Wood
Barrel: 18.5 in.
Chokes: 5, interchangeable
Weight: 7 lb. 11 oz.
Bore/Gauge: 12
Magazine: 2 shells
Features: Beavertail design; rubber recoil pad; adjustable blade trigger in three positions; adjustable comb; hand polished and blued barrel finishing; available in black or nickel receiver; optional upgraded Alien2025 stock, which is made by an Italian crafter and improves recoil by reducing vibrations
MSRP **$1950.00**
With Alien2025 Stock: **$4450.00**

SHOTGUNS

Marocchi

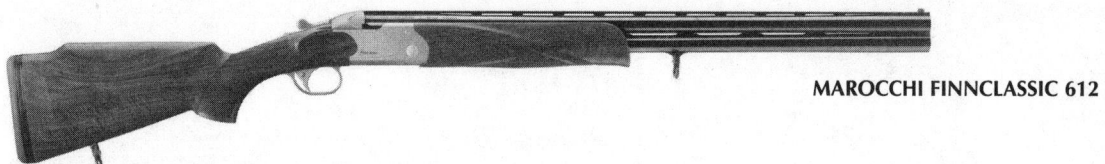

MAROCCHI FINNCLASSIC 612

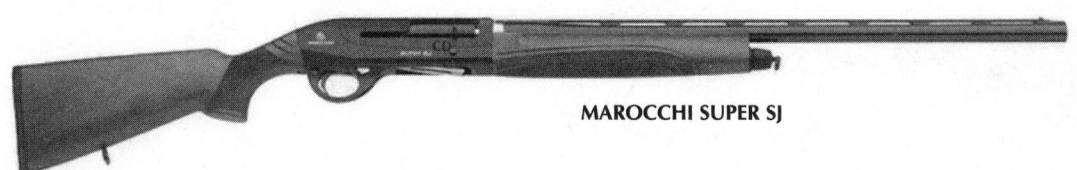

MAROCCHI SUPER SJ

FINNCLASSIC 612

Action: Over/under
Stock: Wood
Barrel: 24 in., 28 in., 30 in.
Chokes: 5 choke tube Maxi 70 plus key
Weight: 6 lb. 8 oz.
Bore/ Gauge: 12
Magazine: 2 shells
Features: 3-in. chamber; available Maxi 90 choke tubes; special steel, proof tested by the Italian National Proof House; scroll work
MSRP $1375.00

SUPER SJ

Action: Semiautomatic
Stock: Wood or synthetic
Barrel: 28 in., 30 in.
Chokes: Various
Weight: 6 lb. 13 oz.
Bore/Gauge: 12
Magazine: 4+1 shells
Features: Inertia operated; five chokes, chokes key, and distance pieces to change the angle of stock; available in standard, camo, or nickel; Complus version for reduced recoil available
MSRP $1495.00

Merkel

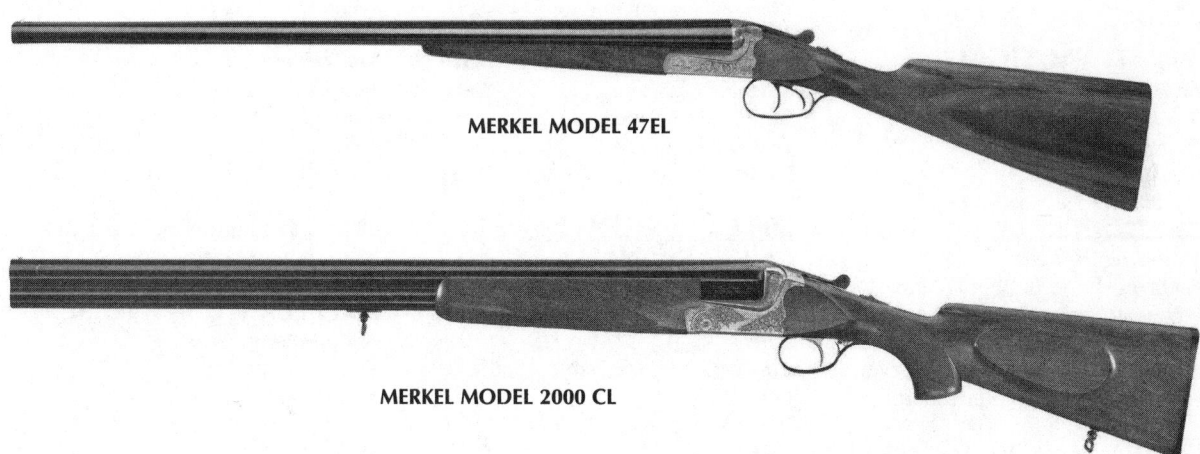

MERKEL MODEL 47EL

MERKEL MODEL 2000 CL

MODEL 147EL

Action: Side-by-side
Stock: Wood
Barrel: 27 in., 28 in.
Chokes: Steel-shot proofed chokes
Weight: 6 lb. 3 oz.
Bore/Gauge: 12, 20
Magazine: None
Features: English stock finished with fine hand-cut checkering at buttplate; silver monogram plate; steel action is gray nitrated; Anson & Deeley locks; Greener-style cross bolt and double bottom bite; double trigger; automatic safety
MSRP $8295.00

MODEL 2000 CL

Action: Over/under
Stock: Wood
Barrel: 27 in., 28 in.
Chokes: 2 interchangeable chokes steel-shot proofed
Weight: 6 lb. 13 oz.
Bore/Gauge: 16, 20, 28
Magazine: 2 shells
Features: Disconnectable ejectors; arabesque engraving; Anson & Deeley locks in steel receiver; Kersten cross-bolt; selective single trigger, adjustable in length; manual safety; wood stock with pistol grip and cheekpiece
MSRP . . . . $11995.00–$12995.00

SHOTGUNS

Mossberg (O. F. Mossberg & Sons)

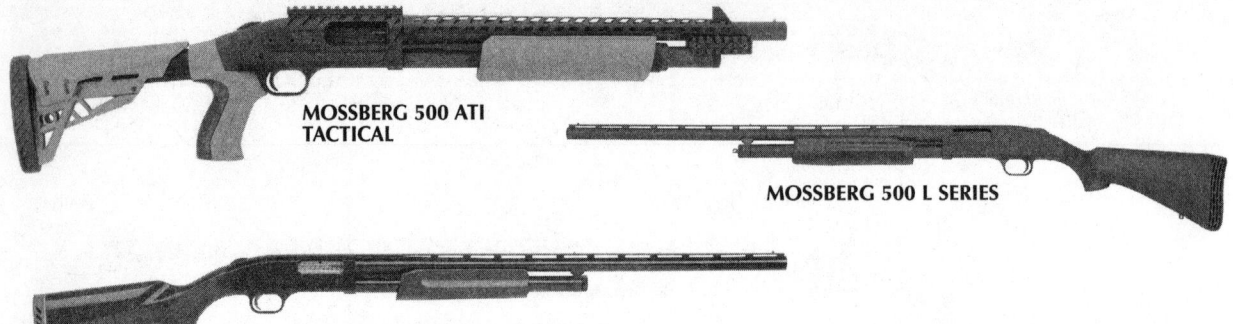

MOSSBERG 500 ATI TACTICAL

MOSSBERG 500 L SERIES

MOSSBERG 500 CLASSIC ALL-PURPOSE FIELD

MOSSBERG 500 FLEX ALL-PURPOSE SERIES

MOSSBERG 500 FLEX HUNTING SERIES

500 ATI TACTICAL

Action: Pump
Stock: Synthetic
Barrel: 18.5 in.
Chokes: Cylinder
Weight: 6 lb. 12 oz.
Bore/Gauge: 12
Magazine: 6 shells
Features: T2 adjustable TactLite stock with pistol grip; ambidextrous safety; dual extractors; Halo add-a-shell side saddle/top rail; Halo Heatshield/rails; single-point sling mount; Scorpion recoil ATI Akita fore-end; six-position adjustable buttstock in Flat Dark Earth
MSRP $588.00

500 L-SERIES

Action: Pump
Barrel: 18.5 in., 24 in., 26 in., 28 in.
Chokes: Accuset, none
Weight: 6 lb. 8 oz.–7 lb. 8 oz.
Bore/Gauge: 12
Magazine: 6 shells
Features: L-Series are left-handed configurations; available in All-Purpose (black synthetic stock), Hunting Field/Deer Combo (wood stock, 28-in. vent rib barrel, 24-in. rifled barrel), Slugster (wood stock,

24-in. rifled barrel), cantilever scope mount, Turkey (Mossy Oak Obsession stock, adjustable fiber optic sights on a 24-in. barrel), and Tactical (18.5-in. barrel with sythetic full and pistol grip stocks; also available in 20-gauge)

All-Purpose: . . . . . . $432.60–$433.00
Combo: $520.80
Slugster: $466.20
Tactical 12-gauge: $498.40
Tactical 20-gauge: $499.00
Turkey: $499.80

500 CLASSIC ALL-PURPOSE FIELD

Action: Pump
Stock: Walnut, synthetic
Barrel: 28 in.
Chokes: Interchangeable Accu-Choke tubes
Weight: 7 lb. 8 oz.
Bore/Gauge: 12
Magazine: 6 shells
Features: High-gloss walnut stock and forend; fine checkering on the pistol grip and wrapping around the underside of the forend; classic red recoil pad with white Pachmayr line spacer; distinctive jeweled bolt, gold trigger, and high polished blued metal finish; non-binding twin action bars; anodized aluminum receiver; vent rib Accu-Choke barrel; ambidextrous top-mounted safety; available in MO Break-up Infinity
MSRP $480.20

500 FLEX ALL-PURPOSE SERIES

Action: Pump
Stock: Synthetic
Barrel: 26 in., 28 in.
Chokes: Accu-Set
Weight: 7 lb. 8 oz.
Bore/Gauge: 12
Magazine: 6 shells
Features: Matte metal finishes or Marinecote finish; stock with medium recoil pad; stock and forend constructed of synthetic with black matte finish; twin bead sights
28-in. barrel blue: $488.60
26-in. barrel Marinecote: . . . $533.40

500 FLEX HUNTING SERIES

Action: Pump
Stock: Synthetic
Barrel: 24 in., 26 in., 28 in.
Chokes: Accu-Set
Weight: 6 lb. 12 oz.–7 lb. 8 oz.
Bore/Gauge: 12, 20
Magazine: 6 shells
Features: Three variations: 12-gauge with 28-in. barrel, Realtree Advantage Max-4 stock, adjustable sights, and tan-finished metal work; 20-gauge with 26-in barrel and black synthetic stock, matte blue metal work; 20-gauge with 24-in. barrel, Mossy Oak Break-Up Infinity stock, and OD green metal work
12-gauge: $557.20
20-gague black stock: $489.00
20-gauge camo: $598.00

SHOTGUNS

Mossberg (O. F. Mossberg & Sons)

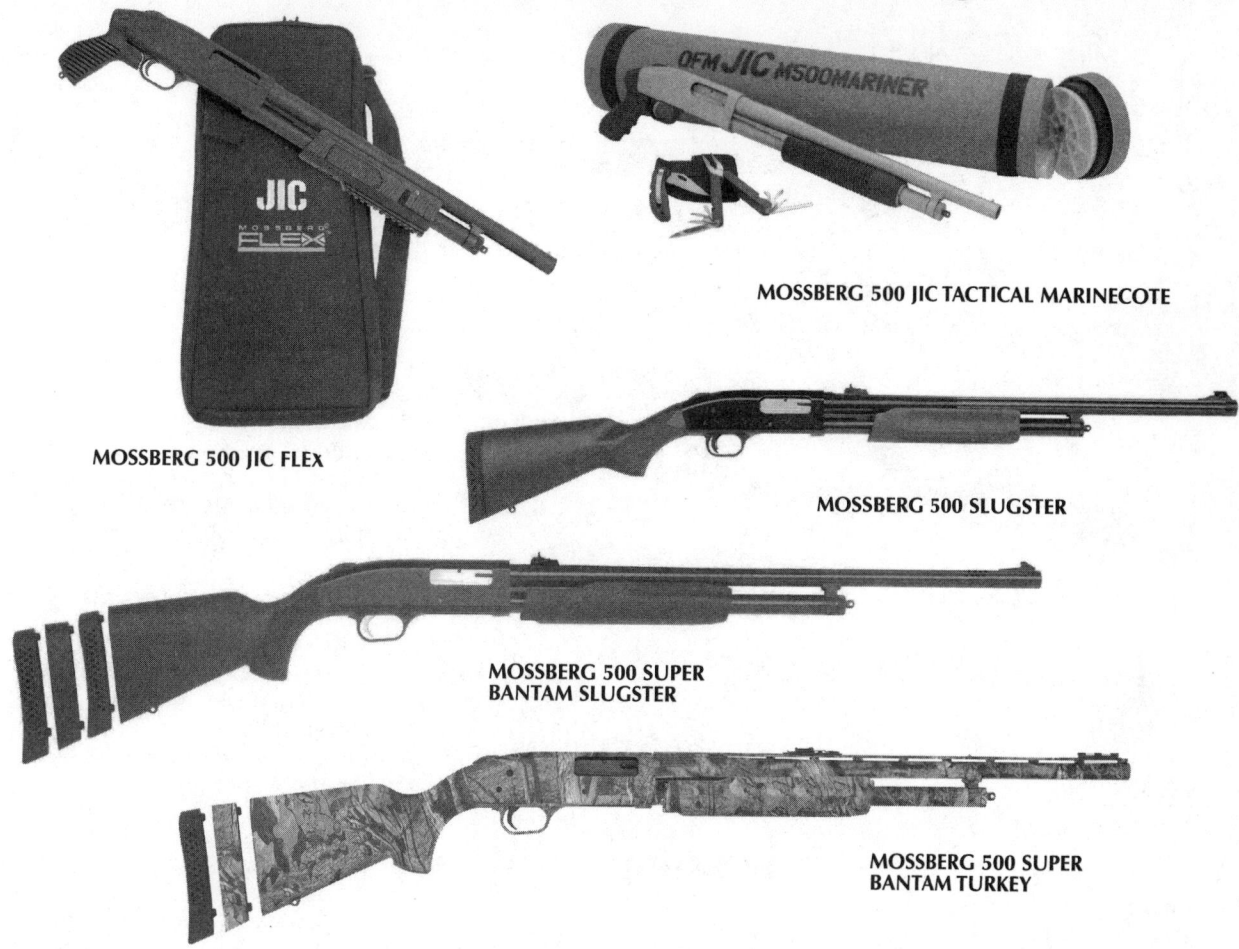

MOSSBERG 500 JIC FLEX

MOSSBERG 500 JIC TACTICAL MARINECOTE

MOSSBERG 500 SLUGSTER

MOSSBERG 500 SUPER BANTAM SLUGSTER

MOSSBERG 500 SUPER BANTAM TURKEY

500 JIC FLEX
Action: Pump
Stock: Synthetic
Barrel: 18.5 in.
Chokes: C
Weight: 5 lb. 8 oz.
Bore/Gauge: 12
Magazine: 6 shells
Features: Bead sights; FLEX pistol grip; 3-in. barrel with matte black finish
MSRP $506.80

500 JIC TACTICAL MARINECOTE
Action: Pump
Stock: Synthetic
Barrel: 18.5 in.
Chokes: Cylinder bore chokes
Weight: 5 lb. 8 oz.
Bore/Gauge: 12
Magazine: 6 shells
Features: Bead sight; Marinecote metal finish; comes with multi-tool, survival knife and cordura carrying case; gun lock; swivel studs; black synthetic stock; only pump-action shotguns to pass all U.S. Military Mil-Spec 3443 standards
MSRP $646.80

500 SLUGSTER
Action: Pump
Stock: Wood, synthetic
Barrel: 24 in.
Chokes: None or rifle sights
Weight: 6 lb. 12 oz.–7 lb. 4 oz.
Bore/Gauge: 12, 20
Magazine: 6 shells
Features: Fully-rifled bore; integral scope base; ported barrel; ambidextrous thumb-operated safety ; available with dual comb set, and choice of integral cantilever scope base or rifled sights; 20-gauge available in Mossy Oak Break-Up Country
MSRP . . . . $418.60–$513.80

500 SUPER BANTAM SLUGSTER
Action: Pump
Stock: Synthetic
Barrel: 24 in.
Chokes: Fully rifled bore
Weight: 5 lb. 4 oz.
Bore/Gauge: 20
Magazine: 6 shells
Features: Available with integral canti-lever scope mount or adustable fiber optic sights; black synthetic stock has shim spacer kit
MSRP $418.60

500 SUPER BANTAM TURKEY
Action: Pump
Stock: Synthetic
Barrel: 22 in.
Chokes: Interchangeable Accu-Choke (X-full and wrench)
Weight: 5 lb. 4 oz.
Bore/Gauge: 20
Magazine: 6 shells
Features: Adjustable synthetic stock in Mossy Oak Obsession; adjustable fiber optic sights; drilled and tapped for scopes; gun lock
MSRP $486.00

Mossberg (O. F. Mossberg & Sons)

MOSSBERG 500 TURKEY

MOSSBERG 510 YOUTH MINI SUPER BANTAM ALL-PURPOSE FIELD

MOSSBERG 590 7-SHOT

MOSSBERG 590A1 7-SHOT GHOST RING IN KRYPTEK TYPHON CAMO

MOSSBERG 590A1 ADJUSTABLE TACTICAL TRI-RAIL 9 SHOT

MOSSBERG 590A1 L SERIES

MOSSBERG 835 ULTI-MAG

500 TURKEY
Action: Pump
Stock: Synthetic
Barrel: 20 in., 24 in.
Chokes: X-Factor
Weight: 6 lb. 12 oz.–7 lb. 4 oz.
Bore/Gauge: 12
Magazine: 6 shells
Features: 12-gauge models available with 20- or 24-in. barrels, 20-gauge with 20- or 22-in. barrels; both have choice of fixed or six-position adjustable stocks, all in Mossy Oak Obsession
MSPR . . . . $485.80–$704.20

510 YOUTH MINI SUPER BANTAM ALL-PURPOSE FIELD
Action: Pump
Stock: Synthetic
Barrel: 18.5 in.
Chokes: Accu-set, Fixed-Mod.
Weight: 5 lb.
Bore/Gauge: 20, .410
Magazine: 3 (.410) or 4 (20 Ga.) shells
Features: Feature shim-adjustable synthetic stocks in black, MO Break-Up Country, or Moonshine Muddy Girl; all have vent ribs. Field models have dual beads, Muddy Girl versions just one bead
MSRP . . . . $419.00–$471.00

590 7-SHOT
Action: Pump
Stock: Synthetic
Barrel: 18.5 in.
Chokes: Cylinder
Weight: 7 lb. 4 oz.
Bore/Gauge: 12
Magazine: 7 shells
Features: Front bead sight; matte blue metal barrel with Heatshield; black synthetic stock; top-mounted safety for amidextrous operation; tri-rail forend
MSRP $455.00

590A1 7-SHOT GHOST RING
Action: Pump
Stock: Synthetic
Barrel: 18.5 in.
Chokes: Cylinder
Weight: 6 lb. 12 oz.–7 lb. 8 oz.
Bore/Gauge: 12
Magazine: 7 shells
Features: Mil-Spec construction; heavy-walled barrel; metal trigger guard and safety buttons; Parkerized, Marinecoate, and Kryptec Thphon Camo finishes available; ghost ring or bead sight; Cylinder bore on all mod-

els but the black 7-Shot Ghost ring, which comes with Cylinder choke tube and takes other AccuChoke tubes
MSRP . . . . $605.00–$756.00

590A1 ADJUSTABLE TACTICAL TRI-RAIL 9 SHOT
Action: Pump
Stock: Synthetic
Barrel: 18.5 in.
Chokes: Cylinder bore
Weight: 7 lb. 8 oz.
Bore/Gauge: 12
Magazine: 9 shells
Features: Six-position adjustable stock with a tri-rail forend; ghost ring sights; Parkerized finish; speedfeed, black stock; heavy barrel wall; Blackwater logo
MSRP $880.00

590A1 L SERIES
Action: Pump
Stock: Synthetic
Barrel: 20 in.
Chokes: Cylinder bore
Weight: 7 lb.
Bore/Gauge: 12
Magazine: 9 shells
Features: Feature black synthetic stocks; non-binding twin action bars; positive steel-to-steel lock-up and anti-jam elevator; dual extractors; ambidextrous top-mounted safety
MSRP $692.00

835 ULTI-MAG
Action: Pump
Stock: Synthetic
Barrel: 20 in., 24 in., 28 in.
Chokes: Ulti-full tube chokes, Accu-Mag Set, or Modified Tube
Weight: 7 lb. 8 oz.–7 lb. 12 oz.
Bore/Gauge: 12
Magazine: 6 shells
Features: Features $3\frac{1}{2}$-in. chambers, dual extractors, and overbored and ported barrels; variations include Turkey/Waterfowl combo (24- and 28-in barrels, MO Break-Up Country); Turkey/Deer combo (one Ulti-Ful 24-in. barrel, one fully rifled 24-in. barrel, MO Break-Up Country); Turkey (20- or 24-in. barrels, MO Obsession); and Waterfowl (28-in. barrel, matte blue/black or MO Shadow Grass Blades)
Single barrels: . . . . $518.00–$619.00
Combos: . . . . $660.80–$701.40

Mossberg (O. F. Mossberg & Sons)

MOSSBERG 835 ULTI-MAG-RECOIL REDUCTION SYSTEM

MOSSBERG 930 PRO SERIES SPORTING

MOSSBERG 930, 935 MAGNUM PRO-SERIES WATERFOWL

MOSSBERG 935 MAGNUM TURKEY

MOSSBERG SA-20 AUTOLOADER

MOSSBERG SILVER RESERVE II FIELD

835 ULTI-MAG-RECOIL REDUCTION SYSTEM

Action: Pump
Stock: Recoil Reduction System/Mathews
Barrel: 24 in.
Chokes: Ulti-full tube
Weight: 8 lb. 8 oz.
Bore/ Gauge: 12
Magazine: 6 shells
Features: Exclusive stock incorporating Mathews Harmonic Damper Technology; two interchangeable low and high profile combs; 3.5 in. chamber; ported barrels; free gun lock and 10-year limited warranty
MSRP $655.20

930 PRO SERIES SPORTING

Action: Semiautomatic
Stock: Walnut
Barrel: 28 in.
Chokes: 3 chokes (F, M, IC)
Weight: 7 lb. 12 oz.
Bore/Gauge: 12
Magazine: 5 shells
Features: Chambered in 2 ¾ in. and 3 in.; engraved Cerakote receiver;

beveled loading gate; Briley extended chokes; vented rib ported barrel; boron nitride-coated gas piston, piston rings, magazine tube, hammer, and sear prevents corrosion and facilitates cleaning
MSRP $1062.00

930, 935 MAGNUM PRO-SERIES WATERFOWL

Action: Semiautomatic
Stock: Synthetic
Barrel: 28 in.
Chokes: 3 chokes (F, M, IC)
Weight: 7 lb. 12 oz.
Bore/Gauge: 12
Magazine: 5 shells
Features: Synthetic stock covered in Mossy Oak Shadowgrass Blades; overbored vent rib barrel; Stock Drop System; Pro Series Waterfowl engraved receivers. 930 model has 3-in. chamber, 935 has 3.5-in chamber
930: $874.00
935: $959.00

935 MAGNUM TURKEY

Action: Semiautomatic
Stock: Synthetic

Barrel: 22 in.
Chokes: Vent rib. overbored
Weight: 7 lb. 8 oz.
Bore/Gauge: 12
Magazine: 5 shells
Features: Semiautomatic chambers 3 ½-in. shells; overbored barrels, dual vent system, Quick Empty magazine release button, stock spacer system, and drilled and tapped receivers. Variations include: Combo Deer/Turkey and Combo Turkey/Waterfowl in Mossy Oak Break-Up Country; Turkey in Mossy Oak Obsession; and Waterfowl in black or Mossy Oak Shadow Grass Blades; sights will vary between adjustable fiber optics and fixed fiber optics
Single barrels: . . . $761.00–$1032.00
Combos: $1004.00

SA-20 AUTOLOADER

Action: Semiautomatic
Stock: Walnut
Barrel: 26 in.
Chokes: 5 chokes (C, IC, M, IM, F)
Weight: 5 lb. 12 oz.
Bore/Gauge: 20
Magazine: 5 shells
Features: Smooth cycling gas-operated system; bead sight; blue finish on barrel; available in walnut or synthetic stocked All-Purpose Field, pink Muddy Girl synthetic stock, a Turkey version in Mossy Oak Obsession, railed versions with and without pistol grips in black synthetic stock, and in a 13-in. length of pull Youth Bantam version with a black synthetic stock
MSRP . . . . $568.40–$653.80

SILVER RESERVE II FIELD

Action: Over/under
Stock: Walnut, satin
Barrel: 26 in., 28 in.
Chokes: 5, Field set or fixed mod–fixed full
Weight: 6 lb. 8 oz.–7 lb. 8 oz.
Bore/Gauge: 12, 20, 28, .410
Magazine: 2 shells
Features: Corrosion-resistant chrome-lined chambers and barrels, tang-mounted safties with integrated barrel selector, dual locking lugs, and wrap-around receiver engraving; variations include: Combo 12/20 Field, Combo 20/28 Field; all single gauges with extractors
Combos: $1162.00
Single gauge: $773.00

Perazzi

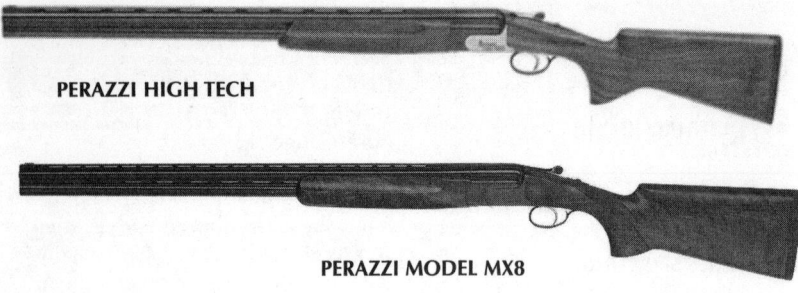

PERAZZI HIGH TECH

PERAZZI MODEL MX8

HIGH TECH
Action: Over/under
Stock: Wood
Barrel: 27–31 in.
Chokes: Can be specified or made interchangeable
Weight: N/A
Bore/Gauge: 12
Magazine: 2 shells
Features:High Tech has a sporty and futuristic look; a large logo engraved in black smoke color on both sides of the receiver, under clear varnish, in contrast to the rest of the receiver; hinge pins are engraved with a checkered design; action is two-tone and varnished "in the white" only in the areas where the logo appears; frame has a greater weight than other Perazzi models and it is distributed within the median line between the grip of the hands, which both improves the fluidity of handling and further reduces recoil; divergent rib that goes from 7mm wide at the action to 10mm at the front end of the barrels allows you to greatly speed up your perception of the target and also expands your field of vision.
MSRP . . . . $12110.00–$40315.00

MX8 SPORTING CLAYS
Action: Over/under
Stock: Walnut
Barrel: 29 in., 30 in., 31 in.
Chokes: Interchangeable chokes
Weight: 7 lb. 5 oz.
Bore/Gauge: 12, 20
Magazine: 2 shells
Features: Custom walnut stock with beavertail forend; half-ventilated side ribs on barrel; removable trigger with flat or coil springs; blue or nickel plating; Sporting, Skeet and Trap models; 28 Ga. and .410 models also available
MSRP . . . .$11420.00–$113300.00

Pointer by Legacy Sports

POINTER (BY LEGACY SPORTS) BLACK SYNTHETIC

POINTER BREAK-ACTION

POINTER 1000 FIELD

POINTER (BY LEGACY SPORTS) SYNTHETIC HOME DEFENSE

BLACK SYNTHETIC
Action: Over/under
Stock: Synthetic
Barrel: 28 in.
Chokes: 5 chokes (C, IC, M, IM, F)
Weight: 7 lb.
Bore/Gauge: 12, 20
Magazine: 2 shells
Features: Chambered in 2 ¾ in. and 3 in. magnum; chrome-moly lined, carbon-steel barrel; fiberoptic front sight; raised, ventilated rib. 12-ga. available in 18- and 28-in. barrels, 20-ga. in 28-in barrels only.
MSRP $609.00

BREAK-ACTION
Action: Break action
Stock: Synthetic
Barrel: 28 in.
Chokes: Fixed
Weight: 4.8–5.4 lb.
Bore/Gauge: 12, 20, .410
Magazine: 1 shell
Features: Fixed, modified choke; matte black finish; black synthetic stock and forend; brass bead sight; manual safety, hammer safety and transfer bar safety
MSRP . . . . $189.00–$199.00

1000 FIELD
Action: Over/under
Stock: Wood
Barrel: 26 in.–28 in.
Chokes: Multi-5
Weight: 6 lb.–7 lb 8 oz.
Bore/Gauge: 12, 20, 28, .410
Magazine: 2 shells
Features: Ventilated raised rib; carbon steel barrel with chrome moly lined bore; brass bead sight; comes with five choke tubes (.410 Ga. is fixed); satin blued barrel finish; high luster Turkish walnut stock
MSRP . . . . $674.00–$715.00

SYNTHETIC HOME DEFENSE
Action: Over/under
Stock: Synthetic
Barrel: 18 in.
Chokes: 5 chokes (C, IC, M, IM, F)
Weight: 6 lb. 9 oz.
Bore/Gauge: 12
Magazine: 2 shells
Features: Chambered in 2¾ in. and 3 in. magnum; fiber optic front sight; Picatinny rail on top receiver and lower barrel
MSRP $600.00

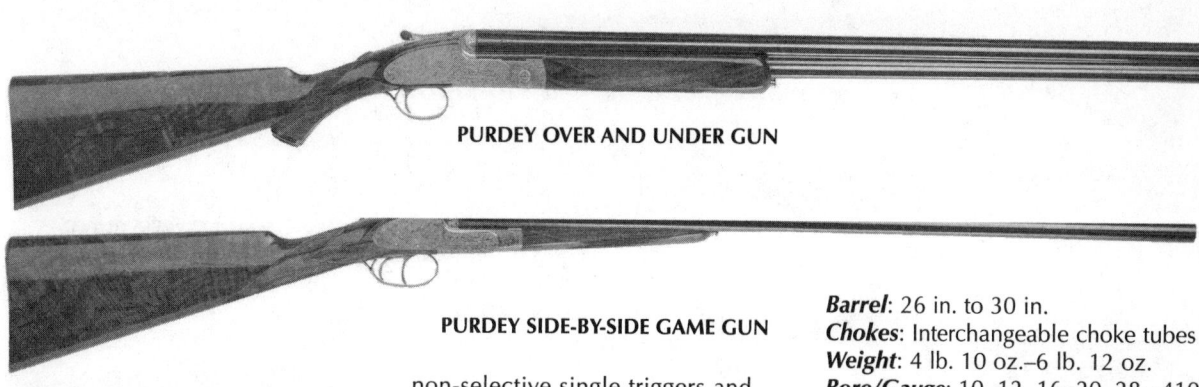

PURDEY OVER AND UNDER GUN

PURDEY SIDE-BY-SIDE GAME GUN

OVER AND UNDER GUN

Action: Over/under
Stock: Walnut
Barrel: 26 in.–30 in.
Chokes: Interchangeable choke tubes
Weight: 4 lb. 14 oz.–7 lb. 8 oz.
Bore/Gauge: 12, 16, 20, 28, .410
Magazine: 2 shells
Features: Available in round, square, or ultra-round action shapes; available with double or non-selective single triggers and automatic safety catch; demi-bloc construction; solid game rib with hand matted finish; Turkish walnut with straight, semi, or full pistol grip; gold oval or inlaid gold letters; sporter scroll engraving
MSRP . . . . . . Contact manufacturer for pricing

SIDE-BY-SIDE GAME GUN

Action: Side-by-side
Stock: Walnut
Barrel: 26 in. to 30 in.
Chokes: Interchangeable choke tubes
Weight: 4 lb. 10 oz.–6 lb. 12 oz.
Bore/Gauge: 10, 12, 16, 20, 28, .410
Magazine: 2 shells
Features: Built on self-opening system; available with double or non-selective single triggers and automatic safety catch; Turkish walnut in straight, semi or full pistol grip; gold oval or inlaid gold letters; sporter scroll engraving; traditional splinter or beavertail forend available
MSRP . . . . . . Contact manufacturer for pricing

Remington Arms Company

REMINGTON MODEL 11-87 SPORTSMAN FIELD

REMINGTON MODEL 870 EXPRESS

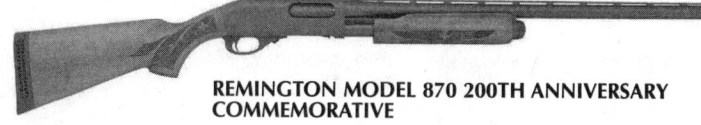

REMINGTON MODEL 870 200TH ANNIVERSARY COMMEMORATIVE

MODEL 11-87 SPORTSMAN FIELD

Action: Semiautomatic
Stock: Walnut
Barrel: 26 in., 28 in.
Chokes: Rem. modified choke
Weight: 7 lb. 4 oz.–8 lb. 4 oz.
Bore/Gauge: 12, 20
Magazine: None
Features: Solid walnut stock and forend with satin finish and fleur-de-lis checkering; nickel-plated bolt and gold-plated trigger; vent rib with dual bead sights
MSRP $815.92

MODEL 870 200TH ANNIVERSARY COMMEMORATIVE

Action: Pump
Stock: Walnut
Barrel: 28 in.
Chokes: Vent Rib Rem Choke
Weight: 7 lb.
Bore/Gauge: 12
Magazine: 4 shells
Features: A-grade walnut stock with fleur de lis checkering; matte black finish; medallion in grip
MSRP $599.00

MODEL 870 EXPRESS

Action: Pump
Stock: Hardwood, synthetic, laminate, or camo
Barrel: 18 in.–28 in.
Chokes: Modified Remington choke, extra full Rem.
Weight: 5 lb. 12 oz.–7 lb. 8 oz.
Bore/Gauge: 12, 20
Magazine: 2–7 shells depending on model
Features: Single bead sight; standard express finish on barrel and receiver; rubber recoil pad; twin action bars ensure smooth, reliable non-binding action; solid steel receiver; optional thumbhole stock in some models
Express: . . . . $417.00–$468.00
Deer: $417.00
Turkey Camo: $492.00

SHOTGUNS

Remington Arms Company

REMINGTON MODEL 870 EXPRESS HARDWOOD HOME DEFENSE

REMINGTON MODEL 870 EXPRESS SUPER MAGNUM TURKEY WATERFOWL

REMINGTON MODEL 870 EXPRESS SYNTHETIC TACTICAL

REMINGTON MODEL 870 SHURSHOT SYNTHETIC TURKEY

REMINGTON MODEL 870 SP MARINE MAGNUM

REMINGTON MODEL 870 SPS SUPER SLUG

MODEL 870 EXPRESS HARDWOOD HOME DEFENSE

Action: Pump
Stock: Hardwood
Barrel: 18.5 in.
Chokes: Cylinder bore
Weight: 7 lb. 8 oz.
Bore/Gauge: 12
Magazine: 4 shells
Features: Traditional dark stain hardwood stock; accepts standard 870 replacement barrels without modification; single bead front sight
MSRP . . . . **$420.00–$443.00**

MODEL 870 EXPRESS SUPER MAGNUM

Action: Pump
Stock: Hardwood, synthetic, or camo
Barrel: 26 in.
Chokes: Wingmaster HD Waterfowl and Turkey Extra Full Rem chokes
Weight: 7 lb. 4 oz.
Bore/Gauge: 12
Magazine: None
Features: Synthetic stock available in full Mossy Oak Bottomland or Duck Blind camo; HiVix fiber-optics; SuperCell recoil pad; drilled and tapped receiver
Express Super Mag: **$469.00**
Synthetic: **$469.00**
Turkey/Waterfowl: **$629.00**
Waterfowl Camo: **$629.00**

MODEL 870 EXPRESS SYNTHETIC TACTICAL

Action: Pump
Stock: Synthetic
Barrel: 18.5 in.
Chokes: Screw-in tube
Weight: 7 lb. 8 oz.
Bore/Gauge: 12
Magazine: 4–7 shells
Features: Synthetic stock available in A-tacs digitized camo; Tactical Rem. choke SpeedFeed IV; pistol grip stock; SuperCell recoil pad; adjustable XS Ghost Ring sight rail with removable with bead front sight; Picatinny-style rail
Express Tactical: **$420.00**
7-Shot: **$443.00**

MODEL 870 SHURSHOT SYNTHETIC TURKEY

Action: Pump
Stock: Synthetic
Barrel: 21 in.
Chokes: Screw-in tubes
Weight: 7 lb. 6 oz.
Bore/Gauge: 12
Magazine: 4 shots
Features: Ambidextrous Shurshot pistol-grip synthetic stock; rubberized overmolding; SuperCell recoil pad; receiver is drilled and tapped; Weaver rail; sling swivels; Mossy Oak camo
MSRP **$536.00**

MODEL 870 SP MARINE MAGNUM

Action: Pump
Stock: Synthetic
Barrel: 18 in.
Chokes: Cylinder chokes
Weight: 7 lb. 8 oz.
Bore/Gauge: 12
Magazine: 6 shells
Features: Single-bead front sight; padded Cordura; sling swivels; electroless nickel plating covers all metal; twin action bars ensure smooth, reliable non-binding action
MSRP **$841.00**

MODEL 870 SPS SUPER SLUG

Action: Pump
Stock: Synthetic
Barrel: 25.5 in.
Chokes: Wingmaster HD extended Rem Choke
Weight: 7 lb. 14 oz.
Bore/Gauge: 12
Magazine: None
Features: Mossy Oak Tree Stand camo; features ShurShot synthetic pistol grip stock; adjustable TruGlo fiber-optic sights; receiver drilled and tapped for scope mounts
MSRP **$829.00**

Remington Arms Company

REMINGTON MODEL 870 WINGMASTER

REMINGTON MODEL 870 WINGMASTER 200TH ANNIVERSARY LIMITED EDITION

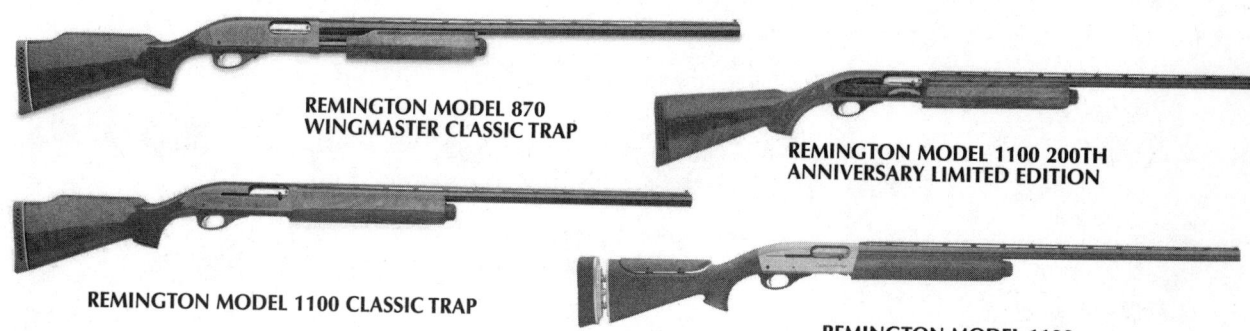

REMINGTON MODEL 870 WINGMASTER CLASSIC TRAP

REMINGTON MODEL 1100 200TH ANNIVERSARY LIMITED EDITION

REMINGTON MODEL 1100 CLASSIC TRAP

REMINGTON MODEL 1100 COMPETITION SYNTHETIC

MODEL 870 WINGMASTER

Action: Pump
Stock: Walnut
Barrel: 25 in., 26 in., 28 in.
Chokes: Screw-in or fixed
Weight: 5 lb. 12 oz.–7 lb.
Bore/Gauge: 12, 20, 28, .410
Magazine: 4 shots
Features: Twin action bars for non-binding action; receiver machined from solid billet of steel; highly polished and richly blued receiver; wide array of barrel and choke options
MSRP . . . . $847.00–$962.00

MODEL 870 WINGMASTER 200TH ANNIVERSARY LIMITED EDITION

Action: Pump
Stock: Walnut
Barrel: 26 in.
Chokes: Vent Rib Rem Choke
Weight: 7 lb.
Bore/Gauge: 12
Magazine: 4 shells
Features: C-grade walnut stock with fleur de lis checkering; classic American-style engraving and 24k gold inlay portraying founder Eliphalet Remington; steel floorplate; medallion in grip; limited to quantity of 2016; special serial number; rifle sights ; custom box
MSRP $1499.00

MODEL 870 WINGMASTER CLASSIC TRAP

Action: Pump
Stock: Walnut

Barrel: 30 in.
Chokes: Screw-in tube, Rem. Choke
Weight: 8 lb. 4 oz.
Bore/Gauge: 12
Magazine: None
Features: American walnut, Monte Carlo stock; forend with deep cut checkering and a high-gloss finish; twin bead sights; three specialized trap Rem. choke tubes; twin action bars ensure smooth, reliable non-binding action; choke vent rib barrel
MSRP $1120.00

MODEL 1100 200TH ANNIVERSARY LIMITED EDITION

Action: Semiautomatic
Stock: Walnut
Barrel: 28 in.
Chokes: None
Weight: 8 lb.
Bore/Gauge: 12
Magazine: 4 shells
Features: C-grade walnut stock with fleur de lis checkering; classic American-style engraving and 24k gold inlay portraying founder Eliphalet Remington; steel floorplate; medallion in grip; limited to quantity of 2016; special serial number; rifle sights ; custom box
MSRP $1999.00

MODEL 1100 CLASSIC TRAP

Action: Semiautomatic
Stock: Walnut
Barrel: 30 in.

Chokes: Screw-in tubes
Weight: 8 lb. 4 oz.
Bore/Gauge: 12
Magazine: None
Features: American walnut stock with cut-checkering; bead blasted top and bottom radius; blued finish on receiver and barrel; gold triggers and gold embellishments on receiver
MSRP $1334.00

MODEL 1100 COMPETITION SYNTHETIC

Action: Semiautomatic
Stock: Synthetic
Barrel: 30 in.
Chokes: 5 extended Briley (Target) choke tubes (Skeet, IC, LM, M, Full)
Weight: 8 lb. 4 oz.
Bore/Gauge: 12
Magazine: None
Features: Nickel-Teflon finish on receiver and all internal parts; barrel has 10mm target-style rib; adjustable comb and cast adjustment options; high-gloss blued barrel; fully adjustable target-style stock with recoil reduction; synthetic polymer stock and forend finished with carbon graphite appearance; twin target-style bead sights
MSRP $1305.00

Remington Arms Company

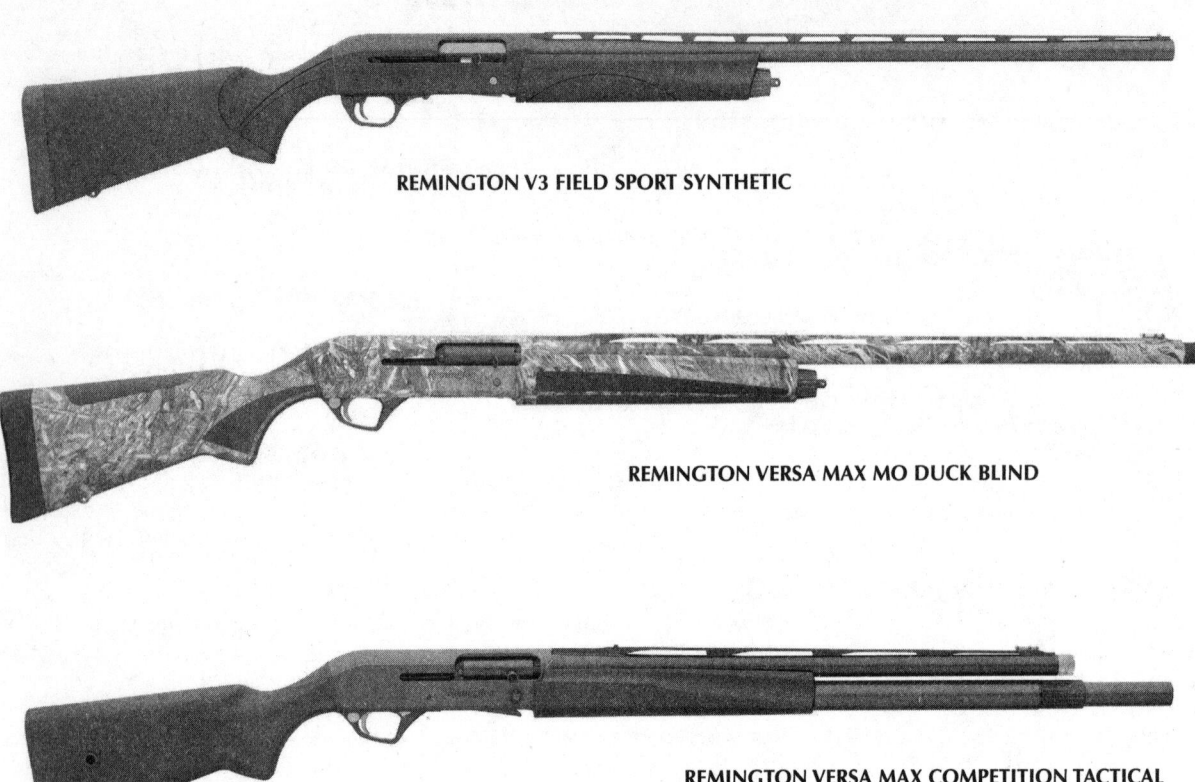

REMINGTON V3 FIELD SPORT SYNTHETIC

REMINGTON VERSA MAX MO DUCK BLIND

REMINGTON VERSA MAX COMPETITION TACTICAL

V3 FIELD SPORT SYNTHETIC

Action: Semiautomatic
Stock: Synthetic
Barrel: 26 in., 28 in.
Chokes: Modified
Weight: 7 lb. 4 oz.
Bore/Gauge: 12
Magazine: 3+1 shells
Features: Reliably cycles 12-gauge rounds from 2 ¾" to 3" magnum; Versaport gas system regulates cycling pressure based on shell length; light contoured barrel with ventilated rib; twin bead sights; synthetic and synthetic camo available in Mossy Oak Break-Up Country and Mossy Oak Blades
MSRP . . . . $895.00–$995.00

VERSA MAX

Action: Semiautomatic
Stock: Synthetic
Barrel: 26 in., 28 in.
Chokes: 5 Flush Mount Pro Bore chokes (F, M, IM, LB, IC)
Weight: 7 lb. 12 oz.
Bore/Gauge: 12
Magazine: 3+1 or 2+1 shells
Features: Remington patented gas-piston system; synthetic stock and forend with gray overmolded grips, comes in black or a Mossy Oak Duck blind camo; drilled and tapped receiver; enlarged trigger guard opening and larger safety for easier use with gloves; TriNyte Barrel and nickel Teflon plated internal components
Black: $1456.00
Camo: $1664.00

VERSA MAX COMPETITION TACTICAL

Action: Semiautomatic
Stock: Synthetic
Barrel: 22 in.
Chokes: IC, M, IM, LM, F
Weight: 8 lb.
Bore/Gauge: 12
Magazine: 8 shells
Features: Enlarged feeding port; "welded" style carrier; enlarged bolt closure button, safety and cocking handle; adjustable XS rear rifle sight; two-shot carbon fiber extension (10+1 shells); QD sling swivel cups on stock and forend
MSRP $1733.00

Remington Arms Company

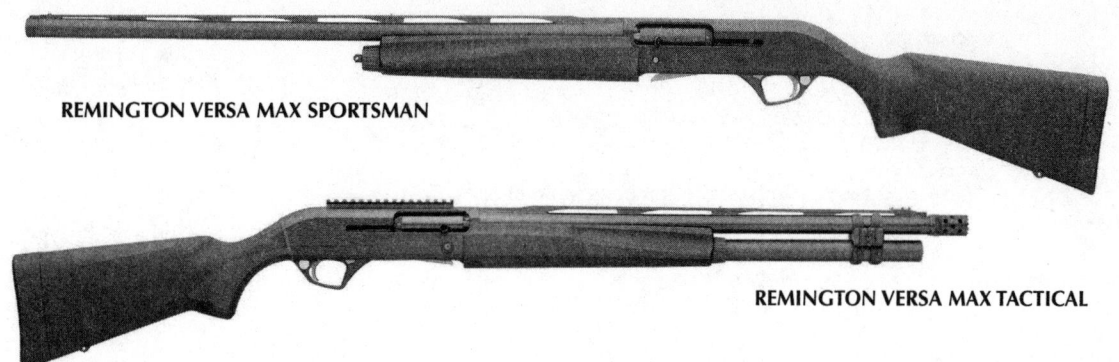

REMINGTON VERSA MAX SPORTSMAN

REMINGTON VERSA MAX TACTICAL

VERSA MAX SPORTSMAN

Action: Semiautomatic
Stock: Synthetic
Barrel: 26 in., 28 in.
Chokes: Modified Pro Bore Flush Mount; Pro Bore Wingmaster Turkey TXF Extended
Weight: 7 lb. 12 oz.
Bore/Gauge: 12
Magazine: 3+1 or 2+1 shells
Features: VersaPort Gas System; 4140 Hammer-Forged barrel; available in Mossy Oak Camo, Realtree AP Camo, and black oxide; SuperCell Recoil Pad; ivory front bead sights, steel mid bead
MSRP **$1066.00**

VERSA MAX TACTICAL

Action: Semiautomatic
Stock: Synthetic
Barrel: 22 in.
Chokes: IC and Tactical ProBore tube
Weight: 7 lb. 12 oz.
Bore/Gauge: 12
Magazine: 8+1 shells
Features: Ventilated rib; fiberoptic HiViz front sight; receiver is drilled and tapped for optics; Picatinny rail; recoil pad; size bolt-release button; oversized trigger guard for easy operation when wearing gloves
MSRP **$1456.00**

Savage Arms

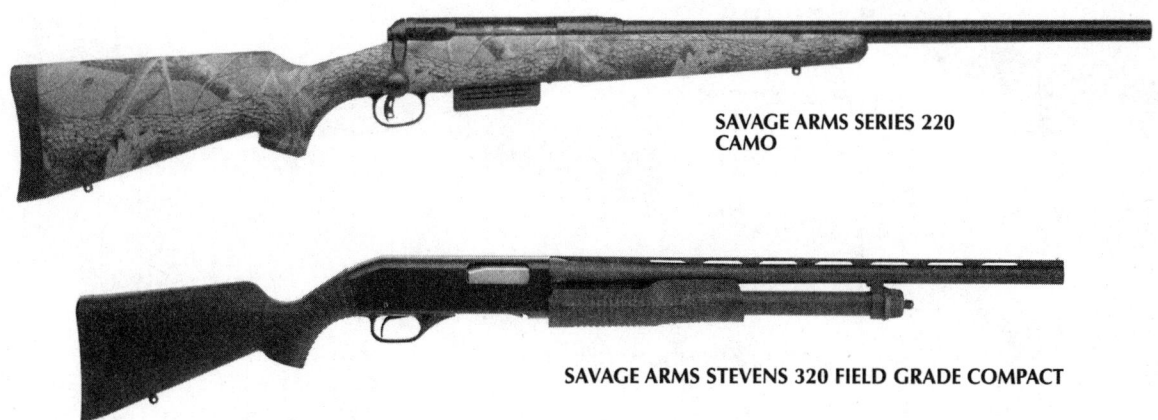

SAVAGE ARMS SERIES 220 CAMO

SAVAGE ARMS STEVENS 320 FIELD GRADE COMPACT

220 COMPACT, 220 CAMO

Action: Bolt
Stock: Synthetic
Barrel: 22 in.
Sights: None
Weight: 7 lb. 8 oz.
Caliber: 20 Ga.
Magazine: 2 shells
Features: Drilled and tapped for scope mounts; carbon steel barrel with matte blued finish; AccuTrigger; synthetic stock in matte black finish or camo
Compact: **$619.00**
Camo: **$685.00**

STEVENS 320 FIELD GRADE COMPACT

Action: Pump
Stock: Synthetic
Barrel: 22 in.
Chokes: N/A
Weight: 7 lb.
Bore/Gauge: 20
Magazine: 2 shells
Features: Carbon steel barrel; compact size and light recoil make it the ideal shotgun for introducing young people to the shooting sports
MSRP **$238.00**

Savage Arms

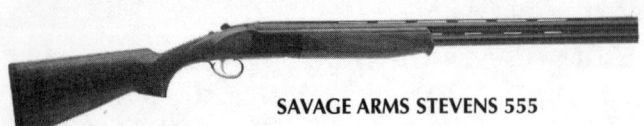

SAVAGE ARMS STEVENS 555

Features: Lightweight alloy receiver, Turkish walnut stock & forearm, single selective trigger, mechanical triggers, extractors, manual safetys
MSRP **$692.00**

STEVENS 555
Action: Over/under
Stock: Wood
Barrel: 28 in.

Chokes: 5 interchangeable chokes
Weight: 6 lb.
Bore/Gauge: 12, 20, 28, .410
Magazine: 2 shells

SRM Arms

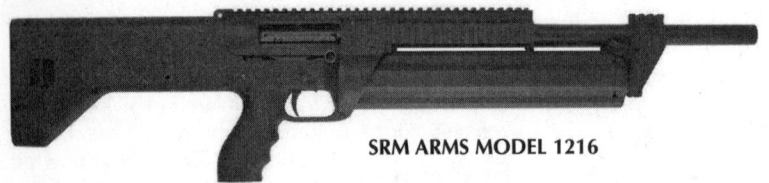

SRM ARMS MODEL 1216

Magazine: 16 shells
Features: Picatinny rail combined with a three face handguard rail; ambidextrous receiver and controls; quad-tube, revolving detachable magazine
MSRP **$1799.95**

MODEL 1216
Action: Semiautomatic
Stock: Synthetic

Barrel: 18 in.
Chokes: N/A
Weight: 7 lb. 4 oz.
Bore/Gauge: 12

Stoeger Industries

STOEGER COACH GUN

STOEGER CONDOR

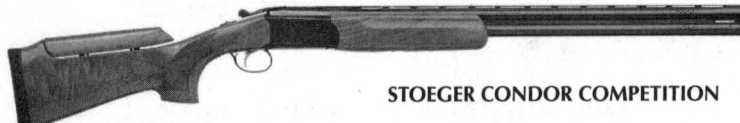

STOEGER CONDOR COMPETITION

Condor Youth: $499.00
Condor Longfowler: $499.00

COACH GUN
Action: Side-by-side
Stock: Walnut, hardwood
Barrel: 20 in.
Chokes: Fixed chokes (IC, M)
Weight: 6 lb. 5 oz.–7 lb.
Bore/Gauge: 12, 20, .410
Magazine: 2 shells
Features: A-grade satin or black finished hardwood stock; brass bead sights; nickel or blued metal finish
MSRP . . . . **$449.00–$549.00**

CONDOR
Action: Over/under
Stock: Walnut
Barrel: 22 in., 24 in., 26 in., 28 in.
Chokes: Screw-in and fixed chokes on 12 Ga., 20 Ga., 28 Ga. (IC, M), 16 Ga. (M, F), .410 (F&F)
Weight: 5 lb. 8 oz.–7 lb. 6 oz.
Bore/Gauge: 12, 16, 20, 28, .410
Magazine: 2 shells
Features: Walnut stock; brass bead sight; single trigger; auto-ejectors
Condor Field: $499.00
Condor Supreme: $649.00

CONDOR COMPETITION
Action: Over/under
Stock: Walnut
Barrel: 30 in.
Chokes: Screw-in (IC, M, F)
Weight: 7 lb. 5 oz.–7 lb. 13 oz.
Bore/Gauge: 12, 20
Magazine: 2 shells
Features: Walnut stock; brass bead with silver mid-bead sight; single selective trigger; automatic ejector; ported barrel
MSRP **$679.00**

SHOTGUNS

Stoeger Industries

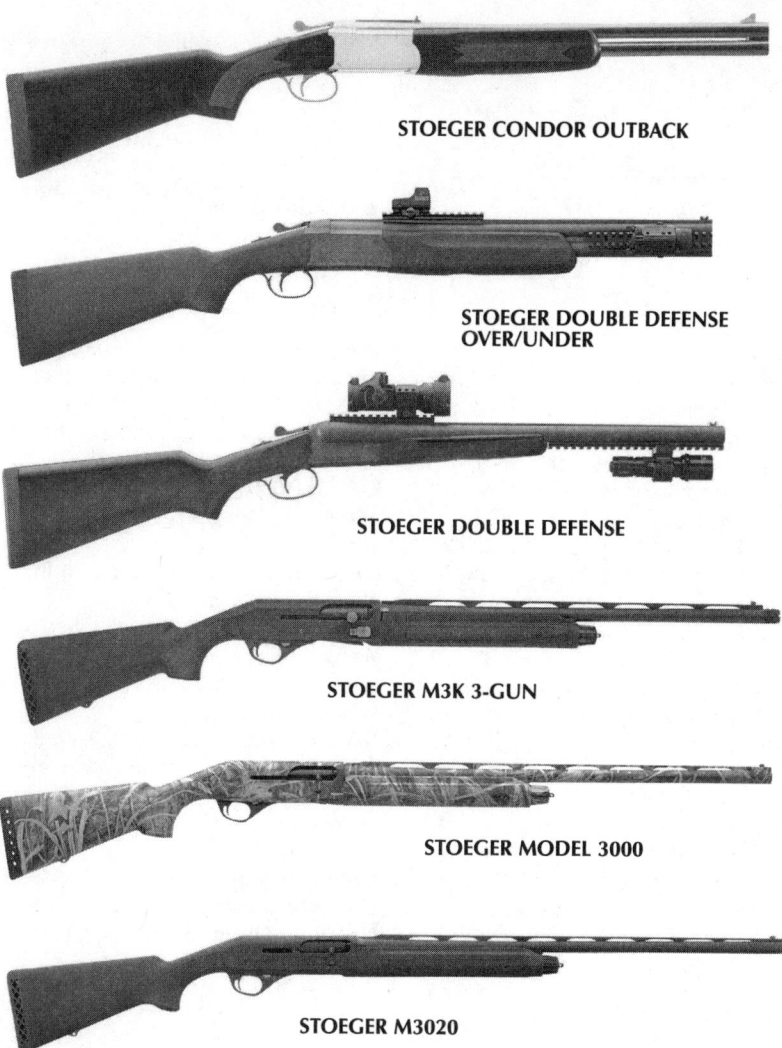

STOEGER CONDOR OUTBACK

STOEGER DOUBLE DEFENSE OVER/UNDER

STOEGER DOUBLE DEFENSE

STOEGER M3K 3-GUN

STOEGER MODEL 3000

STOEGER M3020

M3K 3-GUN
Action: Semiautomatic, inertia-driven
Stock: Synthetic
Barrel: 24 in.
Chokes: XC, IC, M
Weight: 7 lb. 5 oz.
Bore/Gauge: 12
Magazine: 4+1
Features: Fiber optic sights; based on the M3000 line of shotguns; 3-gun ready; oversized anodized aluminum bolt release, oversized safety, and extended tactical-style anodized aluminum bolt handle; elongated carrier and enlarged, beveled loading port for quicker and easier reloading
MSRP **$699.00**

MODEL 3000
Action: Semiautomatic
Stock: Black synthetic, Realtree APG, Realtree APG SteadyGrip
Barrel: 24 in.
Chokes: IC, M, XFT, wrench
Weight: 7 lb. 5 oz.
Bore/ Gauge: 12
Magazine: 4+1 shells
Features: Intertia Driven; red-bar front sight; drilled and tapped; shim kit; 3 in. loads
MSRP . . . . **$599.00–$679.00**

MODEL 3020
Action: Semiautomatic
Stock: Synthetic
Barrel: 26 in., 28 in.
Chokes: IC, M, XFT
Weight: 5 lb. 12 oz.
Bore/Gauge: 20
Magazine: 4 shells
Features: Ideal for waterfowl, turkey and upland game; handles a full range of loads, from 2 ¾-in. to 3-in. magnum; barrels are fitted with a ventilated, stepped rib and fiber-optic front sight; available in black, Realtree APG, or Realtree Max-5
MSRP . . . . **$599.00–$649.00**

CONDOR OUTBACK
Action: Over/under
Stock: Walnut, hardwood
Barrel: 20 in.
Chokes: Screw-in (IC, M)
Weight: 6 lb. 8 oz.–7 lb.
Bore/Gauge: 12, 20
Magazine: 2 shells
Features: Notched rear sight and fixed blade front sight; shell extractor; single trigger; A-grade satin walnut or black finished hardwood
MSRP . . . . $499.00–$549.00

DOUBLE DEFENSE OVER/UNDER
Action: Over/under
Stock: Hardwood
Barrel: 20 in.
Chokes: Screw-in chokes (IC/IC fixed)
Weight: 6 lb. 3 oz.–6 lb. 8 oz.
Bore/Gauge: 12, 20
Magazine: 2 shells
Features: Black hardwood stock; green fiber optic front sight; ported barrels; two Picatinny rails; single trigger design; tang-mounted automatic safety
MSRP $479.00

DOUBLE DEFENSE SIDE-BY-SIDE
Action: Side-by-side
Stock: Hardwood
Barrel: 20 in.
Chokes: Screw-in chokes (IC/IC fixed)
Weight: 6 lb. 8 oz.
Bore/Gauge: 12, 20
Magazine: 2 shells
Features: Black hardwood stock; fiber optic front sight; ported barrels; two Picatinny rails; single trigger design; tang-mounted automatic safety
MSRP $499.00

Stoeger Industries

STOEGER MODEL 3500

STOEGER INDUSTRIES P3000 PUMP

STOEGER THE GRAND

STOEGER UPLANDER

MODEL 3500

Action: Semiautomatic
Stock: Synthetic
Barrel: 24 in., 26 in., 28 in.
Chokes: Screw-in choke tubes (C, IC, M, F, XFT) and wrench
Weight: 7 lb. 7 oz.–7 lb. 10 oz.
Bore/Gauge: 12
Magazine: 4+1 shells
Features: Synthetic stock comes in black or camo finish in Advantage Max-4, Realtree APG, inertia drive system; recoil reducer; red-bar front sight; Weaver scope base; includes shim kit
Black synthetic: $679.00
Realtree: . . . . $779.00–$799.00

P3000 PUMP

Action: Pump
Stock: Synthetic
Barrel: 18.5 in., 26 in., 28 in.

Chokes: M inner choke
Weight: 6 lb. 6 oz.–6 lb. 14 oz.
Bore/Gauge: 12
Magazine: 4+1 shells
Features: Chambered for 2 ¾- and 3-in. shells; in black or Realtree Max-5 camo in long barrel options; 18.5-in. barrel option only in black synthetic but with choice of pistol grip or standard buttstock
MSRP. . . . . $299.00–$399.00

THE GRAND

Action: Break-action
Stock: Wood
Barrel: 30 in.
Chokes: M, IM, F
Weight: 9 lb.
Bore/Gauge: 12
Magazine: 1 shell
Features: Single-barrel target gun designed for shooting trap; stepped ventilated rib and fiber optic front

sight; automatic safety that engages when the lever is activated to open the action
MSRP. $679.00

UPLANDER

Action: Side-by-side
Stock: Walnut
Barrel: 22 in. (youth), 26 in., 28 in., 28 in.
Chokes: Screw-in and fixed tubes
Weight: 6 lb. 8 oz.–7 lb. 8 oz.
Bore/Gauge: 12, 16, 20, 28, .410
Magazine: 2 shels
Features: Brass bead sights; A-grade satin walnut stock; tang-mounted safety; single or double triggers; extractors included
Uplander Field: $499.00
Uplander Supreme: $549.00
Uplander Youth: $499.00
Uplander Longfowler: $499.00

Syren USA

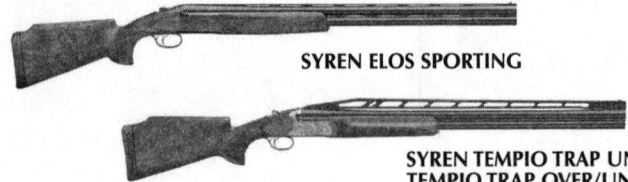

SYREN ELOS SPORTING

SYREN TEMPIO TRAP UNSINGLE AND TEMPIO TRAP OVER/UNDER

ELOS SPORTING

Action: Semiautomatic
Stock: Turkish walnut
Barrel: 30 in.
Chokes: 5 EXIS HP
Weight: 7 lb. 14 oz.
Bore/Gauge: 12
Magazine: 4+1 shells
Features: Turkish walnut stock enhanced by a proprietary TRIWOOD finish, which adds grain and water

resistance; TRIBORE HP barrels for the ultimate in ballistic performance; adjustable trigger; lefthand option; 32-in. barrels can be optioned for additional charge
Right-hand: $2650.00
Left-hand: $2775.00

TEMPIO TRAP UNSINGLE, TEMPIO TRAP OVER/UNDER

Action: Over/under
Stock: Turkish walnut

Barrel: 30 in., 32 in.
Chokes: 3 MAXIS (unsingle); 5 MAXIS (over/under)
Weight: 8 lb. 5 oz.–8 lb. 6 oz.
Bore/Gauge: 12
Magazine: 2 shells
Features: Stock designed to fit the female shooter with specialized dimensions, including length of pull, smaller grip, and increased pitch; calibrated barrel and stock weight; DTS trigger system with two trigger pull weight options, take up, over travel, and length of pull adjustments; hand-polished coin finish with Invisalloy protective finish; 30-in. barreled over/under, 32-in. barrel Unsingle, and combo with both barrel sets
Right-hand: . . . . .$6495.00–$9095.00
Left-hand: . . . . . $6730.00–$9330.00

SHOTGUNS

Taylor's & Co. Firearms

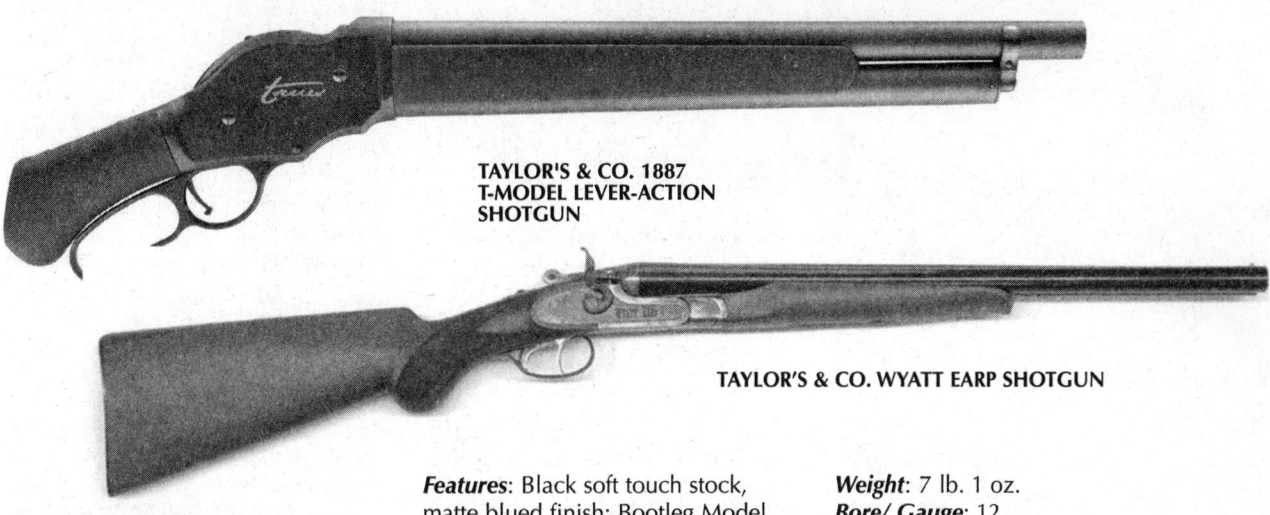

TAYLOR'S & CO. 1887 T-MODEL LEVER-ACTION SHOTGUN

TAYLOR'S & CO. WYATT EARP SHOTGUN

1887 T-MODEL LEVER-ACTION SHOTGUN

Action: Lever
Stock: Synthetic
Barrel: 18.5 in.
Chokes: None
Weight: 7 lb.
Bore/Gauge: 12
Magazine: 5+1 shells

Features: Black soft touch stock, matte blued finish; Bootleg Model
MSRP **$1312.00**

WYATT EARP SHOTGUN

Action: Side-by-side
Stock: Walnut checkered pistol grip
Barrel: 20.06 in.
Chokes: N/A

Weight: 7 lb. 1 oz.
Bore/ Gauge: 12
Magazine: 2 shells
Features: Easily opened with one hand for fast shell loading; case-hardened frame stamped with 'Wyatt Earp'; chromed barrel bores with blued finish
MSRP **$1658.00**

Thompson/Center Arms

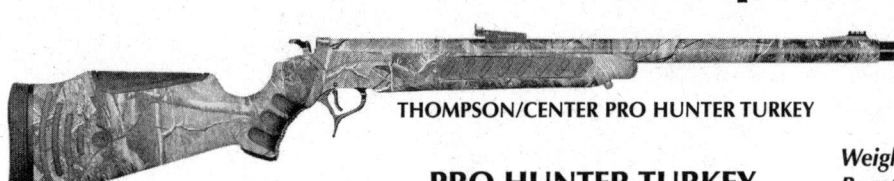

THOMPSON/CENTER PRO HUNTER TURKEY

PRO HUNTER TURKEY

Action: Hinged-breech single-shot
Stock: AP camo with Flextech
Barrel: 24 in. or 26 in.
Chokes: T/C extra full

Weight: 6 lb. 4 oz.–6 lb. 12 oz.
Bore/Gauge: 12, 20
Magazine: 1 shell
Features: Fiber optic sights; 14 in. length pull
MSRP **$892.00**

Tristar Sporting Arms

TRISTAR SPORTING ARMS COBRA FIELD PUMP

COBRA FIELD PUMP

Action: Pump
Stock: Synthetic
Barrel: 24 in., 26 in., 28 in.
Chokes: 1 Berretta-style choke (M)
Weight: 5 lb. 10 oz.–7 lb.
Bore/Gauge: 12, 20

Magazine: None
Features: The standard black synthetic in 12- and 20-gauge chambers 3-in. shells, while a single 12-gauge model chambers 3 ½-in. shells; the Cobra Camo in 12- or 20-gauge is covered in Vista camo or Next camo in a standard stock, while a Vista 12-gauge option is also available with a pistol grip stock and topside Weaver rail; the Youth pump in 20-gauge only comes in black synthetic or choice of Muddy Girl or Vista camos; fiber optic sights, sling swivel studs, Quick Shot plug removal, vent ribs and Beretta-style choke tubes are standard
MSRP . . . . **$350.00–$395.00**
Camo: . . . . **$425.00–$490.00**
Youth: . . . . **$350.00–$425.00**

Tristar Sporting Arms

TRISTAR SPORTING ARMS HUNTER EX LT

TRISTAR SPORTING ARMS RAPTOR A-TAC

TRISTAR SPORTING ARMS SETTER S/T

TRISTAR SPORTING ARMS TT-15

TRISTAR SPORTING ARMS TEC 12

TRISTAR SPORTING ARMS VIPER G2 LH

TRISTAR SPORTING ARMS VIPER G2 YOUTH

HUNTER EX LT
Action: Over/under
Stock: Wood
Barrel: 26 in.
Chokes: SK, IC, M, IM, F
Weight: 4 lb. 13 oz.–6 lb. 13 oz.
Bore/ Gauge: 12, 20, 28
Magazine: 2 shells
Features: Aluminum alloy receiver; steel hinge and firing pins; chambered for 3 in.; fiber optic sight
MSRP $670.00

RAPTOR A-TAC
Action: Semiautomatic
Stock: Synthetic
Barrel: 20 in.
Chokes: N/A
Weight: 7 lb.
Bore/Gauge: 12
Magazine: 5 shells
Features: Gas-operated; bridge-front sight with fiber optic bead; Picatinny rail mounted on of the receiver with a ghost ring sight installed; fixed pistol grip stock, swivel studs, and a tactical style operating handle; comes with an Extended Tactical Beretta/Benelli style choke; available in Kryptec Typhon and digital camo finishes
MSRP $425.00

SETTER S/T
Action: Over/under
Stock: Walnut
Barrel: 26 in., 28 in.
Chokes: 3-Beretta style tubes (IC, M, F)
Weight: 6 lb. 3 oz.–7 lb. 3 oz.
Bore/Gauge: 12, 20, 28, .410
Magazine: 2 shells
Features: Fiber optic front sight; high-gloss wood; single selective trigger; extractors; ventilated rib
MSRP . . . . $535.00–$565.00

TEC 12
Action: Pump or semiautomatic
Stock: Black synthetic
Barrel: 20 in.
Chokes: External Ported Cylinder choke

Weight: 7 lb. 6.4 oz.
Bore/ Gauge: 12
Magazine: N/A
Features: Capable of operating in pump or semiautomatic mode; 3 in. chamber; picatinny rail; ghost ring sight; raised front bridge sight with fiber optic bead; fixed rubber pistol grip; military sling swivels and swivel studs
MSRP $690.00

TT-15
Action: Over/under, top-single, top-unsingle, or combo
Stock: Turkish walnut
Barrel: 30 in., 32 in., 34 in.
Chokes: 3 or 5 extended Benelli/Beretta chokes
Weight: 7 lb. 13 oz.–8 lb. 14 oz.
Bore/Gauge: 12
Magazine: 1 shell, 2 shells
Features: Monte Carlo stock; fully adjustable comb; elegant hand-engraved receiver with nickel finish; fitted with high-standing 3-point adjustable rib, auto-ejectors, and fiber optic front sight
MSRP . . . . $1040.00–$1725.00

VIPER G2 LH
Action: Semiautomatic
Stock: Synthetic
Barrel: 28 in.
Chokes: IC, M, F
Weight: 6 lb. 14.4 oz.
Bore/ Gauge: 12
Magazine: N/A
Features: Chrome lined chambers; barrels threaded for Beretta/Benelli style choke tubes; 3 in. chambers
MSRP . . . . $580.00–$670.00

VIPER G2 YOUTH
Action: Semiautomatic, gas-operated
Stock: Synthetic
Barrel: 26 in.
Chokes: SK, IC, M, F
Weight: 5 lb. 11 oz.–6 lb. 3 oz.
Bore/Gauge: 12, 20
Magazine: 5 shells
Features: Manual E-Z Load magazine cut-off; raised target rib w/ matted sight plane; middle bead and fiber pptic sight; quick shot plug removal; chrome-lined chamber and barrel; adjustable comb; available in wood stock, black synthetic, Advantage Timber, black synthetic two-stock combo, and a black synthetic stock Sport model with red metallic finish on receiver and magazine cap
MSRP . . . . $550.00–$610.00

UTAS UTS-15 BLACK

UTAS XTR-12

UTS-15 BLACK
Action: Pump
Stock: Polymer
Barrel: 18.5 in.
Chokes: N/A
Weight: 6 lb. 15 oz.
Bore/ Gauge: 12
Magazine: 15 shells
Features: Unique pump action chambers up to 3-in. shells, features dual seven-round magazines with alternating or slectible feed, cartridge counter magazine followers, integrated topside Picatinny rail, spring-assisted pin ejector, quick-removal fire control housing, fiber-reinforced buttplate, internally mounted point-and-shoot high-intensity lens focused LED spotlight, and adjustable laser sight; Flat Dark Earth or Tungsten finishes
MSRP $1199.00

XTR-12
Action: Semiautomatic
Stock: Synthetic
Barrel: 20 in.
Chokes: N/A
Weight: 8 lb. 8 oz.
Bore/Gauge: 12
Magazine: 5 shells
Features: Compact forend features a full-length top rail; machined from 7075 aluminum with standard mil-spec fire control parts; AR-style adjustable butt stock; available in matte black, burnt bronze, flat dark earth, OD green, or tungsten finishes
MSRP . . . .$1099.00–$1199.00

Weatherby

WEATHERBY ELEMENT DELUXE

WEATHERBY ELEMENT SYNTHETIC

WEATHERBY ORION I

WEATHERBY PA-08 SYNTHETIC SLUG GUN COMBO

ELEMENT DELUXE
Action: Semiautomatic
Stock: Walnut
Barrel: 26 in., 28 in.
Chokes: IC, M, F
Weight: 6 lb.–6 lb.12 oz.
Bore/Gauge: 12, 20, 28
Magazine: 3+1 or 4+1 shells
Features: Fiber optic front sight; "AA" grade American walnut stock; aircraft grade aluminum; chrome-lined bores; drop-out trigger system; dual purpose bolt release; chrome-plated bolt; inertia-operated action; chrome-lined barrel; ventilated top rib; integral multi choke system with three application specific tubes (IC, Mod, Full)
MSRP $1099.00

ELEMENT SYNTHETIC
Action: Semiautomatic
Stock: Synthetic
Barrel: 26 in., 28 in.
Chokes: 4 application specific chokes (IC, Mod, Full, Long Range Steel)
Weight: 6 lb. 4 oz.–6 lb. 12 oz.
Bore/Gauge: 12, 20
Magazine: 4+1 shells
Features: Griptonite stock features pistol grip and forend inserts gray/black design color; matte, bead blasted finish
MSRP $749.00

ORION I
Action: Over/under
Stock: Walnut
Barrel: 26 in., 28 in.
Chokes: IC, M, F
Weight: 7 lb.
Bore/Gauge: 12
Magazine: 2 shells
Features: Brass front sights; ambidextrous top tang safety; automatic ejectors; low profile receiver; chrome-lined bores; matte ventilated top rib with brass bead front sight; traditional boxlock action; integral multi choke system with three application specific tubes (IC, Mod, Full)
MSRP $1099.00

PA-08 SYNTHETIC SLUG GUN COMBO
Action: Pump
Stock: Synthetic
Barrel: 24 in., 28 in.
Chokes: Interchangeable tubes (IC, M, F)
Weight: 7 lb. 4 oz.
Bore/Gauge: 12
Magazine: 4+1 or 5+1 shells
Features: Lightweight and durable injection-molded synthetic stock; comes with 28 in. field barrel and 24 in. rifled barrel with cantilever scope mount base; swivel studs; aircraft-grade aluminum alloy action; chrome-plated bolt in operating action
MSRP $549.00

SHOTGUNS

Weatherby

WEATHERBY PA-08 TURKEY XTRA GREEN

WEATHERBY PA-08 UPLAND

WEATHERBY PA-08 UPLAND SLUG GUN COMBO

WEATHERBY SA-08 WATERFOWLER MAX-5 COMPACT

WEATHERBY SA-08 DELUXE

WEATHERBY SA-459 TURKEY XTRA GREEN

PA-08 TURKEY XTRA GREEN
Action: Pump
Stock: Synthetic
Barrel: 22 in.
Chokes: Removeable choke tube (F)
Weight: 6 lb. 12 oz.
Bore/Gauge: 12
Magazine: 4+1 or 5+1 shells
Features: Dependable dual action bar system; features Realtree Xtra Green camouflage pattern; special "dipping" process adheres camo directly to all stock components; swivel studs included; chrome-lined barrels
MSRP **$429.00**

PA-08 UPLAND
Action: Pump
Stock: Walnut
Barrel: 26 in., 28 in.
Chokes: Screw in tubes (IC, M, F)
Weight: 6 lb. 8 oz.–7 lb. 4 oz.
Bore/Gauge: 12, 20
Magazine: None
Features: Walnut stock with gloss finish; gloss black finish on metalwork; vented top dissipates heat and aids in target acquisition; chrome-lined barrels
MSRP **$449.00**

PA-08 UPLAND SLUG GUN COMBO
Action: Pump
Stock: Walnut
Barrel: 24 in., 28 in.
Chokes: Interchangeable tubes (IC, M, F)
Weight: 7 lb. 4 oz.
Bore/Gauge: 12
Magazine: 4+1 or 5+1 shells
Features: Walnut stock with gloss finish; receiver with 28 in. field barrel is gloss black for a distinctive look; 24 in. rifled barrel with cantilever scope mount base in matte black; swivel studs; aircraft-grade aluminum alloy action; chrome-plated bolt in operating action
MSRP **$629.00**

SA-08 DELUXE
Action: Semiautomatic
Stock: Walnut
Barrel: 26 in., 28 in.
Chokes: Screw in tubes (IC, M, F)
Weight: 6 lb.–6 lb. 12 oz.
Bore/Gauge: 12, 20
Magazine: None
Features: Walnut stock with high–gloss finish and metalwork; vented top rib dissipates heat and aids in target acquisition; dual valve system
MSRP **$849.00**

SA-08 WATERFOWLER MAX-5 COMPACT
Action: Semiautomatic
Stock: Synthetic
Barrel: 24 in.
Chokes: 3 chokes (Full, Mod, IC)
Weight: 5 lb. 12 oz.
Bore/Gauge: 20
Magazine: 5+1 shells
Features: Realtree Max-5 camo pattern, adheres directly to all metalwork and stock components; shorter 12.5 in. length of pull with 24 in. barrel fits young shooters or those that want the benefits of a compact shotgun; swivel studs included
MSRP **$799.00**

SA-459 TURKEY XTRA GREEN
Action: Gas-operated semiautomatic
Stock: Synthetic
Barrel: 21.25 in.
Chokes: Interchangeable tubes (X-F)
Weight: 6 lb. 4 oz.–6 lb. 12 oz.
Bore/Gauge: 12, 20
Magazine: 4+1 or 5+1 shells
Features: Trimmer forend for easier handling; swivel studs; Mil-Spec Picatinny rail for mounting optics; LPA-style ghost ring rear sight that is adjustable for windage and elevation; front blade sight with fiber optic insert; over-size hourglass-shaped bolt handle for quick and positive chambering; pistol grip stock
MSRP **$799.00**

SHOTGUNS

Winchester Repeating Arms

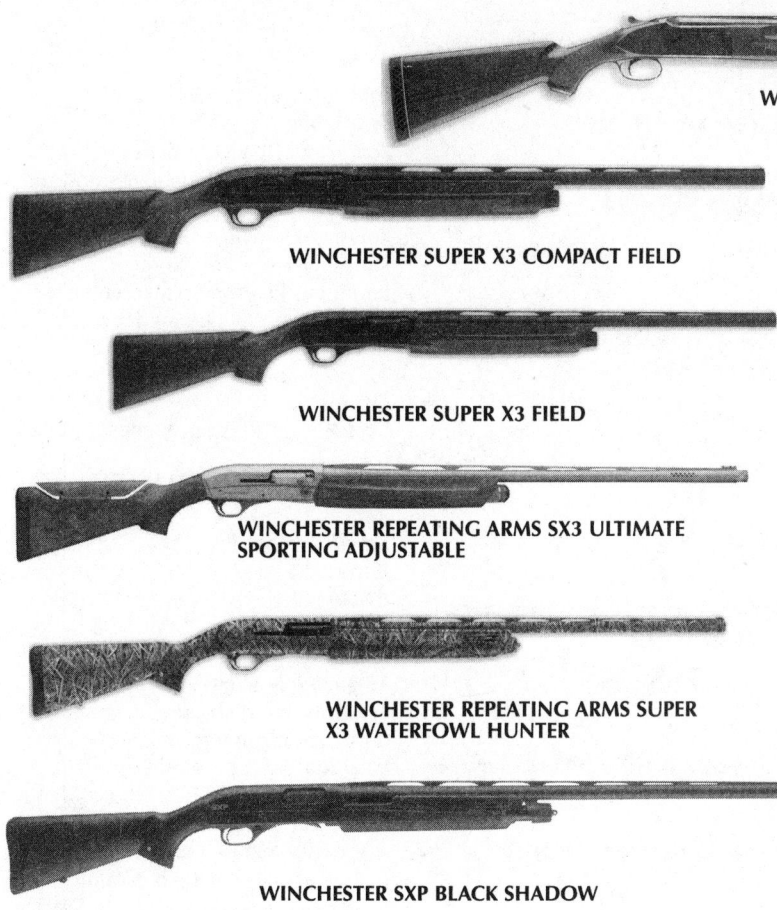

WINCHESTER MODEL 101 FIELD

WINCHESTER SUPER X3 COMPACT FIELD

WINCHESTER SUPER X3 FIELD

WINCHESTER REPEATING ARMS SX3 ULTIMATE SPORTING ADJUSTABLE

WINCHESTER REPEATING ARMS SUPER X3 WATERFOWL HUNTER

WINCHESTER SXP BLACK SHADOW

MODEL 101
Action: Over/under
Stock: Walnut
Barrel: 26 in., 28 in., 30 in., 32 in.
Chokes: Invector-Plus choke system, 3 tubes
Weight: 6 lb. 12 oz.–7 lb. 6 oz.
Bore/Gauge: 12
Magazine: 2 shells
Features: Solid brass bead front sight on Field; Truglo front sight on Sporting; deep relief receiver engraving; high-gloss grade II/III walnut stock; vented Pachmayr Decelerator pad with classic white line spacer
Field: $1899.99
Sporting: $2379.99

SUPER X3 COMPACT FIELD
Action: Semiautomatic
Stock: Walnut
Barrel: 24 in., 26 in., 28 in.
Chokes: Invector Plus
Weight: 6 lb. 4 oz.–6 lb. 14 oz.
Bore/Gauge: 12, 20
Magazine: 4 shells

Features: Stock dimensions trimmed for smaller-frame shooters and hunters with a 13-inch length of pull; satin oil finish walnut stock with classic cut checkering; matte black receivers in lightweight aluminum alloy
MSRP . . . . $1069.99–$1139.99

SUPER X3 FIELD
Action: Semiautomatic
Stock: Walnut
Barrel: 26 in., 28 in.
Chokes: Invector Plus
Weight: 6 lb. 6 oz.–6 lb. 14 oz.
Bore/Gauge: 12, 20
Magazine: 4 shells
Features: Satin oil finish walnut stock with classic cut checkering; matte black receivers in lightweight aluminum alloy; Invector Plus choke system
MSRP . . . . $1069.99–$1139.99

SUPER X3 ULTIMATE SPORTING ADJUSTABLE
Action: Semiautomatic
Stock: Walnut

Barrel: 28 in., 30 in., 32 in.
Chokes: Extended Signature Invector-Plus Choke Tubes
Weight: 7 lb. 6 oz.
Bore/Gauge: 12
Magazine: 4 shells
Features: Adjustable comb; cut checkering; matte nickel-plated receiver; signature Red Briley bolt handle, bolt release button, and magazine cap; back-bored technology; ported Perma-Cote gray barrel; vent rib; Tru-Glo fiber optic sight with white mid-bead; hard chrome-plated chamber and bore; active valve system; Pachmayr Decelerator recoil pad; ambidextrous crossbolt safety; drop-out trigger group
MSRP $1869.99

SUPER X3 WATERFOWL HUNTER
Action: Semiautomatic
Stock: Synthetic
Barrel: 26 in., 28 in.
Chokes: Invector-Plus tube
Weight: 6 lb. 10 oz.–7 lb. 2 oz.
Bore/Gauge: 12, 20
Magazine: None
Features: Mossy Oak Shadow Grass Blades; .742 Back-Bored technology; hard chrome chamber and bore; vent rib; TruGlo Long Bead fiber optic front sight; Active Valve Gas System; Quadra-Vent Ports; ambidextrous crossbolt safety
MSRP . . . . $1139.99–$1199.99

SXP BLACK SHADOW
Action: Pump
Stock: Synthetic
Barrel: 26 in., 28 in.
Chokes: Invector Plus
Weight: 6 lb. 12 oz.–7 lb.
Bore/Gauge: 12, 20
Magazine: 4 shells
Features: Hard chrome chamber and bores; drop-out trigger group for easy cleaning; synthetic stock with non-glare black matte finish on barrel and receiver
MSRP . . . . $379.99–$429.99

Winchester Repeating Arms

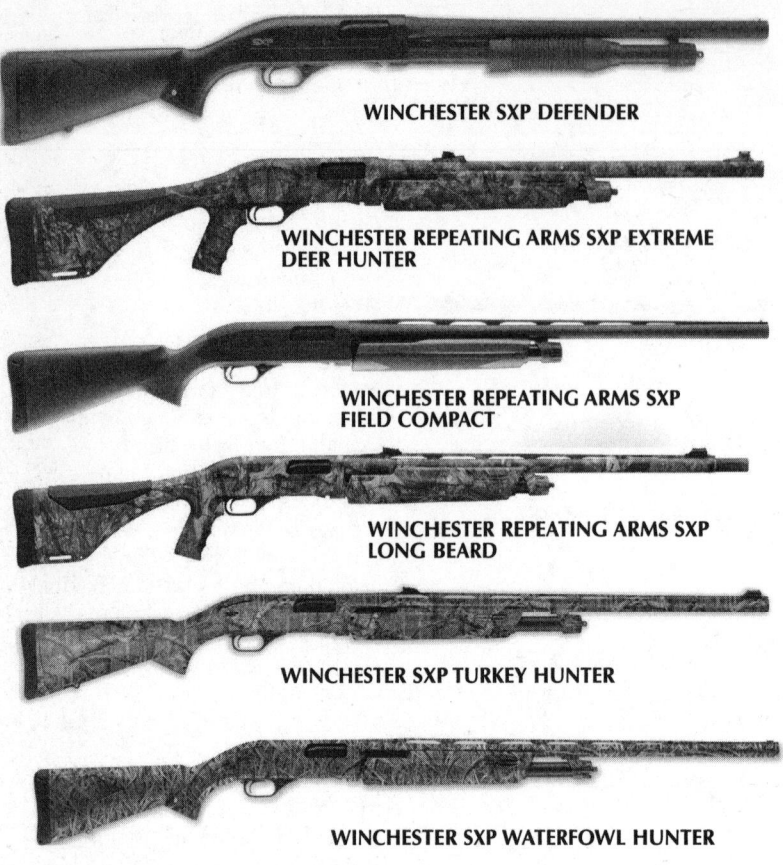

WINCHESTER SXP DEFENDER

WINCHESTER REPEATING ARMS SXP EXTREME DEER HUNTER

WINCHESTER REPEATING ARMS SXP FIELD COMPACT

WINCHESTER REPEATING ARMS SXP LONG BEARD

WINCHESTER SXP TURKEY HUNTER

WINCHESTER SXP WATERFOWL HUNTER

SXP DEFENDER
Action: Pump
Stock: Composite
Barrel: 18 in.
Chokes: Fixed cylinder choked barrel
Weight: 6 lb.–6 lb. 5 oz.
Bore/Gauge: 12, 20
Magazine: 5+1 shells
Features: Uses Foster-type slugs; non-glare metal surfaces with a tough black composite stock; deeply grooved forearm for control and stability
MSRP . . . . **$349.99–$379.99**

SXP EXTREME DEER HUNTER
Action: Pump
Stock: Composite
Barrel: 22 in.
Chokes: Invector-Plus flush, extra full
Weight: 7 lb.
Bore/Gauge: 12
Magazine: 4 shells
Features: Synthetic pistol grip stock with textured gripping surfaces; two interchangeable comb pieces; black chrome protection on the bolt; TRUGLO fiber optic front sight and adjustable rear sight; alloy receiver drilled and tapped for scope mounts; easily operated crossbolt safety; inflex technology recoil pad
MSRP **$619.99**

SXP FIELD COMPACT
Action: Pump
Stock: Satin finish
Barrel: 24 in., 26 in., 28 in.
Chokes: Three Invector-Plus chokes
Weight: 6 lb. 4 oz.–6 lb. 10 oz.
Bore/ Gauge: 12, 20
Magazine: None
Features: Aluminum alloy receiver; matte black finish; hard chrome chamber and bore; Speed plug system; brass bead front sight; Inflex technology recoil pad
MSRP . . . . **$399.99–$429.99**

SXP LONG BEARD
Action: Pump
Stock: Composite
Barrel: 24 in.
Chokes: Invector-Plus flush, extra full
Weight: 6 lb. 14 oz.–7 lb.

Bore/Gauge: 12, 20
Magazine: 4 shells
Features: TRUGLO fiber optic sights; two user-interchangeable combs and height adjust spacers; Extra-Full Turkey tube with a fluted body, knurled friction ring and camo front band; hard chrome-plated chamber and bore; easily operated crossbolt safety; inflex technology recoil pad; 12-ga. available in 3- and 3.5-in. chambers
MSRP . . . . **$529.99–$559.99**

SXP TURKEY HUNTER
Action: Pump
Stock: Synthetic
Barrel: 24 in.
Chokes: Invector Plus
Weight: 6 lb. 4 oz.–6 lb. 10 oz.
Bore/Gauge: 12, 20
Magazine: 4 shells
Features: Hard chrome chamber and bores; drop-out trigger group for easy cleaning; Invector Plus Extra-Full Turkey Choke Tube; crossbolt safety; Inflex technology recoil pad; synthetic stock with textured gripping surfaces in Mossy Oak Break-Up Country
MSRP **$519.99**

SXP WATERFOWL HUNTER
Action: Pump
Stock: Synthetic
Barrel: 26 in., 28 in.
Chokes: Invector Plus
Weight: 6 lb. 8 oz.–7 lb.
Bore/Gauge: 12, 20
Magazine: 4 shells
Features: Hard chrome chamber and bores; drop-out trigger group for easy cleaning; synthetic stock with textured gripping surfaces in Mossy Oak Shadow Grass Blades
MSRP . . . . **$459.99–$499.99**

Accu-Tek

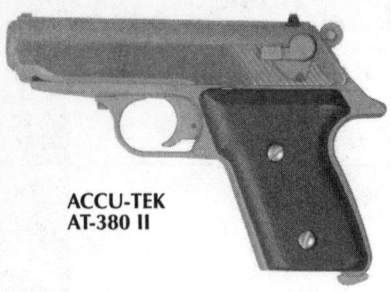

**ACCU-TEK
AT-380 II**

ACCU-TEK HC-380

**ACCU-TEK
FIREARMS
LT-380**

AT-380 II
Action: Semiautomatic
Grips: Composite
Barrel: 2.8 in.
Sights: Target
Weight: 23.5 oz.
Caliber: .380 ACP
Capacity: 6+1 rounds
Features: Stainless steel construction; adjustable rear sight; one hand manual safety blocks; stainless steel magazine
MSRP $289.00

HC-380
Action: Semiautomatic
Grips: Composite
Barrel: 2.8 in.
Sights: Target
Weight: 26 oz.
Caliber: .380 ACP
Capacity: 13 rounds
Features: Adjustable rear sight; black checkered grip; one-hand manual safety block; includes two magazines and cable lock
MSRP $330.00

LT-380
Action: SA semiautomatic
Grips: Composite
Barrel: 2.8 in.
Sights: Adjustable rear sight
Weight: 15 oz.
Caliber: .380 ACP
Capacity: 6 rounds
Features: Aluminum frame; stainless steel slide; exposed hammer; manual safety; European type magazine release
MSRP $324.00

American Derringer

**AMERICAN DERRINGER
LM4 SIMMERLING**

**AMERICAN
DERRINGER LM5**

**AMERICAN DERRINGER
MODEL 1**

LM4 SIMMERLING
Action: Hinged breech
Grips: Mesquite, Rosewood, custom
Barrel: 2 in.
Sights: Open, fixed
Weight: 24 oz.
Caliber: .45 ACP
Capacity: 5 rounds
Features: Vest pocket pistol; first round carried in the chamber; only 1in. thick; stainless steel
MSRP . . . Contact manufacturer for price

LM5
Action: Hinged breech
Grips: Rosewood

Barrel: 2 in.
Sights: Open, fixed
Weight: 15 oz.
Caliber: .25 ACP
Capacity: 5
Features: Stainless steel; cam lock safety
MSRP . . . Contact manufacturer for price

MODEL 1
Action: Hinged breech
Grips: Rosewood or stag
Barrel: 3 in.
Sights: Fixed, open
Weight: 15 oz.
Caliber: .45 Colt, .410, .45-70, .45 ACP, .45 Win. Mag., .44-40 Win., .44

Mag., .44 Spl., .41 Mag., .40 S&W, .380 ACP, .38 Spl., .38 Super, .357 Mag., .32-20, .32 Mag. S&W Long, .30-30 Win., .30 Carbine, .22 LR, .22 WMR, 10mm, 9mm, .223
Capacity: 2 rounds
Features: Single-action; automatic barrel selection; manually operated hammer-block safety
MSRP . . . Contact manufacturer for price

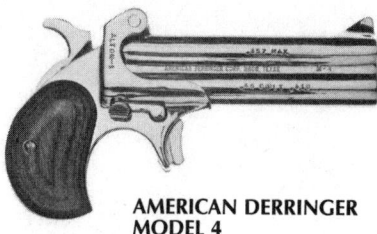

AMERICAN DERRINGER MODEL 4

AMERICAN DERRINGER MODEL 8

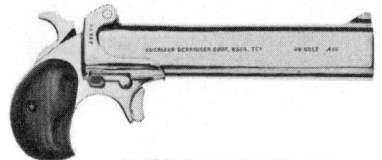

AMERICAN DERRINGER MODEL 6

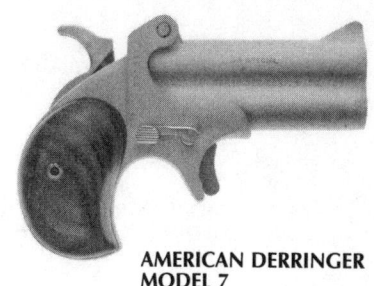

AMERICAN DERRINGER MODEL 7

MODEL 4

Action: Hinged breech
Grips: Rosewood
Barrel: 4.1 in
Sights: Fixed open
Weight: 16.5 oz.
Caliber: .375 Mag., 357 Max., .45-70 Govt.,
.45 Colt/.410, .44 Mag.
Capacity: 2 rounds
Features: Satin or high polish stainless steel finish; single-action; automatic barrel selection; manually operated hammer-block type safety
MSRP . . . Contact manufacturer for price

MODEL 6

Action: Hinged breech
Grips: Rosewood, walnut, black

Barrel: 6 in.
Sights: Fixed open
Weight: 21 oz.
Caliber: .22 WMR, .357 Mag., .45 ACP, .45 Colt/.410
Capacity: 2 rounds
Features: Satin or high polish stainless steel finish; single-action; automatic barrel selection; manually operated hammer-block type safety
MSRP . . . Contact manufacturer for price

MODEL 7 LIGHTWEIGHT & ULTRA LIGHTWEIGHT

Action: Hinged breech
Grips: Blackwood
Barrel: 3 in.
Sights: Fixed open
Weight: 7.5 oz.
Caliber: .44 Spl., .380 ACP, .38 Spl., .32 Mag./.32 S&W Long, .22 LR, .22 Mag.
Capacity: 2 rounds
Features: Grey matte finish; single-action; automatic barrel selection; manually operated hammer-block type safety

MSRP . . . Contact manufacturer for price

MODEL 8

Action: Hinged breech
Grips: Rosewood, walnut, black
Barrel: 6 in.
Sights: Optional Adco red dot scope
Weight: 24 oz.
Caliber: .45 Colt/.410
Capacity: 2 rounds
Features: Satin or high polish stainless steel finish; single-action; automatic barrel selection; manually operated hammer-block type safety
MSRP . . . Contact manufacturer for price

American Tactical Imports

AMERICAN TACTICAL IMPORTS FIREPOWER XTREME HYBRID 45ACP FXH-45 1911

AMERICAN TACTICAL IMPORTS FIREPOWER XTREME 45ACP G1 1911 (FX SERIES)

FIREPOWER XTREME HYBRID 45ACP FXH-45 1911 (FX SERIES)

Action: SA semiautomatic
Grips: Polymer
Barrel: 5 in.
Sights: Fixed
Weight: 27.5 oz.
Caliber: .45 ACP
Capacity: 8 rounds
Features: Polymer frame with 2 metal inserts for added stability and durability; steel match grade barrel and a custom designed steel slide; ergonomic frame with built-in finger grooves; accepts Glock front and rear sights, including aftermarket night sights
MSRP $599.95

FIREPOWER XTREME 45ACP G1 1911 (FX SERIES)

Action: Semiautomatic
Grips: Mahogany
Barrel: 4.25 in.
Sights: Fixed
Weight: 33.5 oz.
Caliber: .45 ACP
Capacity: 7+1 rounds
Features: Steel parts; black matte military-style fixed front and rear sights; military-style slide stop and thumb safety, solid mahogany grip panels
MSRP $449.95

American Tactical Imports

AMERICAN TACTICAL IMPORTS FX FIREPOWER XTREME 45ACP MILITARY 1911 (FX SERIES)

AMERICAN TACTICAL IMPORTS FIREPOWER XTREME THUNDERBOLT 1911 (FX SERIES)

AMERICAN TACTICAL IMPORTS FIREPOWER XTREME THUNDERBOLT ENHANCED 1911 (FX SERIES)

AMERICAN TACTICAL IMPORTS GSG 922 CALIFORNIA COMPLIANT

FIREPOWER XTREME 45ACP MILITARY 1911 (FX SERIES)

Action: Semiautomatic
Grips: Mahogany
Barrel: 5 in.
Sights: Fixed
Weight: 37 oz.
Caliber: .45 ACP
Capacity: 7+1 rounds
Features: Steel parts; black matte military-style fixed front and rear sights; military-style slide stop and thumb safety, solid mahogany grip panels
MSRP. **$449.95**

FIREPOWER XTREME THUNDERBOLT 1911 (FX SERIES)

Action: Semi-automatic
Grips: Mahogany
Barrel: 5 in.
Sights: Fixed
Weight: 37 oz.
Caliber: .45 ACP
Capacity: 8+1 rounds
Features: Picatinny rail; steel parts; Solid mahogany grips
MSRP. **$857.95**

FIREPOWER XTREME THUNDERBOLT ENHANCED 1911 (FX SERIES)

Action: Semiautomatic
Grips: Mahogany
Barrel: 5 in.
Sights: Adjustable 3-dot combat sights
Weight: 37 oz.
Caliber: .45 ACP

Capacity: 8 +1 rounds
Features: Picatinny rail; ambidextrous safety; grip checkering; enhanced model has barrel porting for less recoil
MSRP. **$899.95**

GSG 922 CALIFORNIA COMPLIANT

Action: Semiautomatic
Grips: Plastic
Barrel: 3.2 in.
Sights: Click-adjustable target
Weight: 31 oz.
Caliber: .22 LR
Capacity: 10 rounds
Features: Frame is constructed of Zamak-5 zinc alloy; loaded chamber indicator, grip safety, magazine safety, firing-pin-block, external hammer; optional AD OP's faux suppressor
MSRP. **$384.95**

Anderson Rifles

AM15-7.5 PISTOL

Action: Semiautomatic
Grips: Synthetic
Barrel: 7.5 in. extended barrel
Sights: None
Weight: 4 lb. 14 oz.
Caliber: .223 Rem./5.56 NATO
Capacity: Detachable box, 30 rounds
Features: Picatinny rail; Anderson Knight Stalker flash hider; Magpul grip; available treated with proprietary no lube RF85 treatment
MSRP. **$599.99**

ANDERSON RIFLES AM15-7.5 PISTOL

Armscor/Rock Island Armory

ARMSCOR/ROCK ISLAND ARMORY BABY ROCK

ARMSCOR/ROCK ISLAND ARMORY GI STANDARD FS HC-45ACP

ARMSCOR/ROCK ISLAND ARMORY GI STANDARD MS-45ACP

ARMSCOR/ROCK ISLAND ARMORY PRO MATCH ULTRA 6-IN-10MM

ARMSCOR/ROCK ISLAND ARMORY PRO MATCH ULTRA HC

ARMSCOR/ROCK ISLAND ARMORY TCM TAC ULTRA FS HC COMBO-22TCM/9MM

BABY ROCK

Action: Semiautomatic
Grips: Rubber
Barrel: 4 in.
Sights: Fixed
Weight: 1 lb. 8 oz.
Caliber: .380 ACP
Capacity: 7 rounds
Features: Parkerized frame; front post, Novak-style rear sight
MSRP.................**$460.00**

GI STANDARD FS HC-45ACP

Action: Semiautomatic
Grips: Rubber
Barrel: 5 in.
Sights: Fixed
Weight: 2 lb. 9 oz.
Caliber: .45 ACP
Capacity: 10 rounds
Features: Parkerized frame; 1:16 in. twist; 4–6 lb. trigger pull
MSRP.................**$608.00**

GI STANDARD MS-45ACP

Action: Semiautomatic
Grips: Wood
Barrel: 4.25 in.
Sights: Fixed
Weight: 2 lb. 6 oz.
Caliber: .45 ACP
Capacity: 8 rounds
Features: Parkerized frame; 1:16 in. twist; 4–6 lb. trigger pull
MSRP.................**$537.00**

PRO MATCH ULTRA 6-IN. 10MM

Action: Semiautomatic
Grips: Rubber
Barrel: 6 in.
Sights: Dovetail mounted fiber optic front, LPA TRT1 adjustable rear
Weight: 2 lb. 8 oz.
Caliber: 10mm
Capacity: 8 rounds
Features: Parkerized frame; orange fiber-optic front sight, tactical adjustable rear sight; comes with 9mm conversion kit; 1:16 twist; 4–6 lb. trigger pull; ambidextrous safety; combat hammer; extended beavertail
MSRP.................**$1168.00**

PRO MATCH ULTRA HC-10MM, HC-40S&W

Action: Semiautomatic
Grips: G10
Barrel: 5 in., 6 in.
Sights: Dovetail mounted fiber-optic front, LPA TRT-type rear
Weight: 2 lb. 14 oz.
Caliber: .40 S&W, 10mm
Capacity: 17 rounds
Features: Parkerized frame; orange fiber-optic front sight, tactical adjustable rear sight; comes with 9mm conversion kit; 1:16 twist; 4–6 lb. trigger pull; ambidextrous safety; combat hammer; extended beavertail
.40 S&W: **$1077.00**
10mm: **$1322.00**

Armscor/Rock Island Armory

ARMSCOR/ROCK ISLAND ARMORY TCM TAC ULTRA MS HC COMBO - 22TCM/9MM

ARMSCOR/ROCK ISLAND ARMORY XT 22 MAGNUM

Capacity: 17 rounds
Features: Parkerized frame; orange fiber-optic front sight, tactical adjustable rear sight; comes with 9mm conversion kit; 1:16 twist; 4–6 lb. trigger pull; ambidextrous safety; combat hammer; extended beavertail
MSRP $960.00

XT 22 MAGNUM
Action: Semiautomatic
Grips: Rubber
Barrel: 5 in.
Sights: Fixed
Weight: 2 lb. 3 oz.
Caliber: .22 Mag.
Capacity: 22 rounds
Features: Parkerized frame; single action
MSRP $598.00

TCM TAC ULTRA FS HC COMBO-22TCM/9MM
Action: Semiautomatic
Grips: G10
Barrel: 5 in.
Sights: Dovetail fiber optic front sight, LPA MPS1-type adjustable rear
Weight: 3 lb.
Caliber: .22 TCM, 9mm
Capacity: 17 rounds
Features: Parkerized frame; orange fiber-optic front sight, tactical adjustable rear sight; comes with 9mm conversion kit; 1:16 twist; 4–6

lb. trigger pull; ambidextrous safety; combat hammer; extended beavertail
MSRP $960.00

TCM TAC ULTRA MS HC COMBO - 22TCM/9MM
Action: Semiautomatic
Grips: G10
Barrel: 4.25 in.
Sights: Dovetailed mounted fixed front sight, LPA MPS1-type adjustable rear
Weight: 2 lb. 8 oz.
Caliber: .22 TCM/9mm

Arsenal Firearms

ARSENAL FIREARMS AF-1 STRIKE ONE

ARSENAL FIREARMS AF2011 DUELLER

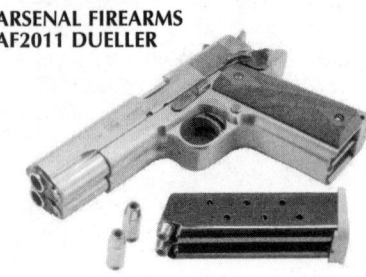

AF-1 STRIKE ONE
Action: Semiautomatic
Grips: 3D polymer
Barrel: 5 in.
Sights: Fixed or adjustable
Weight: 26.4 oz. (poly), 31.4 oz. (ergal)
Caliber: 9mm Para, 9mm IMI, .357 SIG, .40 S&W
Capacity: 17 rounds
Features: Geometric lock, semiautomatic hammerless pistol; short recoil, in-line barrel, patented locking block system; automatic safety; single-action only trigger; ambidextrous magazine release button; reinforced polymer or ergal light alloy frame in ordnance black, desert tan, and olive drab with 360 degree integral mini-skirt; underbarrel integral Picatinny rail; interchangeable back plate/sight, fixed or adjustable, or Micro-Dot ready; available with a Long Range Conversion
MSRP . . . .**Price on request**

AF2011 DUELLER
Action: Semiautomatic double barrel
Grips: Steel, rubber, or walnut
Barrel: 4.9 in.
Sights: Fixed or adjustable
Weight: 65.3 oz.
Caliber: .45 ACP
Capacity: 18 rounds
Features: First industrial double barrel semiautomatic pistol; single slide, single frame, single spur double hammer; single grip safety; single body double mainspring housing and single double cavity magazine floorplate (two single magazines); long and double magazine latch; most internal parts are interchangeable with standard 1911 replacement parts; can be ordered with two independent triggers and one sear group or with two triggers permanently joined and one or two sear groups; deep blued mirror finish or 3400 Vickers surface hardness white ash nitrite coating
MSRP $5319.00

Arsenal, Inc.

ARSENAL, INC. SAM7K

SAM7K
Action: Semiautomatic
Grips: Black polymer
Barrel: 10.5 in.
Sights: Peep rear
Weight: 128 oz.
Caliber: 7.62x39 Warsaw
Capacity: 5 rounds
Features: Milled receiver; short gas system; front sight block; gas block system; chrome-lined hammer-forged barrel; ambidextrous safety lever; scope rail; sling included
MSRP $1199.00

Auto-Ordnance

AUTO-ORDNANCE 1911PKZSE

AUTO-ORDNANCE 1911TC THOMPSON CUSTOM 1911 STAINLESS

1911PKZSE
Action: Semiautomatic
Grips: Brown checkered plastic, checkered wood grips
Barrel: 5 in.
Sights: Blade front, rear drift adjustable sight
Weight: 39 oz.
Caliber: .45 ACP
Capacity: 7+1 rounds
Features: Single-action 1911 Colt design; WWII parkerized; stainless steel or blued metal finish
MSRP $688.00

1911TC THOMPSON CUSTOM 1911 STAINLESS
Action: Semiautomatic
Grips: Checkered laminate
Barrel: 5 in.
Sights: Low-profile iron sights
Weight: 39 oz.

Caliber: .45 ACP
Capacity: 7+1 rounds
Features: Frames machined on high precision computerized machinery from a 420 stainless steel casting; slide is machined from a solid stainless steel billet utilizing specialized tooling to reduce set-up and refixturing; matte finish on slide and frame; front and rear sights are black with serrations; extended beavertail grip safety; extended magazine release
MSRP $866.00

Beretta USA

21A BOBCAT
Action: Semiautomatic
Grips: Plastic
Barrel: 2.4 in.
Sights: Fixed, open
Weight: 11.5 oz.
Caliber: .22 LR, .25 ACP
Capacity: 7 or 8 rounds
Features: Double-action; tip-up barrel; stainless steel slide and barrel; alloy gray frame; other metal parts come in black or Inox finish
MSRP: $410.00

92A1
Action: Semiautomatic
Grips: Plastic
Barrel: 4.9 in.
Sights: 3-Dot System
Weight: 34.4 oz.
Caliber: 9mm, .40 S&W
Capacity: 12 or 17 rounds, restricted capacity 10 rounds
Features: Removable front sight; Picatinny rail, internal recoil buffer; captive recoil spring assembly
MSRP $775.00

BERETTA 21A BOBCAT

BERETTA 92A1

Beretta USA

BERETTA 92FS TYPE M9A1

BERETTA BU-9 NANO

BERETTA PICO

BERETTA 3032 TOMCAT INOX

BERETTA M9

BERETTA PX4 STORM COMPACT

BERETTA PX4 COMPACT CARRY

92FS TYPE M9A1

Action: Semiautomatic
Grips: Plastic
Barrel: 4.9 in.
Sights: 3-Dot System
Weight: 33.9 oz.
Caliber: 9mm
Capacity: 15+1 rounds, restricted capacity 10+1 rounds
Features: Picatinny rail; magazine well bevel; sand-resistant magazine
MSRP.................**$750.00**

3032 TOMCAT INOX

Action: Semiautomatic
Grips: Plastic
Barrel: 2.5 in.
Sights: Fixed, open
Weight: 14.5 oz.
Caliber: .32 ACP, .380 ACP
Capacity: 7+1 round
Features: Double-action; tip-up barrel latch; Inox has stainless steel slide and barrel; titanium alloy frame in black or gray; double- or single-trigger
MSRP.................**$485.00**

BU-9 NANO

Action: Semiautomatic
Grips: Technopolymer
Barrel: 3.07 in.

Sights: 3-dot low profile
Weight: 17.67 oz.
Caliber: 9mm
Capacity: 6+1 rounds
Features: Interchangeable sights; ambidextrous magazine release button; serialized sub-chassis; patent-pending striker deactivator; technopolymer grip frame; four variations available include black, pink, Flat Dark Earth, and an option with a Crimson Trace built-in laser
Black, pink, Flat Dark Earth: . . **$450.00**
Crimson Trace laser: **$650.00**

M9

Action: Semiautomatic
Grips: Plastic
Barrel: 4.9 in.
Sights: Dot-and-Post system
Weight: 33.3 oz.
Caliber: 9mm
Capacity: 15 rounds, restricted capacity 10+1 rounds
Features: Has distinctive military style markings; chrome-lined bore; double-action; automatic firing pin block; ambidextrous manual safety; lightweight forged aluminum alloy frame w/ combat-style trigger guard
MSRP.................**$675.00**

PICO

Action: Semiautomatic
Grips: Technopolymer
Barrel: 2.7 in.
Sights: Front and rear adjustable
Weight: 11.5 oz.
Caliber: .380 ACP
Capacity: 6+1 rounds
Features: Stainless steel sub-chassis engraved with serial number; snag-

free slide and frame; barrel can be replaced with a .32 ACP barrel; dovetail quick-change sights; frames available in flat dark earth, white, or purple
MSRP.................**$400.00**

PX4 STORM COMPACT

Action: Semiautomatic
Grips: Plastic
Barrel: 3.2 in.
Sights: 3-Dot System
Weight: 27.3 oz.
Caliber: 9mm, .40 S&W
Capacity: 12 or 15 rounds; full size magazines 9mm: 17 or 20 rounds, .40 S&W: 14 or 17 rounds; restricted capacity 10 rounds
Features: Ambidextrous side stop lever; integral Picatinny rail; bruiton non-reflective black coating; visible automatic firing pin block
MSRP.................**$650.00**

PX4 STORM COMPACT CARRY

Action: DA/SA
Grips: Synthetic
Barrel: 3.2 in.
Sights: High-visibility night sights
Weight: 27.3 oz.
Caliber: 9mm
Capacity: 15 rounds
Features: Rotating barrel; grey Cerakote slide; Picatinny rail; competition trigger; double stack magazine; Talon grips; reversible magazine release; lightweight polymer frame; stealth levers decock only
MSRP.................**$899.00**

Beretta USA

BERETTA PX4 STORM FULL SIZE

BERETTA U22 NEOS

Weight: 27.7 oz.
Caliber: 9mm, .40 S&W, .45 ACP
Capacity: 14 or 17 rounds, restricted capacity 10 rounds
Features: Picatinny rail; innovative locked-breech with a rotating barrel system; visible automatic firing pin block; ambidextrous safety; reversible magazine release; available in Inox finish
MSRP **$650.00**

PX4 STORM FULL SIZE

Action: Semiautomatic
Grips: Plastic
Barrel: 4 in.
Sights: 3-Dot System

U22 NEOS

Action: Semiautomatic
Grips: Plastic
Barrel: 4.5 in., 6 in.
Sights: Target

Weight: 31.7–36.2 oz.
Caliber: .22 LR
Capacity: 10+1 rounds
Features: Single-action; removable colored grip inserts; deluxe model features adjustable trigger, replaceable sights; optional 7.5 in. barrel
Standard: **$325.00**
Inox: **$350.00**

Bersa

BERSA BP CONCEALED CARRY SERIES

BERSA THUNDER 9 PRO XT

BERSA THUNDER 9 ULTRA COMPACT PRO

BP CONCEALED CARRY SERIES

Action: Short reset DAO
Grips: Integral to frame
Barrel: 3.3 in.
Sights: Interchangeable front and rear
Weight: 21.5 oz.
Caliber: 9mm, .380 ACP, .40 S&W
Capacity: 6+1 or 8+1 rounds
Features: Bersa polymer concealed carry; high impact polymer frame; Picatinny rail, polygonal rifling, and loaded chamber indicator; ambidextrous magazine release; striker fired; micro-polished bore with sharp, deep rifling; 3-dot sight system; integral locking system; automatic firing pin safety; 9mm available in matte black, duotone, or frames in olive drab, flat dark earth or urban gray; .40 S&W availble in matte black; .380 ACP available in matte black and duotone;

some limited edition 9mm in matte black or duotone available with turquoise blue frame
MSRP . . . . **$423.00–$440.00**

THUNDER 9 PRO XT

Action: DA/SA
Grips: Checkered black polymer
Barrel: 4.96 in.
Sights: Fiber optic front sight, adjustable rear
Weight: 33.9 oz.
Caliber: 9mm
Capacity: 10–17 rounds
Features: Dovetailed front fiber optic sight; windage and elevation adjustable rear sights; ambidextrous controls for easy handling; 5-inch competition barrel fitted to slide for maximum precision; Cerakote finish to protect against abrasion, wear, and corrosion
MSRP **$923.00**

THUNDER 9 ULTRA COMPACT PRO

Action: Semiautomatic
Grips: Black polymer
Barrel: 3.25 in.
Sights: 3-Dot system
Weight: 23 oz.
Caliber: 9mm
Capacity: 10+1 or 13+1 rounds
Features: Picatinny rail; precision machined lightweight alloy; ambidextrous safety; lifetime service contract; integral locking system; anatomically designed polymer grips; double-action; available in matte or duotone finish
MSRP . . . . **$508.00–$516.00**

Bersa

THUNDER 40 ULTRA COMPACT PRO

Action: Semiautomatic
Grips: Black polymer
Barrel: 3.25 in.
Sights: 3-Dot system
Weight: 23 oz.
Caliber: .40 S&W
Capacity: 10+1 rounds
Features: Picatinny rail; precision machined lightweight alloy; ambidextrous safety; lifetime service contract; integral locking system; anatomically designed polymer grips; double-action; available in matte
MSRP. **$508.00**

THUNDER 45 ULTRA COMPACT PRO

Action: Semiautomatic
Grips: Black polymer
Barrel: 3.6 in.
Sights: 3-Dot system
Weight: 27 oz.
Caliber: .45 ACP
Capacity: 7+1 rounds
Features: Double-action; Picatinny rail; precision machined lightweight alloy; ambidextrous safety; lifetime service contract; integral locking system; anatomically designed polymer grips; available in matte or duotone finish
MSRP. . . . . **$508.00–$516.00**

THUNDER 380

Action: Semiautomatic
Grips: Black polymer
Barrel: 3.5 in.
Sights: 3-Dot system
Weight: 20 oz.
Caliber: .380 ACP
Capacity: 7+1 rounds
Features: Combat style trigger guard; extended slide release; micro-polished bore with sharp, deep rifling; integral locking system; available in matte, matte with pink rubber wraparound grips, duotone, or Cerakote nickel
MSRP. . . . . **$324.00–$356.00**

THUNDER 380 COMBAT PLUS

Action: DA/SA
Grips: Olive rubber wrap-around
Barrel: 3.5 in.
Sights: Dovetail front, notched-bar dovetail rear

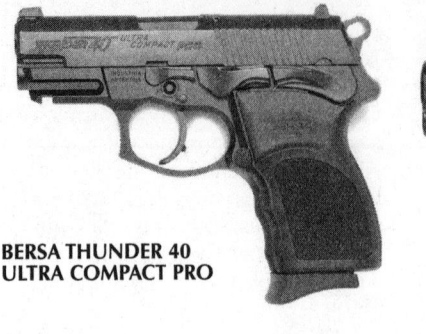

BERSA THUNDER 40 ULTRA COMPACT PRO

BERSA THUNDER 45 ULTRA COMPACT PRO

BERSA THUNDER 380

Weight: 20.5 oz.
Caliber: .380 ACP
Capacity: 8+1, 15+1
Features: Decocker for safer conceal carry; flat-bottom 8 shot magazine; integral locking system for the ultimate in safety; micro-polished bore with sharp, deep rifling for greater accuracy; slim side release for a lower profile; u-shaped combat rear sight for optimum sighting in low-light situations
MSRP. **$424.00**

THUNDER 380 CONCEALED CARRY

Action: Semiautomatic
Grips: Black polymer
Barrel: 3.2 in.
Sights: Blade front and notched-bar dovetailed rear
Weight: 16.4 oz.
Caliber: .380 ACP
Capacity: 8+1 rounds
Features: Extra low profile sights; combat style trigger guard; slim slide release; integral locking system
MSRP. . . . . **$336.00–$346.00**

BERSA THUNDER 380 COMBAT PLUS

BERSA THUNDER 380 CONCEALED CARRY

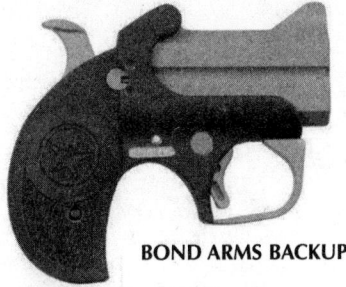

BOND ARMS BACKUP

BOND ARMS CENTURY 2000

BOND ARMS MAMA BEAR

BOND ARMS MINI 45

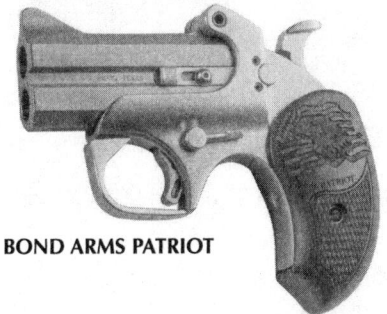

BOND ARMS PATRIOT

BOND ARMS GIRL MINI

BOND ARMS SNAKE SLAYER

BACKUP

Action: SA semiautomatic
Grips: Rubber
Barrel: 2.5 in.
Sights: Blade front, fixed rear
Weight: 18.5 oz.
Caliber: .357 Mag., .38 Spl., .40 S&W, .45 ACP, .45 Colt
Capacity: 2 rounds
Features: Interchangable barrels; rebounding hammer; retracting firing pins; crossbolt safety
MSRP $490.00

CENTURY 2000

Action: SA
Grips: Custom laminated black ash or rosewood
Barrel: 3.5 in.
Sights: Blade front, fixed rear
Weight: 21 oz.
Caliber: .357 Mag./.38 Spl., .410/.45 LC
Capacity: 2 rounds
Features: Interchangeable barrels; automatic extractor; rebounding hammer; retracting firing pins;

crossbolt safety; spring-loaded cammed locking lever; trigger guard; stainless steel with satin polish finish
MSRP $517.00

MAMA BEAR

Action: SA
Grips: Pink wood
Barrel: 2.5 in.
Sights: Blade front, fixed rear
Weight: 18.5 oz.
Caliber: .357 Mag, .38 Spl.
Capacity: 2 rounds
Features: Stainless steel double barrel and frame; automatic spent casing extractor; rebounding hammer; retracting ring pins; crossbolt safety; spring-loaded, cammed locking lever; laser-carved American Flag and bald eagle grips
MSRP $476.00

MINI 45, GIRL MINI

Action: SA
Grips: Rosewood or pink
Barrel: 2.5 in.
Sights: Blade front, fixed rear
Weight: 18 oz.–19 oz.
Caliber: .45 Colt (Mini 45), .357 Mag. (Girl Mini)
Capacity: 2 rounds
Features: The Bond Mini was developed as a special edition gun that is even easier to conceal and carry, but still packs the same power Bond Arms guns are known for; comes in two models the Mini .45 and the Girl Mini; Girl Mini has

slightly smaller barrel included and pink grips
MSRP $469.00

PATRIOT

Action: SA
Grips: Rosewood
Barrel: 3 in.
Sights: Blade front, fixed rear
Weight: 21.5 oz.
Caliber: .45 Colt, .410
Capacity: 2 rounds
Features: Stainless steel double barrel and frame; automatic spent casing extractor; rebounding hammer; retracting ring pins; crossbolt safety; spring-loaded, cammed locking lever; laser-carved American Flag and bald eagle grips
MSRP $598.00

SNAKE SLAYER

Action: SA
Grips: Extended custom rosewood
Barrel: 3.5 in.
Sights: Blade front, fixed rear
Weight: 22 oz.
Caliber: .357 Mag./.38 Spl., .410/.45 LC
Capacity: 2 rounds
Features: Interchangeable barrels; automatic extractor; rebounding hammer; retracting firing pins; crossbolt safety; spring-loaded cammed locking lever; trigger guard; stainless steel with satin polish finish
MSRP $568.00

Bond Arms

BOND ARMS SNAKE SLAYER IV

BOND ARMS TEXAS DEFENDER

BOND TEXAS RANGER - SPECIAL EDITION

SNAKE SLAYER IV

Action: SA
Grips: Extended custom rosewood
Barrel: 4.25 in.
Sights: Blade front, fixed rear
Weight: 23.5 oz.
Caliber: .357 Mag./.38 Spl., .410/.45 LC
Capacity: 2 rounds
Features: Automatic extractor; interchangeable barrels; rebounding hammer; retracting firing pins; crossbolt safety; spring-loaded cammed locking lever; trigger guard; stainless steel with satin polish finish
MSRP..................$613.00

TEXAS DEFENDER

Action: SA
Grips: Custom laminated black ash or rosewood
Barrel: 3 in.
Sights: Blade front and fixed rear
Weight: 20 oz.
Caliber: 45 Colt/.410
Capacity: 2 rounds
Features: Interchangeable barrels; automatic extractor; rebounding hammer; retracting firing pins; crossbolt safety; spring-loaded cammed locking lever; trigger guard; stainless steel with satin polish finish
MSRP..................$493.00

TEXAS RANGER - SPECIAL EDITION

Action: SA
Grips: Texas mesquite
Barrel: 3.5 in.
Sights: Blade front, fixed rear
Weight: 22 oz.
Caliber: .410/.45 LC
Capacity: 2 rounds
Features: Bond Arms has been chosen to represent the prestigious Texas Rangers in their historic 200th Anniversary; gun and knife grips are made from real Texas mesquite wood, the Texas Ranger Stars are handmade by Texas inmates in the Texas Department of Corrections, and it is gold engraved on the barrel; custom glass top display case included
MSRP.................$1420.00

Browning

BROWNING 1911-22 A1 FULL SIZE

BROWNING 1911–22 A1 COMPACT DESERT TAN

1911-22 A1 FULL SIZE

Action: Semiautomatic
Grips: Brown composite
Barrel: 4.25 in.
Sights: Fixed
Weight: 15 oz.
Caliber: 22 LR
Capacity: 10+1 rounds
Features: Alloy frame in matte blued finish; stainless steel barrel block with matte blued finish; blowback action; single-action trigger; detachable magazine; manual thumb safety; grip safety
MSRP..................$599.99

1911-22 A1 COMPACT DESERT TAN

Action: Semiautomatic straight blowback
Grips: Synthetic
Barrel: 3.625 in.
Sights: Fixed
Weight: 13 oz.
Caliber: .22 LR
Capacity: 10 rounds
Features: Machined aircraft-grade aluminum or polymer frame; large manual thumb safety and grip safety
MSRP..................$579.99

Browning

BROWNING 1911-380
BLACK LABEL

BROWNING 1911-380
BLACK LABEL PRO

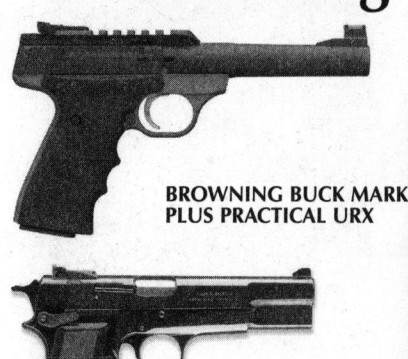

BROWNING BUCK MARK
PLUS PRACTICAL URX

BROWNING BUCK
MARK PLUS UDX

BROWNING BUCK
MARK STANDARD UFX

BROWNING HI-POWER
STANDARD

1911-380 BLACK LABEL

Action: Semiautomatic
Grips: Synthetic
Barrel: 4.25 in.
Sights: Fixed
Weight: 18 oz.
Caliber: .380 ACP
Capacity: 8 rounds
Features: Combat sights; matte black
finish; single-stack magazine
MSRP **$669.99**

1911-380 BLACK LABEL PRO

Action: Semiautomatic
Grips: Synthetic
Barrel: 4.25 in.
Sights: Combat white dot
Weight: 18 oz.
Caliber: .380 ACP
Capacity: 8 rounds
Features: High strength/lightweight
composite frame; machined steel
slide; target crown; extended
ambidextrous manual safety;
skeletonized hammer
MSRP **$799.99**

BUCK MARK PLUS UDX

Action: Semiautomatic
Grips: Brown wood laminate UDX

CABOT GUN COMPANY
AMERICAN JOE 1911

Barrel: 5.5–7.25 in.
Sights: Adjustable pro-target rear
sight, Truglo/Marble fiber-optic front
Weight: 34 oz.
Caliber: 22 LR
Capacity: 10+1 rounds
Features: Matte blued, polished barrel
flats; blowback action; single-action
trigger
MSRP **$549.99**

BUCK MARK PLUS PRACTICAL URX

Action: Semiautomatic
Grips: Ultragrip RX ambidextrous
Barrel: 5.5 in.
Sights: Pro-target adjustable rear;
Truglo/Marble's fiber-optic front
Weight: 34 oz.
Caliber: .22 LR
Capacity: 10+1 rounds
Features: Tapered bull barrel with
matte blued finish; matte gray finish
receiver
MSRP **$479.99**

BUCK MARK SERIES

Action: Semiautomatic
Grips: Composite, black
Barrel: 5.5–7.25 in.
Sights: Adjustable

AMERICAN JOE 1911

Action: Semiautomatic
Grips: Aluminum
Barrel: 5 in.
Sights: Adjustable 2-dot rear
Weight: 40 oz.
Caliber: .45 ACP
Capacity: 8+1 rounds
Features: For this art gun crossing the
rubicon between firearms and art,
Cabot commissioned rock star

Weight: 34–39 oz.
Caliber: .22 LR
Capacity: 10+1 rounds
Features: Alloy, matte blued finish
receiver; tapered barrel; blowback
action; single-action trigger; URX
ambidextrous grip in contour models;
cocobolo, ambidextrous grip on
hunter model; lite gray model has
matte gray barrel finish and truglo/
marble fiber-optic front sight
Camper UFX: **$389.99**
Camper Stainless UFX
   Calif. Compliant: **$429.99**
Hunter: **$499.99**
URX 5.5: **$579.99**

HI-POWER STANDARD

Action: Semiautomatic
Grips: Select walnut, cut checkering
Barrel: 4.6 in.
Sights: Low profile fixed or adjustable
with ramped front post
Weight: 32 oz.
Caliber: 9mm
Capacity: 10+1 rounds
Features: Locked breech action;
single-action trigger; ambidextrous
thumb safety; extra magazine; steel,
polished blued finish barrel
MSRP **$1119.99**

Cabot Gun Company

designer Joe Faris to design art that
represents Detroit and Americana,
and the result is a limited edition run
of a new iconic 1911, the American
Joe; features top slide serrations; 420
stainless steel frame and slide; 20 LPI
front strap checkering; tristar trigger
MSRP **$7450.00**

Canik USA

CANIK USA (BY CENTURY ARMS) TP9SFX PISTOL

TP9SFX PISTOL

Action: SA
Grips: Plastic
Barrel: 5.2 in.
Sights: Industry-standard dovetail sight cuts & four red dot interface plates; removable red dot over
Weight: 29.92 oz.
Caliber: 9mm Luger

Capacity: 20+1 rounds
Features: Improved single action trigger with 3.5–4 lb. pull; lightening cuts on slide to reduce muzzle rise; reversible ambidextrous cocking lever; adjustable length reversible magazine catch; Picatinny rail; Tungsten grey Cerakote over phosphate
MSRP **$549.99**

Charter Arms

BOOMER

Action: DAO revolver
Grips: Rubber
Barrel: 2 in. tapered
Sights: None
Weight: 20 oz.
Caliber: .44 Spl.
Capacity: 5 rounds
Features: Designed specifically for concealed carry; DAO hammer; full rubber combat grips; matte stainless finish; tapered barrel for reduced kick
MSRP **$443.00**

BULLDOG

Action: DA revolver
Grips: Rubber; Crimson Trace lasergrips
Barrel: 2.5 in., 3 in. or 5 in. in target model
Sights: Fixed, adjustable rear on Target model
Weight: 21 oz.
Caliber: .44 Spl.
Capacity: 5 rounds
Features: A larger concealed carry revolver, with DA/SA exposed hammer; available configurations include: Blue Standard; Tiger; Classic with 3-in. barrel, no underlug, exposed crane, and full wood grips; black Nitride; On Duty semi-concealed hammer in all stainless; Stainless Standard; Stainless DAO with concealed hammer; matte stainless with Crimson Trace laser grips; and Target with 4.2-in. barrel, ramp front sight and adjustable rear
MSRP . . . . **$409.00–$690.00**

CHIC LADY

Action: DA/SA, DAO revolver
Grips: Rubber

CHARTER ARMS BOOMER

Barrel: 2 in.
Sights: Fixed
Weight: 12 oz.
Caliber: .38 Spl.
Capacity: 5 rounds
Features: High-polish stainless-steel pink anodized aluminum frame; frame based on Undercover Lite models; DA/SA explosed hammer version also available with Crimson Trace laser grips
DA/SA: **$473.00**
DA/SA with Crimson Trace: . . **$672.00**
DAO: **$483.00**

OFF DUTY

Action: DA revolver
Grips: Crimson Trace lasergrip
Barrel: 2 in.
Sights: Serrated front, rear notch
Weight: 12 oz.
Caliber: .38 Spl. +P
Capacity: 5 rounds
Features: Lightweight, concealed hammer DAO concealed carry revolver of aircraft-grade aluminum and stainless steel; finishes include:

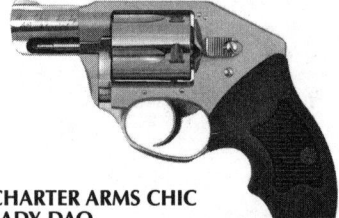

CHARTER ARMS BULLDOG

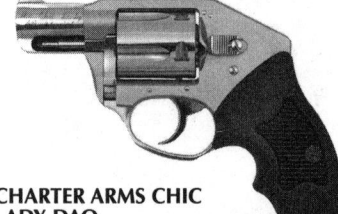

CHARTER ARMS CHIC LADY DAO

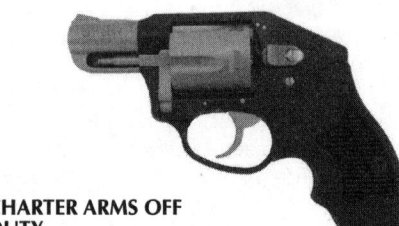

CHARTER ARMS OFF DUTY

black frame/high-polished stainless barrel and cylinder; black frame/matte stainless barrel and cylinder; matte aluminum frame/matte gray barrel and cylinder
MSRP . . . . **$404.00–$436.00**

ON DUTY

Action: DA revolver
Grips: Rubber; Crimson Trace lasergrips
Barrel: 2 in.

Sights: Fixed
Weight: 12 oz.
Caliber: .357 Mag., .38 Spl. +P
Capacity: 5 rounds
Features: Unique semi-concealed hammer design; constructed of heat-treated aluminum; allows single-action and double-action operations while minimizing the risk of snagging the hammer on clothing; standard or Crimson Trace grip
MSRP **$402.00**

PATHFINDER

Action: DA revolver
Grips: Rubber; Crimson Trace lasergrips
Barrel: 2 in., 4.2 in.
Sights: Fixed, adjustable rear on Target model
Weight: 12 oz.–24 oz.
Caliber: .22 LR, .22 Mag.
Capacity: 6 rounds
Features: Choice of stainless steel or aluminum frames, has exposed hammer for DA/SA operation; aluminum frame Lite models in .22 Mag only available in brushed silver frame with matte blue barrel and cylinder; pink frame with matte silver cylinder and barrel; lavender frame with matte silver barrel and cylinder; and matte black frame with matte stainless barrel and cylinder; steel frame models are in .22 LR and .22 WMR, with choice of barrel lengths, all in all stainless
Standard: . . . . **$365.00–$409.00**

PITBULL

Action: DA/SA
Grips: Rubber
Barrel: 2.5 in.
Sights: Fixed
Weight: 22 oz.
Caliber: .40 S&W, 9mm, .45 ACP
Capacity: 5 rounds
Features: Unique design provides a dual coil spring assembly located in the extractor which allows for the insertion and retention of rimless cartridges, so no moon clips are required
MSRP . . . . **$489.00–$522.00**

PITBULL 9MM
BLACKNITRIDE FINISH

Action: DA/SA revolver
Grips: Rubber
Barrel: 2.2 in.

Sights: Fixed
Weight: 22 oz.
Caliber: 9mm
Capacity: 5 rounds
Features: Rimless cartridge extractor assembly system; dual coil spring assembly located in the extractor; nitride adds hardness to the finish and reduces friction and wear; scratch-resistant surface; extended life in the rifling and chambers
MSRP **$522.00**

PITBULL .40 S&W
BLACKNITRIDE FINISH

Action: DA/SA revolver
Grips: Rubber
Barrel: 2.3 in.
Sights: Fixed
Weight: 20 oz.
Caliber: .40 caliber
Capacity: 5 rounds
Features: Dual coil spring assembly located in the extractor; nitride adds hardness to the finish and reduces friction and wear; scratch-resistant surface; extended life in the rifling and chambers
MSRP **$509.00**

PITBULL .45 ACP
BLACKNITRIDE FINISH

Action: DA/SA revolver
Grips: Rubber
Barrel: 2.5 in.
Sights: Fixed
Weight: 22 oz.
Caliber: .45 ACP
Capacity: 5 rounds
Features: Rimless cartridge extractor assembly system; dual coil spring assembly located in the extractor; nitride adds hardness to the finish and reduces friction and wear; scratch-resistant surface; extended life in the rifling and chambers
MSRP **$509.00**

CHARTER ARMS ON
DUTY

CHARTER ARMS
PATHFINDER

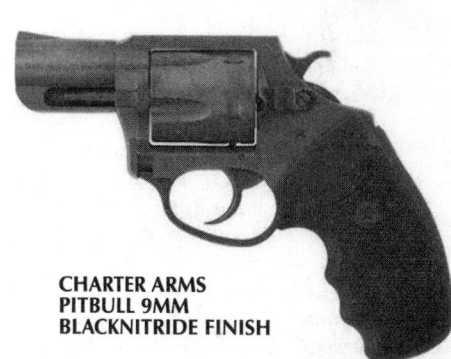

CHARTER ARMS
PITBULL

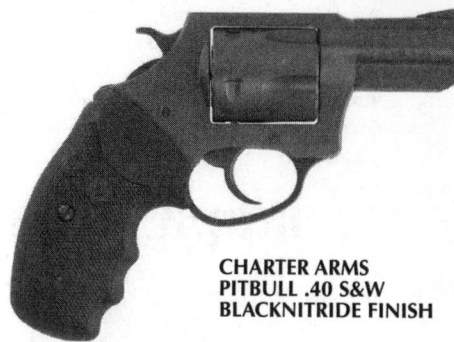

CHARTER ARMS
PITBULL 9MM
BLACKNITRIDE FINISH

CHARTER ARMS
PITBULL .40 S&W
BLACKNITRIDE FINISH

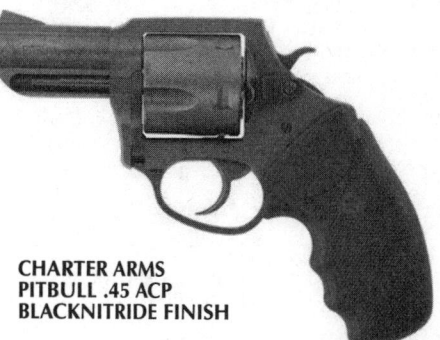

CHARTER ARMS
PITBULL .45 ACP
BLACKNITRIDE FINISH

Charter Arms

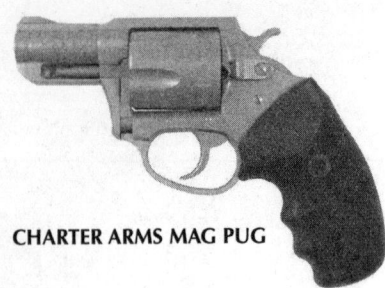

CHARTER ARMS MAG PUG

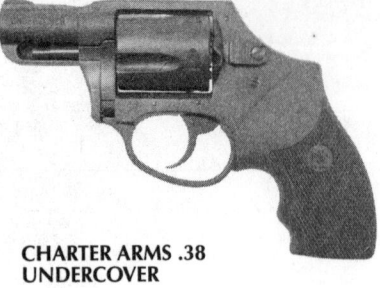

CHARTER ARMS .38 UNDERCOVER

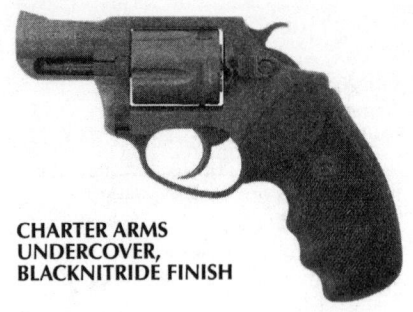

CHARTER ARMS UNDERCOVER, BLACKNITRIDE FINISH

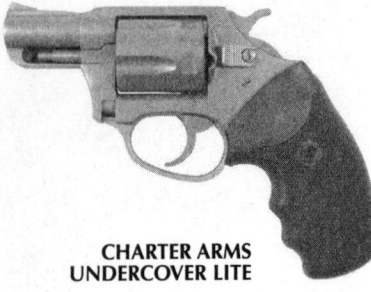

CHARTER ARMS UNDERCOVER LITE

MAG PUG

Action: DA revolver
Grips: Rubber; Crimson Trace lasergrips
Barrel: 2.2 in., 4.2 in.
Sights: Fixed, adjustable rear on Target model
Weight: 23 oz.
Caliber: .357 Mag.
Capacity: 5 rounds
Features: Traditional spurred hammer and full-size grips; optional Crimson Trace grip; stainless steel frame; blued and stainless finish
Standard:. **$394.00**
Crimson: **$609.00**

Green/black stripe:. **$456.00**
Stainless 4.2-in. barrel:. **$470.00**
SS DAO:. **$395.00**

UNDERCOVER

Action: DA revolver
Grips: Checkered compact rubber or Crimson Trace lasergrips
Barrel: 2 in.
Sights: Fixed
Weight: 16 oz.
Caliber: .38 Spl. +P
Capacity: 5 rounds
Features: Stainless steel frame; blued, stainless, tiger & black, DAO available; compact and lightweight, this revolver is ideal for concealed carry situations; 3-point cylinder lock-up
MSRP. . . . . **$346.00–$404.00**

UNDERCOVER, BLACKNITRIDE FINISH

Action: DA/SA revolver
Grips: Rubber
Barrel: 2 in.
Sights: Fixed
Weight: 16 oz.
Caliber: .38 Spl.

Capacity: 5 rounds
Features: Compact and lightweight; ideal for concealed carry due to 2 in. barrel and superior safety features; nitride adds hardness to the finish and reduces friction and wear; scratch-resistant surface; extended life in the rifling and chambers
MSRP. **$379.00**

UNDERCOVER LITE

Action: DA revolver
Grips: Rubber, compact
Barrel: 2 in.
Sights: Fixed
Weight: 12 oz.
Caliber: .38 Spl. +P
Capacity: 5 rounds
Features: Frame is constructed from aircraft-grade aluminum and steel; traditional spurred hammer; optional DAO (double action trigger); many finishes and special editions available
Pink Lady: **$414.00**
Alum. Standard: **$397.00**
Red or Black & SS:. **$414.00**

Chiappa Firearms

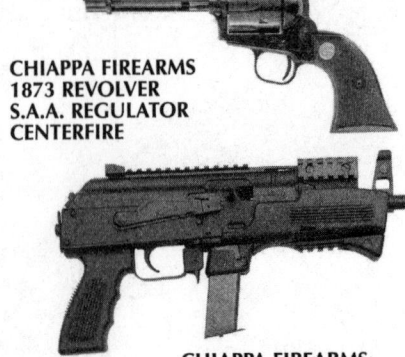

CHIAPPA FIREARMS 1873 REVOLVER S.A.A. REGULATOR CENTERFIRE

CHIAPPA FIREARMS PAK-9 PISTOL

1873 REVOLVER S.A.A. REGULATOR CENTERFIRE

Action: SA revolver
Grips: Black polymer
Barrel: 4.75 in.
Sights: Fixed front
Weight: 32 oz.
Caliber: .38 Spl.
Capacity: 6 rounds
Features: Centerfire cartridge; perfect for competition or plinking
MSRP. **$359.00**

PAK-9 PISTOL

Action: Semiautomatic
Grips: Synthetic
Barrel: 6.3 in.
Sights: Adjustable
Weight: 6 lb.
Caliber: 9mm
Capacity: 10 rounds
Features: Uses more readily available and easier to shoot ammunition; made from steel with exceptional fit and finish; interchangeable magazine adapter
MSRP. **$569**

Chiappa Firearms

MC 14

Action: Semiautomatic
Grips: Rubber
Barrel: 3.82 in.
Sights: Fixed
Weight: 24 oz.
Caliber: .380 ACP
Capacity: 13 rounds
Features: Short recoil; single or double action
MSRP................$519.00

CHIAPPA FIREARMS MC 14

CHIAPPA FIREARMS
RHINO 200DS REVOLVER

RHINO 200DS REVOLVER

Action: Revolver
Grips: Wood
Barrel: 6 in.
Sights: Front blade; adjustable rear
Weight: 37 oz.
Caliber: .357, .40 S&W, .357 Mag/9mm combo
Capacity: 6 rounds
Features: Rhino barrel is aligned with the bottom most chamber, which lowers the center of gravity and yields a centerline of the bore more in line with the shooter's arm allowing for the most natural "point ability" while engaging a target; reduces both recoil and muzzle flip which insures subsequent shots are on target faster; frame available in chrome, black, or gold finish
MSRP.........$849.00–$1079.00

CHIAPPA FIREARMS
SAA 17-10

SAA 17-10

Action: SA revolver
Grips: Plastic
Barrel: 7.5 in.
Sights: Adjustable
Weight: 34 oz.

Caliber: .17 HMR
Capacity: 10 rounds
Features: Black frame
MSRP................$269.00

Cimarron Firearms Co.

CIMARRON 1872 OPEN TOP NAVY

CIMARRON 1911

1872 OPEN TOP NAVY

Action: SA revolver
Grips: Walnut
Barrel: 5.5 in., 7.5 in.
Sights: Fixed, open
Weight: 40 oz.
Caliber: .44 Spl.; .44 Colt, .44 Russian
Capacity: 6 rounds
Features: Forged, color case-hardened frame; Army or Navy grip; charcoal

blued, standard blued, or original barrel finish
MSRP..........$518.70–$547.30

1911

Action: Semiautomatic
Grips: Walnut
Barrel: 5 in.
Sights: Open, fixed
Weight: 39.52 oz.
Caliber: .45 ACP

Capacity: 8+1 rounds
Features: Next generation of firearm widely used in the First World War. Correct historical markings; diamond checkered walnt grips; nickel, polished high luster blued, and standard parkerized finish; optional World War I-style lanyard magazine
MSRP..........$540.80–$676.93

Cimarron Firearms Co.

1911 WILD BUNCH COMBO

Action: Semiautomatic
Grips: Diamond checkered walnut
Barrel: 5 in.
Sights: Fixed
Weight: 39.52 oz.
Caliber: .45 ACP
Capacity: 8+1 rounds
Features: Correct historical markings; the original 1911 frame with a Type 1 smooth mainspring housing; combo includes the 1911 in polished blue finish and the Tanker shoulder holster, a reproduction of the rig used by William Holden in the movie The Wild Bunch
MSRP $842.23

BISLEY MODEL

Action: SA revolver
Grips: Walnut
Barrel: 4.75 in., 5.5 in., 7.5 in.
Sights: Fixed, open
Weight: 42–45 oz.
Caliber: .45 LC, .44 Spl., .44 WCF, .357 Mag.
Capacity: 6 rounds
Features: Reproduction of the original Colt Bisley; forged, color case-hardened frame; blued, charcoal blued, or nickel finish
MSRP $635.70

ELIMINATOR 8

Action: SA
Grips: Wood
Barrel: 4.75 in.
Sights: Fixed
Weight: N/A
Caliber: .357 Mag., .45 LC
Capacity: N/A
Features: Octagonal barrel; short stroke; checkered walnut Army grip; Cimarron low wide hammer; US action job; case hardened pre-war frame; standard blue finish;
MSRP $760.50

ELIMINATOR C

Action: SA
Grips: Wood
Barrel: 4.75 in.
Sights: Fixed
Weight: N/A
Caliber: .357 Mag., .45 LC
Capacity: N/A
Features: Short stroke; checkered walnut grip; Cimarron Cowboy Comp US action job; standard hammer;

frame available in stainless steel pre-war and color case hardened pre-war
MSRP . . . . $715.00–$973.70

FRONTIER

Action: SA
Grips: Ivory
Barrel: 4.75 in., 7.5 in.
Sights: Fixed
Weight: 4 lb. 8 oz.
Caliber: .45 Colt
Capacity: N/A
Features: Old silver frame; standard blue finish; laser engraved; nickel frame and finish available
MSRP . . . . $648.70–$713.70

HOLY SMOKER

Action: SA revolver
Grips: Walnut
Barrel: 4.75 in.
Sights: Open, fixed
Weight: 36 oz.
Caliber: .45 Colt
Capacity: 6 rounds
Features: Revolver made famous in *3:10 to Yuma* film; standard blued finish; case-hardened pre-war frame; gold-plated sterling silver cross inlayed on both sides of one-piece walnut grip
MSRP $773.50

LIGHTNING

Action: SA revolver
Grips: Walnut
Barrel: 3.5 in., 4.75 in., 5.5 in., 6.5 in.
Sights: Fixed, open
Weight: 28.5–30.75 oz.
Caliber: .38 Spl., .22 LR, .41 Colt, .32-20 Win./.32 H&R Dual Cylinder
Capacity: 6 rounds
Features: Forged, pre-war color case-hardened frame; charcoal blued, standard blued, or original barrel finish; walnut stock smooth or checkered
MSRP . . . . $516.10–$648.70

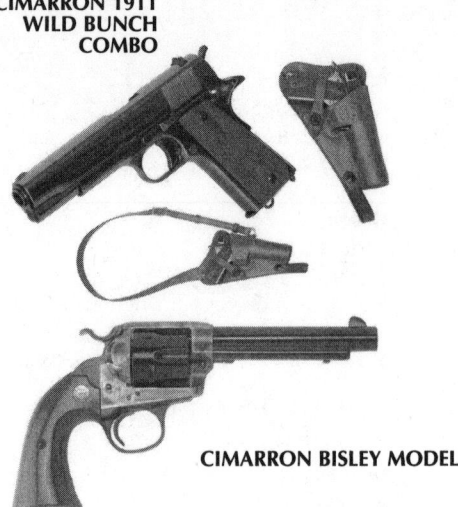

CIMARRON 1911 WILD BUNCH COMBO

CIMARRON BISLEY MODEL

CIMARRON ELIMINATOR 8

CIMARRON ELIMINATOR C

CIMARRON FRONTIER

CIMARRON HOLY SMOKER

CIMARRON LIGHTNING

Cimarron Firearms Co.

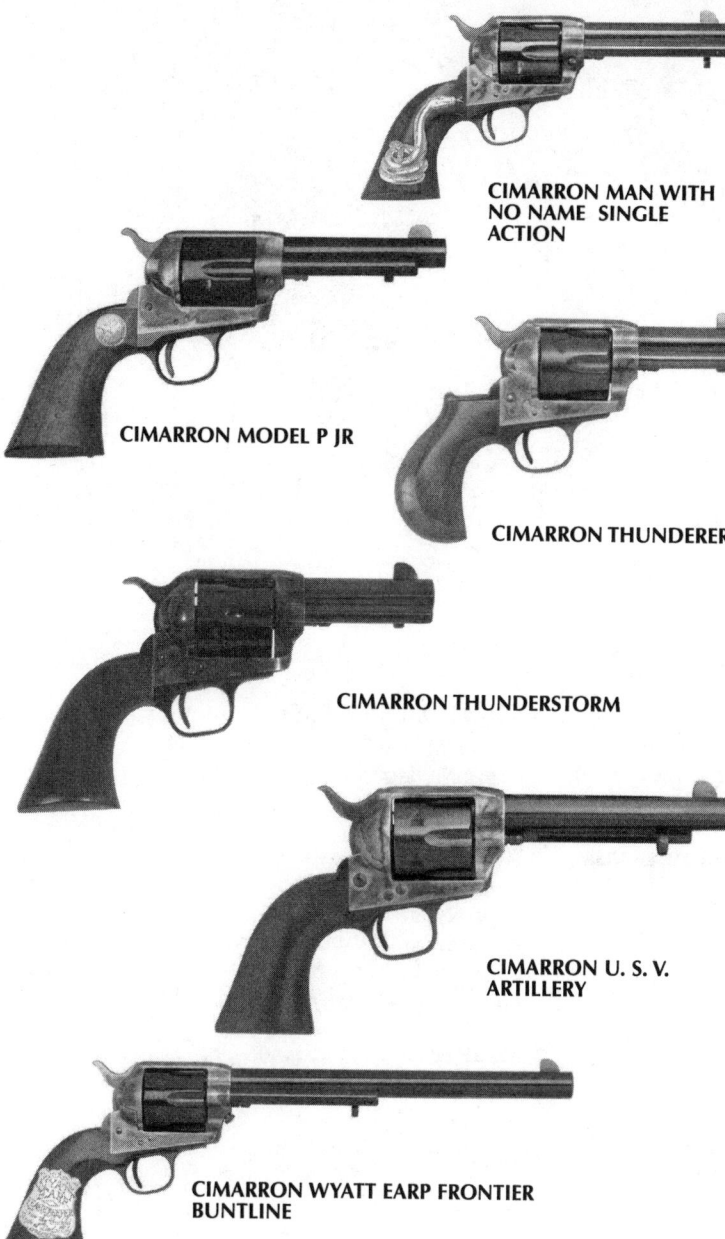

CIMARRON MAN WITH NO NAME SINGLE ACTION

CIMARRON MODEL P JR

CIMARRON THUNDERER

CIMARRON THUNDERSTORM

CIMARRON U. S. V. ARTILLERY

CIMARRON WYATT EARP FRONTIER BUNTLINE

THUNDERER

Action: SA revolver
Grips: Walnut, ivory, mother of pearl or black hard rubber
Barrel: 3.5 in. w/ ejector, 4.75 in., 5.5 in., 7.5 in.
Sights: Fixed, open
Weight: 38–43.60 oz.
Caliber: .45 LC, .44 Spl., .44 WCF, .357 Mag., .45 LC/.45 ACP Dual Cylinder
Capacity: 6 rounds
Features: Designed in 1990 by Cimarron founder & president "Texas Jack" Harvey; forged, color case-hardened frame; blued, charcoal blued or stainless finish
MSRP . . . . $574.60–$747.50

THUNDERSTORM

Action: SA revolver
Grips: Walnut
Barrel: 3.5 in., 4.75 in.
Sights: Front, rear
Weight: 35.7 oz.–39.68 oz.
Caliber: .45 Colt, .357 Mag./.38 Spl.
Capacity: 6 rounds
Features: Checkered grips; stainless steel or standard blued finishes; wide front sights and deep rear notch; smooth action and hand-knurled hammer; available in Model P or Thunderer versions
MSRP . . . . $778.70–$947.70

U. S. V. ARTILLERY

Action: SA revolver
Grips: Walnut
Barrel: 5.5 in.
Sights: Fixed, open
Weight: 40 oz.
Caliber: .45 LC
Capacity: 6 rounds
Features: Old model case-hardened with US Artillery markings; stock is a solid piece of walnut with RAC Cartouche; blued, charcoal blued, or original finish
MSRP . . . . $591.50-$617.50

MAN WITH NO NAME SINGLE ACTION

Action: SA revolver
Grips: Walnut
Barrel: 4.75 in., 5.5 in.
Sights: Open, fixed
Weight: 42.56 oz.–44.16 oz.
Caliber: .45 Colt
Capacity: 6 rounds
Features: Model P in .45 Colt; sterling silver snake on both sides of walnut grip
MSRP $773.50

MODEL P JR.

Action: SA revolver
Grips: Walnut
Barrel: 3.5 in., 4.75 in., 5.5 in.
Sights: Fixed, open
Weight: 35.2 oz.
Caliber: .38 Spl., .22 LR, .32-20 Win./.32 H&R Dual Cylinder
Capacity: 6 rounds
Features: Fashioned after the 1873 Colt SAA but on a smaller scale; color case-hardened frame
MSRP . . . . $479.70–$633.10

WYATT EARP FRONTIER BUNTLINE

Action: SA revolver
Grips: Walnut
Barrel: 10 in.
Sights: Open, fixed
Weight: 43.04 oz.
Caliber: .45 LC
Capacity: 6 rounds
Features: Revolver made famous in the film *Tombstone*; one-piece walnut grips with silver inlaid medallion; choice of blue or case hardened finishes
MSRP . . . . $856.70–$882.70

Citadel by Legacy Sports

M-1911

Action: Semiautomatic
Grips: Full size or compact, wood or Hogue synthetic grips
Barrel: 3.5 in., 5 in.
Sights: Fixed
Weight: 33.6–37.6 oz.
Caliber: 9mm, .45 ACP
Capacity: 7 or 8 rounds
Features: Available in compact and full sized models; matte black, brush nickel, polished nickel, or Cerakote flat dark earth finish; optional Hogue wrap around grip in black, green, or sand; comes with lockable, hard plastic case
MSRP . . . . $609.00–$785.00

CITADEL M-1911 PISTOLS

CMMG, Inc.

CMMG MK47 AKS8 PISTOL

MK47 AKS8 PISTOL

Action: Semiautomatic
Grips: MOE pistol grip
Barrel: 8 in.
Sights: None
Weight: 6 lb. 3 oz.
Caliber: 7.62x39
Capacity: 30 rounds
Features: KRINK muzzle device; pinned on gas block; mid-sized receiver based on CMMG's Mk3 platform; improved 9 in. handguard; lower receiver readily accepts all standard AK magazines
MSRP $1549.95

Cobra

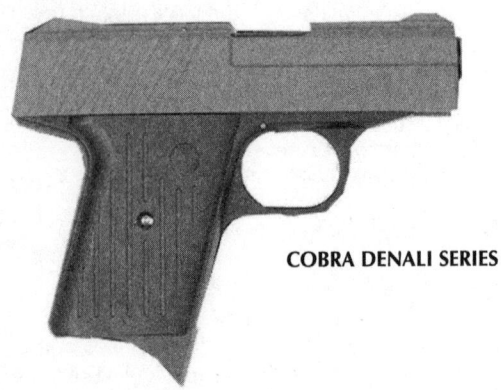

COBRA DENALI SERIES

DENALI SERIES

Action: SA semiautomatic
Grips: Synthetic
Barrel: 2.8 in.
Sights: Fixed
Weight: 17 oz.
Caliber: .380 ACP
Capacity: 5 rounds
Features: Compact, lightweight, and easily concealed; features a durable polymer frame with a pushbutton magazine release; available in black, tactical tan, satin, and OD green Cerakote finishes
MSRP $149.99

Colt's Manufacturing Company

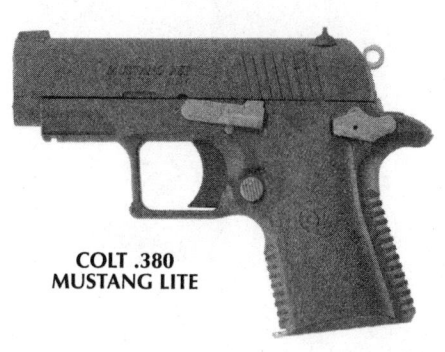

COLT .380 MUSTANG LITE

COLT .380 MUSTANG POCKETLITE

COLT DEFENDER

COLT 1991 SERIES

COLT COMPETITION PISTOL

COLT GOLD CUP TROPHY

.380 MUSTANG LITE

Action: SA semiautomatic
Grips: Polymer
Barrel: 2.75 in.
Sights: Fixed
Weight: 11.8 oz.
Caliber: .380 ACP
Capacity: 6 rounds
Features: Polymer grip frame with tactical grip profile; texturing on front and back straps; front and rear dovetail sights; aluminum alloy frame also available
MSRP. **$499.00**

.380 MUSTANG POCKETLITE

Action: SA semiautomatic
Grips: Composite
Barrel: 2.75 in.
Sights: High-profile
Weight: 12.5 oz.
Caliber: .380 ACP
Capacity: 6+1 rounds
Features: Aluminum alloy frame with a CNC-machined stainless steel slide and barrel; thumb safety and firing-pin-block safety; solid aluminum trigger; lowered ejection port; electroless nickeled aluminum receiver
MSRP. **$599.00**

1991 SERIES

Action: Semiautomatic
Grips: Rosewood or composite
Barrel: 5 in.
Sights: Fixed
Weight: 39 oz.
Caliber: .38 Super, 9mm, .45 ACP
Capacity: 7+1 rounds
Features: Beveled magazine well; single- and double-action; carbon steel, aluminum alloy, or stainless steel frame; standard or beavertail grip safety; blued, brushed stainless steel frame finish
MSRP. . . . . **$799.00–$879.00**

COMPETITION PISTOL

Action: SA
Grips: G10 grips
Barrel: 5 in.
Sights: Fiber optic front, Novak adjustable rear
Weight: 36 oz.
Caliber: .38 Super, .45 ACP, 9mm
Capacity: 8 or 9 rounds
Features: Dual spring recoil system; undercut trigger guard; upswept beavertail grip safety; National Match barrel
.45 ACP, 9mm: **$899.00**
.38 Super **$999.00**

DEFENDER

Action: Semiautomatic
Grips: Rubber finger-grooved
Barrel: 5 in.
Sights: White dot carry front and rear

Weight: 30 oz.
Caliber: .45 ACP, 9mm
Capacity: 7+1 rounds, 8+1 rounds
Features: Beveled magazine well; black skeletonized aluminum trigger; Series 80 firing system; beavertail grip and standard thumb safety; stainless steel slide, Teflon coated receiver; aluminum alloy frame
MSRP. . . . . **$899.00–$949.00**

GOLD CUP TROPHY

Action: Semiautomatic
Grips: Black composite
Barrel: 5 in.
Sights: Dovetail front, adjustable rear
Weight: 39 oz.
Caliber: 9mm, .45 ACP
Capacity: 8+1 rounds
Features: Beveled magazine well; beavertail grip safety; black wrap around grips; wide aluminum 3-Hole trigger adjustable for over travel; stainless steel frame finish and material; enhanced hammer
MSRP. **$1699.00**

Colt's Manufacturing Company

COLT LIGHTWEIGHT COMMANDER

COLT SERIES 70

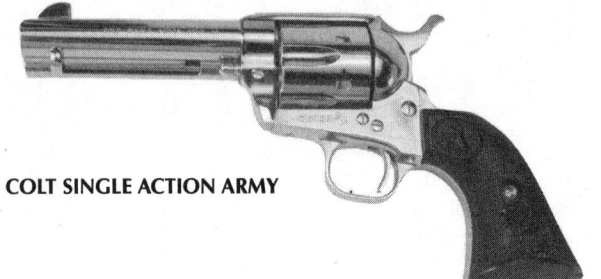

COLT SINGLE ACTION ARMY

LIGHTWEIGHT COMMANDER

Action: SA
Grips: G10 grips
Barrel: 4.25 in.
Sights: Novak sights
Weight: 29.4 oz.
Caliber: .45 ACP, 9mm
Capacity: 8 or 9 rounds
Features: Shorter profile and lower weight than a traditional full-size Government model; dual spring recoil system; undercut trigger guard; upswept beavertail grip safety
MSRP...................$999.00

NEW FRONTIER

Action: SA revolver
Grips: Walnut stock with gold medallions
Barrel: 4.75 in., 5.5 in., 7.5 in.
Sights: Ramp style front; adjustable rear
Weight: 46 oz.
Caliber: .44 Spl., .45 Colt
Capacity: 6 rounds
Features: Royal blued barrel and cylinder; flat top case colored frame
MSRP.................$1699.00

RAIL GUN

Action: Semiautomatic
Grips: Double diamond rosewood or blackened rosewood
Barrel: 5 in.
Sights: White dot, Novak rear
Weight: 39 oz.
Caliber: .45 ACP
Capacity: 8+1 rounds
Features: Stainless steel, blackened receiver and brushed slide, blackened receiver and slide frame finish options; stainless steel frame material; Colt

upswept beavertail with palm swell; enhanced hammer; Picatinny rail; National Match barrel; single-slide tactical thumb safety
MSRP......... $1199.00–$1699.00

SERIES 70

Action: Semiautomatic
Grips: Double diamond rosewood
Barrel: 5 in.
Sights: Fixed
Weight: 39 oz.
Caliber: .45 ACP
Capacity: 7+1 rounds
Features: Spur hammer; single-action; blued or brushed steel finish; carbon steel or stainless steel frame; short steel trigger; original series 70 firing system with titanium firing pin
MSRP.......... $899.00–$979.00

SINGLE ACTION ARMY

Action: SA revolver
Grips: Black composite eagle
Barrel: 4.75 in., 5.5 in., 7.5 in.
Sights: Fixed
Weight: 46 oz.
Caliber: .357 Mag., .45 Colt
Capacity: 6 rounds
Features: Case-colored frame; transfer bar; second generation style cylinder bushing; blued or nickel finish
MSRP......... $1599.00–$1799.00

COLT NEW FRONTIER

COLT RAIL GUN

Coonan, Inc.

CLASSIC
Action: Semiautomatic
Grips: Smooth black walnut
Barrel: 5 in.
Sights: Dovetail front and rear
Weight: 42 oz.
Caliber: .357 Mag.
Capacity: 7+1 rounds
Features: Coonan Classic with compensator barrel; recoil operated; extended slide catch and thumb lock; custom carry case
MSRP . . . . **$1540.00–$2735.00**

COONAN CLASSIC

CZ-USA (Ceska Zbrojovka)

75 B
Action: Semiautomatic
Grips: Plastic
Barrel: 4.6 in.
Sights: Fixed, 3-dot system
Weight: 35.2 oz.
Caliber: .40 S&W, 9mm
Capacity: .40 S&W: 10 rounds, 9mm: 16 rounds
Features: Steel frame; high capacity double column magazines; hammer forged barrels; ergonomic grip and controls; double-action or single-action; firing pin block safety; black polycoat finish
.40 S&W: **$625.00**
9mm: **$612.00**

75 B Ω CONVERTIBLE
Action: DA/SA
Grips: Plastic
Barrel: 4.6 in.
Sights: Fixed
Weight: 35.2 oz.
Caliber: 9mm Luger
Capacity: 10 or 16 rounds
Features: Swappable safety/decocker; interlocking trigger design for easy disassembly and reassembly without tools; low-capacity 10-round magazine option available
MSRP **$570.00**

75 B Ω URBAN GREY SUPPRESSOR-READY
Action: DA/SA
Grips: Plastic
Barrel: 5.2 in.
Sights: High titrium three dot
Weight: 42.1 oz.
Caliber: 9mm Luger
Capacity: 10, 18 rounds

Features: Threaded barrels; high suppressor sights with tritium lamps; extended capacity magazine; swappable safety/decocker; interlocking trigger design for easy disassembly and reassembly without tools; low-capacity 10-round magazine option available
MSRP **$636.00**

75 COMPACT
Action: Semiautomatic
Grips: Plastic
Barrel: 3.8 in.
Sights: Fixed, 3-dot system
Weight: 32.48 oz.
Caliber: 9mm Luger
Capacity: 14 rounds
Features: Black polycoat, dual tone, satin nickel frame finishes; manual safety; steel frame; high capacity double column magazines; hammer forged barrels; low-capacity 10-round magazine version now available
Black polycoat: . . . **$544.00–$581.00**

75 P-01 Ω CONVERTIBLE
Action: DA/SA
Grips: Rubber
Barrel: 3.8 in.
Sights: Fixed
Weight: 28 oz.
Caliber: 9mm Luger
Capacity: 10, 14 rounds
Features: Swappable safety/decocker; interlocking trigger design for easy disassembly and reassembly without tools; compact size and reduced weight ideal for discrete carry; low-capacity 10-round magazine option available
MSRP **$627.00**

CZ-USA 75 B

CZ–USA 75 B Ω CONVERTIBLE

CZ–USA 75 B Ω URBAN GREY SUPPRESSOR-READY

CZ-USA 75 COMPACT

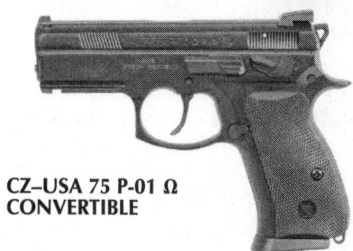
CZ–USA 75 P-01 Ω CONVERTIBLE

CZ-USA (Ceska Zbrojovka)

CZ–USA 75 P-01 Ω URBAN GREY SUPPRESSOR-READY

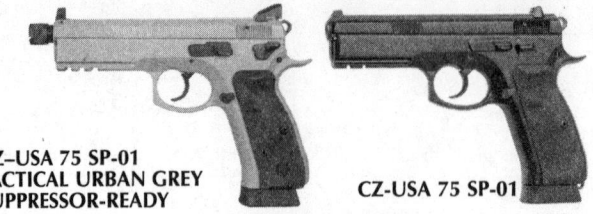

CZ–USA 75 SP-01 TACTICAL URBAN GREY SUPPRESSOR-READY

CZ-USA 75 SP-01

CZ–USA 75 SP-01 SHADOW TARGET II

CZ–USA 75 TACTICAL SPORT ORANGE

CZ-USA 75 TS CZECHMATE

CZ–USA 805 BREN S1 PISTOL

75 P-01 Ω URBAN GREY SUPPRESSOR-READY

Action: DA/SA
Grips: Rubber
Barrel: 4.5 in.
Sights: High titrium three dot
Weight: 30.1 oz.
Caliber: 9mm Luger
Capacity: 10, 16 rounds
Features: Swappable safety/decocker; threaded barrels; high suppressor sights with tritium lamps; extended capacity magazine; interlocking trigger design for easy disassembly and reassembly without tools; compact size and reduced weight ideal for discrete carry; low-capacity 10-round magazine option available
MSRP $653.00

75 SP-01 TACTICAL URBAN GREY SUPPRESSOR-READY

Action: DA/SA
Grips: Rubber
Barrel: 5.2 in.
Sights: High titrium three dot
Weight: 42.1 oz.
Caliber: 9mm Luger
Capacity: 10, 18 rounds
Features: Threaded barrels; high suppressor sights with tritium lamps; extended capacity magazine; ambidextrous decocker; 1913 accessory rail on the dust cover; rubber grip panels; corrosion-resistant black polycoat finish; extended beavertail
MSRP $723.00

75 SP-01

Action: Semiautomatic
Grips: Rubber
Barrel: 4.6 in.

Sights: 3-Dot tritium night
Weight: 38.4 oz.
Caliber: 9mm Luger
Capacity: 18 rounds
Features: Based upon the Shadow Target; decocking lever; safety stop on hammer; firing pin safety; steel frame; low-capacity 10-round magazine version now available
MSRP $680.00

75 SP-01 SHADOW TARGET II

Action: DA/SA
Grips: Thin aluminum checkered
Barrel: 4.61 in.
Sights: Adjustable target rear, fiber optic front
Weight: 38.4 oz.
Caliber: 9mm Luger
Capacity: 18 rounds
Features: Competition-ready Pre-B style SP-01 Shadow, featuring a CZ Custom trigger job with the new short reset single-action trigger, fully-adjustable rear sight, fiber optic front sight, stainless steel guide rod, lighter springs for competition (11 lb recoil and 13 lb main springs), extended magazine release, drop-free magazines and checkered aluminum grips; created by champion shooter Angus Hobdell's CZ Custom Shop to have trigger pulls of 3.0-4.0 lbs in SA and 7.5-8.5 lbs in DA
MSRP $1638.00

TACTICAL SPORT ORANGE

Action: SA
Grips: Thin aluminum
Barrel: 5.4 in.
Sights: Adjustable
Weight: 48 oz.
Caliber: 9mm Luger; .40 S&W
Capacity: 10, 16, 20 rounds
Features: Ambidextrous manual safety; slimmer trigger guard; improved grip geometry; thumb stop; long slide; full-length dust cover; light pull and short reset; low-capacity 10-round magazine option available
MSRP $1784.00

75 TS CZECHMATE

Action: Semiautomatic
Grips: Aluminum
Barrel: 5.4 in.
Sights: Fixed, C-more red dot
Weight: 48 oz.
Caliber: 9mm
Capacity: 20 or 26 rounds
Features: Built upon a modified version of the CZ 75 TS frame; interchangeable parts allow the user to quickly configure the gun for both roles; features a single-action trigger mechanism; red-dot sight; includes spare barrel; includes three 20-round magazines and one 26-round magazine; all-steel pistol is finished in black matte
MSRP $3317.00

97 B

Action: Semiautomatic
Grips: Plastic
Barrel: 4.8 in.
Sights: Fixed
Weight: 40 oz.
Caliber: .45 ACP
Capacity: 10 rounds
Features: Manual safety; cold hammer-forged barrel; single- or double-action
MSRP $707.00

805 BREN S1 PISTOL

Action: Semiautomatic
Grips: Polymer
Barrel: 11 in.
Sights: Flip-up, 2 rear adjustable
Weight: 6 lb. 11 oz.

CZ-USA (Ceska Zbrojovka)

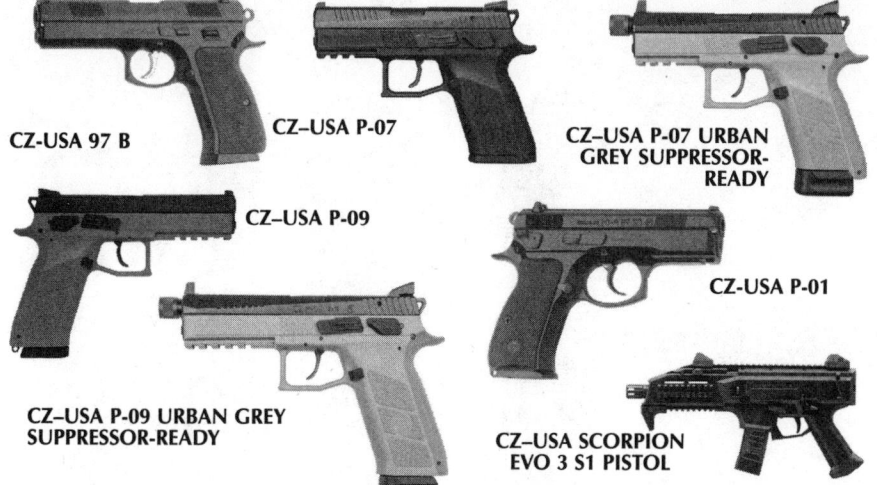

CZ-USA 97 B

CZ–USA P-07

CZ–USA P-07 URBAN GREY SUPPRESSOR-READY

CZ-USA 2075 RAMI

CZ–USA P-09

CZ–USA P-09 URBAN GREY SUPPRESSOR-READY

CZ-USA P-01

CZ–USA SCORPION EVO 3 S1 PISTOL

Caliber: .223/5.56, .300 BLK
Capacity: 10 rounds, 30 rounds
Features: The first civilian-legal form of CZ's 805 Bren; STANAG magazine used in the AR-15/M16; one-piece aluminum upper receiver with a monolithic Picatinny rail; multipurpose rear mounting point, fit from the factory with a single-point sling attachment; accessory arm brace adapter coupled with the effective factory-equipped two-port brake; available in black or Flat Dark Earth
MSRP . . . . $1799.00–$1899.00

2075 RAMI

Action: Semiautomatic
Grips: Rubber
Barrel: 3 in.
Sights: Fixed
Weight: 25.6 oz.
Caliber: 9mm Luger
Capacity: .40 S&W: 7 or 9 rounds, 9mm: 14 rounds
Features: Operates in selective DA and SA mode depending on shooter's preferences; firing pin block; manual safety; double-stack magazine; black polycoat alloy frame; cold hammer forged; available with low-capacity 10-round magazines
MSRP $614.00

P-01

Action: Semiautomatic
Grips: Rubber
Barrel: 3.8 in.
Sights: Fixed
Weight: 28.8 oz.
Caliber: 9mm Luger
Capacity: 10, 14 rounds
Features: Decocking lever; safety stop on hammer; firing pin safety; black

polycoat frame finish; black or pink grips; single- or double-action
MSRP $627.00

P-07

Action: DA/SA semiautomatic
Grips: Synthetic
Barrel: 3.8 in.
Sights: Fixed
Weight: 27 oz.
Caliber: 9mm Luger, .40 S&W
Capacity: 12 or 15 rounds
Features: Ambidextrous safety or decocker; firing pin block; 9mm available with low-capacity 10-round magazines
MSRP . . . . $510.00–$524.00

P-07 URBAN GREY SUPPRESSOR-READY

Action: DA/SA
Grips: Stippled
Barrel: 4.5 in.
Sights: High titrium three dot
Weight: 28 oz.
Caliber: 9mm Luger
Capacity: 10, 17 rounds
Features: Swappable safety/decocker; threaded barrels; high suppressor sights with tritium lamps; extended capacity magazine; interlocking trigger design for easy disassembly and reassembly without tools; nitrated slide finish; increased corrosion resistance; small, medium, and large backstraps; integrated 1913 Picatinny rail on the dust cover; snag-free hammer; forward cocking serrations; low-capacity 10-round magazine option available
MSRP $537.00

P-09

Action: DA/SA semiautomatic
Grips: Synthetic

Barrel: 4.53 in. or 5.23 in. (suppressor model)
Sights: Fixed
Weight: 30 oz.
Caliber: 9mm Luger, .40 S&W
Capacity: 15 (.40 S&W) or 19 rounds
Features: Ambidextrous safety or decocker; firing pin block
MSRP . . . . $530.00–$544.00

P-09 URBAN GREY SUPPRESSOR-READY

Action: DA/SA
Grips: Stippled
Barrel: 5.2 in.
Sights: High titrium three dot
Weight: 30.4 oz.
Caliber: 9mm Luger
Capacity: 21+1 rounds
Features: Threaded barrels; high suppressor sights with tritium lamps; extended capacity magazine; Omega trigger system; swappable safety/decocker; 1913 Picatinny rail
MSRP $629.00

SCORPION EVO 3 S1 PISTOL

Action: SA
Grips: Polymer
Barrel: 7.72 in.
Sights: Low-profile fully adjustable aperture and post, 4 rear aperture sizes
Weight: 5 lb.
Caliber: 9mm Luger
Capacity: 10+1 rounds, 20+1 rounds
Features: Scorpion sub-gun, imported as a pistol; blowback-operated; sights ride on an 11-in. Picatinny rail perfect for mounting optics; ambidextrous controls; non-reciprocating charging handle is swappable and reach to the trigger is adjustable; arm brace adapter quickly and easily adds an AR-style pistol buffer tube to the rear of the action, enabling the use of an arm brace for added stability; barrel threaded at 18x1 to accept the factory flash hider and also at ½x28 underneath flash hider for easy addition of suppressor or after market muzzle device
MSRP $949.00

Dan Wesson Firearms

715

Action: DA semiautomatic
Grips: Rubber
Barrel: 6 in.
Sights: Fixed
Weight: 46 oz.
Caliber: .357 Mag.
Capacity: 6 rounds
Features: Adjustable target rear sight; six inch heavy barrel with ventilated rib; stainless steel construction
MSRP $1558.00

715 PISTOL PACK

Action: DA/SA
Grips: Rubber
Barrel: 4 in., 6 in., 8 in.
Sights: Adjustable
Weight: N/A
Caliber: .357 Mag., .38 Spl.
Capacity: 6 rounds
Features: Swappable barrel assemblies and grips; tensioned barrel; forward crane latch ensures proper cylinder/barrel alignment; clockwise-rotating cylinder reduces stress on the crane
MSRP $1999.00

BRUIN

Action: SA
Grips: Synthetic
Barrel: 6.3 in.
Sights: Adjustable titrium with titrium/ fiber optic front
Weight: 42.9 oz.
Caliber: 10mm Auto; .45 ACP
Capacity: 8 or 9 rounds
Features: Long slide for a long sight radius; 6.3 in. barrel within allows full-power 10mm loads as much time as possible to use their powder charge; tritium/fiber optic combo front sight to make sure the front glows day or night
MSRP . . . . $2064.00–$2194.00

DISCRETION

Action: SA
Grips: Synthetic
Barrel: 5.75 in.
Sights: High tactical ledge titrium
Weight: N/A
Caliber: .45 ACP; 9mm Luger
Capacity: 8 or 10 rounds
Features: Suppressor ready; match-grade stainless barrel; aggressively ported slide; serrated trigger; competition-inspired hammer
MSRP $2142.00

DAN WESSON 715

DAN WESSON BRUIN

DAN WESSON ECO

ECO

Action: SA semiautomatic
Grips: Composite
Barrel: 3.5 in.
Sights: Fixed tritium
Weight: 25 oz.
Caliber: 9mm, .45 ACP
Capacity: 7+1 rounds
Features: Single-stack Officer's size 1991; aluminum alloy frame; undercut trigger guards; 25 lpi checkering; mainspring housing is aluminum with 25 lpi checkering; Ed Brown high rise grip safety; forged steel slide; tritium night sights with tactical ledge rear sight; flush cut ramped bull barrel with target crown
9mm: $1623.00
.45 ACP: $1662.00

ELITE SERIES CHAOS

Action: SA semiautomatic
Grips: Synthetic
Barrel: 5 in.
Sights: Adjustable
Weight: 51 oz.

DAN WESSON 715 PISTOL PACK

DAN WESSON DISCRETION

DAN WESSON ELITE SERIES CHAOS

DAN WESSON GUARDIAN

Caliber: 9mm Luger
Capacity: 21 rounds
Features: Ambidextrous thumb safety; grip safety; double-stack magazine; Picatinny rail; fiber optic sights
MSRP $3829.00

GUARDIAN

Action: SA semiautomatic
Grips: Wood
Barrel: 4.25 in.
Sights: Fixed
Weight: 29 oz.
Caliber: 9mm Luger, .38 Super, .45 ACP
Capacity: 8 (.45 ACP) or 9 rounds
Features: Ambidextrous thumb safety; grip safety; fixed night sights
MSRP . . . . $1558.00–$1619.00

Dan Wesson Firearms

DAN WESSON RAZORBACK RZ-10

DAN WESSON SPECIALIST

DAN WESSON VALKYRIE COMMANDER

DAN WESSON VALOR

DAN WESSON VALOR COMMANDER

Caliber: .45 ACP; 9mm Luger
Capacity: 8 or 9 rounds
Features: Aluminum Commander-length frame; 25 LPI checkering; carry cuts on the slide and tactical tritium sights
MSRP **$2012.00**

RAZORBACK RZ-10

Action: SA semiautomatic
Grips: Diamond-checkered cocobolo
Barrel: 5 in.
Sights: Fixed
Weight: 38.4 oz.
Caliber: 10mm
Capacity: 9 rounds
Features: Razorback is back in 2012 in limited quantities; serrated Clark-style target rib; 1911 model; stainless steel frame; manual thumb safety, grip safety
MSRP **$1480.00**

SPECIALIST

Action: SA semiautomatic
Grips: G10 VZ Operator II grips
Barrel: 5 in.
Sights: Fixed tritium
Weight: 37 oz.
Caliber: .45 ACP, 9mm Luger
Capacity: 8+1 or 10 rounds

Features: Full size single-stack pistol; matte stainless steel or black Duty finishes; forged slide and frame; Clark-style serrated rib with tritium dual-colored night sights stacked in a straight eight-type pattern; tactical ledge rear sight with single rear amber dot and green front with white target ring; Picatinny rail; undercut trigger guard with 25 lpi front strap checkering; ambidextrous thumb safety; two magazines with bumper pads included
SS: **$1701.00**
Black: **$2012.00**

VALKYRIE COMMANDER

Action: SA
Grips: Slim line G10
Barrel: 4.25 in.
Sights: Titrium night sights with tactical rear
Weight: 28.8 oz.

VALOR

Action: SA semiautomatic
Grips: Slim line G10
Barrel: 5 in.
Sights: Tactical ledge titrium
Weight: 38.1 oz.
Caliber: .45 ACP, 9mm Luger, 10mm
Capacity: 8 or 10 rounds
Features: Matte black duty receiver finish; manual thumb safety; forged stainless steel frame
SS: **$1701.00**
Black: **$2012.00**

VALOR COMMANDER

Action: SA semiautomatic
Grips: Slim line G10
Barrel: 4.25 in.
Sights: Tactical ledge titrium
Weight: 35.2 oz.
Caliber: .45 ACP; 9mm Luger
Capacity: 8 or 9 rounds
Features: Manual thumb safety; hand-polished and hand-fitted; non-bobbed
MSRP . . . . **$1701.00–$2012.00**

Del-Ton

LIMA KEYMOD PISTOL

Action: Semiautomatic
Grips: Synthetic
Barrel: 7.5 in.
Sights: None
Weight: 4 lb. 13 oz.
Caliber: 5.56x45mm
Capacity: 8 rounds
Features: Pistol-length Sampson Evolution keymod free floating rail; Mil-spec; chrome-lined carrier interior
MSRP **$876.71**

DEL-TON LIMA KEYMOD PISTOL

Doublestar Corp.

CORP PHD 1911

Action: SA
Grips: Magpul MOE 1911 grip panels
Barrel: 5 in.
Sights: XS Express titrium front sight, XS Express rear sight
Weight: 33 oz.
Caliber: .45 ACP
Capacity: 8 rounds
Features: Aggressive rear cocking serrations for a sure grip in the harshest of environments; flat-topped and serrated slide to reduce glare; round butt and Wilson combat high-ride beavertail grip safety
MSRP $1364.06

DOUBLESTAR CORP PHD 1911

Doubletap Defense LLC

DOUBLETAP

Action: DAO semiautomatic
Grips: Synthetic
Barrel: 3 in.
Sights: Front blade
Weight: 12 oz.–14 oz.
Caliber: .45 ACP, 9mm
Capacity: 2+2 rounds
Features: Titanium frame with a MIL-STD finish that resists corrosion; integral grips house additional two spare rounds; ported barrel reduces muzzle flip and recoil; ambidextrous thumb latch to eject spent rounds; quick-change interchangable barrels; comes with one barrel and you can purchase extra conversion kits; firearm and conversion kit available ported and non-ported
Aluminum: . . . .
    $499.00–$569.00
Conversion kits: . . . .
    $199.00–$269.00

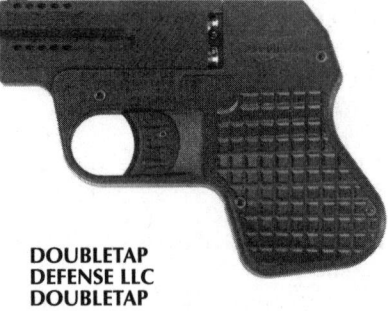

DOUBLETAP DEFENSE LLC DOUBLETAP

Eagle Imports

EAGLE IMPORTS MAC 1911 BOBCUT

EAGLE IMPORTS MAC 1911 BULLSEYE

MAC 1911 BOBCUT

Action: SA semiautomatic
Grips: Hardwood
Barrel: 4.25 in.
Sights: Adjustable rear, dovetail front
Weight: 34.58 oz.
Caliber: .45 ACP
Capacity: 8+1 rounds
Features: 4140 steel frame and hammer forged slide; fully adjustable Novak-type rear sight; dovetail front sight with fiber optic; flared and lowered ejection port; enhanced beavertail grip safety; skeletal hammer; combat trigger; stippled front strap serration; throated forged steel barrel
Deep Blue: **$902.00**
Hard Chrome: **$978.00**

MAC 1911 BULLSEYE

Action: SA semiautomatic
Grips: Hardwood
Barrel: 6 in.
Sights: Adjustable rear, dovetail front
Weight: 46.91 oz.
Caliber: .45 ACP
Capacity: 8+1 rounds
Features: The largest of the MAC 1911 pistol line; 4140 steel frame and hammer forged slide; fully adjustable Bomar-type rear sight; dovetail front sight; flared and lowered ejection port; enhanced beavertail grip safety; skeletal hammer; combat trigger; checkered front strap serration; ramped match grade bull barrel
Deep Blue: **$1219.00**
Hard Chrome: **$1294.00**

MAC 1911 CLASSIC

Action: SA semiautomatic
Grips: Hardwood
Barrel: 5 in.
Sights: Adjustable rear, dovetail front
Weight: 40.56 oz.
Caliber: .45 ACP
Capacity: 8+1 rounds
Features: 4140 steel frame and hammer forged slide; fully adjustable bomar-type rear sight; dovetail front sight with fiber optic; flared and lowered ejection port; enhanced beavertail grip safety; skeletal hammer; combat trigger; checkered front strap serrations; ramped match grade bull barrel
Deep Blue: **$1045.00**
Hard Chrome: **$1120.00**

EAGLE IMPORTS MAC
1911 CLASSIC

EAGLE IMPORTS SPS
PANTERA

SPS PANTERA

Action: SA semiautomatic
Grips: Glass-filled nylon polymer
Barrel: 5 in.
Sights: Adjustable rear, dovetail front
Weight: 36.68 oz.
Caliber: .45 ACP
Capacity: 12+1 rounds
Features: IPSC Standard or Open Competition ready; fully adjustable Bomar-type rear sight, dovetail front sight with fiber optic; light weight polymer trigger; wide front and rear slide serrations; ambidextrous thumb safety; black chrome finish
Blue: **$1730.00**
Black chrome: **$1895.00**
Hard chrome: **$1805.00**

SPS VISTA LONG AND SHORT

Action: SA semiautomatic
Grips: Glass-filled nylon polymer
Barrel: 5 in., 5.5 in.
Sights: Sight mount included
Weight: 41.62 oz.–43.38 oz.
Caliber: 9mm (Short), .38 Super (Long)
Capacity: 21 rounds
Features: Hammer forged steel slide; scope mount for C-MORE optical sight included; checkered front strap serration; ramped match grade threaded barrel; wide magwell; black chrome finish
MSRP **$2450.00**

EAGLE IMPORTS SPS VISTA
LONG AND SHORT

Ed Brown Products

ED BROWN CLASSIC CUSTOM

ED BROWN EXECUTIVE CARRY

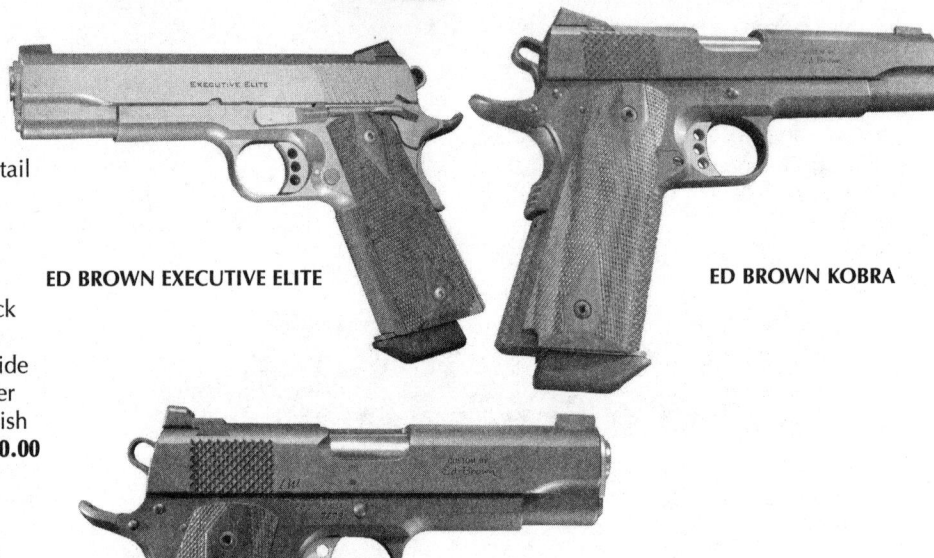

ED BROWN EXECUTIVE ELITE

ED BROWN KOBRA

ED BROWN KOBRA CARRY LIGHTWEIGHT

CLASSIC CUSTOM

Action: Semiautomatic
Grips: Cocobolo wood
Barrel: 5 in.
Sights: Adjustable rear, cross dovetail front
Weight: 40 oz.
Caliber: .45 ACP
Capacity: 7+1 rounds
Features: Single-action; single-stack government model frame; special mirror finished side; two-piece guide rod for smoother cycling and easier disassembly; stainless or blued finish
MSRP **$3420.00**

EXECUTIVE CARRY

Action: Semiautomatic
Grips: Checkered cocobolo wood
Barrel: 4.25 in.
Sights: Fixed, night
Weight: 35 oz.
Caliber: .45 ACP
Capacity: 7+1 rounds
Features: Frame modified with an innovative Ed Brown Bobtail; stainless or blued frame finish with stainless, black or blued slide finish; fixed dovetail 3-dot night sights with high visibility white outlines
MSRP **$2695.00**

EXECUTIVE ELITE

Action: Semiautomatic
Grips: Checkered cocobolo wood
Barrel: 5 in.
Sights: Fixed, night
Weight: 38 oz.
Caliber: .45 ACP
Capacity: 7+1 rounds
Features: Single-stack government model frame; matte finished slide for low glare, with traditional square cut serrations on rear of slide only; blued or stainless finish
MSRP **$2695.00**

KOBRA

Action: Semiautomatic
Grips: Cocobolo wood
Barrel: 5 in.
Sights: Fixed, night
Weight: 38 oz.
Caliber: .45 ACP
Capacity: 7+1 rounds
Features: Single-stack government model frame; John Browning traditional design; exclusive snakeskin treatment on forestrap and mainspring housing; matte finished slide for low glare; 3-dot night sights with high visibility white outlines; blued or stainless finish
MSRP **$2695.00**

KOBRA CARRY LIGHTWEIGHT

Action: Semiautomatic
Grips: Cocobolo wood
Barrel: 4.25 in.
Sights: Fixed dovetail front night with high visibility white outlines
Weight: 27 oz.
Caliber: .45 ACP
Capacity: 7+1 rounds
Features: Lightweight aluminum frame and Bobtail housing; all other components are steel; exclusive snakeskin treatment on forestrap and housing; matte finished Gen III coated slide for low glare
MSRP **$2945.00**

SIGNATURE EDITION

Action: Semiautomatic
Grips: Cocobolo wood
Barrel: 5 in.
Sights: Adjustable rear, cross dovetail front
Weight: 40 oz.
Caliber: .45 ACP
Capacity: 7+1 rounds
Features: The Ed Brown Signature Edition is based on the timeless Classic Custom pistol, with hand relief engraving by our master engraver; single stack government model frame; special mirror finished slide; 50 lpi serrations on back of slide to match serrated adjustable sight; hand relief engraved package; adjustable rear sight buried deep into slide; cross dovetail front sight; blued metal parts
Blued: **$7695.00**
Stainless: **$9995.00**

ED BROWN SIGNATURE EDITION

ED BROWN SPECIAL FORCES CARRY

SPECIAL FORCES CARRY

Action: Semiautomatic
Grips: G10, carbon fiber
Barrel: 4.25 in.
Sights: Fixed dovetail 3-dot night sights

Weight: 35 oz.
Caliber: .45 ACP
Capacity: 7 rounds
Features: Commander model slide, single stack Bobtail frame; chainlink treatment on forestrap; Bobtail housing; slide coated with Gen III low glare protection; high visibility white outlines for sights; available stainless finish
MSRP. . . . . $2695.00–$2795.00

EMF Company, Inc.

1873 GREAT WESTERN II FREEDOM

Action: SA
Grips: Synthetic
Barrel: 4.75 in., 5.5 in.
Sights: Blade front
Weight: 36.8 oz.
Caliber: .45 ACP, .357
Capacity: 6 rounds
Features: Laser engraving/grips
MSRP. **$650.00**

GREAT WESTERN II ALCHIMISTA I, II, III, III STD, III DLX

Action: SA revolver
Grips: Walnut
Barrel: 4.75 in., 5.5 in., 7.5 in.
Sights: Fixed
Weight: 33.6 oz.
Caliber: .357 Mag., .44-40, .45 LC
Capacity: 6 rounds
Features: Standard case-hardening; stainless steel; checkered walnut grips; express grips available ; three variations: Alchimista I has checkered walnut 1860 walnut grips, wide setback trigger, case hardened frame; Alchimista II is similar to I but has lower, wider hammer; Alchimista III STD is similar to the II but with an octagonal barrel and available in STD (case hardened) or DLX (old silver/black) options
MSRP. . . . . $600.00–$725.00

GREAT WESTERN II ALL BLUE PALADIN

Action: Revolver
Grips: Ultra Ivory
Barrel: 3.5 in., 5.5 in., 7.5 in.
Sights: Fixed
Weight: N/A
Caliber: .45 LC
Capacity: 6 rounds
Features: Single action; all blued barrel, cylinder, and frames as seen in Hollywood westerns
MSRP. . . . . $580.00–$590.00

EMF COMPANY, INC. 1873 GREAT WESTERN II "FREEDOM"

EMF GREAT WESTERN II ALCHIMISTA II

EMF GREAT WESTERN II ALL BLUE PALADIN

EMF Company, Inc.

EMF GREAT WESTERN II BUNTLINE

GREAT WESTERN II BUNTLINE

Action: Revolver
Grips: Walnut or Ultra Ivory
Barrel: 12 in.
Sights: Fixed
Weight: N/A
Caliber: .45 LC
Capacity: 6 rounds
Features: Deep color case hardened finish; first version was designed by Colt for Ned Buntline
MSRP . . . . $605.00–$620.00

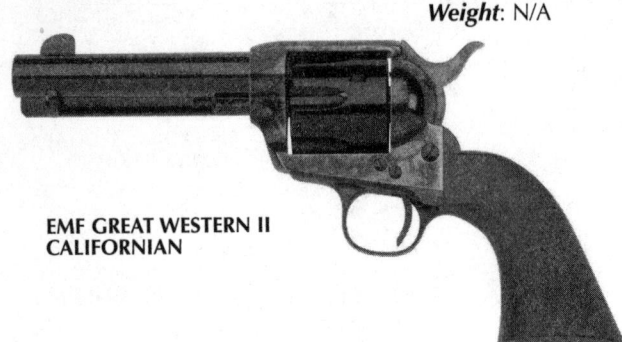

EMF GREAT WESTERN II CALIFORNIAN

EMF GREAT WESTERN II DELUXE ENGRAVED SHERIFF

GREAT WESTERN II CALIFORNIAN

Action: SA revolver
Grips: Walnut
Barrel: 4.75 in., 5.5 in., 7.5 in.
Sights: Fixed
Weight: 48 oz.
Caliber: .357 Mag., .44-40 Win., .45 LC
Capacity: 6 rounds
Features: Standard case-hardening; steel frame
MSRP **$540.00**

GREAT WESTERN II DELUXE ENGRAVED SHERIFF

Action: Revolver
Grips: Ultra Ivory
Barrel: 3 in.
Sights: Fixed
Weight: N/A
Caliber: .357 Mag., 45 LC
Capacity: 6 rounds
Features: Manufactured in Italy; stainless steel with factory laser engraving
MSRP **$860.00**

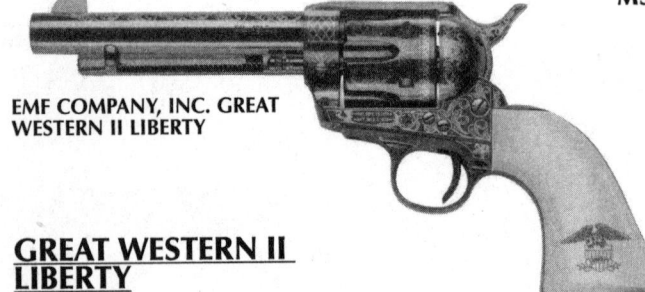

EMF COMPANY, INC. GREAT WESTERN II LIBERTY

E.M.F. GREAT WESTERN II PONY EXPRESS

GREAT WESTERN II LIBERTY

Action: Revolver
Grips: Ultra Ivory
Barrel: 4.75 in., 5.5 in.
Sights: Fixed
Weight: N/A
Caliber: .357 Mag., .45 LC
Capacity: 6 rounds
Features: Manufactured in Italy; all blued barrel, cylinder, and frame; factory laser engraved
MSRP **$630.00**

GREAT WESTERN II PONY EXPRESS

Action: SA revolver
Grips: Walnut express grips
Barrel: 3.5 in.
Sights: Fixed
Weight: 32 oz.
Caliber: .357 Mag., .45 LC
Capacity: 6 rounds
Features: Designed by Dave Anderson, one of the pioneering gunmakers in Cowboy Action Shooting and intended for mounted shooting competitors; available in an Express (bird's head) grip and turned-down hammer or a standard grip and Bisley hammer, both in bright stainless, or in a case hardened version with Express grip
MSRP . . . . $660.00–$930.00

European American Armory (EAA)

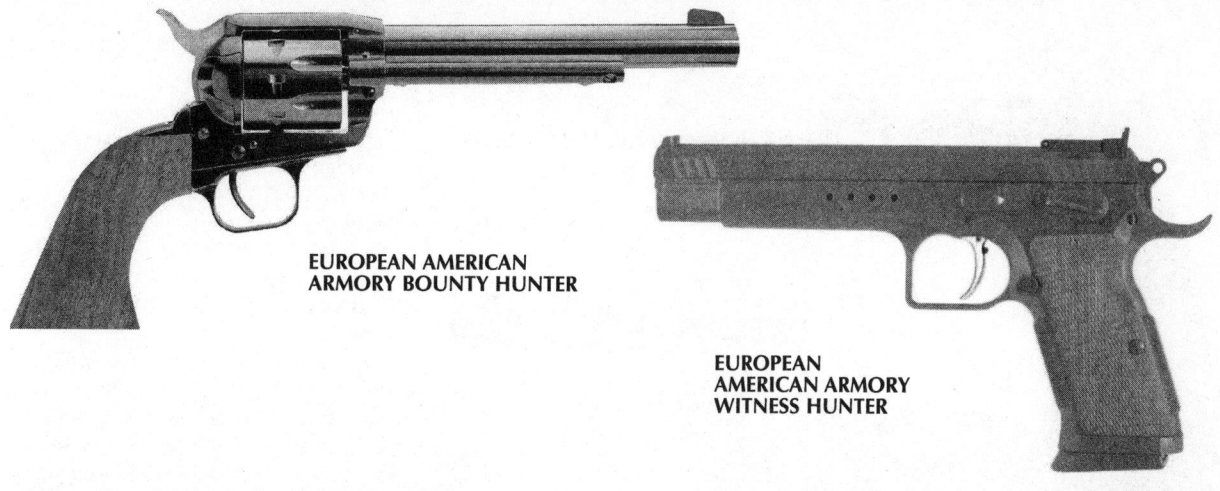

EUROPEAN AMERICAN
ARMORY BOUNTY HUNTER

EUROPEAN
AMERICAN ARMORY
WITNESS HUNTER

EUROPEAN AMERICAN
ARMORY POLYMER
FULL SIZE

EUROPEAN AMERICAN ARMORY
WITNESS STEEL COMPACT

BOUNTY HUNTER

Action: SA revolver
Grips: Walnut
Barrel: 4.5 in., 6.75 in., 7.5 in.
Sights: Fixed, open
Weight: 39–41 oz.
Caliber: .357 Mag.,.44 Mag., .22
LR/.22 WMR, 45 LC
Capacity: 6 or 8 rounds
Features: Transfer bar safety; steel or
alloy frame; in blued or nickel
finishes
MSRP . . . . $374.00–$562.00

WITNESS HUNTER

Action: Semiautomatic
Grips: Rubber
Barrel: 6 in.
Sights: Dovetail front
Weight: 41 oz.
Caliber: 10mm, .45 ACP
Capacity: 10+1 or 15+1 rounds

Features: Single-action with over
travel stop; extended manual safety;
super sight; cone barrel, slide lockup;
checkered non-slip frame; drilled and
tapped for scope mount; auto-firing
pin block
MSRP $1332.00

WITNESS POLYMER FULL SIZE

Action: Semiautomatic
Grips: Rubber
Barrel: 4.5 in.
Sights: 3-Dot
Weight: 33 oz.
Caliber: 9mm, 10mm, .40 S&W, .45
ACP
Capacity: 10+1, 14+1, or 17+1
rounds
Features: Windage adjustable sight;
double- or single-action; polymer
frame; integral accessory rail
MSRP $589.00

WITNESS STEEL COMPACT

Action: Semiautomatic
Grips: Rubber
Barrel: 3.6 in.
Sights: Adjustable
Weight: 30 oz.
Caliber: 9mm, .40 S&W, 10mm, .45
ACP
Capacity: 8+1, 12+1, or 14+1 rounds
Features: Wonder finish, windage
adjustable sight; double- or single-
action; polymer or steel frame;
integral accessory rail; matte stainless
finish
MSRP $665.00

FN America

FN AMERICA FN FIVE-SEVEN SERIES

FN AMERICA FNS-9

FN AMERICA FNX-9

FN AMERICA FNX-45

FN AMERICA FNX-45 TACTICAL

FN FIVE-SEVEN SERIES

Action: SA semiautomatic
Grips: Plastic
Barrel: 4.8 in.
Sights: Adjustable 3-dot
Weight: 20.8 oz.
Caliber: 5.7x28mm
Capacity: 10 or 20 round magazines
Features: Integrated accessory rail for mounting tactical lights or lasers; reversible magazine button; ambidextrous manual safety levers; hammer-forged, chrome lined barrel; adjustable three-dot target sights available with matte or flat dark earth
MSRP................$1399.00

FNS-9/FNS-40

Action: DA semiautomatic
Grips: Polymer
Barrel: 4 in.
Sights: Night sights
Weight: 25.2 oz.
Caliber: 9mm, .40 S&W
Capacity: 17 (FNS-9) or 14 (FNS-40) rounds
Features: Striker-fired semiautomatic; manual safety levers; stainless steel slide in matte black or silver finish; external extractor with loaded chamber indicator; three-dot night sights; hammer-forged stainless steel barrel; black polymer frame; fully ambidextrous
MSRP................. $599.00
Night Sights: $649.00

FNX-9/FNX-40

Action: Semiautomatic
Grips: Interchangeable backstraps with lanyard eyelets
Barrel: 4 in.
Sights: 3-Dot system
Weight: 21.9 oz. (9mm), 24.4 oz. (.40)
Caliber: 9mm, .40 S&W
Capacity: 17 (9mm) or 14 (.40 S&W) rounds
Features: Ergonomic polymer black frame with low bore axis; checkered and ribbed grip panels; stainless steel slide and hammer-forged stainless barrel; DA/SA ambidextrous operating controls
MSRP................ $699.00

FNX-45

Action: DA/SA Semiautomatic
Grips: Interchangeable backstraps with lanyard eyelets
Barrel: 4.5 in.
Sights: Fixed 3-dot
Weight: 33.2 oz.
Caliber: .45 ACP
Capacity: 15 rounds
Features: Polymer frame with stainless steel barrel; external extractor with loaded chamber indicator; front and rear cocking serrations; Picatinny rail; manual, ambidextrous safety; available in black
MSRP................$824.00

FNX-45 TACTICAL

Action: DA/SA semiautomatic
Grips: Textured polymer
Barrel: 5.3 in.
Sights: High-profile night sights
Weight: 33.6 oz.
Caliber: .45 ACP
Capacity: 15 rounds
Features: Stainless steel slide; external extractor with loaded chamber indicator; high-profile combat night sights; red-dot sight optional; hammer-forged stainless steel barrel; flat dark earth or black polymer frame; Picatinny rail; fully ambidextrous
MSRP................$1349.00

Freedom Arms

MODEL 83 PREMIER GRADE

Action: SA revolver
Grips: Hardwood
Barrel: 4.75 in., 6 in., 7.5 in., 10 in.
Sights: Fixed or adjustable
Weight: 52.5 oz.
Caliber: .500 Wyoming Express, .475 Linebaugh, .454 Casull, .44 Rem. Mag., .41 Rem. Mag., .357 Mag.
Capacity: 5 rounds
Features: Adjustable sight models are drilled and tapped for scope mounts; stainless steel, brush finish and impregnated hardwood grips
MSRP . . . . $2743.00–$2848.00

MODEL 83 RIMFIRE

Action: SA revolver
Grips: Hardwood
Barrel: 10 in.
Sights: Adjustable
Weight: 55.5 oz.
Caliber: .22 LR
Capacity: 5 rounds
Features: Drilled and tapped for scope mounts; stainless steel frame; matte finish; match grade chambers
MSRP $2634.00

MODEL 97 PREMIER GRADE

Action: SA revolver
Grips: Laminated hardwood
Barrel: 4.5 in., 5.5 in., 7.5 in., or 10 in.
Sights: Adjustable or fixed

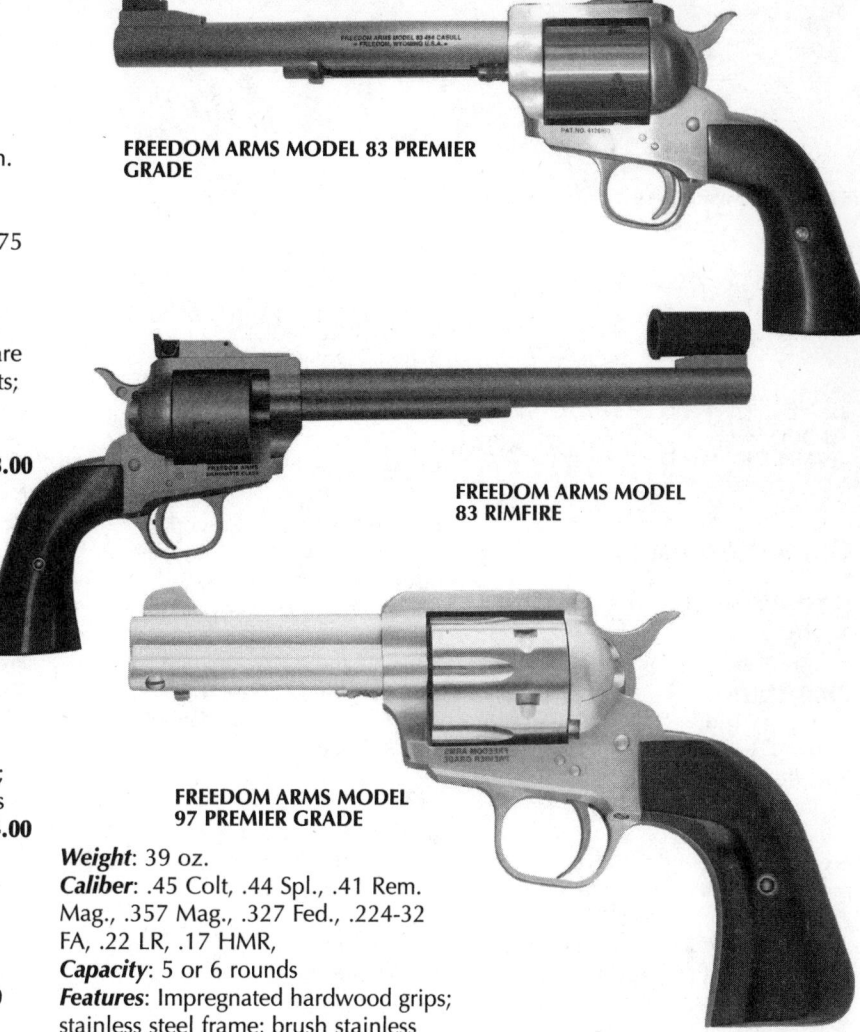

FREEDOM ARMS MODEL 83 PREMIER GRADE

FREEDOM ARMS MODEL 83 RIMFIRE

FREEDOM ARMS MODEL 97 PREMIER GRADE

Weight: 39 oz.
Caliber: .45 Colt, .44 Spl., .41 Rem. Mag., .357 Mag., .327 Fed., .224-32 FA, .22 LR, .17 HMR,
Capacity: 5 or 6 rounds
Features: Impregnated hardwood grips; stainless steel frame; brush stainless finish
MSRP . . . . $2309.00–$2339.00

Gateway Precision Arms

MAXIMUM

Action: Hinged breech
Grips: Walnut
Barrel: 8.5 in., 10.5 in., 14 in.
Sights: Adjustable, open
Weight: 56–67 oz.
Caliber: most rifle chamberings from .22 Hornet to .375 H&H
Capacity: single-shot
Features: Falling block action; free floating barrel; multiple length barrels; receiver tapped for scope mounts
MSRP $1062.00

MOA MAXIMUM

Glock

GLOCK COMPACT G19

GLOCK COMPETITION G34

GLOCK G32 GEN4

GLOCK G34 GEN4

Glock Compact Models

G19, G19 GEN4, G19 GEN4 MOS

Action: Semiautomatic
Grips: Polymer
Barrel: 4.01 in.
Sights: Fixed
Weight: 23.65 oz.
Caliber: 9mm
Capacity: 10, 15, 17, 33 rounds
Features: Striker-fired, polymer framed pistol with safe action system, trigger safety, hexagonal barrel, DAO action; Gen4 has modular backstrap design, rough-textured grip, enlarged and reversible magazine release, and is available in Glock's MOS—Modular Optic System—configuration, which simplifies mounting of many modern pistol red dot and reflex sight optics
MSRP. . . . G19 Gen4 MOS $726.00; G19 Gen4 $649.00; G19 $599.00

G23, G23 GEN4

Action: Semiautomatic
Grips: Polymer
Barrel: 4.01 in.
Sights: Fixed
Weight: 23.65 oz.
Caliber: .40 S&W
Capacity: 10, 15, 22 rounds
Features: Striker-fired, polymer framed pistol with safe action system, trigger safety, hexagonal barrel, DAO action; Gen4 has modular backstrap design, rough-textured grip, enlarged and reversible magazine release
MSRP. G23 Gen4 $649.00; G23 $599.00

G23, G23 GEN4

Action: Semiautomatic
Grips: Polymer
Barrel: 4.01 in.
Sights: Fixed
Weight: 23.65 oz.
Caliber: .40 S&W
Capacity: 10, 15, 22 rounds
Features: Striker-fired, polymer framed pistol with safe action system, trigger safety, hexagonal barrel, DAO action; Gen4 has modular backstrap design, rough-textured grip, enlarged and reversible magazine release
MSRP. G23 Gen4 $649.00; G23 $599.00

G38

Action: Semiautomatic
Grips: Polymer
Barrel: 4.01 in.
Sights: Fixed
Weight: 26.83 oz.
Caliber: .45 G.A.P.
Capacity: 8, 10 rounds
Features: Striker-fired, polymer framed pistol with safe action system, trigger safety, hexagonal barrel, DAO action
MSRP. $614.00

Glock Competition Models

G34, G34 GEN4, G34 GEN4 MOS

Action: Semiautomatic
Grips: Polymer
Barrel: 5.31 in.
Sights: Fixed
Weight: 25.77 oz.
Caliber: 9mm
Capacity: 10, 17, 33 rounds
Features: Striker-fired, polymer framed pistol with safe action system, trigger safety, hexagonal barrel, DAO action; Gen4 has modular backstrap design, rough-textured grip, enlarged and reversible magazine release, and is available in Glock's MOS—Modular Optic System—configuration, which simplifies mounting of many modern pistol red dot and reflex sight optics
MSRP. . . . G34 Gen4 MOS $840.00; G34 Gen4 $729.00; G34 $679.00

G35, G35 GEN4, G35 GEN4 MOS

Photo: 108 page 336
Action: Semiautomatic
Grips: Polymer
Barrel: 5.31 in.
Sights: Fixed
Weight: 27.18 oz.
Caliber: .40 S&W
Capacity: 10, 15, 22 rounds
Features: Striker-fired, polymer framed pistol with safe action system, trigger safety, hexagonal barrel, DAO action; Gen4 has modular backstrap design, rough-textured grip, enlarged and reversible magazine release, and is available in Glock's MOS—Modular Optic System—configuration, which simplifies mounting of many modern pistol red dot and reflex sight optics
MSRP. . . . G35 Gen4 MOS $840.00; G35 Gen4 $729.00; G35 $679.00

G41 GEN4, G41 GEN4 MOS

Photo: 108 page 336
Action: Semiautomatic
Grips: Polymer
Barrel: 5.31 in.
Sights: Fixed
Weight: 27 oz.
Caliber: .45 ACP
Capacity: 10, 13 rounds
Features: Striker-fired, polymer framed pistol with safe action system, trigger safety, hexagonal barrel, DAO action; Gen4 has modular backstrap design, rough-textured grip, enlarged and reversible magazine release, and is available in Glock's MOS—Modular Optic System—configuration, which simplifies mounting of many modern pistol red dot and reflex sight optics
MSRP. . . . G41 Gen4 MOS $840.00; G41 Gen4 $729.00

GLOCK G40 GEN4

GLOCK STANDARD G17

GLOCK G20 GEN4

GLOCK G21 GEN4

Glock Long Slide Models

G40 GEN4 MOS

Action: Semiautomatic
Grips: Polymer
Barrel: 6.02 in.
Sights: Fixed
Weight: 28.15 oz.
Caliber: 10mm
Capacity: 15 rounds
Features: Striker-fired, polymer framed pistol with safe action system, trigger safety, hexagonal barrel, DAO action; Gen4 has modular backstrap design, rough-textured grip, enlarged and reversible magazine release, and is available in Glock's MOS—Modular Optic System—configuration, which simplifies mounting of many modern pistol red dot and reflex sight optics.
MSRP $840.00

Glock Standard Models

G17, G17 GEN4, G17 GEN4 MOS

Action: Semiautomatic
Grips: Polymer
Barrel: 4.48 in.
Sights: Fixed
Weight: 25.06 oz.
Caliber: 9mm
Capacity: 10, 17, 33 rounds
Features: Striker-fired, polymer framed pistol with safe action system, trigger safety, hexagonal barrel, DAO action; Gen4 has modular backstrap design, rough-textured grip, enlarged and reversible magazine release, and is available in Glock's MOS—Modular Optic System—configuration, which simplifies mounting of many modern pistol red dot and reflex sight optics
MSRP . . . . G17 Gen4 MOS $726.00; G17 Gen4 $649.00; G17 $599.00

G22, G22 GEN4

Action: Semiautomatic
Grips: Polymer
Barrel: 4.48 in.
Sights: Fixed
Weight: 25.59 oz.
Caliber: .40 S&W
Capacity: 10, 15, 22 rounds
Features: Striker-fired, polymer framed pistol with safe action system, trigger safety, hexagonal barrel, DAO action; Gen4 has modular backstrap design, rough-textured grip, enlarged and reversible magazine release
MSRP G22 Gen4 $649.00; G22 $599.00

G20SF, G20 GEN4

Action: Semiautomatic
Grips: Polymer
Barrel: 4.6 in.
Sights: Fixed
Weight: 30.71 in.
Caliber: 10mm
Capacity: 10, 15 rounds
Features: Striker-fired, polymer framed pistol with safe action system, trigger safety, hexagonal barrel, DAO action; SF designation model has a reduced circumference backstrap. Gen4 has modular backstrap design, rough-textured grip, enlarged and reversible magazine release
MSRP G20 Gen4 $687.00; G20SF $637.00

G21SF, G21 GEN4

Action: Semiautomatic
Grips: Polymer
Barrel: 4.6 in.
Sights: Fixed
Weight: 29.30 in.
Caliber: .45 ACP
Capacity: 10, 13 rounds
Features: Striker-fired, polymer framed pistol with safe action system, trigger safety, hexagonal barrel, DAO action; SF designation model has a reduced circumference backstrap. Gen4 has modular backstrap design, rough-textured grip, enlarged and reversible magazine release
MSRP G21 Gen4 $687.00; G21SF $637.00

G37, G37 GEN4

Action: Semiautomatic
Grips: Polymer
Barrel: 4.48 in.
Sights: Fixed
Weight: 28.95 oz.
Caliber: .45 G.A.P.
Capacity: 10 rounds
Features: Striker-fired, polymer framed pistol with safe action system, trigger safety, hexagonal barrel, DAO action; Gen4 has modular backstrap design, rough-textured grip, enlarged and reversible magazine release
MSRP G37 Gen4 $664.00; G37 $614.00

G31, G31 GEN4

Action: Semiautomatic
Grips: Polymer
Barrel: 4.48 in.
Sights: Fixed
Weight: 26.12 oz.
Caliber: .357 SIG
Capacity: 10, 15 round
Features: Striker-fired, polymer framed pistol with safe action system, trigger safety, hexagonal barrel, DAO action; Gen4 has modular backstrap design, rough-textured grip, enlarged and reversible magazine release
MSRP . . . G31 Gen4 $649; G31 $599.00

Glock

GLOCK GEN4 G26

GLOCK G29 GEN4

GLOCK SUBCOMPACT
G26

GLOCK G30S

Glock Subcompact Models

G26, G26 GEN4

Action: Semiautomatic
Grips: Polymer
Barrel: 3.42 in.
Sights: Fixed
Weight: 21.71 oz.
Caliber: 9mm
Capacity: 10, 15, 17, 33 rounds
Features: Striker-fired, polymer framed pistol with safe action system, trigger safety, hexagonal barrel, DAO action; Gen4 has modular backstrap design, rough-textured grip, enlarged and reversible magazine release
MSRP........G26 Gen4 $649.00; G26 $599.00

G27, G27 GEN4

Action: Semiautomatic
Grips: Polymer
Barrel: 3.42 in.
Sights: Fixed
Weight: 21.89 oz.
Caliber: .40 S&W
Capacity: 9, 13, 15, 22 rounds
Features: Striker-fired, polymer framed pistol with safe action system, trigger safety, hexagonal barrel, DAO action; Gen4 has modular backstrap design, rough-textured grip, enlarged and reversible magazine release
MSRP........G27 Gen4 $649.00; G27 $599.00

G29SF, G29 GEN4

Action: Semiautomatic
Grips: Polymer
Barrel: 3.77 in.
Sights: Fixed
Weight: 26.83 oz.
Caliber: 10mm
Capacity: 10, 15 rounds
Features: Striker-fired, polymer framed pistol with safe action system, trigger safety, hexagonal barrel, DAO action; SF designation model has a reduced circumference backstrap. Gen4 has modular backstrap design, rough-textured grip, enlarged and reversible magazine release
MSRP........G29 Gen4 $687.00; G29SF $637.00

G30S, G30FS, G30 GEN4

Action: Semiautomatic
Grips: Polymer
Barrel: 3.77 in.
Sights: Fixed
Weight: 22.95 oz.–26.30 oz.
Caliber: .45 ACP
Capacity: 10 rounds
Features: Striker-fired, polymer framed pistol with safe action system, trigger safety, hexagonal barrel, DAO action; S designation denotes slim slide profile. SF designation model has a reduced circumference backstrap. Gen4 has modular backstrap design, rough-textured grip, enlarged and reversible magazine release
MSRP............. G30S $637.00

GLOCK G33 GEN4

GLOCK SUBCOMPACT SLIMLINE G36

GLOCK G42

GLOCK G43 SINGLE STACK

G33, G33 GEN4

Action: Semiautomatic
Grips: Polymer
Barrel: 3.42 in.
Sights: Fixed
Weight: 21.89 oz.
Caliber: .357 SIG
Capacity: 9, 13, 15 rounds
Features: Striker-fired, polymer framed pistol with safe action system, trigger safety, hexagonal barrel, DAO action; Gen4 has modular backstrap design, rough-textured grip, enlarged and reversible magazine release
MSRP G33 Gen4 $649.00; G33 $599.00

G39

Action: Semiautomatic
Grips: Polymer
Barrel: 3.42 in.
Sights: Fixed
Weight: 24.18 oz.
Caliber: .45 G.A.P.
Capacity: 6, 8, 10 rounds

Features: Striker-fired, polymer framed pistol with safe action system, trigger safety, hexagonal barrel, DAO action
MSRP $614.00

Glock Subcompact Slimline Models

G36

Action: Semiautomatic
Grips: Polymer
Barrel: 3.77 in.
Sights: Fixed
Weight: 22.42 oz.
Caliber: .45 ACP
Capacity: 6 rounds
Features: Striker-fired, polymer framed pistol with safe action system, trigger safety, hexagonal barrel, DAO action, single-stack magazine
MSRP $637.00

G42

Action: Semiautomatic
Grips: Polymer

Barrel: 3.25 in.
Sights: Fixed
Weight: 13.76 oz.
Caliber: .380 ACP
Capacity: 6 rounds
Features: Striker-fired, polymer framed pistol with safe action system, trigger safety, hexagonal barrel, DAO action, single-stack magazine
MSRP $480.00

G43

Photo: 108 page 337
Action: Semiautomatic
Grips: Polymer
Barrel: 3.39 in.
Sights: Fixed
Weight: 17.95 oz.
Caliber: 9mm
Capacity:
Features: Striker-fired, polymer framed pistol with safe action system, trigger safety, hexagonal barrel, DAO action, single-stack magazine
MSRP $580.00

Hämmerli

HÄMMERLI MODEL SP20 TARGET PISTOL

HÄMMERLI MODEL X-ESSE LONG

MODEL SP20 TARGET PISTOL

Action: Semiautomatic
Grips: Synthetic
Barrel: 4.86 in.
Sights: Target
Weight: 41 oz.
Caliber: .22 LR, .32 S&W
Capacity: 5 rounds

Features: Front end magazine; counterweight with new recoil reduction system; various grip sizes
MSRP................$1541.00

MODEL X-ESSE

Action: Semiautomatic
Grips: Composite
Barrel: 4.5 in., 5.9 in.

Sights: Adjustable
Weight: 27.9–31 oz.
Caliber: .22 LR
Capacity: 10 rounds
Features: Single-action, two-stage trigger; universal hi-grip
MSRP................ $792.00

Heckler & Koch

HECKLER & KOCH HK45

HECKLER & KOCH HK45 COMPACT

HK45

Action: Semiautomatic
Grips: Polymer
Barrel: 4.53 in.
Sights: Fixed
Weight: 31 oz.
Caliber: .45 ACP
Capacity: 10 rounds
Features: DA/SA with control lever; integral Picatinny rail; ambidextrous controls with dual slide releases; modified Browning linkless recoil operating system; polygonal rifling; open square notch rear sight with contrast points; low profile drift adjustable three-dot sights; available in black, RAL8000 green brown, and olive finishes; supplied with one additional backstrap; night sights optional
MSRP........ $1199.00–$1399.00

HK45 COMPACT

Action: Semiautomatic
Grips: Synthetic
Barrel: 3.94 in.
Sights: Fixed
Weight: 28.48 oz.
Caliber: .45 ACP
Capacity: 8 or 10 rounds
Features: Picatinny rail molded into the polymer frame dust cover; slim-line grip profiles with user replaceable grip panels; ambidextrous controls with dual slide releases and enlarged magazine release; uses the proven modified Browning linkless recoil operating system; O-ring barrel for precise barrel-to-slide lockup and better accuracy; polygonal rifling for longer barrel life and increased

accuracy; improved ergonomic control levers (safety and/or decocking); low profile drift adjustable 3-dot sights; contoured and radiused slide with forward slide (grasping) grooves and anti-glare longitudinal ribs; polymer frame; available in black, RAL8000 green brown, and olive finishes; supplied with one additional backstrap; night sights optional
MSRP........ $1199.00–$1399.00

HECKLER & KOCH HK45 COMPACT TACTICAL

HECKLER & KOCH HK45 TACTICAL

HECKLER & KOCH P30

HECKLER & KOCH MARK 23

HECKLER & KOCH P30 L

HK45 COMPACT TACTICAL

Action: DA/SA semiautomatic
Grips: Textured polymer
Barrel: 4.57 in.
Sights: 3-dot
Weight: 29.12 oz.
Caliber: .45 ACP
Capacity: 10 rounds
Features: Proprietary internal mechanical recoil reduction system; O-ring barrel; cold-hammer-forged barrel; available in black, RAL8000 green brown, and olive finishes; supplied with one additional backstrap; night sights optional
MSRP . . . . $1399.00–$1499.00

HK45 TACTICAL

Action: Semiautomatic
Grips: Polymer with finger grooves
Barrel: 5.16 in.
Sights: 3-dot tritium night sights
Weight: 31.7 oz.
Caliber: .45 ACP
Capacity: 10 rounds
Features: Polymer frame; recoil-operated with modified Browning locking system; threaded barrel; Picatinny rail; key-based HK Lock-Out system; nine different trigger firing

modes; available in black, RAL8000 green brown, and olive finishes; supplied with one additional backstrap; night sights optional
MSRP . . . . $1399.00–$1499.00

MARK 23

Action: Semiautomatic
Grips: Polymer
Barrel: 5.9 in.
Sights: 3-Dot
Weight: 39.4 oz.
Caliber: .45 ACP
Capacity: 12+1 rounds
Features: Threaded O-ring barrel with polygonal bore profile; match grade trigger; one piece machined steel slide; frame mounted decocking lever and separate ambidextrous safety lever; HK recoil reduction system; ambidextrous magazine release lever
MSRP $2299.00

P30

Action: Semiautomatic
Grips: Polymer
Barrel: 3.86 in.
Sights: Fixed
Weight: 26.08 oz.
Caliber: 9mm, .40 S&W

Capacity: 10, 15 rounds
Features: Corrosion proof fiber-reinforced polymer frame; multiple trigger firing modes; HK recoil reduction system; blued finish; Picatinny rail; ambidextrous magazine release levers and side release
MSRP . . . . $1099.00–$1199.00

P30 L

Action: Semiautomatic
Grips: Polymer
Barrel: 4.4 in.
Sights: Fixed
Weight: 27.5 oz.
Caliber: 9mm, .40 S&W
Capacity: 10, 13, or 15 rounds
Features: Interchangeable backstraps and side panel grips in small, medium, and large sizes; ambidextrous slide and magazine releases levers; integral Picatinny rail; modular design allows DA trigger or DA/SA system, with a decocking button
MSRP . . . . $1149.00–$1249.00

Heckler & Koch

HECKLER & KOCH P30SK

P30SK

Action: Semiautomatic
Grips: Rubber
Barrel: 3.27 in.
Sights: Fixed
Weight: 23.99 oz.
Caliber: 9mm
Capacity: 10 rounds
Features: Picatinny rail;
interchangeable backstraps and lateral
grip panels; available in multiple
trigger firing modes including HK's
enhanced double action only Law
Enforcement Modification (LEM);
trigger modes include conventional
double action/single action (DA/SA)
MSRP . . . . **$719.00–$819.00**

P2000 & P2000 SK

Action: Semiautomatic
Grips: Polymer
Barrel: 3.26–3.66 in.
Sights: 3-Dot
Weight: 23.8–25.9 oz.
Caliber: 9mm, .40 S&W
Capacity: 9–13 rounds
Features: LEM trigger system; double-
action; pre-cock hammer;
ambidextrous magazine release and
interchangeable grip straps; mounting
rail
MSRP . . . . **$799.00–$899.00**

USP

Action: Semiautomatic
Grips: Polymer
Barrel: 4.25–4.41 in.
Sights: 3-Dot
Weight: 27.2–31.36 oz.
Caliber: 9mm, .40 S&W, .45 ACP
Capacity: 12, 13, 15 rounds
Features: Browning-type action with a
patented recoil reduction system;
double and single action modes;
available in nine trigger/firing mode
configurations; fiber-reinforced polymer
frame; blued finish; ambidextrous
magazine release trigger
MSRP . . . . **$979.00–$1149.00**

USP COMPACT

Action: Semiautomatic
Grips: Polymer
Barrel: 3.58–3.80 in.
Sights: Fixed
Weight: 25.6–28.2 oz.
Caliber: 9mm, .40 S&W, .45 ACP
Capacity: 8, 12, 13 rounds
Features: Corrosion proof fiber-
reinforced polymer frame;

**HECKLER & KOCH
USP COMPACT**

HECKLER & KOCH USP9 TACTICAL

ambidextrous magazine release lever;
grooved target triggers; can be
converted to any of nine trigger firing
modes
MSRP . . . . **$999.00–$1199.00**

USP9 TACTICAL

Action: Semiautomatic
Grips: Synthetic
Barrel: 4.86 in.
Sights: Adjustable
Weight: 28.16 oz.
Caliber: 9mm
Capacity: 10 or 15 rounds
Features: High profile target sights;
target sights with micrometer
adjustment for windage and elevation;
one piece machined, nitro-carburized
steel slide; nine trigger firing modes;
patented HK recoil reduction system;
corrosion resistant "Hostile
Environment" blued finish; corrosion
proof fiber-reinforced polymer frame;
oversized trigger guard for use with
gloves; choice of flat and extended
floorplate magazines; universal
mounting grooves for installing
accessories; ambidextrous magazine
release lever; extended slide release;

**HECKLER & KOCH
P2000**

**HECKLER & KOCH
USP**

HECKLER & KOCH VP40

extractor doubles as a loaded
chamber indicator; patented Lock-Out
Safety device
MSRP . . . . **$1349.00–$1449.00**

VP9, VP9 TACTICAL, VP40, VP40 TACTICAL

Action: Semiautomatic
Grips: Rubber
Barrel: 4.09 in.
Sights: Fixed
Weight: 26.56 oz.
Caliber: .40 S&W, 9mm
Capacity: 10, 13, 15 rounds
Features: Ergonomic handgun grip
design that includes three changeable
backstraps and six grip side panels;
ambidextrous controls; extended
Picatinny rail molded into the polymer
frame; captive flat recoil spring;
supplied with two additional
backstraps and two additional sets of
lateral grip plates; night sights
optional; specialty versions available
with gray or Flat Dark Earth frames;
tactical versions add threaded barrels
and night sights automatically
MSRP . . . . **$719.00–$899.00**

ROUGH RIDER BIG BORE

Action: SA revolver
Grips: Cocobolo wood
Barrel: 4.5 in., 5.5 in.
Sights: Fixed, open
Weight: 38 oz.
Caliber: .45 LC, .357 Mag.
Capacity: 6 rounds
Features: Patterned after 1873 Colt; blued, nickel, stainless and blued/color-case-hardened finishes are available; frame mounted inertia firing pin and transfer bar
MSRP **$481.03**

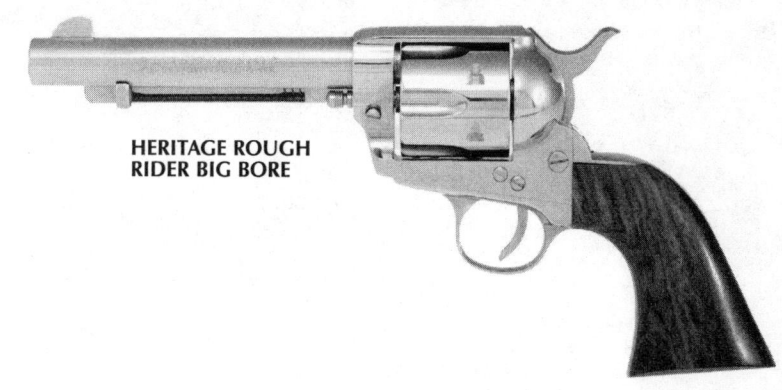

HERITAGE ROUGH RIDER BIG BORE

ROUGH RIDER SMALL BORE

Action: SA revolver
Grips: Cocobolo wood
Barrel: 3.5 in., 4.75 in., 6.5 in., 9 in.
Sights: Fixed
Weight: 31 oz.
Caliber: .22 LR, .22 Mag.
Capacity: 6 rounds
Features: Machined barrel is micro-threaded; optional cocobolo grips include white mother of pearl, black mother of pearl, or green camo laminate grips; frame finish comes in smooth silver satin, deep matte black, low gloss black satin or case-hardened finish
MSRP . . . . **$200.82–$360.48**

HERITAGE ROUGH RIDER SMALL BORE

High Standard

HS-22 VICTOR, CITATION

Action: Semiautomatic
Grips: Walnut
Barrel: 5.5 in.
Sights: Adjustable
Weight: 45 oz.
Caliber: .22 LR
Capacity: 10+1 rounds
Features: Removable aluminum rib; drilled and tapped for scopes; optional slide conversion kit for .22 short; Victor wears a slab-side barrel, Citation model wears a bull barrel; ambidextrous walnut grips or dedicated left- or right-hand walnut grips; available in a flat black oxide or parkerized military gray finish, with choice of flat black, gold, or nickel trim
MSRP **$899.99**

HIGH STANDARD HS-22 VICTOR

Hi-Point Firearms

HI-POINT FIRE-ARMS MODEL JHP45 ACP

HI-POINT FIREARMS MODEL CF-380

HI-POINT FIREARMS MODEL C-9 9MM

MODEL C-9 9MM
Action: Semiautomatic
Grips: Polymer
Barrel: 3.5 in.
Sights: 3-Dots adjustable
Weight: 29 oz.
Caliber: 9mm
Capacity: 8 or 10 rounds
Features: Polymer frame; last round lock open; quick on-off thumb safety; free trigger lock; free extra peep sight; black finish; package options include: with Galco leather holster, with hard case, with nylon holster, with hard case and Kershaw knife; three hydro-dipped camo options (no packages) are also available in Desert digital, pink, and Woodland
Black:. . . . . **$199.00–$235.00**
Camo: **$213.00**

MODEL CF-380
Action: Semiautomatic
Grips: Polymer
Barrel: 3.5 in.
Sights: 3-Dots adjustable
Weight: 29 oz.
Caliber: .380 ACP
Capacity: 8 or 10 rounds
Features: High-impact polymer frame; black powder coat with chrome rail; durable, easy-grip finish; quick on-off thumb safety; free extra rear peep sight; in black with or without hard case or in hydro-dipped pink camo
MSRP. . . . . **$179.00–$195.00**

MODEL JHP45 ACP & JCP 40 S&W
Action: Semiautomatic
Grips: Polymer
Barrel: 4.5 in.
Sights: 3-Dots adjustable
Weight: 35 oz.
Caliber: .40 S&W, .45 ACP
Capacity: 10 rounds
Features: Polymer frame; quick on-off thumb safety; operations safety sheet; +P rated; free extra rear peep sight; free trigger lock; black finish available as standalone gun or with one of three package choices: with Laserlyte, with hard case, with Galco Kydex holster; camo versions (no packages) available in hydro-dipped Desert Digital, pink, or Woodlands
Black:. . . . . **$219.00–$285.00**
Camo: **$235.00**

Iver Johnson Arms, Inc.

IVER JOHNSON EAGLE XL

EAGLE XL
Action: Semiautomatic
Grips: Dymondwood walnut
Barrel: 6 in.
Sights: Adjustable
Weight: 42 oz.
Caliber: .45 ACP, 10mm
Capacity: 8 rounds
Features: Front and rear serrations; extended thumb safety and slide stop; lowered and flared ejection port; beavertail grip safety; three-hole trigger; skeletonized hammer
MSRP. **$845.00**

Kahr Arms

KAHR ARMS CM9

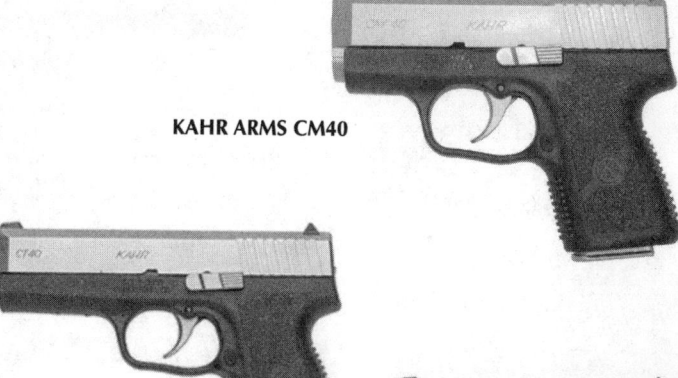

KAHR ARMS CM40

KAHR ARMS CM45

KAHR ARMS CT40

KAHR ARMS CT45

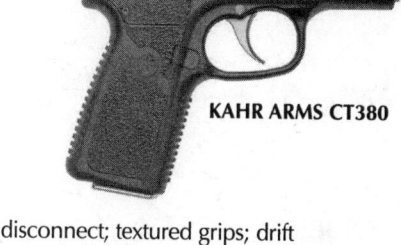

KAHR ARMS CT380

CM9

Action: Semiautomatic
Grips: Textured polymer
Barrel: 3 in.
Sights: Adjustable
Weight: 15.9 oz.
Caliber: 9mm
Capacity: 6+1 rounds
Features: Trigger cocking double-action; lock breech; Browning-type recoil lug; passive striker block; no magazine disconnect; drift adjustable, white bar-dot combat sights; available in Armor Black, Tungsten with Grip Glove frame, or matte stainless slide with front night sight
MSRP . . . . **$487.00–$499.00**

CM40

Action: Semiautomatic
Grips: Textured polymer
Barrel: 3 in.
Sights: Adjustable
Weight: 17.7 oz.
Caliber: .40 S&W
Capacity: 5+1 rounds
Features: Trigger cocking DAO; lock breech; "Browning-type" recoil lug; passive striker block; no magazine disconnect; black polymer frame, matte stainless steel slide
MSRP **$460.00**

CM45

Action: DAO semiautomatic
Grips: Synthetic
Barrel: 3.24 in.
Sights: Fixed
Weight: 17.3 oz.
Caliber: .45 ACP
Capacity: 5+1 rounds

Features: Trigger cocking DAO; lock breech; "Browning-type" recoil lug; passive striker block; no magazine disconnect; textured grips; drift adjustable white bar-dot combat rear sight; pinned in polymer front sight; available with the slide in matte stainless, Armor Black, or Cerakote Tungsten with a Grip Glove frame
MSRP . . . . **$460.00–$499.00**

CT40

Action: DAO semiautomatic
Grips: Synthetic
Barrel: 4 in.
Sights: Fixed
Weight: 21.8 oz.
Caliber: .40 S&W
Capacity: 7+1 rounds
Features: Trigger cocking DAO; lock breech; "Browning-type" recoil lug; passive striker block; no magazine disconnect; textured grips; drift adjustable white bar-dot combat rear sight; pinned in polymer front sight; black polymer frame, matte stainless steel slide
MSRP **$449.00**

CT45

Action: DAO semiautomatic
Grips: Synthetic
Barrel: 4.04 in.
Sights: Fixed
Weight: 23.7 oz.
Caliber: .45 ACP
Capacity: 7+1 rounds
Features: Trigger cocking DAO; lock breech; "Browning-type" recoil lug; passive striker block; no magazine

disconnect; textured grips; drift adjustable white bar-dot combat rear sight; pinned in polymer front sight; black polymer frame, matte stainless steel slide
MSRP **$449.00**

CT380

Action: Semiautomatic
Grips: Synthetic
Barrel: 3 in.
Sights: Fixed
Weight: 11.44 oz.
Caliber: .380 ACP
Capacity: 7+1 rounds
Features: Textured polymer grips; trigger cocking DAO; lock breech; Browning-type recoil lug; passive striker block; no magazine disconnect; drift adjustable white bar-dot combat rear sight; pinned in polymer front sight; available either with a matte stainless slide or with a Cerakote tungsten slide with Grip Glove frame
MSRP . . . . **$419.00–$439.00**

Kahr Arms

KAHR ARMS CT380 TUNGSTEN

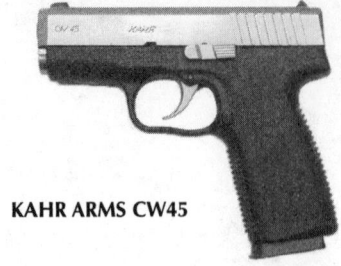

KAHR ARMS CW45

KAHR ARMS CW380 TUNGSTEN

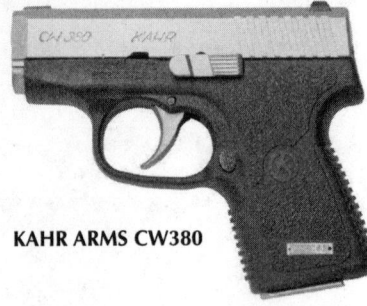

KAHR ARMS CW380

KAHR ARMS P9 SERIES

KAHR ARMS P40 SERIES

CT380 TUNGSTEN

Action: DAO semiautomatic
Grips: Textured polymer
Barrel: 3 in.
Sights: Adjustable rear, fixed front
Weight: 11.44 oz.
Caliber: .380 ACP
Capacity: 7+1
Features: Tungsten Cerakote finish stainless slide; Browning-type recoil lug; passive striker block; drift adjustable white bar–dot combat rear sight with a pinned-in-polymer front sight
MSRP.................$419.00

CW45

Action: Semiautomatic
Grips: Textured polymer
Barrel: 3.64 in.
Sights: Adjustable
Weight: 21.7 oz.
Caliber: .45 ACP
Capacity: 6+1 rounds
Features: Trigger cocking double-action; lock breech; Browning-type

recoil lug; passive striker block; no magazine disconnect; drift adjustable, white bar-dot combat rear sight, pinned in polymer front sight; black frame; matte stainless steel slide
MSRP................. $449.00

CW380

Action: DAO semiautomatic
Grips: Black polymer
Barrel: 2.58 in.
Sights: Adjustable white bar-dot combat rear, pinned in polymer front
Weight: 10.2 oz.
Caliber: .380 ACP
Capacity: 6+1 rounds
Features: Lock breech; modified Browning type recoil lug; "safe cam" action; conventional rifled barrel; metal-injection-molded slide stop lever; slide lock after last round; black and stainless matte finish; available with front night sight
MSRP................ $439.00

CW380 TUNGSTEN

Action: DAO semiautomatic
Grips: Textured polymer
Barrel: 2.58 in.
Sights: Adjustable rear, fixed front
Weight: 10.2 oz.
Caliber: .380 ACP
Capacity: 6+1
Features: Tungsten Cerakote finish stainless slide; Browning-type recoil lug; passive striker block; drift adjustable white bar–dot combat rear

sight with a pinned-in-polymer front sight
MSRP.................$419.00

P9 SERIES

Action: Semiautomatic
Grips: Textured polymer
Barrel: 3.6 in.
Sights: Adjustable
Weight: 16.9 oz.
Caliber: 9mm
Capacity: 7+1 rounds
Features: Trigger cocking DAO; lock breech; Browning-type recoil lug; passive striker block; no magazine disconnect; six versions available: Base P9 with matte stainless slide; with matte stainless slide and night sights; with matte stainless slide, night sights, external thumb safety, and loaded chamber indicator; with matte black slide; with matte black slide and night sights
MSRP..........$762.00–$996.00

P40 SERIES

Action: Semiautomatic
Grips: Textured polymer
Barrel: 3.6 in.
Sights: Adjustable
Weight: 18.7 oz.
Caliber: .40 S&W
Capacity: 6+1 rounds
Features: Trigger cocking DAO; lock breech; Browning-type recoil lug; passive striker block; no magazine disconnect; black polymer frame; six versions available: with matte stainless slide; with matte stainless slide and night sights; with matte black slide; with matte black slide and night sights; with matte stainless slide, external thumb safety, and loaded chamber indicator; and with matte stainless slide, external thumb safety, loaded chamber indicator, and night sights
MSRP..........$762.00–$996.00

Kahr Arms

P45 SERIES

Action: Semiautomatic
Grips: Textured polymer
Barrel: 3.54 in.
Sights: Adjustable
Weight: 18.5 oz.
Caliber: .45 ACP
Capacity: 5+1 or 6+1 rounds
Features: Trigger cocking DAO; lock breech; Browning-type recoil lug; passive striker block; no magazine disconnect; black polymer frame

P45:	**$829.00**
P45 w/ Night Sights:	**$949.00**
P45 Black:	**$880.00**
P45 Black w/ Night sights:	**$999.00**

P380 SERIES

Action: Semiautomatic
Grips: Textured polymer
Barrel: 2.5 in.
Sights: Adjustable
Weight: 11.27 oz.
Caliber: .380 ACP
Capacity: 6+1 rounds
Features: Trigger cocking DAO; Lock breech; Browning-type recoil lug; passive striker block; no magazine disconnect; black polymer frame, matte stainless steel slide; premium Lothar Walther match grade barrel; eight versions available: with matte stainless slide; with matte stainless slide and night sights; with matte stainless slide and Crimson Trace

built-in trigger guard laser; as the Black Rose model with engraved stainless slide; with matte stainless slide and loaded chamber indicator; with matte stainless slide, loaded chamber indicator, and night sights; with matte black slide; and with matte black slide and night sights
MSRP . . . . **$667.00–$949.00**

PM9 SERIES

Action: Semiautomatic
Grips: Textured polymer
Barrel: 3 in.
Sights: Adjustable
Weight: 15.9 oz.
Caliber: 9mm
Capacity: 6+1 or 7+1 rounds
Features: Trigger cocking DAO; lock breech; Browning-type recoil lug; passive striker block; no magazine disconnect; eight versions available: with matte stainless slide; with matte stainless slide and night sights; with matte stainless slide and Crimson Trace built-in trigger guard laser; as the Black Rose model with engraved stainless slide; with matte stainless slide, external thumb safety, and loaded chamber indicator; with matte stainless slide, loaded chamber indicator, external thumb safety, and night sights; with matte black slide; and with matte black slide and night sights
MSRP . . . . **$810.00–$1049.00**

PM40 SERIES

Action: Semiautomatic
Grips: Textured polymer
Barrel: 3 in.
Sights: Adjustable
Weight: 17.7 oz.
Caliber: .40 S&W
Capacity: 5+1 or 6+1 rounds
Features: Trigger cocking DAO; lock breech; "Browning-type" recoil lug; passive striker block; no magazine disconnect; black polymer frame drift adjustable, white bar-dot combat sights; seven versions available: with matte stainless slide; with matte stainless slide and night sights; with matte stainless slide and Crimson Trace built-in trigger guard laser; with matte black slide; with matte black slide and night sights; external thumb safety, and loaded chamber indicator; with matte stainless slide, loaded chamber indicator, external thumb safety, and night sights
MSRP . . . . **$810.00–$987.00**

PM45 SERIES

Action: Semiautomatic
Grips: Textured polymer
Barrel: 3.24 in.
Sights: Adjustable
Weight: 19.3 oz.
Caliber: .45 ACP
Capacity: 6+1 rounds
Features: Trigger cocking double action; lock breech; Browning-type recoil lug; passive striker block; no magazine disconnect; drift adjustable, white bar-dot combat sights; five versions available: with matte stainless slide; with matte stainless slide and night sights; with matte stainless slide and Crimson Trace built-in trigger guard laser; with matte black slide; and with matte black slide with night sights
MSRP . . . . **$880.00–$1053.00**

KAHR ARMS P45 BLACK WITH NIGHT SIGHTS

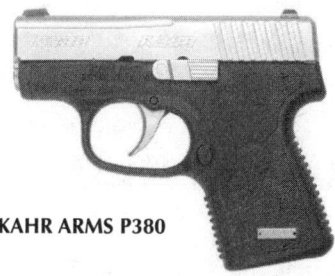

KAHR ARMS P380

KAHR ARMS PM9 SERIES

KAHR ARMS PM40 WITH EXTERNAL SAFETY & LCI

KAHR ARMS PM45

Kel-Tec

KEL-TEC P-11

KEL-TEC PF-9

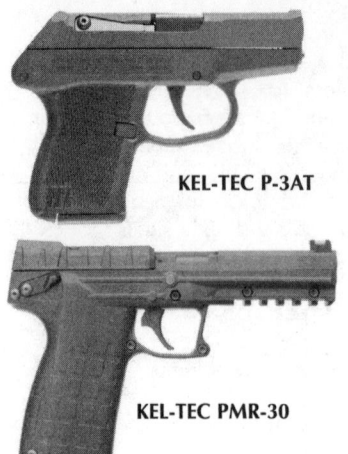

KEL-TEC P-3AT

KEL-TEC PMR-30

KEL-TEC P-32

P-3AT

Action: Semiautomatic
Grips: Polymer
Barrel: 2.7 in.
Sights: Fixed
Weight: 8.3 oz.
Caliber: .380 ACP
Capacity: 6+1 rounds
Features: Double-action only; steel barrel and slide; aluminum frame; transfer bar
MSRP: **$338.18**

P-11

Action: Semiautomatic
Grips: Polymer
Barrel: 3.1 in.
Sights: Fixed
Weight: 14 oz.
Caliber: 9mm

Capacity: 10+1 rounds, optional 12 rounds
Features: Double-action only; steel barrel and slide; aluminum frame; locked breech; high-impact polymer DuPont grips
MSRP: **$347.27**

P-32

Action: Semiautomatic
Grips: Polymer
Barrel: 2.7 in.
Sights: Fixed
Weight: 6.6 oz.
Caliber: .32 ACP
Capacity: 7+1 rounds
Features: Steel barrel and slide; locked breech mechanism
MSRP: **$325.45**

PF-9

Action: Semiautomatic

Grips: Polymer
Barrel: 3.1 in.
Sights: Adjustable
Weight: 12.7 oz.
Caliber: 9mm
Capacity: 7+1 rounds
Features: Firing mechanism is double-action only with an automatic hammer block safety; grips available in black, grey, and olive drab; rear sight is a new design and is adjustable for windage
MSRP: **$356.36**

PMR-30

Action: SA Semiautomatic
Grips: Nylon
Barrel: 4.3 in.
Sights: Picatinny accessory rail under barrel
Weight: 13.6 oz.
Caliber: .22 WMR
Capacity: 30 rounds
Features: Blowback/locked breech system; lightweight but full sized; urethane recoil buffer; disassembles for cleaning with removal of one pin
MSRP: **$454.55**

Kimber

AMETHYST ULTRA II

Action: Semiautomatic
Grips: Micarta thin grips
Barrel: 3 in.
Sights: Fixed titrium night sights
Weight: 25 oz.
Caliber: .45 ACP, 9mm
Capacity: 7 or 8 rounds
Features: Ambidextrous thumb safety; full-length guide rod; amethyst purple PVD coating on small parts and fine engraving; front strap serrations and checkering; ramped barrel; tactical wedge titrium night sights; purple ball-milled Micarta thin grips
MSRP. **$1652.00**

CUSTOM II (TWO-TONE II)

Action: Semiautomatic
Grips: Smooth/checkered rosewood
Barrel: 5 in.
Sights: Fixed, low profile
Weight: 38 oz.
Caliber: .45 ACP, 9mm
Capacity: 7 or 9 rounds
Features: Brushed polished carbon slide; stainless frame; full-length guide rod; sainless steel match-grade barrel
MSRP. **$837.00**

KIMBER AMETHYST ULTRA II

KIMBER CUSTOM II (TWO-TONE II)

Kimber

KIMBER CLASSIC CARRY PRO

KIMBER CUSTOM TLE/ RL II (TFS)

KIMBER GOLD MATCH II

KIMBER GOLD MATCH II

KIMBER MASTER CARRY PRO

KIMBER MICRO 9

KIMBER MICRO CARRY

CLASSIC CARRY PRO

Action: SA semiautomatic
Grips: Solid ivory G10
Barrel: 4 in.
Sights: Fixed low-profile, 3-dot
Weight: 35 oz.
Caliber: .45 ACP
Capacity: 8 rounds
Features: Deep charcoal blued finish; steel frame and slide; match grade bull barrel; serrated flat top slide; night sights; front strap checkering
MSRP **$1785.00**

CUSTOM TLE/RL II (TFS)

Action: Semiautomatic
Grips: G10
Barrel: 5 in.
Sights: Fixed
Weight: 39 oz.
Caliber: .45 ACP, 9mm
Capacity: 7 rounds
Features: Threaded for suppression; Meprolight Tritium 3-dot night sight; Picatinny rail
.45 ACP: **$1175.00**
9mm: **$1195.00**

GOLD MATCH II

Action: Semiautomatic
Grips: Rosewood double diamond

Barrel: 5 in.
Sights: Kimber adjustable
Weight: 38 oz.
Caliber: .45 ACP
Capacity: 8 rounds
Features: Premium aluminum, match grade trigger; full length guide rod; steel frame with highly polished blued finish; stainless steel, match grade barrel
MSRP **$1264.00**

K6S STAINLESS

Action: DAO
Grips: Rubber
Barrel: 2 in.
Sights: Low-profile removable dovetail sights
Weight: 23 oz.
Caliber: .357 Mag.
Capacity: 6 rounds
Features: Stainless steel barrel; low-profile removable front and rear dovetail sights; smooth no-stack double action trigger; superior ergonomic grip contour; serrated backstrap
MSRP **$899.00**

MASTER CARRY PRO

Action: Semiautomatic
Grips: Crimson Trace Lasergrips
Barrel: 3in. (Ultra), 5 in.
Sights: Fixed low profile
Weight: 25 oz.–31 oz.
Caliber: .45 ACP, 9mm
Capacity: 7 or 8 rounds

Features: Aluminum, round-heel frame; satin silver finish; dovetailed night sights; recessed slide-stop pin; serrated mainspring housing; stainless steel slide
.45 ACP: **$1477.00**
9mm: **$1497.00**

MICRO 9

Action: Semiautomatic
Grips: Rosewood
Barrel: 3.15 in.
Sights: Fixed
Weight: 15.6 oz.
Caliber: 9mm
Capacity: 6 rounds
Features: Mild recoil; smooth trigger pull; two-tone slide and frame; single action trigger; small-scale 1911 ergonomics and all-metal construction
Stainless: **$654.00**
Two-Tone: **$654.00**
Crimson Carry: **$894.00**

MICRO CARRY

Action: Semiautomatic
Grips: G10, rosewood, zebrawood
Barrel: 2.75 in.
Sights: Fixed low profile
Weight: 13.4 oz.
Caliber: .380 ACP
Capacity: 6 rounds
Features: Multiple versions: Two-Tone with blued slide, stainless frame; DC, all-blue model with night sights and choice of G10 or Crimson Trace laser grips; CDP with stainless slide, blued

HANDGUNS

Kimber

KIMBER MICRO DC

KIMBER MICRO RCP

KIMBER MICRO STAINLESS ROSEWOOD

KIMBER PRO CARRY HD II (STAINLESS II)

KIMBER SAPPHIRE ULTRA II

KIMBER PRO RAPTOR II

frame and choice of rosewood double diamond grips or rosewood Crimson Trace laser grips; Raptor in all blue or all stainless with scaled scalloping on grips, slide, and mainspring housing, night sights, and zebrawood grips; RCP, in all blue with rosewood grips or rosewood Crimson Trace laser grips; Crimson Carry, with blue slide, stainless frame, and rosewood Crimson Trace laser grips; Stainless Rosewood with satin silver slide, stainless frame, and half smooth/half checkered rosewood grips; Advocate, with blue slides, stainless frames, night sights, extended seven-round mags, and choice of brown/black or purple/black G10 grips; Desert Night with black slide, tan frame, and tan/black G10 grips; 2017 special editions include two stainless frame versions with choice of Amethyst or Sapphire PVD-finished slides (also with engraving), and matchng ball-milled G10 grips, and the Bel Air version with a Bel Air Blue frame, mirror-polished stainless slide, and smooth ivory Micarta grips

Two-Tone:	$597.00
DC:	$877.00–$1095.00
CDP:	$869.00–$1087.00
Raptor:	$815.00–$842.00
RCP:	$775.00–$993.00
Crimson Carry:	$839.00
Stainless Rosewood:	$597.00
Advocate:	$714.00
Desert Night:	$626.00
Special Edition Amethyst:	$1013.00
Special Edition Sapphire:	$1014.00
Special Edition Bel Air:	$802.00

MICRO DC

Action: Semiautomatic
Grips: G10 grips
Barrel: 2.75 in.
Sights: Titrium night sights
Weight: 13.4 oz.
Caliber: .380 ACP
Capacity: 7 rounds
Features: Mild recoil; smooth trigger pull; ambidextrous thumb safety; full-length guide rod; ramped barrel; aggressively textured G10 grips; LG comes with crimson trace lasergrips

MSRP	$877.00
LG:	$1095.00

MICRO RCP

Action: Semiautomatic
Grips: Rosewood
Barrel: 2.75 in.
Sights: None
Weight: 13.4 oz.
Caliber: .380 ACP
Capacity: 6 rounds
Features: Mild recoil; smooth trigger pulls; Carry Melt treatment; ambidextrous thumb safety; full-length guide rod; front strap checkering; ramped barrel; LG comes with crimson trace lasergrips

MSRP	$775.00
LG:	$993.00

MICRO STAINLESS ROSEWOOD

Action: Semiautomatic
Grips: Rosewood
Barrel: 2.75 in.
Sights: Fixed

Weight: 13.4 oz.
Caliber: .380 ACP
Capacity: 6 rounds
Features: Mild recoil; smooth trigger pulls; full-length guide rod; aluminum frame with anodized finish; ramped barrel

MSRP	$597.00

PRO CARRY HD II (STAINLESS II)

Action: Semiautomatic
Grips: Synthetic
Barrel: 4 in.
Sights: Fixed, low profile
Weight: 35 oz.
Caliber: .38 Super, .45 ACP
Capacity: 7 rounds
Features: Aluminum frame with satin silver finish; stainless stell slide; steel match-grade barrel; double-diamond textured grips

.38 Super:	$1094.00
.45 ACP:	$1046.00

PRO RAPTOR II

Action: SA semiautomatic
Grips: Zebra wood, scale pattern
Barrel: 4 in.
Sights: Tactical wedge 3-dot
Weight: 35 oz.
Caliber: .45 ACP
Capacity: 8 rounds
Features: Available in all stainless or all blue; match grade barrel; ambidextrous thumb safety; full-length guide rod

Blue:	$1192.00
Stainless:	$1293.00

SAPPHIRE ULTRA II

Action: SA semiautomatic
Grips: G-10 thin grips
Barrel: 3 in.
Sights: Tactical Wedge night sights
Weight: 25 oz.
Caliber: 9mm
Capacity: 8 rounds
Features: Highly-polished stainless steel slide and small parts are finished with bright blue PVD finish accented with fine engraving; blue/black ball-milled G-10 thin grips and short trigger; ambidextrous thumb safety; Tactical Wedge night sights

MSRP	$1652.00

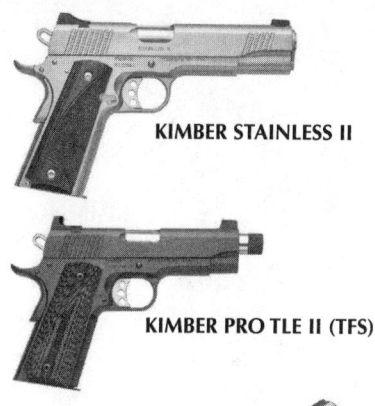

KIMBER STAINLESS II

KIMBER PRO TLE II (TFS)

KIMBER SUPER CARRY PRO

KIMBER STAINLESS GOLD MATCH II

KIMBER STAINLESS ULTRA TLE II

KIMBER TACTICAL ENTRY II

KIMBER STAINLESS PRO TLE II

KIMBER SUPER MATCH II

STAINLESS II

Action: Semiautomatic
Grips: Synthetic
Barrel: 5 in.
Sights: Fixed, low profile
Weight: 38 oz.
Caliber: .45 ACP, 9mm
Capacity: 7 or 9 rounds
Features: Aluminum frame with satin silver finish; stainless stell slide; steel match-grade barrel; double-diamond textured grips
.45 ACP:.................$891.00
9mm:..................$912.00

STAINLESS GOLD MATCH II

Action: Semiautomatic
Grips: Rosewood
Barrel: 5 in.
Sights: Adjustable
Weight: 38 oz.
Caliber: .45 ACP
Capacity: 8 rounds
Features: Ambidextrous thumb safety; full-length guide rod; stainless steel frame with satin silver finish; stainless steel match-grade barrel
MSRP.................$1445.00

STAINLESS PRO TLE II

Action: SA semiautomatic
Grips: Tactical gray double diamond
Barrel: 4 in.
Sights: Meprolight tritium 3-dot night, fixed
Weight: 35 oz.
Caliber: .45 ACP

Capacity: 7 rounds
Features: Full-length guide rod; stainless steel frame with satin silver; Match Grade steel barrel; aluminum Match Grade trigger
MSRP.................$1232.00

PRO TLE II (TFS)

Action: Semiautomatic
Grips: G10 grips
Barrel: 4.5 in.
Sights: Fixed titrium three dot
Weight: 35 oz.
Caliber: .45 ACP, 9mm
Capacity: 7 rounds
Features: Full-length guide rod; front strap checkering; stainless steel match-grade barrel; barrel threaded for suppression; Meprolight tritium 3-dot night sight; textured G10 grips
.45 ACP:...............$1175.00
9mm:.................$1195.00

STAINLESS ULTRA TLE II

Action: SA semiautomatic
Grips: Tactical gray double diamond
Barrel: 3 in.
Sights: Meprolight tritium 3-dot night, fixed
Weight: 25 oz.
Caliber: .45 ACP
Capacity: 7 rounds
Features: Full-length guide rod; front strap checkering; aluminum frame with satin silver finish; steel match grade barrel; aluminum match grade trigger
MSRP.................$1136.00

SUPER MATCH II

Action: Semiautomatic
Grips: Walnut
Barrel: 5 in.
Sights: Adjustable
Weight: 38 oz.
Caliber: .45 ACP
Capacity: 8 rounds
Features: Ambidextrous thumb safety; full-length guide rod; stainless steel frame with satin silver finish; front strap checkering and checkering under trigger guard
MSRP.................$2613.00

SUPER CARRY PRO

Action: SA SA semiautomatic
Grips: Micarta/ laminated rosewood
Barrel: 4 in.
Sights: Night, tritium
Weight: 28 oz.
Caliber: .45 ACP
Capacity: 8 rounds
Features: Ambidextrous thumb safety; carry melt; full-length guide rod; aluminum frame in satin silver; super carry serrations; high cut under trigger guard; steel match grade barrel; aluminum match grade trigger
MSRP.................$1596.00

TACTICAL ENTRY II

Action: SA semiautomatic
Grips: Laminated double diamond, Kimber logo
Barrel: 5 in.
Sights: Meprolight tritium 3-dot night, fixed
Weight: 40 oz.
Caliber: .45 ACP
Capacity: 7 rounds
Features: Ambidextrous thumb safety; full-length guide rod; stainless steel frame and slide; matte gray Kim Pro II frame finish
MSRP.................$1490.00

Kimber

KIMBER ULTRA CARRY II

KIMBER ULTRA CDP

KIMBER ULTRA CRIMSON CARRY II

KIMBER WARRIOR SOC

ULTRA CARRY II
Action: SA semiautomatic
Grips: Black synthetic double diamond
Barrel: 3 in.
Sights: Fixed, low profile
Weight: 25 oz.
Caliber: .45 ACP
Capacity: 7 rounds
Features: Black matte finish; aluminum frame; steel slide; full-length guide rod
MSRP $837.00

ULTRA CDP
Action: Semiautomatic
Grips: Rosewood double diamond
Barrel: 3 in.
Sights: Meprolight tritium 3-dot night, fixed
Weight: 25 oz.
Caliber: .45 ACP
Capacity: 7 rounds
Features: Ambidextrous thumb safety, Carry Melt treatment, aluminum frame with charcoal gray KimPro II finish, stainless slide is flat-topped with satin silver finish
MSRP $1173.00

ULTRA CRIMSON CARRY II
Action: SA semiautomatic
Grips: Rosewood double diamond, Crimson Trace lasergrips
Barrel: 3 in.
Sights: Fixed low profile
Weight: 25 oz.
Caliber: .45 ACP
Capacity: 7 rounds

Features: Full-length guide rod; aluminum frame in satin silver finish; steel match grade barrel; aluminum match grade trigger
MSRP $1180.00

WARRIOR SOC
Action: Semiautomatic
Grips: Kimber G10
Barrel: 5 in.
Sights: Fixed tactical wedge tritium night sights, desert tan Crimson Trace Rail Master laser sight
Weight: 39 oz.
Caliber: .45 ACP
Capacity: 7 rounds
Features: Steel frame; front and rear slide serrations; Picatinny rail; ambidextrous thumb safety; checkered front strap; stainless steel barrel and bushing; beavertail grip; KimPro II dark green finish
MSRP $1533.00

Kriss USA

SPHINX SDP COMPACT ALPHA, ALPHA WOLF, SAND, KRYPTON, COMBAT GREY
Action: DA/SA semiautomatic
Grips: Composite
Barrel: 3.7 in., 4.35 in.
Sights: Fiber optic/tritium front, tritium rear
Weight: 27.5 oz.
Caliber: 9mm
Capacity: 15+1 rounds
Features: Upper frame machined from aeronautic-grade hard-anodized aluminum; integral recoil buffer; Picatinny rail; polymer lower frame; interchangeable grip sizes available; Defiance sights feature fiber optic/tritium day-night green front sight with tritium two-dot red rear sight; internal firing pin safety, drop safety, hammer safety, and integrated slide-position safety; all models listed in this entry have Cerakote finish
Alpha, Alpha Wolfe: $949.00–$999.00
Sand, Krypton: . . $1049.00–$1099.00
Combat Grey: . . .$1049.00–$1119.00

KRISS USA SPHINX SDP COMPACT ALPHA

SPHINX SDP COMPACT BLACK

Action: DA/SA semiautomatic
Grips: Synthetic
Barrel: 3.7 in., 4.35 in.
Sights: Fixed
Weight: 29.27 oz.
Caliber: 9mm
Capacity: 10+1 or 15+1 rounds
Features: Hard anodized aluminum frame; Picatinny rail; ambidextrous decocking lever and magazine release; threaded barrel available
MSRP. . . . . **$999.00–$1049.00**

**KRISS USA SPHINX SDP
COMPACT BLACK**

Les Baer Custom

1911 BLACK BAER 9MM

Action: SA
Grips: Black recon
Barrel: 4.25 in.
Sights: Fixed rear combat night sight, dovetail front night sight
Weight: N/A
Caliber: 9mm
Capacity: 9 rounds
Features: Compact size suitable for comfortable concealed carry; slide fitted to frame; rear serrated slide; speed trigger with crisp 4 lb. pull; tactical extended combat safety; Dupont S coating on complete pistol for maximum corrosion resistance
MSRP. **$2895.00**

**LES BAER 1911 BLACK
BAER 9MM**

Magnum Research

BABY DESERT EAGLE III SERIES

Action: Semiautomatic
Grips: Rubber
Barrel: 3.85 in., 4.43 in.
Sights: Fixed
Weight: 25 oz.–37.9 oz.
Caliber: 9mm, .40 S&W, .45 ACP
Capacity: 10 or 13 Rounds
Features: Polymer or steel frame; available in full size or semi-compact; Weaver rail; double action/single action; ambidextrous, slide-mounted safety and decocker; three dot combat sights
Polymer: **$646.00**
Steel: **$691.00**

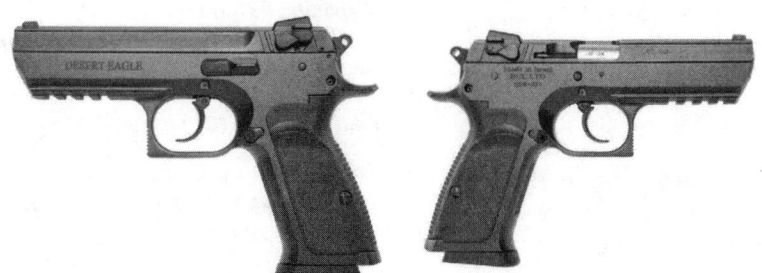

**MAGNUM RESEARCH BABY DESERT
EAGLE III SERIES**

Magnum Research

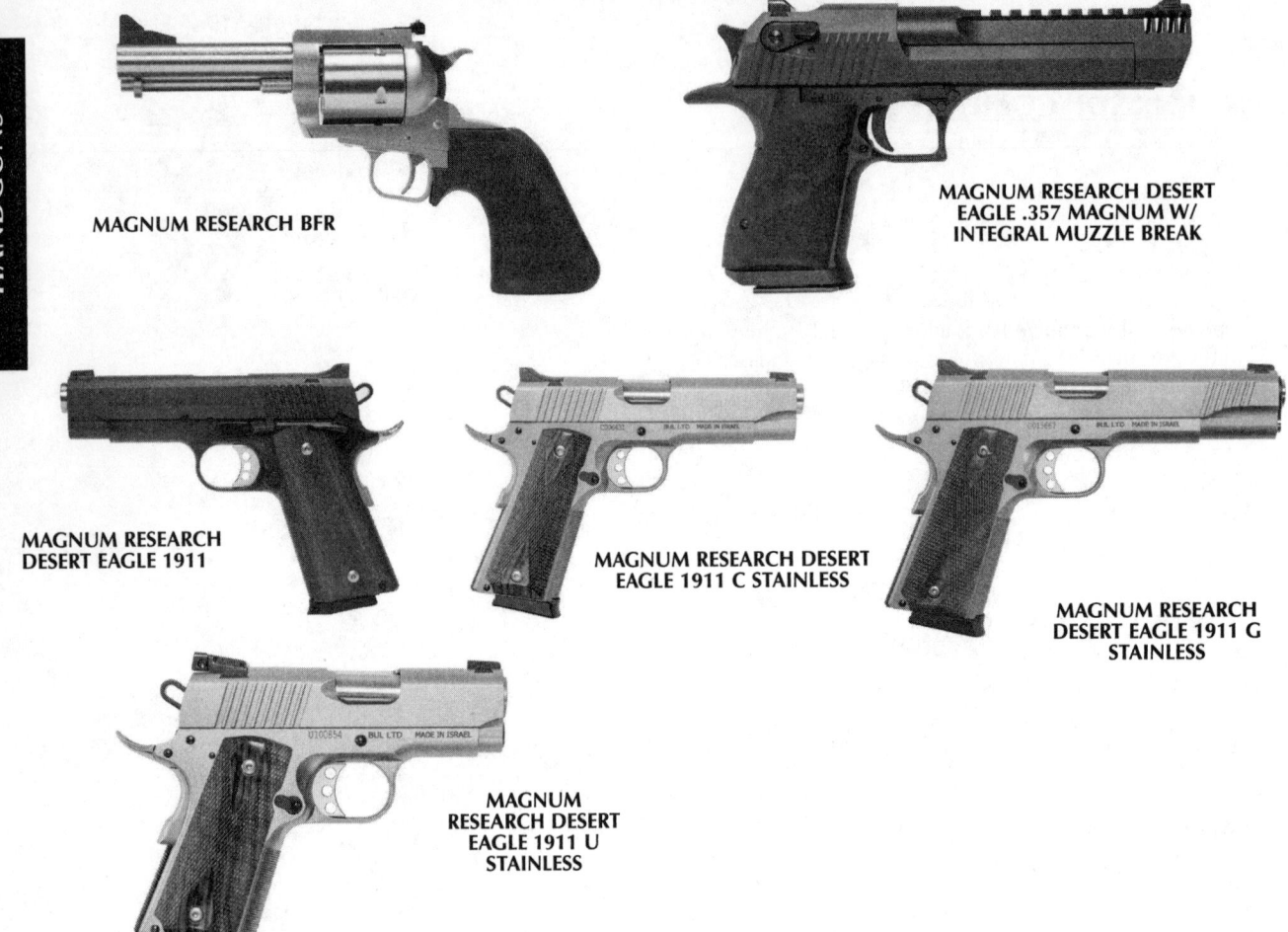

MAGNUM RESEARCH BFR

MAGNUM RESEARCH DESERT EAGLE .357 MAGNUM W/ INTEGRAL MUZZLE BREAK

MAGNUM RESEARCH DESERT EAGLE 1911

MAGNUM RESEARCH DESERT EAGLE 1911 C STAINLESS

MAGNUM RESEARCH DESERT EAGLE 1911 G STAINLESS

MAGNUM RESEARCH DESERT EAGLE 1911 U STAINLESS

BFR (BIG FRAME REVOLVER)

Action: SA revolver
Grips: Rubber, optional wood
Barrel: 5 in., 6.5 in., 7.5 in., 10 in.
Sights: Adjustable rear, fixed front
Weight: 57.6–85 oz.
Caliber: Long Cylinder: .30-30 Win., .444 Marlin, .45 LC/.410, .45-70 Govt., .450 Marlin, .44 Mag., .460 S&W Mag., .500 S&W Mag.; Short Cylinder: .22 Hornet, .454 Casull, .480 Ruger/.475 Linebaugh, .50AE, .500 JRH
Capacity: 5 rounds
Features: Both long and short-cylinder models are made of stainless steel; barrels are stress-relieved and cut rifled; current production revolvers are shipped with rubber grips and Weaver style scope mount
MSRP. **$1184.00**

DESERT EAGLE .357 MAGNUM W/ INTEGRAL MUZZLE BREAK

Action: Semiautomatic
Grips: Rubber
Barrel: 6 in.
Sights: Fixed
Weight: 4 lb. 8.8 oz.
Caliber: .357 Mag.
Capacity: 9 rounds
Features: High quality carbon steel barrel, frame and slide w/ full Weaver style accessory rail and integral muzzle brake; gas-operated, rotating bolt semiautomatic; fixed combat sights
MSRP. **$1710.00**

DESERT EAGLE 1911 SERIES

Action: SA semiautomatic
Grips: Checkered wood
Barrel: 3 in., 5 in., 4.3 in.
Sights: Fixed
Weight: 36 oz. (5 in. barrel), 32 oz. (4.3 in. barrel), 25.8 oz. (3-in. barrel)
Caliber: .45 ACP
Capacity: 6, 8 rounds
Features: Seven variants comprise this series: C has 4.33-in. barrel, allover stainless or blue finish; G has 5.05-in. barrel, allover stainless or blue finish; U Stainless has a 3-in. barrel, allover stainless or blue finish; GR is in allover blue only, with 5.05-in barrel, and accessory rail
MSRP. . . . .**$831.00–$1091.00**

Magnum Research

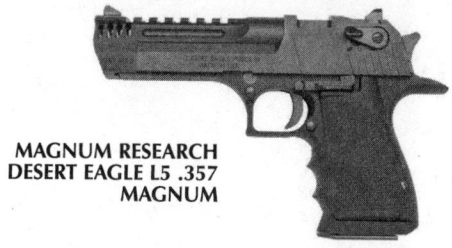

MAGNUM RESEARCH DESERT EAGLE L5 .357 MAGNUM

MAGNUM RESEARCH DESERT EAGLE TUNGSTEN

MAGNUM RESEARCH MARK XIX DESERT EAGLE

MAGNUM RESEARCH MR EAGLE

DESERT EAGLE L5 .357 MAGNUM

Action: SA semiautomatic
Grips: Plastic composite
Barrel: 5 in.
Sights: Fixed combat
Weight: 2 lb. 9 oz.
Caliber: .357 Magnum
Capacity: 9 rounds
Features: Black aluminum frame; black slide/barrel with integral muzzle brake and full Weaver-style accessory rail
MSRP $1790.00

DESERT EAGLE TUNGSTEN

Action: SA semiautomatic
Grips: Plastic composite
Barrel: 6 in.
Sights: Fixed combat
Weight: 4 lb. 6.6 oz.
Caliber: .44 Magnum, .50 A.E.
Capacity: 8 rounds

Features: Tungsten Cerakote finish; high-quality carbon steel barrel; frame and slide with full Weaver-style accessory rail
MSRP $1712.00

DESERT EAGLE 1911USS

Action: Semiautomatic
Grips: Wood
Barrel: 3 in.
Sights: Adjustable rear
Weight: 25.8 oz.
Caliber: .45 ACP
Capacity: 6 rounds
Features: Ships with two eight round magazines; skeletonized hammer; extended magazine release; extended thumb safety; checkered, flat mainspring housing made from aluminum; stainless steel full-length guide rod; bushingless barrel
MSRP $1019.00

MARK XIX DESERT EAGLE

Action: Semiautomatic
Grips: Plastic composite
Barrel: 6 in., 10 in.
Sights: Fixed combat
Weight: 62.4–71.4 oz.
Caliber: .357 Mag., .44 Mag., .50AE
Capacity: 7, 8, 9 rounds
Features: Gas operated; polygonal rifling; integral scope bases; many finishes available, including: black oxide, brushed/matte/polished chrome, bright/satin nickel, 24K gold, titanium gold, and titanium gold with tiger stripes
MSRP . . . . $1710.00–$2195.00

MR40 EAGLE, MR9 EAGLE

Action: Semiautomatic
Grips: Black polymer
Barrel: 4 in. (9mm), 4.15 in. (.40 S&W)
Sights: Adjustable rear, fixed front
Weight: 24.8 oz. (9mm), 26.4 oz. (.40 S&W)
Caliber: 9mm or .40 S&W
Capacity: 10, 15 rounds (9mm), 10, 11 rounds (.40 S&W)
Features: 6-groove filing; hammer forged barrel; full Picatinny rail; ergonomic polymer grip frame; four separate safety devices
MSRP $559.00

MG Arms

MG ARMS WRAITHE

WRAITHE

Action: Semiautomatic
Grips: Custom G10
Barrel: 4.5 in.
Sights: Night or fixed
Weight: 18 oz.–20 oz.
Caliber: .45 ACP, 9mm
Capacity: 8+1, 9+1 rounds
Features: Aluminum alloy bobtail frame; custom grip panels; high ride beavertail safety; two Wilson magazines included, available in olive drab, black or desert tan
MSRP $2895.00

Mossberg (O.F. Mossberg & Sons)

MOSSBERG 715P

715P

Action: Semiautomatic
Grips: Synthetic
Barrel: 6 in.
Sights: Adjustable
Weight: 48 oz.–56 oz.
Caliber: .22 LR
Capacity: 26 rounds
Features: Muzzle brake; adjustable front and rear sights; blued finish; available with red dot sight
Standard sights:. $314.00
Red-dot sight: $359.00

Nighthawk Custom

NIGHTHAWK CUSTOM BOB MARVEL CUSTOM

NIGHTHAWK CUSTOM BROWNING HI-POWER

NIGHTHAWK CUSTOM GA PRECISION

BOB MARVEL CUSTOM

Action: Semiautomatic
Grips: Custom Mil Tac
Barrel: 4.25 in.
Sights: Novak tritium night sight front, tritium adjustable rear
Weight: 38 oz.
Caliber: 9mm, .45 ACP
Capacity: 8+1 rounds
Features: Incorporates new Nighthawk/Marvel Everlast Recoil System allowing for at least 10,000 rounds before a spring change is necessary and reduced recoil and muzzle flip
MSRP. $4295.00

BROWNING HI-POWER

Action: Semiautomatic
Grips: Checkered cocobolo
Barrel: 4.625 in.
Sights: Heinie Slant pro black rear, gold bead front
Weight: 29.65 oz.
Caliber: 9mm
Capacity: 13 rounds
Features: Custom extended beavertail; competition steel hammer, improved sear lever, and trigger job; Cerakote satin rust-resistant finish
MSRP. $3195.00

GA PRECISION

Action: Semiautomatic
Grips: Checkered G10 grips
Barrel: 5 in.
Sights: Night sights
Weight: 38.92 oz.
Caliber: .45 ACP
Capacity: 8 rounds
Features: Fitted and hand-lapped frame and slide; skeletonized aluminum trigger with an adjustable overtravel stop; extended magazine release; single-sided extended safety; precisely fitted beavertail grip safety with a speed bump
MSRP. $3695.00

Nighthawk Custom

NIGHTHAWK CUSTOM GLOBAL RESPONSE PISTOL

NIGHTHAWK CUSTOM PREDATOR T5

NIGHTHAWK CUSTOM HEINIE SIGNATURE RECON

NIGHTHAWK CUSTOM SILENT HAWK SUPPRESSOR READY

NIGHTHAWK CUSTOM HEINIE KESTREL

NIGHTHAWK CUSTOM T3

GLOBAL RESPONSE PISTOL (GRP)

Action: SA Semiautomatic
Grips: Micarta gator grips
Barrel: 5 in.
Sights: Night
Weight: 39 oz.
Caliber: .45 ACP
Capacity: 8 rounds
Features: 1911 design; Lanyard loop integrated into the mainspring housing; forged slide stop axle is cut flush with the frame; Heinie Slant-Pro Night Sights, Novak Low Mount Night Sights, or Novak Extreme Duty Adjustable Night Sights are standard; Perma Kote finish in black, sniper gray, green, coyote tan, titanium blued, and hard chrome
MSRP $2995.00

HEINIE SIGNATURE

Action: Semiautomatic
Grips: Thin proprietary G10
Barrel: 4.25 in., 5 in.
Sights: Tritium front night sight, Heinie Slant-Pro Rear
Weight: 38 oz.–40 oz.
Caliber: 9mm, .45 ACP
Capacity: 7+1 or 8+1 rounds
Features: Features a proprietary thinned frame and mainspring housing that are scalloped to provide a positive grip without the abrasion felt from checkering; new G10 pattern grips are thinned to make concealed carry even easier, and feature a relieved area on the side to allow easy access to the magazine release
Compact: $3695.00
Signature Competition
5-in.: $3695.00
Recon: $3795.00

KESTREL

Action: Semiautomatic
Grips: Ultra-Thin Alumagrips
Barrel: 4.25 in.
Sights: Heinie Slant pro straight eight night sights
Weight: 34.25 oz.
Caliber: .45 ACP, 9mm
Capacity: 7-10 rounds
Features: Reduced overall frame circumference; magazine well beveled for insertion; hand serrated rear of slide; Heinie Signature scalloped front strap and mainspring housing; tactical checkered extended magazine release; standard black nitride finish with stainless controls and optional stainless steel upgrade
MSRP $3695.00

PREDATOR T5

Action: Semitautomatic
Grips: Synthetic
Barrel: 5 in.
Sights: Fixed
Weight: 40.3 oz.
Caliber: 9mm, 10mm, .45 ACP
Capacity: N/A
Features: Stainless steel frame standard; black nitride finish; Nighthawk two-piece magwell; tritium dot front sight; Heinie Slant Pro Straight Eight Tritium rear sight; single-side safety; thinned cocobolo with double diamond checkering
MSRP $3795.00

SILENT HAWK SUPPRESSOR READY

Action: Semiautomatic
Grips: G10 grips
Barrel: 4.25 in.
Sights: Tritium tall suppressor night sights
Weight: 36.91 oz.

Caliber: 9mm
Capacity: 8 rounds
Features: Commander Recon frame and Commander slide; custom checkering on front strap of frame; one piece mainspring housing and magwell; hand serrated rear of the slide; custom slide cocking serrations to match osprey silencer; thick barrel bushing and matching smooth spring plug; nitride black out finish; G10 black and gray spiral cut grips with mag release cut-out
MSRP $4295.00

T3, T3 THIN

Action: SA semiautomatic
Grips: G10 grips
Barrel: 4.25 in.
Sights: Heinie Straight Eight Slant-Pro, night
Weight: 40 oz.
Caliber: .45 ACP, 9mm
Capacity: 7 rounds
Features: Frame based on Officer model; extended magazine well; Heinie Slant-Pro Straight Eights Night Sights are standard; mainspring housing and rear of slide are horizontally serrated to match; top of slide serrated to reduce glare; Nighthawk Custom lightweight aluminum trigger that has been blacked-out using Perma Kote; available in black, gun metal grey, green coyote tan, titanium blued, and hard chrome Perma Kote or stainless steel model; T3 Thin model appears in two-tone with a blued slide and stainless frame, has reduced grip circumference with a thinned front strap, flat mainspring housing, and thin alien grips
Blue: $3450.00
Stainless: $3650.00
Thin: $3650.00

Nighthawk Custom

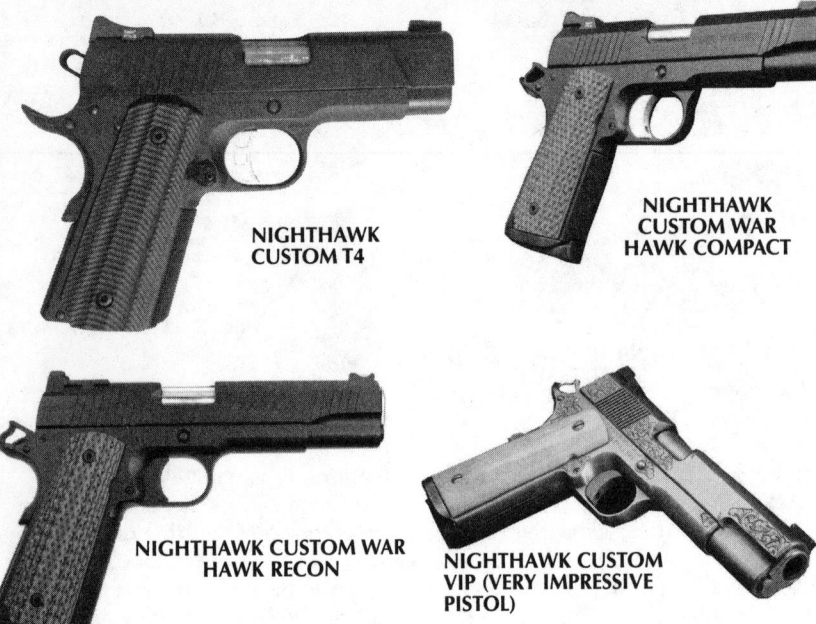

NIGHTHAWK CUSTOM T4

NIGHTHAWK CUSTOM WAR HAWK COMPACT

NIGHTHAWK CUSTOM WAR HAWK GOVERNMENT

NIGHTHAWK CUSTOM WAR HAWK RECON

NIGHTHAWK CUSTOM VIP (VERY IMPRESSIVE PISTOL)

T4
Action: Semiautomatic
Grips: Slim
Barrel: 3.8 in.
Sights: Fixed
Weight: 34.3 oz.
Caliber: 9mm
Capacity: 9 or 10 rounds
Features: Thinned aluminum frame and mainspring housing
MSRP **$3495.00**

WAR HAWK COMPACT
Action: Semiautomatic
Grips: Synthetic
Barrel: 4.25 in.
Sights: Fixed
Weight: 34.7 oz.
Caliber: 9mm, .45 ACP
Capacity: N/A
Features: Unique tri-cut slide with bold angles; serrated arrow style slide top; heavy bevel on bottom of slide; hand serrated rear of slide; barrel is crowned and beveled with the bushing; one-piece fully machined 20 LPI checkered mainspring housing/magwell; high-cut front strap; hightweight solid aluminum match grade trigger; thin G10 in hyena brown; Heinie Slant Pro Straight Eight Tritium night sights; Nighthawk Custom/Marvel EVERLAST recoil system; War Hawk logo engraved on slide; stainless steel frame standard; black nitride finish
MSRP **$3995.00**

WAR HAWK GOVERNMENT
Action: Semiautomatic
Grips: Synthetic
Barrel: 5 in.
Sights: Fixed
Weight: 39.6 oz.
Caliber: 9mm, .45 ACP
Capacity: N/A
Features: Unique multi-faceted slide; serrated arrow style slide top; heavy bevel on bottom of slide; hand serrated rear of slide; barrel is crowned and beveled with the bushing; one-piece fully machined 20 LPI checkered mainspring housing/magwell; high-cut front strap; lightweight aluminum medium solid match trigger; aggressive G10 hyena brown grips; red fiber optic front sights; Tritium dot front sight upgrade available; Jardine Hook rear sight; tactical magazine catch; Nighthawk Custom/Marvel EVERLAST recoil system; War Hawk logo engraved on slide
MSRP **$3995.00**

WAR HAWK RECON
Action: Semiautomatic
Grips: Synthetic
Barrel: 5 in.
Sights: Fixed
Weight: 39.6 oz.
Caliber: 9mm, .45 ACP
Capacity: N/A
Features: Integrated recon accessory rail; unique multi-faceted slide; serrated arrow style slide top; heavy bevel on bottom of slide; hand serrated rear of slide; barrel is crowned and beveled with the bushing; one-piece fully machined 20 LPI checkered mainspring housing/magwell; high cut front strap; lightweight aluminum medium solid match trigger; aggressive G10 hyena brown grips; red fiber optic front sight; Tritium dot front sight upgrade available; Jardine rear hook sight; extended tactical mag catch; Nighthawk Custom/Marvel EVERLAST recoil system; War Hawk logo engraved on slide
MSRP **$4095.00**

VIP (VERY IMPRESSIVE PISTOL)
Action: Semiautomatic
Grips: Giraffe bone
Barrel: 5 in.
Sights: Heinie black rear, 14k gold bead front
Weight: 39.78 oz.
Caliber: .45 ACP
Capacity: 8 rounds
Features: Custom vertical front strap and mainspring serrations; 14k plated gold bead front sight and crowned barrel; deep hand engraving featured throughout; antiqued nickel finish; custom cocobolo hardwood presentation case
MSRP **$7995.00**

North American Arms

NORTH AMERICAN ARMS .32 ACP GUARDIAN

.32 ACP GUARDIAN

Action: DAO semiautomatic
Grips: Polymer
Barrel: 2.5 in.
Sights: Fixed, open
Weight: 13.5 oz.
Caliber: .32 ACP
Capacity: 6+1 rounds
Features: Stainless steel; double action only; integral locking system safety; also available in .25 caliber
MSRP **$409.00**

.380 ACP GUARDIAN

Action: DAO semiautomatic
Grips: Composite
Barrel: 2.49 in.
Sights: Fixed, open
Weight: 18.72 oz.
Caliber: .380 ACP
Capacity: 6+1 rounds

Features: Stainless steel; double action only; integral locking system safety
MSRP **$456.00**

1860 EARL

Action: SA revolver
Grips: Rosewood
Barrel: 6 in.
Sights: Stainless steel post front sight
Weight: 9.7 oz.
Caliber: .22 Mag.
Capacity: 5 rounds
Features: Replica of 1860s Hogleg, with faux loading lever and pin, octagonal barrel, rosewood grips; available with .22 LR conversion cylinder
Standard: **$308.00**
With conversion cylinder: .$344.00

NORTH AMERICAN ARMS .380 ACP GUARDIAN

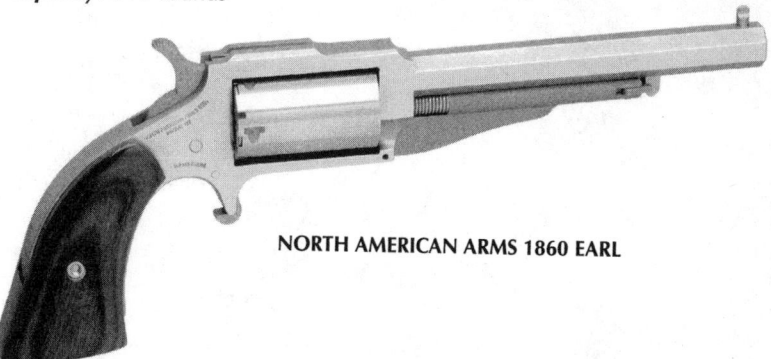

NORTH AMERICAN ARMS 1860 EARL

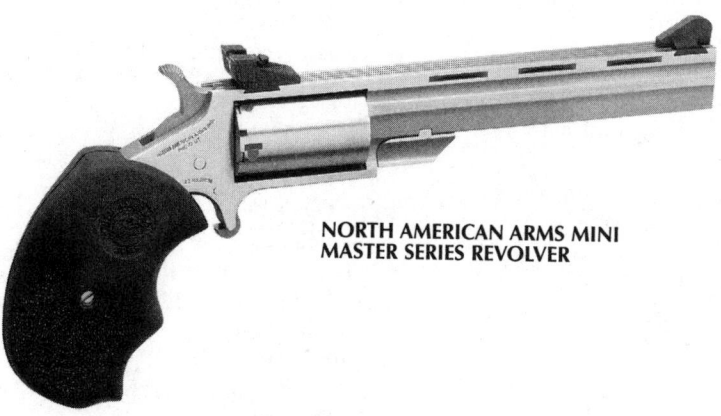

NORTH AMERICAN ARMS MINI MASTER SERIES REVOLVER

MINI MASTER SERIES REVOLVER

Action: SA revolver
Grips: Rubber
Barrel: 4 in.
Sights: Fixed or adjustable
Weight: 10.7 oz.
Caliber: .22 LR, .22 Mag.
Capacity: 5 rounds
Features: Conversion cylinder or adjustable sights available
Fixed sights: **$298.00**
W/ conversion cylinder: . . . **$332.00**
W/ adjustable sights: **$328.00**
W/ conversion and
  adjustable sights: **$363.00**

North American Arms

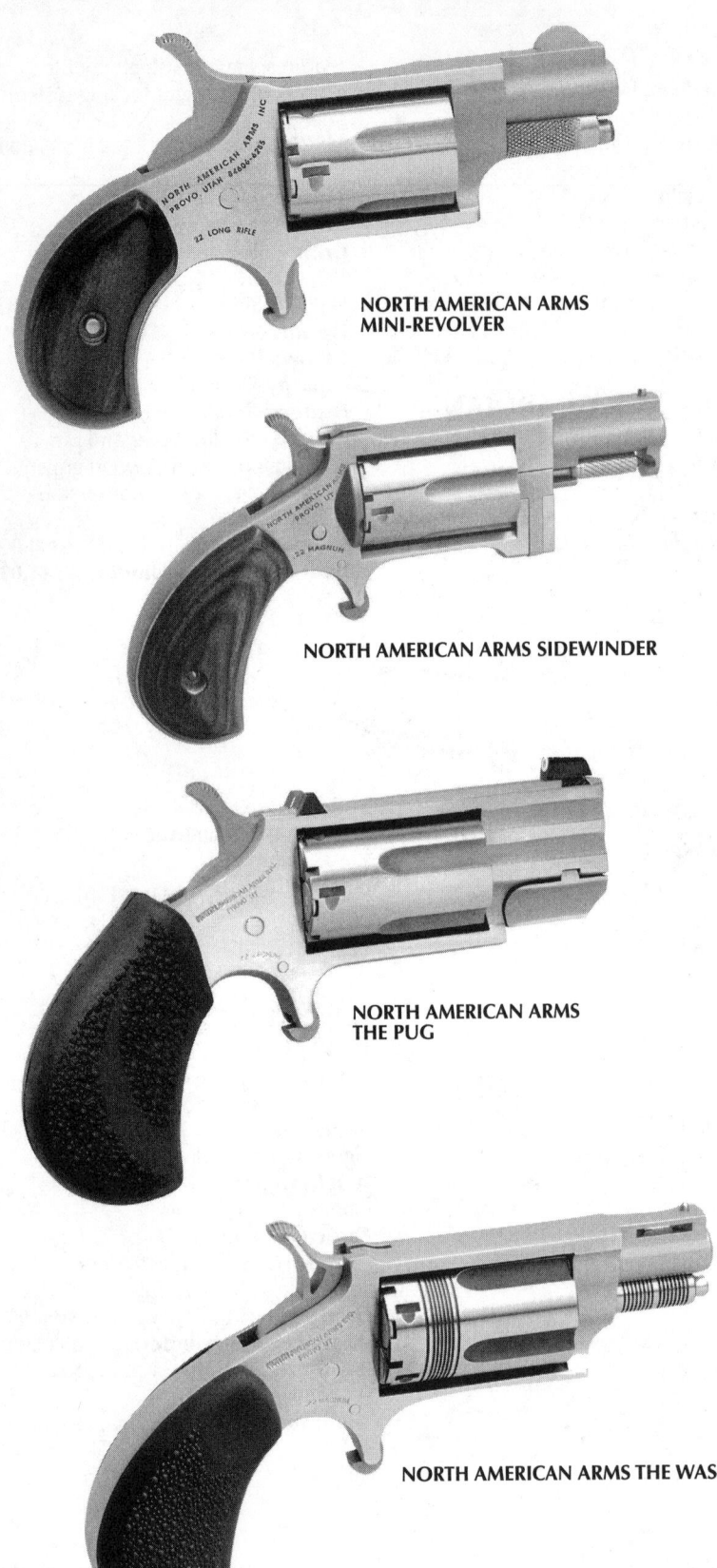

NORTH AMERICAN ARMS MINI-REVOLVER

NORTH AMERICAN ARMS SIDEWINDER

NORTH AMERICAN ARMS THE PUG

NORTH AMERICAN ARMS THE WASP

MINI-REVOLVER

Action: SA revolver
Grips: Laminated rosewood
Barrel: 1.2 in., 1.625 in.
Sights: Fixed, open
Weight: 4 oz.–6.2 oz.
Caliber: .22 Short, .22 LR, .22 Mag.
Capacity: 5 rounds
Features: Features NAA's safety cylinder so mini-revolver can be carried fully loaded; .22 LR available with folding "holster grip." .22 Mag available ported or with folding "holster grip"
.22: $226.00
.22 LR: . . . . $226.00–$256.00
.22 Mag: . . . . $236.00–$291.00

SIDEWINDER

Action: Revolver
Grips: Laminated rosewood
Barrel: 1 in., 2.5 in., 4. in.
Sights: Stainless steel post
Weight: 6.7 oz.
Caliber: .22 Mag.
Capacity: 5 rounds
Features: Features NAA's safety cylinder; stainless steel frame; available .22 LR conversion
MSRP . . . . $350.00–$508.00

THE PUG

Action: Revolver
Grips: Rubber
Barrel: 1 in.
Sights: Tritium and white dot
Weight: 6.4 oz.
Caliber: .22 Mag.
Capacity: 5 rounds
Features: Oversized pebble-textured rubber grips enable the handler to keep a firm grip
White dot sight: $328.00
Tritium sight: $347.00

THE WASP

Action: SA revolver
Grips: Rubber pebble finish
Barrel: 1.125 in., 1.625 in.
Sights: Stainless post
Weight: 5.9 oz.–7.2 oz.
Caliber: .22 Mag.
Capacity: 5 rounds
Features: Stainless steel frame; vent rib barrel; skeleton hammer; .22 LR conversion cylinders available; brushed sides, matte contours, black inlay
MSRP . . . . $266.00–$301.00

Remington Arms Company

MODEL 1911 R1

Action: Semiautomatic
Grips: Double diamond walnut
Barrel: 5 in.
Sights: Fixed
Weight: 38.5 oz.
Caliber: .45 ACP
Capacity: 7 rounds
Features: Short trigger; double diamond walnut grips; modern enhancements include a lowered and flared ejection port; beveled magazine well; loaded chamber indicator; high-profile fixed sights in a three-white-dot pattern; match grade stainless-steel barrel; available in stainless steel
MSRP **$744.00**
SS: **$837.00**

MODEL 1911 R1 200TH ANNIVERSARY COMMEMORATIVE

Action: Semiautomatic
Grips: Walnut
Barrel: 5 in.
Sights: Fixed
Weight: 38.5 oz.
Caliber: .45 Auto
Capacity: 7+1 rounds
Features: Commemorative engraved medalions in grip and grip cap; classic GI-style thumb safety, grip safety, and hammer; stainless steel match-grade barrel; includes 2 magazines; satin black oxide finish on frame
MSRP **$835.00**

MODEL 1911 R1 200TH ANNIVERSARY LIMITED EDITION

Action: Semiautomatic
Grips: Walnut
Barrel: 5 in.
Sights: Fixed
Weight: 38.5 oz.
Caliber: .45 Auto
Capacity: 7+1 rounds
Features: C-grade walnut grips; classic American-style engraving and 24k gold inlay; limited to quantity of 2016; special serial number; bicentennial box with Remington historical timeline
MSRP **$1649.00**

MODEL 1911 R1 CARRY

Action: Semiautomatic
Grips: Cocobolo wood
Barrel: 5 in.

REMINGTON MODEL 1911 R1 CARRY

REMINGTON MODEL 1911 R1 200TH ANNIVERSARY COMMEMORATIVE

REMINGTON MODEL 1911 R1 200TH ANNIVERSARY LIMITED EDITION

REMINGTON MODEL 1911 R1

REMINGTON MODEL 1911 R1 CARRY COMMANDER

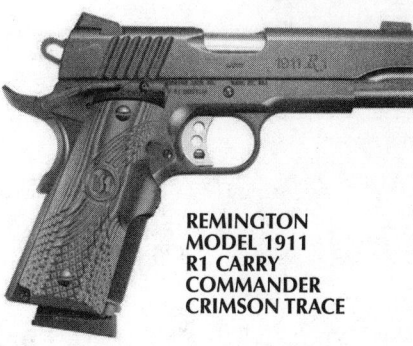

REMINGTON MODEL 1911 R1 CARRY COMMANDER CRIMSON TRACE

Sights: Novak sights with tritium front night sight
Weight: 38.5 oz.
Caliber: .45 ACP
Capacity: 7 or 8 rounds
Features: De-horned forged carbon steel frame and de-horned carbon steel slide; beavertail grip safety with checkered memory bump; checkered front strap and mainspring housing; ambidextrous safety; satin black oxide finish
MSRP **$1067.00**

MODEL 1911 R1 CARRY COMMANDER

Action: Semiautomatic
Grips: Wood
Barrel: 4.25 in.
Sights: Fixed
Weight: 38.5 oz.
Caliber: .45 ACP
Capacity: 7+1 rounds
Features: Satin black oxide finish; beavertail grip safety with checkered

memory bump; ambidextrous safety; Novak sights with Tritium front sight; Cocobolo grips
MSRP **$1067.00**

MODEL 1911 R1 CARRY COMMANDER CRIMSON TRACE

Action: Semiautomatic
Grips: Synthetic
Barrel: 4.25 in.
Sights: Fixed
Weight: 40 oz.
Caliber: .45 ACP
Capacity: 8+1 rounds
Features: Satin black oxide finish; beavertail grip safety with checkered memory bump; ambidextrous safety; Novak sights with Tritium front sight; Crimson Trace lasergrips
MSRP **$1350.00**

Remington Arms Company

REMINGTON MODEL 1911 R1 COMMANDER

REMINGTON MODEL 1911 R1 ENHANCED CRIMSON TRACE

REMINGTON RM380 MICRO CRIMSON TRACE

MODEL 1911 R1 COMMANDER

Action: Semiautomatic
Grips: Wood
Barrel: 4.25 in.
Sights: Fixed
Weight: 38.5 oz.
Caliber: .45 ACP
Capacity: 7+1 rounds
Features: Oversized, flared ejection port; carbon steel frame and slide; 3-dot sights; GI style grip safety; GI style short trigger; black oxide finish; walnut double diamond grips
MSRP $744.00

MODEL 1911 R1 ENHANCED CRIMSON TRACE

Action: Semiautomatic
Grips: Synthetic
Barrel: 5 in.
Sights: Adjustable
Weight: 40 oz.
Caliber: .45 ACP
Capacity: 8+1 rounds
Features: Satin black oxide finish; beavertail grip safety with checkered memory bump; ambidextrous safety; adjustable dovetailed rear sight with fiber optic front sight; Crimson Trace lasergrips
MSRP $1129.00

RM380, RM380 MICRO CRIMSON TRACE

Action: Semiautomatic
Grips: Synthetic
Barrel: 2.9 in.
Sights: Fixed
Weight: 12.2 oz.
Caliber: .380 ACP
Capacity: 6+1 rounds
Features: Fully functional slide stop; all metal construction; DOA trigger; ambidextrous magazine release; checkered front strap and undercut trigger guard; optimized grip handle; 8–9-pound trigger pull
MSRP $436.00
With Crimson Trace: $638.00

Rock River Arms

ROCK RIVER ARMS 1911 POLY

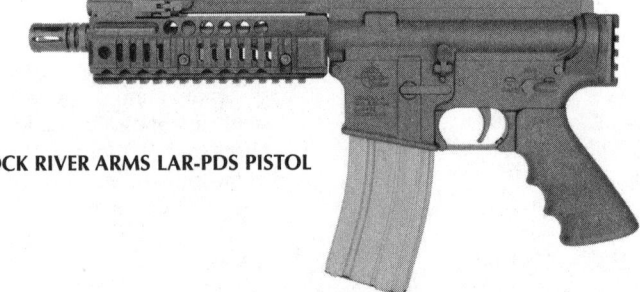

ROCK RIVER ARMS LAR-PDS PISTOL

1911 POLY

Action: SA semiautomatic
Grips: Polymer
Barrel: 5 in.
Sights: Dovetail front and rear
Weight: 32.6 oz.
Caliber: .45 ACP
Capacity: 7 rounds
Features: Chromoly barrel; polymer frame and mainspring housing; steel frame insert; steel slide; parkerized finish on metal; RRA overmolded grips; aluminum speed trigger; beavertail grip safety; RRA dovetail front and rear sights
MSRP $925.00

LAR-PDS PISTOL

Action: Gas-operated semiautomatic
Grips: Hogue rubber
Barrel: 8 in. chromoly
Sights: Picatinny rail
Weight: 80 oz.
Caliber: 5.56 NATO
Capacity: 30 rounds
Features: A2 Flash Hider; aluminum tri-rail handguard; ambidextrous non-reciprocating charging handle
MSRP . . . . $1245.00–$1395.00

Rossi

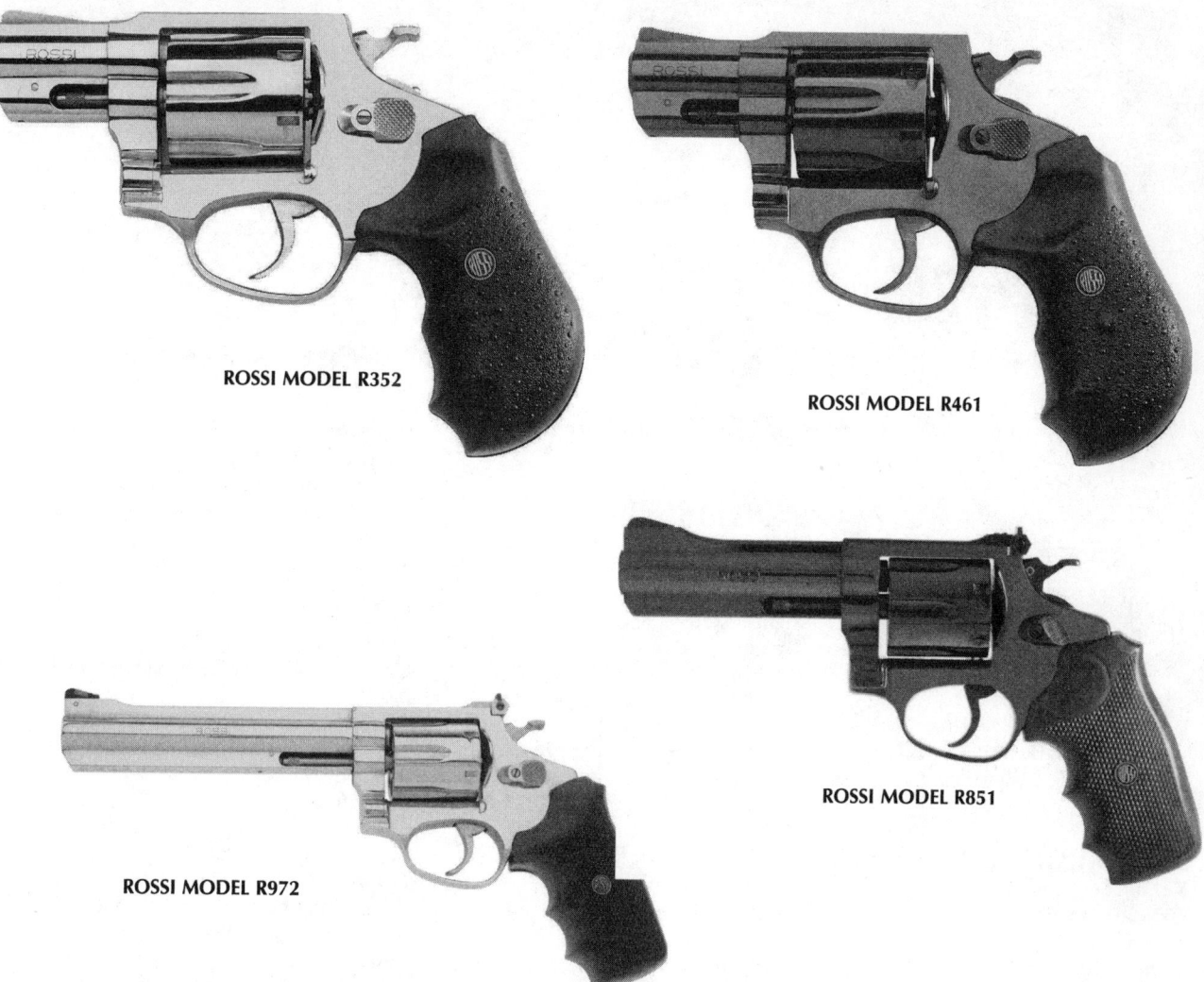

ROSSI MODEL R352

ROSSI MODEL R461

ROSSI MODEL R972

ROSSI MODEL R851

MODEL R351 AND R352
Action: DA revolver
Grips: Rubber
Barrel: 2 in.
Sights: Fixed, open
Weight: 24 oz.
Caliber: .38 Spl., .38 Spl. +P
Capacity: 5 rounds
Features: Blued or stainless steel finish; checkered grips; forged steel frame
R35102: $390.78
R35202: $454.89

MODEL R461 AND R462
Action: DA revolver
Grips: Rubber
Barrel: 2 in.

Sights: Fixed, open
Weight: 26 oz.
Caliber: .357 Mag.
Capacity: 6 rounds
Features: Blued or stainless steel finish; checkered grips; forged steel frame
R46102: $390.78
R46202: $454.89

MODEL R851
Action: DA revolver
Grips: Rubber
Barrel: 4 in.
Sights: Adjustable
Weight: 32 oz.
Caliber: .38 Spl., .38 Spl. +P
Capacity: 6 rounds

Features: Adjustable rear sight; blued finish; forged steel frame
MSRP $390.78

MODEL R971 AND R972
Action: DA revolver
Grips: Rubber
Barrel: 4 in., 6 in.
Sights: Target
Weight: 35 oz.
Caliber: .357 Mag., .38 Spl.
Capacity: 6 rounds
Features: Stainless steel or blued finish; deep contoured finger grooves in the grip for solid grasp and comfort; frame forged from steel
R97104: $454.89
R97206: $511.37

Ruger (Sturm, Ruger & Co.)

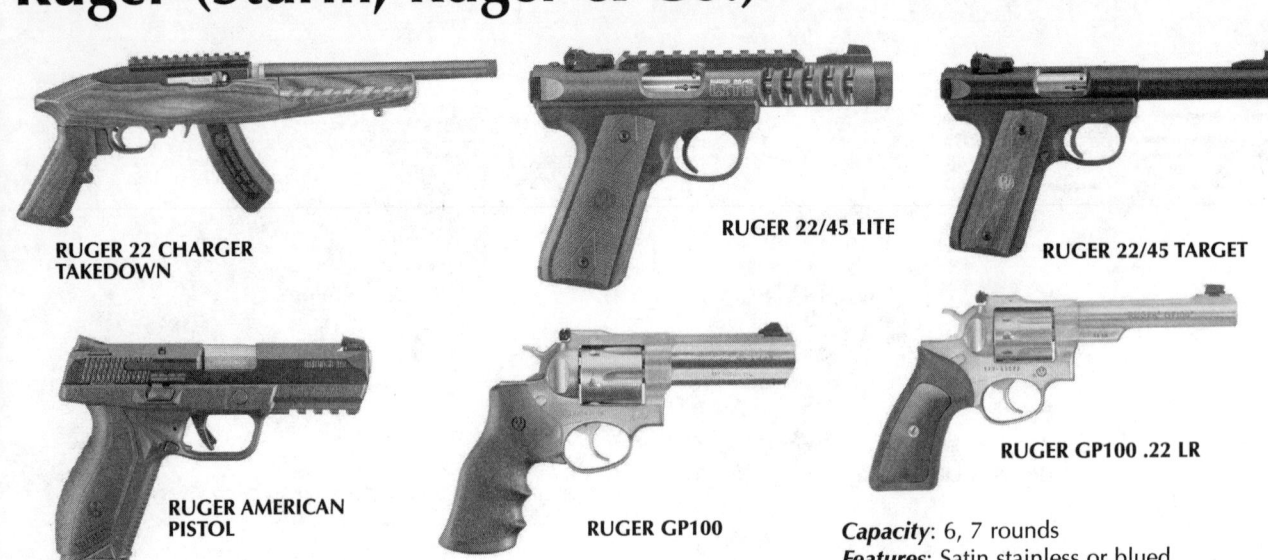

RUGER 22 CHARGER TAKEDOWN

RUGER 22/45 LITE

RUGER 22/45 TARGET

RUGER AMERICAN PISTOL

RUGER GP100

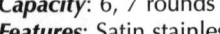

RUGER GP100 .22 LR

RUGER GP100 MATCH CHAMPION

22 CHARGER TAKEDOWN

Action: Semiautomatic
Grips: Synthetic
Barrel: 10 in.
Sights: None
Weight: 3 lb. 4 oz.
Caliber: .22 LR
Capacity: 15 rounds
Features: Cold hammer-forged barrel; threaded barrel; Picatinny rail; A2-style grip; adjustable bipod
MSRP $419.00

22/45 LITE

Action: Semiautomatic
Grips: Synthetic
Barrel: 4.4 in.
Sights: Adjustable
Weight: 22.7 oz.
Caliber: .22 LR
Capacity: 6 rounds
Features: Zytel polymer grip frame; threaded barrel; ccontoured ejection port; loaded chamber indicator; available in black or bronze anodized finishes
MSRP $559.00

22/45 TARGET

Action: SA semiautomatic
Grips: Checkered cocobolo wood
Barrel: 4 in., 5.5 in.
Sights: Adjustable rear
Weight: 31–33 oz.
Caliber: .22 LR
Capacity: 10 rounds
Features: Replaceable panels; Zytel polymer frame; blued finish; classic 1911 style pistol
MSRP $409.00

AMERICAN PISTOL

Action: Semiautomatic
Grips: Ergonomic wrap-around
Barrel: 4.2 in., 4.5 in.
Sights: Three dot
Weight: 30 oz.–31.5 oz.
Caliber: 9mm Luger, .45 ACP
Capacity: 10 or 17 rounds
Features: Trigger features a short takeup with positive reset; recoil-reducing barrel cam; low-mass slide; Novak LoMount Carry three-dot sights; modular wrap-around grip system for adjusting palm swell and trigger reach; ambidextrous slide stop and magazine release; safety features include internal, automatic sear block system, integrated trigger safety and no trigger pull required for takedown
MSRP $579.00

GP100

Action: DA revolver
Grips: Black hogue monogrip
Barrel: 3 in., 4.2 in., 6 in.
Sights: Ramp front, fixed or adjustable rear
Weight: 36 oz.–45 oz.
Caliber: .327 Fed Mag., .357 Mag.

Capacity: 6, 7 rounds
Features: Satin stainless or blued finish; stainless steel or alloy steel frame; cushioned rubber grip; transfer bar; triple-locking cylinder
MSRP . . . . $769.00–$829.00

GP100 .22 LR

Action: DA revolver
Grips: Cushioned rubber with wood insert
Barrel: 5.5 in.
Sights: Fiber optic front, adjustable rear
Weight: 42 oz.
Caliber: .22 LR
Capacity: 10 rounds
Features: Triple-locking cylinder locked into the frame at the front, rear, and bottom; patented grip frame design easily accommodates a wide variety of custom grips; takedown of integrated subassemblies requires no special tools and allows for easy maintenance and assembly; patented transfer bar mechanism provides an unparalleled measure of security against accidental discharge
MSRP $829.00

GP100 MATCH CHAMPION

Action: DA revolver
Grips: Wood
Barrel: 4.2 in.
Sights: Fixed or adjustable
Weight: 38 oz.
Caliber: .357 Mag.
Capacity: 6 rounds
Features: Hogue stippled hardwood; fiber optic front site; triple-locking cylinder; easy takedown; features a slab-sided, half-lug barrel
MSRP $969.00

Ruger (Sturm, Ruger & Co.)

RUGER LC9s

RUGER LC380

RUGER LCP

RUGER LCR

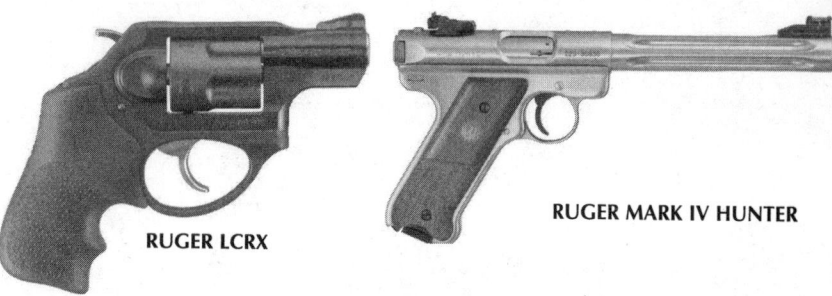

RUGER LCRX

RUGER MARK IV HUNTER

LC380

Action: Semiautomatic
Grips: Black, glass-filled nylon
Barrel: 3.12 in.
Sights: Adjustable 3-dot
Weight: 17.2 oz.
Caliber: .380 ACP
Capacity: 7+1 rounds
Features: Hardened alloy steel slide; checkered grip frame; finger grip extension floorplate; three safeties and loaded chamber indicator; blued finish; California-approved version available
Standard:..............**$479.00**
California approved: **$539.00**

LCP

Action: Semiautomatic
Grips: Glass-filled nylon
Barrel: 2.75 in.
Sights: Integral, Viridian E-Series red laser
Weight: 9.9 oz.
Caliber: .380 ACP
Capacity: 6+1 rounds
Features: Alloy steel barrel and slide; blued finish; fixed/LaserMax CenterFire sights; black, high performance, glass-filled nylon grips
Standard:..............**$259.00**
Laser:.................**$359.00**

LCR

Action: DA/SA

Grips: Rubber
Barrel: 1.87 in.
Sights: Adjustable
Weight: 13.5 oz.–17.2 oz.
Caliber: .38 Spl. +P, 22 LR, 22 WMR, .327 Fed. Mag., .357 Mag., 9mm Luger
Capacity: 5–8 rounds
Features: Hogue Tamer monogrip; adjustable black blade rear sight; Ionbond Diamondblack cylinder finish
MSRP..........**$579.00–$669.00**

LCRX

Action: DA/SA revolver
Grips: Rubber
Barrel: 1.87 in.–3 in.
Sights: Fixed
Weight: 13.5 oz.
Caliber: .38 Spl. +P
Capacity: 5 rounds
Features: High-strength stainless steel cylinder features an Ionbond Diamondblack finish; Grip Peg allows a variety of grip styles to be installed; external hammer that allows for single-action mode; also available with Crimson Trace lasergrips
MSRP..........**$579.00–$669.00**

MARK IV HUNTER

Action: SA semiautomatic
Grips: Checkered laminate
Barrel: 6.88 in.

Sights: Fiber optic front sight, adjustable rear
Weight: 44 oz.
Caliber: .22 LR
Capacity: 10 rounds
Features: Stainless steel frame with satin finish; fluted bull barrel; one-button takedown; drop-free magazine; magazine disconnect
MSRP................**$769.00**

LC9s

Action: Semiautomatic
Grips: Synthetic
Barrel: 3.12 in.
Sights: Drift adjustable white 3-dot, drift adjustable HIVIZ fiber optic
Weight: 17.2 oz.
Caliber: 9mm
Capacity: 7+1 rounds
Features: Dovetailed, high-visibility 3-dot sight system with windage adjustable rear sight and fixed front sigh; striker fire; includes finger grip extension floorplate; blued, alloy steel barrel; integrated trigger safety, manual safety, magazine disconnect, inert magazine for safe disassembly, and a visual inspection port; Pro version has integrated trigger safety only; Standard version now available with green fiber optic front sight and orange fiber optic rear
MSRP..........**$479.00–$499.00**

Ruger (Sturm, Ruger & Co.)

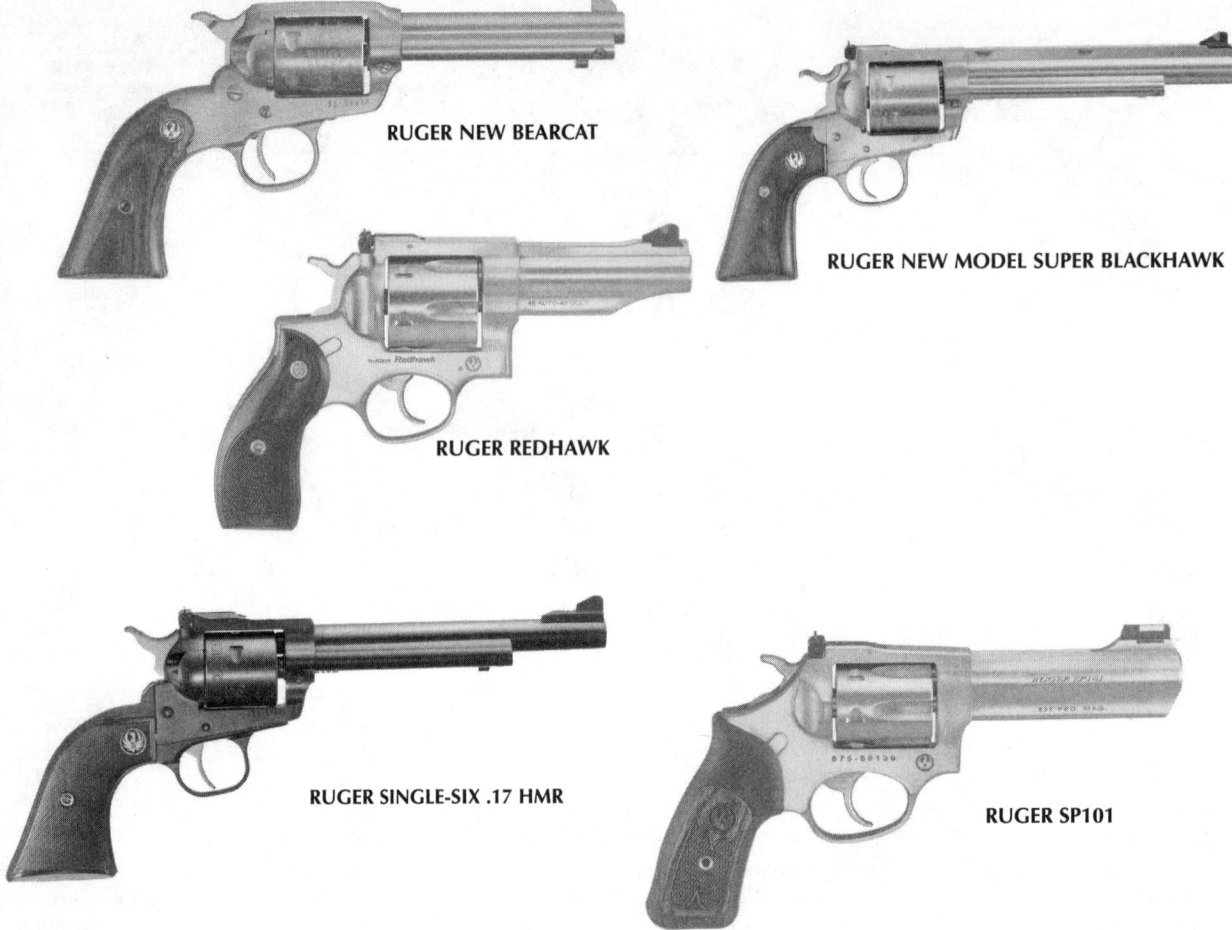

RUGER NEW BEARCAT

RUGER NEW MODEL SUPER BLACKHAWK

RUGER REDHAWK

RUGER SINGLE-SIX .17 HMR

RUGER SP101

NEW BEARCAT
Action: SA revolver
Grips: Hardwood
Barrel: 4.2 in.
Sights: Blade front, integral notch
Weight: 24 oz.
Caliber: .22 LR
Capacity: 6 rounds
Features: Alloy steel with blued finish or stainless steel frame with satin stainless finish; decorative cylinder; transfer bar mechanism; features one piece frame reminiscent of old Remington Civil War-era revolvers
Alloy Steel: **$639.00**
SS: **$689.00**

NEW MODEL SUPER BLACKHAWK
Action: SA revolver
Grips: Hardwood, laminate
Barrel: 4.62 in., 5.5 in., 7.5 in., 10.5 in.
Sights: Ramp front, adjustable rear
Weight: 45–55 oz.
Caliber: .44 Rem. Mag.
Capacity: 6 rounds

Features: Alloy steel or stainless steel frame; blued or satin stainless finish; transfer bar mechanism; western-style grip; Bisley Hunter variation has 7.5-in. barrel, black laminate grips
Standard: **$829.00**
Bisley Hunter: **$959.00**

REDHAWK
Action: DAO
Grips: Wood or Hogue Monogrip
Barrel: 2.75 in.–7.5 in.
Sights: Fixed
Weight: 44 oz.–54 oz.
Caliber: .357 Mag., .44 Rem. Mag., .45 ACP, .45 Colt
Capacity: 6 rounds
Features: Stainless steel construction; triple-lock cylinder; single spring mechanism; adjustable rear sight
MSRP . . . . **$1079.00–$1159.00**

SINGLE-SIX .17 HMR
Action: SA revolver
Grips: Black checkered hard rubber
Barrel: 6.5 in.

Sights: Ramp front, adjustable rear
Weight: 35 oz.
Caliber: .17 HMR
Capacity: 6 rounds
Features: Alloy steel frame with blued finish; transfer bar mechanism
MSRP **$629.00**

SP101
Action: DA/SA
Grips: Wood and rubber
Barrel: 2.25 in.–4.2 in.
Sights: Fixed
Weight: 25 oz.–30 oz.
Caliber: .22 LR, .38 Spl +P, .327 Fed. Mag., .357 Mag.
Capacity: 6 rounds
Features: Features a light-gathering front sight, windage and elevation adjustable rear sight; triple-locking cylinder; easy takedown
MSRP . . . .**$719.00–$769.00**

Ruger (Sturm, Ruger & Co.)

RUGER SR9C

RUGER SR22 RIMFIRE PISTOL

RUGER SR40

RUGER SR45

RUGER SR1911

SR9C

Action: DA semiautomatic
Grips: Black, glass-filled, nylon
Barrel: 3.4 in.
Sights: Adjustable 3-dot
Weight: 23.4 oz.
Caliber: 9mm Luger
Capacity: 10+1 rounds, 17+1 rounds
Features: Compact version of SR9; black alloy or brushed stainless 6-groove rifling; high visibility sights; accessory mounting rail
MSRP $569.00

SR22

Action: DA semiautomatic
Grips: Polymer
Barrel: 3.5 in., 4.5 in.
Sights: Adjustable 3-dot
Weight: 17.5 oz.
Caliber: .22 LR
Capacity: 10 rounds
Features: 3-dot sight system has fixed front sight and adjustable rear sight; polymer frame and two interchangeable rubberized grips; underside Picatinny rail; aluminum slide; ambidextrous manual thumb safety/decocking lever; ambidextrous magazine release; Talo Distributor exclusives were offered in purple,

black, flat dark earth, red titanium Cerakote, yellow Cerakote, and turquoise Cerakote finishes
MSRP $439.00
Silver: $469.00
Threaded Barrel: $479.00

SR40

Action: semiautomatic
Grips: Black, high performance, glass-filled nylon
Barrel: 4.1 in.
Sights: Adjustable 3-dot
Weight: 27.25 oz.
Caliber: .40 S&W
Capacity: 10 or 15 rounds
Features: Glass-filled nylon frame; ambidextrous operating controls; trigger system and reversible; fully adjustable three-dot sights; integral accessory rail; backstraps are identical to SR9; Nitridox pro black or brushed stainless finish
MSRP $569.00

SR45

Action: Semiautomatic
Grips: Black, glass-filled nylon
Barrel: 4.5 in.
Sights: Adjustable 3-dot
Weight: 30.15 oz.
Caliber: .45 ACP

Capacity: 10+1 rounds
Features: Reversible backstrap; ambidextrous safety and magazine release; mouting rail; loaded chamber indicator; black nitride or brushed stainless finish
MSRP $569.00

SR1911

Action: Semiautomatic
Grips: G10, Wood
Barrel: 4.25 in., 5 in.
Sights: Fixed, adjustable
Weight: 29.3 oz.–39 oz.
Caliber: .45 ACP
Capacity: 7+1 rounds, 8+1 rounds
Features: Anodized aluminum frame; stainless steel barrel; standard recoil guide system and flat mainspring housing; rear slide serrations allow for positive grip; now available as a Target model with checkered G10 grips, low-glare stainless finish, and Bomar-style adjustable sights
MSRP . . . . $939.00–$1019.00

Ruger (Sturm, Ruger & Co.)

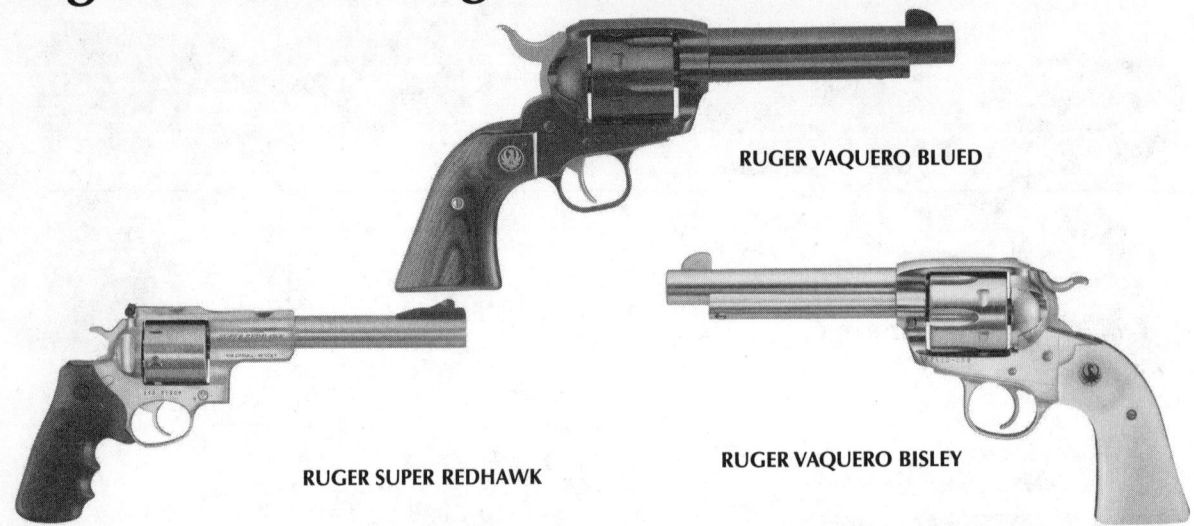

RUGER VAQUERO BLUED

RUGER SUPER REDHAWK

RUGER VAQUERO BISLEY

SUPER REDHAWK

Action: DA revolver
Grips: Black Hogue Tamer monogrip
Barrel: 2.5 in., 7.5 in., 9.5 in.
Sights: Ramp front, adjustable rear
Weight: 53 oz.–58 oz.
Caliber: .44 Mag., .454 Casull, .480 Ruger
Capacity: 6 rounds
Features: Satin stainless finish; triple-locking cylinder; integral scope system; corrosion-resistant; extended frame; dual chambering; transfer bar; Alaskan model has short 2.5-in. barrel
MSRP . . . . $1159.00–$1189.00

VAQUERO BISLEY

Action: SA revolver
Grips: Simulated ivory
Barrel: 5.5 in.
Sights: Fixed
Weight: 41 oz.–45 oz.
Caliber: .45 Colt, .357 Mag.
Capacity: 6 rounds
Features: Stainless steel frame with high-gloss stainless finish
MSRP $899.00

VAQUERO BLUED

Action: SA revolver
Grips: Hardwood
Barrel: 4.62 in., 5.5 in.
Sights: Fixed
Weight: 40 oz.–43 oz.
Caliber: .45 Colt, .357 Mag.
Capacity: 6 rounds
Features: Blued finish alloy steel; reverse Indexing Pawl; ejector rod head; transfer bar mechanism; internal lock
MSRP $829.00

SIG Sauer

SIG SAUER 1911 SPARTAN FULL-SIZE

SIG SAUER 1911 XO FULL-SIZE

1911 SPARTAN FULL-SIZE, SPARTAN CARRY

Action: SAO semiautomatic
Grips: Hogue Spartan
Barrel: 4.2 in., 5 in.
Sights: SIGLite
Weight: 41.6 oz.
Caliber: .45 ACP
Capacity: 8 rounds
Features: Oil-rubbed bronze Nitron finish; gold inlay engraving; 1911 design and ergonomic feel; ancient Greek inscription on slide and grip supposedly spoken by Spartan King Leonidas: "Molon labe," or "Come and take it"
MSRP $1397.00

1911 XO FULL-SIZE

Action: Semiautoamatic
Grips: Ergo XT
Barrel: 5 in.
Sights: Contrast
Weight: 41.6 oz.
Caliber: .45 ACP
Capacity: 8 rounds
Features: SIG's Nitron finish in either black or stainless, match-grade barrel, hammer, sear set, and trigger, beavertail safety, extended thumb safety, firing pin safety, and hammer intercept notch; California-compliant variant availble
Standard: $1010.00
California-compliant: $1083.00

SIG Sauer

SIG SAUER 1911 TWO-TONE ULTRA COMPACT

SIG SAUER P220 NITRON FULL-SIZE

SIG SAUER M11-A1 COMPACT

SIG SAUER P225-A1 COMPACT

SIG SAUER P220 HUNTER

SIG SAUER P226

1911 ULTRA COMPACT, TWO-TONE ULTRA COMPACT

Action: SA semiautomatic
Grips: Black diamondwood, rosewood
Barrel: 3.3 in.
Sights: Low-pro night sights
Weight: 28 oz.
Caliber: .45 ACP
Capacity: 6+1 rounds
Features: Smallest SIG 1911 yet; stainless slide over alloy frame; unique recoil system; 26 lpi front strap checkering; controllable and comfortable small .45; skeletonized trigger; two variants: Nitron (all black with black diamondwood grips) and Two-Tone (natural stainless slide over black hardcoat anodized aluminum frame; rosewood grips)
MSRP **$1119.00**

M11-A1 COMPACT

Action: DA/SA semiautomatic
Grips: Polymer
Barrel: 3.9 in.
Sights: Siglite night sights
Weight: 32 oz.
Caliber: 9mm
Capacity: 10, 15 rounds
Features: Stainless steel slide; Short Reset Trigger; flush fit magazines; phosphate coated internals; Nitron slide finish; black hard anodized
MSRP **$1119.00**

P220 HUNTER

Action: DA/SA
Grips: Hogue G10 grips
Barrel: 5 in.
Sights: Adjustable rear, fiber optic front
Weight: 39.4 oz.
Caliber: 10mm
Capacity: 8 rounds

Features: Kryptek stainless steel slide and frame; match-grade barrel
MSRP **$1629.00**

P220 NITRON FULL-SIZE

Action: Semiautomatic
Grips: Polymer, laminated or custom shop wood
Barrel: 4.4 in.
Sights: Siglite night
Weight: 30.4 oz.–31.2 oz.
Caliber: 10mm, .45 ACP
Capacity: 8 rounds
Features: Nitron finish, light-weight alloy frame; accessory rail; California- and Massachusetts-compliant variation available
Standard: **$1087.00**
**California/Massachusetts-
    compliant:** **$1141.00**

P225-A1 COMPACT

Action: DA/SA
Grips: Checkered G10 with medallion or checkered wood
Barrel: 3.6 in.
Sights: SIGLITE
Weight: 30.5 oz.
Caliber: 9mm
Capacity: 8 rounds
Features: Enhanced trigger; fully machined stainless steel slide with Nitron finish; hard coat anodized frame; two-piece grips with the SIG mark medallion; classic, nitron, and two-tone finishes
MSRP **$1032.00**

P226

Action: DA/SA Semiautomatic
Grips: One-piece ergo grip, extreme model features Hogue custom G10 grips, custom wood

Barrel: 4.4 in.
Sights: Contrast, Siglite night optional
Weight: 23.7 oz.–42.2 oz.
Caliber: 9mm, .357 SIG, .40 S&W
Capacity: 9mm: 10, 15, 20 rounds; .357 SIG: 10 or 12 rounds, .40 S&W: 10 or 12 rounds
Features: The P226 line, now in its 55th year in 2017, continues to evolve; enhanced elite Full-Size has SIG's Short Reset Trigger (SRT), beavertail frame, SIGLITE night sights, front strap checkering (9mm); Legion Full-Size has Legion Gray PVO coating, custom G10 grips, SIG's Electro-Optics X-Ray night sights, X-5 undercut to trigger guard, and an SRT augmented with a Graygun's Inc. P-SAIT trigger; Nitron Full-Size has SIG rail and SIGLITES; RX Full-Size has SIG rail, SIG Romeo1 Reflex Sight, tall SIGLITEs, alloy frame (9mm); Elite Stainless has all-stainless steel finish and custom wood grips (9mm, .40 S&W); TACOPS Full-Size has Nitron finish, SIGLITE rear sight, TRUGLO fiber optic front sight, SRT, beavertail frame, polymer Magwell grips, threaded barrel, SIG rail, and four 20-round magazines (9mm); P226-22 Full-Size is chambered for .22 LR, has adjustable sights, and is convertible to 9mm, .40 S&W, and .357 SIG

Enhanced Elite Full-Size: . . . **$1174.00**
Legion Full-Size: **$1413.00**
Nitron Full-Size: . .**$1087.00–$1141.00**
RX Full-Size: . . . .**$1359.00–$1481.00**
Stainless Elite
    Full-Size: . . . . .**$1413.00–$1495.00**
TACOPS
    Full-Size: . . . . .**$1304.00–$1359.00**
P226-22 Nitron Full-Size: . . .**$630.00**

SIG Sauer

SIG SAUER P226 LEGION

SIG SAUER P226 LEGION SAO

SIG SAUER P226 MK25

SIG SAUER P227

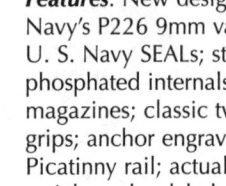

SIG SAUER P229

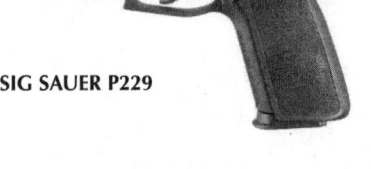

P226 LEGION

Action: DA/SA
Grips: Checkered G10 grips
Barrel: 4.4 in.
Sights: X-ray blacked-out day/night rear
Weight: 34 oz.
Caliber: .357 SIG, .40 S&W, 9mm
Capacity: 10, 12, 15 rounds
Features: Legion gray PVD finish; enhanced action with SRT; low-profile slide catch and decocking levers; reduced and contoured beavertail
MSRP **$1413.00**

P226 LEGION SAO

Action: SAO
Grips: Checkered G10 grips
Barrel: N/A
Sights: X-ray blacked-out day/night rear
Weight: 34.4 oz.
Caliber: 9mm
Capacity: 10, 15 rounds
Features: Legion gray PVD finish; enhanced action with SRT; low-profile slide catch and decocking levers; reduced and contoured beavertail
MSRP **$1413.00**

P226 MK25 FULL-SIZE

Action: SA/DA semiautomatic
Grips: Polymer
Barrel: 4.4 in.
Sights: SIGLITE night sights

Weight: 34 oz.–35 oz.
Caliber: 9mm
Capacity: 10 or 15 rounds
Features: New designation of the Navy's P226 9mm variant issued to U. S. Navy SEALs; still with phosphated internals; (three) 15 round magazines; classic two-piece polymer grips; anchor engraved on slide; Picatinny rail; actual UID scanable serial number label; packaged with FDE grip band and a certificate of authenticity; available in black Nitron or in Desert Tan Nitron; black version can be had with threaded barrel
Black: . . . . **$1187.00–$1255.00**
Desert tan: **$1244.00**

P227

Action: DA/SA semiautomatic
Grips: One-piece polymer
Barrel: 4.4 in.
Sights: SiGLITE, TRUGLO fiber optic
Weight: 30.5 oz.–35 oz.
Caliber: .45 ACP
Capacity: 10 rounds
Features: SIG's premier .45 ACP pistol comes in four versions: Enhanced Elite Full-Size has beavertail frame, front strap checkering, SIGLITE night sights; Nitron Full-Size Nitron-finished slide, SIGLITEs; SAS Gen2 Carry has been dehorned for easy, snag-free carry, has Nitron-finished slide, SIGLITEs; TACOPS Full-Size has SIGLITE rear sight, TRUGLO fiber optic front sight, beavertail frame, front slide cocking serrations, custom G10 grips with magwell, and four 14-round extended magazines
Enhanced Full-Size Elite: . . . **$1174.00**
Nitron Full-Size: **$1087.00**
SAS Gen2 Carry: **$1119.00**
TACOPS Full-Size: **$1413.00**

P229

Action: Semiautomatic
Grips: FDE polymer
Barrel: 3.9 in.

Sights: Contrast, Siglite night optional
Weight: 34.4 oz.
Caliber: 9mm, .40 S&W, .357 SIG
Capacity: 9mm: 10, 13 rounds; .357 SIG: 10, 12 rounds, .40 S&W: 10, 12 rounds
Features: Mid-size 9mm double-stack pistol comes in four versions: Combat Compact passes the military's 240-hour salt spray corrosion test and accuracy requirements, has M1913 Picatinny rail, vertical front strap serrations, SIGLITE night sights, hard-chrome barrel, Nitron-finished slide in matte black, with a tan hard-coat anodized alloy frame (9mm); Enhanced Elite Compact is in all black with Nitron-finished slide and SIG's Short Reset Trigger (SRT), beavertail frame, SIGLITEs, front strap checkering (9mm, .40 S&W); Legion Compact gets Legion Gray PVO coating, custom G10 grips with Legion medallion, SIG's Electro-Optics X-RAY sights, reduced contour beavertail, front strap and under-trigger guard checkering, X-Five undercut, solid steel guide rod, and SRT augmented with Grayguns, Inc. P-SAIT trigger. Nitron Compact has Nitron slide, newly enhanced slide profile, ergonomic grip, SIG rail, and SIGLITEs
Combat Compact: **$1195.00**
Enhanced Elite
   Compact: . . . . . **$1174.00–$1234.00**
Legion Compact: **$1413.00**
Nitron Compact: .**$1087.00–$1141.00**

SIG SAUER P229 LEGION

SIG SAUER P238

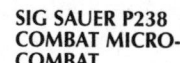

SIG SAUER P238 COMBAT MICRO-COMBAT

SIG SAUER P239

SIG SAUER P250-22 NITRON COMPACT

P229 LEGION FULL-SIZE, COMPACT

Action: DA/SA
Grips: Checkered G10 grips
Barrel: 4.4 in. (Full-Size), 3.9 in. (Compact)
Sights: X-ray blacked-out day/night rear
Weight: 34 oz. (Full-Size), 34.4 oz. (Compact)
Caliber: .357 SIG, .40 S&W, 9mm
Capacity: 10, 12, 15 rounds
Features: Legion gray PVD finish; enhanced action with SRT; low-profile slide catch and decocking levers; reduced and contoured beavertail
MSRP $1413.00

P238

Action: SA semiautomatic
Grips: Fluted polymer, Rosewood Tribal, Pearl, Tribal Engraved Aluminum, Hogue pink rubber
Barrel: 2.7 in.
Sights: Siglite night
Weight: 15.2 oz.
Caliber: .380 ACP (9mm Short)
Capacity: 6 rounds
Features: Microcompact, SA-only .380 carry pistol comes in under one pound. Sixteen versions currently available, including: Rosewood (black Nitron finish, rosewood grips); SAS (dehorned, stainless slide, black frame); Spartan (engraved slide, custom oil-rubbed bronze finish, custom Spartan grips); White Pearl (polished blue engraved slide, custom white pearlescent grips); Army (Army

green frame, Hogue rubber finger groove grip and magazine pinky rest); Black Pearl (similar to White Pearl, but with black pearlescent grips); Desert (two-tone Desert Tan finish, Hogue one-piece FDE rubber finger-groove grips, magazine pinky rest); Blackwood (two-tone stainless slide over black frame, with custom Blackwood grips); Edge (custom EDGE PVO-coated slide and controls, black frame, checkered black G10 grips); Engraved Rosewood (similar to Rosewood, but with polished blue engraved slide, smooth grips with inlaid SIG medallion); Equinox (polished blue slide, matte frame, stainless controls, custom wood grips, TRUGLO front sight/SIGLITE rear); Extreme (allover matte black finish, black/gray G10 Piranha grips, magazine pinky rest); HD (all over stainless steel finish, black G10 grips); Nightmare (allover matte black finish, stainless controls, black G10 grips); Rainbow (high-polished Rainbow Titanium PVO-finished slide, black frame, custom rosewood grips)
MSRP . . . . $679.00–$1013.00

P238 COMBAT MICRO-COMBAT

Action: SAO
Grips: Polymer
Barrel: 3.0 in.
Sights: SIGLITE
Weight: 16 oz.
Caliber: .380 ACP
Capacity: 7 rounds

Features: Nitron stainless steel slide and flat dark earth anodized frame; front cocking serrations
MSRP $760.00

P239

Action: DA semiautomatic
Grips: Polymer, tactical model features black polymer factory grips
Barrel: 3.6 in., 4 in.
Sights: Contrast, Siglite night optional
Weight: 29.5 oz.
Caliber: 9mm, .40 S&W, .357 SIG
Capacity: 8 (9mm) or 7 rounds (.40 S&W, .357 SIG) rounds
Features: Slim-profile, single-stack DA/SA semiauto in two versions: Nitron Compact in 9mm and .40 S&W, both with SIGLITE night sights, both California-compliant; SAS Gen2 Compact in 9mm, .40 S&W, and .357 SIG, with SIG's Short Reset Trigger, SIGLITEs, and dehorned frame
Nitron Compact: $1006.00
SAS Gen2 Compact: $1032.00

P250-22 NITRON COMPACT

Action: Locked breech DAO semiauto
Grips: Interchangeable polymer
Barrel: 3.9 in.
Sights: Adjustable
Weight: 25.1 oz.
Caliber: .22 LR
Capacity: 10 rounds
Features: Interchangeable polymer grip shell with stainless insert; nitron slide finish; interchangeable grip sizes and calibers
MSRP $379.00

SIG Sauer

P320

Action: DAO semiautomatic
Grips: Synthetic
Barrel: 3.6 in.–4.7 in.
Sights: Fixed
Weight: 25 oz.–29.4 oz.
Caliber: .40 S&W, 9mm, .357 SIG, .45 ACP
Capacity: 10–17 rounds
Features: Expansive line of subcompact, compact and full-size modular striker-fired pistols with three-point takedown and interchangeable grip sets; nine models: TACOPS Carry has threaded barrel, full-length grip, tall SIGLITE night sights, four 21-round magazines (9mm); RX Full-Size has full-size slide and grip, ROMEO1 reflex sight, SIGLITEs (9mm); RX Compact is similar to Full-Size, but with shorter barrel; TACOPS Full has full-sized frame, slide, and grip length, TFO front sight, SIGLITE rear, four 21-round magazines (9mm); Nitron Sub-Compact has subcompact grip and slide, SIGLITE or contrast sights, optional accessory rail (9mm, .40 S&W); Nitron Full-Size has full-size grip and slide, choice of contrast or SIGLITE sights (9mm, .40 S&W, .357 SIG, .45 ACP); Nitron Compact is mid-sized version of the Full-Size, available in same calibers; Nitron Carry has frame designed for improved concealed carry, similar otherwise to Nitron Compact including calibers; FDE Compact, identical to the Nitron Compact but in an allover Flat Dark Earth finish

TACOPS Carry:	**$830.00**
RX Full-Size, Compact:	**$869.00**
TACOPS Full:	**$762.00**
Nitron Subcompact:	**$679.00**
Nitron Full-Size:	**$679.00–$869.00**
Nitron Compact, Carry:	**$679.00–$747.00**
FDE Compact:	**$679.00**

P938

Action: SA semiautomatic
Grips: Synthetic or wood
Barrel: 3 in.
Sights: SIGLITE night sights, TFO front on Equinox
Weight: 16 oz.
Caliber: 9mm
Capacity: 6+1, 7+1 rounds
Features: 9mm version of the P238

SIG SAUER P320

SIG SAUER P290

SIG SAUER P938 BLACKWOOD

SIG SAUER P938 COMBAT MICRO-COMBAT

SIG SAUER SP2022

family, with similar aesthetics; twelve current offerings include Blackwood, BRG (dark matte finish with Hogue finger grips and magazine pinky rest), Combat, Edge, Engraved Rosewood, Equinox, Extreme, Nightmare, Nitron, Rosewood, SAS, P938-22 Target (.22 LR with extended magazine finger rest)
MSRP . . . . **$651.00–$855.00**

P938 COMBAT MICRO-COMBAT

Action: SAO
Grips: Rubber
Barrel: 3 in.
Sights: SIGLITE
Weight: 16 oz.
Caliber: 9mm

Capacity: 7 rounds
Features: Nitron stainless steel slide and flat dark earth anodized frame; front cocking serrations
MSRP **$760.00**

SP2022

Action: Semiautomatic
Grips: Polymer
Barrel: 3.9 in., 4.4 in.
Sights: Contrast, Siglite Night optional
Weight: 29 oz.
Caliber: 9mm, .40 S&W
Capacity: 10 or 15 rounds (9mm), 10 or 12 rounds (.40 S&W)
Features: SIG's original full-size polymer pistol, available in three versions: Nitron Full-Size (all black finish, contrast sights (9mm, .40 S&W); Two-Tone Full-Size, stainless slide, black frame, SIGLITE night sights (9mm); FDE Full-Size, allover Flat Dark Earth finish, SIGLITEs (9mm, .40 S&W)

Nitron:	**$568.00–$597.00**
Two-Tone, FDE:	**$638.00**

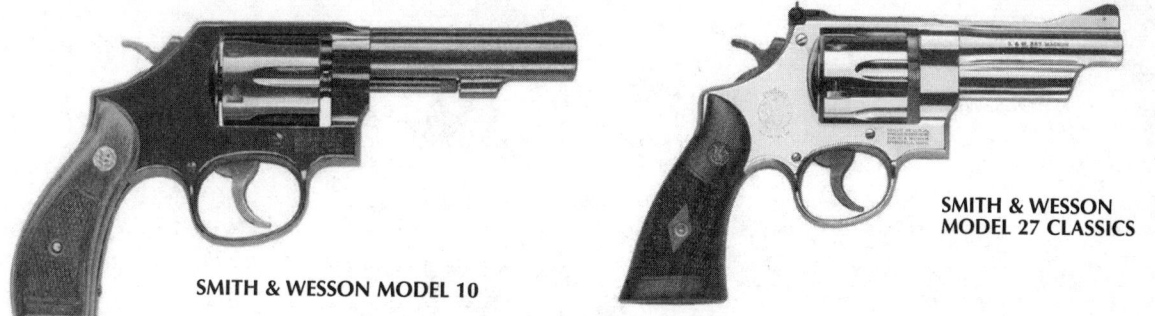

SMITH & WESSON MODEL 10

SMITH & WESSON
MODEL 27 CLASSICS

SMITH & WESSON
MODEL 29 CLASSICS

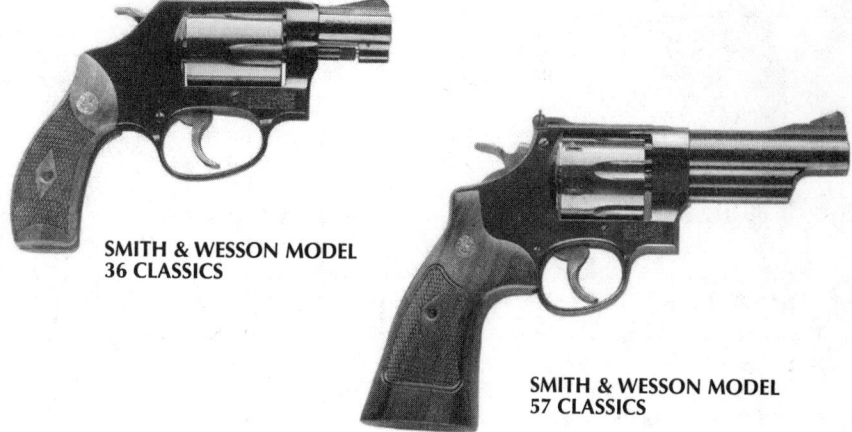

SMITH & WESSON MODEL
36 CLASSICS

SMITH & WESSON MODEL
57 CLASSICS

MODEL 10
Action: SA/DA revolver
Grips: Wood
Barrel: 4 in.
Sights: Black blade, fixed
Weight: 36 oz.
Caliber: .38 S&W Spl. +P
Capacity: 6 rounds
Features: Carbon steel frame; carbon steel cylinder; blued finish; medium size frame; exposed hammer
MSRP................ **$739.00**

MODEL 27 CLASSICS
Action: SA/DA revolver
Grips: Checkered square butt walnut
Barrel: 4 in.
Sights: Pinned serrated ramp front; Micro adjustable with cross serrations
Weight: 48.5 oz.
Caliber: .357 Mag., .38 S&W Spl. +P
Capacity: 6 rounds
Features: Carbon steel frame; bright blued or blued finish
MSRP................**$1019.00**

MODEL 29 CLASSICS
Action: Revolver
Grips: Checkered square butt walnut; 6 in. model features Altamont Service walnut grips
Barrel: 4 in.
Sights: Red ramp, micro adjustable rear
Weight: 48.5 oz.
Caliber: .44 Mag., .44 S&W Spl.
Capacity: 6 rounds
Features: Carbon steel frame with blued finish
MSRP................ **$999.00**

MODEL 36 CLASSICS
Action: Revolver
Grips: Wood
Barrel: 1.8 in.
Sights: Integral front, fixed rear
Weight: 19.5 oz.
Caliber: .38 S&W Spl. +P
Capacity: 5 rounds

Features: Small sized frame; exposed hammer; carbon steel frame and cylinder; blued finish; single or double action
MSRP................ **$749.00**

MODEL 57 CLASSICS
Action: DA N-frame revolver
Grips: Checkered square-butt walnut
Barrel: 6 in.
Sights: Pinned red ramp front, micro adjustable white outline rear;
Weight: 4.8 oz.
Caliber: .41 Mag.
Capacity: 6 rounds
Features: Bright blued or nickel finish; carbon steel frame; classic style thumbpiece; color case wide spur hammer; color case wide serrated target trigger
MSRP: **$1009.00**

Smith & Wesson

SMITH & WESSON MODEL 60

SMITH & WESSON MODEL 66

SMITH & WESSON MODEL 69

SMITH & WESSON MODEL 586 CLASSICS

SMITH & WESSON MODEL 442 ENGRAVED

MODEL 60
Action: Revolver
Grips: Synthetic, wood
Barrel: 2.125 in., 3 in.
Sights: Black blade front, adjustable rear
Weight: 21.4 oz.–23.2 oz.
Caliber: .357 Mag., .38 S&W Spl. +P
Capacity: 5 rounds
Features: Satin stainless finish; single- or double-action; stainless steel fame and cylinder
2.125-in. barrel: **$729.00**
3-in. barrel: **$759.00**

MODEL 66
Action: DA/SA revolver
Grips: Synthetic
Barrel: 4.25 in.
Sights: Adjustable
Weight: 36.9 oz.–37.4 oz.
Caliber: .38 S&W Spl. +P, .357 Mag.
Capacity: 6 rounds
Features: Full top strap and barrel serration; ball-detent lock-up; two-piece barrel; matte stainless finish
MSRP **$849.00**

MODEL 69, MODEL 69 COMBAT MAGNUM
Action: DA/SA revolver
Grips: Synthetic
Barrel: 2.75 in., 4.25 in.
Sights: Adjustable

Weight: 34.4 oz.–37.4 oz.
Caliber: .44 Mag., .44 Spl.
Capacity: 5 rounds
Features: Full top strap and barrel serration; ball-detent lock-up; two-piece barrel
MSRP **$849.00**

MODEL 442 ENGRAVED
Action: DA revolver
Grips: Engraved wood
Barrel: 1.875 in.
Sights: Integral front, fixed rear
Weight: 14.2 oz.
Caliber: .38 S&W Spl. +P
Capacity: 5 rounds
Features: Aluminum alloy frame; stainless steel barrel/cylinder; matte black
MSRP **$749.00**

MODEL 586 CLASSICS
Action: SA/DA revolver
Grips: Wood
Barrel: 6 in.
Sights: Adjustable
Weight: 46.3 oz.
Caliber: .357 Mag., .38 S&W Spl. +P
Capacity: 6 rounds
Features: Carbon steel frame and cylinder with blued finish; adjustable white outline rear sight and red ramp front sight; square-butt design; checkered wood grips
MSRP **$839.00**

MODEL 460XVR, PERFORMANCE CENTER 460XVR, PERFORMANCE CENTER HIVIZ 460XVR
Action: SA/DA revolver
Grips: Synthetic
Barrel: 3.5 in., 7 in., 8.38-in., 10.5 in., 12 in., 14 in.
Sights: Vary with model
Weight: 72.02 oz.–79.3 oz.
Caliber: .460 S&W Mag., .45 LC, .454 Casull, .460 S&W Mag.
Capacity: 5 rounds
New Features: Highest muzzle velocity revolver in the world, gain-twist rifling; Performance Center HIVIZ gets muzzle brake, integral scope base, unfluted cylinder, HIVIZ fiber optic front sight and adjustable white outline rear, PC-tuned action, full underlug on 7.5-in. barrel; Performance Center 14-in. Barrel with Bipod gets bipod, black ramp front sight, adjustable rear sight, muzzle brake, top and bottom accessory/optics rails, chrome hammer, chrome trigger with trigger stop, PC-tuned action (.460 S&W Mag); there are four versions of models known only as Performance Center Model 460XVR: 1) removable compensator, adjustable white-outline rear sight with interchangeable front sight (8.38-in. barrel, non-tapered, full underlug; .45 LC, .454 Casull, .460 S&W Mag.); 2) chrome hammer and trigger, PC-tuned action, removable patridge

Smith & Wesson

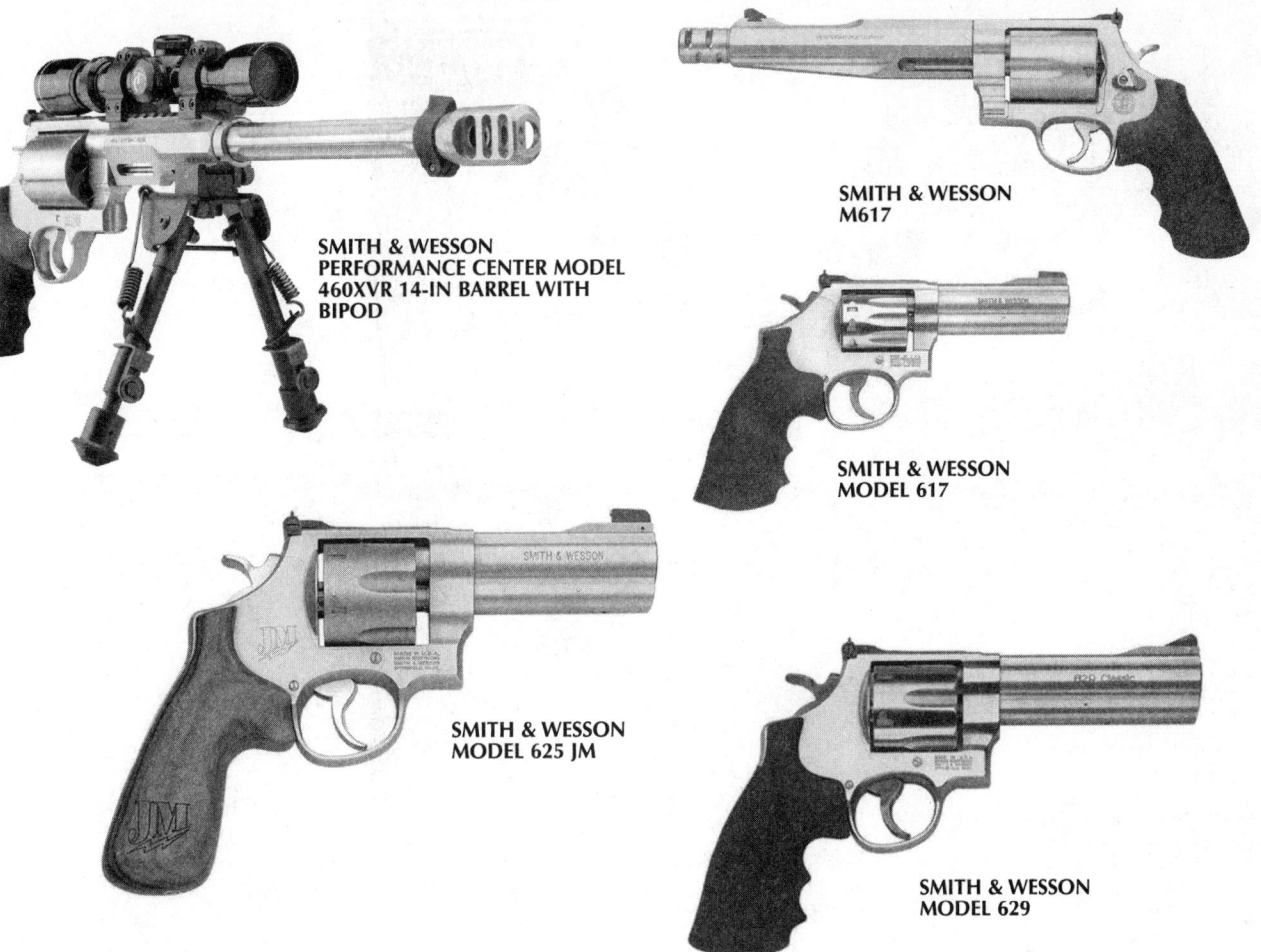

SMITH & WESSON
PERFORMANCE CENTER MODEL
460XVR 14-IN BARREL WITH
BIPOD

SMITH & WESSON
M617

SMITH & WESSON
MODEL 617

SMITH & WESSON
MODEL 625 JM

SMITH & WESSON
MODEL 629

front sight with adjustable rear, sling swivels (12-in. fluted barrel shrouded for several inches in front of frame to accommodate accessory rails top and bottom; .460 S&W Mag.); 3) chrome hammer, chrome trigger with trigger stop, muzzle brake, PC-tuned action, interchangeable fiber optic front sight, adjustable rear, sling swivels (10.5-in. barrel with full, tapered underlug; .460 S&W); 4) in matte silver with an unfluted cylinder, green HIVIZ fiber optic front sight, adjustable rear sight, chrome teardrop hammer, chrome trigger with trigger stop, PC-tuned action (3.5-in. barrel; .460 S&W Mag.)

Performance Center
  HIVIZ: $1779.00
Performance Center
  14-in. barrel and bipod: . $1559.00
Performance Center
  8.38-in. barrel: $1369.00
Performance Center
  12-in. barrel: $1689.00
Performance Center

  10.5-in. barrel: $1629.00
Performance Center
  3.5-in. barrel: $1609.00

MODEL 617
Action: SA/DA revolver
Grips: Synthetic
Barrel: 4 in., 6 in.
Sights: Partridge front, adjustable rear
Weight: 38.9 oz.–44.1 oz.
Caliber: .22 LR
Capacity: 10 rounds
Features: Stainless steel frame and cylinder with satin stainless finish; medium size frame with exposed hammer
MSRP **$829.00**

MODEL 625 JM
Action: SA/DA revolver
Grips: Jerry Miculek wood
Barrel: 4 in.
Sights: Gold bead partridge front, adjustable rear
Weight: 40.3 oz.
Caliber: .45 ACP

Capacity: 6 rounds
Features: JM model named for champion professional S&W team shooter Jerry Miculek, features Jerry Miculek wood grip, Miculek-style .265-in. wide grooved speed trigger, gold bead patridge front sight on an interchangeable base, adjustable rear sight, allover bead-blast matte finish, full underlug
MSRP **$979.00**

MODEL 629
Action: SA/DA revolver
Grips: Synthetic
Barrel: 5 in.
Sights: Red ramp, adjustable white outline
Weight: 44.3 oz.
Caliber: .44 Mag, .44 S&W Spl.
Capacity: 6 rounds
Features: Stainless steel frame and cylinder with satin stainless finish; exposed hammer
MSRP **$989.00**

Smith & Wesson

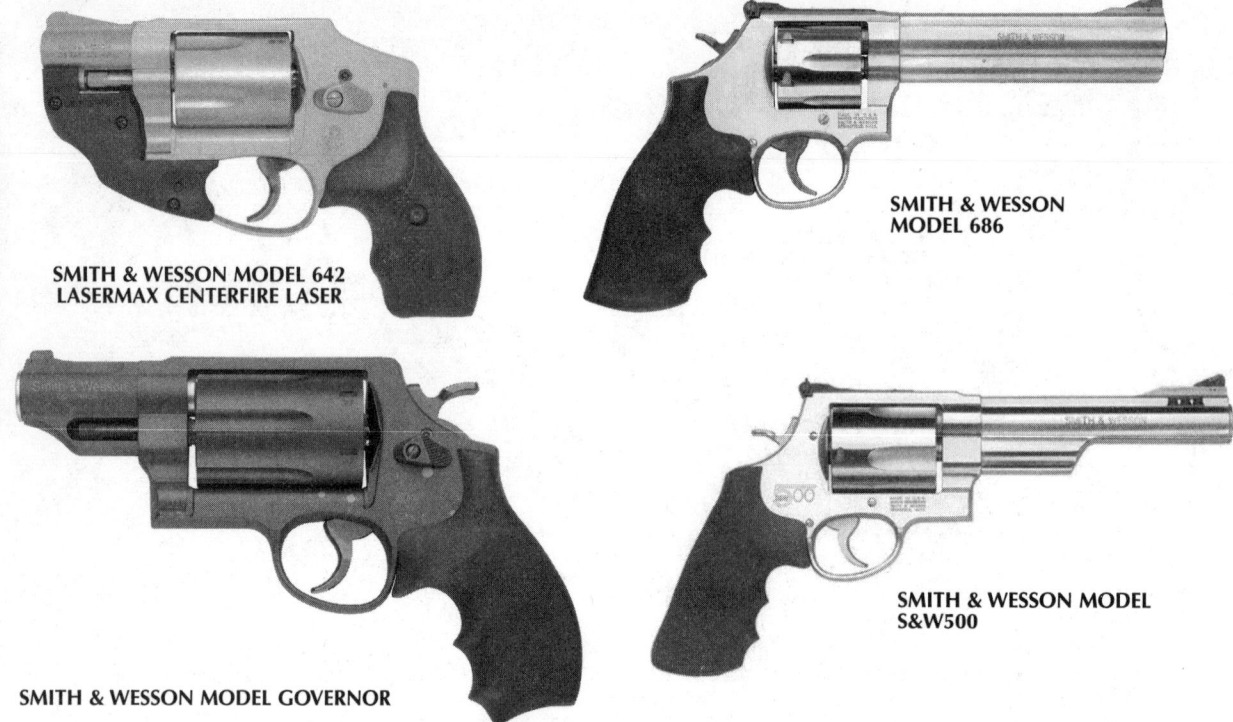

**SMITH & WESSON MODEL 642
LASERMAX CENTERFIRE LASER**

**SMITH & WESSON
MODEL 686**

**SMITH & WESSON MODEL
S&W500**

SMITH & WESSON MODEL GOVERNOR

MODEL 642 LASERMAX CENTERFIRE LASER

Action: DAO
Grips: Synthetic
Barrel: 1.88 in.
Sights: Fixed front, integral rear
Weight: 15.5 oz.
Caliber: .38 S&W Special +P
Capacity: 5 rounds
Features: Enables positive target acquisition and enhances accuracy in low-light conditions; no-snag, hammerless design; rapid target acquisition of the LaserMax sighting system; matte silver finish
MSRP $539.00

MODEL 686

Action: Revolver
Grips: Synthetic
Barrel: 4.125 in., 6 in.
Sights: Varies with model
Weight 39.7 oz.–44.8 oz.
Caliber: .357 Mag.
Capacity: 6 rounds
New Features: L-frame six-shot revolver in satin stainless finish with red ramp front sight, adjustable white outline rear, synthetic grips, full underlug
MSRP $829.00

MODEL GOVERNOR

Action: SA/DA revolver
Grips: Synthetic, Crimson Trace
Barrel: 2.75 in.
Sights: Fixed
Weight: 30.3 oz.
Caliber: .45 Colt, .45 ACP, .410
Capacity: 6 rounds
Features: Patented heat-treated scandium frame; PVD coated cylinder; dovetailed Tritium front night sight; fixed rear sight; matte silver finish; furnished with two full moon clips and three two-shot moon clips for use with .45 ACP
MSRP $809.00

MODEL S&W500

Action: SA/DA revolver
Grips: Synthetic
Barrel: 3.5 in., 4 in., 6.5 in., 7.5 in., 8.38-in., 10.5 in.
Sights: Vary with model
Weight 55.6 oz.–79.6 oz.
Caliber: .500 S&W Mag.
Capacity: 5 rounds
Features: First X-frame developed by S&W and debuted in 2003; most powerful production revolver in the world; base variant has 6.5-in barrel, red ramp front sight/adjustable white outline rear, half-lug, top-vent muzzle compensation; variant with 8.38-in.

barrel has full underlug, choice of interchangeable front sight and top-vent compensator, or HIVIZ red interchangeable front sight with side-vent compensator; variant with 4-in. barrel has full underlug, removable side-vent compensator, red ramp front sight, adjustable rear, satin stainless finish; Performance Center 10.5-in. barrel has full tapered underlug, orange ramp front sights, sling swivels, top-side Weaver optics rail, muzzle brake; Performance Center HIVIZ 3.5-in. barrel has green HIVIZ fiber optic front sight, white outline adjustable rear sight, overall satin finish, unfluted cylinder, trigger overtravel stop; Performance Center 7.5-in. barrel with flats has full tapered underlug, orange ramp front sight, adjustable black blade rear sight, matte silver finish, full muzzle brake
6.5-in. barrel: $1299.00
8.38-in. barrel: . . . $1299.00–$1369.00
4-in. barrel: $1369.00
Performance Center
10.5-in. barrel: $1599.00
Performance Center
HIVIZ 3.5-in. barrel: $1609.00
Performance Center
7.5-in. barrel: $1579.00

SMITH & WESSON PERFORMANCE CENTER MODEL 325 THUNDER RANCH

SMITH & WESSON PERFORMANCE CENTER MODEL 327

SMITH & WESSON PERFORMANCE CENTER MODEL 327 TRR8

SMITH & WESSON PERFORMANCE CENTER MODEL 629 V-COMP

SMITH & WESSON PERFORMANCE CENTER MODEL 625

PERFORMANCE CENTER MODEL 325 THUNDER RANCH

Action: SA/DA revolver
Grips: Synthetic
Barrel: 4 in.
Sights: Interchangeable gold bead front; adjustable rear
Weight: 31 oz.
Caliber: .45 ACP
Capacity: 6 rounds
Features: Scandium alloy frame; stainless steel cylinder; matte black; accommodates accessory rail
MSRP $1329.00

PERFORMANCE CENTER MODEL 327

Action: Revolver
Grips: Wood
Barrel: 2 in.
Sights: Orange ramp front sight, integral "U" rear
Weight: 23.1 oz.
Caliber: .357 Mag., .38 S&W Spl. +P
Capacity: 8 rounds
Features: Color case with overtravel stop; color case tear drop with pinned sear; large frame size; exposed hammer; matte black finish; scandium alloy frame and titanium alloy

cylinder; polish button rifling; smooth double action with Wolff Mainspring
MSRP $1309.00

PERFORMANCE CENTER MODEL 327 TRR8

Action: SA/DA revolver
Grips: Synthetic
Barrel: 5 in.
Sights: Interchangeable front; adjustable V-notch rear
Weight: 35.3 oz.
Caliber: .357 Mag., .38 S&W Spl. +P
Capacity: 8 rounds
Features: Scandium alloy frame; stainless steel cylinder; matte black; large size frame; exposed hammer; equipment rails
MSRP $1329.00

PERFORMANCE CENTER MODEL 625

Action: SA/DA revolver
Grips: Altamont laminate, red, white & blue
Barrel: 4 in.
Sights: Gold bead S&W interchangeable front; Black adjustable rear
Weight: 42 oz.
Caliber: .45 ACP

Capacity: 6 rounds
Features: Performance Center version sports Altamont red-white-and-blue laminate grips, stainless steel frame and cylinder with satin stainless finish],deep cut broached rifling, chamfered charge holes, custom teardrop hammer, interchangeable gold bead front sight, adjustable black rear sight, ¾ underlug
MSRP $1079.00

PERFORMANCE CENTER MODEL 629 V-COMP

Action: SA/DA revolver
Grips: Synthetic
Barrel: 4 in.
Sights: Adjustable orange dovetail front, adjustable black rear
Weight: 43.8 oz.
Caliber: .44 Mag., .44 S&W Spl.
Capacity: 6 rounds
Features: Stainless steel frame and cylinder with matte finish; removable compensator and cap muzzle protector; chamfered charge holes; ball detent lock-up; chromed hammer and trigger with overtravel stop
MSRP $1559.00

Smith & Wesson

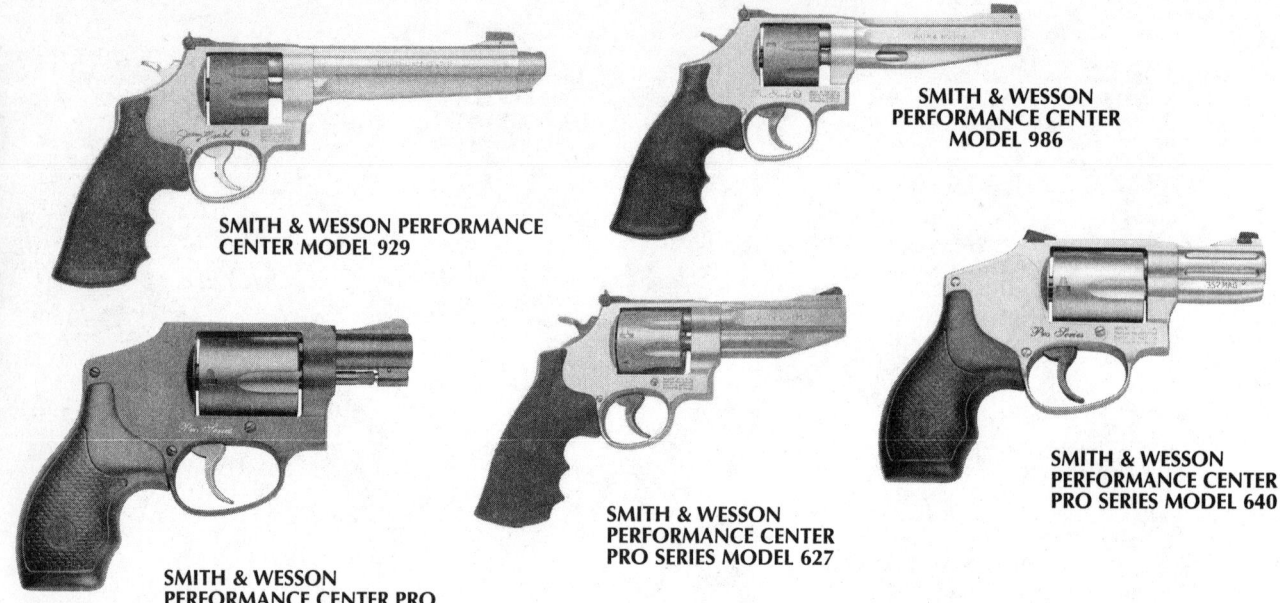

SMITH & WESSON PERFORMANCE CENTER MODEL 929

SMITH & WESSON PERFORMANCE CENTER MODEL 986

SMITH & WESSON PERFORMANCE CENTER PRO SERIES MODEL 442 MOON CLIP

SMITH & WESSON PERFORMANCE CENTER PRO SERIES MODEL 627

SMITH & WESSON PERFORMANCE CENTER PRO SERIES MODEL 640

PERFORMANCE CENTER MODEL 929

Action: DA/SA revolver
Grips: Synthetic
Barrel: 6.5 in.
Sights: Adjustable
Weight: 44.2 oz.
Caliber: 9mm
Capacity: 8 rounds
Features: Removable compensator; titanium cylinder; Jerry Miculek signature; chrome teardrop hammer; chrome trigger with stop
MSRP $1189.00

PERFORMANCE CENTER MODEL 986

Action: DA/SA revolver
Grips: Synthetic
Barrel: 5 in.
Sights: Adjustable
Weight: 34.9 oz.
Caliber: 9mm
Capacity: 7 rounds
Features: Titanium, fluted cylinder; precision crowned barrel; cylinder cut for moonclips
MSRP $1149.00

PERFORMANCE CENTER PRO SERIES MODEL 442 MOON CLIP

Action: DA revolver
Grips: Synthetic
Barrel: 1.87 in.
Sights: Integral front, fixed rear

Weight: 15 oz.
Caliber: .38 S&W Spl. +P
Capacity: 5 rounds
Features: Aluminum alloy frame; stainless steel cylinder; matte black finish; small size frame; internal hammer; cylinder cut for moon clips
MSRP $499.00

PERFORMANCE CENTER PRO SERIES MODEL 627

Action: SA/DA revolver
Grips: Synthetic
Barrel: 2.625 in., 4 in., 5 in.
Sights: varies with model
Weight: 37.8 oz.–46.7 oz.
Caliber: .357 Mag.
Capacity: 8 rounds
Features: Performance Center Pro Series with 4-in. barrel has matte silver finish, chamfered charge holes, custom barrel with recessed precision crown, bossed mainspring, Hogue grips, interchangeable front sight, adjustable rear; Performance Center V-Comp variant has 5-in. barrel, removable compensator, two-tone black frame and barrel/matte stainless cylinder and controls, Hogue grips, adjustable orange dovetail front sight, adjustable rear sight, chrome hammer, chrome trigger with trigger stop; two variants known simply as Performance Center Model 627: 1) Has 2.625-in. barrel, unfluted cylinder, wood gripsdovetail red ramp front sight,

adjustable white outline rear, ball detent lockup, chrome flashed custom tear drop hammer, chrome flashed trigger with stop, cylinder cut for moon clips; 2) Performance Center 5-in. barrel similar to Pro Series with tapering underlug, but with both wood and synthetic grips, gold bead front sight, adjustable rear sight, matte silver finish
Performance Center Pro Series 4-in. barrel: . . . $999.00
Performance Center V-Comp 5-in. barrel: $1599.00
Performance Center 2.625-in. barrel: $1079.00
Performance Center 5-in. barrel: $1289.00

PERFORMANCE CENTER PRO SERIES MODEL 640

Action: DA revolver
Grips: Synthetic
Barrel: 2.1 in.
Sights: Black blade front, fixed rear
Weight: 23 oz.
Caliber: .357 Mag.
Capacity: 5 rounds
Features: Stainless steel frame, barrel, and cylinder, front and rear dovetail tritium night sights, concealed hammer, cylinder cut for moon clips, satin stainless finish
MSRP $839.00

SMITH & WESSON PERFORMANCE CENTER PRO SERIES MODEL 686 SSR

SMITH & WESSON M&P BODYGUARD 380

SMITH & WESSON M&P PRO SERIES C.O.R.E. PISTOL PERFORMANCE CENTER

SMITH & WESSON M&P SHIELD

SMITH & WESSON M&P9 SHIELD CRIMSON TRACE GREEN LASER-GUARD

PERFORMANCE CENTER PRO SERIES MODEL 686 SSR

Action: Revolver
Grips: Wood
Barrel: 4 in.
Sights: Interchangeable front, adjustable rear
Weight: 38.3 oz.
Caliber: .357 Mag., .38 S&W Spl. +P
Capacity: 6 rounds
Features: Stainless steel frame and barrel with satin finish; exposed hammer; chamfered charge holes; bossed mainspring; ergonomic grip to force high-hand hold; custom barrel with recessed precision crown
MSRP $999.00

SEMIAUTOMATIC

M&P BODYGUARD 380

Action: DA semiautomatic
Grips: Synthetic
Barrel: 2.75 in.
Sights: Adjustable
Weight: 11.85 oz.
Caliber: .380 ACP
Capacity: 6+1 rounds
Features: Stainless steel drift adjustable sights; ergonomic grip; high-strength polymer frame; external takedown lever and slide stop;

manual thumb safety; double action fire control (2nd strike compatibility); stainless steel barrel and slide; available in Flat Dark Earth with or without integral Crimson Trace laser; in Armornite finish without thumb safety, without thumb safety but with integral Crimson Trace laser, with thumb safety (no other enhancements), and with thumb safety and choice of Crimson Trace green Laserguard; and with an engraved stainless slide.
MSRP . . . . $379.00–$519.00

M&P PRO SERIES C.O.R.E. PISTOL PERFORMANCE CENTER

Action: Striker Fire Double Action
Grips: Polymer
Barrel: 4.25 in., 5 in.
Sights: White dot dovetail front, fixed 2-dot rear
Weight: 24 oz.–26 oz.
Caliber: 9mm, .40 S&W
Capacity: 17+1, 15+1 rounds
Features: Competition Optics Ready Equipment; mounting platform on slide; engineered as a competition platform; polymer frame; ambidextrous operating controls; interchangeable back strap; Performance Center sear; Melonite finish

MSRP . . . . $689.00–$769.00

M&P SHIELD

Action: Striker Fired
Grips: Polymer
Barrel: 3.1 in.
Sights: White dot front, white 2-dot rear
Weight: 19 oz.
Caliber: 9mm, .40 S&W
Capacity: 6, 7, 8 rounds
Features: Slim, concealable, and lightweight defense firearm; high-strength polymer frame; Melonite coated; consistent 6.5 lb. trigger pull; loaded chamber indicator; many variants available, including Flat Dark Earth and Armornite finishes, with night sights, with and without thumb safety, with Crimson Trace green Laserguard, and California- and Massachusetts-compliant models; Performance Center versions in each caliber get PC sear, enhanced trigger, ported barrel and slide, HIVIZ fiber optic sights or night sights
Without laser: . . . . $449.00–$549.00
Laserguard: $589.00
Performance
Center: . . . . $519.00–$742.00

M&P9 SHIELD CRIMSON TRACE GREEN LASERGUARD

Action: Semiautomatic
Grips: Synthetic
Barrel: 3.1 in.
Sights: Fixed
Weight: 19 oz.
Caliber: 9mm
Capacity: 7 or 8 rounds
Features: Striker fire action; white dot front sight; stainless steel slide and barrel
MSRP $589.00

Smith & Wesson

**SMITH & WESSON
SD9 VE**

**SMITH & WESSON
SW22 VICTORY**

**SMITH & WESSON
SW1911 ENGRAVED**

SD9 VE AND SD40 VE

Action: Striker Fired
Grips: Textured polymer
Barrel: 4 in.
Sights: White dot front, fixed 2-dot rear
Weight: 22.7 oz.
Caliber: 9mm, .40 S&W
Capacity: 10+1, 14+1, 16+1 rounds
Features: Lightweight polymer frame; front and rear slide serrations; Self Defense Trigger; ergonomic grip; Picatinny rail; two-tone finish
**Standard and low capacity: . .$389.00
California- and Massachusetts-
   compliant: $409.00**

SW22 VICTORY

Action: SA
Grips: Polymer
Barrel: 5.5 in.
Sights: Green fiber optic front, adjustable fiber optic rear
Weight: 36 oz.
Caliber: .22 LR
Capacity: 10+1 rounds
Features: Removable interchangeable match-grade barrel; steel reinforced polymer thumb safety; Picatinny-style rail included; adjustable trigger stop; stainless steel frame; textured grip panels with finger cuts for easy magazine removal; available in Kryptek Highlander finish or in a

stainless version with threaded barrel
**Stainless: $409.00
Stainless w/ threaded barrel:$429.00
Kryptec: $459.00**

SW1911 ENGRAVED

Action: SA
Grips: Wood laminate E-Series
Barrel: 5 in.
Sights: White dot front, white two dot rear
Weight: 39.1 oz.
Caliber: .45 ACP
Capacity: 8+1 rounds
Features: Glass bead finish; machine scroll engraving; engraved, wooden presentation case
MSRP. $1219.00

Springfield Armory

**SPRINGFIELD
ARMORY 1911
LOADED**

**SPRINGFIELD ARMORY
1911 MARINE CORPS
OPERATOR**

**SPRINGFIELD
ARMORY 1911 EMP
LIGHTWEIGHT
CHAMPION**

1911 EMP 4-IN. LIGHTWEIGHT CHAMPION

Action: SA semiautomatic
Grips: Cocobolo
Barrel: 4 in.
Sights: Three dot iron w/ fiber optic front and white dot rear
Weight: 31 oz. (9mm), 37 oz. (.40 S&W)
Caliber: 9mm, .40 S&W
Capacity: 9, 10 rounds
Features: Ambidextrous safety levers; match-grade barrel; Posi-Lock grip texture to the front strap; forged aluminum alloy frame with black hardcoat anodized finish
MSRP. $1179.00

1911 LOADED

Action: Semiautomatic
Grips: Synthetic
Barrel: 5 in.
Sights: Fixed
Weight: 43 oz.
Caliber: .45 ACP
Capacity: 8 rounds
Features: Forged steel; integral accessory rail; black Armory Kote; low profile combat, 3-dot tritium; GI style recoil system
MSRP. $1399.00

1911 MARINE CORPS OPERATOR

Action: Semiautomatic
Grips: Synthetic
Barrel: 5 in.
Sights: Fixed
Weight: 43 oz.
Caliber: .45 ACP
Capacity: 7 rounds
Features: Forged steel; integral accessory rail; olive drab Armory Kote; low profile combat, 3-dot tritium; GI style recoil system
MSRP. $1299.00

Springfield Armory

SPRINGFIELD ARMORY
1911 RANGE OFFICER

SPRINGFIELD ARMORY
1911 RANGE OFFICER
CHAMPION

SPRINGFIELD ARMORY
1911 RANGE OFFICER
OPERATOR

SPRINGFIELD ARMORY
1911 RANGE OFFICER
STAINLESS

SPRINGFIELD
ARMORY EMP

SPRINGFIELD ARMORY
LIGHTWEIGHT
CHAMPION OPERATOR

SPRINGFIELD ARMORY
MIL-SPEC FULL SIZE
STAINLESS

1911 RANGE OFFICER

Action: Semiautomatic
Grips: Cocobolo
Barrel: 5 in.
Sights: Adjustable
Weight: 41 oz.
Caliber: .45 ACP, 9mm
Capacity: 9 rounds
Features: Designed for competitive shooters, with GI-style recoil system, national match stainless barrel with fully supported ramp, forged carbon steel frame and slide, Cross Cannon double diamond cocobolo grips, fiber optic front sight in a shielded tube, flat mainspring housing, aluminum match trigger skeletonized hammer, and accessory rail; parkerized or stainless finishes
Parkerized: **$945.00**
Stainless: **$1055.00**

1911 RANGE OFFICER CHAMPION

Action: Semiautomatic
Grips: Wood
Barrel: 4 in.
Sights: Fixed
Weight: 30 oz.
Caliber: .45 ACP
Capacity: 7 rounds
Features: Grips are Cross Cannon double diamond cocobolo; fiber optic front and low profile combat rear; dual spring recoil system with full length guide rod
MSRP **$908.00**

1911 RANGE OFFICER OPERATOR

Action: Semiautomatic
Grips: Double-diamond cocobolo
Barrel: 5 in.
Sights: Fiber optic front, low-profile combat rear
Weight: 40 oz. (.45 ACP), 41 oz. (9mm)
Caliber: .45 ACP, 9mm
Capacity: 9 rounds
Features: Fully supported ramp provides an extended sight radius; Parkerized finish that looks sharp and will ward off corrosion and rust; flat mainspring housing is checkered for positive grip; extended beavertail safety includes a memory bump for positive activation; aluminum match-grade trigger; skeletonized hammer; rail for light or laser
MSRP **$1039.00**

1911 RANGE OFFICER STAINLESS

Action: Semiautomatic
Grips: Double-diamond cocobolo
Barrel: 5 in.
Sights: Fully adjustable target with fiber optic front
Weight: 40 oz. (.45 ACP), 41 oz. (9mm)
Caliber: .45 ACP, 9mm
Capacity: 9 rounds
Features: Forged stainless steel slide and frame; Cross Cannon double-diamond cocobolo grips; GI-style recoil system
MSRP **$1055.00**

EMP (ENHANCED MICRO PISTOL)

Action: Semiautomatic
Grips: Thin line cocobolo wood
Barrel: 3 in.

Sights: Fixed low profile combat rear, dovetail
Weight: 26 oz.–33 oz.
Caliber: 9mm, .40 S&W
Capacity: 3–9 (9mm) or 3–8 (.40 S&W) rounds
Features: Forged stainless steel, satin finish; dual spring recoil system with full length guide rod
MSRP . . . . **$1104.00–$1249.00**

LIGHTWEIGHT CHAMPION OPERATOR

Action: Semiautomatic
Grips: Cocobolo wood
Barrel: 4 in.
Sights: Fixed low profile combat rear, dovetail
Weight: 31 oz.
Caliber: .45 ACP
Capacity: 2–7 rounds
Features: Stainless steel match grade, fully supported ramped bull barrel; long aluminum Match Grade trigger; forged aluminum alloy with integral accessory rail; black hard coat anodized; dual spring with full length guide rod
MSRP **$1050.00**

MIL-SPEC FULL SIZE

Action: Semiautomatic
Grips: Cocobolo wood and black plastic
Barrel: 5 in.
Sights: Fixed combat, 3-dot
Weight: 39 oz.
Caliber: .45 ACP
Capacity: 2–7 rounds
Features: Forged stainless steel, matte rounds with polished flats; GI style recoil system; available Parkerized finish or stainless
Parkerized: **$726.00**
Stainless: **$828.00**

Springfield Armory

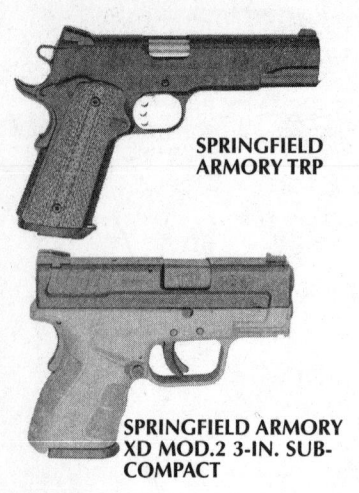

SPRINGFIELD ARMORY TRP

SPRINGFIELD ARMORY XD (M)

SPRINGFIELD ARMORY XD MOD.2 4-IN. SERVICE MODEL

SPRINGFIELD ARMORY XD MOD.2 3-IN. SUB-COMPACT

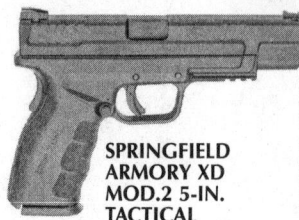

SPRINGFIELD ARMORY XD MOD.2 5-IN. TACTICAL

SPRINGFIELD ARMORY XD(M) 4.5" FULL SIZE WITH THREADED BARREL

SPRINGFIELD ARMORY XD (M) COMPACT

TRP (TACTICAL RESPONSE PISTOL)

Action: Semiautomatic
Grips: G10 composite
Barrel: 5 in.
Sights: Front tritium 3-dot, fixed low profile combat rear, dovetail
Weight: 42 oz.
Caliber: .45 ACP
Capacity: 2–7 rounds
Features: Forged steel frame with black armory kote; two piece full length guide rod; wide-mouth magazine well; tuned trigger; available in Armory Kote and stainless
MSRP $1646.00

XD (M)

Action: DA semiautomatic
Grips: Polymer
Barrel: 3.8 in., 4.5 in., 5.25 in.
Sights: 3-dot
Weight: 27.5 oz.–32 oz.
Caliber: 9mm, .40 S&W, .45 ACP
Capacity: 19 (9mm), 16 (.40 S&W) or 13 (.45 ACP) rounds
Features: "M" features include carrying case, two magazines, paddle holster, magi loader, double magi pouch and three interchangeable backstraps and two magazines; "all-terrain" texture and deep slide serrations are standard
4.5-in. .45 ACP: $651.00
3.8-in., 4.5-in
9mm, .40 S&W: $624.00
Competition: . . . . . $769.00–$796.00

XD MOD.2 4-IN. SERVICE MODEL

Action: Semiautomatic
Grips: Polymer

Barrel: 4 in.
Sights: Fiber optic front, low-profle combat rear
Weight: 27.5 oz. (9mm), 29.5 oz. (.40 S&W), 30 oz. (.45 ACP)
Caliber: 9mm, .40 S&W, .45 ACP
Capacity: 16 rounds
Features: Polymer frame with GripZone texture; available in black (all calibers) and bi-tone (9mm, .40 S&W), or Tactical Gray (9mm only) finishes; striker status indicator; loaded chamber indicator; forged steel slide with Melonite finish; accessory rail in front of trigger guard; internal firing pin block; Ultra Safety Assurance Action Trigger System
MSRP . . . . $565.00–$599.00

XD MOD.2 3-IN. SUB-COMPACT

Action: Semiautomatic
Grips: Polymer
Barrel: 3 in.
Sights: Fiber optic front, low-profle combat rear
Weight: 26 oz.
Caliber: .40 SW, 9mm
Capacity: 9, 10, 12, 13, 16 rounds
Features: Ultra-compact carry gun has Melonite finish steel barrel and slide, full-length guide rod; available in black, bi-tone, and Flat Dark Earth
MSRP . . . . $565.00–$599.00

XD MOD.2 5-IN. TACTICAL

Action: Semiautomatic
Grips: Polymer
Barrel: 5 in.
Sights: Three dot iron w/ fiber optic front and white dot rear
Weight: 29 oz.
Caliber: 9mm, .45 ACP
Capacity: 10, 13, 16 rounds

Features: Double-stack design; full 5 in. hammer forged carbon steel barrel; Melonite-treated to stand up to moisture, sweat, and other undesirable conditions; High-Hand grip near the beavertail and below the trigger guard; GripZone contours and texturing
MSRP . . . . $608.00–$637.00

XD(M) 4.5" FULL SIZE WITH THREADED BARREL

Action: DA semiautomatic
Grips: Polymer
Barrel: 4.5 in.
Sights: Dovetail front, rear three dot
Weight: 29 oz.
Caliber: .45 ACP, 9mm
Capacity: 19 rounds
Features: One-piece full-length guide rod; forged steel slide with Melonite finish; suppressor-height three-dot dovetail sights; flat dark earth polymer finish
MSRP . . . . $645.00–$673.00

XD (M) COMPACT

Action: Semiautomatic
Grips: Synthetic
Barrel: 3.8 in., 5.25 in.
Sights: Fiber optic front, adjustable rear
Weight: 27 oz.–32 oz.
Caliber: 9mm, .45 ACP, .40 S&W
Capacity: 13, 19 rounds
Features: A handgun with improved accuracy, lessened recoil, faster shot recovery and greater sight radius of its newly enhanced performance; lightening cut in the slide reduces reciprocating mass which allows for faster cycling and allows a larger variety of loads to be used
MSRP . . . . $659.00–$694.00

Springfield Armory

SPRINGFIELD ARMORY XD MOD.2 SUB-COMPACT WITH GRIP ZONE

SPRINGFIELD ARMORY XD-S

SPRINGFIELD ARMORY XD-S SINGLE STACK .40 SW

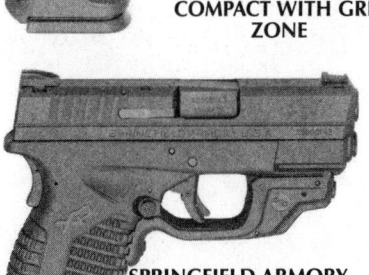

SPRINGFIELD ARMORY XD-S SINGLE STACK WITH CRIMSON LASERGUARD

XD MOD.2 SUB-COMPACT WITH GRIP ZONE

Action: Semiautomatic
Grips: Rubber
Barrel: 3 in., 4 in., 5 in.
Sights: Fixed
Weight: 26–27 oz.
Caliber: 9mm
Capacity: 9 or 13 rounds
Features: Captive recoil spring with full length guide rod; fiber optic front and low profile combat rear; available in black and bi-tone all barrel lengths, Flat Dark Earth in 3-in. barrel, Gray in 4-in. barrel
MSRP . . . . $565.00–$651.00

XD-S

Action: DAO semiautomatic
Grips: Polymer
Barrel: 3.3 in., 4 in.
Sights: Steel dovetail rear, fiber optic front
Weight: 21.5 oz.
Caliber: .40 S&W, .45 ACP, 9mm
Capacity: 5+1 rounds
Features: Slim contour, single stack frame; Ultra Safety Assurance trigger system; loaded chamber indicator; fail-safe disassembly; Picatinny rail system; Mould-Tru backstraps; Melonite finish; 9mm and .45 ACP available in both barrel lengths; .40 S&W available only in 3.3-in. barrel; available in black, bi-tone, Flat Dark Earth, and gray
MSRP . . . . $499.00–$593.00

XD-S 3.3-IN.

Action: DAO semiautomatic
Grips: Polymer
Barrel: 3.3 in.
Sights: Fiber optic front, dovetail rear
Weight: 21.5 oz.–23 oz.
Caliber: .40 SW, 9mm, .45 ACP
Capacity: 5, 6, 7, 8 rounds

Features: Single-stack, striker-fired, polymer frame sub-compact pistol with Melonite-finished barrel and slide; in black, bi-tone, and Flat Dark Earth (all calibers) and Tactical Gray (9mm only); interchangeable backstraps, loaded chamber indicator
MSRP . . . . $499.00–$593.00

XD-S 3.3-IN. WITH CRIMSON TRACE LASERGUARD

Action: DAO semiautomatic
Grips: Polymer
Barrel: 3.3 in.
Sights: Fiber optic front, dovetail rear
Weight: 23 oz.
Caliber: 9mm, .45 ACP
Capacity: 5, 6, 7, 8 rounds
Features: Similar to XD-S 3.3-in. model, but with fully integrated Crimson Trace Laserguard; available in black only
MSRP . . . . $608.00–$652.00

Steyr Arms

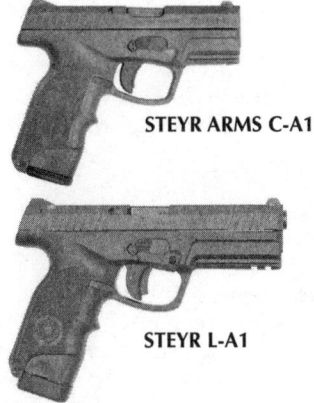

STEYR ARMS C-A1

STEYR L-A1

C-A1

Action: Striker-fired semiautomatic
Grips: Textured polymer
Barrel: 3.6 in.
Sights: Fixed triangular/trapezoid
Weight: 25.6 oz.
Caliber: 9mm, .40 S&W
Capacity: 12, 17 rounds
Features: Polymer frame; trigger, internal striker, internal gun-lock safeties; polygonal rifling; black matte Mannox finish; Picatinny rail
MSRP $560.00

L-A1

Action: Semiautomatic
Grips: Synthetic
Barrel: 4.5 in.
Sights: Fixed triangular/trapezoid
Weight: 28.6 oz.
Caliber: 9mm, .40 S&W
Capacity: 12 or 17 rounds
Features: Rectangular sights with or without Trilux, match sights; full size service pistol; matte finish
From $560.00

STI International

**STI INTERNATIONAL
APEIRO**

**STI
INTERNATIONAL
DVC OPEN**

**STI INTERNATIONAL
EDGE**

**STI INTERNATIONAL
GUARDIAN 2011**

**STI INTERNATIONAL
TACTICAL DS 2011**

**STI
INTERNATIONAL
TROJAN 5.0**

APEIRO

Action: Semiautomatic
Grips: STI patented modular polymer
Barrel: 5 in.
Sights: Dawson fiber optic front mounted on barrel, STI adjustable rear
Weight: 39 oz.
Caliber: 9mm, .40 S&W, .45 ACP
Capacity: 11+1, 14+1, 17+1 rounds
Features: Full length stainless steel bar stock slide features STI's unique sabertooth rear cocking serrations; Schuemann barrel; STI recoil master; STI long curved trigger; blued finish with two toned blued/stainless steel slide
MSRP **$2999.00**

DVC OPEN

Action: Semitautomatic
Grips: Synthetic
Barrel: 5 in.
Sights: None
Weight: 48 oz.
Caliber: .38 Super, 9mm

Capacity: 15, 17, 20, 26 rounds
Features: 2.5 lb. trigger; Dawson toolless guide rod; hard chrome finish; titanium nitride finish barrel and compensator; reversible, dual detent slide racker; mounted C-More 6 MOA dot sight
MSRP **$3999.00**

EDGE

Action: Semiautomatic
Grips: STI patented modular polymer with aluminum mag well
Barrel: 5 in.
Sights: STI front, STI adjustable rear
Weight: 37.6 oz.
Caliber: 9mm, .38 Super, .40 S&W, .45 ACP
Capacity: 11+1, 14+1, 17+1 rounds
Features: STI fully supported, ramped bull barrel; stainless STI grip and ambi slided thumb; STI recoil master guide rod; blued finish
MSRP **$2199.00**

GUARDIAN 2011

Action: Semiautomatic
Grips: Plastic
Barrel: 3.9 in.
Sights: TAS rear, white dot front and rear
Weight: N/A
Caliber: 9mm, .45 ACP
Capacity: 15 rounds
Features: Lightweight aluminum,

narrow frame; shorter VIP grip for easier concealment in light cover; single side safety lever
MSRP **$1899.00**

TACTICAL DS 2011

Action: Semiautomatic
Grips: 2011 Molded
Barrel: 4.15 in., 5.0 in.
Sights: Fixed ledge rear, ramped front; tall tritium suppressor sights
Weight: N/A
Caliber: 9mm, .45 ACP
Capacity: 13, 21 rounds
Features: Features bull barrel in choice of two lengths, threaded barrel option, ambidextrous safety lever, tactical magwell, long tactical dust cover, Picatinny under-rail, steel frame, Recoil Master system, black Cerakote finish
Standard barrel: **$2199.00**
Threaded barrel: **$2399.00**

TROJAN 5.0

Action: Semiautomatic
Grips: STI logo, checkered, cocobolo wood, thin
Barrel: 5 in.
Sights: Fiber optic front sight, LPA adjustable rear
Weight: 36 oz.
Caliber: 9mm, .45 ACP
Capacity: 8, 9 rounds
Features: STI standard blue grip and single-slided thumb safeties; STI one-piece steel guide rod; flat blued finish
MSRP **$1499.00**

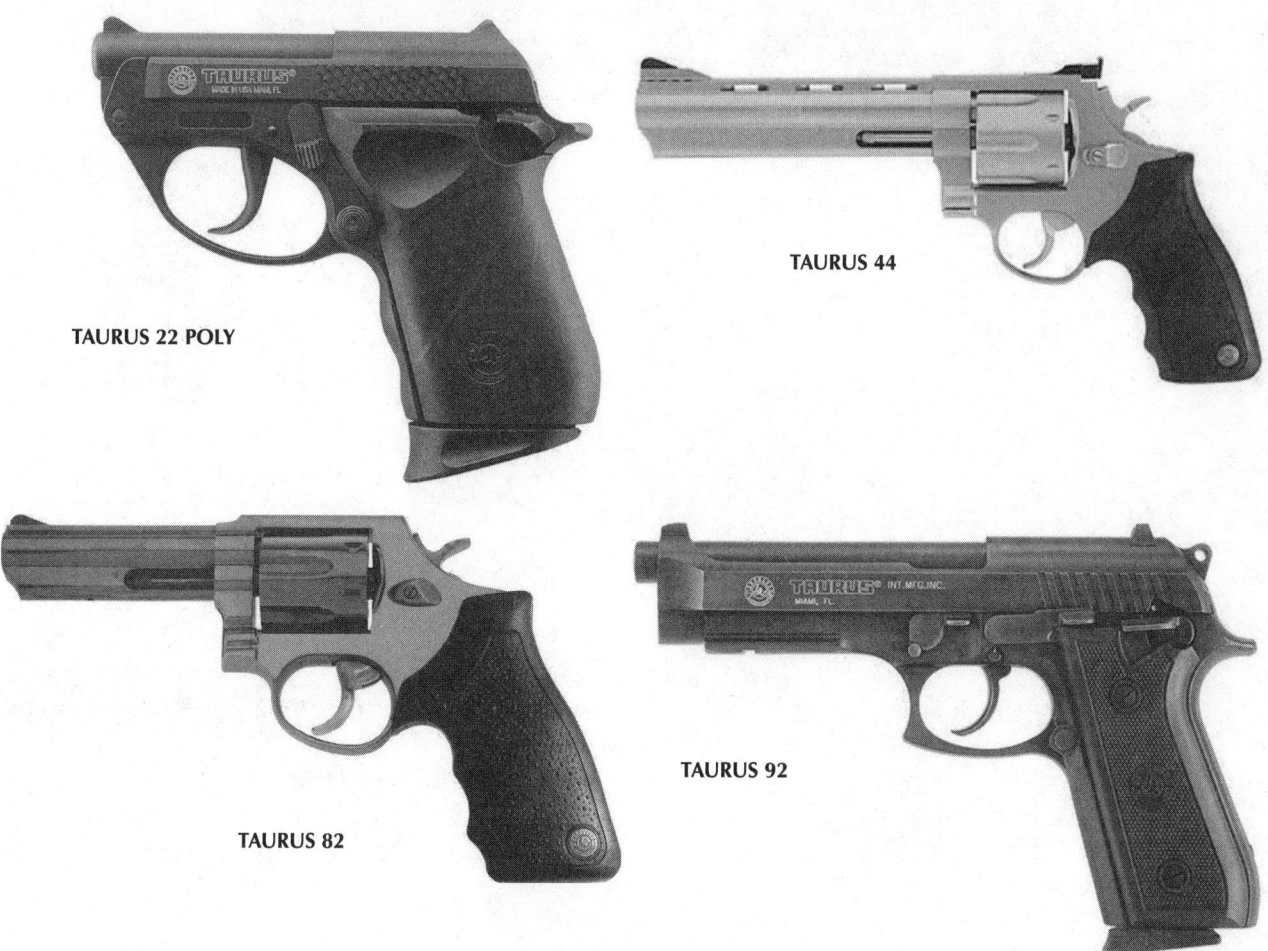

TAURUS 22 POLY

TAURUS 44

TAURUS 82

TAURUS 92

22 POLY
Action: DA semiautomatic
Grips: Polymer
Barrel: 2.3 in.
Sights: Fixed
Weight: 11.3 oz.
Caliber: .22 LR
Capacity: 8+1
Features: Polymer/blued steel construction; blued steel finish; tip-up barrel
Blue slide: **$263.74**
Stainless slide:. **$279.35**

44
Action: Revolver
Grips: Soft rubber
Barrel: 4 in., 6.5 in., 8.4 in.
Sights: Fixed
Weight: 45–57 oz.
Caliber: .44 Mag.

Capacity: 6 rounds
Features: Transfer bar; ported barrel; matte stainless steel finish; double and single-action
4 in.: **$726.59**
6.5 in.: **$741.86**
8.4 in.: **$741.86**

82
Action: Revolver
Grips: Rubber
Barrel: 4 in.
Sights: Fixed
Weight: 36.5 oz.
Caliber: .38 Spl. +P
Capacity: 6 rounds
Features: Transfer bar; steel construction with blued finish; single/double-action trigger
Blued: **$471.67**

92
Action: Semiautomatic
Grips: Checkered rubber
Barrel: 5 in.
Sights: Fixed-1 dot front, fixed-2 dots rear
Weight: 34 oz.
Caliber: 9mm
Capacity: 10+1 or 17+1 rounds
Features: Blued, stainless steel finish; steel/alloy construction; firing pin block, hammer decocker, manual safety
Blued: **$497.83**
Stainless: **$653.32**

Taurus

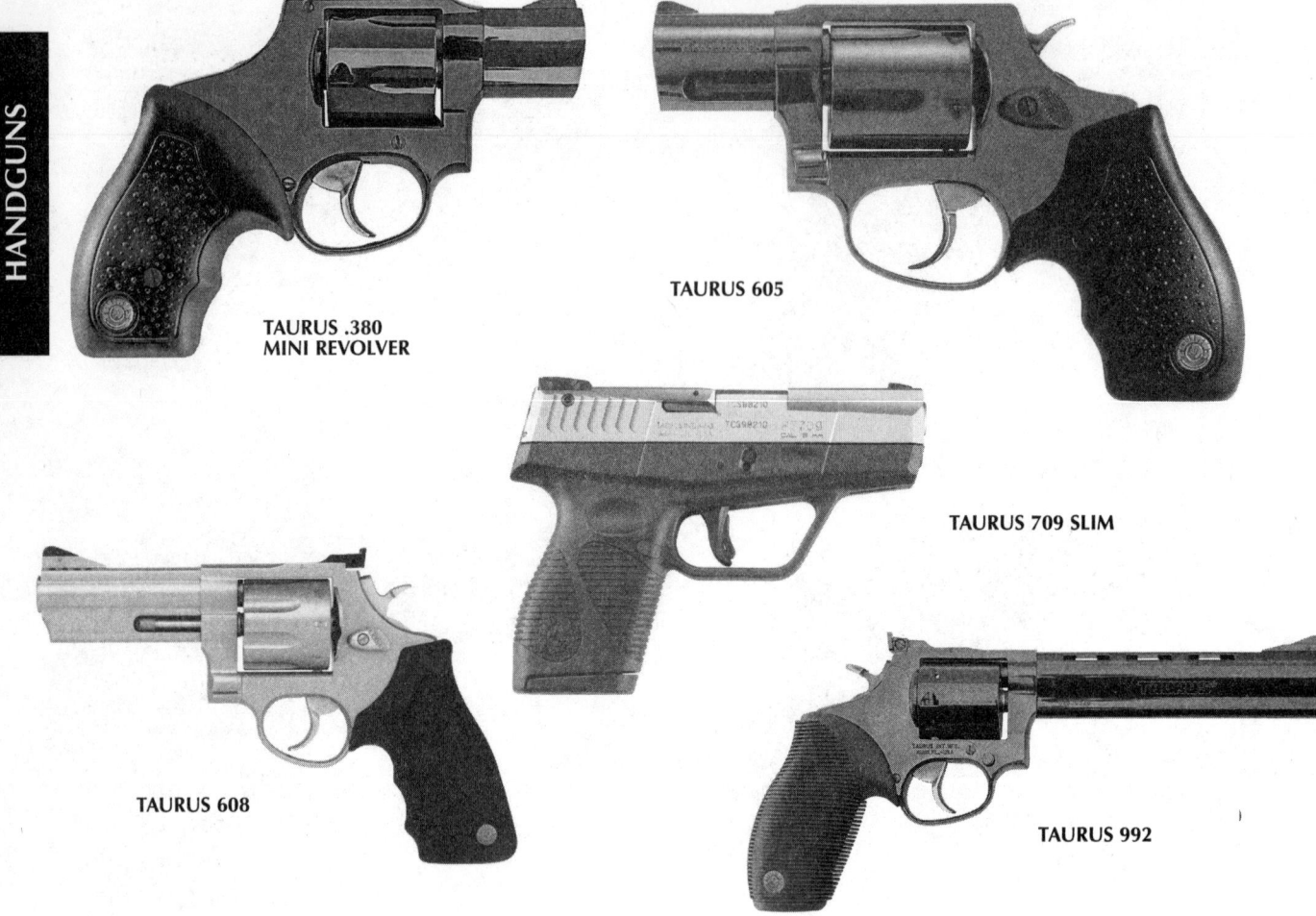

**TAURUS .380
MINI REVOLVER**

TAURUS 605

TAURUS 709 SLIM

TAURUS 608

TAURUS 992

.380 MINI REVOLVER
Action: Revolver
Grips: Rubber
Barrel: 1.75 in.
Sights: Adjustable rear
Weight: 15.5 oz.
Caliber: .380 ACP
Capacity: 5 rounds
Features: Double-action trigger; fully enclosed hammer; blued or matte stainless finish; bobbed hammer
Blued: **$433.52**
Stainless: **$465.56**

605
Action: Revolver
Grips: Rubber
Barrel: 2 in.
Sights: Fixed
Weight: 24 oz.
Caliber: .357 Mag
Capacity: 5 rounds
Features: Transfer bar safety; steel construction with blued or stainless finish; single-double action trigger

Blued: **$356.06**
Stainless: **$371.21**

608
Action: Revolver
Grips: Rubber
Barrel: 4 in., 6.5 in.
Sights: Fixed front, adjustable rear
Weight: 44 oz.–51 oz.
Caliber: .357 Mag
Capacity: 8 rounds
Features: Matte stainless steel finish; transfer bar; large frame; steel frame; Taurus security system; porting
MSRP: **$688.43**

709 SLIM
Action: Semiautomatic
Grips: Checkered polymer
Barrel: 3 in.
Sights: Fixed
Weight: 19 oz.
Caliber: 9mm
Capacity: 7+1 rounds
Features: Steel construction; blued or

stainless finish; single- and double-action
MSRP **$319.00**

992
Action: SA/DA revolver
Grips: Taurus Ribber
Barrel: 4 in., 6.5 in.
Sights: Adjustable
Weight: 55 oz.
Caliber: .22 LR
Capacity: 9 rounds
Features: The versatile Tracker 992 easily transforms from .22 LR to .22 Magnum in seconds with its breakthrough removable cylinder; perfect for plinking, target practice, or varmint hunting
Blued: **$590.68**
Stainless: **$627.41**

Taurus

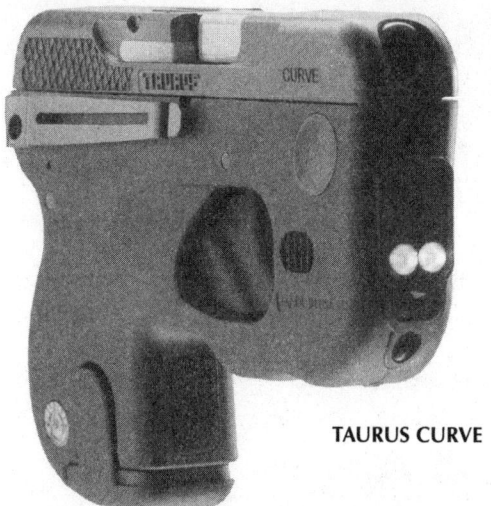

TAURUS CURVE

TAURUS MILLENIUM G2

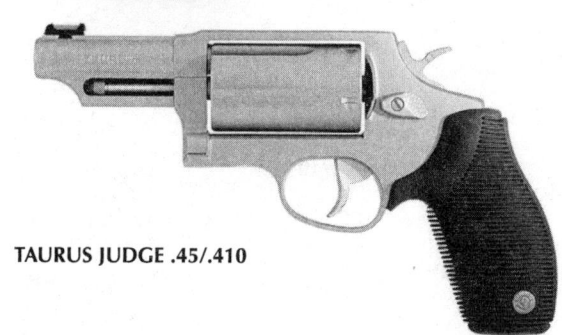

TAURUS JUDGE .45/.410

TAURUS RAGING BULL 444

CURVE

Action: DAO
Grips: Polymer
Barrel: 2.5 in.
Sights: None
Weight: 10.2 oz.
Caliber: .380 ACP
Capacity: 6+1 rounds
Features: Curved form; features Taurus Security System (TSS); light and laser built in
MSRP . . . . **$369.00–$419.00**

JUDGE .45/.410

Action: DA/SA revolver
Grips: Taurus rubber grips
Barrel: 3 in.
Sights: Red fiber optic, fixed
Weight: 29–36.8 oz.
Caliber: .45 Colt/.410
Capacity: 5 rounds
Features: Firing pin block, transfer bar safety; compact frame; matte stainless steel finish; steel construction
Blued: **$589.00**
Stainless: **$629.00**

MILLENIUM G2

Action: Semiautomatic
Grips: Polymer
Barrel: 3.2 in.
Sights: Adjustable
Weight: 22 oz.
Caliber: 9mm, .40 S&W
Capacity: 10, 12 rounds
Features: Loaded chamber indicator; blue finish; Taurus Security System; accessory rail
Blued slide: **$319.00**
Stainless slide: **$339.00**

RAGING BULL 444

Action: Revolver
Grips: Rubber w/cushioned insert
Barrel: 6.5 in., 8.38 in.
Sights: Partridge front, adjustable rear
Weight: 53 oz.–63 oz.
Caliber: .44 Mag.
Capacity: 6 rounds
Features: Steel construction with blued or stainless steel finish; transfer bar; dual lockup cylinder; porting; Taurus security system
Blued: **$752.54**
Stainless: **$799.86**

Taurus

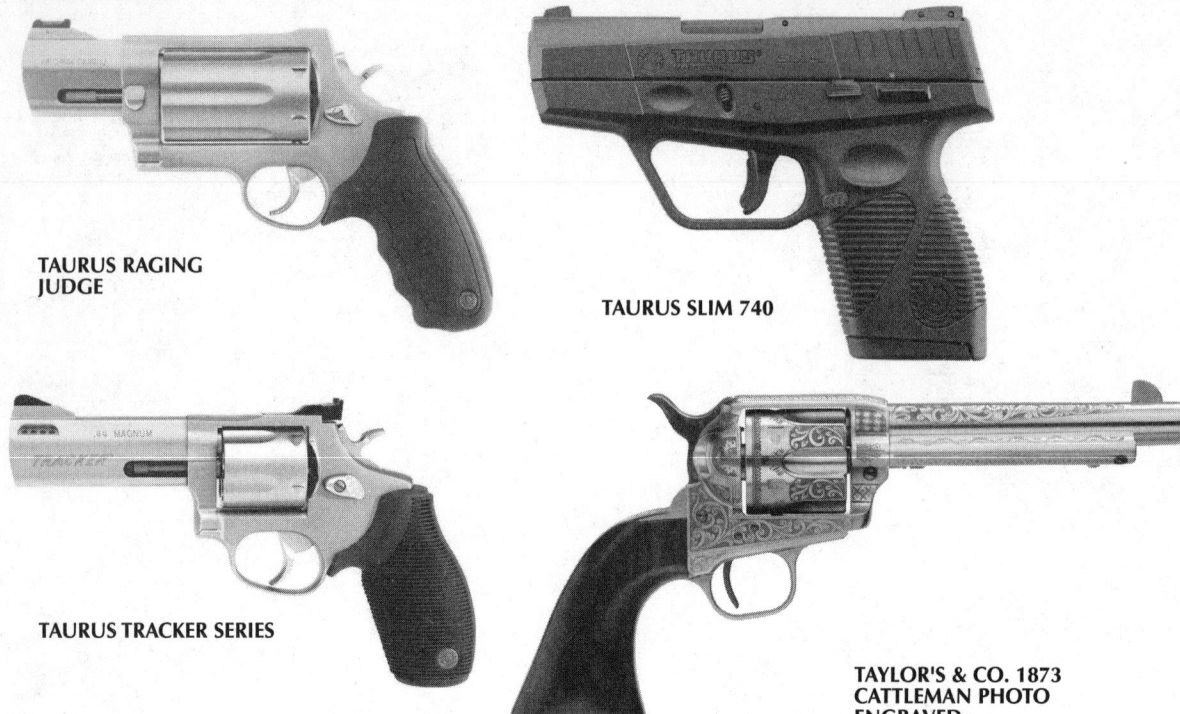

TAURUS RAGING JUDGE

TAURUS SLIM 740

TAURUS TRACKER SERIES

TAYLOR'S & CO. 1873 CATTLEMAN PHOTO ENGRAVED

RAGING JUDGE
Action: DA/SA revolver
Grips: Rubber with soft cushion insert
Barrel: 3 in., 6.5 in.
Sights: Fiber optic front, fixed rear
Weight: 60.6 oz.–73 oz.
Caliber: .410/.45 Colt, .454 Casull
Capacity: 6 rounds
Features: Stainless steel finish; "Raging Bull" backstrap for added cushioning
MSRP $1037.99

SLIM 740
Action: DA/SA semiautomatic
Grips: Polymer metallic inserts
Barrel: 3.2 in.
Sights: Adjustable rear
Weight: 19 oz.
Caliber: .40 S&W

Capacity: 6+1 rounds
Features: Sub-compact pistol in blued, black Tenifer, or stainless steel; loaded chamber indicator; low-profile sights; short, crisp DA/SA trigger pull
Blued: $319.00
Stainless: $339.00

TRACKER SERIES
Action: Revolver
Grips: Rubber with ribs
Barrel: 4 in., 4.5 in., 6.5 in.
Sights: Fixed front, adjustable rear
Weight: 28.8 oz.–46 oz.
Caliber: .22 LR, .22 Mag., .357 Mag., .44 Mag.
Capacity: 5, 7, 9 rounds
Features: Matte stainless steel or blued finish; transfer bar; steel frame; porting

.44 Mag.: . . . . $645.70–$693.02
.357 Mag.: $670.11
.22 LR, .22 Mag.: $555.00

1873 CATTLEMAN PHOTO ENGRAVED
Action: SA revolver
Grips: Walnut
Barrel: 4.75 in., 5.5 in., 7.5 in.
Sights: Fixed
Weight: 2 lb. 4 oz.–3 lb. 6 oz.
Caliber: .357 Mag., .45 LC
Capacity: 6 rounds
Features: White, heat-treated steel finish with charcoal blued screws; laser-engraved and hand chased; forged frame
MSRP . . . . $883.00–$912.00

Taylor's & Co. Firearms

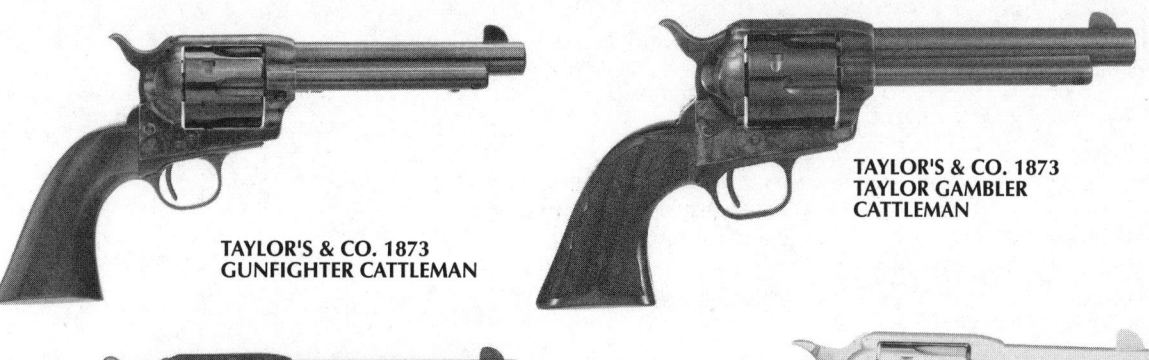

TAYLOR'S & CO. 1873
GUNFIGHTER CATTLEMAN

TAYLOR'S & CO. 1873
TAYLOR GAMBLER
CATTLEMAN

TAYLOR'S & CO. 1873
TAYLOR MARSHALL
CATTLEMAN

TAYLOR'S & CO.
RUNNIN' IRON

TAYLOR'S & CO. THE
SMOKE WAGON

1873 GUNFIGHTER CATTLEMAN

Action: SA revolver
Grips: Walnut
Barrel: 5.5 in.
Sights: Fixed
Weight: 2 lb. 5 oz.
Caliber: .357 Mag., .45 Colt
Capacity: 6 rounds
Features: Special Army-sized grip; steel trigger guard and backstrap; blued finish with case-hardened frame; forged frame
MSRP . . . . $540.00–$575.00

1873 TAYLOR GAMBLER CATTLEMAN

Action: SA revolver
Grips: Walnut
Barrel: 5.5 in.
Sights: Fixed
Weight: 2 lb. 5 oz.
Caliber: .357 Mag., .45 Colt
Capacity: 6 rounds

Features: Fancy checkered walnut grip; blued color case-hardened forged frame
MSRP $565.00

1873 TAYLOR MARSHALL CATTLEMAN

Action: SA revolver
Grips: White PVC
Barrel: 5.5 in.
Sights: Fixed
Weight: 2 lb. 5 oz.
Caliber: .45 Colt
Capacity: 6 rounds
Features: Checkered white PVC grip; blued color case-hardened forged frame
MSRP $661.00

RUNNIN' IRON

Action: SA revolver
Grips: Checkered walnut
Barrel: 3.5 oz.–5.5 in.
Sights: Wider fixed, open
Weight: 39 oz.
Caliber: .45 Colt, .357 Mag.
Capacity: 6 rounds
Features: Designed for the sport of mounted shooting; offered in stainless

or blued finish with low, wide hammer spur; checkered, one-piece gunfighter style grips in walnut or black polymer; wide trigger and extra clearance at front and rear of cylinder
Stainless: . . . . **$766.00–$924.00**
Blued: . . . . **$590.00–$778.00**
Black Rock: . . . . . . **$658.00–$804.00**

SMOKE WAGON

Action: SA revolver
Grips: Checkered wood
Barrel: 3.5 in., 5.5 in.
Sights: Open rear sight groove, wide angle front sight blade
Weight: 40 oz.
Caliber: .357 Mag., .45 Colt, .44-40 Win.
Capacity: 6 rounds
Features: Low profile hammer; deluxe edition model includes custom tuning, custom hammer and base pin springs; jig-cut positive angles on trigger and sears; wire bolt and trigger springs
Standard: . . . . **$565.00–$571.00**
Deluxe: . . . . **$711.00–$717.00**

Thompson/Center Arms

G2 CONTENDER

Action: Single shot, break open design
Grips: Walnut or rubber
Barrel: 12 in., 14 in.
Sights: Adjustable rear; ramp front blade
Weight: 56–60 oz.
Caliber: .22 LR Match, .357 Mag., .44 Rem. Mag., .45 Colt/410 Vent Rib, .223 Rem., .17 HMR, .204 Ruger, 6.8 mm Rem., 7-30 Waters, .45-70 Govt., .30-30 Win.
Capacity: 1 round
Features: .45/410 models include removable choke tube and wrench; stainless steel or walnut frame; manual firing pin selector; button rifled; drilled and tapped for T/C scope mounts
MSRP. **$729.00**

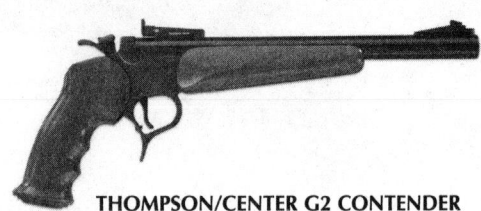

THOMPSON/CENTER G2 CONTENDER

Traditions Firearms

TRADITIONS FIREARMS
FRONTIER

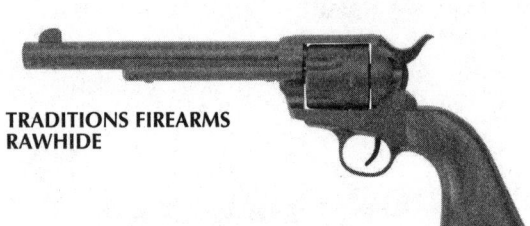

TRADITIONS FIREARMS
RAWHIDE

FRONTIER SERIES

Action: SA revolver
Grips: Simulated ivory or walnut
Barrel: 3.5 in., 4.75 in., 5.5 in., 7.5 in.
Sights: Front blade
Weight: N/A
Caliber: .357 Mag., .44 Mag., .45 Colt, .44-40 Win.
Capacity: 6 rounds
Features: 1873 single action revolvers; deep bluing and nickel frames and barrel or color case hardened frame; transfer bar safety system provides the highest lever of safety offered in an 1873 single action
MSRP. . . . . **$499.00–$659.00**

RAWHIDE SERIES

Action: SA revolver
Grips: Walnut
Barrel: 4.75 in., 5.5 in., 7.5 in.
Sights: Front blade
Weight: N/A
Caliber: .45 Colt, .357 Mag., .22 LR, and .22 LR/.22 Mag.
Capacity: 6 rounds
Features: Quality single action shooter features at an affordable price; matte black finish that provides excellent corrosion resistance; transfer bar system provides the highest level of safety offered in an 1873 single action
MSRP. . . . . **$474.00–$504.00**

Tristar Sporting Arms

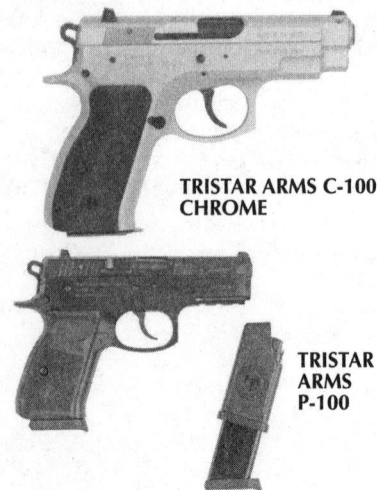

TRISTAR ARMS C-100
CHROME

TRISTAR
ARMS
P-100

C-100

Action: DA/SA semiautomatic
Grips: Polymer
Barrel: 3.9 in.
Sights: Rear dovetail, fixed front
Weight: 24.48 oz.–26.08 oz.
Caliber: 9mm, .40 S&W
Capacity: 11, 15 rounds
Features: Produced to NATO specs; rear snag-free dovetail sights; fixed blade front sight; black polycoat finish; black polymer checkered grips; includes two magazines and a hard plastic case
MSRP. . . . . **$460.00–$480.00**

P-100

Action: Semiautomatic
Grips: Polymer
Barrel: 3.7 in.
Sights: Fixed front, rear dovetail
Weight: 2 lb. 5 oz.
Caliber: 9mm, .40 S&W
Capacity: Detachable box, 11–15 rounds
Features: Steel frame and steel slide; double/single action; rear snag free dovetail sights and fixed blade front sight; Picatinny rail built into frame; Cerakote finish and black polymer checkered grips
MSRP. **$490.00**

Tristar Sporting Arms

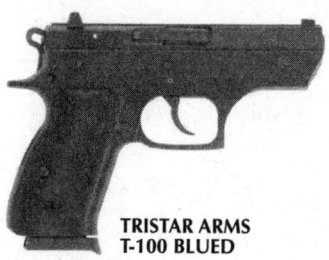

TRISTAR ARMS T-100 BLUED

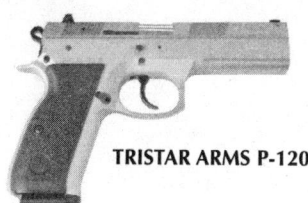

TRISTAR ARMS P-120

T-100

Action: DA/SA semiautomatic
Grips: Polymer
Barrel: 3.7 in.
Sights: Rear dovetail, fixed front
Weight: 26.24 oz.
Caliber: 9mm
Capacity: 15 rounds
Features: Compact pistol perfect for concealed carry; constructed from steel alloy; blued or chrome finish; rear snag-free dovetail sights; fixed blade front sight; includes two magazines, cleaning kit, gun lock, and a black carrying case
MSRP **$460.00**

P-120

Action: DA/SA semiautomatic
Grips: Polymer
Barrel: 4.7 in.
Sights: Rear dovetail, fixed front
Weight: 29.9 oz.
Caliber: 9mm

Capacity: 17 rounds
Features: Originally created for military use; constructed from steel alloy; blued or chrome finish; rear snag-free dovetail sights; fixed blade front sight; includes two magazines, cleaning kit, gun lock, and a black carrying case
MSRP . . . . **$490.00–$510.00**

Turnbull Manufacturing

TURNBULL MANUFACTURING COMMANDER HERITAGE MODEL 1911

TURNBULL MANUFACTURING COMMANDER MODEL 1911

TURNBULL MANUFACTURING GOVERNMENT HERITAGE MODEL 1911

TURNBULL MANUFACTURING GOVERNMENT MODEL 1911

COMMANDER HERITAGE MODEL 1911

Action: Semiautomatic
Grips: Double-diamond walnut
Barrel: 4.25 in.
Sights: Titrium Kensights
Weight: 34.5 oz.
Caliber: .45 ACP
Capacity: 7 rounds
Features: Beavertail grip safety; steel parts, blue finished slide; color case hardened frame; checkered front strap
MSRP . . . . . . **Call Maker for Pricing**

COMMANDER MODEL 1911

Action: Semiautomatic
Grips: Double-diamond walnut
Barrel: 4.25 in.
Sights: Titrium Kensights
Weight: 34.5 oz.
Caliber: .45 ACP
Capacity: 7 rounds

Features: Beavertail grip safety; steel parts, blue finished slide; blued frame; checkered front strap
MSRP . . . . . . **Call Maker for Pricing**

GOVERNMENT HERITAGE MODEL 1911

Action: Semiautomatic
Grips: Double-diamond walnut
Barrel: 5 in.
Sights: Titrium Kensights
Weight: 38 oz.
Caliber: .45 ACP
Capacity: 7 rounds
Features: Beavertail grip safety; steel parts, blue finished slide; color case hardened frame; checkered front strap
MSRP . . . . . . **Call Maker for Pricing**

GOVERNMENT MODEL 1911

Action: Semiautomatic
Grips: Double-diamond walnut
Barrel: 5 in.
Sights: Titrium Kensights
Weight: 38 oz.
Caliber: .45 ACP
Capacity: 7 rounds
Features: Beavertail grip safety; steel parts, blue finished slide; blued frame; checkered front strap
MSRP . . . . . . **Call Maker for Pricing**

Uberti

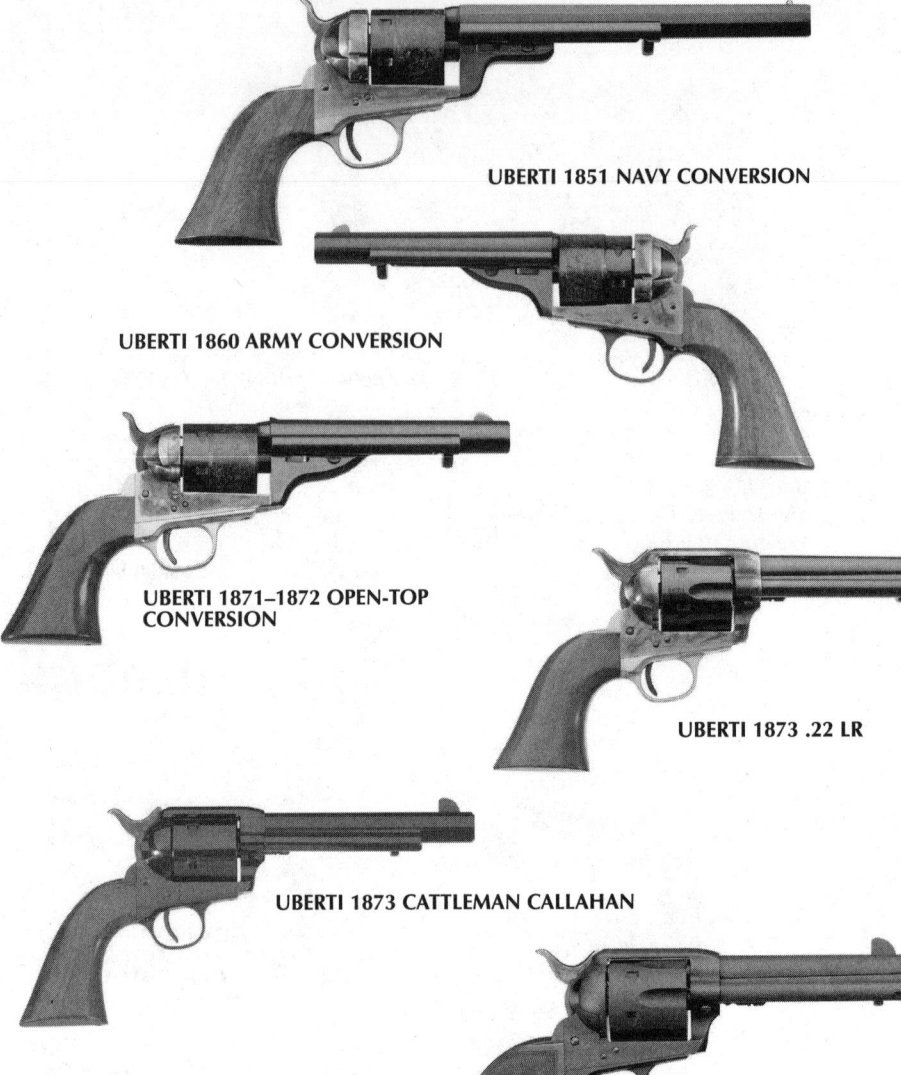

UBERTI 1851 NAVY CONVERSION

UBERTI 1860 ARMY CONVERSION

UBERTI 1871–1872 OPEN-TOP CONVERSION

UBERTI 1873 .22 LR

UBERTI 1873 CATTLEMAN CALLAHAN

UBERTI 1873 CATTLEMAN CHISHOL

1851 NAVY CONVERSION

Action: SA revolver
Grips: Walnut
Barrel: 4.75 in., 5.5 in., 7.5 in.
Sights: Fixed, open
Weight: 42 oz.
Caliber: .38 Spl.
Capacity: 6 rounds
Features: Case-hardened frame octagonal barrel; brass backstrap and trigger guard; conversion revolver frames are retro-fitted with loading gates to accommodate metallic cartridges like the originals
MSRP $569.00

1860 ARMY CONVERSION

Action: SA revolver
Grips: Walnut
Barrel: 4.75 in., 5.5 in., 8 in.
Sights: Fixed, open
Weight: 42 oz.
Caliber: .38 Spl., .45 Colt
Capacity: 6 rounds
Features: Case-hardened frame; round barrel; steel backstrap and trigger guard; conversion revolver frames are retro-fitted with loading gates to accommodate metallic cartridges like the originals
MSRP $589.00

1871–1872 OPEN-TOP CONVERSION

Action: SA revolver
Grips: Walnut
Barrel: 4.75 in., 5.5 in., 7.5 in.
Sights: Fixed, open
Weight: 42 oz.
Caliber: .38 Spl., .45 Colt
Capacity: 6 rounds
Features: 1872 model has steel backstrap and trigger guard; 1871 model has brass backstrap and trigger guard; case-hardened frame; round barrel; blued finish conversion revolver frames are retro-fitted with loading gates to accommodate metallic cartridges like the originals
1871: $539.00
1872: $569.00

1873 CATTLEMAN .22 LR

Action: SA revolver
Grips: Walnut
Barrel: 4.75 in., 5.5 in., 7.5 in.
Sights: Fixed, open
Weight: 36.8 oz.
Caliber: .22 LR

Capacity: 6 and 12 round models
Features: Ideal for cowboy-action shooting practice; light recoil; six-shot comes with brass or steel backstrap and trigger guard; available in six- or twelve-shot; case-hardened frame; blued finish
MSRP . . . . $509.00–$579.00

1873 CATTLEMAN CALLAHAN

Action: SA revolver
Grips: Walnut, black or mother-of-pearl synthetic
Barrel: 4.75 in., 6 in., 7.5 in.
Sights: Fixed
Weight: 42 oz.
Caliber: .44 Mag.
Capacity: 6 rounds
Features: Blued, stainless, case-hardened or Old West finish; target model has angled front target sight

and adjustable notched rear blade sight
MSRP $629.00

1873 CATTLEMAN CHISHOLM

Action: SA revolver
Grips: Checkered walnut
Barrel: 4.75 in., 5.5 in.
Sights: Fixed, open
Weight: 37 oz.
Caliber: .45 Colt
Capacity: 6 rounds
Features: Complete matte finished steel; fluted barrel
MSRP $559.00

UBERTI 1873 CATTLEMAN DESPERADO

UBERTI 1873 CATTLEMAN MATCHING SET

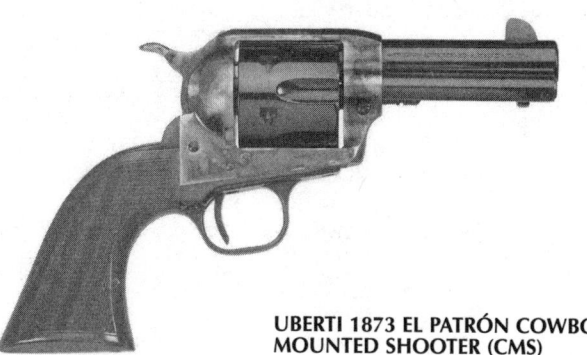

UBERTI 1873 EL PATRÓN COWBOY
MOUNTED SHOOTER (CMS)

UBERTI 1873 SA CATTLEMAN

1873 CATTLEMAN DESPERADO

Action: SA revolver
Grips: Bison horn style
Barrel: 4.75 in., 5.5 in.
Sights: Fixed, open
Weight: 37 oz.
Caliber: .45 Colt
Capacity: 6 rounds
Features: Full nickel-plated steel; fluted barrel
MSRP $829.00

1873 CATTLEMAN MATCHING SETS

Action: SA revolver
Grips: Walnut
Barrel: 5.5 in.
Sights: Fixed, open
Weight: 37 oz.
Caliber: .45 Colt
Capacity: 6 rounds
Features: Fluted barrel; blued case-hardened frame; steel backstrap; trigger guard; the set shares matching serial numbers; available in nickel and ivory-style grip
MSRP $1679.00

1873 EL PATRÓN COWBOY MOUNTED SHOOTER (CMS)

Action: SA revolver
Grips: Checkered walnut
Barrel: 3.5 in., 4 in.
Sights: EasyView
Weight: 37 oz.
Caliber: .45 Colt, .357 Mag.
Capacity: 6 rounds
Features: Blued or stainless steel finish; optional case-hardened frame; fluted barrel; fitted with U.S.-made Wolff springs; numbered cylinders
MSRP: $649.00
Stainless steel: $789.00

1873 SINGLE-ACTION CATTLEMAN

Action: SA revolver
Grips: Walnut
Barrel: 4.75 in., 5.5 in., 7.5 in.
Sights: Fixed, open
Weight: 37 oz.
Caliber: .45 Colt, .44-40 Win., .357 Mag.
Capacity: 6 rounds
Features: Case-hardened frame; brass or steel backstrap and trigger guard; blued, nickel or stainless steel finish; fluted barrel
MSRP . . . . $649.00–$699.00

Uberti

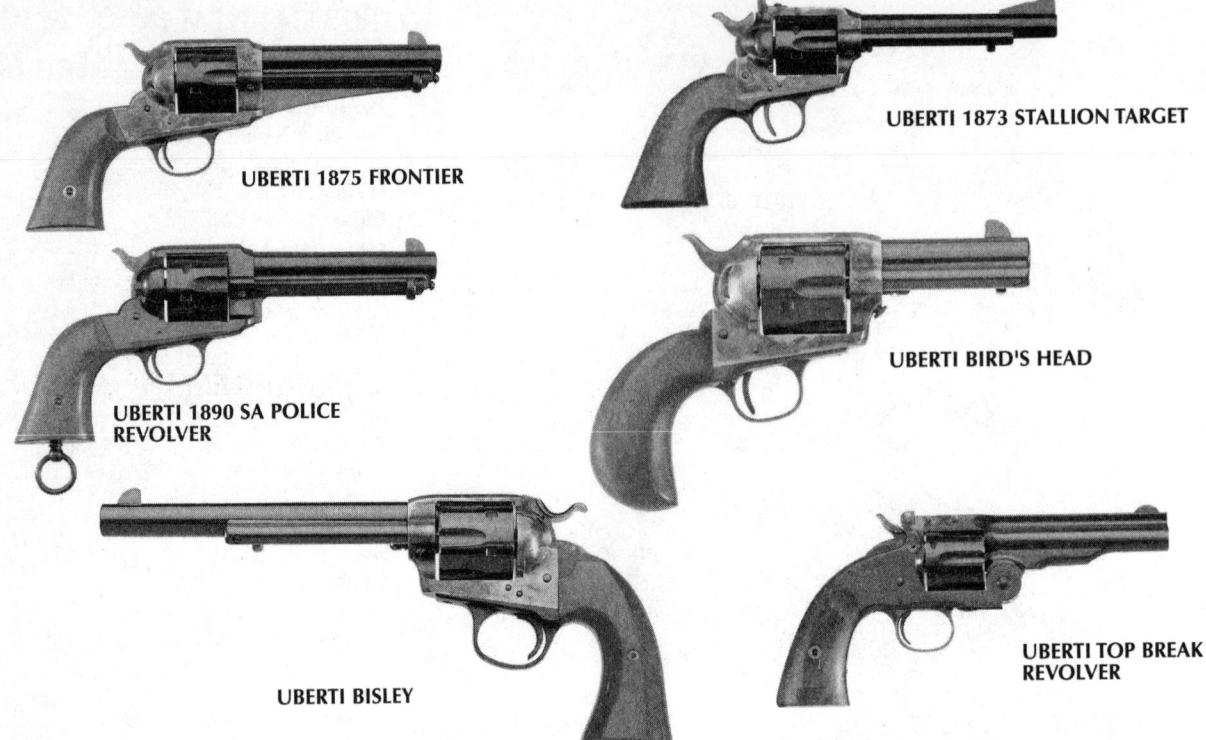

UBERTI 1875 FRONTIER

UBERTI 1873 STALLION TARGET

UBERTI 1890 SA POLICE REVOLVER

UBERTI BIRD'S HEAD

UBERTI BISLEY

UBERTI TOP BREAK REVOLVER

1873 STALLION/STALLION TARGET

Action: SA revolver
Grips: Walnut
Barrel: 4.75 in., 5.5 in.
Sights: Fixed, open
Weight: 32 oz.
Caliber: .22 LR, .22 LR/Mag.
Capacity: 6 or 10 round
Features: Case-hardened frame; brass or steel backstrap and trigger guard; blued finish; fluted barrel
MSRP . . . . $559.00–$599.00

1875 OUTLAW & FRONTIER

Action: SA revolver
Grips: Walnut
Barrel: 5.5 in. (Frontier), 7.5 in.
Sights: Fixed, open
Weight: 40–45 oz.
Caliber: .45 Colt
Capacity: 6 rounds
Features: Case-hardened or full nickel plated steel frame; steel backstrap and trigger guard; fluted barrel
Outlaw: **$559.00**
Outlaw Nickel: **$659.00**
Frontier: **$559.00**

1890 SINGLE ACTION POLICE REVOLVER

Action: SA revolver
Grips: Walnut with lanyard ring
Barrel: 5.5 in.
Sights: Fixed, open
Weight: 42 oz.
Caliber: .45 Colt, .357 Mag.
Capacity: 6 rounds
Features: Blued steel frame, backstrap and trigger guard; fluted barrel
MSRP $579.00

BIRD'S HEAD

Action: SA revolver
Grips: Walnut
Barrel: 3.5 in., 4 in., 4.75 in., 5.5 in.
Sights: Fixed, open
Weight: 35 oz.
Caliber: .38 Spl., .45 Colt, .357 Mag.
Capacity: 6 rounds
Features: Case-hardened frame; steel backstrap and trigger guard; blued finish; bird head shape grip; Bird's Head Stallion Old West Defense is chambered in .38 Spl., has full matte finish, 3.5-in. barrel
Standard: **$569.00**
Stallion Old West Defense: . . **$589.00**

BISLEY

Action: SA revolver
Grips: Bisley target style walnut
Barrel: 4.75 in., 5.5 in., 7.5 in.
Sights: Fixed, open
Weight: 40 oz.
Caliber: .45 Colt, .357 Mag.
Capacity: 6 rounds
Features: Case-hardened frame; steel backstrap and trigger guard; blued finish; fluted barrel
MSRP $609.00

TOP BREAK REVOLVERS

Action: SA revolver
Grips: Walnut or pearl-style
Barrel: 3.5 in., 5 in., 7 in.
Sights: Fixed, open
Weight: 40 oz.
Caliber: .45 Colt, .38 Spl., .44-40 Win.
Capacity: 6 rounds
Features: Full nickel plated steel or blued steel frame and blackstrap; case-hardened trigger guard; fluted barrel
Pearl-style grip: **$1509.00**
Walnut grip: **$1109.00**

Walther Arms

WALTHER CCP (CONCEALED CARRY PISTOL)

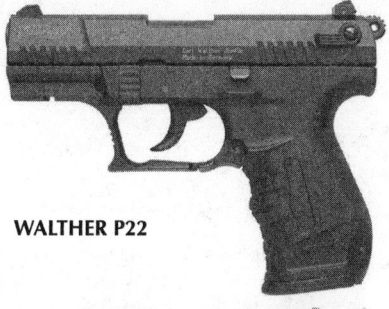

WALTHER P22

WALTHER P99AS

WALTHER PKK/S

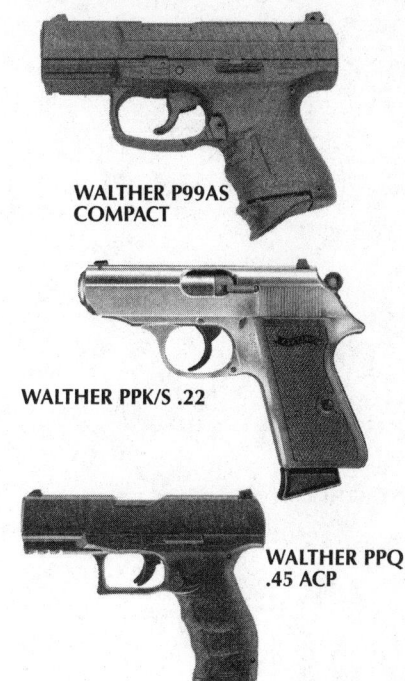

WALTHER P99AS COMPACT

WALTHER PPK/S .22

WALTHER PPQ .45 ACP

CCP (CONCEALED CARRY PISTOL)

Action: Semiautomatic
Grips: Synthetic
Barrel: 3.54 in.
Sights: Adjustable
Weight: 22.33 oz.
Caliber: 9mm
Capacity: 8+1 rounds
Features: Available in black or stainless steel; interchangeable front sight with white dot; adjustable rear sight; reversible magazine release
MSRP . . . . $469.00–$489.00

P22

Action: DA/SA semiautomatic
Grips: Polymer
Barrel: 3.42 in., 5 in.
Sights: 3-dot adjustable low-profile
Weight: 17 oz., 22 oz.
Caliber: .22 LR
Capacity: 10 rounds
Features: Threaded barrel, interchangeable with target barrel; loaded chamber indicator; external slide stop; 3 safeties; two magazine styles; ergonomic grip; ambidextrous magazine release lever; available with integrated laser-set; available in black, nickel, and military finish; Black model now available with laser, Target models with 5-in. barrels available in black or nickel
MSRP . . . . $319.00–$339.00

P99AS

Action: DA semiautomatic
Grips: Black polymer frame and grips
Barrel: 4 in. stainless steel with Tenifer finish
Sights: Front and rear tritium night
Weight: 24 oz.–25.6 oz.
Caliber: 9mm, .40 S&W

Capacity: 15 (9mm) or 12 (.40 S&W) rounds
Features: The first pistol with a firing pin block combines advantages of a traditional DA pull with SA trigger and a decocking button safety integrated into slide, allowing users the ability to decock the striker, preventing inadvertent firing in both DA and SA mode
From: $629.00

P99AS COMPACT

Action: Striker-fired semiautomatic
Grips: Polymer
Barrel: 3.5 in.
Sights: 3-dot adjustable low-profile
Weight: 20.8 oz.–22.4 oz.
Caliber: 9mm, .40 S&W
Capacity: 10 (9mm) or 8 (.40 S&W) rounds
Features: Flat-bottom magazine buttplate, finger rest magazine buttplate; molded with a Weaver-style rail; interchangeable backstraps; hammerless striker system and integral safety devices come standard
From: $629.00

PPK AND PPK/S

Action: DA/SA semiautomatic
Grips: Polymer
Barrel: 3.3 in.
Sights: Fixed, open
Weight: 22.4 oz. (PPK), 24 oz. (PPK/S)
Caliber: .380 ACP
Capacity: 6 (PPK) or 7 (PPK/S) rounds
Features: Firing pin safety; manual safety with decocking function; double- and single-action trigger;

extended beaver tail; nickel plated or blued finish
MSRP . . . . $379.00–$399.00

PPK/S .22

Action: DA/SA semiautomatic
Grips: Polymer
Barrel: 3.3 in.
Sights: Fixed, open
Weight: 24 oz.
Caliber: .22 LR
Capacity: 10 rounds
Features: Manual safety; top strap waved to reduce glare; internal slide stop; iconic PPK/S frame; beaver tail extension; nickel plated or black finish
MSRP . . . . $379.00–$399.00

PPQ .45 ACP

Action: Striker-fired semiautomatic
Grips: Ergonomic polymer
Barrel: 4.25 in.
Sights: Three dot polymer
Weight: 28 oz.
Caliber: .45 ACP
Capacity: 12 rounds
Features: Custom Picatinny accessory rail; quick-defense trigger; ergonomic, non-slip, cross-directional grip surface; three safeties; Tenifer coating on slide and barrel; front and rear slide serrations; ambidextrous slide stop
MSRP $699.00

Walther Arms

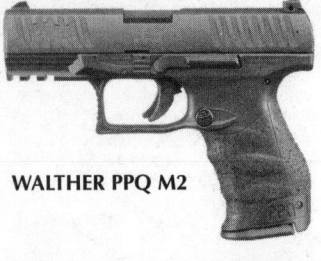

WALTHER PPQ M2

WALTHER PPS

WALTHER PPS M2

WALTHER PPX

PPQ M2

Action: Striker-fired semiautomatic
Grips: Polymer
Barrel: 4 in., 4.1 in., 4.6 in., 5 in.
Sights: 3-dot adjustable low-profile
Weight: 24 oz. (9mm), 25.6 oz. (.40 S&W)
Caliber: 9mm, 9mm (Navy SD), .40 S&W
Capacity: 15 (9mm), 15/17 (9mm Navy SD) or 11 (.40 S&W) rounds
Features: Quick defense trigger; three safeties; ergonomic grip with checkered trigger guard; ambidextrous slide stop and magazine release button; Tenifer coated slide and barrel with matte finish
MSRP.......... **$649.00–$749.00**

PPS (POLICE PISTOL SLIM)

Action: Striker-fired semiautomatic
Grips: Black polymer
Barrel: 3.2 in.
Sights: 3-dot low profile contoured
Weight: 20.8 oz.
Caliber: 9mm, 40 S&W
Capacity: 6 or 8 rounds (9mm), 5 or 7 rounds (.40 S&W)
Features: Ambidextrous magazine release; loaded chamber and cocking indicators; small and large backstrap; trigger safety; Walther QuickSafe safety
MSRP................ **$449.00**

PPS M2

Action: Striker-fired semiautomatic
Grips: Ergonomic polymer
Barrel: 3.18 in.
Sights: Three dot metal
Weight: 21.1 oz.
Caliber: 9mm
Capacity: 6, 7, 8 rounds
Features: Front and rear slide serrations; smooth, light trigger; ergonomic, non-slip, cross-directional grip surface; cocking indicator; chamber viewport; slide stop; magazine release conveniently placed for thumb operation; three magazine options; LE (Law Enforcement) variation comes equipped with phosphoric sights and three magazines
Standard:............... **$469.00**
LE: **$499.00**

PPX

Action: Hammer fire action autoloader
Grips: Polymer
Barrel: 4 in., 4.6 in. (9MM SD)
Sights: 3-dot adjustable low-profile
Weight: 27.2 oz.
Caliber: 9mm, 9mm (SD), .40 S&W
Capacity: 16 rounds (9mm), 14 rounds (.40 S&W)
Features: Constant 6.5 lb. trigger pull; three safeties; ergonomic grip; ambidextrous slide stop and reversible push button magazine release; loaded chamber viewport; Mil-Std-1913 Picatinny accessory mounting rail; Tenifer coated slide and barrel; available in black and stainless
Standard:............... **$469.00**
LE: **$499.00**

Windham Weaponry

WINDHAM WEAPONRY 300 BLACKOUT PISTOL

300 BLACKOUT PISTOL

Action: Semiautomatic gas impingment system
Grips: Rubber
Barrel: 9 in.
Sights: None
Weight: 4 lb. 14 oz.
Caliber: .300 BLK
Capacity: Detachable box, 30+1 rounds
Features: Quick-detach swing swivel; 1:7 inch twist; Picatinny rail; hardcoat black anodize reciever finish with laser caliber identification; chrome-Lined barrel with A2-type flash suppressor
MSRP................ **$1160.00**

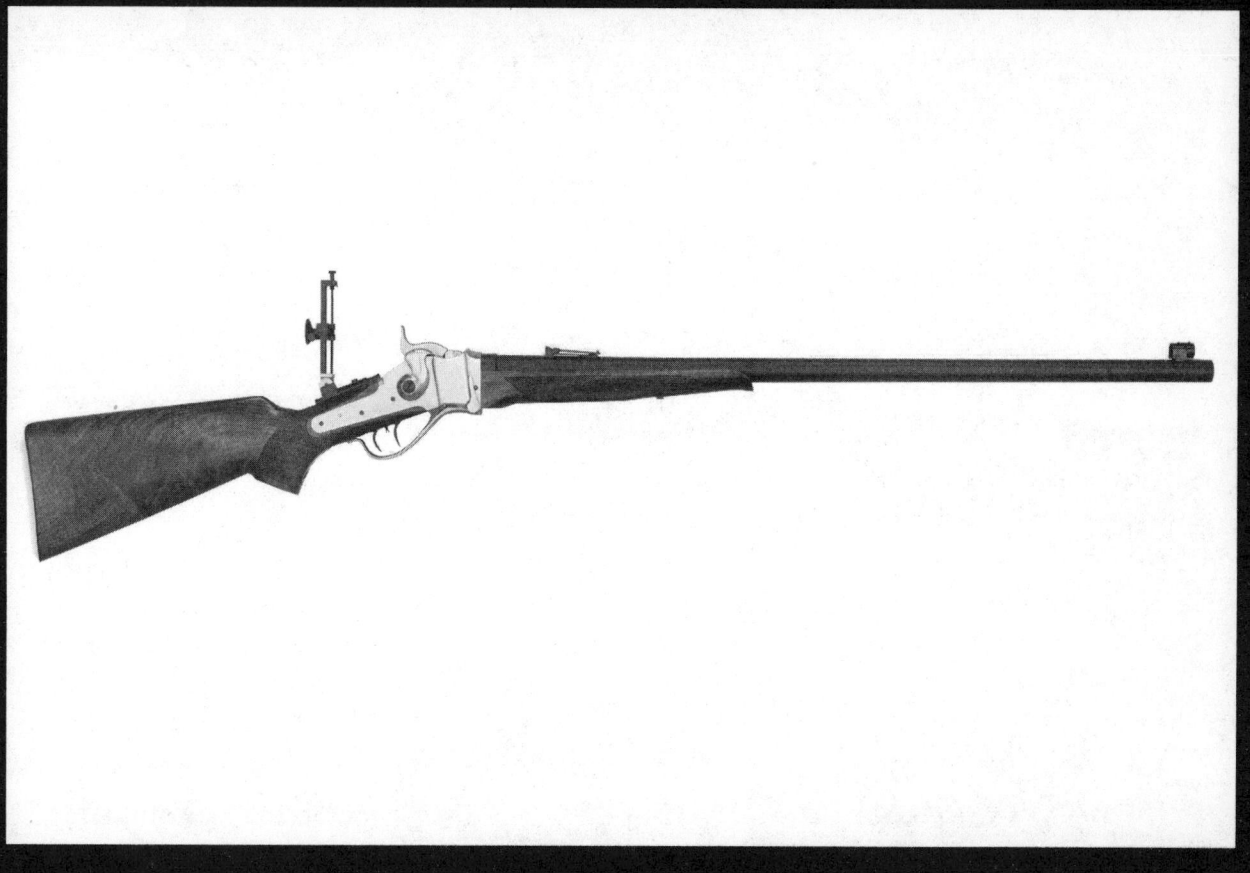

Connecticut Valley Arms (CVA)

CVA ACCURA MR

CVA ACCURA V2

CVA ACCURA V2 NORTHWEST

ACCURA MR

Lock: Break-action in-line
Stock: Synthetic
Barrel: 25 in.
Sights: Scope mount
Weight: 6 lb. 6 oz.
Bore/Caliber: .50
Features: Aluminum frame; quick release breech plug; trigger guard actuated breeching action; Bergara barrel; neutral center of gravity trigger; premium SoftTouch stock with rubber grip panels; WeatherGuard barrel finish on the stainless steel barrel; Realtree Max-1 or black stock finishes; Quake Claw sling included; DuraSight Dead-On scope mount
Black and Nitride: $520.00
Nitride stainless Realtree
   Max-1 HD: $585.00

ACCURA V2

Lock: Break-action muzzleloading
Stock: Composite stock in standard or thumbhole
Barrel: 27 in.
Sights: DuraSight fiber optic
Weight: 7 lb. 5 oz.
Bore/Caliber: .50
Features: 416 stainless Bergara barrel; quick-release breech plug; CrushZone recoil pad; drilled and tapped for scope mount; SoftTouch coating and rubber grip panels; Quake Claw sling; with a variety of configuration choices, including standard or thumbhole stock, black or Realtree APG finishes, scope mount or fiber optic sights, black or stainless Nitride finished barrels
MSRP. . . . . $460.00–$610.00

ACCURA V2 NORTHWEST

Lock: Break-action muzzleloading
Stock: Synthetic
Barrel: 27 in.
Sights: Fiber optics
Weight: 7 lb. 5 oz.
Bore/Caliber: .50
Features: Meets open-breech/ignition requirements of Idaho, Oregan, and Washington; CrushZone recoil pad; quick release breech plug; standard or thumbhole stocks, in Realtree APG with fiber optic sights
MSRP. $580.00

Connecticut Valley Arms (CVA)

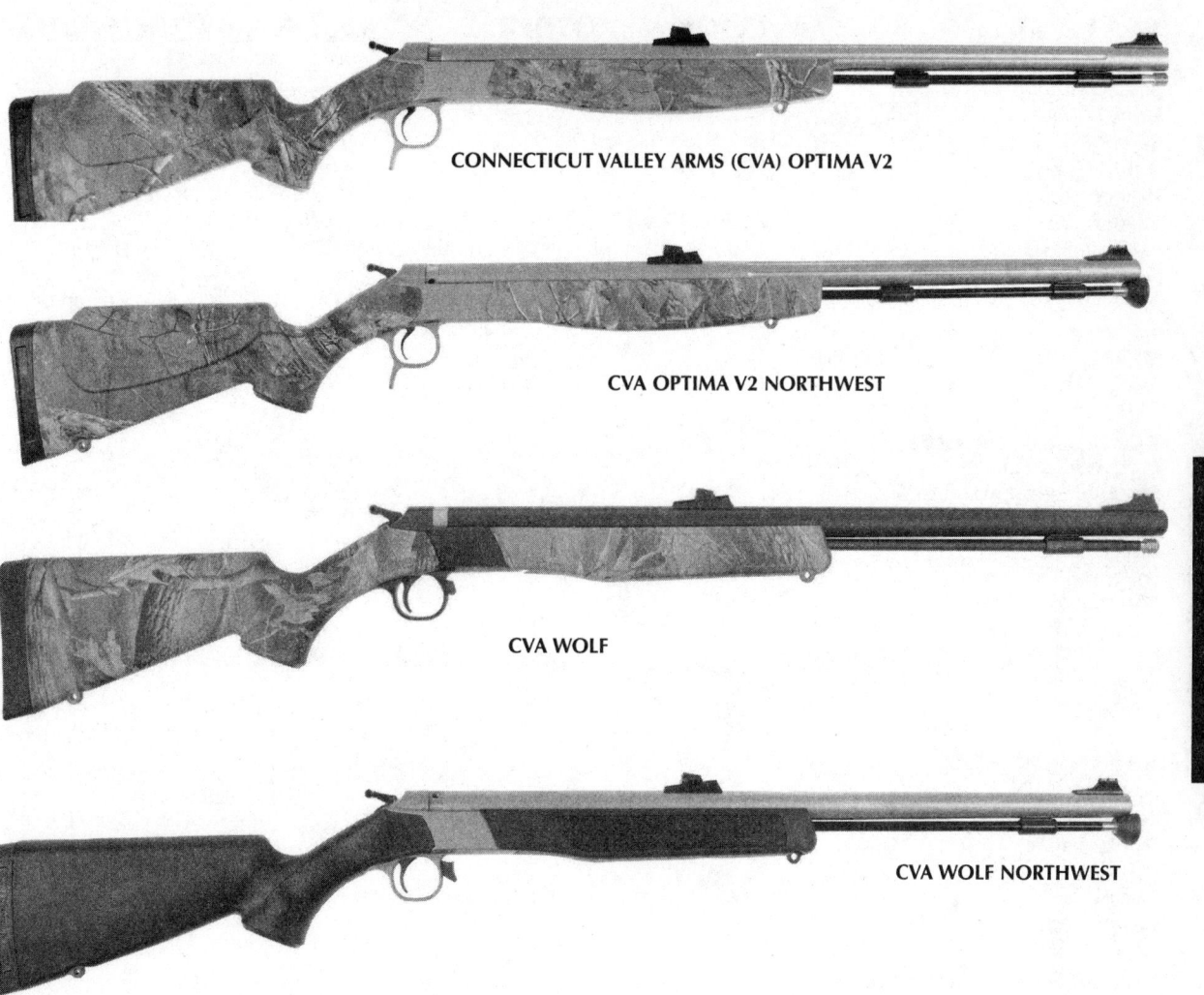

CONNECTICUT VALLEY ARMS (CVA) OPTIMA V2

CVA OPTIMA V2 NORTHWEST

CVA WOLF

CVA WOLF NORTHWEST

OPTIMA V2
Lock: Break-action muzzleloading
Stock: Realtree Xtra Green or black
Barrel: 26 in.
Sights: Fiber optic sights or mount
Weight: 6 lb. 10 oz.
Bore/Caliber: .50
Features: Modeled on the Accura V2; stainless steel barrel; quick release breech plug; 100 percent ambidextrous stock; includes DuraSight Dead-On scope mount and ramrod
Blued/black:. **$290.00**
Stainless/black: . . . **$320.00–$330.00**
**Stainless/Realtree Xtra
    Green:** . . . . **$380.00–$400.00**
**Nitride/Realtree Xtra
    Green:** . . . . **$420.00–$450.00**

OPTIMA V2 NORTHWEST
Lock: Break-action muzzleloading

Stock: Synthetic
Barrel: 26 in.
Sights: Fiber optics
Weight: 6 lb. 10 oz.
Bore/Caliber: .50
Features: Meets open-breech/ignition requirements of Idaho, Oregan, and Washington; CrushZone recoil pad; quick release breech plug; stainless steel hardware and Realtree Xtra Green standard stock
MSRP. **$375.00**

WOLF
Lock: Break-action in-line
Stock: Synthetic
Barrel: 24 in.
Sights: DuraSight fiber optic; includes 3–9x40mm duplex scope
Weight: 6 lb. 4 oz.
Bore/Caliber: .50
Features: Bullet-guiding muzzle; new tool-free QR breech plug system;

ambidextrous compact or standard stock in black or camo; CrushZone recoil pad; reversible hammer spur; blued or stainless barrel
MSRP. . . . .**$225.00–$310.00**

WOLF NORTHWEST
Lock: Break-action muzzleloading
Stock: Synthetic
Barrel: 24 in.
Sights: Fiber optics
Weight: 6 lb. 4 oz.
Bore/Caliber: .50
Features: Meets open-breech/ignition requirements of Idaho, Oregan, and Washington; CrushZone recoil pad; quick release breech plug
MSRP. **$260.00**

Davide Pedersoli & C.

1763 LEGER (1766) CHARLEVILLE

Action: Dropping block
Stock: Walnut
Barrel: 44.7 in.
Sights: Open
Weight: 10 lb. 2 oz.
Caliber: .69
Magazine: None
Features: Creedmoor sight; tunnel front sight; replica of French infantry musket
MSRP **$1530.00**

1805 HARPER'S FERRY PERCUSSION PISTOL

Lock: Percussion cap
Stock: American walnut
Barrel: 10.06 in.
Sights: Bead front
Weight: 2 lb. 10.6 oz.
Bore/Caliber: .54
Features: Brass furniture; smooth bore; chromed and satin finished barrel; old silver case hardened lock
MSRP **$630.00**

BAKER CAVALRY SHOTGUN

Lock: Percussion
Stock: Walnut
Barrel: 11.25 in.
Sights: None
Weight: 5 lb. 12 oz.
Bore/Caliber: 20 Ga.
Features: Single trigger back action, side-by-side shotgun; reproduces a gun made by London gunsmith Ezekiel Baker in 1850; case-hardened locks
MSRP . . . . **$1170.00–$1225.00**

BOUTET 1ER EMPIRE

Lock: Flintlock
Stock: Hardwood
Barrel: 10 in.
Sights: Fixed
Weight: 2 lb. 14 oz.
Bore/Caliber: .45
Features: Napoleon often wrote with flattering appreciation about the style and prestige of the Boutet guns, which Pedersoli now proudly introduces with fine checkering on the sides; metal buttplate; ramrod has a horn tip; single set trigger; on the lock two lines are engraved with MANUF RE/a Versailles.
MSRP . . . . **$1320.00–$3055.00**

COOK & BROTHER ARTILLERY CARBINE

Lock: Caplock
Stock: Walnut
Barrel: 24 in.
Sights: None
Weight: 6 lb. 10 oz.
Bore/Caliber: .58
Features: Inspired by English model guns; originally produced by Cook & Brother beginning in 1861; brass garnitures; blued barrel; case-hardened lock
MSRP **$1055.00**

COOK & BROTHER RIFLE

Lock: Muzzleloading
Stock: Wood
Barrel: 33 in.
Chokes: IC, M, F
Sights: Fixed
Weight: 8 lb. 10 oz.
Bore/Gauge: .58
Features: Brass garnitures; brown colour barrel; walnut stock
MSRP . . . . **$1115.00–$1195.00**

PEDERSOLI 1805 HARPER'S FERRY PERCUSSION PISTOL

PEDERSOLI 1763 LEGER (1766) CHARLEVILLE

PEDERSOLI BAKER CAVALRY SHOTGUN

PEDERSOLI BOUTET 1ER EMPIRE

PEDERSOLI COOK & BROTHER ARTILLERY CARBINE

PEDERSOLI COOK & BROTHER RIFLE

PEDERSOLI DERRINGER PHILADELPHIA

BLACK POWDER

Davide Pedersoli & C.

PEDERSOLI ENFIELD 3 BAND P1853 RIFLE MUSKET

PEDERSOLI ENFIELD 3 BAND P1853 WHITWORTH WITH HEXAGONAL RIFLING

PEDERSOLI GIBBS SHOTGUN

PEDERSOLI HAWKEN HUNTER RIFLE

PEDERSOLI HOWDAH HUNTER PISTOL

PEDERSOLI KODIAK EXPRESS MK VI

PEDERSOLI LA BOHEMIENNE SIDE-BY-SIDE SHOTGUN

DERRINGER PHILADELPHIA

Lock: Percussion
Stock: Walnut
Barrel: 3.06 in.
Sights: None
Weight: 8.6 oz.
Bore/Caliber: .45
Features: Reproduction of the popular pocket pistols originally manufactured by John Henry Derringer; brass furniture; case-hardened lock; original markings on the lock: Derringer/Philadelphia
MSRP . . . . $545.00–$665.00

ENFIELD 3 BAND P1853 RIFLE MUSKET

Lock: Percussion
Stock: Walnut
Barrel: 39 in.
Sights: Adjustable rear
Weight: 8 lb. 13 oz.
Bore/Caliber: .577
Features: Ladder rear sight with a slider assembled on a base with steps; steel barrel bands; brass furniture; ramrod tip is shaped with characteristic jag slot; barrel is blued and lock case-hardened
MSRP $1195.00

ENFIELD 3 BAND P1853 WHITWORTH WITH HEXAGONAL RIFLING

Lock: Percussion cap
Stock: American walnut
Barrel: 36 in.
Sights: Creedmoor sight, tunnel front sight
Weight: 9 lb. 7.4 oz.
Bore/Caliber: .451
Features: Hammer-forged browned finish hexagonal barrel; lock parts with light colour case hardened finish
MSRP $1995.00

GIBBS SHOTGUN

Lock: Percussion
Stock: Walnut
Barrel: 32.3 in.
Sights: None
Weight: 8 lb. 9 oz.
Bore/Caliber: 12 Ga.
Features: Octagonal to round barrel; case-hardened color-finished lock; grip and forend caps with ebony inserts; pistol grip stock
MSRP $1570.00

HAWKEN HUNTER RIFLE

Lock: Percussion, flintlock
Stock: Wood
Barrel: 28.4 in.
Chokes: IC, M, F
Sights: Adjustable rear, fixed front
Weight: 8 lb. 10 oz.
Bore/Gauge: .50, .54
Features: Blade front sight and a dovetail slot to equip it with the rear sight; ghost ring aperture sight is mounted to the tang; American walnut stock features a microcell thick butt plate; double set triggers
Percussion: $710.00
Flintlock: $765.00

HOWDAH HUNTER PISTOL

Lock: Caplock
Stock: Walnut
Barrel: 11.25 in.
Sights: None
Weight: 5 lb. 1 oz.
Bore/Caliber: 20 Ga., .45 LC, .45/.410, .50, .58
Features: Engraved locks with wild animal scenes; case-hardened color finish; checkered walnut pistol grip with steel butt cap
Shotgun: . . . . $890.00–$1340.00
.50, .58: . . . . $950.00–$1440.00
.45 LC, .45/.410: $1350.00
Combo 20-ga., .50: $940.00

KODIAK EXPRESS MK VI

Lock: Percussion
Stock: Hardwood
Barrel: 24.25 in.
Sights: Creedmore
Weight: 10 lb. 2 oz.
Bore/Caliber: .50, .54, .58
Features: A very manageable gun, perfectly balanced; particularly suitable for wild boar hunting; practical rubber buttplate; half pistol grip stock; equipped with ghost sights
MSRP $1410.00

LA BOHEMIENNE SIDE-BY-SIDE SHOTGUN

Lock: Hinged breech muzzleloading
Stock: Checkered walnut
Barrel: 28 in.
Chokes: cyl/mod choke tubes
Weight: 7 lb.
Bore/Caliber: 12 Ga.
Features: Rust brown finish barrel; interchangeable chokes; color case-hardened frame; hand-engraved locks
MSRP $2140.00

Davide Pedersoli & C.

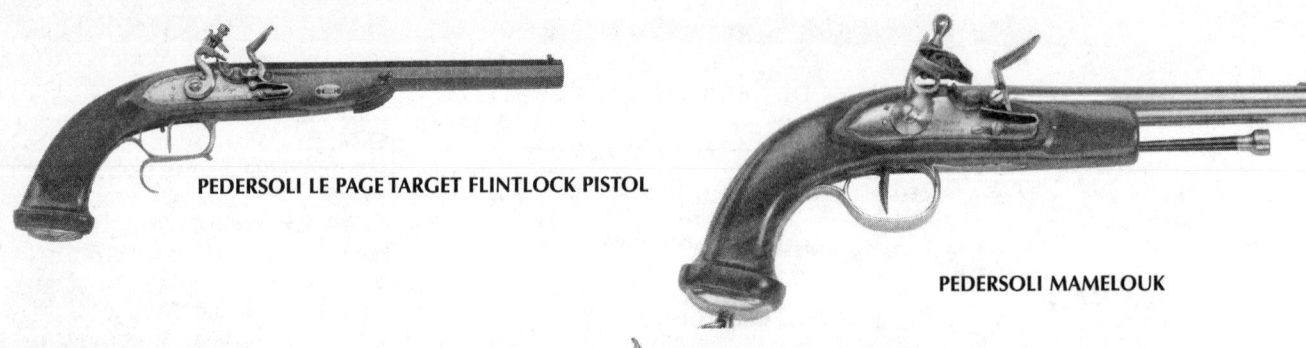

PEDERSOLI LE PAGE TARGET FLINTLOCK PISTOL

PEDERSOLI MAMELOUK

PEDERSOLI MANG IN GRAZ MATCH

PEDERSOLI MISSISSIPPI US MODEL 1841

PEDERSOLI MORTIMER TARGET RIFLE

PEDERSOLI PLAINS SHOTGUN "THE FAST BACK ACTION"

LE PAGE TARGET FLINTLOCK PISTOL

Lock: Traditional flintlock
Stock: Walnut
Barrel: 10.5 in.
Sights: Adjustable
Weight: 2 lb. 10 oz.
Bore/Caliber: .44, .45
Features: Smoothbore .45 available; adjustable single-set trigger; brightly polished lock with a roller frizzen spring
MSRP **$1265.00**

MAMELOUK

Lock: Flintlock
Stock: Hardwood
Barrel: 7.6 in.
Sights: Fixed
Weight: 1 lb. 10 oz.
Bore/Caliber: N/A
Features: Like all the firearms equipping Napoleon's Imperial Guards, the Mameluke pistols were made at the Manufacture of Versailles under the technical management of Nicolas-Noël Boutet; the trigger guard, buttcap, screw washers of the lock, and ramrod tip are brass
MSRP **$985.00**

MANG IN GRAZ MATCH

Lock: Percussion
Stock: Walnut
Barrel: 11.4 in.
Sights: Fixed
Weight: 2 lb. 10 oz.
Bore/Caliber: .38, .44
Features: Fluted grip; octagonal, rifled barrel in brown rust finish; adjustable single set trigger; breech plug shows a typical mask of the period; barrel and tang enriched with gold inlays
MSRP **$1845.00**

MISSISSIPPI US MODEL 1841

Lock: Percussion
Stock: Walnut
Barrel: 33 in.

Sights: Open rear
Weight: 9 lb. 8 oz.
Bore/Caliber: .54, .58
Features: Considered the best-looking ordnance rifle of its period; brass furniture; browned barrel; notched rear sight; case-hardened lock; ramrod with brass tip
MSRP **$1255.00**

MORTIMER TARGET RIFLE

Lock: Flintlock
Stock: English-style European walnut
Barrel: 36.4 in.
Sights: Target
Weight: 10 lb. 2 oz.
Bore/Caliber: .54
Features: Case-colored lock; stock has cheekpiece and hand checkering; 7-groove barrel
MSRP **$1875.00**

PLAINS SHOTGUN "THE FAST BACK ACTION"

Lock: Caplock
Stock: Walnut
Barrel: 27.5 in., 28.5 in.
Sights: None
Weight: 7 lb. 5 oz.–7 lb. 8 oz.
Bore/Caliber: 12, 20 Ga.
Features: Single trigger; side-by-side shotgun; fast second shot, thanks to back action lock reducing minor residues of black powder in lock parts
MSRP **$1260.00**

Davide Pedersoli & C.

PEDERSOLI RICHMOND 1862, TYPE III

PEDERSOLI SPRINGFIELD MODEL 1861 US

PEDERSOLI SWISS MATCH STANDARD FLINTLOCK

PEDERSOLI TATHAM & EGG PISTOL

PEDERSOLI TRADITIONAL HAWKEN TARGET RIFLE

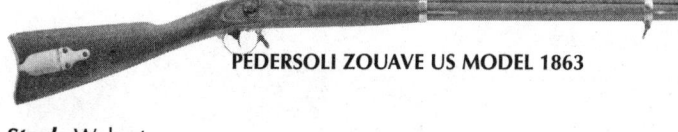

PEDERSOLI ZOUAVE US MODEL 1863

RICHMOND 1862, TYPE III

Lock: Percussion
Stock: Walnut
Barrel: 39.75 in.
Sights: None
Weight: 9 lb. 14 oz.
Bore/Caliber: .58
Features: Manufactured based on the U.S. 1855 Model with the Maynard tape ignition system; except for the lock's profile, the brass buttplate, and the stock nose cap, the gun's appearance resembles the U.S. Model 1861
MSRP $1200.00

SPRINGFIELD MODEL 1861 US

Lock: Caplock
Stock: Walnut
Barrel: 40 in.
Sights: None
Weight: 9 lb. 14 oz.
Bore/Caliber: .58
Features: More efficient than earlier smooth bored muskets used by both sides in the American Civil War; satin finish barrel; stock with three bands; coin-colored finish on the steel furniture
MSRP $1240.00

SWISS MATCH STANDARD FLINTLOCK

Lock: Flintlock
Stock: Walnut
Barrel: 30.8 in.
Sights: Adjustable
Weight: 16 lb. 5 oz.
Bore/Caliber: .40
Features: Octagonal conical profile barrel with rust brown finish; lock is case-hardened; steel ramrod; double-set trigger; steel hook buttplate
MSRP $3400.00

TATHAM & EGG PISTOL

Lock: Flintlock
Stock: Walnut
Barrel: 10.06 in.
Sights: Adjustable rear
Weight: 2 lb. 6.7 oz.
Bore/Caliber: .45 smooth
Features: Ergonomic grip; set trigger; PMG-quality trigger; case-hardened metal parts
MSRP $1390.00

TRADITIONAL HAWKEN TARGET RIFLE

Lock: Percussion, flintlock
Stock: Wood
Barrel: 28.4 in.
Chokes: IC, M, F

Sights: Adjustable rear, fixed front
Weight: 8 lb. 10 oz.
Bore/Gauge: .50, .54
Features: Double set trigger; adjustable buckhorn rear sight; American walnut stock is enriched with a brass patch box; left-handed version available
Percussion: $685.00
Flintlock: $735.00

ZOUAVE US MODEL 1863

Lock: Percussion
Stock: Hardwood
Barrel: 33 in.
Sights: Front, rear
Weight: 9 lb. 4 oz.
Bore/Caliber: .58
Features: Intended for the U.S. Artillery Department and never distributed to any Civil War army division; features brass furnitures; ramrod with a tulip tip; three-leaf rear sight; two sling swivels; the lock shows the Eagle stamp and the U.S. letters in front of the hammer
MSRP $1510.00

Dixie Gun Works

DIXIE GUN WORKS 1853 ENFIELD THREE-BAND

DIXIE GUN WORKS SHARPS 1859 MILITARY CARBINE

DIXIE GUN WORKS SPANISH MUSKET

DIXIE GUN WORKS PEDERSOLI SCREW BARREL PISTOL

1853 ENFIELD THREE-BAND RIFLE MUSKET

Lock: Traditional caplock
Stock: Walnut
Barrel: 39 in.
Sights: Fixed
Weight: 10 lb. 4 oz.
Bore/Caliber: .58
Features: Color case-hardened lock; single trigger; single swivels; steel ramrod
Smoothbore: **$750.00**
Rifled: . . . . **$895.00–$1050.00**

SHARPS 1859 MILITARY CARBINE

Lock: Dropping block
Stock: Walnut
Barrel: 22 in.
Sights: Adjustable open
Weight: 8 lb.
Bore/Caliber: .54
Features: Steel furniture; color case-hardened; single trigger; single barrel band; saddle bar with ring
MSRP **$1400.00**

SPANISH MUSKET

Lock: Flintlock muzzleloading
Stock: Full, European walnut 56 in.
Barrel: 44.75 in.
Sights: Steel stud front
Weight: 10 lb.
Bore/Caliber: .68 round ball

Features: Brass buttplate, trigger guard, and barrel bands; bright steel sideplates; steel ramrod
MSRP **$1400.00**

PEDERSOLI SCREW BARREL PISTOL

Lock: Traditional caplock
Stock: European walnut
Barrel: 3 in.
Sights: None
Weight: 12 oz.
Bore/Caliber: .44
Features: Color case-hardened lock; single folding trigger; combination nipple/barrel wrench included
MSRP **$210.00**

EMF Company, Inc.

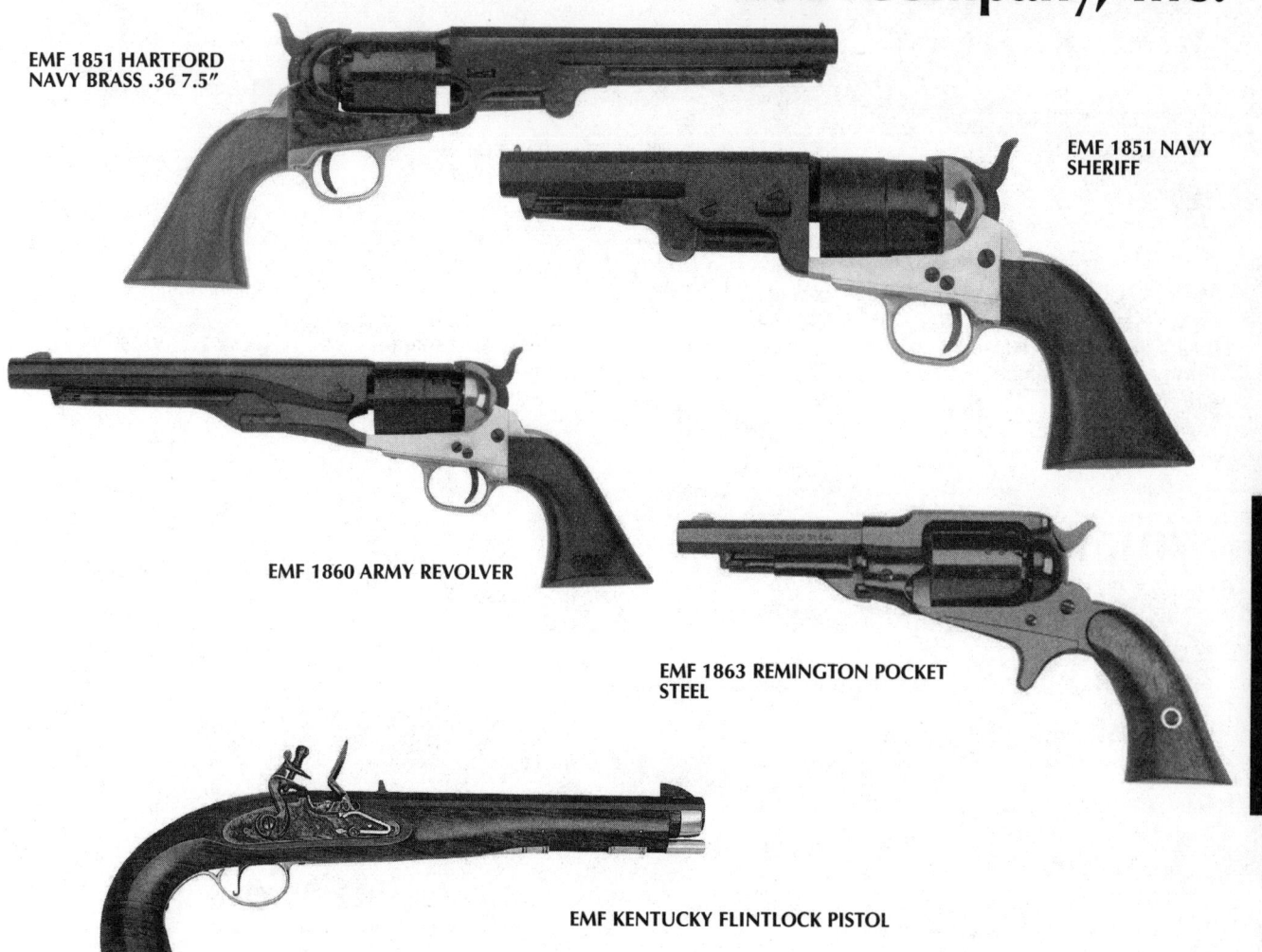

EMF 1851 HARTFORD
NAVY BRASS .36 7.5"

EMF 1851 NAVY
SHERIFF

EMF 1860 ARMY REVOLVER

EMF 1863 REMINGTON POCKET
STEEL

EMF KENTUCKY FLINTLOCK PISTOL

1851 HARTFORD NAVY BRASS

Lock: Caplock revolver
Stock: Walnut
Barrel: 7.5 in.
Sights: Fixed
Weight: 40 oz.
Bore/Caliber: .36, .44
Features: Brass, case-hardened stainless steel frame
MSRP **$210.00**

1851 NAVY SHERIFF

Lock: Caplock revolver
Stock: Walnut
Barrel: 5.5 in.
Sights: None
Weight: 32 oz.
Bore/Caliber: .380 Blank
Features: Brass, case-hardened stainless steel frame; blued barrel optional
MSRP . . . . **$229.95–$259.95**

1860 ARMY REVOLVER

Lock: Caplock revolver
Stock: Walnut
Barrel: 8 in.
Sights: Fixed
Weight: 41.6 oz.
Bore/Caliber: .44
Features: Case-hardened frame; blued barrel
Brass: **$250.00**
Steel: **$285.00**

1863 REMINGTON POCKET STEEL

Lock: Caplock revolver
Stock: Walnut
Barrel: 3.5 in.
Sights: Fixed
Weight: 21 oz.
Bore/Caliber: .36
Features: Steel frame, blued barrel
MSRP **$290.00**

KENTUCKY FLINTLOCK PISTOL

Lock: Flintlock
Stock: Walnut
Barrel: 10.375 in.
Sights: Fixed
Weight: 37 oz.
Bore/Caliber: .45, .50
Features: Classic American pistol during the American Revolution and a favorite of pioneers; case-hardened frame; octagonal rifled blued barrel, polished brass fittings
.45-caliber: **$525.00**
.50-caliber: **$555.00**

EMF Company, Inc.

EMF MISSOURI RIVER HAWKEN

MISSOURI RIVER HAWKEN

Lock: Caplock muzzleloading
Stock: Maple or walnut
Barrel: 30 in.
Sights: Open

Weight: 9 lb. 4 oz.
Bore/Caliber: .45, .50
Features: Replica percussion rifle; available in maple or walnut stock in rust brown color finish; barrel features an octagonal cross-section; case-hard-

ened color lock; equipped with a double-set trigger
Maple:............... **$1486.00**
Walnut:............... **$1261.00**

Lyman

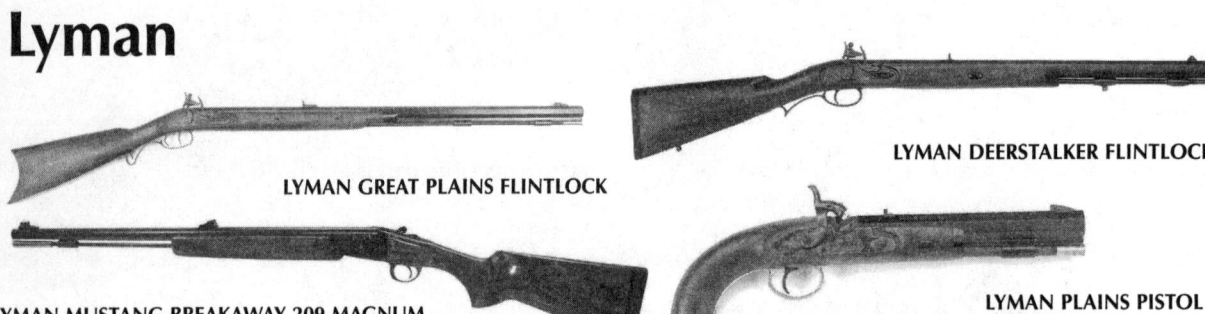

LYMAN GREAT PLAINS FLINTLOCK

LYMAN DEERSTALKER FLINTLOCK

LYMAN MUSTANG BREAKAWAY 209 MAGNUM

LYMAN PLAINS PISTOL

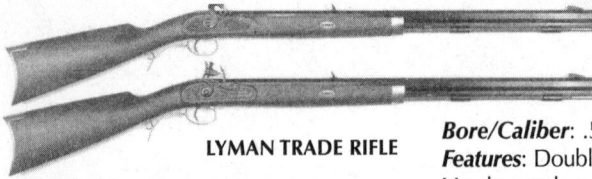

LYMAN TRADE RIFLE

DEERSTALKER RIFLE

Lock: Traditional cap or flint
Stock: Walnut
Barrel: 24 in.
Sights: Fiber optic front and rear
Weight: 10 lb. 6 oz.
Bore/Caliber: .50, .54
Features: Quiet single trigger; metal blackened to avoid glare; black rubber recoil pad; left-hand available
Flintlock:........ **$480.99–$510.99**
Percussion:............. **$435.00**

GREAT PLAINS RIFLE

Lock: Traditional cap or flint
Stock: Walnut
Barrel: 32 in.
Sights: Adjustable open
Weight: 11 lb. 10 oz.

Bore/Caliber: .50, .54
Features: Double-set triggers; Hawken style percussion "snail" with clean-out screw; separate ramrod entry thimble and nose cap; left-hand available
Flintlock:...... **$682.99–$696.99**
Percussion:.... **$629.99–$656.99**

MUSTANG BREAKAWAY 209 MAGNUM

Lock: In-line
Stock: Hardwood
Barrel: 26 in.
Sights: Fiber optic front and rear
Weight: 11 lb.
Bore/Caliber: .50
Features: Pachmayr "Decelerator" recoil pad; comes drilled and tapped for Weaver style bases
MSRP............... **$419.00**

PLAINS PISTOL

Lock: Traditional caplock
Stock: Walnut
Barrel: 6 in.
Sights: Fixed
Weight: 3 lb. 2 oz.
Bore/Caliber: .50, .54
Features: Blackened iron furniture; polished brass trigger guard and ramrod tips; hooked patent breech takes down quickly for easy cleaning
Pistol:.......... **$334.99–$346.99**
Kit:.................... **$282.99**

TRADE RIFLE

Lock: Traditional cap or flint
Stock: Walnut
Barrel: 28 in.
Sights: Adjustable open
Weight: 10 lb. 13 oz.
Bore/Caliber: .50, .54
Features: Brass furniture; originally developed for the early Indian fur trade
Flintlock:............... **$517.99**
Percussion:............. **$457.99**

Shiloh Rifle

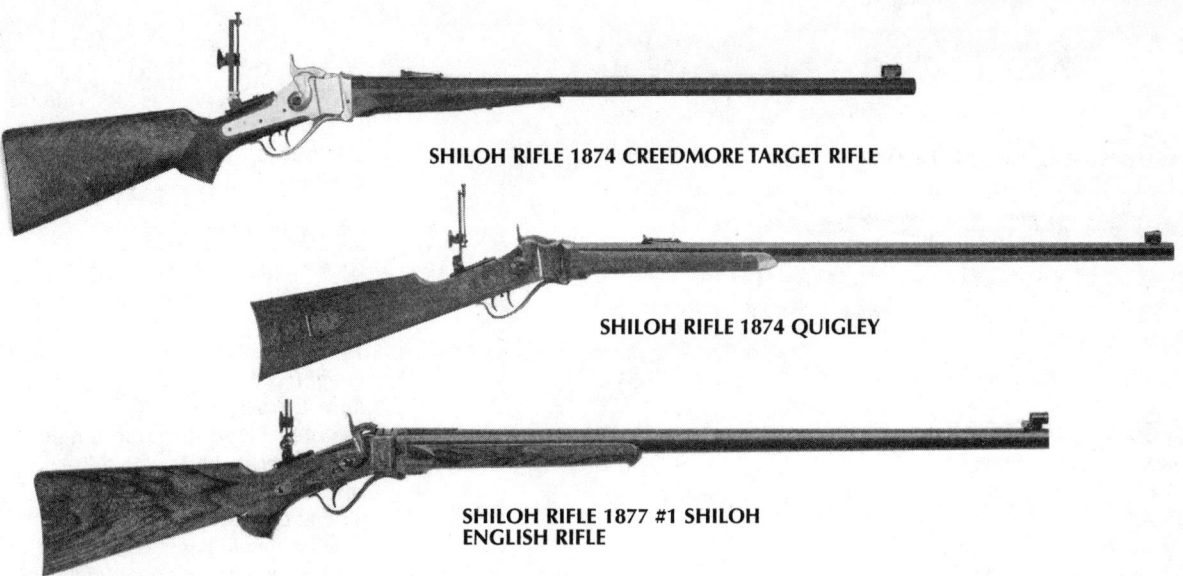

SHILOH RIFLE 1874 CREEDMORE TARGET RIFLE

SHILOH RIFLE 1874 QUIGLEY

SHILOH RIFLE 1877 #1 SHILOH ENGLISH RIFLE

1874 CREEDMORE TARGET RIFLE
Lock: Blackpowder cartridge
Stock: Walnut
Barrel: 32 in.
Sights: V aiming rear; blade front
Weight: 9 lb.
Bore/Caliber: All popular black powder cartridges from .38-55 to .50-90
Features: Pistol grip; single trigger; AA finish on American black walnut; polished barrel; octagon barrel; pewter tip
MSRP $3105.00

1874 QUIGLEY
Lock: Falling block
Stock: Walnut
Barrel: 34 in.
Sights: Semi buckhorn rear, midrange vernier tang, #111 globe aperture front
Weight: 12 lb. 8 oz.
Bore/Caliber: .45-70 Govt. or .45-110
Features: Military buttstock; patchbox; heavy octagonal barrel; pewter tip; Hartford collars; double set triggers; antique or standard color finish; gold inlay initials in gold oval
MSRP $3533.00

1877 #1 SHILOH ENGLISH RIFLE
Lock: Muzzleloading
Stock: Wood
Barrel: 26 in.–34 in.
Sights: Adjustable
Weight: N/A
Bore/Caliber: .38-55, .40-50BN, .40-50ST, .40-65, .40-70ST, .40-70BN, .40-90BN, .45-70, .45-90, .45-100
Features: Standard pistol grip; standard forearm; standard color cased; full or semi buckhorn rear sight; blade front sight; single trigger
MSRP $2250.00

Taylor's & Co. Firearms

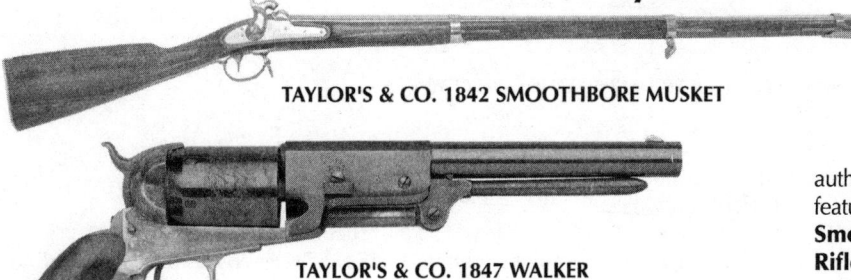

TAYLOR'S & CO. 1842 SMOOTHBORE MUSKET

TAYLOR'S & CO. 1847 WALKER

1842 SMOOTHBORE MUSKET
Lock: Percussion
Stock: Walnut
Barrel: 42 in.
Sights: Military style
Weight: 9 lb. 12 oz.
Bore/Caliber: .69
Features: The Springfield replica has all the features of the original, including a one-piece, oil-finished walnut stock; original-style barrel bands; and completely interchangeable parts; the percussion lock has a V-style mainspring; features the lock with stamping noting 1842 and Springfield; NSSA approved, with certificate of authenticity and a brass medallion featuring the model and serial number
Smoothbore: $1034.00
Rifled: $1082.00

1847 WALKER
Lock: Caplock revolver
Stock: Walnut
Barrel: 9 in.
Sights: Fixed
Weight: 4 lb. 12 oz.
Bore/Caliber: .44
Features: Blued finish; round barrel
Complete firearm: $433.00
Kit: $388.00

Taylor's & Co. Firearms

TAYLOR'S & CO. 1848 DRAGOONS

1848 DRAGOONS

Lock: Caplock revolver
Stock: Walnut
Barrel: 7.5 in.
Sights: Fixed
Weight: 4 lb.–4 lb. 14 oz.
Bore/Caliber: .44
Features: First used by the U.S. Army's Mounted Rifles 1st Cavalry in 1833 and they went on to see considerable use during the 1850 and during the Civil War; blued finish; six-round capacity; available in 1st, 2nd, and 3rd models, as well as the Whitney variation
1st, 2nd, 3rd: **$437.00**
Whitney: **$443.00**

LE MAT CAVALRY

Lock: Caplock revolver
Stock: Walnut
Barrel: 8 in.
Sights: Fixed
Weight: 5 lb.
Bore/Caliber: .44 or 20 Ga.
Features: Blued steel finish; nine-shot .44 caliber revolver with a 20 Ga. single-shot barrel was a favorite among Confederate cavalry troops; case-hardened hammer and trigger; lanyard ring; trigger guard with spur
MSRP **$1086.00**

Thompson/Center Arms

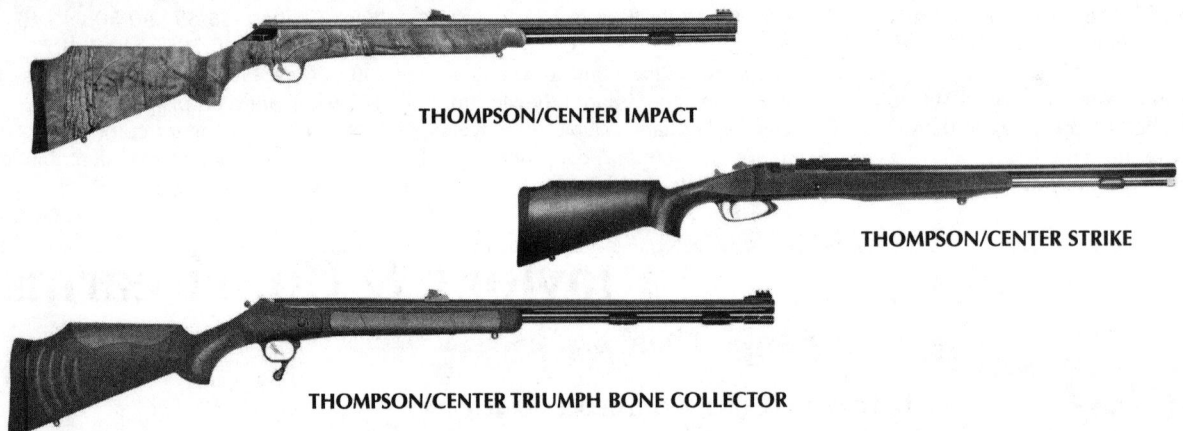

THOMPSON/CENTER IMPACT

THOMPSON/CENTER STRIKE

THOMPSON/CENTER TRIUMPH BONE COLLECTOR

IMPACT

Lock: Hinged breech muzzleloading
Stock: Black or LongLeaf camo
Barrel: 28 in.
Sights: Fiber optic
Weight: 6 lb. 8 oz.
Bore/Caliber: .50
Features: Triple lead thread breech plug; 1-inch adjustable buttstock
MSRP . . . . **$263.00–$324.00**

STRIKE

Lock: Adapt Breech system
Stock: Composite or walnut
Barrel: 24 in.
Sights: None
Weight: 7 lb. 8 oz.
Bore/Caliber: .50
Features: The Adapt Breech system moves the threads to the outside of the barrel, eliminating seized breech plugs and simplifying the cleaning process; Armornite corrosion-protectant metal finish on both inside and outside of barrel; Stealth Striker ambidextrous cocking system; match-grade trigger; finishes include black composite, walnut, or composite G2 camo
MSRP . . . . **$499.00–$599.00**

TRIUMPH BONE COLLECTOR

Lock: In-line
Stock: Composite, black or Realtree AP HD camo
Barrel: 28 in.
Sights: Adjustable fiber optic
Weight: 6 lb. 8 oz.
Bore/Caliber: .50
Features: Blued, stainless, and weather shield finish; speed breech XT
MSRP . . . . **$638.00–$720.00**

BLACK POWDER

Traditions Firearms

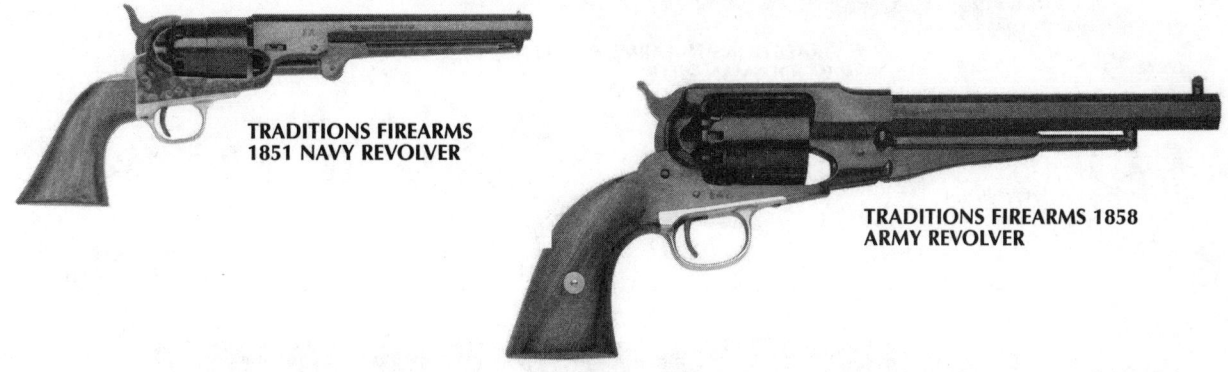

**TRADITIONS FIREARMS
1851 NAVY REVOLVER**

**TRADITIONS FIREARMS 1858
ARMY REVOLVER**

**TRADITIONS FIREARMS 1860
ARMY REVOLVER**

TRADITIONS FIREARMS BUCKSTALKER

TRADITIONS FIREARMS DEERHUNTER RIFLE

BLACK POWDER

1851 NAVY REVOLVER
Lock: Caplock revolver
Stock: Walnut
Barrel: 7.5 in.
Sights: Fixed
Weight: 2 lb. 8 oz.
Bore/Caliber: .44
Features: Octagonal barrel and lever-style loader; brass, antiqued, or old silver frame and guard
Brass:....................**$244.00**
Steel:.....................**$274.00**

1858 ARMY REVOLVER
Lock: Caplock
Stock: Walnut
Barrel: 8 in.

Sights: Fixed
Weight: 2 lb. 12 oz.
Bore/Caliber: .44
Features: Octagonal barrel and lever style loader; steel, brass, or stainless steel frame and guard; top strap and post sights
Steel:..................... **$359.00**
Brass:..................... **$289.00**

1860 ARMY REVOLVER
Lock: Caplock
Stock: Simulated ivory, walnut
Barrel: 8 in.
Sights: Fixed
Weight: 2 lb. 12 oz.
Bore/Caliber: .44

Features: Blued barrel; steel frame; brass guard; hammer/blade sights
Walnut/Steel:........... **$319.00**
Walnut/Brass:........... **$269.00**

BUCKSTALKER
Lock: Break-action muzzleloading
Stock: Synthetic
Barrel: 24 in.
Sights: Tru-Glo fiber optics
Weight: 7 lb. 8 oz.
Bore/Caliber: .50
Features: Dual safety system; nickel guard coating; synthetic black or G1 Vista camo stock; nickel or blued finish barrel; Monte Carlo stock; drilled and tapped for a scope; sling swivel studs
MSRP..........**$219.00–$369.00**

DEERHUNTER RIFLE
Lock: Traditional cap or flint
Stock: Synthetic or hardwood
Barrel: 24 in.
Sights: Lite Optic adjustable
Weight: 6 lb.
Bore/Caliber: .32, .50, .54
Features: Octagonal performance barrels; blued or nickel barrel finish; percussion models are drilled and tapped to accept scope mounts; non-slip recoil pad; stock comes in black synthetic, Mossy Oak Tree Stand camo, or hardwood
MSRP..........**$269.00–$419.00**

Traditions Firearms

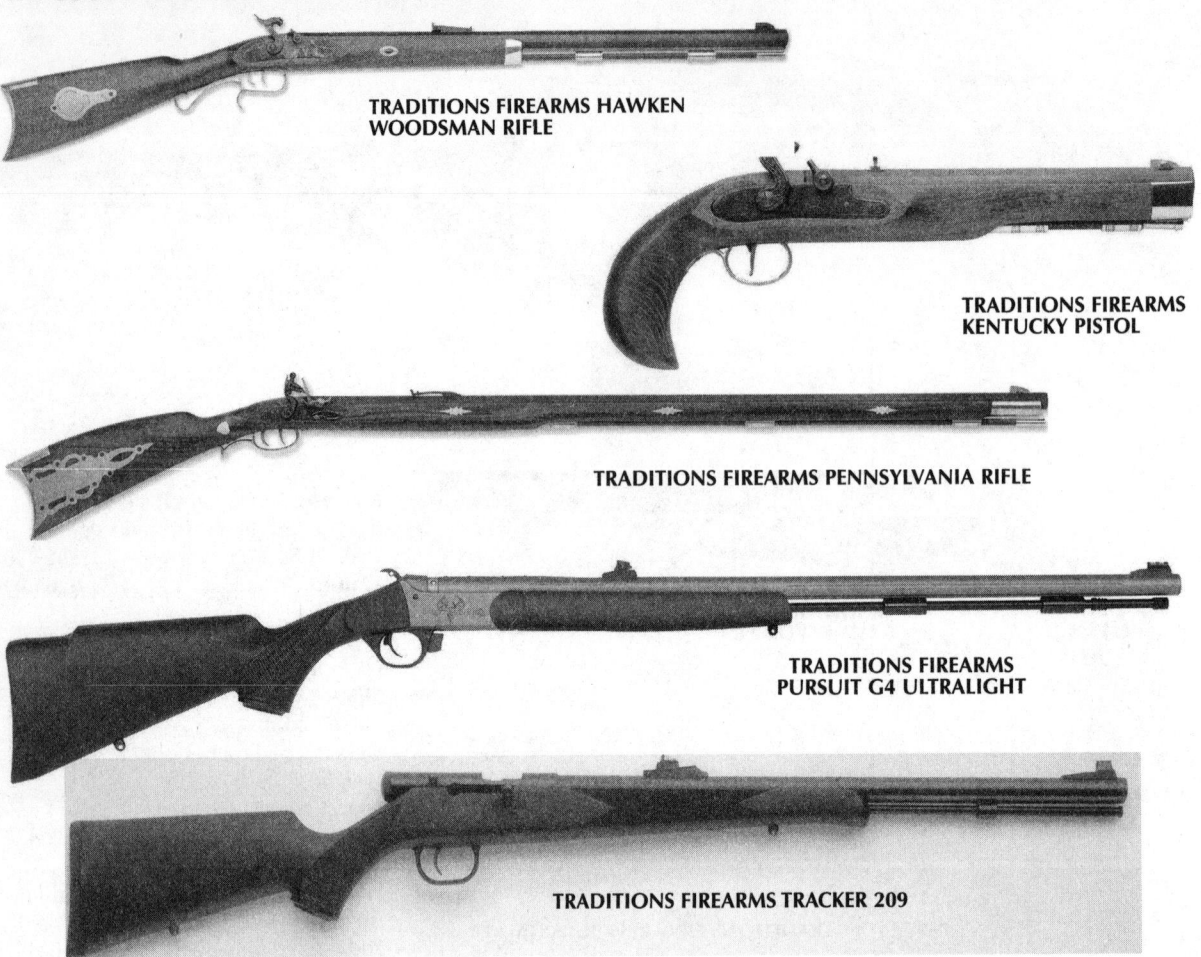

TRADITIONS FIREARMS HAWKEN WOODSMAN RIFLE

TRADITIONS FIREARMS KENTUCKY PISTOL

TRADITIONS FIREARMS PENNSYLVANIA RIFLE

TRADITIONS FIREARMS PURSUIT G4 ULTRALIGHT

TRADITIONS FIREARMS TRACKER 209

HAWKEN WOODSMAN RIFLE
Lock: Traditional cap or flint
Stock: Hardwood
Barrel: 28 in.
Sights: Adjustable rear hunting
Weight: 7 lb. 13 oz.
Bore/Caliber: .50
Features: Hooked breech for easy barrel removal; double-set triggers in an oversized glove-fitting trigger guard; inletted solid brass patch box; left-hand model available; octagonal blued barrel
Flint: **$519.00**
Percussion: **$479.00**

KENTUCKY PISTOL
Lock: Traditional caplock
Stock: Hardwood
Barrel: 10 in.
Sights: Fixed
Weight: 2 lb. 8 oz.
Bore/Caliber: .50
Features: Brass furniture; case-colored sidelock and brass ramrod thimble
MSRP. **$244.00**

PENNSYLVANIA RIFLE
Lock: Traditional cap or flint
Stock: Walnut
Barrel: 20 in.
Sights: Adjustable primitive style rear
Weight: 8 lb. 8 oz.
Bore/Caliber: .50
Features: Brass stock inlay ornamentation and toe plate; cheekpiece; solid brass patch box
Percussion: **$794.00**
Flint: **$824.00**

PURSUIT G4 ULTRALIGHT
Lock: Muzzleloading
Stock: Synthetic
Barrel: 26 in.
Chokes: IC, M, F
Sights: Fixed front, adjustable rear
Weight: 5 lb. 12 oz.
Bore/Gauge: .50
Features: Wider forend for better grip and hand position; Accelerator Breech Plug; Ultralight Chromoly Tapered, Fluted Barrel with Premium CeraKote Finish; LT-1 Alloy Frame; dual safety system - internal hammer block safety and trigger block safety; speed load system; Quick-T Ramrod Handle; soft touch camo stocks; Quick Relief Recoil Pad; Williams Fiber Optic Metal Sights; fast action release button; 1:28" twist rifling; extended ambidextrous hammer extension; drilled and tapped for a scope; sling swivel studs; 209 shotgun primer ignition; solid aluminum ramrod
MSRP. **$344.00**

TRACKER 209
Lock: In-line
Stock: Synthetic, camo
Barrel: 22 in.
Sights: Light optic adjustable
Weight: 6 lb. 8 oz.
Bore/Caliber: .50
Features: Removable 209 primer ignition; projectile alignment system; in-line bolt with a quiet thumb safety; removable breech plug system; rugged synthetic ramrod
MSRP. **$184.00**

Traditions Firearms

TRADITIONS FIREARMS TRAPPER PISTOL

TRAPPER PISTOL
Lock: Traditional cap or flint
Stock: Hardwood
Barrel: 9.75 in.
Sights: Primitive-style adjustable rear
Weight: 2 lb. 14 oz.
Bore/Caliber: .50
Features: Octagonal blued barrel; double set triggers
MSRP . . . . **$329.00–$369.00**

TRADITIONS FIREARMS VORTEK PISTOL - HARDWOOD

TRADITIONS FIREARMS VORTEK ULTRALIGHT LDR

TRADITIONS FIREARMS VORTEK ULTRALIGHT

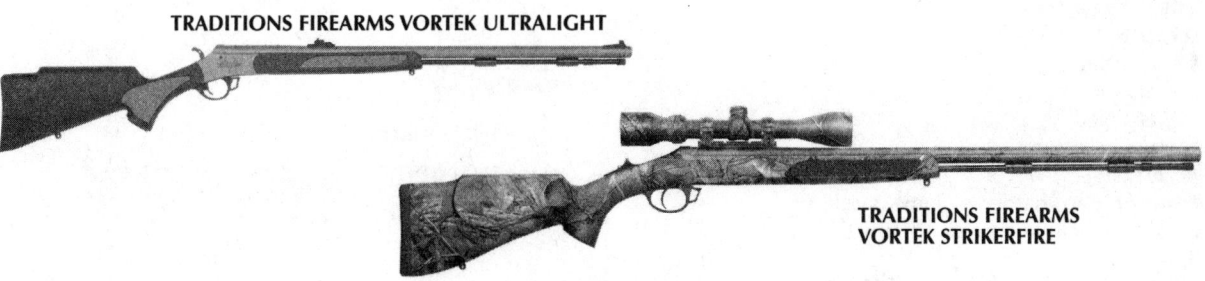

TRADITIONS FIREARMS VORTEK STRIKERFIRE

BLACK POWDER

VORTEK PISTOL
Lock: Hinged breech muzzleloading
Stock: Select hardwood, Realtree AP camo, Reaper Buck camo
Barrel: 13 in.
Sights: Fixed open
Weight: 3 lb. 4 oz.
Bore/Caliber: .50
Features: 209 primer ignition, accelerator breech plug; CeraKote finish on frame and barrel
MSRP: . . . . **$324.00–$374.00**

VORTEK STRIKERFIRE
Lock: Break-action muzzleloading
Stock: Soft Touch synthetic
Barrel: 28 in.
Sights: Fiber optic
Weight: N/A
Bore/Caliber: .50
Features: This patent-pending rifle takes in-line muzzleloaders to the next level by taking away the external hammer and using an internal StrikerFire System; to cock the gun,

simply slide the striker button forward until it locks and fire; the recessed de-cocking buttons allows for quick and quiet de-cocking of the firearm and the gun is also equipped with an automatic de-cocking mechanism—when the gun is opened, it is automatically de-cocked; also includes: two-stage trigger; CeraKote finish; Realtree Xtra, black, Mossy Oak New Treestand, Mossy Oak Break-Up Country, Kryptek Highlander; most options available with 3-9x40mm Traditions Duplex scopes and case; Drury and Crush packages get upgrade to Nikon scope and come with sling and case
MSRP: . . . . **$493.00–$854.00**

VORTEK ULTRALIGHT
Lock: Hinged breech muzzleloading
Stock: Synthetic black Hogue over-mold, Realtree AP camo, or Reaper Buck camo
Barrel: 28 in.

Sights: Fixed, green
Weight: 6 lb. 4 oz.
Bore/Caliber: .50
Features: Drop-out trigger assembly; recoil pad; 3-pound factory trigger; frame and barrel have CeraKote finish
MSRP . . . . **$449.00–$634.00**

VORTEK ULTRALIGHT LDR
Lock: Hinged breech muzzleloading
Stock: Synthetic, Reaper Buck camo
Barrel: 30 in.
Sights: Drilled and tapped for scopes
Weight: 6 lb. 13 oz.
Bore/Caliber: .50
Features: The only break-action muzzleloader with a 30-in. barrel on the market; accelerator breech plug; LT-1 alloy frame with Premium CeraKote finish; ultralight chromoly tapered, fluted barrel; Hogue comfort grip over-molding; Soft Touch camo stocks
MSRP . . . . **$479.00–$554.00**

Black Powder • **417**

Uberti

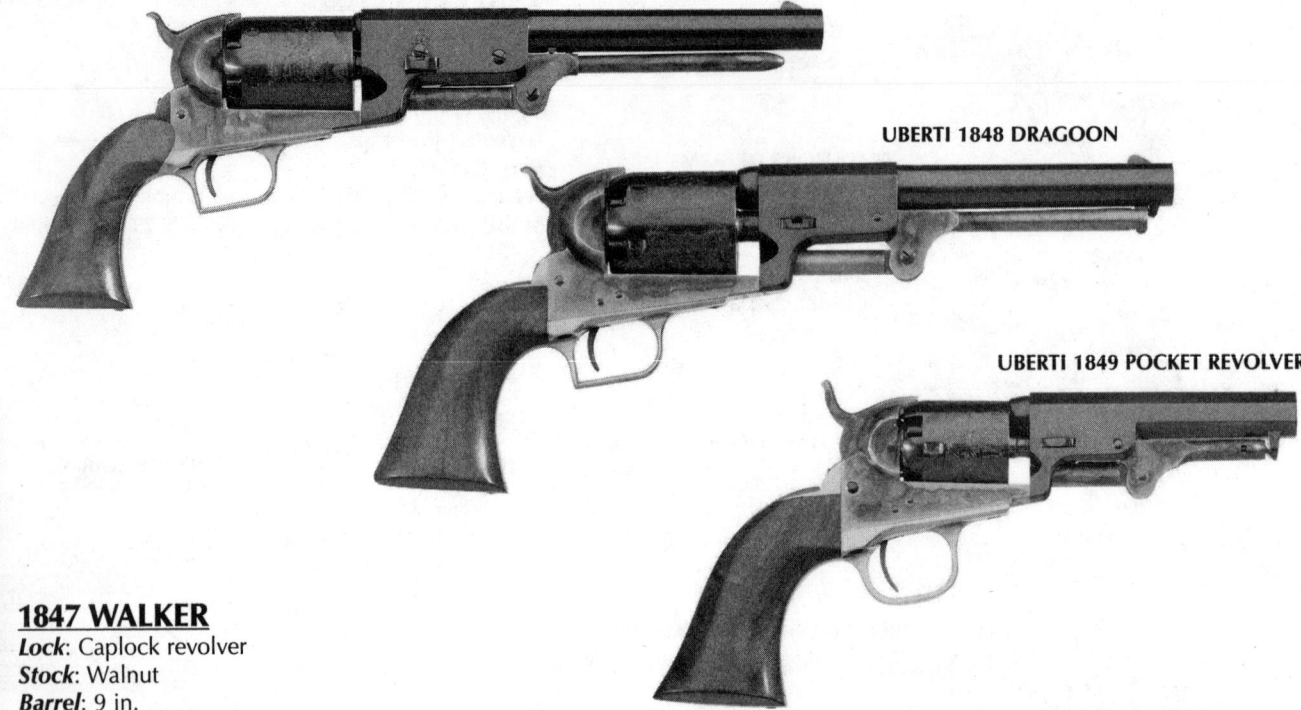

UBERTI 1847 WALKER

UBERTI 1848 DRAGOON

UBERTI 1849 POCKET REVOLVER

UBERTI 1851 NAVY REVOLVER

UBERTI 1858 NEW ARMY REVOLVER

BLACK POWDER

1847 WALKER
Lock: Caplock revolver
Stock: Walnut
Barrel: 9 in.
Sights: Fixed, open
Weight: 4 lb. 8 oz.
Bore/Caliber: .44
Features: Case-hardened frame, steel backstrap, brass trigger guard; blued finish
MSRP $459.00

1848 DRAGOON
Lock: Caplock revolver
Stock: Walnut
Barrel: 7.5 in.
Sights: Fixed, open
Weight: 4 lb. 2 oz.
Bore/Caliber: .44
Features: Case-hardened frame; steel or brass backstrap and trigger guard; engraved
MSRP . . . . $449.00–$459.00

1849 POCKET REVOLVER
Lock: Caplock revolver
Stock: Walnut
Barrel: 4 in.
Sights: Fixed, open
Weight: 1 lb. 8 oz.
Bore/Caliber: .31
Features: Case-hardened frame; brass backstrap and trigger guard; blued octagonal barrel; engraved
MSRP $369.00

1851 NAVY REVOLVER
Lock: Caplock revolver
Stock: Walnut
Barrel: 7.5 in.
Sights: Fixed, open
Weight: 2 lb. 10 oz.
Bore/Caliber: .36
Features: Color case-hardened frame; oval or squareback trigger guard; brass or steel backstrap and trigger guard; octagonal barrel (Leech-Rigdon model has round barrel)
MSRP . . . . $349.00–$379.00

1858 NEW ARMY REVOLVER
Lock: Caplock revolver
Stock: Walnut
Barrel: 8 in.
Sights: Fixed, open
Weight: 2 lb. 11 oz.
Bore/Caliber: .44
Features: Blued or stainless steel frame and backstrap; brass trigger guard; octagonal barrel
Blued: $369.00
Stainless Steel: $459.00

Uberti

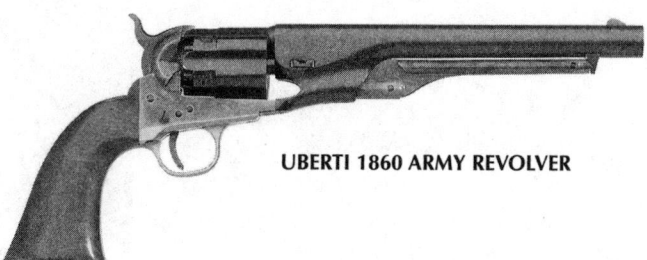

UBERTI 1860 ARMY REVOLVER

UBERTI 1861 NAVY REVOLVER

UBERTI 1862 POCKET NAVY REVOLVER

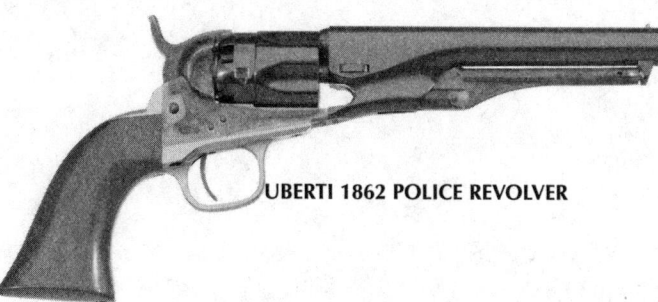

UBERTI 1862 POLICE REVOLVER

UBERTI 1885 HIGH WALL BIG
GAME SINGLE SHOT

1860 ARMY REVOLVER
Lock: Caplock revolver
Stock: Walnut
Barrel: 7.5 in.
Sights: Fixed, open
Weight: 2 lb. 10 oz.
Bore/Caliber: .44
Features: Case-hardened frame, steel backstrap, brass trigger guard; blued, round barrel
Brass, steel: **$369.00**
Fluted steel: **$379.00**

1861 NAVY REVOLVER
Lock: Caplock revolver
Stock: Walnut
Barrel: 7.5 in.
Sights: Fixed, open
Weight: 2 lb. 10 oz.
Bore/Caliber: .36
Features: Case-hardened frame, steel or brass backstrap and trigger guard
Steel: **$369.00**
Brass: **$379.00**

1862 POCKET NAVY REVOLVER
Lock: Caplock revolver
Stock: Walnut
Barrel: 5.5 in., 6.5 in.
Sights: Fixed, open
Weight: 1 lb. 11 oz.
Bore/Caliber: .36
Features: Case-hardened frame; brass backstrap and trigger guard; octagonal, blued barrel
MSRP **$389.00**

1862 POLICE REVOLVER
Lock: Caplock revolver
Stock: Walnut
Barrel: 5.5 in., 6.5 in.
Sights: Fixed, open
Weight: 1 lb. 10 oz.
Bore/Caliber: .36
Features: Case-hardened frame; brass backstrap and trigger guard; fluted round barrel
MSRP **$389.00**

1885 HIGH WALL BIG GAME SINGLE SHOT
Lock: Falling block
Stock: Walnut
Barrel: 22 in.
Sights: Fixed front, adjustable dovetail rear
Weight: 6 lb. 11 oz.
Bore/Caliber: .45-70
Features: Stock and forend designed for use with modern sporting optics; Picatinny rail; accurate 22-inch blued barrel; crisp trigger; satin walnut stock with checkered fore end and pistol grip; soft rubber butt pad to lessen felt recoil
MSRP **$1119.00**

OPTICS

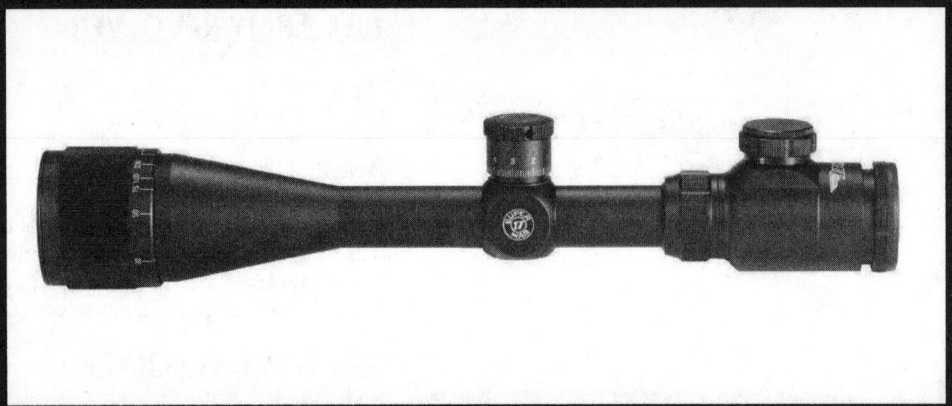

APEX XP AR MODEL 4065

Weight: 15 oz.
Length: 10.7 in.
Power: 1–6X
Obj. Dia.: 24mm
Main Dia.: 30mm
Exit Pupil: 12.5–4mm
Field of View: 108–18 ft @ 100 yds
Twilight Factor: 4.9–12
Eye Relief: 3.75 in.
Features: AR-BDC reticle; water- and fogproof; fully multi-coated; fast focus eyepiece; matte black; zero adj. W/E
MSRP **$1000.00**

APEX XP MODEL 4052 3–9X40MM

Weight: 14 oz.
Length: 12.5 in.
Power: 3–9X
Obj. Dia.: 40mm
Main Dia.: 1 in.
Exit Pupil: 13–4.5mm
Field of View: 35–12 ft @ 100 yds
Twilight Factor: 10.95–18.97
Eye Relief: 3.5 in.
Features: Fully multi-coated lens; WBDC-A reticle; matte black finish; fast-focus; side focus adjust; illuminated red-dot reticle
MSRP **$513.00**

APEX XP MODEL 4058 6–24X50MM

Weight: 24 oz.
Length: 15.5 in.
Power: 6–24X
Obj. Dia.: 50mm
Main Dia.: 30mm
Exit Pupil: 8–2mm
Field of View: 16–4 ft @ 100 yds
Twilight Factor: 17.3–34.6
Eye Relief: 3.5 in.
Features: Matte black; WBDC-TACT reticle available; also in 1.5–6x42, and in red-dot illuminated-reticle 1.5–6x42, 2.5–10x50, and 4–16x56; 6–24x50 and the 4–16x56 have ⅛

MOA adjustment increments, while the others have ¼ MOA
MSRP **$733.00**

KODIAK MODEL 2060 3.5–10X50MM

Weight: 21 oz.
Length: 13.2 in.
Power: 3.5–10X
Obj.Dia.: 50mm
Main Dia.: 1 in.
Exit Pupil: 13.5–4.9mm
Field of View: 35–12 ft @ 100 yds
Twilight Factor: 13.2–22.4
Eye Relief: 3 in.
Features: Multi-coated optical design;

oversized zero-reset windage and elevation dials adjustable in ¼ MOA (⅛ MOA in the 6–24x50) clicks; AccuPlex Tapered duplex-style reticle; fast-focus eye piece; matte black; also in 1.5–4x32, 3–9x32, 4x32, 3–9x40, 4–12x40, and 6–24x50
MSRP: **$240.00**

ALPEN APEX XP AR MODEL 4065

ALPEN APEX XP MODEL 4052 3–9X40MM

ALPEN APEX XP MODEL 4058 6–24X50MM

ALPEN KODIAK MODEL 2060 3.5–10X50MM

Barska

AR6 1–6X24MM

Weight: 17.6 oz.
Length: 11 in.
Power: 1–6X
Obj. Dia.: 24mm
Main Dia.: 30mm
Exit Pupil: 4–11mm
Field of View: 75.78–12.79 ft @ 100 yds

Twilight Factor: 4.9–12
Eye Relief: 3.7 in.
Features: Water- and fogproof; red or green illuminated reticle; dual cantilever ring scope mount, flip-up scope caps
MSRP **$239.99**

BARSKA AR6 1–6X24MM

British Small Arms Co. (BSA)

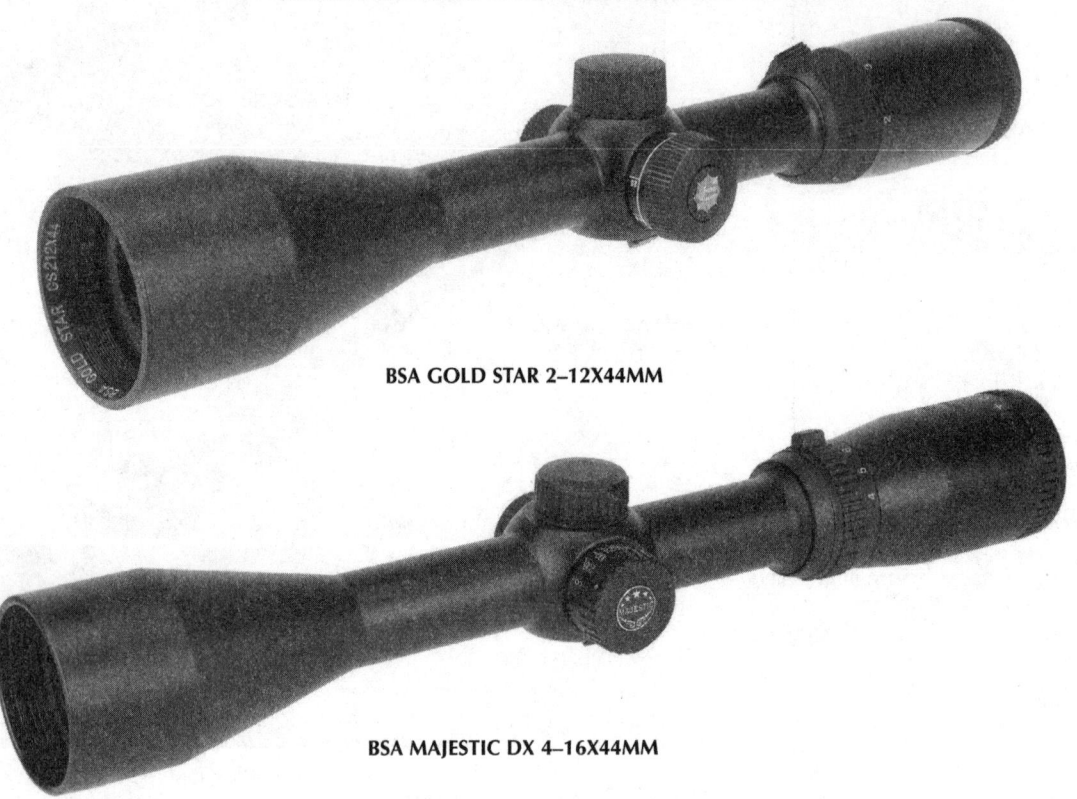

BRITISH SMALL ARMS CO. 17 SUPERMAG SERIES 4.5–14X44MM

BSA GOLD STAR 2–12X44MM

BSA MAJESTIC DX 4–16X44MM

17 SUPERMAG SERIES 4.5–14X44MM

Weight: 21.7 oz.
Length: 13.9 in.
Power: 4.5–14X
Obj. Dia.: 44mm
Main Dia.: 1 in.
Exit Pupil: 6.6–2.3mm
Field of View: 16.6–4.8 ft @ 100 yds
Twilight Factor: 14.07–24.82
Eye Relief: 4 in.
Features: Shock-, water-, and fogproof; adjustable parallax; red, green, or blue glass-etched reticle; designed for use with .17 WSM; 6–24x44 also available
MSRP . . . .$139.95–$159.95

GOLD STAR 2–12X44MM

Weight: 18 oz.
Length: 13.15 in.
Power: 2–12X
Obj.Dia.: 44mm
Main Dia.: 1 in.
Exit Pupil: 22–3.6mm
Field of View: 60–10 ft @ 100 yds
Twilight Factor: 9.38–22.98
Eye Relief: 4 in.
Features: The Gold Star line of riflescopes represent the pinnacle of BSA performance optics, exceptional clarity and resolution; 6x zoom system; perfected optical design; EZ Hunter reticle; precision W/E adjustment; side parallax available on some models; also available in 1-6x20mm and 3-18x44mm
MSRP $140.00

MAJESTIC DX 4–16X44MM

Weight: 17.6 oz.
Length: 12.66 in.
Power: 4–16X
Obj. Dia.: 44mm
Main Dia.: 1 in.
Exit Pupil: 8–4mm
Field of View: 45–7.3 ft @ 100 yds
Twilight Factor: 13.27–26.53
Eye Relief: 4 in.
Features: Newly redesigned one piece tube; fully multi-coated optics; ballistic compensating EZ Hunter reticle; 92 percent light transmission; fast-focus eyepiece ; Majestic line also includes 3-9x40mm, 3.5-10x44mm, 3.5-10x50mm, 6-24x44mm, a 4.5-12x44mm, and an illuminated reticle 3-9x40
MSRP $120.00

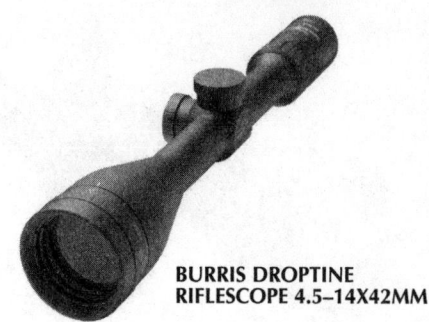

BURRIS 2–7X SCOUT SCOPE

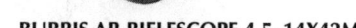

BURRIS AR RIFLESCOPE 4.5–14X42MM

BURRIS DROPTINE RIFLESCOPE 4.5–14X42MM

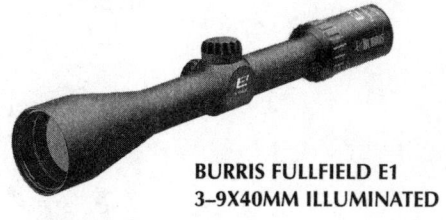

BURRIS C4 PLUS RIFLESCOPE 4.5X–14X42MM

BURRIS ELIMINATOR III 4–16X50MM

BURRIS FULLFIELD E1 3–9X40MM ILLUMINATED

2–7X SCOUT SCOPE
Weight: 13 oz.
Length: 9.7 in.
Power: 2–7X
Obj. Dia.: 32mm
Main Dia.: 1 in.
Exit Pupil: 16–4.6mm
Field of View: 21–7 ft @ 100 yds
Twilight Factor: 8–15
Eye Relief: 11–21 in.
Features: Ballistic Plex reticle; fully multi-coated; variable power; low mounting capabilities; black matte finish; Scout also available in a fixed-power 2.75x20mm
MSRP. . . . . $299.00–$479.00

AR RIFLESCOPE 4.5–14X42MM
Weight: 18 oz.
Length: 13 in.
Power: 4.5–14X
Obj. Dia.: 42mm
Main Dia.: 1 in.
Exit Pupil: 9–3mm
Field of View: 22–7.5 ft @ 100 yds
Twilight Factor: 13.75–24.25
Eye Relief: 3.1 in.–3.8 in.
Features: Shock-, water-, and fog-proof; nitrogen filled; C4 Wind MOA reticle; adjustable parallax; anti-reflection device included; 5.56 and 7.62 calibrated custom clickers included
MSRP. $479.00

C4 PLUS RIFLESCOPE 4.5X–14X42MM
Weight: 18 oz.
Length: 12.2 in.
Power: 4.5–14X

Obj. Dia.: 42mm
Main Dia.: 1 in.
Exit Pupil: 9–3mm
Field of View: 23–8 ft @ 100 yds
Twilight Factor: 13.7–24.2
Eye Relief: 3.2–3.9 in.
Features: Custom knob to match elevation adjustment and a specified catridge and bullet; index matched Hi-Lume multi-coatings; ergonomic power rings; black matte finish; available in 3x–9x40 and 4.5–14x42 in both 1-in. and 30mm tubes
MSRP. . . . . $449.00–$749.00

DROPTINE RIFLESCOPE 4.5–14X42MM
Weight: 18 oz.
Length: 13 in.
Power: 4.5–14X
Obj. Dia.: 42mm
Main Dia.: 1 in.
Exit Pupil: 9–3mm
Field of View: 22–7.5 ft @ 100 yds
Twilight Factor: 13.75–24.25
Eye Relief: 3.1 in.–3.8 in.
Features: Shock-, water-, and fog-proof; nitrogen filled; multi-coated lenses; Ballistic Plex reticle or G2B Mil-Dot reticle; adjustable parallax; 2–7x35, 3–9x40, and 3–9x50 also available
MSRP. . . . . $179.00–$299.00

ELIMINATOR III 4–16X50MM
Weight: 26 oz.
Length: 15.75 in.
Power: 4–16X

Obj. Dia.: 50mm
Main Dia.: 39mm
Exit Pupil: 12.5–3.1mm
Field of View: 25–7 ft @ 100 yds
Twilight Factor: 14.1–28.3
Eye Relief: 3.5–4 in.
Features: Laser rangefinder with wind compensation; range of 1,200+ yards; accurate at any magnification; ergonomic activation buttons; parallax adjustment 50 yards-infinity; black matte finish; fully multi-coated; also available in 3-12x44mm
MSRP. . . . . $1559.00–$2039.00

FULLFIELD E1 3–9X40MM ILLUMINATED
Weight: 12 oz.
Length: 11.4 in.
Power: 3–9X
Obj. Dia.: 40mm
Main Dia.: 1 in.
Exit Pupil: 17–5mm
Field of View: 45–13 ft @ 100 yds
Twilight Factor: 10.95–18.97
Eye Relief: 3.1–4.1 in.
Features: A series of cascading dots to the left and right of the reticle help compensate for crosswinds. The dots represent a 10 mph crosswind (+/- 1.5-in. at 400 yds) for most hunting cartridges. For a 5 mph crosswind, halve the distance between dot and reticle. For 20 mph crosswind, simply double the distance. Also available in 2–7x35, 3–9x50, 4.5–14x42, and 6.5–20x50
MSRP. . . . . $239.00–$599.00

OPTICS

Burris

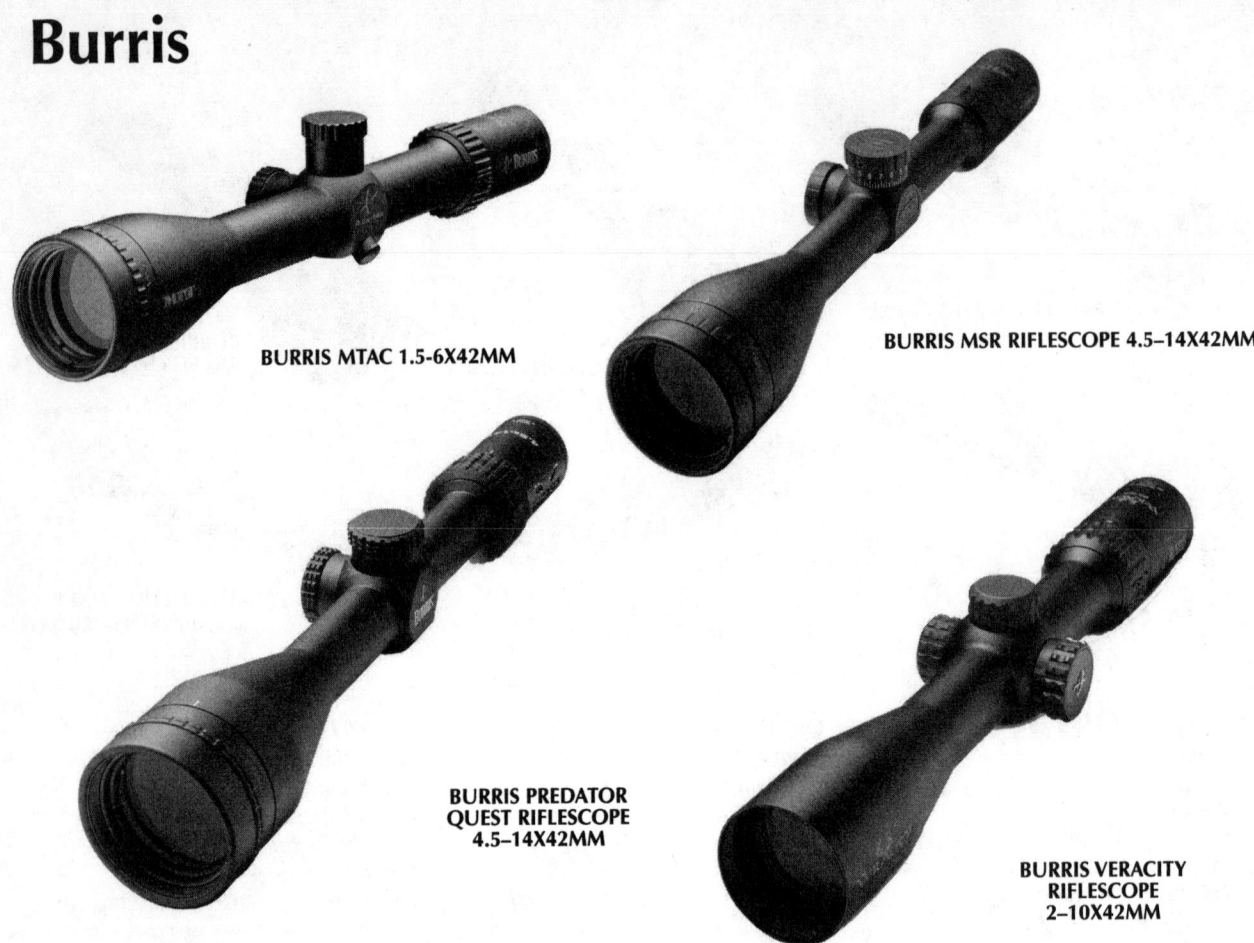

BURRIS MTAC 1.5-6X42MM

BURRIS MSR RIFLESCOPE 4.5–14X42MM

BURRIS PREDATOR
QUEST RIFLESCOPE
4.5–14X42MM

BURRIS VERACITY
RIFLESCOPE
2–10X42MM

MSR RIFLESCOPE 4.5–14X42MM

Weight: 18 oz.
Length: 13 in.
Power: 4.5–14X
Obj. Dia.: 42mm
Main Dia.: 1 in.
Exit Pupil: 9–3mm
Field of View: 22–7.5 ft @ 100 yds
Twilight Factor: 13.75–24.25
Eye Relief: 3.1–3.8 in.
Features: Shock-, water-, and fog-proof; nitrogen filled; multi-coated lenses; Ballistic Plex reticle; adjustable parallax; 3–9x40 also available
MSRP . . . . **$239.00–$323.00**

MTAC 1.5-6X42MM

Weight: 15.5 oz.
Length: 12.2 in.
Power: 1.5–6X
Obj. Dia.: 46mm
Main Dia: 30mm
Exit Pupil: 27–7mm
Twilight Factor: N/A
Eye Relief: 3.1–3.8 in.

Features: Features glare-resistant glass, snag-free profile, solid one-piece tube, internal double spring tension assembly, .5-MOA clicks, finger-adjustable mil-rad target knobs, night-vision technology compatibility, 10 brightness settings. Choice of Ballistic CQ or Ballistic AR reticles; also available in 1-4x24mm in both a standard black finish and in SkullTec graphic finish, with Burris Fast Fire III red dot and AR-P.E.P.R. mount
MSRP . . . . **$479.00–$755.00**

PREDATOR QUEST RIFLESCOPE 4.5–14X42MM

Weight: 18 oz.
Length: 13 in.
Power: 4.5–14X
Obj. Dia.: 42mm
Main Dia.: 1 in.
Exit Pupil: 9–3mm
Field of View: 22–7.5 ft @ 100 yds
Twilight Factor: 13.75–24.25
Eye Relief: 3.1 in.–3.8 in.
Features: Shock-, water-, and fog-

proof; nitrogen filled; Hi-Lume multi-coated lenses; Ballistic Plex E1 reticle (illuminated optional); adjustable parallax; anti-reflection device included; camo or matte black; 2–7x35 and 3–9x40 also available
MSRP . . . . **$275.00–$419.00**

VERACITY RIFLESCOPE 2–10X42MM

Weight: 22.7 oz.
Length: 13.5 in.
Power: 2–10X
Obj. Dia.: 42mm
Main Dia.: 30mm
Exit Pupil: 21–4.2mm
Field of View: 52–10.5 ft @ 100 yds
Twilight Factor: 9.17–20.49
Eye Relief: 3.5 in.–4.25 in.
Features: Shock-, water-, and fog-proof; nitrogen filled; Ballistic E1 FFP MOA reticle with PTC technology; E1 Hunter knobs; parallax adjustment; 3–15x50, 4–20x50, and 5–25x50 also available
MSRP . . . . **$719.00–$1079.00**

Burris

BURRIS XTR II 1–5X24MM

BURRIS XTR II 2–10X42MM

XTR II 2–10X42MM
Weight: 22.7 oz.
Length: 13.5 in.
Power: 2–10X
Obj. Dia.: 42mm
Main Dia.: 34mm
Exit Pupil: 12–4.2mm

Field of View: 52–10.5 ft @ 100 yds
Twilight Factor: 9.17–20.49
Eye Relief: 3.5 in.–4.25 in.
Features: Shock-, water-, and fog-proof; nitrogen filled; Hi-Lume multi-coated lenses; Zero Click Stop technology; G2B Mil-Dot illuminated FFP

reticle; adjustable parallax; 3–15x50, 4–20x50, 5–25x50, 1-5x24, 1.5-8x28, 8-40x50mm, and 1-8x24mm also available
MSRP . . . . **$959.00–$1679.00**

Bushnell Outdoor Products

BUSHNELL AK

BUSHNELL AR OPTICS 2–7X32MM RIMFIRE

BUSHNELL AR OPTICS 1–4X24MM THROW DOWN PCL

AK
Available in: 1–4x24mm
Weight: 18.4 oz.
Length: 11.3 in.
Power: 1–4X
Obj. Dia.: 24mm
Main Dia.: 30mm
Exit Pupil: 12.7mm
Field of View: 140 ft @ 100 yds
Twilight Factor: N/A
Eye Relief: 3.5 in.
Features: Outstanding close-quarters accuracy at 1X; illuminated 7.62x39 BDC reticle for mid-range precision; second focal plane; fully multi-coated optics
MSRP **$249.99**

AR OPTICS 1–4X24MM THROW DOWN PCL
Weight: 17.3 oz.
Length: 3.6 in.
Power: 1–4X
Obj. Dia.: 24mm
Main Dia.: 30mm
Exit Pupil: 13–6mm
Field of View: 110–36 ft @ 100 yds
Twilight Factor: 4.9–9.8
Eye Relief: 3.6 in.
Features: Optional illuminated BTR-1 reticle; first focal plane; Throw Down PCL lever for power changes; fully multi-coated optics; holdovers out to 500 yds; target turrets; matte finish
MSRP **$229.00**

AR OPTICS 2–7X32MM RIMFIRE
Weight: 19.6 oz.
Length: 11.3 in.
Power: 2–7X
Obj. Dia.: 32mm
Main Dia.: 1 in.
Exit Pupil: 13.5–4.6mm
Field of View: 50–17 ft @ 100 yds
Twilight Factor: 8–15
Eye Relief: 3.7 in.
Features: Target turrets; Drop Zone 22 LR BDC reticle; fully multi-coated optics; matte finish
MSRP **$119.99**

Bushnell Outdoor Products

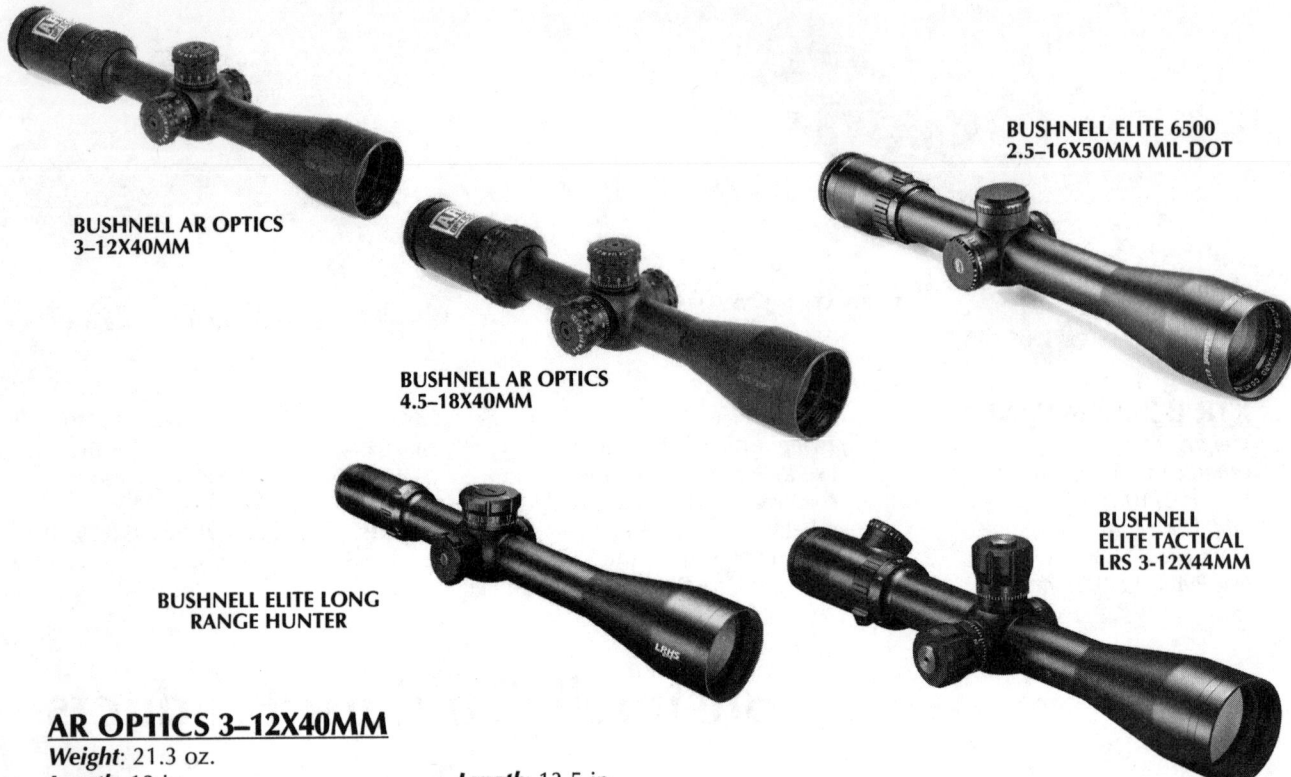

BUSHNELL AR OPTICS 3–12X40MM

BUSHNELL AR OPTICS 4.5–18X40MM

BUSHNELL ELITE 6500 2.5–16X50MM MIL-DOT

BUSHNELL ELITE LONG RANGE HUNTER

BUSHNELL ELITE TACTICAL LRS 3-12X44MM

AR OPTICS 3–12X40MM
Weight: 21.3 oz.
Length: 12 in.
Power: 3–12X
Obj. Dia.: 40mm
Main Dia.: 1 in.
Exit Pupil: 13.7–3.7mm
Field of View: 33–11 ft @ 100 yds
Twilight Factor: 11–21.9
Eye Relief: 3.7 in.
Features: Target turrets; side parallax adjustment; Drop Zone 223 BDC reticle; second focal plane; fully multi-coated optics; 600 yard range; matte finish
MSRP..................**$179.99**

AR OPTICS 4.5–18X40MM
Weight: 21.5 oz.
Length: 12.4 in.
Power: 4.5–18X
Obj. Dia.: 40mm
Main Dia.: 1 in.
Exit Pupil: 8.6–2.3mm
Field of View: 22–7.3 ft @ 100 yds
Twilight Factor: 13.4–26.8
Eye Relief: 3.7 in.
Features: Target turrets; side parallax adjustment; Drop Zone 223 BDC reticle; second focal plane; fully multi-coated optics; 600 yard range; matte finish
MSRP..................**$229.99**

ELITE 6500 2.5–16X50MM MIL-DOT
Weight: 21 oz.
Length: 13.5 in.
Power: 2.5–16X
Obj.Dia.: 50mm
Main Dia.: 30mm
Exit Pupil: 20–3.12mm
Field of View: 42–7 ft @ 100 yds
Twilight Factor: 11.18–28.28
Eye Relief: 3.9 in.
Features: Lenses with 60-layer "Ultra Wide Band Coating"; 91 percent total light transmission through the scope; RainGuard HD; windage and elevation adjustments in ¼ MOA audible increments; also in 2.5–16x42 and 4.5–30x50
MSRP........ **$1053.45–$1334.45**

ELITE LONG RANGE HUNTER SERIES
Weight: 24.4 oz., 26.5 oz.
Length: 13.4 in., 14.2 in.
Power: 4.5–18X
Obj. Dia.: 44mm
Main Dia.: 30mm
Exit Pupil: 12.1–3.7mm, 9.2–2.5mm
Field of View: 24.9–8.96 ft @ 100 yds, 23.5–6 ft @ 100 yds
Twilight Factor: 11.49–22.98, 14.07–28.14
Eye Relief: 3.74 in., 3.94 in.
Features: Fully multi-coated and ultra wide band coating; first focal plane; G2H mil or G2M MOA
MSRP..................**$2100.45**

ELITE TACTICAL LRS 3–12X44MM
Weight: 24.4 oz.
Length: 13 in.
Power: 3–12X
Obj.Dia.: 44mm
Main Dia.: 30mm
Exit Pupil: 14.66–3.66mm
Field of View: 36–10 ft @ 100 yds
Twilight Factor: 11.48–22.97
Eye Relief: 3.75 in.
Features: Tactical treatment of Elite 6500 riflescope; tactical target-adjustment turrets and non-glare black-matte finish as well as "blacked-out" cosmetics for concealment; Bushnell "Ultra Wide Band Coating" optics; RainGuard HD coating; choice of Illuminated Mil-Dot or G2 reticle; scope is first focal plane; includes two sun shades; aso available in 4.5-18x44, 10x40 SFP, 5-15x40 SFP, 4.5-30x50, 2.5-16x42 SFP (SFP = second focal plane)
MSRP..................**$1364.00**

Bushnell Outdoor Products

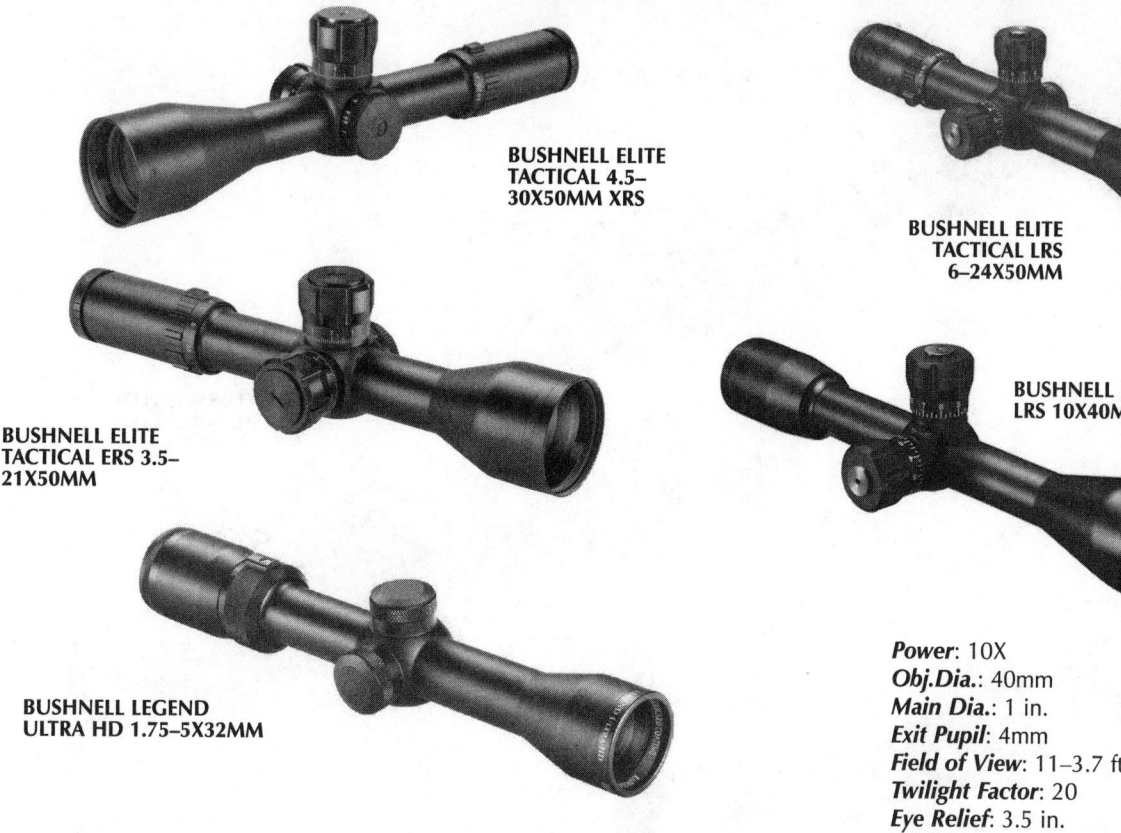

BUSHNELL ELITE TACTICAL 4.5–30X50MM XRS

BUSHNELL ELITE TACTICAL LRS 6–24X50MM

BUSHNELL ELITE TACTICAL ERS 3.5–21X50MM

BUSHNELL ELITE TACTICAL LRS 10X40MM SFP

BUSHNELL LEGEND ULTRA HD 1.75–5X32MM

ELITE TACTICAL 4.5–30X50MM XRS

Weight: 37 oz.
Length: 10.2 in.
Power: 4.5–30X
Obj. Dia.: 50mm
Main Dia.: 34mm
Exit Pupil: 9–1.7mm
Field of View: 24–3.6 ft @ 100 yds
Twilight Factor: 15–38.7
Eye Relief: 3.7 in.
Features: T-Lok locking target turrets; Z-Lok zero stop; G2 reticle; first focal plane; side parallax adjustment; .1 Mil clicks, 10 Mils/rev; blacked-out finish
MSRP. **$3253.00**

ELITE TACTICAL LRS 6–24X50MM

Weight: 27 oz.
Length: 13.5 in.
Power: 6–24X
Obj.Dia.: 50mm
Main Dia.: 30mm
Exit Pupil: 7.5–2.1mm
Field of View: 17.5–4.5 ft @ 100 yds
Twilight Factor: 17.32–24
Eye Relief: 4 in.
Features: Exceptional brightness and extended-range magnification with

side parallax; RainGuard HD; fully multi-coated optics; ultra-strong, one-piece tube; .1 Mil click value; 3-in. sunshade; side parallax adjustment; available in Mil-Dot, Illuminated Mil-Dot, G2, and Illuminated BTR-Mil reticles
MSRP. **$1523.00**

ELITE TACTICAL ERS 3.5–21X50MM

Weight: 35 oz.
Length: 13 in.
Power: 3.5–21X
Obj. Dia.: 50mm
Main Dia.: 34mm
Exit Pupil: 10–2.4mm
Field of View: 26–5 ft @ 100 yds
Twilight Factor: 13.2–32.4
Eye Relief: 3.7 in.
Features: T-Lok locking turrets; Z-Lok zero stop; G2 reticle; first focal plane; side parallax adjustment; .1 Mil click, 10 rev; available in matte black or flat dark earth finishes
MSRP. **$2976.00**

ELITE TACTICAL LRS 10X40MM SFP

Weight: 15.9 oz.
Length: 11.5 in.

Power: 10X
Obj.Dia.: 40mm
Main Dia.: 1 in.
Exit Pupil: 4mm
Field of View: 11–3.7 ft @ 100 yds
Twilight Factor: 20
Eye Relief: 3.5 in.
Features: Fixed-power target scope with Mil-Dot reticle and target turret; RainGuard HD; ultra wide band coating; fully multi-coated optics; blacked-out finish; target turrets; second focal plane optic
MSRP. **$391.00**

LEGEND ULTRA HD 1.75–5X32MM DOA 200

Weight: 13 oz.
Length: 10.25 in.
Power: 1.75–5X
Obj. Dia.: 32mm
Main Dia.: 30mm
Exit Pupil: 18.2–6.4mm
Field of View: 49–17 ft @ 100 yds
Twilight Factor: 7.48–12.65
Eye Relief: 4.5 in.
Features: The perfect scope for medium range hunting with a shotgun; RainGuard HD; fully multi-coated optics; ultra-strong, one-piece tube; parallax set at 75 yds; fast-focus eyepiece; also in 1.75–5x32 Multi-X/DOA Crossbow, 3–9x40 Multi-X/DOA 600, 3–9x50 Multi-X/DOA 600, 4.5–14x44 Multi-X/Mil-Dot
MSRP. **$379.00**

Bushnell Outdoor Products

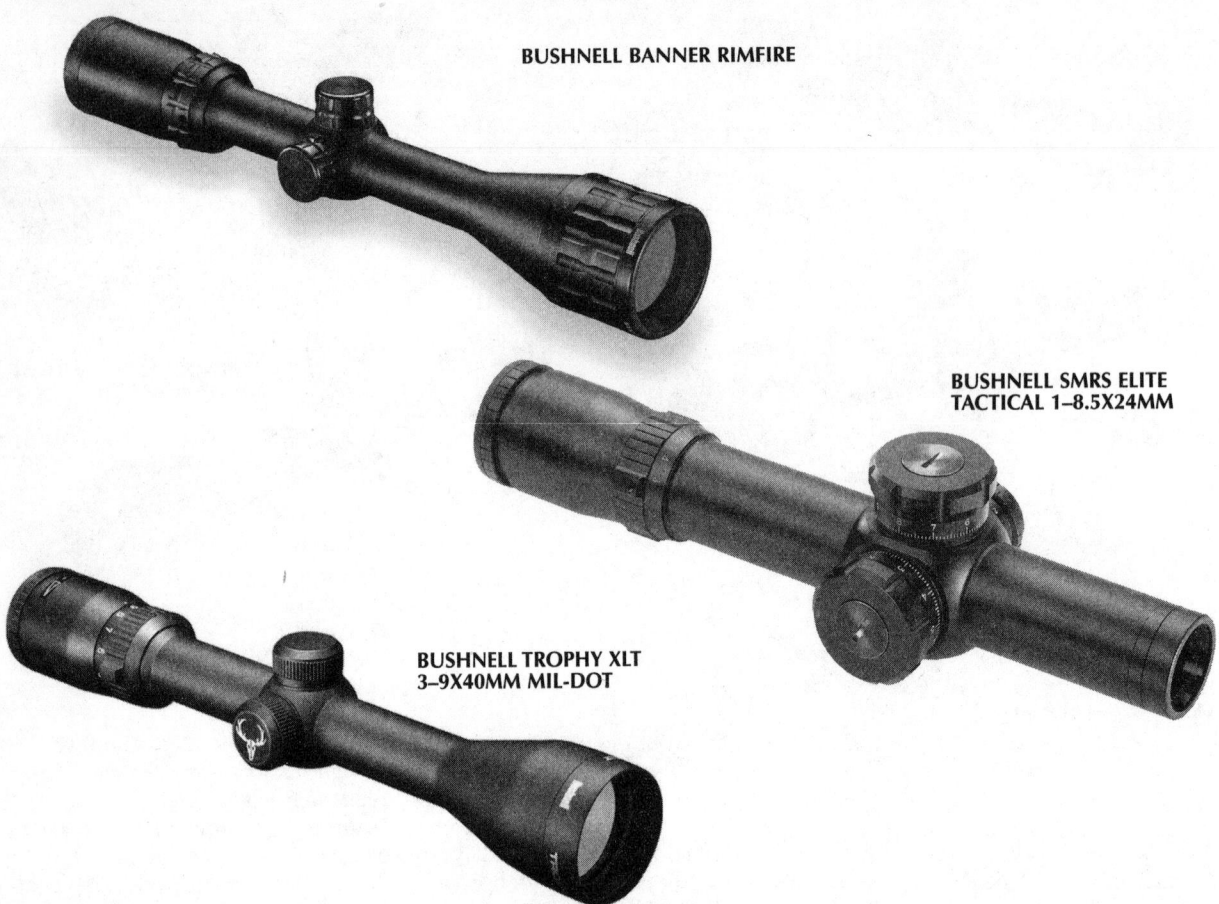

BUSHNELL BANNER RIMFIRE

**BUSHNELL SMRS ELITE
TACTICAL 1–8.5X24MM**

**BUSHNELL TROPHY XLT
3–9X40MM MIL-DOT**

RIMFIRE SERIES

Weight: 20.4 oz., 20 oz., 15 oz., 15 oz., 20.3 oz.
Length: 12.2 in., 12 in., 12.5 oz., 12 in., 12.4 in.
Power: 3–9X, 3–12X, 3.5–10X, 4–12X, 6–18X
Obj. Dia.: 40mm, 40mm, 36mm, 40mm, 40mm
Main Dia.: 1 in.
Exit Pupil: 13–4.4mm, 13–7mm, 10.3–3.6mm, 10–3.3mm, 6.6–2.2mm
Field of View: 31–9.4 ft @ 100 yds, 33–10 ft @ 100 yds, 30–10.4 ft @ 100 yds, 29–11 ft @ 100 yds, 18–5.5 ft @ 100 yds
Twilight Factor: 10.95–18.97, 10.95–21.91, 11.23–20.78, 12.65–21.91, 15.49–26.83
Eye Relief: 3.9 in., 3.9 in., 3.4 in., 3.3 in., 3.9 in.
Features: Second focal plane; adjustable objective; multi-coated lenses; Multi-X reticle; multi-X reticle; side parallax adjustment; ¼ MOA; .22 LR and .17 HRM turrets included
MSRP . . . . $148.95–$194.95

SMRS ELITE TACTICAL 1–8.5X24MM

Weight: 23 oz.
Length: 10.2 in.
Power: 1–8.5X
Obj. Dia.: 24mm
Main Dia.: 34mm
Exit Pupil: 13.2–3.2mm
Field of View: 105–14 ft @ 100 yds
Twilight Factor: 4.9–14.3
Eye Relief: 3.5 in.
Features: Illuminated BTR-2 reticle; first focal plane; .1 Mil click value; eleven brightness settings; T-Lok turrets; black matte finish
MSRP $1977.08

TROPHY XLT 3–9X40MM MIL-DOT

Weight: 14.1 oz.
Length: 11.9 in.
Power: 3–9X
Obj.Dia.: 40mm
Main Dia.: 1 in.
Exit Pupil: 13.3–4.4mm
Field of View: 40–13 ft @ 100 yds
Twilight Factor: 10.95–18.97
Eye Relief: 4 in.
Features: 91percent total light transmission; one-piece tube with integrated saddle; ¼ MOA fingertip windage and elevation adjustments with range of adjustment of 80 MOA; Butler Creek flip-up scope covers; some scopes available in gloss, matte, silver, or camo finishes; also in 3–9x40 DOA 250, 3–9x40 DOA 600, 3–9x40 Multi-X, 3–9x40 Circle-X, 3–9x50, 4–12x40 DOA 600, 4–12x40 Multi-X, 1–4x24, 1.5–6x42, 1.5–6x44, 3–12x56, 1.75–4x32, 2–6x32, 2–7x36 DOA Crossbow, 2–7x36 DOA 200, 3–9x40 DOA 200, 6–18x50
MSRP $205.00

OPTICS

CABELA'S INSTINCT EURO RIFLESCOPE DUPLEX 3–9X42MM

CABELA'S LEVER ACTION 3–9X40MM

CABELA'S RIMFIRE RIFLESCOPE 3–9X40MM

INSTINCT EURO RIFLESCOPE DUPLEX 3–9X42MM

Weight: 16 oz.
Length: 12.4 in.
Power: 3–9X
Obj.Dia.: 42mm
Main Dia.: 1 in.
Exit Pupil: 14–4.66mm
Field of View: 36.3–12.1 ft @ 100 yds
Twilight Factor: 11.22–19.44
Eye Relief: 3.75 in.
Features: CNC machined from a single billet of aircraft-aluminum; ELOX (electrolytic oxidation) anodization for a reduced-glare black matte, abrasion-resistant finish; fully multi-coated lenses; fast-focus eyepieces; elevation and windage turrets are finger adjustable in ¼ MOA clicks; also with EXT reticle, and in 4–12x50 and 6–18x50 with Duplex reticles: and now available in in a 4.5-14x44mm
MSRP . . . . $499.99–$699.99

LEVER ACTION 3–9X40MM

Weight: 14.64 oz.
Length: 13 in.
Power: 3–9X
Obj.Dia.: 40mm
Main Dia.: 1 in.
Exit Pupil: 13.33–4.44mm
Field of View: 30.55–9.6 ft @ 100 yds
Twilight Factor: 10.95–18.97
Eye Relief: 5.5 in.
Features: Ballistic glass reticles specifically engineered for use with a particular Hornady LEVERevolution round; tube is machined aluminum and lenses are multi-coated; windage and elevation are adjustable in ¼ MOA clicks; in .45-70 Govt., .44 Mag., and .30-30 Win. reticles
MSRP $99.99

RIMFIRE RIFLESCOPE 3–9X40MM

Weight: 13.4 oz.
Length: 12 in.
Power: 3–9X
Obj.Dia.: 40mm
Main Dia.: 1 in.
Exit Pupil: 13.33–4.44mm
Field of View: 37.7–12.4 ft @ 100 yds
Twilight Factor: 10.95–18.97
Eye Relief: 4 in.
Features: For hunting, target shooting, or plinking with a rimfire rifle; parallax-free at 50 yards; multi-coated glass optics; extended eye relief and an expanded exit pupil; low-profile windage and elevation turrets; Duplex reticle; also available in 2-7x32, 4X
MSRP . . . . $49.99–$79.99

Carl Zeiss Sports Optics

CONQUEST HD5 2–10X42MM
Weight: 17.5 oz.
Length: 13.19 in.
Power: 2–10X
Obj. Dia.: 50mm
Main Dia.: 25.4mm
Exit Pupil: 10.6–4.2mm
Field of View: 52–10 ft @ 100 yds
Twilight Factor: 6.5–20.5
Eye Relief: 3.5 in.
Features: Versatile in close encounters from cover to mid-range; parallax free to 100 yds; available reticles include Reticle 20 (non-illuminated), and Rapid-Z 600, 800, 1000, or Varmint configurations
MSRP **$929.99 $929.99**

CONQUEST HD5 3–15X42MM
Weight: 18.4 oz.
Length: 13.8 in.
Power: 3–15X
Obj. Dia.: 50mm
Main Dia.: 25.4mm
Exit Pupil: 10–2.8mm
Field of View: 35–7 ft @ 100 yds
Twilight Factor: 9.5–25.1
Eye Relief: 3.5 in.
Features: Mid- to long-range; low profile; parallax adjustment; Z-Plex reticle; hunting turret or lockable target turret; available reticles include Reticle 20 (non-illuminated), and Rapid-Z 600, 800, 1000, or Varmint configurations
MSRP . . . . **$1049.99–$1199.99**

CONQUEST HD5 3–15X50MM
Weight: 24.7 oz.
Length: 13.78 in
Power: 3–15X
Obj. Dia.: 50mm
Main Dia.: 1 in.
Exit Pupil: 10–3.3mm
Field of View: 34.1–6.8 ft @ 100 yds
Twilight Factor: 12.25–27.39
Eye Relief: 3.5 in.
Features: Rear focal plane; water resistant; nitrogen filled; available reticles include Reticle 20 (non-illuminated), and Rapid-Z 600, 800, 1000, or Varmint configurations
MSRP . . . . **$1099.99–$1249.99**

CONQUEST HD5 5–25X50MM
Weight: 26.6 oz.
Length: 14 in.
Power: 5–25X
Obj. Dia.: 60mm
Main Dia.: 25.4mm
Exit Pupil: 8.5–2mm
Field of View: 21–4.2 ft @ 100 yds
Twilight Factor: 14.5–35.4
Eye Relief: 3.5 in.
Features: Mid- to extra-long range; wide magnification range provide flexibility; side parallax adjustment; available reticles include Reticle 20 (non-illuminated), and Rapid-Z 600, 800, 1000, or Varmint configurations matte finish
MSRP . . . . **$1199.99–$1299.99**

TERRA 3X 3–9X42MM
Weight: 14.8 oz.
Length: 12.4 in.
Power: 3–9X
Obj. Dia.: 42mm
Main Dia.: 25.4mm
Exit Pupil: 13.8–4.6mm
Field of View: 35.9–12.3 ft @ 100 yds
Twilight Factor: 11.2–19.4
Eye Relief: 3.5 in.
Features: MC anti-reflective coatings; Reticle 20 Z-Plex; all-purpose scope; larger objective for better low light situations; waterproof; matte finish
MSRP . . . . **$299.99–$359.99**

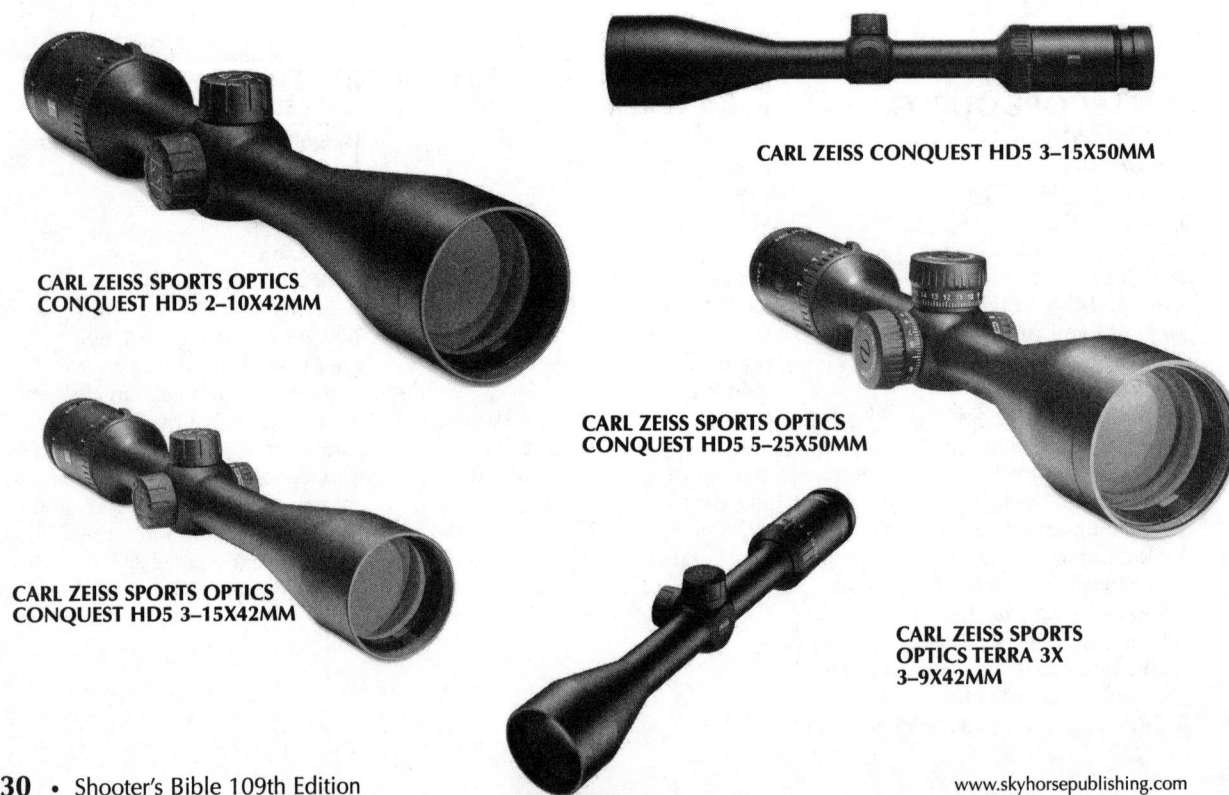

CARL ZEISS CONQUEST HD5 3–15X50MM

CARL ZEISS SPORTS OPTICS CONQUEST HD5 2–10X42MM

CARL ZEISS SPORTS OPTICS CONQUEST HD5 5–25X50MM

CARL ZEISS SPORTS OPTICS CONQUEST HD5 3–15X42MM

CARL ZEISS SPORTS OPTICS TERRA 3X 3–9X42MM

OPTICS

Carl Zeiss Sports Optics

CARL ZEISS TERRA 3X 3–9X50MM

CARL ZEISS VICTORY HT 2.5–10X50MM

CARL ZEISS SPORTS OPTICS VICTORY V8

TERRA 3X 3–9X50MM

Weight: 17.5 oz.
Length: 13.2 in.
Power: 3–9X
Obj. Dia.: 50mm
Main Dia.: 1 in.
Exit Pupil: 12.4–4.16mm
Field of View: 34.8–11.3 ft @ 100 yds
Twilight Factor: 12.25–21.21
Eye Relief: 3.55 in.
Features: Water resistant; nitrogen filled; Reticle 20 Z-Plex
MSRP . . . . $359.99–$399.99

VICTORY HT 2.5–10X50MM

Weight: 20.2 oz.
Length: 13.66 in.
Power: 3–12X
Obj. Dia.: 63mm
Main Dia.: 30mm
Exit Pupil: 14.9–4.7mm
Field of View: 37.5–25.9 ft @ 100 yds
Twilight Factor: 8.5–25.9

Eye Relief: 3.54 in.
Features: The largest of the VICTORY HT line, this 3–12x56 model makes targets visible in the very last of shooting light; the combination of the advanced HT glass, high-performance 56mm objective lens, the super-fine illuminated dot, and ASV+ turret option makes this scope deadly accurate at any distance, in any light; LotuTec lens coating; available with illuminated Reticle 54 or Reticle 60
MSRP . . . . $2599.99–$2899.99

VICTORY V8

Available in: 1–8x30mm, 1.8–14x50mm, 2.8–20x56mm, 4.8–35x60mm
Weight: 21 oz.–34 oz.
Length: 12 in.–15.75 in.
Power: 1–8X, 1.8–13.5X, 2.8–20X, 4.8–35X
Obj. Dia.: 30mm, 50mm, 56mm, 60mm

Main Dia.: 36mm
Exit Pupil: 9.9–3.9mm, 10.3–3.7mm, 9.8–2.8mm, 9.9–1.4mm
Field of View: 110–15 ft @ 100 yds, 63–8.5 ft @ 100 yds, 42–5.7 ft @ 100 yds, 24–3.3 ft @ 100 yds
Twilight Factor: 3.1–15.5; 5.1–26; 7.9–33; 13.6–45.8
Eye Relief: 3.75 in.
Features: Largest zoom range; interaction of 92 percent transmission; fluoride lens elements and SCHOTT HT glass ensures outstanding image quality and target resolution; large exit pupils and extremely large fields of view ensure fast target acquisition, an excellent overview of the hunting situation, no shadowing, and an immediate round image; compact design; generous adjustment range of 100 clicks enables you to stay on target at distances up to 600 yds; a fiber optic thinner than a human hair provides the finest illuminated dot in the world, resulting in 0.1188 in. subtension at 100 yds
MSRP . . . . $2599.99–$3699.99

C-More Systems

C-MORE SYSTEMS C3 1–6X24MM COMPETITION

SYSTEMS C3 1–6X24MM COMPETITION

Available in: 1–6x24mm
Weight: 22 oz.
Length: 10.5 in.
Power: 1–6X
Obj. Dia.: 24mm
Main Dia.: 30mm
Exit Pupil: 12–4.1mm
Field of View: 108.3–19.8 ft @ 100 yds
Twilight Factor: N/A

Eye Relief: 4.25 in.
Features: Lockable windage and elevation turrets; TJ1I competition ballistic reticle with 1.5 in. illuminated red dot; 11 entensity settings; nitrogen filled; waterproof, fogproof, and shockproof; quick-zoom power adjustment ring; coated optics
MSRP $1999.99

EoTech

VUDU SERIES

Available in: 1–6x24mm, 2.5–10x44mm, 3.5–18x50mm
Weight: 19.75 oz.–33.23 oz.
Length: 10.63 in.–14.84 in.
Power: 1–6X, 2.5–10X, 3.5–18X
Obj. Dia.: 24mm–50mm
Main Dia.: 30mm, 34mm
Exit Pupil: 11.4–4mm, 11.4–4.4mm, 10–2.4mm
Field of View: 105.8–17.7 ft @ 100 yds, 44–11 ft @100 yds, 30–6 ft @100 yds
Twilight Factor: N/A
Eye Relief: 3.15–4 in., 3.43–3.94 in., 3.39–3.94 in.

Features: Allows for fast target engagement at low power; at higher power provides the resolution and accuracy required to tackle longer shots; extremely clear XC High-Density glass; first focal plane optical design; oversized and precision-machined turrets; EZ Chek zero stop feature; side-mounted parallax adjustment
MSRP . . . . **$1399.00–$1799.00**

EOTECH VUDU SERIES

Kahles

KAHLES K16I 1–6X24MM

KAHLES K624I 6–24X56MM

KAHLES K1050 10–50X56MM

K16I 1–6X24MM

Weight: 16.9 oz.
Length: 10.9 in.
Power: 1–6X
Obj. Dia.: 24mm
Main Dia.: 30mm
Exit Pupil: 9.65–3.81mm
Field of View: 127–20.1 ft @ 100 yds
Twilight Factor: 4.9–12
Eye Relief: 3.74 in.
Features: Rear focal plane; illuminated; integrated magnification throw lever allows for instant magnification changes even in the most adverse environmental conditions
MSRP **$2221.00**

K624I 6–24X56MM

Weight: 33.5 oz.
Length: 15.9 in.
Power: 6–24X
Obj. Dia.: 56mm
Main Dia.: 34mm
Exit Pupil: 9.3–2.3mm
Field of View: 20–5.1 ft @ 100 yds
Twilight Factor: 18.33–36.66
Eye Relief: 3.54 in.
Features: Front focal plane; illuminated; adjustable parallax; specifically engineered for long range precision
MSRP **$3332.00**

K1050 10–50X56MM

Weight: 31.4 oz.
Length: 16.9 in.
Power: 10–50X
Obj. Dia.: 56mm
Main Dia.: 30mm
Exit Pupil: 15.1–5mm
Field of View: 9.5–2 ft @ 100 yds
Twilight Factor: 23.66–52.92
Eye Relief: 3.75 in.
Features: Rear focal plane; adjustable parallax; ultra-precise 1/8 MOA adjustments constructed of hardened steel
MSRP **$3110.00**

OPTICS

Konus

KONUS KONUSHOT
4X32MM

KONUS KONUSPRO 275 3–9X40MM

KONUS
KONUSPRO 550
3–9X40MM

KONUS KONUSPRO M-30 4.5–16X40MM

KONUSHOT SERIES
Weight: 12.6 oz., 11.2 oz., 13.7 oz.
Length: 12.2 in., 12.2 in., 13.3 in.
Power: 4X, 3–9X, 3–12X
Obj. Dia.: 32mm, 32mm, 40mm
Main Dia.: 1 in.
Exit Pupil: 8mm, 10.7–3.9mm, 13.3–3.3mm
Field of View: 25.5 ft @ 100 yds, 33.54–11.56 ft @ 100 yds, 27.4–6.9 ft @ 100 yds
Twilight Factor: 11.31, 9.8–16.97, 10.95–21.91
Eye Relief: 3.4 in., 3 in., 3 in.
Features: Shock-, water-, and fogproof; nitrogen filled
MSRP . . . . **$89.99–$119.99**

KONUSPRO 275 SERIES
Weight: 14.4 oz., 23.8 oz.
Length: 12.2 in., 12.9 in.
Power: 3–9X, 3–10X
Obj. Dia.: 40mm, 44mm
Main Dia.: 1 in.
Exit Pupil: 10–4.4mm, 14.7–4.4mm
Field of View: 35.1–10.8 ft @ 100 yds
Twilight Factor: 10.95–18.97, 11.49–20.98

Eye Relief: 3 in.
Features: Rear focal plane; shock-, water-, and fogproof; nitrogen filled; designed specifically for muzzle-loaders
MSRP . . . . **$179.99–$249.99**

KONUSPRO 550 SERIES
Weight: 14.1 oz., 14.4 oz., 22.9 oz.
Length: 12.4 in., 12.2 in., 15.5 in.
Power: 3–9X, 3–9X, 4–16X
Obj. Dia.: 40mm, 40mm, 50mm
Main Dia.: 1 in.
Exit Pupil: 10–4.4mm, 10–4.4mm, 10–3.1mm
Field of View: 36.9–12.3 ft @ 100 Yds, 36.9–12.3 ft @ 100 yds, 23.4–5.87 ft @ 100 Yds
Twilight Factor: 10.95–18.97, 10.95–18.97, 14.14–28.28
Eye Relief: 3 in.
Features: Rear focal plane; shock-, water-, and fogproof; nitrogen filled; illuminated reticle dots
MSRP . . . . **$179.99–$219.99**

KONUSPRO M-30 SERIES
Weight: 17.6 oz., 28.2 oz., 35.2 oz., 28.2 oz., 28.9 oz., 31.7 oz., 31.7 oz.

Length: 10.8 in., 14.1 in., 16.4 in., 15.2 in., 16.4 in., 17.6 in., 18.4 in.
Power: 1–4X, 2.5–10X, 3–12X, 4.5–16X, 6.5–25X, 8.5–32X, 10–40X
Obj. Dia.: 24mm, 52mm, 56mm, 40mm, 44mm, 52mm, 52mm
Main Dia.: 30mm
Exit Pupil: 12–6mm, 12.7–2.5mm, 12.7–4.7mm, 8.9–2.5mm, 6.8–1.8mm, 6.1–1.6mm, 5.2–1.4mm
Field of View: 100–25 ft @ 100 yds, 40–11 ft @ 100 yds, 32–8.5 ft @ 100 yds, 23–6.5 ft @ 100 yds, 17–4.5 ft @ 100 yds, 13–3.3 ft @ 100 yds, 11–2.8 ft @ 100 yds
Twilight Factor: 4.9–9.8, 11.4–22.8, 12.96–25.92, 13.42–25.3, 16.91–33.17, 21–40.79, 22.8–45.61
Eye Relief: 3.9 in., 3.5 in., 3.9 in., 3.9–3.4 in., 3.9–3.4 in., 3.9–3.4 in., 3.4 in.
Features: Rear focal plane; shock-, water-, and fogproof; nitrogen filled; illuminated reticle; level bubble; adjustable parallax
MSRP . . . . **$379.99–$719.99**

OPTICSOPTICS

Konus

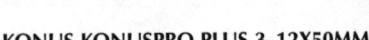

KONUS KONUSPRO PLUS 3–12X50MM

KONUS KONUSPRO RIFLESCOPES 3–10X44MM

KONUSPRO PLUS SERIES

Weight: 23.2 oz., 24.3 oz., 25.7 oz.
Length: 12.2 in., 13.8 in., 16.06 in.
Power: 1.5–6X, 3–12X, 6–24X
Obj. Dia.: 44mm, 50mm, 50mm
Main Dia.: 30mm, 1 in., 1 in.
Exit Pupil: 18–7.3mm, 16.6–42mm, 8.3–2.1mm
Field of View: 64–15.7 ft @ 100 yds, 31.4–8.1 ft @ 100 yds, 16.2–4.45 ft @ 100 yds
Twilight Factor: 8.12–16.25, 12.25–24.49, 17.32–34.64
Eye Relief: 3.9 in., 3 in., 3.4 in.
Features: Rear focal plane; shock-, water-, and fogproof; nitrogen filled; illuminated reticle
MSRP . . . . **$339.99–$349.99**

KONUSPRO RIFLESCOPES SERIES

Weight: 11.6 oz., 10.4 oz., 16 oz., 14.8 oz., 12 oz., 17 oz., 17.2 oz., 15.8 oz., 18 oz., 17.6 oz., 19 oz., 213 oz.
Length: 10.9 in., 9.4 in., 12 in., 11.8 in., 11.8 in., 12.4 in., 12.9 in., 12.5 in., 13.6 in., 12.9 in., 14 in., 15.5 in.
Power: 2.5X, 4X, 4X, 1.5–5X, 2–7X, 3–9X, 3–9X, 3–9X, 3–9X, 3–10X, 3–12X, 6–24X
Obj. Dia.: 32mm, 32mm, 32mm, 32mm, 32mm, 32mm, 40mm, 40mm, 50mm, 44mm, 50mm, 44mm
Main Dia.: 1 in.
Exit Pupil: 12.8mm, 8mm, 8mm, 21.3–6.4mm, 8–4mm, 10.6–3.5mm, 3.3–4.4mm, 3.3–4.4mm, 16.7–5.5mm, 14.7–4.4mm, 16.7–4.2mm, 7.4–2mm
Field of View: 37 ft @ 100 yds, 29 ft @ 100 yds, 29.2 ft @ 100 yds, 60–20 ft @ 100 yds, 43–12.6 ft @ 100 yds, 32.4–12.4 ft @ 100 yds, 38–12.5 ft @ 100 yds, 32.4–12.4 ft @ 100 yds, 38–12.5 ft @ 100 yds, 35–10.8 ft @ 100 yds, 31–7.8 ft @ 100 yds, 16.5–4.1 ft @ 100 yds
Twilight Factor: 8.94, 11.31, 11.31, 6.93–12.65, 8–14.97, 9.8–16.97, 10.95–18.97, 10.95–18.97, 12.25–21.21, 11.49–20.98, 12.25–24.5, 16.25–32.5
Eye Relief: 4.9 in., 4.5 in., 3.4 in., 2.9 in., 3 in., 2.9 in., 3 in., 3 in., 3 in., 3 in., 2.9 in., 2.9 in.
Features: Shock-, water-, and fogproof; nitrogen filled; 3–9x50mm available with a 30mm main tube
MSRP . . . . **$119.99–$269.99**

Leapers, Inc.

UTG T8 SERIES

Available in: 1–8x28mm (Circle Dot & QD rings, Mil-dot, or Mil-dot & QD rings), 2–16x44mm
Weight: 18 oz.–22.6 oz.
Length: 10.2 in.–12.4 in.
Power: 1–8X, 2–16X
Obj. Dia.: 28mm, 44mm
Main Dia.: 30mm
Exit Pupil: 26.5–3.4mm, 22–2.7mm
Field of View: 99.5–13 ft @ 100 yds, 44.5–6.3 ft @ 100 yds
Twilight Factor: N/A
Eye Relief: 3.35–5 in., 3.5–4.1 in.
Features: Completely sealed and nitrogen filled; shockproof, fogproof, and rainproof; multi emerald–coated lenses for maximum light and edge-to-edge clarity; innovative EZ-TAP Illumination Enhancing (IE) System

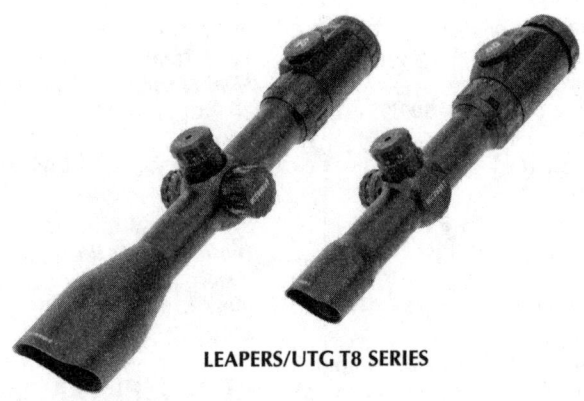

LEAPERS/UTG T8 SERIES

with red/green dual-color mode and 36 colors in multi-color mode to accommodate all weather/light conditions; one-click high-tech illumination memory feature
MSRP . . . . **$229.97–$299.97**

OPTICS

Leatherwood/Hi-Lux

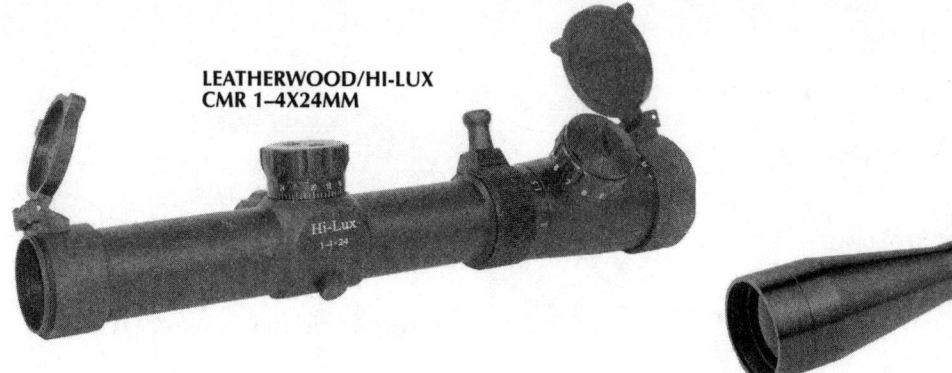

LEATHERWOOD/HI-LUX CMR 1–4X24MM

LEATHERWOOD/HI-LUX M40 TACTICAL HUNTER 3-9X40MM

LEATHERWOOD/HI-LUX M73G4 2.5X16MM

LEATHERWOOD/HI-LUX M-1000 ART 2.5–10X44MM

CLOSE MEDIUM RANGE (CMR) 1–4X24MM

Weight: 16.5 oz.
Length: 10.2 in.
Power: 1–4X
Obj.Dia.: 24mm
Main Dia.: 30mm
Exit Pupil: 11.1–6mm
Field of View: 94.8–26.2 ft @ 100 yds
Twilight Factor: 4.89–9.79
Eye Relief: 3 in.
Features: Zero-locking turrets; large external target-style windage and elevation adjustment knobs; power-ring extended lever handle for power change; CMR ranging reticle for determining range and also BDC hold over value good for .223, .308, and other calibers; red illuminated reticle; turrets adjustable in ½ MOA clicks
MSRP **$365.00**

M40 TACTICAL HUNTER 3-9X40MM

Weight: 16.2 in.
Length: 12.5 in.
Power: 3–9X
Obj. Dia.: 40mm

Main Dia.: 1 in.
Exit Pupil: 13.3–4.4mm
Field of View: 37.7–12.6 ft @ 100 yds
Twilight Factor: 10.95–18.97
Eye Relief: 3.25 in.
Features: Built with the same ranging system that Marine Corps snipers relied on in Vietnam, only improved; auto-range system and BDC reticle; fully multi-coated lenses; military flip-up lens covers
MSRP **$420.00**

M73G4 2.5X16MM

Weight: 11.8 in.
Length: 8.3 oz.
Power: 2.5X
Obj. Dia.: 16mm
Main Dia.: ¾ in.
Exit Pupil: 4mm
Field of View: 24.9 ft @ 100 yds
Twilight Factor: 6.33
Eye Relief: 3.54 in.
Features: Built to bring the vintage sniper rifle competition shooter a top quality scope that surpasses the quality of the WWII originals used on the M1903A4 sniper rifles; modern erec-

tor tube and quality multi-coated lenses for superior light transmission; offers a minimum total of 60 MOA with either windage or elevation when those adjustments are at center
MSRP **$359.00**

M1000 AUTO RANGING TRAJECTORY (ART) 2.5–10X44MM

Weight: 25.2 oz.
Length: 13.2 in.
Power: 2.5–10X
Obj.Dia.: 44mm
Main Dia.: 1 in.
Exit Pupil: 10.2–4mm
Field of View: 47.2–11.9 ft @ 100 yds
Twilight Factor: 10.5–21
Eye Relief: 3.1 in.
Features: Compensates for the bullet drop automatically by using an external cam system; can be calibrated for most centerfire rifle cartridges–from .223 to .50 BMG; comes with mount and rings; "No-Math Mil-Dot" reticle
MSRP **$459.00**

Leatherwood/Hi-Lux

LEATHERWOOD/HI–LUX OPTICS M1200 ART

LEATHERWOOD/HI-LUX MALCOLM 8X USMC SNIPER SCOPE

LEATHERWOOD/HI-LUX TOBY BRIDGES MUZZLELOADING

LEATHERWOOD/HI-LUX WM. MALCOLM SERIES LONG 6X32 INCH

M1200 ART
Weight: 29 oz.
Length: 15.5 in.
Power: 6–24X
Obj. Dia.: 50mm
Main Dia.: 30mm
Exit Pupil: 8.5–2mm
Field of View: 12–4 ft @ 100 yds
Twilight Factor: 17.32–34.64
Eye Relief: 3.25 in.
Features: Auto-ranging trajectory; multi-coated lenses; second focal plane; nitrogen gas filled; waterproof; ZRO-LOK system
MSRP $649.00

MALCOLM 8X USMC SNIPER SCOPE
Weight: 25.4 oz.
Length: 22.1 in.
Power: 8X
Obj. Dia.: 31mm
Main Dia.: .75 in.
Exit Pupil: 4.2mm
Field of View: 11 ft @ 100 yds
Twilight Factor: 15.75

Eye Relief: 3.15 in.
Features: Fully multi-coated lens; fine cross reticle; elevation and wind adjustment ¼ MOA per click at the mounts
MSRP $549.00

TOBY BRIDGES SERIES HIGH PERFORMANCE MUZZLELOADING 3–9X40MM MATTE BLACK
Weight: 15.8 oz.
Length: 12.5 in.
Power: 3–9X
Obj.Dia.: 40mm
Main Dia.: 1 in.
Exit Pupil: 13.3–4.4mm
Field of View: 39–13 ft @ 100 yds
Twilight Factor: 10.9–19
Eye Relief: 3.25 in.
Features: The TB/ML scope is designed for in-line ignition muzzleloaders and saboted bullets. It offers multiple reticles for shooting at ranges out to 250 yards.
MSRP $179.00

W. M. MALCOLM SERIES LONG 6X32 INCH
Weight: 32.5 oz.
Length: 30.5 in.
Power: 6X
Obj.Dia.: 16mm
Main Dia.: .75 in.
Exit Pupil: 5.8mm
Field of View: 10 ft @ 100 yds
Twilight Factor: 9.79
Eye Relief: 4 in.
Features: A modern copy of the Model 1855 W. Malcolm riflescopes; early-style mounts for scoping original and replica 19th century breechloading rifles (Sharps, rolling block, high wall, etc.) or late period long-range percussion muzzleloading bullet rifles; ¾-in. (steel) scope tube; interchangeable front extension tubes to mount on rifles with barrels of 30 to 34 inches; also in 3x17-in. and 6x18-in. short Malcolms
MSRP $461.00

Leupold & Stevens

LEUPOLD FX-3 COMPETITION HUNTER 6X42MM

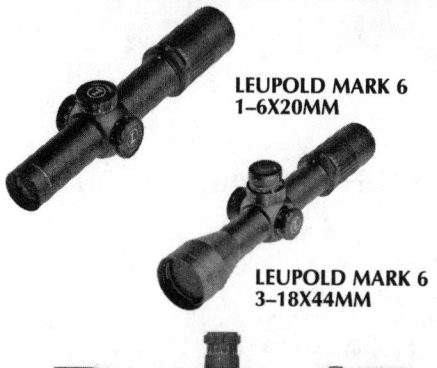

LEUPOLD MARK 6
1–6X20MM

LEUPOLD MARK 6
3–18X44MM

LEUPOLD MARK 4 MR/T 2.5–8X36MM M1

LEUPOLD RIFLEMAN 3–9X40MM

LEUPOLD VX-2 3–9X40MM

FX-3 COMPETITION HUNTER 6X42MM
Weight: 15 oz.
Length: 12.2 in.
Power: 6X
Obj.Dia.: 42mm
Main Dia.: 1 in.
Exit Pupil: 7mm
Field of View: 17.3 ft @ 100 yds
Twilight Factor: 15.87
Eye Relief: 4.4 in.
Features: Fixed-power riflescope; Xtended Twilight Lens System; DiamondCoat 2; blackened lens edges; windage and elevation adjustments are ¼ MOA
MSRP **$614.00**

MARK 4 MR/T 2.5–8X36MM M1
Weight: 16 oz.
Length: 11.33 in.
Power: 2.5–8X
Obj.Dia.: 36mm
Main Dia.: 30mm
Exit Pupil: 14.4–4.5mm
Field of View: 35.5–13.6 ft @ 100 yds
Twilight Factor: 9.48–16.97
Eye Relief: 3.7–3 in.
Features: Xtended Twilight Lens System and DiamondCoat 2; M1 dials are ¼ MOA for windage and elevation; finger-adjustable with audible, tactile clicks; illuminated Mil-Dot, Tactical Milling Reticle (TMR),and non-illuminated TMR versions available; flip-open lens covers; also available 1.5–5x20 and 2.5–8x36
MSRP . . . . **$844.00–$1559.00**

LEUPOLD VX-3I

MARK 6 1–6X20MM
Weight: 17 oz.
Length: 10.3 in.
Power: 1–6X
Obj. Dia.: 20mm
Main Dia.: 1.34 in.
Exit Pupil: 10.2–3.3mm
Field of View: 103.2–17.4 ft @ 100 yds
Twilight Factor: 4.5–11
Eye Relief: 3.7 in.
Features: Xtended Twilight Lens System with Diamond Coat 2; illuminated front focal plane reticles; zerolock adjustments with available BDC; matte finish
MSRP **$2859.00**

MARK 6 3–18X44MM
Weight: 23.6 oz.
Length: 11.9 in.
Power: 3–18X
Obj. Dia.: 44mm
Main Dia.: 1.34 in.
Exit Pupil: 10.3–2.4mm
Field of View: 36.8–6.3 ft @ 100 yds
Twilight Factor: 11.5–28.1
Eye Relief: 3.8–3.9 in.
Features: Xtended Twilight Lens System with Diamond Coat 2; M5B2 Autolocking Pinch & Turn; Elevation Zero Stop with Revolution Indicator; factory or custom quick change BDC rings available; waterproof; matte finish
MSRP . . . . **$2859.00–$5719.00**

RIFLEMAN 3–9X40MM
Weight: 12.6 oz.
Length: 12.33 in.
Power: 3–9X
Obj.Dia.: 40mm
Main Dia.: 1 in.
Exit Pupil: 12–4.7mm
Field of View: 329–131 ft @ 1000 yds
Twilight Factor: 10.95–18.97
Eye Relief: 4.2–3.7 in.
Features: Fully coated lenses for excellent low light brightness; durable waterproof construction; also in 2–7x33, 4–12x40, and 3–9x50
MSRP . . . . **$249.00–$389.00**

VX-2 3–9X40MM
Weight: 12 oz.
Length: 12.4 in.
Power: 3–9X
Obj.Dia.: 40mm
Main Dia.: 1 in.
Exit Pupil: 12–4.6mm
Field of View: 323–140 ft @ 1000 yds
Twilight Factor: 10.95–18.97
Eye Relief: 4.7–3.7 in.
Features: Multi-coated 4 Lens System for 92 percent light transmission; coin click ¼ MOA windage and elevation dials; also in 1-4x20, 1.5-4x28 IER Scout, 2-7x33, 3-9x50, 4-12x40, 4-12x50, 6-18x40
MSRP . . . . **$389.00–$649.00**

VX-3I
Available in: 1.5-5x20mm, 1.75-6x32mm, 2.5-8x36mm, 3.5-10x50mm, 3.5-10x56mm, 3.5-10x40mm, 4.5-14x50mm, 4.5-14x40mm, 4.5-14x56mm, 6.5-20x40mm, 6.5-20x50mm, 8.5-25x50mm
Weight: 9.3 oz–20.4 oz.
Length: 9.5 in.–14.4 in.
Power: 1.5–5X, 2.5–8X, 3.5–10x, 4.5–15X, 6.5–20X
Obj. Dia.: 1 in.–2.3 in.
Main Dia.: 1 in.–1.18 in.
Exit Pupil: N/A
Field of View: Varies with model
Twilight Factor: N/A
Eye Relief: Varies with model
Features: Twilight Max Light Management System provides maximum brightness in all colors and intensified contrast across the entire field of view; Dual Spring Precision Adjustments perform with match grade precision; easy turn power selector can be quickly turned, even with gloves on, while watertight seals ensure fog-free performance for a lifetime; 4.5-14x50mm and 4.5-14x40mm models available with 30mm tubes, side focus and side focus Custom Dial System options; 6.5-20x40mm available with side focus
MSRP . . . . **$519.99–$1299.99**

Leupold & Stevens

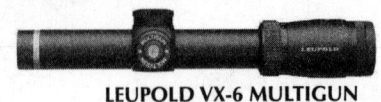

LEUPOLD VX-6

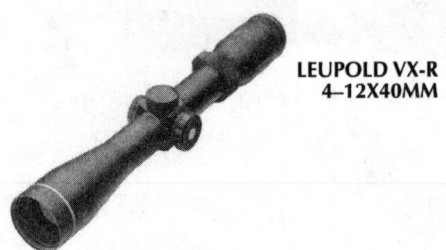

LEUPOLD VX-R
4–12X40MM

LEUPOLD VX-6 MULTIGUN

VX-6
Available in: 2–12x42mm, 3–18x44mm, 3–18x50mm
Weight: 17.8 oz.–20.7 oz.
Length: 13 in.–13.5 in.
Power: 2–12X, 3–18X
Obj. Dia.: 2 in.–2.3 in.
Main Dia.: 1.18 in.
Exit Pupil: N/A
Field of View: 57–10 ft @ 100 yds, 38–7 ft @ 100 yds
Twilight Factor: N/A
Eye Relief: 3.8 in., 3.7–3.8 in.
Features: Quantum optical system; Xtended Twilight lens system; DiamondCoat 2; second generation argon/krypton waterproofing; lead free; 6:1 zoom ratio
MSRP . . . .$1559.99–$1949.99

VX-6 MULTIGUN
Available in: 1–6x24mm
Weight: 14.6 oz.
Length: 12.3 in.
Power: 1–6X24
Obj. Dia.: 1.8 in.
Main Dia.: 1 in.
Exit Pupil: N/A
Field of View: 116–19 ft @ 100 yds
Twilight Factor: N/A
Eye Relief: 3.8 in.
Features: Quantum optical system; Xtended Twilight lens system; DiamondCoat 2; second generation argon/krypton waterproofing; lead free; 6:1 zoom ratio; blackened lens edges; custom dial system; motion sensor technology
MSRP . . . . $1429.99–$1559.99

VX-R 4–12X40MM
Weight: 15.1 oz.
Length: 12.4 in.
Power: 4–12X
Obj.Dia.: 40mm
Main Dia.: 30mm
Exit Pupil: 8.6–3.3mm
Field of View: 21.5–10 ft @ 100 yds
Twilight Factor: 14.2–23.1
Eye Relief: 3.7 in.
Features: Fire Dot reticle system with fiber optic technology; DiamondCoat lens coatings; finger click adjustments; index matched lens system; proprietary Motion Sensor Technology; also available in 1.25-4x20, 1.5-5x33, 2-7x33, 3-9x40, 3-9x50, 4-12x50
MSRP . . . . $649.00–$974.00

Lucid Optics, LLC

LUCID L5 6-24X50 RIFLE SCOPE

LUCID L5 4-16X44MM RIFLE SCOPE

LUCID L7 1–6X24MM

L5 6-24X50 RIFLE SCOPE
Weight: 24.5 oz.
Length: 15.5 in.
Power: 6–24X
Obj. Dia.: 50mm
Main Dia.: 30mm
Exit Pupil: 8.3–2mm
Field of View: 16.5–4.3 ft @ 100 yds
Twilight Factor: 17.32–34.64
Eye Relief: 4.25–3.25 in.
Features: Sniper-style rifle scope with the new L5 reticle; multi-coated lenses; 1/8 MOA turret click value; water-, fog-, and shockproof; matte black finish; available in STRELOK
MSRP $449.00

L5 4-16X44MM RIFLE SCOPE
Weight: 18 oz.
Length: 13.25 in.
Power: 4–16X
Obj. Dia.: 44mm
Main Dia.: 34mm
Exit Pupil: 11–3mm
Field of View: 25.5–8.5 ft @ 100 yds
Twilight Factor: 13.27–8

Eye Relief: 4.25 in.–3.25 in.
Features: Shock-, water-, and fogproof; adjustable parallax; etched-glass reticle
MSRP $419.00

L7 1–6X24MM
Available in: 1–6x24mm
Weight: 20.40 oz.
Length: 10.75 in.
Power: 1–6X
Obj. Dia.: 34mm
Main Dia.: 30mm
Exit Pupil: 15–4mm
Field of View: 56–20 ft @ 100 yds
Twilight Factor: N/A
Eye Relief: 3.75–4 in.
Features: Edge-to-edge sharp, crisp image resolution through the entire magnification range; Lucid blue reticle illumination; windage and elevation turrets offer 60MOA either side of optical center; selectable magnification lever for fast changes to the zoom function
MSRP $449.00

OPTICS

Meopta USA

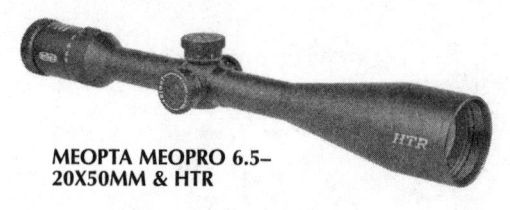

MEOPTA MEOPRO 6.5–20X50MM & HTR

MEOPTA MEOSTAR R1 RD 1.5–6X42MM

MEOPTA MEOSTAR R2 1–6X24MM

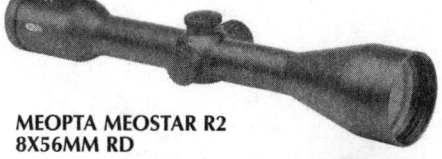

MEOPTA MEOSTAR R2 8X56MM RD

MEOPTA ZD 6–24X56MM RD

MEOPRO 6.5–20X50MM HTR
Available in: 6.5–20x50mm
Weight: 21.83 oz.
Length: 15.59 in.
Power: 6.5–20X
Obj. Dia.: 50mm
Main Dia.: 1 in.
Exit Pupil: 7.7–2.5mm
Field of View: 17.7–5.7 ft @ 100 yds
Twilight Factor: 18–31.9
Eye Relief: 3.5mm
Features: MeoBright ion-assisted lens multi-coating; fast-focus eyepiece; third turret mounted parallax control; erector system developed to provide maximum holding force to withstand heavy caliber recoil and eliminate backlash; MeoTrak TRZ elevation and windage turrets; waterproof, fogproof, and shockproof
MSRP . . . . $1149.99–$1264.99

MEOSTAR R1 SERIES
Weight: 18.87 oz., 20.6 oz., 15.87 oz., 21.87 oz., 18.27 oz., 24.16 oz.
Length: 12.09 in., 13.54 in., 13.03 in., 14.37 in., 12.91 in., 15.16 in..
Power: 1–4X, 1.5–6X, 3–10X, 3–12X, 4–12X, 4–16X
Obj. Dia.: 22mm, 42mm, 50mm, 56mm, 40mm, 44mm
Main Dia.: 30mm
Exit Pupil: 13.5–5.5mm, 14.8–7mm, 16.7–5mm, 14.8–4.6mm, 10–3.3mm, 11–2.8mm
Field of View: 117.78–28.22 ft @ 100 yds, 73.49–22.31 ft @ 100 yds, 43.64–13.12 ft @ 100 yds, 36–11.15 ft @ 100 yds, 33.14–11.15 ft @ 100 yds, 16–4.46 ft @ 100 yds
Twilight Factor: 4.69–9.38, 7.94–15.88, 12.25–22.36, 12.96–25.92, 12.65–21.91, 13.27–26.53
Eye Relief: 3.31–3.47 in., 3.23–3.74 in., 3.15–3.23 in., 3.03–3.27 in., 3.58–3.15 in., 3.94–3.15 in.
Features: Water- and fogproof; illuminated reticle; adjustable parallax; optional illuminated reticle also available
MSRP . . . . $1379.99–$1552.49

MEOSTAR R2 SERIES
Weight: 17.64 oz., 20.32 oz., 21.02 oz., 22.93 oz.
Length: 11.69 in. 3.31–3.47 in., 3.23–3.74 in., 3.15–3.23 in., 3.03–3.27 in., 3.58–3.15 in., 3.94–3.15 in.
Power: 1–6X, 2–8X
Obj. Dia.: 24mm, 56mm
Main Dia.: 30mm
Exit Pupil: 11–4mm, 11.1–4.2mm, 11.2–4.3mm, 11–3.73mm
Field of View: 121.72–20.34 ft @ 100 yds, 71.85–12.14 ft @ 100 yds, 61–10.17 ft @ 100 yds, 48.56–8.2 ft @ 100 yds
Twilight Factor: 4.9–12, 8.45–20.49, 10–24.5, 11.83–28.98
Eye Relief: 3.54 in., 3.54 in., 3.86–3.7 in., 3.86–3.74 in., 3.54 in.
Features: Water- and fogproof; illuminated reticle also available
MSRP . . . . $1494.99–$1954.99

MEOSTAR R2 8X56MM RD
Available in: 8x56mm
Weight: 20.7 oz.
Length: 13.9 in.
Power: 8X
Obj. Dia.: 56mm
Main Dia.: 30mm
Exit Pupil: 7mm
Field of View: 13.5 ft @ 100 yds
Twilight Factor: 21.2
Eye Relief: 9.9mm
Features: MeoLux ion-assisted multi-coating; MeoDrop hydrophobic lens coating repels water, grease, skin oils, and lens surface contaminaters; fast-focus eyepiece; MeoTrak II elevation and windage control; RedZone user selectable red-dot illumination system with 8 levels of reticle intensity; etched glass reticle; waterproof and fogproof
MSRP . . . . $1299.99–$1494.99

ZD 6–24X56MM RD
Available in: 6–24x56mm
Weight: 30.6 oz.
Length: 15.2 in.
Power: 6–24X
Obj. Dia.: 56mm
Main Dia.: 30mm
Exit Pupil: 9.1–2.3mm
Field of View: 18–5 ft @ 100 yds
Twilight Factor: 18.3–36.7
Eye Relief: 3.5–3mm
Features: RD illuminated reticle system; MeoBright ion-assisted lens multi-coating; MeoTrak II elevation and windage control; etched glass reticle; fast-focus eyepiece; waterproof, fogproof, and shockproof
MSRP $2184.99

OPTICS

Millett Tactical

MILLETT DMS 1–4X24MM

MILLETT DMS 1-6X24MM

MILLETT LRS 6–25X56MM ILLUMINATED .1 MIL

MILLETT TRS 4–16X50MM .1 MIL

LRS 6–25X56MM ILLUMINATED .1 MIL
Weight: 35 oz.
Length: 18 in.
Power: 6–25X
Obj.Dia.: 56mm
Main Dia.: 35mm
Exit Pupil: 9.33–2.24mm
Field of View: 45–17 ft @ 100 yds
Twilight Factor: 18.33–37.41
Eye Relief: 3 in.
Features: For extreme-duty and extended-range for calibers such as the .50 BMG and .338 Lapua; one-piece tube; precision controls with 140 MOA range of adjustment; several glass-etched Mil-DotBar reticle and click value configurations; available in a matte or A-TACS finish; also in 6–25x56 Mil-DotBar Reticle .25 or .1 Click Value, 6–25x56 Illuminated Mil-DotBar Reticle A-TACS or Matte Finish
MSRP $752.45

TRS 4–16X50MM .1 MIL
Weight: 29.5 oz.
Length: 16.4 in.
Power: 4–16X
Obj.Dia.: 50mm
Main Dia.: 30mm
Exit Pupil: 12.5–3.12mm
Field of View: 29–8 ft @ 100 yds
Twilight Factor: 14.14–28.28
Eye Relief: 3.5 in.
Features: Mil-DotBar reticle system functions as a standard Mil-Dot with the addition of a thin line for easier alignment for rangefinding and hold-over; illuminated reticle is green and adjustable; scope has side-focus parallax adjustment knob; also in fixed 10x50 model and several 4–16x50 models finished in either matte or A-TACS
MSRP $498.95

DMS 1–4X24MM
Weight: 18 oz.
Length: 11.8 in.
Power: 1–4X
Obj.Dia.: 24mm
Main Dia.: 30mm
Exit Pupil: 24–6mm
Field of View: 90–23 ft @ 100 yds
Twilight Factor: 4.89–9.79
Eye Relief: 3.5 in.
Features: Designated Marksman Riflescope (DMS) features a Donut Dot illuminated reticle; "donut" subtending 18 MOA for ranges as close as three meters; illuminated dot 1 MOA for medium to extended ranges out to 500 yards; available in matte or ATAC finish; 1–6x24 available

Matte: $356.45
ATAC: $397.45

DMS 1-6X24MM
Weight: 20.7 oz.
Length: 10.5 in.
Power: 1–6X
Obj. Dia.: 24mm
Main Dia.: 30mm
Exit Pupil: 46.99–11.75mm
Field of View: 90–23 ft @ 100 yds
Twilight Factor: 4.9–12
Eye Relief: 3.5 in.
Features: Fully multi-coated; illuminated reticle; matte black finish
MSRP $479.95

OPTICS

MINOX ZE 5I 1–5X24MM

MINOX ZE 5I 2–10X50MM

MINOX ZE 5I 5–25X56MM

MINOX ZE 5I 3–15X56MM

MINOX ZV 3 SERIES 3–9X40MM

MINOX ZP TAC SERIES 1–8X24MM

MINOX ZX5/ZX5I SERIES

ZE 5I 1–5X24MM

Weight: 16.9 oz.
Length: 11.2 in.
Power: 1–5X
Obj. Dia.: 24mm
Main Dia.: 30mm
Exit Pupil: 11.4–4.8mm
Field of View: 110.6–23.1 ft @ 100 yds
Twilight Factor: 4.9–11
Eye Relief: 3.94 in.
Features: Illuminated central red-dot with eleven brightness settings; automatic shut down to conserve battery; German A4, BDC, and Dot reticles available; finished with Minox's M* coating; waterproof; shockproof; Z-rail mount
MSRP. **$1649.00**

ZE 5I 2–10X50MM

Weight: 22.9 oz.
Length: 13.2 in.
Power: 2–10X
Obj. Dia.: 50mm
Main Dia.: 30mm
Exit Pupil: 11.4–5.1mm
Field of View: 55.2–11.5 ft @ 100 yds
Twilight Factor: 10–22.4
Eye Relief: 3.94 in.
Features: Illuminated central red-dot with eleven brightness settings; automatic shut down to conserve battery; German A4, BDC, and Dot reticles available; finished with Minox's M* coating; waterproof; shockproof; Z-rail mount
MSRP. **$1849.00**

ZE 5I 3–15X56MM

Weight: 26.1 oz.
Length: 14.6 in.
Power: 3–15X
Obj. Dia.: 56mm
Main Dia.: 30mm
Exit Pupil: 11.4–3.8mm
Field of View: 36.3–7.6 ft @ 100 yds
Twilight Factor: 13–29
Eye Relief: 3.94 in.
Features: Illuminated central red-dot with eleven brightness settings; automatic shut down to conserve battery; German A4, BDC, and Dot reticles available; finished with Minox's M* coating; Z-rail mount
MSRP. **$1949.00**

ZE 5I 5–25X56MM

Weight: 27.9 oz.
Length: 16.9 in.
Power: 5–25X
Obj. Dia.: 56mm
Main Dia.: 30mm
Exit Pupil: 10.9–2.5mm
Field of View: 21.6–4.5 ft @ 100 yds
Twilight Factor: 16.7–37.4
Eye Relief: 3.94 in.
Features: Illuminated central red-dot with eleven brightness settings; automatic shut down to conserve battery; German A4, BDC, and Dot reticles available; finished with Minox's M* coating; Z-rail mount
MSRP. **$2049.00**

ZP TAC SERIES 1–8X24MM

Weight: 24.5 oz.
Length: 11.6 in.
Power: 1–8X
Obj. Dia.: 24mm
Main Dia.: 34mm
Exit Pupil: 10.3–3mm
Field of View: 112.5–14.4 ft @ 100 yds
Twilight Factor: 4.9–13.86
Eye Relief: 3.5 in.
Features: Front focal plane; illuminated reticle; 3–15x50 and 5–25x56 also available
MSRP. . . . . **Starting at $2899.00**

ZV 3 SERIES 3–9X40MM

Weight: 13.6 oz.
Length: 12.2 in.
Power: 3–9X
Obj. Dia.: 40mm
Main Dia.: 1 in.
Exit Pupil: 13.3–4.4mm
Field of View: 35.4–11.5 ft @ 100 yds
Twilight Factor: 10.95–18.97
Eye Relief: 3.8 in.
Features: Fully multi-coated lenses; lightweight aluminum body; nitrogen filled and waterproof; available with a Plex or BDC reticle; 3–9x50 and 4.5–14x44 also available
MSRP. . . . . **$269.00–$349.00**

ZX5/ZX5I SERIES

Available in: 1–5x24mm, 2–10x45mm, 2–10x50mm, 3–15x50mm, 3–15x56mm, 5–25x50mm, 5–25x56mm
Weight: 16.2 oz.–28.2 oz.
Length: 11.2 in.–16.9 in.
Power: 1–5X, 2–10X, 3–15X, 5–25X
Obj. Dia.: 24mm–56mm
Main Dia.: 30mm
Exit Pupil: 11.4–4.8mm, 11.4–4.5mm, 11.4–5mm, 11.4–3.3mm, 11.3–3.7mm, 10–2mm, 11.2–2.2mm
Field of View: 121.7–26.9 ft @ 100 yds, 62–13.1 ft @ 100 yds, 62–13.1 ft @ 100 yds, 39–8.5 ft @ 100 yds, 39–8.5 ft @ 100 yds, 23.6–5.2 ft @ 100 yds, 23.6–5.2 ft @ 100 yds
Twilight Factor: N/A
Eye Relief: 100mm
Features: Available with or without illuminated reticle; large field of view enables quick aiming and a reliable target acquisition; inner components protected by an exceptionally shock-resistant body made of special anodized aluminium; purged with nitrogen gas
MSRP. . . . . **$579.99–$849.99**

OPTICS

Nightforce Optics, Inc.

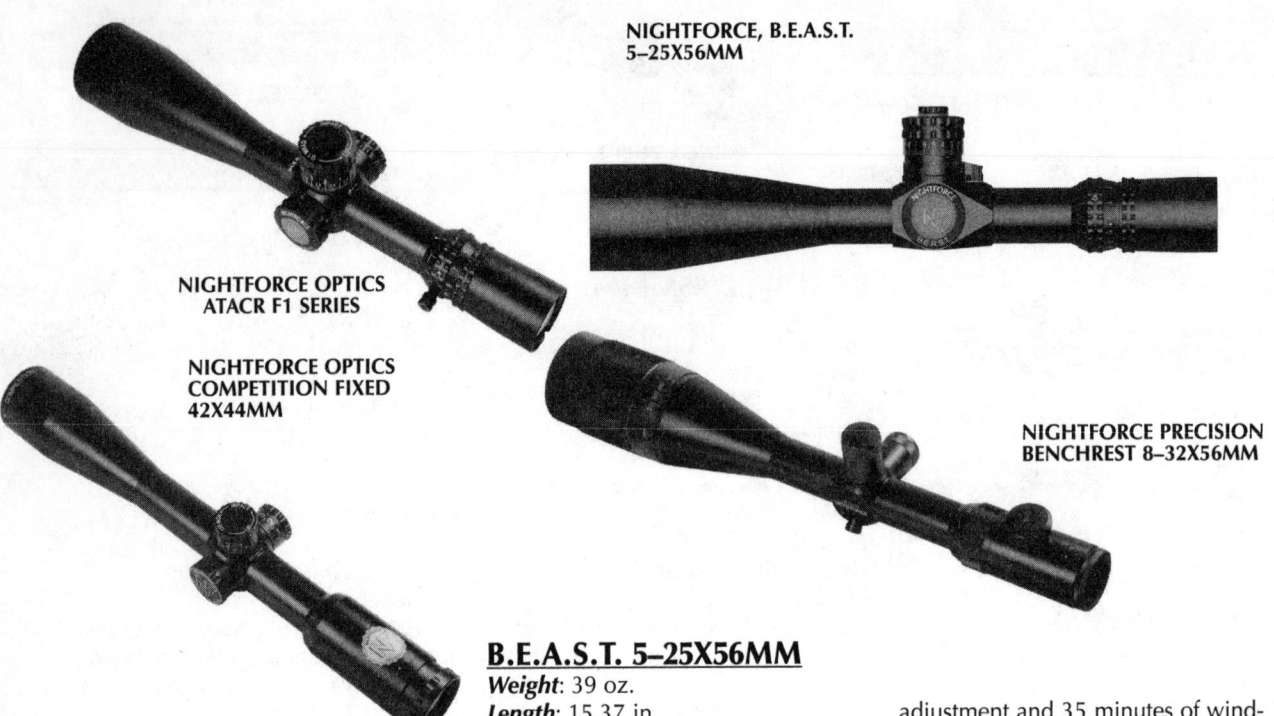

NIGHTFORCE, B.E.A.S.T.
5–25X56MM

NIGHTFORCE OPTICS
ATACR F1 SERIES

NIGHTFORCE OPTICS
COMPETITION FIXED
42X44MM

NIGHTFORCE PRECISION
BENCHREST 8–32X56MM

ATACR F1 SERIES

Weight: 30 oz., 38 oz.
Length: 12.6 in., 15.37 in.
Power: 4–16X, 5–25X, 7-35X
Obj. Dia.: 42mm, 56mm
Main Dia.: 34mm
Exit Pupil: 10.3–2.7mm, 8.3–2.3mm, 6–1.6mm
Field of View: 26.9–6.9 ft @ 100 yds, 18.7–4.92 ft @ 100 yds, 14.97–3.44 ft @ 100 yards
Twilight Factor: 12.96–25.92, 16.73–10.58
Eye Relief: 3.35–3.54 in., 3.26–3.58 in.
Features: Front focal plane; multicoated lenses; eyepiece features enhanced engraving, an integrated Power Throw Lever (PTL) and an XtremeSpeed thread for making a fast diopter adjustment; adjustments are standard with the patented Nightforce Hi-Speed ZeroStop, and available in .1 Mrad (12 Mils per revolution) or .25 MOA (30 MOA per revolution) increments; 4-16X and 5-25X come equipped with non-illuminated H59 or TReMoR3 reticles, or Digillum illuminated MOAR or MIL-R reticles.7-35X has illuminated MOAR reticle
4-16X:. . . . . **$2500.00–$2900.00**
5-25X:. . . . . **$3100.00–$3500.00**
7-35X:. . . . . **$3600.00–$4000.00**

B.E.A.S.T. 5–25X56MM

Weight: 39 oz.
Length: 15.37 in.
Power: 5–25X
Obj. Dia.: 56mm
Main Dia.: 34mm
Exit Pupil: 8.3–2.3mm
Field of View: 18.7–4.92 ft @ 100 yds
Twilight Factor: 16.7–37.4
Eye Relief: 3.35–3.54 in.
Features: First focal plane precision; 90 percent + light transmission; i4F intelligent four-function elevation control, ZeroStop system; XtremeSpeed adjustments; available with non-illuminated H59 or TReMoR3 reticles, or Digillum illuminated MOAR or MIL-R reticles
From:. . . . . **$4100.00–$4500.00**

COMPETITION FIXED 42X44MM

Weight: 20.7 oz.
Length: 15.2 in.
Power: 42X
Obj. Dia.: 44mm
Main Dia.: 30mm
Exit Pupil: 1.05mm
Field of View: 2.87 ft @ 100 yds
Twilight Factor: N/A
Eye Relief: 88mm
Features: 1/8 MOA per click, 10 MOA per revolution; premium ED glass; enhanced high-contrast engraving is easier to see with larger numbers than most other riflescopes in its class; 45 minutes of angle of elevation adjustment and 35 minutes of windage adjustment available
MSRP. **$1290.00**

PRECISION BENCHREST 8–32X56MM, 12-42X56MM

Weight: 36 oz.
Length: 16.6 in.
Power: 8–32X, 12-42X
Obj.Dia.: 56mm
Main Dia.: 30mm
Exit Pupil: 5.6–1.7mm, 4–1.4mm
Field of View: 9.4–3.1 ft @ 100 yds, 6.7–2.3 ft. @ 100 yds
Twilight Factor: 21.16–42.33
Eye Relief: 2.9 in.
Features: Superior resolution; adjustable objective allows extra-fine focus for parallax adjustment from 25 yards to infinity; target adjustments are calibrated in true $1/8$ click) MOA values, and can be re-indexed to zero after sighting in; eyepiece allows for fast reticle focusing; both models have second plane reticles in a choice of NP-R2 or NP-2DD configurations with analog illumination
8-32X:. **$1326.00**
12-42X:. **$1473.00**

Nightforce Optics, Inc.

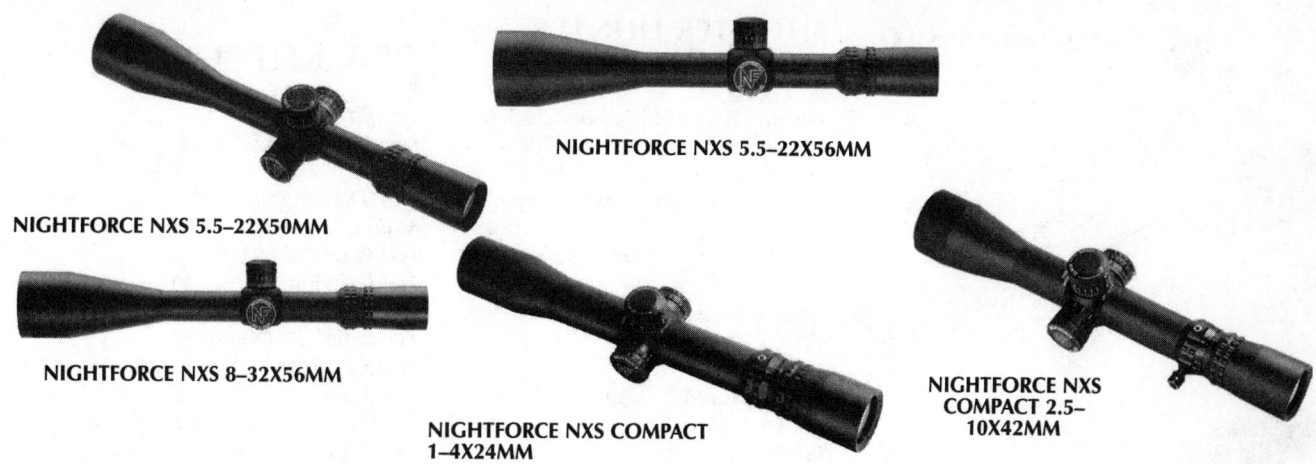

NIGHTFORCE NXS 5.5–22X50MM

NIGHTFORCE NXS 5.5–22X56MM

NIGHTFORCE NXS 8–32X56MM

NIGHTFORCE NXS COMPACT 1–4X24MM

NIGHTFORCE NXS COMPACT 2.5–10X42MM

NXS 5.5–22X50MM
Weight: 31 oz.
Length: 15.1 in.
Power: 5.5–22X
Obj.Dia.: 50mm
Main Dia.: 30mm
Exit Pupil: 9.1–2.3mm
Field of View: 17.5–4.7 ft @ 100 yds
Twilight Factor: 16.58–33.16
Eye Relief: 3.8 in.
Features: Originally developed for the U.S. military's extreme long range shooting and hard target interdiction; 100 MOA of elevation travel make it ideal for use on the .50 BMG, allowing accurate shots to 2000 yards and beyond; slim profile, easily adaptable to a wide range of mounting systems
MSRP $1821.00
ZeroStop: . . . . . $2020.00–$2107.00

NXS 5.5–22X56MM
Weight: 32 oz.
Length: 15.2 in.
Power: 5.5–22X
Obj.Dia.: 56mm
Main Dia.: 30mm
Exit Pupil: 10.2–2.5mm
Field of View: 17.5–4.7 ft @ 100 yds
Twilight Factor: 17.54–35.09
Eye Relief: 3.9 in.
Features: Advanced field tactical riflescope for long-range applications; maximum clarity and resolution across the entire magnification range, exceptional low-light performance; available with ZeroStop technology and ⅛ and ¼ MOA or .1 Mil-Radian adjustments; available with MOAR, MOAR-T, MIL-R, or MIL-DOT reticles, as well as HV.5, HVM, HVM.5, UHV, and UHV.5, all with analog illumina-

tion; all reticles are second focal plane
MSRP $2090.00

NXS 8–32X56MM
Weight: 34 oz.
Length: 15.9 in.
Power: 8–32X
Obj.Dia.: 56mm
Main Dia.: 30mm
Exit Pupil: 7–1.8mm
Field of View: 12.1–3.1 ft @ 100 yds
Twilight Factor: 21.16–42.33
Eye Relief: 3.8 in.
Features: For long-range hunting, competition, and target shooting; choice of five different reticles for the shooter's chosen application; offered with .125 MOA, .250 MOA or .1 Mil-Radian Hi-Speed adjustments; equipped with ZeroStop; second focal plane reticles available in MOAR, MOAR-T, NP-2DD, MIL-R, or MIL-DOT, all with analog illumination
MSRP $2190.00

NXS COMPACT 1–4X24MM
Weight: 17 oz.
Length: 8.8 in.
Power: 1–4X
Obj.Dia.: 24mm
Main Dia.: 30mm
Exit Pupil: 1–6mm
Field of View: 100–25 ft @ 100 yds
Twilight Factor: 4.89–9.79
Eye Relief: 3.5 in.
Features: Ideal for the hunter pursuing dangerous or running game at close quarters; low profile complements big bore bolt action and double rifles; as quick as open sights yet vastly more precise; shooter can keep both eyes open for instant target acquisition in

high-stress situations; second focal plane reticles available in FC-3G or IHR designs with external illumination adjustment; ZeroStop elevation is optional
MSRP $1370.00
ZeroStop: $1561.00

NXS COMPACT 2.5–10X42MM
Weight: 20.5 oz.
Length: 11.9 in.
Power: 2.5–10X
Obj. Dia.: 42mm
Main Dia.: 30mm
Exit Pupil: 15.5–4.4mm
Field of View: 44–11 ft @ 100 yds
Twilight Factor: 10.25–20.49
Eye Relief: 3.5 in.
Features: Optimal low-light performance in a small package, with side parallax adjustment, Power Throw Lever; second focal plane reticles available in a non-illumnated IHR design or in Digillum illuminated MOAR, IHR, MIL-DOT, LV, MV, HV, or MIL-R configurations; ZeroStop is optional
Without ZeroStop: $1950.00
With ZeroStop: $2000.00

OPTICS

Nightforce Optics, Inc.

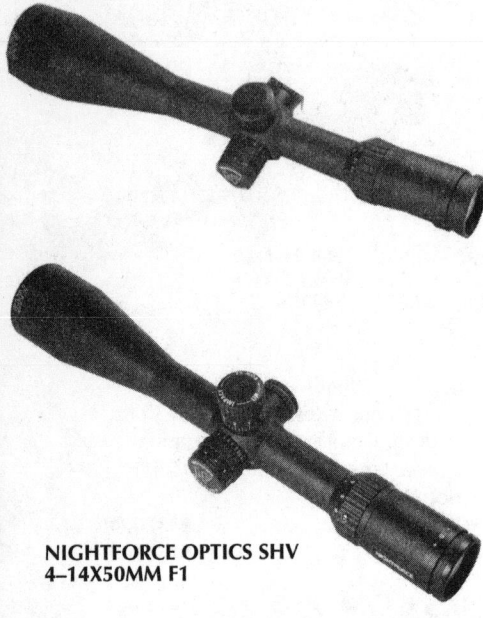

NIGHTFORCE SHOOTER HUNTER VARMINTER (SHV) 4–14X56MM

NIGHTFORCE OPTICS SHV 4–14X50MM F1

SHOOTER HUNTER VARMINTER (SHV) SERIES

Weight: 20.8 oz., 26.9 oz., 29.1 oz.
Length: 11.6 in., 14.8 in., 15.2 in.
Power: 3–10X, 4–14X, 5–20X
Obj. Dia.: 42mm, 56mm, 56mm
Main Dia.: 30mm
Exit Pupil: 10.7–4.4mm, 12–3.6mm, 8.7–2.5mm
Field of View: 34.9–11 ft @ 100 yds, 24.9–7.3 ft @ 100 yds, 17.9–5 ft @ 100 yds
Twilight Factor: 11.22–20.49, 14.97–28, 16.73–33.47
Eye Relief: 3.5 in., 3.15–3.54 in., 3.15–3.54 in.
Features: European-style fast-focus eyepiece, side parallax adjustment, capped .25-MOA adjustments, and multiple reticle choices, including illuminated options, at a consumer-friendly price point; 4-14x50mm is a first focal plane reticle, all others are second focal plane
3-10X: $900.00
4-14X56mm: . . . . . $950.00–$1128.00
5-20X: . . . . $1195.00–$1345.00
4-14X50mm: $1290.00

OPTICS SHV 4–14X50MM F1

Weight: 30 oz.
Length: 14.8 in.
Power: 4–14X
Obj. Dia.: 50mm
Main Dia.: 30mm
Exit Pupil: 10.8–3.3mm
Field of View: 25.1–7.4 ft @ 100 yds
Twilight Factor: N/A
Eye Relief: 70–80mm
Features: First focal plane option; maximum adjustment range of 90 minutes or 26 Mil-radians; Nightforce ZeroSet feature; exposed elevation adjustment allows quick access; capped windage prevents accidental adjustments during travel or in the field; Parallax is adjustable from 25 yds to infinity without any backlash or hesitation; twelve brightness settings on external lumination dial; fast-focus eyepiece design
MSRP . . . . $1795.00 W

Nikko Stirling

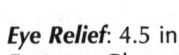

NIKKO STIRLING DIAMOND LONG RANGE

NIKKO STIRLING PANAMAX LONG RANGE SERIES

DIAMOND LONG RANGE

Available in: 4–16x50mm, 6–24x50mm, 10-40x56m
Weight: 16.5 oz.
Length: 14.2 in.
Power: 4–16X, 6–24X, 10-40X
Obj. Dia.: 50mm, 56mm
Main Dia.: 30mm
Exit Pupil: N/A
Field of View: 32.1–8 ft @ 100 yds, 21.4–5.4 ft @ 100 yds, 10.5–2.6 ft.@100 yds
Twilight Factor: N/A

Eye Relief: 4.5 in.
Features: Glass-etched HOLDFAST reticle; fully multi-coated lens; zero-stop turrets; dual-color red/green illumination settings
MSRP . . . . $390.00–$559.00

PANAMAX LONG RANGE SERIES

Weight: 23.6 oz., 24 oz.W
Length: 14.1 in., 14.5 in.
Power: 6–18X, 8–24X
Obj. Dia.: 50mm
Main Dia.: 1 in.
Exit Pupil: N/A
Field of View: 22–7.3 ft @ 100 yds, 16.5–5.5 ft @ 100 yds

Twilight Factor: 17.32–30, 20–34.64
Eye Relief: 3.1 in.
Features: ¼ MOA Increments (7mm @ 100m); centerfire, rimfire and airgun rated; AO models - adjustable objective from 10 yards up to infinity; IR models - illuminated reticle models features red/green illumination; half mil dot reticle; illuminated models features glass etched reticles; fast eye focus; shock- and waterproof; nitrogen filled; multicoated lenses
6-18X: $275.00
8-24X: $309.00

Nikko Stirling

NIKKO STIRLING
PANAMAX SERIES

NIKKO STIRLING
TARGEMASTER SERIES
10–50X60MM

NIKON INLINE XR
3–9X40MM BDC 300

NIKON M-308
4–16X42MM

NIKON MONARCH
3 1–4X20MM BDC

PANAMAX SERIES

Weight: 13.1 oz., 16.6 oz., 19.6 oz.
Length: 12 in., 12.1 in., 12.5 in.
Power: 3–9X, 3–9X, 4–12X
Obj. Dia.: 40mm, 50mm, 50mm
Main Dia.: 1 in.
Exit Pupil: N/A
Field of View: 44.1–14.7 ft @ 100 yds, 44.1–14.7 ft @ 100 yds, 32.9–10.9 ft @ 100 yds
Twilight Factor: 10.95–18.97, 12.25–21.21, 14.15–24.49
Eye Relief: 3.1 in.
Features: ¼ MOA Increments (7mm @ 100m); centerfire, rimfire and airgun rated; AO models available - adjustable objective from 10 yards up to infinity; half mil dot reticle; fast eye focus, illuminated reticle models available; shock- and waterpoof; nitrogen filled; multicoated lenses
MSRP . . . . **$140.00–$240.00**

TARGETMASTER SERIES

Weight: 18.3 oz., 20 oz., 23.6 oz., 25 oz., 27.2 oz., 30.3 oz.
Length: 11.6 in., 13.1 in., 14.6 in., 15.3 in., 16.7 in., 17.3 in.
Power: 1.25-5X, 2.5-10X, 4–16X, 5–20X, 6–24X, 10–50X
Obj. Dia.: 20mm, 42mm, 44mm, 50mm, 56mm, 60mm
Main Dia.: 30mm
Exit Pupil: N/A
Field of View: 26.4–6.6 ft @ 100 yds, 21.6–5.4 ft @ 100 yds, 20–80 ft. @ 100 yds, 15.6–3.9 ft @ 100 yds, 10–40 ft. @ 100 yds, 9.2–1.9 ft @ 100 yds
Twilight Factor: 13.27–26.53, 15.81–31.62, 18.33–36.66, 24.49–54.77
Eye Relief: 3.5 in.–3.9 in.
Features: Adjustable parallax; ETE Mirolux coated lenses; illuminated reticle
MSRP . . . . **$239.00–$530.00**

INLINE XR 3–9X40MM BDC 300

Weight: 13.8 oz.
Length: 11.3 in.
Power: 3–9X
Obj. Dia.: 40mm
Main Dia.: 1 in.
Exit Pupil: 4.4–13.3mm
Field of View: 8.4–25.2 ft @ 100 yds
Twilight Factor: 11–19
Eye Relief: 5 in.
Features: Long range muzzleloader; BDC 300 reticle; ¼ MOA adjustments; Spring-Loaded Zero-Reset Turrets; available in silver, matte black, or Realtree Xtra Green; waterproof; fogproof; shockproof
From: . . . . **$199.95–$219.95**

M-308 4–16X42MM

Weight: 19 oz.
Length: 13.5 in.
Power: 4–16X
Obj. Dia.: 42mm
Main Dia.: 1 in.
Exit Pupil: 10.5–2.6mm

Field of View: 25.2–6.3 ft @ 100 yds
Twilight Factor: 12.96–25.92
Eye Relief: 4–3.7 in.
Features: Available with the all-new BDC 800 reticle or Nikoplex reticle with Rapid Action Turrets; developed specifically for the trajectory of the .308 Win./7.62 NATO round with 168-grain hollow point boat-tail Match bullet; Ultra ClearCoat optical system; Eye Box technology; smooth zoom control
MSRP **$499.95**

MONARCH 3 1–4X20MM BDC

Weight: 12.2 oz.
Length: 10.35 in.
Power: 1–4X
Obj. Dia.: 20mm
Main Dia.: 1 in.
Exit Pupil: 5–20mm
Field of View: 23.1–92.9 ft @ 100 yds
Twilight Factor: 4.5–8.9
Eye Relief: 4 in.
Features: BDC reticle; designed for big game hunting; Spot On Ballistic Match technology; Spring Loaded Instant Zero-Reset Turrets; quick-focus eyepiece; enhanced mount ring spacing; waterproof; fogproof
MSRP **$279.95**

OPTICS

Nikon

**NIKON MONARCH 3
2.5–10X42MM NIKOPLEX**

**NIKON MONARCH 3
4–16X42MM SIDE FOCUS
MILDOT**

**NIKON MONARCH 3 BDC
DISTANCE LOCK**

NIKON MONARCH 7 SF IL MATTE

MONARCH 3 2.5–10X42MM NIKOPLEX
Weight: 16.6 oz.
Length: 12.6 in.
Power: 2.5–10X
Obj.Dia.: 42mm
Main Dia.: 1 in.
Exit Pupil: 16.8–4.2mm
Field of View: 40.3–10.1 ft @ 100 yds
Twilight Factor: 10.24–20.49
Eye Relief: 4.0–3.8 in.
Features: Enhanced ring spacing for mounting on rifles including magnum-length actions; see-through "ballistic circle" BDC reticle available; Ultra ClearCoat optical system; customized with accessory target-style windage and elevation adjustment knobs and caps; available in 2-8x32mm, 5-20x44mm (side] focus), 4-16x50mm (side focus), 6-24x50mm (side focus), 2.5-10x50mm, and 4-16x42mm (side focus), in matte and silver with ED glass, SF Mil-Dot, and fine crosshair with dot
MSRP . . . . **$299.95–$699.95**

MONARCH 3 4–16X42MM SIDE FOCUS MILDOT
Weight: 19 oz.
Length: 13.5 in.
Power: 4–16X
Obj. Dia.: 42mm

Main Dia.: 1 in.
Exit Pupil: 2.6–10.5mm
Field of View: 6.3–25.2 ft @ 100 yds
Twilight Factor: 13–25.9
Eye Relief: 4 in.
Features: Mildot reticle; Max Adj. 40 MOA; Spring Loaded Instant Zero-Reset Turrets; Spot On Ballistic Match technology; Monarch 3 Eyebox technology; matte finish
MSRP **$469.95**

MONARCH 3 BDC DISTANCE LOCK
Available in: 3–12x42mm, 4–16x42mm, 4–16x50mm
Weight: 18 oz.–19.4 oz.
Length: 13.1 in.–14.7 in.
Power: 3–12X, 4–16X
Obj. Dia.: 42mm, 50mm
Main Dia.: 25.4mm
Exit Pupil: 3.5 in., 2.6 in., 3.1 in.
Field of View: 31.8–8 ft @ 100 yds, 23.9–6 ft @ 100 yds
Twilight Factor: N/A
Eye Relief: 4–3.7 in.
Features: First focal plane optical system; fully multi-coated optical system; hand-turn reticle adjustments with spring-loaded instant zero-reset turrets; one-piece main body tube; spot-on ballistic match technology optimized; smooth zoom control with magnification reference numbers viewable from the shooter's position;

quick focus eyepiece; side focus parallax adjustment; waterproof/fogproof/shockproof
MSRP . . . . **$549.95–$629.95**

MONARCH 7 SF IL MATTE
Available in: 4–16x50mm
Weight: 25.8 oz.
Length: 14.8 in.
Power: 4–16X
Obj. Dia.: 50mm
Main Dia.: 30mm
Exit Pupil: 3.1 in.
Field of View: 29.6–7.4 ft @ 100 yds
Twilight Factor: N/A
Eye Relief: 3.7 in.
Features: Illuminated advanced BDC reticle with dot with an innovative wind-compensating feature that integrates windage marks to the left and right of the lower sighting post; remarkably wide field of view; large-diameter eyepiece with long eye relief throughout the magnification range ensures comfortable targeting; features a 30mm tube diameter and 4x zoom ratio; fully multicoated lenses; hand-turn windage and elevation adjustments with instant zero-reset function; side focus with locking system for parallax adjustment; quick-focus eyepiece for extremely simple adjustment; lightweight and durable one-piece main body
MSRP **$1099.95**

NIKON MONARCH 7 SF MATTE

NIKON PROSTAFF 3–9X40MM NIKOPLEX

NIKON PROSTAFF 5 2.5–10X50MM MATTE BDC

NIKON P-300 BLK 2–7X32MM BDC SUPERSUB

NIKON PROSTAFF 5 3.5–14X50MM ILLUMINATED NIKOPLEX

MONARCH 7 SF MATTE

Available in: 2.5–10x50mm, 3–12x56mm, 4–16x50mm
Weight: 22.9 oz.–23.8 oz.
Length: 13.7 in.–14.8 in.
Power: 2.5–10X, 3–12X, 4–16X
Obj. Dia.: 50mm, 56mm
Main Dia.: 30mm
Exit Pupil: 5 in., 4.7 in., 3.1 in.
Field of View: 47.4–11.8 ft @ 100 yds, 39.4–9.8 ft @ 100 yds, 29.6–7.4 ft @ 100 yds
Twilight Factor: N/A
Eye Relief: 3.8–3.6 in.
Features: Advanced BDC reticle with an innovative wind-compensating feature that integrates windage marks to the left and right of the lower sighting post; remarkably wide field of view; large-diameter eyepiece with long eye relief throughout the magnification range ensures comfortable targeting; fully multi-coated lenses enhance light transmission for bright, clear images with well-balanced color; hand-turn windage and elevation adjustments with instant zero-reset function; side focus with locking system for parallax adjustment; quick-focus eyepiece; lightweight and durable one-piece main body
MSRP . . . . $849.95–$999.95

P-300 BLK 2–7X32MM BDC SUPERSUB

Weight: 16.1 oz.
Length: 11.5 in.

Power: 2–7X
Obj. Dia.: 32mm
Main Dia.: 1 in.
Exit Pupil: 4.6–16mm
Field of View: 12.7–44.5 ft @ 100 yds
Twilight Factor: 8–15
Eye Relief: 3.8 in.
Features: BDC SuperSub reticle; optimized for use with supersonic and subsonic ammo; Max Adj. 80 MOA; waterproof; fogproof; matte black
MSRP $199.95

PROSTAFF 3–9X40MM NIKOPLEX

Weight: 15 oz.
Length: 12.4 in.
Power: 3–9X
Obj.Dia.: 40mm
Main Dia.: 1 in.
Exit Pupil: 13.3–4.4mm
Field of View: 33.8–11.3 ft @ 100 yds
Twilight Factor: 10.95–18.97
Eye Relief: 3.6–3.6 in.
Features: ¼ MOA hand-turn reticle adjustments with "Zero-Reset" turrets; quick-focus eyepiece; also in 2–7x32– and in Shotgun Hunter with BDC 200 reticle and 3–9x50 in silver, RealTree APG, and with BDC reticle
MSRP $179.95

PROSTAFF 5 2.5–10X50MM MATTE BDC

Weight: 18 oz.
Length: 13.7 in.
Power: 2.5–10X

Obj. Dia.: 50mm
Main Dia.: 1 in.
Exit Pupil: 5–20mm
Field of View: 9.9–40.4 ft @ 100 yds
Twilight Factor: 11.2–22.4
Eye Relief: 4 in.
Features: Hand-turn reticle adjustments with Spring-Loaded Zero-Reset turrets; BDC reticle; multi-coated optics; Max Adj. 70 MOA; waterproof; fogproof; parallax setting
MSRP $329.95

PROSTAFF 5 3.5–14X50MM ILLUMINATED NIKOPLEX

Weight: 19.9 oz.
Length: 14.3 in.
Power: 3.5–14X
Obj. Dia.: 50mm
Main Dia.: 1 in.
Exit Pupil: 2.9–14.3mm
Field of View: 7.2–28.6 ft @ 100 yds
Twilight Factor: 13.2–26.5
Eye Relief: 4 in.
Features: Illuminated reticle; hand-turn reticle adjustments with Spring-Loaded Zero-Reset turrets; waterproof; fogproof; parallax adjustment; matte finish
MSRP $579.95

Nikon

NIKON PROSTAFF 5 BDC DISTANCE LOCK

NIKON PROSTAFF TARGET EFR 3–9X40MM

PROSTAFF 5 BDC DISTANCE LOCK

Available in: 3.5–14x40mm, 4.5–18x40mm
Weight: 16.8 oz.–18.9 oz.
Length: 13.6 in.–14.3 in.
Power: 3.5–14X, 4.5–18X
Obj. Dia.: 40mm
Main Dia.: 25.4mm
Exit Pupil: 2.9 in., 2.2 in.
Field of View: 25.7–6.5 ft @ 100 yds, 20.1–5 ft @ 100 yds
Twilight Factor: N/A
Eye Relief: 4 in.
Features: First focal plane optical system; fully multi-coated optical system; hand-turn reticle adjustments with spring-loaded instant zero-reset turrets; one-piece main body tube; spot-on ballistic match technology optimized; generous, consistent eye relief; quick focus eyepiece; side focus parallax adjustment; waterproof/fogproof/shockproof
MSRP . . . . **$359.95–$459.95**

PROSTAFF TARGET EFR 3–9X40MM

Weight: 15.7 oz.
Length: 12.5 in.
Power: 3–9X
Obj. Dia.: 40mm
Main Dia.: 1 in.
Exit Pupil: 13.3–4.4mm
Field of View: 16.9–5.7 ft @ 50 yds
Twilight Factor: 10.95–18.97
Eye Relief: 3.6–3.6 in.
Features: Designed and engineered for .22 LR, air rifle, and other applications where the versatility of focusing at extended ranges is desired; new Nikon Precision Reticle featuring a fine crosshair with dot; adjustable objective lens that allows parallax adjustments; large ocular with quick focus eyepiece; zero-reset turrets
MSRP **$189.95**

Redfield

REDFIELD REVOLUTION/TAC 3–9X40MM

REDFIELD REVOLUTION 3–9X40MM

REVOLUTION SERIES

Weight: 11.1 oz., 12.6 oz., 14.5 oz., 13.1 oz.
Length: 11 in., 12.3 in., 12.4 in., 12.3 in.
Power: 2–7X, 3–9X, 4–12X
Obj. Dia.: 33mm, 40mm, 50mm
Main Dia.: 1 in.
Exit Pupil: N/A
Field of View: 43.2–17.3 ft @ 100 yds, 32.9–13.1 ft @ 100 yds, 33–13.1 ft @ 100 yds, 19.9–9.4 ft @ 100 yds
Twilight Factor: 8.12–15.2, 10.95–18.97, 12.25–21.21, 12.65–21.91
Eye Relief: 3.7–4.2 in., 3.7–4.2 in., 3.7–4.2 in., 3.7–4.9 in.
Features: Black matte finish and either a 4-Plex or Accu-Range reticle; Illuminator Lens System with premium lenses and vapor-deposition multi-coatings; Accu-Trac windage and elevation adjustment system has resettable stainless steel ¼ MOA finger click adjustments; "Rapid Target Acquisition" (RTA) lockable eyepiece
4-Plex: . . . .**$249.99–$314.99**
Accu-Range: . . . . .**$264.99–$324.99**

REVOLUTION/TAC 3–9X40MM

Weight: 12.6 oz.
Length: 12.3 in.
Power: 3–9X
Obj. Dia.: 40mm
Main Dia.: 1 in.
Exit Pupil: 12.1–4.7mm
Field of View: 32.9–13.1 ft @ 100 yds
Twilight Factor: 10.95–18.97
Eye Relief: 3.7 in.–4.2 in.
Features: Shock-, water-, and fogproof; nitrogen filled; vapor deposited, multi-coated illuminator lens system
MSRP **$349.99**

OPTICS

SCHMIDT & BENDER 1.1–4X20MM PM II SHORT DOT

1.1–4X20MM PM II SHORT DOT
Weight: 20.11 oz.
Length: 10.6 in.
Power: 1.1–4X
Obj.Dia.: 20mm
Main Dia.: 30mm
Exit Pupil: 14–5mm
Field of View: 96–30 ft @ 100 yds
Twilight Factor: 4.69–8.94
Eye Relief: 3.5 in.
Features: Includes locking turrets and CQB reticle; M855, 75 gr. TAP, and M118LR calibration rings standard; also in 1.5–6x20mm, 1-8x24mm (with dual CC or CC), and 1.5-8x26mm
MSRP **$2200.00**

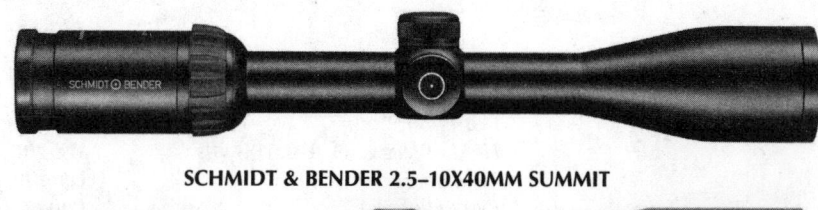

SCHMIDT & BENDER 2.5–10X40MM SUMMIT

SCHMIDT & BENDER 3–12X42MM KLASSIK

SCHMIDT & BENDER 3-12X50 ZENITH FLASH DOT

2.5–10X40MM SUMMIT
Weight: 16.8 oz.
Length: 13.2 in.
Power: 2.5–10X
Obj.Dia.: 40mm
Main Dia.: 1 in.
Exit Pupil: 16–4mm
Field of View: 40.4–12.3 ft @ 100 yds
Twilight Factor: 14–20
Eye Relief: 3.93 in.
Features: Built for the American market with its 1 inch tube; adjustments are ¼ MOA
MSRP **$2068.25**

3–12X42MM KLASSIK
Weight: 19.9 oz.
Length: 13.66 in.
Power: 3–12X
Obj.Dia.: 42mm

Main Dia.: 30mm
Exit Pupil: 3.5–14mm
Field of View: 31.5–11.4 ft @ 100 yds
Twilight Factor: 8.5–22.4
Eye Relief: 3.5 in.
Features: Enhanced model 3–12x42 Klassik designed for longer ranges; P3 reticle with bullet-drop compensated elevation knob; adjustments are in ⅓ MOA; third-turret parallax adjustment; also available in 2.5-10x56mm, 3-12x50mm, 4-16x50mm
MSRP **$2447.16**

3-12X50 ZENITH FLASH DOT
Weight: N/A
Length: N/A
Power: 3–12X
Obj. Dia.: 50mm
Main Dia.: 30mm

Exit Pupil: 42.2–14.1mm
Field of View: 3.5–13.5 ft @ 110 yds (1 meter)
Twilight Factor: N/A
Eye Relief: 3.5 in.
Features: Traditionally styled scope with enhanced luminous sensitivity, making this scope particularly suitable for use at dusk; fixed parallax, first focal plane reticles; flash dot reticles available in FD1, FD4, FD7, and FD9 designs. Also available with non-illuminated reticles A1, A4, A7, and A9
Flash Dot: . . . . . **$2688.25–$2808.09**
Non-illuminated reticle: . . **$1995.00**

Schmidt & Bender

SCHMIDT & BENDER 3–12X50MM KLASSIK ILLUMINATED

SCHMIDT & BENDER 6X42MM
KLASSIK FIXED

SCHMIDT & BENDER 12.5–
50X56MM FIELD TARGET II

SCHMIDT & BENDER PM II DIGITAL BT

SCHMIDT & BENDER PM II HIGH POWER

3–12X50MM KLASSIK ILLUMINATED

Weight: 21.66 oz.
Length: 13.75 in.
Power: 3–12X
Obj.Dia.: 50mm
Main Dia.: 30mm
Exit Pupil: 4.2–14.4mm
Field of View: 33.3–11.4 ft @ 100 yds
Twilight Factor: 8.5–24.5
Eye Relief: 3.14 in.
Features: All of the Klassik variables have generous objectives for greater light transmission; variety of reticles in illuminated, non-illuminated, and varmint; also in illuminated-reticle 2.5–10x56 and 3–12x42, and in non-illuminated 2.5–10x40, 3–12x42, and 4–16x50
Illuminated
   reticle: . . . . . . $2474.67–$2612.23
Non-illuminated
   reticle: . . . . . . $1924.44–$2132.83

6X42MM KLASSIK FIXED

Weight: 16.67 oz.
Length: 13.7 in.
Power: 6X
Obj.Dia.: 42mm
Main Dia.: 1 in.

Exit Pupil: 7mm
Field of View: 21 ft @ 100 yds
Twilight Factor: 15.8
Eye Relief: 3.14 in.
Features: Fixed 6-power magnification applicable to a wide range of hunting situation; windage and elevation adjustments are in $\frac{1}{3}$ MOA increments.; classic European 8x56 configuration offers maximum light transmission
MSRP. $1293.47

12.5–50X56MM FIELD TARGET II

Weight: 40.56 oz.
Length: 16.4 in.
Power: 12.5–50X
Obj.Dia.: 56mm
Main Dia.: 30mm
Exit Pupil: 4.55–1.18mm
Field of View: 10.5–2.7 ft @ 100 yds
Twilight Factor: 26.5–53
Eye Relief: 2.75 in.
Features: High-magnification scope has a shallow depth of field, so the parallax side-focus wheel can be used as a reference for gauging the distance to the target and adjusting the trajectory; extra-large focus wheel to range distances from 7–70m; illuminated reticle with brightness settings adjustable from 1 to 11
MSRP. . . . . $3700.00–$4085.00

PM II DIGITAL BT

Available in: 5–25x56mm
Weight: 44.5 oz.
Length: 16.7 in.
Power: 5–25X
Obj. Dia.: 56mm
Main Dia.: 34mm
Exit Pupil: 11–2.3mm
Field of View: 5.8–1.6 ft @ 100 yds
Twilight Factor: 16.7–37.4
Eye Relief: 90mm
Features: Information from compatible external devices—laser rangefinders, ballistics computers, etc.—can be projected into the shooter's field of view at the touch of a button
MSRP. . . . . $3740.73–$4142.55

PM II HIGH POWER

Available in: 5–45x56mm
Weight: 39.01 oz.
Length: 17.09 in.
Power: 5–45X
Obj. Dia.: 56mm
Main Dia.: 34mm
Exit Pupil: 8.9–1.8mm
Field of View: 23.4–2.58 ft @ 100 yds
Twilight Factor: 16.7–50.2
Eye Relief: 90mm
Features: Nine-fold zoom and upper magnification of 45; the ultra-flat elevation turret allows use of a back-packed red-dot sight for close distances; maximum optical brilliance for perfect target recognition at longest distances
MSRP. . . . . $6382.14–$7217.76

OPTICS

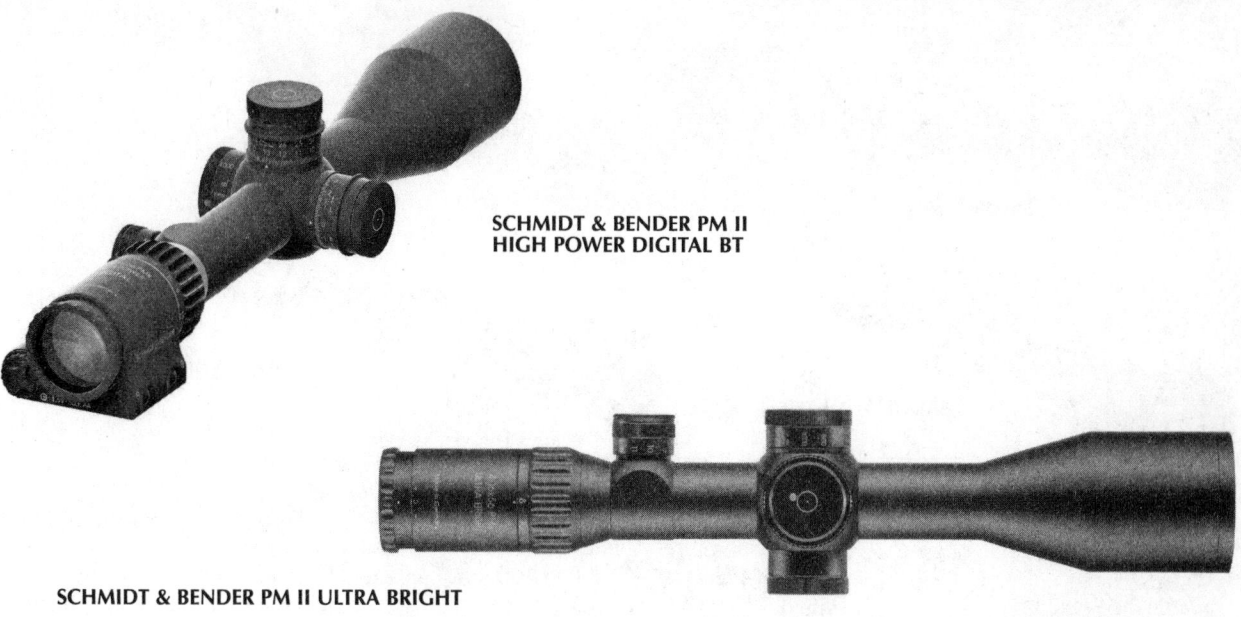

**SCHMIDT & BENDER PM II
HIGH POWER DIGITAL BT**

SCHMIDT & BENDER PM II ULTRA BRIGHT

**SCHMIDT & BENDER
POLAR T96**

PM II HIGH POWER DIGITAL BT

Available in: 3–27x56mm
Weight: 39.82 oz.
Length: 15.51 in.
Power: 3–27X
Obj. Dia.: 56mm
Main Dia.: 34mm
Exit Pupil: 8.6–2mm
Field of View: 39–4.2 ft @ 100 yds
Twilight Factor: 13–38.9
Eye Relief: 90mm
Features: Bluetooth interface allows projection of data from external devices, such as laser rangefinders, into the field of view, which significantly increases the probability of first round hits; the telescopic sight can also be used conventionally without external devices
MSRP . . . . $6162.97–$6998.58

PM II ULTRA BRIGHT

Available in: 3–12x54mm,
4–16x56mm
Weight: 32.52 oz.–34.32 oz.
Length: 13.8 in.–15.2 in.
Power: 3–12X, 4–16X
Obj. Dia.: 54mm, 56mm
Main Dia.: 34mm
Exit Pupil: 11.9–4.6mm
Field of View: 37.5–9.3 ft @ 100 yds, 28.2–6.9 ft @ 100 yds
Twilight Factor: 12.7–25.5, 15–29.9
Eye Relief: 90mm
Features: Transmission of 96 percent; precise shooting under low light conditions at medium and long distances; more rounded shapes and flat turrets
MSRP . . . . $4245.17–$4966.99

POLAR T96

Weight: 22.9 oz., 23.7 oz., 28.6 oz.
Length: 13.2 in., 14 in., 15.2 in.
Power: 2.5–10X, 3-12X, 4-16X
Obj. Dia.: 50mm, 54mm, 56mm
Main Dia.: 34mm
Exit Pupil: 15–5mm, 12–3.5mm
Field of View: 15–3.75m @ 100m, 12.5–3.1m @ 100m, 9.4–2.3m @ 100m
Twilight Factor: 11.18–22.36
Eye Relief: 3.5 in.
Features: Waterproof; front or rear focal plane; illuminated; exterior parts made of anodized aluminum; first or second plane illuminated reticles available on all models in L7 (first focal plane) or D7 and D4 (second focal plane) configurations; 3-12X can option side parallax adjustment; side parallax adjustment is standard on 4-16X
2.5-10x50mm: . . . . . $2333.06–$2443.63
3-12x54mm: . . . . . $2333.06–$2689.34
4-16x56mm:. . . . . . $$2615.63–$2726.20

SIG Sauer

SIG SAUER TANGO4

SIG SAUER TANGO6

SIG SAUER WHISKEY3

SIG SAUER WHISKEY5

TANGO4

Available in: 1–4x24mm, 3–12x42mm, 4–16x44mm, 6–24x50mm
Weight: 20.1 oz.–26.9 oz.
Length: 10 in.–15.6 in.
Power: 1–4X, 3–12X, 4–16X, 6–24X
Obj. Dia.: 24mm–50mm
Main Dia.: 30mm
Exit Pupil: 15.4–6.1mm, 13.3–3.4mm, 22.9–5.1mm, 8–2.1mm
Field of View: 98–24 ft @ 100 yds, 32.8–8.4 ft @ 100 yds, 24.3–6.1 ft @ 100 yds, 16.8–4.2 ft @ 100 yds
Twilight Factor: N/A
Eye Relief: 3.3 in.
Features: Low dispersion glass provides industry-leading optical clarity for any situation; offered in first focal plane with multiple, illuminated reticle options; MOTAC (Motion Activated Illumination) powers up when it senses motion and powers down when it does not; provides for optimum operational safety and enhanced battery life; dependable waterproof (IPX-7 rated for complete immersion up to 1 meter) and fogproof performance; LockDown Zero System features a resettable zero, zero-stop, and auto-locks down at zero
MSRP . . . . $719.99–$1199.99

TANGO6

Available in: 1–6x24mm, 2–12x40mm, 3–18x44mm, 4-24X50mm, 5–30x56mm
Weight: 25.4 oz.–39.5 oz.
Length: 11.1 in.–15.3 in.
Power: 1–6X, 2–12X, 3–18X, 4-24X, 5–30X
Obj. Dia.: 24mm–56mm
Main Dia.: 30mm

Exit Pupil: 11.3–4mm, 11.4–3.3mm, 11.4–2.4mm, 8.8–1.9mm
Field of View: 107–17.7 ft @ 100 yds, 53–8.8 ft @ 100 yds, 35.3–5.9 ft @ 100 yds, 20.2–3.4 ft @ 100 yds
Twilight Factor: N/A
Eye Relief: 3.5–3.9 in.
Features: Offered in first and second focal plane with multiple, illuminated reticle options; HellFire electronic-illuminated reticle system using advanced fiber optic technology to vary the light intensity of the central aiming point in any light condition; HDX optics extra-low dispersion glass combined with high transmittance glass provide industry-leading light transmission and optical clarity for any situation; MOTAC (Motion Activated Illumination) powers up when it senses motion and powers down when it does not; provides for optimum operational safety and enhanced battery life; dependable waterproof (IPX-7 rated for complete immersion up to 1 meter) and fogproof performance; LockDown Zero System features a resettable zero, zero-stop, and is lockable at any location
MSRP . . . . $1679.99–$3119.99

WHISKEY3

Available in: 2–7x32mm, 3–9x40mm, 3–9x50mm, 4–12x40mm, 4–12x50mm
Weight: 14.8 oz.–18.8 oz.
Length: 11.2 in.–14 in.
Power: 2–7X, 3–9X, 4–12X
Obj. Dia.: 32mm–50mm
Main Dia.: 25.4mm
Exit Pupil: 15–4.5mm, 15–4.8mm, 15.1–5.6mm, 10–3.3mm
Field of View: 45.4–13.1 ft @ 100 yds, 33.9–11.3 ft @ 100 yds, 23.6–7.9 ft @ 100 yds

Twilight Factor: N/A
Eye Relief: 3.5 in.
Features: 3X optical zoom offered in second focal plane (SFP) with multiple reticle options; low dispersion glass provides industry-leading optical clarity for any situation; European-style eyepiece for a smooth, fast, and precise reticle adjustment; dependable waterproof (IPX-7 rated for complete immersion up to 1 meter) and fogproof performance
MSRP . . . . $229.99–$539.99

WHISKEY5

Available in: 1–5x20mm, 2-10x42mm, 2.4–12x56mm, 3–15x44mm, 3–15x52mm, 5–25x52mm
Weight: 17.2 oz.–29 oz.
Length: 10.6 in.–14.6 in.
Power: 1–5X, 2–10X, 2.4–12X, 3–15X, 5–25X
Obj. Dia.: 20mm–56mm
Main Dia.: 25.4mm
Exit Pupil: 10.6–4mm, 10.7–4.2mm, 11.6–4.7mm, 10–2.9mm, 10–3.5mm, 8.3–2.1mm
Field of View: 100.4–20.2 ft @ 100 yds, 49.1–9.9 ft @ 100 yds, 43.1–9.3 ft @ 100 yds, 34.1–6.8 ft @ 100 yds, 20.2–4 ft @ 100 yds
Twilight Factor: N/A
Eye Relief: 3.8–4.1 in.
Features: Illuminated and non-illuminated reticles; proprietary HDX optical system provides industry-leading brightness and extreme optical clarity for any situation; offered in second focal plane with multiple reticle options; dependable waterproof (IPX-7 rated for complete water immersion up to 1 meter) and fogproof performance
MSRP . . . . $839.99–$1439.99

Simmons

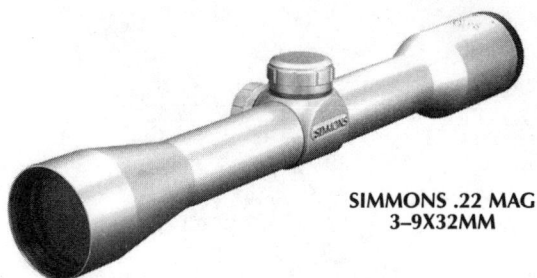

SIMMONS .22 MAG
3–9X32MM

SIMMONS .44 MAG.
3–10X44MM

SIMMONS 8-POINT 3–9X40MM

SIMMONS PREDATOR/VARMINT
SERIES

.22 MAG 3–9X32MM

Weight: 10 oz.
Length: 12 in.
Power: 3–9X
Obj. Dia.: 32mm
Main Dia.: 1 in.
Exit Pupil: 10.7–3.6mm
Field of View: 31.4–10.5 ft @ 100 yds
Twilight Factor: 9.8–17
Eye Relief: 3.75 in.
Features: One piece tube construction; fully coated optics; waterproof; fogproof; shockproof; Truplex reticle; RF Rings with available Adjustable Objective; also available in 4x32; matte or silver finish
3-9X: . . . .$63.95–$92.45
4X: $52.95

.44 MAG. 3–10X44MM

Weight: 11.3 oz.
Length: 12 in.
Power: 3–10X
Obj.Dia.: 44mm
Main Dia.: 1 in.
Exit Pupil: 14.66–4.4mm
Field of View: 33–9.4 ft @ 100 yds
Twilight Factor: 11.48–20.97

Eye Relief: 3.75 in.
Features: Wide field of view with brightness delivered via multi-coated optics; QTA (Quick Target Acquisition) eyepiece; TrueZero windage and elevation adjustment system; also in 4–12x44, 6–21x44, 6–24x44
MSRP . . . . $146.45–$230.95

8-POINT 3–9X40MM

Weight: 10 oz.
Length: 13.125 in.
Power: 3–9X
Obj. Dia.: 40mm
Main Dia.: 1 in.
Exit Pupil: 10.7–3.6mm
Field of View: 31.4–10.5 ft @ 100 yds
Twilight Factor: 11–19
Eye Relief: 3.75 in.
Features: TrueZero fingertip adjustments; Quick Target Acquisition; fully coated optics; waterproof; fogproof; recoilproof; Truplex reticle; also available in 4x32, 3–9x32, and 3–9x50; matte finish
From: . . . .$46.45–$75.95

PREDATOR/VARMINT SERIES

Weight: 20.5 oz.
Length: 10.7 in.
Power: 1–6X
Obj. Dia.: 24mm
Main Dia.: 30mm
Exit Pupil: 11–4mm
Field of View: 105–18 ft @ 100 yds
Twilight Factor: 4.9–12
Eye Relief: 3.9 in.
Features: Strike Zone 223 Reticle is calibrated for common .223/5.56 hunting loads; 11 illumination settings for low-light predator hunting; fully multi-coated optics provide bright, high-contrast images; SureGrip rubber on all adjustments surfaces; also available in 6-24x50mm and 4.5-18x44mm
MSRP . . . . $266.95–$359.95

Steiner

STEINER GS3 SERIES 2–10X42MM

STEINER T5XI SERIES

STEINER NIGHTHUNTER EXTREME SERIES 1–5X24MM

GS3 2–10X42MM
Weight: 18 oz.
Length: 13.5 in.
Power: 2–10X
Obj. Dia.: 42mm
Main Dia.: 30mm
Exit Pupil: 16.8–4.2mm
Field of View: 52–10.5 ft @ 100 yds
Twilight Factor: 9.17–20.49
Eye Relief: 3.5 in.–4.25 in.
Features: Rear focal plane; water- and fog-proof; nitrogen filled; 3–15x50, 3–15x56, and 4–20x50 also available
MSRP . . . . $919.99–$1149.99

NIGHTHUNTER EXTREME SERIES 1–5X24MM
Weight: 20.4 oz.
Length: 11.5 in.
Power: 1–5X

Obj. Dia.: 24mm
Main Dia.: 30mm
Exit Pupil: 11.5–4.8mm
Field of View: 108–21.5 ft @ 100 yds
Twilight Factor: 4.9–10.95
Eye Relief: 3.54 in.
Features: Rear focal plane; water- and fog-proof; nitrogen filled; illuminated reticle; rubber armoring; 1.6–8x42, 2–10x50, and 3–15x56 also available
MSRP . . . . $2587.49–$3219.99

T5XI SERIES
Weight: 19.4 oz., 29.8 oz., 33 oz.
Length: 11.3 in., 13.1 in., 16.6 in.
Power: 1–5X, 3–15X, 5–25X
Obj. Dia.: 24mm, 50mm, 56mm
Main Dia.: 30mm, 34mm, 34mm
Exit Pupil: 11–4.8mm, 12–3.4mm, 11.2–2.3mm

Field of View: 108–21 ft @ 100 yds, 36–7.3 ft @ 100 yds, 21.5–4.3 ft @ 100 yds
Twilight Factor: 4.9–10.95, 12.25–27.39, 16.73–37.42
Eye Relief: 3.5–4.3 in.
Features: The 1-5–24 is designed as a close-combat scope; medium-range 3–15x50 and long-range 5–25x56 scope come with illuminated etched glass featuring the new Special Competition Reticle (SCR) and Second Rotation Indicator that shows each mil of elevation through the indication window on the elevation turret; front focal plane
MSRP . . . . $1609.99–$3615.99

Swarovski Optik

SWAROVSKI OPTIK X5(I)

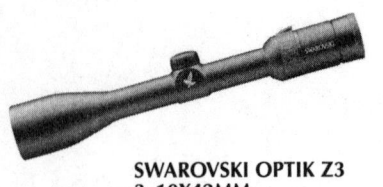

SWAROVSKI OPTIK Z3 3–10X42MM

X5(I)
Weight: 28.6 oz.–32.1 oz.
Length: 14.4 in.–14.8 in.
Power: 3.5–18X, 5–25X
Obj. Dia.: 50mm, 56mm
Main Dia.: 30mm
Exit Pupil: 9.5–2.8mm, 9.5–2.3mm
Field of View: 30–6.3 ft @ 100 yds, 21–4.5 ft @ 100 yds
Twilight Factor: 11–30, 15.5–37.4
Eye Relief: 3.7 in.
Features: The X5(i) from SWAROVSKI OPTIK redefines accuracy; new spring retention system and turrets are part of the total package promoting accuracy and offering across the entire adjustment range an accurate impact point adjustment of ¼ or 1/8 MOA in terms of both elevation and windage (X5/X5i 5-25x56 P), even in the most extreme situations; use the SUBZERO function to go below the sight-in distance
MSRP . . . . $3666.00–$3888.00

Z3 3–10X42MM
Weight: 12.7 oz.
Length: 12.6 in.
Power: 3–10X
Obj.Dia.: 42mm
Main Dia.: 1 in.
Exit Pupil: 12.6–4.2mm
Field of View: 33–11.7 ft @ 100 yds
Twilight Factor: 11.22–20.49
Eye Relief: 3.5 in.
Features: Z3 riflescopes have a 3x zoom factor and are the lightest riflescopes in the Swarovski Optik line; perfect fit for many of today's lightweight rifles; reticles for the Z3 include the 4A, Plex, BRX/BRH (3–10x and 4–12x), and ML in the 3–10x; also available in a 3-9x36mm with 4A Plex reticle
MSRP . . . . $866.00–$1211.00

Swarovski Optik

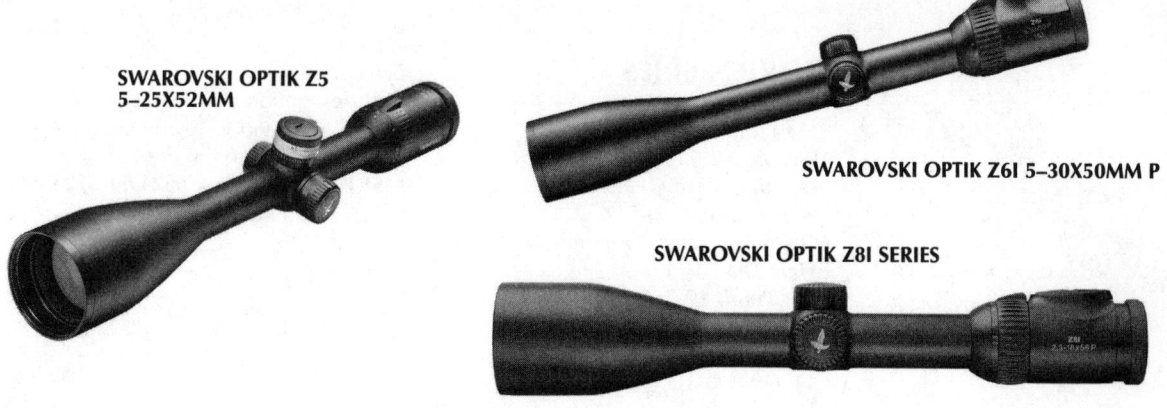

**SWAROVSKI OPTIK Z5
5–25X52MM**

SWAROVSKI OPTIK Z6I 5–30X50MM P

SWAROVSKI OPTIK Z8I SERIES

Z5 5–25X52MM
Weight: 17.5 oz.
Length: 14.6 in.
Power: 5–25X
Obj.Dia.: 52mm
Main Dia.: 1 in.
Exit Pupil: 9.6–2.1mm
Field of View: 21.9–4.5 ft @ 100 yds
Twilight Factor: 16.12–36.05
Eye Relief: 3.75 in.
Features: The Z5 Riflescope line features a 5x zoom factor; a third parallax-adjustment turret; and long eye relief; with reticles available in #4, Plex, Fine in the 5–25x, and BRX/BRH; also available with the ballistic turrets; also in 3.5–18x44
MSRP . . . . **$1366.00–$1554.00**

Z6I 5–30X50MM P
Weight: 22.6 oz.
Length: 15.67 in.
Power: 5–30X
Obj. Dia.: 48.2–50mm

Main Dia.: 30mm
Exit Pupil: 9.5–1.7mm
Field of View: 23.7–3.9 ft @ 100 yds
Twilight Factor: 14.1–38.7
Eye Relief: 3.74 in.
Features: New 2nd Generation scopes feature slimmer design that enables a clearer view of the controls and of the hunting situation; parallax turret also features a lock-in position at the 100 yds mark; more prominent ribbing on the magnification ring; 4A-1, 4W, Plex, and BRH reticles available; also available in 1–6x24, 1–6x24 BRT, 1–6x24 EE, 1.7–10x42, 2–12x50, 2.5–15x44 P, 2.5–15x56 P, 3–18x50 P
MSRP . . . . **$2110.00–$2999.00**

OPTIK Z8I SERIES
Available in: 1–8x24mm, 1.7–13.3x42mm, 2–16x50mm, 2.3–18x56mm
Weight: 18.2 oz.–25.6 oz.

Length: 11.9 in.–14.3 in.
Power: 1–8X, 1.7–13.3X, 2–16X, 2.3–18X
Obj. Dia.: 24mm–56mm
Main Dia.: 30mm
Exit Pupil: 8.1–3mm, 8.1–3.1mm
Field of View: 127.5–15.9 ft @ 100 yds, 75.6–9.3 ft @ 100 yds, 63–7.8 ft @ 100 yds, 55.8–6.9 ft @ 100 yds
Twilight Factor: 2.9–13.9, 4.8–23.6, 5.7–28.3, 6.5–31.8
Eye Relief: 95mm
Features: Ballistic turret flex and FLEXCHANGE, the first switchable reticle, provide you with maximum versatility in every hunting situation; slim 30mm central tube blends seamlessly with any hunting firearm
MSRP . . . . **$2899.00–$3521.00**

Tangent Theta

**TANGENT THETA PROFESSIONAL
MARKSMAN SERIES 5–25X56MM**

PROFESSIONAL MARKSMAN SERIES 5–25X56MM
Weight: 40.57 oz.
Length: 16.73 in.
Power: 5–25X
Obj. Dia.: 56mm
Main Dia.: 34mm
Exit Pupil: 11–2.3mm
Field of View: 7.6–1.6m @ 100m
Twilight Factor: 16.73–37.42
Eye Relief: 3.54 in.
Features: Water- and shockproof; adjustable parallax; illuminated reticle; 3–15x50 also available
MSRP . . . . **$2998.00–$4250.00**

Tract Optics

TRACT TORIC SERIES

TORIC SERIES
Available in: 2–10x42mm, 3–15x42mm, 3–15x50mm
Weight: 18.6 oz.–22.3 oz.
Length: 13.2 in.–13.9 in.
Power: 2–10X, 3–15X, 3–15X
Obj. Dia.: 42mm–50mm
Main Dia.: 1 in.
Exit Pupil: 10.7–4.2mm, 10–2.8mm, 10–3.3mm
Field of View: 49–9.9 ft @ 100 yds, 34–6.9 ft @ 100 yds, 34.3–6.8 ft @ 100 yds
Twilight Factor: N/A

Eye Relief: 4 in.
Features: Schott HT glass; glass etched BDC and T-Plex reticle (w/ windage correction in the BDC)
MSRP . . . . **$624.00–$724.00**

Trijicon

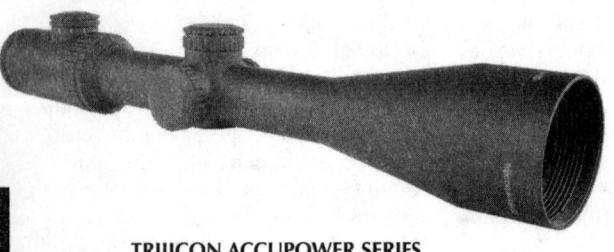

TRIJICON ACCUPOWER SERIES

TRIJICON ACCUPOINT 1–6X24

ACCUPOINT SERIES
Weight: 14.4 oz.–26.9 oz.
Length: 10.3 in.–13.8 in.
Power: 1–4X, 1–6x, 2.5–10X, 2.5–12.5X, 3–9X, 5–20X
Obj. Dia.: 24mm–56mm
Main Dia.: 30mm
Exit Pupil: 17.5–5.1mm, 12–4.1mm, 16.3–5.6mm, 10.6–3.3mm, 13.3–4.4mm, 10–2.5mm
Field of View: 97.5–24.2 ft @ 100 yds, 117.5–18.8 ft @ 100 yds, 37.6–10.1 ft @ 100 yds, 41.3–3.8 ft @ 100 yds, 6.45–2.15 ft @ 100 yds, 19.1–5.1 ft @ 100 yds
Twilight Factor: N/A
Eye Relief: 3.2 in., 3.9 in., 2.8–4.1 in, 3.9 in., 3.6 in., 3.8–4.1 in.

Features: Waterproof; rear focal plane; adjustable parallax; titrium and fiber battery-free dual-illuminated; manual brightness adjustment; reticles include BAC Triangle, Standard Cross-Hair with Dot, Mil-Dot Cross-Hair with Dot, and German #4 in red, green, and amber illumination
MSRP . . . . **$899.00–$1399.00**

ACCUPOWER SERIES
Weight: 16.2 oz, 17 oz., 23.6 oz, 23.3 oz.
Length: 10.2 in., 12.3 in., 13.8 in., 14.2 in.
Power: 1–4X, 3–9X, 2.5–10X, 4–16X
Obj. Dia.: 24mm, 40mm, 56mm, 50mm
Main Dia.: 30mm, 1 in., 30mm,

30mm
Exit Pupil: 15–5mm, 13.3–4.4mm, 16.5–5.6mm, 9.3–3.1mm
Field of View: 97.5–24.2 ft @ 100 yds, 35.5–11.8 ft @ 100 yds, 37.9–10.2 ft @ 100 yds, 25.8–6.4 ft @ 100 yds
Twilight Factor: N/A
Eye Relief: 3.5 in., 3.7–3.5 in., 4 in., 3.6–3.7 in.
Features: Waterproof; illuminated; several reticle options; adjustable parallax; rear focal plane
MSRP . . . . **$699.00–$1699.00**

OPTICS

Trijicon

ACOG WITH .300 BLK RETICLE 3X30MM
Weight: 11.64 oz.
Length: 6.1 in.
Power: 3X
Obj. Dia.: 30mm
Main Dia.: N/A
Exit Pupil: 10mm
Field of View: 19.3 ft @ 100 yds
Twilight Factor: 9.5
Eye Relief: 1.9 in.
Features: TA60 Mount; designed for law enforcement and military applications; .300 BLK Ballistic Reticle for subsonic and supersonic rounds; bullet drop compensator; Bindon Aiming Concept (BAC), fiber optics & tritium illuminated; available with amber, green, or red crosshair reticle
MSRP $1407.00

TARS 3–15X50MM
Weight: 47 oz., 51 oz. with sunshade
Length: 13.9in, 16.9 in. with sunshade
Power: 3–15X
Obj. Dia.: 50mm
Main Dia.: 34mm
Exit Pupil: 16.8–3.3mm
Field of View: 37.5–7.5 ft @ 100 yds
Twilight Factor: 10.1–22.6

TRIJICON ACOG WITH .300 BLK RETICLE 3X30MM

TRIJICON VCOG 1–6X24MM RIFLESCOPE

Eye Relief: 3.3 in.
Features: Tactical Advanced RifleScope is built for long-range shooting demands; multi-layer coated lenses; aircraft grade hard anodized aluminum; side-focus parallax compensation, powered by 1 CR2032 battery; constant eye relief; available with MOA, Duplex, JW MIL-Square reticles and MOA or MIL adjusters
MSRP $4464.00

TRIJICON TARS 3–15X50MM

VCOG 1–6X24MM RIFLESCOPE
Weight: 23.2 oz.
Length: 10.05 in.
Power: 1–6X
Obj. Dia.: 24mm
Main Dia.: N/A
Exit Pupil: 10.4–3.8mm
Field of View: 95–15.9 ft @ 100 yds
Twilight Factor: 12
Eye Relief: 4 in.
Features: Designed and built in the U.S.; Mil Spec, hard-coat finish; 90 MOA of windage and elevation adjustment; fully multi-coated lenses; waterproof; seven different reticle choices, between centered crosshair and horseshoe/dot reticle; red illuminated reticle; six brightness settings; matte finish
MSRP . . . . $2800.00–$3050.00

Truglo

TRUGLO TACTICAL IR 3–9X42MM

TRUGLO TRU-BRITE 30 SERIES

TRUGLO TRU-BRITE XTREME DUAL-COLOR TACTICAL COMPACT 4X32MM

TACTICAL IR 3–9X42MM
Weight: 17.6 oz.
Length: 9.92 in.
Power: 3–9X
Obj. Dia.: 42mm
Main Dia.: 30mm
Exit Pupil: N/A
Field of View: 31–10.47 ft @ 100 yds
Twilight Factor: 11.23–19.44
Eye Relief: 3.46 in.–3.94 in.
Features: Two-color IR MilDot illuminated reticle; BDC can be calibrated to most .223 and .308 cartridges and accommodate targets up to 600 yards away
MSRP $209.00

TRU-BRITE 30 SERIES
Available in: 1–4x24mm, 1–6x24mm
Weight: 13.4 oz.–15.1 oz.
Length: 9.88 in.–10.39 in.
Power: 1–4X, 1–6X
Obj. Dia.: 24mm
Main Dia.: 30mm
Exit Pupil: N/A
Field of View: 93.6–23.03 @ 100 yds,
103.71–18.15 ft @ 100 yds
Twilight Factor: N/A
Eye Relief: 3.75 in.
Features: Includes two pre-calibrated BDC turrets in calibers .223 (55 grain) and .308 (168 grain) to engage targets up to 800 yards away; ½ MOA windage/elevation adjustments
MSRP . . . . $184.00–$270.00

TRU-BRITE XTREME DUAL-COLOR TACTICAL COMPACT 4X32MM
Weight: 15.4 oz.
Length: 9.8 in.
Power: 4X
Obj. Dia.: 32mm
Main Dia.: 1 in.
Exit Pupil: N/A
Field of View: 20.79 ft @ 100 yds
Twilight Factor: 11.31
Eye Relief: 5.5 in.
Features: Illuminated reticle; fully coated lenses; durable, scratch-resistant, non-reflective matte finish
MSRP . . . . $91.00–$117.00

Vortex Optics

VORTEX CROSSFIRE II 30MM SERIES 3–12X56MM

VORTEX CROSSFIRE II SCOUT

VORTEX DIAMONDBACK HP SERIES 2–8X32MM

VORTEX GOLDEN EAGLE HD

VORTEX RAZOR HD AMG

VORTEX RAZOR HD GEN II SERIES 4.5–27X56MM

CROSSFIRE II 30MM 3–12X56MM

Weight: 21.1 oz.
Length: 14.3 in.
Power: 3–12X
Obj. Dia.: 56mm
Main Dia.: 30mm
Exit Pupil: N/A
Field of View: 36.7–9.2 ft @ 100 yds
Twilight Factor: 12.96–25.92
Eye Relief: 3.5 in.
Features: Rear focal plane; shock-, water-, and fogproof; illuminated reticle; 6-24x50mm adjustable objective (AO), 4-16x50 AO, and 1-4x24mm available in 30mm tube; Crossfire IIs with 1-in. tubes are also available in 6-18x44mm AO, 4-12x50mm AO, 4-12x40mm AO, 4-12x44mm, 3-9x50mm, 3-9x40mm, 2-7x32mm, 2-7x32mm Scout, 2-7x32mm Rimfire, and 1X24mm muzzleloader
MSRP..........**$169.00–$369.99**

CROSSFIRE II SCOUT

Available in: 2–7x32mm
Weight: 12 oz.
Length: 10.5 in.
Power: 2–7X
Obj. Dia.: 32mm
Main Dia.: 25.4mm
Exit Pupil: N/A
Field of View: 18.3–5.2 ft @ 100 yds
Twilight Factor: N/A
Eye Relief: 9.45 in.
Features: Fully multi-coated; second focal plane reticle; single-piece tube; capped reset turrets
MSRP.................**$199.99**

DIAMONDBACK HP 2–8X32MM

Weight: 15.9 oz.
Length: 11.6 in.
Power: 2–8X
Obj. Dia.: 32mm
Main Dia.: 1 in.
Exit Pupil: N/A
Field of View: 41.9–12.2 ft @ 100 yds
Twilight Factor: 8–16
Eye Relief: 4.6 in.
Features: Rear focal plane; shock-, water-, and fogproof; adjustable parallax; 3–12x42 and 4–16x42 also available
MSRP..........**$369.00–$479.99**

GOLDEN EAGLE HD

Available in: 15–60x52mm
Weight: 29.7 oz.
Length: 16.1 in.
Power: 15–60X
Obj. Dia.: 52mm
Main Dia.: 30mm
Exit Pupil: N/A
Field of View: 6.3–1.7 ft @ 100 yds
Twilight Factor: N/A
Eye Relief: 3.9 in.
Features: Apochromatic objective lens system uses index-matched lenses to correct color across the entire visual spectrum; extra-fine resolution turret
MSRP.................**$1899.99**

RAZOR HD AMG

Available in: 6–24x50mm
Weight: 28.8 oz.
Length: 15.2 in.
Power: 6–24X
Obj. Dia.: 50mm
Main Dia.: 30mm
Exit Pupil: N/A
Field of View: 20.4–5.1 ft @ 100 yds
Twilight Factor: N/A
Eye Relief: 3.6 in.
Features: ALO proprietary automated laser optical alignment process; apochromatic objective lens system uses index-matched lenses to correct color across the entire visual spectrum; optically indexed lenses; premium high-density, extra-low dispersion glass; fully multi-coated; first focal plane reticle; illuminated reticle; waterproof, fogproof, and shockproof; side focus adjustment
MSRP................**$3399.00**

RAZOR HD GEN II 4.5–27X56MM

Weight: 48.5 oz.
Length: 14.4 in
Power: 4.5–27X
Obj. Dia.: 56mm
Main Dia.: 34mm
Exit Pupil: N/A
Field of View: 25.3–4.4 ft @ 100 yds
Twilight Factor: 15.87–38.88
Eye Relief: 3.7 in.
Features: Front focal plane; shock-, water-, and fogproof; adjustable parallax; illuminated reticle; glass-etched reticle; 1–6x24 RFP and 3–18x50 also available
MSRP.........**$1999.00–$3399.00**

OPTICS

VORTEX RAZOR HD LH SERIES

VORTEX STRIKE EAGLE

VORTEX HS LR RFP SERIES 4–16X44MM

VORTEX VIPER HS-T SERIES 6–24X50MM

VORTEX VIPER PST RFP SERIES 1–4X24MM

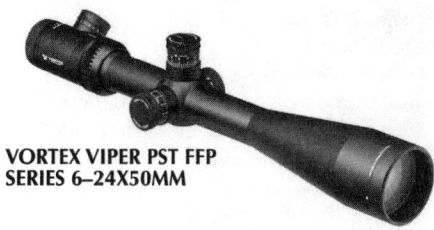

VORTEX VIPER PST FFP SERIES 6–24X50MM

RAZOR HD LH SERIES

Available in: 1.5–8x32mm, 2–10x40mm, 3–15x42mm
Weight: 13.4 oz.–16.5 oz.
Length: 11 in.–13.5 in.
Power: 1.5–8X, 2–10X, 3–15X
Obj. Dia.: 32mm–42mm
Main Dia.: 25.4mm
Exit Pupil: N/A
Field of View: 72.2–13.2 ft @ 100 yds, 56.2–10.8 ft @ 100 yds, 35.8–7.1 ft @ 100 yds
Twilight Factor: N/A
Eye Relief: 3.8 in.
Features: Premium extra-low dispersion glass; optically indexed lenses; fully multi-coated; single-piece tube; waterproof, fogproof, and shockproof; hard anodized finish; large diameter turrets
MSRP . . . . $949.99–$1099.99

STRIKE EAGLE

Weight: 17.6 oz.
Length: 10.5 in.
Power: 1–6X
Obj. Dia.: 24mm
Main Dia.: 30mm
Exit Pupil: N/A
Field of View: 116.5–19.2 ft @ 100 yds
Twilight Factor: N/A
Eye Relief: 3.5 in.
Features: Fully multi-coated lens; illuminated, glass etched, rear focal plane reticle; water-, fog-, and shockproof; hard anodized finish; fast focus eyepiece; also available in a 1-8X24mm
MSRP . . . . $449.99–$569.99

VIPER HUNTING SHOOTING LONG RANGE (HS LR) 4–16X44MM

Weight: 19.8 oz.
Length: 13.7 in.
Power: 4–16X
Obj. Dia.: 44mm
Main Dia.: 30mm
Exit Pupil: N/A
Field of View: 27.4–7.4 ft @ 100 yds
Twilight Factor: 13.27–26.53
Eye Relief: 4 in.
Features: Rear focal plane; shock-, water-, and fogproof; adjustable parallax; 4–16x50 also available
MSRP . . . . $649.00–$749.99

VIPER HUTING SHOOTING TACTICAL (HS-T) 6–24X50MM

Weight: 22.6 oz.
Length: 15.5 in.
Power: 6–24X
Obj. Dia.: 50mm
Main Dia.: 30mm
Exit Pupil: N/A
Field of View: 17.8–5.1 ft @ 100 yds
Twilight Factor: 17.32–34.64
Eye Relief: 4 in.
Features: Rear focal plane; shock-, water-, and fogproof; adjustable parallax; 4–16x44 also available
MSRP . . . . $719.99–$789.99

VIPER PRECISION SHOOTING TACTICAL (PST) 1–4X24MM

Weight: 16.2 oz.
Length: 9.7 in.
Power: 1–4X
Obj. Dia.: 24mm

Main Dia.: 30mm
Exit Pupil: N/A
Field of View: 98–27.5 ft @ 100 yds
Twilight Factor: 4.9–14.7
Eye Relief: 4 in.
Features: Rear focal plane; shock-, water-, and fogproof; illuminated reticle; adjustable parallax on some models; 2.5–10x44, 4–16x50, and 6–24x50 also available
MSRP . . . . $649.00–$949.00

VIPER PRECISION SHOOTING TACTICAL (PST) FFP SERIES 6–24X50MM

Weight: 23.4 oz.
Length: 15.5 in.
Power: 6–24X
Obj. Dia.: 50mm
Main Dia.: 30mm
Exit Pupil: N/A
Field of View: 17.8–5.1 ft @ 100 yds
Twilight Factor: 17.32–34.64
Eye Relief: 4 in.
Features: Front focal plane; shock-, water-, and fogproof; adjustable parallax; illuminated reticle; glass-etched reticle; 2.5–10x32 and 4–16x50 also available
MSRP . . . . $999.00–$1149.00

OPTICS

Weaver

40/44 3–10X44MM
Weight: 13.93 oz.
Length: 12.09 in.
Power: 3–10X
Obj.Dia.: 44mm
Main Dia.: 1 in.
Exit Pupil: 14.7–4.4mm
Field of View: 33.5–10.3 ft @ 100 yds
Twilight Factor: 11.49–20.98
Eye Relief: 3 in.
Features: Ballistic-X reticle on some models; one-piece tube construction; aspherical lens system on some models; also available in 2.8–10x44, 3–9x40, 3.8–12x44, 4–12x44, 6.5–20x44; silver finish on some models
MSRP . . . . $218.95–$331.95

CLASSIC HANDGUN 2.5–8X28MM
Weight: 9.1 oz.
Length: 9.29 in.
Power: 2.5–8X
Obj.Dia.: 28mm
Main Dia.: 1 in.
Exit Pupil: 11.2–3.5mm
Field of View: 11–4.5 ft @ 100 yds
Twilight Factor: 8.37–14.97
Eye Relief: 24.53 in.
Features: Handguns demand a scope that is built to withstand the brutal pounding from today's most powerful revolvers and single-shot pistols. Designed for the tremendous recoil of 1,000 rounds from a .454 Casull revolver; black or silver; also in 1.5–4x20, 2x28
MSRP . . . . $272.95–$386.45

CLASSIC K-SERIES 4X28MM
Weight: 14.2 oz.
Length: 9.17 in.
Power: 4X
Obj.Dia.: 38mm
Main Dia.: 1 in.
Exit Pupil: 7mm
Field of View: 8.5 ft @ 100 yds
Twilight Factor: 12.33
Eye Relief: 9.45 in.
Features: Crafted from a one-piece aircraft-grade aluminum tube; built to take heavy recoil punishment and hold zero to 10,000 rounds from a .375 H&H magnum rifle; presents a consistent field of view that's perfect for open field hunting and are among the easiest scopes any instinctive shooter will ever use; also in 4x28mm, 6x38mm
MSRP . . . . $244.45–$302.45

WEAVER 40/44 3–10X44MM

WEAVER CLASSIC HANDGUN 2.5–8X28MM

WEAVER CLASSIC K SERIES 4X28MM

CLASSIC RIMFIRE 3–9X32MM

Weight: 12 oz.
Length: 11.5 in.
Power: 3–9X
Obj.Dia.: 28mm
Main Dia.: 1 in.
Exit Pupil: 10.6mm
Field of View: 33.2–11 ft @ 100 yds
Twilight Factor: 9.17–15.87
Eye Relief: 3.58 in.
Features: Variable and fixed power models; non-glare lenses that produce edge-sharp, low-light brightness; rugged, aircraft-grade, one-piece aluminum construction; parallax is set at 50 yards; also in 2.5–7x28 (matte, silver) and 4x28
MSRP . . . . $221.45–$412.45

GRAND SLAM 3–12X50MM

Weight: 16.6 oz.
Length: 12.6 in.
Power: 3–12X
Obj. Dia.: 50mm
Main Dia.: 1 in.
Exit Pupil: 13.6–4.2mm
Field of View: 32.7–8.4 ft @ 100 yds
Twilight Factor: 12.2–24.5
Eye Relief: 3.19–3.46 in.
Features: 4x magnification ranges; ground, fully multi-coated lenses; fog-proof; side focus parallax adjustments on select models; multiple reticle options; available in 2–8x36, 3–12x42, 4–16x44, and 5-20x50; matte finish
MSRP . . . . $572.95–$879.95

KASPA HUNTER SERIES 3–9X40MM

Weight: 11.5 oz.
Length: 12.4 in.
Power: 3–9X
Obj. Dia.: 40mm
Main Dia.: 1 in.
Exit Pupil: 13–4.4mm
Field of View: 32.6–11 ft @ 100 yds
Twilight Factor: 10.95–18.97
Eye Relief: 4.37 in.–3.81 in.
Features: Fogproof; nitrogen purged; illuminated Dual-X reticle; available in 2-7x32mm, 1X20mm, 3-12x50mm, 4-16x44mm (side focus, illuminated reticle available), 6-18x44mm, 1-4x24mm (30mm tube and 30mm turkey options); 3-9x40mm also available with non-illuminated Dual-X reticle
MSRP . . . . $132.45–$298.45

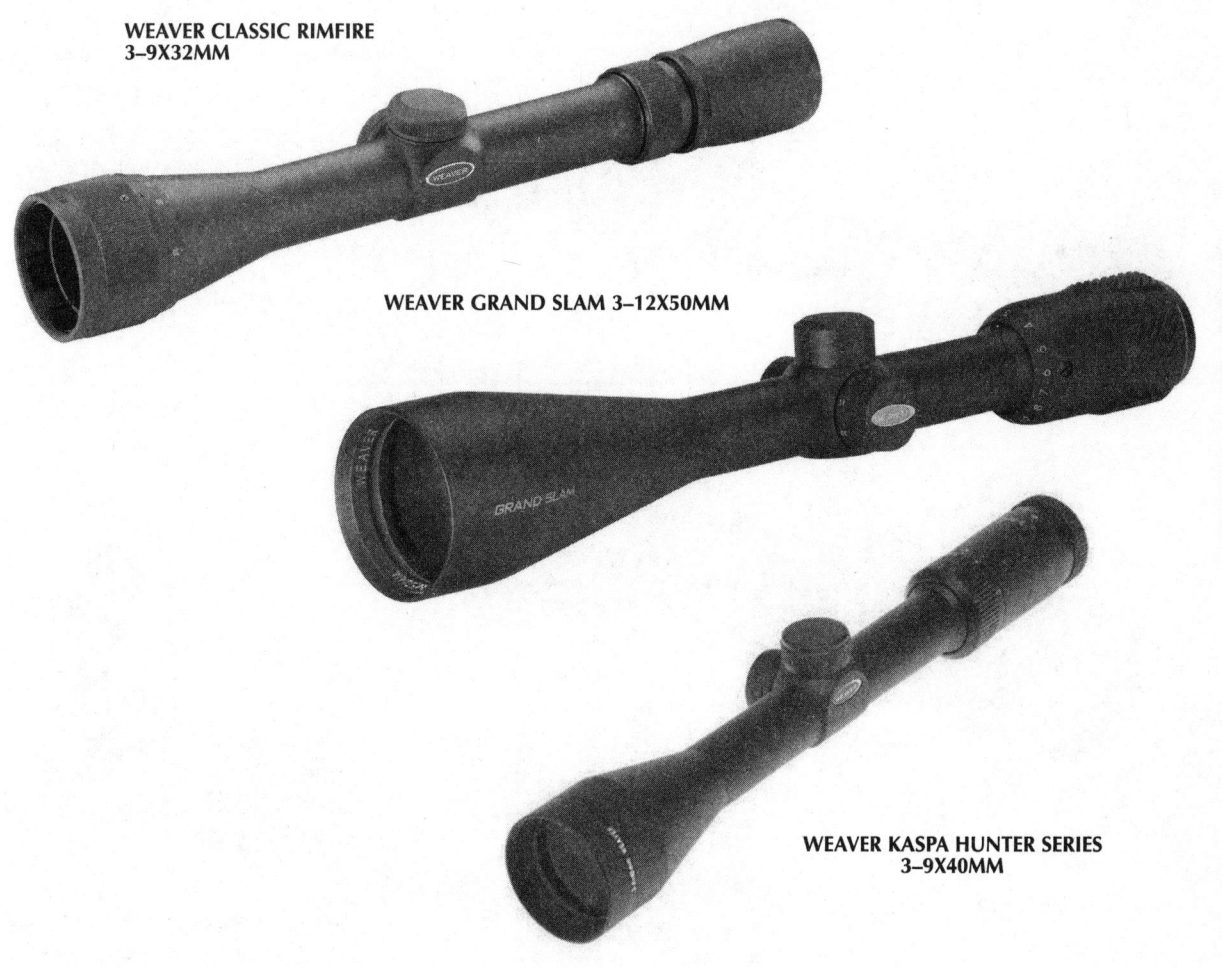

WEAVER CLASSIC RIMFIRE 3–9X32MM

WEAVER GRAND SLAM 3–12X50MM

WEAVER KASPA HUNTER SERIES 3–9X40MM

Weaver

KASPA TACTICAL 1–4X24MM

Weight: N/A
Length: 10.5 in.
Power: 1–4X
Obj. Dia.: 24mm
Main Dia.: 30mm
Exit Pupil: 6–13mm
Field of View: 27–109 ft @ 100 yds
Twilight Factor: 4.9–9.8
Eye Relief: 3.54–4 in.
Features: Illuminated Dual-X reticle; tactical 30mm tube; ¼ MOA adjustments; fully multi-coated lenses; fogproof; matte finish; also available, all with illuminated reticles, in 1.5-6x32mm (IRB-X reticle), 2.5-10x50mm (Mil-Dot reticle), 3-12x44mm (EMDR or TB-X reticles); side focus is available on the 2.4-10x and 3-12x models, and Dark Earth finish is available on 1.5-6x and 3-12x.
MSRP . . . . $280.95–$372.95

SUPER SLAM 4–20X50MM

Weight: 24 oz.
Length: 13.31 in.
Power: 4–20X
Obj.Dia.: 50mm
Main Dia.: 1 in.
Exit Pupil: 10.5–2.44mm
Field of View: 24.5–4.9 ft @ 100 yds
Twilight Factor: 14.14–31.62
Eye Relief: 3.98 in.
Features: Line of premier riflescopes designed for the serious big game hunter and shooter; side focus adjustable parallax; pull-up turrets; also in 1–5x24, 3–15x42 in matte black
MSRP . . . . $802.49–$1039.49

TACTICAL 1–5X24MM

Weight: 14.46 oz.
Length: 10.31 in.
Power: 1–5X
Obj.Dia.: 24mm
Main Dia.: 30mm
Exit Pupil: 11.4–4.9mm
Field of View: 100–19.9 ft @ 100 yds
Twilight Factor: 4.9–10.95
Eye Relief: 4.25 in.
Features: Rugged riflescopes designed specifically for tactical applications; extra hard coating on exterior lenses; first focal plane reticles; side focus parallax adjustment; reset-to-zero turrets; one-piece tube construction; available in 4-20x50mm (side focus, Mil Dot reticle), 3-15x50mm (side focus, Mil Dot reticle), 3-15x50mm (illuminated EMDR reticle), 6-30x56mm (34mm tube, SmartZero feature, IMDR reticle), and 1-7x24mm (34mm tube, dual focal plane, illuminated 4 MOA red dot reticle with Mil Dot ranging)
MSRP . . . . $1196.95–$2171.95

WEAVER SUPER SLAM 4–20X50MM

WEAVER TACTICAL 1–5X24MM

WEAVER KASPA TACTICAL 1–4X24MM

9000SC
Weight: 7.4 oz.
Length: 6.3 in.
Obj. Dia.: 38mm
Features: Ideal for short length action rifles, semi-automatic firearms, and magnum handguns; ACET technology for longer battery life; available in 2 or 4 MOA dot sizes; two-ring configuration for mounting; waterproof; matte finish
Standard: $498.00
Night-vision compatible: . . .$747.00

ACO
Weight: 7.8 oz.
Length: 5.1 in.
Power: 1X
Field of View: N/A
Eye Relief: N/A
Features: Developed with the modern sporting rifle owner in mind, the ACO is ready to mount and shoot directly out of the box; 30mm aluminum alloy sight tube is paired with a rugged fixed height mount designed to provide absolute co-witness with AR-15 backup iron sights; 2 MOA red-dot to allow maximum target acquisition speed and accuracy at all distances; exclusive ACET technology allows for up to one year of constant-on use from a single DL1/3N battery; completely waterproof housing.
MSRP $393.00

MICRO H-1 AND T-1
Weight: 3 oz.
Length: 2.4 in.
Power: 1X
Features: High quality compact red-dot sight; sealed design ensures that no foreign matter will come between the emitter and the lens; can be mounted on nearly any individual weapon platform including: pistols, carbines, personal defense weapons, and sub-machineguns; also available in 4 MOA red-dot
H-1: . . . . $700.00–$1076.00
T-1: . . . . $780.00–$916.00

MICRO H-2 AND T-2
Weight: 4.6 oz.–4.8 oz.
Length: 2.7 in.–3.16 in.
Power: 1X
Field of View: N/A
Eye Relief: N/A

Features: Advanced optical lenses for even better light transmission; can be used on shotguns, rifles, handguns or archery tackle; transparent front and rear flip-up lens covers are included; reinforced protection of the turrets for even greater ruggedness; 12 daylight settings; available in 2 MOA dot size; can be "piggybacked" on larger magnifying optics using an adapter.
H-2: . . . . $789.00–$1176.00
T-2: . . . . $843.00–$981.00

PRO
Weight: 7.8 oz.
Length: 5.1 in.
Power: 1X
Features: Parallax free optic; 2 MOA dot for accurate target engagement at all distances; four night vision settings and six daylight settings; modular QRP2 mount includes removable spacer that indexes the sight at optimal height for co-witness, with the standard iron sights on AR15/M16/M4 carbine style weapons
MSRP $485.00

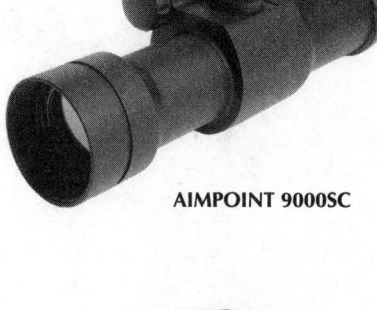
AIMPOINT 9000SC

AIMPOINT ACO

AIMPOINT MICRO H-1

AIMPOINT PRO

AIMPOINT MICRO H-2

OPTICS

British Small Arms Co. (BSA)

**BSA STEALTH TACTICAL
ILLUMINATED SIGHT**

STEALTH TACTICAL ILLUMINATED SIGHT

Weight: 5 oz.
Length: 5.4 in.
Power: 1X
Field of View: 65 ft @ 100 yds
Eye Relief: Unlimited
Features: Glass fully multicoated; multi-purpose twist-cap technology; 5/8-inch Weaver-style rail; illuminated red dot; also available with a user-choice red/blue/green dot and built-in flashlight
Red dot:. \$179.95
Red/green/blue dot:. \$199.95

TACTICAL WEAPON ILLUMINATED SIGHT

Weight: 22 oz.
Length: 8.75 in.
Power: 1X
Field of View: 3.7–19.3 ft @ 100 yds
Eye Relief: 2 in.
Features: Fully multicoated optics; easy one-piece mounting; 5/8-inch Weaver-style rail; illuminated red dot; rubber eye guard; output power: 5mW; wave length: 650 nm; also available with an attachable 140 lumen LED flashlight
MSRP \$99.95
With flashlight: \$139.95

**BSA TACTICAL WEAPON
ILLUMINATED SIGHT**

Browning

BROWNING 2–1 HUNTING SIGHTS

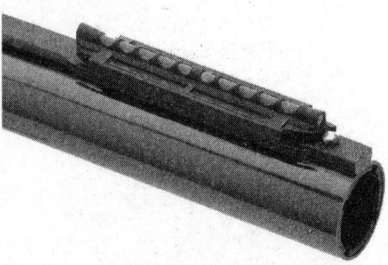

BUCK MARK REFLEX SIGHT

Weight: N/A
Power: 1X
Field of View: 47 ft @ 100 yds
Eye Relief: Unlimited
Features: The Buck Mark has an aluminum housing, four red reticle patterns, a seven-position brightness rheostat powered by a lithium battery, and mounts on a standard Weaver-styled base
MSRP \$69.99

2–1 HUNTING SIGHTS

Features: Magnetic base attaches to shotgun rib; features both red and green LitePipes; comes with both round and triangular LitePipe systems; designed for guns with narrow ribs
MSRP \$29.99

**BROWNING BUCK MARK
REFLEX SIGHT**

OPTICS

BURRIS AR-536

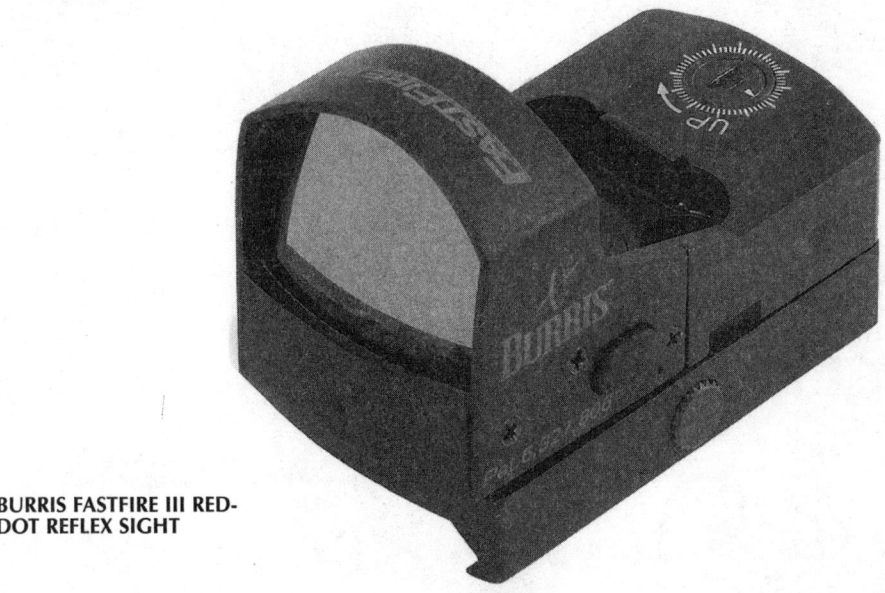

BURRIS FASTFIRE III RED-DOT REFLEX SIGHT

AR-536

Weight: 18.75 oz.
Length: 5.75 in.
Power: 5X
Obj. Dia.: 36mm
Field of View: 20 ft @ 100 yds
Eye Relief: 2.5–3.5 in.
Features: Ballistic/CQTM lighted reticle; 600 yard range; multi-coated lenses; adjustable diopter; three Picatinny rail mounting points; black matte finish; max adj. 60 MOA; one-year warranty
MSRP . . . . $479.00–$659.00

FASTFIRE III RED-DOT REFLEX SIGHT

Weight: 0.9 oz.
Power: 1.07X
Features: Upgraded features such as windage and elevation adjustments that don't require a special tool; 3 or 8 MOA Dot; power button with three levels of brightness; low battery warning indicator and see-through protective cap; ideally suited for use on pistols and AR-15s where fast target acquisition is desired, the FastFire red-dot sight will also match up well with carbines, lever guns, and shotguns; available picatinny mount
MSRP . . . . $287.00–$299.00

Bushnell Outdoor Products

BUSHNELL AK RED DOT

BUSHNELL AR OPTICS 2X MP

AK RED DOT
Weight: 3.7 oz.
Length: 2.4 in.
Power: 1X
Field of View: Unlimited
Eye Relief: Unlimited
Features: 3 MOA red dot; multi-coated optics; Amber-Bright high-contrast lens coating; 100 percent waterproof/fogproof/shockproof construction; CR2032 battery
MSRP **$136.95**

AR OPTICS 2X MP
Weight: 15.6 oz.
Length: 6.75 in.
Power: 2X
Obj. Dia.: 32mm
Exit Pupil: 32mm
Field of View: 44 ft @ 100 yds
Eye Relief: Unlimited
Features: With the ability to display the T-dot reticle in green during low light and red during bright light, the 2X MP offers the versatility shooters demand from electronic sights. With two power

magnification and multi-coated optics, the sight is ideal for acquiring close- to mid-range targets.
MSRP **$341.00**

AR OPTICS 1X28MM
Weight: 6 oz.
Length: 5.5 in.
Power: 1X
Obj. Dia.: 28mm
Exit Pupil: 28mm
Field of View: 68 ft @ 100 yds
Eye Relief: unlimited
Features: 6 MOA red dot sight; eleven brightness settings; tactical rings for variably mounts and heights; matte finish
MSRP: **$117.00**

**BUSHNELL AR
OPTICS 1X28MM
RED DOT**

BUSHNELL FIRST STRIKE RED DOT

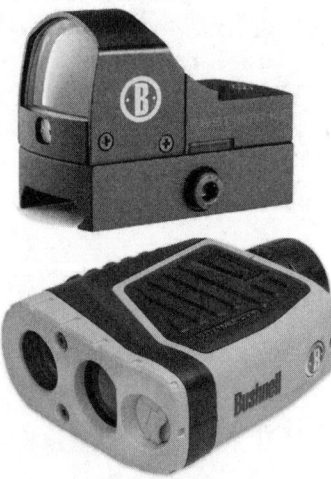

BUSHNELL ELITE 1 MILE ARC

**BUSHNELL SCOUT
DX 1000 ARC**

BUSHNELL THE TRUTH WITH CLEARSHOT

ELITE 1 MILE ARC
Weight: 12.1 oz.
Power: 7X
Obj. Dia.: 26mm
Range: 5–1760 yd
Features: Waterproof; built-in tripod mount; fully multi-coated lenses
MSRP **$599.00**

FIRST STRIKE RED DOT
Weight: 2.1 oz.

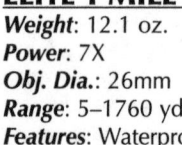

Length: 2.4 in.
Field of View: Unlimited
Eye Relief: Unlimited
Features: 5 MOA red dot reticle; multi-coated optics; self-regulating brightness; integrated mount; waterproof; fogproof; shockproof; matte finish
MSRP **$209.00**

SCOUT DX 1000 ARC
Weight: 6.6 oz.
Power: 6X
Features: Built-in inclinometer; ARC Bow and Rifle Modes; Variable Sight-in; range up to 1,000 yds; diopter adjustment; waterproof; compatible with magnetic attachment system; available in black or RealTree AP
MSRP **$477.00**

THE TRUTH WITH CLEARSHOT
Weight: 6 oz.
Power: 4X
Obj. Dia.: 28mm
Range: 7–850 yd
Features: Rainproof and pocket-sized
MSRP **$280.00**

Bushnell Outdoor Products

**BUSHNELL
TRS-25 HIRISE**

TRS-25 HIRISE
Weight: 6 oz.
Length: 2.4 in.
Power: 1X
Obj. Dia.: 25mm
Exit Pupil: 22mm
Field of View: unlimited
Eye Relief: unlimited
Features: 3 MOA red dot reticle; elev-

en brightness settings; multi-coated; waterproof; fogproof; shockproof; riser block; matte finish
MSRP $171.00

Cabela's

**CABELA'S TACTICAL
REFLEX SIGHT**

TACTICAL REFLEX SIGHT
Features: Automatically turns on when cap is lifted; automatic reticle-brightness control; multi-coated optics with 5 MOA center-dot reticle; waterproof; shockproof; mounts to any Picatinny rail; runs for up to 300 hours on one battery
MSRP $99.99

Carl Zeiss Sports Optics

VICTORY COMPACT POINT
Weight: 2.64 oz.
Length: 2.28 in.
Power: 1.05X
Features: LotuTec coating; single button on/off and five level brightness; 25 percent wider than conventional reflex sites for natural viewing with both eyes
MSRP $549.99

**CARL ZEISS VICTORY
COMPACT POINT**

**CARL ZEISS
VICTORY Z-POINT**

VICTORY Z-POINT
Weight: 5.65 oz.
Length: 2.5 in.
Power: 1X
Features: Acquisition sight for shotguns, rifles, and handguns; dual-source illuminated: a solar cell for daylight hours and battery power for dark; red dot automatically adapts to brightness of surroundings and can be regulated manually; available for Weaver or Picatinny mounts
MSRP $599.99

Davide Pedersoli & C.

150 UNIVERSAL CREEDMOOR SIGHT, MIDDLE AND LONG RANGE, MODELS USA 465 AND 430

Features: Tang sight with elevation and windage adjustment in the eye piece; for long-distance target shooting both with muzzle-loading and breech-loading rifles; 2.1875–2.3125-in. between two mounting holes; 2- and 3-in. elevation adjustments

USA 430 Long Range: **$220.00**
USA 465 Middle Range: **$215.00**

ENGLISH REAR SIGHT, MODEL USA 428

Features: Rear sight with convex base, with two adjustable and folding leaves

From: **$125.00**

FIBER OPTIC FRONT AND REAR SIGHT, MODEL USA 409

Features: Front sight and rear sight set for muzzleloading rifles (Model 410 for breechloaders); front sight with dovetail base; rear sight with base for octagonal barrel

From: **$125.00**

FOLDING FRONT SIGHT

Features: Globe sight for long-range when raised, or fold down for built-in blade for close range; ball/detent locking mechanism; 3/8-in. dovetail base; 1/2-in. high

From: **$95.00**

GHOST CREEDMOOR SIGHT-USA 422

Features: A tang sight inspired by some models in use in the 1800s, economic, functional, and useful for hunting; adjustable in elevation and windage; can fit several gun types; small eye piece ring enables a quick, instinctive aim at the target; when quickly shouldering the rifle, the open ring provides a clear sight picture with low light condition; distance between the two mounting holes is 1 3/4-in.

From: **$80.00**

"SOULE TYPE" MIDDLE RANGE SET, MODEL USA 170

Features: Wooden-box set including Soule XL Middle Range Sight; tunnel front sight with a micrometric screw for windage adjustment, spirit level, and fifteen interchangeable inserts; professional "Hadley Style" eyepiece with eight varying diameter viewing holes, depending on available light, on a rotating disk which can be selected without disassembling or loosening the eyepiece, and a rubber ring on the eyepiece; six interchangeable glass bubbles (spirit level) with different colors for varying light conditions; 3-in. elevation adjustment

From: **$735.00**

SPIRIT LEVEL TUNNEL SIGHT ADJUSTABLE WITH 12 INSERTS SET, MODEL USA 425

Features: Spirit level tunnel sight with micrometer adjustment for windage, equipped with twelve interchangeable inserts; also available in 15 and 18 insert sets

From: **$25.00**

U.S. MODEL 1879 SPRINGFIELD TRAPDOOR REAR SIGHT, MODEL USA 473

Features: Sometimes referred to as "Buckhorn" style; used on Trapdoor rifles from 1874 until superseded by Buffington style in 1884; side ramps are graduated to 500 yds and the ladder to 1500 yds; slide has windage adjustment

From: **$130.00**

PEDERSOLI UNIVERSAL CREEDMOOR SIGHT–430

PEDERSOLI ENGLISH REAR SIGHT–428

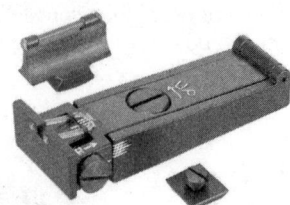

FIBER OPTIC FRONT AND REAR SIGHT–409

PEDERSOLI FOLDING FRONT SIGHT

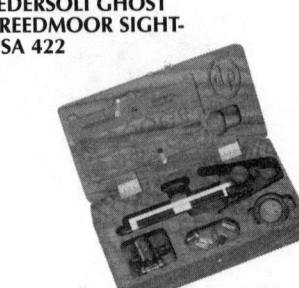

PEDERSOLI GHOST CREEDMOOR SIGHT-USA 422

PEDERSOLI "SOULE TYPE" MIDDLE RANGE SET-170

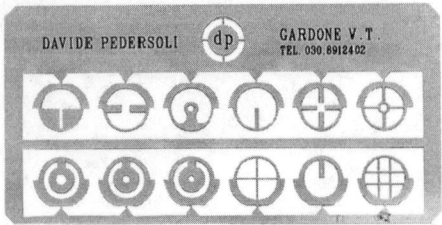

PEDERSOLI U.S. MODEL 1879 SPRINGFIELD TRAPDOOR REAR SIGHT–473

PEDERSOLI SPIRIT LEVEL TUNNEL SIGHT ADJUSTABLE–425

EOTech

HOLOGRAPHIC HYBRID SIGHT (HHS)

Power: 3X
Eye Relief: 2.2 in.
Features: The HHS kits combine the speed of the EXPS holographic weapon sight and the extended range versatility of the G33 magnifier; available in three configurations: Sight I houses the EXPS3 red dot; Sight II houses the EXPS2 red dot; and the Sight III houses with the 518.2 red-dot that takes AA batteries

Sight I:	**$1179.00**
Sight II:	**$1079.00**
Sight III:	**$1039.00**

EOTECH
HOLOGRAPHIC
HYBRID SIGHT

MODEL 300 BLACKOUT

Weight: 9 oz.
Length: 3.8 in.
Power: 1X
Field of View: 90 ft @ 100 yds
Eye Relief: Unlimited
Features: Designed with tactical shooters in mind, this optic offers a two-dot ballistic drop reticle that allows the shooter to zero either subsonic or supersonic rounds in the same reticle pattern; offered in the XPS2 platform, it is the shortest and lightest HWS sight available; its size and weight make it convenient for hunters, military and law enforcement officers to carry; the single compact lithium 123 battery configuration opens up more space on the rail for rear iron sights or magnifiers
MSRP **$549.00**

EOTECH MODEL
300 BLACKOUT

EOTECH MODEL
512 LASER
BATTERY CAP

MODEL 512 LASER BATTERY CAP2

Weight: 12.6 oz.
Length: 5.4 in.
Power: 1X
Field of View: N/A
Twilight Factor:
Eye Relief: N/A
Features: Submersible to 10 feet; twenty daylight settings; fully adjustable windage and elevation
MSRP **$729.00**

MODEL 552 LASER BATTERY CAP

Weight: 13.4 oz.
Length: 5.4 in.
Power: 1X
Field of View: N/A
Eye Relief: N/A
Features: Submersible to 33 feet; twenty daylight settings, ten additional settings for Gen I through III+ night vision devices; fully adjustable windage and elevation
MSRP **$979.00**

EOTECH MODEL
552 LASER
BATTERY CAP2

XPS2-RF

Weight: 7 oz.
Length: 3.8 in.
Power: 1X
Eye Relief: Unlimited
Features: Holographic sight specifically for the rimfire rifle; integrated $^3/_8$-in. dovetail mount (not compatible with 1-in. Weaver or Picatinny rails); lightweight for smaller platforms; single transverse 123 battery to reduce sight length; shortened base; this model is only intended and warranted for calibers .22 LR or smaller
MSRP **$405.00**

EOTECH XPS2-RF

OPTICS

Konus

KONUS SIGHTPRO ATOMIC 2.0

KONUS SIGHTPRO ATOMIC QR

KONUS SIGHTPRO PTS1

KONUS SIGHTPRO TR

KONUS SIGHTPRO FISSION 2.0

SIGHTPRO ATOMIC 2.0
Weight: 3.8 oz.
Length: 2.4 in.
Power: 1X
Field of View: 76 ft @ 100 yds
Eye Relief: N/A
Features: Illuminated reticle dots; fits both Picatinny and Weaver rails
MSRP $189.99

SIGHTPRO ATOMIC QR
Weight: 6.5 oz.
Length: 2.5 in.
Power: 1X

Field of View: N/A
Eye Relief: N/A
Features: Illuminated reticle dots; fits both Picatinny and Weaver rails
MSRP $229.99

SIGHTPRO FISSION 2.0
Weight: 1.76 oz.
Length: 1.7 in.
Power: 1X
Field of View: 115 ft @ 100 yds
Eye Relief: N/A

Features: Illuminated reticle dots; fits both Picatinny and Weaver rails
MSRP $199.99

SIGHTPRO PTS1
Weight: 14.1 oz.
Length: 12.2 in.
Power: 3X
Obj. Dia.: 32mm
Field of View: 36.6 ft @ 100 yds
Eye Relief: 4.5 in.
Features: Shock-, water-, and fog-proof; illuminated reticle dots; fits both Picatinny and Weaver rails
MSRP $399.99

SIGHTPRO TR
Weight: 13 oz.
Length: 4.75 in.
Power: 1X
Field of View: N/A
Eye Relief: N/A
Features: Illuminated reticle dots; four different reticle patterns
MSRP $219.99

Leapers, Inc.

LEAPERS/UTG ITA RED/GREEN CLOSE QUARTERS COMBAT (CQB) DOT OR T-DOT SIGHT

UTG ITA RED/GREEN CLOSE QUARTERS COMBAT (CQB) DOT OR T-DOT SIGHT
Weight: 13.1 oz.
Length: 6.1 in.
Power: 1X
Field of View: 85 ft @ 100 yds
Eye Relief: Unlimited
Features: Completely sealed; shockproof, fogproof; and rainproof; 4 MOA red/green single dot reticle or quick-to-acquire red/green T-dot reticle; premium zero lockable and zero resettable target turrets; TactEdge angled integral sunshade reduces glare off the lens while maintaining superb light transmission clarity
MSRP $72.97

Leatherwood/Hi-Lux

**LEATHERWOOD/
HI-LUX TAC-DOT**

TAC-DOT
Weight: 2.1 oz.
Length: 2.5 in.
Power: 1X
Obj. Dia.: 21x16mm
Field of View: 30x22 ft @ 100 yds
Eye Relief: N/A
Features: Elevation and windage adjustments are 50 MOA per revolution; special illumination circuit is designed to control the illuminated dot size in a consistent shape and size; dot size is 4 MOA; light sensor will control the brightness of the dot automatically based on the light situation
MSRP $129.95

Leica

LEICA CRF 2000-B

RANGEMASTER CRF 2000-B
Weight: 7 oz.
Length: 4.25 in.
Power: 7X
Obj. Dia. 24mm
Field of View: 347 ft. @ 1,000 yds
Eye Relief: 15mm
Twilight Factor: 13
Features: A 2,000-yard rangefinder that calculates the corresponding ballistic curve via Leica's new ABC ballistic program, which integrates angle of incline, temperature, barometric pressure, and ammunition type data; user can select readings in meters or yards. Turn-down rubber eye cups, roof prism glass with P4 phase correcting coating, HDC multicoating, Aquadura coating, and carbon fiber-reinforced housing are standard. Watertight to 1 meter
MSRP $799.99

**LEICA RANGEMASTER
CRF 1600-R**

RANGEMASTER CRF 1600-R
Weight: 8.1 oz.
Length: 4.4 in.
Power: 7X
Obj. Dia.: 24mm
Field of View: 345 ft @ 100 yds
Features: Point-of-aim correction, angle, temperature, and barometric pressure readings; ABC intelligent ballistics program; LED display; range up to 1600 yds; waterproof
MSRP $599.00

Leupold & Stevens

LEUPOLD D-EVO

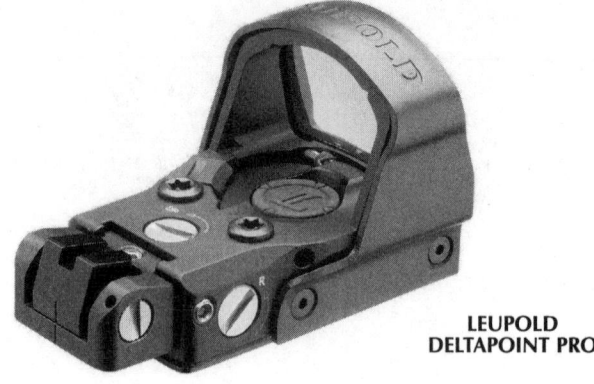

LEUPOLD DELTAPOINT PRO

LEUPOLD LEOPOLD CARBINE OPTIC (LCO)

D-EVO
Weight: 13.8 oz.
Length: 4.6 in.
Power: 6X
Obj. Dia.: 20mm
Field of View: 15.7 ft @ 100 yds
Eye Relief: 3.4 in.
Features: Bullet drop compensation; water- and fogproof; 1/10th MIL click adjustment; 6061-T6 aircraft quality aluminum
MSRP $1949.00

DELTAPOINT PRO
Weight: 1.95 oz.
Length: 1.82 in.
Power: 1X
Field of View: N/A
Eye Relief: Unlimited
Features: Water- and fogproof; DiamondCoat; removable, adjustable rear sight; tool-less, spring actuated battery compartment; illuminated reticle available
MSRP $519.00

LEOPOLD CARBINE OPTIC (LCO)
Weight: 9.5 oz.
Length: 3.6 in.
Power: 1X
Obj. Dia.: 32mm
Field of View: N/A
Eye Relief: Unlimited
Features: Nitrogen filled; water- and fogproof; ½ MOA field click; 6061-T6 aircraft quality aluminum
MSRP $1299.00

Lucid Optics, LLC

LUCID HD7 RED DOT SIGHT

HD7 RED DOT SIGHT
Weight: 13 oz.
Length: 5.5 in.
Power: 1X
Obj.Dia.: 34mm
Field of View: 44 ft @ 100 yds
Eye Relief: Unlimited
Features: Third generation unit; integral Picatinny rail and reversible mounting pins for bullpup-style firearms; manual and a Auto-Brightness with twelve brightness settings; four operator-selectable reticles based on a 2 MOA dot with ½ MOA click adjustments; parallax free, it is powered by one AAA battery; the frame is cast aluminum armored in chemical rubber and is available with a 2x screw-in eyepiece; available in tan
Black: $249.00
Tan: $259.00

OPTICS

Meopta USA

MEOPTA MEORED

MEOPTA MEOSIGHT III

MEORED
Weight: 1.05 oz.
Length: 1.85 in.
Power: 1X
Field of View: N/A
Eye Relief: N/A
Features: Designed for use on handguns with cutout slides, AR platforms, or shotguns, the MeoRed is well suited for tactical use as well as three-gun competitions, target shooting, and hunting close-range moving game such as hogs. It is made from aircraft-grade aluminum alloy and is fully waterproof and shockproof.
MSRP $574.99

MEOSIGHT III
Weight: 1.29 oz.
Length: 1.8 in.
Power: 1X
Field of View: N/A
Eye Relief: N/A
Features: Picatinny quick release mount; illuminated reticle; ideal for handguns, shotguns, and tactical weapons
MSRP $459.99

Millet Tactical

MILLETT SP SERIES RED DOT

SP SERIES RED DOT
Features: Precision-click adjustments; dot intensity control with eleven settings; waterproof; shockproof; available with 1 in. or 30mm tube; available 3 MOA dot, 5 MOA dot, and 3, 5, 8, 10 MOA, multi dot; available in matte or silver
MSRP . . . . $79.95–$109.95

Nikko Stirling

NIKKO STIRLING NSLX2 RED DOT

NSLX2 RED DOT
Weight: 15 oz.
Length: 6 in.
Power: 1X32
Field of View: N/A
Eye Relief: Unlimited
Features: Tactical-style; five brightness-intensity settings; Picatinny and 3/8 in. mounting brackets included
MSRP $199.00

OPTICS

Nikon

ACULON AL11
Weight: 4.4 oz.
Power: 6X
Obj. Dia.: 20mm
Range: 6–550 yd
Features: Ultra-compact for improved portability; multilayered lens coatings for higher light transmittance
MSRP $139.95

NIKON ACULON AL11

NIKON PROSTAFF
7 LASER
RANGEFINDER

PROSTAFF 7 LASER RANGEFINDER
Weight: 5.8 oz.
Length: 4.4 in.
Power: 6X
Obj. Dia.: 21mm
Exit Pupil: 3.5mm
Field of View: 11–600 yds
Eye Relief: 0.7 in.
Features: Multi-coated optics; waterproof; fogproof; Tru Target Technology; switchable display; Nikon's ID Technology; angle compensation
MSRP $299.95

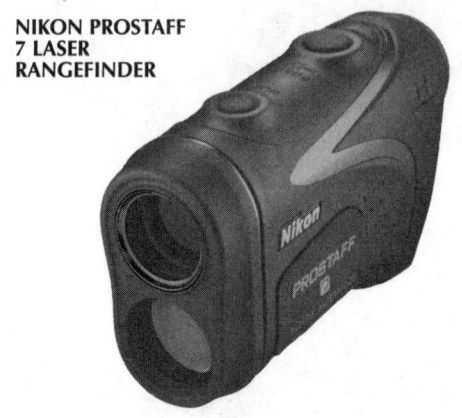

SIG Sauer

SIG SAUER BRAVO4

SIG SAUER ROMEO1

BRAVO4
Weight: 14.8 oz.
Length: 6.25 in.
Power: 4X
Field of View: 53 ft @ 100 yds
Eye Relief: 2.2 in.
Features: MegaView system utilizes an advanced prism and ocular design yielding 43 percent greater field of view than the competitive prismatic battle sights; MOTAC (Motion Activated Illumination) powers up when it senses motion and powers down when it does not; notably flat, distortion-free image for edge-to-edge clarity by means of a combination of low dispersion glass and aspherical lens design; lightweight yet durable magnesium housing with integrated Picatinny top rail for additional accessories such as MRDs and lasers; adjustable eyepiece with +/- 2 diopter correction; dependable IPX-8 waterproof (to 400 mbar or 13 ft) and fogproof performance
MSRP $1559.99

ROMEO1
Weight: 0.8 oz.
Length: 1.8 in.
Power: 1X
Field of View: N/A
Eye Relief: Unlimited
Features: Also available with a universal mount with rear sight dovetail adapters for the most popular handguns on the market; also available with either an M1913 Picatinny or KeyMod Rail interface for use with today's MSR platforms; molded glass aspheric lens with high performance coatings for superior light transmittance and zero distortion; manual illumination controls that remember

OPTICS

SIG Sauer

SIG SAUER ROMEO3

SIG SAUER ROMEO4

SIG SAUER ROMEO7

your last used settings; MOTAC (Motion Activated Illumination) powers up when it senses motion and powers down when it does not; top-loading CR1632 battery, allowing for quick battery replacement without having to remove the sight from the firearm; extremely strong and lightweight aircraft grade CNC magnesium housing ensuring a lifetime of reliable service; dependable waterproof (IPX-7 rated for complete immersion up to 1 meter) and fogproof performance
MSRP . . . . $359.99–$479.99

ROMEO3
Weight: 1.4 oz.
Length: 2.4 in.
Power: 1X
Field of View: N/A
Eye Relief: Unlimited
Features: High transmittance red notch reflector for excellent brightness, light transmittance, and zero distortion; 3 MOA red dot with multiple intensity settings ensures rapid target engagement under a full range of lighting conditions; MOTAC (Motion Activated Illumination) powers up when it senses motion and powers down when it does not; side-loading CR2032 battery, allowing for quick battery replacement without having

to remove the sight from the firearm; extremely strong and lightweight aircraft grade CNC Aluminum housing ensures a lifetime of reliable service; dependable waterproof (IPX-7 rated for complete water immersion up to 1 meter) and fogproof performance
MSRP $479.99

ROMEO4
Weight: 3.2 oz.–3.4 oz.
Length: 2.65 in.
Power: 1X
Field of View: N/A
Eye Relief: Unlimited
Features: Parallax-free so point-of-aim is point-of-impact and the red dot remains parallel to the bore of your firearm; dual reticle option; on select models, toggle between 2 MOA red dot or circle dot; utilizes an ultra-efficient red LED illumination system for daylight visibility with extended runtime and mil-spec objective coatings to limit downrange light leakage in tactical situations; MOTAC (Motion Activated Illumination System) powers up when it senses motion and powers down when it does not; 5000+ hour battery life; side-loading CR2032 battery, allowing for quick battery replacement; extremely strong and lightweight aircraft grade CNC alumi-

num housing ensures a lifetime of reliable service; dependable waterproof (IPX-7 rated for complete water immersion up to 1 atmosphere) and fogproof performance
MSRP $419.99

ROMEO7
Weight: 12.5 oz.
Length: 4.75 in.
Power: 1X
Field of View: N/A
Eye Relief: Unlimited
Features: Low dispersion glass lens design with high-performance coatings for excellent light transmittance and zero distortion; 2 MOA dot is optimal for close quarters battle to mid-range target engagement; MOTAC (Motion Activated Illumination) powers up when it senses motion and powers down when it does not; 62,500 hours of continuous battery life in medium illumination setting; ready to mount with a standard QD mount provided, but can be customized with vertical spacers to fit a variety of systems; dependable waterproof (IPX-7 rated for complete water immersion up to 1 meter) and fogproof performance
MSRP $359.99

Steiner

STEINER MICRO REFLEX SIGHT (MRS)

MICRO REFLEX SIGHT (MRS)
Weight: 2.5 oz.
Length: N/A
Power: 1X
Field of View: N/A
Eye Relief: Unlimited
Features: Picatinny mount; waterproof; holographic sight; adjustable for windage and elevation; illuminated
MSRP $459.99

OPTICS

Trijicon

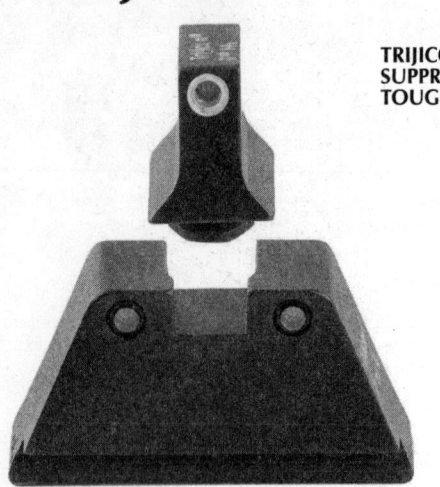

TRIJICON GLOCK SUPPRESSOR BRIGHT & TOUGH NIGHT SIGHTS

TRIJICON MINIATURE RIFLE OPTIC (MRO)

TRIJICON RMR ADJUSTABLE LED RM06

TRIJICON SRS 1X38

clicks allow for quick windage and elevation adjustments; eight brightness settings; reticle can be manually adjusted; also in Dual-Illuminated RMR with 13.0 MOA dot, 7.0 MOA dot, 9.0 MOA dot, and triangle-reticle RMR LED with 3.25 MOA dot and 6.5 MOA dot

Adjustable LED: **$708.00**
Dual Illuminated: **$577.00**
LED: **$655.00**

SRS (SEALED REFLEX SIGHT) 1X38

Weight: 13.8 oz.
Length: 3.75 in.
Power: 1X
Obj. Dia.: 38mm
Features: Body length of only 3.75 inches virtually eliminates the "tube effect" common with other, competitive red-dot sights; field of view provides no obstruction to shooters; LED 1.75 MOA aiming point with 10 brightness settings; SRS powered by solar panel and AA battery; parallax free objective lens; available in Colt-Style flattop mount or Quick Release flattop mount
MSRP: . . . . **$1150.00–$1250.00**

BRIGHT & TOUGH SUPPRESSOR NIGHT SIGHTS

Features: Three-dot iron sights; shock-resistant design; increase night-fire accuracy by as much as 5x; available for a wide variety of Glock, FNH, H&K, SIG Sauer, Smith & Wesson, and Springfield Armory handguns
MSRP **$145.00**

MINIATURE RIFLE OPTIC (MRO)

Weight: 4.1 oz.
Length: 2.6 in.
Power: 1X
Field of View: N/A

Eye Relief: Unlimited
Features: Large viewing area; adjustable brightness settings; ambidextrous brightness control; easy-to-set adjusters; aircraft-grade aluminum housing; surface-flush adjusters; waterproof to 30 meters; single lithium battery
MSRP . . . . **$579.00–$679.00**

RMR ADJUSTABLE LED RM06

Weight: 1.2 oz.
Length: 1.77 in.
Power: 1X
Features: LED sight powered by standard CR2032 battery; rugged forged aluminum; adjusters with audible

Truglo

TRUGLO TRITON 30MM TRI-COLOR TACTICAL TG8230GB

TRUGLO TRU-TEC RED DOT

TRITON 30MM TRI-COLOR TACTICAL RED DOT

Weight: 6.4 oz.
Length: 5.2 in.
Power: 1X
Obj. Dia.: 30mm
Field of View: N/A
Eye Relief: N/A
Features: Weaver style mount; multi-coated lenses; tri-color illuminated reticle; two versions: Model #TG8230B has 5 MOA single dot. Model #TG8230GB has 3 MOA center dot and surrounding aiming ring
MSRP . . . . **$94.00–$110.00**

TRU-TEC RED DOT

Weight: 4.91 oz.–12.9 oz.
Length: 2.4 in.–5.78 in.
Power: 1X
Field of View: 46 ft @ 100 yds, 68 ft @ 100 yds
Eye Relief: Unlimited
Features: Option of 20mm or 30mm objective lens; optional integrated green or red laser with 30mm lens; digital; push-button controls; multiple brightness settings; programmable auto-off feature; click windage and elevation adjustments; wide field of view; shock resistant; waterproof/fog-proof; mounts to standard Picatinny or Weaver-style rails
MSRP . . . . **$233.00–$368.00**

Vortex Optics

VORTEX SPARC II

VORTEX SPARC AR

VORTEX SPITFIRE AR PRISM

SPARC II

Weight: 5.9 oz.
Length: 3.1 in.
Power: 1X
Field of View: N/A
Eye Relief: N/A
Features: Shock-, water-, and fog-proof; illuminated red dot
MSRP **$259.99**

SPARC AR

Weight: 7.5 oz.
Length: 2.9 in.
Power: 1X
Field of View: N/A
Eye Relief: Unlimited
Features: Fully multi-coated; bright red dot highly visible in daylight; ten variable illumination settings; water-proof, fogproof, and shockproof; hard anodized finish; twelve-hour auto-shutdown feature maximizes battery life
MSRP **$259.99**

SPITFIRE AR PRISM

Weight: 11.2 oz.
Length: 4.3 in.
Power: 1X
Field of View: 29 ft @ 100 yds
Eye Relief: 3.8 in.
Features: Fully multi-coated; prism-based design; twelve variable illumination settings; waterpoof and shock-proof; hard anodized finish; red or green reticle option
MSRP **$349.99**

OPTICS

Vortex Optics

VORTEX SPITFIRE PRISM

VORTEX STRIKEFIRE II

VORTEX VENOM

VORTEX VIPER

SPITFIRE PRISM
Weight: 12.2 oz.
Length: 5.5 in.
Power: 3X
Field of View: 31.5 ft @ 100 yds
Eye Relief: 2.8 in.
Features: Shock-, water-, and fogproof; illuminated red dot; 1X available
MSRP . . . . $399.00–$449.99

STRIKEFIRE II
Weight: 7.2 oz.
Length: 5.6 in.
Power: 1X
Field of View: N/A
Eye Relief: N/A
Features: Shock-, water-, and fogproof; illuminated red dot; red/green dot cantilever and low mount models available
MSRP $239.99

VENOM
Weight: 1.1 oz.
Length: 1.9 in.
Power: 1X
Field of View: N/A
Eye Relief: Unlimited
Features: Bright red dot; Picatinny mount; choice of 3 or 6 MOA dots; machined aluminum housing
MSRP $329.99

VIPER
Weight: 1.37 oz.
Length: 1.8 in.
Power: 1X
Field of View: N/A
Eye Relief: Unlimited
Features: Bright red dot; Picatinny mount; 6 MOA dot
MSRP $329.00

Weaver

WEAVER MICRO DOT SIGHT

MICRO DOT SIGHT
Weight: 2.8 oz.
Length: 1.9 in.
Power: 1X
Eye Relief: Unlimited
Features: 4 MOA red dot reticle; matte finish; mounts to most firearms; adjustable brightness
MSRP $123.95

OPTICS

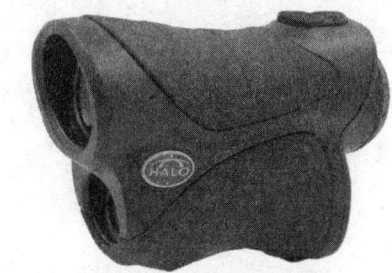

HALO OPTICS XRAY 600

HALO OPTICS XRAY 900

HALO OPTICS XTANIUM 600

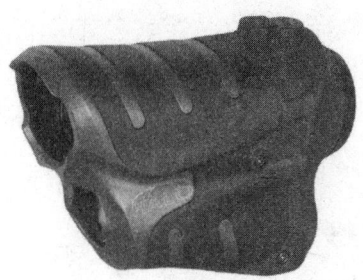

HALO OPTICS XTANIUM 1000

XRAY 600
Weight: 5.3 oz.
Power: 6X
Obj. Dia.: 23mm
Range: up to 600 yd
Features: Water resistent; Angle Intelligence compensation technology
MSRP **$149.99**

XRAY 900
Weight: N/A
Power: 9X
Obj. Dia.: N/A
Range: up to 900 yd
Features: Water resistent; Angle Intelligence compensation technology
MSRP **$199.99**

XTANIUM 600
Weight: N/A
Power: 8X
Obj. Dia.: N/A
Range: up to 600 yd
Features: OLED display for easy use (organic light emitting diode); AI Technology accounts for slope to the target; scan mode allows for constant ranging; precise to +/- 1 yard; water resistant
MSRP **$290.99**

XTANIUM 1000
Weight: N/A
Power: 8X
Obj. Dia.: N/A
Range: up to 1000 yd
Features: OLED display for easy use (organic light emitting diode); AI Technology accounts for slope to the target; scan mode allows for constant ranging; precise to +/- 1 yard; water resistant
MSRP **$299.99**

OPTICS

Leupold & Stevens

RX-850I TBR
Weight: 7 oz.
Power: 6X
Obj. Dia.: N/A
Range: up to 865 yd
Features: Ergonomic design; digitally enhanced accuracy; True Ballistic Range technology; quick set menu; selection of three different reticles; built-in inclinometer
MSRP **$324.00**

RX1001I TBR/W WITH DNA DIGITAL LASER RANGEFINDER
Weight: 7.8 oz.
Power: 6X
Obj. Dia.: N/A
Range: up to 1215 yd
Features: Digitally enhanced accuracy; True Ballistic Range technology; quick set menu; advanced OLED technology; built-in inclinometer; fully multi-coated; fold down rubber eyecups; available in black/gray, Mossy Oak Blaze Camo, and Mossy Oak Infinity finishes
MSRP . . . . **$454.00–$549.00**

LEUPOLD RX-850I TBR

LEUPOLD RX1001I TBR/W
WITH DNA DIGITAL LASER
RANGEFINDER

Redfield

RAIDER 650 AND 650A
Weight: 5.7 oz.
Power: 6X
Obj. Dia.: 23mm
Range: up to 650 yd
Features: Fully multi-coated optics; high contrast LCD display; lightweight; compact; weatherproof; availabe in Mossy Oak in 650A model
MSRP . . . . **$214.99–$279.99**

REDFIELD RAIDER 650 AND 650A

MUZZLELOADING BULLETS

BULLETS

Alexander Arms

ALEXANDER ARMS .50 BEOWULF 200-GRAIN POLYCASE INCEPTOR ARX PROJECTILES

ALEXANDER ARMS .50 BEOWULF 200-GRAIN POLYCASE INCEPTOR ARX PROJECTILES

Features: Muzzle velocity of 2,500 FPS; high muzzle energy of 2,775 foot-pounds; metal-filled polymer; tri-flute design; hydrodynamic shock during impact; wings fracture away creating secondary fragments and additional wound channels
Available in: .50 Beowulf
Box 20: **$33.58**

Barnes Bullets

PRECISION MATCH AMMUNITION

Features: Engineered for precision at extreme distances, with very low standard deviations; Loaded with Barnes match-grade OTM (Open Tip Match) boattail
Available in: 5.56 NATO, .308 Win., .300 Win. Mag., .338 Lapua Mag.
Box 20: . . . .**$26.99–$49.99**

RANGE AR

Features: Higher velocity, flatter trajectory, and ultimate accuracy; factory-fresh brass paired with a lead-free, copper-jacketed, zinc core OTFB (Open Tip Flat Base) provides excellent performance in ARs with quick twist barrels; specialized propellants optimized for ARs of any barrel length
Available in: 5.56x45mm, .300 BLK
Box 20 5.56: **$19.20**
Box 20 .300 AAC: **$21.50**

TAC-XPD AMMUNITION

Features: Loaded with Barnes TAC-XP bullets, the all-copper construction and very large, deep hollow-point cavity expand, penetrate, and perform consistently and optimally for personal and home defense
Available in: .357 Mag., .380 ACP, 9mm Luger +P, .40 S&W, .45 ACP +P
Box 20: . . . .**$24.59–$41.17**

VOR-TX AMMUNITION

Features: Provides maximum tissue and bone destruction, pass-through penetration, and devastating energy transfer; multiple grooves in the bullet's shank reduce pressure and improve accuracy; bullets open instantly on contact causing the nose to peel back into four sharp-edged copper petals destroying tissue, bone, and vital organs for a quick, humane kill
Available in: **Rifle:** .223 Rem., 5.56 NATO, .22-250 Rem., .243 Win., 25-06 Rem. .260 Rem., .270 Win., .270 WSM, 7mm-08 Rem., .280 Rem., 7mm Rem. Mag., .30-30 Win., .300 BLK, .308 Win., .30-06 Spfd., .300 WSM, .300 Win Mag., .300 RUM, .300 Wby. Mag., .338 Win. Mag., .338 Lapua, .35 Whelen, .45-70 Govt., 9.3x62mm, 7x64 Brenneke.
Handgun: .357 Mag., 10mm, .41 Rem. Mag., .44 Mag., .45 Colt, .454 Casull
Safari: .375 H&H Mag., .416 Rem. Mag., .416 Rigby, .458 Win. Mag., .458 Lott, .470 Nitro Express, .500 Nitro Express
Euro: 7x64 Brenneke, .308 Win., .30-06 Spfd., 8x57 JS, 9.3x62mm
Rifle: . . . .**$23.00–$120.58**
Safari: . . . .**$82.84–$165.70**
Handgun: . . . .**$24.59–$41.17**

BARNES BULLETS TAC-XPD AMMUNITION

BARNES BULLETS VOR-TX AMMUNITION

Black Hills Ammunition

Rifle Ammunition
BLACK HILLS GOLD

Features: Coupling the finest components in the industry with bullets by Barnes; lead-free non-toxic rounds; high-performance hunting ammunition
Available in: .22–250 Rem., .243 Win., .25-06 Rem., .260 Rem., .270 Win., 7mm Rem. Mag., .300 Win. Mag., .308 Win., .30-06 Spfd., .338 Lapua
Box 20: . . . .**$33.15–$56.19**

FACTORY NEW RIFLE

Features: Coupling the finest components in the industry with bullets by manufacturers such as Hornady, Barnes, and Nosler; high-performance hunting ammunition; certain calibers available in Molycoat
Available in: .223 Rem., .308 Win. Match, .300 Win. Mag., .338 Lapua, .338 Norma Mag. , .300 Whisper, 5.56 NATO
Box 20, 50: . . . . . .**$30.69–$117.06**

REMANUFACTURED

Features: Ammunition designed with the practice shooter in mind, with

BLACK HILLS FACTORY NEW RIFLE

incredible accuracy for a great price point; the same ammunition used by the U.S. Army Marksmanship Unit in 600 yd matches; has the capability to produce 2-in. groups at 300m
Available in: .223 Rem. (also in Molycoat), .40 S&W
.223 Rem.: . . . .**$28.13–$55.01**
.40 S&W: **$28.74**

Black Hills Ammunition

Handgun Ammunition

COWBOY ACTION
Features: Designed to meet the needs of cowboy-action pistol shooters with its new virgin brass and premium-quality hard-cast bullets; velocities are moderate to provide low recoil and excellent accuracy
Available in: .32 H&R, .32-20 Win., .38 LC, .38 Spl., .38-40 Win., .44-40 Win., .44 Russian, .44 Spl., .44 Colt, .45 Schofield, .45 Colt, .38-55 Win., .357 Mag.
Box 50: . . . . **$32.58–$38.98**

FACTORY NEW HANDGUN
Features: Used by the U.S. Military in all four branches for its reliability
Available in: .32 H&R Mag., .380 ACP, 9mm Luger, .38 Spl., .357 Mag., .40 S&W, .44 Mag., .45 ACP
Box 20: . . . . **$14.57–$53.70**

BLACK HILLS COWBOY ACTION

Brenneke USA

28 GAUGE SLUGS
Features: The moderate recoil makes the 28 Ga. a perfect slug for young hunters who will be introduced to slug shooting; 28 Ga. is a multi-talent: small game, home defense, and all around shooting
Available in: 28 Ga. (2¾ in.)
Box 5: **$11.99**

BLACK MAGIC MAGNUM
Features: The Black Magic Magnum and Black Magic Short Magnum are two of the most powerful cartridges available on the market, offering tremendous knockdown power up to 100/60 yds; clean speed coating reduces lead fouling inside the barrel by almost 100 percent
Available in: 12 Ga. (3 in.)
Box 5: **$12.99**

CLASSIC MAGNUM
Features: Invented by Wilhelm Brenneke in 1898, the classic is the ancestor of all modern shotgun slugs; this state-of-the-art slug provides long-range stopping power, consistently flat trajectories, and a patented B.E.T. wad column
Available in: 12 Ga. (2¾ in.), 16 Ga. (2¾ in.)
Box 5: **$9.99**

CLOSE ENCOUNTER
Features: The .410 Close Encounter is the perfect choice if you are a fan of 2½-in. .410/.45 revolvers. They are powerful without having bad recoil, and they have an incredible frontal area and the legendary Brenneke penetration
Available in: .410 (2½ in.)
Box 5: **$8.99**

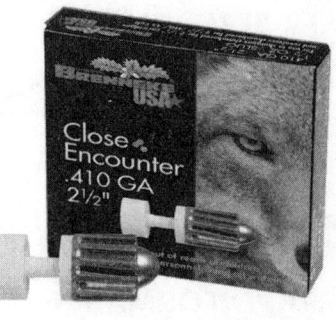

BRENNEKE CLOSE ENCOUNTER

Brenneke USA

HEAVY FIELD SHORT MAGNUM GREEN LIGHTNING

Features: The original "Emerald" slug with patented B.E.T wad and famous stopping power; for all barrel types; range up to 100 yds.
Available in: 12 Ga., 20 Ga. (2¾ in.)
12-gauge: **$9.99**
20-gauge: **$9.49**

K.O. SLUG

Features: The KO is an improved Foster-type slug with excellent penetration; range up to 60 yds; for all barrel types
Available in: 12 Ga. (2¾ in.), 20 Ga. (2 ¾ in.)
20-gauge: **$5.52**
12-gauge: **$6.69**

MAGNUM CRUSH

Features: Delivers a force of more than 3.800 ft/lbs, weighs a full 1 ½ oz. / 666 gr. and the flat trajectory is ideal for bigger game; special coating to reduce lead fouling and broad ribs for optimum groove engagement
Available in: 12 Ga. (3 in.)
Box 5: **$14.99**

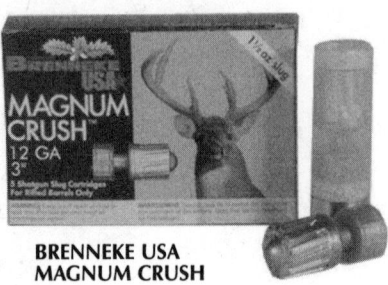

BRENNEKE USA MAGNUM CRUSH

SUPERSABOT

Features: Has a movable core, lead free construction and an effective range up to more than 100 yds; mushrooms up to 1-in.
Available in: 12 Ga. (2¾ in.), 12 Ga. (3 in.)
Box 5: **$18.99**

BRENNEKE HEAVY FIELD SHORT MAGNUM GREEN LIGHTNING SLUGS

Browning Ammunition

BROWNING BPR PERFORMANCE RIMFIRE

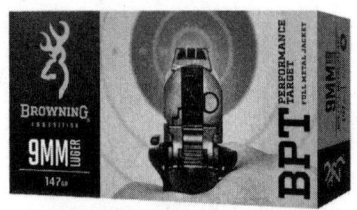

BROWNING BPT PERFORMANCE TARGET

BROWNING BPT TARGET LOAD

BROWNING BXC BIG GAME

BPR PERFORMANCE RIMFIRE

Features: BPR provides reliability and performance in 22 long rifle ammunition that you can expect from The Best There Is in rimfire ammunition.
Available in: .22 LR
Box 100: **$10.99**
Box 1,000: **$104.99**

BPT PERFORMANCE TARGET

Features: BPT Performance Target is a premium training product that can be used to hone your handgun skills. It is a matched training counterpart to BXP Personal Defense.
Available in: .40 S&W, .45 ACP, .380 ACP, 9mm Luger
Box 50 (.380 ACP): . . . . **$17.99–$20.9**
Box 50 (9mm): . . . . . . **$14.99–$17.99**
Box 50 (.40 S&W): . . . **$19.99–$20.99**

Box 50 (.45 ACP): . . . . **$20.99–$23.99**

BPT TARGET LOAD

Features: BPT Performance Target utilizes premium, hard shot to help deliver tight patterns and maximum target breaking energy. The smooth hull allows for a sleek profile and smooth ejection.
Available in: 2¾-in for 12-ga., 16-ga., and 20-ga., No. 7 ½ shot all gauges, No. 8 shot 12- and 20-ga. Handicap and Heavy Target options in 12-ga.
Box 25 (12-ga.): **$9.99**
Box 25 (16-ga.): **$14.99**
Box 25 (20-ga.): **$9.99**

BXC BIG GAME

Features: BXC Controlled Expansion Terminal Tip is designed specifically for use on big game like elk, moose, mule deer, and bear. The Terminal Tip and bonded bullet design allow for deep penetration through thick, tough hide and bone. The brass tip, heavy bullet weight, and boat-tail are integral components to delivering precision accuracy, maximum downrange velocity, and long-range, on-target performance.
Available in: .270 Win., .30-06 Spfd., .300 Win. Mag., .300 WSM, .308 Win., 7mm Rem. Mag.
Box 20: . . . . **$35.99–$44.99**

BXD UPLAND

Features: BXD Upland Extra Distance launches premium-plated shot at high velocities to achieve premium in-the-field performance. Nickel-plated shot helps keep shot round resulting in high velocity retention and energy transfer as well as tighter downrange patterns.
Available in: 12 (2.75 in., 3 in.), 20

Browning Ammunition

BROWNING BXD UPLAND

BROWNING BXD WATERFOWL

BROWNING BXP PERSONAL DEFENSE

BROWNING BXR RAPID EXPANSION

(2.75 in., 3 in.), 16 (2.75 in.). All gauges in No. 6 shot, 12- and 20-ga. also available in No. 5

Box 25 (12-ga.): $18.99
Box 25 (16-ga.): $17.29
Box 25 (20-ga.): . . . . .$17.29–$18.29

BXD WATERFOWL

Features: BXD Waterfowl Extra Distance is launched at high velocities utilizing an optimized long-range wad and plated round steel shot. Combining round steel with a cutting edge wad design results in a lethal combination of energy retention, penetration, and pattern density that is critical in achieving long-range performance. No. 2, 4, and BB shot sizes available in 12-gauge, No. 2 shot only for 20-gauge.
Available in: 12 (3 in., 3.5 in.), 20 (3 in.)

Box 25 (12-ga.): . . . . .$21.99–$27.99
Box 25 (20-ga.): $19.99

BXP PERSONAL DEFENSE

Features: BXP Personal Defense is designed for superior personal defense performance in reliability, expansion, and penetration. The X-Point is designed to shield the hollow point through intermediate barriers.
Available in: .40 S&W, .45 ACP, .380 ACP, 9mm Luger

Box 50 (.380 ACP): $17.99
Box 50 (9mm): $17.99
Box 50 (.40 S&W): . . .$19.99–$20.99
Box 50 (.45 ACP): $20.99

BXR RAPID EXPANSION

Features: BXR Rapid Expansion Matrix Tip is designed specifically for use on whitetail, blacktail, mule deer, and antelope. The proprietary matrix tip design allows for high downrange velocity and energy retention while also initiating rapid positive expansion. The jacket and tip combination yields precision accuracy and rapid energy transfer, and generates massive knockdown power.
Available in: .243 Win., .270 Win., .30-06 Spfd., .30-30 Win., .300 Win. Mag., .300 WSM, .308 Win.
MSRP . . . .$27.99–$33.99

CCI Ammunition

.22 LONG RANGE AR TACTICAL

Features: This load is designed specifically for AR-style guns being offered in .22 Long Rifle chambering; rounds get excellent accuracy including 1.5-in. at 100 yds for ten-shot groups; this target bullet has a copper-plated round nose for smooth feeding; CCI case, priming, and bullet lube combined with clean-burning powder; 375 rounds per box
Available in: .22 Long Rifle (40 gr.)
Box of 300: $29.95

.22 WIN. MAG. MAXI MAG

Features: A favorite of varmint shooters; 40 gr. TMJ flat nose at 1875 fps, or 40 gr. jacketed HP at 1875 fps; both loads give over 1400 fps from a 6-in. revolver; clean-burning propellants keep actions cleaner; sure-fire CCI priming; reusable plastic box with dispenser lid
Available in: .22 Win. Mag.
Box of 50: $14.95

A17 VARMINT TIP

Features: Optimized for feeding and function in the Savage Arms A17 semiautomatic rifle and can be fired through bolt-action .17 HMR firearms; 100 fps faster than other .17 HMR loads of the same weight; Varmint Tip bullet provides rapid expansion; CCI-made and primed case
Available in: .17 HMR
Box of 50: $18.95
Box of 200 : $73.95

COPPER-22

Features: Non-lead, California-legal bullet; constructed from a unique mix of copper particles and polymer compressed into a potent, 21-grain hollow-point bullet
Available in: .22 LR
Box 50: $10.95

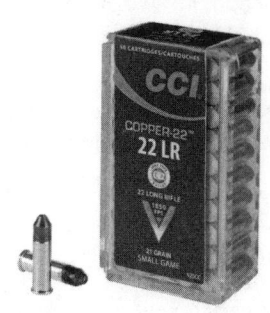

CCI AMMUNITION COPPER-22 (RIMFIRE)

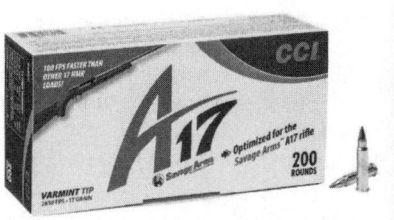

CCI AMMUNITION A17 VARMINT TIP

CCI Ammunition

GREEN TAG

Features: Our first and still most-popular match rimfire product; tight manufacturing and accuracy specs mean you get the consistency and accuracy that the unforgiving field of competition demands; the rimfire match ammo leaves the muzzle sub-sonic which means no buffeting in the transonic zone; clean-burning propellants keep actions cleaner. Sure-fire CCI priming; reusable plastic box with dispenser lid

Available in: .22 LR (40 gr. lead round nose)

Box of 100: . . . . **.$22.95**

HMR TNT

Features: A 17-gr. Speer TNT hollow point answers requests from varmint hunters and gives explosive performance over the .17's effective range; clean-burning propellants keep actions cleaner; sure-fire CCI priming; reusable plastic box with dispenser lid

Available in: .17 HMR (17 gr. TNT hollow point)

Box of 50: . . . . **.$17.95**

LONG HV AND SHORT HV

Features: Designed for rimfire guns that require .22 Long and .22 Short ammunition; clean-burning propellants keep actions cleaner; sure-fire CCI priming; reusable plastic box with dispenser lid

Available in: .22 Short (29 gr. solid lead bullet), .22 Short (27 gr. hollow point bullet), .22 Long (29 gr. solid lead bullet)

MSRP **$11.49**

MINI-MAG.

Features: CCI's first rimfire product and still the most popular; Mini-Mag. hollow points are high-velocity products and offer excellent all-around performance for small game and varmints; clean-burning propellants keep actions cleaner; sure-fire CCI priming; reusable plastic box with dispenser lid

Available in: .22 LR (40 gr. gilded round nose or 36 gr. gilded lead hollow point)

Box of 100: **$9.95**

"Swamp People" Box of 100: . **.$30.95**

PISTOL MATCH

Features: Designed expressly for high-end semiautomatic match pistols; singe-die tooling and great care in assembly lets you wring the last bit of accuracy from your precision pistol; clean-burning propellants keep actions cleaner; sure-fire CCI priming; reusable plastic box with dispenser lid

Available in: .22 LR (40 gr. lead round nose bullet)

Box of 50: . . . . **.$11.95**

QUIET-22

Features: Ideal for bolt-action and single shot .22 LR rifles (and perfectly safe in semiautomatics), this new reduced report cartridge generates ¼ the perceived noise level of standard velocity .22 LR

Available in: .22 LR

Box of 50: **$6.95**

SELECT .22 LR

Features: The .22 Long Rifle Select is built for semiautomatic competition; reliable operation, accuracy, and consistency make Select an ideal choice for competition shooters

Available in: .22 LR

MSRP . . . . **.$19.95**

SUPPRESSOR 22 LONG

CCI GREEN TAG

CCI QUIET-22

RIFLE

Features: Subsonic velocity of 970 fps minimizes sound signature through suppressed firearms; HP bullet; consistent function in semiautomatic firearms; clean-burning powders

Available in: .22 LR

Box 50: **$6.95**

CCI MINI-MAG.

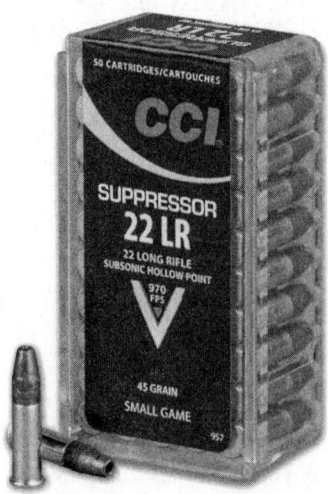

CCI AMMUNITION SUPPRESSOR 22 LONG RIFLE

Cor-Bon

Handgun & Shotgun

.457 WWG
Features: Cor-Bon Ammunition and Wild West Guns teamed up to offer the best in a lever gun big game cartridge
Available in: .457 WWG (350 gr., 460 gr.)
460-grain:. $71.99
350-grain:. $97.99

DPX RIFLE
Features: This is an optimum load for Law Enforcement; lead-free projectile; reduced recoil due to lighter weight projectile; deep penetration on soft tissue 12–17-in.
Available in: .223 Rem., .243 Win., .260 Rem., .270 WSM, .270 Wby Mag., .270 Win., .30-06 Spfd., .300 BLK, .300 H&H Mag., .300 WSM., .300 Wby. Mag., .300 Whisper, .300 Win. Mag., .308 Win., .338 Lapua, .338 RUM, .338 Win. Mag, .340 Wby. Mag., .375 H&H, .444 Marlin, .458 SOCOM, 6.5-284 Norma, 7.62x39mm
Box 20:. . . . . $31.90–$105.89

GLASER SAFETY SLUG
Features: Although slug was originally designed for use by Sky Marshals on airplanes, today the slug is recommended for anyone concerned with over-penetration; uses a copper jacket and is filled with a compressed load of either #12 or #6 lead shot, then capped with a round polymer ball that enhances feeding and reloading
Available in: 10mm, .32 ACP, .357 Mag., .357 SIG, .38 Spl. +P, .38 Super +P, .380 ACP, .40 S&W, .400

CORBON, .44 Mag., .44 Spl., .45 ACP, .45 ACP +P, .45 Colt, .45 Colt +P, 9mm +P
Box 6:. . . . . $18.11–$41.65

MULTI-PURPOSE RIFLE (MPR)
Features: Features a gilding metal jacket with a specially formulated lead core and a green acetal resin tip, which reduces drag, producing extremely high ballistic coefficient, and also creates more reliable feeding in magazine fed firearms; provides rapid, explosive expansion without excessive penetration; aerodynamic resin tip offers extreme accuracy at long-range precision competition and also improves feeding in magazine fed rifles; reliably expands for humane kills on varmints and deer-size game, giving just the right amount of penetration
Available in: .223 Rem., .22-250 Rem., .243 Win., 30-06 Spfd., .300 Whisper, .300 BLK, 300 Win. Mag., .308 Win.
Box 20:. . . . . $23.01–$45.28

HUNTER
Features: Bonded Core Soft Point ammunition retains optimum weight and integrity and provides reliable expansion coupled with deep penetration; features a heavy full-copper jacket enclosed in a hard linotype lead core; Hard Cast bullets are precision cast from hard linotype lead and have the flat, LBT nose design; both loads cause a through and through hole, penetrating the thickest hides and breaking the heaviest bone

Available in: 10mm, .223 Rem., .243 Win., .260 Rem., .270 WSM, .270 Wby. Mag., .270 Win., .30-06 Spfd., .30-30 Win., .300 H&H, .300 WSM, .300 Wby. Mag., .300 Win. Mag., .308 Win., .338 Lapua, .338 Win. Mag., .340 Wby. Mag., .357 Mag., .375 H&H, .41 Rem. Mag., .44 Mag. .45 Colt +P, .45-70 Govt., .454 Casull, .457 WWG, .460 Rowland, .460 S&W, .50 Alaskan, .500 S&W, 6.5x284 Norma, 7mm Rem. Mag.
Box 12, 20:. . . . . $24.67–$139.95

COR-BON AMMUNITION MULTI-PURPOSE RIFLE (MPR)

COR-BON EXPEDITION HUNTER

Handgun

DPX HANDGUN
Features: DPX is a solid copper hollowpoint bullet that combines the best of the lightweight high-speed JHPs and the heavyweight, deep-penetrating JHPs; the copper bullet construction allows it to conquer hard barriers like auto glass and steel while still maintaining its integrity
Available in: 10mm, .32 ACP, .357 Mag., .357 SIG, .375 JDJ, .38 Spl. +P,

.38 Super +P, .380 ACP, .40 S&W, .400 CORBON, .41 Rem. Mag., .44 Mag. .44 Spl., .45 ACP, .45 ACP +P, .45 Colt +P, .454 Casull, .460 S&W, .500 S&W, 9mm, 9mm +P
Box 20:. . . . . $26.61–$95.73

GLASER POW'RBALL
Features: Designed for finicky feeding pistols, Pow'Rball is a great choice for your semiauto pistols or revolvers;

reliable feeding and consistent reliable expansion; deeper soft tissue penetration; custom scored jacket; proprietary polymer ball and patented lead core
Available in: .38 Spl. +P, .38 Super +P, .380 ACP, .40 S&W, .400 CORBON, .45 ACP +P, .45 GAP, 9x23 Win.
Box 20:. . . . . $19.66–$31.98

AMMUNITION

ENVIRON-Metal

HEVI DUTY HOME DEFENSE

Features: Frangible, non-toxic, low recoil home defense load
Available in: 12 Ga. (2¾ in.) Shot sizes: 00
Box 5: . . . . $7.00–$8.00

HEVI-METAL TURKEY

Features: A layered load that combines premium steel shot with HEVI-Shot pellets; timeless testing of various shot load methods found layering to provide the most pellets on target and the best knockdown performance
Available in: 12 Ga. (3 in., 3½ in.), 20 Ga. (3 in.)
Box 5: . . . . $10.99–$12.99

HEVI-SHOT CLASSIC DOUBLES

Features: Optimized for your fixed chokes and fine classic doubles; denser than steel but soft like lead which means you get deeper penetration; USFWS-approved non-toxic shot; 45 percent more on target pellets than steel; belted sphere for maximum pellet mass; buffered and nano-treated pellets for tight patterns; weather-resistant crimp
Available in: 12 Ga. (2¾ in., 3 in.), 16 Ga. (2¾ in.), 20 Ga. (2¾ in., 3 in.), .28 Ga. (2¾ in.), .410 (3 in.)
Box 10: . . . . $24.99–$41.99

HEVI-SHOT DEAD COYOTE!

Features: With these HEVI-Shot T-shot loads, you can be deadly at ranges you never thought possible with a 12 gauge; the 3-in. load pounds out 50 perfectly round pellets at 1,350 fps. 10 percent heavier than lead, 54 percent denser than steel; every 50 rounds includes a dry-storage box.
Available in: 12 Ga. (3 in., 3½ in.)
Box of 10: $49.99

HEVI-SHOT MAGNUM BLEND

Features: Put more lethal pellets in your pattern with a combination of No. 5, 6, and 7 HEVI-13 shot, and boost your lethal range by 14 to 17 percent; buffered and moly-coated pellets produce a denser pattern than conventional shot; HEVI-13 delivers 40 percent more knockdown energy and up to 40 percent longer range than lead shells
Available in: 10 Ga. (3 ½-in.), 12 Ga. (3 in., 3½ in.) 20 Ga. (3 in.)
Box 5: . . . .$20.00–$38.00

SPEED BALL

Features: Speed Ball is an elastomeric ball in the base of the wad that accelerates pellets without boosting chamber pressures; an MV² pellet sits in the base of the shell with a HEVI-Shot layer on top, resulting in higher pellet counts in the 30-in. circle than you get with HEVI-Shot; nearly matches the lethal energy of HEVI-Shot, out to 60 yds (but far exceeds the energy of anything else)
Available in: 12 Ga. (3 in., 3½ in.) 20 Ga. (3 in.); Shot sizes: BB, 1, 3, 5
Box 10: . . . .$26.99–$32.99

HEVI-SHOT TRIPLE BEARD

Features: First all lead turkey load from the makers of HEVI-Shot; speed ball technology for reduced deformation on setback, more uniform pellets, and reduced "pancake" effect of lead; Magnum Blend technology; consistent performance in any temperature
Available in: 12 Ga. (3 in., 3 ½ in.), 20 Ga. (3 in.); Shot sizes: 5, 6, 7
20-ga.: $16.49
12-ga. (3-in.): $17.99
12-ga. (3.5-in.): $20.99

ENVIRON-METAL HEVI-METAL TURKEY

ENVIRON-METAL HEVI DUTY HOME DEFENSE

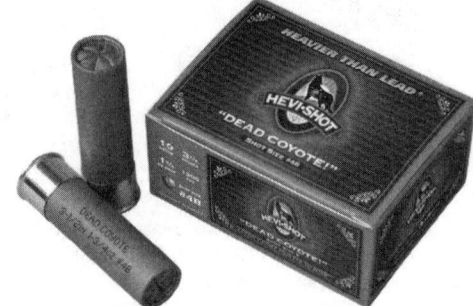

ENVIRON-METAL HEVI-SHOT DEAD COYOTE!

ENVIRON-METAL SPEED BALL

ENVIRON-METAL HEVI-SHOT TRIPLE BEARD

AMMUNITION

Federal Premium Ammunition

Rifle Ammunition
FUSION MSR

Features: Modern sporting rifles (MSRs) represent a very versatile class of firearms, handling a wide range of ammo and game, often built from the ground up and tricked out with accessories to match specific needs; all-new Fusion MSR loads provide that same degree of customization in ammunition
Available in: .223 Rem., 6.5 Grendel, .300 BLK, 6.8 SPC, .308 Win., .338 Fed.
Box 20:. . . . . $25.95–$38.95

CAPE-SHOK WOODLEIGH HYDRO SOLID

Features: Provides safari hunters superb accuracy, consistent performance, and tremendous impact; special heavy jackets provide excellent weight retention, up to 100 percent for solids
Available in: 9.3x62 Mauser, 9.3x74 R, .370 Sako Mag., .375 H&H Mag., .416 Rigby, .416 Rem. Mag., .458 Win. Mag., 458 Lott, .470 NE, .500 NE
Box 20:. . . . . $115.95–$267.95

FUSION RIFLE

Features: This specialized deer bullet electrochemically joins pure copper to an extreme pressure-formed core to ensure optimum performance. The result is high terminal energy on impact that radiates lethal shock throughout the target. This energy is optimized through mass weight retention, a top secretive tip-skiving process and superior bullet integrity.
Available in: .223 Rem., .22-250

Rem., .243 Win., .25-06 Rem., 6.5x55 Swedish Mauser, .260 Rem., .270 Win., .270 WSM, 7mm-08, .280 Rem., 7mm Rem. Mag., 7mm WSM, 7.62x39 Soviet, .30-30 Win. 6.5 Creedmoor, .308 Win., .30-06 Spfd., .300 Win. Mag., .300 WSM, .338 Federal, .338 Win. Mag., .35 Whelen, .45-70 Govt.
Box 20:. . . . . $24.95–$60.95

FUSION SP

Features: Real-world recoil can translate to inaccurate shooting and missed trophies, and because of this bullet weights and velocities have been developed to be lethal on whitetails, without pounding the shooter
Available in: .357 Mag., .41 Rem. Mag., .44 Rem. Mag., .454 Casull, .460 S&W, .500 S&W, 50 Action Express
Box 20:. . . . . $22.95–$44.95

GOLD MEDAL SIERRA MATCHKING BOATTAIL HOLLOWPOINT

Features: Long ranges are its specialty; excellent choice for everything from varmints to big game animals; tapered, boattail design provides extremely flat trajectories; higher downrange velocity for more energy at the point of impact; reduced wind drift
Available in: .223 Rem., .260 Rem.,

.308 Win., .30-06 Spfd., .300 Win. Mag., .338 Lapua Mag.
Box 20:. . . . . $30.95–$147.95

Rifle Ammunition
AMERICAN EAGLE FULL METAL JACKET BOATTAIL

Features: Accurate, non-expanding bullets; flat shooting trajectory, leaves small exit holes in game, and put clean holes in paper; smooth, reliable feeding into semiautomatics
Available in: .223 Rem., .308 Win., .300 BLK, 5.56 NATO, 6.5 Creedmoor
Box of 20 .223:. $11.95
Box of 20 .308:. $26.95

CAPE-SHOK TROPHY BONDED SLEDGEHAMMER SOLID

Features: Use it on the largest, most dangerous game in the world; Jack Carter design maximizes stopping power; bonded bronze solid with a flat nose that minimizes deflection off bone and muscle for a deep straight wound channel
Available in: .375 H&H Mag., .416 Rigby, .416 Rem. Mag., .458 Win. Mag., .458 Lott, .470 NE
Box 20:. . . . . $115.95–$267.95

POWER-SHOK COPPER

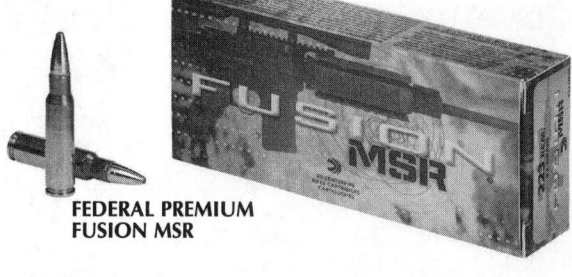

**FEDERAL PREMIUM
FUSION MSR**

FEDERAL PREMIUM FUSION RIFLE

**FEDERAL PREMIUM AMERICAN EAGLE
SYNTECH**

Federal Premium Ammunition

Features: Copper-alloy construction; hollow-point design expands consistently; accurate, reliable performance; large wound channels and efficient energy transfer to the target; lead-free; California-legal; federal brass and primers
Available in: .243 Win. (90 gr.), .270 Win. (130 gr.), .308 Win. (150 gr.), .30-06 Spfd. (150 gr.)
Box 20: . . . . **$26.95–$45.95**

VITAL-SHOK, CAPE-SHOK TROPHY BONDED BEAR CLAW

Features: Ideal for medium to large dangerous game; jacket and core are 100 percent fusion-bonded for reliable bullet expansion from 25 yds to extreme ranges; bullet retains 95 percent of its weight for deep penetration; hard solid copper base tapering to a soft, copper nose section for controlled expansion
Available in: Vital-Shok: 7mm Rem. Mag., .30-06 Spfd., .300 Win. Mag., .338 Win. Mag., .35 Whelen, .375 H&H
Cape-Shok: .375 H&H, .416 Rigby, .416 Rem. Mag.
Vital-Shok: . . . . **$44.95–$90.95**
Cape-Shok: . . . . **$90.95–$245.95**

VITAL SHOK NOSLER PARTITION

Features: Bullet features a partitioned lead core and shank that allows the front half to mushroom while the rear core remains intact for deep penetration and stopping power
Available in: .223 Rem., .22-250 Rem., .243 Win., 6mm Rem., .257 Roberts +P, .25-06 Rem., .270 Win., .270 WSM, 7mm Mauser, 7mm-08, .280 Rem., 7mm Rem. Mag., .30-30 Win., .308 Win. .30-06 Spfd., .300 H&H, .300 Win. Mag., .300 WSM, .300 RUM, .338 Fed., .338 RUM, .375 H&H
Box 20: . . . . **$36.95–$82.95**

VITAL SHOK SIERRA GAMEKING BOATTAIL SOFTPOINT

Features: Proven performer on small game and thin-skinned medium game; aerodynamic tip for a flat trajectory; exposed soft point expands rapidly for hard hits, even as velocity slows at longer ranges
Available in: .243 Win., .25-06 Rem., .260 Rem., .270 Win., 7-30 Waters, 7mm Rem. Mag., .308 Win., .30-06 Spfd.
Box 20: . . . . **$37.95–$45.95**

V-SHOK SPEER TNT GREEN HOLLOWPOINT

Features: Brings non-tox technology to the Federal Premium V-Shok varmint hunting line; a totally lead-free bullet that couples explosive expansion with match-grade accuracy
Available in: .17 HMR, .22 Hornet, .222 Rem., .223 Rem., .22-250 Rem.
Box 20: . . . . **$17.95–$57.95**

VITAL-SHOK TROPHY BONDED TIP

Features: Built on the Trophy Bonded Bear Claw platform to provide deep penetration and high weight retention; sleek profile, with tapered heel and translucent polymer tip; nickel-plated; available as component and in Federal loaded ammunition
Available in: .223 Rem., .270 Win., .270 WSM, .270 Wby. Mag., 7mm-08 Rem., .280 Rem., 7mm Rem. Mag., 7mm WSM, 7mm Wby. Mag., 7mm

FEDERAL PREMIUM POWER-SHOK COPPER

STW, .308 Win., .30-06 Spfd., .300 H&H Mag., .300 Win. Mag., .300 WSM, .300 Wby. Mag., .300 Rem. Ultra Mag., .338 Federal, .338 Win. Mag.
Box 20: . . . . **$27.95–$81.95**

VITAL-SHOK TROPHY COPPER

Features: Tipped bullet cavity for consistent expansion across a broad range of velocities; grooved bullet shank for increased accuracy across a wider range of firearms; copper-alloy design that achieves up to 99 percent weight retention; nickel-plated case
Available in: .243 Win., .25-06 Rem., .270 Win., .270 WSM, 7mm-08, .280 Rem., 7mm Rem. Mag., 7mm WSM, .30-30 Win., 6.5 Creedmoor,.308 Win., .30-06 Spfd., .300 H&H, .300 Win. Mag., .300 WSM, .300 Wby. Mag., .300 RUM, .338 Fed., .338 Win. Mag.
Box 20: . . . . **$36.95–$59.95**

Handgun Ammunition

AMERICAN EAGLE FULL METAL JACKET

Features: Good choice for range practice and reducing lead fouling in the barrel; jacket extends from the nose to the base, preventing bullet expansion and barrel leading; primarily as military ammunition for recreational shooting
Available in: .25 ACP, .32 ACP, .380 ACP, 5.7x28mm, 9mm Luger, .357 SIG, .38 Spl., .40 S&W, 10mm ACP, .45 GAP, .45 ACP
Box 50: . . . . **$17.95–$49.95**

AMERICAN EAGLE LEAD

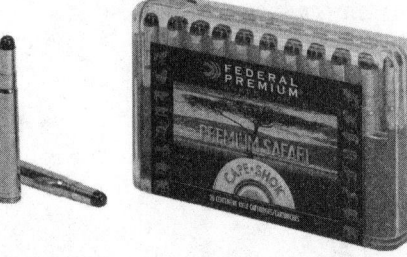

FEDERAL PREMIUM WOODLEIGH HYDRO SOLID

FEDERAL PREMIUM GUARD DOG HOME DEFENSE

Federal Premium Ammunition

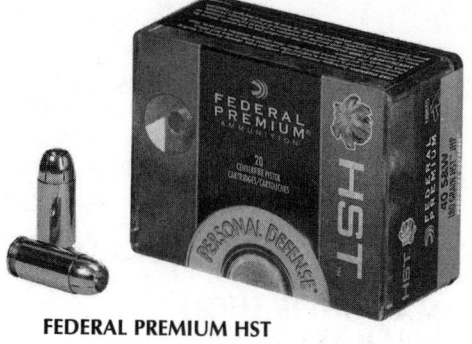

FEDERAL PREMIUM HST

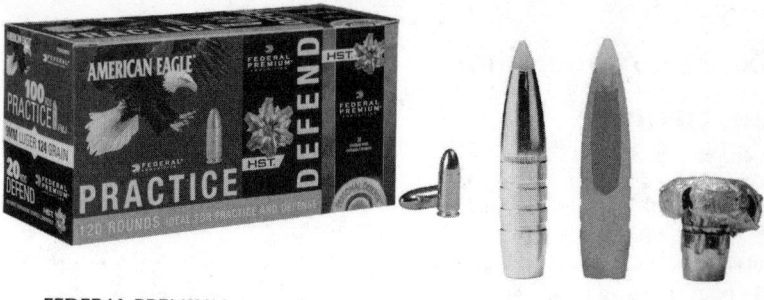

FEDERAL PREMIUM PRACTICE & DEFEND COMBO PACKS

FEDERAL PREMIUM TROPHY BONDED TIP

ROUND NOSE

Features: Great training round for practicing at the range; 100 percent lead with no jacket; excellent accuracy and very economical
Available in: .38 Spl.
MSRP $28.95

AMERICAN EAGLE SYNTECH

Features: Polymer-encapsulated Syntech bullet prevents metal-on-metal contact in the bore, eliminating copper and lead fouling, while extending barrel life; exclusive primer formulation provides reliable, consistent ignition; clean-burning propellants minimize residue and fouling; significantly reduces the required frequency of cleaning; absence of a copper jacket minimizes splash-back on steel targets; less perceived recoil
Available in: .40 S&W, .45 ACP, 9mm Luger
Box 50 (9mm): $19.95
Box 50 (.40 S&W): $26.95
Box 50 (.45 ACP): $33.95

CHAMPION LEAD SEMI-WADCUTTER

Features: Most popular all-around choice for target and personal defense, a versatile design that cuts clean holes in targets and efficiently transfers energy
Available in: .32 H&R Mag.
MSRP $21.95

CHAMPION SEMI-WADCUTTER HOLLOWPOINT

Features: For both small game and personal defense; hollow point design promotes uniform expansion
Available in: .44 Spl., .45 Colt

.44 Spl.: $33.95
.45 Colt: $28.95

GUARD DOG HOME DEFENSE

Features: Protect your home and loved ones with a cartridge designed exclusively for home defense; packs the terminal performance that stops threats while reducing over-penetration through walls
Available in: 9mm Luger, .40 S&W, .45 ACP
Box 20: . . . .$30.00–$33.00

PRACTICE & DEFEND COMBO PACKS

Features: HST bullet design delivers industry-leading performance in FBI protocol testing; American Eagle FMJ target rounds provide consistent accuracy; grain weights of both loads match for familiar feel and realistic practice
Available in: .40 S&W 180 gr. HST/FMJ, .45 Auto 230 gr. HST/FMJ, .380 Auto 99 gr. HST/95 gr. FMJ, 9mm Luger 124 gr. HST/FMJ
Box 20: . . . . $67.95–$96.95

PREMIUM HOME DEFENSE HYDRA-SHOK

Features: Unique center-post design delivers controlled expansion, and the notched jacket provides efficient energy transfer to penetrate barriers while retaining stopping power; deep penetration satisfies even the FBI's stringent testing requirements
Available in: .32 ACP, .327 Fed. Mag., .380 ACP, 9mm Luger, .38 Spl., .38 Spl. +P, .357 Mag., .40 S&W, 10mm ACP, .44 Rem. Mag., .45 GAP, .45 ACP
Box 20: . . . . $23.95–$44.95

PREMIUM PERSONAL DEFENSE HST

Features: Provides near 100 percent weight retention through most barriers; consistent expansion, optimum penetration, and superior terminal performance, it's specially designed hollow point won't plug while passing through a variety of barriers
Available in: .380 ACP, 9mm Luger, .40 S&W, .45 ACP
Box 20: . . . .$26.95–$35.95

PREMIUM PERSONAL DEFENSE JACKETED HOLLOWPOINT

Features: Ideal personal defense round in revolvers and semiautomatics; quick, positive expansion; jacket ensures smooth feeding into autoloading firearms
Available in: .32 H&R Mag., 9mm, .357 SIG, .357 Mag., .40 S&W, .45 ACP
Box 20: . . . .$25.95–$70.95

PREMIUM PERSONAL DEFENSE SHOT SHELLS

Features: The Judge from Taurus has emerged as a very popular handgun for Personal Defense.
Available in: .410 (2½ in.); Shot sizes: 000 Buck, 4
Box 20: $17.49

VITAL-SHOK TROPHY BONDED JSP

Features: 180-grain Trophy Bonded JSP; 1275 fps muzzle velocity
Available in: 10mm Auto
Box 20: $40.95

Federal Premium Ammunition

Shotgun Ammunition

3RD DEGREE

Features: Uses a multi-shot, three-stage payload and the exclusive FLITECONTROL¬Æ wad to deliver forgiving, lethal patterns; FLITECONTROL wad is designed for use with standard choke tubes
Available in: 12 (3 in., 3 ½ in.) 20 (3 in.); Shot sizes: 5, 6, 7
3 in.: . . . .**$21.95–$22.95**
3 1/2 in.: **$25.95**

BLACK CLOUD FS STEEL

Available in: 10 Ga. (3½ in.), 12 Ga. (2¾ in., 3 in., 3½ in.), 20 Ga. (3 in.); Shot sizes: 2, 3, 4, BB, BBB
Box 25: . . . .**$20.95–$36.95**

BLACK CLOUD FS STEEL CLOSE RANGE

Features: Engineered to put more pellets on targets 20 to 30 yards away, achieves a full pattern within a very short distance; comprised of 100 percent Flitestopper Steel for the most lethal payload imaginable, produces more open and optimum patterns; crimp and primer sealed
Available in: 12 Ga., 20 Ga. (3 in.)
Box 25: . . . .**$24.95–$27.95**

BLACK CLOUD HIGH

VELOCITY

Features: The Black Cloud High Velocity line pumps up the speed and lethal performance for waterfowl hunters everywhere.
Available in: 12 Ga. (3 in.); Shot Sizes: 3, 4
Box 25: **$27.95**

GAME-SHOK UPLAND GAME

Available in: 12, 16, 20, 28 Ga. .410 (2¾ in.); Shot sizes: 6, 8, 7.5
Box 25: . . . .**$8.95–$11.95**

GAME-SHOK UPLAND HEAVY FIELD

Available in: 12, 20 Ga. (2¾ in.); Shot sizes: 4, 5, 6, 7.5
Box 25: . . . .**$9.95–$19.95**

GAME-SHOK UPLAND GAME HI-BRASS

Available in: 12, 16, 20 Ga. (2¾ in.), .410 bore (2½ in., 3 in.); Shot sizes: 4, 5, 6, 7.5
Box 25: . . . .**$17.95–$19.95**

GOLD MEDAL GRAND PLASTIC, GOLD MEDAL PLASTIC

Available in: Grand Plastic is 12 Ga. (2¾ in.) only in X-Lite, 2¾ DE, 3 DE, or Handicap loads in 7.5 or 8. Gold Medal Plastic is available in 20, 28 Ga., and .410-bore in 8.5 or 9. 20 Ga. is a 2½ DE, 28 Ga. is a 2 DE, and the .410-bore is a Max Dram loading.

Grand Plastic: **$11.95**
Plastic: . . . .**$11.95–$13.95**

GOLD MEDAL PAPER

Available in: 12 Ga. (2¾ in.) only, in 1 1/8-oz. loads of 7.5 or 8, or 1-oz. load of 8
Box of 25: **$23.95**

MAG-SHOK HIGH VELOCITY WITH FLITECONTROL TURKEY SHOTSHELLS

Available in: 10 Ga. (3½ in.), 12 Ga. (2¾ in., 3 in., 3½ in.) 20 Ga. (3 in.); Shot sizes: 4, 5, 6
Box 10: . . . .**$14.95–$23.95**

MAG-SHOK MAGNUM HEAVYWEIGHT TURKEY

FEDERAL PREMIUM VITAL-SHOK TROPHY BONDED 10MM AUTO

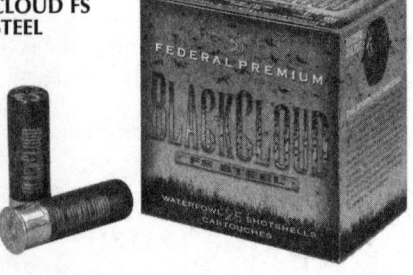

FEDERAL PREMIUM BLACK CLOUD FS STEEL

FEDERAL BLACK CLOUD FS STEEL CLOSE RANGE

FEDERAL PREMIUM 3RD DEGREE

Federal Premium Ammunition

WITH FLITECONTROL TURKEY SHOTSHELLS

Available in: 10 Ga. (3½ in.), 12 Ga. (2¾ in., 3 in., 3½ in.), 20 Ga. (2¾ in., 3 in.); Shot sizes: 5, 6, 7

Box 5:. . . . .$24.95–$41.95

MAG-SHOK MAGNUM LEAD WITH FLITECONTROL TURKEY SHOTSHELLS

Available in: 12 Ga. (3 in., 3 ½ in.); Shot sizes: 4, 5, 6

Box 10:. . . . .$19.95–$23.95

PRAIRIE STORM HIGH VELOCITY STEEL SHOTSHELLS

Available in: 12, 20 Ga. (3 in.); Shot sizes: 3, 4

12-gauge:. $25.95
20-gauge:. $23.95

SPEED-SHOK HIGH VELOCITY STEEL

Available in: 10 Ga. (3½ in.), 12 Ga. (2¾ in., 3 in., 3½ in.), 16 Ga. (2¾ in.), 20 Ga. (2¾ in., 3 in.); Shot sizes: 1, 2, 3, 4, 6, 7, BB, BBB, T

Box 25:. . . . .$15.95–$33.95

STRUT-SHOK MAGNUM LEAD TURKEY SHOTSHELLS

Available in: 12 Ga. (3 in., 3½ in.); Shot sizes: 4, 5, 6

3-in.:. $11.95
3.5-in.:. $18.95

TOP GUN TARGET

Available in: 12 Ga., 20 Ga. (2¾ in.); Shot sizes: 7.5, 8, 9; multiple loadings available, including Extra-Lite 7/8-oz., subsonic, pink hulled, and red-white-and-bue hulls (all 12-ga.), and various dram equivalent loadings in both gauges

Subsonic:. $10.95
All other loadings:. $8.95

TOP GUN TARGET-STEEL

Available in: 12 Ga., 20 Ga. (2¾ in.); Shot size: 7

Box 25:. $10.95

WING-SHOK HIGH VELOCITY

Features: Pheasant and Quail Forever versions available

Available in: 12, 16, 20, 28 Ga., all 2¾ in. and loaded with choice of 4, 5, 6, and 7.5 shot; one 28-ga. load also available in 8

Box 25:. . . . .$20.95–$29.95

WING-SHOK MAGNUM

Available in: 12 Ga. (2¾ in., 3 in.), 20 Ga. (2¾ in., 3 in.); Shot sizes: 4, 5, 6

20-gauge:. $26.95
12-gauge:. $27.95

Shotgun Ammunition Slugs

POWER-SHOK RIFLED SLUG

Features: Hollow point slug type

Available in: 10 Ga. (3½ in.), 12 Ga. (2¾ in., 3 in.), 16 Ga. (2¾ in.), 20 Ga. (2¾ in.), .410 (2½ in.)

Box 5:. . . . .$5.95–$12.95

POWER-SHOK SABOT SLUGS

Features: Sabot hollow point slug type

Available in: 12 Ga., 20 Ga. (2¾ in.)

Box 5:. $9.95

VITAL-SHOK TROPHY COPPER SABOT SLUG

Features: A copper slug that incorporates some of the most advanced technology in the industry; better accuracy, less drop, manageable recoil (similar to a .30-06 Spfd.) and consistent penetration and expansion; unique two-part sabot design achieves accuracy through a clean launch and improved projectile support

Available in: 12 Ga., 20 Ga. (2¾ in., 3 in.)

Box 5: . . . .$15.95–$16.95

VITAL-SHOK RIFLED SLUG

Available in: 12, 20 Ga. (2¾ in., 3 in.)

Box 5:. . . . . $5.95–$6.95

FEDERAL PREMIUM PRAIRIE STORM HIGH VELOCITY STEEL SHOTSHELLS

FEDERAL PREMIUM VITAL-SHOK RIFLED SLUG

Fiocchi USA

Rifle Ammunition

EXTREMA RIFLE HUNTING LINE

Features: Combining the best bullets in the business with our precision-drawn brass cases gives you the best combination of value and performance; uses bullets like the Hornady SST, V Max, and Sierra Game King to provide a combination of accuracy, high ballistic coefficients, and reliable expansion
Available in: .222 Rem., .204 Ruger, .223 Rem., .22-50 Rem., .243 Win., 6.5x55 Swedish, .270 Win., .308 Win., .30-06 Spfd., .300 Win. Mag.
MSRP . . . . N/A

SHOOTING DYNAMICS RIFLE LINE

Features: High-quality reloadable brass cases combined with quality full metal jacket, soft point, or flat soft point (for lever guns) make sure your shooting dollar goes further
Available in: .223 Rem., .22-250 Rem., .243 Win., .270 Win., .30-30 Win., .308 Win., .30-06 Spfd., .300 Win. Mag., 4.6x30 H&K, .222 Rem., 7.62x39 Soviet, .300 BLK
MSRP . . . . N/A

Handgun Ammunition

COWBOY ACTION LINE

Features: Loaded with brass reloadable cases, noncorrosive primers, smokeless powders, and lead bullets coated with lube to reduce leading in the barrel; velocity is on par with what you would expect from period-correct ammo while keeping the recoil to a minimum for timed Cowboy Action competition and to reduce wear and tear on older guns
Available in: .32 S&W Long, .38 S&W Short, .38 S&W Spl., .357 Mag., .44 Spl., .44-40 Win., .45 Long Colt
MSRP . . . . N/A

EXTREMA XTP HANDGUN LINE

Features: Combined with nickel-plated cases for positive feeding and extraction when you need it most, qualified primers and clean powders deliver the maximum performance for the ultimate hunting or self-defense application
Available in: .25 ACP, .32 ACP, .380 ACP, 9mm Luger, .38 Spl., .38 Spl.+P, .357 Mag., .40 S&W, .44 Rem. Mag., .45 ACP
MSRP . . . . N/A

SHOOTING DYNAMICS PISTOL & REVOLVER LINE

Features: Combining quality brass cases with consistent primers, clean powders, and full metal jacket, jacketed hollow point, and soft point bullets in many calibers, Fiocchi loads bullets of the same weight to velocities that are comparable with high-quality defensive loads so you get realistic training-recoil impulse and point of aim/impact
Available in: .25 ACP, .32 ACP, .32 S&W Long, .380 ACP, 9mm Luger, 9mm Makarov, 9mm Steyr, 9x21 IMI, .38 Spl., .357 Mag., .38 Super Auto, .40 S&W, .44 Rem. Mag., .44 Spl., .45 ACP
MSRP . . . . N/A

Shotgun Ammunition

EXACTA TARGET LOADS

Features: Specifically for competitive shooters; the Target Load Line is the offspring of a fifty year tradition of supporting the world of trap, skeet, and now sporting clays, FITASC, and Compaq
Available in: Steel: 12 Ga., 20 Ga. (2¾ in.), Shot size: 7; Helios: 12 Ga. (2¾ in.), Shot sizes: 7, 7.5
MSRP . . . . N/A

GOLDEN PHEASANT LINE

Features: Golden Pheasant shot shells utilize a special hard, nickel-plated lead shot, based on Fiocchi's strict ballistic tolerances that ensure proven shot consistency and result in deeper penetration, longer ranges, and much tighter patterns
Available in: 12 Ga. (2¾ in., 3 in.), 16 Ga. (2¾ in.), 20, 28 Ga. (2¾ in., 3 in.); Shot sizes: 4, 5, 6, 7.5, 8, 9
MSRP . . . . N/A

NICKEL-PLATED BUCKSHOT

Features: Harder pellets from the nickel plating mean better patterns, better penetration, and no buffer needed
Available in: 12 Ga. (2¾ in.); Shot sizes: 00, 4
MSRP . . . . N/A

OPTIMA SPECIFIC HIGH VELOCITY

Features: High brass hulls, one-piece shot cup and cushioned wads, and round shot pellets make sure you get the bang for your buck you have come to expect from Fiocchi
Available in: 12 Ga. (2¾ in., 3 in.), 16 Ga. (2¾ in.), 20 Ga. (2¾ in., 3 in.), 28 Ga. (2¾ in., 3 in.), .410 (3 in.); Shot sizes: 4, 5, 6, 7.5, 8, 9
MSRP . . . . N/A

WATERFOWL STEEL HUNTING

Features: Treated steel pellets, the correct wad, and powders that perform in the cold conditions often encountered in waterfowl hunting deliver the kills a waterfowl hunter wants
Available in: 12 Ga. (2¾ in., 3 in.), 20 Ga. (3 in.); Shot sizes: T, BBB, BB, 1, 2, 3, 4, 5, 6
MSRP . . . . N/A

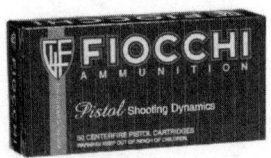

FIOCCHI SHOOTING DYNAMICS PISTOL LINE

FIOCCHI GOLDEN PHEASANT SHOT SHELLS

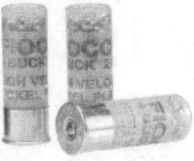

FIOCCHI NICKEL-PLATED BUCKSHOT

RIFLE AMMUNITION

Features: A range of bullets for training and all types of hunting situations worldwide; GECO offers five different bullet types to cover every hunting situation; GECO PLUS for shooting big game, GECO EXPRESS for the long distance shot, GECO SOFTPOINT as the real all-rounder, GECO SWISS MATCH for .223 competitors, and GECO ZERO, a lead-free line for hunters; made in Germany, which means outstanding accuracy and reliable bullet performance

Available calibers: .223 Rem., .243 Win., .270 WSM, .270 Win., .280 Rem., .30-06 Spfd., .300 Win. Mag., .308 Win., 6.5x55 Swedish Mauser, 7mm Rem. Mag., 7x57, 7x57R, 7x64, 7x65R, 8x57 IRS, 8x57 IS, 9.3x62, 9.3x74R, .300 BLK

From: **$20.53**

RIMFIRE AMMUNITION

Features: Target shooters can always depend on the cartridges perfect functioning, consistent performance and good precision.; reliable rimfire ammunition to guarantee required standards of accuracy at a favorable price

Available in: .22 LR Rifle, .22 LR Semi-Auto

From: **$3.60**

PISTOL AMMUNITION

Features: GECO offers 18 loads with cartridges in nine different calibers; these cover all relevant fields of application like precision shooting, dynamic sport disciplines, hunting, protection, and self-defense.

Available in: .38 Super, .40 S&W, .45 ACP, 6.35 Browning, 7.65 Browning (.32 ACP), 9mm Browning Court (.380 ACP), 9mm, 9mm Makarov, 9x21., .357 Mag., .38 Spl.

From: **$10.95**

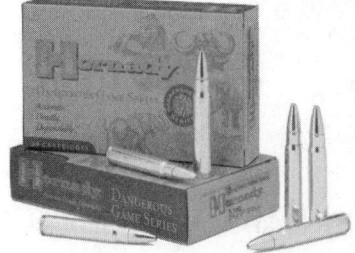

HORNADY DANGEROUS GAME

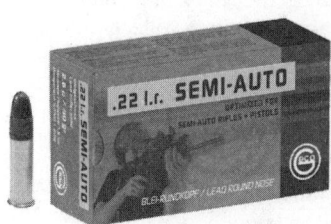

GECO RIMFIRE AMMUNITION

Rifle, Handgun & Shotgun

GECO SUPER MATRIX AMMUNITION

SUPER MATRIX AMMUNITION

Features: The entire line of GECO Super Matrix for pistols, shotguns and rifles, retains the same point of impact, along with the same perceived recoil and muzzle flash as standard duty rounds. By micro-pulverizing into a fine powder upon impact, GECO Super Matrix frangible bullets, buckshot, and slugs will not harm steel targets or other valuable range equipment. By eliminating back splatter, 100% bullet containment in indoor ranges is guaranteed.

Available in: 9mm, .38 Spl., .357 Sig, .40, .45, 12 ga. pellet

MSRP . . . . **N/A**

Hornady Manufacturing

HORNADY AMERICAN GUNNER RIFLE

HORNADY AMERICAN WHITETAIL

HORNADY FULL BOAR

Rifle Ammunition

AMERICAN GUNNER RIFLE

Features: The American Gunner line of ammunition is a collection of tried-and-true, versatile loads that are popular with shooters for their target shooting, hunting, or self-defense needs. Made in the USA with premium components, American Gunner ammunition combines generations of ballistics know-how with modern technology. Hornady introduces new rifle calibers to complement the handgun offerings currently available. These rifle options are loaded with match grade hollow point bullets for a broad range of use including self-defense, target shooting, and varmint/small game hunting.
Available in: .223 Rem., 6.5 Creedmoor, 6.8mm SPC, .300 BLK, .308 Win.
Box 50: . . . . **$34.99–$57.99**

AMERICAN WHITETAIL

Features: Loaded with Hornady InterLock Bullets, optimized loads specifically for deer hunting, and select propellants for greater consistency
Available in: .223 Rem., 6.5 Creedmoor, .243 Win., .25-06 Rem., .270 Win., 7mm-08 Rem., 7mm Rem. Mag, 30-30 Win., .308 Win., 30-06 Spfd., .300 Win. Mag
Box 20: . . . . **$26.92–$38.72**

CUSTOM LITE

Features: CustomLite ammunition is recommended for children, women, and anyone new to the game; offer minimum recoil and a reduced muzzle blast; often paired with SST and RN bullets
Available in: .243 Win, .270 Win., 7mm Rem. Mag., 7mm-08 Rem.,

.30-30 Win., .300 Win. Mag., .308 Win., .30-06 Spfd.
From: . . . . **$29.59–$47.99**

DANGEROUS GAME

Features: These bullets are among the largest offered by Hornady and feature the DGS (Dangerous Game Solid) and the DGX (Dangerous Game eXpanding); made with hard lead/antimony alloy cone and surrounded by a copper-clad steel jacket; straighter penetration comes from a flat meplat that creates more energy than traditional round bullets
Available in: 9.3x62 Mauser, 9.3x74R, .376 Steyr., .375 H&H, .375 Ruger, .450–400 Nitro Express, .404 Jeffery, .416 Rem. Mag., .416 Ruger, .416 Rigby, .458 Win., .450 NE, .458 Lott, .470 NE, .500 NE, .500-416 NE .450 Rigby
From: . . . . **$69.41–$198.19**

FULL BOAR

Features: Hard hitting Hornady GMX bullets for deep penetration and maximum weight retention; monolithic, copper alloy bullets deliver controlled expansion and 95+ percent weight retention; excellent fit, feed and function in ARs and other semi-autos; California compatible and approved for use in other areas requiring the use of non-traditional bullets
Available in: ..25-06 Rem., 6.5 Creedmoor, 7mm-08, .300 BLK, .223 Rem., .30-30 Win., .243 Win., 6.8 PPC, .270 Win., 7mm Rem. Mag., .308 Win., .30-06 Spfd., .300 Win. Mag.
Box 20: . . . . **$29.85–$56.71**

LEVEREVOLUTION

Features: LEVERevolution bullets travel at a speed of 250 fps and have a faster muzzle velocity than most other conventional lever gun loads; are unbelievably accurate and offer incomparable terminal performance; available in FTX and MonoFlex

Available in: .25-35 Win., .30-30 Win., .308 Marlin Express, .32 Win. Spl., .338 Marlin Express, .35 Rem., .357 Mag., .41 Mag., .44 Mag., .444 Marlin, .45 Colt, .45-70 Govt., .450 Marlin
From: . . . .
$26.48–$55.47

MATCH

Features: Match bullets feature a boattail hollow point design that provides both accuracy and speed; these bullets' jackets feature near-zero wall thickness, which leads to uniformity throughout the jacket; case weight and internal capacity are also consistent throughout Match ammunition
Available in: .223 Rem., .260 Rem., 6.5 Grendel, 6.5 Creedmoor, .308 Win., .300 Win. Mag., .338 Lapua, .50 BMG
From: . . . .
$25.65–$125.00

SUPERFORMANCE

Features: Superformance bullets are 100–200 fps faster than any other traditional type of bullet on the market today. In addition to their speed, they also offer minimal recoil, muzzle blast, temperature sensativity, and inaccuracies; these bullets are versatile and can be paired with all types of firearms, including semiautomatics, lever guns, and pump actions
Available in: .223 Rem., .243 Win., .25-06 Rem., .257 Roberts +P, .260 Rem., .270 Win., .280 Rem., .30 TC, .30-06 Spfd., .300 RCM., .300 Savage, .300 Win. Mag., .300 WSM, .308 Win., .338 RCM, .338 Win. Mag., .35 Whelen, .375 H&H, .375 Ruger, .444 Marlin, .458 Win., 5.56 NATO, 6.5 Creedmoor, 6.5x55 Swedish, 6mm. Rem., 7mm Rem. Mag., 7mm-08 Rem., 7x57 Mauser
MSRP . . . .
$31.84–$130.19

Hornady Manufacturing

Handgun Ammunition

AMERICAN GUNNER

Features: XTP (eXtreme Terminal Performance) bullets are exceptionally accurate and deliver excellent versatility and superior ballistic performance; propellants are matched to each load to ensure optimal pressure, velocity, volume and consistency from lot to lot; high quality primers and Hornady cases combine to deliver consistent shooting in the field
Available in: .380 ACP, .40 S&W, .45 ACP, 9mm, 9mm +P, .38 Spl., .357 Mag.
Box 20–75: . . . . $22.17–$63.20

COWBOY

Features: These swaged bullets flatten instead of fragment when they reach their targets; diamond knurling ensures that the entire surface of the bullet is well-lubed

Available in: .44-40 Win., .45 Colt
Box 20: . . . . $23.92–$25.60

CRITICAL DEFENSE

Features: Critical Defense bullets are custom-designed for individual loads, and their shiny silver nickel plating prevents bullet corrosion; Critical Defense ammunition is cannelured and crimped to avoid bullet setback, and clean burning and stable propellants reduce recoil
Available in: .410, .22 WMR, .32 NAA, 32 H&R Mag., 9x18mm Makarov, .380 ACP, 9mm Luger, .38 Spl., .357 SIG., .357 Mag., .38 Spl. +P, 40 S&W, .44 Spl., .45 ACP, .45 Colt
From: . . . . $17.57–$32.60

CRITICAL DUTY

Features: Features FlexLock Bullets, crimped and nickel-plated cases, interlocking bands, and a core made of high-antimony lead; these bullets are among the top choices of law enforcement and military professionals and highly reliable
Available in: .357 Mag., .40 S&W, .45 ACP +P, .357 SIG, 9mm, 9mm Luger +P, 10mm Auto
Box 20–25: . . . . $29.93–$32.77

LEVEREVOLUTION

Features: LEVERevolution bullets travel at a speed of 250 fps and are unbelievably accurate; these bullets feature Flex Tip Technology and should not be stored for long periods of time, as the tips may become deformed; deliver 40 percent more energy than traditional bullets
Available in: .357 Mag., .41 Mag., .44 Mag, .45 Colt
From: . . . . $27.77–$29.53

HORNADY AMERICAN GUNNER

HORNADY CRITICAL DUTY

Hornady Manufacturing
Shotgun Ammunition

AMERICAN WHITETAIL RIFLED SLUG

Features: Rifled slug for smooth-bore barrels; 12 gauge 1-ounce rifled, foster style slug or 325-grain InterLock slug; hollow point, tough lead-alloy core; 1,600 feet per second
Available in: 12 Ga.
Box 5:...................$10.51

AMERICAN WHITETAIL SHOTGUN SLUGS

Features: InterLock ring that locks the core and jacket together to deliver controlled expansion combined with excellent weight retention, energy and accuracy; hollow point bullet design initiates rapid expansion upon impact; serrated lead core and jacket allow for even expansion at low velocities; tough lead alloy core; rigid polycarbonate sabot with exclusive buffer disc combine to open uniformly without compromising accuracy
Available in: 12 Ga. (2 ¾ in.)
Box 5:...................$14.20

BUCKSHOT

Features: Buckshot ammunition is specially designed for unmodified semiauto and pump shotguns; made with Versatite wad technology, these reliable bullets offer a tight, accurate shot; now available in a 00 reduced recoil load
Available in: 12 Ga. (2¾ in.)

Box 10:...........$11.01–$17.92

CUSTOM LITE SHOTGUN SLUGS

Features: Delivers 25 percent less recoil than standard loads; for rifled barrels only; FTX bullet improves ballistic coefficient and aids in expansion; lower recoil and muzzle blast while maintaining accuracy and effectiveness out to 150 yds; innovative sabot design enhances accuracy
Available in: 20 Ga. (2 ¾ in.)
Box 5:...................$16.04

HORNADY AMERICAN WHITETAIL RIFLED SLUG

HORNADY AMERICAN WHITETAIL SHOTGUN SLUGS

HORNADY 00 BUCKSHOT REDUCED RECOIL

HORNADY CUSTOM LITE 20-GAUGE SLUG

AMMUNITION

Hornady Manufacturing

HEAVY MAGNUM COYOTE

Features: Loaded with 1 ½ oz. of nickel plated lead shot in either a BB or 00 buckshot for close range predators; features Hornady Versatite wad for more impact on target; 1,300 fps
Available in: 12 Ga. (3 in., 00 buckshot or BB)
Box 10:. $17.92

HEAVY MAGNUM TURKEY

Features: Each 3-in., 12-ga. shotshell contains 1½ oz. of either #4, #5, or #6 nickel-plated lead; each 20-ga. shotshell is loaded with 1 3/8 oz. of #5 nickel-plated lead shot; loads don't require modified shotguns or specialized turkey chokes
Available in: 12 Ga. (3 in.), 20 Ga. (3 in.); Shot sizes: 4, 5, 6 nickel
Box 10:. . . . . $16.75–$17.81

SST SLUGS

Features: Sharp points at the end of these slugs allow for faster and more accurate shooting; able to reach your target from an impressive 200 yards away; each shot delivers more than 1200 ft.-lbs. of energy
Available in: 12, 20 Ga. (2¾ in)
Box 5:. $15.87

Rimfire Ammunition

17 HMR

Features: The 17 HMR is one of the most accurate rimfire bullets ever made; polymer tip fragments rapidly and dramatically on impact, and its flat trajectory adds to its accuracy and consistency
Available in: .17 HMR
Box 50:. . . . . $17.51–$18.41

17 MACH2

Features: These V-MAX bullets are known for their rapid fragmentation and consistent accuracy; these bullets are made in America and hand inspected; paired with Varmint Express products, ignition is fast and easy
Available in: .17 Mach2
Box 50:. $10.84–12.51

17 WINCHESTER SUPER MAGNUM

Features: 20 grain V-Max bullet that provides tack-driving accuracy; muzzle velocity of 3,000 feet per second; fills the gap between the rimfire 17 HMR and centerfire 17 Hornet
Available in: .17 WSM (20 gr.)
Box 50:. $22.08

22 WMR

Features: The .22 WMR guarantees accurate shooting from more than 125 feet; has a muzzle velocity of 2,200 fps and is one of the most requested products Hornady offers; available in 25, 30, and 45 gr.
Available in: .22 WMR
Box 50:. . . . . $16.25–$17.57

HORNADY SST SLUGS

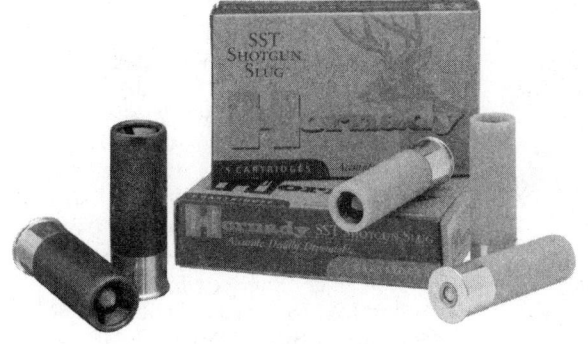

HORNADY HEAVY MAGNUM COYOTE

HORNADY 17 HMR

Jarrett Rifles

TROPHY AMMUNITION

Features: Jarrett's high-performance cartridges are in ten round boxes; cases are from Norma with Jarrett's headstamp

Available in: .243 Win., .270 Win., 7mm Rem. Mag., .30-06 Spfd., .300 WM, .300 Jarrett, .375 H&H, .416 Rem. Mag.

MSRP . . . . $29.12–$82.81

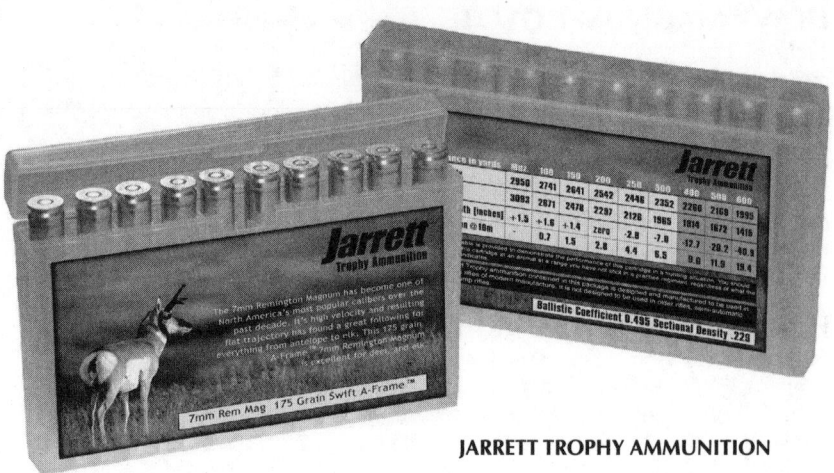

JARRETT TROPHY AMMUNITION

Kynoch Ammunition

KYNOCH RIFLE AMMUNITION

RIFLE AMMUNITION

Features: Kynoch hunting ammunition is now standardized on Woodleigh soft nosed and solid bullets, recognized world wide as the most reliable big game bullets currently manufactured; Kynamco offers virtually the whole range of classic British Nitro Express from its purpose-built factory

Available in: .240 H&H Flanged, .240 Belted NE, 6.5 Mannlicher Schoenauer, 9.5 Mannlicher Schoenauer, .300 H&H Flanged, .300 H&H Belted, .303 British, .310 Cadet, .318 Rimless, .333 Jeffrey Flanged, .333 Rimless NE, .35 Win., .350 Rigby, .400/300 NE, .350 Rigby No. 2, .369 Purdey NE, .400/360 Purdey, .400/360 Westley Richards, .360 No. 2 NE, .375 2 ½ NE, .375 H&H Flanged, .375 H&H Belted, .400/375 Belted NE, .400 Purdey, .450/400 Magnum NE, .450/400 3 ¼ Nitro for Black, .450/400 NE, .404 Jeffery Rimless NE, .405 Win.,, .416 Rigby, .425 Westley Richards, .450 NE, .450 Nitro for Black, .450 No. 2 NE, .450 Rigby, .500/450 NE, .577/450 Martini Henry, .500/465 NE, .458 Win. Mag., .458 Lott, .470 Capstick, .470 NE, .475 NE, .475 No. 2 NE, .476 Westley Richards NE, .500 Jeffery NE, .500 NE 3-in., .500 3-in. Nitro for Black, .500 3 ¼ Nitro for Black, .505 Gibbs, .577 3-in. NE, .577 2 ¾-in. Soft Nose, .577 3-in. Nitro For Black, .577 Snider, .600/577 REWA, .600 NE, .700 NE

From $42.50

Lapua

Rifle Ammunition

CENTERFIRE SPORT

Features: Lapua's extremely accurate target shooting cartridges are loaded with the best target bullets—Scenar, FMJBT, D46 and Lock Base; numerous world championships, Olympic championships, and other top competition gold medals, as well as many official world records in different disciplines, are shot with the Lapua cartridges
Available in: .222 Rem., .223 Rem., .243 Win., 6mm BR Norma, 6.5x47 Lapua, 6.5x55 Swedish, 7.62x39, .308 Win., .30-06 Spfd., 7.62x53R/54R, .338 Lapua Mag.
Box 50: . . . . **$33.49–$141.99**

MEGA BULLETS

Features: Soft point bullet designed for big game hunting; lead core and copper jacket that are mechanically bonded together; long jacket protects core and prevents premature bullet expansion or breakage when bullet goes through light brush or grass cover; up to 97 percent weight retention
Available in: .264, .30, .366
Box of 100: **$56.99–$77.99**

NATURALIS

Features: Bullet mushrooming begins immediately on impact; bullet expands symmetrically and without shattering; gives a maximal shock effect to the hunted game; top premium copper bullet; retains up to 100 percent of its weight after the impact
Available in: .224, .243, .264, .284, .30, .323, .338, .366
Box of 50: . . . . **$75.99–$128.99**

CLEANRANGE

Features: CleanRange ammunition was developed to eliminate airborne lead and the need for lead retrieval at indoor ranges by using a state-of-the-art combination of high-tech, lead-free primers and specially designed Fully Encapsulated Bullets, a unique mix that eliminates lead and heavy metal exposure at the firing point.
Available in: .45 ACP, 9mm Luger
Box 50: . . . . **$20.99–$31.99**

COWBOY ACTION

Features: "Old West" Cowboy Action loads were developed specifically for cowboy action shooting ; these flat-nose bullets deliver reliable knock-down power that puts steel targets down on the first shot
Available in: .357 Mag., .44 Spl., .45 Colt
Box 50: . . . . **$27.99–$33.99**

FIRST DEFENSE

Features: Magtech First Defense rounds are designed with a 100 percent solid copper bullet, unlike traditional hollow points that contain a lead core covered by a copper jacket; First Defense solid copper bullets have no jacket to split or tear away, ensuring every round you fire meets its target with maximum impact and effectiveness
Available in: 9mm Luger, .300 BLK, .40 S&W, .45 ACP
Box 20: . . . . **$18.99–$31.99**

GUARDIAN GOLD

Features: Thanks to its tremendous stopping power, deep penetration, awesome mushrooming, and dead-on accuracy, Guardian Gold is fast-becoming a favorite among those seeking reliable, affordable personal protection
Available in: 9mm Luger, .32 ACP, .380 ACP, .357 Mag., .40 S&W, .45 ACP, .45 GAP
Box 20: . . . . **$12.99–$19.99**

SPORT SHOOTING

Features: The 100 percent solid copper hollow-point projectile features a six-petal hollow-point specifically designed to deliver tight groups, superior expansion, virtually 100 percent weight retention, and increased penetration over jacketed lead-core bullets
Available in: .25 ACP, .30 Carbine, .308 Win., .32 ACP, .32 S&W, .32 S&W L, .357 Mag., .380 ACP, .38 Spl., .38 Spl. S, .38 Super Auto, .38 S&W, .40 S&W, .44-40 Win., .44 Rem. Mag., .454 Casull, .45 ACP, .45 GAP, .500 S&W, 9mm Luger
From: . . . . **$13.49–$46.99**

LAPUA CENTERFIRE SPORT

LAPUA NATURALIS

Magtech Ammunition

MAGTECH AMMUNITION

Norma Ammunition

Rifle Ammunition

AFRICAN PH

Features: Based on many generations of experience of reputable African Professional Hunters, this range of cartridges has been developed to optimize ballistic criteria such as bullet momentum, sectional density and deep, straight-line, bone-breaking penetration; loaded cartridges with Woodleigh softnose and solid bullets

Available in: .375 Flanged Mag. NE, .375 H&H Mag., .404 Jeffery, .416 Rem. Mag., .416 Rigby, .500/.416 NE, .450 Rigby Rimless, .458 Lott, .470 NE, .500 Jeffery, .500 NE 3, .505 Mag. Gibbs

Box 10: . . . . **$74.00–$207.00**

AMERICAN PH

Features: In the "American" style, this line of ammunition features lighter bullets, higher muzzle velocity, and longer average ranges

Available in: .223 Rem., .243 Win., .257 Roberts, 6.5 Jap, 6.5 Carcano, 6.5x55 Swedish, 6.5-284 Norma, .270 Win., .270 WSM; 7mm-08 Rem., .280 Rem., 7mm Rem. Mag, .308 Win., .30-06 Spfd., .308 Norma Magnum, .300 Win. Mag, .300 WSM, .300 RUM, 7.65 Arg, 7.7 Jap, .338 Win. Mag, 9.3x62 Mauser, 9.3x74R, .375 H&H Mag, .338 Lapua Mag, .257 Wby., .270 Wby., 7mm Wby., .300 Wby., .30-378 Wby., .340 Wby.

From: . . . . **$45.00–$152.00**

KALAHARI

Features: The Kalahari is loaded with selected lots of powder to ensure the highest possible velocity, best possible ballistic coefficient, and lowest wind drift achievable at normal hunting ranges; bullet expansion is controlled and restricted–only the front third of the bullet will expand into six razor-edged petals, leaving the rear part of the bullet unimpeded, guaranteeing deep penetration

Available in: .270 Win., .270 WSM, .280 Rem., 7x64 Brenneke, 7mm Rem. Mag., .308 Win., .30–06 Spfd., .300 Win. Mag., .300 WSM

Box 20: . . . . **$55.00–$79.00**

ORYX

Features: The Oryx has a thin forward jacket with internal splitting zones; the bonding and the thicker rear jacket wall ensure a high residual weight after impact (often over 90 percent) and excellent penetration

Available in: .222 Rem., .223 Rem., .22–250 Rem., .220 Swift, 6mm Norma BR, 6XC, .243 Win., 6.5x55 Swedish, 6.5x284 Norma, .270 Wby., .270 Win., .270 WSM, .280 Rem., 7x57 R Mauser, 7x57 Mauser, 7x64 Brenneke, 7x65 R, 7mm Rem. Mag., 7mm Blaser Mag., 7.5x55 Swiss, .308 Win., .30-06 Spfd., .300 Win. Mag., .300 WSM, .300 Blaser Mag., .308 Norma Mag., .338 Blaser Mag., .338 Win. Mag., .35 Whelen, .358 Norma Mag., 8x57 JRS, 8x57 JS, 9.3x57, 9.3x62 Mauser, 9.3x74 R, .375 Blaser Mag., .375 H&H Mag.

Box 20: . . . . **$45.00–$152.00**

NORMA AMERICAN PH

NORMA ORYX

NORMA KALAHARI

AMMUNITION

Nosler

Rifle Ammunition

MATCH GRADE

Features: Match Grade Ammunition consists of Nosler's precisely-designed Custom Competition bullet along with NoslerCustom Brass; each piece of brass is checked for correct length, neck-sized, chamfered, trued and flash holes are checked for proper alignment; powder charges are meticulously weighed and finished rounds are visually inspected and polished
Available in: .223 Rem., .22 Nosler, .26 Nosler, .28 Nosler, .30 Nosler, .300 BLK, .308 Win., .33 Nosler, .338 Lapua Mag., 6.5 Creedmoor, 6.5-284 Norma
Box 20: . . . . **$24.50–$81.90**

SAFARI

Features: Loaded with either the Partition or Nosler Solid and designed for the same point of impact with either bullet, Safari Ammunition provides the ultimate versatility for any dangerous game situation
Available in: Available in both Partition and Solid Dangerous Game: .375 Flanged, .375 H&H, .375 Ruger, .404 Jeffery, .416 Rem. Mag., .416 Rigby, .450 Rigby, .458 Lott, .458 Win. Mag., 9.3x62 Mauser; SD only: .470 NE, .500 Jeffery, .500 NE, .505 Gibbs; PT only: .500/.416 NE
Box 20: . . . . **$139.60–$224.00**

TROPHY GRADE

Features: Manufactured to Nosler's strictest quality standards, Trophy Grade Ammunition uses Nosler Custom Brass and Nosler Bullets to attain optimum performance, no matter where your hunting trip takes you. Whether you want your ammunition loaded with AccuBond, Partition Ballistic Tip or, E-Tip, NoslerCustom Trophy Grade Ammunition will have the right load for the right game.
Available in: .223 Rem., .22 Nosler, .243 Win., .25-06 Rem., .257 Roberts +P, .257 Wby., 6.5 Creedmoor, 6.5x55 Swedish, .260 Rem., .26 Nosler, .28 Nosler, .280 Rem., .260 Rem., 6.5-284 Norma, .264 Win. Mag., .270 Win., .270 WSM, 7mm-08 Rem., .280 Ack. Imp., 7mm SAUM, 7mm Rem. Mag., 7mm STW, 7mm RUM, 7x57 Mauser, 9.3x62 Mauser., 308 Win., .30–06 Spfd., .300 H&H Mag., .300 Win., .300 Win. Mag., Mag, .300 WSM, .300 SAUM, .300 RUM, .300 Wby., .325 WSM, .338 Lapua Mag., .338 RUM, .338 Win. Mag., .340 Wby., .33 Nosler, .35 Whelen, .375 H&H, .375 H&H Mag., .375 Ruger, .30 Nosler, .416 Rem. Mag.
Box 20: . . . . **$29.95–$98.10**

TROPHY GRADE VARMINT

Features: Trophy Grade VARMINT Ammunition consists of the venerable Ballistic Tip VARMINT bullet or the frangible Ballistic Tip Lead Free along with NoslerCustom Brass
Available in: .204 Ruger, .223 Rem., .22 Nosler, .22-250 Rem.
Box 20: . . . . **$24.40–$41.30**

VARMAGEDDON

Features: Featuring a highly accurate polymer tip or hollow point combined with flat base design, Varmageddon products were created for the high-volume varmint shooter who requires the utmost precision; loaded with Nosler Custom Brass, Varmageddon ammunition provides the highest levels of performance for any varmint hunter
Available in: .17 Rem., .22 Hornet, .22 Nosler, .204 Ruger, .221 Rem. Fireball, .222 Rem., .22-250 Rem., .223 Rem., .243 Win., .300 BLK, .308 Win.
Box 20: . . . . **$21.30–$41.95**

NOSLER SAFARI AMMUNITION

NOSLER TROPHY GRADE VARMINT AMMUNITION

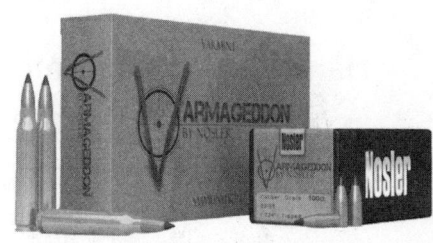

NOSLER VARMAGEDDON AMMUNITION & BULLETS

Handgun Ammunition

DEFENSE HANDGUN

Features: Bonded 'Performance' bullets for higher weight retention and maximum barrier penetration; either jacketed hollow point or polymer tipped configuration
Available in: 9mm Luger +P, .40 S&W, 45 ACP +P
MSRP . . . . **$20.50–$22.80**

NOSLER DEFENSE HANDGUN

PMC Ammunition

Rifle Ammunition

BRONZE LINE - RIFLE

Features: For shooters and hunters who appreciate affordable quality ammunition, the PMC Bronze Line offers reliable performance for every shooting application; Full Metal Jacket (FMJ) bullet types
Available in: .223 Rem, .223 Soft Point, .308 Soft Point, .308 Win., 7.62x39, .50
Box 20: . . . .**$8.00–$49.00**

X-TAC

Features: PMC's exacting adherence to precise specifications of military and law enforcement organizations assures that X-TAC ammunition will perform perfectly in that fraction of a second when a serious threat arises and your life is on the line
Available in: 5.56 NATO, 7.62
Box 20: . . . .**$9.00–$11.00**

X-TAC MATCH

Features: X-TAC ammo performance comined with Sierra Bullets' ballistics
Available in: .223 Rem., .308 Win., .50
Box 20: . . . .**$28.00–$40.00**

Handgun Ammunition

BRONZE LINE - HANDGUN

Features: The same quality and dependability built into our Starfire ammunition is incorporated through-out our extensive line of PMC training ammunition and standard hollow point or soft point ammunition.
Available in: .25 ACP, .32 ACP, .380 ACP, .38 Spl., .38 Super +P, 9mm Luger, .357 Mag., 10mm ACP, .40 S&W, .44 S&W Spl., .44 Rem. Mag., .45 ACP
From: . . . .**$14.00–$39.00**

ERANGE

Features: PMC's eRange environmentally friendly ammunition utilizes a reduced hazard primer that is the first of this type in the industry, an encapsulated metal jacket (EMJ) bullet which completely encloses the surface of the bullet core with precision made copper alloy, and powder with clean-burning characteristics and smooth fire for increased barrel life
Available in: .380 ACP, .38 Spl., .38 Spl. +P, .357 Mag., 9mm Luger, .40 S&W, .44 Rem., .45 ACP
From: **$27.00**

GOLD LINE - STARFIRE

Features: The secret of Starfire's impressive performance lies in a unique, patented rib-and-flute hollow point cavity design; upon impact, the pre-notched jacket mouth begins to peel back, separating into five uniform copper petals and allowing expansion to begin
Available in: .380 ACP, .38 Spl. +P, .357 Mag., 9mm Luger, .40 S&W, .44 Rem. Mag., .45 ACP
From: . . . .**$13.00–$26.00**

PMC BRONZE LINE - HANDGUN

PMC AMMUNITION X-TAC MATCH

PMC ERANGE

AMMUNITION

Remington Arms Company

Rifle Ammunition

.30 REM. AR

Features: A short, .30-caliber round whose 125-grain bullets match the speed of .308 150s, for hunting deer-size game with the AR-15 modular repeating rifle; ammo comes in Core-Lokt, Premier Accu-Tip, UMC, and Hog Hammer loads
Box 20: . . . . **$22.00–$45.00**

CORE-LOKT

Features: The bonded bullet retains up to 95 percent of its original weight with maximum penetration and energy transfer; features a progressively tapered jacket design, the Core-Lokt Ultra Bonded bullet initiates and controls expansion nearly 2x
Available in: 6mm Rem., .25-06 Rem., .25-20 Win., .250 Savage, 6.5x55 Swedish Mauser, .260 Rem., .264 Win. Mag., .270 Win., .270 WSM, .280 Rem., 7mm-08, 7mm Rem. Mag., 7mm RUM, 7x64, 7mm Mauser, .30 Carbine, .30-30 Win., .30-40 Krag, .30-06 Spfd., .300 Savage, .30 Rem. AR, .300 WSM, .300 Win. Mag., .300 RUM, .300 Wby. Mag., .303 British, 7.62x39, .308 Marlin Express, .308 Win., 8mm Mauser, .32 Win. Spec., .338 Win. Mag., .338 RUM, .35 Rem., .35 Whelen, .444 Marlin, .45-70 Govt
Box 20: . . . . **$20.00–$92.00**

HOG HAMMER

Features: Penetrating even the thickest-skinned pigs with a Barnes TSX Bullet at its heart, the all copper construction provides for 28 percent deeper penetration than standard lead-core bullets; offers near 100 percent weight-retention on-hog, while expanding rapidly to deliver devastating wound channels; utilizes a flash-suppressed propellant for nighttime or low light hunts, and uses nickel-plated cases for reliable feeding
Available in: .300 BLK, .223 Rem., .30 Rem. AR, .30–30 Win., .30–06 Spfd., .308 Win.
Box 20: . . . . **$27.00–$41.00**

HYPERSONIC

Features: Delivers more than just laser-flat trajectories and higher downrange energies due to its advanced bonded bullet design, Core-Lokt Ultra Bonded
Available in: .223 Rem., .243 Win., .30-06 Spfd., .300 Win. Mag., .308 Win., 7mm Rem. Mag., .270 Win.
Box 20: . . . . **$27.00–$41.00**

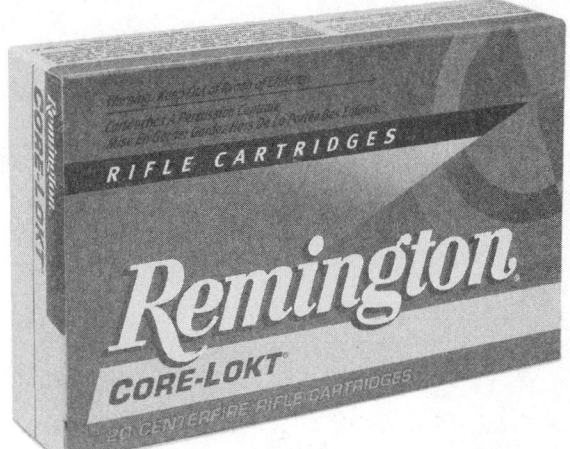

REMINGTON AMMUNITION HOG HAMMER

REMINGTON CORE-LOKT

REMINGTON AMMUNITION HYPERSONIC

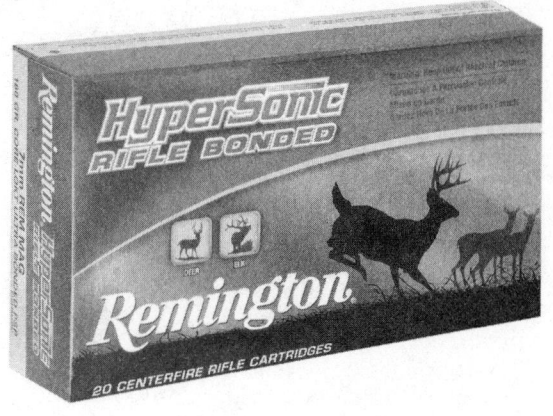

Remington Arms Company

MANAGED RECOIL
Features: Managed-Recoil Ammunition delivers Remington Field proven hunting performance out to 200 yards with half the recoil; bullets provide 2x expansion with over 75 percent weight retention on shots inside 50 yards and out to 200 yards.
Available in: .260 Rem., .270 Win., .30-06 Spfd., .300 Rem. Ultra Mag., .30-30 Win., .300 Win. Mag., 7mm Rem. Mag., 7mm-08 Rem., .308 Win.
Box 20:. . . . .$20.00–$41.00

PREMIER ACCUTIP
Features: Featuring precision-engineered polymer tip bullets designed for match-grade accuracy (sub MOA), Premier AccuTip offers an unprecedented combination of super-flat trajectory and deadly down-range performance
Available in: .30 Rem. AR, .300 BLK, .300 Rem. Ultra Mag., .270 WSM, .300 WSM, .223 Rem., .243 Win., .260 Rem., .270 Win., .280 Rem., 7mm Rem. Mag., .30-06 Spfd., .300 Win. Mag., .308 Win., 7mm-08 Rem., .45 Bushmaster
Box 20:. . . . .$20.00–$28.00

PREMIER MATCH
Features: Loaded with match-grade bullets, this ammunition employs special loading practices to ensure world-class performance and accuracy with every shot
Available in: .308 Win., .223 Rem., 6.8mm Rem. SPC, .300 BLK
Box 20:. . . . .$33.00–$39.00

REMINGTON
AMMUNITION
PREMIER
ACCUTIP

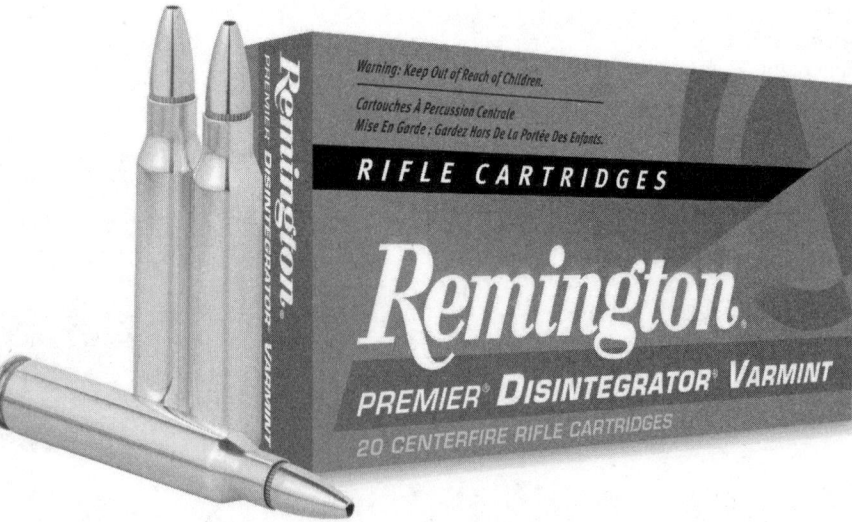

REMINGTON
PREMIER
DISINTEGRATOR
VARMINT

AMMUNITION

Remington Arms Company

Handgun Ammunition

ULTIMATE DEFENSE, COMPACT, FULL-SIZE

Features: Designed with the concealed carry permit holder in mind; delivers big gun terminal performance out of shorter barreled pistols and revolvers; engineered to provide optimal penetration and expansion at lower velocities for maximum stopping power
Available in: 9mm, .380 ACP, .38 Spl. +P, .40 S&W, .45 ACP. Full-size line also includes .357 Mag., 9mm +P
Box 20:. $23.00

Rimfire Ammunition

.22 RIMFIRE TARGET

Features: Whether it's getting young shooters started, practice plinking, small-game hunting, or keeping match shooters scoring high, Remington's rimfire quality stands tall
Available in: .22 LR
From:. . . . .$5.00–$10.00

MAGNUM RIMFIRE

Features: Premier Gold Box Rimfire ammunition features sleek AccuTip-V bullets; Magnum rimfire ammunition gives shooters the choice of either a Jacketed Hollow Point for quick expansion or a Pointed Soft Point for optimum penetration
Available in: .22 Win. Mag.
MSRP. $16.00

REMINGTON-ELEY COMPETITION RIMFIRE MATCH EPS

Features: Remington and Eley offer three grades of their premier .22 Long Rifle ammunition; this match grade load features Eley's innovative Tenex EPS-profile bullet—ideal for aspiring top class shooters and training at the highest level
Available in: .22 LR
Box 50:. . . . .$11.00–$22.00

Shotgun Ammunition

AMERICAN CLAY AND FIELD

Features: Nothing that flies stands a chance against these dual-purpose

rounds. Expect the densest, most consistent patterns possible, no matter the day's pursuit. Featuring a premium STS primer, reloadable hull, our patented Power Piston wad, and high-hardness lead shot, they deliver flawless performance and consistent patterning, whether your target is winged or clay.

REMINGTON AMMUNITION
ULTIMATE DEFENSE COMPACT

REMINGTON
PREMIER NITRO
SPORTING CLAYS

REMINGTON AMMUNITION
AMERICAN CLAY AND FIELD

Available in: 12, 20, 28, .410
MSRP. . . . . N/A

GUN CLUB TARGET

Features: Loaded with Gun Club Grade Shot, Premier STS Primers, and Power Piston One-Piece Wads, these high-quality shells receive the same care in loading as top-of-the-line Premier STS and Nitro .27 shells
Available in: 12, 20 Ga. (2¾ in.); Shot sizes: 7.5, 8, 9
Box 25:. $8.00

Remington Arms Company

EXPRESS EXTRA LONG RANGE

Features: Long considered to be some of the best-balanced, best-patterning upland field loads available, our family of shotshells offer great selections for upland bird hunting; the hunter's choice for a wide variety of game-bird applications, from 12-gauge to .410 bore, with shot-size options ranging from BB's all the way down to 9s; suitable for everything from quail to farm predators
Available in: 12, 16, 20, 28 Ga. (2¾ in.), .410 (2½ in., 3 in.); Shot sizes: 2, 4, 5, 6, 7.5, 9
From:............$16.00–$18.00

HEAVY DOVE

Features: A sure bet for all kinds of upland game, ShurShot loads have earned the reputation as one of the best-balanced, best-pattering upland field loads available; shells combine an ideal balance of powder charge and shot payload to deliver effective velocities and near-perfect patterns with mild recoil for high-volume upland hunting situations
Available in: 12, 20 Ga. (2¾ in.); Shot sizes: 6, 7.5, 8
From:.................. $9.00

HYPERSONIC STEEL

Features: With unprecedented velocity and the highest downrange pattern energies ever achieved, Remington HyperSonic Steel takes lethality to new heights and lengths
Available in: 10 Ga. (3½ in.), 12 Ga. (3 in., 3½ in.), 20 Ga. (3 in.); Shot sizes: BB, BBB, 1, 2, 3, 4
From:............$24.00–$36.00

LEAD GAME

Features: For a wide variety of field gaming, these budget-stretching loads include the same quality components as other Remington shotshells, and are available in four different gauges to match up with your favorite upland shotguns
Available in: 12, 16, 20 Ga. (2¾ in.), .410 (2½ in.); Shot sizes: 6, 7.5, 8
From:.............$8.00–$16.00

PREMIER HIGH-VELOCITY MAGNUM COPPER-PLATED

Features: Utilizing a specially-blended powder recipe, Remington's advanced Power Piston one-piece wad, and hardened copper plated shot, these new high-velocity loads result in extremely dense patterns and outstanding knockdown power at effective ranges
Available in: 12 Ga. (3 in., 3½ in.); Shot sizes: 4, 5, 6
From:............$18.00–$22.00

PREMIER MAGNUM COPPER-PLATED BUFFERED

Features: Premier Magnum Turkey Loads provide that extra edge to reach out with penetrating power and dense, concentrated patterns; the magnum-grade, Copper-Lokt shot is protected by our Power Piston wad and cushioned with special polymer buffering
Available in: 10 Ga. (3½ in.), 12 Ga. (2¾ in., 3 in., 3½ in.), 20 Ga. (3 in.).; Shot sizes: 4, 5, 6
Box 10:............$13.00–$22.00

PREMIER NITRO 27 TARGET

Features: Designed specifically for back-fence trap and long-range sporting clays; delivers consistent handicap velocity and pattern uniformity; new, improved powder loading significantly reduces felt recoil while retaining high velocity; both factors allow avid trap shooters to stay fresh for the shoot off.
Available in: 12 Ga. (2¾ in.); Shot Sizes: 7.5, 8
From:................. $12.00

PREMIER NITRO SPORTING CLAYS

Features: To meet the special demands of avid sporting clays shooters, Remington developed a new Premier Nitro Gold Sporting Clays target load, and at 1300 fps, the extra velocity gives you an added advantage for those long crossers—making target leads closer to normal for ulti-mate target-crushing satisfaction
Available in: 12, 28 Ga. (2¾ in.), .410 (2½ in.); Shot sizes: 7.5, 8
From:............$12.00–$16.00

PREMIER STS TARGET

Features: STS Target Loads have taken shot-to-shot consistency to a new performance level, setting the standard at all major skeet, trap, and sporting clays shooting across the country, while providing handloaders with unmatched reloading ease and hull longevity; available in most gauges, Premier STS shells are the most reliable, consistent, and reloadable shells you can shoot
Available in: 12, 20, 28 Ga. (2¾ in.), .410 (2½ in.); Shot sizes: 7.5, 8, 8.5, 9
From:............$12.00–$16.00

NITRO MAG. BUFFERED MAGNUM

Features: The original buffered magnum shotshells from Remington, the shot charge is packed with a generous amount of shock-absorbing polymer buffering and surrounded by our patented Power Piston wad to protect the specially hardened shot all the way down the barrel for dense, even patterns and uniform shot strings
Available in: 12, 20 Ga. (2¾ in., 3 in.); Shot sizes: 2, 4, 6
Box 25:............$26.00–$38.00

NITRO PHEASANT

Features: Uses Remington's own Copper-Lokt copper-plated lead shot with high antimony content; hard shot stays rounder for truer flight, tighter patterns, and greater penetration; available in both high-velocity and magnum loadings
Available in: 12, 20 Ga. (2¾ in., 3 in.); Shot sizes: 4, 5, 6
From:............$20.00–$23.00

AMMUNITION

Remington Arms Company

NITRO-STEEL HIGH-VELOCITY

Features: Greater hull capacity means heavier charges and larger pellets, which makes these loads ideal for large waterfowl; delivers denser patterns for greater lethality and is zinc plated to prevent corrosion
Available in: 10 Ga. (3½ in.), 12 Ga. (2¾ in., 3 in., 3½ in.), 16 Ga. (2¾ in.), 20 Ga. (2¾ in., 3 in.); Shot sizes: T, BBB, BB, 1, 2, 3, 4
From:. . . . .**$21.00–$30.00**

NITRO TURKEY

Features: These loads contain Nitro Mag. extra-hard lead shot that is as hard and round as copper-plated shot; will pattern as well as other copper-plated, buffered loads without the higher cost
Available in: 12 Ga. (2¾ in., 3 in., 3½ in.), 20 Ga. (3 in.); Shot sizes: 4, 5, 6
Box 10:. . . . .**$9.00–$17.00**

PHEASANT

Features: For the broadest selection in game-specific Upland shotshells, Remington Upland Loads are the perfect choice with high-velocity and long-range performance for any pheasant hunting situation; standard high-base payloads feature Power Piston one-piece wads
Available in: 12, 16, 20 Ga. (2¾ in.); Shot sizes: 4, 5, 6, 7.5
From:. . . . .**$13.00–$17.00**

SPORTSMAN HI-SPEED STEEL

Features: Sportsman Hi-Speed Steel's sealed primer, high-quality steel shot, and consistent muzzle velocities combine to provide reliability in adverse weather, while delivering exceptional pattern density and retained energy; a high-speed steel load that is ideal for short-range high-volume shooting during early duck seasons or over decoys
Available in: 10 Ga. (3½ in.), 12 Ga. (2¾ in., 3 in., 3½ in.), 20 Ga. (2¾ in.); Shot sizes: BB, 1, 2, 3, 4, 6, 7
From:. . . . .**$11.00–$29.00**

Shotgun Slugs & Buckshot

EXPRESS, EXPRESS MAGNUM BUCKSHOT

Features: A combination of heavy cushioning behind the shot column and a granulated polymer buffering helps maintain pellet roundness for tight, even patterns
Available in: 12 (2¾ in., 3 in., 3½ in.), 20 Ga. (2¾ in.); Shot sizes: 000, 00, 0, 1, 3, 4
From:. . . . .**$5.00–$12.00**

MANAGED-RECOIL BUCKSHOT

Features: With less felt recoil than full velocity loads, Express Managed-Recoil Buckshot is an ideal close-range performer; less recoil means second shot recovery is quicker, allowing the user to get back on target more easily; loads are buffered for dense patterns, allowing for highly effective performance at up to 40 yards
Available in: 12 Ga. (2¾ in.); Shot size: 00
From:. **$5.00**

PREMIER ACCUTIP BONDED SABOT

Features: Guided by our new Power Port Tip, the AccuTip Bonded Sabot Slug delivers a degree of accuracy and terminal performance unmatched by any other we tested; yields over 95 percent weight retention thanks to its spiral nose cuts, bonded construction, and high-strength cartridge brass jacket; designed for fully-rifled barrels only
Available in: 12, 20 Ga. (2¾ in., 3 in.)
From:. . . . .**$15.00–$17.00**

REMINGTON HYPERSONIC STEEL

REMINGTON EXPRESS BUCKSHOT

Remington Arms Company

PREMIER COPPER SOLID SABOT
Features: Ultra-high velocities deliver devastating on-game performance and the tightest groups (1.8-in.) of any shotgun slug with ultra-flat trajectories; patented spiral nose cuts ensure consistent 2x expansion over a wide range of terminal velocities; 385-grain bonded bullet yields near 100 percent weight retention; flattest shooting slug in existence—10 percent better than the nearest competition; designed for use in fully-rifled barrels only
Available in: 12, 20 Ga. (2¾ in.)
From: $23.00

SLUGGER HIGH VELOCITY
Features: This is the first high-velocity Foster-style lead slug which exits the barrel at 1800 fps, 13 percent faster than standard 1-oz. slugs; the ⁷/₈ oz. Slugger High Velocity delivers 200 ft.-

lbs. more energy at 50 yards with flatter trajectory on deer than standard 1-oz. slugs; designed for the avid deer hunter using smooth bore guns
Available in: 12 Ga. (2¾ in., 3 in.), 20 Ga. (2¾ in.)
From: . . . . $5.00–$7.00

SLUGGER MANAGED-RECOIL RIFLED
Features: Slugger Managed-Recoil Rifled Slugs offer remarkably effective performance but with 45 percent less felt recoil than full velocity Sluggers; with effective energy out of 80 yards, these 1-oz. slugs easily handle the majority of shotgun deer hunting ranges
Available in: 12 Ga. (2¾ in.)
From: $5.00

SLUGGER RIFLED
Features: Remington redesigned their 12-gauge Slugger Rifled Slug for a 25 percent improvement in accuracy; at 1760 fps muzzle velocity, the 3-in. 12-gauge Magnum slug shoot 25 percent flatter than regular 12 gauge slugs
Available in: 12 Ga. (2¾ in., 3 in.), 16 Ga. (2¾ in.), 20 Ga. (2¾ in.), .410 (2½ in.)
From: . . . . $5–$7.00

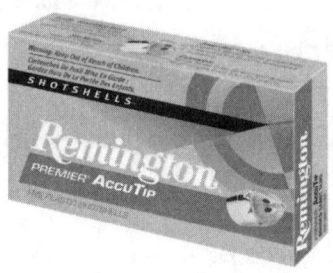

REMINGTON PREMIER ACCUTIP BONDED SABOT

Rottweil

LASER SABOT SLUGS
Features: Everything from the powder to the pellets must be perfectly balanced to produce a shotshell that delivers the required performance.

With Rottweil shotshells components and excellent quality control ensure that Rottweil shotgun cartridges not only perform, but perform safely: one expects no less from this renowned German manufacturer.

Available in: 12 Ga., 20 Ga.
MSRP: . . . . $10.75–$11.50

Ruger (Sturm, Ruger & Co.)

POLYCASE ARX
Features: High speed, yet low recoil, for maximum force to target and fast, repeated target acquisition; advanced material copper-polymer matrix performs in a wide range of firearms, including suppressed weapons; ARX

technology acts as a force multiplier, dispersing energy forward and laterally
Available in: .357 Mag., .40 S&W, .45 ACP, .380 ACP, 9mm Luger
Box 20,25: . . . .$19.99–$20.99

RUGER POLYCASE ARX

Weatherby

WEATHERBY MAGNUM
Features: Weatherby Magnum cartridges are loaded with a variety of popular bullet types for a wide range of shooting purposes

Available in: .224, .240, 6.5-300, .257, .270, 7mm, .300, .340, .30–378, .338–378, .375, .378, .416, .460
MSRP . . . . $44.00–$209.00

WEATHERBY 6.5-300 WEATHERBY MAGNUM

**WINCHESTER AMMUNITION
17 WINCHESTER SUPER MAGNUM**

**WINCHESTER AMMUNITION 17
WINCHESTER SUPER MAGNUM 20-GRAIN
SUPER X POWER-CORE RIMFIRE**

**WINCHESTER AMMUNITION M-22
SUBSONIC**

**WINCHESTER
AMMUNITION DEER
SEASON XP**

**WINCHESTER AMMUNITION EXPEDITION
BIG GAME**

Rifle Ammunition
17 WINCHESTER SUPER MAGNUM

Features: A .27 caliber shellcase necked down to a .17 caliber bullet; surpasses the downrange velocity, energy, trajectory and wind bucking characteristics of both the .17 HMR and .22 WMR; available in Varmint HE, Varmint HV, SuperX, and VarmintX lines.
Available in: .17 WSM
Box 50: **$15.00**

17 WINCHESTER SUPER MAGNUM 20-GRAIN SUPER X POWER-CORE RIMFIRE

Features: The 17 Win Super Mag caliber ballistically exceeds the velocity, energy, trajectory, and wind drift characteristics of all rimfire products currently available. The Power-Core lead-free bullet provides another option in this versatile caliber.
Available in: .17 WSM
Box 50: **$23.99**

BALLISTIC SILVERTIP

Features: Solid-based boattail design delivers excellent long-range accuracy; in .22 calibers, the ballistic plastic polycarbonate Silvertip bullet initiates rapid fragmentation; in medium to larger calibers, special jacket contours extend range and reduce cross-wind drift; harder lead core ensures proper bullet expansion
Available in: .22-250 Rem., .223 Rem., .204 Ruger, .223 WSSM, .243 Win., .243 WSSM, .25-06 Rem., .25 WSSM, .270 Win., .270 WSM, .280 Rem., .300 Win. Mag., .30–06 Spfd., .300 WSM, .30–30 Win., .308 Win., .325 WSM, .338 Win. Mag., 7mm Rem. Mag., 7mm-08 Rem., 7mm WSM
Box 20: . . . . **$22.00–$60.00**

DEER SEASON XP

Features: Large diameter polymer tip accelerates bullet expansion; built specifically for deer hunting and taking down big bucks; alloyed leather core; contoured jacket
Available in: .223 Rem., 6.5 Creedmoor, .243 Win., .270 Win., 270 WSM, .30-06 Spfd., .30-30 Win., .300 Win. Mag., .300 BLK, .300 WSM, .308 Win., 7mm Rem. Mag., 7mm-08 Rem.
Box: . . . . **N/A**

DEFENDER CENTERFIRE RIFLE

Features: Given the recent popularity of modern sporting rifles (MSR) among shooters and hunters, Winchester has designed a product using Split Core Technology (SCT) for personal defense; SCT technology, using a quick expansion front lead core and a deep driving bonded rear lead core, creates the ultimate .223 Rem. Home Defense load
Available in: .223 Rem., .308 Win., 7.62x39
Box 20: . . . . **$30.00–$40.00**

E-TIP LEAD-FREE

Features: The E-Tip lead-free bullet is developed for big-game hunters and complies with current state non-toxic regulations; co-developed with Nosler, the bullet features an E2 energy expansion cavity, which promotes consistent upset, and is made of gliding metal instead of pure copper, which helps prevent barrel fouling
Available in: .270 WSM, .270 Win., .30-06 Spfd., .300 WSM, .300 Win. Mag., .308 Win., 7mm Rem. Mag.
Box 20: . . . . **$43.00–$57.00**

EXPEDITION BIG GAME

Features: Polymer tip; bonded alloyed lead core; jacket technology; Lubalox (black oxide) coating; controlled expansion
Available in: .25-06 Rem., .25 WSSM, .270 Win., .270 WSM, .30-06 Spfd., .300 Win. Mag., .300 WSM, .325 WSM, .338 Win. Mag., .338 Lapua Mag., 7mm Rem. Mag., 7mm WSM
Box 20: . . . . **$33.99–$90.99**

M-22 SUBSONIC

Features: Specifically designed to reliably function semiautomatic rifles and pistols at subsonic velocities. Subsonic velocities offer low noise in both suppressed and non-supressed firearms. Bullet is a black copper-plated roundnose.
Available in: .22 LR (45 gr.)
Box 100 Mini Mag: **$10.99**
Box 800: **$58.99**

Winchester Ammunition

MATCH

Features: Combining proven Winchester technology with proven bullets, the hollow point boat tail design provides the precision match shooters demand; sleek bullet profile, large boattail and small hollow point maximizes long-range accuracy
Available in: .223 Rem., 5.56 NATO, 6.5 Creedmoor, .308 Win., .338 Lapua
Box: . . . .$28.00–$92.00

RAZOR BOAR XT

Features: Razor Boar XT is designed specifically for the rugged demands of boar hunting; drives through thick hide and bone to deliver lethal force; the lead-free bullet has a beveled profile and is made of solid gilding metal with a hollow point for delayed expansion on extremely tough wild hogs; flash suppressed powders make Razor Boar XT perfect for use in low light or after dark with night vision technology
Available in: .223 Rem., .270 Win., .30–06 Spfd., .308 Win., 7.62x39
Box 20: . . . .$27.00–$40.00

SUPER CLEANNT

Features: Super Clean ammunition is completely lead free, utilizing a lead-free primer and a full metal jacket bullet with a zinc core that delivers superior accuracy and reliable performance. Designed for training on indoor and outdoor ranges.
Available in: .40 S&W, 9mm Luger, .38 Spl., .45 ACP
Box 50: . . . .$15.99–$57.99

SUPER-X HOLLOW POINT

Available in: .204 Ruger, .218 Bee, .22 Hornet, .30-30 Win.
Box 20: . . . .$20.00–$59.00

SUPER-X HOLLOW SOFT POINT

Available in: .30 Carbine, .44 Rem. Mag.
Box 20: $24.00

SUPER-X JACKETED SOFT POINT

Available in: .357 Mag.
Box 50: $48.00

SUPER-X JHP

Available in: .45-70 Govt.
Box 20: $36.00

SUPER-X LEAD

Available in: .32-20 Win.
Box 50: $45.00

SUPER-X POSITIVE EXPANDING POINT

Available in: .25-06 Rem., .25 WSSM
Box 20: . . . .$33.00–$35.00

SUPER-X POWER CORE 95/5

Features: Start with a 95/5 copper alloy, integrate a highly engineered contoured cavity—and you have a new benchmark in lead-free big-game cartridges; features a devastating effective bullet with massive initial impact shock plus deep penetration and virtually 100 percent retained weight to assure maximum trauma to bone and vitals
Available in: .223 Rem., .243 Win., .270 Win., .270 WSM, .30-06 Spfd., .300 Win. Mag., .300 WSM, .30-30 Win., .308 Win., 7mm-08 Rem., 7mm Rem. Mag., 7mm WSM
Box 20: . . . .$28.00–$47.00

SUPER-X POWER-POINT

Available in: .22-250 Rem., .223 Rem., .223 WSSM, .243 Win., .243 WSSM, .257 Roberts +P, .264 Win. Mag., .270 Win., .270 WSM, .284 Win., .300 Savage, .30-06 Spfd., .300 WSM, .30–30 Win., .303 British, .30-40 Krag, .307 Win., .308 Win., .300 Win. Mag., .325 WSM, .32 Win. Spl., .338 Win. Mag., .356 Win., 35 Rem., .375 Win., .44-40 Win., 6mm Rem., 7mm-08 Rem., 7x57 Mauser, 7mm Rem. Mag., 7mm WSM, 8x57 Mauser, 6.5x55 Swede, 7.62x39mm
Box 20: . . . .$17.00–$60.00

SUPER-X SILVERTIP HOLLOW POINT

Available in: 44 Rem. Mag.
Box 20: $29.00

SUPER-X SOFT POINT

Available in: .22 Hornet, .25-20 Win., .25-35 Win., .38-40 Win., .38-55 Win., .458 Win.
Box 50: . . . . $46.00–$82.00

USA FORGED

Features: High-quality American-made 9mm ammunition that uses premium Winchester components to provide great performance at a value price, this ammunition utilizes precision-manufactured steel shellcases featuring a proprietary surface treatment optimized for high-volume range sessions with the performance and functionality you expect from Winchester. Cartridge wears 115-gr. brass-jacketed lead core bullet.
Available in: 9mm Luger Cartridge wears 115-gr. brass-jacketed lead core bullet.
Box 150: $35.99

WINCHESTER AMMUNITION USA FORGED

WINCHESTER AMMUNITION SUPER CLEAN

WINCHESTER AMMUNITION MATCH

WINCHESTER RAZOR BOAR XT

Winchester Ammunition

VARMINT X

Features: Polymer tip, alloy jacket, lead core, and rapid fragmentation
Available in: .17 Hornet, .22 Hornet, .204 Ruger; .22-250 Rem.; .223 Rem.; .243 Win.
Box 20: . . . . **$18.00–$27.00**

Handgun Ammunition

DEFENDER HANDGUN

Features: The Winchester Supreme Elite Bonded PDX1, which was chosen by the FBI as their primary service round, is engineered to maximize terminal ballistics, as defined by the demanding FBI test protocol, which simulates real-world threats
Available in: .357 Mag., .357 SIG, .380 ACP, .38 Spl., +P, .40 S&W, .45 Colt, .45 ACP, 9mm Luger +P, 9mm Luger
From: . . . . **$18.00–$32.00**

DUAL BOND

Features: Dual Bond offers a large hollow point cavity, which provides consistent upsets at a variety of ranges and impact velocities; the heavy outer jacket is mechanically bonded to the inner bullet; inner bullet utilizes a proprietary bonding process for a combination of knockdown power, solid penetration, and significant tissue damage
Available in: .44 Rem. Mag., .454 Cassull, .460 S&W Mag., .500 S&W Mag.
Box 20: . . . . **$38.00–$68.00**

FULL METAL JACKET

Available in: .45 ACP, .38 Spl., 9mm Luger, .25 ACP, .38 Super Auto +P, .380 ACP, .40 S&W, .32 ACP, .45 GAP, 9mm Luger
From: . . . . **$15.00–$33.00**

LEAD FLATNOSE

Available in: .38 Spl., .44-40 Win., .44 S&W Spl., .45 Colt
Box 50: . . . . **$34.00–$42.00**

SUPER-X BLANK-BLACK POWDER

Available in: .32 S&W
Box 50: **$34.00**

SUPER-X BLANK-SMOKELESS

Available in: .38 Spl.
Box 50: **$41.00**

SUPER-X EXPANDING POINT

Available in: .25 ACP
Box 50: **$41.00**

SUPER-X HOLLOW SOFT POINT

Available in: .30 Carbine, .44 Rem. Mag.
Box 20: **$24.00**

SUPER-X JACKETED SOFT POINT

Available in: .357 Mag., .38 Spl.
Box 50: . . . . **$26.00–$48.00**

SUPER-X JHP

Available in: .357 Mag., .38 Spl. +P, .454 Casull, .45 Win. Mag., .460 S&W Mag.
Box 20: . . . . **$35.00–$53.00**

SUPER-X LEAD ROUND NOSE

Available in: .32 Short Colt, .32 S&W Long, .32 S&W, .38 Spl., .38 S&W, .44 S&W Spl., .45 Colt
From: **$37.00**

SUPER-X LEAD SEMI-WAD CUTTER

Available in: .38 Spl.
Box 50: **$37.00**

SUPER-X LEAD SEMI-WAD CUTTER HP

Available in: .38 Spl. +P
Box 50: **$38.00**

SUPER-X MATCH

Available in: .38 Spl. Super Match
Box 50: **$34.00**

PLATINUM TIP HOLLOW POINT

Features: Patented notched reserve taper bullet jacket, plated heavy wall jacket, and two-part hollow point cavity for uniform bullet expansion, massive energy depot
Available in: .41 Rem. Mag., .44 Rem. Mag., .454 Casull, .500 S&W
Box 20: . . . . **$31.00–$63.00**

SUPER-X SILVERTIP HOLLOW POINT

Available in: 10mm Auto, .32 ACP, .357 Mag., .380 ACP, .38 Super Auto +P, .38 Spl. +P, .38 Spl., .40 S&W, .41 Rem. Mag., .44 Rem. Mag., .44 S&W Spl., .45 ACP, .45 Colt, .45 GAP, 9x23 Win., 9mm Luger
Box 20, 50: . . . . **$22.00–$55.00**

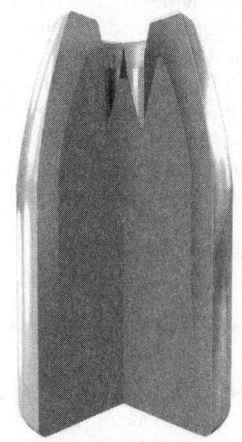

WINCHESTER SUPER-X PLATINUM TIP HOLLOW POINT

WINCHESTER DUAL BOND

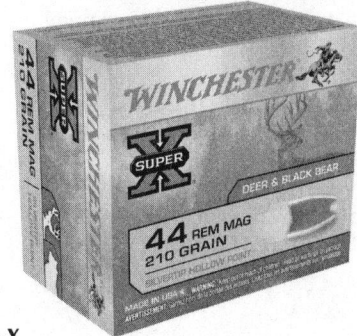

WINCHESTER SUPER-X SILVERTIP HOLLOW POINT

Winchester Ammunition

W TRAIN & DEFEND

Features: A straightforward solution for new shooters interested in training to become more proficient with their personal defense ammunition; ballistically-matched ammunition pairs range-ready TRAIN (T) rounds with threat-stopping, technologically-driven DEFEND (D) rounds, each designed for less felt recoil

Available in: .38 Spl., .380 ACP, .40 S&W, 9mm, .45 ACP

Box 50 (Train): . . . . . . $16.00–$25.00
Box 20 (Defend): . . . . $18.00–$26.00

WIN3GUN PISTOL

Features: Built specifically for high-volume, fast-paced competition and time spent training at the range

Available in: .40 S&W, .45 ACP, 9mm

Box 50: . . . . $17.00–$28.00

WIN1911

Features: Provides a choice of personal defense or training ammunition that has been matched for ballistic performance and engineered for the same feel and function; high-accuracy, ballistically matched full metal jacket and jacketed hollow point offerings make this an ideal ammunition choice

Available in: .45 ACP

Box 50: . . . . $28.00–$40.00

Rimfire Ammunition

DEFENDER .22 RIMFIRE

Features: Rifle load for personal defense; Defender 22 rimfire features a 40-gr. JHP jacketed hollow-point bullet and is designed to deliver the ideal personal defense combination of optimum penetration and maximum projectile expansion for maximum energy transfer

Available in: .22 Win. Mag.

Box 50 . . . .$31.00

DYNA POINT - PLATED

Available in: .22 Win. Mag.

Box 250: $46.00

WINCHESTER AMMUNITION W TRAIN & DEFEND

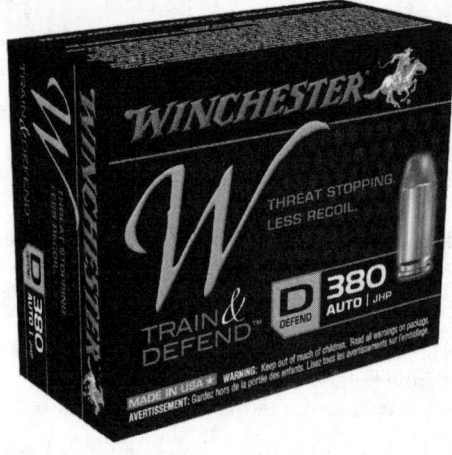

WINCHESTER AMMUNITION WIN3GUN PISTOL

WINCHESTER AMMUNITION WIN1911

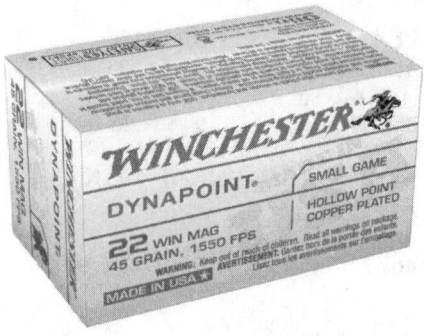

WINCHESTER DYNA POINT - PLATED

AMMUNITION

Winchester Ammunition

SUPER-X #12 SHOT
Available in: .22 LR
Box 50:................. $11.00

SUPER-X BLANK
Available in: .22 Short
Box 50:................. $9.00

SUPER-X FULL METAL JACKET
Available in: .22 Win. Mag.
Box 50:.................$11.00

SUPER-X JHP
Available in: .17 HMR, .17 Win. Super Mag., .22 Win. Mag.
Box 50, 250: ....$15.00–$57.00

SUPER-X LEAD HOLLOW POINT
Available in: .22 LR
Box 100:........... $8.00–$9.00

SUPER-X LEAD ROUND NOSE
Available in: .22 LR, .22 Long, .22 Short
Box 100:................ $7.00

SUPER-X LEAD ROUND NOSE, STANDARD VELOCITY
Available in: .22 LR
Box 100:........... $3.00–$6.00

SUPER-X POWER-POINT, LEAD HOLLOW POINT
Available in: .22 LR
Box 50:................. $4.00

VARMINT HIGH ENERGY
Available in: .22 LR, .22 Win. Mag., .17 WSM
Box 250, 500: ..... $29.00–$155.00

VARMINT HIGH VELOCITY
Available in: .22 Win. Mag., .17 HMR, .17 WSM
Box 500: .... $136.00–$146.00

VARMINT LEAD FREE
Available in: .22 Mag., .22 LR
Box 500:.................$113.00

WILDCAT 22 LEAD ROUND NOSE
Available in: .22 LR
Box 500: $26.00

XPERT LEAD HOLLOW POINT
Available in: .22 LR
Box 500: $32.00

Shotgun Ammunition
AA STEEL
Features: Steel shot; high-strength hull; AA wads
Available in: 12 (2¾ in.); Shot sizes: 7.5, 8
Box: .... N/A

AA TARGET LOADS
Features: The hunter's choice for a wide variety of game bird applications, available in an exceptionally broad selection of loadings, from 12-gauge to .410 bore, with shot size options ranging from BBs all the way down to 9s—suitable for everything from quail to farm predators
Available in: 12, 20, 28 Ga. (2¾ in.), .410 (2½ in.); Shot sizes: 7.5, 8, 8.5, 9
Box 25:............$9.00–$11.00

AA TRAACKER
Features: Stay centered in the pattern all the way to the target; Shot-trap core design captures a portion of the shot to stabilize the wad; unique dove-tail petals allows the wad to spin-stabilize and track in the center of the pattern; available in bright orange for low light conditions and in black for bright light conditions
Available in: 12 Ga. (2 ¾ in.), 20 Ga. (2 ¾ in.)
Box 25:..................$10.00

WINCHESTER AMMUNITION AA TRAACKER

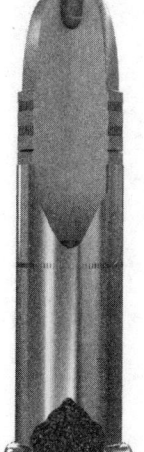

WINCHESTER VARMINT LEAD FREE

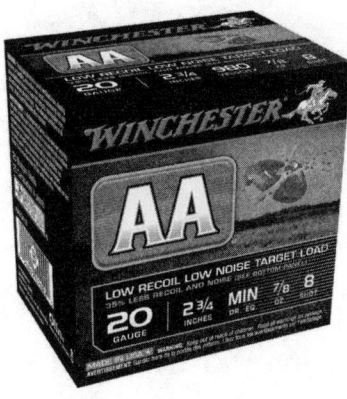

WINCHESTER AA FEATHERLITE

WINCHESTER AMMUNITION AA STEEL

Winchester Ammunition

BLIND SIDE

Features: Blind Side ammunition combines ground-breaking, stacked HEX Shot technology and the Diamond Cut Wad in the most deadly Winchester waterfowl load available. Loaded with 100 percent HEX Shot, you get more pellets on target, a larger kill zone, and more trauma inducing pellets than ever before, meaning quick kill shots
Available in: 12 Ga. (2¾ in., 3 in., 3½ in.), 20 Ga. (3 in.); Shot size: BB, 1, 2, 3, 5, 6
Box 25: . . . .**$20.00–$27.00**

BLIND SIDE MAGNUM PHEASANT

Features: High Packing density for increased powder charge with hinged wad results in 1675 fps; high velocity HEX Shot allows reduced leads and increased pellet energy; diamond cut wad design provides choke responsiveness for increased kill zone; Drylok Super Steel System keeps your powder dry
Available in: 12 (2 ¾ in., 3 in.)
Box: . . . .**N/A**

BLIND SIDE MAGNUM WATERFOWL

Features: High Packing density for increased powder charge with hinged wad results in 1675 fps; high velocity HEX Shot allows reduced leads and increased pellet energy; diamond cut wad design provides choke responsiveness for increased kill zone; Drylok Super Steel System keeps your powder dry
Available in: 12 (2 ¾ in., 3 in., 3 ½ in.), 20 (3 in.)
Box: . . . .**N/A**

LONG BEARD XR

Features: Features Shot-Lok technology; offers the tightest patterns and longest shot capability of any traditional turkey load with twice the pellets in a 10-in. circle out to 60 yds
Available in: 12 Ga. (3 in., 3 ½ in.), 20 Ga. (3 in.)
Box 10: . . . . **$18.00–$23.00**

ROOSTER LOK'D & LETHAL XR

Features: Protects shot during in-bore acceleration; shot launches from barrel near perfectly round for extremely tight long-range patterns; greater penetration over standard lead loads beyond 50 yards; devastating terminal on-target performances
Available in: 12 (2 ¾ in., 3 in.)
Box: . . . .**N/A**

SUPER TARGET LOADS

Available in: 12, 20 Ga. (2¾ in.); Shot sizes: 7, 7.5, 8, 9
Box 25: **$7.00**

SUPER PHEASANT LOADS

Available in: 12 Ga. (2¾ in., 3 in.), 20 Ga. (3 in.); Shot sizes: 4, 5, 6
Box 25: . . . . **$19.00–$23.00**

SUPER PHEASANT STEEL LOADS

Available in: 12 Ga. (3 in.); Shot size: 4
Box 25: . . . . **$20.00–$23.00**

SUPER-X TRIALS AND BLANKS

Available in: 10 Ga. (2⁷/₈ in.), 12 Ga. (2¾ in.)
Box 25: **$20.00**

SUPER-X TURKEY LOADS

Available in: 12 Ga. (2¾ in., 3 in.); Shot sizes: 4, 5, 6
Box 10: . . . . **$9.00–$12.00**

WINCHESTER BLIND SIDE

WINCHESTER AMMUNITION LONG BEARD XR

WINCHESTER AMMUNITION ROOSTER LOK'D & LETHAL XR

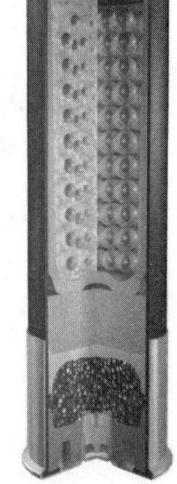

WINCHESTER AMMUNITION ROOSTER XR

WINCHESTER AMMUNITION WIN3GUN SHOTGUN

AMMUNITION

Winchester Ammunition

SUPER-X XPERT HI-VELOCITY STEEL LOADS

Available in: 12 Ga. (2¾ in., 3 in.), 20 Ga. (3 in.); Shot sizes: BB, 1, 2, 3, 4

Box 25:. . . . .$12.00–$18.00

SUPER-X XPERT STEEL LOADS

Available in: 12, 20, 28 Ga., .410 bore (2¾ in.); Shot sizes: 6, 7

Box 25:. $8.00

VARMINT-X SHOT-LOK SHOTGUN

Features: Shot-Lok technology; 50 percent more pellets in a 10 in. circle at 40 yds; greater penetration over standard lead loads beyond 40 yds; devastating terminal on-target performance

Available in: 12

Box 10:. $16.99

Shotgun Ammunition– Slugs & Buckshot

PDX1 12 SLUG AND BUCK

Features: The 12-gauge PDX1 Defender ammunition features a distinctive black hull, black oxide high-base head and three pellets of Grex buffered 00 plated buckshot nested on top of a 1 oz. rifled slug; an ideal, tight patterning personal defense load; slug/buckshot combination provides optimum performance at short and long ranges while compensating for aim error

Available in: 12 Ga. (2¾ in.)

Box 10:. $15.00

PDX1 DEFENDER SEGMENTING SLUG

Features: The uniquely designed slug segments into three pieces when fired into FBI protocol barriers such as bare, light cloth, and heavy cloth covered ballistic gelatin; the round is designed to compensate for aim error over traditional slugs.

Available in: 12 Ga. (2¾ in.), 20 Ga. (2¾ in.)

Box 10: $15.00

RACKMASTER RIFLED SLUGS

Features: The RackMaster system design consists of a hard-hitting lead nose and the innovative WinGlide rear projectile stabilizer, engineered specifically to improve in-bore alignment and enhance down-range accuracy; delivers high accuracy, hard-hitting knockdown performance to hunters shooting shotguns with either smooth bore, rifled choke tube or fully-rifled barrels

Available in: 12 Ga. (2¾ in., 3 in.), 20 Ga. (2¾ in.)

Box 5:. . . . .$7.00–$10.00

SUPER-X BUCKSHOT

Available in: 12 Ga. (2¾ in., 3 in., 3½ in.), 20 Ga. (2¾ in.), .410 (2½ in., 3 in.); Shot sizes: 4, 3, 1, 00, 000

Box 5:. . . . .$5.00–$14.00

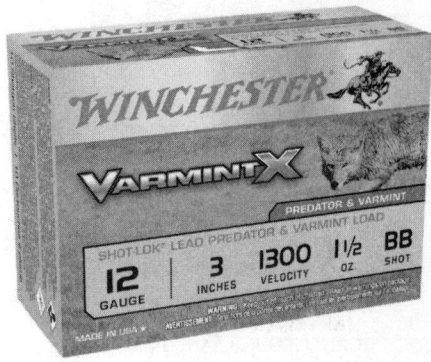

WINCHESTER AMMUNITION VARMINT-X

WINCHESTER SUPER-X BUCKSHOT

WINCHESTER PDX1 DEFENDER SEGMENTING SLUG

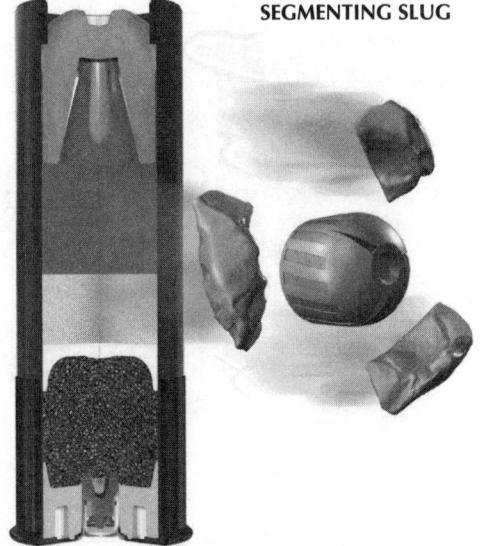

AMMUNITION

MUZZLELOADING BULLETS

Barnes Bullets

H15045BR

HARVESTER MUZZLELOADING CRUSHED RIB SABOT

CRUSHED RIB SABOT
Features: 50 percent less loading friction; consistent ignition and superb accuracy
Available in: .45 (.400); .50 (.400, .429–.430, .451–.452)
Box 50: . . . .$9.49–$10.49

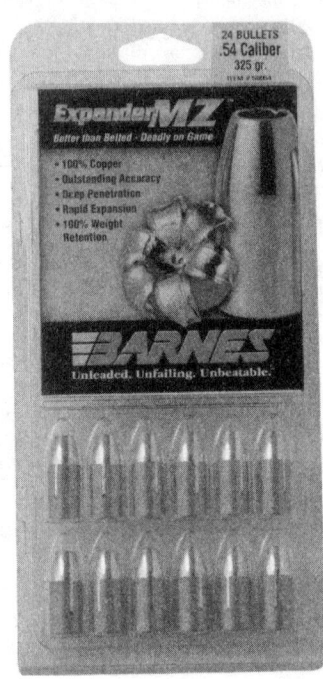

BARNES BULLETS EXPANDER MZ

EXPANDER MZ
Features: 100 percent copper with a large, hollow cavity; six copper petals with double-diameter expansion; full weight retention
Available in: .45 (195 gr.), .50 (250, 300 gr.), .54 (275, 325 gr.)
Box of 15:. . . . .$16.90–$21.05
Box of 24:. . . . .$22.69–$27.23

SPIT-FIRE MZ
Features: A streamlined semi-spitzer give, boattail base and tack-driving accuracy; six razor-sharp copper petals create massive shock, deep penetration, and double-diameter expansion; retains virtually 100 percent of its original weight; available in 15 and 24-bullet packs
Available in: .50 (245, 285 gr.)
Box of 15:. . . . .$18.97–$19.38
Box of 24:. . . . .$23.92–$24.75

SPIT-FIRE TMZ
Features: 100 percent copper boattail design with streamlined polymer tip for faster expansion; expands at 1050 fps.; remains intact at extreme velocities; redesigned sabot loads faster while retaining tight gas seal
Available in: .50 (250, 290 gr.)
Box of 15:. . . . .$18.56–$18.97
Box of 24:. . . . . $26.40-$28.05

BARNES BULLETS SPIT-FIRE TMZ

BARNES BULLETS SPIT-FIRE MZ

AMMUNITION

Harvester Muzzleloading (J-Ron, Inc.)

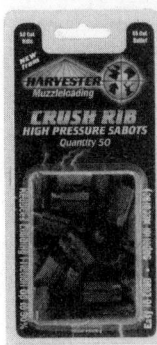

H15045BR

HARVESTER MUZZLELOADING CRUSHED RIB SABOT

HARVESTER SABER TOOTH BELTED

HARVESTER SCORPION FUNNEL POINT MAG

HARVESTER SCORPION PT GOLD

CRUSHED RIB SABOT

Features: 50 percent less loading friction; consistent ignition and superb accuracy
Available in: .45 (.400); .50 (.400, .429–.430, .451–.452)
Box 50: . . .$9.49–$10.49

SABER TOOTH BELTED

Features: Copper-clad belted bullets in Harvester Crush Rib Sabot
Available in: .50 (250, 270, 300, 350 gr.)
MSRP $15.99

SCORPION FUNNEL POINT MAG

Features: Electroplated copper plating does not separate from lead core; loaded in Harvester Crush Rib Sabots
Available in: .50 (240, 260, 300 gr.); .54 (240, 260, 300 gr.)
MSRP . . . .$9.99–$13.99

SCORPION PT GOLD

Features: Scorpion PT Gold Ballistic Tip Bullets are electroplated with copper plating that does not separate from lead core; offers greater accuracy at longer ranges than a hollow point; 3 percent antimony makes the bullet harder than pure lead
Available in: .45 (240, 260, 300 gr.); .50 ((240, 260, 300 gr.)
MSRP . . . .$14.99–$25.99

Hornady Manufacturing

HORNADY GREAT PLAINS - PA CONICAL

HORNADY HP/XTP BULLET/SABOT

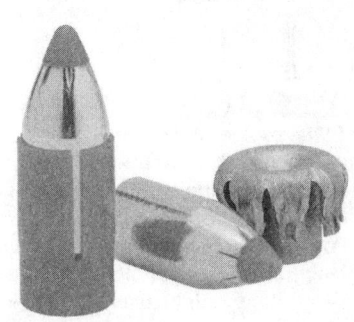

HORNADY MONOFLEX ML

GREAT PLAINS - PA CONICAL

Features: Delivers greater accuracy and more knock-down power; PA bullets are prelubed with special knurled grooves on the bearing surface to hold the lubricant on the bullet—no need for a patch or sabot
Available in: .50 (240, 385 gr.); .54 (425 gr.)
.50 Box of 20: $11.71
.50 Box of 50: $18.33
.54 Box of 20: $12.12

HP/XTP BULLET/SABOT

Features: Hornady XTP bullet/sabot combination with controlled expansion XTP bullet
Available in: .50 sabot with .44 (240 gr.) XTP bullet or .45 sabot with 200 gr. SST ML bullet
.45: $15.95
.50: $13.25

MONOFLEX ML

Features: Constructed with the Hornady Flex Tip and retaining 95 percent of its original weight, it's available in both a High Speed/Low Drag sabot and Lock-N-Load Speed Sabot
Available in: .50 cal. sabot with .45 cal. (250 gr.) bullet
High Speed/Low Drag: $25.87
Lock-N-Load: $27.81

Knight Rifles

BLOODLINE BULLETS
Features: Individually machined, double knurled bullets for increased visual blood trails
Available in: .45 (185, 200 gr.); .50 (220, 250, 275, 300, 350 gr.); .52 (220, 275, 300, 350 gr.); .54 (325 gr.)
Box 20: . . . .**$29.99–$37.99**

RED HOT BULLETS
Features: Saboted Barnes solid copper bullet with superior expansion

Available in: .45 (175, 195 gr.); .50 (250, 300, 350 gr.); .52 (275, 350, 375 gr.)
MSRP. . . . .**$26.99–$37.99**

SPIT-FIRE BOAT TAIL BULLETS
Features: Sabot loaded with Barnes Spit-Fire Boat-tail bullet; 18 pack
Available in: .50 (245, 250, 285 gr.)
MSRP. **$29.99**

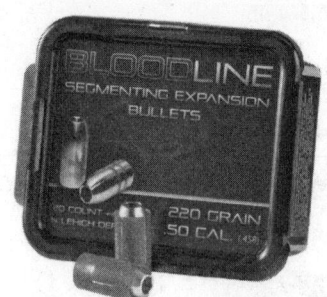

KNIGHT RIFLES BLOODLINE BULLETS

PowerBelt Bullets

POWERBELT AEROLITE

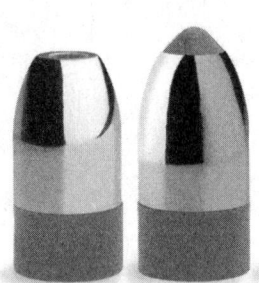

POWERBELT COPPER

POWERBELT PLATINUM AEROTIP

POWERBELT PURE LEAD HOLLOW POINT

AEROLITE
Features: Designed specifically for use with standard 100-grain loads; AeroLite's shape is noticeably longer and more aerodynamic than other PowerBelts of similar weight; longer length is made possible by the massive hollow point cavity that is filled by an oversized polycarbonate point
Available in: .45 (250 gr.), .50 (250, 300 gr.)
MSRP. . . . .**$32.95–$33.40**

COPPER
Features: Thin copper plating reduces bore friction while allowing for optimal bullet expansion; available in four tip designs: Hollow Point,

AeroTip, Flat Point, and Steel Tip
Available in: .45 (195, 225, 275 gr.); .50 (223, 245, 295, 348, 405, 444 gr.); .54 (295, 348 gr.)
MSRP. . . . .**$23.95–$28.95**
50-packs: . . . .**$59.95–$70.95**

PLATINUM AEROTIP
Features: Proprietary hard plating and aggressive bullet taper design for improved ballistic coefficient; large-size fluted gas check produces higher and more consistent pressures
Available in: .45 (223, 300 gr.); .50 (270, 300, 338 gr.)
MSRP. . . . .**$30.95–$32.95**

PURE LEAD
Features: Pure lead, available in four different grain weights in Hollow Point and 444 in Flat Point
Available in: .50 (295, 348, 405, gr.); .54 (295, 405 gr.)
MSRP. . . . .**$23.95–$24.95**

Swift

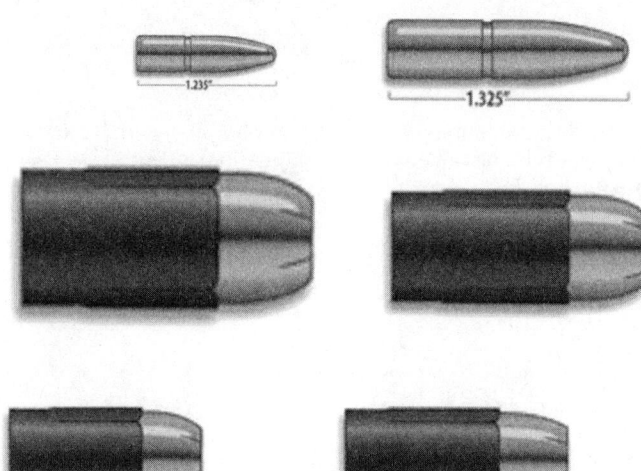

A-FRAME MUZZLELOADING BULLETS

Features: Muzzleloader and heavy revolver A-Frame bullets are one in the same; initiate expansion at 950 feet per second, expand to .65x their original caliber, and maintain 97% of their weight; virtually indestructible at velocities in excess of 3000 feet per second
Available in: .50 (240, 300 gr.); .54 (265, 325 gr.)
Box:.........................**S18.00**

SWIFT A-FRAME MUZZLELOADING BULLETS

Thompson/Center Arms

MAXI-BALL

Features: An exceptionally accurate bullet and the preferred bullet for penetration needed for large game like elk; lubricating grooves (maxi wide grooves)
Available in: .50 (275, 350 gr.)
Box 20:.............**$28.00–$29.00**

SHOCK WAVE SABOTS

Features: Polymer tip spire point bullet with sabot; incorporates harder lead core with walls interlocked with the jacket for maximum weight retention and expansion; available with spire point or bonded bullets
Available in: Bonded Core in Super Glide Sabots .50 (250, 300 gr.); Controlled Expansion in Super Glide Sabot .50 (250, 300 gr.); Bonded Core in Mag Express Sabots .50 (250, 300 gr.); Controlled Expansion in Mag Express Sabots .50 (200, 250, 300) and .45 (200 gr.)
Bonded Core Super Glide:...........**$31.00–$32.00**
Controlled Expansion Super Glide:......**$23.00–$24.00**
Bonded Core Mag Express:.........**$31.00–$32.00**
Controlled Expansion Mag Express:.....**$22.00–$35.00**

SUPER 45 XR SABOTS

Features: Centerfire weight performance without the recoil, Super 45 XR sabots have a flatter trajectory, provide deep penetration, and nearly 2 times the expansion of its original diameter.
Available in: .45 (155 gr.)
Box 30:.................**$26.00**

THOMPSON/CENTER SHOCK WAVE SABOTS

THOMPSON/CENTER SUPER 45 XR SABOTS

     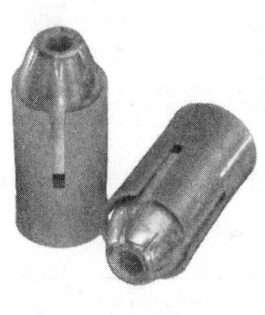

THOMPSON/CENTER MAXI-BALL

BULLETS

Barnes Bullets

Barnes continues to develop leading-edge products with a wide range of workability and functionality using an incredibly broad range of purpose-built components and ammunition. Barnes's most popular hunting bullets, the all-copper TSX line, also comes with a streamlined polymer tip. The Barnes Buster line can be used for both rifles and handguns.

Rifle Bullets

BANDED SOLIDS

Caliber & Description	6MM S BT	25 S BT	6.5MM S BT	270 S BT	7MM S BT	30 S BT	338 RN	9.3MM RN	9.3MM RN	375 RN	375 RN	375 RN	450/400 FN	416 RN
Diameter, Inches	.243	.257	.264	.277	.284	.308	.338	.366	.366	.375	.375	.375	.410	.416
Weight, Grains	75	90	110	120	140	165	250	250	286	270	300	350	400	350
Density	.181	.195	.225	.223	.248	.248	.313	.267	.305	.274	.305	.356	.340	.289
Ballistic Coefficient	.341	.325	.452	.438	.464	.438	.247	.214	.247	.207	.230	.283	.292	.217
Catalog Number	24375	25793	26422	27763	28464	30816	33825	30466	30467	37512	37525	37527	40935	30520

Caliber & Description	505 GIBBS RN	500 NITRO FN	500 JEFF RN	50 BMG BORE RIDER	50 BMG BORE RIDER	577 NITRO FN	600 NITRO FN
Diameter, Inches	.504	.509	.510	.510	.510	.583	.618
Weight, Grains	525	570	535	750	800	750	900
Density	.295	.314	.294	.412	.439	.315	.337
Ballistic Coefficient	.267	.243	-	1.070	1.095	.257	.380
Catalog Number	30685	30690	30694	30703	30707	30713	30714

From: $30.00–$59.00

> **LEGEND**
> **Type of Bullet**
> BT — Boattail
> FB — Flat Base
> FN — Flat Nose
> RN — Round Nose
> S — Spitzer
> SP — Soft Point
> SS — Semi-Spitzer

BARNES BUSTER

Caliber & Description	44 MAG. FN FB	454 CASULL FN FB	45/70 FN FB	500 S&W FN FB
Diameter, Inches	.429	.451	.458	.500
Weight, Grains	300	325	400	400
Density	.233	.228	.272	.229
Ballistic Coefficient	.241	.206	.242	.220
Catalog Number	30545	30572	30644	30672

Box 50: $50.00–$60.00

AMMUNITION

Barnes Bullets

BARNES ORIGINAL

Caliber & Description	348 WIN FN SP	348 WIN FN SP	375 WIN FN SP	38/55 FN SP	38/55 FN SP	"45/70 SSSP"	45/70 FN SP	45/70 SSSP	45/70 FN SP	50/110 WIN FN SP	50/110 WIN FN SP
Diameter, Inches	.348	.348	.375	.375	.377	.458	.458	.458	.458	.510	.510
Weight, Grains	220	250	255	255	255	300	300	400	400	300	450
Jckt.	.032	.032	.032	.032	.032	.032	.032	.032	.032	.032	.032
Density	.260	.295	.259	.259	.256	.204	.204	.272	.272	.165	.247
Ballistic Coefficient	.301	.327	.290	.290	.290	.291	.227	.389	.302	.183	.274
Catalog Number	30437	30438	30496	30498	30611	30612	30612	30613	30614	30682	30683

From: $20.00–$56.00

LRX BULLETS

Caliber & Description	6.5MM BT	270 BT	7MM BT	7MM BT	30 BT	30 BT	338 LAPUA BT	338 LAPUA BT
Diameter, Inches	.264	.277	.284	.284	.308	.308	.338	.338
Weight, Grains	127	129	145	168	175	200	265	280
Density	.257	.240	.257	.257	.264	.301	.331	.350
Ballistic Coefficient	.468	.463	.486	.550	.508	.546	.575	.667
Catalog Number	30228	30262	30282	30284	30318	30374	30434	30432

Box 50: $37.00–$49.00

MATCH BURNER BULLETS

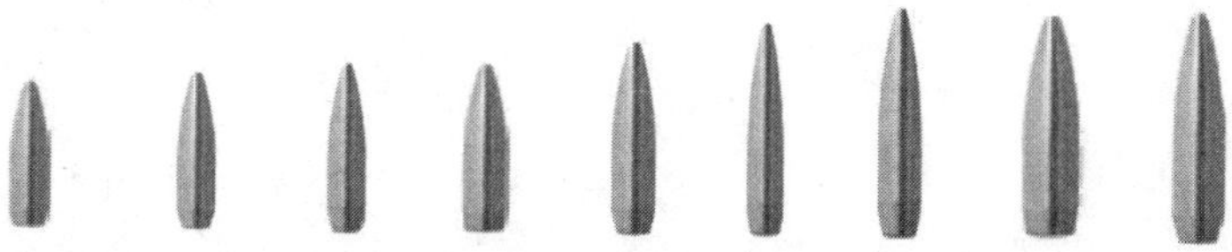

Caliber & Description	22 FB	22 BT	22 BT	6MM FB	6MM BT	6.5MM BT	7MM BT	"30 PALMA FB"	30 BT
Diameter, Inches	.224	.224	.224	.243	.243	.264	.284	.308	.308
Weight, Grains	52	69	85	68	105	140	171	155	175
Density	.148	.196	.242	.165	.254	.287	.303	.233	.264
Ballistic Coefficient	.224	.339	.410	.267	.511	.586	.645	.467	.521
Catalog Number	30160	30162	30164	30205	30206	30230	30285	30381	30385

Box 100: $20.00–$33.00

LEGEND

Type of Bullet

- BT – Boattail
- FB – Flat Base
- FN – Flat Nose
- RN – Round Nose
- S – Spitzer
- SP – Soft Point
- SS – Semi-Spitzer

AMMUNITION

Barnes Bullets

M/LE Reduced Ricochet, Limited Penetration (RRLP) Bullets

Caliber & Description	223/5.56 FB	6.8MM FB	30 FB	7.62X39 FB
Diameter, Inches	.224	.277	.308	.310
Weight, Grains	55	85	150	108
Density	.157	.158	.226	.161
Ballistic Coefficient	.225	.229	.357	.243
Catalog Number	80161	30252	30313	30390

From: $19.00–31.00

M/LE TAC-TX Bullets

Caliber & Description	6.5mm BT	6.5mm BT	6.8mm BT	300 BLK	300 BLK	30 FB	30 BT	338 BT	338 BT	458 SOCOM BT
Diameter, Inches	.264	.264	.277	.308	.308	.308	.308	.338	.338	.458
Weight, Grains	100	120	95	110	120	110	168	225	265	300
Density	.205	.246	.177	.166	.181	.166	.253	.281	.331	.204
Ballistic Coefficient	-	.443	.292	.289	.358	.295	.470	.514	.575	.236
Catalog Number	30236	30237	30253	30321	30813	30358	30359	30420	30419	30640

From: $34.00–$52.00

Multi-Purpose Green (MPG) Bullets

Caliber & Description	223 FB	6.8MM FB	30 FB	7.62X39 FB
Diameter, Inches	.224	.277	.308	.310
Weight, Grains	55	85	150	108
Density	.157	.158	.226	.161
Ballistic Coefficient	.225	.229	.357	.243
Catalog Number	30195	30249	30331	30388

From: $19.00–$31.00

LEGEND
Type of Bullet
BT – Boattail
FB – Flat Base
FN – Flat Nose
RN – Round Nose
S – Spitzer
SP – Soft Point
SS – Semi-Spitzer

TSX Bullets

Caliber & Description	22 FB	22 FB	22 FB	22 FB	22 BT	22 BT	6MM BT	25 BT	25 FB	6.5MM BT	6.5MM FB	6.8MM FB	6.8MM BT	270 BT	270 BT
Diameter, Inches	.224	.224	.224	.224	.224	.224	.243	.257	.257	.264	.264	.277	.277	.277	.277
Weight, Grains	45	50	53	55	62	70	85	100	115	120	130	85	110	130	140
Density	.128	.142	.151	.157	.177	.199	.206	.216	.249	.246	.266	.158	.205	.242	.261
Ballistic Coefficient	.188	.197	.204	.209	.287	.314	.333	.336	.335	.381	.365	.246	.323	374	.404
Catalog Number	30176	30174	30180	30182	30190	30193	30212	30222	30224	30244	30246	30254	30260	30264	30266

Barnes Bullets

Caliber & Description	270 FB	7MM BT	7MM BT	7MM BT	7MM FB	7MM FB	30 FN FB	30 FB	30 BT	30 BT	30 BT	30 BT	30 BT	30 FB	7.62X39 BT
Diameter, Inches	.277	.284	.284	.284	.284	.284	.308	.308	.308	.308	.308	.308	.308	.308	.310
Weight, Grains	150	120	140	150	160	175	150	110	130	150	165	168	180	200	123
Density	.279	.213	.248	.266	.283	.310	.226	.166	.196	.226	.248	.253	.271	.301	.183
Ballistic Coefficient	.386	.349	.394	.408	.392	.417	.184	.264	.340	.369	.398	.404	.453	.423	.275
Catalog Number	30269	30287	30289	30293	30291	30294	30334	30341	30345	30347	30349	30351	30353	30356	30391

Caliber & Description	303/7.65MM FB	8MM BT	8MM BT	338 BT	338 BT	338 FB	338 FB	338 LAPUA BT	35 FB	35 FB	9.3MM FB	9.3MM FB	375 FB	375 FB	375 FB
Diameter, Inches	.311	.323	.323	.338	.338	.338	.338	.338	.358	.358	.366	.366	.375	.375	.375
Weight, Grains	150	180	200	185	210	225	250	285	200	225	250	286	235	270	300
Density	.222	.246	.274	.231	.263	.281	.313	.356	.223	.251	.267	.305	.239	.274	.305
Ballistic Coefficient	.322	.381	.421	.352	.404	.386	.425	.585	.284	.359	.361	.411	.270	.326	.357
Catalog Number	30393	30396	30398	30408	30410	30412	30415	30417	30455	30457	30469	30473	30486	30489	30491

Caliber & Description	375 FB	405 WIN FB	416 FB	416 FB	416 FB	404 JEFFERY FB	458 FB	458 FB	458 FB	458 FB	45/70 FN	45/70 FN	470 NITRO FB
Diameter, Inches	.375	.411	.416	.416	.416	.422	.458	.458	.458	.458	.458	.458	.474
Weight, Grains	350	300	300	350	400	400	300	350	450	500	250	300	500
Density	.356	.254	.248	.289	.330	.321	.204	.238	.306	.341	.170	.204	.318
Ballistic Coefficient	.425	.281	.298	.345	.392	.378	.234	.278	.369	.412	.136	.163	.363
Catalog Number	30494	30516	30527	30529	30532	30537	30615	30617	30619	30622	30629	30630	30647

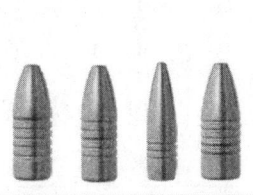

Caliber & Description	505 GIBBS FB	500 NITRO FB	50 BMG BT	577 NITRO FB
Diameter, Inches	.505	.509	.510	.583
Weight, Grains	525	570	647	750
Density	.294	.314	.355	.315
Ballistic Coefficient	.320	.369	.572	.402
Catalog Number	30688	30692	30700	30712

From: $19.00–$62.00

VARMIN-A-TOR

Caliber & Description	20 FB	22 FB	22 FB	6mm FB	6mm FB
Diameter, Inches	.204	.224	.224	.243	.243
Weight, Grains	32	40	50	58	72
Density	.110	.114	.142	.140	.174
Ballistic Coefficient	.159	.153	.192	.173	.208
Catalog Number	30092	30168	30178	30207	30210

From: $20.00–$23.00

VARMINT GRENADE

Caliber & Description	20 FB	22 HORNET FB	22 FB	223 FB	6MM FB
Diameter, Inches	.204	.224	.224	.224	.243
Weight, Grains	26	30	36	50	62
Density	.089	.085	.102	.142	.150
Ballistic Coefficient	.131	.101	.149	.183	.199
Catalog Number	30090	30170	30171	30198	30214

Box 100: $18.00–$59.00

Barnes Bullets

Handgun Bullets

M/LE TAC-XP PISTOL BULLETS

Caliber & Description	380 ACP	9MM	9MM	.357 SIG	38 SPL.	357 MAG.	10MM/40 S&W	10MM/40 S&W	10MM/40 S&W	44 SPL.	45 ACP/45 GAP	45 ACP
Diameter, Inches	.355	.355	.355	.355	.355	.357	.400	.400	.400	.429	.451	.451
Weight, Grains	80	95	115	125	110	125	125.	140	155	200	160	185
Density	.091	.108	.130	.142	.123	.140	.112	.125	.138	.155	.112	.130
Ballistic Coefficient	.107	.120	.167	.159	.156	.160	-	.128	.189	.138	.133	.167
Catalog Number	30440	30444	30442	30446	30449	30451	30500	30502	30504	30539	30550	30552

Box 40: $28.00–$49.00

XPB PISTOL BULLETS

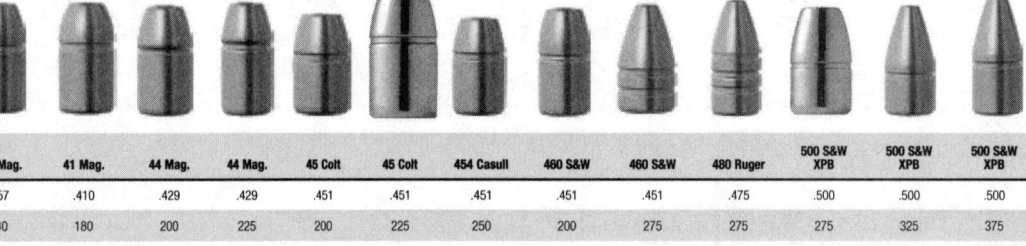

Caliber & Description	357 Mag.	41 Mag.	44 Mag.	44 Mag.	45 Colt	45 Colt	454 Casull	460 S&W	460 S&W	480 Ruger	500 S&W XPB	500 S&W XPB	500 S&W XPB
Diameter, Inches	.357	.410	.429	.429	.451	.451	.451	.451	.451	.475	.500	.500	.500
Weight, Grains	140	180	200	225	200	225	250	200	275	275	275	325	375
Density	.157	.153	.155	.175	.140	.158	.176	.140	.193	.174	.157	.186	.214
Ballistic Coefficient	.150	.126	.138	.166	-	.146	.141	.160	.215	.155	.141	.228	.261
Catalog Number	30453	30512	30541	30543	30556	30558	30562	30554	30548	30659	30663	30665	30667

Box 20: $16.00–$26.00

Berger Bullets

Famous for their superior performance in benchrest matches, Berger bullets also include hunting designs. From .17 to .30, all Bergers feature fourteen jackets with a wall concentricity tolerance of .0003. Lead cores are 99.9 percent pure and swaged in dies to within .0001 of a round. Berger's line includes several profiles: Match, Low Drag, Very Low Drag, Length Tolerant, and Maximum-Expansion, besides standard flat-base and boattail.

HUNTING

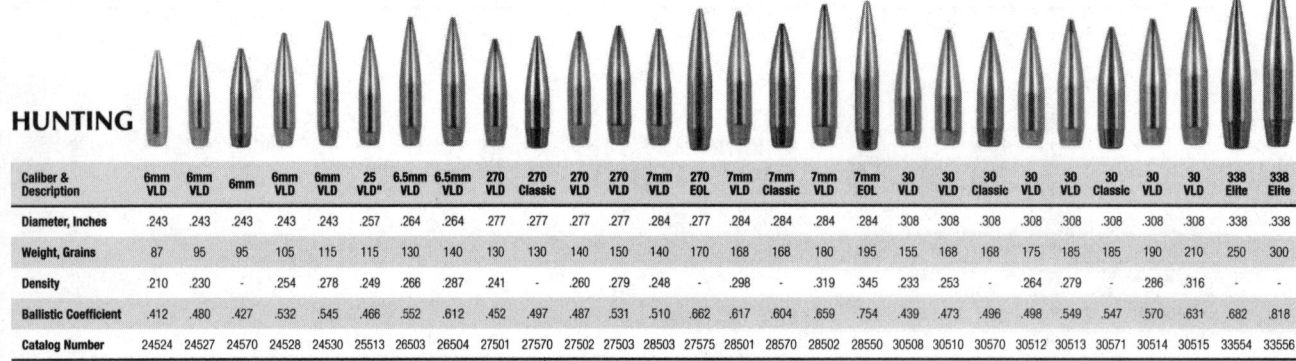

Caliber & Description	6mm VLD	6mm VLD	6mm	6mm VLD	6mm VLD	25 VLD"	6.5mm VLD	6.5mm VLD	270 VLD	270 Classic	270 VLD	270 VLD	7mm VLD	270 EOL	7mm VLD	7mm Classic	7mm VLD	7mm EOL	30 VLD	30 VLD	30 Classic	30 VLD	30 VLD	30 Classic	30 VLD	30 VLD	338 Elite	338 Elite
Diameter, Inches	.243	.243	.243	.243	.243	.257	.264	.264	.277	.277	.277	.277	.284	.277	.284	.284	.284	.284	.308	.308	.308	.308	.308	.308	.308	.308	.338	.338
Weight, Grains	87	95	95	105	115	115	130	140	130	130	140	150	140	170	168	168	180	195	155	168	168	175	185	185	190	210	250	300
Density	.210	.230	-	.254	.278	.249	.266	.287	.241	-	.260	.279	.248	-	.298	-	.319	.345	.233	.253	-	.264	.279	-	.286	.316	-	-
Ballistic Coefficient	.412	.480	.427	.532	.545	.466	.552	.612	.452	.497	.487	.531	.510	.662	.617	.604	.659	.754	.439	.473	.496	.498	.549	.547	.570	.631	.682	.818
Catalog Number	24524	24527	24570	24528	24530	25513	26503	26504	27501	27570	27502	27503	28503	27575	28501	28570	28502	28550	30508	30510	30570	30512	30513	30571	30514	30515	33554	33556

Box 100: $40.00–$91.00

AMMUNITION

Berger Bullets

TARGET

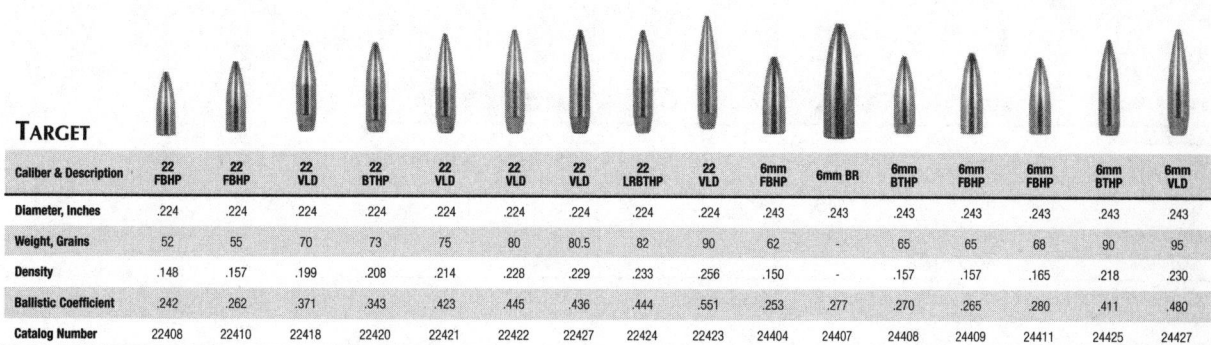

Caliber & Description	22 FBHP	22 FBHP	22 VLD	22 BTHP	22 VLD	22 VLD	22 VLD	22 LRBTHP	22 VLD	6mm FBHP	6mm BR	6mm BTHP	6mm FBHP	6mm FBHP	6mm BTHP	6mm VLD
Diameter, Inches	.224	.224	.224	.224	.224	.224	.224	.224	.224	.243	.243	.243	.243	.243	.243	.243
Weight, Grains	52	55	70	73	75	80	80.5	82	90	62	-	65	65	68	90	95
Density	.148	.157	.199	.208	.214	.228	.229	.233	.256	.150	-	.157	.157	.165	.218	.230
Ballistic Coefficient	.242	.262	.371	.343	.423	.445	.436	.444	.551	.253	.277	.270	.265	.280	.411	.480
Catalog Number	22408	22410	22418	22420	22421	22422	22427	22424	22423	24404	24407	24408	24409	24411	24425	24427

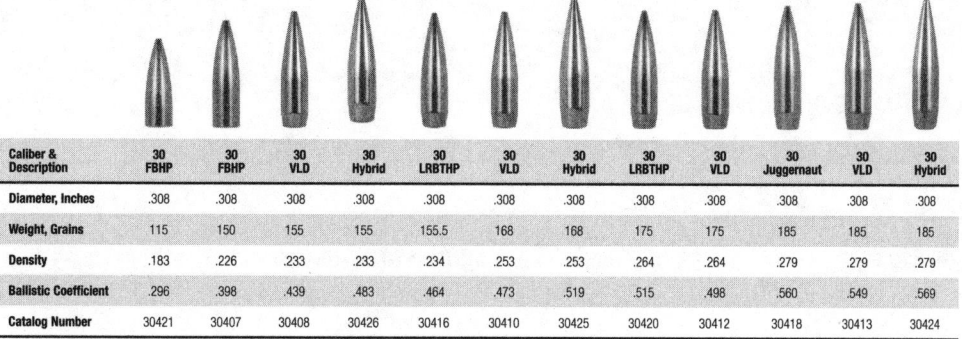

Caliber & Description	6mm BTHP	6mm VLD	6mm Hybrid	6mm BTHP	6mm VLD	6.5mm BTHP	6.5mm VLD	6.5mm VLD	6.5mm LRBTHP	6.5mm Hybrid	7mm VLD	7mm VLD	7mm Hybrid
Diameter, Inches	.243	.243	.243	.243	.243	.264	.264	.264	.264	.264	.284	.284	.284
Weight, Grains	105	105	105	108	115	120	130	140	140	140	168	180	180
Density	.254	.254	.254	.261	.278	.245	.266	.287	.287	.287	.298	.319	.319
Ballistic Coefficient	.493	.495	.547	.551	.545	.453	.552	.612	.592	.618	.617	.659	.674
Catalog Number	24428	24429	24433	24431	24430	26402	26403	26401	26409	26414	28401	28405	28407

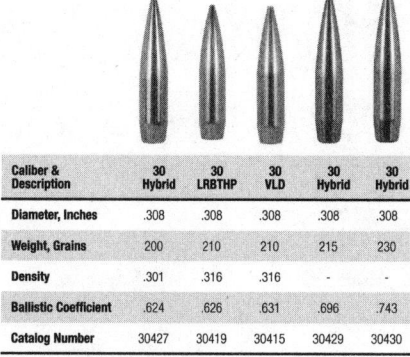

Caliber & Description	30 FBHP	30 FBHP	30 VLD	30 Hybrid	30 LRBTHP	30 VLD	30 Hybrid	30 LRBTHP	30 VLD	30 Juggernaut	30 VLD	30 Hybrid
Diameter, Inches	.308	.308	.308	.308	.308	.308	.308	.308	.308	.308	.308	.308
Weight, Grains	115	150	155	155	155.5	168	168	175	175	185	185	185
Density	.183	.226	.233	.233	.234	.253	.253	.264	.264	.279	.279	.279
Ballistic Coefficient	.296	.398	.439	.483	.464	.473	.519	.515	.498	.560	.549	.569
Catalog Number	30421	30407	30408	30426	30416	30410	30425	30420	30412	30418	30413	30424

Caliber & Description	30 Hybrid	30 LRBTHP	30 VLD	30 Hybrid	30 Hybrid
Diameter, Inches	.308	.308	.308	.308	.308
Weight, Grains	200	210	210	215	230
Density	.301	.316	.316	-	-
Ballistic Coefficient	.624	.626	.631	.696	.743
Catalog Number	30427	30419	30415	30429	30430

Box 100: $31.00–$72.00

LEGEND

Type of Bullet		
BT	–	Boattail
FB	–	Flat Base

HP	–	Hollow Point
LD	–	Low Drag
LR	–	Long Range
VLD	–	Very Low Drag

Berger Bullets

Varmint

Caliber & Description	17 FBHP	20 FBHP	20 BTHP	20 LRBTHP	22 FBHP	22 FBHP	22 FBHP	22 FBHP	22 FBHP	6mm LDHP	6mm FBHP	6mm LDHP
Diameter, Inches	.172	.204	.204	.204	.224	.224	.224	.224	.224	.243	.243	.243
Weight, Grains	25	35	40	55	40	52	55	60	64	69	80	88
Density	.121	.120	.137	.188	.114	.148	.157	.171	.182	.167	.194	.213
Ballistic Coefficient	.150	.176	.225	.381	.155	.197	.210	.278	.294	.291	.306	.391
Catalog Number	17308	20303	20304	20306	22303	22309	22311	22312	22316	24313	24321	24323

Box 100: $31.00–$64.00

Hornady Bullets

Hornady's product line includes over 300 bullets, ranging from .17 caliber all the way up to the .50 caliber A-MAX bullet for the .50 BMG. Hornady is always working to originate the next technological innovation. From prairie dogs to dangerous game, they have the perfect bullet to meet every hunting and shooting need.

Rifle Bullets

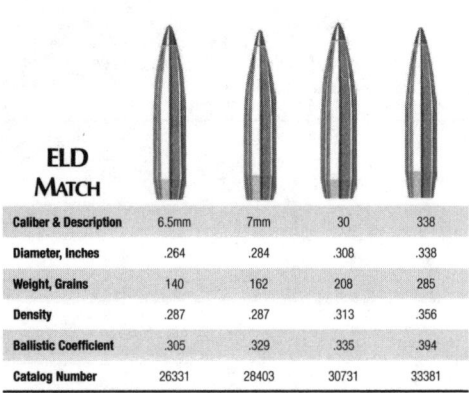

ELD Match

Caliber & Description	6.5mm	7mm	30	338
Diameter, Inches	.264	.284	.308	.338
Weight, Grains	140	162	208	285
Density	.287	.287	.313	.356
Ballistic Coefficient	.305	.329	.335	.394
Catalog Number	26331	28403	30731	33381

MSRP $45.00–$53.28

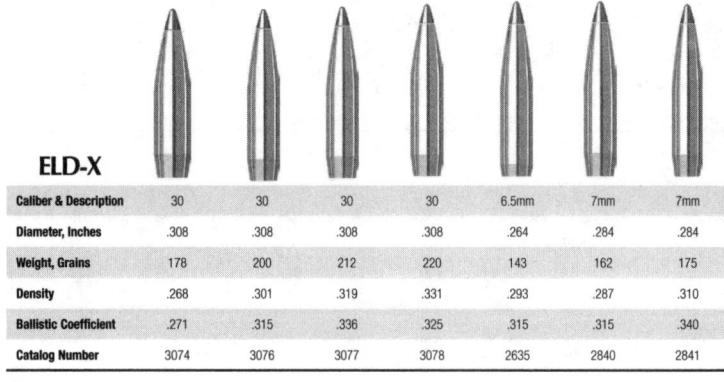

ELD-X

Caliber & Description	30	30	30	30	6.5mm	7mm	7mm
Diameter, Inches	.308	.308	.308	.308	.264	.284	.284
Weight, Grains	178	200	212	220	143	162	175
Density	.268	.301	.319	.331	.293	.287	.310
Ballistic Coefficient	.271	.315	.336	.325	.315	.315	.340
Catalog Number	3074	3076	3077	3078	2635	2840	2841

MSRP $48.33–$54.08

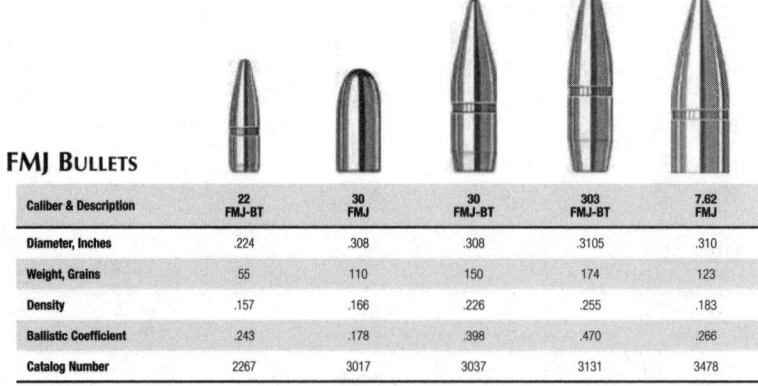

FMJ Bullets

Caliber & Description	22 FMJ-BT	30 FMJ	30 FMJ-BT	303 FMJ-BT	7.62 FMJ
Diameter, Inches	.224	.308	.308	.3105	.310
Weight, Grains	55	110	150	174	123
Density	.157	.166	.226	.255	.183
Ballistic Coefficient	.243	.178	.398	.470	.266
Catalog Number	2267	3017	3037	3131	3478

MSRP $19.00–$42.00

Hornady Bullets

InterBond

Caliber & Description	6mm BT	25 BT	6.5mm BT	270 BT	270 BT	7mm BT	7mm BT	30 BT	30 BT	30 BT	338 BT	416 RN
Diameter, Inches	.243	.257	.264	.277	.277	.284	.284	.308	.308	.308	.338	.416
Weight, Grains	85	110	129	130	150	139	154	150	165	180	225	400
Density	.206	.238	.264	.242	.279	.246	.525	.226	.248	.271	.281	.330
Ballistic Coefficient	.395	.390	.485	.460	.525	.486	.273	.415	.447	.480	.515	.311
Catalog Number	24539	25419	26209	27309	27409	28209	28309	30309	30459	30709	33209	41659

MSRP $61.00–$89.00

InterLock

Caliber & Description	22 SP	6mm BT SP	25 SP	25 BTSP	25 RN	25 HP	6.5mm SP	6.5mm SP	6.5mm RN	6.5mm Carcano RN	270 SP	270 BTSP	270 SP	7mm BTSP	7mm SP	7mm SP	7mm BTSP	7mm RN	7mm SP
Diameter, Inches	.227	.243	.257	.257	.257	.257	.264	.264	.264	.268	.277	.277	.277	.284	.284	.284	.284	.284	.284
Weight, Grains	70	100	100	117	117	120	129	140	160	160	130	140	150	139	139	154	162	175	175
Density	.194	.242	.216	.253	.253	.260	.264	.287	.328	.321	.242	.261	.279	.246	.246	.273	.287	.310	.310
Ballistic Coefficient	.296	.405	.357	.391	.243	.394	.445	.465	.283	.275	.409	.486	.462	.453	.392	.433	.514	.285	.462
Catalog Number	2280	2453	2540	2552	2550	2560	2620	2630	2640	2645	2730	2735	2740	2825	2820	2830	2845	2855	2850

Caliber & Description	30 BTSP	30 RN	30 SP	30 BTSP	30 SP	30 FP	30 BTSP	30 RN	30 SP	30 BTSP	30 RN	7.62 SP	303 SP	303 RN	32 FP	8mm SP
Diameter, Inches	.308	.308	.308	.308	.308	.308	.308	.308	.308	.308	.308	.310	.312	.312	.321	.323
Weight, Grains	150	150	150	165	165	170	180	180	180	190	220	123	150	174	170	150
Density	.226	.226	.226	.248	.248	.256	.271	.271	.271	.286	.331	.183	.220	.255	.236	.205
Ballistic Coefficient	.349	.186	.338	.435	.387	.189	.452	.241	.425	.491	.300	.252	.361	.262	.249	.290
Catalog Number	3033	3035	3031	3045	3040	3060	3072	3075	3070	3085	3090	3140	3120	3130	3210	3232

Hornady Bullets

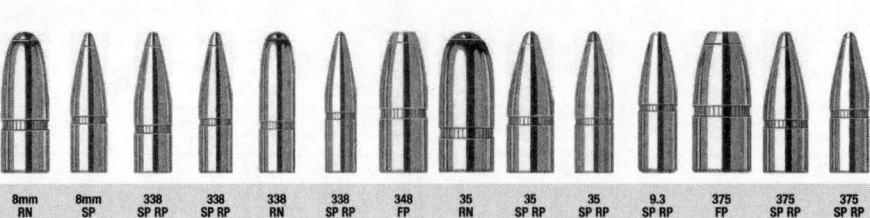

Caliber & Description	8mm RN	8mm SP	338 SP RP	338 SP RP	338 RN	338 SP RP	348 FP	35 RN	35 SP RP	35 SP RP	9.3 SP RP	375 FP	375 SP RP	375 SP RP
Diameter, Inches	.323	.323	.338	.338	.338	.338	.348	.358	.358	.358	.366	.375	.375	.375
Weight, Grains	170	195	200	225	250	250	200	200	200	250	286	220	225	270
Density	.233	.267	.250	.281	.313	.313	.236	.223	.223	.279	.305	.223	.229	.229
Ballistic Coefficient	.217	.410	.361	.397	.291	.431	.246	.195	.282	.375	.410	.217	.320	.380
Catalog Number	3235	3236	3310	3320	3330	3335	3410	3515	3510	3520	3560	3705	3706	3711

Caliber & Description	405 FP	405 SP	416 RN	44 FP	45 HP	45 FP	45 RN	45 RN
Diameter, Inches	.411	.411	.416	.430	.458	.458	.458	.458
Weight, Grains	300	300	400	265	300	350	350	500
Density	.251	.251	.330	.205	.204	.238	.238	.341
Ballistic Coefficient	.215	.250	.311	.186	.197	.195	.189	.287
Catalog Number	41050	41051	4165	4300	4500	4503	4502	4504

MSRP $29.00–$69.00

MATCH A-MAX

Caliber & Description	6.5mm	22	22	22	6mm	6.5mm	6.5mm	6.5mm	7mm	30	30	30 MOLY	30	30	338 BT	50
Diameter, Inches	.264	.224	.224	.224	.243	.264	.264	.264	.284	.308	.308	.308	.308	.308	.338	.510
Weight, Grains	100	52	75	80	105	120	123	140	162	155	168	168	178	208	285	750
Density	.246	.148	.214	.228	.254	.246	.252	.287	.287	.233	.253	.253	.268	.313	.356	.412
Ballistic Coefficient	.390	.247	.435	.453	.500	.465	.510	.585	.625	.435	.475	.475	.495	.325	720	1.050
Catalog Number	26101	22492	22792	22832	24562	26172	26171	26332	28402	30312	30502	30504	30712	30732	3338	5165

MSRP $26.00–$64.00

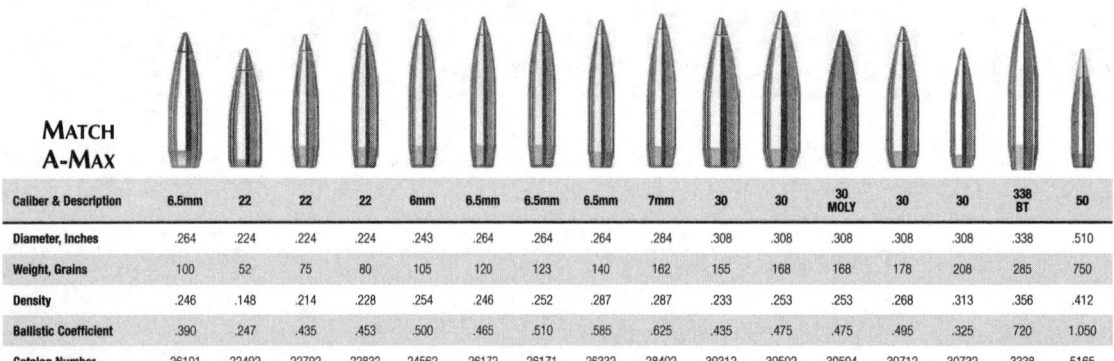

SST

Caliber & Description	6mm	25	6.5mm	6.5mm	6.5mm	270	270	270	270	7mm SST	7mm SST	7mm SST	30	30	30	30
Diameter, Inches	.243	.257	.264	.264	.264	.277	.277	.277	.277	.284	.284	.284	.308	.308	.308	.308
Weight, Grains	95	117	123	129	140	120	130	140	150	139	154	162	125	150	150	165
Density	.230	.253	.252	.264	.287	.223	.242	.261	.279	.246	.273	.287	.185	.226	.226	.248
Ballistic Coefficient	.355	.390	.510	.485	.520	.400	.460	.495	.525	.486	.525	.550	.305	.415	.370	.447
Catalog Number	24532	25522	26173	26202	26302	2716	27302	27352	27402	28202	28302	28452	3019	30302	30303	30452

Hornady Bullets

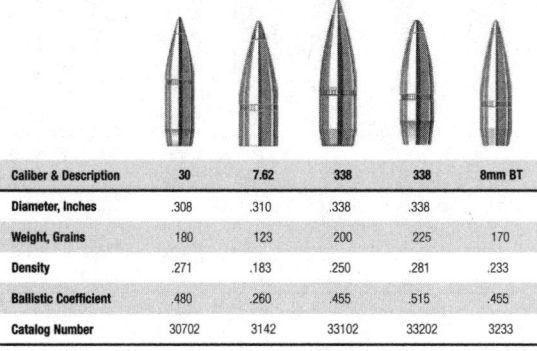

Caliber & Description	30	7.62	338	338	8mm BT
Diameter, Inches	.308	.310	.338	.338	
Weight, Grains	180	123	200	225	170
Density	.271	.183	.250	.281	.233
Ballistic Coefficient	.480	.260	.455	.515	.455
Catalog Number	30702	3142	33102	33202	3233

MSRP $40.00–$54.00

TRADITIONAL VARMINT

Caliber & Description	17 HP	20 SP	22 JET	22 Hornet	22 Hornet	22 HP BEE	22 SP	22 SP SX	22 SP	22 SP	22 SP SX	22 HP	22 SP	6mm HP
Diameter, Inches	.172	.204	.222	.223	.224	.224	.224	.224	.224	.224	.224	.224	.224	.243
Weight, Grains	25	45	40	45	45	45	50	50	55	55	55	60	60	75
Density	.121	.155	.116	.129	.128	.128	.142	.142	.157	.157	.157	.171	.171	.181
Ballistic Coefficient	.187	.245	.104	.202	.202	.108	.214	.214	.235	.235	.235	.271	.264	.294
Catalog Number	1710	22008	2210	2220	2230	2229	2245	2240	2265	2266	2260	2275	2270	2420

Caliber & Description	6mm BTHP	6mm SP	25 FP	25 HP	25 SP	270 SP	270 HP	270 BTHP	7mm HP	30 Short Jacket	30 SP	30 RN	30 SP
Diameter, Inches	.243	.243	.257	.257	.257	.277	.277	.277	.284	.308	.308	.308	.308
Weight, Grains	87	87	60	75	87	100	110	110	120	100	110	110	130
Density	.210	.210	.130	.162	.188	.186	.205	.205	.213	.151	.166	.166	.196
Ballistic Coefficient	.376	.327	.101	.257	.322	.307	.352	.360	.334	.152	.256	.150	.295
Catalog Number	2442	2440	2510	2520	2530	2710	2720	27200	2815	3005	3010	3015	3020

MSRP $18.00–$38.00

AMMUNITION

Hornady Bullets

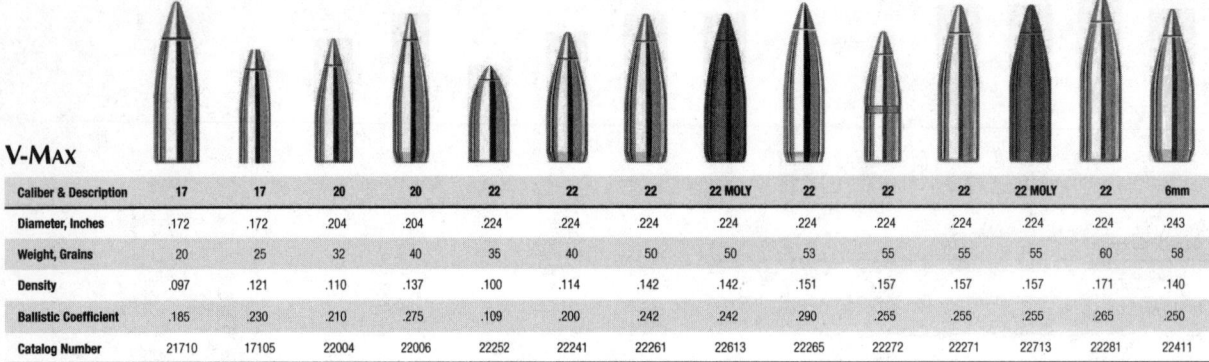

V-Max

Caliber & Description	17	17	20	20	22	22	22	22 MOLY	22	22	22	22 MOLY	22	6mm
Diameter, Inches	.172	.172	.204	.204	.224	.224	.224	.224	.224	.224	.224	.224	.224	.243
Weight, Grains	20	25	32	40	35	40	50	50	53	55	55	55	60	58
Density	.097	.121	.110	.137	.100	.114	.142	.142	.151	.157	.157	.157	.171	.140
Ballistic Coefficient	.185	.230	.210	.275	.109	.200	.242	.242	.290	.255	.255	.255	.265	.250
Catalog Number	21710	17105	22004	22006	22252	22241	22261	22613	22265	22272	22271	22713	22281	22411

Caliber & Description	6mm	6mm	6mm	25	6.5mm	270	7mm	30
Diameter, Inches	.243	.243	.243	.257	.264	.277	.284	.308
Weight, Grains	65	75	87	75	95	110	120	110
Density	.157	.181	.210	.162	.195	.205	.213	.166
Ballistic Coefficient	.280	.330	.400	.290	.365	.370	.365	.290
Catalog Number	22415	22420	22440	22520	22601	22721	22810	23010

> **LEGEND**
> **Type of Bullet**
> BT – Boat Tail
> CT – Combat Target
> FMJ – Full Metal Jacket
> FP – Flat Point
> HB – Hollow Base
> L – Lead
> RN – Round Nose
> SP – Spire Point
> SX – Super Explosive
> SWC – Semi-Wadcutter
> WC – Wadcutter

MSRP $24.00–$38.00

Handgun Bullets

FMJ BULLETS

Caliber & Description	9mm FMJ-RN	9mm FMJ-RN	10mm FMJ- FP	45 SWC	45 FMJ-RN	9mm FMJ	9mm FMJ-RN	10mm FMJ-FP	45 FMJ-CT
Diameter, Inches	.355	.355	.400	.451	.451	.355	.355	.400	.451
Weight, Grains	115	124	180	185	230	100	147	200	200
Density	.130	.141	N/A	.130	.162	.141	.167	.179	.140
Ballistic Coefficient	.140	.145	N/A	.068	.184	.158	.212	.182	.115
Catalog Number	35557	355771	400471	45137	45177	35527B	35597B	40077B	45157B

MSRP $23.00–$33.00

FRONTIER LEAD BULLETS

Caliber & Description	32 HBWC	32 SWC	38	38 HBWC	38 LRN	38 SWC	38 SWC HP	44 Cowboy	44 Cowboy
Diameter, Inches	.314	.314	.358	.358	.358	.358	.358	.427	.430
Weight, Grains	90	90	140	148	158	158	158	205	180
Density	.130	.130	.157	.165	.176	.176	.176	.161	.139
Ballistic Coefficient	.040	.096	.127	.047	.159	.135	.139	.123	.114
Catalog Number	10028	10008	10078	10208	10508	10408	10428	11208	11058

AMMUNITION

Hornady Bullets

FRONTIER/LEAD BULLETS (CONT.)

Caliber & Description	44 SWC	44 SWC HP	45 L-C/T	45 SWC	45 LRN	45 FP Cowboy
Diameter, Inches	.430	.430	.452	.452	.452	.454
Weight, Grains	240	240	200	200	230	255
Density	.185	.185	.140	.140	.162	.177
Ballistic Coefficient	.182	.204	.081	.070	.207	.117
Catalog Number	11108	11118	12208	12108	12308	12458

MSRP $32.00–$51.00

HAP BULLETS

Caliber & Description	9mm	9mm	10mm	45	45	10mm	45
Diameter, Inches	.356	.356	.400	.451	.451	.400	.451
Weight, Grains	115	125	180	185	230	200	200
Density	.130	.141	.161	.130	.162	.179	.140
Ballistic Coefficient	.129	.158	.164	.139	.188	.199	151
Catalog Number	355281	355721	400421	451051	451611	40061B	45159B

MSRP $78.00–$139.00

LEGEND
Type of Bullet

BT	–	Boat Tail
CT	–	Combat Target
FMJ	–	Full Metal Jacket
FP	–	Flat Point
HB	–	Hollow Base
L	–	Lead
RN	–	Round Nose
SP	–	Spire Point
SX	–	Super Explosive
SWC	–	Semi-Wadcutter
WC	–	Wadcutter

XTP BULLETS

Caliber & Description	30 RN	30 HP	32 HP	32 HP	32 HP	9mm HP	9mm HP	38 HP	9mm HP	38 FP	9mm HP	38 HP	38 HP	38 FP	38 HP	38 HP	9x18mm HP	10mm HP	10mm HP
Diameter, Inches	.308	.309	.312	.312	.312	.355	.355	.357	.355	.357	.355	.357	.357	.357	.357	.357	.365	.400	.400
Weight, Grains	86	90	60	85	100	90	115	110	124	125	147	125	140	158	158	180	95	155	180
Density	.130	.136	.088	.125	.147	.102	.130	.123	.141	.140	.167	.140	.157	.177	.177	.202	.102	.138	.161
Ballistic Coefficient	.105	.115	.090	.145	.170	.099	.129	.131	.165	.148	.212	.151	.169	.199	.206	.230	.127	.137	.164
Catalog Number	3100	31000	32010	32050	32070	35500	35540	35700	35571	35730	35580	35710	35740	35780	35750	35771	36500	40000	40040

Caliber & Description	10mm HP	41 HP	44 HP	44 HP	44 HP	44 HP	45 HP	45 HP	45 HP	45	45 HP	45 HP	45	475 MAG	50	500 MAG	500 FP
Diameter, Inches	.400	.410	.430	.430	.430	.300	.451	.451	.451	.452	.452	.452	.452	.475	.500	.500	.500
Weight, Grains	200	210	180	200	240	300	185	200	230	240	250	300	300	325	300	350	500
Density	.179	.178	.139	.155	.185	.232	.130	.140	.162	.168	.175	.210	.210	.206	.171	.192	.275
Ballistic Coefficient	.199	.182	.138	.170	.205	.245	.139	.151	.188	.160	.146	.180	.200	.150	.120	.145	.185
Catalog Number	40060	41000	44050	44100	44200	44280	45100	45140	45160	45220	45200	45230	45235	47500	50101	50100	50105

MSRP $22.00–$61.00

Lapua

Rifle Bullets

Lapua precision bullets are made from the best raw materials and meet the toughest precision specifications. Each bullet is subject to visual inspection and tested with advanced measurement devices.

D46
Manufactured to the strictest tolerances for concentricity, uniformity of shape, and weight; 7.62mm (.308) available
Box 100: **$50.00**

D166
Superbly accurate FMJBT bullet for 7.62mm (.311) cartridges
Box 100: **$52.00**

FMJ
Ten rounds loaded with Lapua's .30 S374 8.0/123gr FMJ bullet from 100m can easily achieve groupings less than; 30mm .224, 6.5mm, 7.62mm (.308, .311) available
Box 100: . . . . **$35.00–$44.00**

LOCK BASE
A distinctive Full Metal Jacket Boat Tail bullet that has many applications from sport shooting to battlefield; streamlined ballistic shape combined with patented base design; 7.62mm and .338 available
Box 100: . . . . **$50.00–$77.00**

MEGA
Soft point bullet with a protective copper jacket bullet at its best in the field and typically more than duplicates on impact; mechanical bonding locks the lead alloy in place; 6.5mm, 7.62mm, and 9.3mm available
Box 100: . . . . **$52.00–$72.00**

LAPUA NATURALIS THIRD GENERATION
Market leaders in terminal ballistic performance, and they can be used in hunting areas where lead-core bullets are prohibited. 5.69 (50 gr.), 6mm (90 gr.), 6.5mm (140 gr.), 7mm (155 gr.), 8mm (180 gr.), 9.3mm (250 gr.), .338 (231 gr.) available.
Box 50: . . . . **$66.99–$113.99**

SCENAR
Scenar Hollow Point Boat Tail bullets have the IBS World Record in 600 yard Heavy Gun 5-shot group (.404") and hold the official world ISSF record of 600 out of 600 possible; also available in Coated Silver Jacket version; .244, 6mm, 6.5mm, 7.62mm, and .338 available
Box 100: . . . . **$37.00–$88.00**

SCENAR-L
A refinement in all manufacturing steps that has resulted in closer weight tolerances, tighter jacket wall concentricity standards, and greater uniformity in every dimension, including the gilding metal cup, lead wire and jacket forming, ending up to core-jacket assembly, boat tail pressing, and tipping ; 6mm, 6.5mm, 7mm, and 7.62mm (.308) available
Box 100: . . . . **$49.00–$58.00**

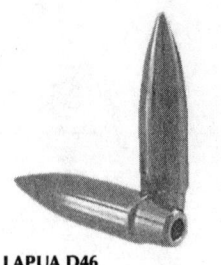

LAPUA D46

LAPUA D166

LAPUA FMJ S

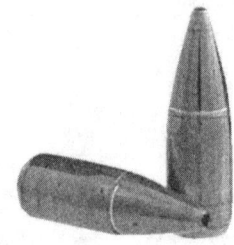

LAPUA HP

LAPUA LOCK BASE

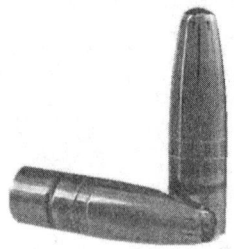

LAPUA MEGA

LAPUA NATURALIS THIRD GENERATION

LAPUA SCENAR

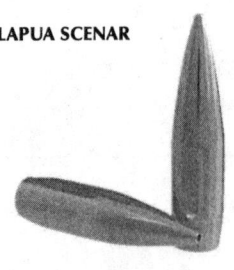

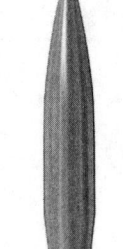

LAPUA SCENAR-L

Rifle Bullets

 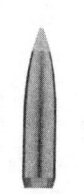       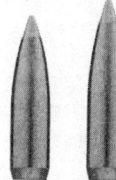

ACCUBOND

Caliber & Description	6mm S	25 SWT	6.5mm SWT	6.5mm	270 SWT	270 SWT	7mm SWT	7mm SWT	30 SWT	30 SWT	30 S	30 SWT	30 SWT
Diameter, inches	.243	.257	.264	.264	.277	.277	.277	.277	.284	.284	.308	.308	.308
Weight, Grains	90	110	130	140	100	110	130	140	140	160	125	150	165
Density	.218	.238	.266	.287	.186	.205	.242	.261	.248	.283	.188	.226	.248
Ballistic Coefficient	.376	.418	.488	.509	.323	.370	.435	.496	.485	.531	.366	.435	.475
Catalog Number	56357	53742	56902	57873	57845	54382	54987	54765	59992	54932	52165	56719	55602

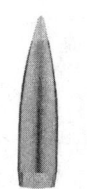  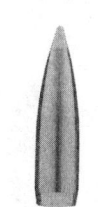     

Caliber & Description	30 S	30 S	8mm S	338 S	338 S	338 S	338 S	338 S	35 Whelen S	35 Whelen S	9.3mm S	375 S	375 S
Diameter, inches	.308	.308	.323	.338	.338	.338	.338	.338	.358	.358	.366	.375	.375
Weight, Grains	180	200	200	180	200	225	250	300	200	225	250	260	300
Density	.271	.301	.274	.225	.250	.281	.313	.375	.223	.251	.267	.264	.305
Ballistic Coefficient	.507	.588	.450	.372	.414	.550	.575	.720	.365	.421	.494	.473	.485
Catalog Number	54825	54618	54374	57625	56382	54357	57287	54851	54425	50712	59756	54413	53662

Box 50, 100: $27.00–$63.00

 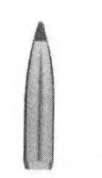 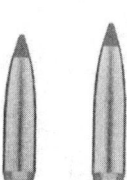  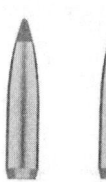  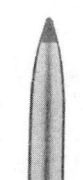  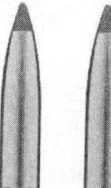

BALLISTIC TIP HUNTING

Caliber & Description	6mm S	6mm S	25 S	25 S	6.5mm S	6.5mm S	6.5mm S	270 S	270 S	270 S	7mm S	7mm S
Diameter, inches	.243	.243	.257	.257	.264	.264	.264	.277	.277	.277	.284	.284
Weight, Grains	90	95	100	115	100	120	140	130	140	150	120	140
Density	.218	.230	.216	.249	.205	.246	.287	.242	.261	.279	.213	.248
Ballistic Coefficient	.365	.379	.393	.453	.350	.458	.509	.433	.456	.496	.417	.485
Catalog Number	24090	24095	25100	25115	26100	26120	26140	27130	27140	27150	28120	28140

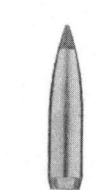 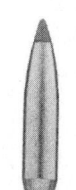   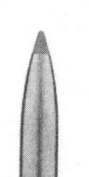 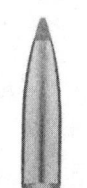 

Caliber & Description	7mm S	30 S	30 S	30 S	30 S	30 S	8mm S
Diameter, inches	.284	.308	.308	.308	.308	.308	.323
Weight, Grains	150	125	150	165	168	180	180
Density	.266	.188	.226	.248	.253	.271	.247
Ballistic Coefficient	.493	.366	.435	.475	.490	.507	.394
Catalog Number	28150	30125	30150	30165	30168	30180	32180

Box 50: $17.00–$30.00

LEGEND

Type of Bullet		Type of Tip	
BT	– Boat Tail	PT	– Purple Tip
HP	– Hollow Point	BT	– Blue Tip
J	– Jacketed	BrT	– Brown Tip
PP	– Protected Point	BuT	– Buckskin Tip
RN	– Round Nose	GT	– Green Tip
S	– Spitzer	GuT	– Gunmetal Tip
SS	– Semi Spitzer	MT	– Maroon Tip
W	– Whelen	OT	– Olive Tip
		RT	– Red Tip
		SLT	– Soft Lead Tip
		YT	– Yellow Tip

AMMUNITION

Nosler Bullets

Ballistic Tip Varmint

Caliber & Description	204 S	204 S	22 S	22 S	22 S	22 S	6mm S	6mm S	6mm S	25 S
Diameter, inches	.204	.204	.224	.224	.224	.224	.243	.243	.243	.257
Weight, Grains	32	40	40	50	55	60	55	70	80	85
Density	.110	.137	.114	.142	.157	.171	.133	.169	.194	.184
Ballistic Coefficient	.206	.239	.221	.238	.27	.270	.276	.310	.329	.329
Catalog Number	35216	52111	39510	39522	39526	34992	24055	39532	24080	43004

Box 100: $23.00–$36.00

CT Ballistic Silvertip Hunting

Caliber & Description	6mm S	25 S	270 S	270 S	7mm S	7mm S	30 S	30 RN	30 S	30 S	8mm S	45-70 RN	338 S
Diameter, inches	.243	.257	.277	.277	.284	.284	.308	.308	.308	.308	.323	.458	.338
Weight, Grains	95	115	130	150	140	150	150	150	168	180	180	300	200
Density	.230	.249	.242	.279	.248	.266	.226	.226	.253	.271	.247	.204	.250
Ballistic Coefficient	.379	.453	.433	.496	.485	.493	.435	.232	.490	.507	.394	.191	.414
Catalog Number	51040	51050	51075	51100	51105	51110	51150	51165	51160	51170	51693	51834	51200

Box 50: $27.00

Custom Competition

Caliber & Description	22 HPBT	22 HPBT	22 HPBT	22 HPBT	6mm HPBT	6mm HPBT	6.5mm HPBT	6.5mm HPBT	6.8mm HPBT	7mm HPBT	30 HPBT	30 HPBT	30 HPBT	30 HPBT	30 HPBT	45 JHP
Diameter, Inches	.224	.224	.224	.224	.243	.243	.264	.264	.277	.284	.308	.308	.308	.308	.308	.451
Weight, Grains	52	69	77	80	105	107	123	140	115	168	140	155	168	175	190	185
Density	.148	.196	.219	.228	.254	.259	.252	.287	.214	.298	.211	.233	.253	.264	.286	.130
Ballistic Coefficient	.220	.305	.340	.415	.517	.525	.510	.529	.375	.520	.396	.450	.462	.505	.530	.142
Catalog Number	53294	17101	22421	25116	53614	49742	53415	26725	45357	53418	53152	53155	53164	53952	53412	44847

Box 100, 250: $19.00–$36.00

E-TIP

Caliber & Description	6mm S	25 S	6.8mm S	270 S	7mm S	7mm S	30 S	30 S	30 S	8mm S	338 S	6.5MM S
Diameter, Inches	.243	.257	.277	.277	.284	.284	.308	.308	.308	.323	.338	264
Weight, Grains	90	100	85	130	140	150	150	168	180	180	200	120
Density	.218	.216	.158	.242	.248	.266	.226	.253	.271	.246	.250	.246
Ballistic Coefficient	.403	.409	.273	.459	.489	.498	.469	.503	.523	.427	.425	.497
Catalog Number	59165	59456	59543	59298	59955	59426	59378	59415	59180	59265	59186	59765

Box 50: $29.00–$49.00

AMMUNITION

Nosler Bullets

Partition

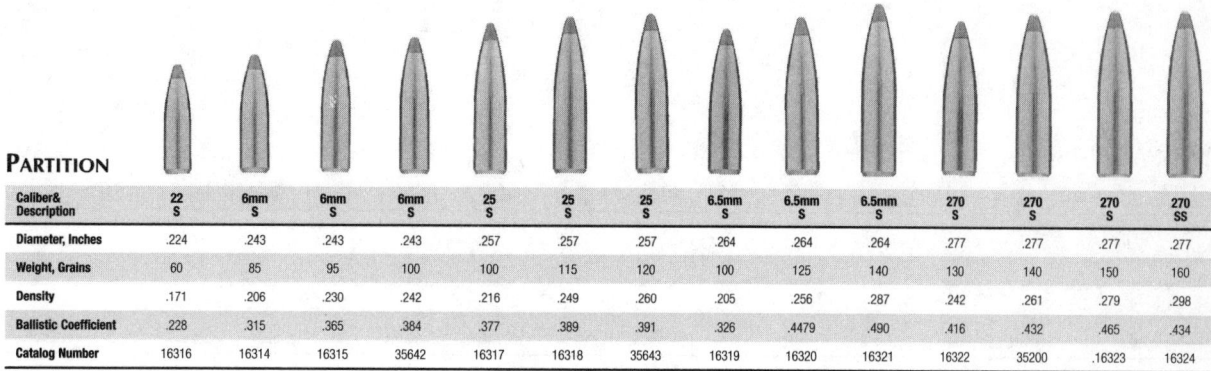

Caliber& Description	22 S	6mm S	6mm S	6mm S	25 S	25 S	25 S	6.5mm S	6.5mm S	6.5mm S	270 S	270 S	270 S	270 SS
Diameter, Inches	.224	.243	.243	.243	.257	.257	.257	.264	.264	.264	.277	.277	.277	.277
Weight, Grains	60	85	95	100	100	115	120	100	125	140	130	140	150	160
Density	.171	.206	.230	.242	.216	.249	.260	.205	.256	.287	.242	.261	.279	.298
Ballistic Coefficient	.228	.315	.365	.384	.377	.389	.391	.326	.4479	.490	.416	.432	.465	.434
Catalog Number	16316	16314	16315	35642	16317	16318	35643	16319	16320	16321	16322	35200	.16323	16324

Caliber & Description	7mm S	7mm S	7mm S	7mm S	30 S	30 S	30 RN	30 PP	30 S	30 S	30 SS	8mm S	338 S	338 S
Diameter, Inches	.284	.284	.284	.284	.308	.308	.308	.308	.308	.308	.308	.323	.338	.338
Weight, Grains	140	150	160	175	150	165	170	180	180	200	220	200	210	225
Density	.248	.266	.283	.310	.226	.248	.256	.271	.271	.301	.331	.274	.263	.281
Ballistic Coefficient	.434	.456	.475	.519	.387	.410	.252	.361	.474	.481	.351	.426	.400	.454
Catalog Number	16325	16326	16327	35645	16329	16330	16333	25396	16331	35626	16332	35277	16337	16336

Caliber & Description	338 S	35 S	35 S	9.3mm S	375 S	375 S	416 S	458 PP
Diameter, Inches	.338	.358	.358	.366	.375	.375	.416	.458
Weight, Grains	250	225	250	286	260	300	400	500
Density	.313	.251	.279	.307	.264	.305	.330	.389
Ballistic Coefficient	.473	.430	.446	.482	.314	.398	.390	.341
Catalog Number	35644	44800	44801	44750	44850	44845	45200	44745

Box 25, 50: $26.00–$119.00

Solid

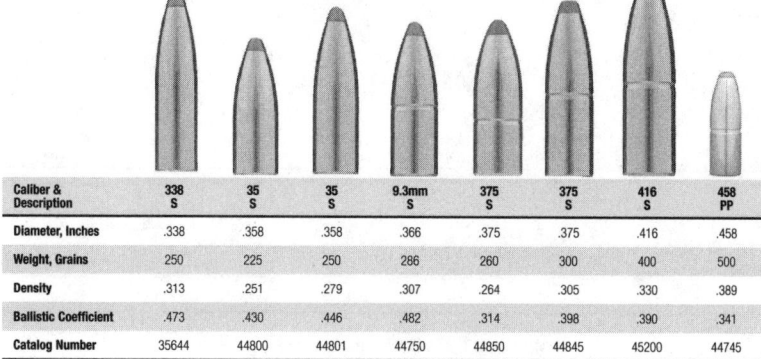

Caliber & Description	9.3mm Solid	375 Solid	375 Solid	416 Solid	458 Solid	470 NE Solid
Diameter, Inches	.366	.375	.375	.416	.458	.474
Weight, Grains	286	260	300	400	500	500
Density	.305	.264	.305	.330	.341	.318
Ballistic Coefficient	.350	.254	.300	.289	.246	.237
Catalog Number	29825	29755	28451	23654	27452	28455

MSRP $70.00–$89.00

AMMUNITION

Nosler Bullets

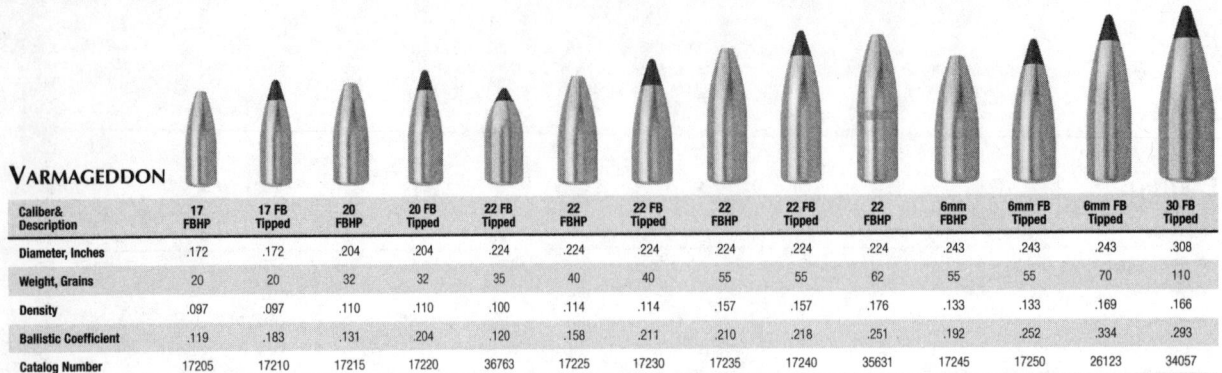

VARMAGEDDON

Caliber & Description	17 FBHP	17 FB Tipped	20 FBHP	20 FB Tipped	22 FB Tipped	22 FBHP	22 FB Tipped	22 FBHP	22 FB Tipped	22 FBHP	6mm FBHP	6mm FB Tipped	6mm FB Tipped	30 FB Tipped
Diameter, Inches	.172	.172	.204	.204	.224	.224	.224	.224	.224	.224	.243	.243	.243	.308
Weight, Grains	20	20	32	32	35	40	40	55	55	62	55	55	70	110
Density	.097	.097	.110	.110	.100	.114	.114	.157	.157	.176	.133	.133	.169	.166
Ballistic Coefficient	.119	.183	.131	.204	.120	.158	.211	.210	.218	.251	.192	.252	.334	.293
Catalog Number	17205	17210	17215	17220	36763	17225	17230	17235	17240	35631	17245	17250	26123	34057

Box 100, 250: $15.00–$25.00

Handgun Bullets

SPORTING PISTOL

Caliber & Description	9mm JHP	9mm JHP	10mm JHP	10mm JHP	10mm JHP	10mm JHP	45 JHP	45 FMJ
Diameter, Inches	.355	.355	.400	.400	.400	.400	.451	.451
Weight, Grains	115	124	135	150	180	200	230	230
Density	.109	.141	.093	.106	.161	.179	.1625	.162
Ballistic Coefficient	.130	.118	.121	.134	.147	.163	.175	.183
Catalog Number	44848	43123	44852	44860	44885	44952	44922	44964

Box 250: $42.00–$60.00

LEGEND

Type of Bullet

BT	–	Boattail
FB	–	Flat Base
FN	–	Flat Nose
RN	–	Round Nose
S	–	Spitzer
SP	–	Soft Point
SS	–	Semi-Spitzer

SPORTING REVOLVER

Caliber & Description	38 JHP	41 JHP	44 JHP	44 JHP	44 JHP	44 JHP	45 Colt JHP
Diameter, Inches	.357	.410	.429	.429	.429	.429	.451
Weight, Grains	158	210	200	240	240	300	250
Density	.182	.170	.151	.173	.177	.206	.177
Ballistic Coefficient	.177	.178	155	.186	.186	.233	.176
Catalog Number	44841	43012	44846	44842	44868	42069	43013

Sierra Bullets

Box 100, 250: $28.00–$58.00

Rifle Bullets

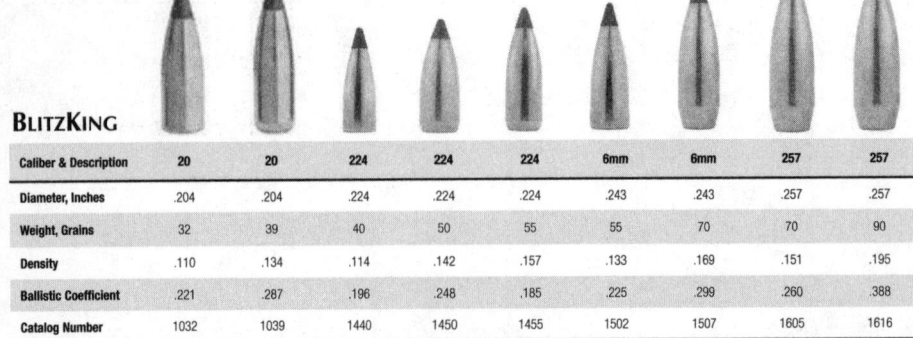

BLITZKING

Caliber & Description	20	20	224	224	224	6mm	6mm	257	257
Diameter, Inches	.204	.204	.224	.224	.224	.243	.243	.257	.257
Weight, Grains	32	39	40	50	55	55	70	70	90
Density	.110	.134	.114	.142	.157	.133	.169	.151	.195
Ballistic Coefficient	.221	.287	.196	.248	.185	.225	.299	.260	.388
Catalog Number	1032	1039	1440	1450	1455	1502	1507	1605	1616

From: $28.00–$34.00

AMMUNITION

GameKing

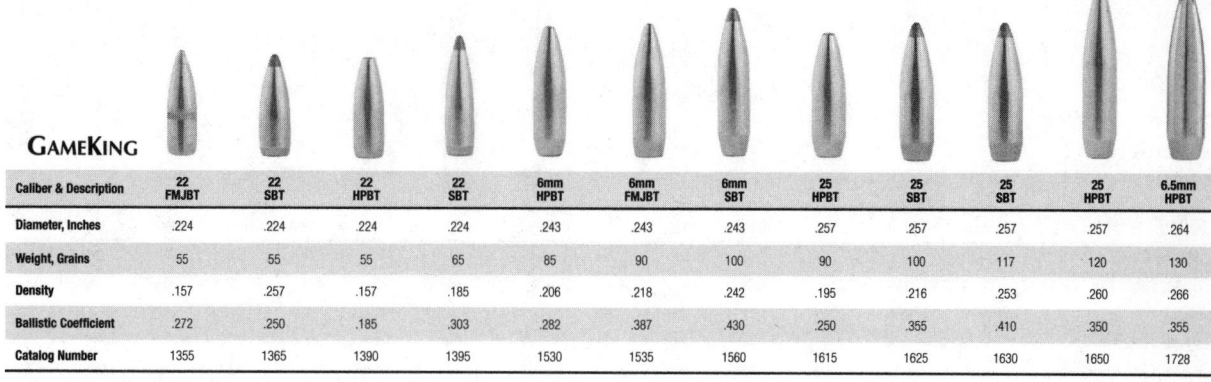

Caliber & Description	22 FMJBT	22 SBT	22 HPBT	22 SBT	6mm HPBT	6mm FMJBT	6mm SBT	25 HPBT	25 SBT	25 SBT	25 HPBT	6.5mm HPBT
Diameter, Inches	.224	.224	.224	.224	.243	.243	.243	.257	.257	.257	.257	.264
Weight, Grains	55	55	55	65	85	90	100	90	100	117	120	130
Density	.157	.257	.157	.185	.206	.218	.242	.195	.216	.253	.260	.266
Ballistic Coefficient	.272	.250	.185	.303	.282	.387	.430	.250	.355	.410	.350	.355
Catalog Number	1355	1365	1390	1395	1530	1535	1560	1615	1625	1630	1650	1728

Caliber & Description	6.5mm SBT	270 SBT	270 HPBT	270 SBT	270 SBT	7mm HPBT	7mm SBT	7mm SBT	7mm SBT	7mm HPBT	7mm SBT	30 FMJBT
Diameter, Inches	.264	.277	.277	.277	.277	.284	.274	.284	.284	.284	.284	.308
Weight, Grains	140	130	140	140	150	140	140	150	160	160	175	150
Density	.287	.242	.261	.261	.279	.248	.248	.266	.283	.283	.310	.226
Ballistic Coefficient	.495	.436	.337	.457	.483	.375	.416	.436	.455	.384	.533	.408
Catalog Number	1730	1820	1835	1845	1840	1912	1905	1913	1920	1925	1940	2115

Caliber & Description	30 SBT	30 HPBT	30 SBT	30 SBT	30 SBT	8mm SBT	338 SBT	338 SBT	35 SBT	375 SBT	375 SBT
Diameter, Inches	.308	.308	.308	.308	.308	.323	.338	.338	.358	.375	.375
Weight, Grains	150	165	165	180	200	220	215	250	225	250	300
Density	.226	.248	.248	.271	.301	.301	.269	.313	.251	.254	.305
Ballistic Coefficient	.380	.363	.404	.501	.560	.521	.485	.565	.370	.353	.475
Catalog Number	2125	2140	2145	2160	2165	2420	2610	2600	2850	2950	3000

From: $21.00–$45.00

MatchKing

Caliber & Description	22 HPBT	22 HP	22 HPBT	22 HPBT	22 HPBT	22 HPBT	6mm HPBT	6mm HPBT	6mm HPBT	25 HPBT	6.5mm HPBT	6.5mm HPBT	6.5mm HPBT	6.5mm HPBT
Diameter, Inches	.224	.224	.224	.224	.224	.224	.243	.243	.243	.257	.264	.264	.264	.264
Weight, Grains	52	53	69	77	80	90	70	107	95	100	107	120	123	140
Density	.148	.151	.196	.219	.228	.256	.169	.259	.230	.216	.219	.246	.252	.287
Ballistic Coefficient	.225	.224	.301	.372	.420	.504	.259	.527	.480	.394	.430	.421	.510	.535
Catalog Number	1410	1400	1380	9377T	9390T	9290T	1505	1570	1537	1628	1715	1725	1727	1740

Sierra Bullets

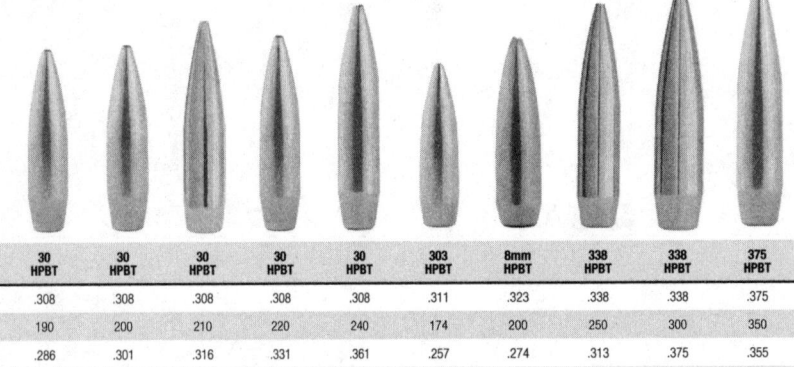

MatchKing (cont.)

Caliber & Description	6.5mm HPBT	270 HPBT	270 HPBT	7mm HPBT	7mm HPBT	7mm HPBT	7mm HPBT	7mm HPBT	7mm HPBT	30 HP	30 HPBT	30 HPBT	30 HPBT	30 HPBT	30 HPBT	30 HPBT
Diameter, Inches	.264	.277	.277	.284	.284	.284	.284	.284	.284	.308	.308	.308	.308	.308	.308	.308
Weight, Grains	142	115	135	130	150	168	175	180	183	125	135	150	155	168	175	180
Density	.291	.214	.251	.230	.266	.298	.310	.319	.324	.188	.203	.226	.233	.253	.264	.271
Ballistic Coefficient	.595	.318	.488	.395	.429	.488	.608	.660	.707	.349	.390	.417	.450	.462	.505	.475
Catalog Number	1742	1815	1833	1903	1915	1930	1975	1980	1983	2121	2123	2190	2155	2200	2275	2220

Caliber & Description	30 HPBT	30 HPBT	30 HPBT	30 HPBT	30 HPBT	303 HPBT	8mm HPBT	338 HPBT	338 HPBT	375 HPBT
Diameter, Inches	.308	.308	.308	.308	.308	.311	.323	.338	.338	.375
Weight, Grains	190	200	210	220	240	174	200	250	300	350
Density	.286	.301	.316	.331	.361	.257	.274	.313	.375	.355
Ballistic Coefficient	.533	.565	.645	.629	.711	.499	.520	.587	.768	.805
Catalog Number	2210	2230	9240T	2240	9245T	2315	2415	2650	9300T	9350T

From: $25.00–$54.00

LEGEND
- **BT** – Boattail
- **FMJ** – Full Metal Jacket
- **FN** – Flat Nose
- **HC** – Hollow Cavity
- **HP** – Hollow Point
- **J** – Jacketed
- **RN** – Round Nose
- **S** – Spitzer
- **SMP** – Semi-Pointed
- **SP** – Soft Point

Pro-Hunter

Caliber & Description	6mm S	25 S	25 S	6.5mm S	270 S	270 S	7mm S	7mm S	30 HP/FN	30 FN	30 FN
Diameter, Inches	.243	.257	.257	.264	.277	.277	.284	.284	.308	.308	.308
Weight, Grains	100	100	117	120	110	130	120	140	125	150	170
Density	.242	.216	.253	.246	.205	.242	.213	.248	.188	.226	.256
Ballistic Coefficient	.373	.330	.388	.356	.318	.370	.328	.377	.119	.185	.205
Catalog Number	1540	1620	1640	1720	1810	1830	1900	1910	2020	2000	2010

Caliber & Description	30 RN	30 FMJ	30 S	30 S	30 RN	30 S	30 RN	30 RN
Diameter, Inches	.308	.308	.308	.308	.308	.308	.308	.308
Weight, Grains	110	110	125	150	150	180	180	220
Density	.166	.166	.188	.226	.226	.271	.271	.331
Ballistic Coefficient	.144	.144	.279	.336	.200	.407	.240	.310
Catalog Number	2100	2105	2120	2130	2135	2150	2170	2180

Sierra Bullets

PRO-HUNTER (CONT.)

Caliber & Description	303 S	303 S	303 S	8mm S	8mm S	338 S	35 RN	375 FN	45-70 HP/FN
Diameter, Inches	.311	.311	.311	.323	.323	.338	.358	.375	.458
Weight, Grains	125	150	180	150	175	225	200	200	300
Density	.185	.222	.266	.205	.240	.281	.223	.203	.204
Ballistic Coefficient	.274	.344	.411	.336	.381	.462	.148	.195	.120
Catalog Number	2305	2300	2310	2400	2410	2620	2800	2900	8900

From: $20.00–$37.00

VARMINTER

Caliber & Description	22 Hornet	22 Hornet	22 Hornet	22 Hornet	22 HP
Diameter, Inches	.223	.223	.224	.224	.224
Weight, Grains	40	45	40	45	40
Density	.115	.129	.114	.128	.114
Ballistic Coefficient	.117	.132	.116	.131	.155
Catalog Number	1100	1110	1200	1210	1385

Caliber & Description	22 S	22 S	22 S	22 Blitz	22 Blitz	22 SMP	22 S	22 HP	22 SMP	6mm HP	6mm HP	6mm SBT Blitz	6mm S	25 HP	25 S	6.5mm HP	6.5mm HP	270 HP	7mm HP	30 HP
Diameter, Inches	.224	.224	.224	.224	.224	.224	.224	.224	.224	.243	.243	.243	.243	.257	.257	.264	.264	.277	.284	.308
Weight, Grains	45	50	50	50	55	55	55	60	63	60	75	80	85	75	87	85	100	90	100	110
Density	.128	.142	.142	.142	.157	.157	.157	.171	.179	.145	.181	.194	.206	.162	.188	.174	.205	.168	.177	.166
Ballistic Coefficient	.210	.192	.222	.222	.237	.204	.237	.246	.231	.182	.217	.319	.315	.189	.293	.225	.259	.195	.209	.177
Catalog Number	1310	1320	1330	1340	1345	1350	1360	1375	1370	1500	1510	1515	1520	1600	1610	1700	1710	1800	1895	2110

From: $20.00–$32.00

TIPPED MATCHKING

Caliber & Description	224	224	243	264	284	308	308	308	308
Diameter, Inches	.224	.224	.243	.264	.284	.308	.308	.308	.308
Weight, Grains	69	77	95	130	160	125	155	168	175
Density	.196	.219	.243	.264	.284	.188	.233	.253	.264
Ballistic Coefficient	.375	.420	.500	.518	.600	.343	.519	.535	.545
Catalog Number	7169	7177	7295	7430	7660	7725	7755	7768	7775

From: $30.54–$48.44

Handgun Bullets

SPORTS MASTER

Caliber & Description	30 RN	32 JHC	9mm JHP	9mm JHP	9mm JHP	38 JHP Blitz	38 JHP	38 JSP	38 JHP	38 JHC	38 JSP	10mm JHP	10mm JHP
Diameter, Inches	.308	.312	.355	.355	.355	.357	.357	.357	.357	.357	.357	.400	.400
Weight, Grains	85	90	90	115	125	110	125	125	140	158	158	135	150
Density	.128	.132	.102	.130	.142	.123	.140	.140	.157	.177	.177	.121	.134
Ballistic Coefficient	.102	.125	.095	.107	.124	.120	.133	.133	.0776	.100	.100	.105	.120
Catalog Number	8005	8030	8100	8110	8125	8300	8320	8310	8325	8360	8340	8425	8430

Sierra Bullets

Handgun Bullets

Caliber & Description	10mm JHP	10mm JHP	41 JHC	41 JHC	44 JHC	44 JHC	44 JHC	44 JSP	45 JHP	45 JHP	45 JHC	45 JSP	50 JHP	50 JSP
Diameter, Inches	.400	.400	.410	.410	.4295	.4295	.4295	.4295	.4515	.4515	.4515	.4515	.500	.500
Weight, Grains	165	180	170	210	180	210	240	300	185	230	240	300	350	400
Density	.147	.161	.144	.178	.139	.163	.186	.232	.130	.161	.168	.210	.200	.229
Ballistic Coefficient	.130	.140	.123	.165	.130	.160	.185	.230	.100	.145	.150	.192	.155	.185
Catalog Number	8445	8460	8500	8520	8600	8620	8610	8630	8800	8805	8820	8830	5350	5400

From: $22.00–$37.00

V-Crown

Caliber & Description	9mm JHP	9mm JHP	9mm JHP	10mm JHP	45 JHP
Diameter, Inches	.355	.355	.355	.400	.4515
Weight, Grains	90	124	125	165	200
Density	.109	.160	.168	.147	.143
Ballistic Coefficient	.094	.120	.122	.132	.118
Catalog Number	9990	9924	9925	9465	9820

Box 100: . . . . . . $24.46–$34.80

Speer Bullets

Rifle Bullets

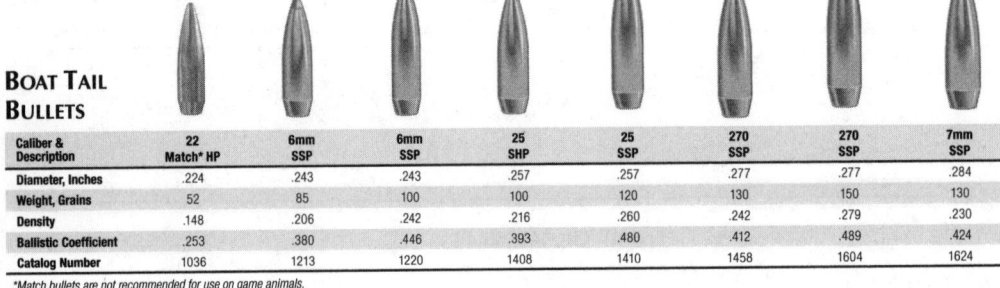

Boat Tail Bullets

Caliber & Description	22 Match* HP	6mm SSP	6mm SSP	25 SHP	25 SSP	270 SSP	270 SSP	7mm SSP
Diameter, Inches	.224	.243	.243	.257	.257	.277	.277	.284
Weight, Grains	52	85	100	100	120	130	150	130
Density	.148	.206	.242	.216	.260	.242	.279	.230
Ballistic Coefficient	.253	.380	.446	.393	.480	.412	.489	.424
Catalog Number	1036	1213	1220	1408	1410	1458	1604	1624

Match bullets are not recommended for use on game animals.

Caliber & Description	7mm SSP	7mm Match* HP	7mm SSP	30 SSP	30 SSP	30 Match* HP	30 SSP	338 SSP	375 SSP
Diameter, Inches	.284	.284	.284	.308	.308	.308	.308	.338	.375
Weight, Grains	145	145	160	150	165	168	180	225	270
Density	.257	.257	.284	.226	.248	.253	.271	.281	.274
Ballistic Coefficient	.472	.468	.519	.417	.520	.534	.545	.497	.478
Catalog Number	1628	1631	1634	2022	2034	2040	2052	2406	2472

Match bullets are not recommended for use on game animals.

From: $27.00–$39.00

AMMUNITION

Speer Bullets

GRAND SLAM

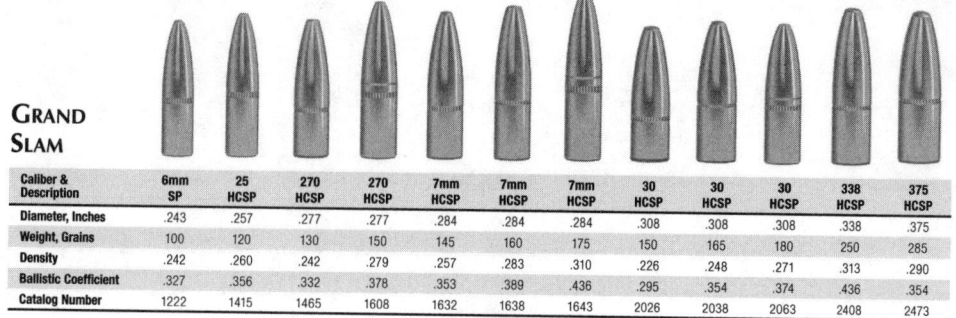

Caliber & Description	6mm SP	25 HCSP	270 HCSP	270 HCSP	7mm HCSP	7mm HCSP	7mm HCSP	30 HCSP	30 HCSP	30 HCSP	338 HCSP	375 HCSP
Diameter, Inches	.243	.257	.277	.277	.284	.284	.284	.308	.308	.308	.338	.375
Weight, Grains	100	120	130	150	145	160	175	150	165	180	250	285
Density	.242	.260	.242	.279	.257	.283	.310	.226	.248	.271	.313	.290
Ballistic Coefficient	.327	.356	.332	.378	.353	.389	.436	.295	.354	.374	.436	.354
Catalog Number	1222	1415	1465	1608	1632	1638	1643	2026	2038	2063	2408	2473

From: $31.00–$66.00

HOT-COR BULLETS*

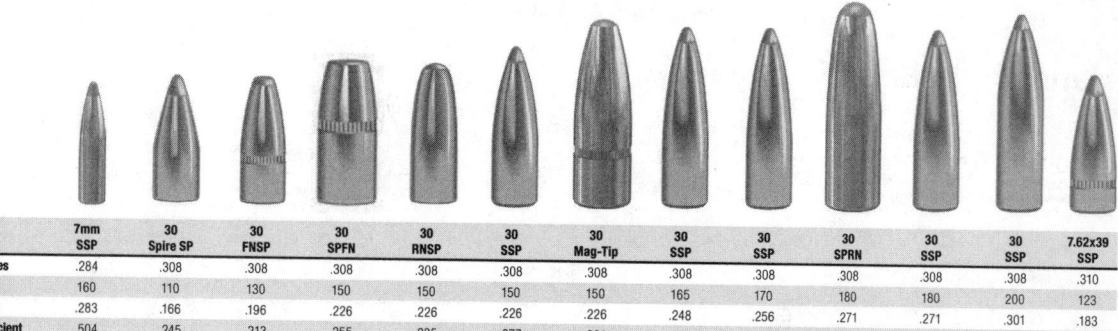

Caliber & Description	6mm SSP	25 SPFN	25 SSP	25 SSP	25 SSP	6.5mm SSP	6.5mm SSP	270 SSP	270 SSP	7mm SSP	7mm SPFN	7mm SSP
Diameter, Inches	.243	.257	.257	.257	.257	.264	.264	.277	.277	.284	.284	.284
Weight, Grains	90	75	87	100	120	120	140	130	150	130	130	145
Density	.218	.162	.188	.216	.260	.246	.287	.242	.279	.230	.230	.257
Ballistic Coefficient	.365	.135	.300	.334	.405	.392	.498	.383	.455	.394	.257	.416
Catalog Number	1217	1237	1241	1405	1411	1435	1441	1459	1605	1623	1625	1629

* Not recommended for lever-action rifles.

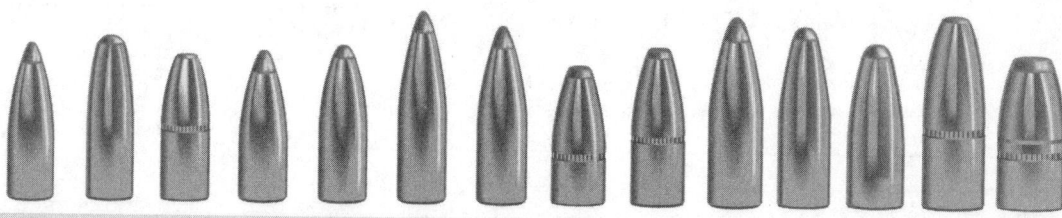

Caliber & Description	7mm SSP	30 Spire SP	30 FNSP	30 SPFN	30 RNSP	30 SSP	30 Mag-Tip	30 SSP	30 SSP	30 SPRN	30 SSP	30 SSP	7.62x39 SSP
Diameter, Inches	.284	.308	.308	.308	.308	.308	.308	.308	.308	.308	.308	.308	.310
Weight, Grains	160	110	130	150	150	150	150	165	170	180	180	200	123
Density	.283	.166	.196	.226	.226	.226	.226	.248	.256	.271	.271	.301	.183
Ballistic Coefficient	.504	.245	.213	.255	.235	.377	.301	.444	.298	.304	.441	.478	.283
Catalog Number	1635	1855	2007	2011	2017	2023	2025	2035	2041	2047	2053	2211	2213

* Not recommended for lever-action rifles.

Caliber & Description	303 SSP	303 RNSP	32 FNSP	8mm SSP	8mm SSSP	8mm SSP	338 SSP	35 FNSP	35 FNSP	35 SSP	9.3mm SSSP	375 SSSP	416 Mag-Tip	45 FNSP
Diameter, Inches	.311	.311	.321	.323	.323	.323	.338	.358	.358	.358	.366	.375	.416	.458
Weight, Grains	150	180	170	150	170	200	200	180	220	250	270	235	350	350
Density	.222	.266	.236	.205	.233	.274	.250	.201	.245	.279	.288	.239	.289	.238
Ballistic Coefficient	.351	.299	.283	.343	.311	.440	.426	.236	.286	.422	.361	.301	.332	.218
Catalog Number	2217	2223	2259	2277	2283	2285	2405	2435	2439	2453	2459	2471	2477	2478

From: $20.00–$44.00

AMMUNITION

Speer Bullets

JACKETED HP BULLETS

Caliber & Description	22 Hornet	45
Diameter, Inches	.224	.458
Weight, Grains	33	300
Density	.094	.204
Ballistic Coefficient	.080	.206
Catalog Number	1014	2482

From: $21.00–$36.00

SPECIAL PURPOSE BULLETS*

Caliber & Description	30 SPRN	30 HP	45 SPFN
Diameter, Inches	.308	.308	.458
Weight, Grains	100	110	400
Density	.151	.166	.272
Ballistic Coefficient	.144	.128	.259
Catalog Number	1805	1835	2479

From: $20.00–$34.00

TNT BULLETS

Caliber & Description	204 HP	22 HP	22 HP	6mm HP	25 HP	6.5mm HP	270 HP	7mm HP	30 HP
Diameter, Inches	.204	.224	.224	.243	.247	.264	.277	.284	.308
Weight, Grains	39	50	55	70	87	90	90	110	125
Density	.134	.142	.157	.169	.188	.184	.168	.195	.188
Ballistic Coefficient	.202	.228	.233	.279	.337	.281	.303	.384	.341
Catalog Number	1015	1030	1032	1206	1246	1445	1446	1616	1986

From: $20.00–$33.00

Handgun Bullets

GOLD DOT BULLETS

Caliber & Description	25 HP	32 Auto HP	327 Fed. Mag. HP	327 Fed. Mag. HP	380 Auto HP	9mm HP	9mm HP	9mm HP	357 SIG HP	38 Spl. HPSB	38 HPSB	357 Mag. HP	40/10mm HP
Diameter, Inches	.251	.312	.312	.312	.355	.355	.355	.355	.355	.357	.357	.357	.400
Weight, Grains	35	60	100	115	90	115	124	147	125	110	135	125	155
Density	.079	.088	.147	.168	.102	.130	.141	.167	.142	.123	.151	.177	.138
Ballistic Coefficient	.091	.118	.137	.180	.101	.125	.134	.164	.141	.117	.141	.140	.123
Catalog Number	3985	3986	3990	3988	3992	3994	3998	4002	4360	4009	4014	4012	4400

Caliber & Description	40/10mm HP	40/10mm HP	40/10mm HPSB	44 Spl. HP	44 Mag. HP	45 Auto HP	45 Auto HP	45 Auto HP	45 HPSB
Diameter, Inches	.400	.400	.400	.429	.429	.451	.451	.451	.451
Weight, Grains	165	180	180	200	210	185	200	230	230
Density	.147	.161	.161	.155	.163	.130	.140	.162	.162
Ballistic Coefficient	.138	.143	.148	.145	.154	.109	.138	.143	.148
Catalog Number	4397	4406	4401	4427	4428	4470	4478	4483	4482

From: $22.00–$36.00

LEGEND

BT	– Boat Tail	S	– Spitzer
FB	– Fusion Bonded	SS	– Semi-Spitzer
FMJ	– Full Metal Jacket	SB™	– For Short-Barrel Firearms
FN	– Flat Nose		
GD	– Gold Dot®	SP	– Soft Point
HC	– Hot-Cor®	TMJ®	– Encased-Core Full Jacket
HP	– Hollow Point		
L	– Lead	RN	– Round Nose
MHP™	– Molybdenum Disulfide Impregnated	SWC	– Semi-Wadcutter
		UC	– Uni-Cor®
		WC	– Wadcutter

AMMUNITION

Speer Bullets

Jacketed Bullets

Caliber & Description	9mm Luger FN JSP	38 Spl./357 Mag. JHP	38 Spl./357 Mag. JSP	38 Spl./357 Mag. JHP	38 Spl./357 Mag. JHP	38 Spl./357 Mag. JHP	38 Spl./357 Mag. JSP
Diameter, Inches	.355	.357	.357	.357	.357	.357	.357
Weight, Grains	124	110	125	125	140	158	158
Density	.141	.123	.140	.140	.157	.177	.177
Ballistic Coefficient	.115	.113	.129	.129	.145	.163	.164
Catalog Number	3997	4007	4011	4013	4203	4211	4217

Caliber & Description	44 Mag. JSP	44 Mag. JSP	45 Colt/460 S&W JHP	45 Colt/460 S&W JSP	50 Action Express JHP
Diameter, Inches	.429	.429	.451	.451	.186
Weight, Grains	240	300	260	300	325
Density	.186	.233	.183	.211	.186
Ballistic Coefficient	.169	.213	.183	.199	.169
Catalog Number	4454	4463	4481	4485	4495

LEGEND
FN – Flat Nose
HB – Hollow Base
HC – Hot-Cor®
HP – Hollow Point
J – Jacketed
RN – Round Nose
S – Spitzer
SP – Soft Point
SS – Semi-Spitzer
SWC – Semi-Wadcutter
WC – Wadcutter

From: $18–$31

Lead Handgun Bullets

Caliber & Description	32 S&W HBWC	9mm Luger RN	38 HBWC	38 SWC	38 SWC HP	38 RN	44 SWC	45 Auto SWC	45 Auto RN	45 Colt SWC
Diameter, Inches	.314	.356	.358	.358	.358	.358	.430	.452	.452	.452
Weight, grains	98	125	148	158	158	158	240	200	230	250
Density	.142	.141	.165	.176	.176	.176	.185	.140	.161	.175
Ballistic Coefficient	.044	.155	.050	.123	.121	.170	.151	.078	.160	.117
Bulk Part No.	4600	4602	4618	4624	4628	4648	4661	4678	4691	4684
Bulk Count	1000	500	500	500	500	500	500	500	500	500

From: $46.00–$84.00

AMMUNITION

Swift Bullets

Rifle Bullets

The Scirocco II rifle bullet starts with a tough, pointed polymer tip that reduces air resistance, prevents tip deformation, and blends into the radius of its secant ogive nose section.

The Scirocco II has a bonded core construction with a pure lead core encased in a tapered, progressively thickening jacket of pure copper. The Swift A-Frame bullet with its midsec-tion wall of copper is less aerodynamic than the Scirocco, but it produces a broad mushroom while carrying almost all its weight through muscle and bone.

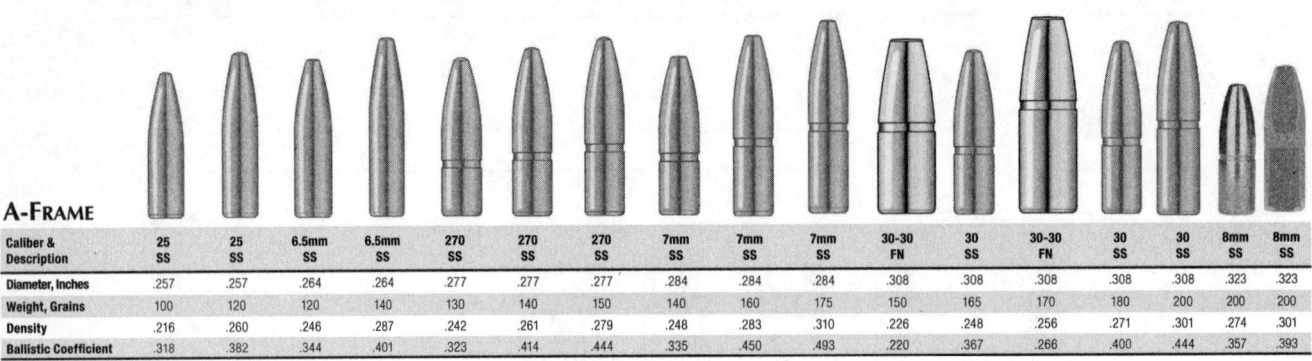

A-FRAME

Caliber & Description	25 SS	25 SS	6.5mm SS	6.5mm SS	270 SS	270 SS	270 SS	7mm SS	7mm SS	7mm SS	30-30 FN	30 SS	30-30 FN	30 SS	30 SS	8mm SS	8mm SS
Diameter, Inches	.257	.257	.264	.264	.277	.277	.277	.284	.284	.284	.308	.308	.308	.308	.308	.323	.323
Weight, Grains	100	120	120	140	130	140	150	140	160	175	150	165	170	180	200	200	200
Density	.216	.260	.246	.287	.242	.261	.279	.248	.283	.310	.226	.248	.256	.271	.301	.274	.301
Ballistic Coefficient	.318	.382	.344	.401	.323	.414	.444	.335	.450	.493	.220	.367	.266	.400	.444	.357	.393

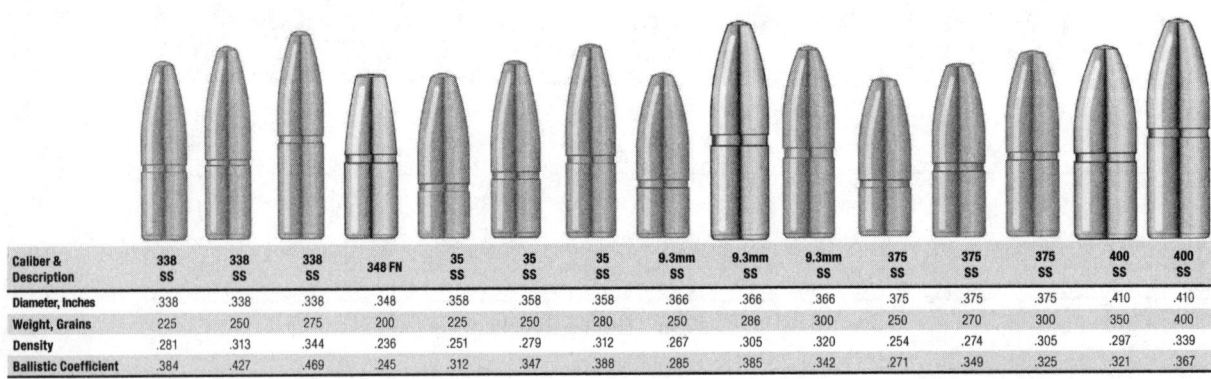

Caliber & Description	338 SS	338 SS	338 SS	348 FN	35 SS	35 SS	35 SS	9.3mm SS	9.3mm SS	9.3mm SS	375 SS	375 SS	375 SS	400 SS	400 SS
Diameter, Inches	.338	.338	.338	.348	.358	.358	.358	.366	.366	.366	.375	.375	.375	.410	.410
Weight, Grains	225	250	275	200	225	250	280	250	286	300	250	270	300	350	400
Density	.281	.313	.344	.236	.251	.279	.312	.267	.305	.320	.254	.274	.305	.297	.339
Ballistic Coefficient	.384	.427	.469	.245	.312	.347	.388	.285	.385	.342	.271	.349	.325	.321	.367

LEGEND

Type of Bullet

BT	–	Boat Tail
CT	–	Combat Target
FMJ	–	Full Metal Jacket
FP	–	Flat Point
HB	–	Hollow Base
L	–	Lead
RN	–	Round Nose
SP	–	Spire Point
SX	–	Super Explosive
SWC	–	Semi-Wadcutter
WC	–	Wadcutter

AMMUNITION

Swift Bullets

Caliber & Description	416 SS	416 SS	404 SS	45-70 FN	458 FN	458 SS	458 SS	470 RN	505 RN	505 RN	50 FN	500 RN	500 RN
Diameter, Inches	.416	.416	.423	.457	.458	.458	.458	.475	.505	.505	.509	.509	.509
Weight, Grains	350	400	400	350	400	450	500	500	535	570	450	535	570
Density	.289	.330	.319	.238	.272	.307	.341	.329	.300	.319	.247	.294	.313
Ballistic Coefficient	.321	.367	.375	.172	.258	.325	.361	.364	.285	.306	.180	.285	.306

MSRP $55.00–$115.00

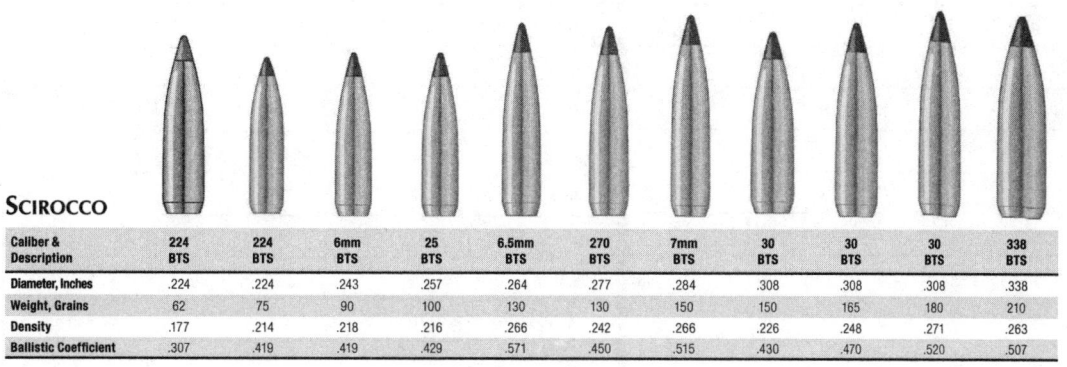

SCIROCCO

Caliber & Description	224 BTS	224 BTS	6mm BTS	25 BTS	6.5mm BTS	270 BTS	7mm BTS	30 BTS	30 BTS	30 BTS	338 BTS
Diameter, Inches	.224	.224	.243	.257	.264	.277	.284	.308	.308	.308	.338
Weight, Grains	62	75	90	100	130	130	150	150	165	180	210
Density	.177	.214	.218	.216	.266	.242	.266	.226	.248	.271	.263
Ballistic Coefficient	.307	.419	.419	.429	.571	.450	.515	.430	.470	.520	.507

MSRP $52.00–$69.00

LEGEND
BT – Boattail
FN – Flat Nose
HP – Hollow Point
RN – Round Nose
S – Spitzer
SS – Semi-Spitzer

Handgun Bullets

A-FRAME HUNTING REVOLVER BULLETS

Caliber & Description	357 HP	357 HP	41 HP	44 HP	44 HP	44 HP	45 HP	45 HP	45 HP	50 HP
Diameter, Inches	.357	.357	.410	.430	.430	.430	.452	.452	.452	.499
Weight, Grains	158	180	210	240	280	300	265	300	325	325
Density	.177	.202	.178	.185	.216	.232	.185	.210	.227	.186
Ballistic Coefficient	.183	.189	.159	.119	.139	.147	.129	.153	.171	.135

MSRP $54.00

LEGEND
BT – Boattail
FN – Flat Nose
HP – Hollow Point
RN – Round Nose
S – Spitzer
SS – Semi-Spitzer

AMMUNITION

Woodleigh Bullets

HYDROSTATICALLY STABILIZED

Hydrostatic stabilization is a method of producing pierced hollow bars to very precise concentricity to produce a bullet that resists deflection and achieves deep straight-line penetration. It's non-toxic and environmentally sensitive. It can be used in most nitro double and magazine rifles.

10–20 per box: $31.00–$80.00

Caliber	Diameter	"Weight, Grains"	Catalog Number
7mm	.284	140	H7mm
308	.308	150	H308A
308	.308	180	H308
303	.312	215	H303
8mm	.323	170	H8mm
338	.338	185	H338A
338	.338	225	H338
358	.358	225	H358
9.3	.366	232	H9.3A
9,3	.366	286	H9.3
375 Win.	.375	235	H375A
375	.375	300	H375
450/400 3"	.410	400	H450/400

Caliber	Diameter	"Weight, Grains"	Catalog Number
416	.416	400	H416
404 Jeffery	.422	400	H404
450	.458	325	H450BPE
45/70	.458	400	H45/70
458	.458	450	H458A
458	.458	480	H458
465	.468	480	H465
470	.474	500	H470
500	.510	570	H500
50 Alaskan	.510	400	H50 Alaskan
505	.505	525	H505
577	.585	750	H577

98% & 95% RETAINED WEIGHT 300 WIN MAG 180GR PP

458 X 500GN SN RECOVERED FROM BUFFALO

270 WIN 150GN PP 86% RETAINED WEIGHT

94% RETAINED WEIGHT 300 WIN MAG 180GR PP

500/465 RECOVERED FROM BUFFALO

Woodleigh Bullets

TRADITIONAL BULLETS

Fashioned from gilding-metal-clad steel 2mm thick, jackets on FMJ bullets are heavy at the nose for extra impact resistance. The jacket then tapers toward the base to assist rifling engraving. Woodleigh Weldcore Soft Nose bullets are made from 90/100 gilding metal (90 percent copper; 10 percent zinc) 1.6 mm thick. **50 per box: $36.00–$86.00**

Caliber Diameter	Type	Weight, Grains	SD	BC	Catalog Number
6.5mm .264	PP SN	140	.287	.444	80
	PP SN	160	.328	.509	80A
	RN SN	160	.328	.285	80B
270 Win .277	PP SN	130	.242	.409	72
	PP SN	150	.279	.463	73
	PP SN	180	.334	.513	73A
7mm .284	PP SN	140	.248	.436	74
	PP SN	160	.283	.486	75
	PP SN	175	.310	.510	76
275 H&H .287	PP SN	160	.277	.474	77
	PP SN	175	.304	.509	78
308 .308	PP SN	130	.189	.302	65I
	PP SN	150	.226	.310	65F
	PP SN	165	.248	.320	65A
	PP SN	180	.271	.376	65B
	RN SN	220	.331	.367	65C
	FMJ	220	.331	.359	65
30-30 .308	FN SN	150	.226	.246	65H
30-06 .308	PP SN	240	.361	.401	65G
300 Win. Mag. .308	PP SN	180	.271	.435	65D
	PP SN	200	.301	.450	65E
303 British .312	PP SN	174	.255	.362	68A
	RN SN	215	.316	.359	68
303/ 7.62x39mm .312	PP SN	130	.180	.295	68B
8mm .323	RN SN	196	.268	.315	64B
	RN SN	220	.301	.355	64C
	RN SN	250	.343	.403	64D
325 Win. (8mm) .323	PP SN	200	.274	.406	64F
	PP SN	220	.301	.448	64G
8x57 .318	RN SN	200	.283	.331	64E
318 WR .330	RN SN	250	.328	.420	63
	FMJ	250	.328	.364	64
333 Jeffery .333	RN SN	250	.322	.335	60
	RN SN	300	.386	.418	61
	FMJ	300	.386	.418	62
338 Fed .338	PP SN	180	.226	.361	56C
	PP SN	200	.251	.401	56D
33 Win. .338	FN SN	200	.246	.234	56E
338 Mag .338	PP SN	225	.281	.425	56A
	RN SN	250	.313	.332	56
	PP SN	250	.313	.431	56B
	FMJ	250	.313	.326	57
	RN SN	300	.375	.416	58
	FMJ	300	.375	.414	59
348 Win. .348	FN SN	250	.295	.281	348

Caliber Diameter	Type	Weight, Grains	SD	BC	Catalog Number
358 .358	RN SN	225	.251	.263	51
	PP SN	225	.251	.372	51A
	FMJ	225	.251	.263	52
	RN SN	250	.279	.300	53
	PP SN	250	.279	.400	53A
	PP SN	275	.307	.450	53B
	RN SN	310	.346	.458	54
	FMJ	310	.346	.458	55
9.3 .366	RN SN	250	.267	.281	47A
	PP SN	250	.267	.381	47C
	RN SN	286	.305	.321	47
	PP SN	286	.305	.396	47B
	FMJ	286	.305	.305	48
	RN SN	320	.341	.359	49
	PP SN	320	.341	.457	49A
	FMJ	320	.341	.341	50
375 Mag. .375	PP SN	235	.239	.310	42A
	RN SN	270	.274	.250	42
	PP SN	270	.274	.370	43A
	RN SN	300	.305	.277	44HD
	RN SN	300	.305	.277	44
	PP SN	300	.305	.380	45A
	FMJ	300	.305	.275	46
	RN SN	350	.356	.321	46B
	RN SN	350	.356	.323	46BHD
	PP SN	350	.356	.400	46C
	FMJ	350	.356	.307	46D
400 Purdey .405	RN SN	230	.200	.181	81
450/400 Nitro .408	RN SN	400	.344	.307	40A
450/400 Nitro .411	RN SN	400	.338	.307	40
450/400 Ruger .410	RN SN	400	.338	.307	40B
450/400 Ruger .408	FMJ	400	.344	.300	41A
.410 Ruger	FMJ	400	.338	.300	41
405 Win. .412	RN SN	300	.252	.194	71
416 Rigby .416	PP SN	340	.281	.330	39
	RN SN	410	.338	.307	37A
	FMJ	410	.338	.300	38
	RN SN	450	.371	.338	37B
	FMJ	450	.371	.330	38B"
416 Rem. .416	RN SN	400	.330	.305	37C
	FMJ	400	.330	.300	38C
	RN SN	450	.371	.338	37N
	FMJ	450	.371	.330	38N
404 Jeffery .422	RN SN	350	.281	.293	35
	RN SN	400	.321	.335	33A
	FMJ	400	.321	.330	34
	RN SN	450	.361	.360	33B
	FMJ	450	.361	.355	34B
10.75x68mm .423	RN SN	347	.277	.290	36
	FMJ	347	.277	.288	36A
444 Marlin .430	FN SN	280	.216	.186	444

AMMUNITION

Woodleigh Bullets

Caliber Diameter	Type	Weight, Grains	SD	BC	Catalog Number
425 WR .435	RN SN	410	.310	.222	31
	FMJ	410	.310	.221	32
11.2 Schuler .440	RN SN	401	.296	.325	67
458 Mag. .458	PP SN	400	.272	.340	30
	RN SN	480	.327	.328	24A
	FMJ	480	.327	.325	25A
	RN SN	500	.341	.310	26
	PP SN	500	.341	.378	26A
	FMJ	500	.341	.310	28
	RN SN	550	.375	.340	27
	FMJ	550	.375	.326	29
450 BPE .458	RN SN	350	.238	.250	30A
45/70 .458	FN SN	405	.276	.204	30B
	FN SN	300	.205	.196	30C
450 Nitro .458	RN SN	480	.327	.328	24
	FMJ	480	.327	.325	25
465 Nitro .468	RN SN	480	.313	.334	22
	FMJ	480	.313	.330	23
470 Nitro .474	RN SN	500	.318	.374	20
	FMJ	500	.318	.370	21
476 WR .476	RN SN	520	.328	.385	18
	FMJ	520	.328	.380	19
475 No. 2 .483	RN SN	480	.294	.309	15
	FMJ	480	.294	.300	16
475 No. 2 Jeffery .488	RN SN	500	.300	.315	13
	FMJ	500	.300	.300	14

Caliber Diameter	Type	Weight, Grains	SD	BC	Catalog Number
500 S&W MAG .500	FN SN	400	.229	.182	83
505 Gibbs .505	RN SN	525	.294	.345	11
	FMJ	525	.294	.340	12
	PP SN	600	.336	.360	11A
	FMJ	600	.336	.360	12A
500 Jeffery .510	RN SN	535	.294	.350	9
	PP SN	535	.294	.310	9A
	FMJ	535	.294	.340	10
	PP SN	600	.330	.350	10B
	FMJ	600	.330	.355	10A
500 BP .510	RN SN	440	.242	.255	8
50 Alaskan & 50/110 Win. .510	FN SN	500	.275	.219	82
500 Nitro .510	RN SN	450	.247	.257	06A
	RN SN	570	.313	.368	6
	FMJ	570	.313	.350	7
577 BP Express .585	RN SN	650	.271	.292	5
577 Nitro .585	RN SN	650	.271	.292	3A
	RN SN	750	.313	.346	3
577 Nitro .584	FMJ	650	.272	.292	4A
	FMJ	750	.314	.351	4
600 Nitro .620	RN SN	900	.334	.371	1
	FMJ	900	.334	.334	2
700 Nitro .700	RN SN	1000	.292	.340	A
	FMJ	1000	.292	.340	B

Centerfire Rifle Ballistics
Comprehensive Ballistics Tables for Currently Manufactured Sporting Rifle Cartridges

No more collecting catalogs and peering at microscopic print to find out what ammunition is offered for a cartridge, and how it performs relative to other factory loads! *Shooter's Bible* has assembled the data for you, in easy-to-read tables, by cartridge.

Data is taken from manufacturers' charts; your chronograph readings may vary. Listings are not intended as recommendations. For example, the data for the .44 Magnum at 400 yards shows its effective range is much shorter. The lack of data for a 285-grain .375 H&H bullet beyond 300 yards does not mean the bullet has no authority farther out. Besides ammunition, the rifle, sights, conditions and shooter ability all must be considered when contemplating a long shot. Accuracy and bullet energy both matter when big game is in the offing.

Barrel length affects velocity, and at various rates

depending on the load. As a rule, figure 50 fps per inch of barrel, plus or minus, if your barrel is longer or shorter than 22 inches.

Bullets are given by make, weight (in grains) and type. Most type abbreviations are self-explanatory: BT=Boat-Tail, FMJ=Full Metal Jacket, HP=Hollow Point, SP=Soft Point—except in Hornady listings, where SP is the firm's Spire Point. TNT and TXP are trademarked designations of Speer and Norma. XLC identifies a coated Barnes X bullet. HE indicates a Federal High Energy load, similar to the Hornady LM (Light Magnum) and HM (Heavy Magnum) cartridges.

Arc (trajectory) is based on a zero range published by the manufacturer, from 100 to 300 yards. If a zero does not fall in a yardage column, it lies halfway between—at 150 yards, for example, if the bullet's strike is "+" at 100 yards and "-" at 200.

.17 HORNET TO .222 REMINGTON

CARTRIDGE BULLET	RANGE, YARDS:	0	100	200	300	400
.17 HORNET						
Hornady 15.5 NXT SPF		0	100	200	300	400
	velocity, fps	3860	2924	2159	1531	1108
	energy, ft-lb	513	294	160	81	42
	arc, inches	-1.5	+1.4	0	-9.1	-33.7
Hornady 20 V-MAX		0	100	200	300	400
	velocity, fps	3650	3077	2574	2122	1721
	energy, ft-lb	592	420	294	200	132
	arc, inches	-1.5	+1.1	0	-6.4	-20.7
.17 REMINGTON						
Rem. 20 AccuTip BT	velocity, ft-lb	4250	3594	3028	2529	2081
	energy, ft-lb	802	574	407	284	192
	arc, inches		+1.3	+1.3	-2.5	-11.8
Rem. 20 Fireball	velocity, fps	4000	3380	2840	2360	1930
	energy, ft-lb	710	507	358	247	165
	arc, inches		+1.6	+1.5	-2.8	-13.5
Rem. 25 HP Power-Lokt	velocity, fps	4040	3284	2644	2086	1606
	energy, ft-lb	906	599	388	242	143
	arc, inches		+1.8	0	-3.3	-16.6
.204 RUGER						
Federal 32 Nosler Ballistic Tip	velocity, fps	4030	3465	2968	2523	2119
	arc, inches		+0.7	0	-4.7	-14.9
Federal 40 Ballistic Tip	velocity, fps	3650	3200	2790	2420	2080
	energy, ft-lb	1185	910	695	520	385
	arc, inches		+1.0	0	-5.4	-16.9
Hornady 32 V-Max	velocity, fps	4225	3632	3114	2652	2234
	energy, ft-lb	1268	937	689	500	355
	arc, inches		+0.6	0	-4.2	-13.4
Hornady 40 V-Max	velocity, fps	3900	3451	3046	2677	2335
	energy, ft-lb	1351	1058	824	636	485
	arc, inches		+0.7	0	-4.5	-13.9
Rem. 32 AccuTip	velocity, fps	4225	3632	3114	2652	2234
	Energy, ft-lb	1268	937	689	500	355
	Arc, inches		+0.6	0	-4.1	-13.1
Rem. 40 AccuTip	velocity, fps	3900	3451	3046	2677	2336
	energy, ft-lb	1351	1058	824	636	485
	arc, inches		+0.7	0	-4.3	-13.2
Win. 32 Ballistic Silver Tip	velocity, fps	4050	3482	2984	2537	2132
	energy, ft-lb	1165	862	632	457	323
	arc, inches		+0.7	0	-4.6	-14.7
Win. 34 HP	velocity, fps	4025	3339	2751	2232	1775
	energy, ft-lb	1223	842	571	376	238
	arc, inches		+0.8	0	-5.5	-18.1

CARTRIDGE BULLET	RANGE, YARDS:	0	100	200	300	400
.218 BEE						
Win. 46 Hollow Point	velocity, fps	2760	2102	1550	1155	961
	energy, ft-lb	778	451	245	136	94
	arc, inches		0	-7.2	-29.4	
.22 HORNET						
Federal 30 Speer TNT	velocity, fps	3150	2150	1390	990	830
	energy, ft-lb	660	310	130	65	45
	arc, inches		+3.3	0	-22.8	-78.7
Federal 45 JSP	velocity, fps	2690	2100	1590	1210	1000
	energy, ft-lb	725	440	255	145	100
	arc, inches		+3.3	0	-17.6	-59.5
Hornady 35 V-Max	velocity, fps	3100	2278	1601	1135	929
	energy, ft-lb	747	403	199	100	67
	arc, inches		+2.8	0	-16.9	-60.4
Rem. 35 AccuTip	velocity, fps	3100	2271	1591	1127	924
	energy, ft-lb	747	401	197	99	66
	arc, inches		+1.5	-3.5	-22.3	-68.4
Rem. 45 Pointed Soft Point	velocity, fps	2690	2042	1502	1128	948
	energy, ft-lb	723	417	225	127	90
	arc, inches		0	-7.1	-30.0	
Rem. 45 Hollow Point	velocity, fps	2690	2042	1502	1128	948
	energy, ft-lb	723	417	225	127	90
	arc, inches		0	-7.1	-30.0	
Win. 34 Jacketed HP	velocity, fps	3050	2132	1415	1017	852
	energy, ft-lb	700	343	151	78	55.
	arc, inches		0	-6.6	-29.9	
Win. 45 Soft Point	velocity, fps	2690	2042	1502	1128	948.
	energy, ft-lb	723	417	225	127	90
	arc, inches		0	-7.7	-31.3	
Win. 46 Hollow Point	velocity, fps	2690	2042	1502	1128	948.
	energy, ft-lb	739	426	230	130	92
	arc, inches		0	-7.7	-31.3	
.221 REMINGTON FIREBALL						
Rem. 50 AccuTip BT	velocity, fps	2995	2605	2247	1918	1622
	energy, ft-lb	996	753	560	408	292
	arc, inches		+1.8	0	-8.8	-27.1
.222 REMINGTON						
Federal 40 Ballistic Tip	velocity, fps	3450	2990	2570	2190	1840
	energy, ft-lb	1055	790	585	425	300
	arc, inches		+1.2	0	-6.5	-20.4

CARTRIDGE BULLET	RANGE, YARDS:	0	100	200	300	400
Federal 43 Speer TNT	velocity, fps:	3400	2750	2180	1680	1290
	energy, ft-lb:	1105	720	450	270	160
	arc, inches:		+1.6	0	-9.2	-31.4
Federal 50 Hi-Shok	velocity, fps:	3140	2600	2120	1700	1350
	energy, ft-lb:	1095	750	500	320	200
	arc, inches:		+1.9	0	-9.7	-31.6
Federal 55 FMJ boat-tail	velocity, fps:	3020	2740	2480	2230	1990
	energy, ft-lb:	1115	915	750	610	484
	arc, inches:		+1.6	0	-7.3	-21.5
Hornady 40 V-Max	velocity, fps:	3600	3117	2673	2269	1911
	energy, ft-lb:	1151	863	634	457	324
	arc, inches:		+1.1	0	-6.1	-18.9
Hornady 50 V-Max	velocity, fps:	3140	2729	2352	2008	1710
	energy, ft-lb:	1094	827	614	448	325
	arc, inches:		+1.7	0	-7.9	-24.4
Norma 50 Soft Point	velocity, fps:	3199	2667	2193	1771	
	energy, ft-lb:	1136	790	534	348	
	arc, inches:		+1.7	0	-9.1	
Norma 50 FMJ	velocity, fps:	2789	2326	1910	1547	
	energy, ft-lb:	864	601	405	266	
	arc, inches:		+2.5	0	-12.2	
Norma 62 Soft Point	velocity, fps:	2887	2457	2067	1716	
	energy, ft-lb:	1148	831	588	405	
	arc, inches:		+2.1	0	-10.4	
PMC 50 Pointed Soft Point	velocity, fps:	3044	2727	2354	2012	1651
	energy, ft-lb:	1131	908	677	494	333
	arc, inches:		+1.6	0	-7.9	-24.5
PMC 55 Pointed Soft Point	velocity, fps:	2950	2594	2266	1966	1693
	energy, ft-lb:	1063	822	627	472	350
	arc, inches:		+1.9	0	-8.7	-26.3
Rem. 50 Pointed Soft Point	velocity, fps:	3140	2602	2123	1700	1350
	energy, ft-lb:	1094	752	500	321	202
	arc, inches:		+1.9	0	-9.7	-31.7
Rem. 50 HP Power-Lokt	velocity, fps:	3140	2635	2182	1777	1432
	energy, ft-lb:	1094	771	529	351	228
	arc, inches:		+1.8	0	-9.2	-29.6
Rem. 50 AccuTip BT	velocity, fps:	3140	2744	2380	2045	1740
	energy, ft-lb:	1094	836	629	464	336
	arc, inches:		+1.6	0	-7.8	-23.9
Win. 40 Ballistic Silvertip	velocity, fps:	3370	2915	2503	2127	1786
	energy, ft-lb:	1009	755	556	402	283
	arc, inches:		+1.3	0	-6.9	-21.5
Win. 50 Pointed Soft Point	velocity, fps:	3140	2602	2123	1700	1350
	energy, ft-lb:	1094	752	500	321	202
	arc, inches:		+2.2	0	-10.0	-32.3

.222 REMINGTON MAGNUM

CARTRIDGE BULLET	RANGE, YARDS:	0	100	200	300	400
Nosler 40 BT	velocity, fps:	3600	3140	2726	2347	2000
	energy, ft-lb:	1150	876	660	489	355
	arc, inches:	-1.5	+1.0	0	-5.7	-17.8
Nosler 50 BT	velocity, fps:	3340	2917	2533	2179	1855
	energy, ft-lb:	1238	945	712	527	382
	arc, inches:	-1.5	+1.3	0	-6.8	-20.9

.223 REMINGTON

CARTRIDGE BULLET	RANGE, YARDS:	0	100	200	300	400
Black Hills 36 Varmint Grenade	velocity, fps:	w3750				
	energy, ft-lb:	1124				
	arc, inches:					
Black Hills 40 Nosler B. Tip	velocity, fps:	3600				
	energy, ft-lb:	1150				
	arc, inches:					
Black Hills 50 V-Max	velocity, fps:	3300				
	energy, ft-lb:	1209				
	arc, inches:					
Black Hills 52 Match HP	velocity, fps:	3300				
	energy, ft-lb:	1237				
	arc, inches:					
Black Hills 55 Softpoint	velocity, fps:	3250				
	energy, ft-lb:	1270				
	arc, inches:					

CARTRIDGE BULLET	RANGE, YARDS:	0	100	200	300	400
Black Hills 55 TSX	velocity, fps:	3200				
	energy, ft-lb:	1250				
	arc, inches:					
Black Hills 60 SP or V-Max	velocity, fps:	3150				
	energy, ft-lb:	1322				
	arc, inches:					
Black Hills 60 Partition	velocity, fps:	3150				
	energy, ft-lb:	1322				
	arc, inches:					
Black Hills 62 TSX	velocity, fps:	3100				
	energy, ft-lb:	1323				
	arc, inches:					
Black Hills 68 Heavy Match	velocity, fps:	2850				
	energy, ft-lb:	1227				
	arc, inches:					
Black Hills 69 OTM	velocity, fps:	2875				
	energy, ft-lb:	1266				
	arc, inches:					
Black Hills 69 Sierra MK	velocity, fps:	2850				
	energy, ft-lb:	1245				
	arc, inches:					
Black Hills 73 Berger BTHP	velocity, fps:	2750				
	energy, ft-lb:	1226				
	arc, inches:					
Black Hills 75 Heavy Match	velocity, fps:	2750				
	energy, ft-lb:	1259				
	arc, inches:					
Black Hills 77 Sierra MKing	velocity, fps:	2750				
	energy, ft-lb:	1293				
	arc, inches:					
Black Hills 77 Tipped MatchKing	velocity, fps:	2750				
	energy, ft-lb:	1293				
	arc, inches:					
Federal 40 Ballistic Tip	velocity, fps:	3700	3210	2770	2370	2010
	energy, ft-lb:	1215	915	680	500	360
	arc, inches:		+0.9	0	-5.5	-17.3
Federal 43 Speer TNT	velocity, fps:	3600	2920	2330	1810	1390
	energy, ft-lb:	1235	810	515	315	185
	arc, inches:		+1.3	0	-7.9	-27.1
Federal 50 Jacketed HP	velocity, fps:	3400	2910	2460	2060	1700
	energy, ft-lb:	1285	940	675	470	320
	arc, inches:		+1.3	0	-7.1	-22.7
Federal 50 Speer TNT HP	velocity, fps:	3300	2860	2450	2080	1750
	energy, ft-lb:	1210	905	670	480	340
	arc, inches:		+1.4	0	-7.3	-22.6
Federal 52 Sierra MatchKing BTHP	velocity, fps:	3300	2860	2460	2090	1760
	energy, ft-lb:	1255	945	700	505	360
	arc, inches:		+1.4	0	-7.2	-22.4
Federal 55 Hi-Shok	velocity, fps:	3240	2750	2300	1910	1550
	energy, ft-lb:	1280	920	650	445	295
	arc, inches:		+1.6	0	-8.2	-26.1
Federal 55 FMJ boat-tail	velocity, fps:	3240	2950	2670	2410	2170
	energy, ft-lb:	1280	1060	875	710	575
	arc, inches:		+1.3	0	-6.1	-18.3
Federal 55 Sierra GameKing BTHP	velocity, fps:	3240	2770	2340	1950	1610
	energy, ft-lb:	1280	935	670	465	315
	arc, inches:		+1.5	0	-8.0	-25.3
Federal 55 Trophy Bonded	velocity, fps:	3100	2630	2210	1830	1500
	energy, ft-lb:	1175	845	595	410	275
	arc, inches:		+1.8	0	-8.9	-28.7
Federal 55 Nosler Bal. Tip	velocity, fps:	3240	2870	2530	2220	1920
	energy, ft-lb:	1280	1005	780	600	450
	arc, inches:		+1.4	0	-6.8	-20.8
Federal 55 Sierra BlitzKing	velocity, fps:	3240	2870	2520	2200	1910
	energy, ft-lb:	1280	1005	775	590	445
	arc, inches:		+-1.4	0	-6.9	-20.9

Centerfire Rifle Ballistics

.223 REMINGTON TO 5.6X52 R

CARTRIDGE BULLET	RANGE, YARDS:	0	100	200	300	400
Federal 60 Partition	velocity, fps:	3160	2740	2350	2000	1680
	energy, ft-lb:	1330	1000	735	530	375
	arc, inches:		+1.6	0	-7.9	-24.8
Federal 62 FMJ	velocity, fps:	3020	2650	2310	2000	1710
	energy, ft-lb:	1225	970	735	550	405
	arc, inches:		+1.7	0	-8.4	-25.5
Federal 64 Hi-Shok SP	velocity, fps:	3090	2690	2325	1990	1680
	energy, ft-lb:	1360	1030	770	560	400
	arc, inches:		+1.7	0	-8.2	-25.2
Federal 69 Sierra MatchKing BTHP	velocity, fps:	3000	2720	2460	2210	1980
	energy, ft-lb:	1380	1135	925	750	600
	arc, inches:		+1.6	0	-7.4	-21.9
Hornady 40 V-Max	velocity, fps:	3800	3305	2845	2424	2044
	energy, ft-lb:	1282	970	719	522	371
	arc, inches:		+0.8	0	-5.3	-16.6
Hornady 53 Hollow Point	velocity, fps:	3330	2882	2477	2106	1710
	energy, ft-lb:	1305	978	722	522	369
	arc, inches:		+1.7	0	-7.4	-22.7
Hornady 55 V-Max	velocity, fps:	3240	2859	2507	2181	1891
	energy, ft-lb:	1282	998	767	581	437
	arc, inches:		+1.4	0	-7.1	-21.4
Hornady 75 BTHP Superformance Match	velocity, fps:	2930	2695	2471	2259	2057
	energy, ft-lb:	1430	1209	1017	850	705
	arc, inches:		+1.7	0	-7.4	-21.6
Hornady 55 TAP-FPD	velocity, fps:	3240	2854	2500	2172	1871
	energy, ft-lb:	1282	995	763	576	427
	arc, inches:		+1.4	0	-7.0	-21.4
Hornady 55 Urban Tactical	velocity, fps:	2970	2626	2307	2011	1739
	energy, ft-lb:	1077	842	650	494	369
	arc, inches:		+1.5	0	-8.1	-24.9
Hornady 60 Soft Point	velocity, fps:	3150	2782	2442	2127	1837
	energy, ft-lb:	1322	1031	795	603	450
	arc, inches:		+1.6	0	-7.5	-22.5
Hornady 60 TAP-FPD	velocity, fps:	3115	2754	2420	2110	1824
	energy, ft-lb:	1293	1010	780	593	443
	arc, inches:		+1.6	0	-7.5	-22.9
Hornady 60 Urban Tactical	velocity, fps:	2950	2619	2312	2025	1762
	energy, ft-lb:	1160	914	712	546	413
	arc, inches:		+1.6	0	-8.1	-24.7
Hornady 75 BTHP Match	velocity, fps:	2790	2554	2330	2119	1926
	energy, ft-lb:	1296	1086	904	747	617
	arc, inches:		+2.4	0	-8.8	-25.1
Hornacy 75 TAP-FPD	velocity, fps:	2790	2582	2383	2193	2012
	energy, ft-lb:	1296	1110	946	801	674
	arc, inches:		+1.9	0	-8.0	-23.2
Hornady 75 BTHP Tactical	velocity, fps:	2630	2409	2199	2000	1814
	energy, ft-lb:	1152	966	805	666	548
	arc, inches:		+2.0	0	-9.2	-25.9
PMC 40 non-toxic	velocity, fps:	3500	2606	1871	1315	
	energy, ft-lb:	1088	603	311	154	
	arc, inches:		+2.6	0	-12.8	
PMC 50 Sierra BlitzKing	velocity, fps:	3300	2874	2484	2106	1809
	energy, ft-lb:	1209	917	685	504	363
	arc, inches:		+1.4	0	-7.1	-21.8
PMC 52 Sierra HPBT Match	velocity, fps:	3200	2808	2447	2117	1817
	energy, ft-lb:	1182	910	691	517	381
	arc, inches:		+1.5	0	-7.3	-22.5
PMC 53 Barnes XLC	velocity, fps:	3200	2815	2461	2136	1840
	energy, ft-lb:	1205	933	713	537	398
	arc, inches:		+1.5	0	-7.2	-22.2
PMC 55 HP boat-tail	velocity, fps:	3240	2717	2250	1832	1473
	energy, ft-lb:	1282	901	618	410	265
	arc, inches:		+1.6	0	-8.6	-27.7
PMC 55 FMJ boat-tail	velocity, fps:	3195	2882	2525	2169	1843
	energy, ft-lb:	1246	1014	779	574	415
	arc, inches:		+1.4	0	-6.8	-21.1
PMC 55 Pointed Soft Point	velocity, fps:	3112	2767	2421	2100	1806
	energy, ft-lb:	1182	935	715	539	398
	arc, inches:		+1.5	0	-7.5	-22.9

CARTRIDGE BULLET	RANGE, YARDS:	0	100	200	300	400
PMC 64 Pointed Soft Point	velocity, fps:	2775	2511	2261	2026	1806
	energy, ft-lb:	1094	896	726	583	464
	arc, inches:		+2.0	0	-8.8	-26.1
PMC 69 Sierra BTHP Match	velocity, fps:	2900	2591	2304	2038	1791
	energy, ft-lb:	1288	1029	813	636	492
	arc, inches:		+1.9	0	-8.4	-25.3
Rem. 50 AccuTip BT	velocity, fps:	3300	2889	2514	2168	1851
	energy, ft-lb:	1209	927	701	522	380
	arc, inches:		+1.4	0	-6.9	-21.2
Rem. 55 Pointed Soft Point	velocity, fps:	3240	2747	2304	1905	1554
	energy, ft-lb:	1282	921	648	443	295
	arc, inches:		+1.5	0	-8.2	-26.2
Rem. 55 HP Power-Lokt	velocity, fps:	3240	2773	2352	1969	1627
	energy, ft-lb:	1282	939	675	473	323
	arc, inches:		+1.5	0	-7.9	-24.8
Rem. 55 AccuTip BT	velocity, fps:	3240	2854	2500	2172	1871
	energy, ft-lb:	1282	995	763	576	427
	arc, inches:		+1.5	0	-7.1	-21.7
Rem. 55 Metal Case	velocity, fps:	3240	2759	2326	1933	1587
	energy, ft-lb:	1282	929	660	456	307
	arc, inches:		+1.6	0	-8.1	-25.5
Remington 62 Core-Lokt Ultra Bonded	velocity, fps:	3100	2695	2324	1983	1676
	energy, ft-lb:	1323	1000	743	541	386
	arc, inches:		+1.7				
Rem. 62 HP Match	velocity, fps:	3025	2572	2162	1792	1471
	energy, ft-lb:	1260	911	643	442	298
	arc, inches:		+1.9	0	-9.4	-29.9
Rem. 69 BTHP Match	velocity, fps:	3000	2720	2457	2209	1975
	energy, ft-lb:	1379	1133	925	747	598
	arc, inches:		+1.6	0	-7.4	-21.9
Win. 40 Ballistic Silvertip	velocity, fps:	3700	3166	2693	2265	1879.
	energy, ft-lb:	1216	891	644	456	314
	arc, inches:		+1.0	0	-5.8	-18.4
Win. 45 JHP	velocity, fps:	3600				
	energy, ft-lb:	1295				
	arc, inches:					
Win. 50 Ballistic Silvertip	velocity, fps:	3410	2982	2593	2235	1907.
	energy, ft-lb:	1291	987	746	555	404
	arc, inches:		+1.2	0	-6.4	-19.8
Win. 53 Hollow Point	velocity, fps:	3330	2882	2477	2106	1770
	energy, ft-lb:	1305	978	722	522	369
	arc, inches:		+1.7	0	-7.4	-22.7
Win. 55 Pointed Soft Point	velocity, fps:	3240	2747	2304	1905	1554.
	energy, ft-lb:	1282	921	648	443	295
	arc, inches:		+1.9	0	-8.5	-26.7
Win. 55 Super Clean NT	velocity, fps:	3150	2520	1970	1505	1165
	energy, ft-lb:	1212	776	474	277	166
	arc, inches:		+2.8	0	-11.9	-38.9
Win. 55 FMJ	velocity, fps:	3240	2854			
	energy, ft-lb:	1282	995			
	arc, inches:					
Win. 55 Ballistic Silvertip	velocity, fps:	3240	2871	2531	2215	1923
	energy, ft-lb:	1282	1006	782	599	451
	arc, inches:		+1.4	0	-6.8	-20.8
Win. 64 Power-Point	velocity, fps:	3020	2656	2320	2009	1724
	energy, ft-lb:	1296	1003	765	574	423
	arc, inches:		+1.7	0	-8.2	-25.1
Win. 64 Power-Point Plus	velocity, fps:	3090	2684	2312	1971	1664
	energy, ft-lb:	1357	1024	760	552	393
	arc, inches:		+1.7	0	-8.2	-25.4
Winchester 69 BTHP Match	velocity, fps:	3060	2740	2442	2163	1902
	energy, ft-lb:	1434	1150	913	716	554
	arc, inches:		+1.6	0	-7.4	-22.4

5.6x52 R

CARTRIDGE BULLET	RANGE, YARDS:	0	100	200	300	400
Norma 71 Soft Point	velocity, fps:	2789	2446	2128	1835	
	energy, ft-lb:	1227	944	714	531	
	arc, inches:		+2.1	0	-9.9	

CARTRIDGE BULLET	RANGE, YARDS:	0	100	200	300	400

.22 PPC

A-Square 52 Berger	velocity, fps:	3300	2952	2629	2329	2049
	energy, ft-lb:	1257	1006	798	626	485
	arc, inches:		+1.3	0	-6.3	-19.1

.225 WINCHESTER

Win. 55 Pointed Soft Point	velocity, fps:	3570	3066	2616	2208	1838.
	energy, ft-lb:	1556	1148	836	595	412
	arc, inches:		+2.4	+2.0	-3.5	-16.3

.224 WEATHERBY MAGNUM

Wby. 55 Pointed Expanding	velocity, fps:	3650	3192	2780	2403	2056
	energy, ft-lb:	1627	1244	944	705	516
	arc, inches:		+2.8	+3.7	0	-9.8

.22-250 REMINGTON

Black Hills 50 Nos. Bal. Tip	velocity, fps:	3700				
	energy, ft-lb:	1520				
	arc, inches:					
Black Hills 60 Nos. Partition	velocity, fps:	3550				
	energy, ft-lb:	1679				
	arc, inches:					
Federal 40 Nos. Bal. Tip	velocity, fps:	4150	3610	3130	2700	2300
	energy, ft-lb:	1530	1155	870	645	470
	arc, inches:		+0.6	0	-4.2	-13.2
Federal 40 Sierra Varminter	velocity, fps:	4000	3320	2720	2200	1740
	energy, ft-lb:	1420	980	660	430	265
	arc, inches:		+0.8	0	-5.6	-18.4
Federal 43 Speer TNT	velocity, fps:	4000	3250	2650	2070	1590
	energy, ft-lb:	1530	1010	655	405	240
	arc, inches:		+0.9	0	-6.1	-20.8
Federal 55 Hi-Shok	velocity, fps:	3680	3140	2660	2220	1830
	energy, ft-lb:	1655	1200	860	605	410
	arc, inches:		+1.0	0	-6.0	-19.1
Federal 55 Sierra BlitzKing	velocity, fps:	3680	3270	2890	2540	2220
	energy, ft-lb:	1655	1300	1020	790	605
	arc, inches:		+0.9	0	-5.1	-15.6
Federal 55 Sierra GameKing BTHP	velocity, fps:	3680	3280	2920	2590	2280
	energy, ft-lb:	1655	1315	1040	815	630
	arc, inches:		+0.9	0	-5.0	-15.1
Federal 55 Trophy Bonded	velocity, fps:	3600	3080	2610	2190	1810.
	energy, ft-lb:	1585	1155	835	590	400.
	arc, inches:		+1.1	0	-6.2	-19.8
Hornady 35 NTX Superformance Varmint	velocity, fps:	4450	3736	3128	2598	2125
	energy, ft-lb:	1539	1085	761	524	351
	arc, inches:		+0.5	0	-4.1	-13.4
Hornady 40 V-Max	velocity, fps:	4150	3631	3147	2699	2293
	energy, ft-lb:	1529	1171	879	647	467
	arc, inches:		+0.5	0	-4.2	-13.3
Hornady 50 V-Max	velocity, fps:	3800	3349	2925	2535	2178
	energy, ft-lb:	1603	1245	950	713	527
	arc, inches:		+0.8	0	-5.0	-15.6
Hornady 50 V-Max Superformance Varmint	velocity, fps:	4000	3517	3086	2696	2337
	energy, ft-lb:	1776	1373	1057	807	606
	arc, inches:		+0.7	0	-4.3	-13.5
Hornady 53 Hollow Point	velocity, fps:	3680	3185	2743	2341	1974.
	energy, ft-lb:	1594	1194	886	645	459
	arc, inches:		+1.0	0	-5.7	-17.8
Hornady 55 V-Max	velocity, fps:	3680	3265	2876	2517	2183
	energy, ft-lb:	1654	1302	1010	772	582
	arc, inches:		+0.9	0	-5.3	-16.1
Hornady 60 Soft Point	velocity, fps:	3600	3195	2826	2485	2169
	energy, ft-lb:	1727	1360	1064	823	627
	arc, inches:		+1.0	0	-5.4	-16.3

CARTRIDGE BULLET	RANGE, YARDS:	0	100	200	300	400
Norma 53 Soft Point	velocity, fps:	3707	3234	2809	1716	
	energy, ft-lb:	1618	1231	928	690	
	arc, inches:		+0.9	0	-5.3	
PMC 50 Sierra BlitzKing	velocity, fps:	3725	3264	2641	2455	2103
	energy, ft-lb:	1540	1183	896	669	491
	arc, inches:		+0.9	0	-5.2	-16.2
PMC 50 Barnes XLC	velocity, fps:	3725	3280	2871	2495	2152
	energy, ft-lb:	1540	1195	915	691	514.
	arc, inches:		+0.9	0	-5.1	-15.9.
PMC 55 HP boat-tail	velocity, fps:	3680	3104	2596	2141	1737
	energy, ft-lb:	1654	1176	823	560	368
	arc, inches:		+1.1	0	-6.3	-20.2
PMC 55 Pointed Soft Point	velocity, fps:	3586	3203	2852	2505	2178
	energy, ft-lb:	1570	1253	993	766	579
	arc, inches:		+1.0	0	-5.2	-16.0
Rem. 50 AccuTip BT (also in EtronX)	velocity, fps:	3725	3272	2864	2491	2147
	energy, ft-lb:	1540	1188	910	689	512
	arc, inches:		+1.7	+1.6	-2.8	-12.8
Rem. 55 Pointed Soft Point	velocity, fps:	3680	3137	2656	2222	1832
	energy, ft-lb:	1654	1201	861	603	410
	arc, inches:		+1.9	+1.8	-3.3	-15.5
Rem. 55 HP Power-Lokt	velocity, fps:	3680	3209	2785	2400	2046.
	energy, ft-lb:	1654	1257	947	703	511
	arc, inches:		+1.8	+1.7	-3.0	-13.7
Rem. 60 Nosler Partition (also in EtronX)	velocity, fps:	3500	3045	2634	2258	1914
	energy, ft-lb:	1632	1235	924	679	488
	arc, inches:		+2.1	+1.9	-3.4	-15.5
Win. 40 Ballistic Silvertip	velocity, fps:	4150	3591	3099	2658	2257
	energy, ft-lb:	1530	1146	853	628	453
	arc, inches:		+0.6	0	-4.2	-13.4
Win. 50 Ballistic Silvertip	velocity, fps:	3810	3341	2919	2536	2182
	energy, ft-lb:	1611	1239	946	714	529.
	arc, inches:		+0.8	0	-4.9	-15.2
Win. 55 Pointed Soft Point	velocity, fps:	3680	3137	2656	2222	1832
	energy, ft-lb:	1654	1201	861	603	410
	arc, inches:		+2.3	+1.9	-3.4	-15.9
Win. 55 Ballistic Silvertip	velocity, fps:	3680	3272	2900	2558	2240
	energy, ft-lb:	1654	1307	1027	799	613
	arc, inches:		+0.9	0	-5.0	-15.4
Win. 64 Power-Point	velocity, fps:	3500	3086	2708	2360	2038
	energy, ft-lb:	1741	1353	1042	791	590
	arc, inches:		+1.1	0	-5.9	-18.0

.220 SWIFT

Federal 52 Sierra MatchKing BTHP	velocity, fps:	3830	3370	2960	2600	2230
	energy, ft-lb:	1690	1310	1010	770	575
	arc, inches:		+0.8	0	-4.8	-14.9
Federal 55 Sierra BlitzKing	velocity, fps:	3800	3370	2990	2630	2310.
	energy, ft-lb:	1765	1390	1090	850	650
	arc, inches:		+0.8	0	-4.7	-14.4
Federal 55 Trophy Bonded	velocity, fps:	3700	3170	2690	2270	1880
	energy, ft-lb:	1670	1225	885	625	430
	arc, inches:		+1.0	0	-5.8	-18.5
Hornady 40 V-Max	velocity, fps:	4200	3678	3190	2739	2329
	energy, ft-lb:	1566	1201	904	666	482
	arc, inches:		+0.5	0	-4.0	-12.9
Hornady 50 V-Max	velocity, fps:	3850	3396	2970	2576	2215.
	energy, ft-lb:	1645	1280	979	736	545
	arc, inches:		+0.7	0	-4.8	-15.1
Hornady 50 SP	velocity, fps:	3850	3327	2862	2442	2060.
	energy, ft-lb:	1645	1228	909	662	471
	arc, inches:		+0.8	0	-5.1	-16.1
Hornady 55 V-Max	velocity, fps:	3680	3265	2876	2517	2183
	energy, ft-lb:	1654	1302	1010	772	582
	arc, inches:		+0.9	0	-5.3	-16.1
Hornady 60 Hollow Point	velocity, fps:	3600	3199	2824	2475	2156
	energy, ft-lb:	1727	1364	1063	816	619
	arc, inches:		+1.0	0	-5.4	-16.3
Norma 50 Soft Point	velocity, fps:	4019	3380	2826	2335	
	energy, ft-lb:	1794	1268	887	605	
	arc, inches:		+0.7	0	-5.1	

Centerfire Rifle Ballistics

.220 SWIFT TO .243 WINCHESTER

CARTRIDGE BULLET	RANGE, YARDS:	0	100	200	300	400
Rem. 50 Pointed Soft Point	velocity, fps:	3780	3158	2617	2135	1710
	energy, ft-lb:	1586	1107	760	506	325
	arc, inches:		+0.3	-1.4	-8.2	
Rem. 50 V-Max boat-tail	velocity, fps:	3780	3321	2908	2532	2185
(also in EtronX)	energy, ft-lb:	1586	1224	939	711	530
	arc, inches:		+0.8	0	-5.0	-15.4
Win. 40 Ballistic Silvertip	velocity, fps:	4050	3518	3048	2624	2238.
	energy, ft-lb:	1457	1099	825	611	445
	arc, inches:		+0.7	0	-4.4	-13.9
Win. 50 Pointed Soft Point	velocity, fps:	3870	3310	2816	2373	1972
	energy, ft-lb:	1663	1226	881	625	432
	arc, inches:		+0.8	0	-5.2	-16.7

.223 WSSM

CARTRIDGE BULLET	RANGE, YARDS:	0	100	200	300	400
Win. 55 Ballistic Silvertip	velocity, fps:	3850	3438	3064	2721	2402
	energy, ft-lb:	1810	1444	1147	904	704
	arc, inches:		+0.7	0	-4.4	-13.6
Win. 55 Pointed Softpoint	velocity, fps:	3850	3367	2934	2541	2181
	energy, ft-lb:	1810	1384	1051	789	581
	arc, inches:		+0.8	0	-4.9	-15.1
Win. 64 Power-Point	velocity, fps:	3600	3144	2732	2356	2011
	energy, ft-lb:	1841	1404	1061	789	574
	arc, inches:		+1.0	0	-5.7	-17.7

6MM PPC

CARTRIDGE BULLET	RANGE, YARDS:	0	100	200	300	400
A-Square 68 Berger	velocity, fps:	3100	2751	2428	2128	1850
	energy, ft-lb:	1451	1143	890	684	516
	arc, inches:		+1.5	0	-7.5	-22.6

6x70 R

CARTRIDGE BULLET	RANGE, YARDS:	0	100	200	300	400
Norma 95 Nosler Bal. Tip	velocity, fps:	2461	2231	2013	1809	
	energy, ft-lb:	1211	995	810	654	
	arc, inches:		+2.7	0	-11.3	

.243 WINCHESTER

CARTRIDGE BULLET	RANGE, YARDS:	0	100	200	300	400
Black Hills 55 Nosler B. Tip	velocity, fps:	3800				
	energy, ft-lb:	1763				
	arc, inches:					
Black Hills 95 Nosler B. Tip	velocity, fps:	2950				
	energy, ft-lb:	1836				
	arc, inches:					
Federal 70 Nosler Bal. Tip	velocity, fps:	3400	3070	2760	2470	2200
	energy, ft-lb:	1795	1465	1185	950	755.
	arc, inches:		+1.1	0	-5.7	-17.1
Federal 70 Speer TNT HP	velocity, fps:	3400	3040	2700	2390	2100
	energy, ft-lb:	1795	1435	1135	890	685
	arc, inches:		+1.1	0	-5.9	-18.0
Federal 80 Sierra Pro-Hunter	velocity, fps:	3350	2960	2590	2260	1950
	energy, ft-lb:	1995	1550	1195	905	675
	arc, inches:		+1.3	0	-6.4	-19.7
Federal 85 Sierra GameKing BTHP	velocity, fps:	3320	3070	2830	2600	2380
	energy, ft-lb:	2080	1770	1510	1280	1070
	arc, inches:		+1.1	0	-5.5	-16.1
Federal 85 Trophy Copper	velocity, fps:	3200	2950	2710	2480	2270
	energy, ft-lb:	1935	1640	1385	1160	970
	arc, inches:		+1.3	0	-6.0	-17.6
Federal 90 Trophy Bonded	velocity, fps:	3100	2850	2610	2380	2160.
	energy, ft-lb:	1920	1620	1360	1130	935
	arc, inches:		+1.4	0	-6.1	-19.2
Federal 100 Hi-Shok	velocity, fps:	2960	2700	2450	2220	1990
	energy, ft-lb:	1945	1615	1330	1090	880
	arc, inches:		+1.6	0	-7.5	-22.0
Federal 100 Sierra GameKing BTSP	velocity, fps:	2960	2760	2570	2380	2210
	energy, ft-lb:	1950	1690	1460	1260	1080
	arc, inches:		+1.5	0	-6.8	-19.8
Federal 100 Nosler Partition	velocity, fps:	2960	2730	2510	2300	2100
	energy, ft-lb:	1945	1650	1395	1170	975.
	arc, inches:		+1.6	0	-7.1	-20.9
Hornady 58 V-Max Superformance Varmint	velocity, fps:	3925	3465	3052	2676	2330
	energy, ft-lb:	1984	1546	1200	922	699
	arc, inches:		+0.7	0	-4.4	-13.8
Hornady 75 Hollow Point	velocity, fps:	3400	2970	2578	2219	1890
	energy, ft-lb:	1926	1469	1107	820	595

CARTRIDGE BULLET	RANGE, YARDS:	0	100	200	300	400
	arc, inches:		+1.2	0	-6.5	-20.3
Hornady 80 GMX Superformance	velocity, fps:	3425	3081	2763	2468	2190
	energy, ft-lb:	2084	1686	1357	1082	852
	arc, inches:		+1.1	0	-5.7	-17.1
Hornady 87 SST Custom Lite	velocity, fps:	2800	2574	2359	2155	1961
	energy, ft-lb:	1514	1280	1075	897	743
	arc, inches:		+1.9	0	-8.1	-23.8
Hornady 95 SST Superformance	velocity, fps:	3185	2908	2649	2404	2172
	energy, ft-lb:	2140	1784	1480	1219	995
	arc, inches:		+1.3	0	-6.3	-18.6
Hornady 100 BTSP	velocity, fps:	2960	2728	2508	2299	2099
	energy, ft-lb:	1945	1653	1397	1174	979
	arc, inches:		+1.6	0	-7.2	-21.0
Hornady 100 BTSP LM	velocity, fps:	3100	2839	2592	2358	2138
	energy, ft-lb:	2133	1790	1491	1235	1014
	arc, inches:		+1.5	0	-6.8	-19.8
Norma 80 FMJ	velocity, fps:	3117	2750	2412	2098	
	energy, ft-lb:	1726	1344	1034	782	
	arc, inches:		+1.5	0	-7.5	
Norma 100 FMJ	velocity, fps:	3018	2747	2493	2252	
	energy, ft-lb:	2023	1677	1380	1126	
	arc, inches:		+1.5	0	-7.1	
Norma 100 Soft Point	velocity, fps:	3018	2748	2493	2252	
	energy, ft-lb:	2023	1677	1380	1126	
	arc, inches:		+1.5	0	-7.1	
Norma 100 Oryx	velocity, fps:	3018	2653	2316	2004	
	energy, ft-lb:	2023	1563	1191	892	
	arc, inches:		+1.7	0	-8.3	
PMC 80 Pointed Soft Point	velocity, fps:	2940	2684	2444	2215	1999
	energy, ft-lb:	1535	1280	1060	871	709
	arc, inches:		+1.7	0	-7.5	-22.1
PMC 85 Barnes XLC	velocity, fps:	3250	3022	2805	2598	2401
	energy, ft-lb:	1993	1724	1485	1274	1088
	arc, inches:		+1.6	0	-5.6	16.3
PMC 85 HP boat-tail	velocity, fps:	3275	2922	2596	2292	2009
	energy, ft-lb:	2024	1611	1272	991	761
	arc, inches:		+1.3	0	-6.5	-19.7
PMC 100 Pointed Soft Point	velocity, fps:	2743	2507	2283	2070	1869
	energy, ft-lb:	1670	1395	1157	951	776
	arc, inches:		+2.0	0	-8.7	-25.5
PMC 100 SP boat-tail	velocity, fps:	2960	2742	2534	2335	2144
	energy, ft-lb:	1945	1669	1425	1210	1021
	arc, inches:		+1.6	0	-7.0	-20.5
Rem. 75 AccuTip BT	velocity, fps:	3375	3065	2775	2504	2248
	energy, ft-lb:	1897	1564	1282	1044	842
	arc, inches:		+2.0	+1.8	-3.0	-13.3
Remington 80 Copper Solid Tipped	velocity, fps:	3350	3011	2696	2403	2128
	energy, ft-lb:	1993	1610	1291	1025	894
	arc, inches:		+1.2	0	-6.1	-18.1
Rem. 80 Pointed Soft Point	velocity, fps:	3350	2955	2593	2259	1951
	energy, ft-lb:	1993	1551	1194	906	676
	arc, inches:		+2.2	+2.0	-3.5	-15.8
Rem. 80 HP Power-Lokt	velocity, fps:	3350	2955	2593	2259	1951
	energy, ft-lb:	1993	1551	1194	906	676
	arc, inches:		+2.2	+2.0	-3.5	-15.8
Rem. 90 Nosler Bal. Tip (also in EtronX) or Scirocco	velocity, fps:	3120	2871	2635	2411	2199
	energy, ft-lb:	1946	1647	1388	1162	966
	arc, inches:		+1.4	0	-6.4	-18.8
Rem. 95 AccuTip	velocity, fps:	3120	2847	2590	2347	2118
	energy, ft-lb:	2053	1710	1415	1162	946
	arc, inches:		+1.5	0	-6.6	-19.5
Rem. 100 PSP Core-Lokt (also in EtronX)	velocity, fps:	2960	2697	2449	2215	1993
	energy, ft-lb:	1945	1615	1332	1089	882
	arc, inches:		+1.6	0	-7.5	-22.1
Rem. 100 PSP boat-tail	velocity, fps:	2960	2720	2492	2275	2069
	energy, ft-lb:	1945	1642	1378	1149	950
	arc, inches:		+2.8	+2.3	-3.8	-16.6
Speer 100 Grand Slam	velocity, fps:	2950	2684	2434	2197	
	energy, ft-lb:	1932	1600	1315	1072	
	arc, inches:		+1.7	0	-7.6	-22.4

556 • Shooter's Bible 108th Edition

www.skyhorsepublishing.com

CARTRIDGE BULLET	RANGE, YARDS:	0	100	200	300	400
Win. 55 Ballistic Silvertip	velocity, fps:	4025	3597	3209	2853	2525
	energy, ft-lb:	1978	1579	1257	994	779
	arc, inches:		+0.6	0	-4.0	-12.2
Win. 80 Pointed Soft Point	velocity, fps:	3350	2955	2593	2259	1951.
	energy, ft-lb:	1993	1551	1194	906	676
	arc, inches:		+2.6	+2.1	-3.6	-16.2
Win. 95 Ballistic Silvertip	velocity, fps:	3100	2854	2626	2410	2203
	energy, ft-lb:	2021	1719	1455	1225	1024
	arc, inches:		+1.4	0	-6.4	-18.9
Win. 95 Supreme Elite XP3	velocity, fps:	3100	2864	2641	2428	2225
	energy, ft-lb:	2027	1730	1471	1243	1044
	a rc, inches		+1.4	0	-6.4	-18.7
Win. 100 Power-Point	velocity, fps:	2960	2697	2449	2215	1993
	energy, ft-lb:	1945	1615	1332	1089	882
	arc, inches:		+1.9	0	-7.8	-22.6.
Win. 100 Power-Point Plus	velocity, fps:	3090	2818	2562	2321	2092
	energy, ft-lb:	2121	1764	1458	1196	972
	arc, inches:		+1.4	0	-6.7	-20.0

6MM REMINGTON

CARTRIDGE BULLET	RANGE, YARDS:	0	100	200	300	400
Federal 80 Sierra Pro-Hunter	velocity, fps:	3470	3060	2690	2350	2040
	energy, ft-lb:	2140	1665	1290	980	735
	arc, inches:		+1.1	0	-5.9	-18.2
Federal 100 Hi-Shok	velocity, fps:	3100	2830	2570	2330	2100
	energy, ft-lb:	2135	1775	1470	1205	985
	arc, inches:		+1.4	0	-6.7	-19.8
Federal 100 Nos. Partition	velocity, fps:	3100	2860	2640	2420	2220
	energy, ft-lb:	2135	1820	1545	1300	1090
	arc, inches:		+1.4	0	-6.3	-18.7
Hornady 95 SST Superformance	velocity, fps:	3235	2955	2693	2445	2211
	energy, ft-lb:	2207	1842	1530	1261	1031
	arc, inches:		+1.3	0	-6.1	-18.0
Hornady 100 SP boat-tail	velocity, fps:	3100	2861	2634	2419	2231
	energy, ft-lb:	2134	1818	1541	1300	1088
	arc, inches:		+1.3	0	-6.5	-18.9
Hornady 100 SPBT LM	velocity, fps:	3250	2997	2756	2528	2311
	energy, ft-lb:	2345	1995	1687	1418	1186
	arc, inches:		+1.6	0	-6.3	-18.2
Rem. 75 V-Max boat-tail	velocity, fps:	3400	3088	2797	2524	2267
	energy, ft-lb:	1925	1587	1303	1061	856
	arc, inches:		+1.9	+1.7	-3.0	-13.1
Rem. 100 PSP Core-Lokt	velocity, fps:	3100	2829	2573	2332	2104.
	energy, ft-lb:	2133	1777	1470	1207	983
	arc, inches:		+1.4	0	-6.7	-19.8
Rem. 100 PSP boat-tail	velocity, fps:	3100	2852	2617	2394	2183.
	energy, ft-lb:	2134	1806	1521	1273	1058
	arc, inches:		+1.4	0	-6.5	-19.1
Win. 100 Power-Point	velocity, fps:	3100	2829	2573	2332	2104
	energy, ft-lb:	2133	1777	1470	1207	983
	arc, inches:		+1.7	0	-7.0	-20.4

.243 WSSM

CARTRIDGE BULLET	RANGE, YARDS:	0	100	200	300	400
Win. 55 Ballistic Silvertip	velocity, fps:	4060	3628	3237	2880	2550
	energy, ft-lb:	2013	1607	1280	1013	794
	arc, inches:		+0.6	0	-3.9	-12.0
Win. 95 Ballistic Silvertip	velocity, fps:	3250	3000	2763	2538	2325
	energy, ft-lb:	2258	1898	1610	1359	1140
	arc, inches:		+1.2	0	5.7	16.9
Win. 95 Supreme Elite XP3	velocity, fps	3150	2912	2686	2471	2266
	energy, ft-lb	2093	1788	1521	1287	1083
	arc, inches		+1.3	0	-6.1	-18.0
Win. 100 Power Point	velocity, fps:	3110	2838	2583	2341	2112
	energy, ft-lb:	2147	1789	1481	1217	991
	arc, inches:		+1.4	0	-6.6	-19.7

.240 WEATHERBY MAGNUM

CARTRIDGE BULLET	RANGE, YARDS:	0	100	200	300	400
Wby. 87 Pointed Expanding	velocity, fps:	3523	3199	2898	2617	2352
	energy, ft-lb:	2397	1977	1622	1323	1069
	arc, inches:		+2.7	+3.4	0	-8.4
Wby. 90 Barnes-X	velocity, fps:	3500	3222	2962	2717	2484
	energy, ft-lb:	2448	2075	1753	1475	1233
	arc, inches:		+2.6	+3.3	0	-8.0
Wby. 95 Nosler Bal. Tip	velocity, fps:	3420	3146	2888	2645	2414
	energy, ft-lb:	2467	2087	1759	1475	1229
	arc, inches:		+2.7	+3.5	0	-8.4
Wby. 100 Pointed Expanding	velocity, fps:	3406	3134	2878	2637	2408
	energy, ft-lb:	2576	2180	1839	1544	1287
	arc, inches:		+2.8	+3.5	0	-8.4
Wby. 100 Partition	velocity, fps:	3406	3136	2882	2642	2415
	energy, ft-lb:	2576	2183	1844	1550	1294
	arc, inches:		+2.8	+3.5	0	-8.4

.25-20 WINCHESTER

CARTRIDGE BULLET	RANGE, YARDS:	0	100	200	300	400
Rem. 86 Soft Point	velocity, fps:	1460	1194	1030	931	858
	energy, ft-lb:	407	272	203	165	141
	arc, inches:		0	-22.9	-78.9	-173.0
Win. 86 Soft Point	velocity, fps:	1460	1194	1030	931	858.
	energy, ft-lb:	407	272	203	165	141
	arc, inches:		0	-23.5	-79.6	-175.9

.25-35 WINCHESTER

CARTRIDGE BULLET	RANGE, YARDS:	0	100	200	300	400
Win. 117 Soft Point	velocity, fps:	2230	1866	1545	1282	1097
	energy, ft-lb:	1292	904	620	427	313
	arc, inches:		+2.1	-5.1	-27.0	-70.1

.250 SAVAGE

CARTRIDGE BULLET	RANGE, YARDS:	0	100	200	300	400
Rem. 100 Pointed SP	velocity, fps:	2820	2504	2210	1936	1684.
	energy, ft-lb:	1765	1392	1084	832	630
	arc, inches:		+2.0	0	-9.2	-27.7
Win. 100 Silvertip	velocity, fps:	2820	2467	2140	1839	1569
	energy, ft-lb:	1765	1351	1017	751	547
	arc, inches:		+2.4	0	-10.1	-30.5

.257 ROBERTS

CARTRIDGE BULLET	RANGE, YARDS:	0	100	200	300	400
Federal 120 Nosler Partition	velocity, fps:	2780	2560	2360	2160	1970
	energy, ft-lb:	2060	1750	1480	1240	1030
	arc, inches:		+1.9	0	-8.2	-24.0
Hornady 117 SP boat-tail	velocity, fps:	2780	2550	2331	2122	1925
	energy, ft-lb:	2007	1689	1411	1170	963
	arc, inches:		+1.9	0	-8.3	-24.4
Hornady 117 SP boat-tail LM	velocity, fps:	2940	2694	2460	2240	2031
	energy, ft-lb:	2245	1885	1572	1303	1071
	arc, inches:		+1.7	0	-7.6	-21.8
Hornady 117 SST Superformance	velocity, fps:	2946	2707	2480	2265	2060
	energy, ft-lb:	2255	1903	1598	1332	1102
	arc, inches:		+1.6	0	-7.3	-21.4
Rem. 117 SP Core-Lokt	velocity, fps:	2650	2291	1961	1663	1404
	energy, ft-lb:	1824	1363	999	718	512
	arc, inches:		+2.6	0	-11.7	-36.1
Win. 117 Power-Point	velocity, fps:	2780	2411	2071	1761	1488
	energy, ft-lb:	2009	1511	1115	806	576.
	arc, inches:		+2.6	0	-10.8	-33.0

.25-06 REMINGTON

CARTRIDGE BULLET	RANGE, YARDS:	0	100	200	300	400
Black Hills 100 Nos. Bal. Tip	velocity, fps:	3200				
	energy, ft-lb:	2273				
	arc, inches:					
Black Hills 100 Barnes XLC	velocity, fps:	3200				
	energy, ft-lb:	2273				
	arc, inches:					
Black Hills 115 Barnes X	velocity, fps:	2975				
	energy, ft-lb:	2259				
	arc, inches:					

Centerfire Rifle Ballistics

.25-06 REMINGTON TO 6.5X55 SWEDISH

CARTRIDGE BULLET	RANGE, YARDS:	0	100	200	300	400
Federal 90 Sierra Varminter	velocity, fps:	3440	3040	2680	2340	2030
	energy, ft-lb:	2365	1850	1435	1100	825
	arc, inches:		+1.1	0	-6.0	-18.3
Federal 100 Barnes XLC	velocity, fps:	3210	2970	2750	2540	2330
	energy, ft-lb:	2290	1965	1680	1430	1205
	arc, inches:		+1.2	0	-5.8	-17.0
Federal 100 Nosler Bal. Tip	velocity, fps:	3210	2960	2720	2490	2280
	energy, ft-lb:	2290	1940	1640	1380	1150.
	arc, inches:		+1.2	0	-6.0	-17.5
Federal 100 Trophy Copper	velocity, fps:	3210	2970	2740	2520	2310
	energy, ft-lb:	2290	1955	1665	1410	1185
	arc, inches:		+1.2	0	-5.9	-17.2
Federal 115 Nosler Partition	velocity, fps:	2990	2750	2520	2300	2100
	energy, ft-lb:	2285	1930	1620	1350	1120
	arc, inches:		+1.6	0	-7.0	-20.8
Federal 115 Trophy Bonded	velocity, fps:	2990	2740	2500	2270	2050
	energy, ft-lb:	2285	1910	1590	1310	1075
	arc, inches:		+1.6	0	-7.2	-21.1
Federal 117 Sierra Pro Hunt.	velocity, fps:	2990	2730	2480	2250	2030
	energy, ft-lb:	2320	1985	1645	1350	1100
	arc, inches:		+1.6	0	-7.2	-21.4
Federal 117 Sierra GameKing BTSP	velocity, fps:	2990	2770	2570	2370	2190
	energy, ft-lb:	2320	2000	1715	1465	1240
	arc, inches:		+1.5	0	-6.8	-19.9
Hornady 90 GMX Superformance	velocity, fps:	3350	3001	2679	2378	2098
	energy, ft-lb:	2243	1799	1434	1130	879
	arc, inches:		+1.2	0	-6.0	-18.3
Hornady 117 SP boat-tail	velocity, fps:	2990	2749	2520	2302	2096
	energy, ft-lb:	2322	1962	1649	1377	1141
	arc, inches:		+1.6	0	-7.0	-20.7
Hornady 117 SP boat-tail LM	velocity, fps:	3110	2855	2613	2384	2168
	energy, ft-lb:	2512	2117	1774	1476	1220
	arc, inches:		+1.8	0	-7.1	-20.3
Hornady 117 SST Superformance	velocity, fps:	3110	2862	2627	2405	2193
	energy, ft-lb:	2513	2127	1793	1502	1249
	arc, inches:		+1.4	0	-6.4	-18.9
PMC 100 SPBT	velocity, fps:	3200	2925	2650	2395	2145
	energy, ft-lb:	2273	1895	1561	1268	1019
	arc, inches:		+1.3	0	-6.3	-18.6
PMC 117 PSP	velocity, fps:	2950	2706	2472	2253	2047
	energy, ft-lb:	2261	1900	1588	1319	1088
	arc, inches:		+1.6	0	-7.3	-21.5
Rem. 100 PSP Core-Lokt	velocity, fps:	3230	2893	2580	2287	2014
	energy, ft-lb:	2316	1858	1478	1161	901
	arc, inches:		+1.3	0	-6.6	-19.8
Rem. 115 Core-Lokt Ultra	velocity, fps:	3000	2751	2516	2293	2081
	energy, ft-lb:	2298	1933	1616	1342	1106
	arc, inches:		+1.6	0	-7.1	-20.7
Rem. 120 PSP Core-Lokt	velocity, fps:	2990	2730	2484	2252	2032
	energy, ft-lb:	2382	1985	1644	1351	1100
	arc, inches:		+1.6	0	-7.2	-21.4
Speer 120 Grand Slam	velocity, fps:	3130	2835	2558	2298	
	energy, ft-lb:	2610	2141	1743	1407	
	arc, inches:		+1.4	0	-6.8	-20.1
Win. 85 Ballistic Silvertip	velocity, fps	3470	3156	2863	2589	2331
	energy, ft-lb:	2273	1880	1548	1266	1026
	arc, inches:		+1.0	0	-5.2	-15.7
Win. 90 Pos. Exp. Point	velocity, fps:	3440	3043	2680	2344	2034
	energy, ft-lb:	2364	1850	1435	1098	827
	arc, inches:		+2.4	+2.0	-3.4	-15.0
Win. 110 AccuBond CT	velocity, fps:	3100	2870	2651	2442	2243
	energy, ft-lb:	2347	2011	1716	1456	1228
	arc, inches:		+1.4	0	-6.3	-18.5
Win. 115 Ballistic Silvertip	velocity, fps:	3060	2825	2603	2390	2188
	energy, ft-lb:	2391	2038	1729	1459	1223
	arc, inches:		+1.4	0	-6.6	-19.2
Win. 120 Pos. Pt. Exp.	velocity, fps:	2990	2717	2459	2216	1987
	energy, ft-lb:	2382	1967	1612	1309	1053
	arc, inches:		+1.6	0	-7.4	-21.8

.25 WINCHESTER SUPER SHORT MAGNUM

CARTRIDGE BULLET	RANGE, YARDS:	0	100	200	300	400
Win. 85 Ballistic Silvertip	velocity, fps:	3470	3156	2863	2589	2331
	energy, ft-lb:	2273	1880	1548	1266	1026
	arc, inches:		+1.0	0	-5.2	-15.7
Win. 110 AccuBond CT	velocity, fps:	3100	2870	2651	2442	2243.
	energy, ft-lb:	2347	2011	1716	1456	1228
	arc, inches:		+1.4	0	-6.3	-18.5
Win. 115 Ballistic Silvertip	velocity, fps:	3060	2844	2639	2442	2254
	energy, ft-lb:	2392	2066	1778	1523	1298
	arc, inches:		+1.4	0	-6.4	-18.6
Win. 120 Pos. Pt. Exp.	velocity, fps:	2990	2717	2459	2216	1987
	energy, ft-lb:	2383	1967	1612	1309	1053
	arc, inches:		+1.6	0	-7.4	-21.8

.257 WEATHERBY MAGNUM

CARTRIDGE BULLET	RANGE, YARDS:	0	100	200	300	400
Federal 115 Nosler Partition 2220	velocity, fps:	3150	2900	2660	2440	
	energy, ft-lb:	2535	2145	1810	1515	1260
	arc, inches:		+1.3	0	-6.2	-18.4
Federal 115 Trophy Bonded	velocity, fps:	3150	2890	2640	2400	2180
	energy, ft-lb:	2535	2125	1775	1470	1210
	arc, inches:		+1.4	0	-6.3	-18.8
Wby. 87 Pointed Expanding	velocity, fps:	3825	3472	3147	2845	2563
	energy, ft-lb:	2826	2328	1913	1563	1269
	arc, inches:		+2.1	+2.8	0	-7.1
Wby. 100 Pointed Expanding	velocity, fps:	3602	3298	3016	2750	2500
	energy, ft-lb:	2881	2416	2019	1680	1388
	arc, inches:		+2.4	+3.1	0	-7.7
Wby. 115 Nosler Bal. Tip	velocity, fps:	3400	3170	2952	2745	2547
	energy, ft-lb:	2952	2566	2226	1924	1656.
	arc, inches:		+3.0	+3.5	0	-7.9
Wby. 115 Barnes X	velocity, fps:	3400	3158	2929	2711	2504
	energy, ft-lb:	2952	2546	2190	1877	1601
	arc, inches:		+2.7	+3.4	0	-8.1
Wby. 117 RN Expanding	velocity, fps:	3402	2984	2595	2240	1921
	energy, ft-lb:	3007	2320	1742	1302	956
	arc, inches:		+3.4	+4.31	0	-11.1
Wby. 120 Nosler Partition	velocity, fps:	3305	3046	2801	2570	2350
	energy, ft-lb:	2910	2472	2091	1760	1471
	arc, inches:		+3.0	+3.7	0	-8.9

6.53 (.257) SCRAMJET

CARTRIDGE BULLET	RANGE, YARDS:	0	100	200	300	400
Lazzeroni 85 Nosler Bal. Tip	velocity, fps:	3960	3652	3365	3096	2844
	energy, ft-lb:	2961	2517	2137	1810	1526
	arc, inches:		+1.7	+2.4	0	-6.0
Lazzeroni 100 Nosler Part.	velocity, fps:	3740	3465	3208	2965	2735
	energy, ft-lb:	3106	2667	2285	1953	1661.
	arc, inches:		+2.1	+2.7	0	-6.7

6.5x50 JAPANESE

CARTRIDGE BULLET	RANGE, YARDS:	0	100	200	300	400
Norma 156 Alaska	velocity, fps:	2067	1832	1615	1423	
	energy, ft-lb:	1480	1162	904	701	
	arc, inches:		+4.4	0	-17.8	

6.5x52 CARCANO

CARTRIDGE BULLET	RANGE, YARDS:	0	100	200	300	400
Norma 156 Alaska	velocity, fps:	2428	2169	1926	1702	
	energy, ft-lb:	2043	1630	1286	1004	
	arc, inches:		+2.9	0	-12.3	

6.5x55 SWEDISH

CARTRIDGE BULLET	RANGE, YARDS:	0	100	200	300	400
Federal 140 Hi-Shok	velocity, fps:	2600	2400	2220	2040	1860
	energy, ft-lb:	2100	1795	1525	1285	1080
	arc, inches:		+2.3	0	-9.4	-27.2

BALLISTICS

CARTRIDGE BULLET	RANGE, YARDS:	0	100	200	300	400
Federal 140 Trophy Bonded	velocity, fps:	2550	2350	2160	1980	1810
	energy, ft-lb:	2020	1720	1450	1220	1015
	arc, inches:		+2.4	0	-9.8	-28.4
Federal 140 Sierra MatchKg. BTHP	velocity, fps:	2630	2460	2300	2140	2000
	energy, ft-lb:	2140	1880	1640	1430	1235
	arc, inches:		+16.4	+28.8	+33.9	+31.8
Hornady 129 SP LM	velocity, fps:	2770	2561	2361	2171	1994
	energy, ft-lb:	2197	1878	1597	1350	1138
	arc, inches:		+2.0	0	-8.2	-23.2
Hornady 140 SP Interlock	velocity, fps:	2525	2341	2165	1996	1836
	energy, ft-lb:	1982	1704	1457	1239	1048
	arc, inches:		+2.4	0	-9.9	-28.5
Hornady140 SP LM	velocity, fps:	2740	2541	2351	2169	1999
	energy, ft-lb:	2333	2006	1717	1463	1242
	arc, inches:		+2.4	0	-8.7	-24.0
Norma 120 Nosler Bal. Tip	velocity, fps:	2822	2609	2407	2213	
	energy, ft-lb:	2123	1815	1544	1305	
	arc, inches:		+1.8	0	-7.8	
Norma 139 Vulkan	velocity, fps:	2854	2569	2302	2051	
	energy, ft-lb:	2515	2038	1636	1298	
	arc, inches:		+1.8	0	-8.4	
Norma 140 Nosler Partition	velocity, fps:	2789	2592	2403	2223	
	energy, ft-lb:	2419	2089	1796	1536	
	arc, inches:		+1.8	0	-7.8	
Norma 156 TXP Swift A-Fr.	velocity, fps:	2526	2276	2040	1818	
	energy, ft-lb:	2196	1782	1432	1138	
	arc, inches:		+2.6	0	-10.9	
Norma 156 Alaska	velocity, fps:	2559	2245	1953	1687	
	energy, ft-lb:	2269	1746	1322	986	
	arc, inches:		+2.7	0	-11.9	
Norma 156 Vulkan	velocity, fps:	2644	2395	2159	1937	
	energy, ft-lb:	2422	1987	1616	1301	
	arc, inches:		+2.2	0	-9.7	
Norma 156 Oryx	velocity, fps:	2559	2308	2070	1848	
	energy, ft-lb:	2269	1845	1485	1183	
	arc, inches:		+2.5	0	-10.6	
PMC 139 Pointed Soft Point	velocity, fps:	2850	2560	2290	2030	1790
	energy, ft-lb:	2515	2025	1615	1270	985
	arc, inches:		+2.2	0	-8.9	-26.3
PMC 140 HP boat-tail	velocity, fps:	2560	2398	2243	2093	1949
	energy, ft-lb:	2037	1788	1563	1361	1181
	arc, inches:		+2.3	0	-9.2	-26.4
PMC 140 SP boat-tail	velocity, fps:	2560	2386	2218	2057	1903
	energy, ft-lb:	2037	1769	1529	1315	1126
	arc, inches:		+2.3	0	-9.4	-27.1
PMC 144 FMJ	velocity, fps:	2650	2370	2110	1870	1650
	energy, ft-lb:	2425	1950	1550	1215	945
	arc, inches:		+2.7	0	-10.5	-30.9
Rem. 140 PSP Core-Lokt	velocity, fps:	2550	2353	2164	1984	1814
	energy, ft-lb:	2021	1720	1456	1224	1023
	arc, inches:		+2.4	0	-9.8	-27.0
Speer 140 Grand Slam	velocity, fps:	2550	2318	2099	1892	
	energy, ft-lb:	2021	1670	1369	1112	
	arc, inches:		+2.5	0	-10.4	-30.6
Win. 140 Soft Point	velocity, fps:	2550	2359	2176	2002	1836
	energy, ft-lb:	2022	1731	1473	1246	1048.
	arc, inches:		+2.4	0	-9.7	-28.1

6.5 GRENDEL

CARTRIDGE BULLET	RANGE, YARDS:	0	100	200	300	400
Hornady 123 A-MAX	velocity, fps:	2590	2420	2256	2099	1948
	energy, ft-lb:	1832	1599	1390	1203	1037
	arc, inches:	-2.4	+1.8	0	-8.6	-25.1
Hornady 123 SST	velocity, fps:	2620	2449	2284	2126	1974

CARTRIDGE BULLET	RANGE, YARDS:	0	100	200	300	400
	energy, ft-lb:	1875	1638	1425	1234	1064
	arc, inches:	-2.4	+1.7	0	-8.4	-24.5

6.5 CREEDMOOR

CARTRIDGE BULLET	RANGE, YARDS:	0	100	200	300	400
Hornady 120 GMX	velocity, fps:	3050	2850	2659	2476	2300
	energy, ft-lb:	2479	2164	1884	1634	1410
	arc, inches:	-1.5	+1.4	0	-6.3	-18.3
Hornady 129 SST	velocity, fps:	2950	2756	2571	2394	2223
	energy, ft-lb:	2493	2176	1894	1641	1415
	arc, inches:	-1.5	+1.5	0	-6.8	-19.7
Hornady 140 A-MAX	velocity, fps:	2710	2557	2410	2267	2129
	energy, ft-lb:	2283	2033	1805	1598	1410
	arc, inches:	-1.5	+1.9	0	-7.9	-22.6
Nosler 140 BT	velocity, fps:	2550	2380	2217	2060	1910
	energy, ft-lb:	2021	1761	1527	1319	1134
	arc, inches:	-1.5	+2.3	0	-9.4	-27.0

.260 REMINGTON

CARTRIDGE BULLET	RANGE, YARDS:	0	100	200	300	400
Federal 140 Sierra GameKing BTSP	velocity, fps:	2750	2570	2390	2220	2060
	energy, ft-lb:	2350	2045	1775	1535	1315
	arc, inches:		+1.9	0	-8.0	-23.1
Federal 140 Trophy Bonded	velocity, fps:	2750	2540	2340	2150	1970
	energy, ft-lb:	2350	2010	1705	1440	1210
	arc, inches:		+1.9	0	-8.4	-24.1
Rem. 120 Nosler Bal. Tip	velocity, fps:	2890	2688	2494	2309	2131
	energy, ft-lb:	2226	1924	1657	1420	1210
	arc, inches:		+1.7	0	-7.3	-21.1
Rem. 120 AccuTip	velocity, fps:	2890	2697	2512	2334	2163
	energy, ft-lb:	2392	2083	1807	1560	1340
	arc, inches:		+1.6	0	-7.2	-20.7
Rem. 125 Nosler Partition	velocity, fps:	2875	2669	2473	2285	2105.
	energy, ft-lb:	2294	1977	1697	1449	1230
	arc, inches:	+1.71	0	-7.4	-21.4	
Rem. 140 PSP Core-Lokt (and C-L Ultra)	velocity, fps:	2750	2544	2347	2158	1979
	energy, ft-lb:	2351	2011	1712	1448	1217
	arc, inches:		+1.9	0	-8.3	-24.0
Speer 140 Grand Slam	velocity, fps:	2750	2518	2297	2087	
	energy, ft-lb:	2351	1970	1640	1354	
	arc, inches:		+2.3	0	-8.9	-25.8

6.5-284

CARTRIDGE BULLET	RANGE, YARDS:	0	100	200	300	400
Norma 120 Nosler Bal. Tip	velocity, fps:	3117	2890	2674	2469	
	energy, ft-lb:	2589	2226	1906	1624	
	arc, inches:		+1.3	0	-6.2	
Norma 140 Nosler Part.	velocity, fps:	2953	2750	2557	2371	
	energy, ft-lb:	2712	2352	2032	1748	
	arc, inches:		+1.5	0	-6.8	

6.5-284 NORMA

CARTRIDGE BULLET	RANGE, YARDS:	0	100	200	300	400
Nosler 120 Ballistic Tip	velocity, fps:	3000	2792	2594	2404	2223
	energy, ft-lb:	2398	2077	1793	1540	1316
	arc, inches:	-1.5	+1.4	0	-6.6	-17.1
Nosler 125 PT	velocity, fps:	3000	2788	2585	2392	2207
	energy, ft-lb:	2497	2157	1855	1588	1352
	arc, inches:	-1.5	+1.5	0	-6.7	-19.5
Nosler 130 AccuBond	velocity, fps:	2900	2709	2526	2351	2182
	energy, ft-lb:	2427	2118	1842	1595	1374
	arc, inches:	-1.5	+1.5	0	-6.9	-18.4

6.5 REMINGTON MAGNUM

CARTRIDGE BULLET	RANGE, YARDS:	0	100	200	300	400
Nosler 125 PT	velocity, fps:	3025	2811	2608	2414	2228
	energy, ft-lb:	2539	2194	1888	1617	1377
	arc, inches:	-1.5	+1.5	0	-6.6	-19.1

Centerfire Rifle Ballistics

BALLISTICS

CARTRIDGE BULLET	RANGE, YARDS:	0	100	200	300	400
Rem. 120 Core-Lokt PSP	velocity, fps:	3210	2905	2621	2353	2102
	energy, ft-lb:	2745	2248	1830	1475	1177
	arc, inches:		+2.7	+2.1	-3.5	-15.5

.264 WINCHESTER MAGNUM

CARTRIDGE BULLET	RANGE, YARDS:	0	100	200	300	400
Nosler 100 Ballistic Tip	velocity, fps:	3400	3105	2829	2569	2324
	energy, ft-lb:	2567	2141	1777	1465	1199
	arc, inches:	-1.5	+1.0	0	-6.0	-16.1
Nosler 130 AccuBond	velocity, fps:	3100	2900	2709	2527	2351
	energy, ft-lb:	2774	2428	2119	1843	1595
	arc, inches:	-1.5	+1.2	0	-6.0	-17.5
Rem. 140 PSP Core-Lokt	velocity, fps:	3030	2782	2548	2326	2114
	energy, ft-lb:	2854	2406	2018	1682	1389
	arc, inches:		+1.5	0	-6.9	-20.2
Win. 140 Power-Point	velocity, fps:	3030	2782	2548	2326	2114.
	energy, ft-lb:	2854	2406	2018	1682	1389
	arc, inches:		+1.8	0	-7.2	-20.8

6.8MM REMINGTON SPC

CARTRIDGE BULLET	RANGE, YARDS:	0	100	200	300	400
Hornady 110 BTHP	velocity, fps:	2570	2332	2107	1895	1697
(16-in. barrel)	energy, ft-lb:	1613	1328	1084	877	703
	arc, inches:	-2.4	+2.0	0	-9.9	-29.5
Hornady 120 SST	velocity, fps:	2460	2250	2051	1863	1687
(16-in. barrel)	energy, ft-lb:	1612	1349	1121	925	758
	arc, inches:	-2.4	+2.3	0	-10.5	-31.1
Rem. 115 Open Tip Match	velocity, fps:	2800	2535	2285	2049	1828
(and HPBT Match)	energy, ft-lb:	2002	1641	1333	1072	853
	arc, inches:		+2.0	0	-8.8	-26.2
Rem. 115 Metal Case	velocity, fps:	2800	2523	2262	2017	1789
	energy, ft-lb:	2002	1625	1307	1039	817
	arc, inches:		+2.0	0	-8.8	-26.2
Rem. 115 Sierra HPBT	velocity, fps:	2775	2511	2263	2028	1809
(2005; all vel. @ 2775)	energy, ft-lb:	1966	1610	1307	1050	835
	arc, inches:		+2.0	0	-8.8	-26.2.
Rem. 115 CL Ultra	velocity, fps:	2775	2472	2190	1926	1683
	energy, ft-lb:	1966	1561	1224	947	723
	arc, inches:		+2.1	0	-9.4	-28.2

.270 WINCHESTER

CARTRIDGE BULLET	RANGE, YARDS:	0	100	200	300	400
Black Hills 130 Nos. Bal. T.	velocity, fps:	2950				
	energy, ft-lb:	2512				
	arc, inches:					
Black Hills 130 Barnes XLC	velocity, ft-lb:	2950				
	energy, ft-lb:	2512				
	arc, inches:					
Federal 130 Barnes XLC	velocity, fps:	3060	2840	2620	2420	2220
And Triple Shock	energy, ft-lb:	2705	2320	1985	1690	1425
	arc, inches:		+1.4	0	-6.4	-18.9
Federal 130 Hi-Shok	velocity, fps:	3060	2800	2560	2330	2110
	energy, ft-lb:	2700	2265	1890	1565	1285
	arc, inches:		+1.5	0	-6.8	-20.0
Federal 130 Nosler Bal. Tip	velocity, fps:	3060	2840	2630	2430	2230
	energy, ft-lb:	2700	2325	1990	1700	1440
	arc, inches:		+1.4	0	-6.5	-18.8
Federal 130 Nos. Partition	velocity, fps:	3060	2830	2610	2400	2200
And Solid Base	energy, ft-lb:	2705	2310	1965	1665	1400
	arc, inches:		+1.4	0	-6.5	-19.1
Federal 130 Sierra GameKing	velocity, fps:	3060	2830	2620	2410	2220
	energy, ft-lb:	2700	2320	1980	1680	1420
	arc, inches:		+1.4	0	-6.5	-19.0
Federal 130 Sierra Pro-Hunt.	velocity, fps:	3060	2830	2600	2390	2190
	energy, ft-lb:	2705	2305	1960	1655	1390
	arc, inches:	+1.4	0	-6.4	-19.0	
Federal 130 Trophy Bonded	velocity, fps:	3060	2810	2570	2340	2130
	energy, ft-lb:	2705	2275	1905	1585	1310
	arc, inches:		+1.5	0	-6.7	-19.8
Federal 130 Trophy Bonded Tip	velocity, fps:	3060	2840	2630	2430	2240
	energy, ft-lb:	2705	2330	2000	1710	1455
	arc, inches:		+1.4	0	-6.4	-18.7
Federal 140 Trophy Bonded	velocity, fps:	2940	2700	2480	2260	2060
	energy, ft-lb:	2685	2270	1905	1590	1315
	arc, inches:		+1.6	0	-7.3	-21.5

CARTRIDGE BULLET	RANGE, YARDS:	0	100	200	300	400
Federal 140 Trophy Bonded Tip	velocity, fps:	2950	2740	2550	2360	2180
	energy, ft-lb:	2705	2340	2015	1730	1475
	arc, inches:		+1.6	0	-6.9	-20.1
Federal 140 Tr. Bonded HE	velocity, fps:	3100	2860	2620	2400	2200.
	energy, ft-lb:	2990	2535	2140	1795	1500
	arc, inches:		+1.4	0	-6.4	-18.9
Federal 140 Nos. AccuBond	velocity, fps:	2950	2760	2580	2400	2230.
	energy, ft-lb:	2705	2365	2060	1790	1545
	arc, inches:		+1.5	0	-6.7	-19.6
Federal 150 Hi-Shok RN	velocity, fps:	2850	2500	2180	1890	1620
	energy, ft-lb:	2705	2085	1585	1185	870
	arc, inches:		+2.0	0	-9.4	-28.6
Federal 150 Sierra GameKing	velocity, fps:	2850	2660	2480	2300	2130
	energy, ft-lb:	2705	2355	2040	1760	1510
	arc, inches:		+1.7	0	-7.4	-21.4
Federal 150 Sierra GameKing HE	velocity, fps:	3000	2800	2620	2430	2260
	energy, ft-lb:	2995	2615	2275	1975	1700
	arc, inches:		+1.5	0	-6.5	-18.9
Federal 150 Nosler Partition	velocity, fps:	2850	2590	2340	2100	1880.
	energy, ft-lb:	2705	2225	1815	1470	1175
	arc, inches:		+1.9	0	-8.3	-24.4
Hornady 120 SST Custom Lite	velocity, fps:	2675	2288	1935	1619	1351
	energy, ft-lb:	1907	1395	998	699	486
	arc, inches:		+2.6	0	-12.0	-37.4
Hornady 130 GMX Superformance	velocity, fps:	3190	2975	2770	2575	2387
	energy, ft-lb:	2937	2554	2215	1913	1645
	arc, inches:		+1.2	0	-5.7	-16.8
Hornady 130 SST (or Interbond)	velocity, fps:	3060	2845	2639	2442	2254
	energy, ft-lb:	2700	2335	2009	1721	1467
	arc, inches:		+1.4	0	-6.6	-19.1
Hornady 130 SST LM (or Interbond)	velocity, fps:	3215	2998	2790	2590	2400
	energy, ft-lb:	2983	2594	2246	1936	1662
	arc, inches:		+1.2	0	-5.8	-17.0
Hornady 130 SST Superformance	velocity, fps:	3200	2984	2779	2583	2396
	energy, ft-lb:	2956	2570	2229	1926	1656
	arc, inches:		+1.2	0	-5.7	-16.7
Hornady 140 SP boat-tail	velocity, fps:	2940	2747	2562	2385	2214
	energy, ft-lb:	2688	2346	2041	1769	1524
	arc, inches:		+1.6	0	-7.0	-20.2
Hornady 140 SP boat-tail LM	velocity, fps:	3100	2894	2697	2508	2327.
	energy, ft-lb:	2987	2604	2261	1955	1684
	arc, inches:		+1.4	0	6.3	-18.3
Hornady 140 SST Superformance	velocity, fps:	3090	2894	2707	2568	2355
	energy, ft-lb:	2968	2604	2278	1986	1724
	arc, inches:		+1.3	0	-6.1	-17.6
Hornady 150 SP	velocity, fps:	2800	2684	2478	2284	2100
	energy, ft-lb:	2802	2400	2046	1737	1469
	arc, inches:		+1.7	0	-7.4	-21.6
Norma 130 SP	velocity, fps:	3140	2862	2601	2354	
	energy, ft-lb:	2847	2365	1953	1600	
	arc, inches:		+1.3	0	-6.5	
Norma 130 FMJ	velocity, fps:	2887	2634	2395	2169	
	energy, ft-lb:					
	arc, inches:		+1.8	0	-7.8	
Norma 150 SP	velocity, fps:	2799	2555	2323	2104	
	energy, ft-lb:	2610	2175	1798	1475	
	arc, inches:		+1.9	0	-8.3	
Norma 150 Oryx	velocity, fps:	2854	2608	2376	2155	
	energy, ft-lb:	2714	2267	1880	1547	
	arc, inches:		+1.8	0	-8.0	
PMC 130 Barnes X	velocity, fps:	2910	2717	2533	2356	2186
	energy, ft-lb:	2444	2131	1852	1602	1379
	arc, inches:		+1.6	0	-7.1	-20.4
PMC 130 SP boat-tail	velocity, fps:	3050	2830	2620	2421	2229
	energy, ft-lb:	2685	2312	1982	1691	1435
	arc, inches:		+1.5	0	-6.5	-19.0
PMC 130 Pointed Soft Point	velocity, fps:	2950	2691	2447	2217	2001
	energy, ft-lb:	2512	2090	1728	1419	1156
	arc, inches:		+1.6	0	-7.5	-22.1
PMC 150 Barnes X	velocity, fps:	2700	2541	2387	2238	2095
	energy, ft-lb:	2428	2150	1897	1668	1461
	arc, inches:		+2.0	0	-8.1	-23.1

Centerfire Rifle Ballistics

.270 WINCHESTER TO .270 WINCHESTER SHORT MAGNUM

CARTRIDGE BULLET	RANGE, YARDS:	0	100	200	300	400
PMC 150 SP boat-tail	velocity, fps:	2850	2660	2477	2302	2134
	energy, ft-lb:	2705	2355	2043	1765	1516.
	arc, inches:		+1.7	0	-7.4	-21.4
PMC 150 Pointed Soft Point	velocity, fps:	2750	2530	2321	2123	1936
	energy, ft-lb:	2519	2131	1794	1501	1248
	arc, inches:		+2.0	0	-8.4	-24.6
Rem. 100 Pointed Soft Point	velocity, fps:	3320	2924	2561	2225	1916
	energy, ft-lb:	2448	1898	1456	1099	815
	arc, inches:		+2.3	+2.0	-3.6	-16.2
Rem. 115 PSP Core-Lokt mr	velocity, fps:	2710	2412	2133	1873	1636
	energy, ft-lb:	1875	1485	1161	896	683
	arc, inches:		+1.0	-2.7	-14.2	-35.6
Rem. 130 PSP Core-Lokt	velocity, fps:	3060	2776	2510	2259	2022
	energy, ft-lb:	2702	2225	1818	1472	1180
	arc, inches:		+1.5	0	-7.0	-20.9
Rem. 130 Bronze Point	velocity, fps:	3060	2802	2559	2329	2110
	energy, ft-lb:	2702	2267	1890	1565	1285
	arc, inches:		+1.5	0	-6.8	-20.0
Rem. 130 Swift Scirocco	velocity, fps:	3060	2838	2677	2425	2232
	energy, ft-lb:	2702	2325	1991	1697	1438
	arc, inches:		+1.4	0	-6.5	-18.8
Rem. 130 AccuTip BT	velocity, fps:	3060	2845	2639	2442	2254
	energy, ft-lb:	2702	2336	2009	1721	1467
	arc, inches:		+1.4	0	-6.4	-18.6
Rem. 140 Swift A-Frame	velocity, fps:	2925	2652	2394	2152	1923
	energy, ft-lb:	2659	2186	1782	1439	1150
	arc, inches:		+1.7	0	-7.8	-23.2
Rem. 140 PSP boat-tail	velocity, fps:	2960	2749	2548	2355	2171
	energy, ft-lb:	2723	2349	2018	1724	1465
	arc, inches:		+1.6	0	-6.9	-20.1
Rem. 140 Nosler Bal. Tip	velocity, fps:	2960	2754	2557	2366	2187
	energy, ft-lb:	2724	2358	2032	1743	1487
	arc, inches:		+1.6	0	-6.9	-20.0
Rem. 140 PSP C-L Ultra	velocity, fps:	2925	2667	2424	2193	1975
	energy, ft-lb:	2659	2211	1826	1495	1212
	arc, inches:		+1.7	0	-7.6	-22.5
Rem. 150 SP Core-Lokt	velocity, fps:	2850	2504	2183	1886	1618
	energy, ft-lb:	2705	2087	1587	1185	872
	arc, inches:		+2.0	0	-9.4	-28.6
Rem. 150 Nosler Partition	velocity, fps:	2850	2652	2463	2282	2108
	energy, ft-lb:	2705	2343	2021	1734	1480
	arc, inches:		+1.7	0	-7.5	-21.6
Speer 130 Grand Slam	velocity, fps:	3050	2774	2514	2269	
	energy, ft-lb:	2685	2221	1824	1485	
	arc, inches:		+1.5	0	-7.0	-20.9
Speer 150 Grand Slam	velocity, fps:	2830	2594	2369	2156	
	energy, ft-lb:	2667	2240	1869	1548	
	arc, inches:		+1.8	0	-8.1	-23.6
Win. 130 Power-Point	velocity, fps:	3060	2802	2559	2329	2110
	energy, ft-lb:	2702	2267	1890	1565	1285.
	arc, inches:		+1.8	0	-7.1	-20.6
Win. 130 Power-Point Plus	velocity, fps:	3150	2881	2628	2388	2161
	energy, ft-lb:	2865	2396	1993	1646	1348
	arc, inches:		+1.3	0	-6.4	-18.9
Win. 130 Silvertip	velocity, fps:	3060	2776	2510	2259	2022.
	energy, ft-lb:	2702	2225	1818	1472	1180
	arc, inches:		+1.8	0	-7.4	-21.6
Win. 130 Ballistic Silvertip	velocity, fps:	3050	2828	2618	2416	2224
	energy, ft-lb:	2685	2309	1978	1685	1428
	arc, inches:		+1.4	0	-6.5	-18.9
Win. 140 AccuBond	velocity, fps:	2950	2751	2560	2378	2203
	energy, ft-lb:	2705	2352	2038	1757	1508
	arc, inches:		+1.6	0	-6.9	-19.9

CARTRIDGE BULLET	RANGE, YARDS:	0	100	200	300	400
Win. 140 Fail Safe	velocity, fps:	2920	2671	2435	2211	1999
	energy, ft-lb:	2651	2218	1843	1519	1242
	arc, inches:		+1.7	0	-7.6	-22.3
Win. 150 Power-Point	velocity, fps:	2850	2585	2336	2100	1879
	energy, ft-lb:	2705	2226	1817	1468	1175
	arc, inches:		+2.2	0	-8.6	-25.0
Win. 150 Power-Point Plus	velocity, fps:	2950	2679	2425	2184	1957
	energy, ft-lb:	2900	2391	1959	1589	1276
	arc, inches:		+1.7	0	-7.6	-22.6
Win. 150 Partition Gold	velocity, fps:	2930	2693	2468	2254	2051
	energy, ft-lb:	2860	2416	2030	1693	1402
	arc, inches:		+1.7	0	-7.4	-21.6
Win. 150 Supreme Elite XP3	velocity, fps:	2950	2763	2583	2411	2245
	energy, ft-lb:	2898	2542	2223	1936	1679
	arc, inches:		+1.5	0	-6.9	-15.5

.270 WINCHESTER SHORT MAGNUM

CARTRIDGE BULLET	RANGE, YARDS:	0	100	200	300	400
Black Hills 140 AccuBond	velocity, fps:	3100				
	energy, ft-lb:	2987				
	arc, inches:					
Federal 130 Nos. Bal. Tip	velocity, fps:	3300	3070	2840	2630	2430
	energy, ft-lb:	3145	2710	2335	2000	1705
	arc, inches:		+1.1	0	-5.4	-15.8
Federal 130 Nos. Partition And Nos. Solid Base And Barnes TS	velocity, fps:	3280	3040	2810	2590	2380
	energy, ft-lb:	3105	2665	2275	1935	1635
	arc, inches:		+1.1	0	-5.6	-16.3
Federal 130 Trophy Copper	velocity, fps:	3280	3060	2850	2650	2460
	energy, ft-lb:	3105	2700	2345	2025	1745
	arc, inches:		+1.1	0	-5.4	-15.8
Federal 140 Nos. AccuBond	velocity, fps	3200	3000	2810	2630	2450
	energy, ft-lb:	3185	2795	2455	2145	1865
	arc, inches:		+1.2	0	-5.6	-16.2
Federal 140 Trophy Bonded	velocity, fps:	3130	2870	2640	2410	2200
	energy, ft-lb:	3035	2570	2160	1810	1500
	arc, inches:		+1.4	0	-6.3	18.7
Federal 140 Trophy Bonded Tip	velocity, fps:	3200	2980	2770	2580	2390
	energy, ft-lb:	3185	2765	2390	2060	1770
	arc, inches:		+1.2	0	-5.8	-16.7
Federal 150 Nos. Partition	velocity, fps:	3160	2950	2750	2550	2370
	energy, ft-lb:	3325	2895	2515	2175	1870
	arc, inches:		+1.3	0	-5.9	-17.0
Norma 130 FMJ	velocity, fps:	3150	2882	2630	2391	
	energy, ft-lb:					
	arc, inches:		+1.5	0	-6.4	
Norma 130 Ballistic ST	velocity, fps:	3281	3047	2825	2614	
	energy, ft-lb:	3108	2681	2305	1973	
	arc, inches:		+1.1	0	-5.5	
Norma 140 Barnes X TS	velocity, fps:	3150	2952	2762	2580	
	energy, ft-lb:	3085	2709	2372	2070	
	arc, inches:		+1.3	0	-5.8	
Norma 150 Nosler Bal. Tip	velocity, fps:	3280	3046	2824	2613	
	energy, ft-lb:	3106	2679	2303	1972	
	arc, inches:		+1.1	0	-5.4	
Norma 150 Oryx	velocity, fps:	3117	2856	2611	2378	
	energy, ft-lb:	3237	2718	2271	1884	
	arc, inches:		+1.4	0	-6.5	
Win. 130 Bal. Silvertip	velocity, fps:	3275	3041	2820	2609	2408
	energy, ft-lb:	3096	2669	2295	1964	1673
	arc, inches:		+1.1	0	-5.5	-16.1
Win. 140 AccuBond	velocity, fps:	3200	2989	2789	2597	2413
	energy, ft-lb:	3184	2779	2418	2097	1810
	arc, inches:		+1.2	0	-5.7	-16.5
Win. 140 Fail Safe	velocity, fps:	3125	2865	2619	2386	2165
	energy, ft-lb:	3035	2550	2132	1769	1457
	arc, inches:		+1.4	0	-6.5	-19.0
Win. 150 Ballistic Silvertip	velocity, fps:	3120	2923	2734	2554	2380.
	energy, ft-lb:	3242	2845	2490	2172	1886.
	arc, inches:		+1.3	0	-5.9	-17.2

.270 WINCHESTER SHORT MAGNUM TO 7MM-08 REMINGTON

BALLISTICS

CARTRIDGE BULLET	RANGE, YARDS:	0	100	200	300	400
Win. 150 Power Point	velocity, fps:	3150	2867	2601	2350	2113
	energy, ft-lb:	3304	2737	2252	1839	1487
	arc, inches:		+1.4	0	-6.5	-19.4
Win. 150 Supreme Elite XP3	velocity, fps:	3120	2926	2740	2561	2389
	energy, ft-lb:	3242	2850	2499	2184	1901
	arc, inches:		+1.3	0	-5.9	-17.1

.270 WEATHERBY MAGNUM

CARTRIDGE BULLET	RANGE, YARDS:	0	100	200	300	400
Federal 130 Nosler Partition	velocity, fps:	3200	2960	2740	2520	2320
	energy, ft-lb:	2955	2530	2160	1835	1550
	arc, inches:		+1.2	0	-5.9	-17.3
Federal 130 Sierra GameKing BTSP	velocity, fps:	3200	2980	2780	2580	2400
	energy, ft-lb:	2955	2570	2230	1925	1655
	arc, inches:		+1.2	0	-5.7	-16.6
Federal 140 Trophy Bonded	velocity, fps:	3100	2840	2600	2370	2150.
	energy, ft-lb:	2990	2510	2100	1745	1440
	arc, inches:		+1.4	0	-6.6	-19.3
Federal 130 Trophy Bonded Tip	velocity, fps:	3200	2970	2760	2560	2360
	energy, ft-lb:	2955	2555	2200	1885	1610
	arc, inches:		+1.2	0	-5.9	-16.9
Wby. 100 Pointed Expanding	velocity, fps:	3760	3396	3061	2751	2462
	energy, ft-lb:	3139	2560	2081	1681	1346
	arc, inches:		+2.3	+3.0	0	-7.6
Wby. 130 Pointed Expanding	velocity, fps:	3375	3123	2885	2659	2444
	energy, ft-lb:	3288	2815	2402	2041	1724
	arc, inches:		+2.8	+3.5	0	-8.4
Wby. 130 Nosler Partition	velocity, fps:	3375	3127	2892	2670	2458.
	energy, ft-lb:	3288	2822	2415	2058	1744
	arc, inches:		+2.8	+3.5	0	-8.3
Wby. 140 Nosler Bal. Tip	velocity, fps:	3300	3077	2865	2663	2470.
	energy, ft-lb:	3385	2943	2551	2204	1896
	arc, inches:		+2.9	+3.6	0	-8.4
Wby. 140 Barnes X	velocity, fps:	3250	3032	2825	2628	2438
	energy, ft-lb:	3283	2858	2481	2146	1848
	arc, inches:		+3.0	+3.7	0	-8.7
Wby. 150 Pointed Expanding	velocity, fps:	3245	3028	2821	2623	2434
	energy, ft-lb:	3507	3053	2650	2292	1973
	arc, inches:		+3.0	+3.7	0	-8.7
Wby. 150 Nosler Partition	velocity, fps:	3245	3029	2823	2627	2439.
	energy, ft-lb:	3507	3055	2655	2298	1981
	arc, inches:		+3.0	+3.7	0	-8.

7-30 WATERS

CARTRIDGE BULLET	RANGE, YARDS:	0	100	200	300	400
Federal 120 Sierra GameKing BTSP	velocity, fps:	2700	2300	1930	1600	1330.
	energy, ft-lb:	1940	1405	990	685	470
	arc, inches:		+2.6	0	-12.0	-37.6

7MM MAUSER (7x57)

CARTRIDGE BULLET	RANGE, YARDS:	0	100	200	300	400
Federal 140 Sierra Pro-Hunt.	velocity, fps:	2660	2450	2260	2070	1890.
	energy, ft-lb:	2200	1865	1585	1330	1110
	arc, inches:		+2.1	0	-9.0	-26.1
Federal 140 Nosler Partition	velocity, fps:	2660	2450	2260	2070	1890.
	energy, ft-lb:	2200	1865	1585	1330	1110
	arc, inches:		+2.1	0	-9.0	-26.1
Federal 175 Hi-Shok RN	velocity, fps:	2440	2140	1860	1600	1380
	energy, ft-lb:	2315	1775	1340	1000	740
	arc, inches:		+3.1	0	-13.3	-40.1
Hornady 139 SP boat-tail	velocity, fps:	2700	2504	2316	2137	1965
	energy, ft-lb:	2251	1936	1656	1410	1192
	arc, inches:		+2.0	0	-8.5	-24.9
Hornady 139 SP Interlock	velocity, fps:	2680	2455	2241	2038	1846
	energy, ft-lb:	2216	1860	1550	1282	1052
	arc, inches:		+2.1	0	-9.1	-26.6
Hornady 139 SP boat-tail LM	velocity, fps:	2830	2620	2450	2250	2070
	energy, ft-lb:	2475	2135	1835	1565	1330
	arc, inches:		+1.8	0	-7.6	-22.1
Hornady 139 SP LM	velocity, fps:	2950	2736	2532	2337	2152.
	energy, ft-lb:	2686	2310	1978	1686	1429
	arc, inches:		+2.0	0	-7.6	-21.5

CARTRIDGE BULLET	RANGE, YARDS:	0	100	200	300	400
Hornady 139 SST Superformance	velocity, fps:	2760	2575	2397	2227	2063
	energy, ft-lb:	2351	2046	1774	1530	1314
	arc, inches:		+1.9	0	-7.9	-22.9
Norma 150 Soft Point	velocity, fps:	2690	2479	2278	2087	
	energy, ft-lb:	2411	2048	1729	1450	
	arc, inches:		+2.0	0	-8.8	
PMC 140 Pointed Soft Point	velocity, fps:	2660	2450	2260	2070	1890
	energy, ft-lb:	2200	1865	1585	1330	1110.
	arc, inches:		+2.4	0	-9.6	-27.3
PMC 175 Soft Point	velocity, fps:	2440	2140	1860	1600	1380
	energy, ft-lb:	2315	1775	1340	1000	740
	arc, inches:		+1.5	-3.6	-18.6	-46.8
Rem. 140 PSP Core-Lokt	velocity, fps:	2660	2435	2221	2018	1827
	energy, ft-lb:	2199	1843	1533	1266	1037
	arc, inches:		+2.2	0	-9.2	-27.4
Win. 145 Power-Point	velocity, fps:	2660	2413	2180	1959	1754
	energy, ft-lb:	2279	1875	1530	1236	990
	arc, inches:		+1.1	-2.8	-14.1	-34.4

7x57 R

CARTRIDGE BULLET	RANGE, YARDS:	0	100	200	300	400
Norma 150 FMJ	velocity, fps:	2690	2489	2296	2112	
	energy, ft-lb:	2411	2063	1756	1486	
	arc, inches:		+2.0	0	-8.6	
Norma 154 Soft Point	velocity, fps:	2625	2417	2219	2030	
	energy, ft-lb:	2357	1999	1684	1410	
	arc, inches:		+2.2	0	-9.3	
Norma 156 Oryx	velocity, fps:	2608	2346	2099	1867	
	energy, ft-lb:	2357	1906	1526	1208	
	arc, inches:		+2.4	0	-10.3	

7MM-08 REMINGTON

CARTRIDGE BULLET	RANGE, YARDS:	0	100	200	300	400
Black Hills 140 AccuBond	velocity, fps:	2700				
	energy, ft-lb:					
	arc, inches:					
Federal 140 Nosler Partition	velocity, fps:	2800	2590	2390	2200	2020
	energy, ft-lb:	2435	2085	1775	1500	1265
	arc, inches:		+1.8	0	-8.0	-23.1
Federal 140 Nosler Bal. Tip And AccuBond	velocity, fps:	2800	2610	2430	2260	2100
	energy, ft-lb:	2440	2135	1840	1590	1360.
	arc, inches:		+1.8	0	-7.7	-22.3
Federal 140 Tr. Bonded HE	velocity, fps:	2950	2660	2390	2140	1900
	energy, ft-lb:	2705	2205	1780	1420	1120
	arc, inches:		+1.7	0	-7.9	-23.2
Federal 140 Trophy Copper	velocity, fps:	2800	2610	2440	2260	2100
	energy, ft-lb:	2435	2125	1845	1595	1370
	arc, inches:		+1.8	0	-7.7	-22.2
Federal 150 Sierra Pro-Hunt.	velocity, fps:	2650	2440	2230	2040	1860
	energy, ft-lb:	2340	1980	1660	1390	1150
	arc, inches:		+2.2	0	-9.2	-26.7
Hornady 120 SST Custom Lite	velocity, fps:	2675	2435	2207	1992	1790
	energy, ft-lb:	1907	1579	1298	1057	854
	arc, inches:		+2.2	0	-9.4	-27.5
Hornady 139 SP boat-tail LM	velocity, fps:	3000	2790	2590	2399	2216
	energy, ft-lb:	2777	2403	2071	1776	1515
	arc, inches:		+1.5	0	-6.7	-19.4
Norma 140 Ballistic ST	velocity, fps:	2822	2633	2452	2278	
	energy, ft-lb:	2476	2156	1870	1614	
	arc, inches:		+1.8	0	-7.6	
PMC 139 PSP	velocity, fps:	2850	2610	2384	2170	1969
	energy, ft-lb:	2507	2103	1754	1454	1197
	arc, inches:		+1.8	0	-7.9	-23.3
Rem. 120 Hollow Point	velocity, fps:	3000	2725	2467	2223	1992
	energy, ft-lb:	2398	1979	1621	1316	1058
	arc, inches:		+1.6	0	-7.3	-21.7
Rem. 140 PSP Core-Lokt	velocity, fps:	2860	2625	2402	2189	1988
	energy, ft-lb:	2542	2142	1793	1490	1228
	arc, inches:		+1.8	0	-7.8	-22.9
Rem. 140 PSP boat-tail	velocity, fps:	2860	2656	2460	2273	2094
	energy, ft-lb:	2542	2192	1881	1606	1363
	arc, inches:		+1.7	0	-7.5	-21.7

BALLISTICS

CARTRIDGE BULLET	RANGE, YARDS:	0	100	200	300	400
Rem. 140 AccuTip BT	velocity, fps	2860	2670	2488	2313	2145
	energy, ft-lb	2543	2217	1925	1663	1431
	arc, inches		+1.7	0	-7.3	-21.2
Rem. 140 Nosler Partition	velocity, fps	2860	2648	2446	2253	2068
	energy, ft-lb	2542	2180	1860	1577	1330
	arc, inches		+1.7	0	-7.6	-22.0
Speer 145 Grand Slam	velocity, fps	2845	2567	2305	2059	
	energy, ft-lb	2606	2121	1711	1365	
	arc, inches		+1.9	0	-8.4	-25.5
Win. 140 Power-Point	velocity, fps	2800	2523	2268	2027	1802.
	energy, ft-lb	2429	1980	1599	1277	1010
	arc, inches		+2.0	0	-8.8	-26.0
Win. 140 Power-Point Plus	velocity, fps	2875	2597	2336	2090	1859
	energy, ft-lb	2570	1997	1697	1358	1075
	arc, inches		+2.0	0	-8.8	26.0
Win. 140 Fail Safe	velocity, fps	2760	2506	2271	2048	1839
	energy, ft-lb	2360	1953	1603	1304	1051
	arc, inches		+2.0	0	-8.8	-25.9
Win. 140 Ballistic Silvertip	velocity, fps	2770	2572	2382	2200	2026
	energy, ft-lb	2386	2056	1764	1504	1276
	arc, inches		+1.9	0	-8.0	-23.8

7x64 BRENNEKE

CARTRIDGE BULLET	RANGE, YARDS:	0	100	200	300	400
Federal 160 Nosler Partition	velocity, fps	2650	2480	2310	2150	2000
	energy, ft-lb	2495	2180	1895	1640	1415
	arc, inches		+2.1	0	-8.7	-24.9
Norma 140 AccuBond	velocity, fps	2953	2759	2572	2394	
	energy, ft-lb	2712	2366	2058	1782	
	arc, inches		+1.5	0	-6.8	
Norma 154 Soft Point	velocity, fps	2821	2605	2399	2203	
	energy, ft-lb	2722	2321	1969	1660	
	arc, inches		+1.8	0	-7.8	
Norma 156 Oryx	velocity, fps	2789	2516	2259	2017	
	energy, ft-lb	2695	2193	1768	1410	
	arc, inches		+2.0	0	-8.8	
Norma 170 Vulkan	velocity, fps	2756	2501	2259	2031	
	energy, ft-lb	2868	2361	1927	1558	
	arc, inches		+2.0	0	-8.8	
Norma 170 Oryx	velocity, fps	2756	2481	2222	1979	
	energy, ft-lb	2868	2324	1864	1478	
	arc, inches		+2.1	0	-9.2	
Norma 170 Plastic Point	velocity, fps	2756	2519	2294	2081	
	energy, ft-lb	2868	2396	1987	1635	
	arc, inches		+2.0	0	-8.6	
PMC 170 Pointed Soft Point	velocity, fps	2625	2401	2189	1989	1801
	energy, ft lb	2601	2175	1808	1493	1224
	arc, inches		+2.3	0	-9.6	-27.9
Rem. 175 PSP Core-Lokt	velocity, fps	2650	2445	2248	2061	1883
	energy, ft-lb	2728	2322	1964	1650	1378
	arc, inches		+2.2	0	-9.1	-26.4
Speer 160 Grand Slam	velocity, fps	2600	2376	2164	1962	
	energy, ft-lb	2401	2006	1663	1368	
	arc, inches		+2.3	0	-9.8	-28.6
Speer 175 Grand Slam	velocity, fps	2650	2461	2280	2106	
	energy, ft-lb	2728	2353	2019	1723	
	arc, inches		+2.4	0	-9.2	-26.2

7x65 R

CARTRIDGE BULLET	RANGE, YARDS:	0	100	200	300	400
Norma 150 FMJ	velocity, fps	2756	2552	2357	2170	
	energy, ft-lb	2530	2169	1850	1569	
	arc, inches		+1.9	0	-8.2	
Norma 156 Oryx	velocity, fps	2723	2454	2200	1962	
	energy, ft-lb	2569	2086	1678	1334	
	arc, inches		+2.1	0	-9.3	

CARTRIDGE BULLET	RANGE, YARDS:	0	100	200	300	400
Norma 170 Plastic Point	velocity, fps	2625	2390	2167	1956	
	energy, ft-lb	2602	2157	1773	1445	
	arc, inches		+2.3	0	-9.7	
Norma 170 Vulkan	velocity, fps	2657	2392	2143	1909	
	energy, ft-lb	2666	2161	1734	1377	
	arc, inches		+2.3	0	-9.9	
Norma 170 Oryx	velocity, fps	2657	2378	2115	1871	
	energy, ft-lb	2666	2135	1690	1321	
	arc, inches		+2.3	0	-10.1	

.284 WINCHESTER

CARTRIDGE BULLET	RANGE, YARDS:	0	100	200	300	400
Win. 150 Power-Point	velocity, fps	2860	2595	2344	2108	1886
	energy, ft-lb	2724	2243	1830	1480	1185
	arc, inches		+2.1	0	-8.5	-24.8

.280 REMINGTON

CARTRIDGE BULLET	RANGE, YARDS:	0	100	200	300	400
Federal 140 Sierra Pro-Hunt.	velocity, fps	2990	2740	2500	2270	2060
	energy, ft-lb	2770	2325	1940	1605	1320
	arc, inches		+1.6	0	-7.0	-20.8
Federal 140 Trophy Bonded	velocity, fps	2990	2630	2310	2040	1730
	energy, ft-lb	2770	2155	1655	1250	925
	arc, inches		+1.6	0	-8.4	-25.4
Federal 140 Trophy Bonded Tip	velocity, fps	2950	2730	2520	2330	2140
	energy, ft-lb	2705	2320	1980	1680	1420
	arc, inches		+1.6	0	-7.0	-20.6
Federal 140 Tr. Bonded HE	velocity, fps	3150	2850	2570	2300	2050
	energy, ft-lb	3085	2520	2050	1650	1310
	arc, inches		+1.4	0	-6.7	-20.0
Federal 140 Nos. AccuBond And Bal. Tip And Solid Base	velocity, fps	3000	2800	2620	2440	2260
	energy, ft-lb	2800	2445	2130	1845	1590
	arc, inches		+1.5	0	-6.5	-18.9
Federal 150 Hi-Shok	velocity, fps	2890	2670	2460	2260	2060
	energy, ft-lb	2780	2370	2015	1695	1420
	arc, inches		+1.7	0	-7.5	-21.8
Federal 150 Nosler Partition	velocity, fps	2890	2690	2490	2310	2130
	energy, ft-lb	2780	2405	2070	1770	1510.
	arc, inches		+1.7	0	-7.2	-21.1
Federal 150 Nos. AccuBond	velocity, fps	2800	2630	2460	2300	2150
	energy, ft-lb	2785	2455	2155	1885	1645
	arc, inches		+1.8	0	-7.5	-21.5
Federal 160 Trophy Bonded	velocity, fps	2800	2570	2350	2140	1940
	energy, ft-lb	2785	2345	1960	1625	1340
	arc, inches		+1.9	0	-8.3	-24.0
Hornady 139 SPBT LMmoly	velocity, fps	3110	2888	2675	2473	2280.
	energy, ft-lb	2985	2573	2209	1887	1604
	arc, inches		+1.4	0	-6.5	-18.6
Hornady 139 SST Superformance	velocity, fps	3090	2891	2700	2518	2343
	energy, ft-lb	2947	2579	2250	1957	1694
	arc, inches		+1.3	0	-6.1	-17.7
Norma 156 Oryx	velocity, fps	2789	2516	2259	2017	
	energy, ft-lb	2695	2193	1768	1410	
	arc, inches		+2.0	0	-8.8	
Norma 170 Plastic Point	velocity, fps	2707	2468	2241	2026	
	energy, ft-lb	2767	2299	1896	1550	
	arc, inches		+2.1	0	-9.1	
Norma 170 Vulkan	velocity, fps	2592	2346	2113	1894	
	energy, ft-lb	2537	2078	1686	1354	
	arc, inches		+2.4	0	-10.2	
Norma 170 Oryx	velocity, fps	2690	2416	2159	1918	
	energy, ft-lb	2732	2204	1760	1389	
	arc, inches		+2.2	0	-9.7	
Rem. 140 PSP Core-Lokt	velocity, fps	3000	2758	2528	2309	2102
	energy, ft-lb	2797	2363	1986	1657	1373
	arc, inches		+1.5	0	-7.0	-20.5
Rem. 140 PSP boat-tail	velocity, fps	2860	2656	2460	2273	2094
	energy, ft-lb	2542	2192	1881	1606	1363
	arc, inches		+1.7	0	-7.5	-21.7
Rem. 140 Nosler Bal. Tip	velocity, fps	3000	2804	2616	2436	2263
	energy, ft-lb	2799	2445	2128	1848	1593
	arc, inches		+1.5	0	-6.8	-19.0

Centerfire Rifle Ballistics

.280 REMINGTON TO 7MM REMINGTON MAGNUM

CARTRIDGE BULLET	RANGE, YARDS:	0	100	200	300	400
Rem. 140 AccuTip	velocity, fps:	3000	2804	2617	2437	2265
	energy, ft-lb:	2797	2444	2129	1846	1594
	arc, inches:		+1.5	0	-6.8	-19.0
Rem. 150 PSP Core-Lokt	velocity, fps:	2890	2624	2373	2135	1912
	energy, ft-lb:	2781	2293	1875	1518	1217
	arc, inches:		+1.8	0	-8.0	-23.6
Rem. 165 SP Core-Lokt	velocity, fps:	2820	2510	2220	1950	1701
	energy, ft-lb:	2913	2308	1805	1393	1060.
	arc, inches:		+2.0	0	-9.1	-27.4
Speer 145 Grand Slam	velocity, fps:	2900	2619	2354	2105	
	energy, ft-lb:	2707	2207	1784	1426	
	arc, inches:		+2.1	0	-8.4	-24.7
Speer 160 Grand Slam	velocity, fps:	2890	2652	2425	2210	
	energy, ft-lb:	2967	2497	2089	1735	
	arc, inches:		+1.7	0	-7.7	-22.4
Win. 140 Fail Safe	velocity, fps:	3050	2756	2480	2221	1977
	energy, ft-lb:	2893	2362	1913	1533	1216
	arc, inches:		+1.5	0	-7.2	-21.5
Win. 140 Ballistic Silvertip	velocity, fps:	3040	2842	2653	2471	2297
	energy, ft-lb:	2872	2511	2187	1898	1640
	arc, inches:		+1.4	0	-6.3	-18.4

.280 ACKLEY IMPROVED

CARTRIDGE BULLET	RANGE, YARDS:	0	100	200	300	400
Nosler 140 AccuBond	velocity, fps:	3150	2947	2753	2567	2389
	energy, ft-lb:	3084	2700	2355	2048	1774
	arc, inches:	-1.5	+1.1	0	-5.0	-16.8
Nosler 150 ABLR	velocity, fps:	2930	2775	2626	2482	2342
	energy, ft-lb:	2858	2565	2297	2052	1827
	arc, inches:	-1.5	+1.5	0	-6.6	-18.7
Nosler 160 Partition	velocity, fps:	2950	2752	2562	2380	2206
	energy, ft-lb:	3091	2690	2332	2013	1729
	arc, inches:	-1.5	+1.5	0	-6.7	-19.4

7MM REMINGTON MAGNUM

CARTRIDGE BULLET	RANGE, YARDS:	0	100	200	300	400
A-Square 175 Monolithic Solid	velocity, fps:	2860	2557	2273	2008	1771
	energy, ft-lb:	3178	2540	2008	1567	1219
	arc, inches:		+1.92	0	-8.7	-25.9
Black Hills 140 Nos. Bal. Tip	velocity, fps:	3150				
	energy, ft-lb:	3084				
	arc, inches:					
Black Hills 140 Barnes XLC	velocity, fps:	3150				
	energy, ft-lb:	3084				
Black Hills 140 Nos. Partition	velocity, fps:	3150				
	energy, ft-lb:	3084				
Federal 140 Nosler Bal. Tip And AccuBond	velocity, fps:	3110	2910	2720	2530	2360.
	energy, ft-lb:	3005	2630	2295	1995	1725
	arc, inches:		+1.3	0	-6.0	-17.4
Federal 140 Nosler Partition	velocity, fps:	3150	2930	2710	2510	2320
	energy, ft-lb:	3085	2660	2290	1960	1670
	arc, inches:		+1.3	0	-6.0	-17.5
Federal 140 Trophy Bonded	velocity, fps:	3150	2910	2680	2460	2250.
	energy, ft-lb:	3085	2630	2230	1880	1575
	arc, inches:		+1.3	0	-6.1	-18.1
Federal 140 Trophy Copper	velocity, fps:	3150	2950	2760	2570	2400
	energy, ft-lb:	3085	2705	2360	2055	1785
	arc, inches:		+1.3	0	-5.9	-16.9
Federal 150 Hi-Shok	velocity, fps:	3110	2830	2570	2320	2090
	energy, ft-lb:	3220	2670	2200	1790	1450
	arc, inches:		+1.4	0	-6.7	-19.9
Federal 150 Nosler Bal. Tip	velocity, fps:	3110	2910	2720	2540	2370
	energy, ft-lb:	3220	2825	2470	2150	1865
	arc, inches:		+1.3	0	-6.0	-17.4
Federal 150 Nos. Solid Base	velocity, fps:	3100	2890	2690	2500	2310
	energy, ft-lb:	3200	2780	2405	2075	1775
	arc, inches:		+1.3	0	-6.2	-17.8
Federal 150 Sierra GameKing BTSP	velocity, fps:	3110	2920	2750	2580	2410
	energy, ft-lb:	3220	2850	2510	2210	1930
	arc, inches:		+1.3 0	-5.9	-17.0	

CARTRIDGE BULLET	RANGE, YARDS:	0	100	200	300	400
Federal 150 Trophy Copper	velocity, fps:	3025	2830	2650	2470	2300
	energy, ft-lb:	3045	2675	2335	2035	1765
	arc, inches:		+1.4	0	-6.4	-18.4
Federal 160 Barnes XLC	velocity, fps:	2940	2760	2580	2410	2240
	energy, ft-lb:	3070	2695	2360	2060	1785
	arc, inches:		+1.5	0	-6.8	-19.6
Federal 160 Sierra Pro-Hunt.	velocity, fps:	2940	2730	2520	2320	2140
	energy, ft-lb:	3070	2640	2260	1920	1620
	arc, inches:		+1.6	0	-7.1	-20.6
Federal 160 Nosler Partition	velocity, fps:	2950	2770	2590	2420	2250.
	energy, ft-lb:	3090	2715	2375	2075	1800
	arc, inches:		+1.5	0	-6.7	-19.4
Federal 160 Nos. AccuBond	velocity, fps:	2950	2770	2600	2440	2280.
	energy, ft-lb:	3090	2730	2405	2110	1845
	arc, inches:		+1.5	0	-6.6	-19.1
Federal 160 Trophy Bonded	velocity, fps:	2940	2660	2390	2140	1900
	energy, ft-lb:	3070	2505	2025	1620	1280.
	arc, inches:		+1.7	0	-7.9	-23.3
Federal 165 Sierra GameKing BTSP	velocity, fps:	2950	2800	2650	2510	2370.
	energy, ft-lb:	3190	2865	2570	2300	2050
	arc, inches:		+1.5	0	-6.4	-18.4
Federal 175 Hi-Shok	velocity, fps:	2860	2650	2440	2240	2060
	energy, ft-lb:	3180	2720	2310	1960	1640
	arc, inches:		+1.7	0	-7.6	-22.1
Federal 175 Trophy Bonded	velocity, fps:	2860	2600	2350	2120	1900
	energy, ft-lb:	3180	2625	2150	1745	1400
	arc, inches:		+1.8	0	-8.2	-24.0
Hornady 139 SPBT	velocity, fps:	3150	2933	2727	2530	2341
	energy, ft-lb:	3063	2656	2296	1976	1692
	arc, inches:		+1.2	0	-6.1	-17.7
Hornady 139 SPBT HMmoly	velocity, fps:	3250	3041	2822	2613	2413
	energy, ft-lb:	3300	2854	2458	2106	1797
	arc, inches:		+1.1 0	-5.7	-16.6	
Hornady 139 SST (or Interbond)	velocity, fps:	3150	2948	2754	2569	2391
	energy, ft-lb:	3062	2681	2341	2037	1764
	arc, inches:		+1.1	0	-5.7	-16.7
Hornady 139 SST Custom Lite	velocity, fps:	2800	2613	2434	2262	2097
	energy, ft-lb:	2420	2108	1829	1579	1357
	arc, inches:		+1.8	0	-7.7	-22.2
Hornady 139 SST LM (or Interbond)	velocity, fps:	3250	3044	2847	2657	2475
	energy, ft-lb:	3259	2860	2501	2178	1890
	arc, inches:		+1.1	0	-5.5	-16.2
Hornady 139 SPBT HMmoly	velocity, fps:	3250	3041	2822	2613	2413
	energy, ft-lb:	3300	2854	2458	2106	1797.
	arc, inches:		+1.1	0	-5.7	-16.6
Hornady 154 Soft Point	velocity, fps:	3035	2814	2604	2404	2212
	energy, ft-lb:	3151	2708	2319	1977	1674
	arc, inches:		+1.3	0	-6.7	-19.3
Hornady 154 SST (or Interbond)	velocity, fps:	3035	2850	2672	2501	2337
	energy, ft-lb:	3149	2777	2441	2139	1867
	arc, inches:		+1.4	0	-6.5	-18.7
Hornady 162 SP boat-tail	velocity, fps:	2940	2757	2582	2413	2251
	energy, ft-lb:	3110	2735	2399	2095	1823
	arc, inches:		+1.6	0	-6.7	-19.7
Hornady 162 SST Superformance	velocity, fps:	3030	2856	2689	2527	2372
	energy, ft-lb:	3302	2933	2600	2298	2023
	arc, inches:		+1.4	0	-6.2	-17.8
Hornady 175 SP	velocity, fps:	2860	2650	2440	2240	2060.
	energy, ft-lb:	3180	2720	2310	1960	1640
	arc, inches:		+2.0	0	-7.9	-22.7
Norma 140 Nosler Bal. Tip	velocity, fps:	3150	2936	2732	2537	
	energy, ft-lb:	3085	2680	2320	2001	
	arc, inches:		+1.2	0	-5.9	
Norma 140 Barnes X TS	velocity, fps:	3117	2912	2716	2529	
	energy, ft-lb:	3021	2637	2294	1988	
	arch, inches:		+1.3	0	-6.0	
Norma 150 Scirocco	velocity, fps:	3117	2934	2758	2589	
	energy, ft-lb:	3237	2869	2535	2234	
	arc, inches:		+1.2	0	-5.8	
Norma 156 Oryx	velocity, fps:	2953	2670	2404	2153	
	energy, ft-lb:	3021	2470	2002	1607	
	arc, inches:		+1.7	0	-7.7	

7MM REMINGTON MAGNUM TO 7MM WINCHESTER SHORT MAGNUM

BALLISTICS

CARTRIDGE BULLET	RANGE, YARDS:	0	100	200	300	400
Norma 170 Vulkan	velocity, fps:	3018	2747	2493	2252	
	energy, ft-lb:	3439	2850	2346	1914	
	arc, inches:		+1.5	0	-2.8	
Norma 170 Oryx	velocity, fps:	2887	2601	2333	2080	
	energy, ft-lb:	3147	2555	2055	1634	
	arc, inches:		+1.8	0	-8.2	
Norma 170 Plastic Point	velocity, fps:	3018	2762	2519	2290	
	energy, ft-lb:	3439	2880	2394	1980	
	arc, inches:		+1.5	0	-7.0	
PMC 140 Barnes X	velocity, fps:	3000	2808	2624	2448	2279
	energy, ft-lb:	2797	2451	2141	1863	1614
	arc, inches:		+1.5	0	-6.6	18.9
PMC 140 Pointed Soft Point	velocity, fps:	3099	2878	2668	2469	2279
	energy, ft-lb:	2984	2574	2212	1895	1614
	arc, inches:		+1.4	0	-6.2	-18.1
PMC 140 SP boat-tail	velocity, fps:	3125	2891	2669	2457	2255
	energy, ft-lb:	3035	2597	2213	1877	1580
	arc, inches:		+1.4	0	-6.3	-18.4
PMC 160 Barnes X	velocity, fps:	2800	2639	2484	2334	2189
	energy, ft-lb:	2785	2474	2192	1935	1703
	arc, inches:		+1.8	0	-7.4	-21.2
PMC 160 Pointed Soft Point	velocity, fps:	2914	2748	2586	2428	2276
	energy, ft-lb:	3016	2682	2375	2095	1840
	arc, inches:		+1.6	0	-6.7	-19.4
PMC 160 SP boat-tail	velocity, fps:	2900	2696	2501	2314	2135
	energy, ft-lb:	2987	2582	2222	1903	1620
	arc, inches:		+1.7	0	-7.2	-21.0
PMC 175 Pointed Soft Point	velocity, fps:	2860	2645	2442	2244	2957
	energy, ft-lb:	3178	2718	2313	1956	1644
	arc, inches:		+2.0	0	-7.9	-22.7
Remington 140 Copper Solid Tipped	velocity, fps:	3175	2964	2762	2570	2385
	energy, ft-lb:	3133	2730	2372	2053	1768
	arc, inches:		+1.4	0	-6.0	-17.6
Rem. 140 PSP Core-Lokt mr	velocity, fps:	2710	2482	2265	2059	1865
	energy, ft-lb:	2283	1915	1595	1318	1081
	arc, inches:		+1.0	-2.5	-12.8	-31.3
Rem. 140 PSP Core-Lokt	velocity, fps:	3175	2923	2684	2458	2243
	energy, ft-lb:	3133	2655	2240	1878	1564
	arc, inches:		+2.2	+1.9	-3.2	-14.2
Rem. 140 PSP boat-tail	velocity, fps:	3175	2956	2747	2547	2356
	energy, ft-lb:	3133	2715	2345	2017	1726
	arc, inches:		+2.2	+1.6	-3.1	-13.4
Rem. 150 AccuTip	velocity, fps:	3110	2926	2749	2579	2415
	energy, ft-lb:	3221	2850	2516	2215	1943
	arc, inches:		+1.3	0	-5.9	-17.0
Rem. 150 PSP Core-Lokt	velocity, fps:	3110	2830	2568	2320	2085
	energy, ft-lb:	3221	2667	2196	1792	1448
	arc, inches:		+1.3	0	-6.6	-20.2
Rem. 150 Nosler Bal. Tip	velocity, fps:	3110	2912	2723	2542	2367
	energy, ft-lb:	3222	2825	2470	2152	1867
	arc, inches:		+1.2	0	-5.9	-17.3
Rem. 150 Swift Scirocco	velocity, fps:	3110	2927	2751	2582	2419
	energy, ft-lb:	3221	2852	2520	2220	1948
	arc, inches:		+1.3	0	-5.9	-17.0
Rem. 160 Swift A-Frame	velocity, fps:	2900	2659	2430	2212	2006
	energy, ft-lb:	2987	2511	2097	1739	1430
	arc, inches:		+1.7	0	-7.6	-22.4
Rem. 160 Nosler Partition	velocity, fps:	2950	2752	2563	2381	2207
	energy, ft-lb:	3091	2690	2333	2014	1730
	arc, inches:		+0.6	-1.9	-9.6	-23.6
Rem. 175 PSP Core-Lokt	velocity, fps:	2860	2645	2440	2244	2057
	energy, ft-lb:	3178	2718	2313	1956	1644
	arc, inches:		+1.7	0	-7.6	-22.1
Speer 145 Grand Slam	velocity, fps:	3140	2843	2565	2304	
	energy, ft-lb:	3174	2602	2118	1708	
	arc, inches:		+1.4	0	-6.7	

CARTRIDGE BULLET	RANGE, YARDS:	0	100	200	300	400
Speer 175 Grand Slam	velocity, fps:	2850	2653	2463	2282	
	energy, ft-lb:	3156	2734	2358	2023	
	arc, inches:		+1.7	0	-7.5	-21.7
Win. 140 Fail Safe	velocity, fps:	3150	2861	2589	2333	2092
	energy, ft-lb:	3085	2544	2085	1693	1361
	arc, inches:		+1.4	0	-6.6	-19.5
Win. 140 Ballistic Silvertip	velocity, fps:	3100	2889	2687	2494	2310
	energy, ft-lb:	2988	2595	2245	1934	1659.
	arc, inches:		+1.3	0	-6.2	-17.9
Win. 140 AccuBond CT	velocity, fps:	3180	2965	2760	2565	2377
	energy, ft-lb:	3143	2733	2368	2044	1756
	arc, inches:		+1.2	0	-5.8	-16.9
Win. 150 Power-Point	velocity, fps:	3090	2812	2551	2304	2071
	energy, ft-lb:	3181	2634	2167	1768	1429
	arc, inches:		+1.5	0	-6.8	-20.2
Win. 150 Power-Point Plus	velocity, fps:	3130	2849	2586	2337	2102
	energy, ft-lb:	3264	2705	2227	1819	1472
	arc, inches:		+1.4	0	-6.6	-19.6
Win. 150 Ballistic Silvertip	velocity, fps:	3100	2903	2714	2533	2359
	energy, ft-lb:	3200	2806	2453	2136	1853
	arc, inches:		+1.3	0	-6.0	-17.5
Win. 160 AccuBond	velocity, fps:	2950	2766	2590	2420	2257
	energy, ft-lb:	3091	2718	2382	2080	1809
	arc, inches:		+1.5	0	-6.7	-19.4
Win. 160 Partition Gold	velocity, fps:	2950	2743	2546	2357	2176
	energy, ft-lb:	3093	2674	2303	1974	1682
	arc, inches:		+1.6	0	-6.9	-20.1
Win. 160 Fail Safe	velocity, fps:	2920	2678	2449	2331	2025
	energy, ft-lb:	3030	2549	2131	1769	1457
	arc, inches:		+1.7	0	-7.5	-22.0
Win. 175 Power-Point	velocity, fps:	2860	2645	2440	2244	2057
	energy, ft-lb:	3178	2718	2313	1956	1644
	arc, inches:		+2.0	0	-7.9	-22.7

7MM REMINGTON SHORT ULTRA MAGNUM

CARTRIDGE BULLET	RANGE, YARDS:	0	100	200	300	400
Rem. 140 PSP C-L Ultra	velocity, fps:	3175	2934	2707	2490	2283
	energy, ft-lb:	3133	2676	2277	1927	1620.
	arc, inches:		+1.3	0	-6.0	-17.7
Rem. 150 PSP Core-Lokt	velocity, fps:	3110	2828	2563	2313	2077
	energy, ft-lb:	3221	2663	2188	1782	1437
	arc, inches:		+2.5	+2.1	-3.6	-15.8
Rem. 160 Partition	velocity, fps:	2960	2762	2572	2390	2215
	energy, ft-lb:	3112	2709	2350	2029	1744
	arc, inches:		+2.6	+2.2	-3.6	-15.4
Rem. 160 PSP C-L Ultra	velocity, fps:	2960	2733	2518	2313	2117
	energy, ft-lb:	3112	2654	2252	1900	1592
	arc, inches:		+2.7	+2.2	-3.7	-16.2

7MM WINCHESTER SHORT MAGNUM

CARTRIDGE BULLET	RANGE, YARDS:	0	100	200	300	400
Federal 140 Nos. AccuBond	velocity, fps:	3250	3040	2840	2660	2470
	energy, ft-lb:	3285	2875	2515	2190	1900
	arc, inches:		+1.1	0	-5.5	-15.8
Federal 140 Nos. Bal. Tip	velocity, fps:	3310	3100	2900	2700	2520
	energy, ft-lb:	3405	2985	2610	2270	1975
	arc, inches:		+1.1	0	-5.2	15.2
Federal 150 Nos. Solid Base	velocity, fps:	3230	3010	2800	2600	2410
	energy, ft-lb:	3475	3015	2615	2255	1935
	arc, inches:		+1.3	0	-5.6	-16.3
Federal 150 Trophy Copper	velocity, fps:	3140	2940	2750	2570	2400
	energy, ft-lb:	3285	2885	2525	2205	1915
	arc, inches:		+1.3	0	-5.9	-16.9
Federal 160 Nos. AccuBond	velocity, fps:	3120	2940	2760	2590	2430
	energy, ft-lb:	3460	3065	2710	2390	2095
	arc, inches:		+1.3	0	-5.9	-16.8
Federal 160 Nos. Partition	velocity, fps:	3160	2950	2750	2560	2380.
	energy, ft-lb:	3545	3095	2690	2335	2015.
	arc, inches:		+1.2	0	-5.9	-16.9

Centerfire Rifle Ballistics

7MM WINCHESTER SHORT MAGNUM TO 7MM REMINGTON ULTRA MAGNUM

CARTRIDGE BULLET	RANGE, YARDS:	0	100	200	300	400
Federal 160 Barnes TS	velocity, fps:	2990	2780	2590	2400	2220
	energy, ft-lb:	3175	2755	2380	2045	1750
	arc, inches:		+1.5	0	-6.6	-19.4
Federal 160 Trophy Bonded	velocity, fps:	3120	2880	2650	2440	2230
	energy, ft-lb:	3460	2945	2500	2105	1765
	arc, inches:		+1.4	0	-6.3	-18.5
Federal 160 Trophy Bonded Tip	velocity, fps:	3000	2820	2640	2470	2310
	energy, ft-lb:	3195	2820	2480	2170	1895
	arc, inches:		+1.5	0	-6.4	-18.5
Win. 140 Bal. Silvertip	velocity, fps:	3225	3008	2801	2603	2414
	energy, ft-lb:	3233	2812	2438	2106	1812
	arc, inches:		+1.2	0	-5.6	-16.4
Win. 140 AccuBond CT	velocity, fps:	3225	3008	2801	2604	2415
	energy, ft-lb:	3233	2812	2439	2107	1812
	arc, inches:		+1.2	0	-5.6	-16.4
Win. 150 Power Point	velocity, fps:	3200	2915	2648	2396	2157
	energy, ft-lb:	3410	2830	2335	1911	1550
	arc, inches:		+1.3	0	-6.3	-18.6
Win. 160 AccuBond	velocity, fps:	3050	2862	2682	2509	2342
	energy, ft-lb:	3306	2911	2556	2237	1950
	arc, inches:		1.4	0	-6.2	-17.9
Win. 160 Fail Safe	velocity, fps:	2990	2744	2512	2291	2081
	energy, ft-lb:	3176	2675	2241	1864	1538
	arc, inches:		+1.6	0	-7.1	-20.8

7MM WEATHERBY MAGNUM

CARTRIDGE BULLET	RANGE, YARDS:	0	100	200	300	400
Federal 160 Nosler Partition	velocity, fps:	3050	2850	2650	2470	2290
	energy, ft-lb:	3305	2880	2505	2165	1865
	arc, inches:		+1.4	0	-6.3	-18.4
Federal 160 Sierra GameKing BTSP	velocity, fps:	3050	2880	2710	2560	2400
	energy, ft-lb:	3305	2945	2615	2320	2050
	arc, inches:		+1.4	0	-6.1	-17.4
Federal 160 Trophy Bonded	velocity, fps:	3050	2730	2420	2140	1880.
	energy, ft-lb:	3305	2640	2085	1630	1255
	arc, inches:		+1.6	0	-7.6	-22.7
Federal 160 Trophy Bonded Tip	velocity, fps:	3100	2910	2730	2560	2390
	energy, ft-lb:	3415	3015	2655	2330	2035
	arc, inches:		+1.3	0	-6.0	-17.2
Hornady 139 GMX Superformance	velocity, fps:	3300	3091	2891	2701	2519
	energy, ft-lb:	3361	2948	2580	2252	1958
	arc, inches:		+1.1	0	-5.2	-15.2
Hornady 154 Soft Point	velocity, fps:	3200	2971	2753	2546	2348.
	energy, ft-lb:	3501	3017	2592	2216	1885
	arc, inches:		+1.2	0	-5.8	-17.0
Hornady 154 SST (or Interbond)	velocity, fps:	3200	3009	2825	2648	2478
	energy, ft-lb:	3501	3096	2729	2398	2100
	arc, inches:		+1.2	0	-5.7	-16.5
Hornady 175 Soft Point	velocity, fps:	2910	2709	2516	2331	2154
	energy, ft-lb:	3290	2850	2459	2111	1803
	arc, inches:		+1.6	0	-7.1	-20.6
Wby. 139 Pointed Expanding	velocity, fps:	3340	3079	2834	2601	2380.
	energy, ft-lb:	3443	2926	2478	2088	1748
	arc, inches:		+2.9	+3.6	0	-8.7
Wby. 140 Nosler Partition	velocity, fps:	3303	3069	2847	2636	2434
	energy, ft-lb:	3391	2927	2519	2159	1841
	arc, inches:		+2.9	+3.6	0	-8.5
Wby. 150 Nosler Bal. Tip	velocity, fps:	3300	3093	2896	2708	2527
	energy, ft-lb:	3627	3187	2793	2442	2127
	arc, inches:		+2.8	+3.5	0	-8.2
Wby. 150 Barnes X	veloctiy, fps:	3100	2901	2710	2527	2352
	energy, ft-lb:	3200	2802	2446	2127	1842
	arc, inches:		+3.3	+4.0	0	-9.4
Wby. 154 Pointed Expanding	velocity, fps:	3260	3028	2807	2597	2397
	energy, ft-lb:	3634	3134	2694	2307	1964
	arc, inches:		+3.0	+3.7	0	-8.8
Wby. 160 Nosler Partition	velocity, fps:	3200	2991	2791	2600	2417
	energy, ft-lb:	3638	3177	2767	2401	2075.
	arc, inches:		+3.1	+3.8	0	-8.9
Wby. 175 Pointed Expanding	velocity, fps:	3070	2861	2662	2471	2288
	energy, ft-lb:	3662	3181	2753	2373	2034
	arc, inches:		+3.5	+4.2	0	-9.9

7MM DAKOTA

CARTRIDGE BULLET	RANGE, YARDS:	0	100	200	300	400
Dakota 140 Barnes X	velocity, fps:	3500	3253	3019	2798	2587
	energy, ft-lb:	3807	3288	2833	2433	2081
	arc, inches:		+2.0	+2.1	-1.5	-9.6
Dakota 160 Barnes X	velocity, fps:	3200	3001	2811	2630	2455
	energy, ft-lb:	3637	3200	2808	2456	2140
	arc, inches:		+2.1	+1.9	-2.8	-12.5

7MM STW

CARTRIDGE BULLET	RANGE, YARDS:	0	100	200	300	400
A-Square 140 Nos. Bal. Tip	velocity, fps:	3450	3254	3067	2888	2715
	energy, ft-lb:	3700	3291	2924	2592	2292
	arc, inches:		+2.2	+3.0	0	-7.3
A-Square 160 Nosler Part.	velocity, fps:	3250	3071	2900	2735	2576.
	energy, ft-lb:	3752	3351	2987	2657	2357
	arc, inches:		+2.8	+3.5	0	-8.2
A-Square 160 SP boat-tail	velocity, fps:	3250	3087	2930	2778	2631
	energy, ft-lb:	3752	3385	3049	2741	2460
	arc, inches:		+2.8	+3.4	0	-8.0
Federal 140 Trophy Bonded	velocity, fps:	3330	3080	2850	2630	2420
	energy, ft-lb:	3435	2950	2520	2145	1815
	arc, inches:		+1.1	0	-5.4	-15.8
Federal 150 Trophy Bonded	velocity, fps:	3250	3010	2770	2560	2350.
	energy, ft-lb:	3520	3010	2565	2175	1830
	arc, inches:		+1.2	0	-5.7	-16.7
Federal 160 Sierra GameKing BTSP	velocity, fps:	3200	3020	2850	2670	2530.
	energy, ft-lb:	3640	3245	2890	2570	2275
	arc, inches:		+1.1	0	-5.5	-15.7
Federal 160 Trophy Bonded Tip	velocity, fps:	3100	2910	2730	2560	2390
	energy, ft-lb:	3415	3015	2655	2330	2035
	arc, inches:		+1.3	0	-6.0	-17.2
Nosler 175 ABLR	velocity, fps:	2900	2760	2625	2493	2366
	energy, ft-lb:	3267	2960	2677	2416	2175
	arc, inches:	-1.5	+1.5	0	-6.6	-18.8
Rem. 140 PSP Core-Lokt	velocity, fps:	3325	3064	2818	2585	2364
	energy, ft-lb:	3436	2918	2468	2077	1737
	arc, inches:		+2.0	+1.7	-2.9	-12.8
Rem. 140 Swift A-Frame	velocity, fps:	3325	3020	2735	2467	2215
	energy, ft-lb:	3436	2834	2324	1892	1525
	arc, inches:		+2.1	+1.8	-3.1	-13.8
Speer 145 Grand Slam	velocity, fps:	3300	2992	2075	2435	
	energy, ft-lb:	3506	2882	2355	1909	
	arc, inches:		+1.2	0	-6.0	-17.8
Win. 140 Ballistic Silvertip	velocity, fps:	3320	3100	2890	2690	2499
	energy, ft-lb:	3427	2982	2597	2250	1941
	arc, inches:		+1.1	0	-5.2	-15.2
Win. 150 Power-Point	velocity, fps:	3250	2957	2683	2424	2181
	energy, ft-lb:	3519	2913	2398	1958	1584
	arc, inches:		+1.2	0	-6.1	-18.1
Win. 160 Fail Safe	velocity, fps:	3150	2894	2652	2422	2204
	energy, ft-lb:	3526	2976	2499	2085	1727
	arc, inches:		+1.3	0	-6.3	-18.5

7MM REMINGTON ULTRA MAGNUM

CARTRIDGE BULLET	RANGE, YARDS:	0	100	200	300	400
Nosler 175 ABLR	velocity, fps:	3040	2896	2756	2621	2490
	energy, ft-lb:	3590	3258	2952	2669	2409
	arc, inches:	-1.5	+1.3	0	-5.9	-16.9
Rem. 140 PSP Core-Lokt	velocity, fps:	3425	3158	2907	2669	2444
	energy, ft-lb:	3646	3099	2626	2214	1856
	arc, inches:		+1.8	+1.6	-2.7	-11.9
Rem. 140 Nosler Partition	velocity, fps:	3425	3184	2956	2740	2534
	energy, ft-lb:	3646	3151	2715	2333	1995
	arc, inches:		+1.7	+1.6	-2.6	-11.4
Rem. 160 Nosler Partition	velocity, fps:	3200	2991	2791	2600	2417
	energy, ft-lb:	3637	3177	2767	2401	2075
	arc, inches:		+2.1	+1.8	-3.0	-12.9

7.21 (.284) FIREHAWK

CARTRIDGE BULLET	RANGE, YARDS:	0	100	200	300	400
Lazzeroni 140 Nosler Part.	velocity, fps:	3580	3349	3130	2923	2724
	energy, ft-lb:	3985	3488	3048	2656	2308
	arc, inches:		+2.2	+2.9	0	-7.0
Lazzeroni 160 Swift A-Fr.	velocity, fps:	3385	3167	2961	2763	2574
	energy, ft-lb:	4072	3565	3115	2713	2354
	arc, inches:		+2.6	+3.3	0	-7.8

7.5x55 SWISS

CARTRIDGE BULLET	RANGE, YARDS:	0	100	200	300	400
Norma 180 Soft Point	velocity, fps:	2651	2432	2223	2025	
	energy, ft-lb:	2810	2364	1976	1639	
	arc, inches:		+2.2	0	-9.3	
Norma 180 Oryx	velocity, fps:	2493	2222	1968	1734	
	energy, ft-lb:	2485	1974	1549	1201	
	arc, inches:		+2.7	0	-11.8	

7.62x39 RUSSIAN

CARTRIDGE BULLET	RANGE, YARDS:	0	100	200	300	400
Federal 123 Hi-Shok	velocity, fps:	2300	2030	1780	1550	1350
	energy, ft-lb:	1445	1125	860	655	500.
	arc, inches:		0	-7.0	-25.1	
Federal 124 FMJ	velocity, fps:	2300	2030	1780	1560	1360
	energy, ft-lb:	1455	1135	875	670	510
	arc, inches:		+3.5	0	-14.6	-43.5
PMC 123 FMJ	velocity, fps:	2350	2072	1817	1583	1368
	energy, ft-lb:	1495	1162	894	678	507
	arc, inches:		0	-5.0	-26.4	-67.8
PMC 125 Pointed Soft Point	velocity, fps:	2320	2046	1794	1563	1350
	energy, ft-lb:	1493	1161	893	678	505.
	arc, inches:		0	-5.2	-27.5	-70.6
Rem. 125 Pointed Soft Point	velocity, fps:	2365	2062	1783	1533	1320
	energy, ft-lb:	1552	1180	882	652	483
	arc, inches:		0	-6.7	-24.5	
Win. 123 Soft Point	velocity, fps:	2365	2033	1731	1465	1248
	energy, ft-lb:	1527	1129	818	586	425
	arc, inches:		+3.8	0	-15.4	-46.3

.30 CARBINE

CARTRIDGE BULLET	RANGE, YARDS:	0	100	200	300	400
Federal 110 Hi-Shok RN	velocity, fps:	1990	1570	1240	1040	920
	energy, ft-lb:	965	600	375	260	210
	arc, inches:		0	-12.8	-46.9	
Federal 110 FMJ	velocity, fps:	1990	1570	1240	1040	920
	energy, ft-lb:	965	600	375	260	210
	arc, inches:		0	-12.8	-46.9	
Hornady 110 FTX	velocity, fps:	2000	1601	1279	1067	
(20-inch barrel)	energy, ft-lb:	977	626	399	278	
	arc, inches:		0	-12.9	-47.2	
Magtech 110 FMC	velocity, fps:	1990	1654			
	energy, ft-lb:	965	668			
	arc, inches:		0			
PMC 110 FMJ	(and RNSP)velocity, fps:	1927	1548	1248		
	energy, ft-lb:	906	585	380		
	arc, inches:		0	-14.2		
Rem. 110 Soft Point	velocity, fps:	1990	1567	1236	1035	923
	energy, ft-lb:	967	600	373	262	208
	arc, inches:		0	-12.9	-48.6	
Win. 110 Hollow Soft Point	velocity, fps:	1990	1567	1236	1035	923
	energy, ft-lb:	967	600	373	262	208
	arc, inches:		0	-13.5	-49.9	

.30 T/C HORNADAY

CARTRIDGE BULLET	RANGE, YARDS:	0	100	200	300	400
Hornady 150	velocity, fps	3000	2772	2555	2348	
	energy, ft-lb	2997	2558	2176	1836	
	arc, inches	-1.5	+1.5	0	-6.9	
Hornady 165	velocity, fps	2850	2644	2447	2258	
	energy, ft-lb	2975	2560	2193	1868	
	arc, inches	-1.5	+1.7	0	-7.6	

.30-30 WINCHESTER

CARTRIDGE BULLET	RANGE, YARDS:	0	100	200	300	400
Federal 125 Hi-Shok HP	velocity, fps:	2570	2090	1660	1320	1080
	energy, ft-lb:	1830	1210	770	480	320
	arc, inches:		+3.3	0	-16.0	-50.9
Federal 150 Hi-Shok FN	velocity, fps:	2390	2020	1680	1400	1180
	energy, ft-lb:	1900	1355	945	650	460
	arc, inches:		+3.6	0	-15.9	-49.1
Federal 170 Hi-Shok RN	velocity, fps:	2200	1900	1620	1380	1190
	energy, ft-lb:	1830	1355	990	720	535
	arc, inches:		+4.1	0	-17.4	-52.4
Federal 170 Sierra Pro-Hunt.	velocity, fps:	2200	1820	1500	1240	1060
	energy, ft-lb:	1830	1255	845	575	425
	arc, inches:		+4.5	0	-20.0	-63.5
Federal 170 Nosler Partition	velocity, fps:	2200	1900	1620	1380	1190
	energy, ft-lb:	1830	1355	990	720	535
	arc, inches:		+4.1	0	-17.4	-52.4
Hornady 150 Round Nose	velocity, fps:	2390	1973	1605	1303	1095
	energy, ft-lb:	1902	1296	858	565	399
	arc, inches:		0	-8.2	-30.0	
Hornady 160 Evolution	velocity, fps:	2400	2150	1916	1699	
	energy, ft-lb:	2046	1643	1304	1025	
	arc, inches:		+3.0	0.2	-12.1	
Hornady 170 Flat Point	velocity, fps:	2200	1895	1619	1381	1191
	energy, ft-lb:	1827	1355	989	720	535
	arc, inches:		0	-8.9	-31.1	
Norma 150 Soft Point	velocity, fps:	2329	2008	1716	1459	
	energy, ft-lb:	1807	1344	981	709	
	arc, inches:		+3.6	0	-15.5	
PMC 150 Starfire HP	velocity, fps:	2100	1769	1478		
	energy, ft-lb:	1469	1042	728		
	arc, inches:		0	-10.8		
PMC 150 Flat Nose	velocity, fps:	2300	1943	1627		
	energy, ft-lb:	1762	1257	881		
	arc, inches:		0	-7.8		
PMC 170 Flat Nose	velocity, fps:	2150	1840	1566		
	energy, ft-lb:	1745	1277	926		
	arc, inches:		0	-8.9		
Rem. 55 PSP (sabot)	velocity, fps:	3400	2693	2085	1570	1187
"Accelerator"	energy, ft-lb:	1412	886	521	301	172
	arc, inches:		+1.7	0	-9.9	-34.3
Rem. 150 SP Core-Lokt	velocity, fps:	2390	1973	1605	1303	1095
	energy, ft-lb:	1902	1296	858	565	399
	arc, inches:		0	-7.6	-28.8	
Rem. 170 SP Core-Lokt	velocity, fps:	2200	1895	1619	1381	1191
	energy, ft-lb:	1827	1355	989	720	535
	arc, inches:		0	-8.3	-29.9	
Rem. 170 HP Core-Lokt	velocity, fps:	2200	1895	1619	1381	1191.
	energy, ft-lb:	1827	1355	989	720	535
	arc, inches:		0	-8.3	-29.9	
Speer 150 Flat Nose	velocity, fps:	2370	2067	1788	1538	
	energy, ft-lb:	1870	1423	1065	788	
	arc, inches:		+3.3	0	-14.4	-43.7
Win. 150 Hollow Point	velocity, fps:	2390	2018	1684	1398	1177
	energy, ft-lb:	1902	1356	944	651	461
	arc, inches:		0	-7.7	-27.9	
Win. 150 Power-Point	velocity, fps:	2390	2018	1684	1398	1177
	energy, ft-lb:	1902	1356	944	651	461
	arc, inches:		0	-7.7	-27.9	
Win. 150 Silvertip	velocity,fps:	2390	2018	1684	1398	1177
	energy, ft-lb:	1902	1356	944	651	461
	arc, inches:		0	-7.7	-27.9	

Centerfire Rifle Ballistics

.30-30 WINCHESTER TO .308 WINCHESTER

CARTRIDGE BULLET	RANGE, YARDS:	0	100	200	300	400
Win. 150 Power-Point Plus	velocity, fps:	2480	2095	1747	1446	1209
	energy, ft-lb:	2049	1462	1017	697	487
	arc, inches:		0	-6.5	-24.5	
Win. 170 Power-Point	velocity, fps:	2200	1895	1619	1381	1191
	energy, ft-lb:	1827	1355	989	720	535.
	arc, inches:		0	-8.9	-31.1	
Win. 170 Silvertip	velocity, fps:	2200	1895	1619	1381	1191
	energy, ft-lb:	1827	1355	989	720	535
	arc, inches:		0	-8.9	-31.1	

.300 SAVAGE

CARTRIDGE BULLET	RANGE, YARDS:	0	100	200	300	400
Federal 150 Hi-Shok	velocity, fps:	2630	2350	2100	1850	1630
	energy, ft-lb:	2305	1845	1460	1145	885
	arc, inches:		+2.4	0	-10.4	-30.9
Federal 180 Hi-Shok	velocity, fps:	2350	2140	1940	1750	1570
	energy, ft-lb:	2205	1825	1495	1215	985
	arc, inches:		+3.1	0	-12.4	-36.1
Hornady 150 SST	velocity, fps:	2740	2499	2272	2056	1852
	energy, ft-lb:	2500	2081	1718	1407	1143
	arc, inches:		+2.1	0	-8.8	-25.8
Rem. 150 PSP Core-Lokt	velocity, fps:	2630	2354	2095	1853	1631
	energy, ft-lb:	2303	1845	1462	1143	806.
	arc, inches:		+2.4	0	-10.4	-30.9
Rem. 180 SP Core-Lokt	velocity, fps:	2350	2025	1728	1467	1252
	energy, ft-lb:	2207	1639	1193	860	626
	arc, inches:		0	-7.1	-25.9	
Win. 150 Power-Point	velocity, fps:	2630	2311	2015	1743	1500
	energy, ft-lb:	2303	1779	1352	1012	749
	arc, inches:		+2.8	0	-11.5	-34.4

.307 WINCHESTER

CARTRIDGE BULLET	RANGE, YARDS:	0	100	200	300	400
Win. 180 Power-Point	velocity, fps:	2510	2179	1874	1599	1362
	energy, ft-lb:	2519	1898	1404	1022	742
	arc, inches:		+1.5	-3.6	-18.6	-47.1

.30-40 KRAG

CARTRIDGE BULLET	RANGE, YARDS:	0	100	200	300	400
Rem. 180 PSP Core-Lokt	velocity, fps:	2430	2213	2007	1813	1632.
	energy, ft-lb:	2360	1957	1610	1314	1064
	arc, inches, s:		0	-5.6	-18.6	
Win. 180 Power-Point	velocity, fps:	2430	2099	1795	1525	1298
	energy, ft-lb:	2360	1761	1288	929	673
	arc, inches, s:		0	-7.1	-25.0	

7.62x54R RUSSIAN

CARTRIDGE BULLET	RANGE, YARDS:	0	100	200	300	400
Norma 150 Soft Point	velocity, fps:	2953	2622	2314	2028	
	energy, ft-lb:	2905	2291	1784	1370	
	arc, inches:		+1.8	0	-8.3	
Norma 180 Alaska	velocity, fps:	2575	2362	2159	1967	
	energy, ft-lb:	2651	2231	1864	1546	
	arc, inches:		+2.9	0	-12.9	
Winchester 180 FMJ	velocity, fps:	2580	2401	2230	2066	1909
	energy, ft-lb:	2658	2304	1987	1706	1457
	arc, inches:	-1.5	+2.6	0	-9.6	-27.3
Winchester 180 SP	velocity, fps:	2625	2302	2003	1729	1485
	energy, ft-lb:	2751	2117	1603	1195	882
	arc, inches:	-1.5	+2.9	0	-11.6	-34.9

.308 MARLIN EXPRESS

CARTRIDGE BULLET	RANGE, YARDS:	0	100	200	300	400
Hornady 160	velocity, fps	2660	2438	2226	2026	1836
	energy, ft-lb	2513	2111	1761	1457	1197
	arc, inches	-1.5	+3.0	+1.7	-6.7	-23.5
Hornady 140 MonoFlex	velocity, fps:	2800	2532	2279	2040	1818

CARTRIDGE BULLET	RANGE, YARDS:	0	100	200	300	400
	energy, ft-lb:	2437	1992	1614	1294	1027
	arc, inches:	-1.5	+2.0	0	-8.7	-25.8

.308 WINCHESTER

CARTRIDGE BULLET	RANGE, YARDS:	0	100	200	300	400
Black Hills 150 Nosler B. Tip	velocity, fps:	2800				
	energy, ft-lb:	2611				
	arc, inches:					
Black Hills 165 Nosler B. Tip (and SP)	velocity, fps:	2650				
	energy, ft-lb:	2573				
	arc, inches:					
Black Hills 168 Barnes X (and Match)	velocity, fps:	2650				
	energy, ft-lb:	2620				
	arc, inches:					
Black Hills 175 Match	velocity, fps:	2600				
	energy, ft-lb:	2657				
	arc, inches:					
Black Hills 180 AccuBond	velocity, fps:	2600				
	energy, ft-lb:	2701				
Federal 150 Barnes XLC	velocity, fps:	2820	2610	2400	2210	2030
	energy, ft-lb:	2650	2265	1925	1630	1370
	arc, inches:		+1.8 0	-7.8	-22.9	
Federal 150 FMJ Boat-Tail	velocity, fps:	2820	2620	2430	2250	2070
	energy, ft-lb:	2650	2285	1965	1680	1430
	arc, inches:		+1.8 0	-7.7	-22.4	
Federal 150 Hi-Shok	velocity, fps:	2820	2530	2260	2010	1770
	energy, ft-lb:	2650	2140	1705	1345	1050
	arc, inches:		+2.0	0	-8.8	-26.3
Federal 150 Nosler Bal. Tip.	velocity, fps:	2820	2610	2410	2220	2040
	energy, ft-lb:	2650	2270	1935	1640	1380
	arc, inches:		+1.8	0	-7.8	-22.7
Federal 150 Trophy Copper	velocity, fps:	2820	2630	2440	2260	2090
	energy, ft-lb:	2650	2295	1980	1700	1455
	arc, inches:		+1.8	0	-7.6	-22.2
Federal 155 Sierra MatchKg. BTHP	velocity, fps:	2950	2740	2540	2350	2170
	energy, ft-lb:	2995	2585	2225	1905	1620
	arc, inches:		+1.9	0	-8.9	-22.6
Federal 165 Sierra GameKing BTSP	velocity, fps:	2700	2520	2330	2160	1990
	energy, ft-lb:	2670	2310	1990	1700	1450
	arc, inches:		+2.0	0	-8.4	-24.3
Federal 165 Trophy Bonded	velocity, fps:	2700	2440	2200	1970	1760
	energy, ft-lb:	2670	2185	1775	1425	1135
	arc, inches:		+2.2	0	-9.4	-27.7
Federal 165 Tr. Bonded HE	velocity, fps:	2870	2600	2350	2120	1890
	energy, ft-lb:	3020	2485	2030	1640	1310
	arc, inches:		+1.8	0	-8.2	-24.0
Federal 168 Sierra MatchKg. BTHP	velocity, fps:	2600	2410	2230	2060	1890
	energy, ft-lb:	2520	2170	1855	1580	1340.
	arc, inches:		+2.1	0	+8.9	+25.9
Federal 180 Hi-Shok	velocity, fps:	2620	2390	2180	1970	1780
	energy, ft-lb:	2745	2290	1895	1555	1270
	arc, inches:		+2.3	0	-9.7	-28.3
Federal 180 Nosler Partition	velocity, fps:	2620	2430	2240	2060	1890
	energy, ft-lb:	2745	2355	2005	1700	1430.
	arc, inches:		+2.2	0	-9.2	-26.5
Federal 180 Nosler Part. HE	velocity, fps:	2740	2550	2370	2200	2030
	energy, ft-lb:	3000	2600	2245	1925	1645
	arc, inches:		+1.9	0	-8.2	-23.5
Federal 180 Sierra Pro-Hunt.	velocity, fps:	2620	2410	2200	2010	1820
	energy, ft-lb:	2745	2315	1940	1610	1330
	arc, inches:		+2.2	0	-9.3	-27.1
Federal 180 Trophy Bonded Tip	velocity, fps:	2620	2450	2280	2120	1960
	energy, ft-lb:	2745	2390	2070	1790	1535
	arc, inches:		+2.2	0	-8.9	-25.5
Hornady 110 TAP-FPD	velocity, fps:	3165	2830	2519	2228	1957
	energy, ft-lb:	2446	1956	1649	1212	935
	arc, inches:		+1.4	0	-6.9	-20.9
Hornady 110 Urban Tactical	velocity, fps:	3170	2825	2504	2206	1937
	energy, ft-lb:	2454	1950	1532	1189	916
	arc, inches:		+1.5	0	-7.2	-21.2

BALLISTICS

CARTRIDGE BULLET	RANGE, YARDS:	0	100	200	300	400
Hornady 125 SST Custom Lite	velocity, fps:	2675	2389	2121	1871	1642
	energy, ft-lb:	1986	1584	1248	971	748
	arc, inches:		+2.3	0	-10.1	-30.1
Hornady 150 SP boat-tail	velocity, fps:	2820	2560	2315	2084	1866
	energy, ft-lb:	2648	2183	1785	1447	1160
	arc, inches:		+2.0	0	-8.5	-25.2
Hornady 150 SP LM	velocity, fps:	2980	2703	2442	2195	1964
	energy, ft-lb:	2959	2433	1986	1606	1285
	arc, inches:	+1.6 0	-7.5	-22.2		
Hornady 150 SST (or Interbond)	velocity, fps:	2820	2593	2378	2174	1984
	energy, ft-lb:	2648	2240	1884	1574	1311
	arc, inches:		+1.9	0	-8.1	-22.9
Hornady 150 SST LM (or Interbond)	velocity, fps:	3000	2765	2541	2328	2127
	energy, ft-lb:	2997	2545	2150	1805	1506
	arc, inches:		+1.5	0	-7.1	-20.6
Hornady 155 A-Max	velocity, fps:	2815	2610	2415	2229	2051
	energy, ft-lb:	2727	2345	2007	1709	1448
	arc, inches:		+1.9	0	-7.9	-22.6
Hornady 155 TAP-FPD	velocity, fps:	2785	2577	2379	2189	2008
	energy, ft-lb:	2669	2285	1947	1649	1387
	arc, inches:		+1.9	0	-8.0	-23.3
Hornady 165 GMX Superformance	velocity, fps:	2750	2550	2358	2174	1999
	energy, ft-lb:	2771	2381	2037	1732	1464
	arc, inches:		+1.9	0	-8.2	-23.8
Hornady 165 SP boat-tail	velocity, fps:	2700	2496	2301	2115	1937
	energy, ft-lb:	2670	2283	1940	1639	1375
	arc, inches:		+2.0	0	-8.7	-25.2
Hornady 165 SPBT LM	velocity, fps:	2870	2658	2456	2283	2078
	energy, ft-lb:	3019	2589	2211	1877	1583
	arc, inches:		+1.7	0	-7.5	-21.8
Hornady 165 SST LM (or Interbond)	velocity, fps:	2880	2672	2474	2284	2103
	energy, ft-lb:	3038	2616	2242	1911	1620
	arc, inches:		+1.6	0	-7.3	-21.2
Hornady 168 BTHP Match	velocity, fps:	2700	2524	2354	2191	2035.
	energy, ft-lb:	2720	2377	2068	1791	1545
	arc, inches:		+2.0	0	-8.4	-23.9
Hornady 168 BTHP Match LM	velocity, fps:	2640	2630	2429	2238	2056
	energy, ft-lb:	3008	2579	2201	1868	1577
	arc, inches:		+1.8	0	-7.8	-22.4
Hornady 168 A-Max Match	velocity fps:	2620	2446	2280	2120	1972
	energy, ft-lb:	2560	2232	1939	1677	1450
	arc, inches:		+2.6	0	-9.2	-25.6
Hornady 168 A-Max	velocity, fps:	2700	2491	2292	2102	1921
	energy, ft-lb:	2719	2315	1959	1648	1377
	arc, inches:		+2.4	0	-9.0	-25.9
Hornady 168 TAP-FPD	velocity, fps:	2700	2513	2333	2161	1996
	energy, ft-lb:	2719	2355	2030	1742	1486
	arc, inches:		+2.0	0	-8.4	-24.3
Hornady 178 BTHP Match	velocity, fps:	2600	2436	2278	2125	1979
	energy, ft-lb:	2672	2345	2050	1785	1548
	arc, inches:		+2.2	0	-8.9	-25.5
Hornady 180 A-Max Match	velocity, fps:	2550	2397	2249	2106	1974
	energy, ft-lb:	2598	2295	2021	1773	1557
	arc, inches:		+2.7	0	-9.5	-26.2
Norma 150 Nosler Bal. Tip	velocity, fps:	2822	2588	2365	2154	
	energy, ft-lb:	2653	2231	1864	1545	
	arc, inches:		+1.6	0	-7.1	
Norma 150 Soft Point	velocity, fps:	2861	2537	2235	1954	
	energy, ft-lb:	2727	2144	1664	1272	
	arc, inches:		+2.0	0	-9.0	
Norma 165 TXP Swift A-Fr.	velocity, fps:	2700	2459	2231	2015	
	energy, ft-lb:	2672	2216	1824	1488	
	arc, inches:		+2.1	0	-9.1	

CARTRIDGE BULLET	RANGE, YARDS:	0	100	200	300	400
Norma 180 Plastic Point	velocity, fps:	2612	2365	2131	1911	
	energy, ft-lb:	2728	2235	1815	1460	
	arc, inches:		+2.4	0	-10.1	
Norma 180 Nosler Partition	velocity, fps:	2612	2414	2225	2044	
	energy, ft-lb:	2728	2330	1979	1670	
	arc, inches:		+2.2	0	-9.3	
Norma 180 Alaska	velocity, fps:	2612	2269	1953	1667	
	energy, ft-lb:	2728	2059	1526	1111	
	arc, inches:		+2.7	0	-11.9	
Norma 180 Vulkan	velocity, fps:	2612	2325	2056	1806	
	energy, ft-lb:	2728	2161	1690	1304	
	arc, inches:		+2.5	0	-10.8	
Norma 180 Oryx	velocity, fps:	2612	2305	2019	1755	
	energy, ft-lb:	2728	2124	1629	1232	
	arc, inches:		+2.5	0	-11.1	
Norma 200 Vulkan	velocity, fps:	2461	2215	1983	1767	
	energy, ft-lb:	2690	2179	1747	1387	
	arc, inches:		+2.8	0	-11.7	
PMC 147 FMJ boat-tail	velocity, fps:	2751	2473	2257	2052	1859
	energy, ft-lb:	2428	2037	1697	1403	1150
	arc, inches:		+2.3	0	-9.3	-27.3
PMC 150 Barnes X	velocity, fps:	2700	2504	2316	2135	1964
	energy, ft-lb:	2428	2087	1786	1518	1284
	arc, inches:		+2.0	0	-8.6	-24.7
PMC 150 Pointed Soft Point	velocity, fps:	2750	2478	2224	1987	1766
	energy, ft-lb:	2519	2045	1647	1315	1039
	arc, inches:		+2.1	0	-9.2	-27.1
PMC 150 SP boat-tail	velocity, fps:	2820	2581	2354	2139	1935
	energy, ft-lb:	2648	2218	1846	1523	1247.
	arc, inches:		+1.9	0	-8.2	-24.0
PMC 168 Barnes X	velocity, fps:	2600	2425	2256	2095	1940
	energy, ft-lb:	2476	2154	1865	1608	1379
	arc, inches:		+2.2	0	-9.0	-26.0
PMC 168 HP boat-tail	velocity, fps:	2650	2460	2278	2103	1936
	energy, ft-lb:	2619	2257	1935	1649	1399
	arc, inches:		+2.1	0	-8.8	-25.6
PMC 168 Pointed Soft Point	velocity, fps:	2559	2354	2160	1976	1803
	energy, ft-lb:	2443	2067	1740	1457	1212
	arc, inches:		+2.4	0	-9.9	-28.7
PMC 168 Pointed Soft Point	velocity, fps:	2600	2404	2216	2037	1866
	energy, ft-lb:	2476	2064	1709	1403	1142
	arc, inches:		+2.3	0	-9.8	-28.7
PMC 180 Pointed Soft Point	velocity, fps:	2550	2335	2132	1940	1760
	energy, ft-lb:	2599	2179	1816	1504	1238.
	arc, inches:		+2.5	0	-10.1	-29.5
PMC 180 SP boat-tail	velocity, fps:	2620	2446	2278	2117	1962
	energy, ft-lb:	2743	2391	2074	1790	1538
	arc, inches:		+2.2	0	-8.9	-25.4
Rem. 125 PSP C-L MR	velocity, fps:	2660	2348	2057	1788	1546
	energy, ft-lb:	1964	1529	1174	887	663
	arc, inches:		+1.1	-2.7	-14.3	-35.8
Rem. 150 PSP Core-Lokt	velocity, fps:	2820	2533	2263	2009	1774
	energy, ft-lb:	2648	2137	1705	1344	1048
	arc, inches:		+2.0	0	-8.8	-26.2
Rem. 150 PSP C-L Ultra	velocity, fps:	2620	2404	2198	2002	1818
	energy, ft-lb:	2743	2309	1930	1601	1320
	arc, inches:		+2.3	0	-9.5	-26.4
Rem. 150 Swift Scirocco	velocity, fps:	2820	2611	2410	2219	2037
	energy, ft-lb:	2648	2269	1935	1640	1381
	arc, inches:		+1.8	0	-7.8	-22.7
Rem. 165 AccuTip	velocity, fps:	2700	2501	2311	2129	1958.
	energy, ft-lb:	2670	2292	1957	1861	1401.
	arc, inches:		+2.0	0	-8.6	-24.8
Rem. 165 PSP boat-tail	velocity, fps:	2700	2497	2303	2117	1941.
	energy, ft-lb:	2670	2284	1942	1642	1379
	arc, inches:		+2.0	0	-8.6	-25.0
Rem. 165 Nosler Bal. Tip	velocity, fps:	2700	2613	2333	2161	1996
	energy, ft-lb:	2672	2314	1995	1711	1460
	arc, inches:		+2.0	0	-8.4	-24.3

Centerfire Rifle Ballistics

.308 WINCHESTER TO .30-06 SPRINGFIELD

BALLISTICS

CARTRIDGE BULLET	RANGE, YARDS:	0	100	200	300	400
Rem. 165 Swift Scirocco	velocity, fps:	2700	2513	2233	2161	1996
	energy, fps:	2670	2313	1994	1711	1459
	arc, inches:		+2.0	0	-8.4	-24.3
Rem. 168 HPBT Match	velocity, fps:	2680	2493	2314	2143	1979
	energy, ft-lb:	2678	2318	1998	1713	1460
	arc, inches:		+2.1	0	-8.6	-24.7
Rem. 180 SP Core-Lokt	velocity, fps:	2620	2274	1955	1666	1414
	energy, ft-lb:	2743	2066	1527	1109	799
	arc, inches:		+2.6	0	-11.8	-36.3
Rem. 180 PSP Core-Lokt	velocity, fps:	2620	2393	2178	1974	1782
	energy, ft-lb:	2743	2288	1896	1557	1269
	arc, inches:		+2.3	0	-9.7	-28.3
Rem. 180 Nosler Partition	velocity, fps:	2620	2436	2259	2089	1927.
	energy, ft-lb:	2743	2371	2039	1774	1485
	arc, inches:		+2.2	0	-9.0	-26.0
Speer 150 Grand Slam	velocity, fps:	2900	2599	2317	2053	
	energy, ft-lb:	2800	2249	1788	1404	
	arc, inches:		+2.1	0	-8.6	-24.8
Speer 165 Grand Slam	velocity, fps:	2700	2475	2261	2057	
	energy, ft-lb:	2670	2243	1872	1550	
	arc, inches:		+2.1	0	-8.9	-25.9
Speer 180 Grand Slam	velocity, fps:	2620	2420	2229	2046	
	energy, ft-lb:	2743	2340	1985	1674	
	arc, inches:		+2.2	0	-9.2	-26.6
Win. 150 Power-Point	velocity, fps:	2820	2488	2179	1893	1633
	energy, ft-lb:	2648	2061	1581	1193	888
	arc, inches:		+2.4	0	-9.8	-29.3
Win. 150 Power-Point Plus	velocity, fps:	2900	2558	2241	1946	1678
	energy, ft-lb:	2802	2180	1672	1262	938
	arc, inches:		+1.9	0	-8.9	-27.0
Win. 150 Partition Gold	velocity, fps:	2900	2645	2405	2177	1962
	energy, ft-lb:	2802	2332	1927	1579	1282.
	arc, inches:		+1.7	0	-7.8	-22.9
Win. 150 Ballistic Silvertip	velocity, fps:	2810	2601	2401	2211	2028
	energy, ft-lb:	2629	2253	1920	1627	1370.
	arc, inches:		+1.8	0	-7.8	-22.8
Win. 150 Fail Safe	velocity, fps:	2820	2533	2263	2010	1775
	energy, ft-lb:	2649	2137	1706	1346	1049
	arc, inches:		+2.0	0	-8.8	-26.2
Win. 150 Supreme Elite XP3	velocity, fps:	2825	2616	2417	2226	2044
	energy, ft-lb:	2658	2279	1945	1650	1392
	arc, inches:		+1.8	0	-7.8	-22.6
Win. 168 Ballistic Silvertip	velocity, fps:	2670	2484	2306	2134	1971
	energy, ft-lb:	2659	2301	1983	1699	1449
	arc, inches:		+2.1	0	-8.6	-24.8
Win. 168 HP boat-tail Match	velocity, fps:	2680	2485	2297	2118	1948
	energy, ft-lb:	2680	2303	1970	1674	1415
	arc, inches:		+2.1	0	-8.7	-25.1
Win. 180 Power-Point	velocity, fps:	2620	2274	1955	1666	1414
	energy, ft-lb:	2743	2066	1527	1109	799
	arc, inches:		+2.9	0	-12.1	-36.9
Win. 180 Silvertip	velocity, fps:	2620	2393	2178	1974	1782
	energy, ft-lb:	2743	2288	1896	1557	1269
	arc, inches:		+2.6	0	-9.9	-28.9

.30-06 SPRINGFIELD

CARTRIDGE BULLET	RANGE, YARDS:	0	100	200	300	400
A-Square 180 M & D-T	velocity, fps:	2700	2365	2054	1769	1524
	energy, ft-lb:	2913	2235	1687	1251	928
	arc, inches:		+2.4	0	-10.6	-32.4
A-Square 220 Monolythic Solid	velocity, fps:	2380	2108	1854	1623	1424
	energy, ft-lb:	2767	2171	1679	1287	990
	arc, inches:		+3.1	0	-13.6	-39.9
Black Hills 150 Nosler B. Tip	velocity, fps:	2900				

CARTRIDGE BULLET	RANGE, YARDS:	0	100	200	300	400
	energy, ft-lb:	2770				
	arc, inches:					
Black Hills 165 Nosler B. Tip	velocity, fps:	2750				
	energy, ft-lb:	2770				
	arc, inches:					
Black Hills 168 Hor. Match	velocity, fps:	2700				
	energy, ft-lb:	2718				
	arc, inches:					
Black Hills 180 Barnes X	velocity, fps:	2650				
	energy, ft-lb:	2806				
	arc, inches:					
Black Hills 180 AccuBond	velocity, ft-lb:	2700				
	energy, ft-lb:					
	arc, inches:					
Federal 125 Sierra Pro-Hunt.	velocity, fps:	3140	2780	2450	2140	1850
	energy, ft-lb:	2735	2145	1660	1270	955
	arc, inches:		+1.5	0	-7.3	-22.3
Federal 150 Hi-Shok	velocity, fps:	2910	2620	2340	2080	1840
	energy, ft-lb:	2820	2280	1825	1445	1130
	arc, inches:		+1.8	0	-8.2	-24.4
Federal 150 Sierra Pro-Hunt.	velocity, fps:	2910	2640	2380	2130	1900
	energy, ft-lb:	2820	2315	1880	1515	1205
	arc, inches:		+1.7	0	-7.9	-23.3
Federal 150 Sierra GameKing BTSP	velocity, fps:	2910	2690	2480	2270	2070
	energy, ft-lb:	2820	2420	2040	1710	1430
	arc, inches:		+1.7	0	-7.4	-21.5
Federal 150 Nosler Bal. Tip	velocity, fps:	2910	2700	2490	2300	2110
	energy, ft-lb:	2820	2420	2070	1760	1485
	arc, inches:		+1.6	0	-7.3	-21.1
Federal 150 FMJ boat-tail	velocity, fps:	2910	2710	2510	2320	2150
	energy, ft-lb:	2820	2440	2100	1800	1535
	arc, inches:		+1.6	0	-7.1	-20.8
Federal 165 Sierra Pro-Hunt.	velocity, fps:	2800	2560	2340	2130	1920
	energy, ft-lb:	2875	2410	2005	1655	1360
	arc, inches:		+1.9	0	-8.3	-24.3
Federal 165 Sierra GameKing BTSP	velocity, fps:	2800	2610	2420	2240	2070.
	energy, ft-lb:	2870	2490	2150	1840	1580
	arc, inches:		+1.8	0	-7.8	-22.4
Federal 165 Sierra GameKing HE	velocity, fps:	3140	2900	2670	2450	2240.
	energy, ft-lb:	3610	3075	2610	2200	1845
	arc, inches:		+1.5	0	-6.9	-20.4
Federal 165 Nosler Bal. Tip	velocity, fps:	2800	2610	2430	2250	2080
	energy, ft-lb:	2870	2495	2155	1855	1585
	arc, inches:		+1.8	0	-7.7	-22.3
Federal 165 Trophy Bonded	velocity, fps:	2800	2540	2290	2050	1830.
	energy, ft-lb:	2870	2360	1915	1545	1230
	arc, inches:		+2.0	0	-8.7	-25.4
Federal 165 Tr. Bonded HE	velocity, fps:	3140	2860	2590	2340	2100
	energy, ft-lb:	3610	2990	2460	2010	1625.
	arc, inches:		+1.6	0	-7.4	-21.9
Federal 165 Trophy Copper	velocity, fps:	2800	2620	2450	2280	2120
	energy, ft-lb:	2870	2515	2190	1900	1645
	arc, inches:		+1.8	0	-7.6	-22.0
Federal 168 Sierra MatchKg. BTHP	velocity, fps:	2700	2510	2320	2150	1980
	energy, ft-lb:	2720	2350	2010	1720	1460
	arc, inches:		+16.2	+28.4	+34.1	+32.3
Federal 180 Barnes XLC	velocity, fps:	2700	2530	2360	2200	2040
	energy, ft-lb:	2915	2550	2220	1930	1670
	arc, inches:	+2.0	0	-8.3	-23.8	
Federal 180 Hi-Shok	velocity, fps:	2700	2470	2250	2040	1850
	energy, ft-lb:	2915	2435	2025	1665	1360
	arc, inches:		+2.1	0	-9.0	-26.4
Federal 180 Sierra Pro-Hunt. RN	velocity, fps:	2700	2350	2020	1730	1470
	energy, ft-lb:	2915	2200	1630	1190	860
	arc, inches:		+2.4	0	-11.0	-33.6
Federal 180 Nosler Partition	velocity, fps:	2700	2500	2320	2140	1970
	energy, ft-lb:	2915	2510	2150	1830	1550
	arc, inches:		+2.0	0	-8.6	-24.6

BALLISTICS

CARTRIDGE BULLET	RANGE, YARDS:	0	100	200	300	400
Federal 180 Nosler Part. HE	velocity, fps:	2880	2690	2500	2320	2150
	energy, ft-lb:	3315	2880	2495	2150	1845
	arc, inches:		+1.7	0	-7.2	-21.0
Federal 180 Sierra GameKing BTSP	velocity, fps:	2700	2540	2380	2220	2080
	energy, ft-lb:	2915	2570	2260	1975	1720
	arc, inches:		+1.9	0	-8.1	-23.1
Federal 180 Barnes XLC	velocity, fps:	2700	2530	2360	2200	2040.
	energy, ft-lb:	2915	2550	2220	1930	1670
	arc, inches:		+2.0	0	-8.3	-23.8
Federal 180 Sierra Pro-Hunt. RN	velocity, fps:	2700	2350	2020	1730	1470
	energy, ft-lb:	2915	2200	1630	1190	860
	arc, inches:		+2.4	0	-11.0	-33.6
Federal 180 Trophy Bonded	velocity, fps:	2700	2460	2220	2000	1800
	energy, ft-lb:	2915	2410	1975	1605	1290
	arc, inches:		+2.2	0	-9.2	-27.0
Federal 180 Tr. Bonded HE	velocity, fps:	2880	2630	2380	2160	1940
	energy, ft-lb:	3315	2755	2270	1855	1505
	arc, inches:		+1.8	0	-8.0	-23.3
Federal 180 Trophy Bonded Tip	velocity, fps:	2700	2520	2350	2190	2030
	energy, ft-lb:	2915	2540	2219	1910	1645
	arc, inches:		+2.0	0	-8.4	-23.9
Federal 200 Trophy Bonded	velocity, fps:	2540	2320	2120	1920	1740
	energy, ft-lb:	2865	2395	1990	1640	1345
	arc, inches:		+2.5	0	-10.1	-29.9
Federal 220 Sierra Pro-Hunt. RN	velocity, fps:	2410	2130	1870	1630	1420
	energy, ft-lb:	2835	2215	1705	1300	985
	arc, inches:		+3.1	0	-13.1	-39.3
Hornady 125 SST Custom Lite	velocity, fps:	2700	2412	2143	1891	1660
	energy, ft-lb:	2023	1615	1274	993	765
	arc, inches:		+2.3	0	-9.9	-29.5
Hornady 150 GMX Superformance	velocity, fps:	3080	2848	2628	2418	2218
	energy, ft-lb:	3159	2701	2300	1948	1639
	arc, inches:		+1.4	0	-6.4	-18.8
Hornady 150 SP	velocity, fps:	2910	2617	2342	2083	1843
	energy, ft-lb:	2820	2281	1827	1445	1131
	arc, inches:		+2.1	0	-8.5	-25.0
Hornady 150 SP LM	velocity, fps:	3100	2815	2548	2295	2058
	energy, ft-lb:	3200	2639	2161	1755	1410
	arc, inches:		+1.4	0	-6.8	-20.3
Hornady 150 SP boat-tail	velocity, fps:	2910	2683	2467	2262	2066.
	energy, ft-lb:	2820	2397	2027	1706	1421
	arc, inches:		+2.0	0	-7.7	-22.2
Hornady 150 SST (or Interbond)	velocity, fps:	2910	2802	2599	2405	2219
	energy, ft-lb:	3330	2876	2474	2118	1803
	arc, inches:		+1.5	0	-6.6	-19.3
Hornady 150 SST LM	velocity, fps:	3100	2860	2631	2414	2208
	energy, ft-lb:	3200	2724	2306	1941	1624
	arc, inches:		+1.4	0	-6.6	-19.2
Hornady 165 GMX Superformance	velocity, fps:	2940	2731	2532	2341	2158
	energy, ft-lb:	3167	2732	3248	2007	1706
	arc, inches:		+1.5	0	-7.0	-20.4
Hornady 165 SP boat-tail	velocity, fps:	2800	2591	2392	2202	2020
	energy, ft-lb:	2873	2460	2097	1777	1495
	arc, inches:		+1.8	0	-8.0	-23.3
Hornady 165 SPBT LM	velocity, fps:	3015	2790	2575	2370	2176
	energy, ft-lb:	3330	2850	2428	2058	1734
	arc, inches:		+1.6	0	-7.0	-20.1
Hornady 165 SST (or Interbond)	velocity, fps:	2800	2598	2405	2221	2046
	energy, ft-lb:	2872	2473	2119	1808	1534
	arc, inches:		+1.9	0	-8.0	-22.8
Hornady 165 SST LM	velocity, fps:	3015	2802	2599	2405	2219
	energy, ft-lb:	3330	2878	2474	2118	1803.
	arc, inches:		+1.5	0	-6.5	-19.3
Hornady 168 A-Max Garand Match	velocity, fps:	2710	2523	2343	2171	2006
	energy, ft-lb:	2739	2374	2048	1758	1501
	arc, inches:		+2.3	0	-8.6	-24.6
Hornady 168 HPBT Match	velocity, fps:	2790	2620	2447	2280	2120.
	energy, ft-lb:	2925	2561	2234	1940	1677.
	arc, inches:		+1.7	0	-7.7	-22.2
Hornady 180 SP	velocity, fps:	2700	2469	2258	2042	1846
	energy, ft-lb:	2913	2436	2023	1666	1362
	arc, inches:		+2.4	0	-9.3	-27.0
Hornady 180 SPBT LM	velocity, fps:	2880	2676	2480	2293	2114
	energy, ft-lb:	3316	2862	2459	2102	1786
	arc, inches:		+1.7	0	-7.3	-21.3

CARTRIDGE BULLET	RANGE, YARDS:	0	100	200	300	400
Norma 150 Nosler Bal. Tip	velocity, fps:	2936	2713	2502	2300	
	energy, ft-lb:	2872	2453	2085	1762	
	arc, inches:		+1.6	0	-7.1	
Norma 150 Soft Point	velocity, fps:	2972	2640	2331	2043	
	energy, ft-lb:	2943	2321	1810	1390	
	arc, inches:		+1.8	0	-8.2	
Norma 180 Alaska	velocity, fps:	2700	2351	2028	1734	
	energy, ft-lb:	2914	2209	1645	1202	
	arc, inches:		+2.4	0	-11.0	
Norma 180 Nosler Partition	velocity, fps:	2700	2494	2297	2108	
	energy, ft-lb:	2914	2486	2108	1777	
	arc, inches:		+2.1	0	-8.7	
Norma 180 Plastic Point	velocity, fps:	2700	2455	2222	2003	
	energy, ft-lb:	2914	2409	1974	1603	
	arc, inches:		+2.1	0	-9.2	
Norma 180 Vulkan	velocity, fps:	2700	2416	2150	1901	
	energy, ft-lb:	2914	2334	1848	1445	
	arc, inches:		+2.2	0	-9.8	
Norma 180 Oryx	velocity, fps:	2700	2387	2095	1825	
	energy, ft-lb:	2914	2278	1755	1332	
	arc, inches:		+2.3	0	-10.2	
Norma 180 TXP Swift A-Fr.	velocity, fps:	2700	2479	2268	2067	
	energy, ft-lb:	2914	2456	2056	1708	
	arc, inches:		+2.0	0	-8.8	
Norma 180 AccuBond	velocity, fps:	2674	2499	2331	2169	
	energy, ft-lb:	2859	2497	2172	1881	
	arc, inches:		+2.0	0	-8.5	
Norma 200 Vulkan	velocity, fps:	2641	2385	2143	1916	
	energy, ft-lb:	3098	2527	2040	1631	
	arc, inches:		+2.3	0	-9.9	
Norma 200 Oryx	velocity, fps:	2625	2362	2115	1883	
	energy, ft-lb:	3061	2479	1987	1575	
	arc, inches:		+2.3	0	-10.1	
PMC 150 X-Bullet	velocity, fps:	2750	2552	2361	2179	2005
	energy, ft-lb:	2518	2168	1857	1582	1339
	arc, inches:		+2.0	0	-8.2	-23.7
PMC 150 Pointed Soft Point	velocity, fps:	2773	2542	2322	2113	1916
	energy, ft-lb:	2560	2152	1796	1487	1222.
	arc, inches:		+1.9	0	-8.4	-24.6
PMC 150 SP boat-tail	velocity, fps:	2900	2657	2427	2208	2000
	energy, ft-lb:	2801	2351	1961	1623	1332
	arc, inches:		+1.7	0	-7.7	-22.5
PMC 150 FMJ	velocity, fps:	2773	2542	2322	2113	1916
	energy, ft-lb:	2560	2152	1796	1487	1222
	arc, inches:		+1.9	0	-8.4	-24.6
PMC 168 Barnes X	velocity, fps:	2750	2569	2395	2228	2067
	energy, ft-lb:	2770	2418	2101	1818	1565
	arc, inches:		+1.9	0	-8.0	-23.0
PMC 180 Barnes X	velocity, fps:	2650	2487	2331	2179	2034
	energy, ft-lb:	2806	2472	2171	1898	1652
	arc, inches:		+2.1	0	-8.5	-24.3
PMC 180 Pointed Soft Point	velocity, fps:	2650	2430	2221	2024	1839
	energy, ft-lb:	2807	2359	1972	1638	1351
	arc, inches:		+2.2	0	-9.3	-27.0
PMC 180 SP boat-tail	velocity, fps:	2700	2523	2352	2188	2030
	energy, ft-lb:	2913	2543	2210	1913	1646
	arc, inches:		+2.0	0	-8.3	-23.9
PMC 180 HPBT Match	velocity, fps:	2800	2622	2456	2302	2158
	energy, ft-lb:	3133	2747	2411	2118	1861
	arc, inches:		+1.8	0	-7.6	-21.7
Rem. 55 PSP (sabot) "Accelerator"	velocity, fps:	4080	3484	2964	2499	2080
	energy, ft-lb:	2033	1482	1073	763	528.
	arc, inches:		+1.4	+1.4	-2.6	-12.2
Rem. 125 PSP C-L MR	velocity, fps:	2660	2335	2034	1757	1509
	energy, ft-lb:	1964	1513	1148	856	632
	arc, inches:		+1.1	-3.0	-15.5	-37.4
Rem. 125 Pointed Soft Point	velocity, fps:	3140	2780	2447	2138	1853
	energy, ft-lb:	2736	2145	1662	1269	953.
	arc, inches:		+1.5	0	-7.4	-22.4
Rem. 150 AccuTip	velocity, fps:	2910	2686	2473	2270	2077
	energy, ft-lb:	2820	2403	2037	1716	1436
	arc, inches:		+1.8	0	-7.4	-21.5

Centerfire Rifle Ballistics

.30-06 SPRINGFIELD TO .300 BLK

CARTRIDGE BULLET	RANGE, YARDS:	0	100	200	300	400
Rem. 150 PSP Core-Lokt	velocity, fps:	2910	2617	2342	2083	1843
	energy, ft-lb:	2820	2281	1827	1445	1131
	arc, inches:		+1.8	0	-8.2	-24.4
Rem. 150 Bronze Point	velocity, fps:	2910	2656	2416	2189	1974
	energy, ft-lb:	2820	2349	1944	1596	1298
	arc, inches:		+1.7	0	-7.7	-22.7
Rem. 150 Nosler Bal. Tip	velocity, fps:	2910	2696	2492	2298	2112.
	energy, ft-lb:	2821	2422	2070	1769	1485
	arc, inches:		+1.6	0	-7.3	-21.1
Rem. 150 Swift Scirocco	velocity, fps:	2910	2696	2492	2298	2111
	energy, ft-lb:	2820	2421	2069	1758	1485
	arc, inches:		+1.6	0	-7.3	-21.1
Rem. 165 AccuTip	velocity, fps:	2800	2597	2403	2217	2039
	energy, ft-lb:	2872	2470	2115	1800	1523
	arc, inches:		+1.8	0	-7.9	-22.8
Rem. 165 PSP Core-Lokt	velocity, fps:	2800	2534	2283	2047	1825.
	energy, ft-lb:	2872	2352	1909	1534	1220
	arc, inches:		+2.0	0	-8.7	-25.9
Rem. 165 PSP boat-tail	velocity, fps:	2800	2592	2394	2204	2023
	energy, ft-lb:	2872	2462	2100	1780	1500
	arc, inches:		+1.8	0	-7.9	-23.0
Rem. 165 Nosler Bal. Tip	velocity, fps:	2800	2609	2426	2249	2080.
	energy, ft-lb:	2873	2494	2155	1854	1588
	arc, inches:		+1.8	0	-7.7	-22.3
Rem. 168 PSP C-L Ultra	velocity, fps:	2800	2546	2306	2079	1866
	energy, ft-lb:	2924	2418	1984	1613	1299
	arc, inches:		+1.9	0	-8.5	-25.1
Rem. 180 SP Core-Lokt	velocity, fps:	2700	2348	2023	1727	1466
	energy, ft-lb:	2913	2203	1635	1192	859
	arc, inches:		+2.4	0	-11.0	-33.8
Rem. 180 PSP Core-Lokt	velocity, fps:	2700	2469	2250	2042	1846
	energy, ft-lb:	2913	2436	2023	1666	1362
	arc, inches:		+2.1	0	-9.0	-26.3
Rem. 180 PSP C-L Ultra	velocity, fps:	2700	2480	2270	2070	1882
	energy, ft-lb:	2913	2457	2059	1713	1415
	arc, inches:		+2.1	0	-8.9	-25.8
Rem. 180 Bronze Point	velocity, fps:	2700	2485	2280	2084	1899.
	energy, ft-lb:	2913	2468	2077	1736	1441
	arc, inches:		+2.1	0	-8.8	-25.5
Rem. 180 Swift A-Frame	velocity, fps:	2700	2465	2243	2032	1833
	energy, ft-lb:	2913	2429	2010	1650	1343
	arc, inches:		+2.1	0	-9.1	-26.6
Rem. 180 Nosler Partition	velocity, fps:	2700	2512	2332	2160	1995
	energy, ft-lb:	2913	2522	2174	1864	1590
	arc, inches:		+2.0	0	-8.4	-24.3
Rem. 220 SP Core-Lokt	velocity, fps:	2410	2130	1870	1632	1422
	energy, ft-lb:	2837	2216	1708	1301	988
	arc, inches, s:		0	-6.2	-22.4	
Speer 150 Grand Slam	velocity, fps:	2975	2669	2383	2114	
	energy, ft-lb:	2947	2372	1891	1489	
	arc, inches:		+2.0	0	-8.1	-24.1
Speer 165 Grand Slam	velocity, fps:	2790	2560	2342	2134	
	energy, ft-lb:	2851	2401	2009	1669	
	arc, inches:		+1.9	0	-8.3	-24.1
Speer 180 Grand Slam	velocity, fps:	2690	2487	2293	2108	
	energy, ft-lb:	2892	2472	2101	1775	
	arc, inches:		+2.1	0	-8.8	-25.1
Win. 125 Pointed Soft Point	velocity, fps:	3140	2780	2447	2138	1853
	energy, ft-lb:	2736	2145	1662	1269	953
	arc, inches:		+1.8	0	-7.7	-23.0
Win. 150 Power-Point	velocity, fps:	2920	2580	2265	1972	1704
	energy, ft-lb:	2839	2217	1708	1295	967
	arc, inches:		+2.2	0	-9.0	-27.0
Win. 150 Power-Point Plus	velocity, fps:	3050	2685	2352	2043	1760
	energy, ft-lb:	3089	2402	1843	1391	1032
	arc, inches:		+1.7	0	-8.0	-24.3
Win. 150 Silvertip	velocity, fps:	2910	2617	2342	2083	1843
	energy, ft-lb:	2820	2281	1827	1445	1131
	arc, inches:		+2.1	0	-8.5	-25.0

CARTRIDGE BULLET	RANGE, YARDS:	0	100	200	300	400
Win. 150 Partition Gold	velocity, fps:	2960	2705	2464	2235	2019
	energy, ft-lb:	2919	2437	2022	1664	1358.
	arc, inches:		+1.6	0	-7.4	-21.7
Win. 150 Ballistic Silvertip	velocity, fps:	2900	2687	2483	2289	2103
	energy, ft-lb:	2801	2404	2054	1745	1473
	arc, inches:		+1.7	0	-7.3	-21.2
Win. 150 Fail Safe	velocity, fps:	2920	2625	2349	2089	1848
	energy, ft-lb:	2841	2296	1838	1455	1137
	arc, inches:		+1.8	0	-8.1	-24.3
Win. 165 Pointed Soft Point	velocity, fps:	2800	2573	2357	2151	1956
	energy, ft-lb:	2873	2426	2036	1696	1402
	arc, inches:		+2.2	0	-8.4	-24.4
Win. 165 Fail Safe	velocity, fps:	2800	2540	2295	2063	1846
	energy, ft-lb:	2873	2365	1930	1560	1249
	arc, inches:		+2.0	0	-8.6	-25.3
Win. 168 Ballistic Silvertip	velocity, fps:	2790	2599	2416	2240	2072
	energy, ft-lb:	2903	2520	2177	1872	1601
	arc, inches:		+1.8	0	-7.8	-22.5
Win. 180 Ballistic Silvertip	velocity, fps:	2750	2572	2402	2237	2080
	energy, ft-lb:	3022	2644	2305	2001	1728
	arc, inches:		+1.9	0	-7.9	-22.8
Win. 180 Power-Point	velocity, fps:	2700	2348	2023	1727	1466
	energy, ft-lb:	2913	2203	1635	1192	859
	arc, inches:		+2.7	0	-11.3	-34.4
Win. 180 Power-Point Plus	velocity, fps:	2770	2563	2366	2177	1997
	energy, ft-lb:	3068	2627	2237	1894	1594
	arc, inches:		+1.9	0	-8.1	-23.6
Win. 180 Silvertip	velocity, fps:	2700	2469	2250	2042	1846
	energy, ft-lb:	2913	2436	2023	1666	1362
	arc, inches:		+2.4	0	-9.3	-27.0
Win. 180 AccuBond	velocity, fps:	2750	2573	2403	2239	2082
	energy, ft-lb:	3022	2646	2308	2004	1732
	arc, inches:		+1.9	0	-7.9	-22.8
Win. 180 Partition Gold	velocity, fps:	2790	2581	2382	2192	2010
	energy, ft-lb:	3112	2664	2269	1920	1615
	arc, inches:		+1.9	0	-8.0	-23.2
Win. 180 Fail Safe	velocity, fps:	2700	2486	2283	2089	1904
	energy, ft-lb:	2914	2472	2083	1744	1450
	arc, inches:		+2.1	0	-8.7	-25.5
Win. 150 Supreme Elite XP3	velocity, fps:	2925	2712	2508	2313	2127
	energy, ft-lb:	2849	2448	2095	1782	1507
	arc, inches:		+1.6	0	-7.2	-20.8
Win. 180 Supreme Elite XP3	velocity, fps:	2750	2579	2414	2256	2103
	energy, ft-lb:	3022	2658	2330	2034	1768
	arc, inches:		+1.9	0	-7.8	-22.5

.300 BLK (.300 WHISPER)

CARTRIDGE BULLET	RANGE, YARDS:	0	100	200	300	400
Barnes 110 Tac/TX	velocity, fps:	2350	1810	1369		
	energy, ft-lb:	1349	800	458		
	arc, inches:	-1.5	-6.7	-55.5		
Black Hills 125 OTM	velocity, fps:	2200				
	energy, ft-lb:	1343				
	arc, inches					
Black Hills 220 OTM	velocity, fps:	1000				
	energy, ft-lb:	488				
	arc, inches					
Hornady 110 V-Max (16-inch barrel)	velocity, fps:	2375	2094	1834	1597	1389
	energy, ft-lb:	1378	1071	821	623	471
	arc, inches:		+3.20	0	-13.7	-41.0
Hornady 110 V-MAX	velocity, fps:	2375	2094	1834	1597	
	energy, ft-lb:	1378	1071	821	623	
	arc, inches:	-1.5	+3.2	0	-13.7	
Hornady 208 A-MAX	velocity, fps:	1020	987	959		
	energy, ft-lb:	480	450	424		
	arc, inches:	-1.5	0	-34.1		

CARTRIDGE BULLET	RANGE, YARDS:	0	100	200	300	400
.300 H&H MAGNUM						
Federal 180 Barnes TSX	velocity, fps:	2880	2680	2480	2290	2120
	energy, ft-lb:	3315	2860	2460	2105	1790
	arc, inches:	-1.5	+1.7	0	-7.3	-21.3
Federal 180 Nosler Partition	velocity, fps:	2880	2620	2380	2150	1930
	energy, ft-lb:	3315	2750	2260	1840	1480
	arc, inches:		+1.8 0	-8.0	-23.4	
Federal 180 Trophy Bonded Tip	velocity, fps:	2880	2700	2520	2350	2180
	energy, ft-lb:	3315	2900	2530	2200	1900
	arc, inches:		+1.6	0	-7.1	-20.6
Handload, 165 Sierra HP	velocity, fps:	3000	2784	2579	2382	2195
	energy, ft-lb:	3297	2840	2436	2079	1764
	arc, inches:	-1.5	+1.5	0	-6.7	-19.5
Handload, 190 Hornady	velocity, fps:	2800	2615	2437	2266	2102
	energy, ft-lb:	3307	2884	2505	2166	1864
	arc, inches:	-1.5	+1.8	0	-7.7	-22.1
Hornady 180 InterBond	velocity, fps:	2870	2678	2493	2316	2146
	energy, ft-lb:	3292	2865	2484	2144	1841
	arc, inches:	-1.5	+1.	0	-7.3	-21.0
Win. 180 Fail Safe	velocity, fps:	2880	2628	2390	2165	1952
	energy, ft-lb:	3316	2762	2284	1873	1523
	arc, inches:		+1.8 0	-7.9	-23.2	
.308 NORMA MAGNUM						
Norma 180 TXP Swift A-Fr.	velocity, fps:	2953	2704	2469	2245	
	energy, ft-lb:	3486	2924	2437	2016	
	arc, inches:		+1.6	0	-7.3	
Norma 180 Oryx	velocity, fps:	2953	2630	2330	2049	
	energy, ft-lb:	3486	2766	2170	1679	
	arc, inches:		+1.8	0	-8.2	
Norma 200 Vulkan	velocity, fps:	2903	2624	2361	2114	
	energy, ft-lb:	3744	3058	2476	1985	
	arc, inches:	0	+1.8	0	-8.0	
Nosler 180 AB	velocity, fps:	2975	2787	2608	2435	2269
	energy, ft-lb:	3536	3105	2718	2371	2058
	arc, inches:	-1.5	+1.5	0	-6.6	-19.1
.300 WINCHESTER MAGNUM						
A-Square 180 Dead Tough	velocity, fps:	3120	2756	2420	2108	1820
	energy, ft-lb:	3890	3035	2340	1776	1324
	arc, inches:		+1.6	0	-7.6	-22.9
Black Hills 180 Nos. Bal. Tip	velocity, fps:	3100				
	energy, ft-lb:	3498				
	arc, inches:					
Black Hills 180 Barnes X	velocity, fps:	2950				
	energy, ft-lb:	3498				
	arc, inches:					
Black Hills 180 AccuBond	velocity, fps:	3000				
	energy, ft-lb:	3597				
	arc, inches:					
Black Hills 190 Match	velocity, fps:	2950				
	energy, ft-lb:	3672				
	arc, inches:					
Federal 150 Sierra Pro Hunt.	velocity, fps:	3280	3030	2800	2570	2360.
	energy, ft-lb:	3570	3055	2600	2205	1860
	arc, inches:		+1.1	0	-5.6	-16.4
Federal 150 Trophy Bonded	velocity, fps:	3280	2980	2700	2430	2190
	energy, ft-lb:	3570	2450	2420	1970	1590
	arc, inches:		+1.2	0	-6.0	-17.9
Federal 165 Trophy Copper	velocity, fps:	3050	2860	2680	2500	2330
	energy, ft-lb:	3410	2995	2620	2290	1990
	arc, inches:		+1.4	0	-6.3	-18.0
Federal 180 Sierra Pro Hunt.	velocity, fps:	2960	2750	2540	2340	2160
	energy, ft-lb:	3500	3010	2580	2195	1860
	arc, inches:		+1.6	0	-7.0	-20.3

CARTRIDGE BULLET	RANGE, YARDS:	0	100	200	300	400
Federal 180 Barnes XLC	velocity, fps:	2960	2780	2600	2430	2260
	energy, ft-lb:	3500	3080	2700	2355	2050
	arc, inches:		+1.5	0	-6.6	-19.2
Federal 180 Trophy Bonded	velocity, fps:	2960	2700	2460	2220	2000
	energy, ft-lb:	3500	2915	2410	1975	1605
	arc, inches:		+1.6	0	-7.4	-21.9
Federal 180 Tr. Bonded HE	velocity, fps:	3100	2830	2580	2340	2110
	energy, ft-lb:	3840	3205	2660	2190	1790
	arc, inches:		+1.4	0	-6.6	-19.7
Federal 180 Nosler Partition	velocity, fps:	2960	2700	2450	2210	1990
	energy, ft-lb:	3500	2905	2395	1955	1585
	arc, inches:		+1.6	0	-7.5	-22.1
Federal 190 Sierra MatchKg. BTHP	velocity, fps:	2900	2730	2560	2400	2240
	energy, ft-lb:	3550	3135	2760	2420	2115
	arc, inches:		+12.9	+22.5	+26.9	+25.1
Federal 200 Sierra GameKing BTSP	velocity, fps:	2830	2680	2530	2380	2240
	energy, ft-lb:	3560	3180	2830	2520	2230
	arc, inches:		+1.7	0	-7.1	-20.4
Federal 200 Nosler Part. HE	velocity, fps:	2930	2740	2550	2370	2200
	energy, ft-lb:	3810	3325	2885	2495	2145
	arc, inches:		+1.6	0	-6.9	-20.1
Federal 200 Trophy Bonded	velocity, fps:	2800	2570	2350	2150	1950
	energy, ft-lb:	3480	2935	2460	2050	1690
	arc, inches:		+1.9	0	-8.2	-23.9
Hornady 150 SP boat-tail	velocity, fps:	3275	2988	2718	2464	2224
	energy, ft-lb:	3573	2974	2461	2023	1648
	arc, inches:		+1.2	0	-6.0	-17.8
Hornady 150 SST (and Interbond)	velocity, fps:	3275	3027	2791	2565	2352
	energy, ft-lb:	3572	3052	2593	2192	1842
	arc, inches:		+1.2	0	-5.8	-17.0
Hornady 150 SST Custom Lite	velocity, fps:	2800	2582	2375	2178	1988
	energy, ft-lb:	2611	2220	1878	1578	1316
	arc, inches:		+1.9	0	-8.0	-23.5
Hornady 165 SP boat-tail	velocity, fps:	3100	2877	2665	2462	2269.
	energy, ft-lb:	3522	3033	2603	2221	1887
	arc, inches:		+1.3	0	-6.5	-18.5
Hornady 165 SST	velocity, fps:	3100	2885	2680	2483	2296
	energy, ft-lb:	3520	3049	2630	2259	1930
	arc, inches:		+1.4	0	-6.4	-18.6
Hornady 180 SP boat-tail	velocity, fps:	2960	2745	2540	2344	2157
	energy, ft-lb:	3501	3011	2578	2196	1859
	arc, inches:		+1.9	0	-7.3	-20.9
Hornady 180 SST	velocity, fps:	2960	2764	2575	2395	2222
	energy, ft-lb:	3501	3052	2650	2292	1974
	arc, inches:		+1.6	0	-7.0	-20.1.
Hornady 180 SPBT HM	velocity, fps:	3100	2879	2668	2467	2275
	energy, ft-lb:	3840	3313	2845	2431	2068
	arc, inches:		+1.4	0	-6.4	-18.7
Hornady 190 BTHP Match	velocity, fps:	2930	2760	2596	2438	2286
	energy, ft-lb:	3717	3297	2918	2574	2262
	arc, inches:		+1.5	0	-6.7	-19.3
Hornady 190 SP boat-tail	velocity, fps:	2900	2711	2529	2355	2187
	energy, ft-lb:	3549	3101	2699	2340	2018
	arc, inches:		+1.6	0	-7.1	-20.4
Norma 150 Nosler Bal. Tip	velocity, fps:	3250	3014	2791	2578	
	energy, ft-lb:	3519	3027	2595	2215	
	arc, inches:		+1.1	0	-5.6	
Norma 150 Barnes TS	velocity, fps:	3215	2982	2761	2550	
	energy, ft-lb:	3444	2962	2539	2167	
	arc, inches:		+1.2	0	-5.8	
Norma 165 Scirocco	velocity, fps:	3117	2921	2734	2554	
	energy, ft-lb:	3561	3127	2738	2390	
	arc, inches:		+1.2	0	-5.9	
Norma 180 Soft Point	velocity, fps:	3018	2780	2555	2341	
	energy, ft-lb:	3641	3091	2610	2190	
	arc, inches:		+1.5	0	-7.0	
Norma 180 Plastic Point	velocity, fps:	3018	2755	2506	2271	
	energy, ft-lb:	3641	3034	2512	2062	
	arc, inches:		+1.6	0	-7.1	
Norma 180 TXP Swift A-Fr.	velocity, fps:	2920	2688	2467	2256	
	energy, ft-lb:	3409	2888	2432	2035	
	arc, inches:		+1.7	0	-7.4	

Centerfire Rifle Ballistics

.300 WINCHESTER MAGNUM TO .300 REMINGTON SHORT ULTRA MAGNUM

CARTRIDGE BULLET	RANGE, YARDS:	0	100	200	300	400
Norma 180 AccuBond	velocity, fps:	2953	2767	2588	2417	
	energy, ft-lb:	3486	3061	2678	2335	
	arc, inches:		+1.5	0	-6.7	
Norma 180 Oryx	velocity, fps:	2920	2600	2301	2023	
	energy, ft-lb:	3409	2702	2117	1636	
	arc, inches:		+1.8	0	-8.4	
Norma 200 Vulkan	velocity, fps:	2887	2609	2347	2100	
	energy, ft-lb:	3702	3023	2447	1960	
	arc, inches:		+1.8	0	-8.2	
Norma 200 Oryx	velocity, fps:	2789	2510	2248	2002	
	energy, ft-lb:	3455	2799	2245	1780	
	arc, inches:		+2.0	0	-8.9	
PMC 150 Barnes X	velocity, fps:	3135	2918	2712	2515	2327
	energy, ft-lb:	3273	2836	2449	2107	1803
	arc, inches:		+1.3	0	-6.1	-17.7
PMC 150 Pointed Soft Point	velocity, fps:	3150	2902	2665	2438	2222
	energy, ft-lb:	3304	2804	2364	1979	1644.
	arc, inches:		+1.3	0	-6.2	-18.3
PMC 150 SP boat-tail	velocity, fps:	3250	2987	2739	2504	2281
	energy, ft-lb:	3517	2970	2498	2088	1733
	arc, inches:		+1.2	0	-6.0	-17.4
PMC 180 Barnes X	velocity, fps:	2910	2738	2572	2412	2258
	energy, ft-lb:	3384	2995	2644	2325	2037
	arc, inches:		+1.6	0	-6.9	-19.8
PMC 180 Pointed Soft Point	velocity, fps:	2853	2643	2446	2258	2077
	energy, ft-lb:	3252	2792	2391	2037	1724
	arc, inches:		+1.7	0	-7.5	-21.9
PMC 180 SP boat-tail	velocity, fps:	2900	2714	2536	2365	2200
	energy, ft-lb:	3361	2944	2571	2235	1935
	arc, inches:		+1.6	0	-7.1	-20.3
PMC 180 HPBT Match	velocity, fps:	2950	2755	2568	2390	2219
	energy, ft-lb:	3478	3033	2636	2283	1968
	arc, inches:		+1.5	0	-6.8	-19.7
Rem. 150 PSP Core-Lokt	velocity, fps:	3290	2951	2636	2342	2068
	energy, ft-lb:	3605	2900	2314	1827	1859
	arc, inches:		+1.6	0	-7.0	-20.2
Rem. 150 PSP C-L MR	velocity, fps:	2650	2373	2113	1870	1646
	energy, ft-lb:	2339	1875	1486	1164	902
	arc, inches:		+1.0	-2.7	-14.3	-35.8
Rem. 150 PSP C-L Ultra	velocity, fps:	3290	2967	2666	2384	2120
	energy, ft-lb:	3065	2931	2366	1893	1496
	arc, inches:		+1.2	0	-6.1	-18.4
Rem. 180 AccuTip	velocity, fps:	2960	2764	2577	2397	2224
	energy, ft-lb:	3501	3053	2653	2295	1976
	arc, inches:		+1.5	0	-6.8	-19.6
Rem. 180 PSP Core-Lokt	velocity, fps:	2960	2745	2540	2344	2157
	energy, ft-lb:	3501	3011	2578	2196	1424
	arc, inches:		+2.2	+1.9	-3.4	-15.0
Rem. 180 PSP C-L Ultra	velocity, fps:	2960	2727	2505	2294	2093
	energy, ft-lb:	3501	2971	2508	2103	1751
	arc, inches:		+2.7	+2.2	-3.8	-16.4
Rem. 180 Nosler Partition	velocity, fps:	2960	2725	2503	2291	2089
	energy, ft-lb:	3501	2968	2503	2087	1744
	arc, inches:		+1.6	0	-7.2	-20.9
Rem. 180 Nosler Bal. Tip	velocity, fps:	2960	2774	2595	2424	2259.
	energy, ft-lb:	3501	3075	2692	2348	2039
	arc, inches:		+1.5	0	-6.7	-19.3
Rem. 180 Swift Scirocco	velocity, fps:	2960	2774	2595	2424	2259
	energy, ft-lb:	3501	3075	2692	2348	2039
	arc, inches:		+1.5	0	-6.7	-19.3
Rem. 190 PSP boat-tail	velocity, fps:	2885	2691	2506	2327	2156
	energy, ft-lb:	3511	3055	2648	2285	1961
	arc, inches:		+1.6	0	-7.2	-20.8

CARTRIDGE BULLET	RANGE, YARDS:	0	100	200	300	400
Rem. 190 HPBT Match	velocity, fps:	2900	2725	2557	2395	2239
	energy, ft-lb:	3547	3133	2758	2420	2115
	arc, inches:		+1.6	0	-6.9	-19.9
Rem. 200 Swift A-Frame	velocity, fps:	2825	2595	2376	2167	1970
	energy, ft-lb:	3544	2989	2506	2086	1722
	arc, inches:		+1.8	0	-8.0	-23.5
Speer 180 Grand Slam	velocity, fps:	2950	2735	2530	2334	
	energy, ft-lb:	3478	2989	2558	2176	
	arc, inches:		+1.6	0	-7.0	-20.5
Speer 200 Grand Slam	velocity, fps:	2800	2597	2404	2218	
	energy, ft-lb:	3481	2996	2565	2185	
	arc, inches:		+1.8	0	-7.9	-22.9
Win. 150 Power-Point	velocity, fps:	3290	2951	2636	2342	2068.
	energy, ft-lb:	3605	2900	2314	1827	1424
	arc, inches:		+2.6	+2.1	-3.5	-15.4
Win. 150 Fail Safe	velocity, fps:	3260	2943	2647	2370	2110
	energy, ft-lb:	3539	2884	2334	1871	1483
	arc, inches:		+1.3	0	-6.2	-18.7
Win. 165 Fail Safe	velocity, fps:	3120	2807	2515	2242	1985
	energy, ft-lb:	3567	2888	2319	1842	1445
	arc, inches:		+1.5	0	-7.0	-20.0
Win. 180 Power-Point	velocity, fps:	2960	2745	2540	2344	2157
	energy, ft-lb:	3501	3011	2578	2196	1859
	arc, inches:		+1.9	0	-7.3	-20.9
Win. 180 Power-Point Plus	velocity, fps:	3070	2846	2633	2430	2236
	energy, ft-lb:	3768	3239	2772	2361	1999
	arc, inches:		+1.4	0	-6.4	-18.7
Win. 180 Ballistic Silvertip	velocity, fps:	2950	2764	2586	2415	2250
	energy, ft-lb:	3478	3054	2673	2331	2023
	arc, inches:		+1.5	0	-6.7	-19.4
Win. 180 AccuBond	velocity, fps:	2950	2765	2588	2417	2253
	energy, ft-lb:	3478	3055	2676	2334	2028
	arc, inches:		+1.5	0	-6.7	-19.4
Win. 180 Fail Safe	velocity, fps:	2960	2732	2514	2307	2110
	energy, ft-lb:	3503	2983	2528	2129	1780
	arc, inches:		+1.6	0	-7.1	-20.7
Win. 180 Partition Gold	velocity, fps:	3070	2859	2657	2464	2280
	energy, ft-lb:	3768	3267	2823	2428	2078
	arc, inches:		+1.4	0	-6.3	-18.3
Win. 150 Supreme Elite XP3	velocity, fps:	3260	3030	2811	2603	2404
	energy, ft-lb:	3539	3057	2632	2256	1925
	arc, inches:		+1.1	0	-5.6	-16.2
Win. 180 Supreme Elite XP3	velocity, fps:	3000	2819	2646	2479	2318
	energy, ft-lb:	3597	3176	2797	2455	2147
	arc, inches:		+1.4	0	-6.4	-18.5

.300 REMINGTON SHORT ULTRA MAGNUM

CARTRIDGE BULLET	RANGE, YARDS:	0	100	200	300	400
Rem. 150 PSP C-L Ultra	velocity, fps:	3200	2901	2672	2359	2112
	energy, ft-lb:	3410	2803	2290	1854	1485
	arc, inches:		+1.3	0	-6.4	-19.l
Rem. 165 PSP Core-Lokt	velocity, fps:	3075	2792	2527	2276	2040
	energy, ft-lb:	3464	2856	2339	1828	1525
	arc, inches:		+1.5	0	-7.0	-20.7
Rem. 180 Partition	velocity, fps:	2960	2761	2571	2389	2214
	energy, ft-lb:	3501	3047	2642	2280	1959
	arc, inches:		+1.5	0	-6.8	-19.7
Rem. 180 PSP C-L Ultra	velocity, fps:	2960	2727	2506	2295	2094
	energy, ft-lb:	3501	2972	2509	2105	1753
	arc, inches:		+1.6	0	-7.1	-20.9
Rem. 190 HPBT Match	velocity, fps:	2900	2725	2557	2395	2239
	energy, ft-lb:	3547	3133	2758	2420	2115
	arc, inches:		+1.6	0	-6.9	-19.9

BALLISTICS

.300 WINCHESTER SHORT MAGNUM

CARTRIDGE BULLET	RANGE, YARDS:	0	100	200	300	400
Black Hills 175 Sierra MKing	velocity, fps:	2950				
	energy, ft-lb:	3381				
	arc, inches:					
Black Hills 180 AccuBond	velocity, fps:	2950				
	energy, ft-lb:	3478				
	arc, inches:					
Federal 150 Nosler Bal. Tip	velocity, fps:	3200	2970	2755	2545	2345
	energy, ft-lb:	3410	2940	2520	2155	1830.
	arc, inches:		+1.2	0	-5.8	-17.0
Federal 160 Trophy Bonded Tip	velocity, fps:	3130	2910	2710	2510	2320
	energy, ft-lb:	3590	3110	2680	2305	1970
	arc, inches:		+1.3	0	-6.0	-17.6
Federal 165 Nos. Partition	velocity, fps:	3130	2890	2670	2450	2250
	energy, ft-lb:	3590	3065	2605	2205	1855.
	arc, inches:		+1.3	0	-6.2	-18.2
Federal 165 Nos. Solid Base	velocity, fps:	3130	2900	2690	2490	2290
	energy, ft-lb:	3590	3090	2650	2265	1920
	arc, inches:		+1.3	0	-6.1	-17.8
Federal 180 Barnes TS And Nos. Solid Base	velocity, fps:	2980	2780	2580	2400	2220
	energy, ft-lbs:	3550	3085	2670	2300	1970
	arc, inches:		+1.5	0	-6.7	-19.5
Federal 180 Grand Slam	velocity, fps:	2970	2740	2530	2320	2130
	energy, ft-lb:	3525	3010	2555	2155	1810
	arc, inches:		+1.5	0	-7.0	-20.5
Federal 180 Trophy Bonded	velocity, fps:	2970	2730	2500	2280	2080
	energy, ft-lb:	3525	2975	2500	2085	1725
	arc, inches:		+1.5	0	-7.2	-21.0
Federal 180 Nosler Partition	velocity, fps:	2975	2750	2535	2290	2126
	energy, ft-lb:	3540	3025	2570	2175	1825
	arc, inches:		+1.5	0	-7.0	-20.3
Federal 180 Nos. AccuBond	velocity, fps:	2960	2780	2610	2440	2280
	energy, ft-lb:	3500	3090	2715	2380	2075
	arc, inches:		+1.5	0	-6.6	-19.0
Federal 180 Hi-Shok SP	velocity, fps:	2970	2520	2115	1750	1430
	energy, ft-lb:	3525	2540	1785	1220	820
	arc, inches:		+2.2	0	-9.9	-31.4
Norma 150 FMJ	velocity, fps:	2953	2731	2519	2318	
	energy, ft-lb:					
	arc, inches:		+1.6	0	-7.1	
Norma 150 Barnes X TS	velocity, fps:	3215	2982	2761	2550	
	energy, ft-lb:	3444	2962	2539	2167	
	arc, inches:		+1.2	0	-5.7	
Norma 180 Nosler Bal. Tip	velocity, fps:	3215	2985	2767	2560	
	energy, ft-lb:	3437	2963	2547	2179	
	arc, inches:		+1.2	0	-5.7	
Norma 180 Oryx	velocity, fps:	2936	2542	2180	1849	
	energy, ft-lb:	3446	2583	1900	1368	
	arc, inches:		+1.9	0	-8.9	
Win. 150 Power-Point	velocity, fps:	3270	2903	2565	2250	1958
	energy, ft-lb:	3561	2807	2190	1686	1277
	arc, inches:		+1.3	0	-6.6	-20.2
Win. 150 Ballistic Silvertip	velocity, fps:	3300	3061	2834	2619	2414
	energy, ft-lb:	3628	3121	2676	2285	1941
	arc, inches:		+1.1	0	-5.4	-15.9
Win. 165 Fail Safe	velocity, fps:	3125	2846	2584	2336	2102
	energy, ft-lb:	3577	2967	2446	1999	1619
	arc, inches:		+1.4	0	-6.6	-19.6
Win. 180 Ballistic Silvertip	velocity, fps:	3010	2822	2641	2468	2301.
	energy, ft-lb:	3621	3182	2788	2434	2116
	arc, inches:		+1.4	0	-6.4	-18.6
Win. 180 AccuBond	velocity, fps:	3010	2822	2643	2470	2304
	energy, ft-lb:	3622	3185	2792	2439	2121
	arc, inches:		+1.4	0	-6.4	-18.5

CARTRIDGE BULLET	RANGE, YARDS:	0	100	200	300	400
Win. 180 Fail Safe	velocity, fps:	2970	2741	2524	2317	2120
	energy, ft-lb:	3526	3005	2547	2147	1797
	arc, inches:		+1.6	0	-7.0	-20.5
Win. 180 Power Point	velocity, fps:	2970	2755	2549	2353	2166
	energy, ft-lb:	3526	3034	2598	2214	1875
	arc, inches:		+1.5	0	-6.9	-20.1
Win. 150 Supreme Elite XP3	velocity, fps:	3300	3068	2847	2637	2437
	energy, ft-lb:	3626	3134	2699	2316	1978
	arc, inches:		+1.1	0	-5.4	-15.8
Win. 180 Supreme Elite XP3	velocity, fps:	3010	2829	2655	2488	2326
	energy, ft-lb:	3621	3198	2817	2473	2162
	arc, inches:		+1.4	0	-6.4	-18.3

.300 RUGER COMPACT MAGNUM

CARTRIDGE BULLET	RANGE, YARDS:	0	100	200	300	400
Hornady 150 SST	velocity, fps:	3310	3065	2833	2613	2404
	energy, ft-lb:	3648	3128	2673	2274	1924
	arc, inches:	-1.5	+1.1	0	-5.4	-16.0
Hornady 165 GMX	velocity, fps:	3130	2911	2703	2504	2314
	energy, ft-lb:	3589	3105	2677	2297	1963
	arc, inches:	-1.5	+1.3	0	-6.1	-17.7
Hornady 180 SST	velocity, fps:	3040	2840	2649	2466	2290
	energy, ft-lb:	3693	3223	2804	2430	2096
	arc, inches:	-1.5	+1.4	0	-6.4	-18.5

.300 WEATHERBY MAGNUM

CARTRIDGE BULLET	RANGE, YARDS:	0	100	200	300	400
A-Square 180 Dead Tough	velocity, fps:	3180	2811	2471	2155	1863.
	energy, ft-lb:	4041	3158	2440	1856	1387
	arc, inches:		+1.5	0	-7.2	-21.8
A-Square 220 Monolythic Solid	velocity, fps:	2700	2407	2133	1877	1653
	energy, ft-lb:	3561	2830	2223	1721	1334
	arc, inches:		+2.3	0	-9.8	-29.7
Federal 180 Nosler Partition	velocity, fps:	3190	2980	2780	2590	2400
	energy, ft-lb:	4055	3540	3080	2670	2305
	arc, inches:		+1.2	0	-5.7	-16.7
Federal 180 Nosler Part. HE	velocity, fps:	3330	3110	2810	2710	2520
	energy, ft-lb:	4430	3875	3375	2935	2540
	arc, inches:		+1.0	0	-5.2	-15.1
Federal 180 Sierra GameKing BTSP	velocity, fps:	3190	3010	2830	2660	2490
	energy, ft-lb:	4065	3610	3195	2820	2480
	arc, inches:		+1.2	0	-5.6	-16.0
Federal 180 Trophy Bonded	velocity, fps:	3190	2950	2720	2500	2290
	energy, ft-lb:	4065	3475	2955	2500	2105
	arc, inches:		+1.3	0	-5.9	-17.5
Federal 180 Tr. Bonded HE	velocity, fps:	3330	3080	2850	2750	2410
	energy, ft-lb:	4430	3795	3235	2750	2320
	arc, inches:		+1.1	0	-5.4	-15.8
Federal 180 Trophy Copper	velocity, fps:	3100	2910	2740	2560	2400
	energy, ft-lb:	3840	3395	2990	2625	2300
	arc, inches:		+1.3	0	-6.0	-17.1
Federal 200 Trophy Bonded	velocity, fps:	2900	2670	2440	2230	2030
	energy, ft-lb:	3735	3150	2645	2200	1820
	arc, inches:		+1.7	0	-7.6	-22.2
Hornady 150 SST (or Interbond)	velocity, fps:	3375	3123	2882	2652	2434
	energy, ft-lb:	3793	3248	2766	2343	1973
	arc, inches:		+1.0	0	-5.4	-15.8
Hornady 165 GMX Superformance	velocity, fps:	3140	2921	2713	2515	2325
	energy, ft-lb:	3612	3126	2697	2317	1980
	arc, inches:		+1.3	0	-6.0	-17.5
Hornady 180 SP	velocity, fps:	3120	2891	2673	2466	2268.
	energy, ft-lb:	3890	3340	2856	2430	2055
	arc, inches:		+1.3	0	-6.2	-18.1
Hornady 180 SST	velocity, fps:	3120	2911	2711	2519	2335
	energy, ft-lb:	3890	3386	2936	2535	2180
	arc, inches:		+1.3	0	-6.2	-18.1
Rem. 180 PSP Core-Lokt	velocity, fps:	3120	2866	2627	2400	2184
	energy, ft-lb:	3890	3284	2758	2301	1905
	arc, inches:		+2.4	+2.0	-3.4	-14.9

Centerfire Rifle Ballistics

.300 WEATHERBY MAGNUM TO .303 BRITISH

CARTRIDGE BULLET	RANGE, YARDS:	0	100	200	300	400
Rem. 190 PSP boat-tail	velocity, fps:	3030	2830	2638	2455	2279
	energy, ft-lb:	3873	3378	2936	2542	2190.
	arc, inches:		+1.4	0	-6.4	-18.6
Rem. 200 Swift A-Frame	velocity, fps:	2925	2690	2467	2254	2052
	energy, ft-lb:	3799	3213	2701	2256	1870
	arc, inches:		+2.8	+2.3	-3.9	-17.0
Speer 180 Grand Slam	velocity, fps:	3185	2948	2722	2508	
	energy, ft-lb:	4054	3472	2962	2514	
	arc, inches:		+1.3	0	-5.9	-17.4
Wby. 150 Pointed Expanding	velocity, fps:	3540	3225	2932	2657	2399
	energy, ft-lb:	4173	3462	2862	2351	1916
	arc, inches:		+2.6	+3.3	0	-8.2
Wby. 150 Nosler Partition	velocity, fps:	3540	3263	3004	2759	2528
	energy, ft-lb:	4173	3547	3005	2536	2128
	arc, inches:		+2.5	+3.2	0	-7.7
Wby. 165 Pointed Expanding	velocity, fps:	3390	3123	2872	2634	2409
	energy, ft-lb:	4210	3573	3021	2542	2126
	arc, inches:		+2.8	+3.5	0	-8.5
Wby. 165 Nosler Bal. Tip	velocity, fps:	3350	3133	2927	2730	2542
	energy, ft-lb:	4111	3596	3138	2730	2367
	arc, inches:		+2.7	+3.4	0	-8.1
Wby. 180 Pointed Expanding	velocity, fps:	3240	3004	2781	2569	2366
	energy, ft-lb:	4195	3607	3091	2637	2237
	arc, inches:		+3.1	+3.8	0	-9.0
Wby. 180 Barnes X	velocity, fps:	3190	2995	2809	2631	2459
	energy, ft-lb:	4067	3586	3154	2766	2417
	arc, inches:		+3.1	+3.8	0	-8.7
Wby. 180 Bal. Tip	velocity, fps:	3250	3051	2806	2676	2503
	energy, ft-lb:	4223	3721	3271	2867	2504
	arc, inches:		+2.8	+3.6	0	-8.4
Wby. 180 Nosler Partition	velocity, fps:	3240	3028	2826	2634	2449
	energy, ft-lb:	4195	3665	3193	2772	2396
	arc, inches:		+3.0	+3.7	0	-8.6
Wby. 200 Nosler Partition	velocity, fps:	3060	2860	2668	2485	2308
	energy, ft-lb:	4158	3631	3161	2741	2366
	arc, inches:		+3.5	+4.2	0	-9.8
Wby. 220 RN Expanding	velocity, fps:	2845	2543	2260	1996	1751.
	energy, ft-lb:	3954	3158	2495	1946	1497
	arc, inches:		+4.9	+5.9	0	-14.6

.300 DAKOTA

CARTRIDGE BULLET	RANGE, YARDS:	0	100	200	300	400
Dakota 165 Barnes X	velocity, fps:	3200	2979	2769	2569	2377
	energy, ft-lb:	3751	3251	2809	2417	2070
	arc, inches:		+2.1	+1.8	-3.0	-13.2
Dakota 200 Barnes X	velocity, fps:	3000	2824	2656	2493	2336
	energy, ft-lb:	3996	3542	3131	2760	2423
	arc, inches:		+2.2	+1.5	-4.0	-15.2

.300 PEGASUS

CARTRIDGE BULLET	RANGE, YARDS:	0	100	200	300	400
A-Square 180 SP boat-tail	velocity, fps:	3500	3319	3145	2978	2817
	energy, ft-lb:	4896	4401	3953	3544	3172
	arc, inches:		+2.3	+2.9	0	-6.8
A-Square 180 Nosler Part.	velocity, fps:	3500	3295	3100	2913	2734
	energy, ft-lb:	4896	4339	3840	3392	2988
	arc, inches:		+2.3	+3.0	0	-7.1
A-Square 180 Dead Tough	velocity, fps:	3500	3103	2740	2405	2095
	energy, ft-lb:	4896	3848	3001	2312	1753
	arc, inches:		+1.1	0	-5.7	-17.5

.300 REMINGTON ULTRA MAGNUM

CARTRIDGE BULLET	RANGE, YARDS:	0	100	200	300	400
Federal 180 Trophy Bonded	velocity, fps:	3250	3000	2770	2550	2340
	energy, ft-lb:	4220	3605	3065	2590	2180
	arc, inches:		+1.2	0	-5.7	-16.8
Federal 180 Trophy Copper	velocity, fps:	3150	2960	2780	2610	2440
	energy, ft-lb:	3965	3505	3090	2715	2380
	arc, inches:		+1.2	0	-5.8	-16.6

CARTRIDGE BULLET	RANGE, YARDS:	0	100	200	300	400
Federal 200 Partition	velocity, fps:	3070	2870	2680	2490	2320
	energy, ft-lb:	4185	3655	3180	2760	2380
	arc, inches:		+1.4	0	-6.2	-18.0
Rem. 150 Swift Scirocco	velocity, fps:	3450	3208	2980	2762	2556
	energy, ft-lb:	3964	3427	2956	2541	2175
	arc, inches:		+1.7	+1.5	-2.6	-11.2
Remington 165 Copper Solid	velocity, fps:	3250	3035	2821	2617	2422
	energy, ft-lb:	3893	3373	2916	2602	2390
	arc, inches:		+1.4	0	-5.8	-16.7
Rem. 180 Nosler Partition	velocity, fps:	3250	3037	2834	2640	2454
	energy, ft-lb:	4221	3686	3201	2786	2407
	arc, inches:		+2.4	+1.8	-3.0	-12.7
Rem. 180 Swift Scirocco	velocity, fps:	3250	3048	2856	2672	2495
	energy, ft-lb:	4221	3714	3260	2853	2487
	arc, inches:		+2.0	+1.7	-2.8	-12.3
Rem. 180 PSP Core-Lokt	velocity, fps:	3250	2988	2742	2508	2287
	energy, ft-lb:	3517	2974	2503	2095	1741
	arc, inches:		+2.1	+1.8	-3.1	-13.6
Rem. 200 Nosler Partition	velocity, fps:	3025	2826	2636	2454	2279
	energy, ft-lb:	4063	3547	3086	2673	2308
	arc, inches:		+2.4	+2.0	-3.4	-14.6

.30-378 WEATHERBY MAGNUM

CARTRIDGE BULLET	RANGE, YARDS:	0	100	200	300	400
Nosler 210 ABLR	velocity, fps:	3040	2907	2778	2653	2531
	energy, ft-lb:	4308	3940	3599	3282	2987
	arc, inches:	-1.5	+1.3	0	-5.8	-16.6
Wby. 165 Nosler Bal. Tip	velocity, fps:	3500	3275	3062	2859	2665
	energy, ft-lb:	4488	3930	3435	2995	2603
	arc, inches:		+2.4	+3.0	0	-7.4
Wby. 180 Nosler Bal. Tip	velocity, fps:	3420	3213	3015	2826	2645
	energy, ft-lb:	4676	4126	3634	3193	2797
	arc, inches:		+2.5	+3.1	0	-7.5
Wby. 180 Barnes X	velocity, fps:	3450	3243	3046	2858	2678.
	energy, ft-lb:	4757	4204	3709	3264	2865
	arc, inches:		+2.4	+3.1	0	-7.4
Wby. 200 Nosler Partition	velocity, fps:	3160	2955	2759	2572	2392.
	energy, ft-lb:	4434	3877	3381	2938	2541
	arc, inches:		+3.2	+3.9	0	-9.1

7.82 (.308) WARBIRD

CARTRIDGE BULLET	RANGE, YARDS:	0	100	200	300	400
Lazzeroni 150 Nosler Part.	velocity, fps:	3680	3432	3197	2975	2764
	energy, ft-lb:	4512	3923	3406	2949	2546.
	arc, inches:		+2.1	+2.7	0	-6.6
Lazzeroni 180 Nosler Part.	velocity, fps:	3425	3220	3026	2839	2661
	energy, ft-lb:	4689	4147	3661	3224	2831
	arc, inches:		+2.5	+3.2	0	-7.5
Lazzeroni 200 Swift A-Fr.	velocity, fps:	3290	3105	2928	2758	2594.
	energy, ft-lb:	4808	4283	3808	3378	2988
	arc, inches:		+2.7	+3.4	0	-7.9

7.65x53 ARGENTINE

CARTRIDGE BULLET	RANGE, YARDS:	0	100	200	300	400
Norma 174 Soft Point	velocity, fps:	2493	2173	1878	1611	
	energy, ft-lb:	2402	1825	1363	1003	
	arc, inches:		+2.0	0	-9.5	
Norma 180 Soft Point	velocity, fps:	2592	2386	2189	2002	
	energy, ft-lb:	2686	2276	1916	1602	
	arc, inches:		+2.3	0	-9.6	

.303 BRITISH

CARTRIDGE BULLET	RANGE, YARDS:	0	100	200	300	400
Federal 150 Hi-Shok	velocity, fps:	2690	2440	2210	1980	1780
	energy, ft-lb:	2400	1980	1620	1310	1055
	arc, inches:		+2.2	0	-9.4	-27.6
Federal 180 Sierra Pro-Hunt.	velocity, fps:	2460	2230	2020	1820	1630
	energy, ft-lb:	2420	1995	1625	1315	1060
	arc, inches:		+2.8	0	-11.3	-33.2
Federal 180 Tr. Bonded HE	velocity, fps:	2590	2350	2120	1900	1700
	energy, ft-lb:	2680	2205	1795	1445	1160
	arc, inches:		+2.4	0	-10.0	-30.0
Hornady 150 Soft Point	velocity, fps:	2685	2441	2210	1992	1787
	energy, ft-lb:	2401	1984	1627	1321	1064
	arc, inches:		+2.2	0	-9.3	-27.4

CARTRIDGE BULLET	RANGE, YARDS:	0	100	200	300	400
Hornady 150 SP LM	velocity, fps:	2830	2570	2325	2094	1884.
	energy, ft-lb:	2667	2199	1800	1461	1185
	arc, inches:		+2.0	0	-8.4	-24.6
Hornady 174 BTHP	velocity, fps:	2430	2252	2082	1919	1765
	energy, ft-lb:	2281	1959	1674	1423	1204
	arc, inches:		+2.7	0	-10.7	-30.9
Norma 150 Soft Point	velocity, fps:	2723	2438	2170	1920	
	energy, ft-lb:	2470	1980	1569	1228	
	arc, inches:		+2.2	0	-9.6	
PMC 174 FMJ (and HPBT)	velocity, fps:	2400	2216	2042	1876	1720
	energy, ft-lb:	2225	1898	1611	1360	1143
	arc, inches:		+2.8	0	-11.2	-32.2
PMC 180 SP boat-tail	velocity, fps:	2450	2276	2110	1951	1799
	energy, ft-lb:	2399	2071	1779	1521	1294
	arc, inches:		+2.6	0	-10.4	-30.1
Rem. 180 SP Core-Lokt	velocity, fps:	2460	2124	1817	1542	1311
	energy, ft-lb:	2418	1803	1319	950	687
	arc, inches, s:		0	-5.8	-23.3	
Win. 180 Power-Point	velocity, fps:	2460	2233	2018	1816	1629
	energy, ft-lb:	2418	1993	1627	1318	1060
	arc, inches, s:		0	-6.1	-20.8	

7.7x58 JAPANESE ARISAKA

CARTRIDGE BULLET	RANGE, YARDS:	0	100	200	300	400
Norma 174 Soft Point	velocity, fps:	2493	2173	1878	1611	
	energy, ft-lb:	2402	1825	1363	1003	
	arc, inches:		+2.0	0	-9.5	
Norma 180 Soft Point	velocity, fps:	2493	2291	2099	1916	
	energy, ft-lb:	2485	2099	1761	1468	
	arc, inches:		+2.6	0	-10.5	

.32-20 WINCHESTER

CARTRIDGE BULLET	RANGE, YARDS:	0	100	200	300	400
Rem. 100 Lead	velocity, fps:	1210	1021	913	834	769
	energy, ft-lb:	325	231	185	154	131
	arc, inches:		0	-31.6	-104.7	
Win. 100 Lead	velocity, fps:	1210	1021	913	834	769
	energy, ft-lb:	325	231	185	154	131
	arc, inches:		0	-32.3	-106.3	

.32 WINCHESTER SPECIAL

CARTRIDGE BULLET	RANGE, YARDS:	0	100	200	300	400
Federal 170 Hi-Shok	velocity, fps:	2250	1920	1630	1370	1180
	energy, ft-lb:	1910	1395	1000	710	520
	arc, inches:		0	-8.0	-29.2	
Hornady 165 FTX	velocity, fps:	2410	2145	1897	1669	
	energy, ft-lb:	2128	1685	1318	1020	
	arc, inches:	-1.5	+3.0	0	-12.8	
Rem. 170 SP Core-Lokt	velocity, fps:	2250	1921	1626	1372	1175
	energy, ft-lb:	1911	1393	998	710	521
	arc, inches:		0	-8.0	-29.3	
Win. 170 Power-Point	velocity, fps:	2250	1870	1537	1267	1082
	energy, ft-lb:	1911	1320	892	606	442
	arc, inches:		0	-9.2	-33.2	

8MM MAUSER (8x57)

CARTRIDGE BULLET	RANGE, YARDS:	0	100	200	300	400
Federal 170 Hi-Shok	velocity, fps:	2360	1970	1620	1330	1120
	energy, ft-lb:	2100	1465	995	670	475
	arc, inches:		0	-7.6	-28.5	
Hornady 195 SP	velocity, fps:	2550	2343	2146	1959	1782
	energy, ft-lb:	2815	2377	1994	1861	1375
	arc, inches:		+2.3	0	-9.9	-28.8.
Hornady 195 SP (2005)	velocity, fps:	2475	2269	2074	1888	1714
	energy, ft-lb:	2652	2230	1861	1543	1271
	arc, inches:		+2.6	0	-10.7	-31.3
Norma 123 FMJ	velocity, fps:	2559	2121	1729	1398	
	energy, ft-lb:	1789	1228	817	534	
	arc, inches:		+3.2	0	-15.0	

CARTRIDGE BULLET	RANGE, YARDS:	0	100	200	300	400
Norma 196 Oryx	velocity, fps:	2395	2146	1912	1695	
	energy, ft-lb:	2497	2004	1591	1251	
	arc, inches:		+3	0	-12.6	
Norma 196 Vulkan	velocity, fps:	2395	2156	1930	1720	
	energy, ft-lb:	2497	2023	1622	1289	
	arc, inches:		3.0	0	-12.3	
Norma 196 Alaska	velocity, fps:	2395	2112	1850	1611	
	energy, ft-lb:	2714	2190	1754	1399	
	arc, inches:		0	-6.3	-22.9	
Norma 196 Soft Point (JS)	velocity, fps:	2526	2244	1981	1737	
	energy, ft-lb:	2778	2192	1708	1314	
	arc, inches:		+2.7	0	-11.6	
Norma 196 Alaska (JS)	velocity, fps:	2526	2248	1988	1747	
	energy, ft-lb:	2778	2200	1720	1328	
	arc, inches:		+2.7	0	-11.5	
Norma 196 Vulkan (JS)	velocity, fps:	2526	2276	2041	1821	
	energy, ft-lb:	2778	2256	1813	1443	
	arc, inches:		+2.6	0	-11.0	
Norma 196 Oryx (JS)	velocity, fps:	2526	2269	2027	1802	
	energy, ft-lb:	2778	2241	1789	1413	
	arc, inches:		+2.6	0	-11.1	
PMC 170 Pointed Soft Point	velocity, fps:	2360	1969	1622	1333	1123
	energy, ft-lb:	2102	1463	993	671	476
	arc, inches:		+1.8	-4.5	-24.3	-63.8
Rem. 170 SP Core-Lokt	velocity, fps:	2360	1969	1622	1333	1123
	energy, ft-lb:	2102	1463	993	671	476
	arc, inches:		+1.8	-4.5	-24.3	-63.8.
Win. 170 Power-Point	velocity, fps:	2360	1969	1622	1333	1123
	energy, ft-lb:	2102	1463	993	671	476
	arc, inches:		+1.8	-4.5	-24.3	-63.8

.325 WSM

CARTRIDGE BULLET	RANGE, YARDS:	0	100	200	300	400
Win. 180 Ballistic ST	velocity, fps:	3060	2841	2632	2432	2242
	energy, ft-lb:	3743	3226	2769	2365	2009
	arc, inches:		+1.4	0	-6.4	-18.7
Win. 200 AccuBond CT	velocity, fps:	2950	2753	2565	2384	2210
	energy, ft-lb:	3866	3367	2922	2524	2170
	arc, inches:		+1.5	0	-6.8	-19.8
Win. 220 Power-Point	velocity, fps:	2840	2605	2382	2169	1968
	energy, ft-lb:	3941	3316	2772	2300	1893
	arc, inches:		+1.8	0	-8.0	-23.3

8MM REMINGTON MAGNUM

CARTRIDGE BULLET	RANGE, YARDS:	0	100	200	300	400
A-Square 220 Monolythic Solid	velocity, fps:	2800	2501	2221	1959	1718
	energy, ft-lb:	3829	3055	2409	1875	1442
	arc, inches:		+2.1	0	-9.1	-27.6
Nosler 180 BT	velocity, fps:	3200	2923	2662	2416	2183
	energy, ft-lb:	4092	3414	2832	2333	1905
	arc, inches:	-1.5	+1.3	0	-6.2	-18.4
Rem. 200 Swift A-Frame	velocity, fps:	2900	2623	2361	2115	1885
	energy, ft-lb:	3734	3054	2476	1987	1577
	arc, inches:		+1.8	0	-8.0	-23.9

.338 FEDERAL

CARTRIDGE BULLET	RANGE, YARDS:	0	100	200	300	400
Federal 180 AccuBond	velocity, fps:	2830	2590	2350	2130	1930
	energy, ft-lb:	3200	2670	2215	1820	1480
	arc, inches:	-1.5	+1.8	0	-8.2	-23.9
Federal 185 Barnes TSX	velocity, fps:	2750	2500	2260	2030	1820
	energy, ft-lb:	3105	2560	2090	1695	1355
	arc, inches:	-1.5	+2.0	0	-8.9	-26.2
Federal 200 Tr. Bonded T	velocity, fps:	2630	2430	2240	2060	1890
	energy, ft-lb:	3070	2625	2230	1885	1580
	arc, inches:	-1.5	+2.2	0	-9.2	-26.3
Federal 210 Partition	velocity, fps:	2630	2410	2200	2010	1820
	energy, ft-lb:	3225	2710	2265	1880	1545
	arc, inches:	-1.5	+2.3	0	-9.4	-27.3

Centerfire Rifle Ballistics

.338 MARLIN EXPRESS TO .340 WEATHERBY MAGNUM

.338 MARLIN EXPRESS

CARTRIDGE BULLET	RANGE, YARDS:	0	100	200	300	400
Hornady 200 FTX	velocity, fps:	2565	2365	2174	1992	`1820
	energy, ft-lb:	2922	2484	2099	1762	1471
	arc, inches:	-1.5	+3.0	+1.2	-7.9	-25.9

.338-06

CARTRIDGE BULLET	RANGE, YARDS:	0	100	200	300	400
A-Square 200 Nos. Bal. Tip	velocity, fps:	2750	2553	2364	2184	2011
	energy, ft-lb:	3358	2894	2482	2118	1796
	arc, inches:		+1.9	0	-8.2	-23.6
A-Square 250 SP boat-tail	velocity, fps:	2500	2374	2252	2134	2019
	energy, ft-lb:	3496	3129	2816	2528	2263
	arc, inches:		+2.4	0	-9.3	-26.0
A-Square 250 Dead Tough	velocity, fps:	2500	2222	1963	1724	1507
	energy, ft-lb:	3496	2742	2139	1649	1261
	arc, inches:		+2.8	0	-11.9	-35.5
Nosler 180 AB	velocity, fps:	2950	2698	2460	2234	2020
	energy, ft-lb:	3477	2909	2418	1994	1631
	arc, inches:	-1.5	+1.6	0	-7.4	-21.8
Nosler 225 AB	velocity, fps:	2600	2441	2287	2139	1997
	energy, ft-lb:	3376	2976	2614	2286	1992
	arc, inches:	-1.5	+2.2	0	-8.8	-25.3
Wby. 210 Nosler Part.	velocity, fps:	2750	2526	2312	2109	1916
	energy, ft-lb:	3527	2975	2403	2074	1712
	arc, inches:		+4.8	+5.7	0	-13.5

.338 RUGER COMPACT MAGNUM

CARTRIDGE BULLET	RANGE, YARDS:	0	100	200	300	400
Hornady 185 GMX	velocity, fps:	2980	2755	2542	2338	2143
	energy, ft-lb:	3647	3118	2653	2242	1887
	arc, inches:	-1.5	+1.5	0	-6.9	-20.3
Hornady 200 SST	velocity, fps:	2950	2744	2547	2358	2177
	energy, ft-lb:	3846	3342	2879	2468	2104
	arc, inches:	-1.5	+1.6	0	-6.9	-20.1
Hornady 225 SST	velocity, fps:	2750	2575	2407	2245	2089
	energy, ft-lb:	3778	3313	2894	2518	2180
	arc, inches:	-1.5	+1.9	0	-7.9	-22.7

.338 WINCHESTER MAGNUM

CARTRIDGE BULLET	RANGE, YARDS:	0	100	200	300	400
A-Square 250 SP boat-tail	velocity, fps:	2700	2568	2439	2314	2193
	energy, ft-lb:	4046	3659	3302	2972	2669
	arc, inches:		+4.4	+5.2	0	-11.7
A-Square 250 Triad	velocity, fps:	2700	2407	2133	1877	1653
	energy, ft-lb:	4046	3216	2526	1956	1516
	arc, inches:		+2.3	0	-9.8	-29.8
Federal 200 Trophy Bonded Tip	velocity, fps:	2930	2720	2520	2320	2140
	energy, ft-lb:	3810	3280	2810	2395	2025
	arc, inches:		+1.6	0	-7.1	-20.7
Federal 210 Nosler Partition	velocity, fps:	2830	2600	2390	2180	1980
	energy, ft-lb:	3735	3160	2655	2215	1835
	arc, inches:		+1.8	0	-8.0	-23.3
Federal 225 Sierra Pro-Hunt.	velocity, fps:	2780	2570	2360	2170	1980
	energy, ft-lb:	3860	3290	2780	2340	1960
	arc, inches:		+1.9	0	-8.2	-23.7
Federal 225 Trophy Bonded	velocity, fps:	2800	2560	2330	2110	1900
	energy, ft-lb:	3915	3265	2700	2220	1800
	arc, inches:		+1.9	0	-8.4	-24.5
Federal 225 Tr. Bonded HE	velocity, fps:	2940	2690	2450	2230	2010
	energy, ft-lb:	4320	3610	3000	2475	2025
	arc, inches:		+1.7	0	-7.5	-22.0
Federal 225 Barnes XLC	velocity, fps:	2800	2610	2430	2260	2090
	energy, ft-lb:	3915	3405	2950	2545	2190
	arc, inches:		+1.8	0	-7.7	-22.2
Federal 250 Nosler Partition	velocity, fps:	2660	2470	2300	2120	1960
	energy, ft-lb:	3925	3395	2925	2505	2130.
	arc, inches:		+2.1	0	-8.8	-25.1

CARTRIDGE BULLET	RANGE, YARDS:	0	100	200	300	400
Federal 250 Nosler Part HE	velocity, fps:	2800	2610	2420	2250	2080
	energy, ft-lb:	4350	3775	3260	2805	2395
	arc, inches:		+1.8	0	-7.8	-22.5
Hornady 185 GMX Superformance	velocity, fps:	3080	2851	2633	2426	2228
	energy, ft-lb:	3897	3338	2848	2417	2038
	arc, inches:		+1.4	0	-6.4	-18.8
Hornady 200 SST Superformance	velocity, fps:	3030	2820	2620	2429	2246
	energy, ft-lb:	4077	3532	3049	2621	2240
	arc, inches:		+1.4	0	-6.5	-18.9
Hornady 225 Soft Point HM	velocity, fps:	2920	2678	2449	2232	2027
	energy, ft-lb:	4259	3583	2996	2489	2053
	arc, inches:		+1.8	0	-7.6	-22.0
Norma 225 TXP Swift A-Fr.	velocity, fps:	2740	2507	2286	2075	
	energy, ft-lb:	3752	3141	2611	2153	
	arc, inches:		+2.0	0	-8.7	
Norma 230 Oryx	velocity, fps:	2756	2514	2284	2066	
	energy, ft-lb:	3880	3228	2665	2181	
	arc, inches:		+2.0	0	-8.7	
Norma 250 Nosler Partition	velocity, fps:	2657	2470	2290	2118	
	energy, ft-lb:	3920	3387	2912	2490	
	arc, inches:		+2.1	0	-8.7	
PMC 225 Barnes X	velocity, fps:	2780	2619	2464	2313	2168
	energy, ft-lb:	3860	3426	3032	2673	2348.
	arc, inches:		+1.8	0	-7.6	-21.6
Rem. 200 Nosler Bal. Tip	velocity, fps:	2950	2724	2509	2303	2108
	energy, ft-lb:	3866	3295	2795	2357	1973
	arc, inches:		+1.6	0	-7.1	-20.8
Rem. 210 Nosler Partition	velocity, fps:	2830	2602	2385	2179	1983
	energy, ft-lb:	3734	3157	2653	2214	1834
	arc, inches:		+1.8	0	-7.9	-23.2
Rem. 225 PSP Core-Lokt	velocity, fps:	2780	2572	2374	2184	2003
	energy, ft-lb:	3860	3305	2815	2383	2004
	arc, inches:		+1.9	0	-8.1	-23.4
Rem. 225 PSP C-L Ultra	velocity, fps:	2780	2582	2392	2210	2036
	energy, ft-lb:	3860	3329	2858	2440	2071
	arc, inches:		+1.9	0	-7.9	-23.0
Rem. 225 Swift A-Frame	velocity, fps:	2785	2517	2266	2029	1808
	energy, ft-lb:	3871	3165	2565	2057	1633
	arc, inches:		+2.0	0	-8.8	-25.2
Rem. 250 PSP Core-Lokt	velocity, fps:	2660	2456	2261	2075	1898
	energy, ft-lb:	3927	3348	2837	2389	1999
	arc, inches:		+2.1	0	-8.9	-26.0
Speer 250 Grand Slam	velocity, fps:	2645	2442	2247	2062	
	energy, ft-lb:	3883	3309	2803	2360	
	arc, inches:		+2.2	0	-9.1	-26.2
Win. 200 Power-Point	velocity, fps:	2960	2658	2375	2110	1862
	energy, ft-lb:	3890	3137	2505	1977	1539
	arc, inches:		+2.0	0	-8.2	-24.3
Win. 200 Ballistic Silvertip	velocity, fps:	2950	2724	2509	2303	2108
	energy, ft-lb:	3864	3294	2794	2355	1972
	arc, inches:		+1.6	0	-7.1	-20.8
Win. 225 AccuBond	velocity, fps:	2800	2634	2474	2319	2170
	energy, ft-lb:	3918	3467	3058	2688	2353
	arc, inches:		+1.8	0	-7.4	-21.3
Win. 230 Fail Safe	velocity, fps:	2780	2573	2375	2186	2005
	energy, ft-lb:	3948	3382	2881	2441	2054
	arc, inches:		+1.9	0	-8.1	-23.4
Win. 250 Partition Gold	velocity, fps:	2650	2467	2291	2122	1960
	energy, ft-lb:	3899	3378	2914	2520	2134
	arc, inches:		+2.1	0	-8.7	-25.2

.340 WEATHERBY MAGNUM

CARTRIDGE BULLET	RANGE, YARDS:	0	100	200	300	400
A-Square 250 SP boat-tail	velocity, fps:	2820	2684	2552	2424	2299
	energy, ft-lb:	4414	3999	3615	3261	2935
	arc, inches:		+4.0	+4.6	0	-10.6
A-Square 250 Triad	velocity, fps:	2820	2520	2238	1976	1741
	energy, ft-lb:	4414	3524	2781	2166	1683
	arc, inches:		+2.0	0	-9.0	-26.8
Federal 225 Trophy Bonded	velocity, fps:	3100	2840	2600	2370	2150
	energy, ft-lb:	4800	4035	3375	2800	2310
	arc, inches:		+1.4	0	-6.5	-19.4

.340 WEATHERBY MAGNUM TO .35 REMINGTON

CARTRIDGE BULLET	RANGE, YARDS:	0	100	200	300	400
Wby. 200 Pointed Expanding	velocity, fps:	3221	2946	2688	2444	2213
	energy, ft-lb:	4607	3854	3208	2652	2174
	arc, inches:		+3.3	+4.0	0	-9.9
Wby. 200 Nosler Bal. Tip	velocity, fps:	3221	2980	2753	2536	2329
	energy, ft-lb:	4607	3944	3364	2856	2409
	arc, inches:		+3.1	+3.9	0	-9.2
Wby. 210 Nosler Partition	velocity, fps:	3211	2963	2728	2505	2293
	energy, ft-lb:	4807	4093	3470	2927	2452
	arc, inches:		+3.2	+3.9	0	-9.5
Wby. 225 Pointed Expanding	velocity, fps:	3066	2824	2595	2377	2170
	energy, ft-lb:	4696	3984	3364	2822	2352
	arc, inches:		+3.6	+4.4	0	-10.7
Wby. 225 Barnes X	velocity, fps:	3001	2804	2615	2434	2260
	energy, ft-lb:	4499	3927	3416	2959	2551
	arc, inches:		+3.6	+4.3	0	-10.3
Wby. 250 Pointed Expanding	velocity, fps:	2963	2745	2537	2338	2149
	energy, ft-lb:	4873	4182	3572	3035	2563
	arc, inches:		+3.9	+4.6	0	-11.1
Wby. 250 Nosler Partition	velocity, fps:	2941	2743	2553	2371	2197
	energy, ft-lb:	4801	4176	3618	3120	2678
	arc, inches:		+3.9	+4.6	0	-10.9

.330 DAKOTA

CARTRIDGE BULLET		0	100	200	300	400
Dakota 200 Barnes X	velocity, fps:	3200	2971	2754	2548	2350
	energy, ft-lb:	4547	3920	3369	2882	2452
	arc, inches:		+2.1	+1.8	-3.1	-13.4
Dakota 250 Barnes X	velocity, fps:	2900	2719	2545	2378	2217
	energy, ft-lb:	4668	4103	3595	3138	2727
	arc, inches:		+2.3	+1.3	-5.0	-17.5

.338 REMINGTON ULTRA MAGNUM

CARTRIDGE BULLET		0	100	200	300	400
Federal 210 Nosler Partition	velocity, fps:	3025	2800	2585	2385	2190
	energy, ft-lb:	4270	3655	3120	2645	2230
	arc, inches:		+1.5	0	-6.7	-19.5
Federal 250 Trophy Bonded	velocity, fps:	2860	2630	2420	2210	2020
	energy, ft-lb:	4540	3850	3245	2715	2260.
	arc, inches:		+0.8	0	-7.7	-22.6
Rem. 250 Swift A-Frame	velocity, fps:	2860	2645	2440	2244	2057
	energy, ft-lb:	4540	3882	3303	2794	2347
	arc, inches:		+1.7	0	-7.6	-22.1
Rem. 250 PSP Core-Lokt	velocity, fps:	2860	2647	2443	2249	2064
	energy, ft-lb:	4540	3888	3314	2807	2363
	arc, inches:		+1.7	0	-7.6	-22.0

.338 NORMA MAGNUM

CARTRIDGE BULLET		0				
Black Hills 300 MatchKing	velocity, fps:	2725				
	energy, ft-lb:	4946				
	arc, inches					

.338 LAPUA

CARTRIDGE BULLET		0	100	200	300	400
Black Hills 250 Sierra MKing	velocity, fps:	2950				
	energy, ft-lb:	4831				
	arc, inches:					
Black Hills 300 Sierra MKing	velocity, fps:	2800				
	energy, ft-lb:	5223				
	arc, inches:					
Hornady 250 BTHP Match	velocity, fps:	2900	2761	2626	2495	2368
	energy, ft-lb:	4668	4230	3827	3455	3112
	arc, inches:		+1.5	0	-6.6	-18.8
Hornady 285 BTHP	velocity, fps:	2745	2616	2491	2369	2251
	energy, ft-lb:	4768	4331	3926	3552	3206
	arc, inches:	-1.5	+1.8	0	-7.4	-21.0

CARTRIDGE BULLET	RANGE, YARDS:	0	100	200	300	600
Lapua 250 Scenar	velocity, fps:	2970	2823	2680	2539	2141
	energy, ft-lb:	4896	4424	3985	3579	2545
	arc, inches:	-1.5	+3.0	+4.0	0	-47.0
Lapua 300 Scenar	velocity, fps:	2723	2600	2482	2367	2042
	energy, ft-lb:	4938	4504	4102	3731	2778
	arc, inches:	-1.5	+4.0	+5.0	0	-54.0

CARTRIDGE BULLET	RANGE, YARDS:	0	100	200	300	400
Nosler 225 AB	velocity, fps:	3000	2826	2659	2498	2342
	energy, ft-lb:	4495	3990	3532	3117	2741
	arc, inches:	-1.5	+1.4	0	-6.3	-18.3

.338-378 WEATHERBY MAGNUM

CARTRIDGE BULLET		0	100	200	300	400
Wby. 200 Nosler Bal. Tip	velocity, fps:	3350	3102	2868	2646	2434
	energy, ft-lb:	4983	4273	3652	3109	2631
	arc, inches:	0	+2.8	+3.5	0	-8.4
Wby. 225 Barnes X	velocity, fps:	3180	2974	2778	2591	2410.
	energy, ft-lb:	5052	4420	3856	3353	2902
	arc, inches:	0	+3.1	+3.8	0	-8.9
Wby. 250 Nosler Partition	velocity, fps:	3060	2856	2662	2475	2297
	energy, ft-lb:	5197	4528	3933	3401	2927
	arc, inches:	0	+3.5	+4.2	0	-9.8

8.59 (.338) TITAN

CARTRIDGE BULLET		0	100	200	300	400
Lazzeroni 200 Nos. Bal. Tip	velocity, fps:	3430	3211	3002	2803	2613
	energy, ft-lb:	5226	4579	4004	3491	3033
	arc, inches:		+2.5	+3.2	0	-7.6
Lazzeroni 225 Nos. Partition	velocity, fps:	3235	3031	2836	2650	2471
	energy, ft-lb:	5229	4591	4021	3510	3052
	arc, inches:		+3.0	+3.6	0	-8.6
Lazzeroni 250 Swift A-Fr.	velocity, fps:	3100	2908	2725	2549	2379
	energy, ft-lb:	5336	4697	4123	3607	3143
	arc, inches:		+3.3	+4.0	0	-9.3

.338 A-SQUARE

CARTRIDGE BULLET		0	100	200	300	400
A-Square 200 Nos. Bal. Tip	velocity, fps:	3500	3266	3045	2835	2634
	energy, ft-lb:	5440	4737	4117	3568	3081
	arc, inches:		+2.4	+3.1	0	-7.5
A-Square 250 SP boat-tail	velocity, fps:	3120	2974	2834	2697	2565.
	energy, ft-lb:	5403	4911	4457	4038	3652
	arc, inches:		+3.1	+3.7	0	-8.5
A-Square 250 Triad	velocity, fps:	3120	2799	2500	2220	1958
	energy, ft-lb:	5403	4348	3469	2736	2128
	arc, inches:		+1.5	0	-7.1	-20.4.

.338 EXCALIBER

CARTRIDGE BULLET		0	100	200	300	400
A-Square 200 Nos. Bal. Tip	velocity, fps:	3600	3361	3134	2920	2715
	energy, ft-lb:	5755	5015	4363	3785	3274
	arc, inches:		+2.2	+2.9	0	-6.7
A-Square 250 SP boat-tail	velocity, fps:	3250	3101	2958	2684	2553
	energy, ft-lb:	5863	5339	4855	4410	3998
	arc, inches:		+2.7	+3.4	0	-7.8
A-Square 250 Triad	velocity, fps:	3250	2922	2618	2333	2066
	energy, ft-lb:	5863	4740	3804	3021	2370
	arc, inches:		+1.3	0	-6.4	-19.2

.348 WINCHESTER

CARTRIDGE BULLET		0	100	200	300	400
Win. 200 Silvertip	velocity, fps:	2520	2215	1931	1672	1443.
	energy, ft-lb:	2820	2178	1656	1241	925
	arc, inches:		0	-6.2	-21.9	

.357 MAGNUM

CARTRIDGE BULLET		0	100	200	300	400
Federal 180 Hi-Shok HP Hollow Point	velocity, fps:	1550	1160	980	860	770
	energy, ft-lb:	960	535	385	295	235
	arc, inches:		0	-22.8	-77.9	-173.8
Win. 158 Jacketed SP	velocity, fps:	1830	1427	1138	980	883
	energy, ft-lb:	1175	715	454	337	274
	arc, inches:		0	-16.2	-57.0	-128.3

.35 REMINGTON

CARTRIDGE BULLET		0	100	200	300	400
Federal 200 Hi-Shok	velocity, fps:	2080	1700	1380	1140	1000
	energy, ft-lb:	1920	1280	840	575	445
	arc, inches:		0	-10.7	-39.3	

Centerfire Rifle Ballistics

.35 REMINGTON TO 9.3X74 R

CARTRIDGE BULLET	RANGE, YARDS:	0	100	200	300	400
Hornady 200 Evolution	velocity, fps:	2225	1963	1721	1503	
	energy, ft-lb:	2198	1711	1315	1003	
	arc, inches:		+3.0	-1.3	-17.5	
Rem. 150 PSP Core-Lokt	velocity, fps:	2300	1874	1506	1218	1039
	energy, ft-lb:	1762	1169	755	494	359
	arc, inches:		0	-8.6	-32.6	
Rem. 200 SP Core-Lokt	velocity, fps:	2080	1698	1376	1140	1001
	energy, ft-lb:	1921	1280	841	577	445
	arc, inches:		0	-10.7	-40.1	
Win. 200 Power-Point	velocity, fps:	2020	1646	1335	1114	985
	energy, ft-lb:	1812	1203	791	551	431
	arc, inches:		0	-12.1	-43.9	

.356 WINCHESTER

CARTRIDGE BULLET	RANGE, YARDS:	0	100	200	300	400
Win. 200 Power-Point	velocity, fps:	2460	2114	1797	1517	1284
	energy, ft-lb:	2688	1985	1434	1022	732
	arc, inches:		+1.6	-3.8	-20.1	-51.2

.358 WINCHESTER

CARTRIDGE BULLET	RANGE, YARDS:	0	100	200	300	400
Hornady 200 SP	velocity, fps:	2475	2180	1906	1655	1434
	energy, ft-lb:	2720	2110	1612	1217	913
	arc, inches:	-1.5	+2.9	0	-12.6	-37.9
Win. 200 Silvertip	velocity, fps:	2490	2171	1876	1610	1379
	energy, ft-lb:	2753	2093	1563	1151	844
	arc, inches:		+1.5	-3.6	-18.6	-47.2

.35 WHELEN

CARTRIDGE BULLET	RANGE, YARDS:	0	100	200	300	400
Federal 225 Trophy Bonded	velocity, fps:	2600	2400	2200	2020	1840
	energy, ft-lb:	3375	2865	2520	2030	1690.
	arc, inches:		+2.3	0	-9.4	-27.3
Hornady 200 SP	velocity, fps:	2910	2585	2283	2001	1742
	energy, ft-lb:	3760	2968	2314	1778	1347
	arc, inches:	-1.5	+1.9	0	-8.6	-25.9
Rem. 200 Pointed Soft Point	velocity, fps:	2675	2378	2100	1842	1606
	energy, ft-lb:	3177	2510	1958	1506	1145
	arc, inches:		+2.3	0	-10.3	-30.8
Rem. 250 Pointed Soft Point	velocity, fps:	2400	2197	2005	1823	1652
	energy, ft-lb:	3197	2680	2230	1844	1515
	arc, inches:		+1.3	-3.2	-16.6	-40.0

.350 REMINGTON MAGNUM

CARTRIDGE BULLET	RANGE, YARDS:	0	100	200	300	400
Nosler 225 PT	velocity, fps:	2550	2349	2158	1976	1804
	energy, ft-lb:	3248	2758	2327	1951	1626
	arc, inches:	-1.5	+2.4	0	-9.9	-28.7

.358 NORMA MAGNUM

CARTRIDGE BULLET	RANGE, YARDS:	0	100	200	300	400
A-Square 275 Triad	velocity, fps:	2700	2394	2108	1842	1653
	energy, ft-lb:	4451	3498	2713	2072	1668
	arc, inches:		+2.3	0	-10.1	-29.8
Norma 250 TXP Swift A-Fr.	velocity, fps:	2723	2467	2225	1996	
	energy, ft-lb:	4117	3379	2748	2213	
	arc, inches:		+2.1	0	-9.1	
Norma 250 Woodleigh	velocity, fps:	2799	2442	2112	1810	
	energy, ft-lb:	4350	3312	2478	1819	
	arc, inches:		+2.2	0	-10.0	
Norma 250 Oryx	velocity, fps:	2756	2493	2245	2011	
	energy, ft-lb:	4217	3451	2798	2245	
	arc, inches:		+2.1	0	-9.0	

.358 STA

CARTRIDGE BULLET	RANGE, YARDS:	0	100	200	300	400
A-Square 275 Triad	velocity, fps:	2850	2562	2292	2039	1764
	energy, ft-lb:	4959	4009	3208	2539	1899.
	arc, inches:		+1.9	0	-8.6	-26.1

9.3x57

CARTRIDGE BULLET	RANGE, YARDS:	0	100	200	300	400
Norma 232 Vulkan	velocity, fps:	2329	2031	1757	1512	
	energy, ft-lb:	2795	2126	1591	1178	
	arc, inches:		+3.5	0	-14.9	
Norma 232 Oryx	velocity, fps:	2362	2058	1778	1528	
	energy, ft-lb:	2875	2182	1630	1203	
	arc, inches:		+3.4	0	-14.5	
Norma 285 Oryx	velocity, fps:	2067	1859	1666	1490	
	energy, ft-lb:	2704	2188	1756	1404	
	arc, inches:		+4.3	0	-16.8	
Norma 286 Alaska	velocity, fps:	2067	1857	1662	1484	
	energy, ft-lb:	2714	2190	1754	1399	
	arc, inches:		+4.3	0	-17.0	

9.3x62

CARTRIDGE BULLET	RANGE, YARDS:	0	100	200	300	400
Federal 286 Swift A-Frame	velocity, fps:	2360	2150	1950	1760	1580
	energy, ft-lb:	3535	2930	2405	1960	1590
	arc, inches:		+2.9	0	-11.6	-31.0
Federal 286 TSX	velocity, fps:	2360	2160	1970	1790	
	energy, ft-lb:	3535	2965	2465	2035	
	arc, inches:	-1.5	+3.0	0	-12.0	
Federal 286 Woodleigh Hydro	velocity, fps:	2360	2050	1760	1510	
	energy, ft-lb:	3535	2665	1975	1445	
	arc, inches::	-1.5	+3.4	0	-14.7	
Hornady 286 SP-HP	velocity, fps:	2350	2155	1961	1778	
	energy, ft-lb:	3537	2949	2442	2008	
	arc, inches:	-1.5	+3.0	0	-12.1	
Norma 232 Oryx	velocity, fps:	2625	2294	1988	1708	
	energy, ft-lb:	3535	2700	2028	1497	
	arc, inches:	-1.5	+2.5	0	-11.4	
Norma 250 A-Frame	velocity, fps:	2625	2322	2039	1778	
	energy, ft-lb:	3826	2993	2309	1755	
	arc, inches:	-1.5	+2.5	0	-10.9	
Norma 286 Plastic Point	velocity, fps:	2362	2141	1931	1736	
	energy, ft-lb:	3544	2911	2370	1914	
	arc, inches:	-1.5	+3.1	0	-12.4	
Nosler 250 AccuBond	velocity, fps:	2550	2376	2208	2048	1894
	energy, ft-lb:	3609	3133	2707	2328	1992
	arc, inches:	-1.5	+2.3	0	-9.5	-27.2
Nosler 286 Partition	velocity, fps:	2350	2179	2015	1859	1711
	energy, ft-lb:	3506	3014	2578	2194	1859
	arc, inches:	-1.5	+2.9	0	-11.5	-33.1

9.3x64

CARTRIDGE BULLET	RANGE, YARDS:	0	100	200	300	400
A-Square 286 Triad	velocity, fps:	2700	2391	2103	1835	1602
	energy, ft-lb:	4629	3630	2808	2139	1631
	arc, inches:		+2.3	0	-10.1	-30.8

.370 SAKO

CARTRIDGE BULLET	RANGE, YARDS:	0	100	200	300	400
Federal 286 TSX	velocity, fps:	2550	2370	2190	2020	1860
	energy, ft-lb:	4130	3555	3045	2595	2195
	arc, inches:	-1.5	+2.4	0	-9.6	-27.5

370 SAKO MAGNUM

CARTRIDGE BULLET	RANGE, YARDS:	0	100	200	300	400
Federal 286 Swift A-Frame	velocity, fps:	2550	2330	2120	1920	1730
	energy, ft-lb:	4130	3440	2845	2330	1900
	arc, inches:		+2.5	0	-10.1	-30.0
Federal 286 TSX	velocity, fps:	2550	2370	2190	2020	1860
	energy, ft-lb:	4130	3555	3045	2595	2195
	arc, inches:		+2.4	0	-9.5	-27.5
Federal 286 Woodleigh Hydro Solid	velocity, fps:	2550	2230	1920	1650	1410
	energy, ft-lb:	4130	3145	2350	1730	1265
	arc, inches:		+2.8	0	-12.4	-37.5

9.3x74 R

CARTRIDGE BULLET	RANGE, YARDS:	0	100	200	300	400
A-Square 286 Triad	velocity, fps:	2360	2089	1844	1623	
	energy, ft-lb:	3538	2771	2157	1670	
	arc, inches:		+3.6	0	-14.0	
Federal 286 Swift A-Frame	velocity, fps:	2360	2150	1950	1760	1580
	energy, ft-lb:	3535	2930	2405	1960	1590
	arc, inches:		+2.9	0	-11.6	-31.0
Federal 286 TSX	velocity, fps:	2360	2160	1970	1790	1630
	energy, ft-lb:	3535	2965	2465	2035	1675
	arc, inches:		+2.9	0	-11.1	-29.9
Federal 286 Woodleigh Hydro Solid	velocity, fps:	2360	2050	1760	1510	1300
	energy, ft-lb:	3535	2665	1975	1445	1065
	arc, inches:		+3.4	0	-14.7	-45.0
Hornady 286	velocity, fps	2360	2136	1924	1727	1545
	energy, ft-lb	3536	2896	2351	1893	1516
	arc, inches	-1.5	0	-6.1	-21.7	-49.0
Norma 232 Vulkan	velocity, fps:	2625	2327	2049	1792	
	energy, ft-lb:	3551	2791	2164	1655	
	arc, inches:		+2.5	0	-10.8	
Norma 232 Oryx	velocity, fps:	2526	2191	1883	1605	
	energy, ft-lb:	3274	2463	1819	1322	
	arc, inches:		+2.9	0	-12.8	

CARTRIDGE BULLET	RANGE, YARDS:	0	100	200	300	400
Norma 285 Oryx	velocity, fps:	2362	2114	1881	1667	
	energy, ft-lb:	3532	2829	2241	1758	
	arc, inches:		+3.1	0	-13.0	
Norma 286 Alaska	velocity, fps:	2362	2135	1920	1720	
	energy, ft-lb:	3544	2894	2342	1879	
	arc, inches:		+3.1	0	-12.5	
Norma 286 Plastic Point	velocity, fps:	2362	2135	1920	1720	
	energy, ft-lb:	3544	2894	2342	1879	
	arc, inches:		+3.1	0	-12.5	

.375 WINCHESTER

CARTRIDGE BULLET	RANGE, YARDS:	0	100	200	300	400
Win. 200 Power-Point	velocity, fps:	2200	1841	1526	1268	1089
	energy, ft-lb:	2150	1506	1034	714	
	arc, inches:		0	-9.5	-33.8	

.375 FLANGED

CARTRIDGE BULLET	RANGE, YARDS:	0	100	200	300	400
Nosler 300 PT	velocity, fps:	2400	2191	1993	1806	1632
	energy, ft-lb:	3836	3198	2646	2173	1775
	arc, inches:	-1.5	+2.9	0	-11.7	-34.0

.375 H&H MAGNUM

CARTRIDGE BULLET	RANGE, YARDS:	0	100	200	300	400
A-Square 300 SP boat-tail	velocity, fps:	2550	2415	2284	2157	2034
	energy, ft-lb:	4331	3884	3474	3098	2755
	arc, inches:		+5.2	+6.0	0	-13.3
A-Square 300 Triad	velocity, fps:	2550	2251	1973	1717	1496
	energy, ft-lb:	4331	3375	2592	1964	1491
	arc, inches:		+2.7	0	-11.7	-35.1
Federal 250 Trophy Bonded	velocity, fps:	2670	2360	2080	1820	1580
	energy, ft-lb:	3955	3100	2400	1830	1380
	arc, inches:		+2.4	0	-10.4	-31.7
Federal 270 Hi-Shok	velocity, fps:	2690	2420	2170	1920	1700
	energy, ft-lb:	4340	3510	2810	2220	1740
	arc, inches:		+2.4	0	-10.9	-33.3
Federal 300 Hi-Shok	velocity, fps:	2530	2270	2020	1790	1580
	energy, ft-lb:	4265	3425	2720	2135	1665
	arc, inches:		+2.6	0	-11.2	-33.3
Federal 300 Nosler Partition	velocity, fps:	2530	2320	2120	1930	1750
	energy, ft-lb:	4265	3585	2995	2475	2040
	arc, inches:		+2.5	0	-10.3	-29.9
Federal 300 Trophy Bonded	velocity, fps:	2530	2280	2040	1810	1610
	energy, ft-lb:	4265	3450	2765	2190	1725
	arc, inches:		+2.6	0	-10.9	-32.8
Federal 300 Tr. Bonded HE	velocity, fps:	2700	2440	2190	1960	1740
	energy, ft-lb:	4855	3960	3195	2550	2020
	arc, inches:		+2.2	0	-9.4	-28.0
Federal 300 Trophy Bonded Sledgehammer Solid	velocity, fps:	2530	2160	1820	1520	1280.
	energy, ft-lb:	4265	3105	2210	1550	1090
	arc, inches, s:		-6.0	-22.7	-54.6	
Federal 300 TSX	velocity, fps:	2470	2240	2010	1800	1610
	energy, ft-lb:	4065	3325	2700	2170	1735
	arc, inches:		+2.7	0	-11.3	-33.6
Federal 300 Woodleigh Hydro Solid	velocity, fps:	2500	2180	1880	1610	1380
	energy, ft-lb:	4165	3160	2355	1735	1270
	arc, inches:		+2.9	0	-20.1	-46.3
Hornady 250 GMX Superformance	velocity, fps:	2890	2675	2471	2275	2088
	energy, ft-lb:	4636	3973	3388	2873	2421
	arc, inches:		+1.7	0	-7.4	-21.5
Hornady 270 SP HM	velocity, fps:	2870	2620	2385	2162	1957
	energy, ft-lb:	4937	4116	3408	2802	2296
	arc, inches:		+2.2	0	-8.4	-23.9
Hornady 300 FMJ RN HM	velocity, fps:	2705	2376	2072	1804	1560
	energy, ft-lb:	4873	3760	2861	2167	1621
	arc, inches:		+2.7	0	-10.8	-32.1
Norma 300 Soft Point	velocity, fps:	2549	2211	1900	1619	
	energy, ft-lb:	4329	3258	2406	1747	
	arc, inches:		+2.8	0	-12.6	
Norma 300 TXP Swift A-Fr.	velocity, fps:	2559	2296	2049	1818	
	energy, ft-lb:	4363	3513	2798	2203	
	arc, inches:		+2.6	0	-10.9	

CARTRIDGE BULLET	RANGE, YARDS:	0	100	200	300	400
Norma 300 Oryx	velocity, fps:	2559	2292	2041	1807	
	energy, ft-lb:	4363	3500	2775	2176	
	arc, inches:		+2.6	0	-11.0	
Norma 300 Barnes Solid	velocity, fps:	2493	2061	1677	1356	
	energy, ft-lb:	4141	2829	1873	1234	
	arc, inches:		+3.4	0	-16.0	
PMC 270 PSP	velocity, fps:					
	energy, ft-lb:					
	arc, inches:					
PMC 270 Barnes X	velocity, fps:	2690	2528	2372	2221	2076
	energy, ft-lb:	4337	3831	3371	2957	2582
	arc, inches:		+2.0	0	-8.2	-23.4
PMC 300 Barnes X	velocity, fps:	2530	2389	2252	2120	1993
	energy, ft-lb:	4263	3801	3378	2994	2644
	arc, inches:		+2.3	0	-9.2	-26.1
Rem. 270 Soft Point	velocity, fps:	2690	2420	2166	1928	1707
	energy, ft-lb:	4337	3510	2812	2228	1747
	arc, inches:		+2.2	0	-9.7	-28.7
Rem. 300 Swift A-Frame	velocity, fps:	2530	2245	1979	1733	1512
	energy, ft-lb:	4262	3357	2608	2001	1523
	arc, inches:		+2.7	0	-11.7	-35.0
Speer 285 Grand Slam	velocity, fps:	2610	2365	2134	1916	
	energy, ft-lb:	4310	3540	2883	2323	
	arc, inches:		+2.4	0	-9.9	
Speer 300 African GS Tungsten Solid	velocity, fps:	2609	2277	1970	1690	
	energy, ft-lb:	4534	3453	2585	1903	
	arc, inches:		+2.6	0	-11.7	-35.6
Win. 270 Fail Safe	velocity, fps:	2670	2447	2234	2033	1842
	energy, ft-lb:	4275	3590	2994	2478	2035
	arc, inches:		+2.2	0	-9.1	-28.7
Win. 300 Fail Safe	velocity, fps:	2530	2336	2151	1974	1806
	energy, ft-lb:	4265	3636	3082	2596	2173
	arc, inches:		+2.4	0	-10.0	-26.9

.375 DAKOTA

CARTRIDGE BULLET	RANGE, YARDS:	0	100	200	300	400
Dakota 270 Barnes X	velocity, fps:	2800	2617	2441	2272	2109
	energy, ft-lb:	4699	4104	3571	3093	2666
	arc, inches:		+2.3	+1.0	-6.1	-19.9
Dakota 300 Barnes X	velocity, fps:	2600	2316	2051	1804	1579
	energy, ft-lb:	4502	3573	2800	2167	1661
	arc, inches:		+2.4	-0.1	-11.0	-32.7

.375 RUGER

CARTRIDGE BULLET	RANGE, YARDS:	0	100	200	300	400
Hornady 250 GMX Superformance	velocity, fps:	2890	2675	2471	2275	2088
	energy, ft-lb:	4636	3973	3388	2873	2421
	arc, inches:		+1.7	0	-7.4	-21.5
Hornady 270 SP	velocity, fps:	2840	2600	2372	2156	1951
	energy, ft-lb:	4835	4052	3373	2786	2283
	arc, inches:	-1.5	+1.8	0	-8.0	-23.6
Hornady 300 Solid	velocity, fps	2660	2344	2050	1780	1536
	energy, ft-lb	4713	3660	2800	2110	1572
	arc, inches	-1.5	+2.4	0	-10.8	-32.6
Nosler 260 AB	velocity, fps:	2900	2703	2514	2333	2160
	energy, ft-lb:	4854	4217	3649	3143	2693
	arc, inches:	-1.5	+1.6	0	-7.1	-20.7

.375 WEATHERBY MAGNUM

CARTRIDGE BULLET	RANGE, YARDS:	0	100	200	300	400
A-Square 300 SP boat-tail	velocity, fps:	2700	2560	2425	2293	2166
	energy, ft-lb:	4856	4366	3916	3503	3125
	arc, inches:		+4.5	+5.2	0	-11.9
A-Square 300 Triad	velocity, fps:	2700	2391	2103	1835	1602
	energy, ft-lb:	4856	3808	2946	2243	1710
	arc, inches:		+2.3	0	-10.1	-30.8
Wby. 300 Nosler Part.	velocity, fps:	2800	2572	2366	2140	1963
	energy, ft-lb:	5224	4408	3696	3076	2541
	arc, inches:		+1.9	0	-8.2	-23.9

Centerfire Rifle Ballistics

.375 JRS TO .416 REMINGTON MAGNUM

CARTRIDGE BULLET	RANGE, YARDS:	0	100	200	300	400
.375 JRS						
A-Square 300 SP boat-tail	velocity, fps:	2700	2560	2425	2293	2166.
	energy, ft-lb:	4856	4366	3916	3503	3125
	arc, inches:		+4.5	+5.2	0	-11.9
A-Square 300 Triad	velocity, fps:	2700	2391	2103	1835	1602
	energy, ft-lb:	4856	3808	2946	2243	1710
	arc, inches:		+2.3	0	-10.1	-30.8
.375 REMINGTON ULTRA MAGNUM						
Nosler 260 AB	velocity, fps:	2950	2750	2560	2377	2202
	energy, ft-lb:	5023	4367	3783	3262	2799
	arc, inches:	-1.5	+1.6	0	-6.9	-19.9
Nosler 300 PT	velocity, fps:	2750	2524	2309	2105	1912
	energy, ft-lb:	5036	4244	3553	2953	2435
	arc, inches:	-1.5	+2.0	0	-8.5	-24.9
Rem. 270 Soft Point	velocity, fps:	2900	2558	2241	1947	1678
	energy, fps:	5041	3922	3010	2272	1689
	arc, inches:		+1.9	0	-9.2	-27.8
Rem. 300 Swift A-Frame	velocity, fps:	2760	2505	2263	2035	1822
	energy, ft-lb:	5073	4178	3412	2759	2210
	arc, inches:		+2.0	0	-8.8	-26.1
.375 A-SQUARE						
A-Square 300 SP boat-tail	velocity, fps:	2920	2773	2631	2494	2360
	energy, ft-lb:	5679	5123	4611	4142	3710
	arc, inches:		+3.7	+4.4	0	-9.8
A-Square 300 Triad	velocity, fps:	2920	2596	2294	2012	1762
	energy, ft-lb:	5679	4488	3505	2698	2068
	arc, inches:		+1.8	0	-8.5	-25.5
.376 STEYR						
Hornady 225 SP	velocity, fps:	2600	2331	2078	1842	1625
	energy, ft-lb:	3377	2714	2157	1694	1319
	arc, inches:		+2.5	0	-10.6	-31.4
Hornady 270 SP	velocity, fps:	2600	2372	2156	1951	1759
	energy, ft-lb:	4052	3373	2787	2283	1855
	arc, inches:		+2.3	0	-9.9	-28.9
.378 WEATHERBY MAGNUM						
A-Square 300 SP boat-tail	velocity, fps:	2900	2754	2612	2475	2342
	energy, ft-lb:	5602	5051	4546	4081	3655
	arc, inches:		+3.8	+4.4	0	-10.0
A-Square 300 Triad	velocity, fps:	2900	2577	2276	1997	1747
	energy, ft-lb:	5602	4424	3452	2656	2034
	arc, inches:		+1.9	0	-8.7	-25.9
Wby. 270 Pointed Expanding	velocity, fps:	3180	2921	2677	2445	2225
	energy, ft-lb:	6062	5115	4295	3583	2968
	arc, inches:		+1.3	0	-6.1	-18.1
Wby. 270 Barnes X	velocity, fps:	3150	2954	2767	2587	2415
	energy, ft-lb:	5948	5232	4589	4013	3495
	arc, inches:		+1.2	0	-5.8	-16.7
Wby. 300 RN Expanding	velocity, fps:	2925	2558	2220	1908	1627.
	energy, ft-lb:	5699	4360	3283	2424	1764
	arc, inches:		+1.9	0	-9.0	-27.8
Wby. 300 FMJ	velocity, fps:	2925	2591	2280	1991	1725
	energy, ft-lb:	5699	4470	3461	2640	1983
	arc, inches:		+1.8	0	-8.6	-26.1
.38-40 WINCHESTER						
Win. 180 Soft Point	velocity, fps:	1160	999	901	827	
	energy, ft-lb:	538	399	324	273	
	arc, inches:		0	-23.4	-75.2	

CARTRIDGE BULLET	RANGE, YARDS:	0	100	200	300	400
.38-55 WINCHESTER						
Black Hills 255 FN Lead	velocity, fps:	1250				
	energy, ft-lb:	925				
	arc, inches:					
Win. 255 Soft Point	velocity, fps:	1320	1190	1091	1018	
	energy, ft-lb:	987	802	674	587	
	arc, inches:		0	-33.9	-110.6	
.41 MAGNUM						
Win. 240 Platinum Tip	velocity, fps:	1830	1488	1220	1048	
	energy, ft-lb:	1784	1180	792	585	
	arc inches:		0	-15.0	-53.4	
.450/.400 NITRO EXPRESS						
A-Square 400 Triad	velocity, fps:	2150	1910	1690	1490	
	energy, ft-lb:	4105	3241	2537	1972	
	arc, inches:		+4.4	0	-16.5	
Hornady 400 DGS, DGX	velocity, fps:	2050	1820	1609	1420	
	energy, ft-lb:	3732	2940	2298	1791	
	arc, inches:	-0.9	0	-9.7	-32.8	
.404 JEFFERY						
A-Square 400 Triad	velocity, fps:	2150	1901	1674	1468	1299
	energy, ft-lb:	4105	3211	2489	1915	1499
	arc, inches:		+4.1	0	-16.4	-49.1
Hornady 400 DGS, DGX	velocity, fps:	2300	2046	1809	1592	
	energy, ft-lb:	4698	3717	2906	2251	
	arc, inches:	-1.5	0	-6.9	-24.4	
Norma 450 Woodleigh SP	velocity, fps:	2150	2048	1949	1853	1760
	energy, ft-lb:	4620	4191	3795	3430	3096
	arc, inches:	-1.5	+.2	0	-2.5	-7.6
.405 WINCHESTER						
Hornady 300 Flatpoint	velocity, fps:	2200	1851	1545	1296	
	energy, ft-lb:	3224	2282	1589	1119	
	arc, inches:		0	-8.7	-31.9	
Hornady 300 SP Interlock	velocity, fps:	2200	1890	1610	1370	
	energy, ft-lb:	3224	2379	1727	1250	
	arc, inches:		0	-8.3	-30.2	
.416 TAYLOR						
A-Square 400 Triad	velocity, fps:	2350	2093	1853	1634	1443
	energy, ft-lb:	4905	3892	3049	2371	1849
	arc, inches:		+3.2	0	-13.6	-39.8
.416 HOFFMAN						
A-Square 400 Triad	velocity, fps:	2380	2122	1879	1658	1464
	energy, ft-lb:	5031	3998	3136	2440	1903
	arc, inches:		+3.1	0	-13.1	-38.7
.416 REMINGTON MAGNUM						
A-Square 400 Triad	velocity, fps:	2380	2122	1879	1658	1464
	energy, ft-lb:	5031	3998	3136	2440	1903
	arc, inches:		+3.1	0	-13.2	-38.7
Federal 400 Trophy Bonded Sledgehammer Solid	velocity, fps:	2400	2150	1920	1700	1500
	energy, ft-lb:	5115	4110	3260	2565	2005
	arc, inches:		0	-6.0	-21.6	-49.2
Federal 400 Trophy Bonded	velocity, fps:	2400	2180	1970	1770	1590
	energy, ft-lb:	5115	4215	3440	2785	2245
	arc, inches:		0	-5.8	-20.6	-46.9
Rem. 400 Swift A-Frame	velocity, fps:	2400	2175	1962	1763	1579
	energy, ft-lb:	5115	4201	3419	2760	2214
	arc, inches:		0	-5.9	-20.8	

.416 RIGBY

CARTRIDGE BULLET	RANGE, YARDS:	0	100	200	300	400
A-Square 400 Triad	velocity, fps:	2400	2140	1897	1673	1478
	energy, ft-lb:	5115	4069	3194	2487	1940
	arc, inches:		+3.0	0	-12.9	-38.0
Federal 400 Trophy Bonded	velocity, fps:	2370	2150	1940	1750	1570
	energy, ft-lb:	4990	4110	3350	2715	2190
	arc, inches:		0	-6.0	-21.3	-48.1
Federal 400 Trophy Bonded Sledgehammer Solid	velocity, fps:	2370	2120	1890	1660	1460
	energy, ft-lb:	4990	3975	3130	2440	1895
	arc, inches:		0	-6.3	-22.5	-51.5
Federal 410 Woodleigh Weldcore	velocity, fps:	2370	2110	1870	1640	1440
	energy, ft-lb:	5115	4050	3165	2455	1895
	arc, inches:		0	-7.4	-24.8	-55.0
Federal 410 Solid	velocity, fps:	2370	2110	2870	1640	1440
	energy, ft-lb:	5115	4050	3165	2455	1895
	arc, inches:		0	-7.4	-24.8	-55.0
Hornady 400 DGX, DGS	velocity, fps:	2415	2156	1915	1691	
	energy, ft-lb:	5180	4130	3256	2540	
	arc, inches:	-1.5	0	-6.0	-21.6	
Norma 400 TXP Swift A-Fr.	velocity, fps:	2350	2127	1917	1721	
	energy, ft-lb:	4906	4021	3266	2632	
	arc, inches:		+3.1	0	-12.5	
Norma 400 Barnes Solid	velocity, fps:	2297	1930	1604	1330	
	energy, ft-lb:	4687	3310	2284	1571	
	arc, inches:		+3.9	0	-17.7	

.416 RUGER

CARTRIDGE BULLET	RANGE, YARDS:	0	100	200	300	400
Hornady 400 DGS, DGX	velocity, fps:	2400	2151	1917	1700	
	energy, ft-lb:	5116	4109	3264	2568	
	arc, inches:	-1.5	0	-6.0	-21.6	

.500/416 NITRO EXPRESS

CARTRIDGE BULLET	RANGE, YARDS:	0	50	100	150	200
Norma 450 Woodleigh SP	velocity, fps:	2100	1991	1886	1785	1688
	energy, ft-lb:	4408	3963	3556	3185	2849
	arc, inches:	-1.5	+.3	0	-2.7	-8.2

.416 DAKOTA

CARTRIDGE BULLET	RANGE, YARDS:	0	100	200	300	400
Dakota 400 Barnes X	velocity, fps:	2450	2294	2143	1998	1859
	energy, ft-lb:	5330	4671	4077	3544	3068
	arc, inches:		+2.5	-0.2	-10.5	-29.4

.416 WEATHERBY

CARTRIDGE BULLET	RANGE, YARDS:	0	100	200	300	400
A-Square 400 Triad	velocity, fps:	2600	2328	2073	1834	1624
	energy, ft-lb:	6004	4813	3816	2986	2343
	arc, inches:		+2.5	0	-10.5	-31.6
Wby. 350 Barnes X	velocity, fps:	2850	2673	2503	2340	2182
	energy, ft-lb:	6312	5553	4870	4253	3700
	arc, inches:		+1.7	0	-7.2	-20.9
Wby. 400 Swift A-Fr.	velocity, fps:	2650	2426	2213	2011	1820
	energy, ft-lb:	6237	5227	4350	3592	2941
	arc, inches:		+2.2	0	-9.3	-27.1
Wby. 400 RN Expanding	velocity, fps:	2700	2417	2152	1903	1676
	energy, ft-lb:	6474	5189	4113	3216	2493
	arc, inches:		+2.3	0	-9.7	-29.3
Wby. 400 Monolithic Solid	velocity, fps:	2700	2411	2140	1887	1656
	energy, ft-lb:	6474	5162	4068	3161	2435
	arc, inches:		+2.3	0	-9.8	-29.7

10.57 (.416) METEOR

CARTRIDGE BULLET	RANGE, YARDS:	0	100	200	300	400
Lazzeroni 400 Swift A-Fr.	velocity, fps:	2730	2532	2342	2161	1987
	energy, ft-lb:	6621	5695	4874	4147	3508
	arc, inches:		+1.9	0	-8.3	-24.0

.425 EXPRESS

CARTRIDGE BULLET	RANGE, YARDS:	0	100	200	300	400
A-Square 400 Triad	velocity, fps:	2400	2136	1888	1662	1465
	energy, ft-lb:	5115	4052	3167	2454	1906
	arc, inches:		+3.0	0	-13.1	-38.3

.44-40 WINCHESTER

CARTRIDGE BULLET	RANGE, YARDS:	0	100	200	300	400
Rem. 200 Soft Point	velocity, fps:	1190	1006	900	822	756
	energy, ft-lb:	629	449	360	300	254
	arc, inches:		0	-33.1	-108.7	-235.2
Win. 200 Soft Point	velocity, fps:	1190	1006	900	822	756
	energy, ft-lb:	629	449	360	300	254
	arc, inches:		0	-33.3	-109.5	-237.4

.44 REMINGTON MAGNUM

CARTRIDGE BULLET	RANGE, YARDS:	0	100	200	300	400
Federal 240 Hi-Shok HP	velocity, fps:	1760	1380	1090	950	860
	energy, ft-lb:	1650	1015	640	485	395
	arc, inches:		0	-17.4	-60.7	-136.0
Rem. 210 Semi-Jacketed HP	velocity, fps:	1920	1477	1155	982	880
	energy, ft-lb:	1719	1017	622	450	361
	arc, inches:		0	-14.7	-55.5	-131.3
Rem. 240 Soft Point	velocity, fps:	1760	1380	1114	970	878
	energy, ft-lb:	1650	1015	661	501	411
	arc, inches:		0	-17.0	-61.4	-143.0
Rem. 240 Semi-Jacketed Hollow Point	velocity, fps:	1760	1380	1114	970	878
	energy, ft-lb:	1650	1015	661	501	411
	arc, inches:		0	-17.0	-61.4	-143.0
Rem. 275 JHP Core-Lokt	velocity, fps:	1580	1293	1093	976	896
	energy, ft-lb:	1524	1020	730	582	490
	arc, inches:		0	-19.4	-67.5	-210.8
Win. 210 Silvertip HP	velocity, fps:	1580	1198	993	879	795
	energy, ft-lb:	1164	670	460	361	295
	arc, inches:		0	-22.4	-76.1	-168.0
Win. 240 Hollow Soft Point	velocity, fps:	1760	1362	1094	953	861
	energy, ft-lb:	1650	988	638	484	395
	arc, inches:		0	-18.1	-65.1	-150.3
Win. 250 Platinum Tip	velocity, fps:	1830	1475	1201	1032	931
	energy, ft-lb:	1859	1208	801	591	481
	arc, inches:		0	-15.3	-54.7	-126.6.

.444 MARLIN

CARTRIDGE BULLET	RANGE, YARDS:	0	100	200	300	400
Rem. 240 Soft Point	velocity, fps:	2350	1815	1377	1087	941
	energy, ft-lb:	2942	1755	1010	630	472
	arc, inches:		+2.2	-5.4	-31.4	-86.7
Hornady 265 Evolution	velocity, fps:	2325	1971	1652	1380	
	energy, ft-lb:	3180	2285	1606	1120	
	arc, inches:		+3.0	-1.4	-18.6	
Hornady 265 FP LM	velocity, fps:	2335	1913	1551	1266	
	energy, ft-lb:	3208	2153	1415	943	
	arc, inches:		+ 2.0	-4.9	-26.5	
Hornady 265 InterLock FP	velocity, fps:	2400	1974	1601	1295	
	energy, ft-lb:	3389	2294	1508	987	
	arc, inches:		+3.8	0	-17.5	
Rem. 240 Soft Point	velocity, fps:	2350	1815	1377	1087	941
	energy, ft-lb:	2942	1755	1010	630	472
	arc, inches:		+2.2	-5.4	-31.4	-86.7

.45-70 GOVERNMENT

CARTRIDGE BULLET	RANGE, YARDS:	0	100	200	300	400
Black Hills 405 FPL	velocity, fps:	1250				
	energy, ft-lb:					
	arc, inches:					
Federal 300 Sierra Pro-Hunt. HP FN	velocity, fps:	1880	1650	1430	1240	1110
	energy, ft-lb:	2355	1815	1355	1015	810
	arc, inches:		0	-11.5	-39.7	-89.1
PMC 350 FNSP	velocity, fps:					
	energy, ft-lb:					
	arc, inches:					
Rem. 300 Jacketed HP	velocity, fps:	1810	1497	1244	1073	969
	energy, ft-lb:	2182	1492	1031	767	625
	arc, inches:		0	-13.8	-50.1	-115.7

Centerfire Rifle Ballistics

.45-70 GOVERNMENT TO .460 WEATHERBY MAGNUM

CARTRIDGE BULLET	RANGE, YARDS:	0	100	200	300	400
Rem. 405 Soft Point	velocity, fps	1330	1168	1055	977	918
	energy, ft-lb	1590	1227	1001	858	758
	arc, inches:		0	-24.0	-78.6	-169.4
Win. 300 Jacketed HP	velocity, fps	1880	1650	1425	1235	1105
	energy, ft-lb	2355	1815	1355	1015	810
	arc, inches:		0	-12.8	-44.3	-95.5
Win. 300 Partition Gold	velocity, fps	1880	1558	1292	1103	988
	energy, ft-lb	2355	1616	1112	811	651
	arc, inches:		0	-12.9	-46.0	-104.9.

.450 BUSHMASTER

CARTRIDGE BULLET	RANGE, YARDS:	0	100	200	300	400
Hornady 250 SST-ML	velocity, fps	2200	1840	1524	1268	
	energy, ft-lb	2686	1879	1289	893	
	arc, inches:	-2.0	+2.5	-3.5	-24.5	

.450 MARLIN

CARTRIDGE BULLET	RANGE, YARDS:	0	100	200	300	400
Hornady 325 FTX	velocity, fps	2225	1887	1585	1331	
	energy, ft-lb	3572	2569	1813	1278	
	arc, inches:	-1.5	+3.0	-2.2	-21.3	
Hornady 350 FP	velocity, fps	2100	1720	1397	1156	
	energy, ft-lb	3427	2298	1516	1039	
	arc, inches:		0	-10.4	-38.9	

.450 NITRO EXPRESS (3¼")

CARTRIDGE BULLET	RANGE, YARDS:	0	100	200	300	400
A-Square 465 Triad	velocity, fps	2190	1970	1765	1577	
	energy, ft-lb	4952	4009	3216	2567	
	arc, inches:		+4.3	0	-15.4	
Hornady 480 DGS, DGX	velocity, fps	2150	1881	1635	1418	
	energy, ft-lb	4927	3769	2850	2144	
	arc, inches:	-1.5	0	-8.4	-29.9	

.450 #2

CARTRIDGE BULLET	RANGE, YARDS:	0	100	200	300	400
A-Square 465 Triad	velocity, fps	2190	1970	1765	1577	
	energy, ft-lb	4952	4009	3216	2567	
	arc, inches:		+4.3	0	-15.4	

.458 WINCHESTER MAGNUM

CARTRIDGE BULLET	RANGE, YARDS:	0	100	200	300	400
A-Square 465 Triad	velocity, fps	2220	1999	1791	1601	1433
	energy, ft-lb	5088	4127	3312	2646	2121
	arc, inches:		+3.6	0	-14.7	-42.5
Federal 350 Soft Point	velocity, fps	2470	1990	1570	1250	1060
	energy, ft-lb	4740	3065	1915	1205	870
	arc, inches:		0	-7.5	-29.1	-71.1
Federal 400 Trophy Bonded	velocity, fps	2380	2170	1960	1770	1590
	energy, ft-lb	5030	4165	3415	2785	2255
	arc, inches:		0	-5.9	-20.9	-47.1
Federal 500 Solid	velocity, fps	2090	1870	1670	1480	1320
	energy, ft-lb	4850	3880	3085	2440	1945
	arc, inches:		0	-8.5	-29.5	-66.2
Federal 500 Trophy Bonded	velocity, fps	2090	1870	1660	1480	1310
	energy, ft-lb	4850	3870	3065	2420	1915
	arc, inches:		0	-8.5	-29.7	-66.8
Federal 500 Trophy Bonded Sledgehammer Solid	velocity, fps	2090	1860	1650	1460	1300
	energy, ft-lb	4850	3845	3025	2365	1865
	arc, inches:		0	-8.6	-30.0	-67.8
Federal 510 Soft Point	velocity, fps	2090	1820	1570	1360	1190
	energy, ft-lb	4945	3730	2790	2080	1605
	arc, inches:		0	-9.1	-32.3	-73.9
Hornady 500 FMJ-RN HM	velocity, fps	2260	1984	1735	1512	
	energy, ft-lb	5670	4368	3341	2538	
	arc, inches:		0	-7.4	-26.4	
Norma 500 TXP Swift A-Fr.	velocity, fps	2116	1903	1705	1524	
	energy, ft-lb	4972	4023	3228	2578	
	arc, inches:		+4.1	0	-16.1	

CARTRIDGE BULLET	RANGE, YARDS:	0	100	200	300	400
Norma 500 Barnes Solid	velocity, fps	2067	1750	1472	1245	
	energy, ft-lb	4745	3401	2405	1721	
	arc, inches:		+4.9	0	-21.2	
Rem. 450 Swift A-Frame PSP	velocity, fps	2150	1901	1671	1465	1289
	energy, ft-lb	4618	3609	2789	2144	1659
	arc, inches:		0	-8.2	-28.9	
Speer 500 African GS Tungsten Solid	velocity, fps	2120	1845	1596	1379	
	energy, ft-lb	4989	3780	2828	2111	
	arc, inches:		0	-8.8	-31.3	
Speer African Grand Slam	velocity, fps	2120	1853	1609	1396	
	energy, ft-lb	4989	3810	2875	2163	
	arc, inches:		0	-8.7	-30.8	
Win. 510 Soft Point	velocity, fps	2040	1770	1527	1319	1157
	energy, ft-lb	4712	3547	2640	1970	1516
	arc, inches:		0	-10.3	-35.6	

.458 LOTT

CARTRIDGE BULLET	RANGE, YARDS:	0	100	200	300	400
A-Square 465 Triad	velocity, fps	2380	2150	1932	1730	1551
	energy, ft-lb	5848	4773	3855	3091	2485
	arc, inches:		+3.0	0	-12.5	-36.4
Federal 500 TSX	velocity, fps	2280	2090	1900	1730	1560
	energy, ft-lb	5770	4825	4000	3305	2715
	arc, inches:		0	-6.4	-22.7	-50.7
Hornady 500 RNSP or solid	velocity, fps	2300	2022	1776	1551	
	energy, ft-lb	5872	4537	3502	2671	
	arc, inches:		+3.4	0	-14.3	
Hornady 500 InterBond	velocity, fps	2300	2028	1777	1549	
	energy, ft-lb	5872	4535	3453	2604	
	arc, inches:		0	-7.0	-25.1	

CARTRIDGE BULLET	RANGE, YARDS:	0	50	100	150	200
Norma 500 Woodleigh SP	velocity, fps	2100	1982	1868	1758	1654
	energy, ft-lb	4897	4361	3874	3434	3039
	arc, inches:	-1.5	+.3	0	-2.8	-8.4

.450 ACKLEY

CARTRIDGE BULLET	RANGE, YARDS:	0	100	200	300	400
A-Square 465 Triad	velocity, fps	2400	2169	1950	1747	1567
	energy, ft-lb	5947	4857	3927	3150	2534
	arc, inches:		+2.9	0	-12.2	-35.8

.450 RIGBY

CARTRIDGE BULLET	RANGE, YARDS:	0	50	100	150	200
Norma 550 Woodleigh SP	velocity, fps	2100	1992	1887	1787	1690
	energy, ft-lb	5387	4847	4352	3900	3491
	arc, inches:	-1.5	+.3	0	-2.7	-8.2

.460 SHORT A-SQUARE

CARTRIDGE BULLET	RANGE, YARDS:	0	100	200	300	400
A-Square 500 Triad	velocity, fps	2420	2198	1987	1789	1613
	energy, ft-lb	6501	5362	4385	3553	2890
	arc, inches:		+2.9	0	-11.6	-34.2

.450 DAKOTA

Dakota 500 Barnes Solid	velocity, fps	2450	2235	2030	1838	1658
	energy, ft-lb	6663	5544	4576	3748	3051
	arc, inches:		+2.5	-0.6	-12.0	-33.8

.460 WEATHERBY MAGNUM

A-Square 500 Triad	velocity, fps	2580	2349	2131	1923	1737
	energy, ft-lb	7389	6126	5040	4107	3351
	arc, inches:		+2.4	0	-10.0	-29.4
Wby. 450 Barnes X	velocity, fps	2700	2518	2343	2175	2013
	energy, ft-lb	7284	6333	5482	4725	4050
	arc, inches:		+2.0	0	-8.4	-24.1

BALLISTICS

CARTRIDGE BULLET	RANGE, YARDS:	0	100	200	300	400
Wby. 500 RN Expanding	velocity, fps:	2600	2301	2022	1764	1533.
	energy, ft-lb:	7504	5877	4539	3456	2608
	arc, inches:		+2.6	0	-11.1	-33.5
Wby. 500 FMJ	velocity, fps:	2600	2309	2037	1784	1557
	energy, ft-lb:	7504	5917	4605	3534	2690
	arc, inches:		+2.5	0	-10.9	-33.0

.500/.465

CARTRIDGE BULLET	RANGE, YARDS:	0	100	200	300	400
A-Square 480 Triad	velocity, fps:	2150	1928	1722	1533	
	energy, ft-lb:	4926	3960	3160	2505	
	arc, inches:		+4.3	0	-16.0	

.470 NITRO EXPRESS

CARTRIDGE BULLET	RANGE, YARDS:	0	100	200	300	400
A-Square 500 Triad	velocity, fps:	2150	1912	1693	1494	
	energy, ft-lb:	5132	4058	3182	2478	
	arc, inches:		+4.4	0	-16.5	
Federal 500 Trophy Bond	velocity, fps:	2150	1890	1660	1450	
(and Sledgehammer solid)	energy, ft-lb:	5130	3975	3045	2320	
	arc, inches:	-1.5	0	-9.4	-29.3	
Hornady 500 DGX, DGS	velocity, fps:	2150	1885	1643	1429	
	energy, ft-lb:	5132	3946	2998	2267	
	arc, inches:	-1.5	0	-8.9	-30.9	

CARTRIDGE BULLET	RANGE, YARDS:	0	50	100	150	200
Norma 500 Woodleigh	velocity, fps:	2100	2002	1906	1814	1725
(soft and solid)	energy, ft-lb:	4897	4449	4035	3654	3304
	arc, inches:	-1.5	+.3	0	-2.7	-8.0

.470 CAPSTICK

CARTRIDGE BULLET	RANGE, YARDS:	0	100	200	300	400
A-Square 500 Triad	velocity, fps:	2400	2172	1958	1761	1553
	energy, ft-lb:	6394	5236	4255	3445	2678
	arc, inches:		+2.9	0	-11.9	-36.1

.475 #2

CARTRIDGE BULLET	RANGE, YARDS:	0	100	200	300	400
A-Square 480 Triad	velocity, fps:	2200	1964	1744	1544	
	energy, ft-lb:	5158	4109	3240	2539	
	arc, inches:		+4.1	0	-15.6	

.475 #2 JEFFERY

A-Square 500 Triad	velocity, fps:	2200	1966	1748	1550	
	energy, ft-lb:	5373	4291	3392	2666	
	arc, inches:		+4.1	0	-15.6	

.495 A-SQUARE

A-Square 570 Triad	velocity, fps:	2350	2117	1896	1693	1513
	energy, ft-lb:	6989	5671	4552	3629	2899
	arc, inches:		+3.1	0	-13.0	-37.8

.50 BMG

Hornady 750 A-Max	velocity, fps:	2815	2727	2641	2557	2474
	energy, ft-lb:	13,196	12,386	11,619	10,889	10,196
	arc, inches:		+1.4	0	-6.4	-18.2

.500 NITRO EXPRESS (3")

A-Square 570 Triad	velocity, fps:	2150	1928	1722	1533	
	energy, ft-lb:	5850	4703	3752	2975	
	arc, inches:		+4.3	0	-16.1	

CARTRIDGE BULLET	RANGE, YARDS:	0	100	200	300	400
Federal 570 TSX	velocity, fps:	2100	1890	1700	1520	1370
	energy, ft-lb:	5580	4530	3655	2935	2355
	arc, inches:	0	-8.4	-28.7	-64.2	
Hornady 570 DGX, DGS	velocity, fps:	2150	1881	1635	1419	
	energy, ft-lb:	5850	4477	3384	2547	
	arc, inches:	-.9	0	-9.0	-31.1	

CARTRIDGE BULLET	RANGE, YARDS:	0	50	100	150	200
Norma 570 Woodleigh SP	velocity, fps:	2100	2000	1903	1809	1719
	energy, ft-lb:	5583	5064	4585	4145	3742
	arc, inches:	-1.5	+.3	0	-2.7	-8.0
50 BMG						
Hornady 750 A-MAX	velocity, fps:	2815	2727	2641	2557	2474
	energy, ft-lb:	13196	12386	11619	10889	10196
	arc, inches:	-1.8	+1.4	0	-6.4	-18.2

.500 JEFFERY

CARTRIDGE BULLET	RANGE, YARDS:	0	50	100	150	200
Norma 570 Woodleigh SP	velocity, fps:	2200	2097	1997	1901	1807
	energy, ft-lb:	6127	5568	5050	4573	4134
	arc, inches:	-1.5	+.2	0	-2.4	-7.1

.500 A-SQUARE

CARTRIDGE BULLET	RANGE, YARDS:	0	100	200	300	400
A-Square 600 Triad	velocity, fps:	2470	2235	2013	1804	1620
	energy, ft-lb:	8127	6654	5397	4336	3495
	arc, inches:		+2.7	0	-11.3	-33.5

.505 GIBBS

A-Square 525 Triad	velocity, fps:	2300	2063	1840	1637	
	energy, ft-lb:	6166	4962	3948	3122	
	arc, inches:		+3.6	0	-14.2	

CARTRIDGE BULLET	RANGE, YARDS:	0	50	100	150	200
Norma 600 Woodleigh SP	velocity, fps:	2100	1998	1899	1803	1711
	energy, ft-lb:	5877	5319	4805	4334	3904
	arc, inches:	-1.5	+.3	0	-2.7	-8.1

.577 NITRO EXPRESS

CARTRIDGE BULLET	RANGE, YARDS:	0	100	200	300	400
A-Square 750 Triad	velocity, fps:	2050	1811	1595	1401	
	energy, ft-lb:	6998	5463	4234	3267	
	arc, inches:		+4.9	0	-18.5	

.577 TYRANNOSAUR

A-Square 750 Triad	velocity, fps:	2460	2197	1950	1723	1516
	energy, ft-lb:	10077	8039	6335	4941	3825
	arc, inches:		+2.8	0	-12.1	-36.0

.600 NITRO EXPRESS

A-Square 900 Triad	velocity, fps:	1950	1680	1452	1336	
	energy, ft-lb:	7596	5634	4212	3564	
	arc, inches:		+5.6	0	-20.7	

.700 NITRO EXPRESS

A-Square 1000 Monolithic Solid	velocity, fps:	1900	1669	1461	1288	
	energy, ft-lb:	8015	6188	4740	3685	
	arc, inches:		+5.8	0	-22.2	

Long Range Rifle

6.6 CREEDMOOR TO .338 LAPUA

CARTRIDGE BULLET	RANGE, YARDS:	0	400	600	800	1000
6.6 CREEDMOOR						
Nosler 140 HPBT	velocity, fps:	2550	2229	1932	1662	1426
	energy, ft-lb:	2021	1544	1160	859	632
	arc, inches:	-1.5	0	-26.7	-90.9	-205.9
.264 WINCHESTER MAGNUM						
Nosler 130 AccuBond	velocity, fps:	3100	2709	2350	2019	1718
	energy, ft-lb:	2773	2118	1594	1176	852
	arc, inches:	-1.5	0	-17.6	-60.6	-137.9
6.5-284 NORMA						
Nosler 129 AccuBond	velocity, fps:	2965	2633	2324	2036	1771
Long Range	energy, ft-lb:	2517	1985	1547	1188	899
	arc, inches:	-1.5	0	-18.7	-63.2	-141.6
.270 WSM						
Nosler 150 AccuBond	velocity, fps:	2960	2661	2381	2118	1873
Long Range	energy, ft-lb:	2917	2358	1888	1495	1169
	arc, inches:	-1.5	0	-18.2	-61.1	-135.1
7MM REMINGTON MAGNUM						
Nosler 168 AccuBond	velocity, fps:	2880	2598	2333	2084	1851
Long Range	energy, ft-lb:	3093	2518	2030	1620	1278
	arc, inches:	-1.5	0	-19.2	-64.0	-141.0
7MM STW						
Nosler 175 AccuBond	velocity, fps:	2900	2625	2366	2122	1893
Long Range	energy, ft-lb:	3267	2677	2175	1750	1393
	arc, inches:	-1.5	0	-18.8	-62.4	-137.1
7MM REMINGTON ULTRA MAG						
Nosler 175 AccuBond	velocity, fps:	3040	2756	2490	2239	2002
Long Range	energy, ft-lb:	3590	2952	2409	1948	1558
	arc, inches:	-1.5	0	-16.9	-56.2	-123.5
.308 WINCHESTER						
Barnes 175 OTM						
	velocity, fps:	2650	2318	2011	1730	1480	1272
	energy, ft-lb:	2730	2089	1571	1163	852	629
	arc, inches:	-1.5	0	-24.6	-83.8	-189.9	-360.0
.300 WSM						
Nosler 190 AccuBond	velocity, fps:	2875	2588	2319	2066	1830
Long Range	energy, ft-lb:	3486	2826	2269	1801	1413
	arc, inches:	-1.5	0	-19.3	-64.7	-142.7

CARTRIDGE BULLET	RANGE, YARDS:	0	400	600	800	1000
.300 WINCHESTER MAGNUM						
Barnes 220 OTM						
	velocity, fps:	2700	2420	2158	1912	1685	1481
	energy, ft-lb:	3562	2862	2275	1786	1387	1072
	arc, inches:	-1.5	0	-22.4	-74.7	-165.4	-305.3
Nosler 190 AccuBond	velocity, fps:	2870	2583	2314	2062	1826
Long Range	energy, ft-lb:	3474	2816	2260	1794	1407
	arc, inches:	-1.5	0	-19.4	-64.9	-143.3
.300 WEATHERBY MAGNUM						
Nosler 210 AccuBond	velocity, fps:	2825	2575	2339	2115	1905
Long Range	energy, ft-lb:	3720	3092	2551	2087	1691
	arc, inches:	-1.5	0	-19.5	-64.6	-140.8
.300 REMINGTON ULTRA MAG						
Nosler 210 AccuBond	velocity, fps:	2920	2665	2424	2196	1980
Long Range	energy, ft-lb:	3975	3311	2740	2248	1828
	arc, inches:	-1.5	0	-18.1	-60.0	-130.8
.30-378 WEATHERBY MAGNUM						
Nosler 210 AccuBond	velocity, fps:	3040	2778	2531	2297	2076
Long Range	energy, ft-lb:	4308	3599	2987	2461	2009
	arc, inches:	-1.5	0	-16.6	-54.9	-119.7
.338 REMINGTON ULTRA MAG						
Nosler 300 AccuBond	velocity, fps:	2600	2359	2131	1916	1716
	energy, ft-lb:	4502	3707	3026	2447	1963
	arc, inches:	-1.5	0	-23.6	-77.9	-170.2
.338 LAPUA						
Barnes 300 OTM						
	velocity, fps:	2600	2375	2161	1958	1767	1591
	energy, ft-lb:	4504	3757	3110	2554	2081	1687
	arc, inches:	-1.5	0	-23.2	-76.4	-165.9	-300.1
Nosler 300 AccuBond	velocity, fps:	2650	2406	2176	1959	1755
	energy, ft-lb:	4677	3857	3154	2555	2053
	arc, inches:	-1.5	0	-22.6	-74.7	-163.1

Rimfire Ballistics

Rimfire cartridges have had a longer run than any centerfire you can name. Horace Smith and Daniel Wesson came up with the first successful .22 rimfires in the United States in 1857. Thirty years later the .22 Long Rifle arrived, courtesy of the J. Stevens Arms & Tool Company. It used 5 grains of black powder to drive a 40-grain bullet, shortly making the transition to smokeless in a case crimped on a heeled bullet. Remington produced the first modern high-speed load in 1930. Current .22 ammo includes myriad Long Rifle listings. The Long (essentially a Short bullet in a Long Rifle case), like the CB and WRF cartridges, is going the way of the dodo. The shot load of #12 "dust" has faded too, though it has dispatched many snakes, and was once hailed as just the ticket for barn mice and rats when you didn't want to perforate the boards. New rimfires have joined the versatile Long Rifle. The .22 WMR (Winchester Magnum Rimfire) came in 1959. More than four decades passed before Hornady necked down the WMR case to form the .17 HMR. A sibling on the CCI Stinger variation of the .22 LR appeared in 2004. Hornady dubbed it the .17 Mach 2. The newest .17, Winchester's Super Mag, arrived in 2013. The .17s and the .22 WMR feature jacketed hollowpoint and polymer-tipped bullets, just like centerfires.

This list is incomplete. For convenience (and given space constraints), it omits duplicate loads—those by the same manufacturer but under different labels). Units: velocity in feet per second, energy in foot-pounds, drop in inches.

.22 TO .17 HORNADY MAGNUM RIMFIRE

CARTRIDGE BULLET	LOAD	MUZZLE VEL./ENERGY	100-YD. VEL./ENERGY
.22			
CCI .22 CB Short	29-gr. RN	710/32	607/24
CCI .22 CB Long	29-gr. RN	710/32	607/24
CCI .22 Short	27-gr. HP	1105/73	868/45
CCI .22 Short	29-gr. RN	1080/75	857/47
CCI .22 Short	29-gr. Target RN	830/44	704/32
CCI .22 Long	29-gr. RN	1215/95	908/53
CCI .22 LR	21-gr. Short Range Green HP	1650/127	912/38
CCI .22 LR	31 gr. #12 birdshot	1000	
CCI .22 LR	32-gr. Stinger HP	1640/191	1066/81
CCI .22 LR	36-gr. HP	1260/127	1003/80
CCI .22 LR	40-gr. Tactical RN	1200/128	964/82
CCI .22 LR	40-gr. Mini-Mag RN	1235/135	998/88
CCI .22 LR	40-gr. Sub-sonic HP	1050/98	897/72
CCI .22 LR	40-gr. Velocitor HP	1435/183	1084/104
CCI .22 LR	40-gr. Small Game Bullet LFN	1235/135	992/87
CCI .22 LR	40-gr. Quiet-22 HP	710/45	640/36
CCI .22 LR	40-gr. Select RN	1200/128	964/82
CCI .22 LR	40-gr. Green Tag RN	1070/102	908/73
CCI .22 LR	45-gr. HP Suppressor	970/95	892/75
Federal .22 LR	25 gr. #12 birdshot		
Federal .22 LR	31-gr. Game-Shok HP	1430/140	1050/75
Federal .22 LR	36-gr. Champion HP	1260/125	1000/80
Federal .22 LR	38-gr. Game-Shok HP	1260/135	1010/85
Federal .22 LR	38-gr. Amer. Eagle HP	1260/135	1010/85
Federal .22 LR	40-gr. Prem. Gold Medal	1200/130	990/85
Federal .22 LR	40-gr. Game-Shok HP	1240/135	1010/90
Federal .22 LR	40-gr. Champion	1240/135	1010/90
Federal .22 LR	45-gr. Amer. Eagle Suppressed	1050/105	910/75
Lapua .22 LR	40-gr. Polar Biathlon	1106/109	914/74
Remington .22 Short	29-gr. RN	1095/77	903/52
Remington .22 LR	33-gr. CBee Low Noise HP	740/40	638/30
Remington .22 LR	33-gr. Yellow Jacket T. C.	1500/165	1075/85

CARTRIDGE BULLET	LOAD	MUZZLE VEL./ENERGY	100-YD. VEL./ENERGY
Remington .22 LR	36-gr. Viper Truncated Cone	1410/159	1056/89
Remington .22 LR	36-gr. Cyclone HP	1280/131	1010/82
Remington .22 LR	38-gr. Sub-sonic HP	1050/93	901/69
Remington .22 LR	40-gr. Target	1150/117	976/85
Remington .22 LR	40-gr. Thunderbolt	1255/140	1017/92
Remington .22 LR	40-gr. Competition RN	1085/105	941/79
Winchester .22 Short	29-gr. RN	1095/77	903/52
Winchester .22 Long	29-gr. RN	770/38	681/30
Winchester .22 LR	31-gr. #12 birdshot	1000	
Winchester .22 LR	26-gr. Varmint LF HP	1650/157	1023/60
Winchester .22 LR	32-gr. Xpediter HP	1640/191	1078/83
Winchester .22 LR	29-gr. Super-X sub-sonic	770/38	681/30
Winchester .22 LR	36-gr. HP	1280/131	975/76
Winchester .22 LR	37-gr. Super-X HP	1280/135	1015/85
Winchester .22 LR	37-gr. Super Speed HP	1330/154	1038/88
Winchester .22 LR	37-gr. Varmint HE HP	1435/169	1080/96
Winchester .22 LR	40-gr. Super-X low-report	1065/101	922/76
Winchester .22 LR	40-gr. DynaPoint	1150/117	976/85
Winchester .22 LR	40-gr. M22 LRN Black	1255/140	1017/92
Winchester .22 LR	40-gr. Power-Point HP	1280/145	1001/89
Winchester .22 LR	40-gr. Super-X	1300/150	1038/96
Winchester .22 LR	40-gr. Hyper Speed HP	1435/183	1070/102

.17 HORNADY MAGNUM RIMFIRE

CARTRIDGE BULLET	LOAD	MUZZLE VEL./ENERGY	100-YD. VEL./ENERGY
CCI .17 HMR	16-gr. TNT Green HP	2500/222	1642/96
CCI .17 HMR	17-gr. TNT JHP	2550/245	1757116
CCI .17 HMR	17-gr. Poly-Tip V-Max	2550/245	1915/138
CCI .17 HMR	20-gr. FMJ	2375/250	1776/140
CCI .17 HMR	20-gr. JSP	2375/250	1754/137
Federal .17 HMR	17-gr. Prem. V-Shok TNT JHP	2530/240	1800/125
Federal .17 HMR	17-gr. Prem. Hornady V-Max	2530/240	1880/135
Hornady .17 Mach 2	15.5-gr. NTX Lead-Free	2050/149	1450/75
Hornady .17 Mach 2	17-gr. V-Max	2100/166	1530/88

Rimfire Ballistics

.17 HORNADY MAGNUM RIMFIRE TO .22 WINCHESTER RIMFIRE

BALLISTICS

CARTRIDGE BULLET	LOAD	MUZZLE VEL./ENERGY	100-YD. VEL./ENERGY	CARTRIDGE BULLET	LOAD	MUZZLE VEL./ENERGY	100-YD. VEL./ENERGY
Hornady .17 HMR	15.5-gr. NTX Lead-Free	2525/236	1829/119	Remington .22 WMR	40-gr. JHP	1910/324	1350/162
Hornady .17 HMR	17-gr. V-Max	2550/245	1901/136	Remington .22 WMR	40-gr. PSP	1910/324	1340/159
Hornady .17 HMR	20-gr. XTP	2375/250	1776/140	Winchester .22 WMR	28-gr. Varmint LF JHP	2200/301	1394/121
Remington.17 HMR	17-gr. AccuTip-V	2550/245	1901/136	Winchester .22 WMR	30-gr. Varmint HV V-Max	2250/337	1490/148
Winchester .17 HMR	15.5-gr. Varmint LF NTX	2550/224	1901/124	Winchester .22 WMR	30-gr. Varmint HV JHP	2250/337	1450/140
Winchester .17 HMR	17-gr. Poly Tip V-Max	2550/245	1915/138	Winchester .22 WMR	34-gr. Varmint HE JHP	2120/339	1437/156
Winchester .17 HMR	20-gr. Super-X JHP	2375/250	1776/140	Winchester .22 WMR	40-gr. Super-X JHP (and FMJ)	1910/324	1326/156
				Winchester .22 WMR	45-gr. USA DynaPoint	1550/240	1147/131

.22 WINCHESTER MAGNUM RIMFIRE

CCI .22 WMR	30 Maxi Mag HP + V	2200/322	1375/126
CCI .22 WMR	30 Poly-Tip V-Max	2200/322	1571/164
CCI .22 WMR	30 TNT JHP	2200/322	1405/131
CCI .22 WMR	30 TNT Green HP	2050/280	1317/116
CCI .22 WMR	40 Maxi Mag HP	1875/312	1319/155
CCI .22 WMR	40 Maxi Mag TMJ	1875/312	1366/166
CCI .22 WMR	40 GamePoint JSP	1875/312	1385/170
CCI .22 WMR	52 #12 birdshot	1000	
Federal .22 WMR	30-gr. Speer TNT HP	2200/320	1420/135
Federal .22 WMR	40-gr. FMJ	1880/315	1310/155
Hornady .22 WMR	30-gr. V-Max	2200/322	1421/134
Remington .22 WMR	33-gr. AccuTip-V	2000/293	1495/164

.17 WINCHESTER SUPER MAG.

Winchester .17 Super Mag	20-gr. Varmint HV	3000/400	2504/278
Winchester .17 Super Mag	25-gr. Polymer Tip	2600/375	2230/276

.22 WINCHESTER RIMFIRE

CCI .22 WRF	45 JHP	1300/169	1013/103
Winchester .22 WRF	45 FN	1300/169	1023/105

Centerfire Handgun Ballistics

Data shown here is taken from manufacturers' charts; your chronograph readings may vary. Barrel lengths for pistol data vary, and depend in part on which pistols are typically chambered in a given cartridge. Velocity variations due to barrel length depend on the baseline bullet speed and the load. Velocity for the .30 Carbine, normally a rifle cartridge, was determined in a pistol barrel.

Listings are current as of February the year *Shooter's Bible* appears (not the cover year). Listings are not intended as recommendations. For example, the data for the .25 Auto gives velocity and energy readings to 100 yards. Few handgunners would call the little .25 a 100-yard cartridge.

Abbreviations: Bullets are designated by loading company, weight (in grains) and type, with these abbreviations for shape and construction: BJHP= brass-jacketed hollowpoint; FN=Flat Nose; FMC=Full Metal Case; FMJ=Full Metal Jacket; HP=Hollowpoint; L=Lead; LF=Lead-Free; +P=a more powerful load than traditionally manufactured for that round; RN=Round Nose; SFHP=Starfire (PMC) Hollowpoint; SP=Softpoint; SWC=Semi Wadcutter; TMJ=Total Metal Jacket; WC=Wadcutter; CEPP, SXT and XTP are trademarked designations of Lapua, Winchester and Hornady, respectively.

.25 AUTO TO .32 S&W LONG

CARTRIDGE BULLET	RANGE, YARDS:	0	25	50	75	100
.25 AUTO						
Federal 50 FMJ	velocity, fps:	760	750	730	720	700
	energy, ft-lb:	65	60	60	55	55
Hornady 35 JHP/XTP	velocity, fps:	900		813		742
	energy, ft-lb:	63		51		43
Magtech 50 FMC	velocity, fps:	760		707		659
	energy, ft-lb:	64		56		48
PMC 50 FMJ	velocity, fps:	754	730	707	685	663
	energy, ft-lb:	62				
Rem. 50 Metal Case	velocity, fps:	760		707		659
	energy, ft-lb:	64		56		48
Speer 35 Gold Dot	velocity, fps:	900		816		747
	energy, ft-lb:	63		52		43
Speer 50 TMJ (and Blazer)	velocity, fps:	760		717		677
	energy, ft-lb:	64		57		51
Win. 45 Expanding Point	velocity, fps:	815		729		655
	energy, ft-lb	66		53		42
Win. 50 FMJ	velocity, fps:	760		707		
	energy, ft-lb	64		56		
.30 LUGER						
Win. 93 FMJ	velocity, fps:	1220		1110		1040
	energy, ft-lb	305		255		225
7.62x25 TOKAREV						
PMC 93 FMJ	velocity and energy figures not available					
.30 CARBINE						
Win. 110 Hollow SP	velocity, fps:	1790		1601		1430
	energy, ft-lb	783		626		500
.32 AUTO						
Federal 65 Hydra-Shok JHP	velocity, fps:	950	920	890	860	830
	energy, ft-lb:	130	120	115	105	100
Federal 71 FMJ	velocity, fps:	910	880	860	830	810
	energy, ft-lb:	130	120	115	110	105
Hornady 60 JHP/XTP	velocity, fps:	1000		917		849
	energy, ft-lb:	133		112		96
Hornady 71 FMJ-RN	velocity, fps:	900		845		797
	energy, ft-lb:	128		112		100
Magtech 71 FMC	velocity, fps:	905		855		810
	energy, ft-lb:	129		115		103
Magtech 71 JHP	velocity, fps:	905		855		810
	energy, ft-lb:	129		115		103

CARTRIDGE BULLET	RANGE, YARDS:	0	25	50	75	100
PMC 60 JHP	velocity, fps:	980	849	820	791	763
	energy, ft-lb:	117				
PMC 70 SFHP	velocity, fps:	velocity and energy figures not available				
PMC 71 FMJ	velocity, fps:	870	841	814	791	763
	energy, ft-lb:	119				
Rem. 71 Metal Case	velocity, fps:	905		855		810
	energy, ft-lb:	129		115		97
Speer 60 Gold Dot	velocity, fps:	960		868		796
	energy, ft-lb:	123		100		84
Speer 71 TMJ (and Blazer)	velocity, fps:	900		855		810
	energy, ft-lb:	129		115		97
Win. 60 Silvertip HP	velocity, fps:	970		895		835
	energy, ft-lb	125		107		93
Win. 71 FMJ	velocity, fps:	905		855		
	energy, ft-lb	129		115		
.32 S&W						
Rem. 88 LRN	velocity, fps:	680		645		610
	energy, ft-lb:	90		81		73
Win. 85 LRN	velocity, fps:	680		645		610
	energy, ft-lb	90		81		73
.32 S&W LONG						
Federal 98 LWC	velocity, fps:	780	700	630	560	500
	energy, ft-lb:	130	105	85	70	55
Federal 98 LRN	velocity, fps:	710	690	670	650	640
	energy, ft-lb:	115	105	100	95	90
Lapua 83 LWC	velocity, fps:	240		189*		149*
	energy, ft-lb:	154		95*		59*
Lapua 98 LWC	velocity, fps:	240		202*		171*
	energy, ft-lb:	183		130*		93*
Magtech 98 LRN	velocity, fps:	705		670		635
	energy, ft-lb:	108		98		88
Magtech 98 LWC	velocity, fps:	682		579		491
	energy, ft-lb:	102		73		52
Norma 98 LWC	velocity, fps:	787	759	732		683
	energy, ft-lb:	136	126	118		102
PMC 98 LRN	velocity, fps:	789	770	751	733	716
	energy, ft-lb:	135				
PMC 100 LWC	velocity, fps:	683	652	623	595	569
	energy, ft-lb:	102				
Rem. 98 LRN	velocity, fps:	705		670		635
	energy, ft-lb:	115		98		88

Centerfire Handgun Ballistics

.32 S&W LONG TO 9MM LUGER

CARTRIDGE BULLET	RANGE, YARDS:	0	25	50	75	100
Win. 98 LRN	velocity, fps:	705		670		635
	energy, ft-lb:	115		98		88

.32 SHORT COLT

CARTRIDGE BULLET	RANGE, YARDS:	0	25	50	75	100
Win. 80 LRN	velocity, fps:	745		665		590
	energy, ft-lb:	100		79		62

.32-20

CARTRIDGE BULLET	RANGE, YARDS:	0	25	50	75	100
Black Hills 115 FPL	velocity, fps:	800				
	energy, ft-lb:					

.32 H&R MAG

CARTRIDGE BULLET	RANGE, YARDS:	0	25	50	75	100
Black Hills 85 JHP	velocity, fps	1100				
	energy, ft-lb	228				
Black Hills 90 FPL	velocity, fps	750				
	energy, ft-lb					
Black Hills 115 FPL	velocity, fps	800				
	energy, ft-lb					
Federal 85 Hi-Shok JHP	velocity, fps:	1100	1050	1020	970	930
	energy, ft-lb:	230	210	195	175	165
Federal 95 LSWC	velocity, fps:	1030	1000	940	930	900
	energy, ft-lb:	225	210	195	185	170

CARTRIDGE BULLET		0	50 yds.		100.
Hornady 80 FTX	velocity, fps:	1150	1039		963
	energy, ft-lb:	235	192		165

.38 SPECIAL LITE, 4"BBL

CARTRIDGE BULLET	RANGE, YARDS:	0	25	50	75	100
Hornady 90 FTX	velocity, fps:	1200		1037		938
	energy, ft-lb:	288		215		176

9MM MAKAROV

CARTRIDGE BULLET	RANGE, YARDS:	0	25	50	75	100
Federal 90 Hi-Shok JHP	velocity, fps:	990	950	910	880	850
	energy, ft-lb:	195	180	165	155	145
Federal 90 FMJ	velocity, fps:	990	960	920	900	870
	energy, ft-lb:	205	190	180	170	160
Hornady 95 JHP/XTP	velocity, fps:	1000		930		874
	energy, ft-lb:	211		182		161
PMC 100 FMJ-TC	velocity, fps:	velocity and energy figures not available				
Speer 95 TMJ Blazer	velocity, fps:	1000		928		872
	energy, ft-lb:	211		182		161

9x21 IMI

CARTRIDGE BULLET	RANGE, YARDS:	0	25	50	75	100
PMC 123 FMJ	velocity, fps:	1150	1093	1046	1007	973
	energy, ft-lb:	364				

9MM LUGER

CARTRIDGE BULLET	RANGE, YARDS:	0	25	50	75	100
Black Hills 115 JHP	velocity, fps:	1150				
	energy, ft-lb:	336				
Black Hills 115 FMJ	velocity, fps:	1150				
	energy, ft-lb:	336				
Black Hills 115 JHP +P	velocity, fps:	1300				
	energy, ft-lb:	431				
Black Hills 115 EXP JHP	velocity, fps:	1250				
	energy, ft-lb:	400				
Black Hills 124 JHP +P	velocity, fps:	1250				
	energy, ft-lb:	430				
Black Hills 124 JHP	velocity, fps:	1150				
	energy, ft-lb:	363				
Black Hills 124 FMJ	velocity, fps:	1150				
	energy, ft-lb:	363				
Black Hills 147 JHP subsonic	velocity, fps:	975				
	energy, ft-lb:	309				
Black Hills 147 FMJ subsonic	velocity, fps:	975				
	energy, ft-lb:	309				
Federal 105 EFMJ	velocity, fps:	1225	1160	1105	1060	1025
	energy, ft-lb:	350	315	285	265	245

CARTRIDGE BULLET	RANGE, YARDS:	0	25	50	75	100
Federal 115 Hi-Shok JHP	velocity, fps:	1160	1100	1060	1020	990
	energy, ft-lb:	345	310	285	270	250
Federal 115 FMJ	velocity, fps:	1160	1100	1060	1020	990
	energy, ft-lb:	345	310	285	270	250
Federal 124 FMJ	velocity, fps:	1120	1070	1030	990	960
	energy, ft-lb:	345	315	290	270	255
Federal 124 Hydra-Shok JHP	velocity, fps:	1120	1070	1030	990	960
	energy, ft-lb:	345	315	290	270	255
Federal 124 TMJ TMF Primer	velocity, fps:	1120	1070	1030	990	960
	energy, ft-lb:	345	315	290	270	255
Federal 124 Truncated FMJ Match	velocity, fps:	1120	1070	1030	990	960
	energy, ft-lb:	345	315	290	270	255
Federal 124 Nyclad HP	velocity, fps:	1120	1070	1030	990	960
	energy, ft-lb:	345	315	290	270	255
Federal 124 FMJ +P	velocity, fps:	1120	1070	1030	990	960
	energy, ft-lb:	345	315	290	270	255
Federal 135 Hydra-Shok JHP	velocity, fps:	1050	1030	1010	980	970
	energy, ft-lb:	330	315	300	290	280
Federal 147 Hydra-Shok JHP	velocity, fps:	1000	960	920	890	860
	energy, ft-lb:	325	300	275	260	240
Federal 147 Hi-Shok JHP	velocity, fps:	980	950	930	900	880
	energy, ft-lb:	310	295	285	265	255
Federal 147 FMJ FN	velocity, fps:	960	930	910	890	870
	energy, ft-lb:	295	280	270	260	250
Federal 147 TMJ TMF Primer	velocity, fps:	960	940	910	890	870
	energy, ft-lb:	300	285	270	260	245
Hornady 115 JHP/XTP	velocity, fps:	1155		1047		971
	energy, ft-lb:	341		280		241
Hornady 124 JHP/XTP	velocity, fps:	1110		1030		971
	energy, ft-lb:	339		292		259
Hornady 124 TAP-FPD	velocity, fps:	1100		1028		967
	energy, ft-lb:	339		291		257
Hornady 147 JHP/XTP	velocity, fps:	975		935		899
	energy, ft-lb:	310		285		264
Hornady 147 TAP-FPD	velocity, fps:	975		935		899
	energy, ft-lb:	310		285		264
Lapua 116 FMJ	velocity, fps:	365		319*		290*
	energy, ft-lb:	500		381*		315*
Lapua 120 FMJ CEPP Super	velocity, fps:	360		316*		288*
	energy, ft-lb:	505		390*		324*
Lapua 120 FMJ CEPP Extra	velocity, fps:	360		316*		288*
	energy, ft-lb:	505		390*		324*
Lapua 123 HP Megashock	velocity, fps:	355		311*		284*
	energy, ft-lb:	504		388*		322*
Lapua 123 FMJ	velocity, fps:	320		292*		272*
	energy, ft-lb:	410		342*		295*
Lapua 123 FMJ Combat	velocity, fps:	355		315*		289*
	energy, ft-lb:	504		397*		333*
Magtech 115 JHP +P	velocity, fps:	1246		1137		1056
	energy, ft-lb:	397		330		285
Magtech 115 FMC	velocity, fps:	1135		1027		961
	energy, ft-lb:	330		270		235
Magtech 115 JHP	velocity, fps:	1155		1047		971
	energy, ft-lb:	340		280		240
Magtech 124 FMC	velocity, fps:	1109		1030		971
	energy, ft-lb:	339		292		259
Norma 84 Lead Free Frangible (Geco brand)	velocity, fps:	1411				
	energy, ft-lb:	371				
Norma 124 FMJ (Geco brand)	velocity, fps:	1120				
	energy, fps:	341				
Norma 123 FMJ	velocity, fps:	1099	1032	980		899
	energy, ft-lb:	331	292	263		221
Norma 123 FMJ	velocity, fps:	1280	1170	1086		972
	energy, ft-lb:	449	375	323		259

Centerfire Handgun Ballistics

9MM LUGER TO .380 AUTO

CARTRIDGE BULLET	RANGE, YARDS:	0	25	50	75	100
PMC 75 Non-Toxic Frangible	velocity, fps:	1350	1240	1154	1088	1035
	energy, ft-lb:	303				
PMC 95 SFHP	velocity, fps:	1250	1239	1228	1217	1207
	energy, ft-lb:	330				
PMC 115 FMJ	velocity, fps:	1157	1100	1053	1013	979
	energy, ft-lb:	344				
PMC 115 JHP	velocity, fps:	1167	1098	1044	999	961
	energy, ft-lb:	350				
PMC 124 SFHP	velocity, fps:	1090	1043	1003	969	939
	energy, ft-lb:	327				
PMC 124 FMJ	velocity, fps:	1110	1059	1017	980	949
	energy, ft-lb:	339				
PMC 124 LRN	velocity, fps:	1050	1006	969	937	908
	energy, ft-lb:	304				
PMC 147 FMJ	velocity, fps:	980	965	941	919	900
	enerby, ft-lb:	310				
PMC 147 SFHP	velocity, fps:	velocity and energy figures not available				
Rem. 101 Lead Free Frangible	velocity, fps:	1220		1092		1004
	energy, ft-lb:	334		267		226
Rem. 115 FN Enclosed Base	velocity, fps:	1135		1041		973
	energy, ft-lb:	329		277		242
Rem. 115 Metal Case	velocity, fps:	1135		1041		973
	energy, ft-lb:	329		277		242
Rem. 115 JHP	velocity, fps:	1155		1047		971
	energy, ft-lb:	341		280		241
Rem. 115 JHP +P	velocity, fps:	1250		1113		1019
	energy, ft-lb:	399		316		265
Rem. 124 JHP	velocity, fps:	1120		1028		960
	energy, ft-lb:	346		291		254
Rem. 124 FNEB	velocity, fps:	1100		1030		971
	energy, ft-lb:	339		292		252
Rem. 124 BJHP	velocity, fps:	1125		1031		963
	energy, ft-lb:	349		293		255
Rem. 124 BJHP +P	velocity, fps:	1180		1089		1021
	energy, ft-lb:	384		327		287
Rem. 124 Metal Case	velocity, fps:	1110		1030		971
	energy, ft-lb:	339		292		259
Rem. 147 JHP subsonic	velocity, fps:	990		941		900
	energy, ft-lb:	320		289		264
Rem. 147 BJHP	velocity, fps:	990		941		900
	energy, ft-lb:	320		289		264
Speer 90 Frangible	velocity, fps:	1350		1132		1001
	energy, ft-lb:	364		256		200
Speer 115 JHP Blazer	velocity, fps:	1145		1024		943
	energy, ft-lb:	335		268		227
Speer 115 FMJ Blazer	velocity, fps:	1145		1047		971
	energy, ft-lb:	341		280		241
Speer 115 FMJ	velocity, fps:	1200		1060		970
	energy, ft-lb:	368		287		240
Speer 115 Gold Dot HP	velocity, fps:	1200		1047		971
	energy, ft-lb:	341		280		241
Speer 124 FMJ Blazer	velocity, fps:	1090		989		917
	energy, ft-lb:	327		269		231
Speer 124 FMJ	velocity, fps:	1090		987		913
	energy, ft-lb:	327		268		230
Speer 124 TMJ-CF (and Blazer)	velocity, fps:	1090		989		917
	energy, ft-lb:	327		269		231
Speer 124 Gold Dot HP	velocity, fps:	1150		1030		948
	energy, ft-lb:	367		292		247
Speer 124 Gold Dot HP+P	velocity, ft-lb:	1220		1085		996
	energy, ft-lb:	410		324		273
Speer 147 TMJ Blazer	velocity, fps:	950		912		879
	energy, ft-lb:	295		272		252

CARTRIDGE BULLET	RANGE, YARDS:	0	25	50	75	100
Speer 147 TMJ	velocity, fps:	985		943		906
	energy, ft-lb:	317		290		268
Speer 147 TMJ-CF (and Blazer)	velocity, fps:	985		960		924
	energy, ft-lb:	326		300		279
Speer 147 Gold Dot	velocity, fps:	985		960		924
	energy, ft-lb:	326		300		279
Win. 105 Jacketed FP	velocity, fps:	1200		1074		989
	energy, ft-lb:	336		269		228
Win. 115 Silvertip HP	velocity, fps:	1225		1095		1007
	energy, ft-lb:	383		306		259
Win. 115 Jacketed HP	velocity, fps:	1225		1095		
	energy, ft-lb:	383		306		
Win. 115 FMJ	velocity, fps:	1190		1071		
	energy, ft-lb:	362		293		
Win. 115 EB WinClean	velocity, fps:	1190		1088		
	energy, ft-lb:	362		302		
Win. 124 FMJ	velocity, fps:	1140		1050		
	energy, ft-lb:	358		303		
Win. 124 EB WinClean	velocity, fps:	1130		1049		
	energy, ft-lb:	352		303		
Win. 147 FMJ FN	velocity, fps:	990		945		
	energy, ft-lb:	320		292		
Win. 147 SXT	velocity, fps:	990		947		909
	energy, ft-lb:	320		293		270
Win. 147 Silvertip HP	velocity, fps:	1010		962		921
	energy, ft-lb:	333		302		277
Win. 147 JHP	velocity, fps:	990		945		
	energy, ft-lb:	320		291		
Win. 147 EB WinClean	velocity, fps:	990		945		
	energy, ft-lb:	320		291		

9 x 23 WINCHESTER

CARTRIDGE BULLET	RANGE, YARDS:	0	25	50	75	100
Win. 124 Jacketed FP	velocity, fps:	1460		1308		
	energy, ft-lb:	587		471		
Win. 125 Silvertip HP	velocity, fps:	1450		1249		1103
	energy, ft-lb:	583		433		338

.38 S&W

CARTRIDGE BULLET	RANGE, YARDS:	0	25	50	75	100
Rem. 146 LRN	velocity, fps:	685		650		620
	energy, ft-lb:	150		135		125
Win. 145 LRN	velocity, fps:	685		650		620
	energy, ft-lb:	150		135		125

.38 SHORT COLT

CARTRIDGE BULLET	RANGE, YARDS:	0	25	50	75	100
Rem. 125 LRN	velocity, fps:	730		685		645
	energy, ft-lb:	150		130		115

.38 LONG COLT

CARTRIDGE BULLET	RANGE, YARDS:	0	25	50	75	100
Black Hills 158 RNL	velocity, fps:	650				
	energy, ft-lb:					

.380 AUTO

CARTRIDGE BULLET	RANGE, YARDS:	0	25	50	75	100
Black Hills 90 JHP	velocity, fps:	1000				
	energy, ft-lb:	200				
Black Hills 95 FMJ	velocity, fps:	950				
	energy, ft-lb:	190				
Federal 90 Hi-Shok JHP	velocity, fps:	1000	940	890	840	800
	energy, ft-lb:	200	175	160	140	130
Federal 90 Hydra-Shok JHP	velocity, fps:	1000	940	890	840	800
	energy, ft-lb:	200	175	160	140	130
Federal 95 FMJ	velocity, fps:	960	910	870	830	790
	energy, ft-lb:	190	175	160	145	130
Hornady 90 JHP/XTP	velocity, fps:	1000		902		823
	energy, ft-lb:	200		163		135

Centerfire Handgun Ballistics

.380 AUTO TO .38 SPECIAL

CARTRIDGE BULLET	RANGE, YARDS:	0	25	50	75	100
Magtech 85 JHP + P	velocity, fps:	1082		999		936
	energy, ft-lb:	221		188		166
Magtech 95 FMC	velocity, fps:	951		861		781
	energy, ft-lb:	190		156		128
Magtech 95 JHP	velocity, fps:	951		861		781
	energy, ft-lb:	190		156		128
PMC 77 NT/FR	velocity, fps:	1200	1095	1012	932	874
	energy, ft-lb:	223				
PMC 90 FMJ	velocity, fps:	910	872	838	807	778
	energy, ft-lb:	165				
PMC 90 JHP	velocity, fps:	917	878	844	812	782
	energy, ft-lb:	168				
PMC 95 SFHP	velocity, fps:	925	884	847	813	783
	energy, ft-lb:	180				
Rem. 88 JHP	velocity, fps:	990		920		868
	energy, ft-lb:	191		165		146
Rem. 95 FNEB	velocity, fps:	955		865		785
	energy, ft-lb:	190		160		130
Rem. 95 Metal Case	velocity, fps:	955		865		785
	energy, ft-lb:	190		160		130
Rem. 102 BJHP	velocity, fps:	940		901		866
	energy, ft-lb:	200		184		170
Speer 88 JHP Blazer	velocity, fps:	950		920		870
	energy, ft-lb:	195		164		148
Speer 90 Gold Dot	velocity, fps:	990		907		842
	energy, ft-lb:	196		164		142
Speer 95 TMJ Blazer	velocity, fps:	945		865		785
	energy, ft-lb:	190		160		130
Speer 95 TMJ	velocity, fps:	950		877		817
	energy, ft-lb:	180		154		133
Win. 85 Silvertip HP	velocity, fps:	1000		921		860
	energy, ft-lb:	189		160		140
Win. 95 SXT	velocity, fps:	955		889		835
	energy, ft-lb:	192		167		147
Win. 95 FMJ	velocity, fps:	955		865		
	energy, ft-lb:	190		160		
Win. 95 EB WinClean	velocity, fps:	955		881		
	energy, ft-lb:	192		164		

.38 SPECIAL

CARTRIDGE BULLET	RANGE, YARDS:	0	25	50	75	100
Black Hills 125 JHP +P	velocity, fps:	1050				
	energy, ft-lb:	306				
Black Hills 148 HBWC	velocity, fps:	700				
	energy, ft-lb:					
Black Hills 158 SWC	velocity, fps:	850				
	energy, ft-lb:					
Black Hills 158 CNL	velocity, fps:	800				
	energy, ft-lb:					
Federal 110 Hydra-Shok JHP	velocity, fps:	1000	970	930	910	880
	energy, ft-lb:	245	225	215	200	190
Federal 110 Hi-Shok JHP +P	velocity, fps:	1000	960	930	900	870
	energy, ft-lb:	240	225	210	195	185
Federal 125 Nyclad HP	velocity, fps:	830	780	730	690	650
	energy, ft-lb:	190	170	150	130	115
Federal 125 Hi-Shok JSP +P	velocity, fps:	950	920	900	880	860
	energy, ft-lb:	250	235	225	215	205
Federal 125 Hi-Shok JHP +P	velocity, fps:	950	920	900	880	860
	energy, ft-lb:	250	235	225	215	205
Federal 125 Nyclad HP +P	velocity, fps:	950	920	900	880	860
	energy, ft-lb:	250	235	225	215	205
Federal 129 Hydra-Shok JHP+P	velocity, fps:	950	930	910	890	870
	energy, ft-lb:	255	245	235	225	215
Federal 130 FMJ	velocity, fps:	950	920	890	870	840
	energy, ft-lb:	260	245	230	215	205
Federal 148 LWC Match	velocity, fps:	710	670	630	600	560
	energy, ft-lb:	165	150	130	115	105
Federal 158 LRN	velocity, fps:	760	740	720	710	690
	energy, ft-lb:	200	190	185	175	170
Federal 158 LSWC	velocity, fps:	760	740	720	710	690
	energy, ft-lb:	200	190	185	175	170
Federal 158 Nyclad RN	velocity, fps:	760	740	720	710	690
	energy, ft-lb:	200	190	185	175	170
Federal 158 SWC HP +P	velocity, fps:	890	870	860	840	820
	energy, ft-lb:	280	265	260	245	235
Federal 158 LSWC +P	velocity, fps:	890	870	860	840	820
	energy, ft-lb:	270	265	260	245	235
Federal 158 Nyclad SWC-HP+P	velocity, fps:	890	870	860	840	820
	energy, ft-lb:	270	265	260	245	235
Hornady 125 JHP/XTP	velocity, fps:	900		856		817
	energy, ft-lb:	225		203		185
Hornady 140 JHP/XTP	velocity, fps:	825		790		757
	energy, ft-lb:	212		194		178
Hornady 140 Cowboy	velocity, fps:	800		767		735
	energy, ft-lb:	199		183		168
Hornady 148 HBWC	velocity, fps:	800		697		610
	energy, ft-lb:	210		160		122
Hornady 158 JHP/XPT	velocity, fps:	800		765		731
	energy, ft-lb:	225		205		188
Lapua 123 HP Megashock	velocity, fps:	355		311*		284*
	energy, ft-lb:	504		388*		322*
Lapua 148 LWC	velocity, fps:	230		203*		181*
	energy, ft-lb:	254		199*		157*
Lapua 150 SJFN	velocity, fps:	325		301*		283*
	energy, ft-lb:	512		439*		388*
Lapua 158 FMJLF	velocity, fps:	255		243*		232*
	energy, ft-lb:	332		301*		275*
Lapua 158 LRN	velocity, fps:	255		243*		232*
	energy, ft-lb:	332		301*		275*
Magtech 125 JHP +P	velocity, fps:	1017		971		931
	energy, ft-lb:	287		262		241
Magtech 148 LWC	velocity, fps:	710		634		566
	energy, ft-lb:	166		132		105
Magtech 158 LRN	velocity, fps:	755		728		693
	energy, ft-lb:	200		183		168
Magtech 158 LFN	velocity, fps:	800		776		753
	energy, ft-lb:	225		211		199
Magtech 158 SJHP	velocity, fps:	807		779		753
	energy, ft-lb:	230		213		199
Magtech 158 LSWC	velocity, fps:	755		721		689
	energy, ft-lb:	200		182		167
Magtech 158 FMC-Flat	velocity, fps:	807		779		753
	energy, ft-lb:	230		213		199
PMC 85 Non-Toxic Frangible	velocity, fps:	1275	1181	1109	1052	1006
	energy, ft-lb:	307				
PMC 110 SFHP +P	velocity, fps:	velocity and energy figures not available				
PMC 125 SFHP +P	velocity, fps:	950	918	889	863	838
	energy, ft-lb:	251				
PMC 125 JHP +P	velocity, fps:	974	938	906	878	851
	energy, ft-lb:	266				
PMC 132 FMJ	velocity, fps:	841	820	799	780	761
	energy, ft-lb:	206				
PMC 148 LWC	velocity, fps:	728	694	662	631	602
	energy, ft-lb:	175				
PMC 158 LRN	velocity, fps:	820	801	783	765	749
	energy, ft-lb:	235				
PMC 158 JSP	velocity, fps:	835	816	797	779	762
	energy, ft-lb:	245				

CARTRIDGE BULLET	RANGE, YARDS:	0	25	50	75	100
PMC 158 LFP	velocity, fps:	800		761		725
	energy, ft-lb:	225		203		185
Rem. 101 Lead Free Frangible	velocity, fps:	950		896		850
	energy, ft-lb:	202		180		162
Rem. 110 SJHP	velocity, fps:	950		890		840
	energy, ft-lb:	220		194		172
Rem. 110 SJHP +P	velocity, fps:	995		926		871
	energy, ft-lb:	242		210		185
Rem. 125 SJHP +P	velocity, ft-lb:	945		898		858
	energy, ft-lb:	248		224		204
Rem. 125 BJHP	velocity, fps:	975		929		885
	energy, ft-lb:	264		238		218
Rem. 125 FNEB	velocity, fps:	850		822		796
	energy, ft-lb:	201		188		176
Rem. 125 FNEB +P	velocity, fps:	975		935		899
	energy, ft-lb:	264		242		224
Rem. 130 Metal Case	velocity, fps:	950		913		879
	energy, ft-lb:	261		240		223
Rem. 148 LWC Match	velocity, fps:	710		634		566
	energy, ft-lb:	166		132		105
Rem. 158 LRN	velocity, fps:	755		723		692
	energy, ft-lb:	200		183		168
Rem. 158 SWC +P	velocity, fps:	890		855		823
	energy, ft-lb:	278		257		238
Rem. 158 SWC	velocity, fps:	755		723		692
	energy, ft-lb:	200		183		168
Rem. 158 LHP +P	velocity, fps:	890		855		823
	energy, ft-lb:	278		257		238
Speer 125 JHP +P Blazer	velocity, fps:	945		898		858
	energy, ft-lb:	248		224		204
Speer 125 Gold Dot +P	velocity, fps:	945		898		858
	energy, ft-lb:	248		224		204
Speer 158 TMJ +P (and Blazer)	velocity, fps:	900		852		818
	energy, ft-lb:	278		255		235
Speer 158 LRN Blazer	velocity, fps:	755		723		692
	energy, ft-lb:	200		183		168
Speer 158 Trail Blazer LFN	velocity, fps:	800		761		725
	energy, ft-lb:	225		203		184
Speer 158 TMJ-CF +P (and Blazer)	velocity, fps:	900		852		818
	energy, ft-lb:	278		255		235
Win. 110 Silvertip HP	velocity, fps:	945		894		850
	energy, ft-lb:	218		195		176
Win. 110 Jacketed FP	velocity, fps:	975		906		849
	energy, ft-lb:	232		201		176
Win. 125 Jacketed HP	velocity, fps:	945		898		
	energy, ft-lb:	248		224		
Win. 125 Jacketed HP +P	velocity, fps:	945		898		858
	energy, ft-lb:	248		224		204
Win. 125 Jacketed FP	velocity, fps:	850		804		
	energy, ft-lb:	201		179		
Win. 125 Silvertip HP + P	velocity, fps:	945		898		858
	energy, ft-lb:	248		224		204
Win. 125 JFP WinClean	velocity, fps:	775		742		
	energy, ft-lb:	167		153		
Win. 130 FMJ	velocity, fps:	800		765		
	energy, ft-lb:	185		169		
Win. 130 SXT +P	velocity, fps:	925		887		852
	energy, ft-lb:	247		227		210
Win. 148 LWC Super Match	velocity, fps:	710		634		566
	energy, ft-lb:	166		132		105
Win. 150 Lead	velocity, fps:	845		812		
	energy, ft-lb:	238		219		
Win. 158 Lead	velocity, fps:	800		761		725
	energy, ft-lb:	225		203		185

CARTRIDGE BULLET	RANGE, YARDS:	0	25	50	75	100
Win. 158 LRN	velocity, fps:	755		723		693
	energy, ft-lb:	200		183		168
Win. 158 LSWC	velocity, fps:	755		721		689
	energy, ft-lb:	200		182		167
Win. 158 LSWC HP +P	velocity, fps:	890		855		823
	energy, ft-lb:	278		257		238

.38-40

CARTRIDGE BULLET	RANGE, YARDS:	0	25	50	75	100
Black Hills 180 FPL	velocity, fps:	800				
	energy, ft-lb:					

.38 SUPER

CARTRIDGE BULLET	RANGE, YARDS:	0	25	50	75	100
Federal 130 FMJ +P	velocity, fps:	1200	1140	1100	1050	1020
	energy, ft-lb:	415	380	350	320	300
PMC 115 JHP	velocity, fps:	1116	1052	1001	959	923
	energy, ft-lb:	318				
PMC 130 FMJ	velocity, fps:	1092	1038	994	957	924
	energy, ft-lb:	348				
Rem. 130 Metal Case	velocity, fps:	1215		1099		1017
	energy, ft-lb:	426		348		298
Win. 125 Silvertip HP +P	velocity, fps:	1240		1130		1050
	energy, ft-lb:	427		354		306
Win. 130 FMJ +P	velocity, fps:	1215		1099		
	energy, ft-lb:	426		348		

.357 SIG

CARTRIDGE BULLET	RANGE, YARDS:	0	25	50	75	100
Federal 125 FMJ	velocity, fps:	1350	1270	1190	1130	1080
	energy, ft-lb:	510	445	395	355	325
Federal 125 JHP	velocity, fps:	1350	1270	1190	1130	1080
	energy, ft-lb:	510	445	395	355	325
Federal 150 JHP	velocity, fps:	1130	1080	1030	1000	970
	energy, ft-lb:	420	385	355	330	310
Hornady 124 JHP/XTP	velocity, fps:	1350		1208		1108
	energy, ft-lb:	502		405		338
Hornady 147 JHP/XTP	velocity, fps:	1225		1138		1072
	energy, ft-lb:	490		422		375
PMC 85 Non-Toxic Frangible	velocity, fps:	1480	1356	1245	1158	1092
	energy, ft-lb:	413				
PMC 124 SFHP	velocity, fps:	1350	1263	1190	1132	1083
	energy, ft-lb:	502				
PMC 124 FMJ/FP	velocity, fps:	1350	1242	1158	1093	1040
	energy, ft-lb:	512				
Rem. 104 Lead Free Frangible	velocity, fps:	1400		1223		1094
	energy, ft-lb:	453		345		276
Rem. 125 Metal Case	velocity, fps:	1350		1146		1018
	energy, ft-lb:	506		422		359
Rem. 125 JHP	velocity, fps:	1350		1157		1032
	energy, ft-lb:	506		372		296
Speer 125 TMJ (and Blazer)	velocity, fps:	1350		1177		1057
	energy, ft-lb:	502		381		307
Speer 125 TMJ-CF	velocity, fps:	1350		1177		1057
	energy, ft-lb:	502		381		307
Speer 125 Gold Dot	velocity, fps:	1375		1203		1079
	energy, ft-lb:	525		402		323
Win. 105 JFP	velocity, fps:	1370		1179		1050
	energy, ft-lb	438		324		257
Win. 125 FMJ FN	velocity, fps:	1350		1185		
	energy, ft-lb	506		390		

.357 MAGNUM

CARTRIDGE BULLET	RANGE, YARDS:	0	25	50	75	100
Black Hills 125 JHP	velocity, fps:	1500				
	energy, ft-lb:	625				
Black Hills 158 CNL	velocity, fps:	800				
	energy, ft-lb:					
Black Hills 158 SWC	velocity, fps:	1050				
	energy, ft-lb:					

Centerfire Handgun Ballistics

.357 MAGNUM TO .40 S&W

CARTRIDGE BULLET	RANGE, YARDS:	0	25	50	75	100
Black Hills 158 JHP	velocity, fps:	1250				
	energy, ft-lb:					
Federal 110 Hi-Shok JHP	velocity, fps:	1300	1180	1090	1040	990
	energy, ft-lb:	410	340	290	260	235
Federal 125 Hi-Shok JHP	velocity, fps:	1450	1350	1240	1160	1100
	energy, ft-lb:	580	495	430	370	335
Federal 130 Hydra-Shok JHP	velocity, fps:	1300	1210	1130	1070	1020
	energy, ft-lb:	490	420	370	330	300
Federal 158 Hi-Shok JSP	velocity, fps:	1240	1160	1100	1060	1020
	energy, ft-lb:	535	475	430	395	365
Federal 158 JSP	velocity, fps:	1240	1160	1100	1060	1020
	energy, ft-lb:	535	475	430	395	365
Federal 158 LSWC	velocity, fps:	1240	1160	1100	1060	1020
	energy, ft-lb:	535	475	430	395	365
Federal 158 Hi-Shok JHP	velocity, fps:	1240	1160	1100	1060	1020
	energy, ft-lb:	535	475	430	395	365
Federal 158 Hydra-Shok JHP	velocity, fps:	1240	1160	1100	1060	1020
	energy, ft-lb:	535	475	430	395	365
Federal 180 Hi-Shok JHP	velocity, fps:	1090	1030	980	930	890
	energy, ft-lb:	475	425	385	350	320
Federal 180 Castcore	velocity, fps:	1250	1200	1160	1120	1080
	energy, ft-lb:	625	575	535	495	465
Hornady 125 JHP/XTP	velocity, fps:	1500		1314		1166
	energy, ft-lb:	624		479		377
Hornady 125 JFP/XTP	velocity, fps:	1500		1311		1161
	energy, ft-lb:	624		477		374
Hornady 140 Cowboy	velocity, fps:	800		767		735
	energy, ft-lb:	199		183		168
Hornady 140 JHP/XTP	velocity, fps:	1400		1249		1130
	energy, ft-lb:	609		485		397
Hornady 158 JHP/XTP	velocity, fps:	1250		1150		1073
	energy, ft-lb:	548		464		404
Hornady 158 JFP/XTP	velocity, fps:	1250		1147		1068
	energy, ft-lb:	548		461		400
Lapua 150 FMJ CEPP Super	velocity, fps:	370		527*		303*
	energy, ft-lb:	664		527*		445*
Lapua 150 SJFN	velocity, fps:	385		342*		313*
	energy, ft-lb:	719		569*		476*
Lapua 158 SJHP	velocity, fps:	470		408*		359*
	energy, ft-lb:	1127		850*		657*
Magtech 158 SJSP	velocity, fps:	1235		1104		1015
	energy, ft-lb:	535		428		361
Magtech 158 SJHP	velocity, fps:	1235		1104		1015
	energy, ft-lb:	535		428		361
PMC 85 Non-Toxic Frangible	velocity, fps:	1325	1219	1139	1076	1025
	energy, ft-lb:	331				
PMC 125 JHP	velocity, fps:	1194	1117	1057	1008	967
	energy, ft-lb:	399				
PMC 150 JHP	velocity, fps:	1234	1156	1093	1042	1000
	energy, ft-lb:	512				
PMC 150 SFHP	velocity, fps:	1205	1129	1069	1020	980
	energy, ft-lb:	484				
PMC 158 JSP	velocity, fps:	1194	1122	1063	1016	977
	energy, ft-lb:	504				
PMC 158 LFP	velocity, fps:	800		761		725
	energy, ft-lb:	225		203		185
Rem. 110 SJHP	velocity, fps:	1295		1094		975
	energy, ft-lb:	410		292		232
Rem. 125 SJHP	velocity, fps:	1450		1240		1090
	energy, ft-lb:	583		427		330
Rem. 125 BJHP	velocity, fps:	1220		1095		1009
	energy, ft-lb:	413		333		283
Rem. 125 FNEB	velocity, fps:	1450		1240		1090
	energy, ft-lb:	583		427		330

CARTRIDGE BULLET	RANGE, YARDS:	0	25	50	75	100
Rem. 158 SJHP	velocity, fps:	1235		1104		1015
	energy, ft-lb:	535		428		361
Rem. 158 SP	velocity, fps:	1235		1104		1015
	energy, ft-lb:	535		428		361
Rem. 158 SWC	velocity, fps:	1235		1104		1015
	energy, ft-lb:	535		428		361
Rem. 165 JHP Core-Lokt	velocity, fps:	1290		1189		1108
	energy, ft-lb:	610		518		450
Rem. 180 SJHP	velocity, fps:	1145		1053		985
	energy, ft-lb:	542		443		388
Speer 125 Gold Dot	velocity, fps:	1450		1240		1090
	energy, ft-lb:	583		427		330
Speer 158 JHP Blazer	velocity, fps:	1150		1104		1015
	energy, ft-lb:	535		428		361
Speer 158 Gold Dot	velocity, fps:	1235		1104		1015
	energy, ft-lb:	535		428		361
Speer 170 Gold Dot SP	velocity, fps:	1180		1089		1019
	energy, ft-lb:	525		447		392
Win. 110 JFP	velocity, fps:	1275		1105		998
	energy, ft-lb:	397		298		243
Win. 110 JHP	velocity, fps:	1295		1095		
	energy, ft-lb:	410		292		
Win. 125 JFP WinClean	velocity, fps:	1370		1183		
	energy, ft-lb:	521		389		
Win. 145 Silvertip HP	velocity, fps:	1290		1155		1060
	energy, ft-lb:	535		428		361
Win. 158 JHP	velocity, fps:	1235		1104		1015
	energy, ft-lb:	535		428		361
Win. 158 JSP	velocity, fps:	1235		1104		1015
	energy, ft-lb:	535		428		361
Win. 180 Partition Gold	velocity, fps:	1180		1088		1020
	energy, ft-lb:	557		473		416

.40 S&W

CARTRIDGE BULLET	RANGE, YARDS:	0	25	50	75	100
Black Hills 155 JHP	velocity, fps:	1150				
	energy, ft-lb:	450				
Black Hills 165 EXP JHP	velocity, fps:	1150 (2005: 1100)				
	energy, ft-lb:	483				
Black Hills 180 JHP	velocity, fps:	1000				
	energy, ft-lb:	400				
Black Hills 180 JHP	velocity, fps:	1000				
	energy, ft-lb:	400				
Federal 135 Hydra-Shok JHP	velocity, fps:	1190	1050	970	900	850
	energy, ft-lb:	420	330	280	245	215
Federal 155 FMJ Ball	velocity, fps:	1140	1080	1030	990	960
	energy, ft-lb:	445	400	365	335	315
Federal 155 Hi-Shok JHP	velocity, fps:	1140	1080	1030	990	950
	energy, ft-lb:	445	400	365	335	315
Federal 155 Hydra-Shok JHP	velocity, fps:	1140	1080	1030	990	950
	energy, ft-lb:	445	400	365	335	315
Federal 165 EFMJ	velocity, fps:	1190	1060	970	905	850
	energy, ft-lb:	520	410	345	300	265
Federal 165 FMJ	velocity, fps:	1050	1020	990	960	935
	energy, ft-lb:	405	380	355	335	320
Federal 165 FMJ Ball	velocity, fps:	980	950	920	900	880
	energy, ft-lb:	350	330	310	295	280
Federal 165 Hydra-Shok JHP	velocity, fps:	980	950	930	910	890
	energy, ft-lb:	350	330	315	300	290
Federal 180 High Antim. Lead	velocity, fps:	990	960	930	910	890
	energy, ft-lb:	390	365	345	330	315
Federal 180 TMJ TMF Primer	velocity, fps:	990	960	940	910	890
	energy, ft-lb:	390	370	350	330	315
Federal 180 FMJ Ball	velocity, fps:	990	960	940	910	890
	energy, ft-lb:	390	370	350	330	315

BALLISTICS

.40 S&W TO .41 REMINGTON MAGNUM

.40 S&W

CARTRIDGE BULLET	RANGE, YARDS:	0	25	50	75	100
Federal 180 Hi-Shok JHP	velocity, fps:	990	960	930	910	890
	energy, ft-lb:	390	365	345	330	315
Federal 180 Hydra-Shok JHP	velocity, fps:	990	960	930	910	890
	energy, ft-lb:	390	365	345	330	315
Hornady 155 JHP/XTP	velocity, fps:	1180		1061		980
	energy, ft-lb:	479		387		331
Hornady 155 TAP-FPD	velocity, fps:	1180		1061		980
	energy, ft-lb:	470		387		331
Hornady 180 JHP/XTP	velocity, fps:	950		903		862
	energy, ft-lb:	361		326		297
Hornady 180 TAP-FPD	velocity, fps:	950		903		862
	energy, ft-lb:	361		326		297
Magtech 155 JHP	velocity, fps:	1025		1118		1052
	energy, ft-lb:	500		430		381
Magtech 180 JHP	velocity, fps:	990		933		886
	energy, ft-lb:	390		348		314
Magtech 180 FMC	velocity, fps:	990		933		886
	energy, ft-lb:	390		348		314
PMC 115 Non-Toxic Frangible	velocity, fps:	1350	1240	1154	1088	1035
	energy, ft-lb:	465				
PMC 155 SFHP	velocity, fps:	1160	1092	1039	994	957
	energy, ft-lb:	463				
PMC 165 JHP	velocity, fps:	1040	1002	970	941	915
	energy, ft-lb:	396				
PMC 165 FMJ	velocity, fps:	1010	977	948	922	899
	energy, ft-lb:	374				
PMC 180 FMJ/FP	velocity, fps:	985	957	931	908	885
	energy, ft-lb:	388				
PMC 180 SFHP	velocity, fps:	985	958	933	910	889
	energy, ft-lb:	388				
Rem. 141 Lead Free Frangible	velocity, fps:	1135		1056		996
	energy, ft-lb:	403		349		311
Rem. 155 JHP	velocity, fps:	1205		1095		1017
	energy, ft-lb:	499		413		356
Rem. 165 BJHP	velocity, fps:	1150		1040		964
	energy, ft-lb:	485		396		340
Rem. 180 JHP	velocity, fps:	1015		960		914
	energy, ft-lb:	412		368		334
Rem. 180 FN Enclosed Base	velocity, fps:	985		936		893
	energy, ft-lb:	388		350		319
Rem. 180 Metal Case	velocity, fps:	985		936		893
	energy, ft-lb:	388		350		319
Rem. 180 BJHP	velocity, fps:	1015		960		914
	energy, ft-lb:	412		368		334
Speer 105 Frangible	velocity, fps:	1380		1128		985
	energy, ft-lb:	444		297		226
Speer 155 TMJ Blazer	velocity, fps:	1175		1047		963
	energy, ft-lb:	475		377		319
Speer 155 TMJ	velocity, fps:	1200		1065		976
	energy, ft-lb:	496		390		328
Speer 155 Gold Dot	velocity, fps:	1200		1063		974
	energy, ft-lb:	496		389		326
Speer 165 TMJ Blazer	velocity, fps:	1100		1006		938
	energy, ft-lb:	443		371		321
Speer 165 TMJ	velocity, fps:	1150		1040		964
	energy, ft-lb:	484		396		340
Speer 165 Gold Dot	velocity, fps:	1150		1043		966
	energy, ft-lb:	485		399		342
Speer 180 HP Blazer	velocity, fps:	985		951		909
	energy, ft-lb:	400		361		330
Speer 180 FMJ Blazer	velocity, fps:	1000		937		886
	energy, ft-lb:	400		351		313
Speer 180 FMJ	velocity, fps:	1000		951		909
	energy, ft-lb:	400		361		330
Speer 180 TMJ-CF (and Blazer)	velocity, fps:	1000		951		909
	energy, ft-lb:	400		361		330
Speer 180 Gold Dot	velocity, fps:	1025		957		902
	energy, ft-lb:	420		366		325
Win. 140 JFP	velocity, fps:	1155		1039		960
	energy, ft-lb:	415		336		286
Win. 155 Silvertip HP	velocity, fps:	1205		1096		1018
	energy, ft-lb	500		414		357
Win. 165 SXT	velocity, fps:	1130		1041		977
	energy, ft-lb:	468		397		349
Win. 165 FMJ FN	velocity, fps:	1060		1001		
	energy, ft-lb:	412		367		
Win. 165 EB WinClean	velocity, fps:	1130		1054		
	energy, ft-lb:	468		407		
Win. 180 JHP	velocity, fps:	1010		954		
	energy, ft-lb:	408		364		
Win. 180 FMJ	velocity, fps:	990		936		
	energy, ft-lb:	390		350		
Win. 180 SXT	velocity, fps:	1010		954		909
	energy, ft-lb:	408		364		330
Win. 180 EB WinClean	velocity, fps:	990		943		
	energy, ft-lb:	392		356		

10 MM AUTO

CARTRIDGE BULLET	RANGE, YARDS:	0	25	50	75	100
Federal 155 Hi-Shok JHP	velocity, fps:	1330	1230	1140	1080	1030
	energy, ft-lb:	605	515	450	400	360
Federal 180 Hi-Shok JHP	velocity, fps:	1030	1000	970	950	920
	energy, ft-lb:	425	400	375	355	340
Federal 180 Hydra-Shok JHP	velocity, fps:	1030	1000	970	950	920
	energy, ft-lb:	425	400	375	355	340
Federal 180 High Antim. Lead	velocity, fps:	1030	1000	970	950	920
	energy, ft-lb:	425	400	375	355	340
Federal 180 FMJ	velocity, fps:	1060	1025	990	965	940
	energy, ft-lb:	400	370	350	330	310
Hornady 155 JHP/XTP	velocity, fps:	1265		1119		1020
	energy, ft-lb:	551		431		358
Hornady 180 JHP/XTP	velocity, fps:	1180		1077		1004
	energy, ft-lb:	556		464		403
Hornady 200 JHP/XTP	velocity, fps:	1050		994		948
	energy, ft-lb:	490		439		399
PMC 115 Non-Toxic Frangible	velocity, fps:	1350	1240	1154	1088	1035
	energy, ft-lb:	465				
PMC 170 JHP	velocity, fps:	1200	1117	1052	1000	958
	energy, ft-lb:	543				
PMC 180 SFHP	velocity, fps:	950	926	903	882	862
	energy, ft-lb:	361				
PMC 200 TC-FMJ	velocity, fps:	1050	1008	972	941	912
	energy, ft-lb:	490				
Rem. 180 Metal Case	velocity, fps:	1150		1063		998
	energy, ft-lb:	529		452		398
Speer 200 TMJ Blazer	velocity, fps:	1050		966		952
	energy, ft-lb:	490		440		402
Win. 175 Silvertip HP	velocity, fps:	1290		1141		1037
	energy, ft-lb:	649		506		418

.41 REMINGTON MAGNUM

CARTRIDGE BULLET	RANGE, YARDS:	0	25	50	75	100
Federal 210 Hi-Shok JHP	velocity, fps:	1300	1210	1130	1070	1030
	energy, ft-lb:	790	680	595	540	495
PMC 210 TCSP	velocity, fps:	1290	1201	1128	1069	1021
	energy, ft-lb:	774				
PMC 210 JHP	velocity, fps:	1289	1200	1127	1068	1020
	energy, ft-lb:	774				
Rem. 210 SP	velocity, fps:	1300		1162		1062
	energy, ft-lb:	788		630		526

Centerfire Handgun Ballistics

.41 REMINGTON MAGNUM TO .45 AUTOMATIC (ACP)

.41 REMINGTON MAGNUM (continued)

CARTRIDGE BULLET	RANGE, YARDS:	0	25	50	75	100
Win. 175 Silvertip HP	velocity, fps:	1250		1120		1029
	energy, ft-lb:	607		488		412
Win. 240 Platinum Tip	velocity, ft-lb:	1250		1151		1075
	energy, ft-lb:	833		706		616

.44 COLT

CARTRIDGE BULLET	RANGE, YARDS:	0	25	50	75	100
Black Hills 230 FPL	velocity, fps:	730				
	energy, ft-lb:					

.44 RUSSIAN

CARTRIDGE BULLET	RANGE, YARDS:	0	25	50	75	100
Black Hills 210 FPL	velocity, fps:	650				
	energy, ft-lb:					

.44 SPECIAL

CARTRIDGE BULLET	RANGE, YARDS:	0	25	50	75	100
Black Hills 210 FPL	velocity, fps:	700				
	energy, ft-lb:					
Federal 200 SWC HP	velocity, fps:	900	860	830	800	770
	energy, ft-lb:	360	330	305	285	260
Federal 250 CastCore	velocity, fps:	1250	1200	1150	1110	1080
	energy, ft-lb:	865	795	735	685	645
Hornady 180 JHP/XTP	velocity, fps:	1000		935		882
	energy, ft-lb:	400		350		311
Magtech 240 LFN	velocity, fps:	750		722		696
	energy, ft-lb:	300		278		258
PMC 180 JHP	velocity, fps:	980	938	902	869	839
	energy, ft-lb:	383				
PMC 240 SWC-CP	velocity, fps:	764	744	724	706	687
	energy, ft-lb:	311				
PMC 240 LFP	velocity, fps:	750		719		690
	energy, ft-lb:	300		275		253
Rem. 246 LRN	velocity, fps:	755		725		695
	energy, ft-lb:	310		285		265
Speer 200 HP Blazer	velocity, fps:	875		825		780
	energy, ft-lb:	340		302		270
Speer 200 Trail Blazer LFN	velocity, fps:	750		714		680
	energy, ft-lb:	250		226		205
Speer 200 Gold Dot	velocity, fps:	875		825		780
	energy, ft-lb:	340		302		270
Win. 200 Silvertip HP	velocity, fps:	900		860		822
	energy, ft-lb:	360		328		300
Win. 240 Lead	velocity, fps:	750		719		690
	energy, ft-lb	300		275		253
Win. 246 LRN	velocity, fps:	755		725		695
	energy, ft-lb:	310		285		265

.44 REMINGTON MAGNUM

CARTRIDGE BULLET	RANGE, YARDS:	0	25	50	75	100
Black Hills 240 JHP	velocity, fps:	1260				
	energy, ft-lb:	848				
Black Hills 300 JHP	velocity, fps:	1150				
	energy, ft-lb:	879				
Federal 180 Hi-Shok JHP	velocity, fps:	1610	1480	1370	1270	1180
	energy, ft-lb:	1035	875	750	640	555
Federal 240 Hi-Shok JHP	velocity, fps:	1180	1130	1080	1050	1010
	energy, ft-lb:	740	675	625	580	550
Federal 240 Hydra-Shok JHP	velocity, fps:	1180	1130	1080	1050	1010
	energy, ft-lb:	740	675	625	580	550
Federal 240 JHP	velocity, fps:	1180	1130	1080	1050	1010
	energy, ft-lb:	740	675	625	580	550
Federal 300 CastCore	velocity, fps:	1250	1200	1160	1120	1080
	energy, ft-lb:	1040	960	885	825	775
Hornady 180 JHP/XTP	velocity, fps:	1550		1340		1173
	energy, ft-lb:	960		717		550
Hornady 200 JHP/XTP	velocity, fps:	1500		1284		1128
	energy, ft-lb:	999		732		565

.44 REMINGTON MAGNUM (continued)

CARTRIDGE BULLET	RANGE, YARDS:	0	25	50	75	100
Hornady 240 JHP/XTP	velocity, fps:	1350		1188		1078
	energy, ft-lb:	971		753		619
Hornady 300 JHP/XTP	velocity, fps:	1150		1084		1031
	energy, ft-lb:	881		782		708
Magtech 240 SJSP	velocity, fps:	1180		1081		1010
	energy, ft-lb:	741		632		623
PMC 180 JHP	velocity, fps:	1392	1263	1157	1076	1015
	energy, ft-lb:	772				
PMC 240 JHP	velocity, fps:	1301	1218	1147	1088	1041
	energy, ft-lb:	900				
PMC 240 TC-SP	velocity, fps:	1300	1216	1144	1086	1038
	energy, ft-lb:	900				
PMC 240 SFHP	velocity, fps:	1300	1212	1138	1079	1030
	energy, ft-lb:	900				
PMC 240 LSWC-GCK	velocity, fps:	1225	1143	1077	1025	982
	energy, ft-lb:	806				
Rem. 180 JSP	velocity, fps:	1610		1365		1175
	energy, ft-lb:	1036		745		551
Rem. 210 Gold Dot HP	velocity, fps:	1450		1276		1140
	energy, ft-lb:	980		759		606
Rem. 240 SP	velocity, fps:	1180		1081		1010
	energy, ft-lb:	721		623		543
Rem. 240 SJHP	velocity, fps:	1180		1081		1010
	energy, ft-lb:	721		623		543
Rem. 275 JHP Core-Lokt	velocity, fps:	1235		1142		1070
	energy, ft-lb:	931		797		699
Speer 240 JHP Blazer	velocity, fps:	1200		1092		1015
	energy, ft-lb:	767		636		549
Speer 240 Gold Dot HP	velocity, fps:	1400		1255		1139
	energy, ft-lb:	1044		839		691
Speer 270 Gold Dot SP	velocity, fps:	1250		1142		1060
	energy, ft-lb:	937		781		674
Win. 210 Silvertip HP	velocity, fps:	1250		1106		1010
	energy, ft-lb:	729		570		475
Win. 240 Hollow SP	velocity, fps:	1180		1081		1010
	energy, ft-lb:	741		623		543
Win. 240 JSP	velocity, fps:	1180		1081		
	energy, ft-lb:	741		623		
Win. 250 Partition Gold	velocity, fps:	1230		1132		1057
	energy, ft-lb:	840		711		620
Win. 250 Platinum Tip	velocity, fps:	1250		1148		1070
	energy, ft-lb:	867		732		635

.44-40

CARTRIDGE BULLET	RANGE, YARDS:	0	25	50	75	100
Black Hills 200 RNFP	velocity, fps:	800				
	energy, ft-lb:					
Hornady 205 Cowboy	velocity, fps:	725		697		670
	energy, ft-lb:	239		221		204
Magtech 225 LFN	velocity, fps:	725		703		681
	energy, ft-lb:	281		247		232
PMC 225 LFP	velocity, fps:	725		723		695
	energy, ft-lb:	281		261		242
Win. 225 Lead	velocity, fps:	750		723		695
	energy, ft-lb:	281		261		242

.45 AUTOMATIC (ACP)

CARTRIDGE BULLET	RANGE, YARDS:	0	25	50	75	100
Black Hills 185 JHP	velocity, fps:	1000				
	energy, ft-lb:	411				
Black Hills 200 Match SWC	velocity, fps:	875				
	energy, ft-lb:	340				
Black Hills 230 FMJ	velocity, fps:	850				
	energy, ft-lb:	368				

CARTRIDGE BULLET	RANGE, YARDS:	0	25	50	75	100
Black Hills 230 JHP	velocity, fps:	850				
	energy, ft-lb:	368				
Black Hills 230 JHP +P	velocity, fps:	950				
	energy, ft-lb:	460				
Federal 165 Hydra-Shok JHP	velocity, fps:	1060	1020	980	950	920
	energy, ft-lb:	410	375	350	330	310
Federal 165 EFMJ	velocity, fps:	1090	1045	1005	975	942
	energy, ft-lb:	435	400	370	345	325
Federal 185 Hi-Shok JHP	velocity, fps:	950	920	900	880	860
	energy, ft-lb:	370	350	335	315	300
Federal 185 FMJ-SWC Match	velocity, fps:	780	730	700	660	620
	energy, ft-lb:	245	220	200	175	160
Federal 200 Exp. FMJ	velocity, fps:	1030	1000	970	940	920
	energy, ft-lb:	470	440	415	395	375
Federal 230 FMJ	velocity, fps:	850	830	810	790	770
	energy, ft-lb:	370	350	335	320	305
Federal 230 FMJ Match	velocity, fps:	855	835	815	795	775
	energy, ft-lb:	375	355	340	325	305
Federal 230 Hi-Shok JHP	velocity, fps:	850	830	810	790	770
	energy, ft-lb:	370	350	335	320	300
Federal 230 Hydra-Shok JHP	velocity, fps:	850	830	810	790	770
	energy, ft-lb:	370	350	335	320	305
Federal 230 FMJ	velocity, fps:	850	830	810	790	770
	energy, ft-lb:	370	350	335	320	305
Federal 230 TMJ TMF Primer	velocity, fps:	850	830	810	790	770
	energy, ft-lb:	370	350	335	315	305
Hornady 185 JHP/XTP	velocity, fps:	950		880		819
	energy, ft-lb:	371		318		276
Hornady 200 JHP/XTP	velocity, fps:	900		855		815
	energy, ft-lb:	358		325		295
Hornady 200 HP/XTP +P	velocity, fps:	1055		982		925
	energy, ft-lb:	494		428		380
Hornady 200 TAP-FPD	velocity, fps:	1055		982		926
	energy, ft-lbs:	494		428		380
Hornady 230 FMJ/RN	velocity, fps:	850		809		771
	energy, ft-lb:	369		334		304
Hornady 230 FMJ/FP	velocity, fps:	850		809		771
	energy, ft-lb:	369		334		304
Hornady 230 HP/XTP +P	velocity, fps:	950		904		865
	energy, ft-lb:	462		418		382
Hornady 230 TAP-FPD	velocity, fps:	950		908		872
	energy, ft-lb:	461		421		388
Magtech 185 JHP +P	velocity, fps:	1148		1066		1055
	energy, ft-lb:	540		467		415
Magtech 200 LSWC	velocity, fps:	950		910		874
	energy, ft-lb:	401		368		339
Magtech 230 FMC	veloctiy, fps:	837		800		767
	energy, ft-lb:	356		326		300
Magtech 230 FMC-SWC	velocity, fps:	780		720		660
	energy, ft-lb:	310		265		222
PMC 145 Non-Toxic Frangible	velocity, fps:	1100	1045	999	961	928
	energy, ft-lb:	390				
PMC 185 JHP	velocity, fps:	903	870	839	811	785
	energy, ft-lb:	339				
PMC 200 FMJ-SWC	velocity, fps:	850	818	788	761	734
	energy, ft-lb:	321				
PMC 230 SFHP	velocity, fps:	850	830	811	792	775
	energy, ft-lb:	369				
PMC 230 FMJ	velocity, fps:	830	809	789	769	749
	energy, ft-lb:	352				
Rem. 175 Lead Free Frangible	velocity, fps:	1020		923		851
	energy, ft-lb:	404		331		281

CARTRIDGE BULLET	RANGE, YARDS:	0	25	50	75	100
Rem. 185 JHP	velocity, fps:	1000		939		889
	energy, ft-lb:	411		362		324
Rem. 185 BJHP	velocity, fps:	1015		951		899
	energy, ft-lb:	423		372		332
Rem. 185 BJHP +P	velocity, fps:	1140		1042		971
	energy, ft-lb:	534		446		388
Rem. 185 MC	velocity, fps:	1015		955		907
	energy, ft-lb:	423		375		338
Rem. 230 FN Enclosed Base	velocity, fps:	835		800		767
	energy, ft-lb:	356		326		300
Rem. 230 Metal Case	velocity, fps:	835		800		767
	energy, ft-lb:	356		326		300
Rem. 230 JHP	velocity, fps:	835		800		767
	energy, ft-lb:	356		326		300
Rem. 230 BJHP	velocity, fps:	875		833		795
	energy, ft-lb:	391		355		323
Speer 140 Frangible	velocity, fps:	1200		1029		928
	energy, ft-lb:	448		329		268
Speer 185 Gold Dot	velocity, fps:	1050		956		886
	energy, ft-lb:	453		375		322
Speer 185 TMJ/FN	velocity, fps:	1000		909		839
	energy, ft-lb:	411		339		289
Speer 200 JHP Blazer	velocity, fps:	975		917		860
	energy, ft-lb:	421		372		328
Speer 200 Gold Dot +P	velocity, fps:	1080		994		930
	energy, ft-lb:	518		439		384
Speer 200 TMJ/FN	velocity, fps:	975		897		834
	energy, ft-lb:	422		357		309
Speer 230 FMJ (and Blazer)	velocity, fps:	845		804		775
	energy, ft-lb:	363		329		304
Speer 230 TMJ-CF (and Blazer)	velocity, fps:	845		804		775
	energy, ft-lb:	363		329		304
Speer 230 Gold Dot	velocity, fps:	890		845		805
	energy, ft-lb:	405		365		331
Win. 170 JFP	velocity, fps:	1050		982		928
	energy, ft-lb:	416		364		325
Win. 185 Silvertip HP	velocity, fps:	1000		938		888
	energy, ft-lb:	411		362		324
Win. 185 FMJ FN	velocity, fps:	910		861		
	energy, ft-lb:	340		304		
Win. 185 EB WinClean	velocity, fps:	910		835		
	energy, ft-lb:	340		286		
Win. 230 JHP	velocity, fps:	880		842		
	energy, ft-lb:	396		363		
Win. 230 FMJ	velocity, fps:	835		800		
	energy, ft-lb:	356		326		
Win. 230 SXT	velocity, fps:	880		846		816
	energy, ft-lb:	396		366		340
Win. 230 JHP subsonic	velocity, fps:	880		842		808
	energy, ft-lb:	396		363		334
Win. 230 EB WinClean	velocity, fps:	835		802		
	energy, ft-lb:	356		329		

.45 GAP

CARTRIDGE BULLET	RANGE, YARDS:	0	25	50	75	100
Federal 185 Hydra-Shok JHP And Federal TMJ	velocity, fps:	1090	1020	970	920	890
	energy, ft-lb:	490	430	385	350	320
Federal 230 Hydra-Shok And Federal FMJ	velocity, fps:	880	870	850	840	820
	energy, ft-lb:	395	380	3760	355	345
Win. 185 STHP	velocity, fps:	1000		938		887
	energy, ft-lb:	411		361		323
Win. 230 JHP	velocity, fps:	880		842		
	energy, ft-lb:	396		363		

Centerfire Handgun Ballistics

.45 GAP TO .500 SMITH & WESSON

CARTRIDGE BULLET	RANGE, YARDS:	0	25	50	75	100
Win. 230 EB WinClean	velocity, fps	875		840		
	energy, ft-lb	391		360		
Win. 230 FMJ	velocity, fps	850		814		
	energy, ft-lb	369		338		

.45 WINCHESTER MAGNUM

CARTRIDGE BULLET	RANGE, YARDS:	0	25	50	75	100
Win. 260 Partition Gold	velocity, fps	1200		1105		1033
	energy, ft-lb	832		705		616
Win. 260 JHP	velocity, fps	1200		1099		1026
	energy, ft-lb	831		698		607

.45 SCHOFIELD

CARTRIDGE BULLET	RANGE, YARDS:	0	25	50	75	100
Black Hills 180 FNL	velocity, fps	730				
	energy, ft-lb					
Black Hills 230 RNFP	velocity, fps	730				
	energy, ft-lb					

.45 COLT

CARTRIDGE BULLET	RANGE, YARDS:	0	25	50	75	100
Black Hills 250 RNFP	velocity, fps	725				
	energy, ft-lb					
Federal 225 SWC HP	velocity, fps	900	880	860	840	820
	energy, ft-lb	405	385	370	355	340
Hornady 255 Cowboy	velocity, fps	725		692		660
	energy, ft-lb	298		271		247
Magtech 250 LFN	velocity, fps	750		726		702
	energy, ft-lb	312		293		274
PMC 250 LFP	velocity, fps	800		767		736
	energy, ft-lb	355		331		309
PMC 300 +P+	velocity, fps	1250	1192	1144	1102	1066
	energy, ft-lb	1041				
Rem. 225 SWC	velocity, fps	960		890		832
	energy, ft-lb	460		395		346
Rem. 250 RLN	velocity, fps	860		820		780
	energy, ft-lb	410		375		340
Speer 200 FMJ Blazer	velocity, fps	1000		938		889
	energy, ft-lb	444		391		351
Speer 230 Trail Blazer LFN	velocity, fps	750		716		684
	energy, ft-lb	287		262		239
Speer 250 Gold Dot	velocity, fps	900		860		823
	energy, ft-lb	450		410		376
Win. 225 Silvertip HP	velocity, fps	920		877		839
	energy, ft-lb	423		384		352
Win. 255 LRN	velocity, fps	860		820		780
	energy, ft-lb	420		380		345
Win. 250 Lead	velocity, fps	750		720		692
	energy, ft-lb	312		288		266

.454 CASULL

CARTRIDGE BULLET	RANGE, YARDS:	0	25	50	75	100
Federal 300 Trophy Bonded	velocity, fps	1630	1540	1450	1380	1300
	energy, ft-lb	1760	1570	1405	1260	1130
Federal 360 CastCore	velocity, fps	1500	1435	1370	1310	1255
	energy, ft-lb	1800	1640	1500	1310	1260
Hornady 240 XTP-MAG	velocity, fps	1900		1679		1483
	energy, ft-lb	1923		1502		1172
Hornady 300 XTP-MAG	velocity, fps	1650		1478		1328
	energy, ft-lb	1813		1455		1175
Magtech 260 SJSP	velocity, fps	1800		1577		1383
	energy, ft-lb	1871		1437		1104
Rem. 300 Core-Lokt Ultra	velocity, fps	1625		1472		1335
	energy, ft-lb	1759		1442		1187

CARTRIDGE BULLET	RANGE, YARDS:	0	25	50	75	100
Speer 300 Gold Dot HP	velocity, fps	1625		1477		1343
	energy, ft-lb	1758		1452		1201
Win. 250 JHP	velocity, fps	1300		1151		1047
	energy, ft-lb	938		735		608
Win. 260 Partition Gold	velocity, fps	1800		1605		1427
	energy, ft-lb	1871		1485		1176
Win. 260 Platinum Tip	velocity, fps	1800		1596		1414
	eneryg, ft-lb	1870		1470		1154
Win. 300 JFP	velocity, fps	1625		1451		1308
	energy, ft-lb	1759		1413		1141

.460 SMITH & WESSON

CARTRIDGE BULLET	RANGE, YARDS:	0	25	50	75	100
Federal 275 Expander	velocity, fps	1800		1640		1500
	energy, ft-lb	1980		1650		1370
Federal 300 A-Frame	velocity, fps	1750		1510		1300
	energy, ft-lb	2040		1510		1125
Hornady 200 SST	velocity, fps	2250		2003		1772
	energy, ft-lb	2248		1395		1081
Win. 260 Supreme Part. Gold	velocity, fps	2000		1788		1592
	energy, ft-lb	2309		1845		2012

.475 LINEBAUGH

CARTRIDGE BULLET	RANGE, YARDS:	0	25	50	75	100
Hornady 400 XTP-MAG	velocity, fps	1300		1179		1093
	energy, ft-lb	1501		1235		1060

.480 RUGER

CARTRIDGE BULLET	RANGE, YARDS:	0	25	50	75	100
Federal 275 Expander	velocity, fps	1350		1190		1080
	energy, ft-lb	1115		870		710
Hornady 325 XTP-MAG	velocity, fps	1350		1191		1076
	energy, ft-lb	1315		1023		835
Hornady 400 XTP-MAG	velocity, fps	1100		1027		971
	energy, ft-lb	1075		937		838
Speer 275 Gold Dot HP	velocity, fps	1450		1284		1152
	energy, ft-lb	1284		1007		810
Speer 325 SP	velocity, fps	1350		1224		1124
	energy, ft-lb	1315		1082		912

.50 ACTION EXPRESS

CARTRIDGE BULLET	RANGE, YARDS:	0	25	50	75	100
Hornady 300 XTP/HP	velocity, fps	1475		1251		1092
	energy, ft-lb	1449		1043		795
Speer 300 Gold Dot HP	velocity, fps	1550		1361		1207
	energy, ft-lb	1600		1234		970
Speer 325 UCHP	velocity, fps	1400		1232		1106
	energy, ft-lb	1414		1095		883

.500 SMITH & WESSON

CARTRIDGE BULLET	RANGE, YARDS:	0	25	50	75	100
Federal 275 Expander	velocity, fps	1660		1440		1250
	energy, ft-lb	1680		1255		950
Federal 325 A-Frame	velocity, fps	1800		1560		1350
	energy, ft-lb	2340		1755		1315
Hornady 350 XTP Mag	velocity, fps	1900		1656		1439
	energy, ft-lb	2805		2131		1610
Hornady 500 FP-XTP	velocity, fps	1425		1281		1164
	energy, ft-lb	2254		1823		1505
Win. 350 Super-X	velocity, fps	1400		1231		1106
	energy, ft-lb	1523		1178		951
Win. 400 Platinum Tip	velocity, fps	1800		1647		1505
	energy, ft-lb	2877		2409		2012

BALLISTICS

Directory of Manufacturers & Suppliers

Accu-Tek Firearms
Ontario, CA
www.accu-tekfirearms.com

Adcor Defense
Baltimore, MD
www.adcordefense.com

Advanced Armament
Lawrenceville, GA
www.advanced-armament.com

Aimpoint
Chantilly, VA
www.aimpoint.com

AirForce Airguns
Fort Worth, TX
www.airforceairguns.com

Alexander Arms
Radford, VA
www.alexanderarms.com

Alpen Optics
Rancho Cucamonga, CA
www.alpenoptics.com

American Derringer
Waco, TX
www.amderringer.com

American Spirit Arms
Scottsdale, AZ
www.americanspiritarms.com

American Tactical Imports
Rochester, NY
www.americantactical.us

Anderson Rifles
Hebron, KY
www.andersonrifles.com

J.G. Anschutz
Ulm, Germany
www.jga.anschuetz-sport.com

Arex (FIME Group)
Šentjernej, Slovenia
www.arex.si

ArmaLite, Inc.
Geneso, IL
www.armalite.com

Armscor
Pahrump, NV
www.armscor.com

Arsenal Firearms
Gardone val Trompia, Italy
www.arsenalfirearms.com

Arsenal, Inc.
Las Vegas, NV
www.arsenalinc.com

Ashbury Precision Ordnance
Charlottesville, VA
www.ashburyprecisionordnance.com

Auto-Ordnance
Worcester, MA
www.auto-ordnance.com

Avidity Arms
Wanamassa, NJ
www.avidityarms.eagleimportsinc.com

AYA
Eibar, Spain
www.aya-fineguns.com

Barnes Bullets
Mona, UT
www.barnesbullets.com

Barrett
Murfreesboro, TN
www.barrett.net

Barska
Pomona, CA
www.barska.com

Beeman Precision Airguns
Santa Fe Springs, CA
www.beeman.com

Benelli USA
Pocomoke, MD
www.benelliusa.com

Beretta USA
Accokeek, MD
www.berettausa.com

Bergara North America
Lawrenceville, GA
www.bergarausa.com

Berger Bullets
Fullerton, CA
www.bergerbullets.com

Bersa
Wanamassa, NJ
www.bersa.com

Black Hills
Rapid City, SD
www.black-hills.com

Blaser USA
San Antonio, TX
www.blaser-usa.com

Boberg Arms Corp.
White Bear Lake, MN
www.barska.com

Bond Arms
Granbury, TX
www.bondarms.com

Brenneke USA
Clinton, IA
www.brennekeusa.com

Browning
Morgan, UT
www.browning.com

BSA Optics
Ft. Lauderdale, FL
www.bsaoptics.com

Burris
Greeley, CO
www.burrisoptics.com

Bushmaster Firearms International
Madison, NC
www.bushmaster.com

Bushnell Outdoor Products
Overland Park, KS
www.bushnell.com

Cabela's, Inc.
Sidney, NE
www.cabelas.com

Cabot Gun Company
Cabot, PA
www.cabotgun.com

Caesar Guerini USA, Inc.
Cambridge, MD
www.gueriniusa.com

Canik USA
Delray Beach, FL
www.canikusa.com

Caracal USA
Boise, ID
www.caracalusa.com

Carl Zeiss Sports Optics
North Chesterfield, VA
www.sportsoptics.zeiss.com

CCI Ammunition
Lewiston, ID
www.cci-ammunition.com

Century International Arms
Delray Beach, FL
www.centuryarms.com

Ceska Zbrojovka Arms (CZ)
Kansas City, KS
www.cz-usa.com

C&H Precision USMC
LaBelle, FL
www.chpws.com

Charles Daly
Miami, FL
www.charlesdaly-us.com

Charter Arms
Shelton, CT
www.charterfirearms.com

Chiappa Firearms
Dayton, OH
www.chiappafirearms.com

Chipmunk Rifles
Milton, PA
www.chipmunkrifles.com

Christensen Arms
Gunnison, UT
www.christensenarms.com

Cimarron Firearms Co.
Fredericksburg, TX
www.cimarron-firearms.com

Citadel by Legacy Sports
see Legacy Sports

CMMG
Fayette, MO
www.cmmginc.com

C-More Systems
Warrenton, VA
www.cmore.com

Cobra Firearms
Salt Lake City, UT
www.cobrapistols.net

Colt Competition Rifle
Breckenridge, TX
www.coltcompetitionrifle.com

Colt's Manufacturing Company
Hartford, CT
www.coltsmfg.com

Connecticut Shotguns Mfg. Co.
New Britain, CT
www.connecticutshotgun.com

Connecticut Valley Arms (CVA)
Duluth, GA
www.cva.com

Coonan Inc.
Blaine, MN
www.coonaninc.com

Cooper Firearms
Stevensville, MT
www.cooperfirearms.com

CorBon / Glaser
Sturgis, SD
www.corbon.com

Crosman
Bloomfield, NY
www.crosman.com

Daisy
Rogers, AR
www.daisy.com

Dakota Arms
Sturgis, SD
www.dakotaarms.com

Dan Wesson Firearms Co.
Norwich, NY
www.cz-usa.com/products/by-brand/dan-wesson

Daniel Defense
Black Creek, GA
www.danieldefense.com

Del-Ton, Inc.
Elizabethtown, NC
www.del-ton.com

Dixie Gun Works
Union City, TN
www.dixiegunworks.com

DoubleTap Defense LLC
St. Louis, MO
www.doubletapdefense.com

Doublestar Corporation
Winchester, KT
www.star15.com

DPMS Firearms
St. Cloud, MN
www.dpmsinc.com

Eagle Imports
Wanamassa, NJ
www.eagleimportsinc.com

Ed Brown Products, Inc.
Perry, MO
www.edbrown.com

EMF Company, Inc.
Santa Ana, CA
www.emf-company.com

ENVIRON-Metal, Inc.
Sweet Home, OR
www.hevishot.com

EOTech
Ann Arbor, MI
www.eotech-inc.com

E.R. Shaw, Inc.
Bridgeville, PA
www.ershawbarrels.com

Escort by Legacy Sports
see Legacy Sports

European American Armory
Rockledge, FL
www.eaacorp.com

Excel Arms
Ontario, CA
www.excelarms.com

Fabarm
Brescia, Italy
www.fabarm.com

Fausti USA
Fredericksburg, VA
www.faustiusa.com

Federal Premium Ammunition
Anoka, MN
www.federalpremium.com

Fiocchi
Ozark, MO
www.fiocchiusa.com

FN America
McLean, VA
www.fnamerica.com

Franchi USA
Pocomoke, MD
www.franchiusa.com

Freedom Arms
Freedom, WY
www.freedomarms.com

Gamo USA
Ft. Lauderdale, FL
www.gamousa.com

GECO
see RUAG

Glock, Inc.
Smyrna, GA
www.glock.com

Halo Optics
Grand Prarie, TX
www.halooptics.com

Hämmerli
Ulm, Germany
www.haemmerli.info

Hatsan USA
Bentonville, AR
www.hatsanusa.com

Harvester Muzzleloading
Henderson, KY
www.harvestermuzzleloading.com

Heckler & Koch
Columbus, GA
www.hk-usa.com

Henry Repeating Arms
Bayonne, NJ
www.henryrepeating.com

Heritage Mfg., Inc.
Miami, FL
www.heritagemfg.com

High Standard
Houston, TX
www.highstandard.com

Hi-Point
Dayton, OH
www.hi-pointfirearms.com

Hornady Mfg., Co.
Grand Island, NE
www.hornady.com

Howa by Legacy Sports
see Legacy Sports

H-S Precision
Rapid City, SD
www.hsprecision.com

I.O., Inc.
Palm Bay, FL
www.ioinc.us

Ithaca Gun Company
Upper Sandusky, OH
www.ithacagun.com

Iver Johnson
Rockledge, FL
www.iverjohnsonarms.com

Jarrett Rifles
Jackson, SC
www.jarrettrifles.com

J. P. Sauer & Sohn Rifles
San Antonio, TX
www.jpsauer.us/firearms

Kahles
Guntramsdorf, Austria
www.kahles.at

Kahr Arms
Worcester, MA
www.kahr.com

Kel-Tec CNC Industries, Inc.
Cocoa, FL
www.keltecweapons.com

Kimber Mfg. Inc.
Elmsford, NY
www.kimberamerica.com

Knight Rifles
Athens, TN
www.knightrifles.com

Knight's Armament
Titusville, FL
www.knightarmco.com

Konus
Miami, FL
www.konuspro.com/en

Directory of Manufacturers & Suppliers

Krieghoff International, Inc.
Ottsville, PA
www.krieghoff.com

Kriss USA
Virginia Beach, VA
www.kriss-usa.com

K-Var Corp.
Las Vegas, NV
www.k-var.com

Kynoch Ammunition
Englewood, CO
www.kynochusa.com

Lapua Bullets
Lapua, Finland
www.lapua.com

Lazzeroni Arms, Inc.
Tuscon, AZ
www.lazzeroni.com

Leapers, Inc.
Livonia, MI
www.leapers.com

Leatherwood/Hi-Lux Optics
Torrance, CA
www.hi-luxoptics.com
www.leatherwoodoptics.com

Legacy Sports International
Reno, NV
www.legacysports.com

Legends
See Umarex

Leica
Allendale, NJ
www.us.leica-camera.com/sport_optics

Les Baer Custom
LeClaire, IA
www.lesbaer.com

Leupold & Stevens
Beaverton, OR
www.leupold.com

Lewis Machine & Tool Company
Milan, IL
http://www.lewismachine.net/

Lithgow Arms
Lithgow, NSW, Australia
http://www.lithgowarms.com/

Ljutic LLC
Yakima, Washington
www.Ljuticgun.com

Lucid
Riverton, WY
www.mylucidgear.com

LWRC International
Cambridge, MD
www.lwrci.com

Lyman Products
Middletown, CT
www.lymanproducts.com

Magnum Research
Pillager, MN
www.magnumresearch.com

Magtech Ammunition Company, Inc.
Lino Lakes, MN
www.magtechammunition.com

Marlin
Madison, NC
www.marlinfirearms.com

Marocchi Arms
Sarezzo, Italy
www.marocchiarms.com

MasterPiece Arms
Carrollton, GA
www.masterpiecearms.com

Mauser
Isny, Germany
www.mauser.com

McMillian
Phoenix, AZ
www.mcmillanfirearms.com

Meopta
Hauppauge, NY
www.meoptasportsoptics.com/us

Merkel
Trussville, AL
www.merkel-usa.com

MG Arms
Spring, TX
www.mgarmsinc.com

Millet Tactical
Overland Park, KS
www.millettsights.com

Minox
Germany
www.minox.com

Montana Rifle Company
Kalispell, MT
www.montanarifleco.com

Mossberg
North Haven, CT
www.mossberg.com

Nesika Firearms
Sturgis, SD
www.nesikafirearms.com

New Ultra Light Arms
Granville, WV
www.newultralight.com

Nightforce Optics, Inc.
Orofino, ID
www.nightforceoptics.com

Nighthawk Custom
Berryville, AR
www.nighthawkcustom.com

Nikko Stirling
Shanghai, China
www.nikkostirling.com

Nikon Sport Optics
Melville, NY
www.nikonsportoptics.com

Noreen Firearms
Belgrade, MT
www.onlylongrange.com

Norma
Amotfors, Sweden
www.norma-usa.com

North American Arms
Provo, UT
www.naaminis.com

Nosler
Bend, OR
www.nosler.com

Noveske
Grants Pass, OR
www.shopnoveske.com

Patriot Ordnance Factory
Phoenix, Arizona
www.pof-usa.com

Pedersoli & C., Davide
Brescia, Italy
www.davide-pedersoli.com

Perazzi
Azusa, CA
www.perazzi.it

Peregrine Bullets
Pretoria, South Africa
www.peregrinemonolithics.com

P.M.C. Ammunition
Conroe, TX
www.pmcammo.com

Pointer by Legacy Sports
see Legacy Sports

PolyCase Ammunition
Savannah GA
www.polycaseammo.com

PowerBelt Bullets
Nampa, ID
www.powerbeltbullets.com

Primary Weapons Systems
Boise, ID
www.primaryweapons.com

PTR Industries
Aynor, SC
www.ptr91.com

Purdey
London, England
www.purdey.com

Rainier Ballistics Co.
Fife, WA
www.ranierballistics.com

Redfield
Beaverton, OR
www.redfield.com

Remington Arms
Madison, NC
www.remington.com

Rifles, Inc.
Pleasanton, TX
www.riflesinc.com

Ritter&Stark
Feistritz im Rosental, Austria
www.ritterstark.com

Rock Island Armory
Pahrump, NV
us.armscor.com

Rock River Arms
Colona, IL
www.rockriverarms.com

Rossi
Miami, FL
www.rossiusa.com

Rottweill
See RUAG

RUAG
Fürth, Germany
www.ruag-ammotec.com/

Ruger
Newport, NH
www.ruger.com

RWS
see RUAG

Sako
Riihimaki, Finland
www.sako.fi

Savage Arms
Westfield, MA
www.Savagearms.com

Schmidt & Bender
Claremont, NH
www.schmidtundbender.de/en

Shiloh Rifle
Big Timber, MT
www.shilohrifle.com

Sierra Bullets
Sedalia, MO
www.sierrabullets.com

Sig Sauer
Exeter, NH
www.sigsauer.com

Simmons Optics
Overland Park, KS
www.simmonsoptics.com

Smith & Wesson
Springfield, MA
www.smith-wesson.com

Speer Bullets
Lewiston, ID
www.speer-bullets.com

Sphinx (by Kriss)
Interlaken, Switzerland
www.sphinxarms.com

Springfield Armory
Geneso, IL
www.springfield-armory.com

SRM Arms
Meridian, ID
www.srmarms.com

Stag Arms
New Britain, CT
www.stagarms.com

Steiner Division
Creeley, CO
www.steiner-binoculars.com

Steyr Arms
Trussville, AL
www.steyrarms.com

STI International, Inc.
Georgetown, TX
www.stiguns.com

Stoeger Industries
Pocomoke, MD
www.stoegerindustries.com

Swarovski Optik
Cranston, RI
www.swarovskioptik.com

Swift Bullets
Quinter, KS
www.swiftbullets.com

Syren
Cambridge, MD
www.syrenusa.com

Szecsei & Fuchs
Windsor, Ontario, Canada
www.fuchs-fine-guns.com

Tactical Rifles
Zephyrhills, FL
www.tacticalrifles.net

Tangent Theta
Halifax, Nova Scotia, Canada
www.tangenttheta.com

Taurus
Miami, FL
www.taurususa.com

Taylor's & Co.
Winchester, VA
www.taylorsfirearms.com

Thompson/Center
Springfield, MA
www.tcarms.com

Tikka T3
Riihimaki, Finland
www.tikka.fi

TNW Firearms
Vernonia, OR
www.tnwfirearms.com

Tract Optics
Hummelstown, PA
www.tractoptics.com

Traditions Firearms
Old Saybrook, CT
www.traditionsfirearms.com

Trijicon
Wixom, Michigan
www.trijicon.com

Tristar Sporting Arms
North Kansas City, MO
www.tristarsportingarms.com

Troy Defense
West Springfield, MA
www.troydefense.com

Truglo
Richardson, TX
www.truglo.com

Turnbull Mfg. Co.
Bloomfield, NY
www.turnbullmfg.com

Uberti
Pocomoke, MD
www.uberti.com

Umarex
Fort Smith, AR
www.umarexusa.com

UTAS USA
Des Plaines, IL
www.utas-usa.com

Volquartsen Custom
Carroll, IA
www.volquartsen.com

Vortex Optics
Middletown, WI
www.vortexoptics.com

Walther Arms, Inc.
Fort Smith, AR
www.waltherarms.com

Weatherby
Paso Robles, CA
www.weatherby.com

Weaver Optics
Anoka, MN
www.weaveroptics.com

Webley & Scott
Reno, NV
http://webleyandscott.com/us-shotguns

Wilson Combat
Berryville, AR
www.wilsoncombat.com

Winchester Repeating Arms & Ammunition
East Alton, IL
www.winchester.com

Windham Weaponry
Windham, ME
www.windhamweaponry.com

Woodleigh Bullets
Murrabit, Australia
www.woodleighbullets.com.au

Zastava Arms
Kragujevac, Serbia
http://www.zastava-arms.rs/

Zeiss
Thornwood, NY
www.zeiss.com/sports-optics

Gunfinder Index

Gunfinder Index